Lecture Notes in Computer Science   9423

Commenced Publication in 1973
Founding and Former Series Editors:
Gerhard Goos, Juris Hartmanis, and Jan van Leeuwen

More information about this series at http://www.springer.com/series/7412

Alvaro Pardo · Josef Kittler (Eds.)

Progress in Pattern Recognition, Image Analysis, Computer Vision, and Applications

20th Iberoamerican Congress, CIARP 2015
Montevideo, Uruguay, November 9–12, 2015
Proceedings

 Springer

Editors
Alvaro Pardo
University Católica del Uruguay
Montevideo
Uruguay

Josef Kittler
University of Surrey
Guildford
UK

ISSN 0302-9743   ISSN 1611-3349   (electronic)
Lecture Notes in Computer Science
ISBN 978-3-319-25750-1   ISBN 978-3-319-25751-8   (eBook)
DOI 10.1007/978-3-319-25751-8

Library of Congress Control Number: 2015952526

LNCS Sublibrary: SL6 – Image Processing, Computer Vision, Pattern Recognition, and Graphics

Printed on acid-free paper

Springer International Publishing AG Switzerland is part of Springer Science+Business Media
(www.springer.com)

Preface

The 20th Iberoamerican Congress on Pattern Recognition CIARP 2015 (Congreso IberoAmericano de Reconocimiento de Patrones) was the 20th edition of a yearly event organized by scientific associations of Iberoamerican countries in this field.

In this special anniversary edition, as in previous years, the congress received contributions from many countries beyond Iberoamerica. The papers presented research results in the areas of pattern recognition, biometrics, image processing, computer vision, speech recognition, and remote sensing to name a few. The papers tackle theoretical as well as applied contributions in many fields related to the main topics of the conference. In this way, CIARP 2015 continued the tradition of an event that fosters scientific exchange, discussions, and cooperation among researchers.

CIARP 2015 received 185 contributions authored by researchers from 32 countries, 11 of which are Iberoamerican countries. These contributions were reviewed in a double-blind process and 95 papers were accepted.

Following tradition, CIARP 2015 was a single-track conference in which 40 papers were selected for oral presentation and 55 were presented in poster sessions. The type of presentation did not imply quality differences. The poster sessions were organized by topic to encourage discussions among authors and attendees.

A selection of the accepted papers will be published in a special issue of the *IPOL (Image Processing OnLine) Journal*. After the reviewing process an evaluation committee pre-selected a set of papers in the area of image processing and invited the authors to submit an extended version to IPOL. To facilitate the production of all the materials needed to publish the papers in IPOL, these authors were also invited to attend the Training and Hands-On in Reproducible Research Workshop (THORR Workshop) that took place during November 13–14 at the Facultad de Ingeniería, Universidad de la República. This workshop was dedicated to providing the necessary tools for reproducible research (RR) and training on the *IPOL Journal* publication process. Also, a special section of *Pattern Recognition Letters* has been added to include two papers by the researchers selected as the IAPR-CIARP 2015 Best Paper Award and the Aurora Pons-Porrata Award.

The IAPR-CIARP Best Paper Award recognizes outstanding contributions and is aimed at acknowledging excellence and originality of both theoretical contributions and practical applications to the field of pattern recognition and data mining. On the other hand, the CIARP Aurora Pons-Porrata Award is given to a living woman in recognition to her outstanding contribution to the field of pattern recognition or data mining.

Beside the presentation of the 95 selected contributions, four keynotes were given by Professors Magnus Fontes (Lund University, Sweden and Institut Pasteur, France), Rene Vidal (Johns Hopkins University, USA), Guillermo Sapiro (Duke University, USA), and Josef Kittler (University of Surrey, UK).

CIARP 2015 was organized by the Uruguayan IAPR Chapter, including members from Universidad de la República and Universidad Católica del Uruguay, with the endorsement of the International Association for Pattern Recognition (IAPR) and the sponsorphip of the following national associations: Argentine Society for Pattern Recognition (SARP-SADIO), the Special Interest Group of the Brazilian Computer Society (SIGPR-SBC), the Chilean Association for Pattern Recognition (AChiRP), the Cuban Association for Pattern Recognition (ACRP), the Mexican Association for Computer Vision, Neural Computing and Robotics (MACVNR), the Spanish Association for Pattern Recognition and Image Analysis (AERFAI), and the Portuguese Association for Pattern Recognition (APRP).

We acknowledge the work of all members of the Organizing Committee and of the Program Committee for the rigorous work in the reviewing process. We thank the partial funding of the Administración del Mercado Eléctrico (ADME), the Agencia Nacional de Investigación e Innovación (ANII), the French Embassy in Montevideo, Sonda, Universidad Católica del Uruguay, and CSIC - Universidad de la República.

November 2015   Alvaro Pardo
                                                                      Josef Kittler

Organization

CIARP 2015 was organized by the Uruguayan IAPR Chapter, including members from the Universidad de la República and Universidad Católica del Uruguay, with the endorsement of the International Association for Pattern Recognition (IAPR).

Co-chairs

Alvaro Pardo	Universidad Católica del Uruguay, Uruguay
Josef Kittler	University of Surrey, Guildford, UK

Organizing Committee

Alicia Fernández	Universidad de la República, Uruguay
Alvaro Gómez	Universidad de la República, Uruguay
Ignacio Ramírez	Universidad de la República, Uruguay
Federico Lecumberry	Universidad de la República, Uruguay
Pablo Musé	Universidad de la República, Uruguay
Gregory Randall	Universidad de la República, Uruguay

Program Committee

Sergey Ablameyko	Belarusian State University, Belarus
Daniel Acevedo	Universidad de Buenos Aires, Argentina
Cecilia Aguerrebere	Duke University, USA
Andrés Almansa	CNRS - Telecom ParisTech, France
Akira Asano	Kansai University, Japan
Laura Aspirot	Universidad de la República, Uruguay
Rafael Bello	Universidad Central de Las Villas, Cuba
Olga Bellon	Universidade Federal do Parana, Brazil
César Beltrán Castaón	Pontificia Universidad Católica del Perú
Pablo Belzarena	Universidad de la República, Uruguay
Rafael Berlanga	Universitat Jaume I, Spain
Paola Bermolen	Universidad de la República, Uruguay
Marcelo Bertalmio	Universitat Pompeu Fabra, Spain
Isabelle Bloch	ENST - CNRS UMR 5141 LTCI, France
Jean-Francois Bonastre	Université d'Avignon et des Pays de Vaucluse, France
Gunilla Borgefors	Centre for Image Analysis, Uppsala University, Sweden
Mathias Bourel	Universidad de la República, Uruguay
Anders Brun	Uppsala University, Sweden
Maria Elena Buemi	Universidad de Buenos Aires, Argentina
José Ramón Calvo De Lara	CENATAV, Cuba
Pablo Cancela	Universidad de la República, Uruguay

Ignacio Ramirez	Universidad de la República, Uruguay
Gregory Randall	Universidad de la República, Uruguay
Marítn Rocamora	Universidad de la República, Uruguay
Jose Ruiz-Shulcloper	CENATAV, Cuba
Cesar San Martín	Universidad de la Frontera, Chile
Gonzalo Sanguinetti	TUE, The Netherlands
Rafael Sotelo	Universidad de Montevideo, Uruguay
Axel Soto	Dalhousie University, Canada
Pablo Sprechmann	New York University, USA
Carmen Paz Suárez-Araujo	Universdad de Las Palmas de Gran Canaria, Spain
Mariano Tepper	Duke University, USA
Leonardo Val	Universidad Católica del Uruguay, Uruguay
Gustavo Vázquez	Universidad Católica del Uruguay, Uruguay
Sergio A. Velastin	Universidad de Santiago de Chile

Additional Reviewers

Michael Affenzeller
Pablo Arias
Mariano Bianchi
André Bindilatti
Pierre-Michel Bousquet
José Ramón Calvo De Lara
Antoine Deblonde
Luis Di Martino
Francesco Fontanella
Enzo Ferrante
Elisabet García
Haokun Geng
Victor Gradin
Nadia Heredia
Gabriel Hernandez Sierra
Jonas Hilty
Ngoc Tu Huynh
Florencia Iglesias
Ignacio Irigaray
Florian Kleber
Federico Larroca
Jatuporn Leksut

José Lezama
Dongwei Liu
Luciano Lorenti
Rosana Matuk Herrera
Enric Meinhardt-Llopis
Sergio Martínez
Driss Matrouf
Leonardo Moreno
Seyednaser Nourashrafeddin
Carlos Ismael Orozco
Raydonal Ospina
Adrián Pastor López Monroy
Juan Pechiar
Pedro Penna
Osvaldo Andrés Pérez García
Jorg Portegies
Christopher Pramerdorfer
Lara Raad
Heitor S. Ramos
Martin Rais
Dayana Ribas González
Benigno Rodríguez

Jorge Sánchez
Cid Santos
Alessandra Scotto di Freca
Stefan Sigle
Alberto Taboada Crispi
Junli Tao

Sergio Torres
Christopher Tralie
Juan Vallelisboa
Mitko Veta
Sebastian Zambanini

Contents

Applications of Pattern Recognition

Computer Vision

Gesture Recogntion

Segmentation, Analysis of Shape and Textur

Signals Analysis and Processing

Theory of Pattern Recognition

Video Analysis, Segmentation and Tracking

Applications of Pattern Recognition

Evaluating Imputation Techniques for Missing Data in ADNI: A Patient Classification Study

Sergio Campos[1]([envelope]), Luis Pizarro[3], Carlos Valle[1], Katherine R. Gray[2], Daniel Rueckert[2], and Héctor Allende[1]

[1] Departamento de Informática,
Universidad Técnica Federico Santa María, Valparaíso, Chile
sergio0.1@gmail.com
[2] Department of Computer Science, University College London, London, UK
[3] Department of Computing, Imperial College London, London, UK

Abstract. In real-world applications it is common to find data sets whose records contain missing values. As many data analysis algorithms are not designed to work with missing data, all variables associated with such records are generally removed from the analysis. A better alternative is to employ data imputation techniques to estimate the missing values using statistical relationships among the variables. In this work, we test the most common imputation methods used in the literature for filling missing records in the ADNI (Alzheimer's Disease Neuroimaging Initiative) data set, which affects about 80% of the patients–making unwise the removal of most of the data. We measure the imputation error of the different techniques and then evaluate their impact on classification performance. We train support vector machine and random forest classifiers using all the imputed data as opposed to a reduced set of samples having complete records, for the task of discriminating among different stages of the Alzheimer's disease. Our results show the importance of using imputation procedures to achieve higher accuracy and robustness in the classification.

Keywords: Missing data · Imputation · Classification · ADNI · Alzheimer

1 Introduction

Alzheimer's disease (AD) is the most common type of dementia in the elderly, representing about 80% of all dementia patients and the sixth cause of death in the USA. 26.6 million people worldwide were estimated to suffer from some degree of dementia in 2006, and 100 million impaired people are expected by 2050 [1]. Unfortunately, no drug treatment reducing the risk of developing AD or delaying its progression has been discovered so far. The Alzheimer's Disease Neuroimaging Initiative[1] (ADNI), launched in 2004, contributes to the development of biomarkers for the early detection (diagnostic) and tracking (prognostic)

---

[1] http://adni.loni.usc.edu/

© Springer International Publishing Switzerland 2015
A. Pardo and J. Kittler (Eds.): CIARP 2015, LNCS 9423, pp. 3–10, 2015.
DOI: 10.1007/978-3-319-25751-8_1

of AD using longitudinal clinical, imaging, genetic and biochemical data from patients with AD, mild cognitive impairment, and healthy controls. Its major achievements have been reviewed in [2]. Pattern recognition techniques have been instrumental in identifying disease patterns. Tasks such as classification, prediction, feature extraction and selection, multimodal data fusion, dimensionality reduction, among others, are at the core of this ongoing multidisciplinary research initiative. Pattern analysis is, however, hampered by *missing data* in the ADNI dataset, i.e. patients with incomplete records, cases where the different data modalities are partially or fully absent due to several reasons: high measurement cost, equipment failure, unsatisfactory data quality, patients missing appointments or dropping out of the study, and unwillingness to undergo invasive procedures. The missing data problem can be handled in two ways. Firstly, all samples having a missing record are removed before any analysis takes place. This is a reasonable approach when the percentage of removed samples is low so that a possible bias in the study can be discarded. Secondly, the missing values can be estimated from the incomplete measured data. This approach is known as *imputation* [3] and is recommended when the adopted data analysis techniques are not designed to work with missing entries. About 80% of the ADNI patients have missing records. Despite this, such patients are discarded in the vast majority of ADNI studies, which is a disuse of valuable incomplete information. Only recently, pattern recognition and machine learning techniques that can cope with missing entries or perform data imputation have been investigated. This article focuses on the task of patient classification into clinical groups. In particular, we conduct a comparative study of different imputation techniques and evaluate their impact on classification performance. We train support vector machine and random forest classifiers using all the imputed data as opposed to a reduced set of samples having complete records, for the task of discriminating among different stages of AD. We show the importance of including imputation and data analysis procedures to achieve more accurate and robust classification results.

In section 2 we provide further background on the classification task for ADNI patients and briefly describe the imputation and classification methods we used in this study. Section 3 details the experimental settings on which we tested the different methods against imputation error and classification performance, discussing our findings. Final remarks and future work are examined in section 4.

2   Methods

2.1   Classification with Incomplete Data

The ADNI study provides a database of multimodal entries for 819 subjects: 229 participants with normal cognition as healthy controls (HC), 397 with mild cognitive impairment (MCI), and 193 with mild Alzheimer's disease. Individuals with MCI are divided into two groups: those who remained in a *stable* condition (sMCI) and those who later *progressed* to AD (pMCI). It is therefore crucial to diagnose the patients into these clinical categories correctly in order to choose an appropriate treatment and further monitoring the disease. This task is especially difficult when approximately 80% of the participants have missing observations.

Let $X \in \mathbb{R}^{n \times p}$ be an incomplete matrix with n samples (subjects) and p variables (features). X can be seen as two matrices, one containing the observed data X_o, and the other one representing the missing data to be estimated X_m. Most classification methods from the literature discard all samples having at least one missing value. Only a few works that use all the available data exist, such as [4–7] where direct data imputation is avoided, and [8] where a subset of the missing data is estimated based on variable and sample selection. It is then important to investigate the different causes of the missing data to evaluate the utilisation of adequate imputation methods. Little and Rubin [3] define three missing data mechanisms: i) missing completely at random, MCAR: missing values are independent of both observed and unobserved data; ii) missing at random, MAR: given the observed data, missing values are independent of unobserved data; and iii) missing not at random, MNAR: missing values depend on the unobserved data. A recent longitudinal study [9] found that missing data in ADNI are not MCAR, but rather conditional to other features in addition to cognitive function. Moreover, the authors found evidence of different missing data mechanisms between different biomarkers and clinical groups.

2.2 Imputation Methods

Efforts to define a taxonomy of imputation methods have been reported in [3,10]. In this work we compare some common techniques used in the literature.

1. *Zero.* This method consists of imputing missing data with 0 (zero) values.
2. *Mean.* Missing values filled with the mean of the observed values per variable.
3. *Median.* Missing values filled with the median of the observed values per variable. The median is more robust against outliers than the mean. It tolerates up to 50% of outliers [11].
4. *Winsorised mean.* Provides a more robust estimate for the mean, which is calculated after replacing a given percentage (α) of the largest and smallest values with the closest observations to them. We used $\alpha = 10\%$. This method also controls the effect of outliers.
5. *k-nearest neighbours (kNN).* Missing values filled with the mean of the k-nearest observed samples based on the Euclidean distance. We use a modified cross-validation approach [12] to find the parameter k in the range $[1, \sqrt{n_{obs}}]$.
6. *Regularised expectation maximisation (RegEM).* Proposed by Schneider [13], this imputation method makes two important assumptions: the data follow a Normal distribution, and the missing values are generated by a MAR process. The missing entries are estimated by the linear regression model $x_m = \mu_m + (x_o - \mu_o)B + e$, where $x_o \in \mathbb{R}^{1 \times p_o}$ and $x_m \in \mathbb{R}^{1 \times p_m}$ are row vectors of the observed data matrix X_o and the estimated missing data matrix X_m, respectively; μ_o and μ_m are their corresponding means; $B \in \mathbb{R}^{p_o \times p_m}$ is the regression coefficients matrix, and $e \in \mathbb{R}^{1 \times p_m}$ is a zero-mean random residual vector with unknown covariance matrix $C \in \mathbb{R}^{p_m \times p_m}$. Initially, the algorithm

estimates the missing data with the Mean method, followed by i) E-step: compute the expected mean μ and covariance matrix Σ of X, ii) M-step: compute the maximum likelihood estimates of the regression parameters B and C, conditional to the estimates (μ, Σ), and iii) impute missing values using the regression model. These three steps are iterated until convergence, i.e., until the estimates (μ, Σ) stabilise. We run Schneider's implementation[2] using the individual ridge regression model.

3   Experimental Results

3.1   Data

In this work, we consider three baseline ADNI modalities: cerebrospinal fluid (CSF), magnetic resonance imaging (MRI) and positron emission tomography (PET). The modalities were preprocessed according to [14], with 43 out of 819 subjects excluded for not passing the quality control. The CSF source contains 3 variables that measure the levels of some proteins and amino acids that are crucially involved in AD. The MRI source provides volumetric features of 83 brain anatomical regions. The PET source (with FDG radiotracer) provides the average brain function, in terms of the rate of cerebral glucose metabolism, within the 83 anatomical regions. Hence, each subject consists of 169 features.

3.2   Imputation

In this section we work with the 147 subjects who have complete records: 35 HC, 75 MCI and 37 AD. We synthesise different patterns of missing data, considering the individual modalities and pairs of them: CSF, MRI, PET, CSF-MRI, CSF-PET and MRI-PET. For each pattern we removed such features from a given percentage $\{10, 20, 30, 40, 50\}\%$ of subjects that were chosen randomly. The performance of the different imputation methods is assessed between three clinically relevant pairs of diagnostic groups: AD/HC, MCI/HC and pMCI/sMCI.

Due to space limitations, Fig. 1 only shows the results for the experiment AD/HC (72 subjects) with the CSF-PET missing data pattern. 95% confidence intervals were computed for the Pearson correlation (PC) and the relative error (RE) over 100 runs. As expected, we observed that the PC of the imputed variables decreases with the amount of missing data. It is noteworthy that the PC for the Zero method is the lowest because this technique does not consider any additional information for estimating the data. Moreover, the RE for each method seems rather constant. Since it is computed as $\mathrm{RE} = |x_o - x_m|/x_o$, the Zero method will always produce $\mathrm{RE} = 1$. Filling CSF data produces an error of about 45% for the Median, Winsorised mean and kNN methods, which outperform the Mean and EM methods. Filling PET data produces an error of about 13% for most techniques, except for the Zero method. This low error can be explained by inspecting the actual PET values. Fig. 2 shows the histograms

---

[2] www.clidyn.ethz.ch/imputation

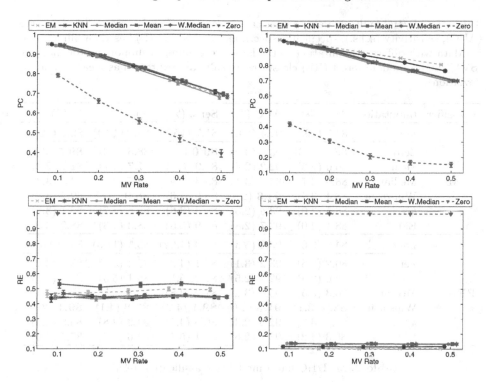

Fig. 1. Imputation performance. Pearson correlation (*bottom*) and relative error (*top*) for the imputation of missing values (MV) in CSF (*left panels*) and PET (*right panels*) for the CSF-PET missing data pattern.

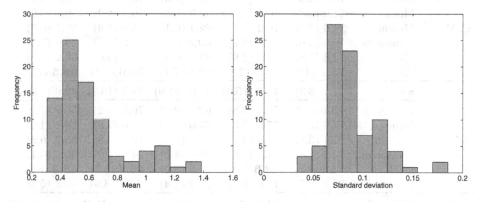

Fig. 2. Mean (*left*) and standard deviation (*right*) histograms over all 83 PET variables.

of the mean and standard deviation over all 83 PET variables. These small quantities indicate that the PET values are bunched up close to the mean. For this reason, the methods tend to provide estimates around this value even if they do not directly impute using the mean.

Table 1. AD/HC multi-modality classification accuracy (acc.), area under the curve (AUC), sensitivity (sens.), specificity (spec.), and F-measure (F) based on filling missing data with different imputation methods before training a support vector machine (SVM) and a random forest (RF) classifiers. Results are expressed as mean (standard deviation).

Classifier	Imputation	Acc. (%)	AUC (%)	Sens. (%)	Spec. (%)	F (%)
	none	83.5 (10.7)	92.4 (8.0)	81.7 (15.7)	86.1 (12.4)	82.2 (12.2)
SVM	Zero	**88.7** (3.3)	93.9 (3.0)	**89.0** (4.7)	88.6 (5.2)	**89.5** (3.1)
	Mean	86.6 (2.3)	92.2 (2.4)	85.9 (5.6)	87.7 (4.7)	87.7 (2.4)
	Median	88.5 (3.7)	93.7 (3.1)	88.3 (3.9)	88.5 (6.7)	89.3 (3.3)
	Winsor m.	88.4 (3.4)	**94.3** (2.4)	88.6 (4.6)	**88.9** (5.5)	89.2 (3.2)
	*k*NN	88.5 (3.0)	93.5 (2.5)	88.3 (3.6)	88.8 (4.7)	89.1 (3.2)
	EM	88.1 (4.0)	93.7 (2.8)	87.9 (5.6)	88.3 (4.3)	88.9 (3.8)
	none	84.8 (9.0)	93.2 (5.3)	85.9 (13.2)	85.5 (11.3)	84.3(9.6)
RF	Zero	86.2 (3.5)	93.2 (3.1)	87.1 (4.9)	85.4 (5.4)	87.1 (3.2)
	Mean	86.6 (2.8)	92.7 (2.5)	87.2 (5.5)	86.1 (5.3)	87.5 (2.7)
	Median	86.3 (3.5)	93.6 (3.2)	87.2 (3.8)	85.2 (6.7)	87.3 (3.1)
	Winsor m.	**88.4** (3.1)	**94.3** (2.0)	**89.1** (4.2)	**87.8** (4.1)	**89.1** (2.8)
	*k*NN	85.3 (3.3)	92.5 (2.3)	86.5 (4.7)	84.2 (4.8)	85.9 (3.4)
	EM	86.3 (4.2)	93.1 (2.6)	87.1 (5.1)	85.6 (5.9)	87.1 (4.0)

Table 2. MCI/HC multi-modality classification results.

Classifier	Imputation	Acc. (%)	AUC (%)	Sens. (%)	Spec. (%)	F (%)
	none	69.1 (11.8)	69.5 (14.6)	48.3 (21.5)	74.9 (13.4)	44.3 (22.8)
SVM	Zero	70.9 (3.3)	74.4 (11.1)	59.8 (5.6)	76.3 (4.3)	56.6 (5.4)
	Mean	71.9 (3.8)	76.1 (12.2)	62.5 (6.8)	76.7 (4.0)	58.8 (6.0)
	Median	71.0 (3.9)	76.3 (4.1)	62.4 (6.1)	75.8 (4.9)	59.1 (6.5)
	Winsor m.	72.0 (3.6)	77.9 (3.7)	**63.4** (5.6)	76.2 (4.6)	59.0 (5.1)
	*k*NN	72.6 (3.8)	78.8 (3.6)	63.3 (6.3)	77.3 (5.6)	58.9 (6.7)
	EM	**73.1** (4.2)	**78.9** (2.8)	62.8 (7.1)	**78.6** (5.1)	**59.5** (7.3)
	none	71.1 (8.3)	75.3 (10.6)	65.0 (21.9)	74.3 (10.2)	42.6 (14.9)
RF	Zero	**73.6** (3.2)	78.3 (3.8)	**67.1** (8.0)	76.1 (4.2)	56.7 (7.1)
	Mean	71.9 (3.3)	77.6 (5.0)	65.0 (8.0)	75.0 (2.8)	56.1 (4.5)
	Median	71.4 (3.8)	76.5 (4.7)	66.1 (7.3)	73.5 (3.8)	55.7 (6.3)
	Winsor m.	72.2 (3.8)	77.5 (3.6)	66.9 (4.2)	74.3 (4.9)	55.5 (6.1)
	*k*NN	73.2 (4.2)	**78.6** (4.6)	65.5 (8.0)	**76.7** (5.4)	**58.5** (6.1)
	EM	72.6 (3.7)	77.6 (3.8)	63.2 (7.4)	**76.7** (3.9)	56.8 (5.3)

3.3 Classification

We now use all 776 subjects to assess the impact of the different imputation methods on patient classification. The whole data set has 33% of missing values, from which 97% correspond to PET values. The remaining 3% are CSF values, while the MRI source is complete. We consider two experiments: AD/HC with

395 subjects (185 AD and 210 HC) and MCI/HC with 591 subjects (381 MCI and 210 HC). In each experiment we used 75% of the data to train two classifiers, namely a ν-Support Vector Machine (ν-SVM) and a Random Forest (RF), evaluated over 25 runs. The other 25% of the data was used for testing. We employed the implementations found in the scikit-learn library[3]. The ν and σ parameters for ν-SVM and the number of trees and number of features for RF were tuned using 5-fold CV.

Tables 1 and 2 show the classification results for the experiments AD/HC and MCI/HC, respectively. We juxtapose both classifiers, SVM and RF, for the different imputation methods. For completeness, we include the results when the classifiers are trained solely with the reduced set of subjects having complete records and thus no imputation is needed. It can be noticed that the classification improves considerably when the full data set is used, imputing the missing values. This clearly provides more information to discriminate among the different diagnostic groups. These experiments suggest that the Winsorised mean, the kNN and the EM methods should be preferred as imputation methods as they provide more stable performance. The Zero method seems competitive, which is explained again by the fact that the most of the missing data come from the PET source which presents low dispersion values close to zero. Both classifiers present similar performances in each scenario. A remarkable point, is that their robustness (low variance) is increased in cases with imputation.

4 Conclusions and Future Work

We have seen how imputation techniques allow for the utilisation of additional information, that would otherwise be discarded, to better distinguish between different diagnostic groups. The development of biomarkers using more evidence could result in more accurate diagnosis and prognosis of Alzheimer's patients. Our results showed that training classifiers with imputed data is better than constructing a predictive model with a reduced number of subjects with complete records. This is supported by the fact that all imputation techniques increase both performance metrics and robustness of the classifiers. An apparently unexpected finding is that the Zero method is competitive with the other methods, according to the performance metrics used in this article. It is expected that more sophisticated methods such as kNN and EM would deliver better results. However, as we stated before, possibly more relevant than the quality of the imputation algorithms is the nature of the data, which plays an important role in the performance as we have seen.

Future work includes studying other imputation and classification techniques, as well as exploring multi-class extensions and alternative ways of treating the feature space to handle data-dependent imputation pitfalls. There is interest in comparing imputation methods with methods that can internally handle the missing values, as Artificial Neural Networks (ANN) [15] and SVM [16].

---

[3] scikit-learn.org/stable

References

1. Brookmeyer, R., Johnson, E., Ziegler-Graham, K., Arrighi, H.M.: Forecasting the global burden of Alzheimer's disease. Alzheimer's & Dementia 3(3), 186–191 (2007)
2. Weiner, M.W., et al.: The Alzheimer's Disease Neuroimaging Initiative: A review of papers published since its inception. Alzheimer's & Dementia 9(5), 111–194 (2013)
3. Little, R.J.A., Rubin, D.B.: Statistical Analysis with Missing Data, 2nd edn. Wiley-Interscience (2002)
4. Wang, C., Liao, X., Carin, L., Dunson, D.B.: Classification with incomplete data using Dirichlet process priors. JMLR 11, 3269–3311 (2010)
5. Ingalhalikar, M., Parker, W.A., Bloy, L., Roberts, T.P.L., Verma, R.: Using multiparametric data with missing features for learning patterns of pathology. In: Ayache, N., Delingette, H., Golland, P., Mori, K. (eds.) MICCAI 2012, Part III. LNCS, vol. 7512, pp. 468–475. Springer, Heidelberg (2012)
6. Yuan, L., Wang, Y., Thompson, P.M., Narayan, V.A., Ye, J.: Multi-source feature learning for joint analysis of incomplete multiple heterogeneous neuroimaging data. NeuroImage 61(3), 622–632 (2012)
7. Xiang, S., Yuan, L., Fan, W., Wang, Y., Thompson, P.M., Ye, J.: Bi-level multisource learning for heterogeneous block-wise missing data. NeuroImage 102, Part 1, 192–206 (2014)
8. Thung, K.-H., Wee, C.-Y., Yap, P.-T., Shen, D.: Neurodegenerative disease diagnosis using incomplete multi-modality data via matrix shrinkage and completion. NeuroImage 91, 386–400 (2014)
9. Lo, R.Y., Jagust, W.J.: Predicting missing biomarker data in a longitudinal study of Alzheimer disease. Neurology 78, 1376–1382 (2012)
10. García-Laencina, P.J., Sancho-Gómez, J.-L., Figueiras-Vidal, A.R.: Pattern classification with missing data: A review. Neural Computing and Applications 19(2), 263–282 (2010)
11. Maronna, R.A., Martin, D.R., Yohai, V.J.: Robust Statistics: Theory and Methods. John Wiley and Sons, New York (2006)
12. Arlot, S., Celisse, A.: A survey of cross-validation procedures for model selection. Statistics Surveys 4, 40–79 (2010)
13. Schneider, T.: Analysis of incomplete climate data: Estimation of mean values-sand covariance matrices and imputation of missing values. Journal of Climate 14, 853–871 (2001)
14. Gray, K., Aljabar, P., Heckemann, R.A., Hammers, A., Rueckert, D.: Random forest-based similarity measures for multi-modal classification of Alzheimer's disease. NeuroImage 65, 167–175 (2013)
15. Báez, P.G., Araujo, C.P.S., Viadero, C.F., García, J.R.: Automatic prognostic determination and evolution of cognitive decline using artificial neural networks. In: Yin, H., Tino, P., Corchado, E., Byrne, W., Yao, X. (eds.) IDEAL 2007. LNCS, vol. 4881, pp. 898–907. Springer, Heidelberg (2007)
16. Pelckmans, K., Brabanter, J.D., Suykens, J.A.K., Moor, B.D.: Handling missing values in support vector machine classifiers. Neural Networks 18(5–6), 684–692 (2005)

Genetic Prediction in Bovine Meat Production: Is Worth Integrating Bayesian and Machine Learning Approaches? a Comprenhensive Analysis

Maria Ines Fariello[1]($\boxtimes$), Eileen Amstrong[2], and Alicia Fernandez[3]

[1] IMERL, Facultad de Ingenieria, UdelaR & UBi, Institut Pasteur de Montevideo, Montevideo, Uruguay
fariello@fing.edu.uy
[2] Facultad de Veterinaria, UdelaR, Montevideo, Uruguay
[3] IIE, Facultad de Ingeniería, UdelaR, Montevideo, Uruguay

Abstract. Genomic prediction is a still growing field, as good predictions can have important economic impact in both, agronomics and health. In this article, we make a brief review and a comprehensive analysis of classical predictors used in the area. We propose a strategy to choose and ensemble of methods and to combine their results, to take advantage of the complementarity that some predictors have.

Keywords: Parametric · Non parametric · Genomic · Selection · Prediction · Fusion

1 Introduction

Beef consumers increasingly demand meat of high and consistent quality. As a consequence, research has focused on understanding muscle biology to control quality traits. In the past two decades, molecular genetics has changed dramatically animal production research. Genome sequencing has facilitated the identification of polymorphisms (here we focus on Single Nucleotide Polymorphisms: SNPs), that can be used as genetic markers in animal breeding. Genes involved in the physiological regulation of energy, body weight, triglyceride synthesis and growth are candidates that may have effects on economically important carcass and meat quality traits ([7] [6]). On the other hand, such avalanche of information has increased in a considerable way the complexity of the analysis, making obvious that the usual statistical methods may not be enough ([10] [18]). In this paper we try to predict the carcass weight from genomic information. A review of the state of the art in genetic prediction shows the interest in performance comparison between lineal regression models as Bayesian Ridge regression, Bayesian Lasso, Bayes A, B and C with non-linear models as Bayesian Regularized Neural Networks (BRNN), Reproducing Kernel Hilbert Spaces Regresion (RKHS) and Support Vector Machine Regression (SVR).

© Springer International Publishing Switzerland 2015
A. Pardo and J. Kittler (Eds.): CIARP 2015, LNCS 9423, pp. 11–18, 2015.
DOI: 10.1007/978-3-319-25751-8_2

In [16], the superiority of nonlinear regression methods versus linear ones is analyzed in the case of wheat genomic prediction. In [11] a comparison between Best Linear Unbiasd Prediction (BLUP) and SVR shows discrepancy between prediction accuracies obtained by cross-validation procedures and correlation ones, beeing more accurate BLUP when a limited set of training samples are available. In [13], a comparison of five methods to predict genomic breeding values of dairy bulls from genome-wide SNP markers is done. Fixed regression using least squares (FRLS), BLUP, bayesian regression (BayesR), partial least squares regression and SVR are compared in Australian Selection Index and protein percentage prediction. Although the selected methods have inherent differences in the underlying assumptions, they show similar performances (except FRLS, which is not recomended). In [14] methods with large conceptual differences also reached very similar predictive performances, although re-ranking of methods was observed depending on the analyzed phenotype. In [19] the effects of feature selection methods on prediction performance for different methods was observed. The authors found that feature selection and prediction algorithms should be carefully selected depending on the phenotypes. A nice review of kernel-based whole-genome prediction of complex trait is presented by [12]. They concluded that research involving analysis of raw phenotypes coupled with enviromental variables needs more attention. In recent works, like [17], the impact of predictive modes averaging is analyzed. It is proposed to combine several RKHS models with different t-kernels, but no improvements were found compared with one kernel models. Although several works compared different approaches for genomic prediction (born in breeding animal, statistics and machine learning), they use performance measures, as the prediction error, that are global statistical averages, which can hide the differences and complementarities between methods. In particular, these differences are what can make it worth a combination of methods. In pattern recognition, it is well known that the best scenario is to combine when individual methods have similar performance but bring diversity, *i.e.* different behavior in different individuals [1,2,8,9].

In this paper we study the behavior of a set of known approaches for genomic prediction of carcass weight in Aberdeen Angus cattle from Uruguay. A comparative analysis of the behavior of the different methods in the sample space is presented. We propose a method to choose a subset of predictors, once their performances are computed. The proposed analysis aims to provide knowledge of the specific problematic, but also give elements for a greater understanding of the similarities and differences between approaches and to know in advance if it is worthy to use an ensemble of methods.

2   Methodology

Data Set Characterization. The database used comprise several phenotypic measures [15] from a total of 705 Aberdeen Angus animals of different age-sex categories. The animals came from ten commercial herds and were slaughtered in different slaughter houses. The database is complex, due both to the amount of data and the diversity thereof. Apart from genotypic variables, it includes environmental effects such as age, sex and origin. To avoid dealing with fixed effects, we just considered the individuals of the most numerous herd. The trait analyzed here is carcass weight. A total of 160 SNPs were selected for genotyping from the bibliography and public genomic databases. They are located in candidate genes that take part in metabolic pathways and physiological processes related to energy expenditure, triglyceride and fatty acid synthesis, body weight and growth. After removing SNPs with minor allele frequency lower than 0.05 (to avoid bias of the data), and individuals with more than 20% of missing values or with no phenotype, there were 79 SNPs and 93 individuals left.

Prediction Methods. In genome-wide association studies the objective is to predict an individual's breeding value (here, carcass weight) from its genotype. The association between genotypes and phenotypes is modeled in a group of individuals with phenotypic and genetic information (training set). The model is then used to predict the individual phenotypes in individuals for whom only information from genetic markers is available.

The basic prediction model, that seeks to minimize the mean square error (Ordinary Least Squares (OLS)), has prediction coefficients that are unbiased estimates with variance dependent on the sample size (n), the number of coefficients prediction (p) and interdependence between the predictor variables. One way to address "the curse of dimensionality" (p large in relation to n) of OLS, which generates high variance and therefore a large mean square error (MSE), is applying regularization in the regression. This is done adding a penalty term in the optimization seeking to balance the goodness of the approximation to the complexity of the model. Ridge Regression (RR) adds an extra term to the likelihood function that reduces the regression coefficients in an amount which depends on the variance of the co-variates. The regularization introduces bias, but reduces the variance of the estimate, reducing potentially MSE estimation of the prediction coefficients. Other individual cases of regularization are Least Absolute Shrinkage and Selection Operator (LASSO) in which the penalty is the absolute value of the coefficients, instead of the squares of them (as in RR), which introduces sparcity.

In a Bayesian approach, different penalty methods can be introduced changing the priors from where the regression coefficients are sampled and the likelihood functions. The Bayesian equivalent of RR, BRR (Bayesian Ridge Regression), allows to deploy G-BLUP (BLUP using a genomic distance's matrix), which is one of the most commonly used models in genomic prediction. A set of methods that share the same likelihood function but differ in the priors, which suppose different effects of the markers is known as the Bayesian alphabet ([3]).

The problem becomes almost intractable with large p. An alternative strategy is to use semi-parametric models as proposed by Gianola [4] as RKHS (Reproducing Kernel Hilbert Space), in which the model is determined by the choice of a kernel which fixes the space in which the regression is performed, and the parameter that determines shrinkage similar to that used in RR. An alternative method to capture additive, dominance and epitasis integrating linear and non-linear functions are complex neural networks (NN [5]). One of the distinguishing characteristics of neural networks is the flexibility to capture complex nonlinear patterns, the drawback are that increasing p with multiple neurons, increases strongly the computational requirements and tends to overfitting.

Having a set of tools as described previously, we faced the problem of defining how to use them efficiently, taking full advantage of the benefits and minimizing weaknesses. To do this we needed to define a set of measures for evaluating the performance of complementarity and/or the diversity they bring to the set. In particular, it lead us to investigate the advantages of assembly methods and how to make the assemble.

Comprehensive Analysis of Diversity of Predictors. As was shown before, different strategies have been proposed to deal with gene-trait association and genetic prediction. The studies showed that there is no method that is always superior to others in all data sets. These works make focus in MSE and they do not make a deeper comparative analysis about the diversity between the methods. They hide how the individual strategies work in the data space and if they have enough diversity between them that it could be worth embeding. Dealing with complex data sets where the traits have high dependence on enviroment introduce specific problems that have to be taken with care and different methods have to be used. We will discuss the relevance that different methods give to the variables, making focus in similarities and differences. We propose to study the relation between the genomic array, using its first two principal components and the error distribution in the sampling space.

Diversity Meassure in Ensamble. For regression ensembles the "diversity" can be measured and quantified explicitly. The MSE can be expressed in a bias-variance-covariance decomposition for the predictors ensembles. In an assemble of methods, the predictive error depends on the bias and variance of individual predictors but also on the covariance between individuals (shown in [2]).

The default method for the assembly of regression methods is the average of the predictions of the different methods. Given that the average error is a function of the average bias, variances and covariances between methods. An improvement in performance would be expected against the individual methods.The optimal assemble choice is the one that balances the trade-off between these terms to reduce the overall MSE. Given a set of methods with similar performance in terms of individual MSE or correlation between the predicted and the real values in the training set, the ones that provide smaller covariance, $i.e.$ are the most diverse, are worth to be ensemble.

Based on the above analysis, it is proposed as a criterion for the ensemble to seek "diversity" measured by the covariance between methods: (i) Select the two methods with less covariance, (ii) in an iterative way select the method with less covariance with respect to the already selected provided that the covariance

Table 1. Correlation Matrix of Predictors and the real value y: MMR: Multiple Marker Regression, RR:Ridge Regression, BC: Bayes C, BB2: Bayes B with $\pi = 10^{-4}$, RK: Regression Kernel in Hilbert Spaces, NN: Neural Networks

	y	MMR	RR	BC	BB2	RK	NN
y	1.00	-0.13	0.20	0.15	0.18	0.16	0.19
MMR	-0.13	1.00	-0.11	-0.18	-0.20	-0.16	-0.04
RR	0.20	-0.11	1.00	0.88	0.70	0.77	0.76
BC	0.15	-0.18	0.88	1.00	0.92	0.96	0.75
BB2	0.18	-0.20	0.70	0.92	1.00	0.98	0.63
RK	0.16	-0.16	0.77	0.96	0.98	1.00	0.71
NN	0.19	-0.04	0.76	0.75	0.63	0.71	1.00

is lower than a threshold, (iii) weighted average of the indiviual predictions is given as result.

3   Results

Relationship Between Errors and Genetic Structure. To investigate if the prediction error was related to the genomic relationship between each individual and the rest of the population, a Principal Component Analysis of the genomic matrix of the population was done. PCA is also helpful to investigate if there is a hidden substructure in the population, which could introduce confounding effects in our analyisis. We suppose that if the error of a predictor is related with the genetic composition of the individuals, then individuals with the same type of errors would cluster together. Although different bayesian approches were used, in Figure 1 only BayesC is shown because the predictors were highly correlated ($\approx 99\%$).

No obvious clusterization is observed in Figure 1. From the individual error point of view, there are some variations on the individual errors between methods, but in general the error structure remains the same, but for the multi marker regression. This predictor was negatively correlated with the real values and with the other predictors in the testing set (Table 1), so it is no longer considered in the analyisis.

Combining Predictors. Although the differences between the error structure of the predictors were slight (Fig. 1), the algorithm proposed in 2 was used to investigate if there was a way of embedding predictors that predicted better than the predictors individually.

The first chosen predictors were NN and BB2, for having the smallest positive covariance. Then, the correlation between the mean of those predictors (mNN-BB2) was computed and as a result of that RK was chosen. The predictor was computed as $m2RK = (2*mNN - BB2 + RK)/3$, to avoid underweighting the first chosen predictors. Then, the correlation between m2RK and the remaining

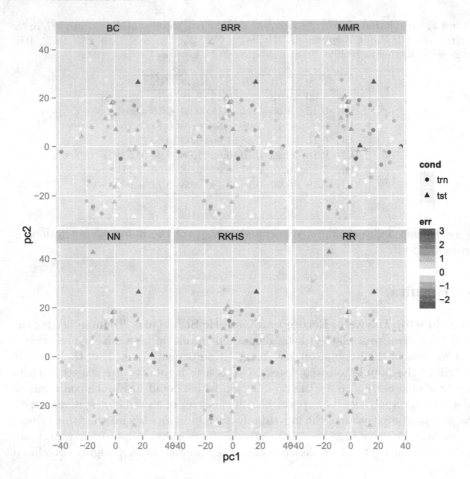

Fig. 1. Principal Component Analysis of Genomic Array. Errors in carcass weight prediction are represented with a color gradient

predictors was computed and RR was chosen. The new predictor m3RR was computed in the same way as the previous one. The correlation between the remaining predictor BC and the new one was 90%, so BC was not integrated to the predictor. The correlations of the previous steps were between 70% and 80%.

Three different combinations of the predictors were evaluated: The mean of them, the weighted mean using the correlations between each predictor (w-mean) and the

Table 2. Mean Squared Error. BRR: Bayesian Ridge Regression (= G-BLUP), BA, BB, BC and BL: Bayes A, B, C and LASSO, mean was taken over RR, BB2, RK, NN, m2RK = (mNN+BB2)/2

MMR	RR	BRR	BA	BL	BC	BB	BB2	RK	NN	mean	w-mean	m2	m2RK	m3RR
0.80	0.72	0.58	0.57	0.57	0.60	0.58	0.57	0.57	0.85	0.58	0.58	0.60	0.57	0.59

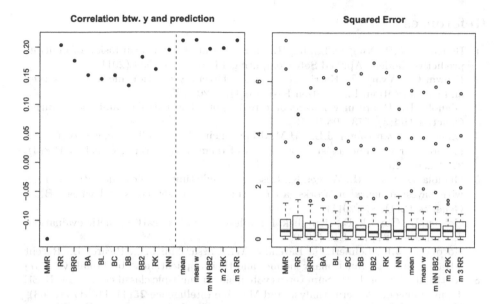

Fig. 2. Correlation between the predicted values using the different predictors and the real value (left) and distribution of the squared errors (right). Results from testing set.

real value and the predictor resulting from the algorithm (m3RR). The new estimators have almost the same MSE than the lowest observed value (0.57), and a slightly better correlation with the real value. The best correlation found between the classical predictors was the one of the Ridge Regression predictor (Fig. 2), but it has one of the worst MSE (0.80, Table 2). The new predictor has the best correlation with the phenotype and almost the lowest MSE.

4   Conclusions

A comprehensive analysis of the performances of the main methods used in genetic prediction of complex traits of high economic impact was done.

Based on the evaluation of diversity among the indivuduals, an ensemble strategy was proposed and evaluated. In particular, it was found that bayesian predictors have low complementarity, while BayesC (or any of the others), Ridge Regression, RKHS and Neural Networks have the highest degree of complementarity. By comparing several ways of combining the predictors, obtained by taking diversity into account, we found that the proposed criteria is consistent.

As it is not possible to know in advance which of the methods would work better, as they do not require much computation after the predictors are computed, and as the shown combinations work at least as well as the best predictor, it is worth to combine the methods.

Further reserch has to be done in order to obtain the best weights for combining these predictors, without loosing interpretability of the results.

Acknowledgment. The work of Maria Ines Fariello was partially supported by ANII Posdoc research scholarship. The authors want to thanks Daniel Gianola for sharing his experience in the genetic prediction field.

References

1. Bonissone, P.P., Xue, F., Subbu, R.: Fast meta-models for local fusion of multiple predictive models. Applied Soft Computing **11**(2), 1529–1539 (2011)
2. Brown, G., Wyatt, J., Harris, R., Yao, X.: Diversity creation methods: a survey and categorisation. Information Fusion **6**(1), 5–20 (2005)
3. Gianola, D.: Priors in whole-genome regression: The bayesian alphabet returns. Genetics **194**(3), 573–596 (2013)
4. Gianola, D., van Kaam, J.B.C.H.M.: Reproducing kernel hilbert spaces regression methods for genomic assisted prediction of quantitative traits. Genetics **178**(4), 2289–2303 (2008)
5. Gianola, D., Okut, H., Weigel, K., Rosa, G.: Predicting complex quantitative traits with bayesian neural networks: a case study with jersey cows and wheat. BMC Genetics **12**(1), 87 (2011)
6. Golden, B., Garrick, D., Benyshek, L.: Milestones in beef cattle genetic evaluation. J. Anim. Sci. **87**, E3–E10 (2009)
7. Hocquette, J.F., Lehnert, S., Barendse, W., Cassar-Malek, I., Picard, B.: Recent advances in cattle functional genomics and their application to beef quality (2007)
8. Kittler, J., Alkoot, F.M.: Sum versus vote fusion in multiple classifier systems. IEEE Transactions on Pattern Analysis and Machine Intelligence **25**(1), 110–115 (2003)
9. Kuncheva, L.I.: A theoretical study on six classifier fusion strategies. IEEE Transactions on Pattern Analysis and Machine Intelligence **24**(2), 281–286 (2002)
10. Lambert, C.G., Black, L.J.: Learning from our gwas mistakes: from experimental design to scientific method. Biostatistics **13**(2), 195–203 (2012)
11. Maenhout, S., De Baets, B., Haesaert, G.: Prediction of maize single-cross hybrid performance: support vector machine regression versus best linear prediction. Theoretical and Applied Genetics **120**(2), 415–427 (2010). http://dx.doi.org/10.1007/s00122-009-1200-5
12. Morota, G., Gianola, D.: Kernel-based whole-genome prediction of complex traits: a review. Frontiers in Genetics **5** (2014)
13. Moser, G., Tier, B., Crump, R.E., Khatkar, M.S., Raadsma, H.W., et al.: A comparison of five methods to predict genomic breeding values of dairy bulls from genome-wide snp markers. Genet. Sel. Evol. **41**(1), 56 (2009)
14. Neves, H.H., Carvalheiro, R., Queiroz, S.A.: A comparison of statistical methods for genomic selection in a mice population. BMC Genetics **13**(1), 100 (2012). http://dx.doi.org/10.1186/1471-2156-13-100
15. Nunes, J.L., Piquerez, M., Pujadas, L., Armstrong, E., Fernández, A., Lecumberry, F.: Beef quality parameters estimation using ultrasound and color images. BMC Bioinformatics **16**(Suppl. 4), S6 (2015)
16. Prez-Rodrguez, P., Gianola, D., Gonzlez-Camacho, J.M., Crossa, J., Mans, Y., Dreisigacker, S.: Comparison between linear and non-parametric regression models for genome-enabled prediction in wheat. G3: Genes—Genomes—Genetics **2**(12), 1595–1605 (2012). http://www.g3journal.org/content/2/12/1595.abstract
17. Tusell, L., Pérez-Rodríguez, P., Forni, S., Gianola, D.: Model averaging for genome-enabled prediction with reproducing kernel hilbert spaces: a case study with pig litter size and wheat yield. Journal of Animal Breeding and Genetics **131**(2), 105–115 (2014)
18. Visscher, P.M., Brown, M.A., McCarthy, M.I., Yang, J.: Five years of gwas discovery. The American Journal of Human Genetics **90**(1), 7–24 (2012)
19. Yoon, D., Kim, Y.J., Park, T.: Phenotype prediction from genome-wide association studies: application to smoking behaviors. BMC Systems Biology **6**(Suppl. 2), S11 (2012). http://www.biomedcentral.com/1752-0509/6/S2/S11

Classification of Low-Level Atmospheric Structures Based on a Pyramid Representation and a Machine Learning Method

Sebastián Sierra[2], Juan F. Molina[1], Angel Cruz-Roa[2], José Daniel Pabón[1,2,3], Raúl Ramos-Pollán[3], Fabio A. González[2], and Hugo Franco[1]([✉])

[1] Computer Engineering Department, Universidad Central,
110321 Bogotá D.C., Colombia
hfranco@ucentral.edu.co
[2] MindLab Research Group, Universidad Nacional de Colombia,
Ciudad Universitaria, 111321 Bogotá, Colombia
[3] Centre for Supercomputing and Scientific Computing,
Universidad Industrial de Santander, Bucaramanga, Colombia

Abstract. The atmosphere is a highly complex fluid system where multiple intrinsic and extrinsic phenomena superpose at same spatial and temporal dominions and different scales, making its characterization a challenging task. Despite the novel methods for pattern recognition and detection available in the literature, most of climate data analysis and weather forecast rely on the ability of specialized personnel to visually detect atmospheric patterns present in climate data plots. This paper presents a method for classifying low-level wind flow configurations, namely: confluences, difluences, vortices and saddle points. The method combines specialized image features to capture the particular structure of low-level wind flow configurations through a pyramid layout representation and a state-of-the-art machine learning classification method. The method was validated on a set of volumes extracted from climate simulations and manually annotated by experts. The best results into the independent test dataset was 0.81 of average accuracy among the four atmospheric structures.

1 Introduction

The superposition of an intricate set of interactions between air, ocean and land components and states yields both regular (periodic or quasiperiodic) and chaotic patterns at different scales for atmospheric relevant variables –i.e. temperature, pressure, humidity, air velocity, density, chemical composition, etc. The dynamics of such patterns and their corresponding physical manifestations (cloud coverage, winds, rain, hail, snow, etc.) configure a continuous from climate (long time and space atmospheric scales) to weather (in short time scale and local domains).

Behind the specific occurrence of each observable atmospheric pattern, there are several physical processes converging at different spatial and temporal scales, determining their distinctive features. Indeed, the relevant structures for both

A. Pardo and J. Kittler (Eds.): CIARP 2015, LNCS 9423, pp. 19–26, 2015.
DOI: 10.1007/978-3-319-25751-8_3

climate and weather description are a compound of several atmospheric variable configurations present in a particular region at the same time.

Weather forecast is carried out by the coupling of mechanistic models, such as WRF (Weather Research and Forecasting Model [6]) and statistical processing of real data. Furthermore, computer simulations and data acquisition (satellite imagery, weather stations, RADAR) are just the first part of the process: a detailed empirical description from classical meteorological approaches allow specialists to visually detect atmospheric structures and manually track their evolution over time to *qualitatively* describe their dynamics and, then, predict the most probable scenarios according to each particular spatio-temporal configuration obtained [7]. Then, low level structure characterizations of the atmosphere are implicitly carried out by meteorologists on a daily basis, with the aid of computer systems that enhance data visualization (isolines, streamlines, data fusion on scalar and vector fields, etc.).

Moreover, the automatic detection of atmospheric structures, even for *low level* configurations (particularly, fluid flow patterns) is a challenging problem, given the high local and global variability of climatic data, no matter if it comes from experimental measurements or modeling and simulation results. Recent works are still exploring new techniques for structure representation and identification [4].

In the data visualization context, the works of Tzeng and Ma [10] and Gruchalla et al. [3] proposed frameworks for 3D fluid structure extraction and rendering by detecting regions of interests (ROIs) containing such patterns in the wavelet domain. Given that low level fluid structures are expected to have quite regular patterns, Rao et al. [9] presented a region-based detection and extraction method based in phase portraits, where the salient ROIs are those where the geometrical pattern of the vector field best matches the solution of the differential equation associated to the analytic structure description. Even the use of such methods in climate and weather data visualization, state of the art climate data analysis and weather forecast depends mainly on the ability and experience of the specialist to detect patterns constituting relevant atmospheric structures.

This work proposes a machine learning approach to support the automatic detection of such *low level* patterns, specifically those related to wind dynamics. The method takes as input a volume, which includes information of atmospheric variables (temperature, pressure, humidity and air velocity) at a given time in a particular region; next, different features based on divergence and curl differential operators are extracted from the volume represented as a spatial pyramid layout (SPL) and fed to a support vector machine classifier, which has been previously trained with a set of annotated volumes for four classes: confluence, difluence, vortex and saddle point (as it is shown in Figure 1); finally, the classifier outputs a prediction that indicates the probability of the presence of a particular low-level wind flow configuration. The method was evaluated over a set of volumes extracted from climate simulations and manually annotated by expert meteorologists.

The rest of paper is organized as follows: Section 2 explains the details of the proposed classification method. Section 3 describes the experimental evaluation –including the dataset description, the experimental setup and results–. Finally, Section 4 concludes with the main remarks and establishes the future work.

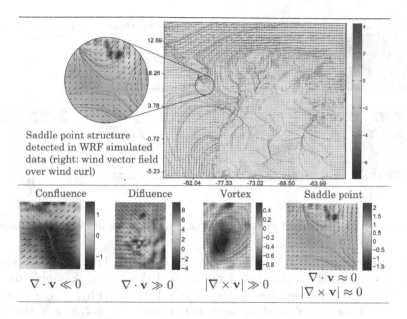

Fig. 1. Representative instances of confluence, difluence, vortex and saddle point wind structures in WRF simulated data for northern South America and the Caribbean. Winds (in m/s) are plotted over this geographical domain and its corresponding latitude and longitude coordinates (upper map) for a spatial resolution of 40 km.

2   Automatic Classification of *Low Level* atmospheric structures

An overview of the method herein proposed is depicted in Figure 2, which starts from a database of *low level* atmospheric structures manually annotated by experts meteorologists. For each annotated sample, an approximation of the differential operators curl and divergence is applied to capture characteristics of the wind velocity vector field into three atmospheric feature maps (curl, divergence, negative of divergence). Then, several histogram representations are built at different resolutions following a SPL. The final concatenation of the resulting histograms is used to train a machine learning classifier (support vector machine, SVM, or random forest, RF) to distinguish between four atmospheric structures (vortex, difluence, confluence and saddle point). The prediction is performed using the trained classifier over a particular ROI. The details of each step are presented in the following subsections.

2.1   Approximation of Differential Operators from Wind Velocity Field

Given $\nabla = \left(\frac{\partial}{\partial x}, \frac{\partial}{\partial y} \right)$ and $\mathbf{v} = (u, v)$, a vector field representing two dimensional components of winds *parallel* to Earth surface within an isobaric layer, it is

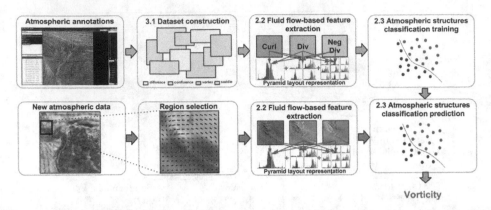

Fig. 2. Overall method description for automatic detection of atmospheric structures.

possible to derive expressions for both *divergence* and *curl* operators, to support further design of a fluid flow-based vector field descriptor. A simple discrete version of a two-dimensional $\mathbf{v}$, is the matrix $V = \{(u,v)_{ij}\}_{M \times N}$ where $i = 1, 2, \ldots, M$ is the index pointing to each row and $j = 1, 2, \ldots, N$ the index pointing to each column of the matrix.

Divergence. The divergence of $\mathbf{v}$ is defined as $\nabla \cdot \mathbf{v} = \frac{\partial u}{\partial x} + \frac{\partial v}{\partial y}$ for the two-dimensional case. Since this is an interior product, divergence is a scalar field. Using the basic centered finite difference approximation to each partial derivative, the 2D divergence can be estimated as $\nabla \cdot \mathbf{v} \approx (u_{i+1,j} - u_{i-1,j})/2h + (v_{i,j+1} - v_{i,j-1})/2h$.

Curl. The curl of a vector field determines how much the vectors within the dominion under study "rotate" around each particular position. In the 2D case, curl is easily build by taking into account only the rotation on the xy plane. Then $\nabla \times \mathbf{v} = \left(\frac{\partial v}{\partial x} - \frac{\partial u}{\partial y} \right) \vec{z}$, which, therefore, is always perpendicular to that plane and can be approximated by $\nabla \times \mathbf{v} \approx (v_{i+1,j} - v_{i-1,j})/2h - (u_{i,j+1} - u_{i,j-1})/2h$.

2.2 Fluid Flow-Based Feature Descriptor

Taking into account that an atmospheric structure can occur in different spatial locations and each phenomenon can have different scales, we propose a set of atmospheric-based feature descriptors able to support translational and scale invariance by using a SPL representation of the region of interest. Over the SPL, we extract features from the differential curl and divergence operators, max-pooling and the histogram of oriented optical flow as explained below.

Spatial Pyramid Layout (SPL) Representation. This representation allows to capture the atmospheric structures in different spatial locations and scales. As it is shown in Figure 3, the image is divided in different regions following a pyramidal layout organization. The first layer of the pyramid corresponds

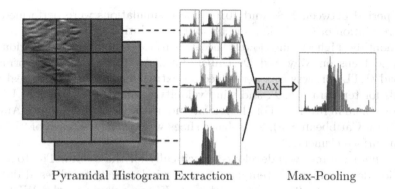

Pyramidal Histogram Extraction   Max-Pooling

Fig. 3. Fluid flow-based feature descriptors. Histograms are extracted in a pyramid layout from the different feature maps. The resulting 14 histograms are further integrated in the max-pooling descriptor, which corresponds to a histogram with the maximum values for all the bins.

to the whole image, the second to a 2×2 division, and the third to a 3×3 division [5]. The image is represented by a concatenation of the resulting 14 normalized histograms for divergence, negative-divergence and curl feature maps.

Max-pooling. The max-pooling works to detect atmospheric structure independently of its location and scale. Max-pooling applies a maximum operator among the 14 histograms of all spatial layouts. This pooling function is typically used for detection tasks exploiting spatial invariances [8].

Histogram of Oriented Optical Flow. As a baseline, we decided to use histograms of oriented optical flow (HOOF) [2] attempting to detect the patterns in the wind flow that better describe each phenomena. Additionally, the SPL was also applied to this image representation.

2.3   Atmospheric Structure Classifier

For automatic prediction of the atmospheric structures, a Support Vector Machine (SVM) classifier and a Random Forest (RF) classifier were trained. For addressing the multiclass problem of classifying the atmospheric structures (vortex, difluence, confluence and saddle points), the SVM uses a one-vs-all strategy. The kernels evaluated for SVM were linear and radial basis function (RBF).

3   Experimental Evaluation

3.1   Atmospheric Structure Dataset Construction

The 4D (3D + time) data used in this study come from WRF regional climate simulations from the climate change study developed by Armenta and Pabón [1] for the period between 1981 and 2010. These simulations were performed at a spatial resolution of $h = 10$ km and temporal resolution of 3 hours.

A monthly highest and lowest ocean surface temperature criterion was applied to focus on May and December data. An Extraction-Transformation and Load (ETL) process was performed to extract and transform to real units 3D fields for temperature, T, and wind velocity components, U, V and W, and then store them in raw files. For the region under study (northern South America and western Caribbean Sea), 27 isobaric slices were extracted, each of 287×280 uniform surface elements.

An annotation tool was developed specifically for these data. The tool loads simulation data and renders temperature and wind velocity for slices at different isobaric levels (up to 27 for each volume). Experts navigate the WRF data using the annotation software by exploring the 3D volumes along a specific time period, and are asked to manually segment the ROI containing one structure and to specify its particular type. The ROI bounding box is then stored in a XML file along with the corresponding class and related information, such as simulation time, isobaric level and divergence and rotational computations on the ROI. The resulting annotated dataset contains 793 annotations, 232 for confluences, 166 for divergences, 177 for saddles and 218 for vortices.

3.2   Experimental Design and Performance Measures

For evaluation purposes, we split the original dataset into two parts for training and testing. The testing dataset comprises a complete and independent 4D data from a simulation of a month with region annotations for all four climate phenomena (vortex = 78, difluence = 47, confluence = 39, saddles = 35). The training set corresponds to remaining simulation 4D data with annotations from four months (vortex = 140, difluence = 119, confluence = 193, saddles = 142). The performance measure used to evaluate the classification was the average accuracy, i.e. the average of the accuracy per class.

For parameter selection, a stratified 5-fold cross-validation scheme was applied over the training dataset for each strategy (combinations of features and classifiers). The same folds distribution was used for all strategies in order to compare them in the same conditions. The parameter combination that obtained the best performance was used to train a model using the whole training dataset. The final performance measure was reported over the independent testing dataset for each strategy for comparison.

The representations evaluated were defined as follows: *pyrHOOF* (baseline) by concatenating the HOOF descriptor for each region obtained from SPL, *histdivcurl* is the concatenation of histogram distribution of the three feature maps of atmospheric operators (curl, divergence and negative divergence), *pyrdivcurl* is the histogram concatenation of the three feature maps for each region obtained from SPL, and *maxpooldivcurl* is the corresponding histogram obtained by applying max-pooling over all concatenated histograms from regions obtained from the SPL.

3.3 Results

Table 1 shows the classification performance of the proposed method evaluated in terms of accuracy for the different representations and classification methods. Notice that these results were obtained from independent data corresponding to a month of simulation. The best performance measure was achieved by the complete SPL representation without max-pooling (*pyrdivcurl*) and using a Support Vector Machine with an RBF kernel obtaining an average accuracy of 0.81. In general, the confluence class shows the highest accuracy for the most configurations whereas saddle point class have the worst performance. Interestingly max-pooling applied over SPL does not help because most of the region annotations are centered in the atmospheric structure. However, preliminary work with larger regions where the atmospheric structure was not at the center, the max-pooling over SPL obtained the best results. Table 1 also shows that performance achieved using SVM with a linear kernel is very close to the reported one using SVM with RBF kernel. Furthermore Random Forest classifiers were trained with 10,000 estimators, indeed during cross validation we could determine that increasing the number of estimators did not improve our results.

Table 1. Classification performance in test dataset in terms of accuracy.

Feature	Classifier	Vortex	Difluence	Confluence	Saddle pt	Avg. Accuracy
pyrdivcurl	SVM-RBF	0.71	0.82	0.92	0.77	0.81
histdivcurl	SVM-RBF	0.69	0.87	0.89	0.6	0.765
maxpooldivcurl	SVM-RBF	0.69	0.87	0.89	0.6	0.765
pyrHOOF	SVM-RBF	0.76	0.87	0.56	0.48	0.672
pyrdivcurl	SVM-Linear	0.74	0.8	0.92	0.71	0.797
histdivcurl	SVM-Linear	0.75	0.78	0.87	0.6	0.753
maxpooldivcurl	SVM-Linear	0.75	0.78	0.87	0.6	0.753
pyrdivcurl	RF	0.73	0.8	0.94	0.6	0.771
maxpooldivcurl	RF	0.69	0.85	0.92	0.51	0.745
histdivcurl	RF	0.69	0.85	0.92	0.45	0.73
pyrHOOF	RF	0.62	0.97	0.58	0.34	0.634

4 Concluding Remarks

This paper presents a successful application of a novel method which combines features based on differential operators and machine learning classifiers to discriminate *low level* wind structures. The feature maps obtained from approximate differential operators help to highlight the relevant atmospheric structures. The SPL show the best classification performance since it includes multi–resolution information, despite the complexity of the structures.

Future work includes to increase the dataset with more annotations of *low level* and new *high level* atmospheric structures, adding more atmospheric variables, enhancing the *low level* structure characterization, as well as to develop a detection method to efficiently analyze whole 4D volumes.

Acknowledgments. This work was funded by project number 1225-569-34920 *"Diseño e implementación de un sistema de cómputo sobre recursos heterogéneos para la identificación de estructuras atmosféricas en predicción climatológica"* through Administrative Department of Science, Technology and Innovation of Colombia (Colciencias). We want to thank Diana Díaz and Darwin Martínez for their valuable hints and discussions.

References

1. Armenta, G., Pabón, J.: Modeling northern South America and Caribbean climate using PRECIS and WRF for climate variability and change studies. In: Proceedings of the CORDEX-LAC1 Workshop - World Climate Research Programme, Lima, Peru (2013)
2. Chaudhry, R., Ravichandran, A., Hager, G., Vidal, R.: Histograms of oriented optical flow and Binet-Cauchy kernels on nonlinear dynamical systems for the recognition of human actions. In: IEEE Conference on Computer Vision and Pattern Recognition, CVPR 2009, pp. 1932–1939, June 2009
3. Gruchalla, K., Rast, M., Bradley, E., Clyne, J., Mininni, P.: Visualization-driven structural and statistical analysis of turbulent flows. In: Adams, N.M., Robardet, C., Siebes, A., Boulicaut, J.-F. (eds.) IDA 2009. LNCS, vol. 5772, pp. 321–332. Springer, Heidelberg (2009)
4. Holmén, V.: Methods for vortex identification. Master's thesis, Lund University (2012)
5. Lazebnik, S., Schmid, C., Ponce, J.: Beyond bags of features: spatial pyramid matching for recognizing natural scene categories. In: 2006 IEEE Computer Society Conference on Computer Vision and Pattern Recognition, vol. 2, pp. 2169–2178 (2006)
6. Michalakes, J., Chen, S., Dudhia, J., Hart, L., Klemp, J., Middlecoff, J., Skamarock, W.: Development of a next generation regional weather research and forecast model. In: Developments in Teracomputing: Proceedings of the Ninth ECMWF Workshop on the Use of High Performance Computing in Meteorology, vol. 1, pp. 269–276. World Scientific (2001)
7. Murphy, A.H.: What is a good forecast? an essay on the nature of goodness in weather forecasting. Weather and Forecasting **8**(2), 281–293 (1993)
8. Nagi, J., Ducatelle, F., Di Caro, G., Ciresan, D., Meier, U., Giusti, A., Nagi, F., Schmidhuber, J., Gambardella, L.: Max-pooling convolutional neural networks for vision-based hand gesture recognition. In: 2011 IEEE International Conference on Signal and Image Processing Applications (ICSIPA), pp. 342–347, November 2011
9. Rao, A.R., Jain, R.C.: Computerized flow field analysis: Oriented texture fields. IEEE Transactions on Pattern Analysis and Machine Intelligence **14**(7), 693–709 (1992)
10. Tzeng, F.Y., Ma, K.L.: Intelligent feature extraction and tracking for visualizing large-scale 4d flow simulations. In: Proceedings of the 2005 ACM/IEEE Conference on Supercomputing, p. 6. IEEE Computer Society (2005)

Inferring Leaf Blade Development from Examples

María Escobar[1], Mary Berdugo[2], Orlando Rangel-Ch[2],
and Francisco Gómez[1]([X])

[1] Computer Science Department, Universidad Central, Bogotá, Colombia
fagomezj@gamil.com
[2] Instituto de Ciencias Naturales, Universidad Nacional, Bogotá, Colombia

Abstract. Morphogenesis is the process by which plant tissues are organized and differentiated to determine the morphological structure of their organs. Understanding leaf blade morphogenesis is a major unsolved challenge in plant sciences. Despite the advances, until now there is no a clear understanding of the physiological mechanisms underlying these morphological changes. In this work, we present a novel automatic approach to infer the geometrical structure of a leaf blade developmental model out of samples of sequences of the leaf development. The main idea is to infer the set of parameters of a non-linear ordinary differential equation model based on relative elementary rates of growth, which better adjusts an empirical leaf blade developmental sequence that was extracted from real images. From the resulting models leaf shape simulations were calculated. These simulations were compared against the 12 real sequences of leaf blade growing. The results show that the proposed method is able properly infer leaf blade parameters of leaf development for a variety of leaf shapes, both in simulated and real sequences.

Keywords: Computational ecology · Leaf morphogenesis modeling · Leaf morphology · Relative growth rate · Dynamic time warping

1 Introduction

Morphogenesis is the process by which plant tissues are organized and differentiated to determine the morphological structure of their organs [2]. The analysis and modeling of plant morphogenesis, and in particular leaf morphogenesis, is a paramount important problem in plant sciences, agriculture, industrial forestry and ecology [4]. A better comprehension of leaf morphology is fundamental to understand plant resilience capacity in response to adverse events, such as, global warming, reductions in the water supply and soil contamination [2,6].

Leaf morphogenesis critically depends on the plant genetic information and metabolic and hormonal regulation [3]. Nevertheless, this process can be severely altered by changes in the environmental conditions and in the supply of substrates and minerals [2]. In general, studies in leaf morphogenesis may require

© Springer International Publishing Switzerland 2015
A. Pardo and J. Kittler (Eds.): CIARP 2015, LNCS 9423, pp. 27–34, 2015.
DOI: 10.1007/978-3-319-25751-8_4

large and complex experimental settings, spanning along extensive time periods [13]. The use of computational models can be a complementary tool suitable for the study to these dynamics in shorter times. In the recent years several models have been proposed to simulate leaf development [7]. These models have shown accurate visual results, however, they are highly dependent of parameters and may lack of biological interpretability. In this paper, we present a novel computational approach to model leaf growing dynamics out of real sample sequences of leaf development. The proposed approach automatically extracts parameters for a model of development, can be used to simulate accurately blade leaf development process and provides a set of biologically interpretable parameters.

2   Background and Related Work

Leaf Morphogenesis. The foliar morphogenesis refers to the set of processes that control the different aspects of the leaf growing [2]. Including, the regulation of the initial grow, the determination of the foliar symmetry, the shape and the definition of the leaf in subregions. The foliar shape is mainly determined by two morphogenetical processes: primary and secondary. The primary one includes the initiation of the lamina, the specification of their different domains (the mid vein, the petiole and the leaf base) and the formation of lamina structures, including, leaflets, lobes and serrations. In the secondary process leaf expansion occurs and specific tissues complete their differentiation [2].

Computational Description of Leaf Growth. Leaf shape may range from simple leaves with elliptical shapes to complex compound leaves with fractal shapes [7]. Because of this large morphological variability understanding of leaf development is still a major unsolved challenge in computational modeling and pattern recognition. Geometry of a biological form results from the growth. Foliar growing can be described in two ways: globally and locally. The first description is based on the idea that forms of related but different organisms can be obtained one from another by changing the coordinate system in which these shapes are expressed. This idea can be computationally implemented by using, for instance, shape deformation and morphing algorithms. These methods have been adapted to model blade leaf growth and development of leaf venation networks [9]. This approach provides consistent visual results, however, it is highly descriptive and it does not provide a biologically interpretable description of the leaf growing. Leaf development can also be described locally by considering how small regions are organized to form more complex objects. In this case, the size and dimensions of the regions can be characterized by using a single number, for example, a growing rate that describe in any moment in space-time the development properties of the unit [7]. This kind of description is commonly used by biologists to study plant development [6].

Geometric modeling of simple leaves was firstly explored by Scholten & Lindenmayer [11]. This model specifies the progression of the leaf shape over time. A similar model was subsequently employed to simulate development of leaf venation patterns [9]. In this case, the complete surface of the leaf blade was propagated across the domain. Branching structures as the ones observed in compound leaves have been also modeled by using recursive structures, based for instance in the L-system formalism [7]. Alternative approaches based on physically based expansion models have been also explored in literature [8]. More recently, the dynamic of morphogens, which controls rate and direction of the organ growth, have been also considered to account for serration patterns commonly observed in leaf borders [3]. These models provide accurate visual results. However, their interpretability in biological terms can be limited.

3   Materials and Methods

The proposed approach is illustrated in figure 1. Firstly, an empirical sequence of the leaf lamina border is extracted out of real samples of the leaf development. Following, a local model of the leaf lamina growing is used to simulate an instance of the leaf growing dynamic, this model is dependent on a set of parameters θ. A cost function $J(\theta)$ that measures the similarity between the empirical sequence and the simulated sequence is computed. Finally, a Monte Carlo based optimization algorithm is used to find the optimal set of parameters θ^* that minimize the cost function.

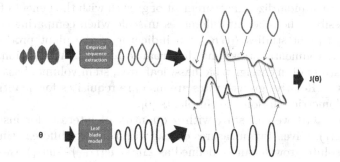

Fig. 1. Proposed approach. An empirical sequence of the leaf lamina border is extracted out of real samples of the leaf development. Following, a local model of the leaf lamina growing is used to simulate an instance of the leaf growing dynamic depending on a set of parameters θ. Finally, a cost function $J(\theta)$ that measures the similarity between the empirical sequence and the simulated sequence is computed.

3.1   Leaves Data and Empirical Sequence Extraction

The sequence of leaf development was sampled for 12 plant species. Each sequence contained 15 different leaf samples organized in an incremental way according to their developmental stage. For each sample in the sequence, foliar lamina was acquired at 300 *ppp* by using desktop scanner (MP250-Canon) [5]. Images were stored in RGB format. Figure 2 shows a sequence of example.

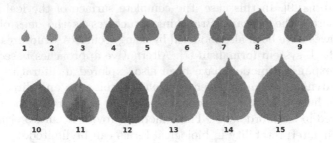

Fig. 2. Example of a leaf development sequence.

The leaf borders were extracted by using binary thresholding and contour tracing algorithms [12]. Spurious regions were removed by using morphological operators. Leaf base for each contour was manually selected. The leaf contours inside a sequence were reoriented to coincide in their basis by using principal component analysis (PCA) and rigid transforms [12].

3.2 Leaf Blade Development Model

To simulate the leaf blade development a relative growth rate (RGR) model was used. RGR is a standardized measurement of growth with the benefit of avoiding, as far as possible, the inherent differences in scale when comparing contrasting organisms. In plant studies RGR is an indicator of the plant productivity as related to environmental stress and disturbance regimes. Applications of RGR include the study of dry weight, biomass, leaf area, stem volume, basal area and stem diameter. Relative growth rates are also pre-requisites for quantifying and modeling allometric relationships in plants [6].

To define RGR we can start with a quantity of interest, for instance, the leaf width $w(t)$. Given two measures of leaf width in two different times t_i and t_{i+1}, the absolute growth can be defined as $\Delta w = w(t_{i+1}) - w(t_i)$, this quantity is dependent on both the time difference $t_{i+1} - t_i$ and the initial size $w(t_{i+1})$. In order to have a growth description independent of these two quantities, the absolute growth can be normalized, i.e., $\frac{\Delta w}{(t_{i+1}-t_i)w(t_i)}$. For instantaneous times, this quantity is called RGR and can be defined at time t as $RGR = \frac{w'(t)}{w(t)}$. RGR is the increase in size of some quantify relative to the size of the quantity present at the start of a given time interval. Different RGR can be specified depending on the growing direction. By using RGR, growth rates can be compared among species and individuals that differ widely in size.

A number of plant growth functions have been proposed in the literature. They are often combinations of power functions and exponential functions [6]. Most functions of relative growth rate have the advantage that they have fewer model parameters than the corresponding functions of absolute growth rate. In this work, we used RGRs proposed by Bilsborough et al [3], which were previously used to model leaf blade growth of *Arabidopsis Thaliana*. In this case, two relative elementary rates of growth ($RERG$) depending on both directions x (lateral) and y (longitudinal) directions are defined as:

$$RERG_x(x,y) = \begin{cases} \alpha_x(1 - \frac{y}{Th_x}) & 0 \leq y < Th_x \\ 0 & otherwise \end{cases} \quad RERG_y(x,y) = \begin{cases} \alpha_y(1 - \frac{y}{Th_y}) & 0 \leq y < Th_y \\ 0 & otherwise \end{cases}$$

where α_x and α_y represent maximum lateral and longitudinal growths, respectively. Th_x and Th_y the longitudinal extents of lateral and longitudinal growth inhibition. $RERG_y(x,y)$ ($RERG_x(x,y)$) are functions that represents the increase in leaf lamina width (length) relative to the size of the width (length) present at the start of a given time interval. Note that these quantities can also be interpreted also as a vector field of RGR. This vector field provides information about the displacement of a wall (i,j) between cells i and j in the transversal direction. This displacement can be obtained from the integration of $RERG_X$ along the x-axis direction $\frac{dx}{dt} = \int_0^x RERG_x(s,y)ds$ with y is the ordinate of the center of the wall between cells i and j. A similar expression can be obtained for displacement for the longitudinal direction, $\frac{dy}{dt} = \int_0^y RERG_y(x,s)ds$. These two integrals can be solved analytically:

$$\frac{dx}{dt} = \begin{cases} \alpha_x(1 - \frac{y}{Th_x})x & 0 \leq y < Th_x \\ 0 & otherwise \end{cases} \quad \frac{dy}{dt} = \begin{cases} \alpha_y(y - \frac{y^2}{2Th_y}) & 0 \leq y < Th_y \\ \alpha_y \frac{Th_y}{2} & otherwise \end{cases}$$

These two equations describe the dynamic of the border displacement. By solving numerically this system a leaf growing instance can be simulated. Note that by choosing a different set of parameters $\theta = (\alpha_x, Th_x, \alpha_y, Th_y)$ a different leaf shape can be obtained. Note that other leaf development models do not account for the REGs parameters. Therefore, this work is focused on REGs based growing models.

3.3   Cost Function

Dynamic Time Warping. As cost function we used dynamic time warping (DTW). This is an algorithm for measuring similarity between two temporal sequences which may vary in time or speed [10]. Suppose we have two time series X and Y^θ not necessarily of the same length, as follows

$$X = x_1, x_2, \ldots, x_n \quad Y^\theta = y_1^\theta, y_2^\theta, \ldots, y_m^\theta$$

here X corresponds to the empirical sequence and Y_θ to the sequence of development obtained by using the blade development model described in section 3.2. To align both sequences first a local dissimilarity function $d(i,j)$ between the empirical blade border x_i and the simulated blade border y_j^θ is computed. Using these distances a matrix distance with $n \times m$ can be constructed. To find the best match between these two sequences a warping path can be defined. A warping path W is a set of elements that defines a mapping between X and Y^θ. The k-th element of W is defined as $w_k = (i,j)_k$, therefore W can be written as $W = w_1, w_2, \ldots, w_K$, $\max(m,n) \leq K < n+m+1$. The warping path is subject

to different constraints, namely, boundary conditions, continuity and monoticity. Boundary conditions refers to the fact that W should start and finish in
the diagonally opposite corner cells of the distance matrix, i.e., $w_1 = (1,1)$ and
$w_K = (n, m)$. Continuity restricts the allowable steps in the warping path to
adjacent cells (including diagonally adjacent cells), i.e., given $w = (a, b)$ then
$w_{k-1} = (a', b')$ where $(a - a') \leq 1$ and $(b - b') \leq 1$. Monoticity forces the
points in W to be monotonically spaced in time, i.e., given $w_k = (a, b)$ then
$w_{k-1} = (a', b')$ where $aa' \geq 0$ and $b - b' \geq 0$. Figure 3 illustrates a path W that
satisfies the above conditions. Given these conditions, we are interested in the
warping that minimizes the following warping costs:

$$DTW(X, Y^\theta) = \min \left\{ \sqrt{\sum_{k=1}^{K} w_k} / K \right\} \tag{1}$$

the K in the denominator compensate warping paths that may have different lengths. An efficient solution to problem 1 can be found by computing the
cumulative distance $\gamma(i, j)$ between cells i and j. This distance can be defined
recursively as the distance $d(i, j)$ found in the current cell and the minimum of
the cumulative distances of the adjacent elements $\gamma(i, j) = d(x_i, y_j^\theta) + \min\{\gamma(i -
1, j - 1), \gamma(i - 1, j), \gamma(i, j - 1)\}$. This problem can be solved by using dynamic
programming [10], the path W can be reconstructed by using a backtracking
algorithm.

To compute the local dissimilarity function $d(i, j)$ we reparametrized both
curves x_i and y_j^θ to have 200 points equally spaced by using a linear interpolation. Following we defined the distance as the Frobenious norm between the
corresponding reparametrized point sequences.

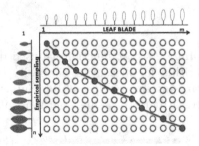

Fig. 3. Distance time warping.

Monte Carlo Optimization. In order to find the set of model parameters $\theta*$
associated to the data the following optimization problem $\theta^* = \arg\min_\theta J(\theta) =$
$\arg\min_\theta DTW(X, Y^\theta)$. Because of the non-linear nature of the blade development
model herein used a Monte Carlo optimization method was used to find the
optimal set of parameters θ^* [1]. In particular, we used Simulated annealing

Fig. 4. Inferred sequences (blue) for an empirical sequences of leaf development (green).

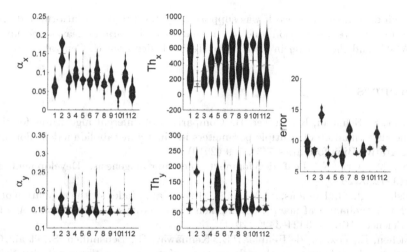

Fig. 5. Distribution plots of the inferred model parameters $(\alpha_x, Th_x, \alpha_y, Th_y)$ and the corresponding error (value of DTW) distribution for each leaf development sequence considered. Red lines indicate mean and standard deviations.

with 100 iterations. For the optimization, model parameters ranged uniformly between 0.01 and 0.18 for α_x, 100 and 700 for th_x, 0.14, 0.25 for α_y and 60 and 250 for th_y. To probe stability of the proposed method this experiment was repeated 30 times.

4   Results

Figure 4 shows three simulated sequences for three examples of the leaf development process. As observed, the method was able to properly infer the general developmental structure for the first two sequences. In the third sequence, the training sequence (green) does not reflect the leaf growing dynamic affecting the algorithm performance. Figure 5 shows the distribution of the model parameters estimated for the 12 development sequences (x-axis) for 30 runs. The proposed strategy provided different and stable parameter estimations for all the parameters. Interestingly, sequences 3 (last sequence of figure 4), 7 and 11 where the training samples do not reflect the leaf growing resulted in a higher approximation errors.

5 Conclusions

We have introduced a method to infer the geometrical structure of a leaf blade developmental model out of samples of sequences of the leaf development out of real leaf samples. The method is based on a non-linear ordinary differential equation model of relative elementary rates of growth. Experimental results indicate that the proposed method is able to extract stable parameters that may properly reconstruct the dynamic of the leaf growing.

Acknowledgments. This work was supported by the projects Platform and Architecture for the representation and data analytics of Páramo leaves morhpology (PARAMO) and the Cluster in Convergent Technologies from U. Central.

References

1. Baker, S., Schallau, K., Junker, B.: Comparison of different algorithms for simultaneous estimation of multiple parameters in kinetic metabolic models. Journal of Integrative Bioinformatics **7**(3), 1–9 (2010)
2. Bar, M., Ori, N.: Leaf development and morphogenesis. Development **141**, 4219–4230 (2014)
3. Bilsborough, G., Runions, A., Michalis, M.B., et al.: Model for the regulation of arabidopsis thaliana leaf margin development. Proceedings of the National Academy of Sciences **108**(8), 3424–3429 (2011)
4. Kuchen, E., Fox, S., de Reuille, P.B., Kennaway, R., Bensmihen, S., et al.: Generation of leaf shape through early patterns of growth and tissue polarity. Science Signalling **335**(6072), 1092 (2012)
5. O'Neal, M., Landis, D., Isaacs, R.: An inexpensive, accurate method for measuring leaf area and defoliation through digital image analysis. Journal of Economic Entomology **95**(6), 1190–1194 (2002)
6. Pommerening, A., Muszta, A.: Methods of modelling relative growth rate. Forest Ecosystems **2**(1), 5 (2015)
7. Prusinkiewicz, P., Runions, A.: Computational models of plant development and form. New Phytologist **193**(3), 549–569 (2012)
8. Rolland, A., Bangham, J., Coen, E.: Growth dynamics underlying petal shape and asymmetry. Nature **422**, 161–163 (2003)
9. Runions, A., Fuhrer, M., Lane, B., et al.: Modeling and visualization of leaf venation patterns. ACM Trans. Graph. **24**(3), 702–711 (2005)
10. Sakoe, H., Chiba, S.: Dynamic programming algorithm optimization for spoken word recognition. IEEE Trans. on Acoust., Speech, and Signal Process. **26**, 43–49 (1978)
11. Scholten, H., Lindermayer, L.: A mathematical model for the laminar development of simple leaves. In: Morphologie-Anatomie und Systematic der Pflanzen, Waegeman, Ninove, Belgium, pp. 29–37 (1981)
12. Szeliski, R.: Computer Vision: Algorithms and Applications, 1st edn. Springer-Verlag New York Inc., New York (2010)
13. Walch-Liu, P., Neumann, G., Bangeerth, F., Engels, C.: Rapid effects of nitrogen form on leaf morphogenesis in tobacco. Journal of Experimental Botanic **51**(343), 227–237 (2000)

Human Skin Segmentation Improved by Texture Energy Under Superpixels

Anderson Santos[(✉)] and Helio Pedrini

Institute of Computing, University of Campinas, Campinas, SP 13083-852, Brazil
acarlos@liv.ic.unicamp.br

Abstract. Several applications demand the segmentation of images in skin and non-skin regions, such as face recognition, hand gesture detection, nudity recognition, among others. Human skin detection is still a challenging task and, although color attribute is a very important clue, it usually generates high rate of false positives. This work proposes and analyzes a skin segmentation method improved by texture energy. Experimental results on a challenging public data set demonstrate significant improvement of the proposed skin segmentation method over color-based state-of-the-art approaches.

Keywords: Skin segmentation · Texture energy · Superpixels

1 Introduction

Several applications require the detection of human skin regions in digital images, such as gesture analysis [17], face detection [4,7], nudity detection [12]. Skin detection can be considered as a binary classification problem, where pixels are assigned to belong to skin or non-skin class.

Human skin segmentation is challenging since it is sensitive to camera properties, illumination conditions, individual appearance such as age, gender and ethnicity, among other factors.

In this work, we propose the use of texture energy to reduce the false positives found by color-based methods. Skin color detection is combined with a skin texture probability to generate a final skin probability map. Experiments conducted on large and challenging data set demonstrate that the proposed method is capable of improving the skin color segmentation approaches available in the literature.

The text is organized as follows. Section 2 briefly reviews some works related to skin detection. Section 3 presents the proposed skin segmentation method based on texture probability. Experiments conducted on public data sets are discussed in Section 4. Finally, Section 5 concludes the paper with final remarks and some directions for future work.

2 Background

Research on skin segmentation is vast, such that the most common is to classify the pixel skin color individually in some color space. Fixed rules over one or

© Springer International Publishing Switzerland 2015
A. Pardo and J. Kittler (Eds.): CIARP 2015, LNCS 9423, pp. 35–42, 2015.
DOI: 10.1007/978-3-319-25751-8_5

more color spaces are the simplest form to define a pixel as skin or non-skin. Sobottka et al. [14] limit the skin to a subsection of the HSV color space. Kovac el al. [7] opt for the RGB space, however, with rules concerning the minimum and maximum values of the channels and their differences. Cheddad et al. [2] propose a transformation of RGB color to a 1-dimensional error signal, where simple low and high threshold values define the skin.

Another approach is to fit a parametric model for the distribution of skin and non-skin color. The most common is to use a single Gaussian [16] or a Gaussian Mixture Model [18]. Jones et al. [5] propose to model both skin ($P(c|skin)$) and non-skin ($P(c|\neg skin)$ in order to define the probability of a pixel as skin given its color (c) to be

$$P(skin|c) = \frac{P(c|skin)P(skin)}{P(c|skin)P(skin) + P(c|\neg skin)P(\neg skin)} \tag{1}$$

as stated by the Bayes' rule.

For a Gaussian Mixture Model, the skin or non-skin prior probability is established as

$$P(c|class) = \sum_{i=1}^{N} w_i \frac{1}{(2\pi)^{\frac{3}{2}}|\Sigma_i|^{\frac{1}{2}}} e^{-\frac{1}{2}(c-\mu_i)^\tau \Sigma_i^{-1}(c-\mu_i)} \tag{2}$$

where c is an RGB color vector, $class$ can be skin or non-skin and the contribution of the i-th Gaussian is determined by a scalar weight w_i, mean vector μ_i, and diagonal covariance matrix Σ_i.

The model can also be achieved in a non-parametric way by histogram density [5], where the prior probabilities are calculated as

$$P(c|class) = \frac{H_{class}(c)}{\sum_{i=1}^{N}(H_{class}(i))} \tag{3}$$

As expected, the color attribute can individually be ambiguous in skin and non-skin regions, referred to as skin-like regions. Thus, these methods usually achieve high rate of false positives. There are some approaches to improving pixel-based methods by adapting the model to particular characteristics of the image through the analysis of the entire image [7,11] or just a part of it, such as detecting a face [3] or precise skin blobs [13]. Region-based methods, such as texture [9], can be applied as a second step and also spatial analysis in the form of interactive segmentation [6,15].

3   Proposed Method

We propose a method for reducing the rate of false positives in skin detection caused by skin-like color. Law's texture energy measure [8] is employed in the

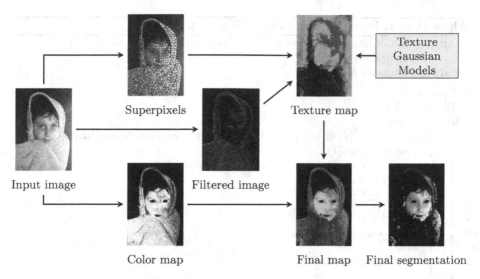

Fig. 1. Main stages of the proposed skin detection method.

process, which works on the response of the intensity image to a special filter mask. The main steps of our skin detection method are illustrated in the flowchart of Figure 1.

The filters defined by Law [8] are built by the product of two vectors obtained from a fixed set of 1D masks designed to detect edges, spots, ripple, among others. A filter is named according to the purpose of the vectors from which it was produced and its size. For example, an E5S5 mask is a 5×5 mask produced by the product of a 1D edge mask and a 1D spot mask. In the following section, we explore the choice of the filter for the proposed method.

To allow the calculation of energy over a region and prevent that the same region covers both skin and non-skin, we use the Simple Linear Iterative Clustering (SLIC) [1] technique for segmenting the image into superpixels (atomic regions, formed by groups of perceptually meaningful pixels). Thus, we calculate the mean energy of each superpixel in the training and test sets.

The goal of the training stage is to obtain two Gaussian models, one for skin and another for non-skin texture energy measures. The images are submitted to superpixels over segmentation and convoluted with a spatial filter. The texture energy is computed for each superpixel, such that mean and standard deviation are extracted for each class (skin and non-skin), forming the two Gaussian models. Algorithm 1 summarizes the training stage.

In the test stage, once the energies of an image have been computed through the same pipeline as in the training step, the skin and non-skin probability densities for each superpixel are obtained. Then, the skin probability given the texture energy is computed in a similar manner to Equation 1, as stated in

---

Algorithm 1. Proposed Skin Texture Training.

---

    input : List of images L, list of ground-truth pixels G, filter mask f, size of
             superpixels sp_size.
    output: Gaussian Models

1 $X_{skin} \leftarrow \emptyset$
2 $X_{\neg skin} \leftarrow \emptyset$
3 **for** $I \in L$ **do**
4      $SP_{list} \leftarrow SLIC(I, sp\_size)$ /* SP_{list} holds the superpixels coordinates */
5      $I_{gray} \leftarrow rgb2gray(I)$
6      $I_f \leftarrow I_{gray} * f$ /* where $*$ denotes a convolution */
7   **for** $x \in SPlist$ **do**
8          $E_\Phi \leftarrow \frac{\sum I_f(x)^2}{length(SP_{list})}$
9   **if** $I(x) \in G$ **then**
10           $X_{skin} \leftarrow \{E_\Phi\}$
11   **else**
12           $X_{\neg skin} \leftarrow \{E_\Phi\}$

13 Compute μ and σ for X_{skin} and $X_{\neg skin}$.
14 **return** $\mu_{skin}, \mu_{\neg skin}, \sigma_{skin}, \sigma_{\neg skin}$

Equation 4

$$P(skin|E_\Phi) = \frac{f(E_\Phi, \mu_{skin}, \sigma_{skin})}{f(E_\Phi, \mu_{skin}, \sigma_{skin}) + f(E_\Phi, \mu_{\neg skin}, \sigma_{\neg skin})} \tag{4}$$

where E_Φ is the energy measure and $f(E_\Phi, \mu_{class}, \sigma_{class})$ is the Gaussian probability density function for the texture energy.

As texture in a face can vary from the rest of the body, the skin probability in the region close to the nose, around the eyes and mouth will be very low. Thus, it is necessary to apply a heuristic to avoid this type of problem. In our work, we perform a postprocessing mechanism, where areas with low probabilities, surrounded by high probabilities, are filled with the mean of these surroundings high probabilities. Finally, the result of this process constitutes the skin texture probability map.

The texture probability map (T_{map}) is combined with a color probability map (C_{map}) through an AND operation, as shown in Equation 5

$$F_{map} = \sqrt{C_{map} \cdot T_{map}} \tag{5}$$

producing the final skin probability map F_{map}.

The color probability map can be calculated from any color skin detector, even binary output methods that produce only probability 0 or 1. At the final stage, the framework outputs a skin map. Thus, the final segmentation can be performed by a simple threshold or a more sophisticated strategy.

4   Experiments

Experiments were conducted on two different data sets to evaluate the proposed methodology. For training, we used 8963 non-skin images and 4666 skin images from the Compaq database [5], which contains images acquired from the Internet in a diverse variety of settings. For evaluation and comparison purposes, we used the ECU database [10] that was divided into 1000 images for validation and 3000 images for test. This ensures a diversity in terms of background scenes, lighting conditions, and skin types. Both data sets contain a manually labeled ground-truth.

The performance of the skin detection method was assessed through a number of metrics: true positive rate (η_{tp} - percentage of skin correctly classified as skin); false positive rate (δ_{fp} - percentage of non-skin classified as skin); F_{score} (harmonic mean between η_{prec} and η_{tp}) and detection error ($\delta_{min} = (1 - \eta_{tp}) + \delta_{fp}$). Additionally, ROC (receiver operating characteristics) curves are computed.

In order to select the filter, we used four 1D vectors:

$$
\begin{array}{lll}
\text{L5 (Level)} & = & [\ \text{-1} \quad 4 \quad 6 \quad 4 \quad 1\ ] \\
\text{E5 (Edge)} & = & [\ \text{-1} \quad \text{-2} \quad 0 \quad 2 \quad 1\ ] \\
\text{S5 (Spot)} & = & [\ \text{-1} \quad 0 \quad 2 \quad 0 \quad 1\ ] \\
\text{R5 (Ripple)} & = & [\ 1 \quad \text{-4} \quad 6 \quad \text{-4} \quad 1\ ]
\end{array}
$$

which generates sixteen 5×5 filters. Each one is convolved with the image; some filters will be just transposed of others, so they are combined to produce only one filter with their mean, resulting in nine features.

From the validation set, we evaluate the gain provided by each feature in relation to the color individually. The filter E5S5/S5E5 produced the best results.

In order to evaluate the proposed method, we selected three widely used skin detectors with different approaches: Cheddad's rule [2] (rule based), Histogram Model [5] (non-parametric) and Gaussian Mixture Model (GMM) [5] (parametric). The Histogram Model was built with 64 bins per channel in the RGB space. For the Gaussian Mixture, we used the 16 kernels trained in the original paper with the same database as used here.

Figure 2 shows comparative ROC curves between the original skin detector and our improvement. It is possible to observe that the proposed method always achieves superior results.

Table 1 shows the result values when considering the closest point to the optimum point (0, 100%) in the ROC curve. For Cheddad's rule, which is a binary method, the tables present isolated point values.

For a more detailed comparison, we provide true positive rate values for a 10% false positive rate in Table 2. In other words, this represents how much of true skin is possible to detect since there is only 10% tolerance for skin-like. In case of the original Cheddad method, we perform a linear approximation preserving the same ratio between η_{tp} and δ_{fp}.

It is worth mentioning that our method always results in higher true positive rates with a considerable advantage over the original approaches.

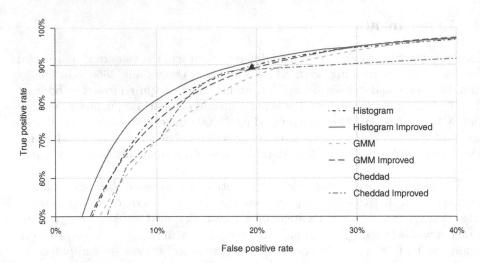

Fig. 2. ROC curve illustrating the results on test data set for the original method and the improvement through our method.

Table 1. Detection results for different methods (ECU data set).

Method	Original				Improved			
	η_{tp} (%)	δ_{fp} (%)	F_{score} (%)	δ_{min} (%)	η_{tp} (%)	δ_{fp} (%)	F_{score} (%)	δ_{min} (%)
Cheddad	89.33	19.51	64.78	30.18	87.32	16.22	67.38	28.90
Gaussian Mixture	87.55	20.30	63.09	32.76	87.37	17.78	65.64	30.41
Histogram Model	87.21	16.54	66.95	29.33	86.96	14.55	**69.17**	**27.59**

Table 2. True positive rates for a fixed value of false positive rate (ECU data set).

Method	$\eta_{tp}(\%)$, $\delta_{fp} = 10\%$	
	Original	Improved
Cheddad	46	71
Gaussian Mixture	70	75
Histogram Model	77	**81**

Figure 3 shows some examples of final segmentation in the tested data set. The first column presents the original image, the second one shows the ground-truth, whereas the remaining columns show the segmentation result for each original method on the left and its corresponding improved segmentation results on the right.

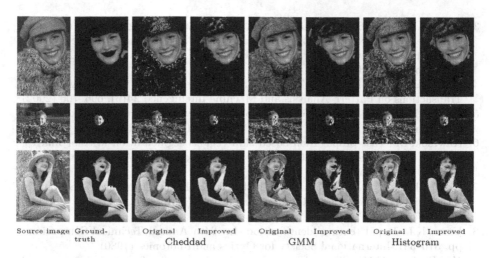

Source image Ground-   Original Improved   Original Improved   Original Improved
              truth   Cheddad   GMM   Histogram

Fig. 3. Examples of skin regions detected through different methods.

5 Conclusions

This work describes a new technique for reducing the high number of false positives in color-based skin segmentation. It can be applied in conjunction with any skin segmentation method, while not adding more sensitive parameters to perform the skin classification.

Experiments conducted on a well-known large test set demonstrated that the proposed technique can provide a significant improvement on the results obtained with different color-based skin detection approaches. Furthermore, the use of texture for skin segmentation is very difficult; although human skin has a distinguishable texture, this can only be noticeable on high resolution images. Age, amount of body hair, expression and pose constitute obstacles in finding a structural pattern for skin.

As directions for future work, we intend to expand the method through multi-resolution analysis to take the variety in terms of image quality and size into account. We also plan to propose a better filter, designed specifically for the skin detection problem.

Acknowledgments. The authors are grateful to FAPESP, CNPq and CAPES for their financial support.

References

1. Achanta, R., Shaji, A., Smith, K., Lucchi, A., Fua, P., Susstrunk, S.: SLIC Superpixels Compared to State-of-the-Art Superpixel Methods. IEEE Transactions on Pattern Analysis and Machine Intelligence **34**(11), 2274–2282 (2012)
2. Cheddad, A., Condell, J., Curran, K., Mc Kevitt, P.: A Skin Tone Detection Algorithm for an Adaptive Approach to Steganography. Signal Processing **89**(12), 2465–2478 (2009)

3. Fritsch, J., Lang, S., Kleinehagenbrock, M., Fink, G.A., Sagerer, G.: Improving adaptive skin color segmentation by incorporating results from face detection. In: 11th IEEE International Workshop on Robot and Human Interactive Communication, pp. 337–343 (2002)
4. Hsu, R.L., Abdel-Mottaleb, M., Jain, A.K.: Face Detection in Color Images. IEEE Transactions on Pattern Analysis and Machine Intelligence 24(5), 696–706 (2002)
5. Jones, M.J., Rehg, J.M.: Statistical Color Models with Application to Skin Detection. International Journal of Computer Vision 46(1), 81–96 (2002)
6. Kawulok, M.: Fast propagation-based skin regions segmentation in color images. In: 10th IEEE International Conference and Workshops on Automatic Face and Gesture Recognition, pp. 1–7 (2013)
7. Kovac, J., Peer, P., Solina, F.: Human skin color clustering for face detection. In: International Conference on Computer as a Tool (Eurocon), vol. 2, pp. 144–148. IEEE, September 2003
8. Laws, K.I.: Rapid texture identification. In: 24th Annual Technical Symposium, pp. 376–381. International Society for Optics and Photonics (1980)
9. Ng, P., Pun, C.M.: Skin color segmentation by texture feature extraction and k-means clustering. In: Third International Conference on Computational Intelligence, Communication Systems and Networks, pp. 213–218. IEEE (2011)
10. Phung, S.L., Bouzerdoum, A., Chai Sr, D.: Skin Segmentation using Color Pixel Classification: Analysis and Comparison. IEEE Transactions on Pattern Analysis and Machine Intelligence 27(1), 148–154 (2005)
11. Phung, S.L., Chai, D., Bouzerdoum, A.: Adaptive skin segmentation in color images. In: International Conference on Multimedia and Expo., vol. 3, pp. III–173 (2003)
12. Platzer, C., Stuetz, M., Lindorfer, M.: Skin sheriff: a machine learning solution for detecting explicit images. In: 2nd International Workshop on Security and Forensics in Communication Systems, pp. 45–56. ACM, New York (2014)
13. Santos, A., Pedrini, H.: A self-adaptation method for human skin segmentation based on seed growing. In: 10th International Conference on Computer Vision Theory and Applications, Berlin, Germany, pp. 455–462, March 2015
14. Sobottka, K., Pitas, I.: A Novel Method for Automatic Face Segmentation, Facial Feature Sxtraction and Tracking. Signal Processing: Image Communication 12(3), 263–281 (1998)
15. Ruiz-del Solar, J., Verschae, R.: Skin detection using neighborhood information. In: Sixth IEEE International Conference on Automatic Face and Gesture Recognition, pp. 463–468. IEEE (2004)
16. Subban, R., Mishra, R.: Human skin segmentation in color images using Gaussian color model. In: Thampi, S.M., Abraham, A., Pal, S.K., Rodriguez, J.M.C. (eds.) Recent Advances in Intelligent Informatics. AISC, vol. 235, pp. 13–21. Springer, Heidelberg (2014)
17. Wachs, J.P., Kölsch, M., Stern, H., Edan, Y.: Vision-based hand-gesture applications. Communications of the ACM 54(2), 60–71 (2011)
18. Yang, M.H., Ahuja, N.: Gaussian mixture model for human skin color and its application in image and video databases. In: SPIE: Storage and Retrieval for Image and Video Databases VII, vol. 3656, pp. 458–466 (1999)

Integrative Functional Analysis Improves Information Retrieval in Breast Cancer

Juan Cruz Rodriguez[✉], Germán González,
Cristobal Fresno, and Elmer A. Fernández[✉]

CONICET-Universidad Católica de Córdoba, Córdoba, Argentina
{jcrodriguez,efernandez}@bdmg.com.ar

Abstract. Gene expression analysis does not end in a list of differentially expressed (DE) genes, but requires a comprehensive functional analysis (FA) of the underlying molecular mechanisms. Gene Set and Singular Enrichment Analysis (GSEA and SEA) over Gene Ontology (GO) are the most used FA approaches. Several statistical methods have been developed and compared in terms of computational efficiency and/or appropriateness. However, none of them were evaluated from a biological point of view or in terms of consistency on information retrieval. In this context, questions regarding "are methods comparable?", "is one of them preferable to the others?", "how sensitive are they to different parameterizations?" All of them are crucial questions to face prior choosing a FA tool and they have not been, up to now, fully addressed.

In this work we evaluate and compare the effect of different methods and parameters from an information retrieval point of view in both GSEA and SEA under GO. Several experiments comparing breast cancer subtypes with known different outcome (i.e. Basal-Like vs. Luminal A) were analyzed. We show that GSEA could lead to very different results according to the used statistic, model and parameters. We also show that GSEA and SEA results are fairly overlapped, indeed they complement each other. Also an integrative framework is proposed to provide complementary and a stable enrichment information according to the analyzed datasets.

1 Introduction

The complexity and heterogeneity of diseases such as cancer reveals that the identification of differentially expressed genes is not enough to decipher the underlying phenomena. A proof of this is the large number of molecular signatures for cancer stratification for the same phenotype with few overlapping genes between them [3]. However, through Functional Analysis (FA) common functionalities have been reported. Functional analysis allows to identify deregulated pathways, biological processes, molecular functions, cellular components, etc. Functional Analysis methods are based on the analysis of gene sets instead of individual ones under the assumption that their coordinated action could be used to infer phenotype association [7]. One of the most used gene sets definition is the one provided by the Gene Ontology (GO) consortium (http://geneontology.org), a popular ontology with controlled

© Springer International Publishing Switzerland 2015
A. Pardo and J. Kittler (Eds.): CIARP 2015, LNCS 9423, pp. 43–50, 2015.
DOI: 10.1007/978-3-319-25751-8_6

vocabulary (molecular functions, biological processes and cellular components) where several genes are associated to each term. This ontology can be interrogated in order to devise which terms might have been affected by the experiment. The most common methods used for FA are Singular and Gene Set Enrichment Analysis (SEA and GSEA respectively). In essence both methodologies try to answer the same question "which are the terms that were affected by the phenotype under consideration?". The main difference between both approaches is that, in SEA, the user should provide a list of differentially expressed genes to test the enrichment of all the terms in the ontology structure. On the other hand, GSEA methods use all the available genes to pursue term enrichment, by means of this it claims to reduce the arbitrariness of selecting a gene list using a "cutoff strategy" [12].

For both approaches several algorithms have been developed, where each author intends to demonstrate or emphasize the superiority of his algorithm over the rest. However, all of the available comparisons rely on the evaluation of statistical performance in terms of appropriateness of the distributional assumptions, p-value estimation, etc., instead of the information retrieval. Questions like "what is being evaluated in GO when using one method or another?", "are these results independent from the method?", "are they complementary?", "are all the method equally useful?" have not been addressed yet in a comprehensive manner. Here, we analyze and compare both SEA and GSEA methods from an information retrieval point of view. The DAVID platform [6] for SEA, and for GSEA both the Subramanian [17] (bGSEA hereafter) and the mGSZ [11] were evaluated under different input parameter options.

2 Methods

In this section we describe: i) FA algorithms, ii) Enrichment consideration criteria, iii) Input data and iv) Consensus analysis.

2.1 Functional Analysis Algorithms

Despite the fact that both SEA and GSEA approaches can potentially be used with any gene set (GS), here we use the GO terms. Every evaluated method presented as output report, at least, the list of enriched/deregulated GS.

Singular Enrichment Analysis
The DAVID web platform (http://david.abcc.ncifcrf.gov) is one of the most used Bioinformatic tool for SEA. The enrichment provided by DAVID is based on Fisher's exact test using a contingency table of DE (not DE) gene vs. in/out the term. Thus, it requires as input, two gene lists: the differentially expressed and the background reference.

Gene set Enrichment Analysis
One of the most used GSEA's strategies is the one proposed by Subramanian et al. [17], which is available at the BROAD Institute website (http://broadinstitute.org).

Here, the enrichment score (ES) is calculated from the rank value of all gene members in the GS. Thus, bGSEA can be feed with both a pre-ranked gene list (from a suitable metric) or the expression matrix in order to rank the genes by means of signal to noise ratio. In this work both strategies were compared. Then the ES is calculated using equation (1):

$$ES(S, i) = \sum_{\substack{g_j \in S \\ j \le i}} \frac{|r_j|^W}{N_R} - \sum_{\substack{g_j \in S \\ j \le i}} \frac{1}{N - N_H}, where\ N_R = \sum_{g_j \in S} |r_j|^W \qquad (1)$$

where S is any gene set, i is the i-th analyzed gene set, g_j is the gene associated to the j-th ranking value r_j of the ordered expression matrix, N_H = #S, N = #genes, , W is a an integer value and ES(S) = max deviation from 0 of (ES(S,i))

In equation (1), W could be set to {0, 1 or 2} thus providing weighted (smoothed) versions of the Kolmogorov-Smirnov (KS) statistic. Then, the significance of the ES statistic is estimated through a permutation strategy over the gene labels or the sample phenotype, and generating a Null distribution of ES to estimate term enrichment p-value. The default option for W is 1, however it is the effect of the other available options is not clear, although software guideline suggest different parameterizations according to data inputs. Here, it was evaluated both permutation strategies as well as the set of W values. Another GSEA method compared here is mGSZ which is claimed to be one of the most appropriate ones, in terms of statistical significance over ES. The method is based on Gene Set Z-scoring function (GSZ) and asymptotic p values using sample and (implicitly) gene permutation thus, requiring to evaluate less permutations.

Ontology Analysis

The GO structure was used to define the GSs. In DAVID platform the GO structure is already included in the database, and as suggested by Fresno et al., we did not limit the size of the GSs. On the contrary, the user needs to input the GSs to bGSEA and mGSZ. We used the *org.Hs.eg.db* R library in order to provide the same GO terms. However, the default options for bGSEA limits the GS size between 15 and 500 genes, whereas, mGSZ only sets the minimum to 6 genes. In order to make a fare comparison, the mGSZ approach was evaluated using its default limits and bGSEA ones.

2.2   Enrichment Consideration Criteria

A term would be considered as enriched according to each author's recommendation (when available):

SEA: p-value <= 0.05
bGSEA phenotype permutation:
     Adjusted False Discovery Rate (FDR) p-value <= 0.25
bGSEA gene   permutation (includes pre-ranked): FDR <= 0.05
mGSZ: p-value <= 0.01

2.3   Input Data

Given the fact that there is no "gold standard", the methods were evaluated on six freely available Breast Cancer (BC) datasets from Bioconductor repository (Table 1). For each dataset, BC identification was carried out using PAM50 algorithm [13] and only the resulting 741 subjects from Luminal A and Basal-Like subtypes were selected for further analysis. These subtypes have very different biological underlying mechanisms, hence it is a priori expected to have many terms enriched. Then, the raw expression matrix of these subjects was built for each dataset. Only the genes with a valid Entrez Gene ID were used.

SEA Input

It has been demonstrated that different lengths of the background reference (BR) list could lead to different results [4]. Here, we evaluate and compare the BR strategies proposed by Fresno et al., and used the genome (BRI) and the reliable genes detected on the experiment (BRIII). In order to automate the query process, the RDAVID-WebService R package [5] was used. The number of genes used in BRIII for each dataset is shown in Table 1.

The second input list is the differentially expressed (DE) genes, which was obtained for each dataset using the treat function from limma R library [15]. The treat method [8] declares a gene as DE if its fold change is significantly (p value < 0.01 in this case) greater to a given fold change (treatLfc). The fold change was chosen in order to provide a gene list length about 5% of the BRIII length (Table 1).

Table 1. Subjects subtype assignation for each dataset

	#Basal	#LumA	#Genes	treatLfc	#DE
Vdx [9, 20]	91	108	13,091	0.75	611 (4.7%)
Nki [18, 19]	70	105	13,108	0.2	568 (4.3%)
Transbig [1]	46	66	13,091	0.6	628 (4.8%)
Upp [10]	34	69	18,528	0.3	932 (5%)
Unt [16]	22	40	18,528	0.25	1059 (5.7%)
Mainz [14]	33	57	13,091	0.45	605 (4.6%)

#: number of subjects, DE stands for differentially expressed genes and treatLfc stands for the absolute log fold-change used in treat function call.

bGSEA Input

Typically bGSEA can be fed with the expression matrix and the sample class label. However, a one column pre-ranked gene list can also be used. In this case, the *treat* with treatLfc=0 was used to assign the statistical p-value (p) for each gene in the dataset. Then, the genes were pre-ranked according to 1-p and -log(p) metrics.

2.4   Consensus Analysis

Since no gold standard exists, for SEA and GSEA results, the enrichment overlap between the different datasets was used as a surrogate index of appropriateness. An enrichment matrix $E^{MxT}=\{e_{ij}\}$ was built, where each column (T) holds for a GO term and each row (M) for a method per dataset combination. Then, each cell e_{ij} of the matrix could be defined as:

$$e_{ij} = \begin{cases} 1 & \text{if GO term}_j \text{ is enriched in } M_i \\ 0 & \text{if GO term}_j \text{ is not enriched in } M_i \\ -1 & \text{if GO term}_j \text{ is not analyzed by } M_i \end{cases}$$

Only the GO terms that were enriched in at least one M_i were kept for consensus analysis. A hierarchical clustering approach was applied on E to group similar enrichment profiles and a heatmap was constructed for visualization purposes.

3   Results

3.1   Overall Analysis

Result integration for the different datasets allow us to provide inter-study validation (i.e., deregulated terms in one dataset might also be deregulated in other datasets) as stated by Edelman et al. [2]. A high variability was found between methods as well as within each method's parameterizations.

The distribution of the number of enriched terms over the different datasets for each method is shown in Fig. 1. The figure shows that bGSEA methods (pre-ranked, gene (gP) and phenotype permutation (pP)) were very sensitive to the weight "W" of equation (1), and also showed very different behavior depending on the method used. For instance, pre-ranked methods (1-p or −log(p)) showed almost no enriched terms when W>0, but for W=0 many terms were present as expected for the biological setting. Both pre-ranking, by means of 1-p or -log(p), enriched the same terms since they provide exactly the same rank order when W=0.

For phenotype permutation with W=0 almost no enriched terms were found as noticed in the pre-ranked case. On the contrary W=2 generates several terms enriched and with very stable results between datasets. In the case of W=1 the median value kept similar to the one of W=2, but a greater variability can be observed. Moreover, only two terms were enriched in common in all datasets. This method also presents the highest extreme value for Nki dataset with 724 and 1058 enriched terms for W=1 and W=2, respectively. The weight effect is inverse for gene permutation, since W=2 produces fewer number of enriched terms and shows greater variability across datasets than using W=0 and W=1. The case with W=0 produces almost the double (565 terms) of enriched terms than W=1, however, only 224 of these terms are commonly enriched in all datasets.

The mGSZ method proved to be very sensitive to GS size. When GS size is limited to [5, ∞] the number of enriched terms double in median as well as in variance their competitor methods. On the other hand, if GS size is limited to [15, 500] the number of enriched terms is very stable through the datasets.

The SEA presents very stable results across the datasets regardless of the chosen reference. Moreover, BRI enriches the same terms as BRIII plus very general (non-specific)3.2 GSs with large number of genes.

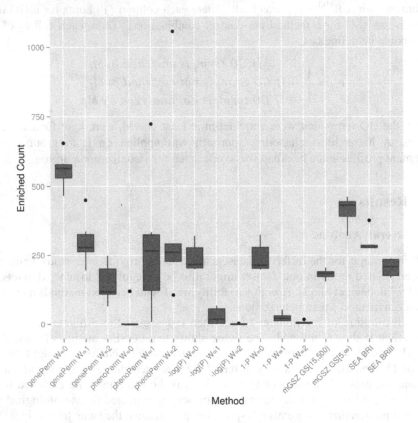

Fig. 1. Boxplots of enrichment count of each method for all datasets.

3.2   Enrichment Comparison

The evidence of the former section suggest that some methods are equivalent or do not provide valid enrichment information. Hence, we dismissed from analysis hereafter the following methods: pre-ranked methods with W>0, gP with W=0 and W=2, pP with W=0 and W=1, SEA with BRI, and mGSZ with GS size of [15, 500]. Heatmap visualization of E matrix is shown in Fig. 2, where dataset and method combinations are clustered by rows and GO terms represented in columns. It can be observed that in each method M_j some terms were not analyzed (in red) but they were analyzed and enriched (yellow) by others. Additionally, high consensus between datasets over each method was observed suggesting the appropriateness of the consensus approach which supports the biological information retrieval approach. The bGSEA strategy shows great enrichment variability (the methods do not cluster together) compared to

SEA and mGSZ over the datasets, suggesting a greater number of spurious enriched terms. On the other hand, SEA and mGSZ methods tend to analyze terms not considered by bGSEA, which seems to provide complementary information (see consensus enrichment columns A, B, C and D in Fig. 2).

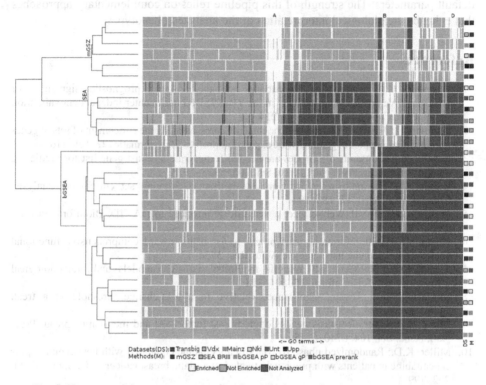

Fig. 2. Heatmap of the consensus matrix of enriched terms for the compared methods.

4   Discussion

A comparison between SEA and GSEA methods was performed from a biological information retrieval perspective. Results suggest that bGSEA is very sensitive to different parameters and data input. For instance, pre-ranked methods with W>0 and phenotype permutation with W=0 almost no terms were enriched for the analyzed datasets. This result is quite unexpected due to the fact that the nature of the BC subtypes under consideration. On the other hand, methods like gene permutation with W=2 and phenotype permutation with W=1 shows great variability in the number of enriched terms. Meanwhile, the number of enriched terms obtained by genotype permutation with W=0 is stable. However, the terms enriched by these last three methods do not show overlap across datasets. From a biological point of view, these methods provide little or contradictory information, and thus their use is discouraged. Moreover, SEA and mGSZ methods enrich not only those GSs that were consistently enriched through all the datasets by bGSEA, but also additional terms that are not considered by this method. Given these considerations, the authors propose to use a pipeline for meta-functional enrichment of gene expression experiments, which consist in the integration of the results obtained with SEA with BRIII and mGSZ with default parameters. The strength of this pipeline relies on complementary approaches that enhance the biological interpretation of the analyzed phenotypes.

References

1. Desmedt, C.: Strong time dependence of the 76-gene prognostic signature for node-negative breast cancer patients in the TRANSBIG multicenter independent validation series. Clin. Cancer Res. **13**, 3207–3214
2. Edelman, E.: Analysis of sample set enrichment scores: assaying the enrichment of sets of genes for individual samples in genome-wide expression profiles. Bioinformatics **22**, 108–116
3. Ein-dor, L.: Thousands of samples are needed to generate a robust gene list for predicting outcome in cancer. Proc. Natl. Acad. Sci. **103**, 5923–5928
4. Fresno, C.: The multi-reference contrast method: facilitating set enrichment analysis. Comput. Biol. Med. **42**, 188–194
5. Fresno, C.: RDAVIDWebService: a versatile R interface to DAVID. Bioinformatics **29**, 2810–2811
6. Huang, D.W.: Bioinformatics enrichment tools: paths toward comprehensive functional analysis of large gene lists. Nucleic Acids Res. **37**, 1–13
7. Maciejewski, H.: Gene set analysis methods: statistical models and methodological differences. Brief. Bioinform. **15**, 504–518
8. McCarthy, D.J.: Testing significance relative to a fold-change threshold in a treat. Bioinformatics **25**, 765–771
9. Minn, A.J.: Lung metastasis genes couple breast tumor size and metastatic spread. Proc. Natl. Acad. Sci. **104**, 6740–6745
10. Miller, K.D.: Randomized phase III trial of capecitabine compared with bevacizumab plus capecitabine in patients with previously treated metastatic breast cancer. J. Clin. Oncol. **23**, 792–799
11. Mishra, P.: Gene set analysis: limitations in popular existing methods and proposed improvements. Bioinformatics **30**, 2747–2756
12. Mootha, V.K.: PGC-1alpha-responsive genes involved in oxidative phosphorylation are coordinately downregulated in human diabetes. Nat. Genet. **34**, 267–273
13. Parker, J.S.: Supervised risk predictor of breast cancer based on intrinsic subtypes. J. Clin. Oncol. **27**, 1160–1167
14. Schmidt, M.: The humoral immune system has a key prognostic impact in node-negative breast cancer. Cancer Res. **68**, 5405–5413
15. Smyth, G.K.: Linear models and empirical bayes methods for assessing differential expression in microarray experiments. Stat. Appl. Genet. Mol. Biol. **3**, 1–25
16. Sotiriou, C.: Gene expression profiling in breast cancer: understanding the molecular basis of histologic grade to improve prognosis. J. Natl. Cancer. Inst. **98**, 262–272
17. Subramanian, A.: Gene set enrichment analysis: A knowledge-based approach for interpreting genome-wide expression profiles. Proc. Natl. Acad. Sci. **102**, 15545–15550
18. Van De Vijver, M.J.: A gene-expression signature as a predictor of survival in breast cancer. N. Engl. J. Med. **347** 1999–2009
19. Van't Veer, L.J.: Gene Expression profiling predicts clinical outcome of breast cancer. Nature **415**, 530–536
20. Wang, Y.: Gene-expression profiles to predict distant metastasis of lymph-node-negative primary breast cancer. Lancet **365**, 671-679

Color Fractal Descriptors for Adaxial Epidermis Texture Classification

André R. Backes[1]([✉]), Jarbas Joaci de Mesquita Sá Junior[2],
and Rosana Marta Kolb[3]

[1] Faculdade de Computação, Universidade Federal de Uberlândia,
Av. João Naves de Ávila, 2121, Uberlândia, MG 38408-100, Brazil
arbackes@yahoo.com.br
[2] Departamento de Engenharia de Computação,
Campus de Sobral - Universidade Federal Do Ceará,
Rua Estanislau Frota, S/N, Centro, Sobral, Ceará 62010-560, Brazil
jarbas_joaci@yahoo.com.br
[3] Departamento de Ciências Biológicas, Faculdade de Ciências E Letras,
Universidade Estadual Paulista, UNESP, Av. Dom Antônio, 2100, Assis, SP
19806-900, Brazil
rosanakolb@hotmail.com

Abstract. The leaves are an important plant organ and source of information for the traditional plant taxonomy. This study proposes a plant
classification approach using the adaxial epidermis tissue, a specific cell
layer that covers the leaf. To accomplish this task, we apply a high
discriminative color texture analysis method based on the Bouligand-
Minkowski fractal dimension. In an experimental comparison, the
success rate obtained by our proposed approach (96.66%) was the highest among all the methods used, demonstrating that the Bouligand-
Minkowski method is very suitable to extract discriminant features from
the adaxial epidermis. Thus, this research can significantly contribute
with other studies on plant classification by using computer vision.

Keywords: Adaxial epidermis tissue · Texture analysis · Color · Fractal
dimension · Bouligand-Minkowski method

1 Introduction

Traditional plant taxonomy cannot neither explore all possible information
sources from plants (for instance, a leaf) nor extract all their discriminative
attributes, such as contour, color and texture. This explains why, in the last
years, there has been an increasing interest in solving problems from this knowledge field by using computer vision approaches. As examples of promising
researches, we have works that aim to extract attributes from leaf contour and
venation [1], the computation of texture signatures from a leaf surface [2], and
the extraction of thickness measures and texture descriptors from various cell
tissues presented in a leaf cross-section [3].

© Springer International Publishing Switzerland 2015
A. Pardo and J. Kittler (Eds.): CIARP 2015, LNCS 9423, pp. 51–58, 2015.
DOI: 10.1007/978-3-319-25751-8_7

Among all the features that can be computed from an image, texture is surely one of the most discriminative and widely studied. Even though texture does not possess a definite concept, it is easily recognized by humans. A suitable definition, yet restricted, is that texture is a model repeated in an exact way or with small changes over a surface [4]. Being texture a great source of information, many methods have been developed to extract signatures from it, such as co-occurrence matrices [5], Gabor filters [6], wavelet descriptors [7], tourist walk [8], local binary patterns (LBP) [9], gravitational models [10], shortest paths in graphs [11] etc.

All these mentioned methods were designed for grayscale textures. However, in recent years, many methods have been developed for color textures to increase the capacity of extracting discriminant signatures. Generally, such methods can be classified into three groups: parallel, sequential and integrative [12]. Parallel approaches consider color and texture as independent phenomena [13]. Sequential approaches divide the process of extracting signatures into two steps: first, the color texture is indexed; then, the indexed image is processed as a grayscale texture [14]. Integrative approaches consider the informative dependency between color and texture [15].

This work aims to contribute to plant taxonomy by applying an integrative state-of-the-art color texture analysis method to a very discriminative leaf tissue called adaxial epidermis. We extend the work proposed in [15], which presented the technique and aimed the classification of synthetic and natural texture. Here we focus on the application of the technique to a biological problem. Textures extracted from biological images do not necessarily present a well-defined pattern, specially in the microscopic scale, where the growing and disposal of cells are influenced by external factors. Thus, this work helps to establish the applicability of this method in biological problems.

Our presentation is organized as follows: Section 2 presents the Bouligand-Minkowski complexity descriptor. Section 3 describes the process of extracting signatures based on fractal errors. Section 4 presents the evaluated image database and the performed experiments. Section 5 shows the obtained results as well as a discussion on them. Finally, Section 6 presents some remarks about this work.

2   Complexity Analysis of Color Textures

A simple and efficient way to estimate the complexity of a shape or texture is through fractal dimension. It is a measurement based on the concept of self-similarity and it describes objects in images in terms of its irregularity and space occupation [15,16].

Among the methods developed throughout the years, the Bouligand-Minkowski method is considered one of the most accurate. This method is able to describe small structural changes in objects due to its great sensitiveness [4,17]. Firstly proposed for shape analysis, this method was extended to texture analysis by mapping the pixels of the image I onto a surface $S \in R^3$ by using the function $f : I(x, y) \to S(x, y, I(x, y))$. Then, each point of the surface is dilated by a sphere of radius r. This results in its influence volume and the Bouligand-Minkowski fractal dimension D is estimated as

$$D = 3 - \lim_{r \to 0} \frac{\log V(r)}{\log r}, \tag{1}$$

where

$$V(r) = \left| \left\{ s' \in R^3 | \exists s \in S : |s - s'| \leq r \right\} \right|, \tag{2}$$

is the influence volume of the surface S dilated using a sphere of radius r.

Usually, we build the surface S from a grayscale image. However, it is possible to map all color channels of a RGB image as different surfaces sharing the same space [15]. Let $I(x, y) = \{R(x, y), G(x, y), B(x, y)\}$ be a RGB color texture. For each color channel $C = \{R, G, B\}$, we are able to compute its respective surface S_C, which can easily be combined to form a single volume $S_{RGB} \in R^3$, as shown in Figure 1. Then, we apply the dilation process over this new volume. The influence volume computed from S_{RGB} enables us to explore how the channels are related to each other, thus taking into consideration the correlations among them and not only the characteristics of a single one.

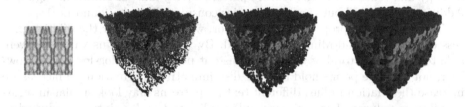

Fig. 1. From left to right: Original image; Computed surface S_{RGB} (each pixel is converted to a point in R^3; Surface dilated using $r = 2$ (each point is replaced by a sphere of radius $r = 2$); Surface dilated using $r = 5$ (each point is replaced by a sphere of radius $r = 5$).

3   Error-Based Fractal Signature

When we compute the fractal dimension D from its log-log curve, the information about fine structural changes are lost. The log-log curve presents a great richness of details and a single value computed through line regression is not able to fully represent it. To overcome this problem, we propose a feature vector which describes the error between the computed line regression and the original log-log curve to represent these curve details.

To compute these descriptors, consider a line with slope a and b its y-intercept estimated from log-log curve. Notice that $D = 3 - a$ is the estimated fractal dimension of the image. This line is just an approximation of the real behavior of the curve. To fully represent its characteristics, we propose a feature vector that represents the error e_i between the estimated line and the original curve at a given point i

$$e_i = a \times \log r_i + b - \log V(r_i), \tag{3}$$

From this definition, we create a feature vector which consists of n equidistant radius values selected from the log-log curve, as shown as follows:

$$\psi(n) = [e_1, e_2, \ldots, e_n]. \tag{4}$$

Additional details about the proposed feature vector can be found in the paper [15].

4   Experiments

To accomplish the adaxial epidermis classification, we used a database composed of 30 texture windows acquired from eight different plant species. Figure 2 shows one example for each species in the database. Each texture is 150 pixels height. The width varies from sample to sample as it is determined by the adaxial surface epidermis thickness. As this variation in the width could influence the performance of the method, we adopted a mosaic of 150×150 pixels size produced by copy and reflection of the texture pattern over y axis, as shown in Figure 3. Additional details about the plant species considered can be found in [18].

To compute the proposed feature vector, we used $r = 8$ for the dilation process of the Bouligand-Minkowski method. By using this radius value, we were able to compute a total of $n = 77$ equidistant points of the log-log curve. However, not all these points hold relevant discriminative information. In fact, as we increase the dilation radius, different texture patterns may look similar in terms of influence volume. The same principle applies to the descriptors computed at this range of radius values. Thus, we evaluate the behavior of the success rate as we increase the number of descriptors used (Figure 4). In general, the success rate increases as the number of descriptors n increases, achieving its maximum at $n = 46$. For $n > 46$, we notice the occurrence of a subtle, but constant, degradation of the discrimination ability of the proposed feature vector. This is due to the similarities in the influence volume. We evaluated the computed feature vectors using Linear Discriminant Analysis (LDA), a supervised statistical classification method, in a *leave-one-out cross-validation* scheme [19].

5   Results and Discussion

Table 1 presents the comparison between our proposed approach and other important color texture analysis methods. The obtained results clearly demonstrate the superior performance of the error-based fractal signature, as it provides the highest success rate (96.66%), with a difference of 0.41% when compared to the second best method. Although it seems a small advantage, it is necessary to take into account that both methods are very close to 100% of success rate, and,

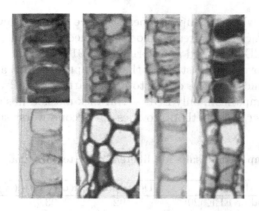

Fig. 2. Adaxial epidermis images of the eight species considered.

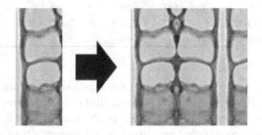

Fig. 3. Process of building a texture mosaic by copy and reflection.

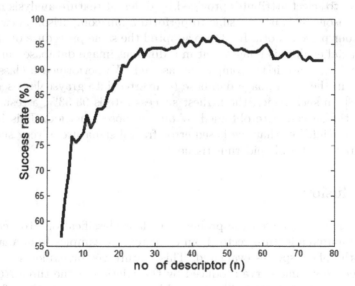

Fig. 4. Classification accuracy observed for different numbers of descriptors (n).

in such condition, whatever superior performance is very relevant. This is corroborated by the fact that three methods obtained less than 90.00% of success rate and Gabor EEE presented a performance 2.91% inferior when compared to our method. Moreover, we must stress that our approach has a small number of attributes (46), which is $7,2\%$ of the total of features used by the second best method. In this comparison, only LBP + Haralick method has a smaller number of features. However, this method provides the second worst success rate.

Table 1. Comparison results for different color texture analysis methods.

Methods	Descriptors	Success rate (%)
Gabor EEE [20]	192	93.75
HRF [21]	-	45.42
MultiLayer CCR [22]	640	96.25
LBP + Haralick [14]	10	84.58
MSD [23]	72	85.83
Proposed approach	46	96.66

We expected to compare our results on adaxial epidermis tissue to other works in literature. However, we were able to find only our three previous papers related to computer vision applied to this problem. This lack of related works confirms that this is a very recent and unexplored research topic. In [24], we used the same eight plant species, but only ten samples per class and Jeffries-Matusita distance [25] to select attributes provided by different texture analysis methods. For these reasons, it is not possible to perform a fair comparison between such paper and our present work. In [3], we adopted the same procedure of the paper [24] for adaxial epidermis images, but in a different image database, and, therefore, we could not use it for comparison as well. We performed a classification experiment in the same image database (converted into grayscale) used in this work in [18]. In such paper, the highest success rate is 93.33%, a result $3,33\%$ inferior to the success rate obtained by our proposed method. This increased performance reinforces that the based-error fractal signature is very suitable to discriminate the adaxial epidermis tissue.

6   Conclusion

In this paper, we addressed the problem of plant classification. To accomplish this, we computed a feature vector from color texture samples from adaxial epidermis of the plant species evaluated. This feature vector explores the details in the influence volume curve produced by the dilation of the three RGB color channels in a single step. Such dilation enables us to incorporate the information about the relationship between channels to the feature vector, thus improving its discrimination power. The comparison of these features with other color texture analysis methods shows that our approach achieves the highest classification results. Moreover, it uses fewer descriptors than methods with similar classification results, corroborating its great ability to discriminate different color patterns.

Acknowledgments. André R. Backes gratefully acknowledges the financial support of CNPq (National Council for Scientific and Technological Development, Brazil) (Grant #301558/2012-4), FAPEMIG and PROPP-UFU. Jarbas Joaci de Mesquita Sá Junior gratefully acknowledges the financial support of FUNCAP.

References

1. Plotze, R.O., Pádua, J.G., Falvo, M., Bernacci, L.C., Oliveira, G.C.X., Vieira, M.L.C., Bruno, O.M.: Leaf shape analysis using the multiscale Minkowski fractal dimension, a new morphometric method: a study with Passiflora. (Passifloraceae). Canadian Journal of Botany - Revue Canadienne de Botanique **83**(3), 287–301 (2005)
2. Casanova, D., Junior, J.J.M.S., Bruno, O.M.: Plant leaf identification using Gabor wavelets. International Journal of Imaging Systems and Technology **19**(1), 236–243 (2009)
3. Sá Junior, J.J.M., Rossatto, D.R., Kolb, R.M., Bruno, O.M.: A computer vision approach to quantify leaf anatomical plasticity: a case study on Gochnatia polymorpha (Less.) Cabrera. Ecological Informatics **15**, 34–43 (2013)
4. Backes, A.R., Casanova, D., Bruno, O.M.: Plant leaf identification based on volumetric fractal dimension. IJPRAI **23**(6), 1145–1160 (2009)
5. Haralick, R.M.: Statistical and structural approaches to texture. Proc. IEEE **67**(5), 786–804 (1979)
6. Manjunath, B.S., Ma, W.Y.: Texture features for browsing and retrieval of image data. IEEE Trans. Pattern Anal. Mach. Intell **18**(8), 837–842 (1996)
7. Laine, A., Fan, J.: Texture classification by wavelet packet signatures. IEEE Transactions on Pattern Analysis and Machine Intelligence **15**(11), 1186–1191 (1993)
8. Backes, A.R., Gonçalves, W.N., Martinez, A.S., Bruno, O.M.: Texture analysis and classification using deterministic tourist walk. Pattern Recognition **43**(3), 685–694 (2010)
9. Ojala, T., Pietikainen, M., Maenpaa, T.: Multiresolution gray-scale and rotation invariant texture classification with local binary patterns. IEEE Trans. Pattern Analysis and Machine Intelligence **24**(7), 971–987 (2002)
10. Sá Junior, J.J.M., Backes, A.R.: A simplified gravitational model to analyze texture roughness. Pattern Recognition **45**(2), 732–741 (2012)
11. Sá Junior, J.J.M., Backes, A.R., Cortez, P.C.: Texture analysis and classification using shortest paths in graphs. Pattern Recognition Letters **34**(11), 1314–1319 (2013)
12. Palm, C.: Color texture classification by integrative co-occurrence matrices. Pattern Recognition **37**(5), 965–976 (2004)
13. Drimbarean, A., Whelan, P.F.: Experiments in colour texture analysis. Pattern Recognition Letters **22**(10), 1161–1167 (2001)
14. Porebski, A., Vandenbroucke, N., Macaire, L.: Haralick feature extraction from LBP images for color texture classification. In: Image Processing Theory, Tools and Applications, pp. 1–8 (2008)

15. Backes, A.R., Casanova, D., Bruno, O.M.: Color texture analysis based on fractal descriptors. Pattern Recognition **45**(5), 1984–1992 (2012)
16. Mandelbrot, B.: The fractal geometry of nature. Freeman & Co. (2000)
17. Tricot, C.: Curves and Fractal Dimension. Springer (1995)
18. Backes, A.R., de M. Sá Junior, J.J., Kolb, R.M., Bruno, O.M.: Plant Species identification using multi-scale fractal dimension applied to images of adaxial surface epidermis. In: Jiang, X., Petkov, N. (eds.) CAIP 2009. LNCS, vol. 5702, pp. 680–688. Springer, Heidelberg (2009)
19. Everitt, B.S., Dunn, G.: Applied Multivariate Analysis. 2nd edition edn. Arnold (2001)
20. Hoang, M.A., Geusebroek, J.M., Smeulders, A.W.M.: Color texture measurement and segmentation. Signal Processing **85**(2), 265–275 (2005)
21. Paschos, G., Petrou, M.: Histogram ratio features for color texture classification. Pattern Recognition Letters **24**(1–3), 309–314 (2003)
22. Bianconi, F., Fernández, A., González, E., Caride, D., Calvino, A.: Rotation-invariant colour texture classification through multilayer CCR. Pattern Recognition Letters **30**(8), 765–773 (2009)
23. Liu, G.H., Li, Z., Zhang, L., Xu, Y.: Image retrieval based on micro-structure descriptor. Pattern Recognition **44**(9), 2123–2133 (2011)
24. Sá Junior, J.J.M., Backes, A.R., Rossatto, D.R., Kolb, R.M., Bruno, O.M.: Measuring and analyzing color and texture information in anatomical leaf cross sections: an approach using computer vision to aid plant species identification. Botany **89**(7), 467–479 (2011)
25. Richards, J.A., Jia, X.: Remote Sensing Digital Image Analysis: An Introduction, 3rd edn. Springer-Verlag New York Inc., Secaucus (1999)

A Multiclass Approach for Land-Cover Mapping by Using Multiple Data Sensors

Edemir Ferreira de Andrade Jr.$^{(\boxtimes)}$, Arnaldo de Albuquerque Araújo,
and Jefersson A. dos Santos

Department of Computer Science, Universidade Federal de Minas Gerais (UFMG),
Av. Antônio Carlos, 6627, Pampulha, Belo Horizonte, MG 31270-901, Brazil
{edemirm,arnaldo,jefersson}@dcc.ufmg.br

Abstract. An usual way to acquire information about monitored
objects or areas in earth surface is by using remote sensing images. These
images can be obtained by different types of sensors (e.g., active and
passive) and according to the sensor, distinct properties can be observed
from the specified data. Typically, these sensors are specialized to encode
one or few properties from the object (e.g. spectral and spatial properties), which makes necessary the use of diverse and different sensors to
obtain complementary information. Given the amount of information collected, it is essential to use a suitable technique to combine the different
features. In this work, we propose a new late fusion technique, a majority
voting scheme, which is able to exploit the diversity of different types of
features, extracted from different sensors. The new approach is evaluated
in an urban classification scenario, achieving statistically better results
in comparison with the proposed baselines.

Keywords: Data fusion · Remote sensing · Late fusion · Land-cover

1 Introduction

Over the years, there has been a growing demand for remotely-sensed data. Specific objects of interest are being monitored with earth observation data, for the
most varied applications. Some examples include ecological science [1], hydrologi-
cal science [2], agriculture [3], military [4], and many other applications. Remote
sensing images (RSIs) have been used as a major source of data, particularly
with respect to the creation of thematic maps. This process is usually modeled
as a supervised classification problem where the system needs to learn the patterns of interest provided by the user and assign a class to the rest of the image
regions. In the last few decades, the technological evolution of sensors has provided remote sensing analysis with countless distinct information, e.g., spatial,
spectral, temporal, thermal.

Typically, these sensors are designed to be specialists in obtaining one or
few properties from the earth surface. Therefore, it is necessary the utilization
of diverse and different sensors to gather the most complementary information

© Springer International Publishing Switzerland 2015
A. Pardo and J. Kittler (Eds.): CIARP 2015, LNCS 9423, pp. 59–66, 2015.
DOI: 10.1007/978-3-319-25751-8_8

as possible. In this scenario, it is essential to use a more suitable technique to combine the different features in a effective way. Mura et al. [5] confirmed the benefit of the use of data fusion in the challenges associated with RSI analysis in competitions. They pointed out that it is difficult to conclude which method has the best performance, since it depends on the foundation of the problem and the nature of the data used.

In this work, we propose a new late fusion technique, able to exploit the diversity of these different types of features, extracted from various sensors. Our approach, called *Dynamic Majority Vote*, uses different learning techniques on the extracted features to create base classifiers. Then, it assigns weights to each classifier according to their ability in identifying individual classes. The weights are calculated regarding the confusion matrix of a classifier in a validation set. Our method exploits the specialty of each classifier to solve multiclass problems.

2 Related Work

Despite the recent advances in feature extraction and representation for RSIs, the combination/fusion of these features, especially when they are extracted by different sensors, requires the development of new techniques.

In this context, Li et al. [6] developed a classification technique based on active learning to combine spatial and spectral information. Petitjean et al. [7] proposed an extraction approach to explore the spatiotemporal characteristics for classification in RSIs. Yang et al. [8] presented a system for evaluating the growth of crops using high resolution images from satellites and airplanes.

Ouma et al. [9] and Wang et al. [10] showed approaches that use multi-scale data to identify land use changes. In Ouma et al. [9], the authors presented a multi-scale segmentation technique with a neural network (unsupervised) for analysis of vegetation. Wang et al.[10] in the other hand, proposed an approach to change detection in urban areas. That method is based on the fusion of characteristics from multiple scales through the average pixel of each scale. The result is a new image corresponding to the combination of scales.

More recently, Gharbia et al. [11] made an analysis of fusion techniques images (Intensity-Hue-Saturation (IHS), Brovey Transform (BT), Principle Component Analysis (PCA)) for remote sensing tasks, at pixel level, showing that all techniques have limitations when used individually. They encourage the use of hybrid systems as a solution. Mura et al. [5] analyzed the approaches used in the past nine years of data fusion competition (Data Fusion Contest). The approaches are separated into three main categories: the level of information/pixels, where the data are combined in the way they were extracted; feature level, where the data are extracted and used as entries for a classification model; and the decision level, which uses a combination of different outputs from various sources, to increase the robustness of final decision (using, e.g., a majority vote). After investigated the last challenges, Mura et al. confirmed the benefits of the use of data fusion in the challenges associated with RSI analysis in competitions. In the majority of cases, the frameworks proposed in the literature are projected to deal with a specific scenario or a particular region, using techniques apart of each domain and object, e.g., roofs are checked with shape features, tree and vegetation are discriminated using a vegetation index. However, it is very difficult to conclude what is the best approach, since it depends on the foundation of the problem, the nature of the data used and the source of information utilized.

The proposed method aim at exploiting multi-sensor data in a more general way. We propose a framework based on a supervised learning scheme, dealing with different scenarios, regions and objects, on the creation of thematic maps for the classification task. For that we propose a new approach, at decision level, to handle with an amount of decisions from different classifiers, and combine them for a final decision for each pixel in the thematic map. Contrary to approaches from the literature, our method uses the kappa index [12] as effectiveness measure to compare two classifiers. This fact brings some advantages since kappa index is more robust in dealing with unbalanced training sets.

3   Proposed Method

The proposed method is projected to receive two images from the same place with different domains as input: an image with very high spatial (VHS) resolution and another one with hyperspectral (HS) resolution. Our method is developed for a multiclass mapping scenario. Its main characteristic is to exploit the expertise of each learning approach over each class in order to find the most specialized classifiers. The result of this process is a *dynamic weight matrix*.

Our approach is divided into five main steps: object representation, feature extraction, training, dynamic weight matrix construction, and predicting. Figure 1 illustrates the proposed framework. We detail each step next.

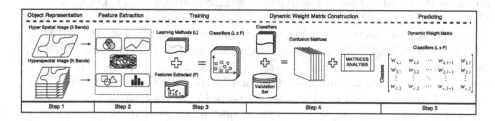

Fig. 1. The Proposed *Dynamic Weight Matrix* (DWM)-based framework

Object Representation. Let Y_R, the set of labels of regions R, be the input dataset, Y_R^t is the training set. In an experimental scenario, $Y_R = Y_R^t \cup Y_R^{t'}$, where $Y_R^{t'}$ is the test set. Let I_{VHS} and I_{HS} be the input images, the first step is to define the objects to be described by the feature extraction algorithms. For the I_{VHS} image, we perform a segmentation process over the regions of Y_R^t in order to split the entire image into more spatially homogeneous objects. It allows the codification of suitable texture features for each part of the image. Due to the low spatial resolution, we consider the pixel as the unique spatial unit for the I_{HS} image.

(a)   (b)

Fig. 2. (a) VHS input image segmented. (b) HS input image with reflectance values.

Anyway, we are more interested in exploiting the spectral signature of each pixel. Figure 2 illustrates the object representation phase for each input image.

Feature Extraction. We use the descriptor definition proposed by Torres et al. [13]. Concerning I_{VHS} image, we have used image descriptors based on visible color and texture information to encode complementary features. For the I_{HS} image, we exploit dimensionality reduction/projection properties from the spectral signature in order to obtain diversity.

Training. Let $Y_R^v \subset Y_R^t$ be a validation set split from the training set. We use the features extracted by each descriptors over the remaining training samples and a set of learning methods to create an amount of classifiers (tuples of descriptor/learning method). We use the obtained classifiers to learn the probability distribution of the training set. Notice that training process requires a mapping between spatial and spectral resolutions, using an interpolation method, since I_{VHS} and I_{HS} images are from different domains.

Dynamic Weight Matrix Construction. Algorithm 1 outlines the proposed steps for the construction of the dynamic weight matrix (W_{dyn}). Let $C = \{c_i \in C, 1 < i \le |C|, i \in \mathbb{N}^*\}$, be a set of trained classifiers c_i over different features from spatial and spectral domains, and evaluated in the Y_R^v. Let $M_C = \{M_i \in M_C, 1 < i \le |C|, i \in \mathbb{N}^*\}$, the set of confusion matrices M_i computed from c_i, be the input of the algorithm. Let $L = \{l_i \in L, 2 < i \le |L|, i \in \mathbb{N}^*\}$, be a set of all classes l_i in the problem. For each l_i, the hits at the class l_i (h_{l_i}) are extracted from M_C, and created a list of pairs (h_{l_i}/c_i) sorted by the h_{l_i} (Line 2), and for every pair (h_{l_i}/c_i) a initial weight is assigned in W_{dyn}, regarding with the position j of the pair (h_{l_i}/c_i) in the sorted list (Line 3-4). In Lines 5-6, the column i of M_i is used to compute: (1) the sparsity S, which indicates the degree of importance of c_i at l_i, given by the ratio of the highest miss value at column i (max_{miss}) and the sum of all predicts, (hits and misses); and (2) the uniform misses expected for each class (m_{exp}), given by the the percentage of misses (p_{miss}) uniformly distributed to the other classes. Finally, at Lines 7-11 the weights of W_{dyn} are updated when the kappa index of c_i (κ_{c_i}) is greater than the mean of all classifiers kappa's index ($\bar{\kappa}$). When S is less than m_{exp}, the weight in W_{dyn} for c_i in l_i is increased and decreased otherwise, regarding with the ratio between κ_{c_i} and $\bar{\kappa}$. The reweight in the W_{dyn} aims to explore the specialty of each classifier in every class, given a gain (or penalty) for those classifiers which

---

Algorithm 1. Construction of the Dynamic Weight Matrix.

1   **Input**: Stack of Confusion Matrices (M_C)
2   **Initializing**: Set $W_{dyn} \leftarrow 0$, individual κ_{c_i} and mean $\bar{\kappa}$ kappa index.
3   **for** each class l_i in L **do**
4   Creating of a sorted list of pairs (h_{l_i}/c_i)
5   **for** every pair (h_{l_i}/c_i) at position j **do**
6   Initial weight in $W_{dyn} \leftarrow (j + 1.0)/|L|$
7   Compute the sparsity $S \leftarrow max_{miss}/(hits + misses)$
8   Compute $m_{exp} \leftarrow p_{miss}/(|L| - 1)$
9   **if** $\kappa_{c_i} > \bar{\kappa}$ **then**
10   **if** $S < 2 * m_{exp}$ **then**
11   Gain at $W_{dyn} \leftarrow (\kappa_{c_i}/\bar{\kappa})*W_{dyn}$
12   **else**
13   Penalty at $W_{dyn} \leftarrow (\bar{\kappa}/\kappa_{c_i})*W_{dyn}$
14   **end for**
15 **end for**

---

show a sparsity (or density) in the predicts by class at the confusion matrix, regarding to the validation set.

Predicting. Once the W_{dyn} is built, the same method of segmentation is used in $Y_R^{t'}$, and the segmented objects are labeled by the classifiers as regions (spatial tuple) or pixel by pixel (spectral tuple) creating a thematic map for each classifier. Once more, since the thematic maps from the I_{HS} image have a different resolution, we apply the same interpolation method as in training phase, to map its outcomes to the spatial resolution domain. Finally, the thematic maps are used as input of the dynamic majority vote technique. We used the weight of each classifier in their respective predicted classes for each labeled pixel in thematic maps with the dynamic weight matrix previously built, and taking the final decision according to the highest final weight class for that pixel in specific. An example of how to use the W_{dyn} is showed in Figure 3.

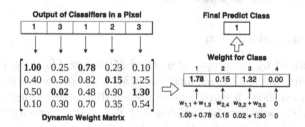

Fig. 3. Given the output of the classifiers in a pixel, the relevance of each prediction is given by the dynamic weight matrix, and chosen the class with the highest final weight.

4 Experiments

4.1 Setup

Dataset. We have used the grss_dfc_2014 [14]. It is an urban classification scenario with two sensors information: (a) Very High Spatial (VHS) resolution; and (2) Hyper Spectral (HS) resolution. **Measures.** We used Overall Accuracy and Kappa index. For the statistical test of significance, we used paired Student t-test (confidence of 95%), with 10 samples for each experiment, since in a statistical way that will still provide the desired confidence for our experiments. **Segmentation.** We used the IFT-Watershed [15] with spatial radius 5 and volume threshold equal to 100. **Feature Extraction.** We used four image descriptors to encode spatial information [16]: BIC, CCV, GCH, and Unser. To extract spectral information, we have used four different approaches: (1) the raw data of HS image (84 Bands), (3) the Fisher Linear Discriminant (FLD) [17] components, (3) the first 3 principal components of PCA [18], and (4) the first 4 PCA components. **Training.** A validation set is split from training set and trained in a Stratified ShuffleSplit cross validation scheme, using a group of 6 weak learners: Gaussian Naive Bayes, k-Nearest Neighbors (3, 5 and 10-Nearest Neighbors), Decision Tree, and a Support Vector Machine with linear kernel, using the features extracted by each descriptors, resulting in the total of 48 classifiers (24 from each domain). We have used the implementation of those learning methods available in the Scikit-Learn Python library. All learning methods were used with default parameters which means we did not optimize them whatsoever. The management of HS data is made using the Spectral Python (SPy) Library, including the extraction of features from spectral domain. We used the Nearest-neighbor interpolation to the mapping in training and predicting phases. **Baselines.** We have implemented a diversity-based fusion framework as proposed by Faria et al. [19], varying the number of classifiers selected, and using the majority vote at the meta learning phase. We setup the framework with 4 different ways: using only the spatial and spectral images, the spatial and spectral images in parallel and fusioning the results, and combining the spatial and spectral domains at the construction of the validation matrix. Refer to [19] for further details about the framework.

4.2 Results and Discussion

The results obtained by the proposed method (*Dynamic Majority Vote*) against the baselines, with the confidence intervals (95%), are presented in Figure 4.

The comparison shows a statistical significant difference among our approach and the baseline proposed at the confidence of 95%, regarding with the t-student test. Since our method is based on the simple majority vote, a special case where all weights in the dynamic weight matrix are equal to 1, was already expected the outperforms results. Our approach has the ability to handle with the issue of instead give to a classifier a fix weight (when used a weight majority vote), assign to each classifier a separated weight for each class predicted. In this way

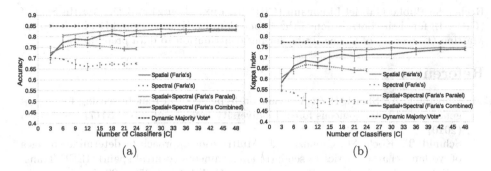

Fig. 4. The results of the proposed approach in comparison with the baselines based on [19], regarding of the accuracy measure in (a) and kappa index in (b).

we exploit these classifiers who have a specialty in some specifics classes, but would be suppressed by the others classifiers in an equal weight scheme.

Another good point in our approach, is the capacity to deal with information from different domains, without being unfair in the weighting, just because the initial weight is assigned without seeing the general performance of the classifier, but only at the specific class. As a drawback, our method do is not handle with the binary classification problem (since the analysis of the sparsity of a classifier with two classes does not make sense), and the initial weight might not be enough to deal with an amount of bad classifiers.

5   Conclusion

In this paper, we proposed a framework called *Dynamic Majority Vote* for remote sensing image classification with data from multiple sensors. Our approach extracts features from different domains, which are trained with different learning techniques. This process creates a set of classifiers with different expertise. Our method assigns a weigh for each classifier according to their expertise in each specific class. The creation of the final thematic maps consists in classifying each non-labeled region by fusioning the predicted output of each classifier according to their weights. We conducted a series of experiments in the grss_dfc_2014 [14] dataset (IEEE GRSS Data Fusion Contest 2014) that demonstrate a significant improvement in comparison with the proposed baselines. For the future work, we intend to extend this framework exploring the use of more descriptors, classifiers, and other late fusions methods. We also plan to test our method with other real scenarios, such as agriculture and environmental monitoring.

Acknowledgments. This work was partially financed by CNPq, CAPES, Fapemig. The authors would like to thank Telops Inc. (Québec, Canada) for acquiring and providing the data used in this study, the IEEE GRSS Image Analysis and Data Fusion Technical Committee and Dr. Michal Shimoni (Signal and Image Centre, Royal Military Academy, Belgium) for organizing the 2014 Data Fusion Contest, the Centre de

Recherche Public Gabriel Lippmann (CRPGL, Luxembourg) and Dr. Martin Schlerf (CRPGL) for their contribution of the Hyper-Cam LWIR sensor, and Dr. Michaela De Martino (University of Genoa, Italy) for her contribution to data preparation.

References

1. Ghiyamat, A., Shafri, H.Z.: A review on hyperspectral remote sensing for homogeneous and heterogeneous forest biodiversity assessment. IJRS **31**(7), 1837–1856 (2010)
2. Schmid, T., Koch, M., Gumuzzio, J.: Multisensor approach to determine changes of wetland characteristics in semiarid environments (central spain). IEEE Transactions on Geoscience and Remote Sensing **43**(11), 2516–2525 (2005)
3. Lanthier, Y., Bannari, A., Haboudane, D., Miller, J.R., Tremblay, N.: Hyperspectral data segmentation and classification in precision agriculture: a multi-scale analysis. In: IGARSS 2008, vol. 2, p. II-585. IEEE (2008)
4. Briottet, X., Boucher, Y., Dimmeler, A., et al.: Military applications of hyperspectral imagery. In: DSS, ISPIE, p. 62390B (2006)
5. Mura, M.D., Prasad, S., Pacifici, F., Gamba, P., Chanussot, J.: Challenges and opportunities of multimodality and data fusion in remote sensing. In: 2013 Proceedings of the 22nd European, EUSIPCO, pp. 106–110. IEEE (2014)
6. Li, J., et al.: Spectral-spatial classification of hyperspectral data using loopy belief propagation and active learning. TGRS on **51**(2), 844–856 (2013)
7. Petitjean, F., Kurtz, C., Passat, N., Gançarski, P.: Spatio-temporal reasoning for the classification of satellite image time series. PRL **33**(13), 1805–1815 (2012)
8. Yang, C., Everitt, J.H., Du, Q., Luo, B., Chanussot, J.: Using high-resolution airborne and satellite imagery to assess crop growth and yield variability for precision agriculture. Proceedings of the IEEE **101**(3), 582–592 (2013)
9. Ouma, Y.O., Josaphat, S., Tateishi, R.: Multiscale remote sensing data segmentation and post-segmentation change detection based on logical modeling: Theoretical exposition and experimental results for forestland cover change analysis. Computers & Geosciences **34**(7), 715–737 (2008)
10. Wang, W.J., Zhao, Z.M., Zhu, H.Q.: Object-oriented change detection method based on multi-scale and multi-feature fusion. In: JURSE, pp. 1–5. IEEE (2009)
11. Gharbia, R., Azar, A.T., Baz, A.E., Hassanien, A.E.: Image fusion techniques in remote sensing. arXiv preprint arXiv:1403.5473 (2014)
12. Congalton, R.G., Green, K.: Assessing the accuracy of remotely sensed data: principles and practices. CRC Press (2008)
13. da Silva Torres, R., Falcão, A.X.: Content-based image retrieval: Theory and applications. RITA **13**(2), 161–185 (2006)
14. 2014 IEEE GRSS Data Fusion Contest. http://www.grss-ieee.org/community/technical-committees/data-fusion/
15. Lotufo, R., Falcao, A., Zampirolli, F.: Ift-watershed from gray-scale marker. In: SIBGRAPI, pp. 146–152 (2002)
16. dos Santos, J.A., Penatti, O.A.B., da Silva Torres, R.: Evaluating the potential of texture and color descriptors for remote sensing image retrieval and classification. In: VISAPP, Angers, France, May 2010
17. Fisher, R.A.: The use of multiple measurements in taxonomic problems. Annals of Eugenics **7**(2), 179–188 (1936)
18. Jolliffe, I.: Principal component analysis. Wiley Online Library (2002)
19. Faria, F.A., Dos Santos, J.A., Rocha, A., Torres, R.D.S.: A framework for selection and fusion of pattern classifiers in multimedia recognition. PRL **39**, 52–64 (2014)

Coffee Crop Recognition Using Multi-scale Convolutional Neural Networks

Keiller Nogueira, William Robson Schwartz, and Jefersson A. dos Santos[✉]

Department of Computer Science,
Universidade Federal de Minas Gerais, Belo Horizonte, Brazil
{keiller.nogueira,william,jefersson}@dcc.ufmg.br

Abstract. Identifying crops from remote sensing images is a fundamental to know and monitor land-use. However, manual identification is expensive and maybe impracticable given the amount data. Automatic methods, although interesting, are highly dependent on the quality of extracted features, since encoding the spatial features in an efficient and robust fashion is the key to generating discriminatory models. Even though many visual descriptors have been proposed or successfully used to encode spatial features, in some cases, more specific description are needed. Deep learning has achieved very good results in some tasks, mainly boosted by the feature learning performed which allows the method to extract specific and adaptable visual features depending on the data In this paper, we propose two multi-scale methods, based on deep learning, to identify coffee crops. Specifically, we propose the Cascade Convolutional Neural Networks, or simply CCNN, that identifies crops considering a hierarchy of networks and, also, propose the Iterative Convolutional Neural Network, called ICNN, which feeds a same network with data several times. We conducted a systematic evaluation of the proposed algorithms using a remote sensing dataset. The experiments show that the proposed methods outperform the baseline consistent of state-of-the-art components by a factor that ranges from 3 to 6%, in terms of average accuracy.

Keywords: Deep learning · Coffee crop · Remote sensing · Feature learning

1 Introduction

The use of Remote Sensing Images (RSIs) as a source of information is very common in several areas, such as agrobusiness. A lot of knowledge can be extracted from these images including geolocation of events (burned forest, for example), productivity forecast, and crop recognition. In this work, we focus on the latter task, specifically, we aim at identifying coffee crops in RSIs.

Considering this kind of plantation, the identification of crops is essential to know and monitor the land-use, helping to define new expansion strategies of the land or to estimate the feasible production amount. Although interesting,

© Springer International Publishing Switzerland 2015
A. Pardo and J. Kittler (Eds.): CIARP 2015, LNCS 9423, pp. 67–74, 2015.
DOI: 10.1007/978-3-319-25751-8_9

recognizing coffee regions in RSIs is not a trivial task. First, because coffee usually grows in mountainous regions, which causes shadows and distortions in the spectral information. Second, the growing of coffee is not a seasonal activity, and, therefore, in the same region, there may be coffee plantations of different ages (high intraclass variance).

The identification process, which, in our case, can be described as locate and classify the crops, is an open problem in the pattern recognition field [5]. The most common strategy uses a combination of segmentation algorithms, visual features extraction techniques and machine learning methods. Some works [6] combine these steps with a multi-scale strategy, resulting in a more robust method. In all these cases, visual features are extracted from regions of a segmented image using some auxiliary method, such as low-level or mid-level one, and, then used with some machine learning approach. Although this method has been successfully applied to RSIs [5], some applications require more specific descriptors. In this way, the neural networks distinguish from other methods, since it can learn specific image features depending on the problem.

As introduced, in this paper, we are particularly interested in identifying coffee crops in RSIs. Therefore, we formulate this task by using a deep learning strategy, i.e., we propose **two** multi-scale methods using Convolutional Neural Network (CNN). First, we propose the **Cascade Convolutional Neural Network**, or simply CCNN, which is, in this case, composed of three network levels that process images with same dimension. Specifically, after every level, unclassified images are decomposed into smaller patches, which are resized into a predefined size and given as input to the subsequent level. The resize step changes the image composition allowing the networks to capture different features at each level. Second, we propose the **Iterative Convolutional Neural Network**, or just ICNN, which has only one neural network that processes the input data three times, being equivalent to the the CCNN method. Actually, after processing the data, unclassified patches are split and resized, going back again into the same network.

Moreover, we are concerned in design a method robust enough to handle real world data (even from different locations), so it can be a useful tool for any activity involving crops recognition around the globe. Thus, the proposed methods were designed and trained using real data of two entire counties, that have distinct image characteristics (mountains, etc). Specifically, the experiments were conducted using one county as training and the other as test.

In practice, we claim the following benefits and contributions over existing solutions: (i) Our main contribution is **two novel algorithms** capable of identify region of interest in real world RSIs using deep learning paradigm, and (ii) a systematic set of experiments, using real world data reveals that our algorithm improves upon a baseline composed of state-of-the-art components, by a factor that ranges from 3% to 6% in terms of average accuracy.

The paper is structured as follows. Related work is presented in Section 2. Section 3 presents the methodology. Experimental protocol as well as obtained results are discussed in Section 4. Finally, in Section 5 we conclude the paper and point promising directions for future work.

2 Related Work

The development of algorithms for spatial extraction information is a hot research topic in the remote sensing community [2], which has been mainly boosted by the recent accessibility of high spatial resolution data provided by new sensor technologies. Even though many visual descriptors have been proposed or successfully used for remote sensing image processing [7], some applications demand more specific description techniques. As an example, very successful low-level descriptors in computer vision applications do not yield suitable results for coffee crop classification, as shown in [7]. Anyway, the general conclusion is that ordinary descriptors can achieve suitable results in most of applications, but not all. However, higher accuracy rates are yielded by the combination of complementary descriptors that exploits late fusion learning techniques. Following this trend, many approaches have been proposed for combination of spatial descriptors [9], including several ones using multi-scale strategy [6,7]. In these approaches, an essential step is extracting the feature at various segmentation scales, which could be expensive, depending on the strategy, since features would need to be extracted from each scale, for example.

However, even the combination of visual descriptors may not achieved satisfactory results and more robust features are needed. In this way, deep learning distinguish from other methods, since it can learn specific image features depending on the problem. Many works have been proposed to learn spatial feature descriptors [13]. Moreover, new effective hyperspectral and spatio-spectral feature descriptors [11] have been developed mainly boosted by the deep learning growth in recently years.

The proposed methods are very different from others in the literature. First, the proposed approach is capable of create a thematic map without any use of auxiliary methods. For the best of our knowledge, there is no other method capable of doing this. Second, as introduced, accuracy is highly dependent on the quality of extracted features. Thus, a method that learns adaptable and specific spatial features based on the images, such as the ones based on deep learning, could exploits better the feasible information available on the data. In this work, we experimentally demonstrate the robustness of our approach by achieving state-of-the-art results in a challenging dataset composed of high resolution remote sensing images.

3 Methodology

In this section, we present the proposed methods for identification of crops. The network architecture is presented first in Section 3.1 while the proposed methods are presented in Section 3.2.

3.1 Network Architecture

To achieve higher discrimination power with deep representations, the final network architecture, presented in Figure 1, is composed of six stacked layers: 3 convolutional (followed by max pooling and Local Response Normalization (LRN)),

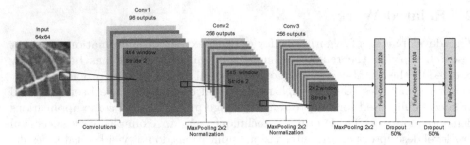

Fig. 1. The proposed Convolution Neural Network architecture with six layers.

2 fully-connected and a final classifier layer. All layers are composed of Rectifier Linear Units (ReLUs). Also, to prevent overfitting, the dropout method [10] was employed. At the end of the network, a softmax was used as classification layer. As mentioned, this architecture was used in both proposed methods, being the base of all the methodology employed in this work, which is presented next.

3.2   Multi-scale Convolutional Neural Network

The first multi-scale method proposed is the **Cascade Convolutional Neural Network model (CCNN)**, which is a hierarchical model composed of three levels[1], that always process tiles of 64×64 pixels, since this is the required input size of the proposed network. As mentioned, the same architecture was employed in all levels but with some differences related to the classification layer and the training data, depending on the level.

Considering the classification layer, in the first two levels, tiles must be classified into three possible classes. A threshold approach, based on the number of coffee pixels of the patch, was employed to select the class of each tile. Thus, a tile could be: (i) coffee, if a patch has, at least, 90% of coffee pixels, (ii) non-coffee, if a patch has, at maximum, 10% of coffee pixels, and mixed (or undefined), otherwise. How the last level must classify the remaining tiles, it has only two possible classes: coffee, patches with at least, 50% of coffee pixels, and non-coffee, otherwise. Considering all available training data, the first level network receive a small amount of patches while the last one is trained with a large amount of data, since between each level a tile is split and resized into a new patch, increasing the amount of available training data for the subsequent level.

Figure 2 presents a overview of the CCNN method. The first level network processes a small amount of tiles and, the ones classified into the mixed class are split into patches of 32×32 pixels, resized, and processed by the second level network. Once more, unclassified tiles are again split into patches of 16×16 pixels and resized. The last level network is responsible to finally classify the remaining tiles. At the end, a class is associated to each tile and a new image may be recomposed, showing the regions of interest, in this case, the coffee crops.

---

[1] In this case, only three network levels were used based on a cost-benefit analysis.

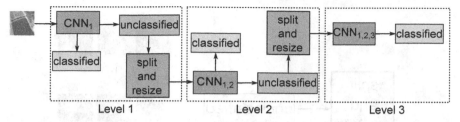

Fig. 2. A overview of the Cascade Convolutional Neural Network model. The subscript number of the convolutional symbolizes the quantity of data available for training each level.

The second method proposed is the **Iterative Convolutional Neural Network (ICNN)**, which has only one neural network that processes the input data three times, being equivalent to the CCNN method. Actually, after processing the data once, unclassified patches are split and resized, going back again into the same network. Just like the CCNN, this method uses the architecture proposed in Section 3.1, trained with all tiles split and resized into 64×64 pixels patches. These patches has three possible classes (coffee, non-coffee and mixed) independent of the iteration. The class of each tile were defined following the same protocol used in the first two levels of the CCNN method. However, by doing this, the last iteration, which must classify all remaining tiles into coffee or non-coffee classes, could classify tiles into a unwanted mixed class. A work around is to change the class of these tiles to the second class with higher probability. Thus, we force the last iteration to classify the remaining tiles, as intended.

A overview of the proposed method is presented in Figure 3a. The first iteration process tiles of 64×64 without resize. Unclassified tiles are split into patches of 32×32 pixels, resized and processed into the same network. The same occurs for the last iteration, which split the tiles into patches of 16×16 pixels, resized and processed, for the last time, into the same network.

4   Experimental Evaluation

In this section, we present the experimental setup and results.

4.1   Setup

Dataset. To evaluate the proposed methods, we used a multispectral high-resolution scene dataset, which is composed of **huge** scenes taken by the SPOT sensor in 2005 over two entire counties in the State of Minas Gerais, Brazil: Guaranésia and Guaxupé. Figure 3 shows some samples of these classes. As mentioned, this dataset was partitioned into tiles of 64×64, 32×32 and 16×16 pixels, generating, for Guaranésia, 21,600, 86,400 and 345,600 tiles, and, for Guaxupé, 17,280, 69,120 and 276,480 regions. Although interesting, this dataset has several challenges, such as: (i) high intraclass variance, caused by different

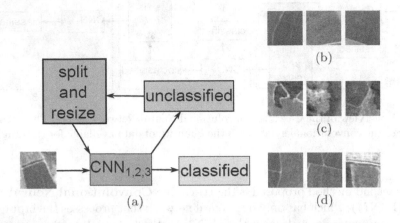

Fig. 3. (a): A overview of the Iterative Convolutional Neural Network model. (b)-(d): Respectively, coffee, non-coffee and mixed samples of the coffee dataset.

crop management techniques, (ii) scenes with different plant ages, since coffee is an evergreen culture and, (iii) images with spectral distortions caused by shadows, since Minas Gerais is a mountainous region.

Baselines. As baseline, we consider the most common strategy that uses a combination of segmentation algorithms, visual features extraction techniques and machine learning methods. In this case, we have used SLIC [1], which has achieving good results for remote sensing images [12]. As visual features, BIC [4], which is the most suitable descriptor to describe coffee crops, as pointed out by [6], was employed. As machine learning technique, RBF-SVM was used. The CCNN paradigm was simulated in the baseline by extracting three different segmentation maps with different granularity.

Experimental Protocol. As introduced, we devised our experiments to evaluate the performance of the proposed methods considering a real world scenario. Thus, the protocol used consider one county for training and other for testing. Since there is much more non-coffee areas than coffee ones, the metric used to evaluate the proposed methods were the average accuracy, which is calculated by averaging the pixel accuracy for each class. The proposed networks were built using Caffe framework [8], since it is more suitable due to its simplicity and support to parallel programming using CUDA. Furthermore, all computational experiments presented were performed on a 64 bits Intel i7 4,960X machine with 3.6GHz of clock, 64 GB of RAM memory and GeForce GTX980. A drawback of deep learning strategy is the large number of parameters, which are, in this case, five different ones: learning rate, weight decay, momentum, maximum iterations and step size (which defines the number of iterations until the learning is divided by a constant value (gamma) equals to 0.1). Select the best value for each parameter, as well as the best network architecture, is totally experimental, which requires a high number of tests and a well-structured protocol. In this case, the networks and its parameters were adjusted by considering a full set of experiments guided by [3]. After all the setup experiments, the best values for the learning rate, weight decay, step size, momentum and max iterations were 0.01, 0.001, 10,000, 0.9 and 30,000, respectively.

4.2 Results and Discussion

For the proposed methods, the processing time, for each county, took around one hour to be completed. At the end, the CCNN method yielded average accuracy around 57% and 63%, for Guaxupé and Guaranésia, respectively. Both results outperforms the baseline by a factor varying from 2 to 6%, in terms of average accuracy. The ICNN method also outperform the baseline, but was less effective than the CCNN approach. However, the baseline is more hand-working, since segments and features need to be extracted first to be, then, used with some machine learning technique, while the proposed methods learns all at once. Furthermore, it is worth to mention that agricultural scenes is very hard to classify since the method must to differentiate among different vegetation [6].

Table 1. Results, in terms of average accuracy (%), of the proposed methods and the baseline for the coffee dataset.

Method	Guaranésia	Guaxupé
SLIC+BIC+SVM-RBF	57.89	55.86
CCNN	**69.33**	**57.98**
ICNN	60.22	56.08

5   Conclusions and Future Work

In this paper, we propose two multi-scale methods based on Convolutional Neural Networks to identifying coffee crops from remote sensing images, considering a real world scenario. Experimental results show that the CCNN method is more effective and robust than all others, achieving state-of-the-art, in terms of average accuracy, for coffee crop identification, considering two entire counties. As future work, we intend to evaluate new datasets and applications. We also consider to use some different strategies, such as fine-tuning.

Acknowledgments. This work was partially financed by Brazilian National Research Council – CNPq (grant 449638/2014-6), the Coordination for the Improvement of Higher Education Personnel – CAPES (DeepEyes Project), the Minas Gerais Research Foundation – FAPEMIG (grants APQ-00768-14 and APQ-00567-14). The authors gratefully acknowledge the support of NVIDIA Corporation with the donation of the GeForce GTX980 GPU used for this research.

References

1. Achanta, R., Shaji, A., Smith, K., Lucchi, A., Fua, P., Susstrunk, S.: Slic superpixels compared to state-of-the-art superpixel methods. IEEE Transactions on Pattern Analysis and Machine Intelligence **34**(11), 2274–2282 (2012)
2. Benediktsson, J., Chanussot, J., Moon, W.: Advances in very-high-resolution remote sensing [scanning the issue] 566–569
3. Bengio, Y.: Practical recommendations for gradient-based training of deep architectures. In: Montavon, G., Orr, G.B., Müller, K.-R. (eds.) Neural Networks: Tricks of the Trade, 2nd edn. LNCS, vol. 7700, 2nd edn, pp. 437–478. Springer, Heidelberg (2012)
4. Stehling, R.O., Nascimento, M.A., Falcao, A.X.: A compact and efficient image retrieval approach based on border/interior pixel classification. In: International Conference on Information and Knowledge Management (2002)
5. dos Santos, J.A., Faria, F.A., Calumby, R.T., Torres, R.S., Lamparelli, R.A.C.: A genetic programming approach for coffee crop recognition. In: IEEE International Geoscience & Remote Sensing Symposium (2010)
6. dos Santos, J.A., Faria, F.A., Torres, R.S., Rocha, A., Gosselin, P.-H., Philipp-Foliguet, S., Falcao, A.: Descriptor correlation analysis for remote sensing image multi-scale classification. In: International Conference on Pattern Recognition, pp. 3078–3081, November 2012
7. dos Santos, J.A., Penatti, O.A.B., Gosselin, P.-H., Falcao, A.X., Philipp-Foliguet, S., Torres, R.S.: Efficient and effective hierarchical feature propagation. IEEE Journal of Selected Topics in Applied Earth Observations and Remote Sensing **7**(12), 4632–4643 (2014)
8. Jia, Y., Shelhamer, E., Donahue, J., Karayev, S., Long, J., Girshick, R., Guadarrama, S., and Darrell, T.: Caffe: Convolutional architecture for fast feature embedding. arXiv preprint arXiv:1408.5093 (2014)
9. Schindler, K.: An overview and comparison of smooth labeling methods for land-cover classification. IEEE Transactions on Geoscience and Remote Sensing **50**(11), 4534–4545 (2012)
10. Srivastava, N., Hinton, G., Krizhevsky, A., Sutskever, I., Salakhutdinov, R.: Dropout: A simple way to prevent neural networks from overfitting. The Journal of Machine Learning Research **15**(1), 1929–1958 (2014)
11. Tuia, D., Flamary, R., Courty, N.: Multiclass feature learning for hyperspectral image classification: Sparse and hierarchical solutions. Journal of Photogrammetry and Remote Sensing 0 (2015)
12. Vargas, J.E., Saito, P.T., Falcao, A.X., de Rezende, P.J., dos Santos, J.A.: Superpixel-based interactive classification of very high resolution images. In: SIBGRAPI Conference on Graphics, Patterns and Images (2014)
13. Zhang, F., Du, B., Zhang, L.: Saliency-guided unsupervised feature learning for scene classification. IEEE Transactions on Geoscience and Remote Sensing **53**(4), 2175–2184 (2015)

A Grading Strategy for Nuclear Pleomorphism in Histopathological Breast Cancer Images Using a Bag of Features (BOF)

Ricardo Moncayo, David Romo-Bucheli, and Eduardo Romero[✉]

CIM@LAB, Universidad Nacional de Colombia,
Carrera 45 No 26-85, Bogotá, Colombia
{ramoncayomar,deromob,edromero}@unal.edu.co
http://cimlaboratory.com/

Abstract. Nuclear pleomorphism is an early breast cancer (BCa) indicator that assesses any nuclear size, shape or chromatin appearance variations. Research involving the ranking by several experts shows that kappa coefficient ranges from 0.3(low) to 0.5 (moderate)[12]. In this work, an automatic grading approach for nuclear pleomorphism is proposed. First, a large nuclei sample is characterized by a multi-scale descriptor that is then assigned to the most similar atom of a previously learned dictionary. An occurrence histogram represents then any Field of View (FoV) in terms of the occurrence of the descriptors with respect to the learned atoms of the dictionary. Finally, a SVM classifier assigns a full pleomorphism grading, between 1 and 3, using the previous histogram. The strategy was evaluated extracting 134 FoV (×20), graded by a pathologist, from 14 BCa slides of 'The Cancer Genome Atlas' (TCGA) database. The obtained precision and recall measures were 0.67 and 0.67.

Keywords: Breast cancer · Histopathology · Biomedical · Nuclear pleomorphism

1 Introduction

Worldwide breast cancer(Bca) is a major cause of women death. In 2012, approximately 522.000 deaths and 1.677.000 new Bca cases were reported [5]. Bca is frequently diagnosed after a suspicious breast mass is found in radiologic studies, by extracting a tissue sample using a fine needle. This sample is analyzed and information about the type of tumor, aggressiveness and receptor status is obtained. The cancer aggressiveness is determined by using one of the available scoring systems. The World Health Organization and the College of American Pathologists endorse the Notthingham grading system. This system assigns and correlates the scores of three features, namely nuclear pleomorphism, mitotic count and tubule formation [4]. This classification provides prognostic and diagnostic information. Both, the biological variability and the pathologist expertise determine the accuracy and reliability of the evaluation performed when assigning the

A. Pardo and J. Kittler (Eds.): CIARP 2015, LNCS 9423, pp. 75–82, 2015.
DOI: 10.1007/978-3-319-25751-8_10

three aforementioned features. There exist many studies reporting low or moderated grading reproducibility: mitotic counts with κ from 0.45 to 0.64 or tubule formation with κ between 0.57 and 0.83. In nuclear pleomorphism, the index agreement (κ) has been reported to be between 0.3 (low) and 0.5($medium$), a very low figure for an important feature in terms of the prognosis [12]. Nuclear pleomorphism serves as an indicator of the cancer evolution and is part of the Nottingham prognostic index [7,8]. Some authors suggest that nuclear morphometry may improve the grading task, but manual quantification is time consuming and impractical in routine diagnostic workflow [14,17]. The expert made a quantitative and qualitative judgment with the epithelial cells, features to be evaluated are: size of nuclei, size of nucleoli, density of chromatin, thickness of nuclear membrane, regularity of nuclear contour, anisonucleosis, then a nuclear pleomorphism grading is give, score ranges from 1 to 3 , in the figure 1 examples the histological images of nuclear pleomorphism are show.

Fig. 1. Nuclear pleomorphism scores. **Left:** Nuclear atypia grade 1. **Center:**, grade 2, **Right:** grade 3

In this paper, an automatic methodology for nuclear pleomorphism grading of breast cancer images is proposed. Unlike other approaches, the proposed method is not based on histomorphometry information such as area, roundness, or texture. Instead, a nuclei detector, a bag of features (BoF) and a multi-scale descriptor are used to characterize the differences among the three nuclear atypia grades. The method is able to learn from a whole FoV, not requiring individual cell annotations. Finally, the BoF representation is used to train a bank of support vector machines (SVM) that assign a pleomorphism grade to a test FoV.

This paper is organized as follows: In Section 2, a brief review of techniques for nuclear atypia (pleomorphism) characterization is presented. Section 3 describes the proposed method. Results of the proposed methodology in the nuclear atypia scoring are presented in Section 4. Finally, we present conclusions and future work on the characterization and feature extraction of nuclear pleomorphism in Section 5.

2   Previous Work

Several algorithms have been proposed to assess nuclear pleomorphism in breast cancer. Automatic nuclear shape and size related measurements are commonly used. Cossato et al. [2] proposed a pleomorphism grading method that starts by

detecting nuclei candidates (related to hematoxylin dye) using a color deconvolution algorithm. Then a 2D difference of gaussians (DoG) is applied to improve
nuclei detection. Each nucleus is segmented by applying an active contour algorithm and outliers are discarded by using some statistical measurements. Morphometric features (such as nuclear area, shape, and texture) are computed for
each segmentation and then used as an input to a SVM classifier to grading each
nucleus between "benign" and "malignant" classes, obtaining a classification performance of 81%. Dalle et al.[3] proposed a similar approach for nuclear pleomorphism grading, but measurements of nucleus roundness(perimeter and area) and
texture were included as features. After computing these features, a multivariate
gaussian model is estimated for each grading score (only atypia grades 2 and 3 were
used). Test images are graded by computing the likelihood of the nuclei grade at a
particular magnification frame. After classifying each nucleus, an overall reported
accuracy error of 7.8% for the classification task. Veta et al.[18] propose a nuclei
segmentation for nuclear pleomorphism method, using a color unmixing process
and only the hematoxylin channel was used. Afterward, the nuclear contours are
found by a fast radial symmetry transform, followed by a post-processing method
to remove regions with not nuclei. Finally the overlapping regions are eliminated.
The sensitivity reported by the method was 0.853.

3 Methodology

An overview of the proposed method is presented in figure 2

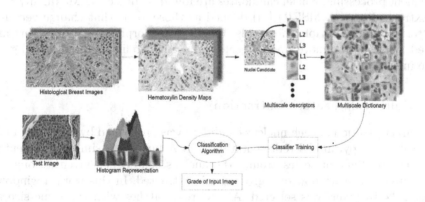

Fig. 2. Diagram of the proposed approach

The first step to detect nuclei candidates is the colour deconvolution in the
H&E image[10]. Then, maximally stable extreme regions (MSER) are used to
identify blobs[11]. Morphological operations, namely opening and closing, are
applied to improve the nuclei detection. A discriminant multi-scale histopathology descriptor [15], centered at each nucleus candidate, is then computed.

The set of selected nuclei descriptors constitutes a dictionary of visual words comprised of samples at different pathological evolution (grading range from 1 to 3 in the nuclear pleomorphism nothingam grading system). The dictionary of visual words is a partition of the space, spanned by the set of collected descriptors or dictionary atoms. Any point of that space may then be represented by a frequential distribution of the basis defined by the partition. The resultant histograms are used to train a bank of binary classifiers or support vector machines (SVM), using the annotated labels associated to the pathological grade of each atom in the dictionary. A new FoV is scored by identifying nuclei candidates that are represented in terms of the dictionary of multiscale nuclei descriptors.

3.1   Candidate Detection Using MSER Descriptors

First, the hematoxylin stain is estimated by using a color deconvolution approach [10]. The process starts by mapping the usual RGB color image to the Optical density space (O_d) using equation 1

$$O_d = -log(I); \quad O_d = VS \rightarrow S = V^{-1}O_d \tag{1}$$

Where I is the RGB color space, O_d is the computed optical density and V, S are matrices of the stain vectors and their saturation, respectively. In the optical density space, the hematoxylin and eosin estimations are modeled by a linear generative model, where two sources are computed.

The hematoxylin contribution map is used in the nuclei detection and the subsequent processing. Nuclei candidates are found by detecting Maximally Stable Extreme Regions (MSER) [11] defined as those areas that change very little after applying multiple thresholds. Finally two morphological operators are applied, opening to remove small objects and closing to fill small holes and gaps in the image.

3.2   Multi-scale Feature Extraction

The characterization of each nucleus candidate was performed by analyzing multiple scales of a pyramidal representation [15]. A nucleus is simply represented by a series of different scales around the nucleus center, i.e., given a point X, a nucleus center, a window of a given size is extracted. In this work a windows size of 16×16 pixels was selected. Afterwards, patches with the same size at lower resolution are obtained by dyadically subsampling the original image after a blurring operation between each scale. These patches are then concatenated for obtaining the feature vector, as depicted in Figure 3.

After collecting a large number of descriptors (equal to the number of nuclei detected in the training set), the space is partitioned with a k-means algorithm [9] using the k-atoms of the dictionary (k was set to 1600 visual words). This dictionary is created with random samples for each grade. The dictionary is thus used to represent each nucleus from any breast cancer at a high magnification

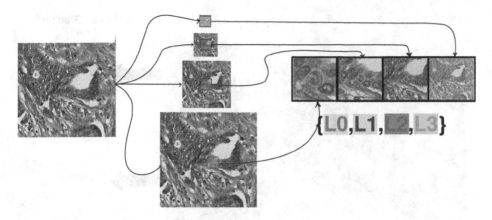

Fig. 3. Multi-Scale Feature Extraction

($\times$ 40), by choosing the most similar atom to a particular nucleus candidate. Then, a feature vector is built by computing a histogram of occurrences, for which each bin stands for each atom of the dictionary. A SVM classifier (with a chi square kernel) is then trained to assign a nuclear pleomorphism grade for a new FoV. SVM classifier with chi square kernel has been extensively used on BoF applications [16].

4   Experimental Setup

4.1   Breast Cancer Dataset

The dataset is comnposed of fourteen(14) breast cancer slides from the TCGA database [13]. The TCGA provides clinical information and the cases were evaluated by different experts since images are provided by 27 different institutions. The associated Nottingham grading to each evaluation is provided (tubule formation, mitotic count, nuclear pleomorphism). Additionally, for each of the database samples, high magnification FoV ($\times$ 20) were selected and graded by an independent expert pathologist. A total of 134 high magnification frames (around 10 FoV per slide) were digitized and the associated nuclear pleomorphism grading was recorded. The Figure 4 shows an example of the dataset: a whole breast cancer Virtual Slide, the manually selected high magnification FoV and the grading assigned by the pathologist.

4.2   Evaluation and Dictionary Setup

The evaluation was carried out using a leave one out scheme, i.e., for a total of 14 cases, 13 were used for training and the remaining one for testing. In this experimentation, the dictionary was initialized by randomly sampling 18 FoV per each grade. After the learning process, the dictionary contains 1600 atoms

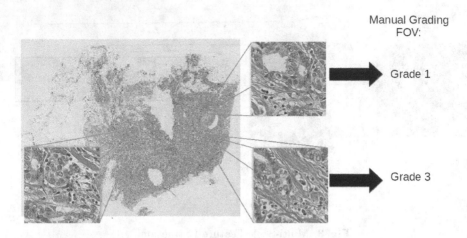

Fig. 4. Breast Cancer Dataset

with 768 dimensions (size patch × scales : 16 × 16 × 3). The SVM classifier was trained by using the multi-scale features extracted from 90 random training images (30 for each grade).

5   Results

The nuclei candidates were processed by extracting three (3) scale levels on a patch size of 16 × 16 pixels. Only the hematoxylin contribution map was used. A set of dictionaries for descriptors of each grade is built and then concatenated. Afterwards a bank of three (3) SVM classifiers was trained. The evaluation was performed as described in section 3.2. The precision, recall and F-measure results with standard deviation (SD) are shown in table 1.

Table 1. Results of Proposed Method. Mean ± standard deviation figures for the precision, recall and f-measure of the nuclear atypia grades are presented.

	grade 1	*grade 2*	*grade 3*	*Mean*
Precision	0.74 ± 0.04	0.58 ± 0.06	0.69 ± 0.03	0.67 ± 0.03
Recall	0.55 ± 0.09	0.62 ± 0.03	0.85 ± 0.04	0.67 ± 0.04
F-measure	0.63 ± 0.06	0.60 ± 0.04	0.76 ± 0.02	0.66 ± 0.04

Atypical grade three (3) obtained larger F-measures. The nuclei related with these grading shows a significant deviation from the shape and size of grade two

(2) and one(1), that is adequately assessed by the proposed method, the intermediate class grade two(2) have the low f-measure.

The Cohen's kappa coefficient (agreement between 2 rater) [1] and the Fleiss' kappa coefficient (multiple rater)[6] were also used to obtain a statistical measure of the agreement between a pathologist, TCGA record diagnosis and the proposed method. The Cohen's kappa coefficient between the TCGA's reported grading and our pathologist was $\kappa = 0.43$(moderate agreement). The kappa coefficient between the proposed method and TCGA diagnosis was $\kappa = 0.51$ (moderate agreement) while the agreement of the proposed method with our pathologist corresponds to $\kappa = 0.31$(fair agreement). Finally, the Fleiss' Kappa was used to establish an agreement among the three raters: the pathologist, the TCGA record and the proposed method. The obtained value was $\kappa = 0.46$ which amounts to a moderate agreement.

6 Conclusion

In this work an automatic method for a complete grading of nuclear pleomorphism in breast cancer images, in accordance to the Nothingham grading system, was proposed. The method does not use morphometric information from manually segmented cells, but builds up a visual dictionary of nuclei that implicitly captures differences in nuclei size and shape, among the different nuclear atypia grades. The descriptor also includes the neighborhood of the nuclei at subsequent lower scales, including context information of the nuclei that is known to be important. Performance measures show that the method is suitable for automatic pleomorphism grading of microscopical FoV.

Future work includes the improvement of candidate nuclei detection and the use of nuclei density information to improve the grading task. Another important topic is the exploration of this representation in the analysis of another potential or recognized diagnostic/prognostic indicators.

References

1. Cohen, J.: A Coefficient of Agreement for Nominal Scales. Educational and Psychological Measurement **20**(1), 37 (1960)
2. Cosatto, E., Miller, M., Graf, H., Meyer, J.: Grading nuclear pleomorphism on histological micrographs, pp. 1–4, December 2008
3. Dalle, J.R., Li, H., Huang, C.H., Leow, W.K., Racoceanu, D., Putti, T.C.: Nuclear pleomorphism scoring by selective cell nuclei detection. In: IEEE Workshop on Applications of Computer Vision Snowbird, Utah, USA (2009)
4. Elston, C.W., Ellis, I.O.: Pathological prognostic factors in breast cancer. I. The value of histological grade in breast cancer: experience from a large study with long-term follow-up. Histopathology 1991; 19; 403–410. Histopathology 41(3a), 151 (2002)

5. Ferlay, J., Soerjomataram, I., Ervik, M., Dikshit, R., Eser, S., Mathers, C., Rebelo, M., Parkin, D., Forman, D., Bray, F.: GLOBOCAN 2012 v1.0, Cancer Incidence and Mortality Worldwide: IARC CancerBase No. 11 (2012). http://globocan.iarc.fr
6. Fleiss, J.: Measuring nominal scale agreement among many raters. Psychological Bulletin **76**(5), 378–382 (1971)
7. Galea, M., Blamey, R., Elston, C., Ellis, I.: The nottingham prognostic index in primary breast cancer. Breast Cancer Research and Treatment **22**(3), 207–219 (1992). http://dx.doi.org/10.1007/BF01840834
8. Green, A.R., Soria, D., Stephen, J., Powe, D.G., Nolan, C.C., Kunkler, I., Thomas, J., Kerr, G., Jack, W., Camreron, D., Piper, T., Ball, G.R., Garibaldi, J.M., Rakha, E.A., Bartlett, J.M., Ellis, I.O.: Nottingham prognostic index plus (npi+): Validation of the modern clinical decision making tool in breast cancer. Cancer Research **75**(9), P5–09 (2015)
9. Hartigan, J.A., Wong, M.A.: Algorithm as 136: A k-means clustering algorithm. Journal of the Royal Statistical Society. Series C (Applied Statistics) **28**(1), 100–108 (1979). http://www.jstor.org/stable/2346830
10. Macenko, M., Niethammer, M., Marron, J., Borland, D., Woosley, J., Guan, X., Schmitt, C., Thomas, N.: A method for normalizing histology slides for quantitative analysis. In: IEEE International Symposium on Biomedical Imaging: From Nano to Macro, 2009. ISBI 2009, pp. 1107–1110, June 2009
11. Matas, J., Chum, O., Urban, M., Pajdla, T.: Robust wide baseline stereo from maximally stable extremal regions. In: Proceedings of the British Machine Vision Conference, pp. 36.1–36.10 (2002) doi:10.5244/C.16.36
12. Meyer, J.S., Alvarez, C., Milikowski, C., Olson, N., Russo, I., Russo, J., Glass, A., Zehnbauer, B.A., Lister, K., Parwaresch, R.: Breast carcinoma malignancy grading by Bloom-Richardson system vs proliferation index reproducibility of grade and advantages of proliferation index. Modern pathology: an official journal of the United States and Canadian Academy of Pathology, Inc **18**(8), 1067–1078 (2005)
13. National Cancer Institute: The Cancer Genoma Atlas. http://cancergenome.nih.gov/
14. Prvulović, I., Kardum-Skelin, I., Sustercić, D., Jakić-Razumović, J., Manojlović, S.: Morphometry of tumor cells in different grades and types of breast cancer. Collegium antropologicum **34**(1), 99–103 (2010)
15. Romo, D., Garcez, P., Romero, E.: A discriminant multi-scale histopathology descriptor using dictionary learning. In: Proc. SPIE 9041, 90410Q–90410Q-6 (2014)
16. Vedaldi, A., Zisserman, A.: Efficient additive kernels via explicit feature maps. IEEE Transactions on Pattern Analysis and Machine Intelligence **34**(3), 480–492 (2012)
17. Veta, M., Kornegoor, R., Huisman, A., Verschuur-Maes, A.H.J., Viergever, M.A., Pluim, J.P.W., van Diest, P.J.: Prognostic value of automatically extracted nuclear morphometric features in whole slide images of male breast cancer. Modern pathology : an official journal of the United States and Canadian Academy of Pathology, Inc **25**(12), 1559–15565 (2012)
18. Veta, M., Van Diest, P.J., Kornegoor, R., Huisman, A., Viergever, M.A., Pluim, J.P.W.: Automatic Nuclei Segmentation in H&E Stained Breast Cancer Histopathology Images. PLoS ONE **8**(7), e70221 (2013)

Optimal and Linear F-Measure Classifiers Applied to Non-technical Losses Detection

Fernanda Rodriguez, Matías Di Martino, Juan Pablo Kosut,
Fernando Santomauro, Federico Lecumberry, and Alicia Fernández(✉)

Instituto de Ingeniería Eléctrica, Facultad de Ingeniería,
Universidad de la República, Julio Herrera Y Reissig 565, Montevideo, Uruguay
alicia@fing.edu.uy

Abstract. Non-technical loss detection represents a very high cost to power supply companies. Finding classifiers that can deal with this problem is not easy as they have to face a high imbalance scenario with noisy data. In this paper we propose to use Optimal F-measure Classifier (OFC) and Linear F-measure Classifier (LFC), two novel algorithms that are designed to work in problems with unbalanced classes. We compare both algorithm performances with other previously used methods to solve automatic fraud detection problem.

Keywords: Class imbalance · One class SVM · F-measure · Recall · Precision · Fraud detection · Level set method

1 Introduction

Improving non-technical loss detection is a huge challenge for electrical companies. In Uruguay the national electric power utility (henceforth call UTE) addresses the problem by manually monitoring a group of customers. A group of experts inspects the monthly consumption curve of each customer and indicates those with some kind of suspicious behavior. This set of customers, initially classified as suspects are then analyzed taking into account other factors (such as fraud history, electrical energy meter type, etc.). Finally a subset of customers is selected to be inspected by an UTE's employee, who confirms (or not) the irregularity (illustrated in Figure 1). The procedure described before has major drawbacks, mainly, the number of customers that can be manually controlled is small compared with the total number of customers (around 500.000 only in Montevideo).

Several pattern recognition approaches have addressed the detection of non-technical losses, both supervised, unsupervised or recently semi-supervised as shown in [36]. Leon et al. review the main research works found in the area between 1990 and 2008 [23]. Here we present a brief review that builds on this work and wide it with new contributions published between 2008 and 2014. Several of these approaches consider unsupervised classification using different techniques such as fuzzy clustering [2], neural networks [25,35], among others. Monedero et al. use regression based on the correlation between time and

© Springer International Publishing Switzerland 2015
A. Pardo and J. Kittler (Eds.): CIARP 2015, LNCS 9423, pp. 83–91, 2015.
DOI: 10.1007/978-3-319-25751-8_11

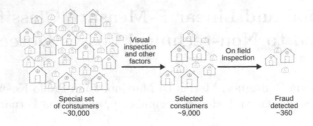

Fig. 1. Scheme of the manual procedure to detect fraudulent customers.

monthly consumption, looking for significant drops in consumption [26]. Then they go through a second stage where suspicious customers are discarded if their consumptions vary according to the moment or the year's season. Only major customers were inspected and 38% were detected as fraudulent. Similar results (40%) were obtained in [14] using a decision tree classifier and customers who had been inspected in the past year. In [9] and [37] SVM is used. In the latter, Modified Genetic Algorithm is employed to find the best parameters of SVM. In [38], is compared the methods Back-Propagation Neural Network (BPNN), Online-sequential Extreme Learning Machine (OS-ELM) and SVM. Biscarri et al. [5] seek for outliers, Leon et al. [23] use Generalized Rule Induction and Di Martino et al. [10] combine CS-SVM , One class SVM, C4.5, and OPF classifiers using various features derived from the consumption. In [34] it is compared the feature sets selected when using different classifiers with two different labelling strategies. Different kinds of features are used among this works, for examples, consumption [5,37], contracted power and consumed ratio [15], Wavelet transformation of the monthly consumption [20], amount of inspections made to each client in one period and average power of the area where the customer resides [2], among others.

This application has to deal with the class imbalance problem, where it is costly to misclassify samples from the minority class and there is a high overlapping between classes.

In almost all the approaches that deal with an imbalanced problem, the idea is to adapt the classifiers that have good accuracy in balanced domains. Many solutions have been proposed to deal with this problem [16,18]: changing class distributions [7,8,21], incorporating costs in decision making [3,4], and using alternative performance metrics instead of accuracy [17] in the learning process with standard algorithms. In [24] a comparative analysis of the two former methodologies is done, showing that both have similar performance and that they could be improved by hybrid procedures that combine the best of both methodologies. In [12] and [11] a different approach to this problem is proposed: designing a classifier based on an optimal decision rule that maximizes the F-measure [33] instead of the accuracy. In contrast with common approaches, this algorithm does not need to change original distributions or arbitrarily assign misclassification costs in the algorithm to find an appropriate decision rule.

In this work we propose to study and compare the following classifiers: Optimal F-measure (OFC) and Linear F-measure (LFC) with some classical approaches as presented in [10] applied to non-technical losses detection. In Section 2 theory is presented. In Section 3 we present non-technical loss problem and the data set used. In Section 4 experimental results are shown and in the last section we share conclusions and future work.

2 Classifiers for Unbalanced Problems

In this section we are going to introduce a brief descriptions of OFC and LFC classifiers. These classifiers were designed to face imbalance problems by looking for maximizing the F-measure value. Since high value of F-measure (F_β) ensures that both Recall and Precision are reasonably high, which is a desirable property since it indicates reasonable values of both true positive and false positive rates. This is relevant to non-technical loss detection problem since it has great imbalance between *normal* and *fraud/suspicious* classes and where, ideally, we want to detect all frauds with a minimum number of inspections to normal clients.

The goal of the OFC is to find class frontiers that guarantee maximum F-measure. The algorithm assumes that there are two classes, one called the **negative** class (ω_-), that represents the majority class, usually associated to the normal scenario (no suspicious, nor fraud), and the other called the **positive** class (ω_+) that represents the minority class (suspicious or fraud). Let us recall some related well known definitions:

$$\text{Accuracy: } \mathcal{A} = \frac{TP+TN}{TP+TN+FP+FN} \qquad \text{Recall: } \mathcal{R} = \frac{TP}{TP+FN}$$

$$\text{Precision: } \mathcal{P} = \frac{TP}{TP+FP} \qquad \text{F-measure: } F_\beta = \frac{(1+\beta^2)\mathcal{R}\,\mathcal{P}}{\beta^2 \mathcal{P}+\mathcal{R}}$$

Where, TP (true positive) is the number of $x \in \omega_+$ correctly classified, TN (true negative) the number of $x \in \omega_-$ correctly classified, FP (false positive) and FN (false negative) the number of $x \in \omega_-$ and $x \in \omega_+$ misclassified respectively.

As we stated before, Precision and Recall are two important measures to evaluate the performance of a given classifier in an imbalance scenario. The Recall indicates the True Positive Rate, while the Precision indicates the Positive Predictive Value. The F-measure combines them with a parameter $\beta \in [0, +\infty)$. With $\beta = 1$, F_β is the harmonic mean between Recall and Precision, meanwhile with $\beta \gg 1$ or $\beta \ll 1$, the F_β approaches the Recall or the Precision respectively.

It can be seen that maximizing F-measure is equivalent to minimizing the quantity:

$$\epsilon = \frac{\beta^2 FN + FP}{TP}. \tag{1}$$

The quantities FN, FP, and TP can be expressed as:

$$FN = P \int_{\Omega_-} f_+(x)dx, \ FP = N \int_{\Omega_+} f_-(x)dx \text{ and } TP = P \int_{\Omega_+} f_+(x)dx$$

where P and N are the number of positive and negative classes in the training database, and $f_+(x)$ and $f_-(x)$ are the probability distribution functions of the positive and negative class respectively.

Therefore, the task of training a classifier $u : \Omega \to \mathbb{R}$, that maximizes the F-measure (and minimizes ϵ) can be approached as finding the regions $\Omega_+(u) = \{x : u(x) \geq 0\}$ and $\Omega_-(u) = \{x : u(x) < 0\}$ that minimize:

$$\epsilon(u) = \frac{\beta^2 \int_{\Omega_-(u)} f_+(x)dx + \int_{\Omega_+(u)} f_-(x)dx}{\int_{\Omega_+(u)} f_+(x)dx}. \tag{2}$$

OFC looks for the classifier u that minimize $\epsilon(u)$ solving the optimization problem using a gradient descent flow, inspired by the level-set method [30]. A complete description of this classifier can be found in [12]. On the other hand, LFC proposes a way to get the regions Ω_+ and Ω_- that minimize energy ϵ thresholds for each dimension in an iterative way. A rectangular partition of the space is found by considering independently probability distributions in each dimension. Following this procedure in all the dimensions, one at a time, a set of hyper-rectangles are defined. The main difference between OFC and LFC, is that in the case of OFC, decision boundaries can have any arbitrary shape while in the case of LFC they are always parallel to input feature space coordinates axes. Although OFC is a more general approach and fewer hypothesis are assumed, LFC has the advantage of been very fast and its implementation is very simple and straightforward. For this reasons, in this work both strategies are considered and compared for the case of automatic fraud detection. A complete description of LFC algorithm can be found in [11].

Finally, as was done in previous analysis, One-Class Support Vector Machine (O-SVM) [19], Cost-Sensitive Support Vector Machine (CS-SVM) [19], Optimum Path Forest (OPF) [32], and a decision tree proposed by Roos Quinlan, C4.5 [31] are also considered and compared with OFC and LFC approaches.

It should be noted briefly that Optimum Path Forest (OPF) was proposed by [32] to be applied to the problem of fraud detection in electricity consumption, showing good results. It consists in creating a graph with the training dataset, associating a cost to each path between two elements, based on the similarity between the elements of the path. This method assumes that the cost between elements of the same class is lower than those belonging to different classes. Next, a representative is chosen for each class, called prototypes. A new element is classified as the class that has lower cost with the corresponding prototype. Since OPF is very sensitive to class imbalance, we change class distribution of the training dataset by under-sampling the majority class.

The decision tree proposed by Ross Quinlan: C4.5 it is widely utilized since it is a very simple method that obtains good results. However, it is very unstable

Table 1. Fraud detection.

Description	Recall (%)	Precision (%)	$F_{measure}$ (%)[$\beta = 1$]
OPF	36	34	35
Tree (C4.5)	33	**37**	35
O-SVM	71	31	44
CS-SVM	74	33	46
LFC	75	32	45
OFC	**77**	34	**47**

and highly dependent on the training set. Thus, a later stage of AdaBoost was implemented, accomplishing more robust results. Just as with the OPF it was needed a resamplig stage to manage the dependency of the C4.5 with the class distribution.

Related to cost-sensitive learning (CS-SVM) and one-class classifier (O-SVM), in the former different costs were assigned to the misclassification of the elements of each class, in order to tackle the unbalanced problem while the second one considers the minority class as the outliers.

3   Experimental Results

In this work we used a data set of 456 industrial profiles obtained from the UTE's database. Each profile is represented by the customers monthly consumption in the last 36 months, with inspection results labels: fraud or not fraud. A pre-processing and normalization step is performed in order to normalizes the data and to avoid peaks from billing errors. A feature set was proposed taking into account UTE's technician expertize in fraud detection by manual inspection and recent papers on non-technical loss detection [1], [28], [29]. Some of them are:

- Consumption ratio for the 3, 6 and 12 months and the average consumption.
- Difference in wavelet coefficients from the last and previous years.
- Euclidean distance of each customer to the *mean customer*, where the *mean customer* is calculated by taking the mean for each month consumption for all the customers.
- Module of the Fourier coefficients of the total consumption.
- Difference in Fourier coefficients from the last and previous years.
- Variance of the consumption curve.
- Slope of the straight line that fits the consumption curve.

It is well known that finding a small set of relevant features can improve the final classification performance [6]; this is the reason why we implemented a feature selection stage. We used two types of evaluation methods: filter and wrapper. Filters methods look for subsets of features with low correlation between them and high correlation with the labels, while wrapper methods evaluate the performance of a given classifier for the given subset of features. In the wrapper methods, we used as performance measure the F-measure. The evaluations were performed using 10 fold cross validation over the training set. As searching method, we used *Bestfirst* [27], since we obtained a good balance between performance and computational costs.

In order to confront the class imbalance problem in O-SVM, CS-SVM, C4.5 and OPF, the strategies of changing class distribution by re-sampling [22] were used.

Table 1 shows the results obtained by the different classifiers using 10-fold cross validation.

In spite of the fact that in this work we used a more complicated and challenging dataset than that analyzed in [13], results are consistent with the reported in [13] if we compare the performance between the classifiers. CS-SVM outperforms O-SVM, C4.5 and OPF, while the novel approaches included in the present work show one of the highest results with very promising performances. OFC approach outperforms LCF as expected but, LFC also seems to be a reasonably option to face automatic fraud detection problem for instance performing similar to the best state of the art algorithm, with computational efficiency. A deeper interpretation of the results, taking into consideration the specific problem of non-technical losses detection, shows that all algorithms obtained a similar value in the rate of fraud detected (TP) per number of inspections (TP + FP). However it can be seen that the OPF and C4.5 get that performance in an operating point which corresponds to a high threshold, where it is detected a low fraudulent registrations percentage, while C-SVM, OFC and LFC are working in an operating point where a high percentage is detected. Working in a more demanding operation point (detecting not only the obvious fraud but those which are more difficult, those similar to normal records) without deteriorating the precision, reaffirms the assessment that the new proposed algorithms have a very good performance and that the use the F-measure as the objective measure to be optimized is suitable for the problem of non-technical losses.

4   Conclusions and Future Work

We propose to use two novel algorithms specially design to deal with class imbalance problems to non-technical loss detection. We compare these algorithms performance with previous strategies used to solve this problem. Performance evaluation shows that OFC and LFC can achieve similar performance to the state of art such as SVM and outperforms C4.5 and OPF classifiers. In future work, we propose to extend OFC and LFC algorithms to semisupervised approach and study the impact of applying them to the non-technical losses detection.

Acknowledgment. This work was supported by the program *Sector Productivo CSIC UTE.*

References

1. Alcetegaray, D., Kosut, J.: One class SVM para la detección de fraudes en el uso de energía eléctrica. Trabajo Final Curso de Reconocimiento de Patrones, Dictado por el IIE-Facultad de Ingeniera-UdelaR (2008)
2. dos Angelos, E., Saavedra, O., Corts, O., De Souza, A.: Detection and identification of abnormalities in customer consumptions in power distribution systems. IEEE Transactions on Power Delivery **26**(4), 2436–2442 (2011)
3. Barandela, R., Garcia, V.: Strategies for learning in class imbalance problems. Pattern Recognition 849–851 (2003)
4. Batista, G., Pratti, R., Monard, M.: A study of the behavior of several methods for balancing machine learning training data. SIGKDD Explorations **6**, 20–29 (2004)
5. Biscarri, F., Monedero, I., Leon, C., Guerrero, J.I., Biscarri, J., Millan, R.: A data mining method based on the variability of the customer consumption - A special application on electric utility companies, vol. AIDSS, pp. 370–374. Inst. for Syst. and Technol. of Inf. Control and Commun. (2008)
6. Bishop, C.: Neural Networks for Pattern Recognition. Oxford University Press, USA (1996)
7. Chawla, Nitesh V., Lazarevic, Aleksandar, Hall, Lawrence O., Bowyer, Kevin W.: SMOTEBoost: improving prediction of the minority class in boosting. In: Lavrač, Nada, Gamberger, Dragan, Todorovski, Ljupčo, Blockeel, Hendrik (eds.) PKDD 2003. LNCS (LNAI), vol. 2838, pp. 107–119. Springer, Heidelberg (2003)
8. Chawla, N., Bowyer, K., Hall, L., Kegelmeyer, W.: Smote: Synthetic minority over-sampling technique. Journal of Artificial Intelligence Research **16**, 321–357 (2002)
9. Depuru, S.S.S.R., Wang, L., Devabhaktuni, V.: Support vector machine based data classification for detection of electricity theft. In: 2011 IEEE/PES Power Systems Conference and Exposition pp. 1–8 (2011)
10. Di Martino, J., Decia, F., Molinelli, J., Fernández, A.: Improving electric fraud detection using class imbalance strategies. In: International Conference In Pattern Recognition Aplications and Methods pp. 135–141 (2012)
11. Di Martino, M., Fernández, A., Iturralde, P., Lecumberry, F.: Novel classifier scheme for imbalanced problems. Pattern Recognition Letters **34**(10), 1146–1151 (2013)
12. Di Martino, M., Hernández, G., Fiori, M., Fernández, A.: A new framework for optimal classifier design. Pattern Recognition **46**(8), 2249–2255 (2013)
13. Di Martino, Matías, Decia, Federico, Molinelli, Juan, Fernández, Alicia: A novel framework for nontechnical losses detection in electricity companies. In: Latorre Carmona, Pedro, Sánchez, JSalvador, Fred, Ana L.N. (eds.) Pattern Recognition - Applications and Methods. AISC, vol. 204, pp. 109–120. Springer, Heidelberg (2013)
14. Filho, J., Gontijo, E., Delaiba, A., Mazina, E., Cabral, J.E., Pinto, J.O.: Fraud identification in electricity company costumers using decision tree pp. 3730–3734 (2004)
15. Galván, J., Elices, E., Noz, A.M., Czernichow, T., Sanz-Bobi, M.: System for detection of abnormalities and fraud in customer consumption. In: Proc. 12th IEEE/PES conf. Electric Power Supply Industry (1998)
16. Garca, V., Mollineda, J.S.S.R.A., Sotoca, R.A.J.M.: The class imbalance problem in pattern classification and learning, pp. 283–291 (2007)
17. García, V., Sánchez, J., Mollineda, R.: On the suitability of numerical performance measures for class imbalance problems. In: International Conference In Pattern Recognition Aplications and Methods, pp. 310–313 (2012)

18. Guo, X., Yin, Y., Dong, C., Yang, G., Zhou, G.: On the class imbalance problem. In: International Conference on Natural Computation, pp. 192–201 (2008)
19. Hsu, C., Chang, C., Lin, C.: A practical guide to support vector classification. National Taiwan University, Taipei (2010)
20. Jiang, R.J.R., Tagaris, H., Lachsz, A., Jeffrey, M.: Wavelet based feature extraction and multiple classifiers for electricity fraud detection. IEEE/PES Transmission and Distribution Conference and Exhibition vol. 3 (2002)
21. Kolez, A., Chowdhury, A., Alspector, J.: Data duplication: an imbalance problem?. Workshop on Learning with Imbalanced Data Sets, ICML (2003)
22. Kuncheva, L.: Combining Pattern Classifiers: Methods and Algorithms. Wiley-Interscience (2004)
23. Leon, C., Biscarri, F.X.E.L., Monedero, I.X.F.I., Guerrero, J.I., Biscarri, J.X.F.S., Millan, R.X.E.O.: Variability and trend-based generalized rule induction model to ntl detection in power companies. IEEE Transactions on Power Systems **26**(4), 1798–1807 (2011)
24. López, V., Fernández, A., del Jesus, M.J., Herrera, F.: Cost sensitive and preprocessing for classification with imbalanced data-sets: Similar behaviour and potential hybridizations. In: International Conference In Pattern Recognition Aplications and Methods, pp. 98–107 (2012)
25. Markoc, Z., Hlupic, N., Basch, D.: Detection of suspicious patterns of energy consumption using neural network trained by generated samples. In: Proceedings of the ITI 2011 33rd International Conference on Information Technology Interfaces, pp. 551–556 (2011)
26. Monedero, Iñigo, Biscarri, Félix, León, Carlos, Guerrero, Juan I., Biscarri, Jesús, Millán, Rocío: Using regression analysis to identify patterns of non-technical losses on power utilities. In: Setchi, Rossitza, Jordanov, Ivan, Howlett, Robert J., Jain, Lakhmi C. (eds.) KES 2010, Part I. LNCS, vol. 6276, pp. 410–419. Springer, Heidelberg (2010)
27. Müller-Merbach, H.: Heuristics: Intelligent search strategies for computer problem solving. European Journal of Operational Research **21**(2), 278–279 (1985)
28. Muniz, C., Vellasco, M., Tanscheit, R., Figueiredo, K.: A neuro-fuzzy system for fraud detection in electricity distribution. In: IFSA-EUSFLAT, pp. 1096–1101 (2009)
29. Nagi, J., Mohamad, M.: Nontechnical loss detection for metered customers in power utility using support vector machines. In: IEEE Transactions on Power Delivery, pp. 1162–1171 (2010)
30. Osher, S., Sethian, J.A.: Fronts propagating with curvature- dependent speed: Algorithms based on Hamilton-Jacobi formulations. Journal of Computational Physics **79**, 12–49 (1988)
31. Quinlan, J.: C4.5: Programs for Machine Learning. C4.5 - programs for machine learning. J. Ross Quinlan. Morgan Kaufmann Publishers (1993). http://books.google.com.uy/books?id=HExncpjbYroC
32. Ramos, C.C.O., Sousa, A.N.D., Papa, J.P., Falcao, A.X.: A new approach for nontechnical losses detection based on optimum-path forest. IEEE Transactions on Power Systems **26**(1), 181–189 (2011)
33. van Rijsbergen, C.J.: Information Retrieval. Butterworth (1979)
34. Rodríguez, F., Lecumberry, F., Fernández, A.: Non technical loses detection - experts labels vs. inspection labels in the learning stage. In: ICPRAM 2014 - Proceedings of the 3rd International Conference on Pattern Recognition Applications and Methods, ESEO, Angers, Loire Valley, France, 6–8 March, 2014, pp. 624–628 (2014). http://dx.doi.org/10.5220/0004823506240628

35. Sforna, M.: Data mining in power company customer database. Electrical Power System Research **55**, 201–209 (2000)
36. Tacón, Juan, Melgarejo, Damián, Rodríguez, Fernanda, Lecumberry, Federico, Fernández, Alicia: Semisupervised approach to non technical losses detection. In: Bayro-Corrochano, Eduardo, Hancock, Edwin (eds.) CIARP 2014. LNCS, vol. 8827, pp. 698–705. Springer, Heidelberg (2014)
37. Yap, K.S., Hussien, Z., Mohamad, A.: Abnormalities and fraud electric meter detection using hybrid support vector machine and genetic algorithm. In: 3rd IASTED Int. Conf. Advances in Computer Science and Technology, Phuket, Thailand, vol. 4 (2007)
38. Yap, K.S., Tiong, S.K., Nagi, J., Koh, J.S.P., Nagi, F.: Comparison of supervised learning techniques for non-technical loss detection in power utility. International Review on Computers and Software (I.RE.CO.S.) **7**(2), 1828–6003 (2012)

A Multimodal Approach for Percussion Music Transcription from Audio and Video

Bernardo Marenco[✉], Magdalena Fuentes, Florencia Lanzaro,
Martín Rocamora, and Alvaro Gómez

Facultad de Ingeniería, Universidad de la República, Montevideo, Uruguay
{bmarenco,mfuentes,carla.florencia.lanzaro,rocamora,agomez}@fing.edu.uy

Abstract. A multimodal approach for percussion music transcription from audio and video recordings is proposed in this work. It is part of an ongoing research effort for the development of tools for computer-aided analysis of Candombe drumming, a popular afro-rooted rhythm from Uruguay. Several signal processing techniques are applied to automatically extract meaningful information from each source. This involves detecting certain relevant objects in the scene from the video stream. The location of events is obtained from the audio signal and this information is used to drive the processing of both modalities. Then, the detected events are classified by combining the information from each source in a feature-level fusion scheme. The experiments conducted yield promising results that show the advantages of the proposed method.

Keywords: Multimodal signal processing · Machine learning applications · Music transcription · Percussion music · Sound classification

1 Introduction

Although music is mainly associated with an acoustic signal, it is inherently a multimodal phenomenon in which other sources of information are involved, for instance visual (images, videos, sheet music) and textual (lyrics, tags). In the recent decades this has lead to research on multimodal music processing, in which signal processing and machine learning techniques are applied for automatically establishing semantic relationships between different music sources [12]. This has several applications, such as sheet music to audio synchronization or lyrics to audio alignment [12], audiovisual musical instrument recognition [11] and cross-modal correlation for music video analysis [6]. Even thought the problem of music transcription has received a lot of attention [10], most existing research focus on audio signals. Among the few works that take multimodal information into account, drum transcription is tackled in [7] using audio and video.

In this work, a multimodal approach for percussion music transcription is proposed. It is tailored to the analysis of audio and video recordings of Candombe

This work was supported by funding agencies CSIC and ANII from Uruguay.

A. Pardo and J. Kittler (Eds.): CIARP 2015, LNCS 9423, pp. 92–99, 2015.
DOI: 10.1007/978-3-319-25751-8_12

drumming performances, with the aim of determining the location of sound events and their classification into a set of different stroke types. A comparison between the performance attained by monomodal classifiers (i.e. audio or video) and the multimodal approach is considered, so as to evaluate the impact of including different sources of information. The ultimate goal of this research is to contribute with automatic software tools for computer-aided music studies.

Candombe drumming is the essential component of an afro-rooted tradition which has evolved for almost two centuries and is at present one of the most characteristic features of Uruguayan popular culture [1]. The rhythm is played marching on the street by groups of drums of which there are three different types: *chico*, *repique* and *piano* [4]. The drumhead is hit with one hand and with a stick in the other, producing different types of sound. The stick is also used to hit the shell of the drum which is made of wood.

The rest of this paper is organized as follows. Next section outlines the proposed multimodal approach for percussion transcription. Then, Section 3 introduces the datasets used for developing and evaluating the system. Section 4 is devoted to explaining the signal processing techniques applied to the audio and video streams. The feature selection techniques and the classification scheme adopted are described in Section 5. Experiments and results are presented in Section 6. Finally, the paper ends with some concluding remarks.

2 Proposed Multimodal Approach

The information coming from the different modalities can be integrated in various ways, for instance by combining the outputs of monomodal classifiers (i.e. decision-level fusion) or by considering the features from each mode into an unified set for classification (i.e. feature-level fusion). In this work, high-level information obtained from one modality is used to drive the processing of both modalities, which as noted in [3] can be a better strategy than merely relying on direct feature-level or decision-level fusion. This is based on the fact that the location of events can be obtained quite reliably using the audio signal alone (known as onset detection [2]), whereas the classification of the type of stroke can be better attained by exploiting the information from both modalities. This is illustrated in Figure 1, where a stroke performed with the stick is shown. The detection of events relies on the Spectral Flux (see Sec. 4.1) of the audio signal and exhibits a clear maximum, while the position of the stick extracted from the video shows a corresponding minimum indicating a stick stroke.

The proposed system is depicted in the diagram of Figure 2. Onset detection guides the feature extraction in both modalities. In order to obtain meaningful information from the video, relevant objects in the scene have to be segmented, namely the stick, the drumhead and the hand. After extracting features from each modality, a feature selection stage is introduced separately, which proved to be more effective than a single selection over the whole feature set. Finally, detected events are classified by combining the information from both modalities in a feature-level fusion scheme.

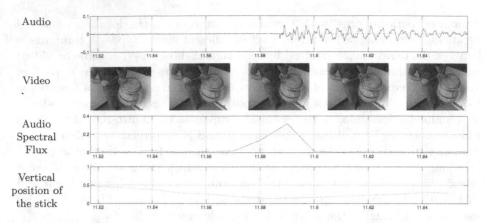

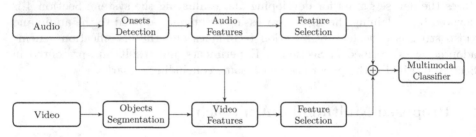

Fig. 1. Example of multimodal information extracted. Event detection is based on the audio signal, but classification exploits information from both modalities.

Fig. 2. Block diagram of the proposed multimodal transcription system. The symbol ⊕ represents the fusion of the features from each modality into an unified set.

3 Datasets

Two recording session were conducted in order to generate the data for this research. High-quality equipment was used for recording audio. Since the performances involve very fast movements, video acquisition was carried out at high-speed rates (120 and 240 fps). Four percussionists took part in the first session, and each of them recorded two improvised performances of the *repique* drum. In the second session, several different configurations of solo drums and ensembles were recorded, performed by five renowned Candombe players.

Recordings from the first dataset were manually labeled by an expert, indicating the location of the strokes and their corresponding type. This data was used for training and evaluating the classification system. Recordings of the second session were mainly used for developing the object segmentation and feature extraction algorithms.

The following six different stroke classes were considered for a *repique* performance: *wood*, in which the stick hits the wooden shell of the drum; *hand*, when the bare hand hits the drumhead; *stick*, that corresponds to a single hit of the drumhead with the stick; *bounce*, in which the stick hits the drumhead several times in a short time interval; *rimshot*, with the stick hitting tangentially to the drumhead; and *flam*, which consists of two single strokes played almost together by alternating the hand and stick (in any order).

4 Signal Processing

4.1 Audio Signal Processing

Onsets Detection. The first step in the proposed system is to automatically find the location of sound events. A typical approach is adopted in this work, namely the Spectral Flux, which emphasizes changes in the energy content of the audio signal in different frequency bands [2]. The Short-Time Fourier Transform of the signal is calculated and mapped to the MEL scale (approximately linear in log frequency) for sequential 20-ms duration windows in hops of 10 ms. The resulting sequences are time-differentiated (via first-order difference), half-wave rectified, and summed along the MEL sub-bands. Finally, a global threshold of 10% of the maximum value is applied to the obtained detection function to determine the location of onsets.

Audio Features. The type of sound, i.e. the *timbre*, is mainly related to the energy distribution along its spectrum. Therefore, two different sets of features commonly used for describing spectral timbre of audio signals were adopted. In addition, two features were proposed to capture the behaviour of strokes which involve several events in a short time interval. A temporal window of 90 ms centered at the detected onset is considered for computing each type of feature.

Spectral Shape Features. A feature set commonly used for general-purpose musical instruments classification was considered, comprising several measures describing the shape of the spectral energy distribution, namely: spectral centroid, spectral spread, spectral skewness, spectral kurtosis, spectral decrease, spectral slope and spectral crest [10].

Mel-frequency Cepstral Coefficients. (MFCC) These are the most widespread features in speech and music processing for describing spectral timbre. A filter bank of 160 bands is applied to the signal frame, whose center frequencies are equally-spaced according to the MEL scale. Then an FFT is calculated and the log-power on each band is computed. The elements of these vectors are highly correlated so a Discrete Cosine Transform is applied and the 40 lowest order coefficients are retained.

Spectral Flux Features. The *bounce* and *flam* strokes involve several events in a short time interval. Therefore, the number of Spectral Flux peaks and the amplitude difference between the first and second peak (set to zero if no second peak exist) are also computed to capture the behaviour of these type of strokes.

4.2   Video Signal Processing

In order to analyze a video recording and to extract features for describing the performance, it is necessary to automatically detect the most important objects that appear in the scene. These are the drumhead, the stick and the hand of the performer. The scene was slightly prepared to simplify the detection and the evaluation process, but taking care not to alter the sound of the drums or disturb the performer. The stick and the contour of the drumhead were painted to ease their segmentation. Besides, in the second recording session some fiducial paper markers were pasted to the drum and the body of the performer for evaluation purposes. This can be seen in Fig. 3(a), which shows a video frame that is used for illustrating the objects segmentation and detection process hereafter.

Objects Segmentation and Detection

Drumhead Detection. While the drumhead is a circle, it becomes an ellipse in the image due to the camera perspective projection. Detecting ellipses in images is a classical problem [13] usually tackled in two steps: (a) edge detection on the image and (b) estimation of the ellipse that best fits the obtained edges. As mentioned before, the drumhead contour was painted, so the first step is achieved by color filtering the image. The fitting of the best ellipse was performed based on [5], using the OpenCV implementatin. Color filtering and ellipse fitting for drumhead detection are shown in Fig. 3(b) and Fig. 3(c), respectively.

Stick Detection. The detection of the stick is also carried out in a two-step way. Only relying in color filtering turned out to be insufficient for segmenting the stick due to the lighting conditions. Since the stick is one of the fast moving objects in the scene, a background subtraction algorithm [14] was used together with the color cue to point out pixel candidates. Then, the stick is identified from the filtered pixels by a line segment detector [8], also implemented in OpenCV. To assure a continuous detection of the stick, coherence is imposed by restricting the segment detection in a frame to a window determined by the movement in previous frames. The moving objects mask is depicted in Fig. 3(d) and the detected stick in Fig. 3(e).

Hand Detection. The detection of the hand that hits the drum is addressed by segmenting the main skin blob above the drumhead. Skin segmentation cannot be accomplished by a simple thresholding of the color space, because there are other regions with similar chromaticity, such as the wooden floor and the drum. To overcome this difficulty, a permissive color filtering is followed by a tree classifier which recognizes skin pixels in the YCbCr color space. Once the skin pixels are identified, some morphological operations are applied, and the bounding box of the largest blob within a certain region above the previously detected drumhead is selected. Kalman filtering of the detections is also applied to impose temporal coherence. The hand detection process is illustrated in Fig. 3: output of the color filter (f), skin detection based on tree classifier (g), mask above the drumhead (h), and the bounding box of the hand blob (i).

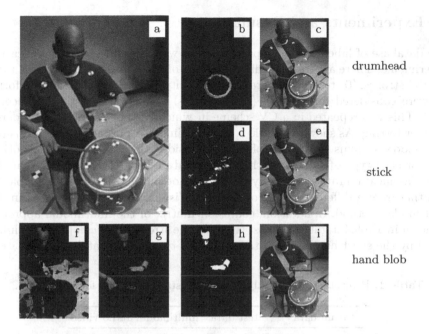

Fig. 3. Objects detection for a video frame (a). Drumhead: color filter (b) and ellipse fitting (c). Stick: moving objects mask (d) and linear segments detection (e). Hand blob: color filter (f), skin detection (g), mask above drumhead (h), bounding box (i).

Video Features. Based on the position of the drumhead, the stick and the hand blob, several features are devised to describe the type of movement of these objects during an audio event. Features are computed within a time window centered at the onset, as shown in Fig. 1. The extracted features for both the stick and hand blob are: the normalized distance to the drumhead, the maximum and minimum value of vertical speed, the zero crossings of vertical speed, and the first ten coefficients of the Discrete Cosine Transform of the vertical position.

5 Multimodal Classification

Feature Selection. Feature selection was carried out within each modality independently, before the feature-level fusion of both sets. This turned out to be more effective than a single selection over the whole feature set. To do that, a correlation-based feature selection method was adopted [9], considering 10-fold cross-validation (CV). For the audio modality 37 features where selected out of 49, and for the video modality 14 out of 30, for a complete set of 51 features.

Classification. Based on the performance attained by different classification techniques in preliminary tests, a Support Vector Machine (SVM) with a Radial Basis Function (RBF) kernel was selected for the implemented system. Optimal values for parameters C and γ were grid-searched in a CV scheme.

6 Experiments and Results

The database of labeled *repique* performances was used for stroke classification experiments. There are two recordings for each of the four performers, for a total of 4132 strokes. To test the generalization ability of the system, three performers were considered for training (6 recordings) and one for testing (2 recordings). This was repeated in a CV scheme in which each performer is considered once for testing. As shown in Table 1, the multimodal approach outperforms the monomodal systems in each fold of the CV. Besides, the advantage is also noticeable for each type of stroke, which is presented in Table 2-left. Notice that the poor classification rate attained by the audio modality for performer 1 (Table 1), resulting from a different tuning of the drum, is effectively compensated in the multimodal method. In addition, confusion matrix of the multimodal approach is shown in Table 2-right. The most troublesome stroke was *flam*, probably influenced by the short number of instances of this type in the database.

Table 1. Percentage of correctly classified instances in each fold of the CV.

train data	test data	multimodal	audio	video
performers 1, 2, 3	performer 4	89.5	83.7	74.3
performers 1, 3, 4	performer 2	95.9	88.2	77.7
performers 1, 2, 4	performer 3	91.2	87.6	75.8
performers 2, 3, 4	performer 1	92.7	60.1	88.0

Table 2. Percentage of correctly classified instances for each type of stroke (left) and confusion matrix for the multimodal approach (right), averaged over all the CV folds.

stroke	multimodal	audio	video
wood	98.2	97.2	91.2
hand	99.2	86.6	98.9
stick	89.9	71.3	74.8
bounce	76.2	71.8	27.0
rimshot	93.7	83.9	57.8
flam	45.9	6.2	23.5

a	b	c	d	e	f	← classified as
556	0	0	0	10	0	a wood
1	1468	2	5	3	2	b hand
0	44	1019	49	20	2	c stick
0	2	76	224	1	4	d bounce
1	4	23	4	524	3	e rimshot
0	13	5	24	4	39	f flam

7 Concluding Remarks

A multimodal approach for percussion music transcription was presented, which focuses on the analysis of audio and video recordings of Candombe drumming. This work is part of an ongoing interdisciplinary research effort for the development of tools for computer-aided music analysis. Recording sessions were conducted in order to generate the data for this research. Due to the fast movements involved in real performances, high video frame rates are mandatory. This generates huge amounts of data, calling for automatic analysis methods. To that end, several signal processing techniques are applied for automatically extracting meaningful information from audio and video recordings.

In the proposed approach, multimodality is exploited two-fold: (a) onsets detected on the audio source are used to drive the processing of both modalities, and (b) classification of the detected events is performed by combining the information from audio and video in a feature-level fusion scheme. Results show that the method is able to improve the performance attained by each modality on its own, which will be further explored in future research.

References

1. Andrews, G.: Blackness in the White Nation: A History of Afro-Uruguay. The University of North Carolina Press, Chapel Hill (2010)
2. Dixon, S.: Onset detection revisited. In: Proceedings of the 9th International Conference on Digital Audio Effects (DAFx-06), Montreal, Canada, pp. 133–137, September 2006
3. Essid, S., Richard, G.: Fusion of multimodal information in music content analysis. In: Müller, M., Goto, M., Schedl, M. (eds.) Multimodal Music Processing, pp. 37–52. Schloss Dagstuhl-Leibniz-Zentrum fuer Informatik, Germany (2012)
4. Ferreira, L.: An afrocentric approach to musical performance in the black south atlantic: The candombe drumming in Uruguay. TRANS-Transcultural Music Review 11, 1–15 (2007)
5. Fitzgibbon, A., Fisher, R.B.: A buyer's guide to conic fitting. In: British Machine Vision Conference, BMVC 1995, Birmingham, pp. 513–522, September 1995
6. Gillet, O., Essid, S., Richard, G.: On the correlation of automatic audio and visual segmentations of music videos. IEEE Transactions on Circuits and Systems for Video Technology 17(3), 347–355 (2007)
7. Gillet, O., Richard, G.: Automatic transcription of drum sequences using audiovisual features. In: Proceedings of the IEEE International Conference on Acoustics, Speech, and Signal Processing, (ICASSP 2005), pp. 205–208, March 2005
8. Grompone von Gioi, R., Jakubowicz, J., Morel, J.-M., Randall, G.: LSD: a Line Segment Detector. Image Processing On Line 2, 35–55 (2012)
9. Hall, M.A.: Correlation-based feature selection for discrete and numeric class machine learning. In: Proceedings of the Seventeenth International Conference on Machine Learning, ICML 2000, San Francisco, CA, USA, pp. 359–366 (2000)
10. Klapuri, A., Davy, M. (eds.): Signal Processing Methods for Music Transcription. Springer, New York (2006)
11. Lim, A., Nakamura, K., Nakadai, K., Ogata, T., Okuno, H.: Audio-visual musical instrument recognition. In: National Convention of Audio-Visual Information Processing Society, March 2011
12. Müller, M., Goto, M., Schedl, M. (eds.): Multimodal Music Processing. Schloss Dagstuhl-Leibniz-Zentrum fuer Informatik, Germany (2012)
13. Tsuji, S., Matsumoto, F.: Detection of ellipses by a modified Hough Transformation. IEEE Transactions on Computers 27(8), 777–781 (1978)
14. Zivkovic, Z.: Improved adaptive gaussian mixture model for background subtraction. In: Proceedings of the 17th International Conference on Pattern Recognition (ICPR 2004), vol. 2, pp. 28–31. IEEE (2004)

Modeling Onset Spectral Features
for Discrimination of Drum Sounds

Martín Rocamora[1]([✉]) and Luiz W.P. Biscainho[2]

[1] Universidad de la República, Montevideo, Uruguay
rocamora@fing.edu.uy
[2] Federal University of Rio de Janeiro, Rio de Janeiro, Brazil
wagner@smt.ufrj.br

Abstract. Motivated by practical problems related to ongoing research on Candombe drumming (a popular afro-rooted rhythm from Uruguay), this paper proposes an approach for recognizing drum sounds in audio signals that models for sound classification the same audio spectral features employed in onset detection. Among the reported experiments involving recordings of real performances, one aims at finding the predominant Candombe drum heard in an audio file, while the other attempts to identify those temporal segments within a performance when a given sound pattern is played. The attained results are promising and suggest many ideas for future research.

Keywords: Audio signal processing · Machine learning applications · Musical instrument recognition · Percussion music · Candombe drumming

1 Introduction

The extraction of musically meaningful content information via automatic analysis of audio recordings has become an important research field in audio signal processing. It encompasses a wide scope of applications, ranging from computer-aided musicology to automatic music transcription and recommendation. Research on automatic music transcription has concentrated mainly on pitched instruments, and only in the past decade percussion instruments have gained interest, most of the work focusing on the standard pop/rock drum kit [4]. The striking of a drum membrane produces a very short waveform that can be modeled as an impulsive function with broad-band spectrum [5], whose accurate characterization and analysis is a challenging problem in signal processing. In this context, the goal of automatic transcription is to determine the type of percussion instrument played (instrument recognition) and the temporal location of the event. Even if the problem of isolated sound classification is widely studied [7], the performance of available methods largely decreases when simultaneous sounds and real performances are considered [11].

This work was supported by CAPES and CNPq from Brazil, and ANII from Uruguay.

A. Pardo and J. Kittler (Eds.): CIARP 2015, LNCS 9423, pp. 100–107, 2015.
DOI: 10.1007/978-3-319-25751-8_13

Existing approaches for percussion transcription can be roughly divided into two types [4]. Most of the proposed solutions apply a pattern recognition approach to sound events. Firstly the audio signal is segmented into meaningful events, either by detecting onsets or by building a pulse grid. Then, audio features are computed for each segment, usually to describe spectral content and its temporal evolution [4, 7]. Finally, the segments are classified using pattern recognition methods. The other usual approach is based on segregating the audio input into streams which supposedly contain events from a single percussion sound class, by means of signal separation techniques [6]. After that, a class is assigned and an onset detection procedure is applied to each stream. Other distinctions can be made, such as if the classification is supervised or not, and whether it takes high-level musicological information into account [4].

In this paper, automatic percussion instrument recognition addresses audio files in which a predominant instrument suffers the interference from some others, aiming to determine the prevailing one. This type of audio file could be either the result of a signal separation technique as previously described, or coming from a microphone placed close to an instrument when a poly-instrument performance is recorded. The latter situation is common practice in some music productions or musicological field studies [10], and is the case of the dataset considered in the reported experiments.

The present work is part of an interdisciplinary collaboration that pursues the development of automatic tools for computer-aided analysis and transcription of Candombe drumming, one of the most defining traits of popular culture in Uruguay. Part of a tradition that has its roots in the culture brought by the African slaves in the 18th century, it evolved during a long historical process and is nowadays practiced by thousands of people and influenced various genres of popular music [1]. The rhythm is produced by groups of people marching in the streets playing drums [3]. There are three drum sizes (see Fig. 1) with respective registers: *chico* (small/high), *piano* (big/low) and *repique* (medium). The minimal ensemble of drums must have at least one of each type. All the drums are played with one hand hitting the drumhead bare and the other holding a stick. The stick is also used to hit the wooden shell of the drum, producing a sound called *madera*, when playing the *clave* pattern. This pattern serves as a mean of temporal organization and synchronization, and is played by all the drums before the rhythm patterns are initiated, and also by the *repique* drum in between phrases. A *repique* performance can also include occasional *madera* sounds as part of the repertoire of strokes used when improvising.

Two types of experiments are conducted in this work, one aiming to recognize the predominant Candombe drum in an audio file, and the other attempting to identify those temporal segments of a *repique* performance when the *clave* pattern is played. The classification is addressed by modeling the same audio features used for onset detection.

The remaining of the document is organized as follows. The dataset of audio recordings is introduced in the next section. Then, Section 3 is devoted to the extraction of audio features. The clustering and classification methods applied are described in Sections 4 and 5 respectively. Experiments and results are presented in Section 6. The paper ends with some critical discussion of the present work and ideas for future research.

2 Datasets

A training dataset containing isolated sounds of Candombe drums was compiled and annotated for this work. To this end, a studio recording session was conducted in which five percussionists played in turns one among a set of three drums (one of each type) called drums-1 hereafter. Automatic onset detection was performed over each audio track, and the resulting events were manually checked and labeled as of a certain sound type. A different class was attributed to each drum type (i.e. *chico, repique, piano*) besides an additional one to *madera* strokes (which sound very similar for all drums). Recording each type of drum separately greatly simplified the manual labeling process, since once *madera* sounds had been identified and labeled in a given track, all remaining events could be assigned to its (known) drum type. Finally, a training dataset of 2000 patterns was built through a stratified random sampling (i.e., 500 of each class).

Fig. 1. Testing dataset recording session. Drums on the left are also used for training (drums-1), while drums on the right belong to the set used only for testing (drums-2).

Another dataset of real performances of drum ensembles was used for testing. This data was collected in other recording session, in which five renowned Candombe drummers took part, playing in groups of three to five. Two of these configurations are depicted in Fig. 1. Audio recordings were done using spot microphones close to each drum.[1] This provides synchronized audio tracks in which a certain drum is predominant, whilst there is interference from the other drums. Complete performances of variable lengths were recorded, approximately from two to four minutes each. The same set of drums, drums-1, used for recording the training samples was used in all three-player performances. Another set of drums, called drums-2, was involved in the four- and five-player recordings. This setup allows for two different types of experiment regarding the generalization ability of the classification system: one in which training and testing drums

---

[1] Except for the *chico* drum in ensembles of five players due to equipment constraints.

are the same, but recording conditions (e.g. room acoustics, microphones) and performance configuration (e.g. drum tuning, percussionist) change; and another in which the instruments are also changed.

3 Extraction of Audio Features

In order to find the occurrence of sound events in recorded audio, usually one implements a detection function that emphasizes note onsets by detecting changes in some signal properties, such as the energy content in different frequency bands [2]. This work adopts a typical approach, the Spectral Flux: first, the Short-Time Fourier Transform of the signal is computed for sequential 80-ms duration windows in hops of 20 ms, and mapped to the MEL scale (approximately linear in log frequency); the resulting sequences are time-differentiated (via first-order difference) and half-wave rectified. To produce the detection function the obtained feature values are summed along all MEL sub-bands. Any peak above 20% of the maximum value in this function is taken as a true onset.

For drum sound classification, this work adopts the same spectral features, specifically the vector containing the first 40 MEL bands (corresponding to frequencies up to 1000 Hz). This value was chosen based on some feature selection experiments.

4 Clustering for Data Exploration

In order to explore the training data, a clustering analysis using the K-means algorithm [8] was carried out. The distance measure for the analysis should reflect the similarity in shape between two spectral feature profiles, and turned out to be a key issue since several measures considered were not appropriate. The Pearson correlation $PearsonCorr(x, y)$, computed as the inner product of two sequences x and y normalized to zero mean and unit standard deviation, can be seen as a shift-invariant cosine similarity. By treating the data points as the correlated sequences, their distances can be measured as $D(x, y) = 1 - PearsonCorr(x, y) \in [0, 2]$. The component-wise mean of its points is the centroid of each cluster.

The results of this clustering analysis applied to the training data when setting the number of clusters K=4 is presented in Fig. 2. The confusion matrix of a cluster-to-class evaluation (top left part) shows that *madera* and *chico* classes are correctly grouped, while *piano* and *repique* exhibit a higher rate of misclassification. A three-dimensional representation computed with Multidimensional Scaling (MDS) using the same distance measure is included (right part) for data visualization, and highlights the overlapping of classes. In particular, *repique* is the most troublesome class, which is not surprising since this is the drum of medium size and register, and thus expected to overlap the other drums' spectra. This issue is confirmed by the cluster centroids (bottom left part), whose shape is consistent with the spectral content of each sound class. The centroid of the *piano* drum class has a clear predominance at low frequencies, whereas the centroid of the *madera* class is dominant at high frequencies. At medium

	chico	repique	piano	madera
chico	474	23	0	3
repique	78	403	3	16
piano	1	79	420	0
madera	2	2	0	496
%	94.8	80.6	84.0	99.2

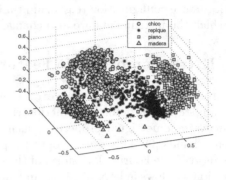

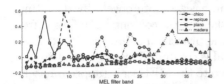

Fig. 2. Clustering analysis of the training data. Confusion matrix of a cluster-to-class evaluation and cluster centroids (left). Three-dimensional MDS representation (right).

frequencies, the centroid of the *repique* class exhibits a maximum towards the lower range, while the centroid of the *chico* class has higher frequency content.

5   Classification Methods

Results of the clustering analysis motivated the idea of testing a very simple classifier based on the obtained centroids: each centroid was considered as a single class prototype in a 1-NN classifier, using the previously introduced Pearson correlation distance. Such a classification scheme can simplify the process of building the training database, since unsupervised clustering can substitute for manual labeling. Furthermore, data coming from different sources, for instance different sets of drums or recording conditions, may be clustered independently so as to better describe classes with more than a single prototype. A k-NN and an RBF-SVM using the same distance measure were also implemented for comparison. SVM parameters were grid-searched in a cross-validation scheme.

6   Experiments and Results

6.1   Predominant Drum Recognition

The predominant drum recognition of a given audio track is tackled in a straightforward manner. First, the Spectral Flux feature is computed, followed by onsets detection, and classification of each detected event into one of the four defined classes. The proportion of onsets in each class gives an indication of the predominant instrument in the audio file. A simple but effective strategy was adopted to improve the detection of the *repique* drum, already identified in the training phase as the most difficult one. Considering that in a real performance, after the rhythm patterns have been initiated (i.e. after the first few seconds), *madera*

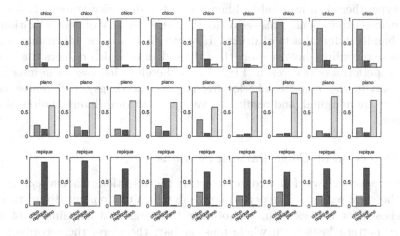

Fig. 3. Results of predominant drum recognition for the three-drum recordings using a 1-NN classifier of training dataset K-means centroids (■ *chico*, ■ *repique*, ▨ *piano*).

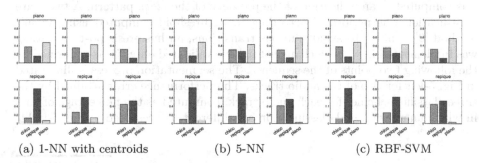

(a) 1-NN with centroids   (b) 5-NN   (c) RBF-SVM

Fig. 4. Predominant drum recognition for `drums-2` set (■ *chico*, ■ *repique*, ▨ *piano*).

sounds are played only by the *repique* drum, the onsets in the *madera* class were included in the *repique* drum class before computing the proportions.

In the first experiment setup all three-drum performances were considered. There are 9 recordings of 3 tracks, totaling 75 minutes and 27 audio files. Note that in this case, the same set of drums of the training samples (`drums-1`) was used. The estimated proportion of onsets for each audio file is shown in Fig. 3, for the 1-NN classifier based on the K-means centroid prototypes. It can be seen that the majority class always indicates the predominant drum. Similar results were obtained with k-NN and RBF-SVM, as shown in the next experiments.

The other set of drums (`drums-2`), not used for training, was employed in another experiment. There are 6 different drums, 3 *piano* and 3 *repique* (no *chico*). A track was processed for each drum, totaling 22 minutes of audio. Classification results are presented in Fig. 4 for a 1-NN of centroid prototypes, a 5-NN, and an RBF-SVM. Although the majority class always reveals the correct drum type, there is a noticeable difference in the disparity among classes w.r.t. the previous experiment. This seems to disclose some lack of generalization ability to handle different sets of drums. However, it has to be taken into account that these recordings involve more than three drums, which reduces the distance between performers (as seen in Fig. 1) and therefore increases the interference (e.g. *chico* in the *piano* tracks for five-player recordings). Differences among classifiers are marginal, and results are very similar for different choices of k-NN neighbors.

6.2 Detection of *Clave* Pattern Sections

A similar approach was followed for detecting those sections when a *repique* drum plays the *clave* pattern. Five performances in which two *repique* drums take part were chosen for this experiment, totaling 10 tracks and 33 minutes of audio. A *clave* pattern lasts for a whole musical bar; therefore, the recordings were manually labeled indicating all bar locations as well as which of them contained the *clave* pattern. The onsets in each track were detected and classified. Then, the proportion of *madera* onsets to the total detected events within each bar was computed as an indication of the presence of the *clave* pattern. A two-state classification was performed according to a threshold computed using Otsu's method [9]. Finally, to avoid spurious transitions, an hysteresis post-processing was implemented in which a change of state is validated only if it is confirmed by the following two points of the sequence. The segmentation process is illustrated in Fig. 5-left for two of the audio tracks. The performance error attained by the three classifier schemes for each audio track, computed as the percentage of bars in which annotation and classification are different, is presented in Fig. 5-right.

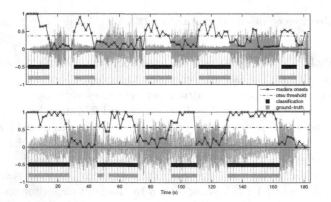

1-NN	5-NN	SVM
8.4	5.9	8.4
1.7	5.4	4.2
2.0	1.0	3.1
2.0	2.0	2.0
9.3	6.5	6.5
1.0	1.0	1.0
2.7	1.4	2.7
2.7	1.4	2.7
0.8	4.7	0.8
11.6	10.9	10.9
4.2	4.0	4.2

Fig. 5. Detection of *clave* pattern for two *repique* tracks of the same performance (left) and classification error for each track of the dataset (right). For each waveform plot: in the upper part, the proportion of *madera* onsets detected within each bar is depicted along with the Otsu threshold; in the lower part, vertical lines indicate the labeled bars, while horizontal thick lines show classification and ground-truth labels.

7 Discussion and Future Research

In this work an approach for predominant drum recognition in audio signals based on modeling onset spectral features was described. It is motivated by practical applications related to ongoing research on Candombe drumming from audio recordings. The reported experiments yielded promising results, even for the 1-NN classifier of centroid prototypes. To this regard, the Pearson correlation measure–which captures the similarity in shape between two spectral profiles– plays an essential role, which will be further assessed in future work.

Automatically detecting *clave* patterns from audio recordings, as proposed in this work, is a valuable tool for studying performance in musicological research. For instance, the interaction of two *repique* drums playing together is clearly visible in Fig. 5. Sections in which a performer plays the *clave* pattern show an almost perfect anti-symmetry between the two tracks. Besides, there exist several variations of the *clave* pattern that deserve a thorough study. To do that, the automatic detection of *clave* sections in a recording could allow dealing with large audio collections. In addition, *clave* pattern serves as a mean of temporal synchronization and can be exploited by automatic rhythm analysis algorithms.

References

1. Andrews, G.: Blackness in the White Nation: A History of Afro-Uruguay. The University of North Carolina Press, Chapel Hill (2010)
2. Dixon, S.: Onset detection revisited. In: Proc. of the 9th International Conference on Digital Audio Effects, Montreal, Canada, pp. 133–137, September 2006
3. Ferreira, L.: An afrocentric approach to musical performance in the black south atlantic: The candombe drumming in Uruguay. TRANS-Transcultural Music Review **11**, 1–15 (2007)
4. Fitzgerald, D., Paulus, J.: Unpitched percussion transcription. In: Klapuri, A., Davy, M. (eds.) Signal Processing Methods for Music Transcription, pp. 131–162. Springer, New York (2006)
5. Fletcher, N.H., Rossing, T.D.: The Physics of Musical Instruments, 2nd edn. Springer, New York (2010)
6. Gillet, O., Richard, G.: Transcription and separation of drum signals from polyphonic music. IEEE Transactions on Audio, Speech, and Language Processing **16**(3), 529–540 (2008)
7. Herrera, P., Dehamel, A., Gouyon, F.: Automatic labeling of unpitched percussion sounds. In: AES 114th Convention, Amsterdam, The Netherlands, pp. 1–14, March 2003. Convention Paper 5806
8. Jain, A.K.: Data Clustering: 50 Years Beyond K-Means. Pattern Recognition Letters **31**(8), 651–666 (2010)
9. Otsu, N.: A threshold selection method from gray-level histograms. IEEE Transactions on Systems, Man, and Cybernetics **9**(1), 62–66 (1979)
10. Polak, R., London, J.: Timing and Meter in Mande Drumming from Mali. Music Theory Online **20**(1), 1–22 (2014)
11. Sillanpää, J.: Drum stroke recognition. Technical report, Tampere University of Technology, Tampere, Finland (2000)

Classification of Basic Human Emotions from Electroencephalography Data

Ximena Fernández[1], Rosana García[1], Enrique Ferreira[1 (✉)],
and Juan Menéndez[2]

[1] Universidad Católica del Uruguay,
Av. 8 de Octubre 2738, 11600 Montevideo, Uruguay
enferrei@ucu.edu.uy
[2] Sentia Labs, 25 de Mayo 604, Of 102, 11100 Montevideo, Uruguay
juan.menendez@sentialabs.com

Abstract. This paper explores the combination of known signal processing techniques to analyze electroencephalography (EEG) data for the classification of a set of basic human emotions. An Emotiv EPOC headset with 16 electrodes was used to measure EEG data from a population of 24 subjects who were presented an audiovisual stimuli designed to evoke 4 emotions (rage, fear, fun and neutral). Raw data was preprocessed to eliminate noise, interference and physiologic artifacts. Discrete Wavelet Transform (DWT) was used to extract its main characteristics and define relevant features. Classification was performed using different algorithms and results compared. The best results were obtained when using meta-learning techniques with classification errors at 5 %. Final conclusions and future work are discussed.

Keywords: Electroencephalography · Discrete Wavelet Transform · Human emotion classification

1 Introduction

Recently, scientific development has been enhanced by the application of the interaction between different research paradigms to help understand complex phenomena in a field of study. For example, the use of neuroscience techniques to model human behavior in different areas [1]. Usually, research on emotion analysis is based on facial expressions and voice analysis (discourse). [6]. However, there are ways to alter those tests by masking real emotions or faking emotions in an interview. To avoid this issue there has been growing interest in the use of physiological data such us the EEG [2]. Ekman [5] and Winton [6] found the first evidences of physiological signal changes in relation to a small set of emotions. Cacioppo [4] identified patterns within the physiological signals with statistical significance to emotional changes on humans. An EEG system records electrical signals on the scalp generated by brain activity [9]. These signals are voltage variations due to ionic currents caused by neuronal activity in the brain [8].

© Springer International Publishing Switzerland 2015
A. Pardo and J. Kittler (Eds.): CIARP 2015, LNCS 9423, pp. 108–115, 2015.
DOI: 10.1007/978-3-319-25751-8_14

EEG signals are usually separated by its frequency content in 5 types. Delta signals with frequencies up to 4 Hz and larger amplitude (250 to 325 μV). Theta signals in the range between 4 an 8 Hz. Alpha signals cover the range between 8 and 14 Hz and characterize relax and alert states. Beta waves, with a frequency range between 14 and 32 Hz is related to motor activity. Gamma waves are the fastest, with a frequency range in between 32 and 100 Hz [8]. With so many interactions between neurons in the brain plus muscular activity and outside interference, these signals have a relatively low signal to noise ratio. To gather useful information from EEG data needs special equipment but also specific signal processing techniques [3,7,15,22]. On the other hand, it is a non invasive technique with a simple setup, relatively low cost and temporal high resolution potential that makes it ideal for engineering and clinical applications. There are commercial products that use EEG data for different applications such as games, rehabilitation [11] but mostly there is not detailed information on how they do it, making it difficult to use on research. This work makes use of a medium range commercial platform to gather EEG data from a designed experiment on 24 subjects and presents a signal processing strategy applying wavelet theory and meta-learning techniques to classify four basic human emotions.

The paper is organized as follows: section 2 explains the methodology used, equipment, population and experiment protocol. Section 3 describes the signal processing techniques employed to classify the emotions present in the data. Results are presented in section 4. Finally, conclusions and future work are presented in section 5.

2 Methodology

2.1 Population

EEG signals were recorded from 24 subjects between 22 and 39 years of age, 16 male and 8 women. None of them had any history of physical or mental illnesses nor were taking any drugs or medication that could affect EEG data. All subjects were informed of the scope and objectives of the test and signed an informed agreement with a detailed explanation of the test. Besides, any subject could leave the experiment at any time if desired.

2.2 Experimental Setup

EEG data was measured and recorded using an Emotiv EPOC headset with 16 channels, although two of them were used as reference [10]. Ag/AgCl electrodes were placed on the subject's scalp using the international 10-20 standard convention [9]. Sampling time selected was 128 Hz. The headset is connected to a PC which receives the time sequences corresponding to each channel. The sequences are preprocessed in the device with 2 notch filters at 50 and 60 Hz to eliminate power line interference and a passband filter of 0.16-45 Hz bandwidth. The device also gives a measure of the contact quality on each channel. Data was discarded if contact quality on a given channel was no good.

2.3   Test Protocol

The subjects were sat in front of a PC running the Psychopy [12] application with the headset correctly placed. A sequence of 12 audiovisual clips was presented to the subjects to elicit 4 emotions: rage, fear, fun and neutral (or absence of emotion), with 3 clips per emotion. The clips were selected from FilmStim [13], a free stimuli database. Each clip, taken from a commercial film, has been validated to elicit a specific emotion, even for spanish speakers [14,18]. The order of clips in the sequence is such that consecutive clips can not evoke the same emotion. In between clips a short survey with 3 SAM images [19] is given for relaxation and in order to neutralize the effects of one clip on the next. Three 12-sequence audiovisual protocols were generated using the same 12 clips in different order, randomly selecting one for each subject. The experimental process is summarized in Fig. 1. The whole test took between 30 to 45 minutes to complete for all subjects.

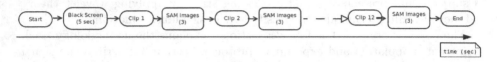

Fig. 1. Test protocol presented to each subject: a sequence of 12 audiovisual clips to elicit a specific emotion alternated with a survey of 3 SAM images.

3   Data Classification Process

3.1   Preprocessing

EEG raw signal is contaminated with noise and artifacts of external and physiologic origin. Emotiv EPOCH acquires and filters the raw data with notch filters in 50 and 60 Hz to eliminate interference from the power line and a passband filter with 0.16-45 Hz bandwidth [10]. There are still non desired artifacts in the channel signal as shown in Fig. 2.

First, the EEG raw data obtained from Emotiv for each subject is segmented in time in 12 pieces corresponding to each clip. To further eliminate artifacts such as eye and eyebrow movements and neck muscle activity the `clean_rawdata()` wrapper function from the Artifacts Subspace Reconstruction (ASR) extension to the EEGLAB Matlab Toolbox was applied [20]. Normalization of the filtered data was performed before extracting the main features to use for classification.

3.2   Feature Extraction

Preprocessed data is still too big and complex to be able to discriminate emotions from them directly. A set of relevant features needs to be extracted to minimize classification mistakes. Because EEG data is a strongly non-stationary signal

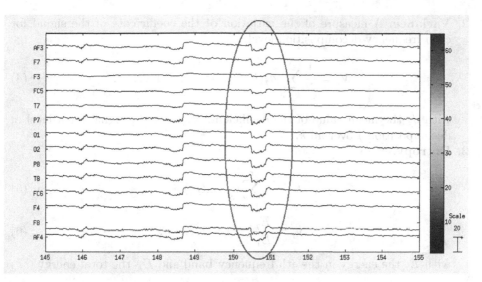

Fig. 2. Raw data from all 14 active headset channels showing ocular artifacts (red oval).

a multi-resolution analysis method using a Wavelet Transform is selected to compress the data without losing too much information from it as proposed in [17, 21, 22]. DWT uses a mother wave $\Psi(t)$ to generate the basis for decomposition of the time sequences recorded from EEG signals. Three mother waves were selected, two from the Daubechies family (db4, db8) and one from the Symlet (sym8) because they provided acceptable time-frequency resolution [23, 24]. The basis is generated using two integer parameters j and k, the scale and translation indexes, giving the wavelets

$$\Psi_{j,k}(t) = \Psi(2^j t - k), \quad j = 1, \ldots, n \quad k = 1, \ldots, N, \tag{1}$$

with N the number of samples and n the number of decomposition levels. Since the sampling frequency is 128 Hz, $n = 14$ decomposition levels were used to have sufficient discrimination for the 5 types of EEG waves. Each EEG preprocessed sampled data per subject, channel and clip $s(t)$ can be expressed in terms of the wavelets as

$$s(t) = \sum_{k=1}^{N} \sum_{j=1}^{n} d_j(k).\Psi_{j,k}(t). \tag{2}$$

The coefficients $d_j(k)$ were computed using the Quadrature Mirror Filter Bank [22]. Based on the coefficients $d_j(k)$ the following features were computed:

1. **Power**. The power of the signal for each frequency decomposition level j.

$$P_j = \frac{1}{N} \sum_{k=1}^{N} |d_j(k)|^2, \quad j = 1, \ldots, n. \tag{3}$$

2. **Variance**. A measure of the variation of the coefficients of the signal for each frequency decomposition level j.

$$V_j = \frac{1}{N} \sum_{k=1}^{N} (d_j(k) - \bar{d}_j)^2, \quad j = 1, \ldots, n. \tag{4}$$

with $\bar{d}_j$ the mean value of the coefficients $d_j(k)$ of the signal for a level of decomposition j over all k.

3. **Entropy**.

$$H = -\sum_{j=1}^{n} p_j \log(p_j) \tag{5}$$

$$p_j = \frac{E_j}{E_T}, \quad j = 1, \ldots, n, \tag{6}$$

with E_j the energy in the jth frequency band and E_T the total energy.

In summary, for each EEG channel and clip, $2n + 1$ features are generated.

3.3 Classification Process

Pattern classification algorithms associate each element, i.e. each set of feature values characterizing the current emotion of a subject, with one of the 4 emotions analyzed. In this work a comparison of the best classifiers used for a similar problem in previous works was carried out [16,21]. Those were: K-nearest neighbors (KNN), AdaBoost and Random Committee. KNN is a nonparametric classifier where a decision for an individual value is taken by looking at which classes its K nearest neighbors are and voting. It is robust to outliers. K values between 2 and 8 were tried to find the optimum (K=3). AdaBoost is a supervised learning algorithm that combines weak classifiers to generate a strong classifier. It is robust to overfitting but sensible to outliers [25,26]. The best results were reached when using the kernel called J48 [28]. RandomCommittee is a technique within the framework of metalearning algorithms. It takes existing classifier systems and generates an ensemble of instances of classifiers using random parameters that are embedded in the base classifiers selected. The classification is made by either voting or averaging the results of the ensemble of classifiers generated.In this work the best results were obtained when using RandomForest as the base classifier and averaging their results [27]. Classification was performed using the tool WEKA [29], using 10-fold cross validation and pattern testing with 10 percent fresh data.

4 Results

The tables below show the results as percentage of correct classification and ROC area for each class, and total percentage of correct classification for the three classifiers selected.

Table 1. Classification accuracy when using KNN method with k=3.

	db4		db8		sym8	
	%	ROC	%	ROC	%	ROC
Correct Classification (%)	79.9		73.4		59.4	
Fear	70.0	0.900	63.8	0.820	44.7	0.734
Rage	80.0	0.819	74.1	0.846	45.8	0.704
Fun	77.4	0.924	64.7	0.845	58.3	0.805
Neutral	98.1	0.992	96.2	0.991	98.2	0.994
Weighted Average	81.0	0.909	74.3	0.874	60.2	0.807

Table 2. Classification accuracy using Random Committee with Random Forest kernel.

	db4		db8		sym8	
	%	ROC	%	ROC	%	ROC
Correct Classification (%)	94.3		91.8		84.6	
Fear	87.5	0.989	83.1	0.978	73.3	0.949
Rage	96.5	0.993	91.5	0.992	89.4	0.939
Fun	94.8	0.990	88.3	0.983	83.0	0.947
Neutral	100	1.00	98.3	1.00	98.0	0.999
Weighted Average	94.5	0.975	92.1	0.960	85.5	0.958

Table 3. Individual Classification Accuracy when using AdaBoostM1 with kernel J48.

	db4		db8		sym8	
	%	ROC	%	ROC	%	ROC
Correct Classification (%)	87.3		82.4		77.9	
Fear	89.5	0.956	76.6	0.932	73.3	0.899
Rage	83.3	0.986	83.6	0.980	69.5	0.899
Fun	81.8	0.974	76.6	0.944	75.8	0.951
Neutral	96.4	0.985	94.5	0.987	98.2	0.995
Weighted Average	87.8	0.975	82.6	0.960	78.2	0.935

Table 4. Confusion matrix for Random Committee for db4 feature set.

	Fear	Rage	Fun	Neutral
Fear	64	0	2	0
Rage	6	53	0	0
Fun	5	0	55	0
Neutral	0	2	0	57

For the three types of wavelets selected the Random Committee classifier obtained the best results. Within each classifier, the wavelet of type Daubechies with 4 vanishing moments (db4) outperform the others, reaching 94.3 % of overall correct classification percentage for the Random Committee classifier. ROC values are mostly acceptable at around 90 % in all cases and higher than 97 % for the best results. Finally, the best classifier reached 87.5 % classification accuracy on the test set. Looking at the emotions themselves, the neutral emotion was the easiest to discriminate for any classifier throughout. On the other hand, the Fear emotion seems to dominate over Rage and Fun according to Table 4.

5 Conclusions

This work presents a system to record, analyze EEG signals and classify basic human emotions. An experiment was conducted using 24 subjects with a validated database of audiovisual clips to induce rage, fear, fun or neutral emotions. Even though the hardware only allowed to sense 16 channels compare to research devices with 64 up to 256 electrodes, by an adequate signal processing using DWT and relevant features, the overall percentage of errors achieved was around 5 % when using meta-learning techniques. Some of the mistakes between classes might be due to a smaller train set or the clips themselves that were in some cases too long and with mixed feelings to clearly represent the emotion assigned even though the dataset has been validated internationally. The study allowed to see the impact in classification of the selection of features, algorithms for eliminating artifact in the signals and wavelets selected. The results are promising to consider an EEG system like this one a relatively low cost new complex sensor device for research into other bioengineering areas. From a practical point of view, the use of shorter clips should be better to have less dispersion in the data. Also, to have more subjects will improve the statistics. Future work includes the use of other techniques to improve the elimination of artifacts such as independent component analysis, to reduce the dimensionality of the problem in the feature space and the application of this sensor in neuromarketing and rehabilitation engineering.

References

1. Lee, N., Broderick, A.J., Chanberlain, L.: What is neuromarketing? A discussion and agenda for future research. Int. J. Psychophysiol. **63**(2), 199–204 (2007)
2. Jatupaiboon, N., Pan-ngum, S., Israsena, P.: Real-Time EEG-Based Happiness Detection System. The Scientific World Journal **2013**, 12 (2013). ID 618649
3. Torres, A.A., Reyes, C.A., Villaseor, L., Ramrez, J.M.: Anlisis de Seales Electroencefalogrficas para la Clasificacin de Habla Imaginada. Revista Mexicana de Ingeniera Biomdica **34**(1), 23–39 (2013)
4. Cacioppo, C.T., Tassinary, L.G.: Inferring Physiological Significance from Physiological Signals. Am. Psychol. **45**(1), 16–28 (1990)
5. Ekman, P., Levenson, R.W., Freison, W.V.: Autonomic Nervous System Activity Distinguishes Among Emotions. J. Exp. Soc. Psychol. **19**, 195–216 (1983)

6. Winton, W.M., Putnam, L., Krauss, R.: Facial and Autonomic Manifestations of the dimensional structure of Emotion. J. Exp. Soc. Psychol. **20**, 195–216 (1984)
7. Murugappan, M., Murugappan, S., Balaganapathy, C.: Wireless EEG signals based neuromarketing system using fast fourier transform (FFT). In: 10th Int. Col. on Signal Processing & its Applications, pp. 25–30. IEEE (2014)
8. Lopes da Silva, F., Niedermeyer, E.: Electroencephalography: Basic Principles, Clinical Applications, and Related Fields, 6th edn. Lippincot Williams & Wilkins (2004). ISBN 0-7817-5126-8
9. Sanei, S., Sanei, S., Chambers, J.A.: EEG Signal Processing. Centre of Digital Signal Processing Cardiff University, UK (2007). ISBN 978-0-470-02581-9
10. (2015). http://www.emotiv.com/
11. (2015). http://neurogadget.com/category/headset-2
12. Pierce, J.W.: PsychoPy. Psychophysics software in Python (2007). http://www.psychopy.org/
13. Schaefer, A., Nils, F., Snchez, X., Philippot, P.: FilmStim, Assessing the effectiveness of a large database of emotion-eliciting films: A new tool for emotion researchers. Cognition and Emotion **24**(7), 1153–1172 (2010)
14. Fernandez Megas, C., Prez Sola, V.: Inducción de emociones en condiciones experimentales: un banco de estímulos audiovisuales. Programa de Doctorado en Psiquiatra Departament de Psiquiatria i Medicin UAB (2012)
15. Murugappan, M., Nagarajan, R., Yaacob, S.: Combining Spatial Filtering and Wavelet Transform for Classifying Human Emotions Using EEG Signals. IEEE Symposium on Industrial Electronics & Applications **2**, 836–841 (2009)
16. Murugappan, M.: Human emotion classification using wavelet transform and KNN. In: Int. Conf. on Pattern Analysis and Intelligent Robotics, vol. 11, pp. 48–153 (2011)
17. Murugappan, M., Nagarajan, R., Yaacob, S.: Comparison of different wavelet features from EEG signals for classifying human emotions. IEEE Symposium on Industrial Electronics & Applications **2**, 836–841 (2009)
18. Fernandez, C., Pascual, J.C., Soler, J., Garca, E.: Validacin espaola de una batera de pelculas para inducir emociones. Psicothema **23**(4), 778–785 (2011)
19. Bradley, M., Lang, P.: Measuring Emotion: the Self-Assessment Semantic Differential. J. Behav. Ther. & Exp. Psvchrar. **25**(1), 49–59 (1994)
20. EEGLAB Wiki. http://sccn.ucsd.edu/wiki/EEGLAB
21. Weber, P., Letelier, J.: Clasificacion de Espigas Extracelulares Basada en la Transformada de Wavelet Discreta. Universidad de Chile (2002). http://repositorio.uchile.cl/tesis/uchile/2002/weber_p/html/index-frames.html
22. Samar, V.J., Bopardikar, A.: Wavelet analysis of neuroelectric waveforms: a conceptual tutorial. Brain and Language **66**(1), 7–60 (1999)
23. Mallat, S.: A wavelet tour of signal processing. Academic Press (1999)
24. Parameswariah, C., Cox, M.: Frequency characteristics of wavelets. IEEE Transactions on Power Delivery **17**(3), 800–804 (2002). ISSN: 0885–8977
25. Witten, H., Frank, I., Hall, M.: DATA MINING Practical Machine Learning Tools and Techniques, 3rd edn, pp. 356–372 (2011)
26. Aha, D., Kibler, D.: Instance-based learning algorithms. Machine Learning **6**(1), 37–66 (1991)
27. Breiman, L.: Random Forests. Machine Learning **45**(1), 5–32 (2001)
28. Quinlan, J.R.: C4.5: Programs for Machine Learning. Machine Learning **16**(3), 235–240 (1994)
29. Hall, M., Frank, E., Holmes, G., Pfahringer, B., Reutemann, P., Witten, I.H.: The WEKA Data Mining Software: An Update. SIGKDD Explorations **11**(1) (2009)

A Non-parametric Approach to Detect Changes in Aerial Images

Marco Túlio Alves Rodrigues[(✉)], Daniel Balbino, Erickson Rangel Nascimento, and William Robson Schwartz

Department of Computer Science, Universidade Federal de Minas Gerais, Av. Antônio Carlos, Pampulha, Belo Horizonte 6627, Brazil
{tulio.rodrigues,balbino,erickson,william}@dcc.ufmg.br

Abstract. Detecting changes in aerial images acquired from a scene at different times, possibly with different cameras and at different view points, is a crucial step for many image processing and computer vision applications, such as remote sensing, visual surveillance and civil infrastructure. In this paper, we propose a novel approach to automatically detect changes based on local descriptors and a non-parametric image block modeling. Differently from most approaches, which are pixel-based, our approach combines contextual information and kernel density estimation to model the image regions to identify changes. The experimental results show the effectiveness of the proposed approach compared to other methods in the literature, demonstrating the robustness of our algorithm. The results also demonstrate that the approach can be employed to generate a summary containing mostly frames presenting significant changes.

Keywords: Change detection · Non-parametric modeling · Aerial images

1 Introduction

The detection of changes in a scene plays a central rule in a myriad of applications, such as disaster management, urban growth, security, burned areas and surveillance to name a few. In addition, detecting structural changes is useful to gather information from the environment, which might present economic impact.

The most common procedure applied to detect changes is to use human operators to watch videos from a monitoring camera and identify changes in images from the scene. However, in general, video monitoring performed by humans is error prone due to lack of attention in repetitive long tasks. Therefore, automated monitoring is a solution to reduce human error and can be used as a filter to locate video segments that should be further analyzed by operators.

The basic task of change detection in images is to locate the pixels from a *reference image* that are different from other images [9], referred to as *test images*. Significant changes may include object removal, movement of objects and shape

© Springer International Publishing Switzerland 2015
A. Pardo and J. Kittler (Eds.): CIARP 2015, LNCS 9423, pp. 116–124, 2015.
DOI: 10.1007/978-3-319-25751-8_15

variation of the scene structures. Changes in image pixels can also be generated by viewpoint change, noise, illumination changes, nonuniform attenuation, atmospheric absorption, swaying trees, rippling water or flickering monitors. Although such effects produce changes in the pixel intensity, they must be ignored by the change detection method, which makes it a hard problem to handle.

In general, two main goals are pursued by change detection systems: (i) location of changes through a mask, referred to as *change mask* and (ii) identification of frames where changes occur without the creation of change masks. While in former, the exact location of the changes is of interest, in the latter, the user is interested in finding the frames that the changes happened, in which a further analysis will be performed. This work focuses on the latter goal to being able to create a shortlist containing frames with high likelihood of presenting changes.

Several approaches focusing on background subtraction and remote sensing techniques have been applied to change detection. In general, the background subtraction performance is highly dependent on building and maintaining a background model. Most of these techniques are pixel-based and they assume independence among pixels. In remote sensing methods, the change detection performance depends on the trade-off between the spatial and spectral resolution [1].

In this paper, we propose a novel approach to identify, from a set of images, which ones present significant differences when compared to a reference image. Our method extracts local feature descriptors from image blocks and estimates the likelihood of a change by using a non-parametric modeling based on Kernel Density Estimation (KDE) [5]. KDE is a statistically-sound method that estimates a continuous distribution from a finite set of points. Unlike background subtraction and remote sensing methods, our technique does not require a complex learning stage (i.e., it just stores samples). Additionally, our method requires a few number of samples (single example from the reference image), being therefore, capable of detecting changes by using only two images (the reference image and a test images), which is hard to perform with parametric approaches due to the lack of samples to estimate parameters.

In the experiments, we compare our method with techniques widely used for change detection. According to the results, the proposed approach outperforms several other methods found in the literature [2,3,10,11,18], mainly due to the fact that our approach is more robust to illumination changes, frequent on aerial images taken at different times. The results also demonstrate that our method is able to filter the video segments generating a video summary containing mostly frames presenting significant changes.

2   Related Work

Over the past years, a large number of change detection techniques have been proposed, mostly based on background subtraction and remote sensing techniques [9]. However, there are still several limitations in change detection techniques since it is hard to separate significant (e.g., object removal, structural changes) from insignificant changes (e.g., noise, illumination changes).

Background subtraction methods consist in learning the background model by using several reference images. In the test phase, all pixels are classified as foreground or background. The foreground pixels indicate changes [8]. Such methods can divided into parametric and non-parametric.

Parametric methods assume that each pixel can be modeled as a random process that can be approximated by some parametric distribution [12]. Regarding non-parametric approaches, the background is modeled by a probability density function (PDF) estimated for each pixel. The main characteristic of these methods is the strong dependence on the data. Although such approaches are capable of adapting to sudden changes, they require to store the pixels. Elgammal et al. [4] presented a non-parametric kernel density estimation to perform the background subtraction. St-Charles et al. [11] proposed an approach based on the adaptation and integration of Local Binary Similarity Pattern (LBSP) features in a non-parametric background model that is then automatically tuned using pixel feedback. The major improvement is related to internal threshold that makes the binary descriptors much more robust to illumination variation.

Similar to background subtraction methods, remote sensing techniques for change detection also requires a learning stage to model the reference image [15]. However, unlike the background subtraction methods, the remote sensing approaches are based on feature extraction, which reduces errors due to pixels noise and small changes in the reference image.

Celik [2] computes the difference between the test image and the reference image by combining PCA and K-means. The change is detected by partitioning the feature vector space into two clusters. The algorithm assigns each pixel to one of the two clusters based on the Euclidean distance between the pixel feature vector and mean feature vector of clusters. To reduce the effect caused by noise in [2], Cheng et al. [3] proposed the use of the fraction Fourier transform (FRFT). Zheng et al. [17] also employ a technique based on a clustering. They apply image subtraction the log ratio operator to generate two types of change maps. Then, a simple combination uses the maps obtained by the mean filter and the median filter to improve the final change map.

Rodrigues et al. [10] investigate the sensibility of pixel to noise and the influence of monotonic transformation in change detection methods. They proposed a solution that is neither based on background subtraction nor on remote sensing techniques, but a combination of super-pixel extraction, hierarchical clustering and segment matching. The drawback of their approach is its sensibility to variations in lighting and camera displacement.

In spite of the significant progress in solving the change detection problem, the aforementioned techniques are highly limited by the large variability of irrelevant changes. Virtually, all described approaches require a learning stage and present high computational cost. Moreover, these techniques do not work properly whenever the background scene suddenly changes or there are not enough samples to estimate the background model. Therefore, they are unfeasible when it is provided only a single reference image.

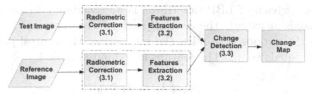

Fig. 1. Steps of the proposed change detection method. When a reference and a test image are presented to the system, we first perform the radiometric normalization and extract the features to estimate the likelihood of changes.

3   Proposed Approach

Let the *reference image* and the *test image* be two registered aerial images acquired from the same geographical area at times t_1 and t_2, respectively, we detect changes in the scene by analyzing the image characteristics and output a score indicating whether there are changes between the two images. As illustrated in Figure 1, the proposed approach in this work is composed of the three main steps: (i) *radiometric correction*, (ii) *feature extraction*, and (iii) *change detection*. These steps are described in details in the following sections.

3.1   Radiometric Correction

The goal of radiometric correction is to remove or compensate for illumination changes. We employ the Self-Quotiente Image (SQI) [14], a popular method used for synthesizing an illumination normalized image from a single image. The SQI normalization is defined by a smoothed image $S(x, y)$ of a image $I(x, y)$ as

$$Q(x, y) = \frac{I(x, y)}{S(x, y)} = \frac{I(x, y)}{F(x, y) * I(x, y)}, \tag{1}$$

where $F(x, y)$ is a low-pass filter and $*$ is the convolution operator.

3.2   Feature Extraction

We use in our method two different local feature descriptors to provide high robustness to lighting changes: the Local Binary Patterns (LBP) [7] and the Local Ternary Patterns (LTP) [13]. These features are invariant to monotonic changes and are extremely fast to compute.

The LBP descriptor for a pixel $C = (x_c, y_c)$ is computed by thresholding the gray value of N sampling pixels defined by the indicator function $s(x_1, x_2)$. The indicator function returns 1 when the intensity value of pixel x_1 is greater than x_2 and 0 otherwise. By considering g_c the intensity of the center pixel and g_p $(p = 0, \ldots, N - 1)$ the corresponding intensity of a pixel value of N sampling points, the final feature vector is given by summing the thresholded values weighted by powers of two.

The major drawback of LBP descriptor is its sensibility to noise, since the operator thresholds at exactly the central pixel g_c. To overcome this limitation, Tan and Triggs [13] proposed to relax the intensity of the central pixel by using a slack of width equals to $\pm t$. The feature is computed as

$$LTP(g_p, g_c, t) = \begin{cases} 1, & g_p \geq g_c + t \\ 0, & |g_p - g_c| < t \\ -1, & g_p \geq g_c - t \end{cases} \quad (2)$$

A coding scheme is used to split the ternary pattern in negative and positive LBP. Here, t is a parameter that makes the LBP more resistant to noise. In this work we use $t = 5$, defined experimentally.

After computing the LBP or LTP (positive and negative) codes for each pixel, the vector descriptor is represented by a 256-bin normalized histogram (in our tests we use $N = 8$ and $t = 5$).

3.3 Change Detection

We use a non-parametric approach to estimate the probability density function, since only one sample is available (the reference image) to learn the background model. Given a set reference image blocks $B = \{b_1, b_2, \ldots, b_N\}$, the density estimate at a new test image block b_t is given by

$$\hat{f}(b_t) = \frac{1}{N} \sum_{i=1}^{N} K_h(b_t, b_i) = \frac{1}{Nh} \sum_{i=1}^{N} K(\frac{b_t - b_i}{h}), \quad (3)$$

where h is the bandwidth, N is the number of samples in the reference image, b_i is a block in reference image and b_t is a block in test image. We used the Gaussian kernel for density estimation. Then, for each block histogram, the density estimate is found.

To evaluate the kernel summations in linear time, we use FigTree [6], which provides an efficient computation of probabilities by KDE by combining the Improved Fast Gaussian Transform (IFGT) [16] with a kd-tree on cluster centers for neighbor searching in multiple dimensions. This method accelerates the Gaussian kernel summation and reduces the computational complexity of the evaluation of the sum of N Gaussians at M points in d dimensions from $O(MN)$ to $O(M + N)$.

4 Experimental Results

To evaluate the effectiveness of the proposed approach, we conduct several experiments considering synthetic and non-synthetic datasets. First, we evaluate the feature extraction using a synthetic dataset (Section 4.1). We then evaluate different setups for the proposed method (Section 4.2). Finally, in Section 4.3, we compare the results with other methods regarding the accuracy and the ability of generating a summary with relevant frames, i.e., frames presenting changes.

We evaluate our approach using the area under the curve (AUC) obtained from the operating characteristic (ROC) curve computed based on the true positive rate and the false positive rate, in which a test image is considered a false positive when the amount of changes is larger than a threshold (used to generate the ROC curve). Due to the lack of space, only the AUC values are shown.

To evaluate parameters of our method, we consider a *synthetic* dataset, in which from a single aerial image, we generated a set of 60 new images by applying several transformations simulating common effects in a capture system: Gaussian noise (with $\sigma = 0.01$), small translations (up to 5 pixels), blur, contrast and brightness changes. Moreover, on 30 of those images, we manually inserted artificial changes. The main purpose of this test set is to validate our algorithm on a controlled environment and also for tunning some of the main parameters. It is important to note that this dataset considers only one image as reference and the remaining as test images.

To compare our approach to other methods in the literature, we use a *non-synthetic* dataset composed of 26 aerial images acquired from PETROBRAS over oil pipes in the southern part of Brazil. Each with their own registered reference image, where in 13 of those have some change and on the other 13 do not contain changes.

4.1   Feature Extraction

To detect changes, our method divides the image into m block regions, from which local feature descriptors are extracted. Moreover, we add the coordinates of the blocks to the descriptors. This includes spatial information to the feature histograms. Six different block size were considered (8×8, 16×16, 32×32, 64×64, 92×92 and 128×128). According to the results obtained in the *synthetic* dataset, the block size 64×64 achieved the best results. Therefore, this block size will be used in the comparisons using non-synthetic dataset.

Three different descriptors were considered: LBP, LTP negative and LTP positive. We use LTP negative as the feature descriptor for the evaluation since it achieved the best results in the *synthetic* dataset (AUC=0.96), compared to the LTP positive (AUC=0.95) and LBP (AUC=0.90).

4.2   Evaluation of the Proposed Approach

In this section, we evaluate three setups for the proposed method. The first employs a simple nearest neighbor (*NN*) search, which is perhaps the most intuitive approach to change detection; the second employs a local KDE (*FigTree Local*), in which each image block is modeled by a single KDE; and the third setup employs a global KDE (*FigTree Global*) considering a single KDE model for the entire image but adding the block coordinates to the feature vector. The last two setups use the FigTree to optimize the search.

Approach	AUC values
Zivkovic [18]	0.50
PCA-kmeans [2]	0.50
FRFT [3]	0.52
MLEW [10]	0.52
LBPSP [11]	0.55
NN	0.70
FigTree Local	0.72
FigTree Global	**0.88**

(a)

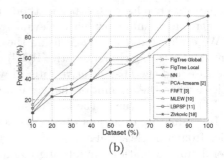

(b)

Fig. 2. Results comparing the proposed approach to other methods. (a) AUC achieved considering the *non-synthetic* dataset (the best results are closer to one); (b) precision as a function of the number of frames selected to show that our approach is able to create a summary containing relevant frames (i.e., frames presenting changes).

The last three rows of Table in Figure 2(a) depict the results achieved by each setup. According to the results, all three approaches achieved good results compared to the remaining methods. The small difference between the *NN* and *FigTree Local* is due the normalization performed by the KDE. They have nearly the same results, however, the complexity computational of *NN* is greater than the *FigTree Local* as discussed in Section 1. This makes the computation for large scale problems prohibitively expensive for *NN*. Finally, when a single KDE model is considered (*FigTree Global*), the results improved significantly, achieving AUC=0.88, compared with AUC=0.72 using *FigTree Local*. The global approach allows the contribution of nearby blocks, different from the *FigTree Local* and *NN*, which consider each block independently. The contribution of nearby blocks is essential to suppress acquisition noise and small errors in image registration, achieving therefore, more accurate results.

We also evaluated the multivariate Gaussian distribution to model the blocks. However, due to the nature of our problem, in which only a reference is available, the employment of a parametric model is not appropriate since the lack of samples does not allow a proper parameter estimation.

4.3   Comparisons

In this section, we compare the proposed approach using the *non-synthetic* dataset with five change detection techniques: Zivkovic [18], LBPSP [11], MLEW [10], PCA-Kmeans [2] and FRFT [3]. According to the results shown in Table of Figure 2(a), the background subtraction approaches (e.g, *Zivkovic* and *LBPSP*) do not work properly due to the lack of samples to estimate the background model. Therefore, they are unfeasible when it is provided only a single reference image. In addition, *PCA-Kmeans*, *FRFT* and *MLEW* achieved poor results due to their lack of robustness to the strong influence of illumination variation. On the other hand, the proposed approach (*FigTree Global*) achieved very accurate results due to its robustness to illumination changes and noises.

The achieved results demonstrate the importance of developing a method robust to illumination changes by performing radiometric correction and using robust feature descriptors. Otherwise, changes due to illumination, common in aerial taken at different times, might be considered as relevant changes, which should not be the case.

Figure 2(b) shows the accuracy measured by AUC as a function of the percentage of frames selected. According to the results achieved by the *FigTree Global*, it is possible to capture 58% of the changes, showing only for 30% of the frames (by displaying 40%, we were able to show 78% of the changes), which are the best results compared to the other approaches. Therefore, the employment of an automatic system can be used as a filter to provide a shortlist with frames that should be further analyzed. This would help the operators in the decision making process regarding actions to be executed.

5 Conclusions

In this paper, we described a combination of radiometric correction and a non-parametric strategy to estimate a probability density function by kernel approaches. The proposed approach uses radiometric correction, features description and Figtree. When compared to baseline techniques, the proposed approach achieved the highest AUC values, demonstrating to be a promising technique to be employed in change detection tasks when a single reference image is provided.

Acknowledgments. The authors would like to thank CNPq, CAPES, FAPEMIG and Petrobras.

References

1. Aplin, P., Atkinson, P.M., Curran, P.J.: Fine spatial resolution simulated satellite sensor imagery for land cover mapping in the United Kingdom. RSE (1999)
2. Celik, T.: Unsupervised Change Detection in Satellite Images Using Principal Component Analysis and k-Means Clustering. IGRSL (2009)
3. Cheng, Y.Q., Li, H.C., Celik, T., Zhang, F.: FRFT-based improved algorithm of unsupervised change detection in SAR images via PCA and K-means clustering. In: IGARSS (2013)
4. Elgammal, A., Harwood, D., Davis, L.: Non-parametric model for background subtraction. In: Vernon, D. (ed.) ECCV 2000. LNCS, vol. 1843, pp. 751–767. Springer, Heidelberg (2000)
5. Morariu, V.I., Srinivasan, B.V., Raykar, V.C., Duraiswami, R., Davis, L.: Automatic online tuning for fast Gaussian summation. In: ANIPRS (2009)
6. Morariu, V.I., Srinivasan, B.V., Raykar, V.C., Duraiswami, R., Davis, L.S.: Automatic online tuning for fast Gaussian summation. In: NIPS (2008)
7. Ojala, T., Pietikäinen, M., Mäenpää, T.: Multiresolution Gray-Scale and Rotation Invariant Texture Classification with Local Binary Patterns. PAMI (2002)
8. Piccardi, M.: Background subtraction techniques: a review. In: ICSMC (2004)

9. Radke, R., Andra, S., Al-Kofahi, O., Roysam, B.: Image change detection algorithms: a systematic survey. IEEE TIP (2005)
10. Rodrigues, M., Milen, L.O., Nascimento, E.R., Schwartz, W.R.: Change detection based on features invariant to monotonic transforms and spatial constrained matching. In: ICASSP (2014)
11. St-Charles, P.L., Bilodeau, G.A., Bergevin, R.: Subsense: A universal change detection method with local adaptive sensitivity (2014)
12. Stauffer, C., Grimson, W.E.L.: Learning patterns of activity using real-time tracking. PAMI (2000)
13. Tan, X., Triggs, B.: Enhanced local texture feature sets for face recognition under difficult lighting conditions. In: Zhou, S.K., Zhao, W., Tang, X., Gong, S. (eds.) AMFG 2007. LNCS, vol. 4778, pp. 168–182. Springer, Heidelberg (2007)
14. Wang, H., Li, S.Z., Wang, Y.: Face recognition under varying lighting conditions using self quotient image. In: ICAFGR (2004)
15. Xu, Q., Karam, L.J.: Change detection on SAR images by a parametric estimation of the KL-divergence between Gaussian mixture models. In: ICASSP (2013)
16. Yang, C., Duraiswami, R., Davis, L.S.: Efficient kernel machines using the improved fast Gauss transform. In: Advances in Neural Information Processing Systems (2004)
17. Zheng, Y., Zhang, X., Hou, B., Liu, G.: Using Combined Difference Image and-Means Clustering for SAR Image Change Detection. GRSS (2014)
18. Zivkovic, Z.: Improved adaptive Gaussian mixture model for background subtraction. In: ICPR. IEEE (2004)

Biometrics

A New Fingerprint Indexing Algorithm for Latent and Non-latent Impressions Identification

José Hernández-Palancar and Alfredo Muñoz-Briseño[✉]

Advanced Technologies Application Center (CENATAV), Havana, Cuba
{jpalancar,amunoz}@cenatav.co.cu

Abstract. In this work, a new fingerprint identification algorithm for latent and non-latent impressions based on indexing techniques is presented. This proposal uses a minutia triplet state-of-the-art representation, which has proven to be very tolerant to distortions. Also, a novel strategy to partition the indexes is implemented, in the retrieving stage. This strategy allows to use the algorithm in both contexts, criminal and non-criminal. The experimental results show that in latent identification this approach has a 91.08% of hit rate at penetration rate of 20%, on NIST27 database using a large background of 267000 rolled impressions. Meanwhile in non-latent identification at the same penetration rate, the algorithm reaches a hit rate of 97.8% on NIST4 database and a 100% of hit rate on FVC2004 DB1A database. These accuracy values were reached with a high efficiency.

Keywords: Fingerprint indexing · Index partition · Polygonal hull

1 Introduction

Biometrics is the science of identifying people from particular physical features such as voice, fingerprints, iris texture or facial structure. One of the techniques used by biometric systems is the comparison of fingerprints due its uniqueness. Depending on the context of implementation of fingerprint recognition systems, two general classes of problems can be distinguished: verification (1 vs 1) and identification (1 vs many). A first approach to the identification of a person, could be to compare the given fingerprint with every one stored in the database. However, the size of current fingerprint databases is in the order of millions of impressions, so this approach is impracticable and some techniques to reduce the search space are needed, e.g., indexing techniques. The methods based on indexing techniques return a list sorted by relevance of potential candidates to match with a given query. An additional complexity is presented when the query is performed using a latent fingerprint. These impressions are taken from crime scenes and generally the images have very bad quality.

In the literature, diverse approaches of indexing algorithms can be found. The differences between these methods are mainly in the selection of the features and in the indexing and retrieving stages. One of the most used features

© Springer International Publishing Switzerland 2015
A. Pardo and J. Kittler (Eds.): CIARP 2015, LNCS 9423, pp. 127–134, 2015.
DOI: 10.1007/978-3-319-25751-8_16

selection strategies is based on choosing triplets of minutiae [1–5] or other more complex geometric structures [6]. Other algorithms extract features directly from ridges [7], from a neighborhood around the each minutia [8,9] or from orientation maps extracted from every fingerprint [10]. On the other hand, there are few works about latent fingerprint indexing algorithms. Among them, the most relevant is an approach introduced by Paulino et al. [11]. In this work, a fusion of many features of level 1 and 2, like MCC [8], singular points and ridge periods, is performed in order to build a candidates list. Also, there is a proposal in the literature [12] that can be used for latent and non-latent impressions and uses polygons matching.

In the present work, a minutia based indexing algorithm is introduced. This proposal uses a previously defined representation of fingerprints [3] based on minutia triplets, which is very tolerant to distortions. There are many differences of our approach regarding the algorithm proposed in [3], among them is the use of other combination of characteristics and a novel strategy to partition the features and indexes. The partition strategy proposed by us allows to search latent and non-latent impressions on the same fingerprint database.

This work is organized as follows. In Section 2 the used representation and features are described. Also, the index construction and partition is defined. The Section 3 is dedicated to the indexing and retrieving stages using the primary and secondary indexes. In Section 4 experiments performed on public databases that validate our proposal are shown. Finally, Section 5 contains the conclusions.

2   Indexes Generation

In order to perform a proper identification, from each fingerprint some indexes representing characteristic information must be extracted. These indexes are conformed by features extracted from the used representation and in posteriors stages they can be used for finding correspondences.

2.1   Fingerprint Representation

The minutia is the most common feature used in fingerprint recognition algorithms. Minutiae are singularities in the ridges pattern, which are commonly used by experts for performing manual comparisons. In latent fingerprint case an expert manually marks the minutae. In this way, some indexing approaches use minutia triplets in order to represent impressions [1–5]. In this work, is used one of these representations, which has proven to be very effective for situations in which some minutiae are not located correctly [3]. This approach defines an expanded triplets set $R = \{t_1, t_2, \cdots, t_n\}$ in which the vertexes of each triplet are conformed by minutiae.

The number of triplets of R is linear with respect to the number of minutiae [3]. This is very desirable since the sets R will be used as a representation for fingerprints in indexing tasks. This property also has the advantage that the identification errors by false acceptance are reduced in comparison with other approaches that use all possible triplets [2] or only a Delaunay triangulation [1].

2.2 Features Used

In the present work, a study of the different features that can be extracted from a triplet of minutiae present on the state-of-the-art, was conducted. As result, the better features for fingerprint recognition in both cases, civil and criminal, were identified. In order to generate indexes, from each $t_i \in R$, where $p_i(x_i, y_i)$, $p_j(x_j, y_j)$ and $p_k(x_k, y_k)$ are the points of t_i , the following features are extracted attending to their robustness:

- s_t: Triangle sign, where $s_t = 0$ if $x_i(y_j - y_k) + x_j(y_k - y_i) + x_k(y_i - y_j) < 0$; otherwise $s_t = 1$.
- θ_i, θ_j and θ_k: Normalized difference of directions of minutiae represented by p_i, p_j and p_k, with respect to their opposite side on t_i.
- L_1 and L_2: Normalized heights of the triplets. Heights of the smallest and the largest side of each t_i with respect to the opposite point in the triplet
- r_i, r_j and r_k: Ridge counters.
- ρ_i, ρ_j and ρ_k: Relative position of p_i, p_j and p_k regarding a reference point.

The order of the minutiae in a triplet is given by the sides length of the triangle that they describe. The features were obtained from the minutiae extracted with VeriFinger 4.2. In the performed studies, was observed that the min-max heights regarding each triangle side although are not easy to calculate, provide a very stable feature. Also, was concluded that the relative position regarding a reference point avoids false correspondences between impressions.

2.3 Index Generation and Partition

Since in this work is introduced an algorithm that can be used with latent and non-latent impressions, and the features may have different identification value in correspondence with this fact, a partition of the index function is proposed, in Primary (PI_i) and Secondary (SI_i) indexes, as can see in Table 1. In this way, PI_i is used in the presence of both, latent and non-latent impressions.

Table 1. Binary representation of triplet features used.

Index part	Feature	Size (bits)
Primary	s_t	1
	θ_i, θ_j and θ_k	$3 + 3 + 3 = 9$
	L_1 and L_2	$3 + 3 = 6$
Secondary	r_i, r_j and r_k	$6 + 6 + 6 = 18$
	ρ_i, ρ_j and ρ_k	$3 + 3 + 3 = 9$

The indexes are constructed by concatenating the binary representation of each involved feature. In Table 1 the amount of bits necessary for representing the used features based on the higher value that each one can reach is shown. As can be deduced from this, each index can be stored in a very compact way.

3 Indexing and Retrieving Processes

In this section, a detailed description of the process of identification is made. For this, a very efficient technique that uses the previously defined primary and secondary indexes is used.

3.1 Indexing

This process is made in preprocessing time, when a fingerprint with an assigned ID is inserted in the database. The first step is the construction of its expanded triplets set R. Then, from each one of these triplet $t_i \in R$, all the mentioned features are extracted and from these, PI_i and SI_i are made up. With this information, a tuple $(PI_i, SI_i, ID, t_i(p_1p_2p_3))$ is built from each t_i. Finally, every one of these tuples is inserted in an index table H, using PI_i as primary index. In this way, H will contain information about all the triplets generated from every fingerprint inserted in the database. It is important to note that H allows to store more than one element under the same key (primary index). In our case, this is very desirable since some triplets may generate the same primary index. However, these triplets may have different secondary index and ID.

3.2 Retrieving

In this stage, a similarity value is computed between the query fingerprint and every impression stored. Then, the candidates list is made up by the elements from the database that archive a similarity value higher than 0, ordered in decreasing way. In order to perform this operation, the expanded triplets set R_q is computed from the query. In this way the primary and secondary indexes PI_{iq} and SI_{iq} from each $t_{iq} \in R_q$ are computed. Then, a query is performed on the index table H using all the PI_{iq} as keys. If we are not in the presence of a latent impression, those elements stored in H that have a secondary index different than SI_{iq} are discarded. On the contrary, if the query is a latent impression, then this second level filtering is not used. As we can see, this strategy allows us to solve both cases in a very efficient manner.

As result of the previously described operation, n tuples with an associated identifier ID_i and with the form $R_{ti} = \{t_1, \ldots, t_k\}$ can be obtained. These tuples are made up from the elements retrieved from H, grouping those triplets that contain the same ID. After this process, a triplets matching strategy very similar to one already defined in the literature can be used for matching the sets R_q and R_{ti} [13]. The correlation tuples between two triplets $t_q(p_{1q}, p_{2q}, p_{3q})$ and $t_t(p_{1t}, p_{2t}, p_{3t})$ are defined as $ct_i = (\alpha_i, \overline{p_{iq}p_{jq}}, \overline{p_{it}p_{jt}})$ with $i, j \in \{1, 2, 3\}$, were α_i represents the normalized difference between the i-th interior angles of t_q and t_t, and $\overline{p_{iq}p_{jq}}, \overline{p_{it}p_{jt}}$ are segments of the triangles represented by the triplets. The process followed to obtain the value of α_i, is very similar to that presented by Chikkerur et al. [9], to obtain the similarity between an edge that connects two minutiae of an impression and one edge joining two minutiae of other fingerprint. In this way, the set $T(R_q, R_{ti}) = \{ct_1, ct_2, \ldots, ct_n\}$ represents the union of all the correlation tuples of every corresponding triangle between R_i and R_j. In the following step, a reduced set $Tr(R_q, R_{ti}) = \{ct_1, ct_2, \ldots, ct_r\}$ is used. This set contains only the correlation tuples whose value of α_i are equal to the statistic mode in $T(R_q, R_{ti})$, for the values of α_i of every ct_i. The main goal of this process is to check the rotation histogram for finding the most probable value of relative rotation between the involved feature models and use only the correlation tuples that are consequent with this.

With the reduced set $Tr(R_q, R_{ti})$ a similarity graph $G_s = \langle V, E, L, s, l \rangle$ is made up where $s : E \to \Re$ is a similarity function that assign a value to every edge, $l : m_i^2 \to L$ is a labeling function given two vertexes and L is a set of vertex labels. s is a similarity function that represents in fuzzy terms the grade of closeness between the two segments $\overline{p_{iq}p_{jq}}$ and $\overline{p_{it}p_{jt}}$ that originated a edge in G_s. In this way, a graph that represents matches between triplet sets R_q and R_{ti} is constructed and weighted with a similarity function. The graph G_s may be not connected. More details of the construction of G_s can be found in a previous work found in the literature [13].

In order to find the spanning tree of every connected components of G_s with the higher value of similarity in their edges, the Kruskal algorithm is applied to G_s. This is a well know method to find a minimum (or maximum in our case) spanning forest of disconnected graphs. Let $\{F_1, F_2, \ldots, F_n\}$ be the set of spanning trees returned by the Kruskal algorithm, sorted in descending order by the amount of edges. A strategy to merge F_1 and F_2 is implemented by trying to add a virtual edge e_v between then. This virtual edge must complain with some geometric restrictions. If this process is successful then $F_1 = F_1 \cup F_2 \cup \{e_v\}$, F_2 is eliminated and $F_i = F_{i-1}, \forall\, i, 3 < i < n$. This process is repeated while F_1 and F_2 can be merged.

The similarity value between the triplets sets R_q and R_{ti} is given by the following expression:

$$similarity(R_q, R_{ti}) = \frac{sim \times |V|}{min(|R_q|, |R_{ti}|)} \tag{1}$$

where $|V|$ is the number of vertexes in the similarity graph G_s, $|R_q|$ and $|R_{ti}|$ are the cardinalities of R_q and R_{ti} respectively, and sim is the sum of the weights of every edge of F_1. Finally, with the process described, a similarity score can be generated between the representation of the query R_q and every impression previously stored in the database that shares correspondences with the query. The final candidates list can be obtained by sorting these impressions by the computed score. In Fig. 1 the flow of the algorithm is shown. As can be seen, the use of primary and secondary indexes provides a great flexibility to this proposal. It is important to note that this work uses an efficient consolidation strategy that does not compromise the response times and that is similar to the used in [13]. This does not mean that we use a matching algorithm, because comparisons 1:1 are not performed, so the results shown are based on an indexing scheme.

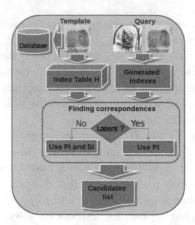

Fig. 1. Flow of the fingerprint identification process.

4 Experimental Evaluation

In this section, an evaluation of the accuracy of our proposal is performed, compared with other state-of-the-art algorithms. For this, the most common measure to evaluate the accuracy of indexing algorithms was used, i.e., the trade off between penetration rate (PR) and Correct Index Power (CIP). The experiments were executed on a PC with a microprocessor i7, 1.7 Ghz and 8 Gb of RAM.

4.1 Latent Case

The NIST Special Database 27 was used to test the accuracy of our proposal. This database contains 258 latent fingerprints from crime scenes and their matching rolled impressions mates. For each latent fingerprint there are four sets of minutiae that have been validated by a professional team of latent examiners. From these, only the set of manually marked minutiae called ideal was used. Also, a large background database of 267000 rolled impressions obtained from NIST databases and a private database of our country was used, in order to fairly compare our results with others works [11,12]. As can be seen in Fig. 2, our proposal outperforms other approaches for almost all values of penetration rate. In particular, we can see that the better results of our algorithm compared to other methods, are reached for a penetration value of 1%. In criminal cases, the searches are performed on the whole database and the decisions are made by human experts. That is why it is important that the searched candidate is included on the firsts positions of the returned candidates list. In latent case this approach was able to perform approximately 50000 comparisons per second.

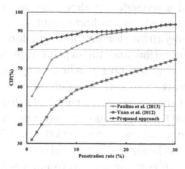

Fig. 2. Experiments performed in the NIST 27 database.

4.2   Non-latent Case

Two well-known databases were used for testing the accuracy of our approach. The first one is FVC2004 DB1 that contains 800 fingerprints (100 fingers and 8 impressions per finger). The second one was the NIST Special Database 4, composed by 4000 rolled impressions (2000 fingers and 2 impressions per finger). The Figures 3(a) and 3(b) show that in general the approach results are very good, and in particular are better than the others proposals for the first values of penetration rate. The algorithm was able to perform 1.5 millions comparisons per second, for this test we used a variation of the same background database employed in latent case.

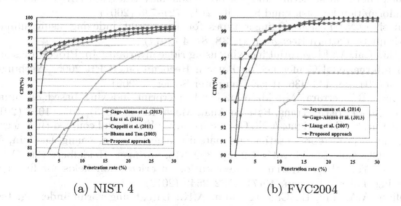

(a) NIST 4   (b) FVC2004

Fig. 3. Experiments performed in different databases.

5   Conclusions

The proposed indexing algorithm introduces a very efficient strategy to identify latent and non-latent fingerprints, implementing two search levels based on the use of a primary index and a secondary index, allowing the searching of latent and non-latent impressions on the same fingerprint database, due to this, it is possible to use the same algorithm for civilian and forensic applications. The features used for index generation and fingerprint representation have a great robustness in the presence of noise. Our method outperforms some of the best approaches in state-of-the-art, reaching a good hit rate at low values of the penetration rate. This is a very desirable characteristic for identification systems since minimizes the response time and was one of our goals in the development of this work. The proposed approach performs 50000 and 1.5 millions comparisons per second for latent and non-latent cases respectively. The cited approaches do not report execution times, so comparisons were not performed.

References

1. Bebis, G., Deaconu, T., Georgiopoulos, M.: Fingerprint identification using delaunay triangulation. In: IEEE International Conference on Intelligence, Information, and Systems (ICIIS 1999), pp. 452–459 (1999)
2. Bhanu, B., Tan, X.: Fingerprint indexing based on novel features of minutiae triplets. IEEE Transactions on Pattern Analysis and Machine Intelligence **25**(5), 616–622 (2003)
3. Gago-Alonso, A., Hernández-Palancar, J., Rodríguez-Reina, E., Muñoz-Briseño, A.: Indexing and retrieving in fingerprint databases under structural distortions. Expert Syst. Appl. **40**(8), 2858–2871 (2013)
4. Khachai, M.Y., Leshko, A.S., Dremin, A.V.: The problem of fingerprint identification: A reference database indexing method based on delaunay triangulation. Pattern Recognit. Image Anal. **24**(2), 297–303 (2014)
5. Liang, X., Bishnu, A., Asano, T.: A robust fingerprint indexing scheme using minutia neighborhood structure and low-order delaunay triangles. IEEE Transactions on Information Forensics and Security **2**(4), 721–733 (2007)
6. Iloanusi, O.N.: Fusion of finger types for fingerprint indexing using minutiae quadruplets. Pattern Recogn. Lett. **38**, 8–14 (2014)
7. Feng, J., Cai, A.: Fingerprint indexing using ridge invariants. In: Proceedings of the 18th International Conference on Pattern Recognition, ICPR 2006, Washington, DC, vol. 04, pp. 433–436. IEEE Computer Society (2006)
8. Cappelli, R., Ferrara, M., Maltoni, D.: Fingerprint indexing based on minutia cylinder-code. IEEE Trans. Pattern Anal. Mach. Intell. **33**(5), 1051–1057 (2011)
9. Chikkerur, S., Cartwright, A.N., Govindaraju, V.: K-plet and coupled BFS: a graph based fingerprint representation and matching algorithm. In: Zhang, D., Jain, A.K. (eds.) ICB 2005. LNCS, vol. 3832, pp. 309–315. Springer, Heidelberg (2005)
10. Liu, M., Yap, P.T.: Invariant representation of orientation fields for fingerprint indexing. Pattern Recogn. **45**(7), 2532–2542 (2012)
11. Paulino, A.A., Liu, E., Cao, K., Jain, A.K.: Latent fingerprint indexing: fusion of level 1 and level 2 features. In: Biometrics: Theory, Applications and Systems (BTAS), Washington, D.C., pp. 1–8 (2013)
12. Yuan, B., Su, F., Cai, A.: Fingerprint retrieval approach based on novel minutiae triplet features. In: Biometrics: Theory, Applications and Systems (BTAS), Arlington, VA, pp. 170–175 (2012)
13. Hernández-Palancar, J., Muñoz-Briseño, A., Alonso, A.G.: Using a triangular matching approach for latent fingerprint and palmprint identification. IJPRAI **28**(7) (2014)

Homogeneity Measure for Forensic Voice Comparison: A Step Forward Reliability

Moez Ajili[1,2]($\boxtimes$), Jean-François Bonastre[1], Solange Rossato[2],
Juliette Kahn[3], and Itshak Lapidot[4]

[1] Laboratoire Informatique d'Avignon (LIA), University of Avignon, Avignon, France
[2] Laboratoire Informatique de Grenoble (LIG), University of Grenoble,
Grenoble, France
[3] Laboratoire National de Métrologie et d'Essais (LNE), Paris, France
[4] Afeka Center for Language Processing (ACLP), Tel Aviv, Israel

Abstract. In forensic voice comparison, it is strongly recommended to
follow the Bayesian paradigm to present a forensic evidence to the court.
In this paradigm, the strength of the forensic evidence is summarized
by a *likelihood ratio* (LR). But in the real world, to base only on the
LR without looking to its degree of reliability does not allow experts to
have a good judgement. This work is mainly motivated by the need to
quantify this reliability. In this concept, we think that the presence of
speaker specific information and its homogeneity between the two signals
to compare should be evaluated. This paper is dedicated to the latter,
the homogeneity. We propose an information theory based homogeneity
measure which determines whether a voice comparison is feasible or not.

Keywords: Forensic voice comparison · Reliability · Homogeneity ·
Speaker recognition

1 Introduction

In forensic comparison, it is strongly recommended to present the forensic evidence to the court following the Bayesian paradigm [1]: *Speaker recognition* (SR) systems should calculate for a given trial a *likelihood ratio* (LR) which represents the degree of support for the prosecutor hypothesis (the two speech extracts are pronounced by the same speaker) rather than the defender hypothesis (the two speech extracts are pronounced by different speakers). Theoretically, a good LR is assumed to contain by itself all the needed information including reliability: in good conditions, the LR should be far from 1 to support comfortably one of the two hypothesis (big LR values, about 10^{10} support H_0 and low values, about 10^{-10} support H_1) while in bad conditions the LR is close to one and consequently, it does not allow a good discrimination between the two hypothesis. But in the real world, forensic processes are working only with an empirical estimation of LRs that could be far from theoretical ones. In this case, LRs are unable to embed reliability information furthermore as there is no concrete evaluation of the disagreement between theoretical and empirical LR. It is particularly true for SR systems which are working as black boxes: They calculate

© Springer International Publishing Switzerland 2015
A. Pardo and J. Kittler (Eds.): CIARP 2015, LNCS 9423, pp. 135–142, 2015.
DOI: 10.1007/978-3-319-25751-8_17

a sort of score in all situations without verifying if there is enough reliable information present in the two records. Then, those scores will be calibrated (i.e. normalized) to be viewed as a LR [2][3]. So, it could be misleading to the court if experts report only the LR and not its degree of reliability. Presently, these issues of validity and reliability are of great concern in forensic science [4] [5] [6] [7] [8] [9]. To cope with this problem, it is interesting to define a *confidence measure* (CM) that indicates the reliability of a system output. Several solutions were proposed in [6] [7] [8] [9][10] [11] where the CM is estimated for each trial from both system decision score and the two speech extracts of a given voice comparison, S_A-S_B. An alternative consists in studying the losses in LR quality which are related to: (i) A lack of discriminative information (as shown in [12]) in S_A and/or S_B. (ii) Sufficient discriminative information are available but the system is unable to output a meaningful (LR) due for example to the mismatch between elements used to build the system (UBM, total variability matrix, PLDA,...) and the pair of voice records S_A-S_B [13][14]. In brief, the loss could be divided into two origins. Our interest concerns the case (i) detailed before.

The final objective of our work is to define a *"Feasibility measure"* (FM) able to measure the presence of speaker discriminant cues and the homogeneity of this information between the pair of voice records S_A-S_B. So, this measure is estimated only from the two in-interest voice records. If it is obvious that the presence of speaker specific information inside S_A and S_B is mandatory, it is not sufficient: examples tied with the same class of cues should be included in both speech recordings in order to be useful.

In this paper, we address more specifically the problem of the evaluation of the homogeneity of two speech signals in terms of information classes, at the acoustic level. We propose an information theory-based homogeneity criterion able to quantify this homogeneity.

This paper is structured as follows. Section 2 presents our new homogeneity measure and details the algorithm to compute it. Section 3 describes the LIA baseline system and presents experiments and results. Then, section 4 presents the conclusion and proposes some extends of the current work.

2   Information Theory Based Homogeneity Measure

In this section, we define an information theory (IT) based homogeneity measure denoted HM(). Its objective is to calculate the amount of acoustic information that appertains to the same class between the two voice records. The set of acoustic frames gathered from the two files S_A and S_B is decomposed into acoustic classes thanks to a Gaussian Mixture Model (GMM) clustering. Then the homogeneity is first estimated in terms of bits as the amount of information embedded by the respective "number of acoustic frames" of S_A and S_B linked to a given acoustic class. Each acoustic class is represented by the corresponding Gaussian component of the GMM model. The occupation vector could be seen as the number of acoustic frames of a given recording belonging to each class m. It is noted: $[\gamma_{g_m}(s)]_{m=1}^{M}$.

Given a Gaussian g_m and two posterior probability vectors of the two voice records S_A and S_B, $[\gamma_{g_m}(A)]_{m=1}^M$ and $[\gamma_{g_m}(B)]_{m=1}^M$, we define also:

- $\chi_A \cup \chi_B = \{x_{1A}, ..., x_{NA}\} \cup \{x_{1B}, ..., x_{NB}\}$ the full data set of S_A and S_B with cardinality $N = N_A + N_B$
- $\gamma(m)$ and $\omega(m)$ are respectively the occupation and the prior of Gaussian m where $\omega(m) = \frac{\gamma(m)}{\sum_{k=1}^M \gamma(k)} = \frac{\gamma(m)}{N}$.
- $\gamma_A(m)$ (respectively $\gamma_B(m)$) is the partial occupations of the mth component due to the voice records S_A (respectively S_B).
- p_m is the probability of the Bernoulli distribution of the mth bit (due to the mth component), $B(p_m)$. $p_m = \frac{\gamma_A(m)}{\gamma(m)}$, $\bar{p}_m = 1 - p_m = \frac{\gamma_B(m)}{\gamma(m)}$.
- $H(p_m)$ the entropy of the mth Gaussian (the unit is bits) given by: $H(p_m) = -p_m log_2(p_m) - \bar{p}_m log_2(\bar{p}_m)$.

The class entropy, $H(p_m)$, has some interesting properties in the context of an homogeneity measure:

* $H(p_m)$ belongs to $[0, 1]$.
* $H(p_m) = 0$ if $p_m = 0$ or $p_m = 1$. It means that when the repartition of the example of a given class m is completely unbalanced between S_A and S_B, $H(p_m)$ is zero (i.e. $H(p_m)$ goes to zero when p_m is close to 0 or 1).
* $H(p_m) = 1$ when $p_m = 0.5$. $H(p_m)$ is maximal when the examples belonging to a given class are perfectly balanced between between S_A and S_B (i.e. $H(p_m)$ goes to the maximum value 1 when the repartition goes to the balanced one).

With these theoretical properties, $H(p_m)$ is definitively a good candidate in order to build a homogeneity measure. Two measures based on $H(p_m)$ are proposed hereafter. The first measure is a normalized version. It ignores the size of the frame sets (i.e. the duration of the recordings) when the second ones 'non-normalized' takes this aspect into account.

The normalized HM denoted "HM_{BEE}" is calculated as shown in Equation 1. It measures the Bit Entropy Expectation (BEE) with respect to the multinomial distribution defined by GMM's priors $\{\omega(m)\}_{i=1}^M$.

$$HM_{BEE} = \sum_{m=1}^M \frac{\gamma(m)}{N} H(p_m) = \sum_{m=1}^M \omega_m H(p_m) \tag{1}$$

By definition HM_{BEE} contains the percentage of the data-homogeneity between S_A and S_B. It does not take into account the quantity of the homogeneous information between the two speech extracts. To integrate this information, a *Non-normalized Homogeneity Measure* (NHM) is proposed. NHM calculates the quantity of homogeneous information between the two voice records as shown in Equation 2. The amount of information is defined in term of number of acoustic frames. NHM measures the BEE with respect of the quantity of information present in each acoustic class $\{\gamma(m)\}_{i=1}^M$.

$$NHM_{BEE} = \sum_{m=1}^{M} (\gamma_A(m) + \gamma_B(m))H(p_m) = \sum_{m=1}^{M} \gamma(m)H(p_m) \qquad (2)$$

As mentioned before, a GMM presenting the different acoustic classes is mandatory to estimate both homogeneity measure. So, it will be reasonable to estimate HM using different representation of the acoustic space. Several avenues are explored in this paper. First, we use a GMM trained only on the two speech signals. The major advantage of this representation is its independence toward the system. Nevertheless, the amount of data involved in the two signals is not always quite sufficient to build stable acoustic classes. An alternative consists in to use a stable representation of the acoustic space, UBM. As it is learnt on a very large data set and its high ability to model the whole acoustic space, the estimation quality of the UBM could be higher than the GMM A-B (learnt only on the two speech recordings).

3   Experiments and Results

In order to evaluate the homogeneity measures presented in section 2, we propose several experiments based on NIST SRE framework.

3.1   Baseline LIA System

In all experiments, we use as baseline the LIA_SpkDet system presented in [15]. This system is developed using the ALIZE/SpkDet open-source toolkit [16]. It uses I-vector approach [17].

Acoustic features are composed of 19 MFCC parameters, its derivatives, and 11 second order derivatives (the frequency window is restricted to 300-3400 Hz). A normalization file-based process is applied, so that the distribution of each cepstral coefficient is 0-mean and 1-variance for a given utterance.

The *Universal Background Model* (UBM) is trained on Fisher database on about 10 millions of speech frames. It has 512 components whose variance parameters are floored to 50% of the global variance (0.5). The total variability matrix T is trained using 15660 sessions from 1147 speakers (using NIST_SRE 2004, 2005, 2006 and Switchboard data). Speaker models are derived by Bayesian adaptation of the Gaussian component means, with a relevance factor of 14. The same database is used to estimate the inter-session matrix W in the I-vector space. The dimension of the I-Vectors in the total factor space is 400.

For scoring, PLDA scoring model [18] is applied. The speaker verification score given two I-vectors w_A and w_B is the likelihood ratio described by:

$$score = log\frac{P(w_A, w_B|H_p)}{P(w_A, w_B|H_d)} \qquad (3)$$

where the hypothesis H_p states that inputs w_A and w_B are from the same speaker and the hypothesis H_d states they are from different speakers.

3.2   Experimental Protocol

All the experiments presented in this work are performed based upon the NIST-SRE 2008 campaign, all trials (det 1), "short2-short3", restricted to male speakers only (referred to as 2008 protocol). This protocol is composed by 39433 tests (8290 target tests, the rest are impostor trials). The utterances contain 2.5 minutes of speech in average.

As seen in section 2, for each trial the set of acoustic frames is clustered thanks to a GMM. This GMM has 512 components and is trained by EM/ML (with a variance flooring ≈ 0).

3.3   Evaluation Process of the Homogeneity Measure

In order to evaluate the proposed homogeneity measures, we apply it on all the trials of our evaluation set and sort the set accordingly. We are expecting that lowest values of homogeneity are correlated with the lowest performance of the speaker recognition system, as well as the opposite behaviour for high values. To compute the speaker recognition performance, we select the *log-likelihood-ratio cost* (C_{llr}), largely used in forensic voice comparison because it is based on likelihood ratios and not on hard decisions like, for example, *equal error rate* (EER) [6,19]. C_{llr} has the meaning of a cost or a loss: lower the C_{llr} is, better is the performance. In order to withdraw the impact of calibration mistakes, we use the minimum value of the C_{llr}, noted C_{llr}^{min}. If a C_{llr} could be computed for a given trial, it makes sense to average the values on a reasonably large set of trials. So, we apply a 1500 trials sliding window, with a step of 1000, on the trials sorted by homogeneity values. On each window, we compute the averaged C_{llr}^{min} to be compared with the HM value (computed here as the median value on the window). To work on such number of trials allows also to compute the percentage of *false rejection* (FR) and *false acceptance* (FA). FR and FA are computed using a threshold estimated onto the whole test set and tuned to correspond at the EER. The C_{llr}^{min} baseline system computed on all trials is equal to 0.2241.

3.4   Evaluation of Homogeneity Measures

- **GMM A-B.** In this subsection, we use a GMM learnt on the pair of speech signals (GMM A-B). From Figure 1, it can be seen that HM_{BEE} value does not have a remarkable impact on C_{llr}^{min}. It is confirmed by a not significant low correlation with C_{llr}^{min}, evaluated to a R^2 equal to -0.39 (p=0.16). It seems that to focus only on BEE, ignoring the involved quantity of examples does not allow to build an homogeneity measure with the desired characteristics.

Experimental results obtained using NHM_{BEE} are reported in Figure 2. The shape of the curve is interesting with C_{llr}^{min} varying from 0.309 to 0.122, indicating a high correlation between NHM_{BEE} and C_{llr}^{min} ($R^2 = -0.942$, p <0.01). Moreover, it seems that NHM_{BEE} brings new information compared to the system outputs. The result is confirmed with a lower R^2 of 0.55 (to be compared with a R^2 equal to 0.73 in the case of HM_{BEE}). Further experiments have been done using NHM_{BEE} only.

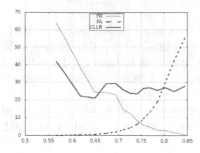

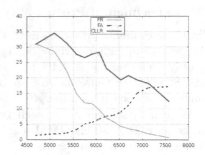

Fig. 1. HM_{BEE} behaviour, estimated with GMM-AB.

Fig. 2. NHM_{BEE} behaviour, estimated with GMM-AB.

- UBM Model. In Figure 3, we present the results obtained using NHM_{BEE} like the previous one but here, we use directly the UBM in order to cluster the acoustic frames of the pair of speech recordings. With a C_{llr}^{min} varying between 0.3 and 0.089 and its high correlation with NHM_{BEE}, evaluated to R^2 equal to -0.950 (p < 0.01), this variant seems to outperform the previous one.

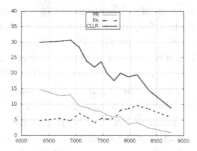

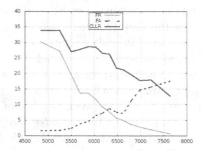

Fig. 3. NHM_{BEE} behaviour, estimated with UBM.

Fig. 4. NHM behaviour using GMM A-B initialized with UBM.

Two more experiences are realized. In Figure 4, we report results when the GMM A-B is now initialized with the UBM (case A), and in Figure 5, we use the UBM mean-adapted (using MAP) by the two speech recordings S_A and S_B (case B). In both cases, NHM is highly correlated with the SR system performance, C_{llr}^{min} (A: $R^2 = -0.963$, p < 0.01 ; B: $R^2 = -0.973$, p < 0.01). Moreover, it seems to be more dependent to the system output compared to the previous one in which we use only the UBM (case A: $R^2 = 0.57$, p<0.01; case B: $R^2 = 0.37$, p<0.01; UBM $R^2 = 0.29$, p<0.01). We notice that using the mean-adapted UBM model to estimate NHM_{BEE} adds more stability to C_{llr}^{min} variation. It can be explained by the fact that adapted UBM model preserves the good modeling of the whole acoustic space and at the same time, takes into account the characteristics of a given trial. Whereas in case A, it is clear that using a GMM A-B with UBM initialization is very close to the case in which we use GMM A-B (without initialization). This result is clear when we see the big similarity between the two NHM behavioural curve (Figure 4 and 2).

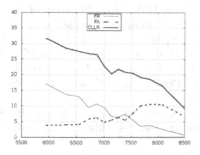

Fig. 5. NHM behaviour estimated using the UBM adapted by S_A and S_B.

4   Discussion and Conclusions

In this paper, we have proposed an IT-based data Homogeneity Measure denoted NHM_{BEE} where the quantity of homogeneous examples presented in both speech extracts is taken into account. NHM_{BEE} belongs to the Bit Entropy Expectation (BEE) computed on a Gaussian Mixture Model view of the couple of speech recordings which composes a given voice comparison trial. A first variant from this measure uses GMM as a model trained by the pair of recordings. It showed interesting properties with a nice relation between the homogeneity values and the C_{llr}^{min}, varying from (HM=4689,C_{llr}^{min}=0.309) to (HM=7579, C_{llr}^{min}=0.1227). A second variant of NHM_{BEE} uses directly the UBM model in order to cluster the pair of speech recordings (without training or adaptation of the UBM). This version has a similar behaviour than the previous one but outperformed it with a behavioural curve moving from (HM=6341, C_{llr}^{min}=0.3) to (HM=8762, C_{llr}^{min}=0.089). In the same direction, the use of a UBM mean-adapted by the pair of recordings adds more stability to the C_{llr}^{min}, varying quite consistently from (HM=5953,C_{llr}^{min}=0.31) to (HM=8490, C_{llr}^{min}=0.09). This result shows that the way to cluster the pair of speech recordings is important. Moreover, the different variant of NHM_{BEE} showed a low correlation with the scores issued by the speaker recognition system. The behavioural curves of NHM_{BEE} and this low correlation encourage us strongly to conclude that NHM_{BEE} is a good candidate in order to measure the data homogeneity between a pair of speech recordings, in the view of voice comparison reliability.

This work will firstly extended by working on other representation of acoustic classes in order to estimate NHM_{BEE}. In addition to this point, the behaviour of our measures depending on the session variability factors should be explored more deeply. Finally, as expressed in the introduction, data homogeneity is a mandatory first step for a voice comparison feasibility measure and we expect to explore this new avenue.

References

1. Champod, C., Meuwly, D.: The inference of identity in forensic speaker recognition. Speech Communication, 193–203 (2000)
2. Brummer, N., van Leeuwen, D.A.: On calibration of language recognition scores. In: Speaker and Language Recognition Workshop, pp. 1–8. IEEE Odyssey (2006)
3. Brummer, N., Doddington, G.: Likelihood-ratio calibration using prior-weighted proper scoring rules (2013). arXiv preprint arXiv:1307.7981
4. Bonastre, J.F., Bimbot, F., Boë, L.J., Campbell, J.P., Reynolds, D.A., Magrin-Chagnolleau, I.: Person authentication by voice: a need for caution. In: INTERSPEECH (2003)
5. Campbell, J.P., Shen, W., Campbell, W.M., Schwartz, R., Bonastre, J.-F., Matrouf, D.: Forensic speaker recognition. Institute of Electrical and Electronics Engineers (2009)
6. Morrison, G.S.: Forensic voice comparison and the paradigm shift. Science & Justice, 298–308 (2009)
7. Rose, P.: Technical forensic speaker recognition: Evaluation, types and testing of evidence. Computer Speech & Language, 159–191 (2006)
8. Morrison, G.S., Zhang, C., Rose, P.: An empirical estimate of the precision of likelihood ratios from a forensic-voice-comparison system. Forensic science international, 59–65 (2011)
9. Morrison, G.S.: Measuring the validity and reliability of forensic likelihood-ratio systems. Science & Justice, 91–98 (2011)
10. Campbell, W.M., Reynolds, D.A., Campbell, J.P., Brady, K.: Estimating and evaluating confidence for forensic speaker recognition. In: ICASSP, pp. 717–720 (2005)
11. Mengusoglu, E., Leich, H.: Confidence Measures for Speech/Speaker Recognition and Applications on Turkish LVCSR. PhD Faculte Polytechnique de Mons (2004)
12. Rao, W., Mak, M.W.: Boosting the performance of i-vector based speaker verification via utterance partitioning. IEEE Transactions on Audio, Speech and Language Processing, 1012–1022 (2013)
13. Greenberg, C.S., Stanford, V.M., Martin, A.F., Yadagiri, M., Doddington, G.R., Godfrey, J.J., Hernandez-Cordero, J.: The 2012 NIST speaker recognition evaluation. In: INTERSPEECH, pp. 1971–1975 (2013)
14. Kahn, J., Audibert, N., Rossato, S., Bonastre, J.F.: Intra-speaker variability effects on speaker verification performance. In: Odyssey, p. 21 (2010)
15. Matrouf, D., Scheffer, N., Fauve, B.G., Bonastre, J.F.: A straightforward and efficient implementation of the factor analysis model for speaker verification. In: INTERSPEECH, pp. 1242–1245 (2007)
16. Larcher, A., Bonastre, J.F., Fauve, B.G., Lee, K.A., Lévy, C., Li, H., Parfait, J.Y.: ALIZE 3.0-open source toolkit for state-of-the-art speaker recognition. In: INTERSPEECH, pp. 2768–2772 (2013)
17. Dehak, N., Kenny, P., Dehak, R., Dumouchel, P., Ouellet, P.: Front-end factor analysis for speaker verification. IEEE Transactions on Audio, Speech, and Language Processing, 788–798 (2011)
18. Prince, S.J.D., Elder, J.H.: Probabilistic linear discriminant analysis for inferences about identity. IEEE 11th International Conference on Computer Vision, ICCV (2007)
19. Brummer, N., du Preez, J.: Application-independent evaluation of speaker detection. Computer Speech and Language, 230–275 (2006)

On Multiview Analysis for Fingerprint Liveness Detection

Amirhosein Toosi, Sandro Cumani, and Andrea Bottino$^{(\boxtimes)}$

Politecnico di Torino, Corso Duca Degli Abruzzi, 24, 10129 Turin, Italy
{amirhosein.toosi,sandro.cumani,andrea.bottino}@polito.it

Abstract. Fingerprint recognition systems, as any other biometric system, can be subject to attacks, which are usually carried out using artificial fingerprints. Several approaches to discriminate between live and fake fingerprint images have been presented to address this issue. These methods usually rely on the analysis of individual features extracted from the fingerprint images. Such features represent different and complementary views of the object in analysis, and their fusion is likely to improve the classification accuracy. However, very little work in this direction has been reported in the literature. In this work, we present the results of a preliminary investigation on multiview analysis for fingerprint liveness detection. Experimental results show the effectiveness of such approach, which improves previous results in the literature.

Keywords: Spoofing detection · Multiview approach · SVM · Multi task learning · Sparse reconstruction

1 Introduction

On September 2014, the new iPhone 6 was unveiled and released on sale. This device is equipped with a Touch ID fingerprint reader allowing users to unlock their device and to authenticate for on-line purchases. Two days after that launch, a group of German hackers showed how to bypass the Touch ID security system [1]. This is just one of the many possible examples of the vulnerability of fingerprint recognition systems, which is a severe issue due to the integration of such devices into a number of forensic, commercial and military applications [2]. The typical scenario depicts an adversary trying to gain unauthorized access by using the biometric traits of a person legitimately enrolled into the system. In the case of fingerprint recognition systems, these attacks are usually carried out using spoof artifacts, i.e. duplicated artificial fingerprints. Artificial fingerprints can be created filling a mold, obtained from a live or a latent fingerprint, with materials such as gelatine, silicone or Play-Doh [3]. It has been shown that the success rate of such spoof attacks can be up to 70% [4].

To address this problem, several methods have been developed to detect the *liveness* of a fingerprint image. Software-based approaches distinguish between live and fake fingerprint relying solely on the digital processing of images acquired

© Springer International Publishing Switzerland 2015
A. Pardo and J. Kittler (Eds.): CIARP 2015, LNCS 9423, pp. 143–150, 2015.
DOI: 10.1007/978-3-319-25751-8_18

from the device, and can be further divided into dynamic and static ones. Dynamic methods are based on the analysis of certain phenomena like skin deformation [5] and perspiration [6] on a temporal image sequence. However, these methods are not general, since their multi-temporal dimension makes them applicable in a minority of operative conditions. Static methods, on the contrary, focus their analysis on a single fingerprint image, which makes them more general and attractive. These methods can be, again, divided into two main categories. Holistic methods process the image as a whole to derive some discriminative global characteristics, such as the texture coarseness [7] or several first and second order statistics (like mean, energy, entropy, variance, skewness [7] or Gray-Level Co-Occurrence Matrices [8]). However, as shown in [9], their discriminative power is quite low, while better performance is given by local methods, which rely on mathematical descriptors summarizing texture features of small regions surrounding an image point. Global image descriptors can then be obtained by summing up the local descriptors into a histogram collected from the whole image or into multiple histograms obtained from image patches.

Several global image descriptors have been experimented in the context of spoof detection, such as basic [10] and multi-scale [11] Local Binary Pattern (LBP), Local Phase Quantization (LPQ) [12], Weber Local Descriptor (WLD) [13] and Binary Statistical Image Features (BSIF) [14]. Recently, Local Contrast Phase Descriptors (LCPD), a novel global descriptor specifically designed to deal with the characteristics of fingerprint images, has been proposed in [9]. Local Contrast Phase Descriptors (LCPD) is composed by a spatial-domain component, derived from WLD, and by a rotation invariant phase component, derived from LPQ.

All these descriptors provide complementary information or, equivalently, complementary views of the objects under analysis. Previous studies in the area of pattern recognition and machine learning have shown that the combination of features of different nature is usually a powerful method to improve the recognition accuracy of the final classifier. Despite that, such integration has not been fully analyzed yet in the context of fingerprint liveness detection. To the best of our knowledge, the only paper tackling this problem was [13], where the integration of WLD plus LPQ and LBP plus LPQ were analyzed. To this end, in this paper we present the preliminary results of an investigation aimed at detecting the fingerprint liveness by analyzing the integration, at feature level, of different attributes summarizing individual fingerprint images from different views.

The remainder of the paper is organized as follows. Section 2 outlines our approach and Section 3 presents and discusses the experimental results. Finally, conclusions are drawn in Section 4.

2   Multiview Approaches to Fingerprint Liveness Detection

When tackling this work, our main research questions were the following. Which are the global descriptors most suited to tell live from fake fingerprints? Which are the best combinations of different descriptors and how can they be effectively combined to improve the classification accuracies? As we already stated in the introduction, in this paper we will provide some preliminary answers to these questions. These answers are supported by the results of our experiments, which show the effectiveness of multiview approaches in developing anti-spoofing software systems.

In the following subsections we will first discuss two possible methods to (i) integrate, at feature level, different attributes (i.e. feature types) extracted from fingerprint images, and (ii) to classify them into live and fake fingerprints. Then, we will describe the set of individual attributes we found most suitable for the problem in analysis.

2.1 Support Vector Machines (SVM) Based Classification

A simple but effective way of combining multiple representations of the same sample is to concatenate the characteristic vector of each representation. Denote $y = [y^1, \ldots, y^K]$ a test sample described under K *tasks*, where each task represents a different view of the sample (i.e. for images, tasks can be colour histograms, edges, local descriptors and so on). Each task $y^k \in \mathbb{R}^{m_k}$, and each sample $y \in \mathbb{R}^m$, where $m = \sum_{k=1}^{K} m_k$.

The samples are then fed to a linear SVM for classification. The choice of linear SVMs was mainly motivated by the properties of the datasets used in our experiments and by the good accuracy the linear kernel achieves. Indeed, linear SVMs tend to be less prone to overfitting, due to the lower complexity of the separation surface. The dimensionality of the input space is sufficiently high to ensure that the linear classifier is able to properly separate the classes (as we will show in the results section). Furthermore, linear SVMs provide huge benefits in terms of time and memory requirements, since the separation hyperplane can be computed offline and scoring reduces to a simple dot-product in feature space. Finally, SMVs provide a good alternative to feature selection, on the condition that the regularization coefficient is properly chosen. The main motivations behind feature selection are the removal of nuisance dimensions and the reduction of overfitting issues. The presence of the regularization term in the SVM objective function tends to favour simpler separation surfaces, thus mitigating the problems of overfitting, especially in presence of large dimensional vectors, thus improving the generalization capabilities of the model [15].

2.2 Multi-Task Joint Sparse Reconstruction Classification (MTJSRC)

Multi-Task Joint Sparse Reconstruction Classification (MTJSRC), introduced in [16], combines multi-task learning and classification based on sparse representation. In brief, sparse coding aims at representing a signal as a linear combination of a set of reference samples enforcing sparsity in the coefficient set. Multi-task or multi-view learning aims at jointly estimating models from multiple representations of the same data.

Suppose we have a training set $X^k = [X_1^k, \ldots, X_J^k]$ for task k, where J is the number of classes and $X_j^k \in \mathbb{R}^{m_k \times n_j}$, with n_j the number of training samples for class j. Given a test sample y, we can reconstruct each of its representation modalities y^k from the corresponding training set X^k as:

$$y^k = \sum_{j=1}^{J} X_j^k w_j^k + \epsilon^k \qquad k = 1, \ldots, K$$

where w_j^k are the reconstruction coefficients associated to class j and task k and ϵ_k is the residual for the kth modality. Defining $w_j = [w_j^1, \ldots, w_j^K]$ as the representation coefficients for the jth class across the different tasks, the multi-task joint sparse representation can be obtained from the solution of the following least square regression problem:

$$\min_{W} \frac{1}{2} \sum_{k=1}^{K} \left\| y^k - \sum_{j=1}^{J} X_j^k w_j^k \right\|_2^2 + \lambda \sum_{j=1}^{J} \|w_j\|_2 \tag{1}$$

where $W = [w_j^k]_{j,k}$ and $\lambda \sum_j \|w_j\|_2$ is a regularization term.

Model Optimization. In [16], the authors proposed Accelerated Proximal Gradient (APG) for model optimization. A drawback of APG is that, to ensure convergence of the objective function in reasonable time, it requires proper selection of the gradient step at each iteration. The main issue in the optimization of (1) is the presence of a non–differentiable regularization term. Several approaches could be modified to handle this regularizer [17]. In practice, we observed that, for the task at hand, convergence can be easily achieved through the use of L–BFGS algorithm [18], provided that the regularizer is replaced by an ϵ–smoothed term (for small values of ϵ): $\sum_j \|w_j\|_2 \approx \sum_j \sqrt{\|w_j\|_2^2 + \epsilon}$

Classification. Once the optimal reconstruction coefficients for a test sample y have been computed, for each task k and each class j it is possible to compute the reconstruction error $\|y^k - X_j^k w_j^k\|_2$. A straightforward way to assign the sample label is then to pick the class minimizing the sum of the reconstruction errors over all the sample modalities:

$$label = \arg \min_{j} \sum_{k=1}^{K} \theta^k \|y^k - X_j^k w_j^k\|_2 \tag{2}$$

where $\Theta = \{\theta^k\}$ are values weighting the relative relevance of the different modalities in the final classification choice. Since our classification problem is binary, it is easy to verify that the label assignment in (2) corresponds to:

$$label = \begin{cases} 1 & \text{if } \sum_k \theta^k \left(\|y^k - X_1^k\|_2 - \|y^k - X_2^k\|_2 \right) < 0 \\ 2 & \text{if } \sum_k \theta^k \left(\|y^k - X_1^k\|_2 - \|y^k - X_2^k\|_2 \right) > 0 \end{cases} \tag{3}$$

Equation (3) can be interpreted as the fusion of K different systems with associated score function:

$$s_k(y^k) = -\theta^k \left(\left\| y^k - X_1^k \right\|_2 - \left\| y^k - X_2^k \right\|_2 \right) . \qquad (4)$$

where higher (resp., lower) values of (4) tend to favour the hypothesis of sample belonging to class one (resp., two). We define the scoring function for the *fused* systems as:

$$s(\Theta, y) = \theta^0 + \sum_k \theta^k s_k(y^k)$$

where an additional term θ^0 is added to act as bias. Given a validation set, the weights are then estimated by training a Logistic–Regression (LR) classifier. The advantage of LR–based fusion with respect to the approach in [16] is that it both allows to improve the discriminative ability of the system, and, instead of simply providing class membership, it produces outputs which can be interpreted as log–likelihood ratios between class hypotheses [19]. Moreover, the LR objective function is convex, and can be easily trained using standard solvers as L–BFGS.

2.3   Feature Extraction

The individual fingerprint images have been characterized with the following attributes: Histogram of Oriented Gradients (HOG) [20], BSIF, LPQ, WLD and several variants of the LBP, such as patch-based or rotation invariant LBP [21].

The results of initial experiments, which we do not report for the sake of brevity, led us to exclude from the list of candidate attributes both HOG and the various LBP formulations since they were consistently providing lower accuracies than other candidates. As for the other attributes, we provide in the following a brief description and pieces of information on their computation.

BSIF are histograms of binary codes computed for each pixel. The pixel code is obtained by projecting local image patches onto a subspace learnt from natural images. From the results in [14], it can be deduced that variations of the local window size actually capture different characteristics of live and fake fingerprint images. Thus, we experimented different window sizes (from 3x3 to 17x17) as complementary attributes, each of which has dimension 4.096. LPQ codes are obtained first computing local phase information on a window surrounding each pixel, by means of different possible filters, and then extracting the quantized phase of selected frequency components. Histograms of LPQ codes in image patches are then computed and concatenated. Each LPQ attribute has size 256. WLD compute for each pixel the differential excitation (the ratio between the sum of neighboring pixel intensity and the intensity of the pixel itself) and the orientation of the pixel gradient. WLD features of the image can be computed at different image scales and then encoded into a histogram that contains, for each scale, 960 elements.

3   Results and Discussion

The accuracies of our liveness detection approach were assessed on LivDet 2011 dataset [3]. This dataset is one of the most used in the literature and, thus, allows for a comparison with a large number of methods. LivDet 2011 consists of four datasets of images acquired from different devices (*Biometrika*, *Digital Persona*, *Italdata* and *Sagem*). For each device, 2000 live images of different subjects and 2000 fake images obtained with different materials (such as gelatine, latex, PlayDoh, silicone and wood glue), were collected. Images were divided into a training and a test set, each containing an equal number of live and fake images, with fake images equally distributed among different materials. LivDet 2011 datasets were acquired using a consensual method [3], where the subject actively cooperated to create a mold of his/her finger, thus obtaining surrogates of better quality, i.e. more difficult to detect, than those created from latent fingerprints.

Experiments were organized as follows. First, we optimized the parameters of each method, i.e. the parameter C of the linear SVM and the task weights for MTJSRC, with a 5-fold cross validation procedure on the training set. Then, we computed the classification capabilities of both individual and grouped attributes. A preliminary result, not detailed for the sake of brevity, is that the individual attributes perform consistently worse than their combination with other attributes, demonstrating the strength of multiview approaches. As for grouped attributes, we tested different combinations of the candidate attributes described in Section 2.3 and, for each candidate attribute, we tested different parameter settings. We found that the best results were obtained for WLD using three different image scales (referred in the results as W3), for BSIF using different windows size, 5x5 (B5), 15x15 (B15) and 17x17 (B17), while for LPQ we obtained similar results computing phase information with either Short Term Fourier Transform (LS) or Gaussian derivative quadrature filter pairs (LG).

Results are summarized in Table 1 where we report error rates for each method and dataset and for the attribute groups that obtained the best results; average error rates over all the datasets are reported as well. The baseline for benchmarking our results was the method [9], which combines feature selection, linear SVM and LCPD outperforming previous results in the literature (see [9]). Bold values in Table 1 are those improving or matching the baseline.

Based on the results, the following remarks can be drawn. We found several attribute groups improving the baseline, and an optimal average error of 5.2% was obtained on SVM with the combination is B5+B17+W3+LG, reducing of 8.8% the error rates of [9]. In general, SVM performs better than MTJSRC. However, this result deserves a closer look to the data, as Italdata accuracies stand out for being definitely higher than the average. In particular, MTJSRC appears to be severely penalized by the performances on this dataset. Indeed, the accuracies of the two methods on the other datasets are definitely comparable (their average difference being 0.4% in favour of SVM). Specifically, if we consider the last three groups in Table 1. i.e. those combining multiple BSIF features, their average accuracies over Biometrika, Digital Persona and Sagem dataset improve the corresponding accuracies of the baseline of 36.2% and 28.6% for,

Table 1. Performance comparision on LivDet 2011.

Feature set	Feat. chaining + linear SVM					MTJSRC				
	Biom	DigP	IData	Sag	Avg	Biom	DigP	IData	Sag	Avg
B5 + W3	5.7	**3.5**	9.3	3.7	**5.6**	8.7	4.5	18.6	3.9	8.9
B5 + W3 + LG	5.6	**3.4**	9.0	3.7	**5.4**	6.2	**4.3**	18.8	4.1	8.3
B5 + B15 + W3 + LF	**3.7**	1.8	13.0	2.8	**5.3**	4.5	2.0	18.2	**2.4**	6.8
B5 + B15 + W3 + LG	**3.8**	1.7	13.3	2.8	**5.4**	4.6	2.2	17.9	2.5	6.8
B5 + B17 + W3 + LG	**4.7**	2.0	11.4	**2.7**	**5.2**	4.3	2.5	19.1	**2.6**	7.1
Baseline(LCPD) [9]	4.9	4.2	11.0	2.7	5.7	4.9	4.2	11.0	2.7	5.7

respectively, SVM and MTJSRC. These last partial result seems also to suggest that performance is mainly related to the design of the feature set rather than to the choice of the classifier itself.

Hence, how can this behaviour on Italadata be interpreted? Actually, similar problems were reported in the literature ([14], [9]), and a possible explanation is that Italdata images seem to be more clear and less natural than those obtained with other sensors. The somewhat contradictory behaviour of this dataset in our experiments supports this conjecture. For SVM, groups scoring well on Italdata performed badly on other datasets, and the other way around. As for MTJSRC, we found that optimal λ values of the regularizer in (1) for Italdata penalized the other dataset accuracies and, again, the opposite.

Concluding, we think that, overall, our preliminary results highlights the benefits of tackling the fingerprint liveness detection problem with multiview approaches.

4   Conclusion and Future Work

We presented the initial results of our investigation on the application of a multiview approach to the problem of fingerprint liveness detection. This approach combines in various ways different and complementary representation modalities of the samples under analysis. Experimental results show the strength of such approach, which is capable of improving, on the same data, previous results in the literature. These preliminary outcomes are promising but, at the same time, highlight the fact that further studies are sorely needed to fully understand the different factors involved in the problem, which will be the objective of our future work.

References

1. International Business Time: iphone 6 touch id fingerprint scanner hacked days after launch (2015). http://tinyurl.com/px33mre. (Accessed June 01, 2015)
2. Marasco, E., Ross, A.: A survey on antispoofing schemes for fingerprint recognition systems. ACM Comput. Surv. **47**(2), 28:1–28:36 (2014)

3. Yambay, D., Ghiani, L., Denti, P., Marcialis, G., Roli, F., Schuckers, S.: Livdet 2011 - fingerprint liveness detection competition 2011. In: 2012 5th IAPR International Conference on Biometrics (ICB), pp. 208–215, March 2012
4. Matsumoto, T., Matsumoto, H., Yamada, K., Hoshino, S.: Impact of artificial "gummy" fingers on fingerprint systems. In: Proceedings of SPIE **4677**, January 2002
5. Antonelli, A., Cappelli, R., Maio, D., Maltoni, D.: Fake finger detection by skin distortion analysis. IEEE Transactions on Information Forensics and Security **1**(3), 360–373 (2006)
6. Schuckers, S.A.C., Parthasaradhi, S.T.V., Derakshani, R., Hornak, L.A.: Comparison of classification methods for time-series detection of perspiration as a liveness test in fingerprint devices. In: Zhang, D., Jain, A.K. (eds.) ICBA 2004. LNCS, vol. 3072, pp. 256–263. Springer, Heidelberg (2004)
7. Abhyankar, A., Schuckers, S.: Fingerprint liveness detection using local ridge frequencies and multiresolution texture analysis techniques. In: 2006 IEEE International Conference on Image Processing, pp. 321–324, October 2006
8. Nikam, S., Agarwal, S.: Co-occurrence probabilities and wavelet-based spoof fingerprint detection. Int. Journal of Image and Graphics **09**(02), 171–199 (2009)
9. Gragnaniello, D., Poggi, G., Sansone, C., Verdoliva, L.: Local contrast phase descriptor for fingerprint liveness detection. Pattern Recognition **48**(4), 1050–1058 (2015)
10. Nikam, S., Agarwal, S.: Texture and wavelet-based spoof fingerprint detection for fingerprint biometric systems. In: First International Conference on Emerging Trends in Engineering and Technology, ICETET 2008, pp. 675–680, July 2008
11. Jia, X., Yang, X., Cao, K., Zang, Y., Zhang, N., Dai, R., Zhu, X., Tian, J.: Multiscale local binary pattern with filters for spoof fingerprint detection. Information Sciences **268**, 91–102 (2014)
12. Ghiani, L., Marcialis, G., Roli, F.: Fingerprint liveness detection by local phase quantization. In: ICPR 2012, pp. 537–540, November 2012
13. Gragnaniello, D., Poggi, G., Sansone, C., Verdoliva, L.: Fingerprint liveness detection based on weber local image descriptor. In: IEEE BIOMS 2013, pp. 46–50, September 2013
14. Ghiani, L., Hadid, A., Marcialis, G., Roli, F.: Fingerprint liveness detection using binarized statistical image features. In: 2013 IEEE Sixth International Conference on Biometrics: Theory, Applications and Systems (BTAS), pp. 1–6, September 2013
15. Burges, C.J.C.: A tutorial on support vector machines for pattern recognition. Data Mining and Knowledge Discovery **2**, 121–167 (1998)
16. Yuan, X.T., Yan, S.: Visual classification with multi-task joint sparse representation. CVPR 2010, 3493–3500, June 2010
17. Schmidt, M., Fung, G., Rosales, R.: Fast optimization methods for l1 regularization: a comparative study and two new approaches. In: Kok, J.N., Koronacki, J., Lopez de Mantaras, R., Matwin, S., Mladenič, D., Skowron, A. (eds.) ECML 2007. LNCS (LNAI), vol. 4701, pp. 286–297. Springer, Heidelberg (2007)
18. Liu, D.C., Nocedal, J.: On the limited memory BFGS method for large scale optimization. Math. Program. **45**(3), 503–528 (1989)
19. Brummer, N.: Fusion of heterogeneous speaker recognition systems in the STBU submission for the NIST speaker recognition evaluation 2006. IEEE Transactions on Audio, Speech, and Language Processing **15**(7), 2072–2084 (2006)
20. Dalal, N., Triggs, B.: Histograms of oriented gradients for human detection. In: CVPR 2005, vol. 1, pp. 886–893, June 2005
21. Nanni, L., Lumini, A., Brahnam, S.: Survey on LBP based texture descriptors for image classification. Expert Systems with Applications **39**(3), 3634–3641 (2012)

Online Signature Verification: Is the Whole Greater Than the Sum of the Parts?

Marianela Parodi$^{(\boxtimes)}$ and Juan Carlos Gómez

Laboratory for System Dynamics and Signal Processing, FCEIA, National University of Rosario, CIFASIS, CONICET, Rosario, Argentina
parodi@cifasis-conicet.gov.ar

Abstract. To choose the best features to model the signatures is one of the most challenging problems in online signature verification. In this paper, the idea is to evaluate whether it would be possible to combine different feature sets selected by different criteria in such a way that their main characteristics could be properly exploited and the verification performance could be improved with respect to the case of using each set individually. In particular, the combination of an automatically selected feature set, a feature set inspired by the ones used by Forensic Handwriting Experts (FHEs), and a set of global features is proposed. Two different fusion strategies are used to perform the combination, namely, a decision level fusion scheme and a pre-classification scheme. Experimental results show that the proposed feature combination approaches result not only in improvements regarding the verification error rates but also the simplicity, flexibility and interpretability of the verification system.

Keywords: Online signature verification · Forensic handwriting examination · Information fusion

1 Introduction

Automatic signature verification is an important research area in the field of biometrics [1], being the most popular method for identity verification. Signatures are recognized as a legal means of identity verification by financial and administrative institutions, and people is familiar with their use in everyday life.

Two categories of signature verification systems can be distinguished, namely, offline (only the image of the signature is available), and online (dynamic information acquired during the signing process is available). The interest in the online approach has increased in recent years due to the widespread use of electronic pen-input devices in many daily applications. In addition, it is reasonable to expect that the incorporation of dynamic information would make signatures more difficult to forge. Nevertheless, there are certain applications that demand the use of the offline approach. For example, Forensic Handwriting Experts (FHEs) only have the signature image available in their daily work, although in the future it might occur that FHEs will also have to deal with online signatures.

© Springer International Publishing Switzerland 2015
A. Pardo and J. Kittler (Eds.): CIARP 2015, LNCS 9423, pp. 151–159, 2015.
DOI: 10.1007/978-3-319-25751-8_19

In online systems, the signature is parameterized by discrete time functions, such as pen coordinates, velocity and pressure, among others. Researchers have long argued about their effectiveness for verification purposes, and the conflicting results make the discussion still open [2], [3]. To decide which features extract from the available time functions is also an important design step. Local (computed for each point in the time sequence) and global (computed from the whole signature) features can be considered [4], [5].

In this paper, the idea is to evaluate whether it would be possible to combine different online feature sets selected by different criteria taking advantage of their main characteristics in order to improve the verification performance with respect to the case of using them individually. The combination of three feature sets that have already proved to have interesting qualities, resulting not only in good verification performances, but also providing different advantages to the verification systems, is then proposed. In particular, an automatically selected feature set, a set of features relevant to FHEs, and a global feature set are combined and the discriminative power of the resulting combination is evaluated. The advantages of using each of these feature sets will be highlighted along this paper. Two different strategies are proposed for the combination of the feature sets. One is based on a decision level fusion strategy and the other one on a pre-classification approach. A well known state-of-the-art classifier, namely, Random Forest (RF), is used to perform the verification experiments. The verification performance of the proposed combination approaches is evaluated for two different signature styles of a publicly available database, namely, Western (Dutch) and Chinese.

2   Feature Selection

Typically, the measured data consists of three discrete time functions: pen coordinates x and y, and pressure p. Several extended time functions are usually computed from them [5], [6]. In this paper, the velocity magnitude v_T and direction θ, the total acceleration a_T and the log-radius curvature ρ are computed. The first and second order time derivatives of these functions are also computed. The different features are then extracted from the above mentioned time functions, as described in the following Subsections.

2.1   Global Features

In [7], a set of widely used global features corresponding to the better ranked ones in [5] and [4] is used. These global features (hereafter referred to as GF) will be the ones considered in this paper (for both, Dutch and Chinese signatures), and they are: signature total time duration T, pen down duration T_{pd}, positive x velocity duration T_{vx}, average pressure $\bar{P}$, maximum pressure P_M and the time of maximum pressure T_{P_M}. To include global features to the combination would simplify and improve the interpretability of the system since they are simple, intuitive and easily to compute and compare.

2.2   Time Function Based Features

A wavelet approximation of the time functions is proposed to model them. The Discrete Wavelet Transform (DWT) decomposes the signal at different resolution levels, splitting it in low (*approximation*) and high (*details*) frequency components. The idea is to use the DWT approximation coefficients to represent the time functions. In particular, the widely used db4 wavelet is employed. Resampling of the time functions, previous to the DWT decomposition, is needed in order to have a fixed-length feature vector.

Automatically Selected Time Function Based Features. In [8], an automatic feature selection based on the variable importance provided by the RF algorithm is performed from the original set of time functions listed at the beginning of Section 2. The automatically selected features are: x, a_T, y, v_T, p, dp, ρ, dx, θ, dy, d^2x, d^2y and dv_T for the Dutch data, and y, x, p, v_T, a_T, dy, dx, d^2y, θ, ρ, dp, d^2x, $d\theta$, d^2p, dv_T, $d\rho$ and $d^2\theta$ for the Chinese data. Here, df and d^2f denote de first and second order time derivatives of the corresponding time function f, respectively. Note that different features are selected for each signature style, then to include these features to the combination will improve its flexibility and capability to adapt to each type of signature. These feature sets will be referred to as ASF.

FHE Based Features. Although FHEs work with the static image of the signature, they can infer some dynamic properties from it. FHEs consider velocity and curvature as distinctive features, since in natural handwriting the stroke velocity is determined by its curvature, while in a forgery process this would not be the case. The pen pressure is not useful for them since it is strongly dependant on external factors such as the writing material and surface, although the pressure fluctuations are highly individualistic to the writer. In this paper, the set of features presented in [8], hereafter referred to as TFFHE, is considered as the one relevant to FHEs: v_T, θ, ρ and dp. To include these features to the combination would make it meaningful for FHEs, then the system could be integrated into toolkits that could be useful for them. This could contribute towards bridging the gap between the FHE and the Pattern Recognition (PR) communities. The TFFHE features have been selected based on FHE criteria for Latin scripts. Since information about FHE criteria for Chinese scripts was not available for the authors, the same TFFHE set is used for both signature styles.

3   Feature Combination Approaches

Two different combination strategies are proposed. One of them is based on a decision level fusion (DLF) approach, while the other is based on a pre-classification (PC) of the signatures so that gross forgeries can be early detected and discarded. They are described in Subsections 3.1 and 3.2, respectively.

3.1 Decision Level Fusion

Traditionally, three main approaches for information fusion can be distinguished, namely, feature, classifier or decision level fusion. In the feature level case, the feature vectors coming from different sources are concatenated to obtain a combined feature vector which is then used in the classification task. In the classifier level approach, a composite classifier is generated by combining the individual classifiers used to process the different signals involved. Finally, in the decision level approach, a final decision is obtained by combining the probability/likelihood scores from the separate classifiers processing the different signals.

In this paper, classifier level fusion is not possible due to the particular classifier being used (RF). Regarding a fusion at feature level, it is clear that since the ASF feature set contains the TFFHE set, feature level fusion of these two sets would not make sense. Two separate experiments fusing GF features with ASF features on one hand, and fusing GF features with TFFHE features on the other, were carried out. The verification results obtained (not shown here) did not improve the ones corresponding to the case of using the ASF and the TFFHE feature sets individually.

Based on the above comments, only DLF is considered in this paper. Three independent RF classifiers are fed by each type of features (GF, ASF and TFFHE) and the final decision is computed as a combination of the likelihood scores associated which each classifier based on the widely used *weighted geometrical combination rule*, that is:

$$P_{fused} = P_{GF}^{\beta} \ P_{ASF}^{\gamma} \ P_{TFFHE}^{(1-\beta-\gamma)}, \tag{1}$$

where P_{fused} is the likelihood score for the combined scheme, P_{GF}, P_{ASF} and P_{TFFHE} are the likelihood scores for the classifiers based on GF, ASF and TFFHE features, respectively, and $0 \leq \beta \leq 1$ and $0 \leq \gamma \leq 1$ are user defined parameters weighting the individual likelihood scores.

3.2 Pre-classification

It would be reasonable to expect that for gross forgeries some features such as global features and the ones based on the FHE criteria, would present a wide variability. This leads to the idea of using GF and TFFHE features for pre-classification in order to quickly recognize and discard gross forgeries.

In this paper, a multivariate version of the univariate PC approach introduced in [9] is proposed. The decision rule is shown in Fig. 1 (right), where $\mathbf{g}_{test}$ denotes the feature vector corresponding to the test signature, $\bar{\mathbf{g}}_{train}$ and Σ_{train} are the feature vector sample mean and sample covariance over the genuine training set, respectively, and α is a coefficient defining the threshold. The decision rule means that signatures whose feature vectors lie outside the hyperellipsoid define as $(\mathbf{g}_{test} - \bar{\mathbf{g}}_{train})^T \Sigma_{train}^{-1} (\mathbf{g}_{test} - \bar{\mathbf{g}}_{train}) = \alpha^2$, are considered as forgeries. Figure 1 (left) illustrates this, for the case of a two-dimensional feature vector. Coefficient α^2 is computed as:

$$\alpha^2 = \max_{A} \max_{A_i} \left\{ (\mathbf{g}_{test} - \bar{\mathbf{g}}_{train})^T \Sigma_{train}^{-1} (\mathbf{g}_{test} - \bar{\mathbf{g}}_{train}) \right\}, \qquad (2)$$

where A is the set of all the authors in the Training Set and A_i denotes the i-th author in the same set.

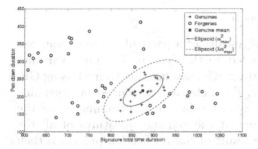

Decision Rule

If $(\mathbf{g}_{test} - \bar{\mathbf{g}}_{train})^T \Sigma_{train}^{-1} (\mathbf{g}_{test} - \bar{\mathbf{g}}_{train}) > \alpha^2$

then signature=FORGERY

else continue classification

Fig. 1. Left: Distribution of the global feature vectors for the genuine (+) and forged (o) signatures of an author in the database. A bounding ellipsoid ((red) solid line) as defined above, and an enlarged ellipsoid ((red) dashed line) as defined in Section 5, are also represented. In this case, the feature vector is composed by T and T_{PD}. Right: Decision rule.

In this paper, two different experiments employing the PC approach are proposed. One of them, referred to as PC-GF, uses GF features for PC while the subsequent classification stage is performed based on a DLF between two RF classifiers fed by ASF and TFFHE features, respectively. The other one, referred to as PC-FHE, uses TFFHE features for PC while for the subsequent classification stage employs a DLF between two RF classifiers fed by ASF and GF features, respectively.

4   Evaluation Protocol

The SigComp2011 Dataset [10] is used for the experiments. Since it contains Dutch and Chinese signatures, the influence of the cultural origin of the signatures in the verification performance can be evaluated, which is crucial in order for the system to be widely accepted. Each dataset is divided into a Training and a Testing Set. Skilled forgeries (simulated signatures in which forgers are allowed to practice the reference signature for as long as they deem it necessary) are available. The measured data are: pen coordinates x and y, and pressure p.

To evaluate the performance, the Equal Error Rate (EER) and the cost of the log-likelihood ratios ($\hat{C}_{llr}$ and $\hat{C}_{llr}^{min}$) are computed. A smaller value of $\hat{C}_{llr}^{min}$ (minimal possible value of $\hat{C}_{llr}$) indicates a better performance of the system. The use of log-likelihood ratios has been recommended by the experts in the lastest main conferences of the area since they allow FHEs to give an opinion on the strength of the evidence.

The optimization of the tunning parameters of the proposed verification systems is performed over the Training Set, while the Testing Set is used for independent testing purposes. To obtain statistically significant results, a 5-fold cross-validation (5-fold CV) is performed over the Testing Set to estimate the verification errors. Forgeries are not usually available in real applications during the training phase, then only genuine signatures are used for training purposes.

4.1 Decision Level Fusion Approach

For each instance of the 5-fold CV, a signature of a particular writer from one of the testing sets in the 5-fold CV is fed to the system. The GF, ASF and TFFHE features are computed. Then, three RF classifiers are trained using GF, ASF and TFFHE features, respectively. Each classifier is trained by a genuine class consisting of the current writer's genuine class in the training set of the 5-fold CV, and a forged class consisting of the genuine signatures of all the remaining writers in the same set. The result of the verification process is then the combination of the outputs of these three RF classifiers computed as in (1).

4.2 Pre-classification Approach

For each instance of the 5-fold CV, a signature of a particular writer from one of the testing sets in the 5-fold CV is fed to the system. The GF (for the PC-GF) or the TFFHE (for the PC-FHE) features are computed to construct g_{test}. Then, the distance between g_{test} and $\bar{g}_{train}$ (sample mean computed over the current writer's genuine signatures available in the training set of the 5-fold CV) is computed. If this distance is larger than the threshold (α^2), the signature is declared to be a forgery. If this is not the case, the signature is subjected to the subsequent classification stage, where two RF classifiers are trained, one of them with the ASF features and the other one with the TFFHE (for the PC-GF) or the GF (for the PC-FHE). Each RF classifier is trained as described in Subsection 4.1. A DLF is performed over the two RF classifier outputs, giving the final output of this classification stage. Then, the result of the verification process is either the result of the PC (the input signature is declared to be a forgery), or the one of the DLF of the two RF classifiers. Note that, in case the result is given by the PC, the verification process is simplified and speeded up.

5   Results and Discussion

The tuning parameters are optimized over the corresponding Training Sets. For both approaches, the number of trees and randomly selected splitting variables in the RF classifiers were set to 500 and $\sqrt{P}$ (being P the feature vector dimension), respectively. The time functions were resampled to a normalized length of 256. Regarding the resolution level, a better approximation accuracy is obtained using a lower resolution level, at the cost of increasing the amount of the modeling DWT coefficients. To increase the amount of DWT coefficients to model each time function is not a limitation when using the TFFHE features since the feature vector contains only four features, although it will significantly increase the feature vector dimension in the case of using the ASF features. Then, the DWT resolution level was set to 2 when computing the TFFHE features, and to 3 in the case of the ASF ones.

For the PC approach, parameter α is computed resorting to (2) over the Training Sets. Experiments carried out over these sets showed that such a computation of α leads to several genuine signatures lying outside the defined hyper-ellipsoid and so wrongly classified as forgeries. This is probably due to the fact that α is always computed over a separate subset of genuine signatures used exclusively for training purposes, without taking into account the forgeries which are also available in the Training Sets. The experiments also showed that it is possible to enlarge the hyper-ellipsoid in such a way that less genuine signatures lie outside it. This is illustrated in Fig. 1, where an enlarged ellipsoid containing the original one has been plotted in (red) dashed line. Then, better results can be obtained by redefining the decision threshold multiplying α^2 by a factor $\lambda > 1$. The parameter λ was also optimized over the Training Sets, being set to $\lambda = 5$ for both PC approaches (PC-GF and PC-FHE), and both datasets. For the DLF approach, the parameters β and γ are optimized by minimizing $\hat{C}_{llr}^{min}$ over the Training Sets, being set to $\beta^{Dutch} = 0.2$ and $\gamma^{Dutch} = 0.5$ for Dutch data, and $\beta^{Chinese} = 0.1$ and $\gamma^{Chinese} = 0.8$ for Chinese data.

The verification results obtained when using the PC-GF approach are shown in the first row of Table 1, for the Dutch (left) and Chinese (right) datasets, respectively, while the ones corresponding to the PC-FHE approach are not good and it does not make sense to include them in Table 1. The verification results corresponding to the case of using the DLF approach are presented in the second row of Table 1. The best verification results for the case of using each feature set individually correspond to the case of using the ASF features, and they are shown in the third row of Table 1. In addition, state-of-the-art results corresponding to the best commercial and non-commercial systems in the SigComp2011 Competition reported over the same datasets [10], are included in the last two rows of Table 1 (information about the EER was not given).

Table 1. Verification results for the Dutch (left) and Chinese (right) Datasets

	Dutch Dataset			Chinese Dataset		
	EER	$\hat{C}_{llr}$	$\hat{C}_{llr}^{min}$	EER	$\hat{C}_{llr}$	$\hat{C}_{llr}^{min}$
PC-GF	3.55	0.172	0.133	5.1	0.194	0.162
DLF	6.95	0.261	0.228	7.31	0.268	0.218
ASF	6.58	0.243	0.205	7.455	0.296	0.248
Comm.	–	0.259	0.123	–	0.413	0.218
Non-comm.	–	0.493	0.237	–	0.565	0.351

It can be observed that the PC-GF approach obtains better verification results than the DLF one, for both datasets. In addition, the PC-GF approach outperforms the ASF one (for both datasets), while the DLF approach outperforms the ASF one only for the Chinese data. Note also that the proposed combinations obtain results comparable to the best ones in the state-of-the-art, being even better than the non-commercial systems. Moreover, in the case of the Chinese data, results are better than the ones corresponding to the commercial system, which is particularly promising since Chinese signatures are usually more complex than Western ones.

Based on the above discussion, the best combination strategy is the PC-GF approach, that is to use GF features for PC and to perform DLF with the remaining information (ASF and TFFHE features).

Finally, the obtained verification results (shown in Table 1) allow to answer the question in the title of the paper for the positive.

6   Conclusions

The feasibility of combining different feature sets selected by different criteria so that their main characteristics could be properly exploited was evaluated. The experimental results show that the best combination strategy is to use GF for PC and to perform DLF with the additional information (ASF and TFFHE features). The results obtained in this case outperforms the ones obtained when using the feature sets individually. In addition, they are comparable to the best results reported in the state-of-the-art. In particular, for Chinese signatures, they are even better than the best result in the state-of-the-art. This is a promising result since this data is usually more difficult to deal with and, for this reason, it is considered more challenging. Finally, since the best combination scheme is based on a PC, the resulting verification process is simplified and speeded up.

References

1. Impedovo, D., Pirlo, G.: Automatic signature verification: The state of the art. IEEE T. on Syst., Man, and Cybern.-Part C: Appl. and Rev. **38**(5), 609–635 (2008)
2. Muramatsu, D., Matsumoto, T.: Effectiveness of pen pressure, azimuth, and altitude features for online signature verification. In: Lee, S.-W., Li, S.Z. (eds.) ICB 2007. LNCS, vol. 4642, pp. 503–512. Springer, Heidelberg (2007)
3. Houmani, N., Salicetti, S.G., Dorizzi, B.: On assessing the robustness of pen coordinates, pen pressure and pen inclination to time variability with personal entropy. In: Proc. IEEE Int. Conf. on Biom.: Theory, Appl., and Syst., USA (2009)
4. Fierrez-Aguilar, J., Nanni, L., Lopez-Peñalba, J., Ortega-Garcia, J., Maltoni, D.: An on-line signature verification system based on fusion of local and global information. In: Proc. IAPR Int. Conf. on Audio- and Video-Based Biomet. Person Authent., Rye Brook, NY, USA, pp. 523–532 (2005)
5. Richiardi, J., Ketabdar, H., Drygajlo, A.: Local and global feature selection for on-line signature verification. In: Proc. Int. Conf. on Doc. Anal. and Recognit., Seoul, Korea (2005)
6. Fierrez-Aguilar, J., Ortega-Garcia, J., Ramos-Castro, D., Gonzalez-Rodriguez, J.: HMM-based on-line signature verification: feature extraction and signature modelling. Pattern Recognit. Lett. **28**, 2325–2334 (2007)

7. Parodi, M., Gomez, J.C.: Using Global Features for Pre-classification in Online Signature Verification Systems. In: Emerging Aspects in Handwritten Signature Verification, pp. 39–52. World Sci. (2014)

8. Parodi, M., Gómez, J.C., Liwicki, M., Alewijnse, L.: Orthogonal function representation for online signature verification: which features should be looked at? IET Biomet. **2**(4), 137–150 (2013)

9. Lee, L.L., Berger, T., Aviczer, E.: Reliable on-line human signature verification systems. IEEE T. on Pattern Anal. and Mach. Intell. **18**(6), 643–647 (1996)

10. Liwicki, M., Malik, M.I., den Heuvel, C.E., Chen, X., Berger, C., Stoel, R., Blumenstein, M., Found, B.: Signature verification competition for online and offline skilled forgeries (SigComp2011). In: Proc. 11th Int. Conf. on Doc. Anal. and Recognit., China (2011)

Fingerprint Matching Using a Geometric Subgraph Mining Approach

Alfredo Muñoz-Briseño[✉], Andrés Gago-Alonso, and José Hernández-Palancar

Advanced Technologies Application Center (CENATAV), Havana, Cuba
{amunoz,agago,jpalancar}@cenatav.co.cu

Abstract. In the present work, a new representation of fingerprints in form of geometric graph, is proposed. This representation is obtained by fusing two previously defined approaches found in the literature and proves to be very tolerant to occlusions and distortions in the minutiae. Also, a novel matching fingerprint algorithm that uses geometric graphs was introduced. The mentioned algorithm applies frequent geometric subgraph mining in order to match fingerprint representations for computing a final similarity score. The introduced proposal reports very promising accuracy values and it applies a new approach allowing many future improvements.

Keywords: Fingerprint matching · Graph mining · Delaunay triangulation · Geometric similarity

1 Introduction

Biometrics can be seen as the automatic use of physical or behavioural characteristics to identify or verify the identity of a person. One of the most commonly used techniques in biometric systems is the comparison of fingerprints. The ridge patterns found in fingers and other parts of the human body are unique, providing enough information to distinguish a specific person from the rest. Also, these patterns can be extracted in a simple manner, which makes the use of fingerprints a very reliable technique. The goal of fingerprint recognition is to determine if two impressions were generated by the same finger or not, and it is a very treated topic in literature. However, even when there are some very effective solutions, this problem can not be considered entirely solved. In fact, the design of more accurate and efficient algorithms is still a topic of interest.

Most fingerprint recognition algorithms use minutiae in order to represent characteristic information. Minutiae are singularities in the ridge patterns, which are classified as bifurcations and terminations. A bifurcation is a point in which a ridge bifurcates, while a termination represents the termination of a ridge. Another very used feature is the direction of minutiae. This characteristic is defined as the angle formed between the horizontal axis and the tangent of the ridge associated to the minutiae, in counter clock wise. Even when there are some features extraction methods that report good results [1], they can fail

© Springer International Publishing Switzerland 2015
A. Pardo and J. Kittler (Eds.): CIARP 2015, LNCS 9423, pp. 160–167, 2015.
DOI: 10.1007/978-3-319-25751-8_20

under occlusion conditions. In this work, minutiae and their directions are used in order to define a fingerprint representation as a geometric graph. Thus, the fusion of two previously defined representations is used. The introduced matching algorithm uses frequent geometric subgraphs between the representation of two impressions, and it states coherence geometric criterion for calculating a similarity score. This approach represents a new perspective for fingerprint matching presenting very promising results. The rest of this work is organized as follows. The Section 2, introduces some theoretical formulations necessary for the understanding of the work. Section 3 is dedicated to the definition of the fingerprints representation. Section 4 introduces the algorithm for finding matches between the representations of two impressions. Finally, the experimental results that validate our proposal are shown in Section 5 and the final conclusions are given in Section 6.

2 Introduction to Geometric Graphs

Undirected geometric graphs are used as base for modeling fingerprints in this work. This kind of graph and their properties are defined as follows:

Definition 1 (Label domain). *Let L_V and L_E be label sets, where L_V is a set of vertex labels and L_E represents a sets of edge labels, the label domain of every label is denoted by $L = L_V \cup L_E$.*

Definition 2 (Geometric graph). *A geometric graph in L is a 5-tuple, $G = (V, E, I, J, K)$ where V is a set of vertexes, $E \subseteq \{\{u,v\} \mid u,v \in V, u \neq v\}$ is a set of edges (the edge $\{u,v\}$ connects the vertexes u and v), $I : V \to L_V$ is a function that assigns labels to vertexes, $J : E \to L_E$ is a function that assigns labels to edges, and finally $K : V \to \mathbb{R}^2$ is a function that assigns coordinates to vertexes, $\mathbb{R}$ represents the set of real numbers, and $K(u) \neq K(v)$ for each $u \neq v$.*

Definition 3 (Topological isomorphism). *Let $G_1 = (V_1, E_1, I_1, J_1, K_1)$ and $G_2 = (V_2, E_2, I_2, J_2, K_2)$ be two geometric graphs, G_1 is a topological subgraph of G_2 if $V_1 \subseteq V_2$, $E_1 \subseteq E_2$, $\forall u \in V_1, I_1(u) = I_2(u)$, and $\forall e \in E_1, J_1(e) = J_2(e)$. ALso, f is a topological isomorphism between G_1 and G_2 if $f : V_1 \to V_2$ is a bijective function where $\forall u \in V_1, I_1(u) = I_2(f(u))$, and $\forall \{u,v\} \in E_1, \{f(u), f(v)\} \in E_2 \wedge J_1(\{u,v\}) = J_2(\{f(u), f(v)\})$.*

When a topological isomorphism exists between G_1 and G_2, we can say that G_1 and G_2 are topologically isomorphic.

In the geometric context, two graphs may be geometrically similar having different vertex coordinates. An example of this can be seen in Figure 1(a). This situation takes place when one of the graphs is rotated, moved or scaled with respect to the other. That is why it is necessary to take in consideration the best geometric transformation for matching the two involved graphs, obtaining a geometric isomorphism. Let $G_1 = (V_1, E_1, I_1, J_1, K_1)$ and $G_2 = (V_2, E_2, I_2, J_2, K_2)$ be two topologically isomorphic geometric graphs. Let f be a topological isomorphism between G_1 and G_2. A geometric transformation in $\mathbb{R}^2$ is defined as a function $T : \mathbb{R}^2 \to \mathbb{R}^2$ which can be characterized by a scale factor λ, a rotation angle ω, and a traslation (t_x, t_y).

On the other hand, the error of a geometric transformation can be computed using the following expression:

$$\epsilon(T) = \frac{\sum_{v \in V_1} \|K_1(v) - T(K_2(f(v)))\|}{\|V_1\|}. \tag{1}$$

Let $G_1 = (V_1, E_1, I_1, J_1, K_1)$ and $G_2 = (V_2, E_2, I_2, J_2, K_2)$ be two topologically isomorphic geometric graphs with n vertexes. Let f be an isomorphism between G_1 and G_2. The geometric transformation T associated to G_1 and G_2 is defined as the transformation that minimizes the error $\epsilon(T)$. Using this measure, the concept of geometric isomorphism can be defined.

Definition 4 (Isomorphism τ-tolerant). *Let T be the transformation associated to the topologically isomorphic geometric graphs G_1 and G_2. We can say that G_1 and G_2 are isomorphic τ-tolerant if $\epsilon(T) < \tau$.*

In this case, the geometric similarity between two graphs G_1 and G_2 τ-tolerant can be defined with the following expression:

$$\phi(G_1, G_2) = \frac{1}{n\tau} \sum_{v \in V_1} \|K_1(v) - T(K_2(f(v)))\|. \tag{2}$$

In this way, given two geometric graphs $G_1 = (V_1, E_1, I_1, J_1, K_1)$ and $G_2 = (V_2, E_2, I_2, J_2, K_2)$, G_1 is a geometric subgraph of G_2 if some topological subgraph of G_2 is isomorphic τ-tolerant with G_1.

In Figure 1(b), an example of a geometric transformation T associated to two graphs, can be seen. The distances between the corresponding vertexes are pointed with arrows. If the average value of these distances is higher than the tolerance threshold τ, the graphs are not isomorphic τ-tolerant. In the illustrated case, the first edge of each graph was used to compute T.

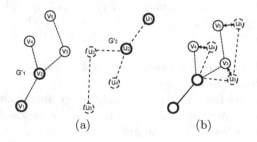

(a)   (b)

Fig. 1. Transformation applied to isomorphic τ-tolerant geometric graphs.

Definition 5 (Support set). *Let $D = \{G_1, G_2, \ldots, G_{|D|}\}$ be a collection of geometric graphs and let δ be a predefined frequency threshold. The support set of a graph g is defined as the set $G_i \in D$ composed by the graphs where g is geometric subgraph. The notations $\Delta(g, D)$ and $\sigma(g, D) = |\Delta(g, D)|$ are used for referring the support set and the frequency of g in D, respectively. A graph g is frequent in a collection D if $\sigma(g, D) \geq \delta$.*

Definition 6 (Geometric occurrence). *Let g and G be two geometric graphs, such that g is a geometric subgraph of G, the topological subgraph g' of G, isomorphic τ-tolerant with g is called geometric occurrence of g in G. If there is more than one subgraph g' fulfilling this condition, the geometric occurrence will be the one that maximizes the expression $\phi(g, g')$.*

Definition 7 (Frequency set). *Let g be a frequent geometric subgraph in a collection D, and let $\Delta(g, D) = \{G_1, \ldots, G_N\}$ be its support set. The frequency set of g is defined as $\Gamma(g, D) = \{g'_1, \ldots, g'_N\}$, where g'_i is the geometric occurrence of g in G_i.*

There are some algorithms finding every frequent geometric subgraph in a given collection [2,3]. Using these approaches, the construction of the frequency set of each occurrence is a simple process. One of the novelties presented in this work is the use of one of these algorithms in fingerprint matching.

3 Fingerprints Representation

In the present work, a fingerprint representation based on the fusion of two previously proposed approaches is introduced. Thus, there are some aspects that need to be mentioned. From a geometric point of view, a triangulation of a set of points $P = \{p_1, \cdots, p_n\}$ in $\mathbb{R}^2$ is a planar subdivision of the plane in triangles $\triangle p_i p_j p_k$. The vertexes of these triangles are made up by points of P. A triangulation is considered of Delaunay, and is denoted as $TD(P)$, if the circumcircle of every triangle contains no points of P [4].

This triangulation is unique for a specific set P, if there is no circumcircle with more than three points of P at its border. This characteristic makes $TD(P)$ very useful in the field of fingerprints recognition. There are some algorithms that use $TD(P)$ computed from the coordinates of the minutiae, for representing the impressions [5]. These representations have some problems since $TD(P)$ can suffer great structural changes when minutiae are slightly displaced or when some of them are missing. Both situations are common in the feature extraction step, mostly because of the skin elasticity or the occlusions of some fingerprints parts. In order to deal with the minutiae displacement, Muñoz-Briseño et al. [6] proposed a representation based on Delaunay triangulations of order k.

Definition 8 (Delaunay triangulation of order k). *Let $P = \{p_1, \cdots, p_n\}$ be a set of points in $\mathbb{R}^2$, for $p_l, p_m, p_n \in P$, $\triangle p_l p_m p_n$ is a Delaunay triangle of order k is its circumcircle contains at most k points of P. Subsequently, a triangulation of P is of Delaunay of order k, and is denoted as $TD_k(P)$, if every one of its triangles is of order k.*

The representation proposed on the previously mentioned work is made up by the set of triangles:

$$ET_k(P) = TD_0(P) \cup TD_k(P) \tag{3}$$

Similarly, Gago-Alonso et al. [7] proposed a representation, denoted as R, that avoids the problems found when a minutia is not detected. Using the Delaunay triangulation of order k, in this work we propose a generalized variant as follows.

Definition 9 (Polygonal hull of order k). *Let $P = \{p_1, \cdots, p_n\}$ be a set of points on $\mathbb{R}^2$, and let $TD_k(P)$ be the Delaunay triangulation of order k of P. Let $p_i \in P$, the set N_i denotes the points adjacent to p_i in $TD_k(P)$. The polygonal hull of order k is defined as the Delaunay triangulation of order k of N_i, and is denoted as Hk_i.*

The final triangle set used in this work is given by the following expression:

$$R_k(P) = ET_k(P) \cup Hk_1(P) \cup \ldots \cup Hk_n(P) \tag{4}$$

Figure 2 shows that a Delaunay triangulation can suffer major structural changes when a point p is not present 2(b) or when its slightly displaced 2(c). However, the proposed triangles set 2(d) preserves many edges in both situations. In this context, this implies that our approach can find correspondences between fingerprints of a same finger, even if some of them have some missing or displaced minutiae. In this way, the set $R_k(P)$ is robust to displacement and absence of minutiae. The defined representation also preserves the linearity of the amount of triangles with respect to the number of minutiae in the impressions. In order to use a geometric subgraph mining algorithm, the associated

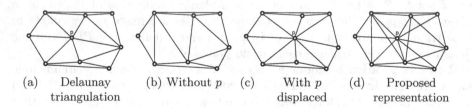

(a)   Delaunay triangulation   (b) Without p (c)   With p displaced   (d)   Proposed representation

Fig. 2. Triangles sets.

graph $G_R = (V_R, E_R, I_R, J_R, K_R)$ of $R_k(P)$ is defined, where V_R represents the points of P, E_R is composed by every edge contained in the triangles of $R_k(P)$ (every edge is represented only once, even if appears in more than one triangle), $I_R : V \rightarrow \{0, 1\}$ is the function that assigns labels to the vertexes (the values of these labels depend on the minutiae type that each vertex represents, bifurcation or termination) and $J_R : E \rightarrow \{0, \ldots, 360\}$ is the function that assigns labels to the edges (computed by subtracting the directions of the minutiae that define each edge). With the impressions represented as geometric graphs, the mining method that is the base of the matching algorithm can be applied.

4   Fingerprint Matching

Let $G_{R1} = (V_{R1}, E_{R1}, I_{R1}, J_{R1}, K_{R1})$ and $G_{R2} = (V_{R2}, E_{R2}, I_{R2}, J_{R2}, K_{R2})$ be the graphs that represent two fingerprints. The goal of applying a matching algorithm to G_{R1} and G_{R2} is to determine if the impressions belong to the same finger, by computing similarity score. For this, the proposal introduced uses a geometric graph mining algorithm found on the literature [3]. This algorithm will be referred as $FreqGeom(D, \delta)$. The idea is to extract correspondences between G_{R1} and G_{R2} using their common geometric subgraphs. The input of $FreqGeom(D, \delta)$ is set by a collection $D = \{G_{R1}, G_{R2}\}$ in which the mining is performed, and a support. In our case $\delta = 2$, since the matching operation involves only two graphs. The output of $FreqGeom(D, \delta)$ is a set of frequent geometric subgraphs $F = \{g_1, \ldots, g_n\}$, and their respective frequency sets $\{\Gamma_1, \ldots, \Gamma_n\}$. Using F, correspondences between the representations are found.

Let $g_i = (V_i, E_i, I_i, J_i, K_i)$ be a geometric subgraph such that $g_i \in F$. The frequency set of g_i is conformed in this context by only two graphs $\Gamma_i(g_i, D) = \{g'_{i1}, g'_{i2}\}$, since $|D| = 2$. Using this information, a similarity tuple can be obtained for each frequent geometric subgraphs found, with the form $s_i = \langle sim_i, T_i \rangle$ where T_i is the geometric transformation associated to g'_{i1} and g'_{i2}, and sim_i is given by the following expression:

$$sim_i = (|V_i| + |E_i|) \times \phi(g'_{i1}, g'_{i2}) \tag{5}$$

The number of edges and vertexes have a great influence in the similarity value previously defined, since bigger correspondences should have more weight. Let $S = \{s_1, \ldots, s_n\}$ be the set of similarity tuples obtained from the frequent geometric subgraphs $F = \{g_1, \ldots, g_n\}$ in D; with the goal of computing the final similarity between G_{R1} and G_{R2}, an overlapped clustering of n clusters P_j of S, is performed, where:

$$P_j = \{s_k \mid d_t(T_j, T_k) < \varepsilon \ \forall \ s_k \in S, 1 \leq j, k \leq M\}, \tag{6}$$

$$d_t(T_j, T_k) = G_s(|\lambda_j - \lambda_k|) + G_s(d_2(t_{xj}, t_{yj}, t_{xk}, t_{yk})) + G_s(|\omega_j - \omega_k|), \tag{7}$$

In this case, $d_2(t_{xj}, t_{yj}, t_{xk}, t_{yk})$ represents the euclidean distance between the translation components of the involved geometric transformations and G_s is the gaussian function:

$$G_s(t) = e^{\frac{t^2}{2d^2}} \tag{8}$$

This process creates n subsets P_j of S, where each P_j in conformed by the closest s_k to each s_j, using the distance function $d_t(T_j, T_k)$. Finally, the similarity of the two representations is given by:

$$simFinal(G_{R1}, G_{R2}) = \sum_{s_i \in P_j} sim_i. \tag{9}$$

where P_j is the subset of S with the higher cardinality. This algorithm is based on the idea that if some frequent geometric subgraphs are found between two

Fig. 3. Frequent geometric subgraphs found between two fingerprints of a same finger.

representations of fingerprints, they must have very similar associated geometric transformations. In Figure 3 an example of a relatively large common subgraph found using the mining algorithm can be seen.

5   Experimental Evaluation

In the first performed experiment, our proposal was compared with one of the best state-of-the-art approaches, Minutia Cylinder Code (MCC) [8]. For this, False Match Rate (FMR) and False Non-Match Rate (FMR) curves were computed with different similarity thresholds values in the FVC2006 DB2 database, with $\varepsilon = 2$. As can be seen in Figure 4(a), the EER reported by MCC (1.46) is slightly smaller than the obtained with our algorithm (1.90). However, the values of FMR and FNMR of MCC increase more abruptly. This fact makes more difficult the reduction of one measure without affecting the other greatly. Also, Cumulative Match Curves (CMC) were computed by using the last 11 impressions of each finger of the FVC2006 DB2 as queries. Since the accuracy of the fingerprint identification algorithms is affected by the number of possible fingerprint candidates, the comparison dataset was established with the remaining 140 fingerprints of the FVC2006 DB2 and with 31258 rolled impressions contained

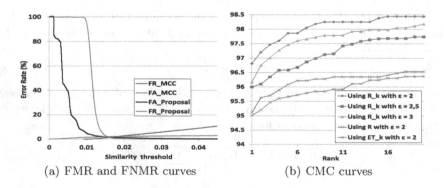

(a) FMR and FNMR curves   (b) CMC curves

Fig. 4. Experimental evaluation.

in the datasets NIST 27, NIST 4 and NIST 14. In Figure 4(b) the CMC curves of our proposal are shown, using different values for ε and representations. The reported accuracy is higher than 96,8% and 98,4% with $\varepsilon = 2$, in the positions 1 and 20, respectively. As can be seen, the best results are reached using the proposed representation R_k. These results are very promising since only minutiae information was used. Also, the mining methods provide many possibilities than can be exploited in the future. Each matching was performed in 28 miliseconds as average, in a PC with a microprocessor i7, 1.7 Ghz and 8 Gb of RAM. These values are lower than the average execution time of the 10 best algorithms reported on FVC2006 competition (53 miliseconds).

6   Conclusions

In this work, a new representation of fingerprints based on the fusion of two previous works, was proposed. The result of this fusion is a labeled geometric graph that is able to eliminate most of the noise generated by the absence of minutiae or the distortions found in the fingerprints. Also, a novel matching algorithm between these representations was defined, by using frequent subgraphs mining. In a consolidation step, a coherence criteria between the resulting subgraphs was applied in order to compute the final similarity. The proposed method shows the usefulness of the data mining, specifically the geometric subgraphs mining, in the field of biometrics. Future works are focused on improving *FreqGeom* in order to use other benefits of using graphs in fingerprint matching algorithms.

References

1. Rajanna, U., Erol, A., Bebis, G.: A comparative study on feature extraction for fingerprint classification and performance improvements using rank-level fusion. Pattern Anal. Appl. **13**(3), 263–272 (2010)
2. Kuramochi, M., Karypis, G.: Discovering frequent geometric subgraphs. Inf. Syst. **32**(8), 1101–1120 (2007)
3. Gago-Alonso, A., Muñoz-Briseño, A., Acosta-Mendoza, N.: A new proposal for graph classification using frequent geometric subgraphs. Data Knowl. Eng. **87**, 243–257 (2013)
4. de Berg, M., van Kreveld, M., Overmars, M., Schwarzkopf, O.: Computational Geometry: Algorithms and Applications, 2nd edn. Springer-Verlag (2000)
5. Bebis, G., Deaconu, T., Georgiopoulos, M.: Fingerprint identification using delaunay triangulation. In: IEEE Int. Conf. on Intell. Inf. Sys., pp. 452–459 (1999)
6. Muñoz-Briseño, A., Gago-Alonso, A., Hernández-Palancar, J.: Fingerprint indexing with bad quality areas. Expert Syst. Appl. **40**(5), 1839–1846 (2013)
7. Gago-Alonso, A., Hernández-Palancar, J., Rodríguez-Reina, E., Muñoz-Briseño, A.: Indexing and retrieving in fingerprint databases under structural distortions. Expert Syst. Appl. **40**(8), 2858–2871 (2013)
8. Cappelli, R.M.F., Maltoni, D.: Minutia cylinder-code: A new representation and matching technique for fingerprint recognition. IEEE Trans. Pattern Anal. Mach. Intell. **32**(12), 2128–2141 (2010)

Improving Writer Identification Through Writer Selection

Diego Bertolini[1](✉), Luiz S. Oliveira[2], and Robert Sabourin[3]

[1] Universidade Tecnologica Federal do Paraná, Campo Mourão (PR), Brazil
diegobertolini@utfpr.edu.br
[2] Universidade Federal do Paraná, Curitiba (PR), Brazil
[3] École de Tecnologie Supérieure, Montreal, Canada

Abstract. In this work we present a method for selecting instances for a writer identification system underpinned on the dissimilarity representation and a holistic representation based on texture. The proposed method is based on a genetic algorithm that surpasses the limitations imposed by large training sets by selecting writers instead of instances. To show the efficiency of the proposed method, we have performed experiments on three different databases (BFL, IAM, and Firemaker) where we can observe not only a reduction of about 50% in the number of writers necessary to build the dissimilarity model but also a gain in terms of identification rate. Comparing the writer selection with the traditional instance selection, we could observe that both strategies produce similar results but the former converges about three times faster.

1 Introduction

The concept of dissimilarity [9] has been used successfully to deal with several pattern recognition problems. In the case of writer identification [2] and signature verification [1], the dissimilarity-based classifiers using a dichotomy transformation have been proved a good alternative since i) they can deal with a large number of classes by reducing any pattern recognition problem to a 2-class pattern, ii) the ability of using disjoint sets for training and testing, and iii) the model is scalable in the sense that we do not need to train it each time a new class (writer) is enrolled into the system. In this approach the feature vectors are extracted from both questioned and reference samples and then the dissimilarity feature vectors are computed. In ideal conditions, if both samples come from the same writer (genuine), then all the components of such a vector should be close to 0, otherwise (forgery), the components should be far from 0. Figure 1 illustrates this transformation.

The difference vectors plotted in Figure 1b compose then the training set T that will be used to train the 2-class classifier. As pointed out in the literature [6], in practice, T contains useless information for the classification task (that is, superfluous instances which can be noisy or redundant) therefore a process to discard them from T is needed. This process is known as instance selection [6] or prototype selection [5].

© Springer International Publishing Switzerland 2015
A. Pardo and J. Kittler (Eds.): CIARP 2015, LNCS 9423, pp. 168–175, 2015.
DOI: 10.1007/978-3-319-25751-8_21

Similarly to feature selection, instance selection algorithms can also be classified into two categories based on whether or not instance selection is performed independently of the learning algorithm used to construct the classifier. If instance selection is done independently of the learning algorithm, the technique is said to follow a filter approach. Otherwise, it is said to follow a wrapper approach. The literature shows that the wrapper approach produce better results, however, it involves the computational overhead of evaluating candidate instance subsets by executing a given learning algorithm on the database using each instance subset under consideration.

The literature shows different strategies for wrapping a classifier into the instance selection process. Several of them formulate the problem as a search problem using different algorithms, such as Tabu Search [11], Sequential Floating Search [7], and Genetic Algorithms [3]. In the case of Genetic Algorithms, the straightforward approach consists in using a binary coded chromosome where the size of the chromosome is the number of instances available for training. This strategy produce good results but it shows its limits as the number of instances available for training gets larger.

In this work we deal with instance selection for writer identification using the dissimilarity representation. To overcome the limitations imposed by large training sets, we proposed selecting writers instead of instances. In other words, if a given writer is not selected, all his instances are removed from the training set. In the proposed method, the selection takes place before the dichotomy transformation, therefore only the instances of the selected writers are used to build the dissimilarity space.

To assess the proposed method we have used the writer identification system described in [2]. In this system the handwriting is first transformed into a texture and then different descriptors are used to generate the vectors in the feature space. Then, it applies the dichotomy transformation to create the dissimilarity representation where a SVM classifier is trained to discriminate between positive (writer) and negative (not writer) classes. Through a set of comprehensive set of experiments on three different databases, using a classifier trained with two textural descriptors (LBP and LPQ), we show that the proposed writer selection method is able to reduce considerably the number of writers necessary to build the dissimilarity model, in about 50%, while improving the identification rates. We also show that the performance of the selection mechanism is related to the number of references available for training and testing. Results show that when few references are available, which is true in most of real problems, the writer selection process appears to be more relevant. Finally, we compare the proposed approach with instance selection and show that it converges much faster producing similar results.

2   The Writer Identification System

As stated before, the method introduced in [2] was used to assess the proposed method. For the sake of clarity we reproduce it in this section. Given a queried

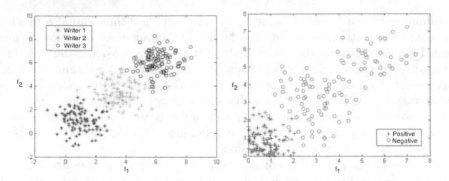

Fig. 1. The dichotomy transformation: (a) three classes in the feature space and (b) two classes in the dissimilarity space

handwritten document and a reference handwritten document, the aim is to determine whether or not the two documents were produced by the same writer. Let V and Q be two vectors in the feature space, labeled l_V and l_Q respectively. Let Z be the dissimilarity feature vector resulting from the dichotomy transformation $Z = |V - Q|$, where $|\cdot|$ is the absolute value. This dissimilarity feature vector has the same dimensionality as V and Q.

In the dissimilarity space, there are two classes that are independent of the number of writers: the within class ($+$) and the between class ($-$). The dissimilarity vector Z is assigned the label l_Z,

$$l_Z = \begin{cases} + \text{ if } l_V = l_Q, \\ - \text{ otherwise} \end{cases} \quad (1)$$

Figure 1 illustrates this transformation. Suppose there are three writers, $\{\omega_1, \omega_2, \omega_3\}$, and each one of them provides some samples. The feature extraction process extracts a vector from each sample, and these are shown in Figure 1a. Then, a dichotomy transformation takes place and computes the dissimilarity between the features of each pair of samples to form vectors. The distribution of such vectors, which we call dissimilarity feature vectors, are shown in Figure 1b.

We can see in Figure 1 that the dichotomy transformation affects the geometry of the distribution. In the feature space, multiple boundaries are needed to separate all the writers. In the dissimilarity space, by contrast, only one boundary is necessary, since the problem is reduced to a 2-class classification problem. The number of samples in the dissimilarity space is larger, because these samples are made up of every pair of feature vectors. We can also see in Figure 1 that, if both samples come from the same writer (genuine), then all the components of such a vector should be close to 0, otherwise they come from different writers (a forgery), in which case the components should be far from 0. This is true under favorable conditions. However, as in any other feature representation, the dissimilarity feature vector can be affected by intra-writer variability. This variability could generate values that are far from zero, even when the dissimilarity between the samples produced by the same writer is measured.

As mentioned earlier, one advantage of this approach is that even writers whose specimens were not used for training can be identified by the system. This characteristic is quite attractive, since it obviates the need to train a new model every time a new writer is introduced. In our experiments, we emphasize this feature by using disjoint sets of writers for training and testing.

The framework underpinning the identification system works as follows. Initially, a handwritten document is converted to a texture image. Then, the texture is split into n equal parts, $R_i(i = 1, 2, \ldots, n)$, which are sent to the feature extraction module. The resulting feature vectors, V_i, are stored in a database. When a queried handwritten document is presented to the system, it is also converted to a texture and split into m equal parts, $S_i(i = 1, 2, \ldots, m)$. These m textures undergo the same feature extraction process, and so creating the feature vectors Q_i. Then, the dissimilarity feature vectors $Z_i = |V_i - Q_i|$ are computed and sent to the SVM classifier, which yields a decision on each dissimilarity feature vector. The final decision, is based on combining these partial decisions, and is obtained by means of a fusion rule.

The dissimilarity framework requires the classifiers to discriminate between genuine (positive) and forgeries (negative). To generate the positive samples to train the SVM classifier, we computed the dissimilarity vectors among the R genuine samples (references) of each writer which resulted in $\binom{R}{2}$ different combinations. The same number of negative samples is generated by computing the dissimilarity between one reference of one writer against one reference of other writers picked at random. In this work we assess the impact of the number of references per writer in the writer selection process.

2.1   Feature Extraction

In order to generate the texture, the document is binarized and scanned top-down and left-right to detect all the connected components of the image. The bounding box of the remaining components is then used to extract the original components of the gray level image. The components in gray levels are then aligned with the new image using the center of mass of the bounding box. This algorithm, described in details in [2], compacts the handwriting generating texture images. Then, the texture is segmented into nine 256×256 blocks. Figure 2 shows two examples of the handwriting texture produced by two different writers.

Fig. 2. Examples of handwriting textures from two different writers.

After creating the textural fragments, the next step consists in dealing with representation. The literature shows us a long story of research in texture representation but recent works have shown that Local Binary Pattern (LBP) and Local Phase Quantization (LPQ) appear to be a very interesting alternatives to represent texture. They have been successfully applied to different problems achieving promising results. Besides, they are quite easy to implement. In this work, we have used the traditional LBP configuration, i.e., $LBP_{8,2}^{u2}$ with 59 components and the 256 dimensional feature vector produced by the LPQ.

3   The Writer Selection Method

The selection mechanism is based on a Genetic Algorithm (GA) with bit representation, one-point crossover, bit-flip mutation, stochastic uniform selection, and elitism which is implemented using a generational procedure. The following parameter setting were employed: population size: 20, number of generations: 100, probability of crossover: 0.8, and probability of mutation: 0.01. In order to define the probabilities of crossover and mutation, we have used the one-max problem, which is probably the most frequently-used test function in research on genetic algorithms because of its simplicity. This function measures the fitness of an individual as the number of bits set to one on the chromosome. The population size was determined through experimentation.

Let $A = W_1, W_2, \ldots, W_n$ be the pool of n writers and B a chromosome of size n of the population. The relationship between A and B is straightforward, i.e., the gene i of the chromosome B is represented by the writer W_i from A. Thus, if a chromosome has all bits selected, all writers of A will be used to train the classifier.

In this work we have adopted a wrapper approach where each solution created by the genetic algorithm is a SVM classifier trained on the training set (TR) using 5-fold cross validation. It uses a Gaussian kernel and the parameters C and γ are determined through a grid search. After training, the solution is assessed on the validation set (VAL#1) where we compute the Equal Error Rate (EER), which is given by Equation 2

$$\text{Equal Error Rate} = \frac{FP + FN}{TP + TN + FP + FN} \tag{2}$$

where FP, FN, TP, and TN stand for False Positive, False Negative, True Positive, and True Negative, respectively. The minimisation of the ERR is the measure of fitness of the genetic algorithm.

During the search the performance of the classifier on VAL#1 may continue to improve, but its performance on a independent validation set will only improve to a point, where the classifier start to overfit VAL#1. To avoid this overfitting, a second validation set (VAL#2) is used to monitor and stop the evolutionary algorithm. Finally the solution the minimises the ERR on VAL#2 is evaluated in the the independent testing set (TS).

4   Experimental Results

In order to build a reliable experimental protocol to assess the proposed selection method we have performed the same experiments on the three aforementioned databases using two different textural descriptors, LBP and LPQ. As described in Section 2, the dissimilarity-based system uses a certain number of references for training (R) and testing (S). To produce a final decision, the system combines all partial decisions produced on S using a fusion rule. Based on previous experiments [2], the fusion rule that provides the best results is the Sum rule.

To show the reproducibility of the proposed strategy, three databases were considered in this work, the Brazilian Forensic Letter (BFL) database (Freitas et al. [4]), the IAM database (Marti and Bunke, [8]), and the Firemaker database [10]. To meet the requirements of the proposed method, all databases were divided into four independent partitions, i.e., training (TR), validation 1 (VAL#1), validation 2 (VAL#2), and testing (TS). The BFL database was divided into four subsets: 25, 60, 60, and 115 writers for TR, VAL#1, VAL#2, and TS, respectively. Each writer is represented by 9 blocks of texture (256 × 256 pixels). The IAM database was divided into four subsets: 50, 125, 125, and 240 writers for TR, VAL#1, VAL#2, and TS, respectively. Each writer is represented by 9 blocks of 256 × 128 pixels. Finally, the Firemaker dataset was divided into four subsets: 20, 45, 45, and 90 writers for TR, VAL#1, VAL#2, and TS, respectively. Each writer is represented by 9 blocks of texture of 256 × 256 pixels.

Our previous experiments also show that the best results were achieved when the number of references available for training and testing are maximised, i.e., $R, S = 9$. One aspect we analyse in these experiments is the impact of the number of references in the writer selection process. To that end, we have performed the experiments using $R, S = [3, 5, 9]$. All experiments were performed three times so the identification rates are the average of three runs. The four partitions of the databases were randomly generated for each experiment.

Table 1 compares the identification rates on the BFL database. It shows that the proposed method is able to reduce in about 50% the number of writers in all scenarios. In the case of the classifier trained with LBP using few references (R,S=3), besides reducing the number of writers the writer selection method also brought an important gain in terms of performance, about 5 percentage points.

In the second experiment we have applied the same protocol in a bigger database, the IAM. Table 2 shows the results for IAM database where we can observe a similar behavior, i.e., reduction of the number of writers in about 50% and improvement in terms of identification rate.

In the third experiments we have considered the Firemaker database, which contains different handwriting styles such as upper-case and copied text and also forgeries. The results for the Firemaker database are reported in Table 3 and follows the same pattern exhibited by the experiments on BFL database. The number of writers was reduced in about 50% and the performance was improved when few references were available.

A final experiment was performed to compare the results of the proposed method with the traditional instance selection approach. In this case we have

174   D. Bertolini et al.

Table 1. Results on the BFL database

	Ref. R,S	With Writer Selection %	σ	# of writers	σ	Without Writer Selection %	# of writers
	3	95.1	0.01	9.6	2.3	89.5	25
LBP	5	95.7	0.02	12	1.0	94.7	25
	9	98.0	0.01	14	4.3	99.8	25
	3	95.5	0.01	11.3	0.6	96.5	25
LPQ	5	98.3	0.01	13	3.5	99.1	25
	9	99.4	0.01	14	1.0	99.0	25

Table 2. Results on the IAM database

	Ref. R,S	With Writer Selection %	σ	# of writers	σ	Without Writer Selection %	# of writers
	3	68.2	0.03	26	2.6	60.0	50
LBP	5	76.5	0.02	25.6	1.38	74.0	50
	9	91.3	0.01	28.6	1.1	91.0	50
	3	77.5	0.08	26.3	1.1	75.0	50
LPQ	5	81.8	0.02	22	1.7	77.0	50
	9	93.1	0.01	27.3	1.15	92.0	50

used the BFL database for R = 9 and the LPQ-based classifier. The size of the chromosome is the number of instances available per writer. Considering the 25 writers times 9 references, the size of the chromosome is 225.

The consequence of dealing with a large search space is a higher computational overhead. Table 4 shows that writer and instance selection arrives to very similar solution, in terms of performance and number of instances, but the proposed strategy uses a considerably reduced amount of time.

Table 3. Results on the Firemaker database

	Ref. R,S	With Writer Selection %	σ	# of writers	σ	Without Writer Selection %	# of writers
	3	96.7	0.02	10.3	1.5	94.4	20
LBP	5	91.9	0.01	9.3	1.5	91.1	20
	9	96.7	0.01	12.3	0.5	97.7	20
	3	98.1	0.01	8.6	0.5	96.6	20
LPQ	5	98.9	0.01	11.6	4.9	96.6	20
	9	97.8	0.02	10.3	1.5	98.8	20

Table 4. Instance versus writer selection on the BFL database for R = 9 and LPQ

Method	Rec. Rate (%)	writers	instances	time (seconds)
Writer Selection	99.4	14	117	84021
Instance Selection	99.4	25	113	215680

5   Conclusion

In this paper we have discussed a method for selecting instances for a writer identification system underpinned on the dissimilarity representation and a holistic representation based on texture. The proposed method is based on a genetic algorithm that surpasses the limitations imposed by large training sets by selecting writers instead of instances.

Our experiments on different databases show that the proposed method is able to reduce in about 50% the number of writers necessary to build the dissimilarity model while improving the identification rates. Comparing the writer selection with the traditional instance selection, we could observe that both strategies produce similar results but the former converges about three times faster.

References

1. Bertolini, D., Oliveira, L.S., Justino, E., Sabourin, R.: Reducing forgeries in writer-independent off-line signature verification through ensemble of classifiers. Pattern Recognition **43**(1), 387–396 (2010)
2. Bertolini, D., Oliveira, L.S., Justino, E., Sabourin, R.: Texture-based descriptors for writer identification and verification. Expert Systems With Applications **40**(6), 2069–2080 (2013)
3. Bezdek, J.C., Kuncheva, L.: Nearest prototype classifier designs: an experimental study. International Journal of Hybrid Intelligent Systems **16**(12), 1445–14473 (2001)
4. Freitas, C., Oliveira, L.S., Sabourin, R., Bortolozzi, F.: Brazilian forensic letter database. In: 11th Int. Workshop on Frontiers on Handwriting Recognition (2008)
5. Garcia, S., Derrac, J., Cano, J.R., Herrera, F.: Prototype selection for nearest neighbor classification: Taxonomy and empirical study. IEEE Trans. on Pattern Anaysis and Machine Intelligence **34**(3), 417–435 (2012)
6. Lopes, J., Ochoa, J., Trinidad, J., Kittler, J.: A review of instance selection methods. Artificial Intelligence Review **34**, 133–143 (2010)
7. Lopes, J., Trinidad, J., Ochoa, J., Kittler, J.: Prototype selection based on sequeintial search. Intelligent Data Analysis **13**(4), 599–631 (2009)
8. Marti, U.V., Bunke, H.: The IAM-database: an english sentence database for offline handwriting recognition. International Journal on Document Analysis and Recognition **5**(1), 39–46 (2002)
9. Pekalska, E., Duin, R.P.W.: Dissimilarity representations allow for building good classifiers. Pattern Recognition **23**, 943–956 (2002)
10. Schomaker, L., Vuurpijl, L.: Forensic writer identification: A benchmark data set and a comparison of two systems. Technical report, Nijmegen, February 2000
11. Zhang, H., Sun, G.: Optimal reference subset selection for nearest neighbor classification by tabu search. Pattern Recognition **35**, 1481–1490 (2002)

One-Shot 3D-Gradient Method Applied to Face Recognition

J. Matías Di Martino$^{(\boxtimes)}$, Alicia Fernández, and José Ferrari

Facultad de Ingeniería, Universidad de la República, Montevideo, Uruguay
{matiasdm,alicia,jferrari}@fing.edu.uy

Abstract. In this work we describe a novel one-shot face recognition setup. Instead of using a 3D scanner to reconstruct the face, we acquire a single photo of the face of a person while a rectangular pattern is been projected over it. Using this unique image, it is possible to extract 3D low-level geometrical features without the explicit 3D reconstruction. To handle expression variations and occlusions that may occur (e.g. wearing a scarf or a bonnet), we extract information just from the eyes-forehead and nose regions which tend to be less influenced by facial expressions. Once features are extracted, SVM hyper-planes are obtained from each subject on the database (one vs all approach), then new instances can be classified according to its distance to each of those hyper-planes. The advantage of our method with respect to other ones published in the literature, is that we do not need and explicit 3D reconstruction. Experiments with the Texas 3D Database and with new acquired data are presented, which shows the potential of the presented framework to handle different illumination conditions, pose and facial expressions.

Keywords: 3D face recognition · Differential 3D reconstruction

1 Introduction

Face recognition is one of the most popular and challenging problems in the field of pattern recognition and computer vision [1]. It has many applications such as security control and prevention, medical and biometrical analysis or gesture understanding. In the last decade, lot of research included three-dimensional (3D) face information to improve recognition rates and make the methods more robust to pose, gesture and illumination variations [3]. Bronstein et al. [4] used 3D facial scanners and achieved a robust recognition framework by modeling facial expressions as surface isometries, and constructing an expression-invariant face representation using the canonical forms approach. The work of Chang et al. [7] was one of the first that combined scores obtained from matching multiple overlapping regions around the nose. A similar method was proposed by Faltemier et al. [11] where 28 different regions around the face were selected and a score-based fusion approach was followed. Kakadiaris et al. [15] presented a 3D deformable model approach where the face was parametrized by the annotated

© Springer International Publishing Switzerland 2015
A. Pardo and J. Kittler (Eds.): CIARP 2015, LNCS 9423, pp. 176–183, 2015.
DOI: 10.1007/978-3-319-25751-8_22

face model (AFM). Mahoor et al. [18] used the principal curvature to represent the face image as a 3D binary image, then Hausdorff distance and iterative closest points (ICP) [2] were used for matching. More recently, Li et al. [17] used facial curves to form a rejection classifier and produce a facial deformation mapping from which adaptively select different face regions for matching. In Y. Zhang et al. [20] each 3D facial surface was mapped onto a 2D lattice that represents local 3D geometrical or textural properties, then traditional 2D face recognition techniques were applied. Lei et al. [16] presented a 3D face recognition approach based on low-level geometric features collected from the eyes-forehead and nose regions, and Support Vector Machine (SVM) algorithm was used to separate different subjects' representation.

In the present work instead of using a 3D scanner we acquire a standard color photo of the face while a rectangular pattern is been projected. We show that from this unique image, it is possible to extract low-level geometrical features without the explicit 3D reconstruction, as well as texture information. To handle expressions variations and occlusions that may occur by wearing a scarf or a bonnet, we extract information just from the eyes-forehead and nose regions which tend to be less influenced by facial expressions, as discussed by Lei et al. [16].

The rest of this work is organized as follows. Section 2 starts with a general description of the proposed framework and then some important specific steps are detailed. Section 3 presents some experimental results, firstly using the Texas 3D Face Recognition Database [12], and secondly, using our own database where all the steps of the proposed framework are involved. In section 4 we present the conclusions and discuss some future work.

2 Description of the Proposed Method

We will start by presenting an overview of the proposed framework, highlighting the main steps and properties. After that, some important individual steps will be described in detail.

The main steps of the proposed technique can be identified as: (i) acquisition; (ii) extraction of geometric and texture information; (iii) localization of the eyes and nose position; (iv) extraction of features from the rigid and semi-rigid regions of the face, and finally; (v) train/classify.

Once the texture and the 3D geometrical information is retrieved, we perform a curvature analysis to localize the nose tip and eyes corners.

From the corners of the eyes and nose tip position, we extract two different areas of the face. The first is a rectangular region that contains both eyes, and the second one is a trapezoidal region that contains the nose. As it was demonstrated in several works, these are the portions of the face more rigid and less affected by facial expressions (see e.g. [3,16] and reference therein).

The next step consists on defining features using the information available in the selected portions of the face. We analyze features computed from the geometrical 3D information and from the texture information. Then using a training dataset we define boundaries in the m-dimensional feature space using the Support Vector Machine (SVM) algorithm.

Figure 1 illustrates the main steps of the proposed framework and the kind of data processed at each step. Before presenting the experimental results, additional explanations and details of some key steps are covered in the following subsections.

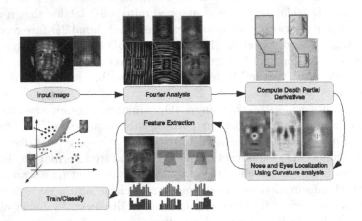

Fig. 1. Illustration of the main steps of the proposed framework. Note: due to image resolution some artifacts can appear, the full images, the code and a demo can be found at authors' web page.

2.1   Nose and Eyes Localization

To achieve a robust localization of the eyes and nose regions, we follow the procedure presented in [9] to estimate those candidate pixels. In our previous work [9] we address the problem of detecting the position of the nose and the eyes using face gradient information. Once candidates points for the nose and eyes are obtained, we remove those false positive nose and eyes detections by follow 2 basic steps. Firstly we estimate from the training set (in which eyes and nose position was manually marked) the likelihood distribution for the distance between the eyes and the distance between each eye and the nose (this step is performed once and in the training step). Secondly, we keep from all the nose and eyes candidates (obtained by curvature inspection) those who present inter-distances with higher likelihood.

2.2   Feature Extraction

Two different regions of the face will be considered for local feature extraction (as illustrated in Fig. 1). The first patch (named PatchA) corresponds to the regions around eyes and the second one (PatchB) corresponds to the region around the nose. The region of the nose, is the portion of the face less distorted by facial expressions, thus is called the rigid region. The area of the eyes is called semi-rigid region [16], and finally, the rest of the face is much more affected due to facial expression, and therefor was not considered in the present work.

Following the approach of [8], we calculate the partial derivatives D_x and D_y of the face depth (D); $D_{x,y}$ are directly obtained (from the acquired image) by measuring the deformation of the projected pattern. Then, using these partial derivative, over the PathA we have to calculate the directional derivatives D_v and $D_{v_\perp}$, where v is a direction parallel to the largest side of PatchA. Analogously D_u and $D_{u_\perp}$ are calculated over PatchB, where u is a direction parallel to the largest side of PatchB. Histograms for these quantities are computed to construct the 3D low level features descriptor, in addition, the LBP description over the Texture image is also taken into account.

2.3   Training and Classifying

The last step of the proposed framework consists on training a classifier for each subject we want to recognize. We decide to use Support Vector Machine (SVM) because it shows to be an efficient and robust algorithm for the sake of face recognition[16]. Recall that for a binary classification problem, where we assume that are known m training samples $x_k \in \mathbb{R}^N$ $(k = 1..m)$, with labels $y_k \in \{-1, 1\}$, SVM finds the hyper-plane with largest margin by solving the optimization problem:

$$\min_{\omega, b, \xi} \left(\frac{1}{2} \omega^T \omega + C \sum_i \xi_i \right) \tag{1}$$
$$\text{s.t. } y_i \left(\omega^T x_i + b \right) \geq 1 - \xi_i, \quad \xi_i \geq 0.$$

The parameter C is a penalty parameter of the error term and must be set; ω is a vector orthogonal to the hyper-plane, b is a constant that sets the location of the hyper-plane and ξ_i are auxiliary variables that allow to handle non separable problems. Depending on the problem, we may replace the constraint $y_i (\omega^T x_i + b) \geq 1 - \xi_i$, $\xi_i \geq 0$ by $y_i (\omega^T \phi(x_i) + b) \geq 1 - \xi_i$, $\xi_i \geq 0$ (Kernel SVM) which allows us to find the hyper-plane in a higher dimensional space. Once the SVM hyper-plane is obtained, one can classify new instances according to its positions with respect to the hyper-plane, i.e. by measuring the signed distance defined as:

$$d(x) = \frac{\omega^T x + b}{\|\omega\|}. \tag{2}$$

For a detailed explanation of the SVM algorithm we refer the reader to [5,10, 14,19].

As in the work of Y. Lei et all. [16] we opted by a *one versus all* approach. That means, that for each subject in the database, we will solve a two class problem in which we try to separate those feature vectors that belong to a given subject (named *positive* class) from the rest of the feature vectors (*negative* class). To find each hyper-plane, we used the implementation of SVM given in [6] and we tried both linear SVM and Kernel-SVM [with a Radial Basis Function kernel (SVM-RBF)]. The cost parameter of SVM algorithm (C) and the kernel parameter (γ) (when the kernel was considered) were estimated performing 5-fold cross validation.

Table 1. Accuracy (percentage) over Train and Test Sets. The superscript (A or B) recalls the patch from which features were extracted. Recall that the patch A corresponds to the region of the eyes while patch B corresponds to the region of the nose. The first two columns shows the results obtained just considering the geometrical information (represent by histograms of depth partial derivatives values). The last three columns shows the accuracy obtained by considering all the features extracted from the path A, patch B and the union of these, respectively.

(Acc %)	D_v^A $D_{v_\perp}^A$	D_u^B $D_{u_\perp}^B$	$LBP_{(Tex.)}^A$	$LBP_{(Tex.)}^B$	All feat. PatchA	All feat. PatchB	All feat.
Train	99.3 ± 0.4	98.4 ± 0.5	77.0 ± 4.2	51.6 ± 3.6	99.8 ± 0.2	99.4 ± 0.3	$\mathbf{100 \pm 0.0}$
Test	91.9 ± 1.7	93.6 ± 1.3	64.9 ± 3.8	44.3 ± 3.8	95.2 ± 0.8	95.1 ± 1.8	$\mathbf{99.4 \pm 0.2}$

3 Experiments and Evaluation

In this section, we perform two different set of experiments; firstly, experiments with the Texas 3D Face Recognition Database [12,13], and secondly, experiments with acquired images where the whole framework is tested.

3.1 Evaluation over the Texas 3D Face Recognition Database

This database contains 1149 pairs of high resolution, pose normalized, preprocessed, and perfectly aligned color and range images of 118 subjects. Additionally, it includes the locations of 25 manually marked anthropometric facial fiducial points. From those 25 fiducial points, just three are used (the nose tip and the corner of the eyes).

Texas database was split in two sets: one used for training (estimating SVM hyper-plane parameters) and the other was reserved for evaluation. Train and test sets contain (each) 486 samples obtained from scans of 25 different subjects. Once the 25 hyper-planes were obtained, the signed distance to each hyper-plane is measured for all the samples in train and test datasets. To each pair of range and color images, the assigned class is the one associated to the hyper-plane that has the higher distance to the respective feature vector.

Results are summarized in Table 1 for different subsets of features. As we can see the area of the nose is the more robust region of the face for the sake of 3D face recognition when we have expression variations. This fact is in agreement with recent research in this field (see e.g. [7,11,16,17]). Furthermore, the geometrical information seems to be more effective than the texture analysis, this is an expectable result as texture is easily affected, e.g. by illumination conditions or gestures. The best results were achieve by the fusion of all the features.

3.2 Evaluation of the Entire System

In a second series of experiments our own one-shot database was used. This database was generated by illuminating the subjects with structured light, as described in section 2. Images were collected over different days, and therefore, illumination conditions, pose and face expressions present significant variations.

The database contains pictures of approximately 120 different subjects, and in most cases there was available only one picture for each person. As the main objective of this second series of experiment is to evaluate the robustness of the proposed framework under different pose and facial expressions, we will focus on the two class problem where multiples images of one of the authors play the role of the positive class and the rest of the subjects represents the negative class.

As training set we used 219 images, with multiples images of the target subject (positive class) and the rest of images from different subjects representing the negative class. The test set is composed of 48 new negative instances (new pictures of people that were not present in the training set) plus 46 new positive instances (pictures of the target subject). In this test dataset, a wide range of facial expressions and pose variations are included as well as some pictures of the subjects with the face partially occluded (i.e. wearing a scarf or a bonnet as illustrated in Fig. 2). Figure 2 shows red/green histograms obtained by measuring the signed distance to the hyper-plane of each negative/positive sample on the test set.

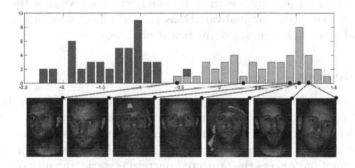

Fig. 2. Number of test instances versus its signed distance to SVM hyperplane. Red and green histograms were obtained by considering the negative and positive samples respectively. Under the histogram, some examples of positive samples are shown. The dashed lines shows the particular distance obtained for each of the example images.

By considering the signed distance of each test sample to the hyper-plane, one can classify each sample as positive if the signed distance [Eq. 2] is higher than certain threshold and negative in the other case. Figure 3 shows the Precision (portion of the samples labeled as positive that actually belong to the positive class), Recall (portion of samples of the positive class correctly classified) and the Precision-Recall curve for different threshold values.

A larger database is required to perform more exhaustive experiments (e.g. by repeating the previous two-class experiment for several subjects) before extracting quantitative conclusions. Despite this, some interesting aspects of the proposed technique can be addressed. Firstly, the proposed approach shows to be

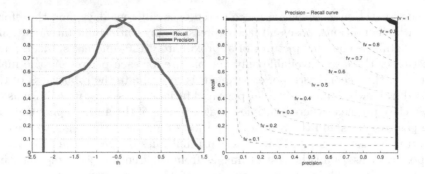

Fig. 3. Left: Recall and Precision for different threshold values. Right: Precision-Recall curve obtained varying the threshold value used for classification. The colored dashed lines shows the lines of constant F-measure (which represents the geometrical mean between Recall and Precision).

robust to facial expression (even exaggerated ones). Secondly, also promising results were achieved when the areas of the face (other than the nose or forehead) were occluded (e.g. by a scarf or bonnet), which shows that the approach is also robust to some intentional variations that a subject may produce such as variations of facial hair (e.g. shave his beard off).

4   Conclusions

A novel one-shot 2D+3D face recognition approach was presented. Instead of using a 3D scanner, we acquire a single photo of the face while a rectangular pattern is been projected over it; from this unique image, it is possible to extract low-level geometrical features without the explicit 3D reconstruction as well as texture information. Also as the projected pattern is static, the proposed method can be applied to dynamic scenes and can be trivially extended to video face analysis. On the other hand, the proposed framework is likely limited to indoor scenarios, and requires a set of images of the subjects we want to be able to identify (for the negative class one single image of many different subjects is enough) as a SVM algorithm must be trained.

Experiments shows the potential of the proposed framework to handle pose and facial expression variations, while requiring very low hardware requirements (as we just need e.g. a rectangular static pattern, a lens, and a led light source).

Acknowledgments. The authors thank PEDECIBA, CSIC and ANII for their financial support.

References

1. Abate, A.F., Nappi, M., Riccio, D., Sabatino, G.: 2d and 3d face recognition: A survey. Pattern Recognition Letters **28**(14), 1885–1906 (2007)
2. Besl, P., McKay, N.D.: A method for registration of 3-d shapes. IEEE Transactions on Pattern Analysis and Machine Intelligence **14**(2), 239–256 (1992)
3. Bowyer, K.W., Chang, K., Flynn, P.: A survey of approaches and challenges in 3D and multi-modal 3D+2D face recognition. Computer Vision and Image Understanding **101**(1), 1–15 (2006)
4. Bronstein, A.M., Bronstein, M.M., Kimmel, R.: Three-Dimensional Face Recognition. International Journal of Computer Vision (IJCV) **64**(1), 5–30 (2005)
5. Chang, C., Lin, C.: LIBSVM: a library for support vector machines (2001)
6. Chang, C.C., Lin, C.J.: LIBSVM: A library for support vector machines. ACM Transactions on Intelligent Systems and Technology **2**, 27:1–27:27 (2011). Software available at http://www.csie.ntu.edu.tw/~cjlin/libsvm
7. Chang, K.I., Bowyer, K.W., Flynn, P.J.: Multiple nose region matching for 3D face recognition under varying facial expression. IEEE Transactions on Pattern Analysis and Machine Intelligence **28**(10), 1695–1700 (2006)
8. Di Martino, J.M., Ayubi, G., Fernández, A., Ferrari, J.A.: Differential 3d shape retrieval. Optics and Laser in Engineering **58C**, 114–118 (2014)
9. Di Martino, J.M., Fernández, A., Ferrari, J.A.: 3d curvature analysis with a novel one-shot technique. In: IEEE International Conference on Image Processing (ICIP2014) (2014)
10. Duda, R., Hart, P., Stork, D.: Pattern Classification, 2nd edn. Wiley, New York (2001)
11. Faltemier, T.C., Bowyer, K.W., Flynn, P.J., Member, S.: A Region Ensemble for 3-D Face Recognition **3**(1), 62–73 (2008)
12. Gupta, S., Castleman, K., Markey, M., Bovik, A.: Texas 3d face recognition database. In: 2010 IEEE Southwest Symposium on Image Analysis Interpretation (SSIAI), pp. 97–100, May 2010
13. Gupta, S., Markey, M., Bovik, A.: Anthropometric 3d face recognition. International Journal of Computer Vision **90**(3), 331–349 (2010)
14. Hsu, C., Chang, C., Lin, C.: A practical guide to support vector classification. National Taiwan University, Taipei 106, Taiwan (2010)
15. Kakadiaris, I.A., Passalis, G., Toderici, G., Murtuza, M.N., Lu, Y., Karampatziakis, N., Theoharis, T.: Three-dimensional face recognition in the presence of facial expressions: an annotated deformable model approach. IEEE Transactions on Pattern Analysis and Machine Intelligence **29**(4), 640–649 (2007)
16. Lei, Y., Bennamoun, M., El-Sallam, A.A.: An efficient 3D face recognition approach based on the fusion of novel local low-level features. Pattern Recognition **46**(1), 24–37 (2013)
17. Li, X., Da, F.: Efficient 3D face recognition handling facial expression and hair occlusion. Image and Vision Computing **30**(9), 668–679 (2012)
18. Mahoor, M.H., Abdel-Mottaleb, M.: Face recognition based on 3d ridge images obtained from range data. Pattern Recognition **42**, 445–451 (2009)
19. Steinwart, I., Christmann, A.: Support Vector Machines, 1st edn. Springer, USA (2006)
20. Zhang, Y.N., Guo, Z., Xia, Y., Lin, Z.G., Feng, D.D.: 2D representation of facial surfaces for multi-pose 3D face recognition. Pattern Recognition Letters **33**(5), 530–536 (2012)

Iris Texture Description Using Ordinal Co-occurrence Matrix Features

Yasser Chacón-Cabrera[1]([⊠]), Man Zhang[2], Eduardo Garea-Llano[1], and Zhenan Sun[2]

[1] Advanced Technologies Application Center, 7ma A ♯21406, Playa, 12200 Havana, Cuba
{ychacon,egarea}@cenatav.co.cu
[2] Center for Research on Intelligent Perception and Computing, Institute of Automation, Chinese Academy of Sciences, 95 Zhongguancun Donglu, Beijing 100190, China
{zhangman,znsun}@nlpr.ia.ac.cn

Abstract. Feature extraction is one of the fundamental steps of any biometric recognition system. The biometric iris recognition is not an exception. In the last 30 years a lot of algorithms have been proposed seeking a better description of the texture image of the human iris. The problem still remains into find features that are robust to the different conditions in which the iris images are captured. This paper proposes a new iris texture description based on ordinal co-occurrence matrix features for iris recognition scheme that increases the recognition accuracy. The novelty of this work is the new strategy in applying robust feature extraction method for texture description in iris recognition. The experiments with the Casia-Interval, Casia-Thousands and Ubiris-v1 databases show that our scheme increases the recognition accuracy and it is robust to different condition of image capture.

Keywords: Feature extraction · Ordinal measures · Iris recognition

1 Introduction

The human iris has been proved to be a good and high-confident biometric characteristic for the person verification and identification due to its reliability, stability and uniqueness. One of the important tasks in iris recognition process is feature extraction from iris texture patterns. Analyzed the variety and large number of techniques found in the literature can say that has been a hot topic. However, the overall performances of such methods can be reduced in non-ideal conditions, such as non-voluntary on-the-move, or non-collaborative setups[1].

For iris feature extraction there are reported methods that perform signal processing in both: (1) spatial domain, using mathematical operators such as Laplacian of Gaussian filters [2] and (2) frequency domain, using transformed as Gabor [3,4] and Wavelets [5,6]. Another group uses statistical processing

© Springer International Publishing Switzerland 2015
A. Pardo and J. Kittler (Eds.): CIARP 2015, LNCS 9423, pp. 184–191, 2015.
DOI: 10.1007/978-3-319-25751-8_23

techniques such as LBP [7], Co-Occurrence [8]. The combined methods such as [9,10] make use of the feature fusion obtained from several individual methods.

In 2009 Sun and Tan [11] proposed Ordinal Measures (OMs) for iris recognition. Unlike traditional approaches that use quantitative values to represent features, OMs focus on qualitative values. These qualitative values may represent the results of ordinal comparisons between, for example, two groups of image regions, taken some intra and inter region parameters. The shape of the region, location of the region, average intensity values of pixels of the region, spatial configuration of the region, the region filtering (using different filters as Gabor, Wavelet, etc.); may be taken as parameters.

Tan, Zhang et al. [9] proposed an integrated scheme (OMs and color histogram for iris texture, texton representation and semantic label for eye patterns) to match visible light iris images in uncontrolled situations. Zhang, Sun et al. [12] used bandpass geometric information and lowpass ordinal features to address deformed iris image matching problem. Recently Rahulkar and Holambe [13] presented the directional ordinal measures scheme using their previous proposed filter new class of triplet half-band checkerboard shaped filter bank.

Motivated by the (promising) results obtained OMs and their flexibility for biometric recognition, in this work we propose and explore the use of ordinal co-occurrence matrix [14] to represent the features of iris texture. The flowchart of this method is shown in Fig. 1. Normalized iris images are taken as input. In feature extraction step normalized iris image is divided into regions. In each region, pixels are labeled based on ordinal comparisons. Then matrices of co occurrence of pairs of label pixel, with specific orientation and distance, are obtained as iris pattern texture features.

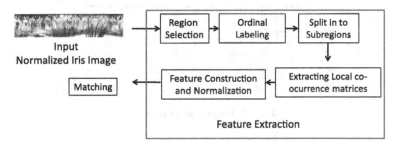

Fig. 1. A general description of proposed algorithm.

The remainder of this paper is organized as follows. Section 2 presents the proposed feature extraction method based on ordinal co-ocurrence matrix. Section 3 presents the principles of the experimental design. Section 4 presents a discussion of the experimental evaluation, and Section 5 gives the conclusion and future of this work.

2   Iris Recognition Process Based on Ordinal Co-ocurrence Matrix Features

A new feature extraction method based on ordinal measure concept and using the ordinal co-ocurrence matrix [14] is proposed to describe the texture of iris patterns. Iris recognition process consists on the general steps (image capture, eye localization, segmentation, noise detection, normalization, feature extraction and matching). Nevertheless, these steps present some peculiarities when Ordinal Co-ocurrence Matrix Features (OCMF) is used in feature extraction stage, see Fig. 1. The main OCMF steps are explained in the followings subsection.

2.1   Region Selection

Normalized iris image T is divided into a set of overlapping regions R_p. $T = \{R_p | p = 1, 2, 3, ..., P\}$, where P is the number of regions in T. The regions are overlapped based on a certain value d of displacement between the central pixels cp of each region. This operation permits the local computation of texture features (see Fig. 2). Local ordinal co-occurrence matrices are then computed over these regions. Taking in to account the rectangular shape of the normalized iris images, we consider subregions to be rectangle blocks of size $n \times m$.

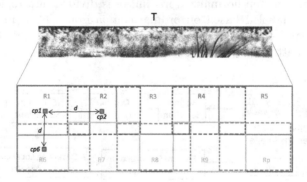

Fig. 2. Region selection.

2.2   Iris Ordinal Labeling

Based on the flexibility of ordinal measures, the selected regions should be labeled in order to retain the ordinal information of each region. The basic idea is to establish a labeling of the region following some criteria of comparison based only on ordinal relations. As in [14], the goal of this step is to represent the ordinal information of the local iris region in a compact manner allowing the efficient feature construction.

Two labels $(0, 1)$ are used to represent the values to be considered in the next step and another label (-1) for values that are not going to be consider, following the next idea: first the mean intensity value V_m of the pixels in the region R_p and standard deviation S_d are calculated. Then intensity value of each pixel V_j is compared with the V_m and S_d, for ordinal labeling, by the following rule (Eq.1):

$$Lb = \begin{cases} 0 & \text{if } (V_m - S_d) \leq V_j < V_m, \\ 1 & \text{if } V_m \leq V_j \leq (V_m + S_d), \\ -1 & \text{if } V_j > (V_m + S_d) \text{ or } V_j < (V_m - S_d). \end{cases} \tag{1}$$

As shown in Eq.1 the pixels which intensity value is out of range $V_m \pm S_d$ are considered as noise pixel. With this strategy is possible extenuate some illumination problem in images taken in uncontrolled environment.

2.3 Split in to Subregions

In order to accelerate the process of feature extraction, each region R_p is subdivided into N subregions Sr_i, $R_p = \{Sr_i | r = 1, ..., N\}$. The regions are divided into rectangular shapes considering the size of each region. The most representative label value of each sub-region is taken as the value of the sub-region.

2.4 Iris Local Ordinal Co-occurrence Matrix

Iris local ordinal co-occurrence matrices can capture the co-occurrence of ordinal relations between label pixel in the representative values of the subregion in the normalized iris image. The columns of the matrices contain the occurrences detected in different directions o. Rows contain the occurrences at different distances d. The number of obtained ordinal matrices will depends on the number of used labels.

The proposed method utilize a binary labeling $(0, 1)$, then the possible patterns combinations, to be consider, between two label pixels are: $00, 01, 10, 11$. For each pattern one co-occurrence matrix is obtained. In total, four matrices representing the local characteristics of possible texture patterns.

Each co-occurrence matrix have a size of $N_o \times N_d$, where N_o, represents the number of orientations between pixels to be compared and N_d, represents the distance. The orientations used are: $235^0, 270^0, 315^0, 360^0$ degrees. With this strategy are not compared twice a couple of pixels, because will always be compared the central pixel with the neighbors pixels at the bottom and right. Further, when the distance is greater than 1 adjacent pixels to the left of each orientation are considered to be compared(see Fig. 3).

2.5 Feature Construction and Normalization

The co-occurrence matrices obtained in each subregion are taken as features. Then to represent the features we built a feature vector, where each position contains the four co-occurrence matrices obtained in the previous stage.

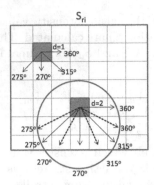

Fig. 3. Orientations and distances between pixels to be compared in each subregion.

3   Experimental Design

The main experimental scheme consisted in comparing the proposed approach with five (Daugman[1] and Masek, Ma, Monro[2] and OMs [11] two-lobe filters) different feature extraction methods in the verification task.

The protocol adopted for the experiments, compares the probe data with all labeled templates in the gallery. This sort of matching is also referred as 1:N matching. The evaluation of accuracy was assessed by the degree of influence on verification accuracy, estimated by Equal Error Rate(EER) and decidability index (d') [3]. The Equal Error Rate (EER) is the location on ROC curve, where the False Reject Rate (FRR) and False Accept Rate (FAR) are the same. The (d') combines the mean and standard deviation of the intra-class and inter-class measurement distributions.

The matching process between two normalized iris images is performed by comparing the correspondent matrices between each subregion of images. Matrices are compared using Euclidean distance and the result of each comparison is summed. The final score will be the sum of scores obtained from the comparison of each local regions.

3.1   Iris Databases

The proposed method was evaluated on three iris databases: CASIA-Interval, CASIA-Thousand and UBIRIS-V1.

CASIA-Interval[3], all iris images were collected under near infrared illumination with high quality, 320×280 pixel resolution and contains 2639 images from 395 subjects. For the experiments we used the whole database.

CASIA-Thousand[3] , contains 20,000 iris images from 1,000 subjects, collected using IKEMB-100 camera. The main sources of intra-class variations in CASIA-

---

[1] OSIRIS v4.1,http://svnext.it-sudparis.eu/svnview2-eph/ref_syst/

[2] USIT - University of Salzburg Iris Toolkit v1.0, http://www.wavelab.at/sources/

[3] CASIA-Interval and CASIA-Thousands, http://biometrics.idealtest.org/

Thousand are eyeglasses and specular reflections. For the experiments we used a subset composed by 3,960 images from the all subjects.

UBIRIS-v1 [15], database is comprised of 1,877 images collected from 241 subjects. This database incorporates images with several noise factors, simulating less constrained image acquisition environments. For the experiments we used a subset composed by 1,207 images from all the subjects.

All databases were segmented and normalized using OSIRIS[1]. Subsets images in (UBIRIS-v1 and Thousand) were chosen based on the quality of the result of this previous step.

4   Experimental Results

This section show the results obtained by the experimental design oriented to explore the capacity of the proposed feature extraction method to increase the recognition rates independently of the image quality.

Table 1 report the results of the recognition accuracy in EER at $\leq 0.01\%$ FAR and (d') on three databases. Fig. 4 show ROC curves.

Table 1. Experimental results on three iris image databases

Database Method	Interval EER(%)	d'	Thousand EER(%)	d'	UBIRIS v1 EER(%)	d'
Daugman	10.13	2.38	12.27	1.97	7.01	3.04
Masek	7.43	2.73	10.80	2.11	7.76	3.01
Ma	17.60	1.81	13.90	1.83	9.57	2.74
Monro	21.11	1.53	21.03	1.39	12.02	2.14
OMs	7.45	2.79	12.77	2.00	7.44	3.20
OCMF	**5.5**	**3.18**	**15.2**	**1.76**	**6.95**	**3.12**

The ROC curves in Fig. 4 show that, the OCMF marked improvement over five compared methods in Interval (top left), slightly perform better than Daugman in UBIRIS (down) and similar performance in Thousands (top right).

The experimental results, as shown in Table 1, indicate that the proposed OCMF allows and reduces the EER and increase the (d'). From the five evaluated feature extraction methods is possible to see that the proposed OCMF method obtains a better performance for two databases (Interval and UBIRIS-v1).

However on Thousands database this behavior is different, though OCMF maintains a similar level of accuracy than the rest of the algorithms outperforming only one of them (Monro) on the value of ERR. This fact could be caused by the presence of eyeglasses and specular reflections in this database. This behavior can also be produced by an incorrect selection of quantity and region distribution in the OCMF representation. This problem should be addressed in our future researches.

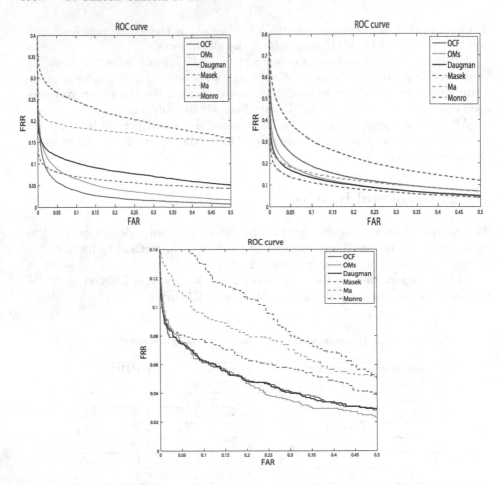

Fig. 4. ROC curves for Interval (top left), Thousand (top right) and UBIRIS-v1 (down).

From the results in the UBIRIS-v1 database containing iris images taken in the visible spectrum, under less controlled conditions than the images of Interval databases, the performance of our method outperforms the rest of the analyzed algorithms. It can also be possible to foresee that it would be a promising technique to address the problem of identification by iris in less cooperative environments and different types of iris sensors.

5   Conclusions and Future Work

In this paper we have presented a new feature extraction method for texture iris representation based on the Ordinal Co-occurrence Matrix Features. The characteristics obtained are invariant to monotonic gray-level changes in the pixel values, therefore can be applied to the iris images which may be obtained, for example, under different illumination conditions.

Experiments conducted on three databases and compared with five state-of-the-art feature extraction algorithms demonstrate the ability of the proposed representation to address the problem of robust feature extraction of iris allowing the recognition of people with greater accuracy.

Some aspects must still be researched to achieve a better performance of the proposed representation. The correct selection of sizes and the number of regions based on the characteristics of the sensor and images taken by it is an area that requires more research and experimentation.

References

1. Labati, R.D., Genovese, A., Piuri, V., Scotti, F.: Iris segmentation: state of the art and innovative methods. In: Liu, C., Mago, V.K. (eds.) Cross Disciplinary Biometric Systems. ISRL, vol. 37, pp. 151–182. Springer, Heidelberg (2012)
2. Chou, C.T., Shih, S.W., Chen, W.S., Cheng, V., Chen, D.Y.: Non-orthogonal view iris recognition system. IEEE Transactions on Circuits and Systems for Video Technology 20(3), 417–430 (2010)
3. Daugman, J.G.: High confidence visual recognition of persons by a test of statistical independence. IEEE Trans. Pattern Anal. Mach. Intell. 15(11), 1148–1161 (1993)
4. Masek, L.: Recognition of human iris patterns for biometric identification. Master thesis, University of Western Australia (2003)
5. He, X., Shi, P.: Extraction of complex wavelet features for iris recognition. In: 19th International Conference on Pattern Recognition, ICPR 2008, pp. 1–4. IEEE (2008)
6. Nasare, R.M., Hase, S.G., More, V.: Iris recognition by complex wavelet transform. International Journal of Engineering and Innovative Technology (IJEIT) 1(4), 119–123 (2012)
7. Sun, Z., Tan, T., Qiu, X.: Graph matching iris image blocks with local binary pattern. In: Zhang, D., Jain, A.K. (eds.) ICB 2005. LNCS, vol. 3832, pp. 366–372. Springer, Heidelberg (2005)
8. Li, P., Liu, X., Zhao, N.: Weighted co-occurrence phase histogram for iris recognition. Pattern Recognition Letters 33(8), 1000–1005 (2012)
9. Tan, T., Zhang, X., Sun, Z., Zhang, H.: Noisy iris image matching by using multiple cues. Pattern Recogn. Lett. 33(8), 970–977 (2012)
10. Santos, G., Hoyle, E.: A fusion approach to unconstrained iris recognition. Pattern Recogn. Lett. 33(8), 984–990 (2012)
11. Sun, Z., Tan, T.: Ordinal measures for iris recognition. IEEE Transactions on Pattern Analysis and Machine Intelligence 31(12), 2211–2226 (2009)
12. Zhang, M., Sun, Z., Tan, T.: Deformed iris recognition using bandpass geometric features and lowpass ordinal features. In: 2013 International Conference on Biometrics (ICB), pp. 1–6 (2013)
13. Rahulkar, A., Holambe, R.: Ordinal measures based on directional ordinal wavelet filters. In: Iris Image Recognition. SpringerBriefs in Electrical and Computer Engineering, pp. 69–82. Springer International Publishing (2014)
14. Partio, M., Cramariuc, B., Gabbouj, M.: An ordinal co-occurrence matrix framework for texture retrieval. J. Image Video Process. 2007(1), 1–1 (2007)
15. Proença, H., Alexandre, L.A.: UBIRIS: a noisy iris image database. In: Roli, F., Vitulano, S. (eds.) ICIAP 2005. LNCS, vol. 3617, pp. 970–977. Springer, Heidelberg (2005)

Confounding Factors in Keystroke Dynamics

Osvaldo Andrés Pérez-García(✉)

Advanced Technologies Application Center (CENATAV),
7ma A #21406 e/214 y 216, Rpto. Siboney, Playa, CP 12200 La Habana, Cuba
osvaldo.perez@cenatav.co.cu

Abstract. Authentication is the verification of the identity of a person to access a resource or perform an activity. Authentication based on keystroke dynamics biometrics validates a legitimate user, comparing his typing on keyboard with his stored template. An important group of factors influences the capture of the raw data generated by the user's typing. These Confounding Factors have been addressed in the literature from different approaches, and most of these studies agree that their influence affects the reliability of Keystroke Dynamics. In this research, a taxonomy of Confounding Factors is proposed, and several mitigation actions are discussed to face them.

Keywords: Keystroke dynamic · Authentication · Behavioral biometric · Confounding factors

1 Introduction

Authentication in computer security is the process of linking a user with their identity. The basis of authentication process is the knowledge that the system must have about authorized users, and the validation of this information. This validation is performed based on (i) What secret a user knows (e.g., password), (ii) What a user has (e.g., a token); (iii) Who is he/she (e.g., biometric traits), or (iv) Where he/she is (e.g., connected from a particular network)[1].

In 1975, Spillane [2] suggested the user authentication based on the user's typing behavior and Gaines, et al. in [3], were the first to study the possibilities of Keystroke Dynamics (KD) for this purpose. After that, KD has been the focus of multiple research works, some of them dedicated to the negative influence of several factors in experiment results and practical systems [4-6].

The present paper discusses KD and its relationship with those negative factors. A taxonomy to facilitate their study is proposed. The existence and poor understanding of these factors, their impact on KD Authentication Systems (KDAS) reliability, and the possibility of their exploitation by impostors, for example, to generate synthetic forgery attacks, were the main motivations to do this work.

According to this, and to accomplish our aim, it is necessary to know the bases of KD briefly. Thus, this paper was organized as follow: KD systems are described in the next section 2. In section 3, the proposed taxonomy, and an explication about abovementioned factors are discussed. At the same time, mitigation actions that may be applied in experimental and real scenarios are proposed. Finally, the conclusions of the study are presented.

© Springer International Publishing Switzerland 2015
A. Pardo and J. Kittler (Eds.): CIARP 2015, LNCS 9423, pp. 192–199, 2015.
DOI: 10.1007/978-3-319-25751-8_24

2   Keystroke Dynamics in Brief

KDAS compare user's templates with keystroke samples. In function of that, the user may type fixed text when a predefined text is required or free text when restrictions about content or length of text are not necessary. KDAS are used in a static manner, for example, at the beginning of a session, or in a dynamic (continuous) way while the user's session lasts.

Five recommended components to be used in KDAS are described in [7]. That is, (a) Data acquisition: Original data are captured and processed. (b) Features extraction: Raw data acquired are processed and users' profiles are conformed, which contain extracted user's traits. (c) Classification and matching: Selected criteria are applied to categorize data. (d) Decision: User's data are compared using selected algorithms (classification or matching). Finally, (e) Adaptation: Although an enrolled user have been correctly recognized by the system, is recommended that the user re-enroll to add new information and update stored user profile.

According to the literature, the features distinctive of the user's typing behavior, but not only, are: (1) the pressure that is exerted on each key; (2) the position adopted by hands when user types; (3) functional relationship between fingers and keys; (4) the sound generated by keystroke; (5) the vibration generated by keystroke; (6) the sequence used to perform an action; (7) quantity of errors committed when writing and methods to correct them; (8) the use of special keys; (9) keystroke speed (total typing); (10) time interval that remains on a pressed a key, and (11) time interval between pressing a key and then another.

The first five features require special devices to be gathered (cameras, pressure sensor, motion sensor or microphone). The rest only needs the keyboard. Most public research is focused on the use of time intervals, viz. 9, 10 and 11. Of these, the two latest features have attracted more interest. For example, in [7] was reported that the 90 percent of the studied works used features based on timing, and only 5 percent of them were focused on pressure. According to literature, all mentioned characteristics are present while users are typing (universality), which helps distinguish one user from another (uniqueness), and they permit to recognize a person for long periods of time (permanence) [1].

Whereas the user types, a sequence of two consecutive events take place: a) Key-Down, when he/she presses the key, and b) Key-Up, when the same key is released. While a keystroke occurs, the KDAS must capture the key's identification (or key's name), Key-Down's timestamp and Key-Up's timestamp. Knowing these data, it is possible to calculate how long it takes the user to press two keys (digraph), three keys (three graphs), or several consecutive keys (n-graph), and a posteriori, it is possible to extract features, and obtain the user's templates.

2.1   Keystroke Dynamics Classification

Classification methods for KD have been treated in the literature through different approximations, using classic statistical methods, machine learning, with emphasizing in neural networks, pattern recognition techniques, and hybrid approaches. In [1, 7-10]

194   O.A. Pérez-García

surveys of these methods are presented. From analysis of these studies, two issues stick out, the variability in the design of experiments and the insufficient amount of public data sets, making it too complex the execution of performance analysis and comparison of algorithms [5]. This complexity increases due to the influence of a group of confounding factors (CF), which are ignored by most of researches when designing experiments, when creating the users' templates database, and worse, when a KDAS is applied in real scenarios. Section 3 is dedicated to explaining CF.

2.2 Evaluation Metrics

To evaluate the performance of a KDAS in experimental scenarios [1], four metrics are applied. (i) False *Rejection Rate* (FRR): percentage of genuine users rejected. (ii) *False Acceptance Rate* (FAR): percentage of impostors accepted. (iii) *Equal Error Rate* (EER): Point on the ROC curve where FRR is equal to FAR, and (iv) *Half-Total Error Rate (HTER)*, which is defined as the mean of both error rates FAR and FRR[11], that is, HTER = (FAR + FRR) / 2.

For systems with very high security needs, it is desired to reduce the value of FAR to the minimum possible [11, 12]. In contrast, if the system needs standard security, but emphasizing in user's acceptation, similar and small values of FAR and FRR are preferred. In addition, selecting the adequate performance metric depend on how you design the authentication system. For example, if the intention is to develop a conti-nuous authentication system, it is necessary to collect continuous or periodically the user's keystrokes, and, on this basis, both ANIA (Average Number of Impostor Actions) as ANGA (Average Number of Genuine Actions) could be most appropriated to evaluate the system performance than the aforementioned metrics [13].

3   Confounding Factors (CF), Background and Related Works

The CF in KDAS are internal or external elements that affect in some way the value of data captured at system's stages, causing error rates unexpected variability, and misinterpretation of outcomes.

Problems associated with the inability to repeat experiments, or variability in the results of applying the same classifier to different data sets, are described in the litera-ture as probable effects of CF. For example, Maxion, in an excellent analysis [14], which explains different CF that according to his criteria had disturbed KD experi-ments conducted up to that time. Maxion's article has two antecedents. First, [15], where the dependence of the KDAS of the internal clock of the computers, and the participation of the operating systems in this dependence are demonstrated. And second, [4], where authors measured the effects of 5 factors over the KDAS's data capture mechanism, and demonstrated how one of them, the Operating System load (I\O load specifically), had affected that process. In that paper, the analyzed factors were included in Environmental class. In contrast, in our work, the same factors are classified into the Technical factors class because, in our opinion, this class does not influence the way of the user's typing, as Environmental factors do. See Figure 1.

Lee et al. [16], referred that keystroke-based authentication systems show much higher error rates than others behavioral biometric systems because of the influence of several factors, between them, types of keyboard, physical status of user, etc. On the other hand, in [17], authors identified six factors that, in their view, "might influence the error rates of keystroke-dynamics detectors". These are, the algorithm, training amount, feature set, updating, impostor practice and typist-too-typist variation; some of them included in Table 1 and grouped as part of the Experimental and System Design class.

3.1   Confounding Factors Taxonomy

According outcomes from review of current papers about KD, what stands out is the fact that the authors correctly identify most of the Confounding Factors, but assuming that those factors are inherent to the environment where the experiment has been applied or the behavior and characteristics of users. Without going to judge the validity of this approach, the premise in this paper is that by mixing the origin of the CF, it is more complicated to determine how to minimize its effects on experimental and real scenarios. Then, in the light of our knowledge, and according to the reviewed literature, there are at least four sources of CF (see Table 1):

1. **Technical Type:** For KDAS, it is very important the precision of raw data captured. As it was aforementioned in section 2, the majority of research works about KDAS have focused on features based on time intervals. The captures of these periods between keystrokes depend on the computer's hardware, Operating System, keyboard and application used in keystrokes acquisition. In [15] and [18], authors reported the incidence of these factors in their measurements, which showed significant variations of error rates, while Villani, et al. in [19] demonstrated the importance of using the same keyboard in experiments

   In order to identify in practice this kind of factors (see Figure 1), it is necessary to understand that they do not affect the way of the user types, but the data value captured by the sensor, which can be considered as the union of the keyboard, the computer hardware, the Operating System and the final application. Knowing how each factor affects the samples, it allows us, from the design phase, to consider how to mitigate their influence, for example, by removing the affected data samples, and include automated controls to detect inappropriate sensors.

   Another important characteristic of Technical Factors is their influence over all users involved in tests. That is, no matter who is the user, his keystroke timing measures will be affected by the combination of the computer's hardware, Operating System, keyboard and the application used in keystrokes acquisition.

2. **Environmental Type:** This class includes every elements belonging to the location where the experiment takes place or where the final application will run, and that they may affect the way the user types: the illumination, keyboard position in relation to the user, room temperature, possibility of interruptions (e.g., colleagues, phone calls), and others. Some authors refer to these CF, but no revised article demonstrates the existence of a relation between them and the error rate variability[20]. On the above, it is logical and obvious to think that the environment influences on the mood of the user, and this, in turn, affects his way of typing. See Figure 1.

Table 1. Confounding factors taxonomy

Confounding Factor			Description
Type	**Factor**		
Technical	Operating System (OS) [11, 15]		Data from keyboard events are recorded running system-calls.
	Keyboard [11, 19]		Keyboard type: shape, language, keys' positions (ZERTY, QWERTY...), technical characteristics (interface), defective device.
	OS load		IO load, multithread, etc.
	RAM and μprocessor [18]		Amount of RAM, type of μprocessor
	Level of data capture		For instance: driver or application level
	Computer		E.g., Laptop or Desktop
Environment	Lighting		Low light
	Keyboard position		Position of keyboard to user
	Interruptions		Colleges, phones, etc.
Behavioral [21]	Transients	Physical tiredness, emotions, stress, drowsiness	Impact on the way of user's typing
	Permanents	User experience	
		User age, soft biometric [22]	
Experimental and system Design	Design	Text · Type	Fix (structured) or Free (unstructured) text
		Text · Length	How many characters
		Monitored · Continuous	While user types
		Monitored · Periodic	Time windows
		Task	Copy from dictated or reading
	Database	Type	Public or private
		Size	How many samples per user?
	Detectors	Classifier and metrics	Statistical, Machine Learning...
		Feature Set	Dimension
	Metrics		Performance metrics to continuous or static authentication
	Subjects (users & impostors)	Subjects number	Class number
		Number of attempts and time between them.	Impact on user experience
		Training amount	More training, less error rate

3. **Behavioral Type:** This kind of factor includes mood, fatigue, and others. In [23] these factors are named Transient factors, but the user experience is not a temporal element, neither the user age, and both affect the way the user types. In [24], the relation between emotional states and the variations in the rhythm of fingering if proved, and in [21], was demonstrated how the user's emotional states affect for short time his/her typing rhythm.

4. **Experimental Type:** These factors are discussed in most of the reviewed papers, but very few of them deal with this topic in the necessary depth, despite their importance. All experiments designed and carried out with the required quality must ensure repeatability, reproducibility and validity. Under those principles, Maxion in [14] proposed to take into account a set of environmental factors (including into this denomination our Technical class) and behavioral factors in the design of experiments, due to the demonstrated influence of these factors on experimental outcomes. Before that, Killourhy and Maxion [5] showed the drawbacks to trying to compare the experimental results published until that moment, precisely due to the influence of several factors described in our taxonomy inside the current class.

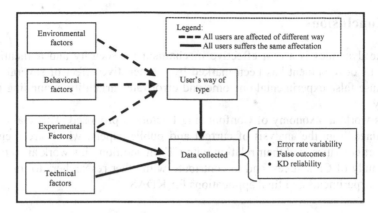

Fig. 1. Influence of Confounding Factors over users and data collection process

3.2   About Mitigations Actions

In general, the correct design of the experiments ensuring their repetition, reproduction and their validity should be the first step in any debate about how to mitigate the influence of CF in KDAS. And second, but not less important, it is essential to understand that CF are probable sources of error, and though their most significant impact is perceived in the assessment of the results, it is practically impossible to recognize their presence without knowledge about their existence.

On this basis, it is necessary to establish as the requirements for the execution of the experiments and developing of an application of KD-based authentication, the use of specific hardware and software (e.g., computer, keyboard, memory RAM, Operating System). In addition, it is essential to include automatic controls to ensure compliance with these requirements inclusive until level code.

For further analysis the following works are recommended: [5], where the authors, Killourhy and Maxion, presented some of the ways to mitigate the influence of Experimental CF; and [25], where Deng and Yu Zhong proposed the application of the Identity Vector (i-vector) method. This is a new approach taken from the voice biometric domain, and they demonstrated how much it could help to mitigate CF actions. The own Killourhy, in [6], proposed a much more comprehensive approach to face CF.

To mitigate the influence of technical factors, it must first understood that they act like a monolithic sensor, affecting each other, while causing changes in the readings of the keyboard event times. Therefore, it can be understood to be the same influence for all users, which is true, but it is not all the time, because it depends on all the variables involved. For example, the characteristics of the microprocessor and RAM are constants whose influence varies according to the load of operating system tasks. And so on, a similar analysis can be performed to all components of such factors.

Then, it is possible to adjust the operating system timer (for example, to 1 millisecond) at the enrollment stage, or use the same trick to the continuous authentication while the user types. To implement both ideas, it is recommended to study carefully its negative effects, and take into account the differences between laptops and desktop computers[26].

4   Conclusions

Keystroke dynamics is a cost effective mechanism for security and authentications systems. Its development has been marked by the negative effect of several factors, which cause false experimental outcome and error rate variability, wounding the KD reliability.

In this work, a taxonomy of Confounding Factors is proposed. This classification was obtained from the analysis of current and public papers, which are focused on KDAS particularities, and their relation with CF. In addition, this work aims to facilitate the study of CF sources, and to contribute with other researchers to improve the design of experiments and final applications for KDAS.

References

1. Zhong, Y., Deng, Y.: A survey on keystroke dynamics biometrics: approaches, advances, and evaluations. In: Zhong, Y., Deng, Y. (eds.) Recent Advances in User Authentication Using Keystroke Dynamics Biometrics. Science Gate Publishing (2015)
2. Spillane, R.: Keyboard apparatus for personal identification. IBM Technical Disclosure Bulletin **17**, 3346 (1975)
3. Gaines, R.S., Lisowski, W., Press, S.J., Shapiro, N.: Authentication by keystroke timing: some preliminary results. DTIC Document (1980)
4. Killourhy, K.S.: The role of environmental factors in keystroke dynamics. In: IEEE/IFIP International Conference on Dependable Systems and Networks (DSN 2009) Supplemental Volume (Student Forum), pp. 125–134 (2009)
5. Killourhy, K.S., Maxion, R.A.: Comparing anomaly-detection algorithms for keystroke dynamics. In: IEEE/IFIP International Conference on Dependable Systems and Networks. DSN 2009, pp. 125–134 (2009)
6. Killourhy, K.S.: A scientific understanding of keystroke dynamics. DTIC Document (2012)
7. Teh, P.S., Teoh, A.B.J., Yue, S.: A survey of keystroke dynamics biometrics. The Scientific World Journal **2013** (2013)
8. Karnan, M., Akila, M., Krishnaraj, N.: Biometric personal authentication using keystroke dynamics: A review. Applied Soft Computing **11**, 1565–1573 (2011)
9. Bhatt, S., Santhanam, T.: Keystroke dynamics for biometric authentication—A survey. In: 2013 International Conference on Pattern Recognition, Informatics and Mobile Engineering (PRIME), pp. 17–23. IEEE (2013)
10. Banerjee, S.P., Woodard, D.L.: Biometric authentication and identification using keystroke dynamics: A survey. Journal of Pattern Recognition Research **7**, 116–139 (2012)
11. Giot, R., El-Abed, M., Rosenberger, C.: Keystroke Dynamics Authentication. Biometrics chapitre 8 (2011)
12. Jain, A.K., Ross, A., Prabhakar, S.: An introduction to biometric recognition. IEEE Transactions on Circuits and Systems for Video Technology **14**, 4–20 (2004)
13. Bours, P., Mondal, S.: Continuous Authentication with Keystroke Dynamics (2015)
14. Maxion, R.: Making experiments dependable. In: Jones, C.B., Lloyd, J.L. (eds.) Dependable and Historic Computing. LNCS, vol. 6875, pp. 344–357. Springer, Heidelberg (2011)

15. Killourhy, K.S., Maxion, R.A.: The effect of clock resolution on keystroke dynamics. In: Lippmann, R., Kirda, E., Trachtenberg, A. (eds.) RAID 2008. LNCS, vol. 5230, pp. 331–350. Springer, Heidelberg (2008)
16. Lee, J.-W., Choi, S.-S., Moon, B.-R.: An evolutionary keystroke authentication based on ellipsoidal hypothesis space. In: Proceedings of the 9th Annual Conference on Genetic and Evolutionary Computation, pp. 2090–2097. ACM (2007)
17. Killourhy, K., Maxion, R.: Why did my detector do *That*?! In: Jha, S., Sommer, R., Kreibich, C. (eds.) RAID 2010. LNCS, vol. 6307, pp. 256–276. Springer, Heidelberg (2010)
18. Bello, L., Bertacchini, M., Benitez, C., Pizzoni, J.C., Cipriano, M.: Collection and publication of a fixed text keystroke dynamics dataset. In: XVI Congreso Argentino de Ciencias de la Computación (2010)
19. Villani, M., Tappert, C., Ngo, G., Simone, J., Fort, H.S., Cha, S.-H.: Keystroke biometric recognition studies on long-text input under ideal and application-oriented conditions. In: 2006 Computer Vision and Pattern Recognition Workshop, CVPRW 2006, p. 39. IEEE (2006)
20. Roy, S., Roy, U., Sinha, D.: Text-based Analysis of Keystroke Dynamics in User Authentication. International Journal of Computer Sciences and Engineering **3** (2015)
21. Lee, P.-M., Chen, L.-Y., Tsui, W.-H., Hsiao, T.-C.: Will user authentication using keystroke dynamics biometrics be interfered by emotions? In: Zhong, Y., Deng, Y. (eds.) Recent Advances in User Authentication Using Keystroke Dynamics Biometrics, GCSR vol. 2, pp. 71–81. Science Gate Publishing (2015)
22. Syed Idrus, S.Z., Cherrier, E., Rosenberger, C., Mondal, S., Bours, P.: Keystroke dynamics performance enhancement with soft biometrics. In: IEEE International Conference on Identity, Security and Behavior Analysis (ISBA), Hong Kong, China (2015)
23. Zhong, Y., Deng, Y., Jain, A.K.: Keystroke dynamics for user authentication. In: 2012 IEEE Computer Society Conference on Computer Vision and Pattern Recognition Workshops (CVPRW), pp. 117–123. IEEE (2012)
24. Lee, P.-M., Tsui, W.-H., Hsiao, T.-C.: The influence of emotion on keyboard typing: an experimental study using visual stimuli. Biomedical Engineering Online **13**, 81 (2014)
25. Deng, Y., Zhong, Y.: Keystroke dynamics user authentication using advanced machine learning methods. In: Zhong, Y., Deng, Y. (eds.) Recent Advances in User Authentication Using Keystroke Dynamics Biometrics, GCSR vol. 2, pp. 23–40. Science Gate Publishing (2015)
26. Microsoft: Timers, Timer Resolution, and Development of Efficient Code (2010). http://www.microsoft.com/whdc/system/pnppwr/powermgmt/Timer-Resolution.msp

Denoising Autoencoder for Iris Recognition in Noncooperative Environments

Eduardo Luz[1]([✉]) and David Menotti[1,2]

[1] Computing Department, Federal University of Ouro Preto, Ouro Preto, MG, Brazil
{eduluz,menottid}@gmail.com
[2] Informatics Department, Federal University of Paraná, Curitiba, PR, Brazil

Abstract. The iris is considered as the most unique phenotype feature visible in a person's face and has been explored in the last three decades. Outstanding approaches are known for iris recognition task when the image is acquired in a well controlled environment. However, the problem is still challenging in a noncooperative environment. Having this context in mind, and from a learning representation perspective, in this paper, we propose the use of denoising autoencoders networks to create descriptors to iris recognition. We extract features from six regions of the iris and also use a specific scheme in the literature that employ a set of thresholds for iris acceptance / rejection. We perform experiments on two well-know databases, by comparing our descriptor with 2D Gabor and Wavelet representations of implementations of us. In both data sets, the proposed descriptor outperforms these features, and presents comparable results with the best performing method in a NICE contest.

Keywords: Learning representation · Denoising autoencoders · Neural networks · Iris recognition · Noncooperative environment

1 Introduction

Modalities acquired from the eye are considered as the most unique phenotype feature visible in a person's face [4]. It is composed of particular and random textures for each individual, which are even different for each eye of the same person, which increases its uniqueness (possibility of 1 among 10^{72} individuals), making even difficult to fraud. In constrained environments, in short distances, and smaller databases, there are currently efficient and effective methods for correct (or almost perfect) iris identification [3,1]. Nonetheless the main question is how to identify it on adverse conditions in natural environments.

Thus a major problem in using iris for person identification is in its recognition on noncooperative environment where the images could be acquired at an uncontrolled distance, moving people, and use of some accessories such as lenses and glasses, among others. Difficulties also increases when the system runs on a large dataset, with degraded images by light reflections and other noise, where a misidentification may cause great damages.

© Springer International Publishing Switzerland 2015
A. Pardo and J. Kittler (Eds.): CIARP 2015, LNCS 9423, pp. 200–207, 2015.
DOI: 10.1007/978-3-319-25751-8_25

In general, an iris recognition system is divided in six main steps such as: image acquisition; iris segmentation; normalization; feature extraction; representation of features; and classification. How to represent the information presented in the iris image (feature extraction step), specifically on degraded ones, are often discussed and investigated in works related to iris recognition in noncooperative environments.

Proença & Alexandre [12] divide the iris into two independent blocks, one composed of four sub-regions and the other composed of two sub-regions. Although the sub-regions of the same block are independent (non-overlapping), there is overlap among the sub-regions of distinct blocks. The rationale for this division is the robustness to noisy environments and loss of biometric signature. From these sub-regions, six dissimilarity values extracted using a 2D Gabor descriptor are obtained and then fused by means of a classification rule, which is also employed in our work and involves an ordered set of optimized thresholds obtained to minimize the false rejection (false negative) and false acceptance (false positive) rates.

Szewczyk et al. [14] initially segmented the iris image and then pre-processed, using the following steps: blue channel removal; conversion to monochrome images; histogram equalization; and removal of reflections, eyelashes, and occlusions caused by eyelid. They also analyze and choose the best Wavelet function for iris feature extraction.

Other works in the literature coping with iris images in noncooperative environment are focused on effectiveness comparison of different strategies. In [5], the features extracted from the LoG-Gabor filters, Haar wavelet, Discrete Cosine Transform (DCT), and Fast Fourier Transform (FFT) are compared. Marsico et. al. [7] combine two techniques, Linear Binary Patterns (LBP), which produces a local texture description, and Discriminable Textons (BLOBs), which highlights uniqueness of the texture (furrows, crypts and spots), and verify that the resulting method increases the final recognition performance.

Despite the large number of techniques presented in the literature for iris recognition in noncooperative environments, here we propose the use of Denoising Autoencoder Neural Network (DAeNN) to extract features following the classification scheme proposed in [12]. To the best of our knowledge the DAeNN technique for iris feature extraction has been used here for the first time. The rationale to use DAeNN in the noncooperative scenario is it capability to deal with noise, and it is the main contribution to the literature of our work and brings promising results as stated below. To validate our proposal the databases CASIA-IrisV4 database [2] and UBIRIS.v2 [11] are used. The CASIA-IrisV4 database is very popular among iris recognition methods and UBIRIS.v2 database includes images captured in unconstrained conditions. By comparing our descriptor with 2D Gabor [12,16] and Wavelet [14] representations of implementations of us, in both data sets, the proposed descriptor outperforms these features, and presents comparable results with the best performing method in a NICE contest [10].

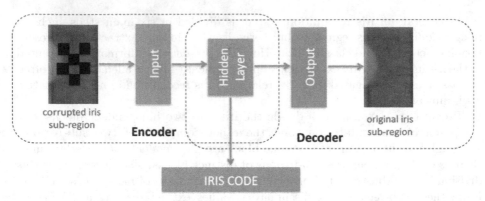

Fig. 1. Denoising Autoencoder for Iris Recognition problem.

2   Proposed Descriptor

In this section, we present the proposed descriptor for iris recognition based on denoising autoencoder representations. The steps of segmentation, normalization, and partition are straightforward and identical to the ones proposed in [12] and due to space constraints are omitted. Although the classification step used here is also similar to [12], a small modification in it is made and then it presented.

2.1   Feature Extraction

A denoising autoencoder network is employed for each iris partitions as Fig. 1 illustrates. Then, six independent biometric signatures are created, each one corresponding to a specific iris region. It is worth mentioning that we used the same autoencoder network topology to all partitions.

Autoencoder Neural Network. The Autoencoder is an unsupervised feature learning technique. Autoencoder can be considered as a neural network aiming to learn an identity function by setting the output equal to the input, with the less possible amount of error. During this process, the inputs are encoded (mapped) to a new representation, i.e., the hidden layer

$$h(x) = f(Wx + b), \tag{1}$$

where $h(x)$ is the hidden layer (the computation result), f is called activation function, x the input values, and W and b parameters are the weight matrix and the bias vector, respectively. The decoder portion of the network maps back the output of $h(x)$ to Y, i.e.,

$$Y(h(x)) = f(W_y(h(x)) + b_y), \tag{2}$$

where Y is the autoencoder output, and it should be considered as a prediction of X. While conceptually simple, the autoencoder technique has been shown to achieve state-of-the-art results in several classification problems [15,8,9], specially when deep/stacked architectures are employed.

The autoencoder architecture used here consists in one input layer, one output layer and one hidden layer. The layers are composed of artificial neurons in which each layer is fully-connected to each other. Each connection from the hidden layer is a weighted output of input neurons (an iris image) and its connections to the output layer should reproduce its own input.

The learning process of a neural network consists of obtaining the suitable weights for the connections by means of a training algorithm. Here we used a well-know backpropagation algorithm. The inner hidden layer outputs are the new feature vector (descriptor), and it can be calculated according to

$$h_{w,b}(x) = f(W^T x) = f(\gamma W_i x_i + b). \tag{3}$$

An approach to make the autoencoder more robust is to use a denoising algorithm [15]. The denoising algorithm consists in training the autoencoder with a corrupted version of the training images as input. According to Vincent et al. [15], the denoising phase is specially important to increase generalisation power of the network, by making it less vulnerable to input noise and other artefacts. Thus, this is the rationale to use autoencoder as feature extraction in noncooperative environment iris recognition, where the iris is often noisy or have some parts obfuscated.

2.2   Classification

Initially, dissimilarities between two images, for all six sub-regions $D_i = HD(I_i^1, I_i^2)$, are calculated in which $i = 1, ..., N$ ($N = 6$ is the number of subregions), I_i^1 the sub-region i of the image 1, I_i^2 the sub-region i of the image 2.

The Euclidean Distance (ED) is used to compute the dissimilarity between images. Given two feature vectors sets $A = \{a_1, ..., a_N\}$ and $B = \{b_1, ..., b_N\}$ the Euclidean Distance is given by

$$ED(A, B) = \sqrt{\sum_{i=1}^{N}(a_i - b_i)^2} \tag{4}$$

Given the sets of dissimilarities $D_i = [D_1, ..., D_N]$ and the thresholds $T_i = [T_1, ..., T_N]$, explained later, the next step is to count the number of $D_j \in D$ that are less or equal to T_i:

$$C(D, T_i) = \sum_{j=1}^{N} \Pi_{\{D_j \leq T_i\}}, \tag{5}$$

where, $\Pi_{\{.\}}$ is the indicator function.

The images I^1 and I^2 are classified as corresponding to the same iris if:

$$\exists_i : C(D, T_i) \geq i, i = 1, \ldots, N. \tag{6}$$

3   Experiments

In this section, we describe the experiments performed in order to validate the proposed method. Initially, we describe details of the iris images and their databases and then the results of the experiments performed are presented. The evaluation of the proposed descriptor employs the use of the *Equal Error Rate* (ERR) which in turn is defined as the point in which the *False Acceptance Rate* (FAR) is equal to the *False Rejection Rate* (FRR) [12,3]. Finally, a brief discussion of the results is made.

3.1   Databases

The CASIA-IrisV4 database [2] is one of the most popular database for iris recognition evaluation. CASIA-Iris.v4 contains a total of 54,601 iris images from more than 1,800 natural individuals and 1,000 virtual individuals. The iris images of this database have low noise influence due to its acquisition protocol, where images are acquired in a very constrained and controlled environment.

In the UBIRIS.v2 [11] database, the images were captured in unconstrained conditions, such as at different distances, in motion and in the visible wavelength, which allow images with more realistic noise factors. The UBIRIS.v2 contains 11,102 iris images from more than 261 individuals.

In our experiments, 800 images of 80 subjects (10 images per individual) of UBIRIS database are used. Same amount of images are considered for CASIA database. Worth mentioning that, for both databases, we randomly select the individuals as done in previous works [12,14,13], which difficults a fair comparison between published works. However, we propose to let available our selection of individuals and also all the source code used in a webpage once the paper is *accepted to publication* to allow further comparisons.

For both databases, images from 40 individuals were used in the training phase for estimating the classifying thresholds, lefting 400 images of the other 40 individuals for testing/evaluation.

3.2   Results

In the followings, we report the results of our experiments. Initially, we evaluate the results obtained by using the Denoising Autoencoder descriptors and, by varying some parameters of the network and the increments used to obtain the classification thresholds. Finally, we took the parameters that obtained the best results for each descriptors and evaluated it on smaller thresholds values.

We stressed that we follows the same evaluation protocol used in previous works on literature to report the results here [12,14,13]. In that sense, we estimate the classification thresholds in the training set, and in the evaluation/testing set all images of each individuals are taken as query image in a scheme similar to leave-one-out.

As several other works in the literature, we use the *equal error rate* (EER) as our effectiveness measure of analysis.

Autoencoder. In single layer denoising autoencoder neural network, several parameters should be adjusted such as: the number of neurons in the layer; the learning rate; the number of training epochs; and the percentage of corruption noise applied on input of network. For this experiment we keep the normalized input image with a fixed sized of 16×128 pixels, and only one hidden layer, as an initial guess. Thus, a gridsearch is applied in order to find the remaining parameters that will produce the best results for the training phase. We vary the number of neurons in each hidden layer in 6 possibilites [15 20 30 40 50 100]. The network learning rate and the percent of corruption noise both vary in the range [0.3-0.1] with a step of 0.1. The number of training epochs used during trainig was [3000 6000]. The gridsearch figures was proposed based on empirical experimentation previously conducted. From the EER values we have obtained, we observed that the higher the number of epochs for training, the better values DAeNN produced. Also, we observed that for CASIA-IrisV4, less input noise level produced best results while UBIRIS.v2 database required higher noise level.

We selected the parameters that have achieved the lowest EER, 0.42% for CASIA V4 and 14.94% for UBIRIS V2. It is worth noticing that best NICE:II participant report EER of approximately 12% on a database similar to UBIRIS V2. We have also run the same methodology on two widely used

Table 1. Results comparison in CASIA

Method	Input	EER (%) incr. 0.025
Proposed descritpor	16×128	0.42
2D Gabor based [12]	16×128	2.55
Wavelet based [14]	16×128	3.84

Table 2. Results comparison in UBIRIS

Method	Input	EER (%) incr. 0.025
Proposed descriptor	16×128	14.94
2D Gabor based [12]	16×128	23.14
Wavelet [14]	16×128	18.48

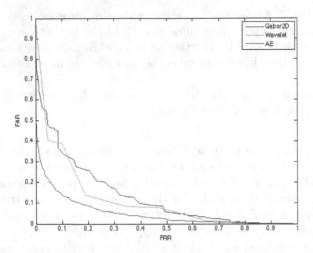

Fig. 2. The ROC curve obtained by the proposed method in the UBIRIS database considering an increment value of 0.025 in the classification threshold step. Autoencoder (AE) parameters: 30 neurons on hidden layer; noise level of 30%; learning rate of 0.1. Mother wavelet used: rbio3.1.

feature extraction techniques for the iris recognition problem: 2D Gabor [12,16] and Wavelet [14,6]. Methods based on 2D Gabor descriptor embedded commercial of-the-shelf systems for iris recognition and according to [14] wavelet transform is one of the most relevant tool for extract features for iris recognition. Fig. 2 illustrates ROC curves for our proposed descriptor and for the others in comparison. The superiority of our proposal is remarkable.

3.3   Discussion

Results presented on Tables 1 and 2 show that DAeNN can be a promising tool for the iris recognition problem, specially in noncooperative environments. Experiments show that for UBIRIS V2 database, 30% of corruption on training images during the DAeNN training phase produces the best results.

4   Conclusion

In this work we addressed the problem of iris image representation in noncooperative environment using the denoising autoencoder technique. We performed experiments on two databases (UBIRIS and CASIA), and the proposed descriptor outperforms popular feature extraction methods, such as 2D Gabor [12,16] and Wavelet transform [14]. The proposed descriptor also showed comparable results, in terms of EER, with the best performing method in a NICE.II contest [10], even on UBIRIS database. Our result suggest that denoising autoencoder can be a promising tool for iris representation. As future work we plan to investigate stacked (deep) autoencoders architectures aiming to improve iris recognition effectiveness in noncooperative environments.

Acknowledgment. The authors would like to thank to UFOP, CAPES, and CNPq (grant #307010/2014-7).

References

1. Bowyer, K.W., Hollingsworth, K., Flynn, P.J.: Image understanding for iris biometrics: A survey. Comp. Vision and Image Understanding **110**(2), 281–307 (2008)
2. Chinese Academy of Sciences (CASIA): CASIA Iris Image Database. http://biometrics.idealtest.org/findTotalDbByMode.do?mode=Iris (accessed April 2015)
3. Daugman, J.: New methods in iris recognition. IEEE Transactions on Systems, Man, and Cybernetics, Part B: Cybernetics **37**(5), 1167–1175 (2007)
4. Daugman, J.: High confidence visual recognition of persons by a test of statistical independence. IEEE TPAMI (1993)
5. Kumar, A., Passi, A.: Comparison and combination of iris matchers for reliable personal authentication. Pattern Recognition **43**, 1016–1026 (2009)
6. Li, P., Ma, H.: Iris recognition in non-ideal imaging conditions. Pattern Recognition Letters (2011)
7. Marsico, M.D., Nappi, M., Riccio, D.: Noisy iris recognition integrated scheme. Pattern Recognition Letters (2011)
8. Mohamed, A.R., Sainath, T.N., Dahl, G., Ramabhadran, B., Hinton, G.E., Picheny, M.A.: Deep belief networks using discriminative features for phone recognition. In: IEEE ICASSP, pp. 5060–5063 (2011)
9. Netzer, Y., Wang, T., Coates, A., Bissacco, A., Wu, B., Ng, A.Y.: Reading digits in natural images with unsupervised feature learning. In: NIPS Workshop on Deep Learning and Unsupervised Feature Learning, vol. 2, p. 5 (2011)
10. Proenca, H., Alexandre, L.: Toward covert iris biometric recognition: Experimental results from the nice contests. IEEE TIFS **7**(2), 798–808 (2012)
11. Proença, Hugo, Alexandre, Luís A.: UBIRIS: a noisy iris image database. In: Roli, Fabio, Vitulano, Sergio (eds.) ICIAP 2005. LNCS, vol. 3617, pp. 970–977. Springer, Heidelberg (2005)
12. Proença, H., Alexandre, L.A.: Toward noncooperative iris recognition: a classification approach using multiple signatures. IEEE TPAMI **29**(4), 607–612 (2007)
13. Song, Y., Cao, W., He, Z.: Robust iris recognition using sparse error correction model and discriminative dictionary learning. Neurocomputing (2014)
14. Szewczyk, R., Grabowski, K., Napieralska, M., Sankowski, W., Zubert, M., Napieralski, A.: A reliable iris recognition algorithm based on reverse biorthogonal wavelet transform. Pattern Recognition Letters (2011)
15. Vincent, P., Larochelle, H., Lajoie, I., Bengio, Y., Manzagol, P.A.: Stacked denoising autoencoders: Learning useful representations in a deep network with a local denoising criterion. The J. Machine Learning Research **11**, 3371–3408 (2010)
16. Wang, Q., Zhang, X., Li, M., Dong, X., Zhou, Q., Yin, Y.: Adaboost and multiorientation 2D Gabor-based noisy iris recognition. Pat. Rec. Letters (2011)

A New Ridge-Features-Based Method
for Fingerprint Image Quality Assessment

Katy Castillo-Rosado$^{(\boxtimes)}$ and José Hernández-Palancar

Advanced Technologies Application Center (CENATAV),
7ma A #21406 e/ 214 Y 216, Rpto. Siboney, Playa, 12200 La Habana, Cuba
{krosado,jpalancar}@cenatav.co.cu

Abstract. Fingerprint is the most widely used biometric trait. Many factors may cause the quality degradation of fingerprint impressions: users, sensors and environmental facts. Most of the fingerprint-based biometric systems need an accurate prediction of fingerprint quality. A fingerprint quality measure can be used in enrollment or recognition stages, for improving the AFIS performances. In this work, a new fingerprint image quality estimation method guided by how experts classify fingerprint images quality is presented. By using six features, a continuous quality value is calculated. Experiments were performed in a well-known database. The proposed approach performance was evaluated by measuring its impact on the recognition stage and comparing it with the NFIQ quality algorithm. The Verifinger 4.2 was used as matching algorithm. The results shown that the proposed approach has a very good performance.

Keywords: Fingerprint · Quality estimation · Orientation map · Coherence value · Ridge frequency

1 Introduction

Biometrics is the study of measurable biological characteristics for automatic authentication purposes. Some of these human characteristics are fingerprints, palms, facial patterns, eye retinas and irises, voice patterns, hands, gait, etc. Currently, fingerprints are one of the most used biometric trait, in both, civilian and forensic applications. Fingerprints can be classified into three types depending on the acquisition methodology: rolled, plain and latent impressions. Rolled and plain fingerprint impressions are acquired with the supervision of an expert. Rolled impressions are obtained by rolling the finger from one side to the other to obtain the entire fingerprint pattern, while plain impressions are captured by pressing down the finger on a flat surface, without rolling it [7]. It is expected that these two kind of impressions have good quality due to their acquisition way. This is different for latent fingerprints, that are lifted from surfaces of objects touched by a person in a crime scene. Normally, latent impressions are partial fingerprints and have poor quality.

© Springer International Publishing Switzerland 2015
A. Pardo and J. Kittler (Eds.): CIARP 2015, LNCS 9423, pp. 208–215, 2015.
DOI: 10.1007/978-3-319-25751-8_26

Automatic Fingerprint Identification Systems (AFIS) can be used in criminal investigations, attendance system, access control and others. Its performances are highly influenced by the quality of the enrolled fingerprints in the database and also by the quality of the query fingerprint. Experts must be involved in the process of acquiring reference fingerprints (database), for recapturing fingerprints in cases where poor quality is noted [3]. But, this process still needs automatic improvements, either to not storing corrupt information in databases or for knowing how reliable the features extracted from fingerprints can be. That is why, an algorithm that correctly estimate a quality value from fingerprint non-latent images is needed.

In this work, a new method for estimating a fingerprint quality value is presented. In section 2 a review of features used in other works of fingerprint quality assessment is given. In section 3, features and a general background of the proposed method are discussed. The new method performance is evaluated and its results are compared with another fingerprint quality algorithm in section 4. Finally, conclusions and future works are presented.

2   Related Work

A lot of approaches have been proposed in order to obtain a fingerprint image quality value. This value can be used in both enrollment and recognition/identification stages depending on user needs. A comparative study of some of the more important works is presented by Alonso-Fernandez et al. [1]. Most of the algorithms found on the literature are based on the extraction of local or global features. An overall quality value is calculated using a combination of these features. Other works address the quality assessment task as a classification problem.

Some features used for quality assessment are based on pixel intensities like Local Clarity Score (LCS) [4], low contrast map [10], gray intensity mean, gray intensity standard deviation [2][8][12], uniformity, smoothness, inhomogenity [2][12] and texture features [13]. Other features are extracted from the spectral domain like power spectrum and the response of Butterworth band-pass filters using Fast Fourier Transform [8], or global spectrum and relative spectral density [9]. Also, features characterizing the wavelength and amplitude are extracted from the wave representation of the ridges [2]. On the other hand, features based on the orientation field are also used. Examples of this are orientation certainty level (OCL) [6], Local Orientation Quality Score (LOQS) [4], direction map, low flow map, high curve map [10], orientation coherence [12], relative spectral orientation continuity [9], orientation certainty and consistency [2] and ridge-line smoothness [11]. Also, penalty due to the backgrounds noise and the quality of the core point position are features used [12]. Recently, minutiae features have been used to obtain a quality measure. Examples of them are the minutiae extractability [11], the number of total minutiae found and a quality minutia histogram [10]. Eight other features based on minutiae number and DFT of their three components have been previously used [13]. Another approach, computes a quality value based on unreasonable minutiae structures detected from the minutiae Delaunay triangulation [14].

Some approaches compute a quality value for each analysed block [2][6][8][10] and in a final step an overall quality value is obtained by combining the blocks classification results. In other cases a combination of the features values is used to estimate the final quality measure [12].

There are cases in which classifiers are used to generate a quality class. In a previous work, a neural network was used to classify a 11-dimensional feature vector extracted, into one of the quality levels defined (poor (5), fair (4), good (3), very good (2), and excellent (1)) [10]. In another proposal, a hierarchical k-means clustering algorithm was utilized to classify the fingerprint image in one of four classes (good, dry, normal or wet) [8]. Also, a genetic algorithm was proposed in another work to computed the quality image metric [13].

3 Proposed Fingerprint Quality Features

The fingerprint quality must be a measure of its efficiency in aiding recognition to a person [3]. In order to obtain a reliable quality value for fingerprint images, both, local and global characteristics of the biometric sample should be examined. The proposed quality estimation is inspired by how experts work. They take into account two principal features to classify the fingerprint quality: completeness of the three ridges systems (marginal, nuclear and basilar) and consistency (clarity) of the ridges pattern. A fingerprint impression has high quality when it has a clear ridge pattern and their three ridges systems are complete. To automatically describe these two characteristics, six features describing them are extracted. First, the region of interest (ROI) is detected using a segmentation method implemented by our investigation group, and a mask is obtained. Then, the minimum rectangle containing the ROI is located. A preprocessing step is applied to the image where a median filter and a normalization are performed to remove small noises in the ROI. The orientation map from the ROI is calculated with the gradients of the fingerprint image [5]. Using the fingerprint image, its ROI mask, and the orientation map, features that characterize the ridges systems completeness and the ridges pattern clarity are extracted. These features are invariant to the image texture, due to the high relation of texture with the enrollment step. Finally, an overall fingerprint image quality is estimated.

3.1 Ridges Pattern Clarity Features

One of the main features extracted from fingerprints is the orientation map. It describes the general flow direction of fingerprint ridges. The orientation map Φ is a matrix where each element Φ_{ij} denotes the average orientation of the ridges in a neighbourhood of pixel (i, j) [7]. A very common way for calculating the ridge orientation is the computation of the square gradients $G_{xx}(i,j)$, $G_{yy}(i,j)$, $G_{xy}(i,j)$ for pixel (i, j) [5].

A measure defined for indicating the behaviour of the local strength of the directional field is the coherence of its orientation vectors Ω_Φ defined in the equation 1 [5].

$$\Omega_\Phi(i,j) = \frac{\sqrt{(G_{xx}(i,j) - G_{yy}(i,j))^2 + 4G_{xy}(i,j)^2}}{G_{xx}(i,j) + G_{yy}()i,j} \quad . \tag{1}$$

This is why, the coherence is used for separating orientation in good or bad. A binary coherence map G_{Ω_Φ} is computed, where $G_{\Omega_\Phi}(i,j)$ takes value 1 (good coherence) if the coherence of the pixel (i, j) is equal or higher than a threshold ξ and 0 (bad coherence) otherwise, as follow:

$$G_{\Omega_\Phi}(i,j) = \begin{cases} 1 \text{ if } \Omega_\Phi(i,j) \geq \xi, \\ 0 \text{ otherwise.} \end{cases} \tag{2}$$

Using this, three features are defined in order to describe the ridges pattern in the fingerprint:

Orientation Strength. Because of the shape of fingerprint ridges, orientation changes must be continuous and smooth. In this work is used the amount of pixels with good coherence for calculating a value between 0 and 1. This value describes the continuity and smoothness of the orientation map of a fingerprint impression, as follow:

$$S_{gos} = \frac{|P_{gos}|}{|P_{ROI}|}, \tag{3}$$

where P_{gos} is the set of pixels (i, j) where $G_{\Omega_\Phi}(i,j)$ has value 1, P_{ROI} is the set of pixels present in the ROI, $|P_{gos}|$ and $|P_{ROI}|$ are the cardinality of each set. While better is the quality of the fingerprint, closer to 1 is P_{gos}.

Orientation Strength in Center Area. Singular points and fingerprint Henry classification are features commonly used by recognition algorithms. For their reliable extraction the center area of the fingerprint must have very good quality. Therefore, a proportion of pixels with bad orientation strength around the center area is presented:

$$S_{bosc} = \frac{|P_{bosc}|}{(w * 2 + 1)^2}, \tag{4}$$

where w is the block size used for choosing the pixels that will be analysed, P_{bosc} is the set of pixels with bad coherence present in the neighbourhood with window size w around the ROI center and $|P_{bosc}|$ is its cardinality. S_{bosc} moves between 0 and 1 and it is inversely proportional to the fingerprint quality.

Ridge Frequency. The ridge frequency is a popular feature extracted from fingerprints and it has been used for enhancement recognition algorithms. This feature describes the ridge distribution in a block. For describing the ridge distribution in the entire fingerprint, a proportion of blocks with good ridge frequency with respect to all analysed blocks is proposed:

$$S_{grf} = \frac{|P_{grf}|}{T_b}, \tag{5}$$

where $|P_{grf}|$ is the set of blocks where its ridge frequency is between two thresholds f_1 and f_2 experimentally chosen, $|P_{grf}|$ is its cardinality and T_b is the total analysed blocks with an empirically estimated size.

3.2   Ridges Systems Completeness Features

In dactyloscopy, experts separate the fingerprint in three ridge systems: marginal, nuclear and basilar as can be seen in figure 1. In this work, the completeness of these ridges systems is used to classify the fingerprint image quality.

Fig. 1. Example of the three ridge systems of a fingerprint: marginal(blue, upper area), nuclear (red, central area) and basilar (green, bottom area).

The completeness of the ridges systems gives an idea of how much of the fingerprint is captured in the impression. The region of interest is the area that will be analysed, so a set of three features were defined to describe its size:

Region of Interest. The *ROI* is the region chosen for being processed in later steps of the biometric systems (feature extraction and matching). Its size is highly important for obtaining an accurate performance on these stages. With the aim of describing it, the proportion of the amount of pixels belonging to *ROI* with respect to the number of pixels present in the minimum rectangle containing this region is calculated:

$$S_{roi} = \frac{|P_{ROI}|}{width * height}, \tag{6}$$

where P_{ROI} is the set of pixels present in the *ROI*, $|P_{ROI}|$ is its cardinality and *width* and *height* are the size of the minimum rectangle containing *ROI*.

Attempting to represent the amount of information that can be extracted from a fingerprint image, two other features are used:

Horizontal Ridge Count. The number of ridges crossing the horizontal line to the central pixel (S_{hrc}) of *ROI*, and

Vertical Ridge Count. The ridges count crossing the vertical line to the central pixel (S_{vrc}) of *ROI*.

3.3 Overall Quality Estimation Function

With the aim of calculating the continuous quality metric proposed, first a Gaussian function (equation 7) is applied to each feature for obtaining a fuzzy value of belonging to a high quality fingerprint,

$$G_f(x) = \begin{cases} 1 & \text{if } \delta_{min} \leqslant x \leqslant \delta_{max}, \\ \alpha_1 e^{-\frac{(x-\mu_1)^2}{2\sigma_1^2}} & x < \delta_{min}, \\ \alpha_2 e^{-\frac{(x-\mu_2)^2}{2\sigma_2^2}} & \text{otherwise}, \end{cases} \tag{7}$$

where α_1, α_2, μ_1, μ_2, σ_1 and σ_2 are the parameters of the Gaussian function.

So as to describe the ridges pattern clarity (Q_{RPC}) and the ridges systems completeness (Q_{RSC}), one dominant feature is chosen for each of these global characteristics by the following equations:

$$Q_{RPC} = min(G_f(S_{gos}), G_f(S_{bosc}), G_f(S_{grf})), \tag{8}$$

$$Q_{RSC} = min(G_f(S_{roi}), G_f(S_{hrc}), G_f(S_{vrc})). \tag{9}$$

Then, the final quality value is calculated by merging Q_{RPC} and Q_{RSC} as shown below:

$$Q_f = Q_{RPC} * Q_{RSC}. \tag{10}$$

4 Experimental Results

The fingerprint quality value is a measure of the biometric sample usability for both, enrollment and recognition stages. An accurate estimation of fingerprint quality is extremely important for improving fingerprint-based biometric systems, because the false non-matches can be reduced. To validate the proposed metric, the experiments measure its impact on the matching stage using the Verifinger 4.2 matching algorithm. Five different matching accuracy measures are used for obtaining the impact of the new fingerprint quality assessment method. Its performance is compared with NFIQ quality method. Experiments were conducted on a well-know public database, FVC2004 DB1-A which contains 100 fingers and 800 images.

In order to perform a comparison with NFIQ algorithm the proposed continuous quality value is quantified in five quality levels: 1, 2, 3, 4, 5, where 1 is the best quality and 5 is the worst quality. The matching accuracy measures are computed by eliminating the comparisons where at least one fingerprint image with bad quality (3, 4, or 5) is involved. A good performance of a quality assessment method should reduce error rates. The methodology used for the matching algorithm is the same proposed by the FVC competitions. Table 1 present a comparison of the three possible scenarios.

In table 1 it is shown that the matching algorithm performance is improved when both quality assessment algorithms are used. It can be clearly seen that the results of the proposed algorithm outperform the results of NFIQ method, even

Table 1. Comparison of the Verifinger algorithm performance, performance of the Verifinger algorithm using NFIQ method and the proposed quality assessment method.

	FVC 2004 db1A		
	Normal	*NFIQ*	Q_f
EER	0.0968	0.0826	0.0782
OP(0.001)	0.1854	0.1633	0.1505
FMR100	0.1504	0.1332	0.1191
FMR10	0.0889	0.0810	0.0782
ZeroFMR	0.2311	0.2003	0.1922

Table 2. Amount of impressions for each quality levels defined by NFIQ and the proposed approach.

Quality Levels	1	2	3	4	5
NFIQ	512	208	70	4	6
Q_f	484	246	39	25	11

Fig. 2. Example of a fingerprint image with NFIQ quality value of 1 (best quality) where the quality value generated by the new proposal is 5 (worst quality).

when the amount of images of higher quality levels is lower with the proposed approach than with NFIQ method as indicated in table 2.

An example of a fingerprint image where NFIQ gives the best posible quality and the proposed approach classifies it in the worst quality level can be seen in figure 2. This occurs because the zone of the fingerprint in the impression presents good quality, and has an acceptable amount of minutiae, but it can be clearly seen that its size is not acceptable for a fingerprint with good quality.

5   Conclusions and Future Work

In this work, a new method for fingerprint image quality assessment based on ridge characteristics, that can perform a continuous classification is presented. Six features that correctly describe the fingerprint quality are proposed. Its performance is evaluated in the recognition stage, using the Verifinger 4.2 matching algorithm. From the experiments carried out it can be concluded that the proposed method can attain accurate quality values for fingerprints and it outperforms the NFIQ results. The function used for obtained the final quality value is quite simple, nevertheless the proposed method achieved very good results. Consequently, a more sophisticated function to calculate the final quality value is being studied. Moreover, some of these features can be used for describing palm impressions quality.

References

1. Alonso-Fernandez, F., Fiérrez-Aguilar, J., Ortega-Garcia, J., Gonzalez-Rodriguez, J., Fronthaler, H., Kollreider, K., Bigün, J.: A comparative study of fingerprint image-quality estimation methods. IEEE Transactions on Information Forensics and Security 2(4), 734–743 (2007)
2. Awasthi, A., Venkataramani, K., Nandini, A.: Image quality quantification for fingerprints using quality-impairment assessment. In: IEEE Workshop on Applications of Computer Vision, WACV, pp. 296–302 (2013)
3. Bharadwaj, S., Vatsa, M., Singh, R.: Biometric quality: a review of fingerprint, iris, and face. EURASIP Journal on Image and Video Processing 2014, 34 (2014)
4. Chen, T.P., Jiang, X., Yau, W.Y.: Fingerprint image quality analysis. In: ICIP, pp. 1253–1256 (2004)
5. Kass, M., Witkin, A.P.: Analyzing oriented patterns. Computer Vision, Graphics, and Image Processing 37(3), 362–385 (1987)
6. Lim, E., Jiang, X., Yau, W.: Fingerprint quality and validity analysis. In: ICIP (1), pp. 469–472 (2002)
7. Maltoni, D., Maio, D., Jain, A.K., Prabhakar, S.: Handbook of fingerprint recognition, 2nd edn. Springer Publishing Company, Incorporated (2009)
8. Munir, M.U., Javed, M.Y., Khan, S.A.: A hierarchical k-means clustering based fingerprint quality classification. Neurocomputing 85, 62–67 (2012)
9. Phromsuthirak, K., Areekul, V.: Fingerprint quality assessment using frequency and orientation subbands of block-based fourier transform. In: International Conference on Biometrics, ICB, pp. 1–7 (2013)
10. Tabassi, E., Wilson, C.L., Watson, C.I.: Fingerprint image quality. Tech. Rep. NISTIR 7151, National Institute of Standars & Technology, August 2004
11. Tiwari, K., Gupta, P.: No-reference fingerprint image quality assessment. In: Huang, D.-S., Jo, K.-H., Wang, L. (eds.) ICIC 2014. LNCS, vol. 8589, pp. 846–854. Springer, Heidelberg (2014)
12. Wu, M., Yong, A., Zhao, T., Guo, T.: A systematic algorithm for fingerprint image quality assessment. In: Huang, D.-S., Gan, Y., Gupta, P., Gromiha, M.M. (eds.) ICIC 2011. LNCS, vol. 6839, pp. 412–420. Springer, Heidelberg (2012)
13. Yao, Z., Bars, J.L., Charrier, C., Rosenberger, C.: Fingerprint quality assessment combining blind image quality, texture and minutiae features. In: 1st International Conference on Information Systems Security and Privacy, ICISSP, pp. 336–343 (2015)
14. Yao, Z., Bars, J.L., Charrier, C., Rosenberger, C.: Quality assessment of fingerprints with minutiae delaunay triangulation. In: 1st International Conference on Information Systems Security and Privacy, ICISSP, pp. 315–321 (2015)

Computer Vision

A Computer Vision Approach for Automatic Measurement of the Inter-plant Spacing

Anderson Brilhador[1], Daniel A. Serrarens[2], and Fabrício M. Lopes[1]([✉])

[1] Federal University of Technology - Paraná, Cornélio Procópio-PR, Brazil
andersonbrilhador@gmail.com, fabricio@utfpr.edu.br
[2] Belagrícola Comércio e Representação de Produtos Agrícolas Ltda - Paraná,
Tamarama, Brazil
daniel.serrarens@belagricola.com.br

Abstract. Global food demand is increasing every year and it is needed to respond to this demand. In addition, some crops such as corn, which is the most produced grain in the world, is used as food, feed, bio-energy and other industrial purposes. Thus, it is needed the development of new technologies that make possible to produce more from less land. In particular, the corn crop is sensitive to its spatial arrangement and any variation in plant distribution pattern can lead to reduction in corn production. Nowadays, the uniformity of the plant spacing is checked manually by agronomists in order to predict possible production losses. In this context, this work proposes an automatic approach for measuring the spacing between corn plants in the early stages of growth. The proposed approach is based on computer vision techniques in order to evaluate the automatic inter-plant spacing measurement from images in a simple and efficient way, allowing its use on devices with low computational power such as smart phones and tablets. An image dataset was built as an additional contribution of this work containing 2186 corn plants in two conditions: tillage after the application of herbicide (TH) with 1387 corn plants and conventional tillage (CT) with 799 corn plants. The dataset is available at url: http://github.com/Brilhador/cornspacing. The experimental results achieve 90% of precision and 92% of sensitivity in corn plant identification. Regarding the automatic measurement of the inter-plant spacing, the results showed no significant differences from the same measurements taken manually, indicating the effectiveness of the proposed approach in two distinct types of planting.

Keywords: Computer vision · Inter-plant spacing · Pattern recognition · Precision agriculture · Image processing

1 Introduction

The world population is increasing every year and it is needed to improve the global food production in order to be able to feed the world. In this way the precision agriculture techniques can maximize food production, minimize environmental impact and reduce cost.

© Springer International Publishing Switzerland 2015
A. Pardo and J. Kittler (Eds.): CIARP 2015, LNCS 9423, pp. 219–227, 2015.
DOI: 10.1007/978-3-319-25751-8_27

In particular, the corn crop is the most produced grain in the world, being used as food, feed and industrial utilities such as ethanol production [3]. It is a major component of livestock feed. The United States produces 40.2% of the world's harvest and other top producing countries include China (31.0%) and Brazil (9.5%). However, the corn production has its own peculiarities including the sensitivity to its spatial arrangement, which is defined as the geometric area available for planting each of the corn plants, i.e., its distribution pattern [21].

Indeed, the plants compete for natural resources such as water, light and nutrients. The uniformity of inter-plant spacing decreases this competition [16]. Some works address the plant spacing variability (PSV) on corn grain yield, which is defined by the standard deviation of consecutive plant-to-plant spacings within rows [12]. It was reported a reduction of about 2.5 bushels per acre for each centimeter increased in the standard deviation of plant spacing[12]. Similar effects was reported, achieving a reduction of 3.4 bushels per acre for every inch increase in standard deviation [4], which points out the PSV as an important factor in grain production. In general, the PSV is evaluated manually with a tape measure positioned along the row of plants, while the spacings are stored numerically in a notebook or as an audio recorder. Manual methods are exhaustive, time consuming and subject to human error.

The spatial arrangement of plants has been analyzed by many researchers as well as its influence on grain production. In this context there are some works that address this important issue. For instance, in [18] it was adopted three morphological features to distinguish between weeds and corn plants. In [17] it was used the shape and the area of the corn plants to measure the population of plants and the space between them. In [19] it was applied morphological features, color and the center of the planting row to measure the spacing between plants. Recent works [10,11] present approaches based on 3D sensors in order to measure corn plants in later stages. However, these techniques requires a very specific hardware/machine in order to capture and/or analyze the images.

This work address the PSV issue presenting a simple and effective approach for measuring the spacing between plants in two different situations of planting (Sec. 2). More specifically, it was adopted only shape descriptors in order to identify the corn plant and its stem and as a result, to evaluate the automatic inter-plant spacing measurement from images in a simple and efficient way. Besides, the proposed approach can be used on devices with low computational power such as smart phones and tablets.

2   Image Dataset

After an exhaustive search from image dataset of corn crops, it was identified that this matter is still little explored by the scientific community. Thus, an image dataset was built as an additional contribution of this work, which is available at url: http://github.com/brilhador/cornspacing.

The image dataset is composed by corn plants, which were acquired through a mobile device considering panoramic images. The image acquisition process

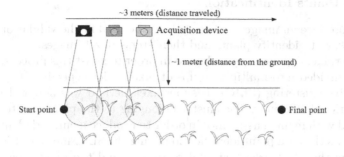

Fig. 1. The image acquisition process.

(Fig. 1) was performed by a person carried a camera at an average height of 1 meter from the ground. The initial starting point for the acquisition was determined randomly and from there it traveled approximately 3 meters capturing the images of corn plants building a panoramic image.

Currently, the image dataset contains 188 panoramic images of corn planting with 24-bit color depth with an average resolution of 3000 x 600 pixels in JPG image format. The image acquisition was performed in a real situation of planting, as a result, the stored images present highly lighting variation and different spacing between corn plants.

The images were acquired in two distinct situations: tillage after the application of herbicide (TH) and conventional tillage (CT). In CT images the soil goes through a mechanical preparation of plowing and harrowing. On the other hand, the TH images there is no mechanical preparation of the soil, in which the ground remains covered with waste from various cultures used in succession or rotation [6]. The elimination of crop residues and weeds are carried out by applying herbicide. These two classes of images are presented in Fig. 4.

The corn plants have phenotypic features related to their growth stages, commonly defined as $V(n)$, where n is the number of leaves fully developed in the plant [15]. This variation of the plant growth modifies the shape of its canopy. The image dataset comprises these phenotypic variations, with images between $V(2)$ and $V(3)$ stages in CT condition and $V(3)$ and $V(4)$ in TH condition. These stages were chosen as they provide better uniformity between plants in the planting row. The $V(1)$ stage presents the initial plant development and some of them remain in a germination process, i.e., buried in the ground.

Another important issue is that the image dataset was built with panoramic images containing corn plants in early stages of development, which turns possible to identify problems in inter-plant spacing at early stages of the plant development, as a result, enables the rapid intervention of the producer avoiding losses in corn crop. Therefore, the proposed image dataset presents real conditions of the plant development in order to provide a suitable benchmark, not only for this work, but for other related works.

2.1   Corn Plants Identification

In order to produce an image dataset that can be used in the validation process, it was necessary to identify plants and their stems in all images.

The superpixel technique was adopted in order to assist this process, in which an image is divided into multiple groups of pixels. More specifically, the simple linear iterative clustering (SLIC) [1] superpixel method was adopted in face of its computational efficiency. The cluster belonging to the plant and to the stem were selected with manual assistance in order to produce a curated identification. Figure 2 shows the corn plant identification using the SLIC method. Figures 2(a) and (c) show the plant area (external rectangle) and the plant stem (internal rectangle). Figures 2(b) and (d) show the plant identification and its parts.

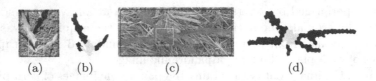

(a)   (b)   (c)   (d)

Fig. 2. Figures (a) and (c) show the plant identification, the external rectangle (blue) is the area of the plant. The internal rectangle (yellow) is the stem of the plant. Figures (b) and (d) is the plant identification by superpixel method, all identified pixels belongs to the plant and the yellow pixels is the stem.

As a result, it were identified 2186 corn plants, in which are distributed as following: 1387 in TH condition and 799 in CT condition. The plant and its stem identification were stored in XML (eXtensible Markup Language) files in order to be used in the classification process.

3   Proposed Approach

The main goal of this work is to address the PSV on corn grain yield through an automatic approach to measure the inter-plant spacing in a simple and efficient way. The schematic flowchart of the proposed approach is presented in Figure 3.

After the image acquisition, it was preprocessed by an average filter in order to reduce the reflections on the leaf surface caused by the sunlight. The next step was the image segmentation, in which the goal is to segment the regions of interest (corn plants) from its background (solo and other crop residues).

It is commonly known that vegetation index is a suitable way to improve the image segmentation from its background (soil, rocks and other residues) when the images contain some vegetation. Various vegetation indices were tested in a recent work [9], in which the CIVE (color index of vegetation extraction) shows better results in images with highly lighting variation, achieving more than 90% of accuracy in average. Thus, it was adopted in the proposed approach. The CIVE [8] starts by rescaling the RGB colors individually in the range [0,1].

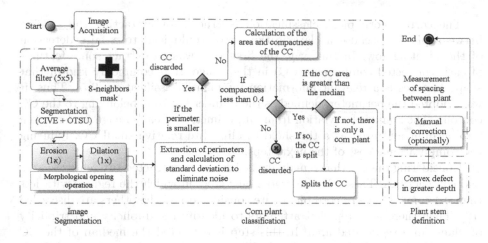

Fig. 3. Flowchart of the proposed approach.

After that, a second rescaling is performed in order to each color band (RGB) gets a relative value, i.e., the fraction of each intensity in relation to the sum of the three bands. This rescaling process is frequently adopted in the agricultural images [7]. As a third step the CIVE index is applied, as a result a grayscale image is produced (Fig. 4 (c) and (d)). In the proposed approach grayscale images were segmented by the Otsu threshold method [13]. However, the acquired images have numerous environmental conditions resulting in noisy segmentation in most of the cases. In order to reduce the noise while preserving the correctly segmented plants it was performed a morphological opening operation[5]. Figures 4 (e) and (f) show the resulting images.

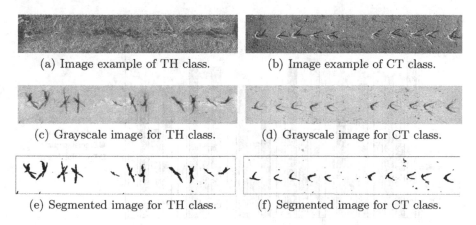

(a) Image example of TH class. (b) Image example of CT class.

(c) Grayscale image for TH class. (d) Grayscale image for CT class.

(e) Segmented image for TH class. (f) Segmented image for CT class.

Fig. 4. (a) and (b) are raw images from proposed dataset. (c) and (d) are grayscale images after performing CIVE. (e) and (f) are binary images after performing threshold.

The correct corn plant classification is crucial for extracting the spacing between plants, because a classification error could lead to a false detection of the planting row. In this way, the first step was to extract some features of each connected component (CC) in the image. It is commonly known that shape features is a relevant information for plants classification [2,5]. Thus, it was adopted the perimeter, defined as the number of pixels belonging to the CC contour. The standard deviation from all perimeters of each image is also taken into account and used as a threshold to eliminate relative small CC, reducing the computational cost of the next steps.

Considering the CC that remain in the image are extracted two features: area and compactness. These CC undergo a new step, in which the regions with less than 0.4 compactness of corn plants are considered and the others are discarded [19]. Then there is a step that attempts to identify the duplicity and triplicity of plants in a segmented area. In this step is extracted the median of the CC areas in the image. If the area of each CC is greater than the median, the CC is divided. This division is recursively applied until that the area of the resulting CC is less than the median.

The plant stem definition is essential for the extraction of the inter-plant spacing with higher accuracy. It was adopted the convex hull, which is commonly adopted for object recognition [14,22]. More specifically, the stem of the corn plant is extracted by identifying the more deeply convex defect, as a result it is found the pixel belonging to the contour with greater distance from the convex hull. Thus, this pixel is used to identify its opposite pixel and then to estimate the average between them as the stem coordinates.

The spatial coordinates of the plant stem are stored and optionally is allowed to the user perform manual corrections to add or remove new plants and move stem coordinates that are outside of its location, ensuring the measurement of distances closer to reality. After this, the inter-plant spacing is measured.

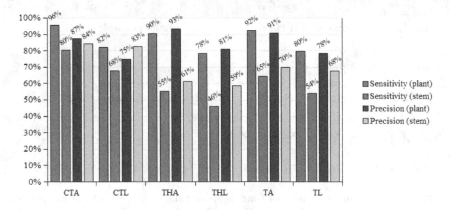

Fig. 5. Classification results.

4   Results and Discussions

This section presents the experimental results in order to evaluate the proposed approach regarding the inter-plant spacing. The experiments were performed addressing two important issues: (1) The automatic corn plants identification; (2) The automatic measurement of the inter-plant spacing.

The automatic corn plants identification was performed considering its area and stem individually (Sec. 2.1) for TH and CT images (Sec. 2). Thus, it were produced six classes: the area for TH images (THA);the stem for TH images (THL);the area for CT images (CTA);the stem for CT images (CTL);the area for CT and TH images (TA); and the stem for CT and TH images (TL).

Figure 5 presents the results by considering the precision and sensitivity measures [20]. It is possible to observe that TA achieve 92% of sensitivity and 91% of precision for plant classification. For TL were obtained 80% e 78%, respectively. The sensitivity was 96% for CTA and 90% for THA with a precision of 87% e 93% respectively. These results were coherent and expected because the area of the plant is larger than its stem. Moreover, the precision for the stem identification was higher in the images in CT condition, achieving 84% (CTA) and 83% (CTL). On the other hand, the results for TH condition were lower than the previous, obtaining 61% (THA) and 59% (THL), which affects partially the inter-plant spacing measurement, since the corn plants were identified with more than 87% of precision and sensitivity in average. This result was due to the stage of maturity of the plants between classes. The CT condition presents corn plants with stages between $V(2)$ and $V(3)$, in which the leaves has a deeper convex defect, while in TH condition contains corn plants with $V(3)$ and $V(4)$, in which this defect can be covered by another branch of the leaf.

The experiments for automatic measurement of the inter-plant spacing were performed comparing the measurements from a manual tape and the measurements inferred by the proposed approach. The obtained differences in average were 1.4 cm for images in CT condition and 1.33 cm for images in TH condition with standard deviations of 0.96 cm and 0.99 cm respectively, presenting very close results. In summary, the results indicate the suitability of the proposed approach for the automatic corn plant identification and the automatic measurement of its inter-plant spacing. Furthermore, the proposed approach present a faster and reliable method than manual analysis for PSV measurement.

5   Conclusions

This work presented an objective approach for the automatic measurement of the inter-plant spacing. An image dataset was built as an additional contribution of this work containing 2186 corn plants in two conditions: tillage after the application of herbicide (TH) with 1387 corn plants and conventional tillage (CT) with 799 corn plants. In addition, both cases present phenotypic variations caused by different stages of plant development.

The experimental results achieve 87% of precision and 96% of sensitivity for CT and 93% of precision and 90% of sensitivity for TH, when considering the automatic corn plants identification. The stem identification achieve 84% of precision when considering the area of the plant and 83% when considering only its stem for CT images. On the other hand, the results for TH images were lower than the previous, obtaining 61% of precision considering the area and 59% considering only the stem, which affects partially the inter-plant spacing measurement, since the corn plants were identified with more than 87% of accuracy and sensitivity in average. Regarding automatic measurement of the inter-plant spacing, the presented results are very close to the manual measurements. In summary, the results indicate the suitability of the proposed approach as an auxiliary tool in preventing grain losses due to variations in spacing between plants caused by the poor performance of planters or low seed quality.

Future work includes to test other strategies for image segmentation and to explore more image features as shape and texture in order to improve the proposed approach, in particular regarding the precision of the stem identification.

Acknowledgements. This work was supported by CNPq, Fund. Araucária, UTFPR and Belagrícola.

References

1. Achanta, R., Shaji, A., Smith, K., Lucchi, A., Fua, P., Susstrunk, S.: Slic superpixels compared to state-of-the-art superpixel methods. Pattern Analysis and Machine Intelligence, IEEE Transactions on **34**(11), 2274–2282 (2012)
2. Brilhador, A., Colonhezi, T.P., Bugatti, P.H., Lopes, F.M.: Combining texture and shape descriptors for bioimages classification: a case of study in ImageCLEF dataset. In: Ruiz-Shulcloper, J., Sanniti di Baja, G. (eds.) CIARP 2013, Part I. LNCS, vol. 8258, pp. 431–438. Springer, Heidelberg (2013)
3. Council, I.G.: Grain market report. Tech. rep. (2015)
4. Doerge, T., Hall, T., Gardner, D.: New research confirms benefits of improved plant spacing in corn. Crop insights **12**(2), 1–5 (2002)
5. da Fontoura Costa, L., Cesar Jr, R.M.: Shape Classification and Analysis: Theory and Practice, 2nd edn. CRC Press, Boca Raton (2009)
6. Freire, F.M., Vasconcellos, C.A., de França, G.E.: Manejo da fertilidade do solo em sistema plantio direto. Embrapa Milho e Sorgo-Artigo (2001)
7. Gée, C., Bossu, J., Jones, G., Truchetet, F.: Crop/weed discrimination in perspective agronomic images. Comput. and Electr. in Agric. **60**(1), 49–59 (2008)
8. Kataoka, T., Kaneko, T., Okamoto, H., Hata, S.: Crop growth estimation system using machine vision. IEEE/ASME AIM **2**, b1079–b1083 (2003)
9. Kazmi, W., Garcia-Ruiz, F.J., Nielsen, J., Rasmussen, J., Andersen, H.J.: Detecting creeping thistle in sugar beet fields using vegetation indices. Computers and Electronics in Agriculture **112**, 10–19 (2015)
10. Nakarmi, A., Tang, L.: Automatic inter-plant spacing sensing at early growth stages using a 3D vision sensor. Comp. and Elect. in Agric. **82**, 23–31 (2012)
11. Nakarmi, A.D., Tang, L.: Within-row spacing sensing of maize plants using 3D computer vision. Biosystems Engineering **125**, 54–64 (2014)
12. Nielsen, R.: Effect of plant spacing variability on corn grain yield (2006)
13. Otsu, N.: A Threshold Selection Method from Gray-level Histograms. IEEE Transactions on Systems, Man and Cybernetics **9**(1), 62–66 (1979)

14. Pedrini, H., Schwartz, W.: Análise de imagens digitais: princípios, algoritmos e aplicações. Thomson Learning (2008)
15. Ritchie, S.W., Hanway, J.J., Benson, G.O., Herman, J.: How a corn plant develops (1993)
16. Sangoi, L., Gracietti, M., Rampazzo, C., Bianchetti, P.: Response of Brazilian maize hybrids from different eras to changes in plant density. Field Crop. Res. **79**(1), 39–51 (2002)
17. Shrestha, D.S., Steward, B.L.: Size and shape analysis of corn plant canopies for plant population and spacing sensing. Appl. Eng. Agric. **21**(2), 295 (2005)
18. Shrestha, D., Steward, B., Birrell, S.: Video processing for early stage maize plant detection. Biosystems Engineering **89**(2), 119–129 (2004)
19. Tang, L., Tian, L.F.: Plant identification in mosaicked crop row images for automatic emerged corn plant spacing measurement. T. ASABE **51**(6), 2181 (2008)
20. Webb, A.R.: Statistical Pattern Recognition, 2nd edn. John Willey & Sons (2002)
21. Willey, R., Rao, M.: A systematic design to examine effects of plant population and spatial arrangement in intercropping, illustrated by an experiment on chickpea/safflower. Experimental Agriculture **17**(01), 63–73 (1981)
22. Zhang, D., Lu, G.: Review of shape representation and description techniques. Pattern Recognition **37**(1), 1–19 (2004)

An EA-Based Method for Estimating the Fundamental Matrix

Daniel Barragan[1]($\boxtimes$), Maria Trujillo[1], and Ivan Cabezas[2]

[1] Universidad del Valle, Melendez Campus, Cali, Colombia
{daniel.barragan,maria.trujillo}@correounivalle.edu.co
[2] Universidad de San Buenaventura, Avenida 10 de Mayo, La Umbria, Cali, Colombia
imcabezas@usbcali.edu.co

Abstract. The camera calibration problem consists in estimating intrinsic and extrinsic parameters. It can be solved by computing a 3x3 matrix enclosing such parameters - the fundamental matrix -, which can be obtained from a set of corresponding points. Nevertheless, in practice, corresponding points may be falsely matched or badly located, due to occlusion and ambiguity. Moreover, if the set of corresponding points does not include information on existing scene depth, the estimated fundamental matrix may not be able to correctly recover the epipolar geometry. In this paper, an EA-based method for accurately selecting estimated corresponding points is introduced. It considers geometric issues that were ignored in previous EA-based approaches. Two selection operators were evaluated and obtained similar results. Additionally, a mutation operator is designed to tackle bad located points by shifting disparity vectors. An inter-technique comparison is performed against a standard camera calibration method. The qualitative evaluation is conducted by analysing obtained epipolar lines, regarding expected appearance, based on a-priori knowledge of camera systems during the capturing process. The quantitative evaluation of the proposed method is based on residuals. Experimental results shown the proposed method is able to correctly reconstruct the epipolar geometry.

Keywords: Camera calibration · Corresponding points · Evolutionary algorithms · Inverse problems · Fundamental matrix

1 Introduction

The camera calibration problem has applications in diverse fields [11,15]. It is related to the estimation of intrinsic and extrinsic camera parameters. Intrinsic parameters characterise inherent optical properties of a camera, including the focal length, the image centre, the image scaling factors and the lens distortion coefficients. Extrinsic camera parameters indicate position and orientation of the camera in relation to the world coordinate system. Intrinsic and extrinsic camera parameters define the projection of a 3D scene into a 2D image plane, by a camera system.

© Springer International Publishing Switzerland 2015
A. Pardo and J. Kittler (Eds.): CIARP 2015, LNCS 9423, pp. 228–235, 2015.
DOI: 10.1007/978-3-319-25751-8_28

Camera calibration can be performed in either a semi-automatic or an automatic way. The former - called photogrammetric calibration - requires of calibration patterns, which have to be accurately known [5]. Moreover, calibration patterns or apparatus have to be used [12]. The latter - called self-calibration - is supported by the epipolar geometry [8]. The epipolar geometry is the intrinsic projective geometry between any two views. The epipolar geometry is encapsulated in the fundamental matrix, F. A set of corresponding points can be used for computing the fundamental matrix. Corresponding points are formed by projecting a 3D point into two slightly different image planes. Thus, if these projections are accurately known, the 3D position of a point can be recovered by triangulation. However, in practice, corresponding points may be inaccurately estimated. In fact, recovering the intrinsic and the extrinsic parameters is an inverse and ill-posed problem. Moreover, if a set of corresponding points does not include information of existing scene depth, the estimated fundamental matrix may not be able to correctly recover the epipolar geometry due to the inverse nature of the problem.

The camera calibration problem has been addressed using Evolutionary Algorithms (EA) and Genetic Algorithms (GA) by several authors [1,6,10,13,17]. The most similar approaches to the presented method are [2,7]. These works represent a chromosome as a set of stereo matching pairs. In [2], a minimal set of matching points is pursued, and there is no guarantee that a single chromosome properly contains information of existing scene depth. Also, there is no clear insight about how the mutation operator works. A chromosome of variable length is used in [7] due to the considered crossover operator. Thus, multiples strategies are required to compute the Fundamental matrix, according to the chromosome's length.

In this paper, the calibration problem is turned into finding an accurately estimated set of corresponding points. Consequently, an EA is used for accurately selecting estimated corresponding points and then estimating the fundamental matrix.

2   Problem Statement

The calibration problem is an ill-posed problem. Thus, small perturbations in the input corresponding points may produce arbitrary large variations in the estimated fundamental matrix. Corresponding points are projections such that:

Definition 1. *For a given pair of stereo images, let m be a point, with coordinates $[u, v, 1]^T$, in the right image, and let m' be a point, with coordinates $[u', v', 1]^T$, in the left image. Points m and m' are corresponding points iff they are projections of a scene point M.*

There is a set of constraints commonly used for estimating corresponding points in order to cope with the ill-posedness, for instance: *Similarity:*   the matching points have to have similar appearance. *Uniqueness:* a given feature point from one image can match no more than one feature point from the other image. *Continuity:* disparity of a matching point should vary smoothly almost everywhere over an image. *Ordering:* if $m_i \leftrightarrow m'_i$ and $m_j \leftrightarrow m'_j$ and if m_i is to the left of m_j then m'_i should also be to the left of m'_j and vice versa. That is, the ordering of points is preserved across images.

Taking into account the inverse and the ill-posed nature of the calibration problem, there is a set of criteria that the estimated corresponding points has to fulfil in order to stabilise the solution.

Definition 2. *Let* $S = \{(m_1, m'_1), (m_2, m'_2), \cdots, (m_i, m'_i), \cdots, (m_n, m'_n)\}$ *be an accurately estimated set of corresponding points, subject to:*

1. *The points* (m_i, m'_i) *have to be projections of scene points* M_i, $\forall\, i = 1, \cdots, n$.
2. *The* $[u_i, v_i]^T$ *and* $[u_{i'}, v'_i]^T$ *coordinates have to correspond to an accurate localisation of* m_i *and* m'_i, $\forall\, i = 1, \cdots, n$.
3. *The cardinality of* S *has to be in relation to existing scene depth.*

The calibration problem can be turned into finding an accurately estimated set of corresponding points. Moreover, the extrinsic and the intrinsic parameters do not depend on the scene content, in the direct problem. However, in the inverse problem, a set corresponding points belonging to existing scene depth may compensate the lack of information about scene depth. The problem addressed in this paper consists in finding a set S which fulfils the above criteria.

3   An EA-Based Fundamental Matrix Estimation

The EA-based method is briefly described as threefold: *1.* estimating a set S^+ of corresponding points, *2.* S^+ evolution by EA, and *3.* calculating the fundamental matrix.

3.1   Estimating a Set S^+ of Corresponding Points

1. **Feature points extraction**: Feature points are extracted using Shi-Tomasi [14].
2. **Matching feature points**: Matching of feature points is performed using the block-matching algorithm with Normalised Cross Correlation (NCC) and two different window sizes: -5×5 *and* $7 \times 7-$. Each point in the reference image is correlated to every point in a 2D search-window in the target image and the bidirectional constraint is enforced during the calculation. A set of matching points is obtained.
3. **Filtering matching points**: Outliers, in the initial set of matching points, are removed by RANSAC, and the distance between a point and its epipolar line is used as a criterion to decide whether or not there is an outlier. Then, the ordering constraint is verified on the remaining matching points. That is, the order of feature points is preserved across images. A filtered set of matching points is obtained.

4. **Clustering filtered matching points**: Filtered matching points are clustered based on estimated disparities, in order to take into account the existing scene depth. The k-means algorithm is used to cluster filtering matching points, using the subtractive clustering method, available in MATLAB, to determine the number of clusters κ. As a result, a set S^+ is formed, where $S^+ = \{(m_j, m'_j, k)\}$, $j = 1, \cdots, n_c$, and $k = 1, \cdots, \kappa$.

3.2 S^+ Evolution by EA

1. **Configuration of initial population**: The initial population is built by sampling with replacement q matching points from each cluster in S^+. Chromosome codification is formulated as follows:

$$\theta = ((m_1, m'_1), \ldots, (m_j, m'_j), \ldots, (m_p, m'_p)), \qquad (1)$$

where θ is a chromosome and p is the size of the chromosome with $p = q \times \kappa$. A chromosome only contains a matching pair of points once.

2. **Chromosome expression and fitness evaluation**: The fitness function enforces the epipolar and the smoothness constraints. The fitness function is given by:

$$g(\theta) = \sum_{i=1}^{p} d(m_i, Fm'_i) + d(m'_i, Fm_i) + C_i. \qquad (2)$$

The epipolar constraint requires the calculation of the fundamental matrix, F, which is estimated using the set of matching points in S^+. The smoothness constraint is reflected in the term C_i, by summing absolute differences among the disparity d_i – where $d_i = [m_i - m'_i]$ – and disparities belonging to the same cluster of (m_i, m'_i):

$$C_i = \sum_{j=1}^{q} \|d_i - d_j\|_1 \ \forall \ i \neq j; \ \ d_j = \left[(u_j - u'_j), (v_j - v'_j)\right]. \qquad (3)$$

The objective function is given by,

$$\theta = argmin \ g(\theta_l). \qquad (4)$$

3. **Elitist preservation**: A number η of the best fitted population individuals is preserved and kept unchanged among consecutive generations.
4. **Selection**: Two selection methods are considered – the proportional roulette wheel and the tournament – to perform parents selection for crossover.
5. **Crossover**: A single point crossover operator exchanges matching points between parents, by combining information associated to the existing scene depth.
6. **Mutation**: Mutation is applied in an informed manner. The matching point with the largest distances to its epipolar line is mutated. Given a pair of matching points, a point is randomly selected from the pair. A number among

0 to 7 is randomly chosen in order to determine the direction ω towards the selected point is moved. The new localisation of the selected point is within an 8-neighbourhood, as it is shown as follows:

$$m_j^* = m_j + \delta_{omega}, \tag{5}$$

where ω is a mutation offset, such as:

$\omega=0$	$\omega=1$	$\omega=2$	$\omega=3$	$\omega=4$	$\omega=5$	$\omega=6$	$\omega=7$
$\delta_{omega}=(-1,-1)$	$\delta_{omega}=(0,-1)$	$\delta_{omega}=(1,-1)$	$\delta_{omega}=(1,0)$	$\delta_{omega}=(1,1)$	$\delta_{omega}=(1,0)$	$\delta_{omega}=(1,-1)$	$\delta_{omega}=(-1,0)$

The uniqueness constraint is verified after a mutation in order to enforce its fulfilment. In case of degeneration of a chromosome, it is discarded.

7. **Validation**: The validation consists in verifying that each chromosome does not contain a matching point two or more times. If a repetition is found, the chromosome is discarded. The validation is conducted on the initial population and after the mutation.

8. **Population replacement**: The population is replaced by introducing new generated chromosomes, and elitist chromosomes are kept.

9. **Stop criterion**: The stop criterion is based on the first occurrence of the convergence principle, over the elitist population, and a maximum number of generations. If the population of the best fitted remains unchanged over a period of τ generations, it is assumed that convergence is reached. In practice τ is taken as a fixed number, and the number of maximum generations is fixed large. The elite population is the set S^*.

3.3   Fundamental Matrix Estimation

The estimation of the fundamental matrix has the elite population S^* as the input to a non-homogeneous linear equation system that is solved using a preconditioned LMedS and SVD based on the Rank-Nullity Theorem.

4   Experimental Evaluation

The performance of the proposed method was evaluated using the following sets of stereo images: Lab – which were acquired during the conducted research – and Corridor [3], Raglan [3] and Kapel [4] – which are available in public repositories. Matlab was used as programming tool. The Video Processing Toolbox was used for performing RANSAC and guided sampling. The scripts for corner detection and matching of Peter Kovesi were used [9]. Obtained results are compared to the calibration method proposed by Zhang and Kanade [18], which is based on the bucketing technique and the LMedS estimator [16]. The EA parameters are: $\eta = 10$, $\tau = 5$, $G_{max} = 20$, $P_{crossover} = 0.7$, and $P_{mutation} = 0.15$.

Initially, the two selection operators were evaluated using as criteria the residuals – calculated as the distance among points and its epipolar lines – and the execution time. Experiments are repeated 10 times using the set S^+.

Table 1. Comparison of the two selection methods.

Selection Method	Average residuals			
	Lab	Corridor	Raglan	Kapel
Tournament	3.34×10^{-7}	3.19×10^{-8}	5.01×10^{-8}	1.42×10^{-7}
Roulette	4.84×10^{-9}	8.45×10^{-9}	2.12×10^{-9}	1.43×10^{-8}

Table 2. Comparison of the two selection methods.

Selection Method	Average execution times in seconds			
	Lab	Corridor	Raglan	Kapel
Tournament	6.02×10^{0}	4.62×10^{0}	7.43×10^{0}	$3.32 \times 10^{+1}$
Roulette	8.30×10^{0}	3.67×10^{0}	7.67×10^{0}	$3.72 \times 10^{+1}$

Table 3. Performance evaluation of the proposed method and the bucketing technique plus LMedS [18].

Method	Average residuals			
	Lab	Corridor	Raglan	Kapel
Proposal	2.11×10^{-6}	1.32×10^{-9}	1.63×10^{-10}	6.10×10^{-9}
Bucketing plus LMedS	1.87×10^{-4}	1.60×10^{-5}	1.21×10^{-4}	1.83×10^{-4}

Tables 1 and 2 show that the proportional roulette wheel yielded smaller residuals than the tournament and they shown similar execution times. The proportional roulette wheel is used as the selection operator of the proposed method.

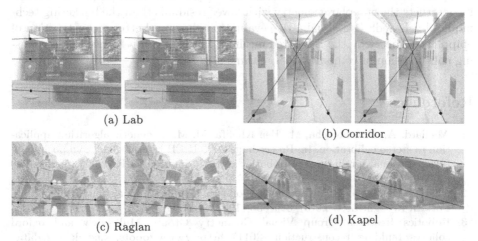

(a) Lab

(b) Corridor

(c) Raglan

(d) Kapel

Fig. 1. Points superimposed on epipolar lines: using the EA-based method at the left and using the bucketing technique plus LMedS at the right.

Performance evaluation of the proposed method is based on residuals. Residual values obtained using the proposed EA-based method are lower than residual values obtained using the bucketing technique plus LMedS [18]. However, computing elapsed times took longer for calculating the EA-based method. Table 3 shows average residual values of 20 trials.

Regarding the epipolar geometry in Figure 1, the Lab, the Raglan and the Kapel are stereo images for which the motion between views is approximately a translation parallel to the x-axis, with no rotation. Although, matching points lie on corresponding epipolar lines, the epipolar geometry is not correctly recovered for the Raglan and the Kapel datasets. In the corridor dataset, one image plane is behind the other. Consequently, the epipole is a fixed point at the same coordinate in both images. The epipolar geometry is recovered.

5 Final Remarks

The proportional roulette wheel is a selection operator simple and easy to implement. It was chosen for being used in the proposed method based on obtained residuals and execution times.

Existing scene depth has to be considered in order not only to avoid degenerate configurations, but also to introduce information to tackle the inverse nature of the problem. In the proposed approach, existing scene depth is taken into account by the means of selecting matching points from clusters.

The proposed EA-based method tackles bad located matching points by introducing a specifically designed mutation operator, capable of shifting disparity vectors. It is also capable of removing false correspondences by a filtering step.

Quantitative experimental evaluation shown that the proposed method reconstructs the epipolar geometry with lower residuals than the bucketing technique plus LMedS [18]. Qualitative evaluation shown a better reconstruction of epipolar geometry by the EA-based method. Future work is focused on optimising consumption of computational resources.

References

1. Abellard, A., Bouchouicha, M., Ben Khelifa, M. M.: A genetic algorithm application to stereo calibration. In: Proceedings 2005 IEEE International Symposium on Computational Intelligence in Robotics and Automation, CIRA 2005, pp 285–290 (2005)
2. Chai, J., De Ma, S.: Robust epipolar geometry estimation using genetic algorithm. Pattern Recogn. Lett. **19**(9), 829–838 (1998)
3. Robotics Research Group Visual Geometry Group. Multi-view and oxford colleges building reconstruction (2011) http://www.robots.ox.ac.uk/vgg/data/data-mview.html
4. Hartley, R., Zisserman, A.: Multiple View Geometry in Computer Vision. Cambridge books online,Cambridge University Press(2003)

5. M.F.A. Hassan, I. Ma'arof, and A.M. Samad. Assessment of camera calibration towards accuracy requirement. In: 2014 IEEE 10th International Colloquium on Signal Processing its Applications (CSPA), pp 123–128, March 2014

6. Hati, S., Sengupta, S.: Robust camera parameter estimation using genetic algorithm. In: Proceedings 1999 IEEE International Conference on Systems, Man, and Cybernetics, SMC1999, vol. 4, pp. 943–947. IEEE (1999)

7. Hu, M., Dodds, G., Yuan, B., Tang, X.: Robust camera calibration with epipolar constraints. In: Proceedings 2004 7th International Conference on Signal Processing, ICSP 2004, vol. 2, pp. 1115–1118, August 2004

8. Ju Jeong, Y., Hwang, H., Nam, D., Jay Kuo, C.C.: Uncalibrated multiview synthesis based on epipolar geometry approximation. In: 2015 IEEE International Conference on Consumer Electronics (ICCE), pp. 542–543, January 2015

9. Kovesi, P.D.: MATLAB and Octave functions for computer vision and image processing. Centre for Exploration Targeting, School of Earth and Environment, The University of Western Australia. http://www.cssc.uwa.edu.au/~pk/Research/MatlabFns/

10. Kumar, S.,Thakur, M., Raman, B.,Sukavanam, N.: Stereo camera calibration using real coded genetic algorithm. In: TENCON 2008–2008 IEEE Region 10 Conference, pp. 1–5, November 2008

11. Liu, J., Li, Y., Chen, S.: Robust camera calibration by optimal localization of spatial control points. IEEE Transactions on Instrumentation and Measurement **63**(12), 3076–3087 (2014)

12. Merras, M., El Akkad, N., Saaidi, A., Nazih, A.G., Satori, K.: Camera self calibration with varying parameters by an unknown three dimensional scene using the improved genetic algorithm. 3D. Research **6**(1), 39: 1–39: 14 (2015)

13. QiShen, L., Li-Cai, L., ZeTao, J.: A camera self-calibration method based on hybrid optimization algorithm. In: Second International Symposium on Electronic Commerce and Security, ISECS 2009, vol. 2, pp. 60–64, May 2009

14. Shi, J., Tomasi, C.: Good features to track. In: Proceeding of the IEEE Conference on Computer Vision and Pattern Recognition (CVPR1994), pp. 593–600 (1994)

15. Song, L., Wu, W., Guo, J., Li, X.: Survey on camera calibration technique. In: 2013 5th International Conference on Intelligent Human-Machine Systems and Cybernetics (IHMSC), vol. 2, pp. 389–392, August 2013

16. Sonnberger, H.: Robust regression and outlier detection. Journal of Applied Econometrics **4**(3), 309–311 (1989)

17. Y. Zhang and Q. Ji. Camera calibration with genetic algorithms. In Robotics and Automation, 2001. Proceedings 2001 ICRA. IEEE International Conference on, volume 3, pages 2177–2182 vol. 3, 2001

18. Zhang, Z., Kanade, T.: Determining the epipolar geometry and its uncertainty: A review. Int. J. Comput. Vision **27**, 161–195 (1998)

Two Applications of RGB-D Descriptors in Computer Vision

Mariano Bianchi[1]([✉]), Nadia Heredia[1], Francisco Gómez-Fernández[1],
Alvaro Pardo[2], and Marta Mejail[1]

[1] University of Buenos Aires, Buenos Aires, Argentina
{mabianchi,nheredia,fgomez,marta}@dc.uba.ar
[2] Universidad Católica Del Uruguay, Montevideo, Uruguay
apardo@ucu.edu.uy

Abstract. In this paper an evaluation of RGB-D descriptors in the context of Object Recognition and Object Tracking is presented. Spin-images, CSHOT and ECV context descriptors were used for detecting objects in point clouds. Empirical evaluation over a dataset with ground truth shows that shape is the most important cue for RGB-D descriptors. However, texture helps discrimination when objects are large or have little structure.

Keywords: RGB-D · Object recognition · Tracking · Point clouds

1 Introduction

The study of feature descriptors has been one of the main areas of research in image processing and computer vision for many years. Nowadays, the introduction of new low-cost sensors capable of capturing 3D scene information, has generated attention to descriptors that combine color and depth.

Traditionally, 2D descriptors capture, for example, color, texture or shape information from the image. RGB and depth sensors (RGB-D), such as the Kinect, allow the extraction of color and depth information of the scene. With this data, 3D descriptors can be used to model the geometry and color appearance of objects. The combination of color and depth allows for more discriminative power, making this an interesting area of research.

In this work, 3D point clouds are used instead of RGB and depth images independently. Working directly with 3D point clouds is a recent trend in computer vision; traditionally applications build polygonal meshes and then discard point cloud data. Here we evaluate different RGB-D descriptors in terms of their performance in two important applications: object recognition and tracking.

There are many works about 3D and RGB-D descriptors [7,11,3,4,9] (to name a few) but generally they do not assess their performance in particular applications. The analysis of their impact on the results of two applications, such as Object Recognition and Tracking, is very important and provides new cues and methodologies to understad which descriptors perform better in real applications.

A. Pardo and J. Kittler (Eds.): CIARP 2015, LNCS 9423, pp. 236–244, 2015.
DOI: 10.1007/978-3-319-25751-8_29

In order to quantitatively analyze object recognition and tracking we make use of a dataset with ground truth [8]. This is a large dataset, thus, first we analyze object recognition with three different descriptors and then the best descriptor is used in the tracking application.

This work is organized as follows. In Section 2 we describe RGB-D sensors and point clouds, then in Section 2.1 we talk about 3D descriptors and the datasets used. After that, in Section 4 and 5 discuss object recognition and tracking contributions respectively. Finally, in Section 6 we present a discussion of the presented work along with the conclusions.

2   RGB-D Sensors and Point Clouds

RGB-D sensors are composed of an RGB camera that captures color information of the scene, and a depth sensor which provides information about the distance from the camera to the objects in the scene.

There are different implementations for this kind of sensors to choose from, each one having its own unique sets of characteristics: image quality, frame rate, depth range. One that has gained popularity in recent years is the Kinect by Microsoft which provides RGB-D images with a default resolution of 640x480 pixels at rate of 30 fps.

Depth information used in conjunction with color information (RGB) allows 3D scene reconstruction. The calibration parameters for the RGB-D sensor can be used to estimate each pixel's position in the 3D scene, forming what is called a point cloud, where each point contains depth and color information.

2.1   Evaluated RGB-D Descriptors

In this work, we use local descriptors for object recognition because they are more robust to noise, clutter and occlusion, typical problems that arise when working with real RGB-D data. We use three histogram-based descriptors: CSHOT [11], Spin-Images [7] and ECV context descriptors [4], each one capturing information about the underlying surface in a different way. The selection of the previous descriptors takes into account the results presented in [1], where the author concludes that CSHOT and histogram-based descriptors are well suited for object recognition.

All descriptors are built for a set of selected input points but they use the entire point cloud to create them.

CSHOT (Color Signatures of Histograms of Orientations) [11]. The SHOT descriptor, first defines a robust local reference frame that is unique and unambiguous, built upon a local sign disambiguation method for the problem of normal estimation. At each input point a 3D grid is superimposed defining 3D volumes where local histograms are computed. Each local histogram accumulates into bins the angles (cosines) between the reference frame and the normal at each point. The Color SHOT (CSHOT) descriptor is an enhanced version of SHOT that also accumulates in a histogram the absolute color difference between points and then is chained together to the SHOT descriptor itself.

Spin-Images [7]. A Spin-Image (SI) is a cumulative 2D histogram which is computed on each oriented point (3D position plus surface normal) over a given set of points over the model's surface mesh or point cloud. At each input point a 2D histogram is built binning neighboring points that are projected on a plane (image) passing through the point's normal. Each bin is defined as a ring product of spinning that plane.

ECV Context Descriptors [4]. Early Cognitive Vision (ECV) systems were first developed with the aim to understand how human visual and cognitive systems work. Image pixels are classified as belonging to either an edge or a texture region and accompanied with an appearance and geometry-based description of their spatial neighborhood. At each input point all point-pair relations are considered, estimating geometric (cosine between orientations) and appearance (color gradients) relations and then binning them into histograms. The geometry part, the 3D position and orientation, is used, where the orientation are the direction along the edge or the normal vector to the local surface.

3   Dataset

Along this work we used sequences of RGB-D images with *ground truth* information with the goal of testing the studied methods and creating a reference to compare and assess the performance of the RGB-D descriptors under evaluation. We took scenes of a database from Kevin Lai et al. [8] where objects and scenes databases were created. Since our work is focused on real world scenarios, we took 3 annotated scenes from the dataset containing 10 different objects. Figure 1 shows the sequences employed for the results. For the objects we construct 3D models from their partial views acquired in a turning table, see Figure 2 for some of them. Note that we discard the flashlight due the impossibility of building the 3D model from its views.

4   Object Recognition

An object recognition system has the purpose of finding objects in images or point clouds. From now on, we will call *model* to the point cloud which has the object to be searched, and *scene* to the point cloud in which we wish to find it.

We divide our object recognition pipeline in the following steps: 1. Keypoint Extraction, 2. Descriptor Generation and 3. Matching. An overview of the steps of the employed procedure to recognize objects is shown in Figure 3a.

1. **Keypoint Extraction:** a subset of points from the original set is extracted. Keypoints are interesting points which are repeatable, there is a high chance that the same point is found in the same scene with different data-acquiring methods. Also, since they are distinctive, they are very useful for achieving

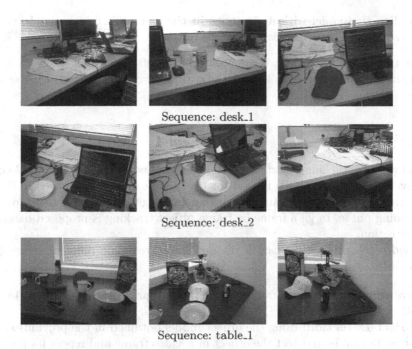

Sequence: desk_1

Sequence: desk_2

Sequence: table_1

Fig. 1. Example frames taken from the sequences of the dataset.

bowl_2_2   cap_1_4   cereal_box_4_1   coffe_mug_1   soda_can_6

Fig. 2. Object models built from partial views.

an effective recognition. This point selection can be done using a keypoint detector, or by simply subsampling the points and using the resulting sub-sampled set as keypoints. In this work, we use subsampling every 1 cm for the model and the scene.

2. **Descriptor Generation:** for each keypoint in the model and the scene, RGB-D descriptors are computed, representing object's information in a distinctive and meaningful way. In our work, we use SI, CSHOT and ECV, described in Section 2.1.

3. **Matching:** descriptors computed for the model and the scene are compared in order to establish associations between them. A match between a pair of descriptors can translate into a match between the corresponding points. Point matches can then be used to determine the roto-translation needed

to align the model with its instance in the scene. To find a match, vector distances are used, such as $\mathcal{L}_1$ and $\mathcal{L}_2$ norms.

For the matching stage, we compare all pair of descriptors using $\mathcal{L}_1$ norm and then we impose a threshold over the ratio between the first and the second nearest match.

5   Tracking

Several ways of tracking objects in 3D images are known. In [10] the well known Iterative Closest Point (ICP) is used for this goal, originally proposed in [12,2]. Then, they improve the obtained results using edge information taken during the training phase. In [5] a frame by frame object tracking is proposed based on edge detection.

A video tracking system can be divided into three main different stages (see Figure 3b):

1. **Training:** consists in obtaining a model or representation of the object to follow.
2. **Object Detection:** using the object model obtained in the previous stage, the main goal is to detect the object in a video frame and report its position in a previously defined coordinate system. It is used as a starting point in the video tracking system and when frame by frame tracking fails.
3. **Tracking:** using the object location in the previous frame, the goal is to track the object frame to frame. This is the most important stage because it is used in most of the video frames. The efficiency of this method will determine the system efficiency.

We use this pipeline because it allows us to test different methods for each stage without much effort and is a modular way of treating the tracking problem.

We choose different methods for each of the proposed stages. First, we reconstruct a complete 3D model of the object to track merging several views of it taken from different angles and all around of it, using an ICP based method. Reconstructions obtained using this method are then improved manually. Figure 2 shows an example of some of the constructed models in the dataset.

Once the model is built, we use the method explained in Section 4 to detect it in the first frame of the scene. Once a matching between the model and the scene is found, we use a KD-Tree to filter the nearest object points from the scene's point cloud. The points obtained by this filter are then used as the model to track in the next stage. This is done to increase robustness in tracking.

The most important features of the tracking stage are efficiency and robustness. The selected method needs to be computationally efficient because the system needs to be fast. Thus, it has to be robust because otherwise we will need to use the object detection method and that would be time consuming, losing the overall efficiency.

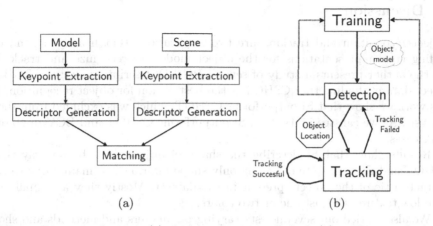

Fig. 3. Diagrams showing: (a) object recognition method, (b) tracking method.

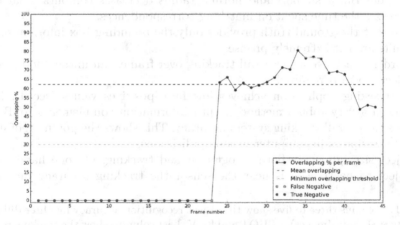

Fig. 4. Frame by frame overlapping analysis. Object: coffee_mug_5. Scene: desk_1. The object to track shows up at frame 24.

In order to have an efficient method to track objects frame by frame it is natural to think of an ICP based method. To apply this method, we take the result from the object recognition stage and take a bounding box twice as big as the detected one. Then apply ICP between this two point clouds. If there is no match, we go back to the previous stage and apply object detection. Otherwise, if a match is found, we filter scene points using a KD-Tree as mentioned before and continue tracking.

In Figure 4, we show an analysis frame by frame of tracked object. We extract the object's bounding box and then compute the overlap between the ground truth bounding box. In order to measure the quality of the computed object area of our method we use a formula taken from [6]. This measure punishes reported areas smaller than or bigger than the ground truth area. We show how our method obtains a mean percentage overlapping of 62.34% in this example.

6   Discussion

Object recognition and tracking are two applications that heavily depend on finding good representations for the object models to recognize and track. In [1], the author presents a study of several RGB-D descriptors over the RGB-D object dataset, finding that CSHOT is the best option for object recognition. In this work we show that SI outperforms CSHOT, which was excluded from their analysis. As we can see in Table 1, SI outperforms CSHOT and ECV in 10 out of 12 cases.

Results show that SI describe the shape of objects in a better way than CSHOT and ECV in spite of having only shape information, mainly due to the characteristic of the objects present in the dataset. Mostly they are small and have low texture, i.e. just one or two colors.

We also carried out several tests varying parameters and methods and show that subsampling is faster than using Harris detector over point clouds. Also, reducing descriptor support and normal radius decreases computational time but increases the time spent on matching correspondences.

Note that the ground truth provides only the bounding box information, so the results are not extremely precise.

In order to achieve a successful tracking over frames, an initial good pose of the object model is required.

Our tracking application achieves low false positives values (see Table 1) resulting in a very robust method. Depth information complements RGB and improves the overall tracking system accuracy. This shows the potential of using RGB-D descriptors in computer vision applications.

Object size influences both recognition and tracking. On one hand, when the object to be tracked is near the sensor the tracking accuracy increases.

Table 1. Columns three to five show the object recognition accuracy for three different descriptors SI (Spin-Images), CSHOT and ECV. Last columns show the tracking results (Tracking Accuracy) and false positive rate (% FP).

Object	Scene	Recognition			Tracking	
		SI	CSHOT	ECV	Accuracy	% FP
cap_4	desk_1	**93.90**	81.71	80.89	97.73	0.00
coffee_mug_5	desk_1	**93.18**	**93.18**	87.12	19.51	40.24
soda_can_6	desk_1	**91.67**	78.33	50.00	58.33	0.00
bowl_3	desk_2	**73.13**	**73.13**	59.38	66.88	3.13
soda_can_4	desk_2	**66.03**	53.85	27.88	19.87	30.13
bowl_2	table_1	**89.91**	86.24	65.14	36.90	0.00
cap_1	table_1	**95.26**	59.48	50.86	55.83	3.07
cap_4	table_1	**70.62**	68.04	47.42	76.61	0.00
cereal_box_4	table_1	81.09	**91.18**	54.58	70.93	2.33
coffee_mug_1	table_1	**44.05**	**44.05**	54.76	48.97	5.15
coffee_mug_4	table_1	**68.10**	65.03	43.56	53.36	0.00
soda_can_4	table_1	46.15	**49.45**	34.07	32.97	9.89

On the other, when the object appears small in the captured image it contains less points to be used for recognition and tracking; less points translates into less discriminative power.

Besides the analysis of the computational performance was not the main focus of this work we found that working with point clouds acquired from commercial RGB-D sensors is mandatory to tune methods and theirs parameters to deal with the noise present in RGB and specially in depth data.

7 Conclusions

Based on our empirical evaluation we showed that shape it is the most important cue for recognizing and tracking 3D objects. Texture plays an important role when objects are large or have simple structure.

In particular, objects from the RGB-D database [8] tend to have very low texture, just one or two colors, making it necessary to have a descriptor that focuses more on the shape of the objects. Our results showed that SI perform better than CSHOT and ECV in spite of having only shape information.

Also, we observed that RGB-D descriptors that work well with object recognition not necessary perform in the same way in a tracking application.

In order to achieve robust tracking we saw that a good initial pose is required and a good object model for the detection phase.

References

1. Alexandre, L.A.: 3D descriptors for object and category recognition: a comparative evaluation. In: IEEE/SRJ Int. Conf. on Intelligent Robots and Systems (IROS), Workshop on Color-Depth Camera Fusion (2012)
2. Besl, P., McKay, N.D.: A method for registration of 3-d shapes. IEEE Trans. on Pattern Analysis and Machine Intelligence 14(2), 239–256 (1992)
3. Bo, L., Ren, X., Fox, D.: Depth kernel descriptors for object recognition. In: Intelligent Robots and Systems (IROS), Int. Conf. on. pp. 821–826 (2011)
4. Buch, A.G., Kraft, D., Kamarainen, J.K., Petersen, H.G., Kruger, N.: Pose estimation using local structure specific shape and appearance context. In: Int. Conf. Robotics and Automation (ICRA), pp. 2080–2087 (2013)
5. Drummond, T., Cipolla, R.: Real-time tracking of complex structures with on-line camera calibration. In: BMVC, pp. 1–10 (1999)
6. Everingham, M., Van Gool, L., Williams, C.K., Winn, J., Zisserman, A.: The pascal visual object classes (voc) challenge. Int. Jour. of Computer Vision 88(2), 303–338 (2010)
7. Johnson, A.E., Hebert, M.: Using spin images for efficient object recognition in cluttered 3D scenes. IEEE Trans. on Pattern Analysis and Machine Intelligence 21(5), 433–449 (1999)
8. Lai, K., Bo, L., Ren, X., Fox, D.: A large-scale hierarchical multi-view rgb-d object dataset. In: 2011 IEEE International Conference on Robotics and Automation (ICRA), pp. 1817–1824 (2011)

9. Nascimento, E.R., Oliveira, G.L., Campos, M.F.M., Vieira, A.W., Schwartz, W.R.: Brand: A robust appearance and depth descriptor for rgb-d images. In: Int. Conf. on. Intelligent Robots and Systems (IROS), pp. 1720–1726 (2012)

10. Park, Y., Lepetit, V., Woo, W.: Texture-less object tracking with online training using an rgb-d camera. In: Int. Symp. Mixed and Augmented Reality (ISMAR), pp. 121–126 (2011)

11. Tombari, F., Salti, S., Di Stefano, L.: Unique signatures of histograms for local surface description. In: Daniilidis, K., Maragos, P., Paragios, N. (eds.) ECCV 2010, Part III. LNCS, vol. 6313, pp. 356–369. Springer, Heidelberg (2010)

12. Zhang, Z.: Iterative point matching for registration of free-form curves and surfaces. International Journal of Computer Vision 13(2), 119–152 (1994)

Gesture Recogntion

Fast and Accurate Gesture Recognition Based on Motion Shapes

Thierry Moreira[1], Marlon Alcantara[1], Helio Pedrini[1(✉)], and David Menotti[2]

[1] Institute of Computing, University of Campinas,
Campinas, SP 13083-852, Brazil
helio@ic.unicamp.br
[2] Department of Informatics, Federal University of Paraná,
Curitiba, PR 81531-980, Brazil

Abstract. As in many other computer vision applications, the large amount of data is an inherent problem in video gesture recognition. A challenging task is to maintain a suitable trade-off between time and accuracy aiming a solution meeting certain requirements and constraints. In this paper, we propose a simple and fast gesture recognition approach that extracts meaningful and discriminative descriptors from hand gesture videos. Experiments conducted on the Sheffield Kinect Gestures (SKIG) data set show that our method achieves competitive accuracies, while processing frames at frequencies higher than those required for real-time applications.

Keywords: Gesture recognition · Image classification · Motion shapes · Feature descriptor · Video cameras

1 Introduction

The automatic gesture recognition field is associated with communication between humans and computers. Gesture, however, can be considered a broad concept, once it may involve hand, head, body, leg, or eye movements, facial expressions, blinks and winks [11]. Each application has different demands and challenges.

Arm and body gestures have received attention [3,13] to allow the development of intelligent interfaces for devices equipped with cameras, which are becoming increasingly popular. Stereo camera devices, such as Microsoft's Kinect that provides RGB-D images, have made this task easier, encouraging research in the area [8].

Some methods search for exploring RGB-D images to their maximum by fusing information on both images. The work described in [10] learns the feature extraction pipeline with graph-based genetic programming (RGGP). The method developed in [4] uses hierarchical feature extraction to compute a similarity measure between gestures and apply it on distance-based classifiers. In [14], the authors apply incremental training to 3DHOF and GHOG features [6] in order to enhance classification accuracy and enable it to online learning.

© Springer International Publishing Switzerland 2015
A. Pardo and J. Kittler (Eds.): CIARP 2015, LNCS 9423, pp. 247–254, 2015.
DOI: 10.1007/978-3-319-25751-8_30

Other methods use only depth data, under the principle that the actor's geometry – in this case, carrying some 3D information – is enough to learn the gestures. This is the case of the work proposed in [5]. Local descriptors are extracted from each pixel of the depth map volume (a 4-dimensional shape), encoding low-level information, such as first and second derivatives, gradients and curvatures. Covariance matrices are used as descriptors, as they carry feature variations and are low-dimensional.

Furthermore, conventional monocular vision algorithms can be applied to stereo vision data sets, ignoring depth data. In [2], the authors apply imprecise hidden Markov models (IHMM) to time series. Distance metrics on mixture pairs are used to measure the dissimilarity between two video sequences.

This paper extends upon the method described in [1,12] to a new domain: gesture recognition. The method has shown good results on human action recognition data sets. It uses depth data to produce shape signatures based on extreme point positions with enough discrimination power to achieve accuracy comparable to state-of-the-art methods, while consuming very little processing time to perform it. Furthermore, our approach contributes with a suitable cost-benefit ratio in terms of time and precision.

This paper is organized as follows. Section 2 explains our gesture recognition methodology. Section 3 presents the results obtained applying it to the SKIG public data set and details the computational environment and the used parameters. Section 4 concludes the paper and include some directions for future work.

2   Proposed Method

Our methodology is composed of the stages illustrated in Fig. 1, extending the approaches developed in [1,12]. Each stage of the pipeline, marked with a letter from (a) to (e), is explained as follows.

First, motion segmentation is applied to the original videos. Ideally, this stage should output a set of silhouettes, however, it often results in unintelligible

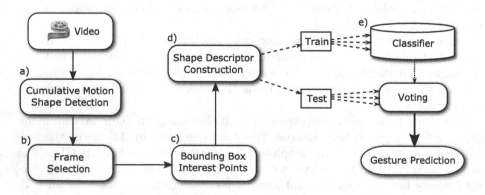

Fig. 1. Diagram illustrating the main stages of the proposed methodology.

broken shapes in real scenarios. This is why we call them *motion shapes*, such that errors and missegmentations are accepted.

To fix some of the resulting artifacts, morphological operations are applied [7]. First, a morphological closing with a 3×3 structuring element is used to join broken parts. Then, an area opening is applied to remove small and/or noisy objects that usually result from small changes in lighting, background movement and noise. The threshold area was experimentally chosen as $1/360$ of the total image area.

After the aforementioned steps, the Cumulative Motion Shapes (CMS) [12] are computed (Fig. 1(a)). CMSs are constructed by means of sliding windows on the temporal dimension of the video volume. For each time window, the processed motion shapes are joined. This is performed as a union set, so that the CMS for the k-th frame of a video sequence is given as

$$\text{CMS}_k = \bigcup_{i=k-n}^{k} S_i, \tag{1}$$

where n is the size of the sliding window and S_i is the motion shape of the i-th frame. Fig. 2 illustrates this process. Images from Fig. 2(a) to Fig. 2(d) show the result of the discussed morphological operations on foreground masks. The arms are hollow since frame difference was used to extract them. Fig. 2(e) shows the constructed CMS from these other frames.

The purpose of CMS is to add temporal motion information, while keeping the representation simple and without raising dimensionality. The CMS can join broken parts of segmented foreground, creating a meaningful shape. It makes silhouette-based methods more robust to problems found in the segmentation process.

The next step, corresponding to Fig. 1(b), consists of excluding faulty frames. Dealing with noise is a difficult task: although some artefacts can be treated with morphological operations, meaningless information is still obtained. A frame is discarded if it fits into one of these criteria: (i) if there is little movement or no movement at all; a threshold is defined to filter small portions of movement; and (ii) if the bounding boxes touch the borders of the frame; this usually indicates

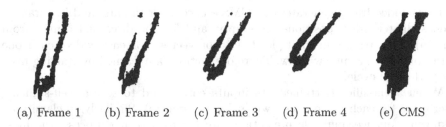

(a) Frame 1   (b) Frame 2   (c) Frame 3   (d) Frame 4   (e) CMS

Fig. 2. CMS construction: (a)-(d) Examples of extracted foreground from the cross action from SKIG [10] data set; (e) CMS from joining previous images.

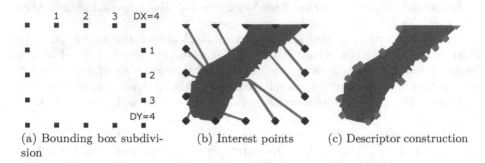

(a) Bounding box subdivision (b) Interest points (c) Descriptor construction

Fig. 3. (a) Control points are defined as equally spaced points along the bounding box. The number of control point divisions in the x and y axes are denoted DX and DY, respectively; (b) characterization of the interest points by the nearest distances to the CMS contour for each control point – this example has 20 interest points; (c) construction of the descriptor from the normalized coordinates of the interest points.

that only a part of the person is visible, and partial information would undermine the training.

Interest points are selected, in step (c) (Fig. 1), as prominent parts of the CMS. These points are found through control points over the bounding box shape, that is, the smallest rectangle that comprises the entire shape, as shown in Fig. 3(a). Control points are equally spaced along the bounding box sides. For each control point, the nearest point to the CMS contour is selected as an interest point, as Fig. 3(b) illustrates. The number of key points can be parameterized.

The descriptor construction (Fig. 1(d)) is performed as follows (Fig. 3(c)):

1. the centroid of the shape is determined as the center of the bounding box;
2. the centroid is assigned as the origin and a coordinate system is created and normalized in relation to the borders of the box, so that the values range from −1 to 1;
3. each point is positioned in the new coordinate system;
4. the final descriptor vector is obtained by concatenating the coordinates of all interest points.

Every video frame generates one CMS – except for the first and last frames, when sliding window positions are empty, and for the discarded frames from step (b). This results in multiple descriptor vectors for each video, each one corresponding to a time window. Therefore, actions are learned by starting from any part of its cycle.

When a classifier is trained, its inputs correspond to several self-sufficing descriptors for each video, as shown in Fig. 1, step (e). Similarly to classify an unknown sequence, multiple predictions are fed to a voting process: the most voted class is chosen. To avoid overpopulating classifiers, a parameterized number of equally spaced samples are selected.

3   Experiments

In this section, we evaluate our method on a public gesture data set and present the results, as well as implementation details such as software libraries and parameters.

The experiments were conducted on the Sheffield KInect Gesture (SKIG) data set [10], which consists of 10 action categories, performed by 6 actors, on 3 hand poses, 3 backgrounds and 2 illumination conditions. This results in 1080 videos. Each video sequence is available as a set of RBG color images and depth maps. The images were acquired with the Microsoft Kinect sensor.

The gestures present in the data set include: circle (clockwise), triangle (anti-clockwise), up-down, right-left, wave, "Z", cross, come here, turn-around and pat. These gestures are illustrated in Figure 4, where color images with arrows to assist understanding are shown on the top row and depth maps on the bottom row.

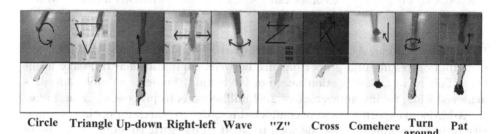

| Circle | Triangle | Up-down | Right-left | Wave | "Z" | Cross | Comehere | Turn around | Pat |

Fig. 4. Samples from each gesture class of SKIG data set. Color images (with arrows indicating the gesture) on the top row and depth maps on the bottom row. Extracted from [10].

The feature extraction module was written in C/C++ programming language using OpenCV (library version 2.4.9). The classification module was written in Python 2.7.6 using the SciKit-Learn package (version 0.15.2), which includes implementation for several classification machines and cross-validation functionalities.

According to the experimental protocol described in [10], we performed a 3-fold cross-validation set up. The data was evaluated through two classification machines: Support Vector Machines (SVM) and K-nearest neighbors (K-NN).

Table 1 shows the feature extraction speed (in frames per second - FPS), the average classification time for a single video (in milliseconds) and the accuracy rates for SVM and K-NN (in percentage). It can be seen that the feature extraction time is very low, allowing for the method to work in real case scenarios, where computational time is an important factor. Time measures correspond to an average of runs. The experiments were conducted in a 2.4GHz Intel i7 processor using no parallelism resources.

Our method achieves 93.52% accuracy using only depth map images, surpassing the baseline results of 76.1% on the depth images, and 88.7% on a color/depth

Table 1. Accuracy rates (in percentage), average feature extraction speed (in frames per second) and average classification time (in milliseconds) for SKIG data set. All time measurements were obtained from an average on five runs.

Approach	Measurements	Results	
Proposed	Feature extraction speed (FPS)		354.37
	Classification time (ms)	SVM	20.80
		KNN	12.70
	Accuracy rate (%)	SVM	93.52
		KNN	91.30
RGGP [10]	Accuracy rate (%)	Depth only	76.1
		RGB-D fusion	88.7
Hierarchical model [4]	Accuracy rate (%)	Depth only	91.3
		RGB-D fusion	91.9
IHMM [2]	Accuracy rate (%)	RGB only	92.8
ABACOC [14]	Accuracy rate (%)	RGB-D fusion	97.5

fusion classification. Although state-of-the-art methods overcome this rate, our contribution results in a proper balance between computational time and accuracy. This correct classification rate, not far behind the best available values, is achieved while taking an average of 2.82 milliseconds to process a single frame.

Additional experiments were conducted in order to search for optimum quantity of interest points. It was decided to set it to 64, with 16 along each side of the bounding box. As each point contributes with 2-dimensional coordinates, the descriptor size is 128. To reduce it, extracting the most discriminative dimensions, principal component analysis (PCA) [9] is applied to the data, keeping 50 dimensions. This value was able to keep the dimensionality low, while still keeping the descriptor discriminative.

Furthermore, since it was observed that the use of many frames would add confusion and redundancy to the classification process, thirty equally spaced samples were taken from each video. This value was also determined empirically.

The sliding window size is the most decisive descriptor parameter. Short gestures require small windows, whereas longer gestures require larger windows. A grid search showed that the best window size for SKIG data set is 25 frames.

Parameter grid searches were run for both SVM and K-NN classifiers. The best results using SVM were on RBF kernels for C and Gamma equal to 100 and 0.1, respectively. These parameters were consistently the best configuration, even changing the number of interest points and number of sample frames. The behavior for the K-NN parameter was not so constant, where its value for the best run was 5.

Figure 5 shows the confusion matrix of the SVM best result, as shown in Table 1. The cell with the highest misclassification is the Pat action, predicted as Up-Down. They are similar actions, both involving hand movements up and down.

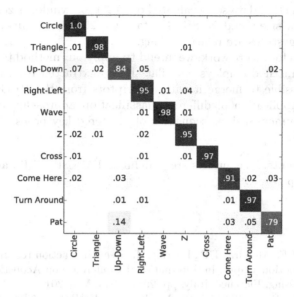

Fig. 5. Confusion matrix for the best result (accuracy of 93.52%) using SVM classifier.

4   Conclusions

This work describes and evaluates a gesture recognition method. The descriptor, originally constructed to represent entire human shapes for action detection [12], demonstrated to be effective on hand movements.

The proposed gesture recognition method shares some common characteristics with other domains, for instance, object detection and activity recognition. Its feature vector has low dimensionality and can be computed in real time. Furthermore, it has enough discriminative power to be competitive with state-of-the-art methods in terms of accuracy.

The most challenging task for shape-based methods is the foreground segmentation. This is mitigated by grouping several frames into one sliding window, which we refer to as cumulative motion shapes (CMS). It is particularly easier for gesture recognition, since it is often done in closed scenes, with one person interacting with the machine. The Kinect sensor also facilitates the task by making depth maps and people detection available.

Experiments showed that the method achieved 93.52% accuracy on SKIG public dataset, while extracting descriptor vectors at an average of 354.37 FPS. These results represent an alternative on the trade-off problem between accuracy and processing time.

Training a classifier with several descriptors for each video allows for the method to detect a gesture in any of its stage, instead of having to wait for it to complete a sequence of states or for an initial pose.

Most of the action data sets evaluated on [12] took window sizes of 12 or less. The best window size found for SKIG data set is 25. This occurs since the time periods for the gestures are relatively long.

As directions for future work, we intend to apply our method to other gesture data sets. Our method employs only flat shapes extracted from depth images. It would be possible to merge it with descriptors from the RBG images. Furthermore, the application of different classification approaches could improve the method accuracy, such as sequences of clustered key poses or probabilistic techniques.

Acknowledgements. The authors are grateful to FAPESP, CNPq and CAPES for their financial support.

References

1. Alcântara, M.F., Moreira, T.P., Pedrini, H.: Real-time action recognition based on cumulative motion shapes. In: International Conference on Acoustics, Speech and Signal Processing, Florence, Italy, pp. 2941–2945, May 2014
2. Antonucci, A., Rosa, R.D., Giusti, A., Cuzzolin, F.: Robust Classification of Multivariate Time Series by Imprecise Hidden Markov Models. International Journal of Approximate Reasoning **56**(Part B), 249–263 (2015)
3. Chaudhary, A., Raheja, J.L., Das, K., Raheja, S.: Intelligent Approaches to Interact with Machines using Hand Gesture Recognition in Natural Way: A Survey. CoRR abs/1303.2292 (2013)
4. Choi, H., Park, H.: A hierarchical structure for gesture recognition using RGB-D sensor. In: Int. Conf. on Human-Agent Interaction, pp. 265–268 (2014)
5. Cirujeda, P., Binefa, X.: 4DCov: a nested covariance descriptor of spatio-temporal features for gesture recognition in depth sequences. In: International Conference on 3D Vision, vol. 1, pp. 657–664, December 2014
6. Fanello, S.R., Gori, I., Metta, G., Odone, F.: Keep It Simple and Sparse: Real-time Action Recognition. Journal Machine Learning Research **14**(1), 2617–2640 (2013)
7. Gonzalez, R.C., Woods, R.E.: Digital Image Processing, 3rd edn. Addison-Wesley Longman Publishing Co. Inc., Boston (2007)
8. Han, J., Shao, L., Xu, D., Shotton, J.: Enhanced Computer Vision With Microsoft Kinect Sensor: A Review. IEEE Trans. on Cybernetics **43**(5), 1318–1334 (2013)
9. Jolliffe, I.: Principal Component Analysis. Springer, 2nd edn. (2002)
10. Liu, L., Shao, L.: Learning discriminative representations from RGB-D video data. In: Int. Joint Conf. on Artificial Intelligence, pp. 1493–1500 (2013)
11. Mitra, S., Acharya, T.: Gesture Recognition: A Survey. IEEE Trans. on Systems, Man, and Cybernetics, Part C: Applications and Reviews **37**(3), 311–324 (2007)
12. Moreira, T.: Real-Time Human Action Recognition Based on Motion Shapes. Master's thesis, Institute of Computing, University of Campinas, April 2014
13. Rautaray, S., Agrawal, A.: Vision based Hand Gesture Recognition for Human Computer Interaction: A Survey. Artificial Intelligence Review **43**(1), 1–54 (2015)
14. Rosa, R.D., et al.: Online action recognition via nonparametric incremental learning. In: British Machine Vision Conference (2014)

Recognition of Facial Expressions
Based on Deep Conspicuous Net

João Paulo Canário$^{(\boxtimes)}$ and Luciano Oliveira

Intelligent Vision Research Lab, Federal University of Bahia,
UFBA, Salvador, Brazil
jopacanario@gmail.com, lreboucas@ufba.br
http://www.ivisionlab.eng.ufba.br/

Abstract. Facial expression has an important role in human interaction and non-verbal communication. Hence more and more applications, which automatically detect facial expressions, start to be pervasive in various fields, such as education, entertainment, psychology, human-computer interaction, behavior monitoring, just to cite a few. In this paper, we present a new approach for facial expression recognition using a so-called deep conspicuous neural network. The proposed method builds a conspicuous map of region faces, training it via a deep network. Experimental results achieved an average accuracy of 90% over the extended Cohn-Kanade data set for seven basic expressions, demonstrating the best performance against four state-of-the-art methods.

Keywords: Conspicuity · Facial expression · Deep learning

1 Introduction

Non-verbal language can be highlighted as one of the first forms of human communication, and consequently a source of countless studies in science. Particularly, facial expression is one of the most powerful, immediate and natural non-verbal ways that humans can use to transmit their emotions and intentions [2]. Also, face is able to express emotions so soon as a person can speak or perceive his/her feelings [5].

Adopting Charles Darwin's starting premise [1], which stated that the mammals understand and show their emotions from a set of facial expressions, Ekman and Friesen [4] initially suggested that there exist six primary emotions plus neutral (e.g, happy, sadness, fear, disgust, surprise and anger), with each one of them having singular and universal facial expressions and characteristics; later, they have also included contempt as a primary expression [8].

In contrast with facial expression recognition, emotion recognition is a pure interpretation of the expression, and it frequently demands a comprehension of a given situation, along with the evaluation of all contextual information surrounding [3]. With that in mind, some research areas, such as affective computing, try to give to computers the ability to recognize and feel emotions. In the near

© Springer International Publishing Switzerland 2015
A. Pardo and J. Kittler (Eds.): CIARP 2015, LNCS 9423, pp. 255–262, 2015.
DOI: 10.1007/978-3-319-25751-8_31

future, it may be possible to give more particular, natural and proper guidance to end-users in the human-computer interaction [6].

Nowadays, starting from facial expression detection to ultimately accomplish emotion recognition, some works have been achieving high accuracy. Chew et al. [9] explored a person-independent system using constrained local models (CLM) to highlight the face shape and recognize facial expression by using local binary pattern (LBP) descriptor with an SVM classifier. Lee and Chellappa [10] introduced a framework for facial motion modeling; they represented the faces as a sparse localized motion dictionaries obtained by a motion flow estimation, which were then classified by an nearest neighborhood (NN) classifier. Nie, Wang and Ji [11] have dealt with facial expression recognition by means of a type of classification problem over multi-dimensional sequence data; they extracted spatio-temporal patterns in high-dimensional motion data using an improved restricted Boltzmann machine (RBM), where pairwise potential energy functions were used; the main goal was to break the assumption of the input data dependence by means of a standard RBM model. Shojaeilangari et al. [12] introduced a histogram of local phase and local orientation of gradients achieved from a sequence of face images, as a descriptor of facial expressions.

Differently from the other works, we propose a method that combine conspicuous maps representation (addressed in Section 2.1), and a deep learning approach to classify that conspicuous regions, as described in Section 2.2. The conspicuous maps highlight the most salient areas of the face, avoiding the classification of unnecessary areas of the face that does not influence on the facial expression (*e.g.*, ears, top of the head and hairs). The convolutional neural network (CNN) helps to learn different high-level features (over the eyes, mouth and nose). This is so, since the deep net can locally sharing weights at high layers providing a greater abstraction power. To assess the performance of the proposed method, the extended Cohn-Kanade (CK+) data set [17] was used as a referential comparison. Over that data set, our method achieved the best performance when compared against four state-of-the-art works [9] [10] [11] [12], reaching an average accuracy of 90%, considering all the expressions.

This paper is structured as follows: In Section 2, our proposed method is described. Section 3 presents the experimental results. Finally, Section 4 draws the conclusions, as well as, suggestions for future works.

2   On Deeply Learning Facial Expressions

2.1   Conspicuity Maps

An object is more usually noticed in a scene based on their behavioral relevance. In case of the facial expressions, the regions that are capable to draw more visual attention are in the t-region of the face (eyes and nose), which ultimately highlight most of the facial movements to be analyzed. To detect the salient regions of the face, similarly to the way to achieve the intense maps in [18], the input image I is progressively downsampled using a Gaussian pyramid [19], which consists of low-pass filtering and sub-sampling versions of the input image, in eight octaves σ. From the Gaussian pyramid, each feature is computed by a set of linear "center-surround" differences, denoted as $\ominus$, and they are implemented in the model, as the difference between fine and coarse scales, whose center is a pixel at scale $c \in \{2, 3, 4\}$, and the surrounding is the corresponding pixel at scale $s = c + \delta$, where $\delta \in \{3, 4\}$. The referred differences are computed in a set of six maps, given by

$$\mathcal{I}(c, s) = \mid I(c) \ominus I(s) \mid . \tag{1}$$

The conspicuity map $\overline{\mathcal{I}}$ is obtained by a cross-scale addition, "$\oplus$", which works by reducing each map to scale 4 and point-by-point addition, according

$$\overline{\mathcal{I}} = \bigoplus_{c=2}^{4} \bigoplus_{s=c+3}^{c+4} \mathcal{N}(\mathcal{I}(c, s)). \tag{2}$$

A normalizing operator $\mathcal{N}(.)$ is used to globally promotes maps where a small number of strong peaks of activity – conspicuous locations – is presented, while globally suppresses maps, which contain numerous comparable peak responses. The normalizing operation consists of: (i) Normalizing the values in the map to a fixed range $[0..M]$, in order to eliminate modality-dependent amplitude differences; (ii) finding the location of the map's global maximum M and computing the average $\overline{m}$ of all its other local maxima; and (iii) globally multiplying the map by $(M - m^2)$. After that, a fixed threshold defined empirically is applied in the map in order to create a binary mask; this binary image finally highlight the salient regions (refer to Fig. 1 for visual examples of the method steps).

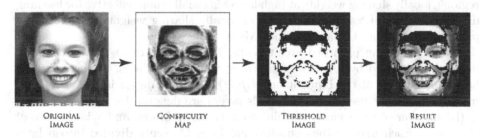

ORIGINAL IMAGE   CONSPICUITY MAP   THRESHOLD IMAGE   RESULT IMAGE

Fig. 1. Generation of the conspicuity regions. Left to right: First image is the original image after alignment, cropping and color normalization. Second image is the generated conspicuity map of the face. Third image is the thresholded image and, finally, the fourth image is the image only with the most salient facial regions.

2.2 Deep Learning

Deep learning can be described as a learning experience at various levels of representation, corresponding to different levels of abstractions. To consider a neural network deep, it is necessary that the input of the deep network pass through several non-linearity filters before being output.

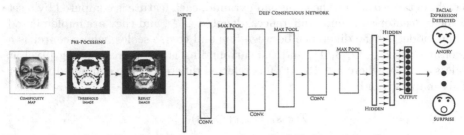

Fig. 2. General architecture of the proposed method. Left to right: Conspicuous map representation and the architecture of the deep CNN.

In this paper, we focus on combining a strategy of a salience map and a deep convolution network. The proposed method is based on a coarse-to-fine approach, by considering the conspicuous maps, the three convolution layers followed by max pooling, two hidden layers fully connected and one output layer, also fully connected, with eight possible outputs, as illustrated on Fig. 2.

Some important aspects of the network architecture have been taken into consideration. First, predicting an expression valence from large input regions is a high-level task. So, because deeper structures help to form high-level information, our convolution networks should be deep, as well. Second, since deep structures tend to be very hard to train, and to obtain performance improvement, the network should locally share weights of neurons. On the other hand, globally sharing weights does not work well on images with fixed spatial layout, such as faces; once eyes and mouth may share low-level features, they are very different at high-level. This way, for networks whose inputs contain different semantic regions, locally sharing weights at high layers is usually more effective for learning different high-level features. The idea of locally sharing weights was originally proposed by Huang, Lee and Learned-Miller [16].

Considering the proposed architecture, the input layer of the deep neural network is denoted by a vector of size hxw where h and w is, respectively, the height and width of the input image $I(h,w)$. Also, the input is 2D since color information is not used. Convolutionals layers are denoted by $C(f, s)$, where f is the number of the square convolution kernels, or filters, and s is the size of the filters. Each map in the convolutional layer is evenly divided into p by q regions, and weights are locally shared in each region. Pooling layer is denoted as $P(ds)$. The parameter ds is the size of the square pooling regions, which are not overlapped. The fully connected layers are denoted as $F(n)$, where n is the number of nodes at the current layer.

2.3   Deep Conpiscuous Neural Net

Before training the convolutional neural network with the data set images, all images were pre-processed. The preprocessing module in Fig. 1 illustrates all steps described below

1. First all the faces images were aligned and cropped to 380x380 pixel wide.
2. Second image normalization was made with a contrast filter and grey-level transformation for those images that were not already in grey-level, yet.
3. Finally, the salient regions of face are obtained by computing conspicuity maps, described in Section 2.1, over each training image.

After the preprocessing phase, the images with salient regions are used to train the deep neural network, and for training validation a stratified K-Folds cross, where the number of folds is equals to 3, is used.

In our work, we evaluate two different deep neural network architectures: (i) The first one is so-called Deep conspicuous network (DCN), built on three convolutional layers and two fully connected layers; each convolutional layer is followed by a 2x2 max-pooling layer; starting with 32 convolutional filters, this number is doubled with every convolutional layer, which has 3x3 and 2x2 filters. The fully connected hidden layers have 500 units and a output layer is a full connected layer with eight possible outputs (one for each detected expression plus neutral). Figure 2 depicts an overview of our system using the DCN approach. (ii) The second architecture evolved from this first one, and it was coined as dropout DDCN (DDCN); in that second architecture, we increased the number of units of the fully connected hidden layers from 500 to 1000 units; also the learning rate and momentum overtime were changed during the training, after Sutskever et al. [14]; dropout layers were added between the existing layers, assigning dropout probabilities to each one of them. Dropout is a popular regularization technique introduced by Hinton et al. [15] to reduce the overfitting on large neural networks.

3 Experimental Results

To assess the performance of the proposed method, we have performed experiments for emotion recognition over the widely adopted CK+ data set [17]. The CK+ facial expression data set is an extension of the original Cohn-Kanade Database [13] and consists in image sequences (frontal view) of 123 students of different ages, gender and ethnicity, performing each one the seven basic facial expressions: Anger – An, Contempt – Co, Disgust – Di, Fear – Fe, Happy – Ha, Sad – Sa and Surprise – Su, plus the Ne – Neutral one. The neutral expression is obtained on the first image of each facial expression sequence and a total of 593 image sequences or 10792 separated images were generated. All images the image were considered, following the same protocol suggested in [17], and followed by all compared works. In the experiments, the CK+ data set was split into random train and test subsets. Four state-of-the-art methods were used to compare the performance of our detector.

According Fig. 3, DCN achieved the following results: Neutral - 93%; Angry 94%; Contempt 82%; Disgust 85%; Fear 92%; Happy 90%; Sadness 96%; Surprise 91%, while, DDCN performance was: Neutral - 93%, Angry 94%; Contempt 88%; Disgust 78%; Fear 92%; Happy 92%; Sadness 97%; Surprise 90%. If keep neutral expressions out, the average accuracy of all the expressions is 90%, which is 2%

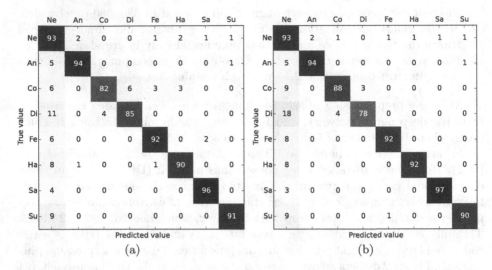

Fig. 3. Confusion matrix of the two trained deep conspicuity facial expression architectures, Fig. (a) represents the DCN architecture, and Fig. (b) represents the DDCN architecture. The analyzed expressions were Neutral – Ne, Anger – An, Contempt – Co, Fear – Fe, Happiness – Ha, Sadness – Sa and Surprise – Su.

Table 1. Classification accuracy (%) of our method and the other four state-of-art approaches, ordered by the average performance. A bold number indicates the best performance method.

Approach	An	Co	Di	Fe	Ha	Sa	Su	Avg.
DCN	94	82	85	**92**	90	96	91	**90**
DDCN	94	**88**	78	**92**	92	**97**	89	**90**
Nie, Wang and Ji [11]	**97**	72	89	84	**100**	78	97	88
Shojaeilangari et al. [12]	90	–	**96**	66	**100**	78	**98**	88
Lee and Chellappa [10]	84	81	89	63	91	80	93	83
Chew et al. [9]	70	52	92	72	94	45	93	74

better than the best state-of-the-art method studied. In Table 1, the comparison of our model with some recent approaches are summarized. Our method reaches the best accuracy on three expressions (contempt, fear and sadness) among all the methods listed. Although our model did not achieve the best accuracy for all expressions, it does not fall behind very much the other detectors.

4   Conclusion

In this paper, we presented a new approach for facial expression recognition called deep conspicuous neural network. The proposed method achieved the best average accuracy of 90% on the CK+ data set, considering seven basic emotions, against four state-of-the-art methods. Our method relied on a salient conspicuous maps classified by a deep neural network.

For that proposed map, we created two model architectures, denoted as DCN and DDCN. Although the average performance of both architecture were the same, it is noteworthy that better results in four expressions (contempt, fear, happy, sadness) were achieved, proving the improvement of DDCN over the DCN. For future work, we are working on a pre-training approach to initialize our network with better epochs, layers and weights. Also, we are exploring the use of concatenated deep network structures that will automatically segment the most conspicuous regions of the face.

References

1. Darwin, C., Ekman, P., Prodger, P.: The Expression of the Emotions in Man and Animals. Oxford University Press, USA (1998)
2. Nakatsu, R., Nicholson, J., Tosa, N.: Emotion recognition and its application to computer agents with spontaneous interactive capabilities. Knowledge-Based Systems **13**, 497–504 (2000)
3. Fasel, B., Luettin, J.: Automatic facial expression analysis: a survey. Pattern Recognition **36**, 259–275 (2003)
4. Ekman, P., Friesen, W.V.: Measuring facial movement. Environmental psychology and nonverbal behavior. Human Sciences Press (1976)
5. Tian, Y.L., Kanade, T., Cohn, J.F.: Recognizing action units for facial expression analysis. IEEE Transactions on Pattern Analysis and Machine Intelligence **23**, 97–115 (2001)
6. Busso, C., Deng, Z., Yildirim, S., Bulut, M., Lee, C.M., Kazemzadeh, A., Lee, S., Neumann, U., Narayanan, S.: Analysis of emotion recognition using facial expressions, speech and multimodal information. In: Proceedings of the 6th International Conference on Multimodal Interfaces, pp. 205–211. ACM (2004)
7. Ekman, P., Friesen, W.V., Ellsworth, P.: Emotion in the human face: Guidelines for research and an integration of findings. Elsevier (2013)
8. Friesen, W.V., Ekman, P.: EMFACS-7: Emotional Facial Action Coding System. Unpublished manuscript, University of California, San Francisco (1983)
9. Chew, S.W., Lucey, P., Lucey, S., Saragih, J., Cohn, J.F., Sridharan, S.: Person-independent facial expression detection using constrained local models. In: IEEE International Conference on Automatic Face & Gesture Recognition and Workshops (FG 2011), pp. 915–920 (2011)
10. Lee, C.S., Chellappa, R.: Sparse localized facial motion dictionary learning for facial expression recognition. In: IEEE International Conference on Acoustics, Speech and Signal Processing (ICASSP), pp. 3548–3552 (2014)
11. Nie, S., Wang, Z., Ji, Q.: A generative restricted boltzmann machine based method for high-dimensional motion data modeling. Computer Vision and Image Understanding (2015)

12. Shojaeilangari, S., Yau, W.Y., Li, J., Teoh, E.K.: Multi-scale Analysis of Local Phase and Local Orientation for Dynamic Facial Expression Recognition. Journal of Multimedia Theory and Application, 1 (2014)
13. Kanade, T., Cohn, J.F., Tian, Y.: Comprehensive database for facial expression analysis. In: Fourth IEEE International Conference on Automatic Face & Gesture Recognition, pp. 46–53 (2000)
14. Sutskever, I., Martens, J., Dahl, G., Hinton, G.E.: On the importance of initialization and momentum in deep learning. In: Proceedings of the 30th International Conference on Machine Learning (ICML 2013), pp. 1139–1147 (2013)
15. Hinton, G.E., Srivastava, N., Krizhevsky, A., Sutskever, I., Salakhutdinov, R.R.: Improving neural networks by preventing co-adaptation of feature detectors. CoRR (2012)
16. Huang, G.B., Lee, H., Learned-Miller, E.: Learning hierarchical representations for face verification with convolutional deep belief networks. In: IEEE Conference on Computer Vision and Pattern Recognition, pp. 2518–2525 (2012)
17. Lucey, P., Cohn, J.F., Kanade, T., Saragih, J., Ambadar, Z., Matthews, I.: The Extended Cohn-Kanade Dataset (CK+): a complete dataset for action unit and emotion-specified expression. In: IEEE Conference on Computer Vision and Pattern Recognition Workshops (CVPRW), pp. 94–101 (2010)
18. Itti, L., Koch, C., Niebur, E.: A model of saliency-based visual attention for rapid scene analysis. IEEE Transactions on Pattern Analysis & Machine Intelligence **20**, 1254–1259 (1998)
19. Greenspan, H., Belongie, S., Goodman, R., Perona, P., Rakshit, S., Anderson, C.H.: Overcomplete steerable pyramid filters and rotation invariance. In: IEEE Conference on Computer Vision and Pattern Recognition, pp. 222–228 (1994)

Facial Expression Recognition with Occlusions Based on Geometric Representation

Jadisha Y. Ramírez Cornejo[1], Helio Pedrini[1]([✉]),
and Francisco Flórez-Revuelta[2]

[1] Institute of Computing, University of Campinas, Campinas, SP 13083-852, Brazil
helio@ic.unicamp.br
[2] Faculty of Science, Engineering and Computing,
Kingston University, Kingston upon Thames KT1 2EE, UK

Abstract. In recent years, emotion recognition based on facial expressions has received increasing attention by the scientific community in several knowledge domains, such as emotional analysis, pattern recognition, behavior prediction, interpersonal relations, human-computer interactions, among others. This work describes an emotion recognition system based on facial expressions robust to occlusions. Initially, the occluded facial expression to be recognized is reconstructed through Robust Principal Component Analysis (RPCA). Then, a fiducial point detection is performed to extract facial expression features, represented by Gabor wavelets and geometric features. The feature vector space is reduced using Principal Component Analysis (PCA) and Linear Discriminant Analysis (LDA). Finally, K-nearest neighbor algorithm (K-NN) and Support Vector Machine (SVM) classifiers are used to recognize the expressions. Three public data sets are used to evaluate our results. The geometric representation achieved high accuracy rates for occluded and non-occluded faces compared to approaches available in the literature.

Keywords: Facial expression · Emotion recognition · Occlusion · Fiducial landmarks

1 Introduction

In recent years, human emotion has been studied in various knowledge fields. Emotion is a physiological reaction or subjective experience of human beings, which can be expressed as facial expressions, body movement, voice intonation, cardiac rhythm, among other forms [13]. However, facial expressions are a universal and non-verbal communication mode that shows emotions in all human beings, which allow to communicate emotional information in an easier, simple and natural way. A facial expression consists of one or more facial musculature movements, which is functionally the same for adults and newborns. Facial expressions are independent on culture, gender and age. Furthermore, there is strong evidence of universal facial expressions for seven emotions: anger, contempt, disgust, fear, happiness, sadness and surprise [3].

© Springer International Publishing Switzerland 2015
A. Pardo and J. Kittler (Eds.): CIARP 2015, LNCS 9423, pp. 263–270, 2015.
DOI: 10.1007/978-3-319-25751-8_32

Research has recently been conducted to develop robust devices that can help to understand emotions and moods of human beings. Furthermore, investigations are carried out to apply these devices in the development of automated tools for behavioral research, airport security, video surveillance systems, aggression detector for CCTV, on-board emotion detector for drivers. Therefore, facial expression recognition plays an important role for affective computing research.

Facial expression recognition can be categorized into two major approaches: frame-based and sequence-based. The former recognizes facial expressions from a single image frame, whereas the latter is based on recognition over an image sequence, taking into account temporal information [13], such as skin color changes, facial muscle movement, head movement, among other factors.

Automatic facial expression recognition systems usually involve three main stages: facial detection, facial expression feature extraction and representation, and expression recognition. A persistent problem on developing facial expression recognition systems is that most of them are based on image collections that do not reflect real and natural scenes. Besides, the majority of them do not deal with occlusions caused by sunglasses, hats, scarves, beard, etc. The omission of these factors during the training stage could affect facial expression recognition accuracy.

In this paper, we propose a novel and effective methodology for facial expression recognition robust to occlusions. The approach is composed of five stages. The first one consists on performing the occluded facial expression reconstruction using the Dual Algorithm, which is based on RPCA principles [4]. The second step resides on detecting the facial fiducial points automatically. The third phase consists on extracting two types of features: Gabor wavelets and geometric representations. The next step performs a feature reduction through PCA and LDA. The latter phase aims to recognize occluded facial expressions using K-NN and SVM classifiers.

Our approach achieved high recognition accuracy rates for occluded and non-occluded images on three data sets, using a geometric representation. The results obtained with the proposed method were compared against other approaches available in the literature. A Gabor representation proposed showed to work better with non-occluded faces. Furthermore, the proposed feature extraction methods did not demand high computational resources.

The remainder of the paper is organized as follows. Section 2 presents the methodology proposed in this work, describing the preprocessing, the facial expression reconstruction, the facial feature extraction and the feature reduction stage. Section 3 describes and discusses the experiments and results. Section 4 concludes the paper with final remarks and directions for future work.

2   Methodology

The proposed methodology for facial expression recognition with occlusions is composed of five main steps: preprocessing, facial expression reconstruction, facial feature extraction, feature reduction and classification. These stages are described as follows.

The image preprocessing stage is crucial to the expression recognition task, whose main purpose is to obtain occluded facial expression images with aligned faces, uniform size and shape, and randomized occluded facial regions. This preprocessing procedure consists in the following seven steps: (1) automatic detection of fiducial points through Chehra Face and Eyes Tracking Software [2]; (2) extraction of eye coordinate features; (3) rotation of the images to align the eye coordinates; (4) scaling of the images proportionally to the minimum distance d between the eyes; (5) cropping of the face region using an appropriate bounding rectangle; (6) conversion of the color images to gray-scale; (7) addition of randomized black rectangles to occlude facial regions, including left eye, right eye, two eyes, bottom left side of the face, bottom right side of the face or bottom side of the face, as illustrated in Figure 1.

Fig. 1. Cropped images with occluded facial regions from the MUG data set.

PCA is widely used as a tool for reducing high-dimensional feature subspaces. However, PCA does not work well with grossly corrupted observations, such as variations of facial expressions, occluded faces, image noise, illumination problems, etc. Instead, RPCA [4] performs robustly with missing data and outliers. RPCA is an extension of the classical PCA procedure and it has been shown to perform better, among other approaches, for the reconstruction of occluded facial expressions [6] and to contribute in achieving better facial expression recognition accuracy [10].

Several experiments conducted over the training set demonstrated the RPCA algorithm to be effective for facial expression reconstruction using 150 iterations and a parameter regularization $\lambda = \frac{1}{\sqrt{\max{(m,n)}}}$ [5], where m and n are the size of matrix D.

After performing the facial expression reconstruction, we project all samples of the testing set onto the space created by RPCA. Thereafter, we fill all occluded facial regions set from the reconstructed faces for both training and testing sets. Hence, we perform the contrast-limited adaptive histogram equalization (CLAHE) over the reconstructed facial regions to enhance the image contrast to facilitate of facial fiducial points detection. Figure 2 shows the process.

Two types of facial features, Gabor wavelet and geometric representation, are extracted for facial expression recognition.

After performing experiments with different sets of Gabor wavelet kernels, we decide to use 20 Gabor wavelet kernels at five scales ($v = \{0, 1, 2, 3, 4\}$) and four orientations ($\mu = \{1, 2, 3, 4\}$), with $\sigma = k_{\max} = \pi$, and $f = \sqrt{2}$. This combination provides a proper recognition accuracy rate.

This set of kernels is used for convolving a facial image region of 15×15 pixels around the location of 22 facial fiducial points: six points for the corners and

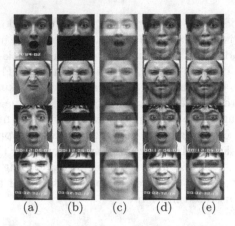

(a)   (b)   (c)   (d)   (e)

Fig. 2. (a) Cropped images without occlusions from the Cohn-Kanade database, (b) faces with occluded regions; (c) reconstructed faces; (d) filling the occluded facial regions from (c); (e) facial fiducial points detected.

middle of the eyebrows; eight points for the corners and middle of the borders of the eyes; four points for the superior and inferior side of the nose; and four points for the left, right, superior and inferior border of the mouth. Figure 3(a) shows the location of these 22 points.

Each convolved image region is divided into 9 (3×3) equivalent blocks of 5×5 pixels, as shown in Figure 3(d), and two measures are calculated from each one: mean and standard deviation [14]. The Gabor wavelet representation is basically the concatenation of the two measures calculated from each block of 5×5 pixels for all the regions around the location of the selected fiducial points, resulting in a feature vector of length $2\times9\times20\times22=7920$. Figure 3 illustrates the process.

As suggested in [11], the geometric representation uses eight 2D facial fiducial points: two points for the middle of the eyebrows (1-2); two points for eye's inner corner (3-4); and four points for the left, right, superior and inferior border of the mouth (5-8). Figure 4 shows the localization of the eight facial points.

We calculated the mean μ and standard deviation σ of the set of facial selected points per each class. Each x- and y-coordinates are projected to a $[0,1]$

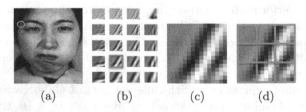

(a)   (b)   (c)   (d)

Fig. 3. (a) 22 facial fiducial points of a cropped image from the JAFFE database, (b) the 20 convolution results of Gabor wavelets of the region around the location of the outer corner of the eyebrow; (c) the convolution results at orientation μ and scale v; (d) the convolution result is divided into 9 sub-blocks.

 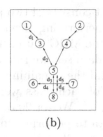

(a)   (b)

Fig. 4. (a) Eight 2D facial fiducial points detected of a cropped image from the Cohn-Kanade database; (b) the six distances calculated from the eight selected facial points. Adapted from [11].

interval, considering the upper left corner as the origin. These points form a feature vector of length 16. This feature vector is normalized as $f'_l = \frac{[(f_i - \mu_i)/2\sigma_i] + 1}{2}$, where f'_l is the normalization form of f_i, the ith ($i = 1, \ldots, 16$) feature across the training data [11].

The geometric representation helps to describe the position of the facial points to each other. Thereby, six distances are calculated from the selected points, as shown in Figure 4 (b). These distances are normalized according to face width. For further consideration, the two distances d_1 and d_2 are the average values of the mirrored distances of each side of the face. The two distances d_5 and d_6 are calculated using the intersection point of the line between the points of the superior and inferior borders of the mouth, and the line between the left and right corner of the mouth. Hence, the set of selected points and distances calculated form a vector of 22 features.

Two approaches for feature reduction, i.e., PCA and LDA, are used sequentially. Thereby, we apply this procedure individually for the texture feature vector and the geometric feature vector. Hence, we used SVM and KNN classification techniques for comparing the recognition rates.

3   Experimental Results

The proposed methodology has been tested on three facial expression data sets: the Cohn-Kanade (CK+) [8] data set, the Japanese Female Facial Expression (JAFFE) [9] data set and the MUG Facial Expression data set [1].

The CK data set is available in two versions, such that we used the second one (CK+) that contains 593 sequential images of posed and non-posed expressions from 123 subjects, labeled as one of seven facial expressions, i.e., anger, contempt, disgust, fear, happy, sadness and surprise. Each image sequence incorporates the onset with a neutral facial expression to peak a facial expression. The CK+ data set also includes some metadata as 68 facial landmarks [8].

The JAFFE data set contains 213 images of seven facial expressions, i.e., anger, disgust, fear, happiness, neutral, sadness and surprise, performed by 10 Japanese female models [9].

The MUG data set consists of two parts, where we used the static image collection of 86 subjects performing seven facial expressions as the JAFFE database, without occlusions. The MUG data set also contains 80 facial points [1].

Initially, for each data set, we randomly choose 80% of samples of each class for the training set and the remaining 20% for the testing set. Then, 50% of the training set samples of each class were occluded and a similar procedure was applied to the testing set. We set 20 different randomized collections of occluded and non-occluded data to perform experiments for each of the three data sets.

From these image collections, we performed experiments using Gabor wavelet and geometric representation following four methods: PCA+K-NN, PCA+LDA+K-NN, PCA+SVM and PCA+LDA+SVM. The results are shown in Tables 1 and 2, whose values represent the average facial expression recognition accuracy rate from performing 20 experiments with different collections. It is relevant to clarify that RPCA is always applied independently of the feature reduction and classification methods applied.

Table 1. Average accuracy, in percentage, for non-occluded facial images using Gabor wavelet and geometric representation.

Method	Gabor Representation			Geometric Representation		
	CK+	JAFFE	MUG	CK+	JAFFE	MUG
PCA + K-NN	59.71	86.20	79.06	36.20	43.93	61.16
PCA + LDA + K-NN	92.76	**95.36**	**91.84**	99.78	99.17	**99.94**
PCA + SVM	86.12	93.21	85.95	95.75	93.34	93.80
PCA + LDA + SVM	**94.03**	95.12	91.33	97.47	96.91	99.24

Table 2. Average accuracy, in percentage, for occluded facial images using Gabor wavelet and geometric representation.

Method	Gabor Representation			Geometric Representation		
	CK+	JAFFE	MUG	CK+	JAFFE	MUG
PCA + K-NN	50.17	48.58	55.76	36.65	32.62	43.49
PCA + LDA + K-NN	84.63	82.51	**81.21**	**98.73**	**98.21**	**99.43**
PCA + SVM	76.87	73.48	67.76	95.30	88.69	92.92
PCA + LDA + SVM	**85.68**	**82.86**	81.02	97.47	95.95	98.67

From our experiments, it is possible to see that the PCA+LDA approach achieves better recognition accuracy than just using PCA. Also, we can observe that the geometric representation reaches higher facial expression recognition accuracy among occluded and non-occluded image collections compared with Gabor wavelet representation. From Tables 1 and 2, we can notice that a recognition accuracy of non-occluded collections is much better than among occluded image collections using a Gabor wavelet representation due to the difficulty on recovering the occlusion images. We can also see that an accuracy rate of non-occluded collections is slightly better than among occluded image collections using a geometric representation.

We compared our methods to others available in the literature that apply random partial occlusions over the faces for both training and testing phases. Table 3 summarizes the best results achieved by our method on each data set, as well as a comparison against other state-of-the-art approaches available in the literature. There are few similar works that consider occlusions on the training stage, then it can be seen that the proposed method - Geometric+PCA+LDA+K-NN - obtains the best results for CK+ and JAFFE datasets, not only for occluded images, even for non-occluded images. Table 3 is sorted in descending order by occluded recognition accuracy rate.

Table 3. Accuracy rates, in percentage, for non-occluded images and for comparable methods that work with random partial occlusions on the faces in both training and testing phases.

Data Set	Approach	Strategy	Non-Occlusion	Occlusion
	Ours	Geometric+PCA+LDA+K-NN	99.78	98.73
CK+	Ours	Gabor+PCA+LDA+SVM	94.03	85.68
	Liu et al. [7]	Maximum Likelihood Estimation Sparse Representation	94.29	85.24
	Ours	Geometric+PCA+LDA+K-NN	99.17	98.21
JAFFE	Liu et al. [7]	Maximum Likelihood Estimation Sparse Representation	93.42	86.73
	Ours	Gabor+PCA+LDA+SVM	95.12	82.86
	Zhang et al. [12]	Gabor template and SVM	81.20	48.80
MUG	Ours	Geometric+PCA+LDA+K-NN	99.94	99.43
	Ours	Gabor+PCA+LDA+K-NN	91.84	81.21

4   Conclusions and Future Work

Using RPCA to perform occluded facial expression reconstruction task allowed to obtain a better accuracy for facial fiducial point detection. Experimental results have shown that geometric representation for facial expression recognition can achieve robustness to occluded and non-occluded faces. A normalized geometric representation for facial expression recognition has proven to be independent on gender, race and age. Furthermore, it has also been shown that discriminant feature selection techniques, such as PCA and LDA, can contribute to increase recognition accuracy significantly.

Despite the fact that the Gabor wavelet representation did not provide a high accuracy for occluded facial expression recognition, the achieved accuracy is superior and competitive compared to other similar works. Also, an accuracy rate achieved for facial expression recognition without occlusions is competitive as well as other similar works. Furthermore, Gabor wavelet representation does not demand high computational resources to generate a feature vector, because of the convolution of small regions around few facial fiducial points.

In order to achieve better accuracy using a Gabor wavelet representation, new facial fiducial point set and facial reconstruction algorithm improvements will be explored. Also, there is a need to research the development of an automatic occlusion detector for facial expression recognition systems robust to occlusions.

Acknowledgements. The authors are grateful to FAPESP, CNPq and CAPES for their financial support.

References

1. Aifanti, N., Papachristou, C., Delopoulos, A.: The MUG facial expression database. In: 11th International Workshop on Image and Audio Analysis for Multimedia Interactive Services, pp. 1–4. Desenzano del Garda, Italy, April 2010
2. Asthana, A., Zafeiriou, S., Cheng, S., Pantic, M.: Incremental face alignment in the wild. In: IEEE International Conference on Computer Vision and Pattern Recognition (2014)
3. Ekman, P.: Facial Expressions. Handbook of Cognition and Emotion, vol. 16, pp. 301–320 (1999)
4. Ganesh, A., Lin, Z., Wright, J., Wu, L., Chen, M., Ma, Y.: Fast algorithms for recovering a corrupted low-rank matrix. In: Computational Advances in Multi-Sensor Adaptive Processing, pp. 213–216, December 2009
5. Guyon, C., Bouwmans, T., Zahzah, E.: Robust principal component analysis for background subtraction: systematic evaluation and comparative analysis. In: Principal Component Analysis, pp. 223–238. INTECH, March 2012
6. Jiang, B., Jia, K.: Research of robust facial expression recognition under facial occlusion condition. In: Zhong, N., Callaghan, V., Ghorbani, A.A., Hu, B. (eds.) AMT 2011. LNCS, vol. 6890, pp. 92–100. Springer, Heidelberg (2011)
7. Liu, S., Zhang, Y., Liu, K.: Facial expression recognition under random block occlusion based on maximum likelihood estimation sparse representation. In: International Joint Conference on Neural Networks, pp. 1285–1290, July 2014
8. Lucey, P., Cohn, J.F., Kanade, T., Saragih, J., Ambadar, Z., Matthews, I.: The Extended Cohn-Kanade Dataset (CK+): A complete dataset for action unit and emotion-specified expression (2010)
9. Lyons, M., Kamachi, M., Gyoba, J.: Japanese Female Facial Expressions (JAFFE), database of Digital Images (1997)
10. Mao, X., Xue, Y.L., Li, Z., Huang, K., Lv, S.: Robust facial expression recognition based on RPCA and AdaBoost. In: 10th Workshop on Image Analysis for Multimedia Interactive Services, pp. 113–116, May 2009
11. Saeed, A., Al-Hamadi, A., Niese, R., Elzobi, M.: Frame-Based Facial Expression Recognition Using Geometrical Features. Advances in Human-Computer Interaction **2014**, 1–13 (2014)
12. Zhang, L., Tjondronegoro, D., Chandran, V.: Random Gabor based Templates for Facial Expression Recognition in Images with Facial Occlusion. Neurocomputing **145**, 451–464 (2014)
13. Zhang, S., Zhao, X., Lei, B.: Facial Expression Recognition Using Sparse Representation. WSEAS Transactions on Systems and Control **11**(8), 440–441 (2012)
14. Zhao, Q.Y., Pan, A.C., Pan, J.J., Tang, Y.Y.: Facial expression recognition based on fusion of Gabor and LBP features. In: International Conference on Wavelet Analysis and Pattern Recognition, pp. 362–367, Hong Kong, August 2008

Automatic Eyes and Nose Detection
Using Curvature Analysis

J. Matías Di Martino$^{(\boxtimes)}$, Alicia Fernández, and José Ferrari

Facultad de Ingeniería, Universidad de la República, Montevideo, Uruguay
{matiasdm,alicia,jferrari}@fing.edu.uy

Abstract. In the present work we propose a method for detecting the nose and eyes position when we observe a scene that contains a face. The main goal of the proposed technique is that it capable of bypassing the 3D explicit mapping of the face and instead take advantage of the information available in the Depth gradient map of the face. To this end we will introduce a simple false positive rejection approach restricting the distance between the eyes, and between the eyes and the nose. The main idea is to use nose candidates to estimate those regions where is expected to find the eyes, and vice versa. Experiments with Texas database are presented and the proposed approach is testes when data presents different power of noise and when faces are in different positions with respect to the camera.

Keywords: Landmark detection · Differential 3d reconstruction · Nose tip detection · Eyes detection

1 Introduction

One of the most popular and challenging problems in the field of pattern recognition and computer vision consists is the analysis and recognition of human faces[1]. It has many applications such as security control and prevention, medical and biometrical analysis or gesture understanding. In the last decade, lot of research included three-dimensional (3D) face information to improve recognition rates and make the methods more robust to pose, gesture and illumination variations[3]. See e.g. the work of Chang et al. [6], Faltemier et al. [10], Mahoor et al. [15], and Li et al. [14]. Most of these approaches, uses features of the face collected from the eyes forehead and nose regions, and hence they require in a initial step to find the position of the eyes and nose on the input images. To achieve a robust localization of the eyes and nose position, we follow a curvature approach (see e.g.[8] and references therein). This methods is very efficient for detecting those possible nose and eyes candidates, despite that, it is important to solve the problem of removing false positive candidates. To solve this issue we will follow a message passing methodology; the main idea behind it is to use nose candidates to estimate those regions where is expected to find the eyes, and vice versa.

© Springer International Publishing Switzerland 2015
A. Pardo and J. Kittler (Eds.): CIARP 2015, LNCS 9423, pp. 271–278, 2015.
DOI: 10.1007/978-3-319-25751-8_33

In order to remove possible false detections many approaches has been proposed; for example, Li and Da [14] fitted a nose template to each nose candidate. Bronstein et al. [4] impose geometric relations between the candidates (e.g. that the nose apex is located between the two eyes, above the nose tip and within certain distance intervals). In the work of Faltemier et al. [10] the nose tip is found as the highest z value after the face surface is aligned using ICP to a template face. Chang et al. [6] impose that the eyes regions must present similar y and z value, and that the nose tip is found starting between the eyes landmark and moving *down* (i.e. along the x direction) along the face. Another example is the work of Colombo et al. [7] in which the idea is to look from all the nose and eyes candidates, all the possible triangles formed by one nose candidate and two eyes candidates. Then, each triangle is described by the distances between the three regions composing it; finally, triangles with abnormal distances are rejected.

While some of the previously described methods make hypothesis regarding the position or orientation of the face (i.e. assuming than the nose is down the two eyes), others are computationally expensive (i.e. requiring ICP registration or checking all possible combination of nose and eyes triangles). But what these methods have in common is that they use the explicit three-dimensional representation of the face, in the present work we aim to bypass the 3D mapping of the face and instead take advantage of the information available in the Depth gradient map of the face. To this end we will introduce a simple false positive rejection approach -that do not need the explicit 3D mapping of the face- and instead restricts the distance (in the image plane) between the eyes, and between the eyes and the nose.

2 Proposed Approach

2.1 Find Nose and Eyes Candidates

Let S be the surface defined by a twice differentiable real valued function $D : \Omega \to \mathbb{R}$, defined on an open set $\Omega \subseteq \mathbb{R}^2$:

$$S = \{(x, y, z) \mid (x, y) \in \Omega;\ z \in \mathbb{R};\ D(x, y) = z\}. \tag{1}$$

For every point $(x, y, D(x, y)) \in S$ we consider two different curvature measures, the Mean (H) and the Gaussian (K) curvature defined as [5, 7]:

$$H(x, y) = \frac{(1 + D_y^2)\, D_{xx} - 2 D_x D_y D_{xy} + (1 + D_x^2)\, D_{yy}}{2 \left(1 + D_x^2 + D_y^2\right)^{3/2}}, \tag{2}$$

$$K(x, y) = \frac{D_{xx} D_{yy} - D_{xy}^2}{\left(1 + D_x^2 + D_y^2\right)^2}. \tag{3}$$

Following the procedure described in [9] we compute the first derivatives of the scene depth. After that, to calculate $H(x, y)$ and $K(x, y)$ it is only necessary to compute the second order derivatives (D_{xx}, D_{yy} and D_{xy}) e.g. using finite differences.

Once the Mean and Gaussian curvatures are computed, it is possible to classify the different areas of the face according to its shape [2]. Depending on H and K values, points on the surface are classified. To remove smooth regions from the areas of interest a thresholding approach was followed[7,11], and then those points with high absolute value of K and H were isolated. For those points with $K > 0$ and $H > 0$ the eye candidate label was assigned, while those with $K > 0$ and $H < 0$ were selected as nose candidates. Figure 1 illustrates some of the nose and eyes candidates obtained.

Fig. 1. Examples of nose (red dots) and eyes (green dots) candidates point detected.

2.2 Remove False Positive Detections

In first place, we estimate the distance between the eyes and between each eye and the nose tip using a training set. We approximate each distance distributions by a Gaussian distributions i.e.

$$d_{ee}(u) = \frac{1}{\sigma_{ee}\sqrt{2\pi}}\, e^{-\left(\frac{(u-\mu_{ee})^2}{2\sigma_{ee}^2}\right)} \qquad (4)$$

$$d_{ne}(u) = \frac{1}{\sigma_{ne}\sqrt{2\pi}}\, e^{-\left(\frac{(u-\mu_{ne})^2}{2\sigma_{ne}^2}\right)}. \qquad (5)$$

where d_{ee} and d_{ne} denote the distance between eyes and the distance between the nose and each eye, respectively. The mean and variance parameters (μ and σ^2) were estimated by fitting the distributions given by Eqs. (4) and (5) to the distributions obtained from a given training set.

Once distance distributions are obtained, they are used to *propagate* where it is feasible to find the nose/eyes considering each of the others nose and eyes candidates.

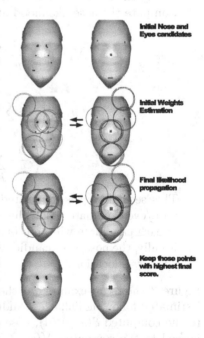

Fig. 2. Illustration of the steps followed to remove false positive detections. The size of each candidate point illustrates the likelihood of that point at each step.

$$\mathcal{K}_{ne}(x,y) = d_{ne}\left(\sqrt{x^2+y^2}\right) \quad \text{and} \quad \mathcal{K}_{ee}(x,y) = d_{ee}\left(\sqrt{x^2+y^2}\right). \quad (6)$$

The next step consists in estimating in which areas is more suitable to have the nose and eyes candidates so we can keep the set of points with higher probability to be the true ones. For this we follow four basic steps -illustrated in Fig. 2-:

1. Estimate initial *nose-likelihood* ($\mathcal{N}$) and *eye-likelihood* ($\mathcal{E}$) functions:

$$\mathcal{N}_0(x,y) = \frac{1}{\#e}\sum_{i=1}^{\#e} \delta_{x_i,y_i} * \mathcal{K}_{ne}(x,y) \quad (7)$$

$$\mathcal{E}_0(x,y) = \left(\frac{1}{\#e}\sum_{i=1}^{\#e}\delta_{x_i,y_i}*\mathcal{K}_{ee}(x,y)\right) \cdot \left(\frac{1}{\#n}\sum_{j=1}^{\#n}\delta_{x_j,y_j}*\mathcal{K}_{ne}(x,y)\right) \quad (8)$$

where $\#e$, $\#n$ is the number of eyes and nose candidates respectively, δ_{x_i,y_i} is the Dirac delta function at each nose/eye candidate location (x_i,y_i); and $\mathcal{K}_{ne/ee}$ the Kernels defined above.

2. Compute the nose-likelihood and eyes-likelihood distributions as,

$$\mathcal{N}(x,y) = \frac{1}{\#e}\sum_{i=1}^{\#e}\mathcal{E}_0(x_i,y_i)\delta_{x_i,y_i}*\mathcal{K}_{ne}(x,y) \quad (9)$$

$$\mathcal{E}(x,y) = \left(\frac{1}{\#e}\sum_{i=1}^{\#e}\mathcal{E}_0(x_i,y_i)\delta_{x_i,y_i}*\mathcal{K}_{ee}(x,y)\right)$$
$$\cdot \left(\frac{1}{\#n}\sum_{j=1}^{\#n}\mathcal{N}_0(x_i,y_i)\delta_{x_j,y_j}*\mathcal{K}_{ne}(x,y)\right). \quad (10)$$

This second step is illustrated in the third row of Fig. 2, the size of each nose/eye candidate point illustrates the value of $\mathcal{N}_0/\mathcal{E}_0$ and the information of each candidate will be propagated with different weight.

3. Finally, the nose/eyes candidate points with higher $\mathcal{N}/\mathcal{E}$ are kept as the true nose/eyes locations.

Figure 3 shows an example of the input image (a), depth gradient field (b-c) [estimated following [9]], eyes candidate points (display as blue dots) overlapped to the computed $\mathcal{E}(x,y)$ (d), nose candidate points (display as blue dots) overlapped to the computed $\mathcal{N}(x,y)$ (e), and finally (f) the output nose and eyes locations obtained .

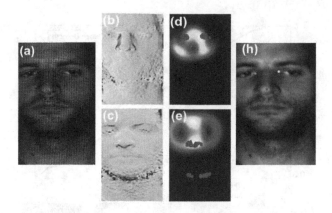

Fig. 3. This figure illustrates the nose and eyes detection procedure. (a) Input image. (b-c) x and y depth partial derivatives obtained by measuring fringes' deformation. (d-e) eyes and nose candidates obtained by curvature thresholding (as blue dots) overlapped with the estimated functions $\mathcal{E}(x,y)$ and $\mathcal{N}(x,y)$ respectively. (h) Nose and eyes located in the image.

3   Experiments and Evaluation

In this section, we perform a set of experiments using the Texas 3D Face Recognition Database [12,13]. This Database contains 1149 pairs of high resolution, pose normalized, preprocessed, and perfectly aligned color and range images of 118 subjects. Additionally, it includes the locations of manually marked anthropometric facial fiducial points which will be used as ground truth. For the experiments, we split the database in two sets: Train and Test sets. The first one was used to estimate the parameters, and the test set was used for evaluation once all the parameters were trained.

In a first experiment, we want to evaluate the robustness of the proposed methodology when we have different power of noise in the input gradient field. Figure 5 shows the accuracy obtained (over the test set) for different levels of noise . The noise added to the input gradient field was Gaussian with zero mean; as we can see, when the variance of noise distribution was below the 20% of the maximum of the signal, the error in both nose and eyes detection was below the 10%.

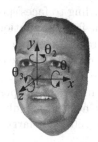

Fig. 4. Definition of θ_1, θ_2 and θ_3.

In a second experiment, we want to test the robustness of the proposed technique when the faces are in a non-frontal position with respect to the camera. We define the angles θ_1, θ_2 and θ_3 as illustrated in Figure 4. Recall that we are measuring the projected euclidean distance in the 3D space over the image plane, because of this it is expected that for databases

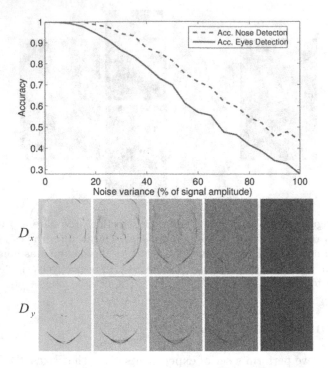

Fig. 5. Result obtained over the test set varying the power of the noise added to the input gradient field.

with larger pose variations, K_{ne} and K_{ee} kernels will become wider and hence more errors should be expected[1].

A new dataset was generated by randomly rotating faces (of the Texas Database) and projecting them back to the image plane. Again this database was spitted in train and test sets to avoid over fitting. The test set was divided according to faces' position, hence we were able to measure the accuracy for different face orientation (i.e. different values of θ_1, θ_2 and θ_3). Figure 6 shows the accuracy for test sets with faces in different positions. Accuracies on eyes and nose recognition are displayed for $|\theta_i| \in [0^o, 55^o]$ $i = 1..3$, the range images below the x axis illustrates the pose obtained with the corresponding value of θ_i. As we can see the proposed approach is independent with respect to the value of θ_3 while accurate results can be achieved when we restrict θ_1 and θ_2 to the interval $[-30^o, 30^o]$, for larger values of θ_1 and θ_2 the performance drops significantly.

---

[1] In this direction we think there is room for interesting future work. For example, an improvement could be to estimate the distance in the 3D space from the distances in the image plane plus the information available in the Depth gradient field (D_x and D_y).

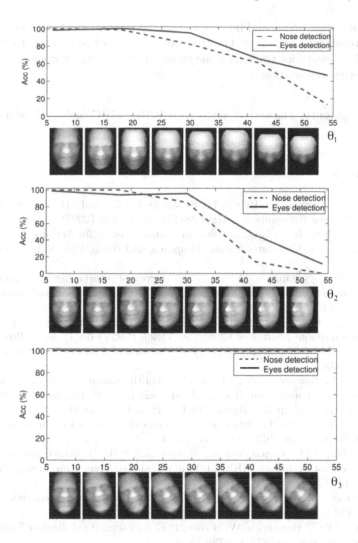

Fig. 6. Results when varying face position.

4   Conclusions

This work proposes an efficient approach to find the location of the eyes and nose position using curvature analysis but bypassing the explicit 3D mapping of the face. In addition a method for removing the false candidates was proposed, which constrain the inter-distances between the set of candidate point to find a robust solution. The proposed method was tested in a public database; in particular the effect of noise in the input gradient field and the position of the face on system performance was studied. In future work we plan to include depth gradient information in order to achieve a more robust estimation of the distance between candidate point, and hence improve the robustness of the method under arbitrary rotations of the face. Other interesting line of research is to apply the proposed framework for tracking some facial landmarks which could be analyzed e.g. for gesture recognition.

Acknowledgments. The authors thank PEDECIBA, CSIC, and ANII for their financial support.

References

1. Abate, A.F., Nappi, M., Riccio, D., Sabatino, G.: 2D and 3D face recognition: A survey. Pattern Recognition Letters **28**(14), 1885–1906 (2007)
2. Besl, P.J., Jain, R.C.: Invariant surface characteristics for 3D object recognition in range images. Computer Vision, Graphics, and Image Processing **33**(1), 33–80 (1986)
3. Bowyer, K.W., Chang, K., Flynn, P.: A survey of approaches and challenges in 3D and multi-modal 3D+2D face recognition. Computer Vision and Image Understanding **101**(1), 1–15 (2006)
4. Bronstein, A.M., Bronstein, M.M., Kimmel, R.: Three-Dimensional Face Recognition. International Journal of Computer Vision (IJCV) **64**(1), 5–30 (2005)
5. do Carmo, M.: Differential Geometry of Curves and Surfaces. Pearson Education Canada (1976)
6. Chang, K.I., Bowyer, K.W., Flynn, P.J.: Multiple nose region matching for 3D face recognition under varying facial expression. IEEE Transactions on Tattern Analysis and Machine Intelligence **28**(10), 1695–1700 (2006)
7. Colombo, A., Cusano, C., Schettini, R.: 3D face detection using curvature analysis. Pattern Recognition **39**(3), 444–455 (2006)
8. Di Martino, J.M., Fernández, A., Ferrari, J.A.: 3D curvature analysis with a novel one-shot technique. IEEE International Conference on Image Processing (ICIP2014) (2014)
9. Di Martino, J.M., Fernández, A., Ferrari, J.A.: One-shot 3D gradient field scanning. Optics and Lasers in Engineering **72**, 26–38 (2015)
10. Faltemier, T.C., Bowyer, K.W., Flynn, P.J., Member, S.: A Region Ensemble for 3-D Face Recognition **3**(1), 62–73 (2008)
11. Gordon, G.G.: Face recognition based on depth maps and surface curvature. SPIE 1570, Geometric Methods in Computer Vision, pp. 234–247, Sep 1991
12. Gupta, S., Castleman, K., Markey, M., Bovik, A.: Texas 3d face recognition database. In: 2010 IEEE Southwest Symposium on Image Analysis Interpretation (SSIAI), pp. 97–100, May 2010
13. Gupta, S., Markey, M., Bovik, A.: Anthropometric 3D face recognition. International Journal of Computer Vision **90**(3), 331–349 (2010)
14. Li, X., Da, F.: Efficient 3D face recognition handling facial expression and hair occlusion. Image and Vision Computing **30**(9), 668–679 (2012)
15. Mahoor, M.H., Abdel-Mottaleb, M.: Face recognition based on 3D ridge images obtained from range data. Pattern Recognition **42**, 445–451 (2009)

Image Classification and Retrieval

A Novel Framework for Content-Based Image Retrieval Through Relevance Feedback Optimization

Reginaldo Rocha, Priscila T.M. Saito, and Pedro H. Bugatti[✉]

Department of Computer Science, Federal University of Technology - Paraná,
Cornélio Procópio, Brazil
reginaldorocha@alunos.utfpr.edu.br, {psaito,pbugatti}@utfpr.edu.br

Abstract. Content-based image retrieval remains an important research topic in many domains. It can be applied to assist specialists to improve the efficiency and accuracy of interpreting the images. However, it presents some intrinsic problems. This occurs due to the semantic interpretation of an image is still far to be reach, because it depends on the user's perception about the image. Besides, each user presents different personal behaviors and experiences, which generates a high subjective analysis of a given image. To mitigate these problems the paper presents a novel framework for content-based image retrieval joining relevance feedback techniques with optimization methods. It is capable to not only capture the user intention, but also to tune the process through the optimization method according to each user. The experiments demonstrate the great applicability and efficacy of the proposed framework, which presented considerable gains of precision regarding similarity queries.

Keywords: Image analysis · CBIR · Relevance feedback · Optimization

1 Introduction

Nowadays there is a continuously growing regarding devices capable of generate different types of images. On the other hand images are a complex data type that brings in itself a number of challenges. This fact leads to a huge volume of images that must be organized and retrieved considering a specific domain [4], regarding the specialist intention. Thus, the great challenge is to find among a large volume of images those which are actually relevant to a given context.

In order to perform this retrieval process the images can be searched based on metadata (i.e. keywords defined for each image). However, this approach is extremely subjective, tiresome and susceptible to errors. This occurs not only in the organization step because someone needs to define the keywords for the images, but also in the search process. Trying to solve these problems, it was developed content-based image retrieval (CBIR) techniques that automatically

---

This work was supported by CAPES, CNPq, Fund. Araucária and UTFPR.

A. Pardo and J. Kittler (Eds.): CIARP 2015, LNCS 9423, pp. 281–289, 2015.
DOI: 10.1007/978-3-319-25751-8_34

extract visual characteristics from the images to describe them, generating feature vectors. The main features extracted are based on color, texture and shape. Thereafter, these features are compared by a measure (i.e. distance function) in order to calculate the similarity between the images. For instance, given a query image, it is possible to retrieve the most similar (relevant) according to it, and solving the problems of the search based on metadata (i.e. text) [4].

On the other hand, CBIR process suffers from the so called semantic gap problem [11], where the results returned by the low-level features (color, texture and shape) automatically extracted from the images and compared by a distance function do not complies with the user (e.g. specialist in a given context) expectation about the search. It occurs because of the gap between the low-level features and the high-level interpretation of the user regarding the similarity between the images.

Hence, to mitigate the semantic gap problem relevance feedback techniques can be aggregated into the process in order to approximate the user from the CBIR approach. This type of technique was adapted from the textual retrieval area to CBIR [11]. Relevance feedback techniques allow the users to label and define the relevance (irrelevance) degree of the images returned by a given query. This labeling process performed by the user provides the CBIR to adapt and adjust the query, taking into account the high-level relevance of the images according to the user needs. Thus, it is an effective technique for mapping the high-level semantics to the low-level features.

In order to improve this process performed by the specialist, obtaining more accurate results, the present paper applies the CBIR approach with the relevance feedback process, joined with optimization strategies (e.g. particle swarm optimization) to diminish the intrinsic problems of semantic gap in image retrieval. Besides, using relevance feedback techniques the approach is capable to closer the user to the CBIR system, capturing the high-level semantics of the specialist, aiding the process and serving as training for fresh specialists.

Experiments showed that the proposed methodology improves the query precision up to 99% and at the same time captures the specialist intentions.

The present paper is organized as follows. Section 2 summarizes the concepts needed to understand our approach. Section 3 presents the methodology applied, while Section 4 discusses the experiments and results. Finally, Section 5 presents the conclusions of the present work.

2   Background

2.1   Feature Extraction

An essential key in similarity search is regarding the feature extraction process, which describes the intrinsic visual features from the images. As aforecited, the features are automatically extracted from the images and organized in feature vectors. There are several methods proposed in the literature to extract image features based on color, texture or shape low-level characteristics.

Edge statistics are computed on the images Prewitt gradient, and includes the mean, median, variance, and eight bins histogram of both the magnitude and the direction components. Other edge features are the total number of edge pixels (normalized to the size of the image) and the direction homogeneity, which is measured by the fraction of edge pixels that are in the first two bins of the direction histogram. Additionally, the edge direction difference is measured as the difference among direction histogram bins at a certain angle [6].

Zernike Moments are used to represent complex shapes, composed of several disjoint regions. It represents shape properties of the image without redundancy of information between moments [7].

2.2   Relevance Feedback

Relevance feedback techniques perform an interactive query modification and fulfill an important role in CBIR systems, since it is capable to gradually reduce the semantic gap through user interactions.

Typically, a relevance feedback approach consists of three steps in the CBIR context: in the first step, it is performed a similarity query and the most similar images are retrieved according to a give image query; at the second step, the users initiate the labeling process, guiding the search, judging the retrieved images in relevant or irrelevant; finally, in third step, the systems capture the user's intention based on the feedback performed in step two and modify the initial query. Steps two and three are repeated until the user is satisfied with the retrieved images.

Different methods can be applied to steps 2 and 3 of the relevance feedback cycle. Considering step 2, the labeling process can consider only relevant (positive examples) images, or relevant and irrelevant (negative examples) images at the same time. In step 3, different techniques can be employed such as based on query point movement (QPM). This type of technique consists in modifying the query point. To accomplish such task, the Rocchio's model [10] can be applied, which approximates the query point from the relevant images and, at the same time, keeps it away from the irrelevant ones. The Rocchio's formula is formally defined by Equation 1.

$$\overrightarrow{q}_m = \alpha \overrightarrow{q}_o + \beta \left(\frac{1}{|D_r|} \sum_{\overrightarrow{d_j} \in D_r} \overrightarrow{d_j} \right) - \gamma \left(\frac{1}{|D_{nr}|} \sum_{\overrightarrow{d_j} \in D_{nr}} \overrightarrow{d_j} \right) \qquad (1)$$

where $\overrightarrow{q}_o$ is the feature vector of the old query center; $|D_r|$ and $|D_{nr}|$ are, respectively, the number of relevant and irrelevant images labeled by the user; $\overrightarrow{d_j}$ is the feature image vector; and α, β and γ are weights used to define the importance of the factors (i.e. old query center, relevant images, irrelevant images) to generate the new query center ($\overrightarrow{q}_m$). Varying the weights of α, β and γ, the results can show large difference. However, to the best of our knowledge, there is no work which focus on the best-suited definition of these weights, according to a given context and user intention. Usually, the values of such parameters are empirically defined without further analysis. The great majority of works focus on the relevance/irrelevance degree definition for each image or in the image features re-weighting, and neglects those parameters.

2.3 Evolutionary Algorithms

In the field of artificial intelligence, evolutionary algorithm (EA) is part of a category called evolutionary computing. The main idea behind this algorithm is to apply the process of natural evolution as a problem solving paradigm. An EA uses mechanisms inspired by biological evolution, such as reproduction, mutation, recombination, and selection.

Genetic algorithm (GA) is one of the most known and most used in the evolutionary computing. It is started with a set of solutions represented by chromosomes, called population. Solutions from one population are taken and used to form a new population. This is motivated by a hope, that the new population will be better than the older one. Solutions which are selected to form new solutions (offspring) are selected according to their fitness - the more suitable they are the more chances they have to reproduce. This is repeated until some condition (for example, number of populations or improvement in the best solution) is satisfied [3].

The Particle Swarm Optimization (PSO) algorithm was created based on migration process of birds in searching for food. The concept behind the process is the particle (i.e. each bird), which is a point in the solution space [9]. The basic idea is to create a group (swarm) of particles that move within a given problem space, searching the location that best suits your needs, in this case, given by the fitness function. The specification of this function depends on the problem to be optimized. Once a problem space is defined, a set of particles is generated and subsequently their positions and their speeds are adjusted iteratively.

In this optimization algorithm, we have a complete connected set, which means that all particles share information. Thus, any particle knows the best position ever visited by any of the swarm. Each particle has a position (2) and a velocity (3), which are defined by Equations 2 and 3.

$$x_{i,d}(it+1) = x_{i,d}(it) + v_{i,d}(it+1) \tag{2}$$

$$\begin{aligned} v_{i,d}(it+1) = v_{i,d}(it) \\ +C_1 * Rnd(0,1) * [pb_{i,d}(it) - x_{i,d}(it)] \\ +C_2 * Rnd(0,1) * [gb_d(it) - x_{i,d}(it)] \end{aligned} \tag{3}$$

where: i is the index used to identify the particle; d is the particle dimension; $x_{i,d}$ is the dimension d of the particle i; $v_{i,d}$ is the velocity of the particle i in the dimension d; it is the iteration number; C_1 is a constant acceleration to the cognitive component (toward the global best solution); Rnd defines a random value between 0 and 1; $pb_{i,d}$ is the dimension d of the best local particle; C_2 defines a constant acceleration for the social component (toward the best solution); and gb_d is the dimension d of the best global particle.

3 Proposed Approach

The proposed framework performs content-based image retrieval through relevance feedback optimization. The framework provides the flexibility to incorporate not only new types of distances, but also feature extraction methods, relevance feedback approaches and optimization algorithms.

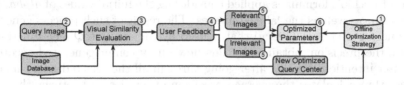

Fig. 1. Pipeline of the proposed framework.

The main idea of the proposed framework consists in using information from the user intention about the similarity query to optimize the relevance feedback process according to it. The great majority of works do not take into account that the initial parameters (e.g. α, β and γ from Rocchio's formula) of the relevance feedback process also needs to evolve according to a given image context and user intention, and maintain their initial values. This fact not only leads to considerable losses in query precision, but also degenerates in a very fast pace the relevance feedback process, trapping the query in less relevant subspaces. In order to mitigate this problem, our proposed framework allows to apply optimization strategies to escape from the subspace trapping, according to the user intention. To do so, we optimize the values of factors α, β and γ from Rocchio's formula, according to the image context (i.e. types of image datasets) and the labeling process accomplished by the user in the relevance feedback approach.

Figure 1 illustrates the pipeline of the current framework instances. Initially, in step 1, it is executed the offline optimization process to get best Rocchio's parameters according to a given dataset. In step 2, the query image is applied to the similarity search process accomplished in step 3. In steps 4 and 5, the user evaluates the retrieved images and labeled them as relevant/irrelevant. Finally, in step 6, the user intention is used as input to recalculate the query center using pre-processed parameters to weight the Rocchio's factors. To the best of our knowledge there are no studies that perform the same approach. In the present paper, we generate two instances of the proposed framework, applying the particle swarm optimization (PSO) and genetic algorithm (GA) approaches (Section 2.3) linked to the definition of the best values to the Rocchio's factors.

As fitness function for the PSO and GA, it was used the average precision of a set of performed similarity queries and relevance feedback iteration.

Algorithm 1 describes the pipeline of the fitness calculation, considering the PSO instance of the proposed framework. Consider G an image dataset, composed by images from different classes, where every image $g \in G$ is described by a feature vector (generated by a given feature extractor e), the proposed method randomly selects an equal number of query images per class (line 3), generating the *RandImages* set. Afterwards, the initial values (employed in the literature) of the factors α, β and γ are defined as the dimensions of the particle (i.e. three dimensions) for the PSO (lines 5 to 7). Given the images from the *RandImages* set, each one of them are used as query centers to an initial k-NN query. So, the retrieved images (*retrievedImages* set) are labeled in relevant or irrelevant by the user (i.e. generating the *labeledImages* set). Then, the query point movement based on Rocchio's formula is applied considering the initial values of *alpha*, *beta* and *gamma*, as well as the labeled images. The result of such process generates a new query center (*newQuery*) that is used by the *evaluateQuery* function to calculate the precision, obtained by this new query center generated according to the user intention. Finally, after going through all the selected query images, the algorithm calculates the average precision of queries and returns the value as fitness for the PSO algorithm. It is important to highlight that the fitness is an offline process, fact that does not generate impact on the computational time of the similarity query.

Algorithm 1. Pipeline of the PSO Fitness Calculation

Require: Image Dataset G, k, distance d, feature extractor e, random query images
    per class n

1: **function** GETFITNESS(particle)
2:    // receive IDs of images
3:    $RandImages \leftarrow$ GETQUERYIMAGES(G, n)
4:    $pr \leftarrow 0$ ▷ initialize precision
5:    $\alpha \leftarrow particle_0$
6:    $\beta \leftarrow particle_1$
7:    $\gamma \leftarrow particle_2$
8:    **for all** img i in $RandImages$ **do**
9:        $retrievedImages \leftarrow k\text{-}NN(img, k, d, e)$
10:       $newQuery \leftarrow$ ROCCHIO($\alpha, \beta, \gamma, labeledImages$)
11:       $pr+ =$ EVALUATEQUERY($newQuery$)
12:    **end for**
13:    $precision \leftarrow pr/$ COUNT(images)
14:    **return** $precision$
15: **end function**

---

4 Experiments

The experiments were performed using our proposed method in comparison with the approach widely employed in the literature (i.e. rocchio without factor's optimization).

In order to evaluate it, and summarize the results, we applied the mean average precision measure [1]. The precision is defined as: $precision = \frac{|R_A|}{|A|}$, where $|R_A|$ is the number of retrieved images that are relevant and $|A|$ is the size of the answer set [1]. To generate the precision values we performed k-nearest neighbor queries using randomly query centers from the dataset, and setting $k = 15$. This value of k was considered since large numbers would make the process not faithful with the common practice employed during daily activities. To perform the k-NN queries, it was considered the Euclidean distance function and all features cited in Section 2, joined with the Rocchio's relevance feedback (Section 2.2). To the experiments, we consider three relevance feedback cycles.

In order to accomplish a fair comparison between our method and the widely employed approach in the literature (i.e. empirically weight definition), we performed experiments setting the initial values of α, β and γ as 1.0, 0.5 and 0.25, respectively, because positive feedback also turns out to be much more valuable than negative feedback, and the most information retrieval systems set $\beta > \gamma$ [5]. Regarding the parameters of the PSO algorithm (Section 2.3), we defined: minimum and maximum values for each particle dimension equal to 0 and 1, respectively; a particle composed of 3 dimensions; maximum velocity equals to 0.5; number of iterations equals to 20; and, finally values of 0.02 to the constants C_1 and C_2. For GA, we defined as parameters: maximum number of generations $= 100$, population size $= 40$, minimum and maximum values, for each dimension, equal to 0 and 1 respectively, convergence rate $= 0.9$, selection type $=$ tournament and size of chromosome $= 21$.

To evaluate the methods, we performed a supervised automated evaluation of the algorithms. For each query, we considered as relevants, the images retrieved belonging to the same class of the image query, and irrelevants those belonging to a different class. The goal of this technique is to simulate the feedback given by the user through this information. This is a common configuration employed in the literature to perform a large number of tests over the algorithm under evaluation.

4.1 Image Dataset Description

For the experiments, we used image datasets containing Regions of Interest (ROI) extracted from images of Computed Tomography of the Chest, more specifically containing lung lesions. The dataset LungCT was obtained from a hospital university [2]. The dataset contains 3264 images of 8-bit depth gray scale with dimensions of 64 x 64 pixels. The images divided into six distinct classes, contain abnormal patterns that characterize diffuse lung lesions. The distribution of the images in each class is: normal - 591 images; consolidation - 452 images; emphysema - 503 images; thickening - 591 images; honeycomb - 531 images; ground-glass - 596 images.

The proposed algorithm was also tested on a public database containing 1000 color images from the Corel database [8], which are from 10 different semantic categories (cat, bonsai, texture six, primates, mineral, leopard, cards, texture one, sunset, rockform), each one containing 100 images.

4.2   Results

Due to space limitations, we present the most representative results obtained considering the aforecited methods and datasets.

Figure 2 shows the results obtained by the proposed approach compared to literature baseline (i.e. Rocchio without optimization) using ctLung and Corel datasets, respectively. The y-axis represents values obtained by MAP and the x-axis represents the iterations of the relevance feedback process (initial query q and i-th relevance feedback cycles, where $i = 1, ..., 10$).

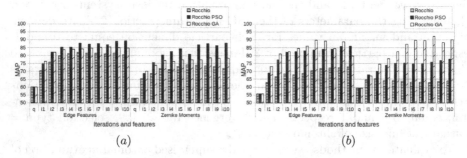

(a) (b)

Fig. 2. Comparison of the baseline Rocchio against the proposed approach. (a) using lungCT dataset. (b) using Corel dataset.

Analyzing the results of Figure 2, we can see that the instances of the proposed approach (i.e. Rocchio PSO and GA) when compared with the approach of the literature (i.e. Rocchio) showed precision gain in all feedback cycles. The proposed approach reached precision gains of up to 23% for Rocchio PSO and 39% for Rocchio GA in the tenth cycle (i_{10}). Besides, the proposed approach presents better performance regarding the query saturation, also leading to higher precisions in the final relevance feedback cycles.

5   Conclusions

In this paper, we presented a novel framework for content-based image retrieval with relevance feedback joined with optimization methods. The framework allows the combination of a set of distance functions, feature extractors and relevance feedback techniques, which are optimized by different strategies. Thus, mitigating the intrinsic problems of the CBIR process, capturing the user intention about a given similarity query and optimizing the relevance feedback component through the optimization strategies.

From the experiments, we can argue that the proposed framework instances (Rocchio PSO and Rocchio GA, as optimization strategies) were capable to improve in a great extent the precision of the similarity queries, reaching gains of up to 39% when compared with the literature approach, and at the same time capturing the user's intention.

References

1. Baeza-Yates, R., Ribeiro-Neto, B., et al.: Modern Information Retrieval, vol. 463. ACM Press, New York (1999)
2. Dias, R.L., Bueno, R., Ribeiro, M.X.: Reducing the complexity of k-nearest diverse neighbor queries in medical image datasets through fractal analysis. In: IEEE CBMS, pp. 101–106 (2013)
3. Gali, R., Dewal, M., Anand, R.: Genetic algorithm for content based image retrieval. In: CICSyN, pp. 243–247 (2012)
4. Liu, Y., Zhang, D., Lu, G., Ma, W.Y.: A survey of content-based image retrieval with high-level semantics. Pattern Recognition 40(1), 262–282 (2007)
5. Manning, C.D., Raghavan, P., Schütze, H.: Introduction to Information Retrieval. Cambridge University Press, New York (2008)
6. Orlov, N., Shamir, L., Macura, T., Johnston, J., Eckley, D.M., Goldberg, I.G.: Wnd-charm: Multi-purpose image classification using compound image transforms. Pattern recognition letters 29(11), 1684–1693 (2008)
7. Singh, C.: Pooja: Improving image retrieval using combined features of hough transform and zernike moments. Optics and Lasers in Engineering 49(12), 1384–1396 (2011)
8. Wang, J.Z., Li, J., Wiederhold, G.: Simplicity: Semantics-sensitive integrated matching for picture libraries. TPAMI 23(9), 947–963 (2001)
9. Xu, X., Zhang, L., Yu, Z., Zhou, C.: The application of particle swarm optimization in relevance feedback. In: International Conf. on FBIE, pp. 156–159 (2009)
10. Zhang, W.J., Wang, J.Y.: The study of methods for language model based positive and negative relevance feedback in information retrieval. In: International Symposium - Information Science and Engineering (ISISE), pp. 39–43 (2012)
11. Zhou, X.S., Huang, T.S.: Relevance feedback in image retrieval: A comprehensive review. Multimedia Systems 8(6), 536–544 (2003)

Graph Fusion Using Global Descriptors for Image Retrieval

Tomás Mardones[1]([✉]), Héctor Allende[1], and Claudio Moraga[2,3]

[1] Universidad Técnica Federico Santa María, CP 110-V, Valparaíso, Chile
tomas.mardones@alumnos.usm.cl
[2] European Centre for Soft Computing, 33600 Mieres, Spain
hallende@inf.utfsm.cl
[3] Faculty of Computer Science, TU Dortmund University, Dortmund, Germany
claudio.moraga@udo.edu

Abstract. This paper addresses the problem of content-based image retrieval in a large-scale setting. Recently several graph-based image retrieval systems to fuse different representations have been proposed with excellent results, however most of them use at least one representation based on local descriptors that does not scale very well with the number the images, hurting time and memory requirements as the database grows. This motivated us to investigate the possibility to retain the performance of local descriptor methods while using only global descriptions of the image. Thus, we propose a graph-based query fusion approach -where we combine several representations based on aggregating local descriptors such as Fisher Vectors- using distance and neighborhood information to evaluate the individual importance of each element in every query. Performance is analyzed in different time and memory constrained scenarios. Experiments are performed on 3 public datasets: the UKBench, Holidays and MIRFLICKR-1M, obtaining state of the art performance.

Keywords: Fisher vector · Graph fusion · Large scale image retrieval · Global descriptors

1 Introduction

Content-based image retrieval (CBIR) is an important area of research in Multimedia, since it is linked to numerous image applications, especially web and mobile image search. Given a query image, the problem consists in finding the most similar images in a database. The image presentation that has received the most attention corresponds to the Bag of Words (BoW) representation [12]. Still it has an important limitation regarding the amount of images it can handle at a time due to its time response and memory usage, becoming impractical when working with a 100M image database (a database with 100 million images).

To overcome the database size limitation, the Fisher Vector (FV) and Vector of Locally Aggregated Descriptors (VLAD) were proposed [7] as a global image

© Springer International Publishing Switzerland 2015
A. Pardo and J. Kittler (Eds.): CIARP 2015, LNCS 9423, pp. 290–297, 2015.
DOI: 10.1007/978-3-319-25751-8_35

descriptor being able to leverage the advantages of powerful local descriptors like RootSIFT. A global descriptor usually implies that the memory usage per image is fixed and is represented by a dense vector. Dense vectors can have their dimension reduced by powerful methods, such as Principal Component Analysis (PCA) and Optimized Product Quantization (OPQ) [2].

To improve the performance of image retrieval systems, global descriptors have been combined with local descriptors representations [17]. Some of these systems achieve State of the Art performance, but the presence of local descriptors representations makes them unsuitable to very large scale image retrieval. Only a few works have used exclusively combination of global descriptors [3,8] and none of them, in our knowledge, have explored the query results fusion area.

Therefore in this work we propose a new unsupervised method to combine query results using only Fisher Vectors as image representations with the objective of meeting a low memory requirement and to enhance the performance achieved by the use of global descriptors.

The rest of the paper is organized as follows. Section 2 reviews relevant work regarding fusion methods using global descriptors. In Section 3 our proposal is detailed and its experimental results are discussed in Section 4. Concluding remarks are given in Section 5.

2   Related Work

2.1   Feature Combination

To build a large scale image retrieval system it is important that a compact image representation is used in addition to the descriptors fusion, such as BoW, FVs or GIST [3,8,17]. In particular, in the work of Zhang et al. [17] a graph method is employed to combine the individual ranking list from a BoW, a GIST and a global color representation. Only a few works have explored the combination of exclusively global descriptors for large-scale image retrieval [3,8]. Gordo et al. [3] proposed to use category-level labels of image classification datasets to learn sub-spaces to reduce the dimension of two concatenated Fisher Vectors based on SIFT and statistical color features respectively. On the other hand, Mardones et al. [8] used three concatenated Fisher Vectors based only on SIFT descriptors, but varying the sampling method used to obtain them, demonstrating that the use of different sampling methods is an important way to introduce diversity in the representations. Both works achieved an important boost in performance compared to results obtained with the individual Fisher Vectors employed.

2.2   Graph Based Methods in Image Retrieval

Utilizing graphs is a natural way to introduce the neighborhood relationships when using several representations as noted in several works [11,17]. The closest inspiring works to ours, regarding the fusion method, include [11] and [17]. Qin et al. work [11] introduced a simple, albeit effective, method based on the analysis of the K-reciprocal nearest neighbor structure in the image space with the objective of re-ranking the retrieval images. Zhang et al. [17] proposed an unsupervised graph fusion method, capable of combining any type of image representations, relying only on a set of ranking list obtained, by exploiting the neighborhood structure. In contrast, since we use only Fisher Vectors we concentrate on how to leverage the use of similar representations - as they have comparable distances - and their neighborhood structures to obtain a new ranking list.

3 Proposed Approach

3.1 Individual Image Representations

As previously stated, Fisher Vectors (FVs) are the selected global descriptors to represent the images in this work. This is a method that aggregates local descriptors of an image to build a vectorial representation of it by comparing the image descriptors with a general probabilistic distribution model of them. To model the distribution of the local descriptors a Gaussian Mixture Model (GMM) is used [7] and the Fisher Vector of an image is the derivative of the likelihood of this image descriptors distribution with respect to the learnt GMM parameters. The FV's part corresponding to the GMM mean and variance parameters will be referred to as the mean and variance component of the Fisher Vector respectively.

3.2 Basic Definitions

In the next subsections a few definitions will be shared. To avoid redundancy or confusion, they will be written here. Most of the notation is similar to the one in [17] for consistency.

Denote q and d as the query image and a database image respectively, and i as either of them. Given a distance function $\text{dist}(\cdot, \cdot)$ between images representation vectors, the rank list corresponds to the sorted list of candidate relevant images by the distances between the query image and every database image. Since this list can be very large depending on the number of database images, normally a short rank list - called shortlist - of the first L images of the rank list will be used. Now it is possible to define the K nearest neighbours (NN) of an image i as $N_K(i)$, where this corresponds to the top-K candidates obtained using i as the query. Finally we define the reciprocal neighbour relation between two images i and i' as:

$$R_K(i, i') = i \in N_K(i') \wedge i' \in N_K(i). \tag{1}$$

3.3 Preprocessing Steps for Ranking Reordering and Similarity Computing

Every representation share a common space -being all of them Fisher Vectors- though their distances are not directly comparable since they are based on different descriptors. To take advantage of this, it is important to normalize the distances list in some way. To do this, the influence of arbitrary long distances is limited by using the query adaptive criterion C_a to transform the distances into similarities [6]. C_a works by replacing the distance of a query and an image by the difference between the distance of the k-th NN match of the query and this distance (or 0 if the difference is negative). This has the effect of aligning the rank-distance curves by a translation using as a reference the distance to the k-th NN match. However, the highest similarity is not bounded, so every non-zero value is divided by the highest similarity. This will be called bounded query adaptive criterion C_{ba}. $C_{ba}^L(q, d)$ will be used to transform the distances between the query and its L-nearest-neighbors (rank shortlist elements) into similarities.

An additional step taken before the graph construction is the use of the *maximum reciprocal rank* (MRR) algorithm [1]. The objective is to increase the number of reciprocal neighbors in the ranking's first positions, thus determining a higher quality shortlist. Using this method, a new ranking list is build inserting first the reciprocal neighbors according to the worst ranking position between the rank of the query in the specific neighbor rank shortlist and the rank of the neighbor the query rank shortlist. When no further reciprocal neighbors are found, the non-recriprocal neighbors are added in the same order of the original ranking list. For further details refer to [1].

3.4 Graph Construction and Fusion

For each representation, a weight undirected graph $G = (V, E, w)$ centered at the query q is initialized, where the nodes are the images. The graph will be constructed using nodes from levels 0, 1 and 2. Each level indicates a set of conditions to select the nodes to add to the graph and the weight of its edge and K is a user defined parameter (in Section 4.4 it will be discussed further):

- *Level 0.* The only level 0 node is the query.
- *Level 1.* Every K-nearest neighbor d of the query that satisfies $R_K(q, d)$ is linked by an edge $(q, d) \in E$ to the query. The weight associated with this edge is $C_{ba}^K(q, d)$.
- *Level 2.* Each K-nearest neighbor i of the level 1 nodes is added to the graph, linked to its respective level 1 node. The attached edge weight is computed using the extended Jaccard similarity coefficient $\bar{J}(d, i)$ [1] between the neighborhoods of the level 1 image d and the level 2 image i,

Using $\bar{J}$, instead of the regular Jaccard similarity coefficient J, has the advantage of taking into account the rank of the neighbors, therefore if the K parameter is high and there is only a strong connection between a few nodes in the first rank positions (important nodes probably), the similarity coefficient will be still high making the method more stable respect to the K parameter.

To design the conditions of every level, a vast amount of possible configurations were tested, combining the use of shared neighborhood measurement (J or $\bar{J}$), reciprocal neighbors criterion ($R_K(i, i')$) and similarity measures (C_{ba}). The first two are strong indicators of the quality of the result, as it has been extensively studied in several works [1,11,17]. The similarity plays a fundamental role when there exists a substancial similarity difference between the first images in the rank and the rest, giving a strong indicator of being a relevant image. Several strategies for the graph construction had similar results. The common factor observed was the combination of adding reciprocal neighbors as the level 1 nodes and using the similarities as their weights. Then adding a second layer of neighbors of the level 1 nodes with or without any condition and using their "neighborhood score" ($\bar{J}$) as their weights.

After obtaining a graph for every m-th representation $G^m = (V^m, E^m, w^m)$, they are fused as described in [17]: the final graph $G = (V, E, w)$ with $V = \cup_m V^m$, $E = \cup_m E^m$ and $w(i, i') = \sum_m w^m(i, i')$ for every existing edge. To obtain the final rank list from the graph, the *Ranking by Maximizing Weighted Density* is used [17].

4 Experiments

4.1 Databases and Evaluation Protocol

The following two public benchmarks are employed. INRIA Holidays [5] consists of 1,491 images of 500 scenes and objects. Each scene / object has a query image and the accuracy is measured as the Mean Average Precision (MAP). The University of Kentucky Benchmark (UKB) [9] consists of 10,200 images of 2,550 objects. Each image is used alternatively as a query to search within the 10,200 images (including itself) and the performance is measured as $4 \times$recall@4 (called Kentucky Score, KS or N-S sometimes) averaged over the 10,200 queries. Therefore, the score goes from zero to four on this dataset.

Ten thousand images of the MIRFLICKR-1M dataset [4] are used to learn the GMM parameters and the PCA matrices of the different Fisher Vector representations, the rest are used as distractor images for the large-scale experiments.

4.2 Implementation Details

Several ROI detectors and descriptors will be employed to introduce diversity on the different Fisher Vectors. The base algorithm -independently of the detector and descriptor used- follows the same guidelines and parameters used in [7].

Features. Two types of descriptors are used in this work: 128-dimensional Root-SIFT descriptors and Color descriptors [3]. Four sampling methods are employed to extract descriptors in most experiments: 3 scales dense sampling (D3), Hessian affine (HA), Hessian Laplace and Perdoch's Hessian affine variation (HAP) interest point detectors [15] [10]. RootSIFT is used with every sampling method, while the Color descriptor is used only with the dense sampling method. In the rest of the section we will loosely refer to the Fisher Vectors based on the RootSIFT descriptors sampled with the previously mentioned methods as HA, HL, HAP, D3M and D3V (M and V stand for mean and variance components respectively) and ColorM and ColorV as the Fisher Vectors based on the Color descriptors.

4.3 Scenarios to Consider

There are two principal scenarios of interest to evaluate the performance of the proposed method. The first one focuses on performance, sacrificing response time and memory usage, while the second focuses on balancing the three aspects. All the times reported were measured when processing with an Intel Core i5 2500S (using a single thread).

Performance Scenario (PS). As time is not a primary concern, 640x480 images are used for every representation. The FVs are just reduced to 1024 dimensions using PCA. Table 1 shows that the query time and the memory usage per image are not excellent, but sufficient depending on the application. The performance is better than the obtained in the next scenario.

Balanced Scenario (BS). A combination of 320x240 and 640x480 images is used. Every FV has its dimension reduced to 32 bytes using PCA and OPQ. In Table 1 it can be seen that this configuration reduces the response time to less than a second and, more important, the memory requirements to 792 bytes and 660 bytes on Holidays and UKBench respectively (each uses different representation mixtures). Given the low memory usage of this scenario, it will also be used for the large-scale experiments in Section 4.5.

4.4 Test Datasets Results

On Holidays and UKB the results are encouraging in both scenarios as seen in Table 1. In the performance scenario, the MAP and KS (on Holidays and UKB respectively) increase respect to their best individual representations (D3V and HΛ respectively) is 18.6% and 0.46 respectively. These results improve over the State of the Art in both datasets when considering methods based only on global descriptors, to the best of our knowledge, and are among the State of the Art in general, as seen in Table 2.

In the balanced scenario the improvement of MAP and KS is equally important over the best individual representations (D3V and ColorV), being 14.9% and 0.54 respectively. These results are close in both datasets to the best in the State of the Art. However the memory usage is much lower compared to the best performing methods, as it is possible to see in Table 2.

It is important to mention that the fine-tuning of the K parameter does not make a sustancial difference, but it should be adjusted depending on the expected number of relevant nearest neighbors. For example, the difference from using K=4 to K=15 results in a loss of MAP and KS of 2.4% and 0.08 respectively. In comparison, if Jaccard is used instead of $\bar{J}$, the loss increases to 3.3% and 0.15.

The use of MRR and C_{ba} also enhanced significantly the performance of the system. On Holidays and UKB, the improvement was of 2.8% and 0.05 KS.

4.5 Large-Scale Experiments

An important point of the proposal is its ability to scale due to the relatively small memory usage per image. Equally important is the performance stability as more

Table 1. Holidays and UKB Results. Mean average precision (Kentucky Score for UKB), memory usage per image and total query time (including feature extraction).

Scenario	Holidays			UKB		
	MAP	Memory	Query Time	KS	Memory	Query Time
Performance	86.0%	29 KB	1853 ms	3.85	29 KB	1875 ms
Balanced	80.2%	792 B	768 ms	3.75	660 B	777 ms
Balanced + 1M	76.9%	792 B	950 ms	3.70	660 B	918 ms

Table 2. Comparison with the State of the Art. Results from Holidays, UKB and average memory per image, if available.

	[16]	[14]	[13]	[17]	[11]	[3]	Ours PS	Ours BS
Holidays, MAP	80.2%	84.1%	88.0%	84.6%	-	78.3%	86.0%	80.2%
UKB, KS	-	-	-	3.83	3.67	3.36	3.85	3.75
Memory	8192 B	≈143 KB	-	≈20.2 KB	-	1024 B	≈29 KB	660-792 B

images are being integrated in the database. In Table 1 it can be observed that the total decrease of MAP and KS - with MIRFLICKR-1M's distractor images - is 3.5% and 0.05 respectively. This shows that the proposed system is very robust to the number of images in the database. We believe that this robustness is due to the relevant neighbor consistency across the different representations, e.g. if a rank list is modified due to the insertion of a new image, there are several other rank lists that are not modified, being robust to insertions. Furthermore, a new insertion in the rank shortlist only implies that two image representations are within a short distance, but not a neighborhood similarity. In additional experiments it was seen that the decrease in precision was more significant with the insertion of the first 50K images, but after that is was much slower.

5   Conclusions

In this paper, a query fusion method for Fisher Vectors based on different features is presented. Multiple RootSIFT and Color features are extracted from the image using multiple sampling methods and a Fisher Vector is computed for each of them. Using the ranking and distance lists from every representation a graph is constructed weighting its edges considering a distance similarity measure and the neighborhood structure. Finally every graph is fused and a ranking list is obtained. Using this proposal, it is shown that by the use of solely global descriptors, State of the Art performance is achievable, while maintaining a fixed low memory usage per image.

Acknowledgements. This work was supported by the following research and fellowship grants: DGIP-UTFSM and MECESUP. The work of C. Moraga was partially supported by the Foundation for the Advance of Soft Computing, Mieres, Spain.

References

1. Delvinioti, A., Jégou, H., Amsaleg, L., Houle, M.E.: Image retrieval with reciprocal and shared nearest neighbors. In: Proc. International Conference on Computer Vision Theory and Applications, pp. 321–328, January 2014
2. Ge, T., He, K., Ke, Q., Sun, J.: Optimized product quantization. IEEE Trans. Pattern Analysis and Machine Intelligence **36**(4), 744–755 (2014)
3. Gordo, A., Rodriguez-Serrano, J.A., Perronnin, F., Valveny, E.: Leveraging category-level labels for instance-level image retrieval. In: Proc. CVPR, pp. 3045–3052 (2012)
4. Huiskes, M.J., Thomee, B., Lew, M.S.: New trends and ideas in visual concept detection: the MIR Flickr retrieval evaluation initiative. In: Proc. ACM International Conference on Multimedia Information Retrieval, pp. 527–536. ACM (2010)
5. Jegou, H., Douze, M., Schmid, C.: Hamming embedding and weak geometric consistency for large scale image search. In: Forsyth, D., Torr, P., Zisserman, A. (eds.) ECCV 2008, Part I. LNCS, vol. 5302, pp. 304–317. Springer, Heidelberg (2008)
6. Jégou, H., Douze, M., Schmid, C.: Exploiting descriptor distances for precise image search. Research report, INRIA, Jun 2011
7. Jégou, H., Perronnin, F., Douze, M., Sánchez, J., Pérez, P., Schmid, C.: Aggregating local image descriptors into compact codes. IEEE Trans. Pattern Analysis and Machine Intelligence **34**(9), 1704–1716 (2012)
8. Mardones, T., Allende, H., Moraga, C.: Combining fisher vectors in image retrieval using different sampling techniques. In: Proc. International Conference on Pattern Recognition Applications and Methods, pp. 128–135, January 2015
9. Nister, D., Stewenius, H.: Scalable recognition with a vocabulary tree. In: Proc. CVPR, pp. 2161–2168 (2006)
10. Perdoch, M., Chum, O., Matas, J.: Efficient representation of local geometry for large scale object retrieval. In: Proc. CVPR, pp. 9–16, Jun 2009
11. Qin, D., Gammeter, S., Bossard, L., Quack, T., Van Gool, L.: Hello neighbor: Accurate object retrieval with k-reciprocal nearest neighbors. In: Proc. CVPR, pp. 777–784, Jun 2011
12. Sivic, J., Zisserman, A.: Efficient visual search of videos cast as text retrieval. IEEE Trans. Pattern Analysis and Machine Intelligence **31**(4), 591–606 (2009)
13. Tolias, G., Avrithis, Y., Jégou, H.: To aggregate or not to aggregate: selective match kernels for image search. In: Proc. IEEE ICCV, pp. 1401–1408 (2013)
14. Tolias, G., Furon, T., Jégou, H.: Orientation covariant aggregation of local descriptors with embeddings. In: Fleet, D., Pajdla, T., Schiele, B., Tuytelaars, T. (eds.) ECCV 2014, Part VI. LNCS, vol. 8694, pp. 382–397. Springer, Heidelberg (2014)
15. Tuytelaars, T., Mikolajczyk, K.: Local invariant feature detectors: A survey. Foundations and Trends in Computer Graphics and Vision **3**(3), 177–280 (2008)
16. Gong, Y., Wang, L., Guo, R., Lazebnik, S.: Multi-scale orderless pooling of deep convolutional activation features. In: Fleet, D., Pajdla, T., Schiele, B., Tuytelaars, T. (eds.) ECCV 2014, Part VII. LNCS, vol. 8695, pp. 392–407. Springer, Heidelberg (2014)
17. Zhang, S., Yang, M., Cour, T., Yu, K., Metaxas, D.: Query specific rank fusion for image retrieval. IEEE Trans. Pattern Analysis and Machine Intelligence **37**(4), 803–815 (2015)

Fisher Vectors for Leaf Image Classification: An Experimental Evaluation

Javier A. Redolfi[1]([✉]), Jorge A. Sánchez[2], and Julián A. Pucheta[3]

[1] CONICET, CIII, UTN, Córdoba, Argentina
jredolfi@frc.utn.edu.ar
[2] CONICET, UNC, Córdoba, Argentina
[3] Laboratorio de Matemática Aplicada al Control, UNC, Córdoba, Argentina

Abstract. In this work we present an experimental evaluation of the exponential family Fisher vector (eFV) encoding applied to the problem of visual plant identification. We evaluate the performance of this model together with a variety of local image descriptors on four different datasets and compare the results with other methods proposed in the literature. Experiments show that the eFV achieves a performance that compares favorably with other state-of-the-art approaches on this problem.

Keywords: Plant identificacion · Exponential family fisher vectors · Image classification

1 Introduction

In recent years there has been an increasing interest in the problem of plant species classification in images [3,7,12,18]. This is motivated, among other reasons, by an increase in the number of endangered species due to climate change, shifts in the agricultural production (higher deforestation rates) and poor urban planing.

In this paper we address the problem of leaf image classification which consists on predicting the species of a plant based on images of its leaves. The problem is very challenging and it is a very difficult task even for trained experts and botanists [5]. The difficulty arises from the large number of species that has to be taken into account, large degrees of intra-class variability and high visual similarities between classes [18].

Here we evaluate a recently proposed image representation known as the exponential family Fisher vector (eFV) [17]. This model is a generalization of the Gaussian Fisher vector [16] (FV) to a broader class of distributions known as the exponential family. This model has the advantage that it allow us to consider local feature spaces other than $\mathbb{R}^n$, e.g. binary or even the space of symmetric positive definite (SPD) matrices.

© Springer International Publishing Switzerland 2015
A. Pardo and J. Kittler (Eds.): CIARP 2015, LNCS 9423, pp. 298–305, 2015.
DOI: 10.1007/978-3-319-25751-8_36

2 Related Work

There exists a large body of work on the leaf image classification problem. Most of it has been focused on the design of different pre-processing [22,23] and feature extraction techniques [12,20] as well as classification algorithms [8,18] designed specifically for this problem. If we consider the feature extraction stage, methods can be grouped into two main categories: those using global image features and those based on local descriptors. Next, we provide some examples for the global and local feature approach, respectively.

In [22,23] the authors propose to use shape and texture global features obtained after a segmentation step for the classification of leaves images. In [12] a system using geometric descriptors, multi-scale distance matrix, invariant moments and a new set of global descriptors is proposed. The computation of such descriptors requires a contour extraction step which –according to the authors– accounts for one of its main limitation. In [18] the authors propose a semi-automatic approach based on global features that requires the user to mark the base and apex of the leaf. The method presented in [3] is based on a set of global descriptors which are not rotations invariant. In this case, the images have to be aligned before computing the descriptors.

In the case of the methods based on local descriptors, Hsiao *et al.* [8] proposed a system based on sparse coding of SIFT descriptors. A similar method but using a combination of local features is presented in [14]. In [1], the authors propose the use of different local descriptors (SURF, Fourier, Rotation Invariant, LBP) encoded with FV to classify images of leaves on a natural background. In [13] the authors use different local descriptors (4 versions of SIFT and a self-similarity descriptor) augmented to take into account the neighborhood structure in feature space. The set of augmented features is encoded with a Gaussian FV. In [4] a FV over SIFT and color moments are combined with a Convolutional Neural Networks (CNN) and a pre-processing step in order to choose the most representative bounding box from the image.

In this work we evaluate the performance of the recently proposed eFV model [17] using a variety of local descriptors that, by its non-Euclidean nature, are not commonly adopted in the literature, namely: raw binary features and covariance patch descriptors. Experiments are performed on four different datasets and results compared against the state-of-the-art.

3 Method Description

Following a common pipeline in FV-based image classification, our approach consists of the following steps: dense feature extraction, eFV signature computation and linear classification. A diagram of the pipeline is shown in figure 1.

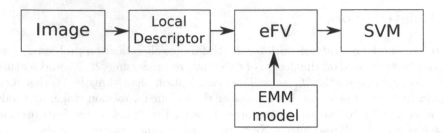

Fig. 1. Block diagram of the proposed system.

3.1 Local Descriptor Extraction

Descriptors are extracted densely on a regular grid with the same step in both directions. To account for variations in scale, local descriptors are extracted from a resolution pyramid of 5 levels and a scale factor of $\frac{1}{\sqrt{2}}$ [17].

In this work, we consider the following types of descriptors: SIFT, binarized SIFT (BinSIFT), BRIEF, LBP and a variation of the patch covariance features (COV) described in [19]. For SIFT and BinSIFT, we reduce its dimensionality to 80 by PCA.

3.2 Exponential Family Fisher Vector

The FV[16] encodes an image as a gradient vector that characterizes the distribution of a set of low-level descriptors with respect to the parameters of a probabilistic generative model which in case of the traditional FV, corresponds to a mixture of multivariate Gaussian pdfs with diagonal covariances. The eFV generalizes the FV by considering mixtures of a more general class of distributions known as the exponential family. This allow the model to deal with input spaces other than $\mathbb{R}^D$ in a principled manner. Next, we provide a brief overview of the eFV representation. More details can be found in [17].

Let $\mathbf{X} = \{\mathbf{X}_1, ..., \mathbf{X}_N\}$, $\mathbf{X}_i \in \mathbb{R}^D$, a set of low-level descriptors extracted from image I. We model its generation process as a mixture distribution of the form:

$$P(\mathbf{X}|\lambda) = \prod_{i=1}^{N} \sum_{k=1}^{K} \mathbf{w_k} p(\mathbf{X_i}|\eta_k), \quad \mathbf{w_k} > 0 \ \forall k, \quad \sum_{k=1}^{K} \mathbf{w_k} = 1 \tag{1}$$

with $\lambda = \{\mathbf{w_k}, \eta_k : k = 1, ..., K\}$ and

$$p(\mathbf{X}|\eta_k) = \mathbf{h}(\mathbf{X}) \exp(\langle \eta_k, \mathbf{T}(\mathbf{X}) \rangle - \psi(\eta_k)) \tag{2}$$

is a member of the exponential family. Here, $T(\mathbf{X})$ is the vector of sufficient statistics, $\psi(\eta_k)$ is known as *partition function* and $h(\mathbf{X})$ is a normalizer which is independent of η_k. Given $P(\mathbf{X}|\lambda)$, the eFV of I is computed as the normalized gradient w.r.t λ of the log-likelihood of $\mathbf{X}$ as:

Table 1. Descriptors and corresponding distribution used for enconding.

Descriptor	Input Domain	Distribution	$T(X)$	$\psi(\eta)$	$h(X)$
SIFT	$\mathbb{R}^D$	Gaussian	$(x_1, x_1^2, \ldots, x_D, x_D^2)$	$-\frac{1}{4}\eta_1^t\,\eta_2^{-1}\eta_1 - \frac{1}{2}\log|-2\eta_2|$	1
BRIEF, BinSIFT, LBP	$\{0,1\}^D$	Bernoulli	X	$\sum_{j=1}^D \log(1+e^{\eta_j})$	1
COV	$D \times D$ SPD	Wishart	X	$\log \Gamma_p(\frac{n}{2}) - \frac{n}{2}\log|\eta|$	$|\eta|^{(n-D-1)/2}$

$$g(\mathbf{X}) \triangleq L_\lambda \nabla_\lambda \log P(\mathbf{X}|\lambda) = \sum_{i=1}^N L_\lambda \nabla_\lambda \log \left(\sum_{k=1}^K w_k p(\mathbf{X}_i|\eta_k) \right) \qquad (3)$$

L_λ is a normalizer obtained from the Cholesky decomposition of the inverse of the Fisher information matrix of $P(\cdot|\lambda)$.

Table 1 show, for each local descriptor we consider in the experiments, the corresponding exponential family distribution and the most relevant terms used for eFV encoding.

3.3 Classifier

For classification we rely on linear SVMs trained on the primal with Stochastic Gradient Descent (SGD) [16,17].

4 Experiments

We performed experiments on four different publicly available datasets and compared the results obtained by our method with different algorithms found in the literature.

4.1 Datasets

We ran experiments on the following datasets: Flavia [21], Foliage [10], Plant-CLEF2012 [6] and PlantCLEF2013 [5].

Flavia contains 1907 images of leaves from 32 classes of trees, with a minimun of 50 samples per class and a maximun of 72. The normal procedure of evaluation is to leave 10 samples of each class for test and train on the rest.

Foliage contains 120 samples for each of 60 species of trees. The recommended procedure of evaluation is to take 100 samples for training and 20 for testing for each class.

PlantCLEF2012 consists of 11572 images of 126 species of trees divided in three types, scan, scan-like and photograph.

PlantCLEF2013 contains 26077 images of 250 tree species of two types, sheet as background and natural background. The NaturalBackground images are divided into 5 types, images of entire plant, flower, fruit, leaf and stem.

Table 2. eFV configurations and short names.

Acronym	Descriptor	PCA	Exponential Mixture Model
BRIEF-BMM-eFV	BRIEF	No	Bernoulli
SIFT-PCA-GMM-eFV [1]	SIFT	Yes	Gaussian
COV-WMM-eFV	Covariance	No	Wishart
LBP-BMM-eFV	LBP	No	Bernoulli
BinSIFT-BMM-eFV	BinSIFT	Yes	Bernoulli

4.2 Experimental Configuration

In all our experiments we compute eFV signatures using mixture models with 256 components. These models were fitted using a set of 1M descriptors randomly sampled from the training set. Table 2 shows a summary of the different configurations and its acronym for further reference.

Furthermore, we propose the use of the results obtained using the descriptores based on CNN proposed in [15] as a baseline for comparison. In that work, the authors show that features obtained from CNN nets should be used as the first candidate in most visual recognition tasks. These descriptors were computed such as the output of the 7th layer (fc7) of the convolutional neural network available in [9] and then classified with an SVM. This baseline is referred in the following as CNN+SVM.

4.3 Results

Table 3 shows the accuracy of different configurations of the proposed method on the Flavia and Foliage datasets together with recent results available in the literature. The accuracy is obtained as the percent of well classified samples.

As can be seen from table 3 the best accuracy of eFV are obtained with SIFT and COV descriptors, and their accuracy on Flavia and Foliage is above the obtained with recent proposed methods in the literature. In the Foliage dataset the baseline CNN+SVM has the best accuracy.

In tables 4 and 5, we compare the results of our algorithm with the best results on the PlantCLEF2012 and PlantCLEF2013 challenges. The score is computed using the scripts provided with the datasets. Top performing results are highlighted in bold. For these two datasets we only show the accuracy for SIFT and COV descriptors.

In PlantCLEF2012 dataset (table 4) the enconding of SIFT descriptors with eFV shows the best performance for Scan-like, Photos and Average, and the baseline system CNN+SVM, shows the best performance for Scan type of images.

For the dataset PlantCLEF2013, the best performance for SheetAsBackground images is obtained with the method proposed in [22] but this method fails for the NaturalBackground images as can be seen in table 5. The cause of

---

[1] This configuration is the traditional FV[16].

Table 3. Accuracy of different configurations of eFV and results in the literature on datasets Flavia and Foliage

Method	Acc. Flavia	Acc. Foliage
CNN+SVM	99.06	**99.33**
SIFT-PCA-GMM-eFV	99.06	98.75
COV-WMM-eFV	**99.38**	98.25
LBP-BMM-eFV	95.62	93.25
BinSIFT-BMM-eFV	89.06	94.33
BRIEF-BMM-eFV	74.06	67.83
GLC [12]	93.00	-
SC [8]	95.47	-
CS [18]	97.00	-
GLS [11]	97.19	95.00
ICM [20]	97.82	-

Table 4. Classification results on PlantCLEF2012 for the 3 types of images and on average.

Method	Scan	Scan-like	Photos	Average
CNN+SVM	**0.65**	0.51	0.40	0.52
SIFT-PCA-GMM-eFV	0.62	**0.74**	**0.44**	**0.60**
COV-WMM-eFV	0.48	0.43	0.24	0.38
SABANCI OKAN [23]	0.58	0.55	0.22	0.16
INRIA [2]	0.39	0.59	0.21	0.40
LSIS DYNI [14]	0.41	0.42	0.32	0.42

this behavior is a preprocessing segmentation step which is inapplicable for NaturalBackground images. For this type of images, one of the best performance is achieved with the method presented in [13] based in a complex scheme of late-fusion of 4 versions of SIFT and self-similarity encoded with a polynomial embedding of descriptors encoded with FV. Also, the last method uses metadata information of the test set, in particular the type of NaturalBackground image, in constrast to ours. Again, the baseline CNN+SVM has the best performance for one type of images.

Table 5. Classification results on PlantCLEF2013 for the 2 types of images.

Method	SheetAsBackground	NaturalBackground
CNN+SVM	0.56	**0.40**
SIFT-PCA-GMM-eFV	0.59	0.37
COV-WMM-eFV	0.36	0.18
SABANCI OKAN [22]	**0.61**	0.18
NlabUTokio [13]	0.50	0.39

5   Conclusions

We presented an empirical evaluation of different eFV configurations applied to the problem of plant identification. We performed experiments in different publicly available datasets and compared our results against other state-of-the-art approaches. The results in some experiments are better than the state of the art and in most of the cases the best eFV configuration is SIFT descriptors encoded with GMM based eFV. But the baseline using CNN and SVM performs also very well and this performance can be explained by the discriminative power of these descriptors.

The advantages of the proposed method are that it does not need a preprocessing step for the leaf contour extraction because it is based on local descriptors, it allows the use of different descriptors in an unified framework, it is not based in handcrafted or ad-hoc descriptors and it is simpler than some of the existing algorithms. Furthermore, unlike other methods it can be applied on images of leaves with a simple background or with complex background as we demonstrated on the experiments.

References

1. Bakic, V., Mouine, S., Ouertani-Litayem, S., Verroust-Blondet, A., Yahiaoui, I., Goëau, H., Joly, A.: Inria's participation at ImageCLEF 2013 plant identification task. CLEF (Online Working Notes/Labs/Workshop) (2013)
2. Bakic, V., Yahiaoui, I., Mouine, S., Ouertani, S.L., Ouertani, W., Verroust-Blondet, A., Goëau, H., Joly, A.: Inria IMEDIA2's participation at ImageCLEF 2012 plant identification task. CLEF (Online Working Notes/Labs/Workshop) (2012)
3. Chaki, J., Parekh, R., Bhattacharya, S.: Plant leaf recognition using texture and shape features with neural classifiers. Pattern Recognition Letters 58, 61–68 (2015)
4. Chen, Q., Abedini, M., Garnavi, R., Liang, X.: IBM research Australia at LifeCLEF 2014: Plant identification task. In: Working notes of CLEF 2014 conference (2014)
5. Goëau, H., Bonnet, P., Joly, A., Bakic, V., Barthélémy, D., Boujemaa, N., Molino, J.F.: The ImageCLEF 2013 plant identification task. In: CLEF (2013)
6. Goëau, H., Bonnet, P., Joly, A., Yahiaoui, I., Bakic, V., Barthélémy, D., Boujemaa, N., Molino, J.F.: The ImageCLEF 2012 plant identification task. In: CLEF (2012)
7. Goëau, H., Joly, A., Bonnet, P., Selmi, S., Molino, J.F., Barthélémy, D., Boujemaa, N.: LifeCLEF plant identification task 2014. CLEF2014 Working Notes. Working Notes for CLEF 2014 Conference, Sheffield, September 15–18, 2014, pp. 598–615 (2014)
8. Hsiao, J.K., Kang, L.W., Chang, C.L., Lin, C.Y.: Comparative study of leaf image recognition with a novel learning-based approach. In: Science and Information Conference (SAI), pp. 389–393. IEEE (2014)
9. Jia, Y., Shelhamer, E., Donahue, J., Karayev, S., Long, J., Girshick, R., Guadarrama, S., Darrell, T.: Caffe: Convolutional architecture for fast feature embedding. In: Proceedings of the ACM International Conference on Multimedia, pp. 675–678. ACM (2014)
10. Kadir, A., Nugroho, L., Susanto, A., Santosa, P.: Neural Network Application on Foliage Plant Identification. International Journal of Computer Applications 29(9), 15–22 (2011)

11. Kadir, A.: A Model of Plant Identification System Using GLCM, Lacunarity and Shen Features (2014). arXiv preprint arXiv:1410.0969
12. Kalyoncu, C., Toygar, ö: Geometric leaf classification. Computer Vision and Image Understanding **133**, 102–109 (2015)
13. Nakayama, H.: Nlab-utokyo at ImageCLEF 2013 plant identification task. In: Working notes of CLEF 2013 conference (2013)
14. Paris, S., Halkias, X., Glotin, H.: Participation of LSIS/DYNI to Image-CLEF 2012 plant images classification task. In: CLEF (Online Working Notes/Labs/Workshop) (2012)
15. Razavian, A.S., Azizpour, H., Sullivan, J., Carlsson, S.: CNN Features off-the-shelf: an Astounding Baseline for Recognition. In: IEEE Conference on Computer Vision and Pattern Recognition Workshops (CVPRW), pp. 512–519. IEEE (2014)
16. Sánchez, J., Perronnin, F., Mensink, T., Verbeek, J.J.: Image Classification with the Fisher Vector: Theory and Practice. International Journal of Computer Vision **105**(3), 222–245 (2013)
17. Sánchez, J., Redolfi, J.: Exponential family Fisher vector for image classification. Pattern Recognition Letters **59**, 26–32 (2015)
18. Sfar, A.R., Boujemaa, N., Geman, D.: Confidence Sets for Fine-Grained Categorization and Plant Species Identification. International Journal of Computer Vision, pp. 1–21 (2014)
19. Tuzel, Oncel, Porikli, Fatih, Meer, Peter: Region covariance: a fast descriptor for detection and classification. In: Leonardis, Aleš, Bischof, Horst, Pinz, Axel (eds.) ECCV 2006. LNCS, vol. 3952, pp. 589–600. Springer, Heidelberg (2006)
20. Wang, Z., Sun, X., Ma, Y., Zhang, H., Ma, Y., Xie, W., Zhang, Y.: Plant recognition based on intersecting cortical model. In: International Joint Conference on Neural Networks (IJCNN), pp. 975–980. IEEE (2014)
21. Wu, S.G., Bao, F.S., Xu, E.Y., Wang, Y.X., Chang, Y.F., Xiang, Q.L.: A leaf recognition algorithm for plant classification using probabilistic neural network. In: IEEE International Symposium on Signal Processing and Information Technology, pp. 11–16. IEEE (2007)
22. Yanikoglu, B., Aptoula, E., Yildiran, S.T.: Sabanci-Okan system at ImageCLEF 2013 plant identification competition. In: Working notes of CLEF 2013 conference (2013)
23. Yanikoglu, B.A., Aptoula, E., Tirkaz, C.: Sabanci-Okan system at ImageClef 2012: Combining features and classifiers for plant identification. In: CLEF (Online Working Notes/Labs/Workshop) (2012)

Hierarchical Combination of Semantic Visual Words for Image Classification and Clustering

Vinicius von Glehn De Filippo[1], Zenilton Kleber G. do Patrocínio Jr.[2]([⊠]), and Silvio Jamil F. Guimarães[2]

[1] Instituto Politécnico, Centro Universitário UNA, Belo Horizonte, Brazil
vinicius.filippo@prof.una.br
[2] Pontifícia Universidade Católica de Minas Gerais, Belo Horizonte, Brazil
{zenilton,sjamil}@pucminas.br

Abstract. Image classification and image clustering are two important tasks related to image analysis. In this work a two-level hierarchical model for both tasks using a hierarchical combination of image descriptors is presented. The construction of a latent semantic representation for images is also presented and its impact on the results of both tasks for the two-level hierarchical model is evaluated. Experiments have shown the superior performance attained by the hierarchical combination of descriptors when compared to the simple concatenation of them or to the use of single descriptors. The hierarchical combination of a latent semantic representation has presented results similar to the other hierarchical combinations, using only a small fraction of the time and space needed by others, which is interesting specially for those with restrictions of computer power and/or storage space.

Keywords: Hierarchical combination of descriptors · Image classification · Image clustering · Semantic visual vocabulary

1 Introduction

Due to the rapid development of computers and networks, the storage and transmission of a large number of images become possible. Thus, nowadays images are widely used. With the increasing use of systems for image retrieval, there is a need to provide efficient mechanisms for storage, indexing, and recovery of this type of media. Content-based image retrieval (CBIR) is regarded as one of the most effective way of accessing visual data [7]. Most of CBIR systems analyze image information by using low level features, such as color, texture, shape, among others, and index each image based on its feature vectors (or descriptors).

The early studies on CBIR have only used a single feature approach. However, it is hard to attain satisfactory results by using a single feature, since images contain various visual characteristics. Thus, CBIR systems have started using a

The authors are grateful to PUC Minas, Centro Universitário UNA, CNPq, CAPES, and FAPEMIG for the partial financial support of this work.

© Springer International Publishing Switzerland 2015
A. Pardo and J. Kittler (Eds.): CIARP 2015, LNCS 9423, pp. 306–313, 2015.
DOI: 10.1007/978-3-319-25751-8_37

combination of visual features. In [6], a method based on the integration of color and texture was proposed yielding on higher retrieval accuracy. In [1], a combination of global and local descriptors through genetic programming was used to outperform the use of single descriptors. Finally, in [2] a novel coding scheme by combining global and local descriptors was proposed, which are applied to improve robustness and to explore the latent structure of the codebook.

In this work, we propose a two-level hierarchical model for image classification and image clustering using a hierarchical combination of descriptors. Moreover, we also evaluated the construction of a latent semantic representation and its impact on both tasks. To the best of our knowledge, there is no other approach in the literature which was designed to solve both tasks at the same time. Experiments have shown the superior performance attained by the hierarchical combination of descriptors when compared to a simple concatenation of them or to the use of single descriptors. The hierarchical combination of semantic representations has presented results similar to the other combinations, spending only a small fraction of the time and space needed by others (which is interesting when restrictions of computer power and/or storage space exist).

2 Image Representations

Both the effectiveness and the efficiency of an image processing system are dependent on *descriptors* (or visual features). A feature extraction algorithm can produce either a single feature vector or a set of feature vectors. In the former case, a single feature vector must capture the entire information of the visual content (named *global descriptor*). In the latter case, a set of feature vectors (or *local descriptors*) is associated with the image visual content.

In order to be able to efficiently deal with a large number of local descriptors, an important task is the construction of a visual dictionary, or codebook. Afterwards, the codebook can be used to create a *mid-level* image descriptor – named *Bag-of-Words* (BoW) – to describe any image using two steps: *coding* (*i.e.*, assignment of descriptors to visual words) and *pooling* (*i.e.*, generation of an image representation). The BoW is simple to build, however it may suffer from two issues: *polysemy* – a single visual word may represent different contents; and *synonymy* – several visual words may characterize the same content.

To cope with these problems, the adoption of latent space models have been proposed to capture co-occurrence information. The analysis of visual word co-occurrence can be considered using similar approaches. Here, Latent Semantic Analysis (LSA) [3] model is used for producing a low-rank approximation of the word-image occurrence matrix. Let A be the occurrence matrix whose rows correspond to t terms (or visual words) and columns correspond to d documents (or images). By selecting the k largest singular values (obtained using sigular value decomposition – SVD), a rank-k approximation of A is given by

$$A \approx A_k = U_k \Sigma_k V_k^T. \tag{1}$$

The column vectors of U_k and V_k span the concept space of terms and the concept space of documents, respectively.

In this work, similar to [4], the traditional approach (used in LSA) of representing documents through rows of V_k was not used. Instead of that, a semantic visual vocabulary is generated by finding clusters of the synonym terms in the term-concept space (U_k). To do that, *K-Means clustering* is used to divide the set of t terms into n clusters. Afterwards, each cluster representative can be seen as a distinct semantic term (*i.e.*, semantic visual word), and they form a semantic visual vocabulary. Using the nearest neighbor search, each original term is related to one of the semantic words for generating a semantic map. And, finally, that semantic map is used to produce a semantic description of the original document, *i.e.*, entries of synonym terms are merged generating a new occurrence matrix A_S in which rows correspond to n semantic visual words. Here, a semantic description of each image is obtained by adding the values of the original BoW vector related to synonym terms.

3 Two-level Hierarchical Model

In this work, we propose a two-level hierarchical model for image classification and clustering using a hierarchical combination of image descriptors. The model consists of two distinct levels of index structures: the upper level – called *category level* – is responsible for representing the image categories and for pointing to the index structures belonging to the lower level – named *object level* – where the information is actually stored.

Content-based image retrieval systems are based on two main operations: the construction of the database from a given set of images (and the insertion of new images) and the retrieval of images for a given query.

3.1 Image Indexing

In the proposed model, each image is described by a pair of descriptors (d_c, d_o), in which d_c is used at the category level – *class descriptor* – while d_o is adopted at the object level – *object descriptor*. This allows any combination of image descriptors, even one that consists of two identical image descriptors. The indexing process is described in the following.

The process begins with the indexing of the class descriptor of the image to be indexed at the category level. To do that, a nearest neighbor search at the category level is made using the image class descriptor. The answer of that search allows to determine the image category (*i.e.*, where the class descriptor should be inserted). If no class descriptor has been inserted before, the image class descriptor is considered the first representative of a group and the first category should be created. Each time that a new category is created, a new reference is generated for another index structure at the object level, where the corresponding object descriptor should be inserted. The criterion used to create a new class is based on the distance between the new class descriptor and its nearest neighbor at the category level. If the distance between them is lower than the threshold r (known as category radius), the image is considered to belong to the same class of its nearest neighbor and its object descriptor is inserted in the same index structure used for storing its nearest neighbor. Otherwise, if the distance between them is greater than the threshold r, a new category should be created, and so on. It is worth to mention that the number of groups is directly related to the value of category radius r (*i.e.*, lesser the value of r, greater the number of categories generated at the end of the process).

The category level is also responsible for pointing to the index structure where the object descriptors of all the images belonging to the same group are stored. So, after indexing the class descriptor of the new image at the category level, the corresponding object descriptor (together with a pointer to the new image) should always be inserted into the associated index structure at the object level, according to the group selected (or created) at the category level. Those steps are repeated for each new image that has to be inserted in the database, until the hierarchical structure is fully created.

3.2   Image Retrieval

For a given query image q, a pair of descriptors should be generated (similar to the indexing procedure). Thus, considering that the query image q is represented by a pair of descriptors (q_c, q_o), in which q_c is the *query class descriptor* and q_o is the *query object descriptor*, the retrieval process is described in the following.

First, a nearest neighbor search is made at the category level using the query class descriptor q_c. The answer to that search indicates the group that may contain images that are similar to the query, thus given also a reference to the lower-level index structure. Using that reference, a K-nearest neighbors search, using the query object descriptor q_o, is made in the lower-level index structure; and, the K-nearest neighbors found are returned as result. One should notice that the search results are approximate, even if an exact access method is used.

4   Experiments

In this section, we present the results of experiments made to assess the performance of the proposed hierarchical model. During experiments, the **FGComp2013**[1] dataset was used. It is a 5-domain subset of the **ILSVRC2013** (*Imagenet Large Scale Visual Recognition Challenge*[2]) and contains 75,533 images (49,052 for training and 28,481 for test). The index structure used at both levels was the Slim-tree (which is an exact metric access method).

The global descriptor GIST and the *mid-level* descriptor BoW were used to describe the visual content. The descriptor BoW (with hard assignment and sum pooling) was built from local image descriptors *Compact Color* SIFT – hereafter called BAG. Most of the works using the GIST descriptor resize the image in a preliminary stage to a size of 32×32 pixels. After resizing, color GIST

---

[1] https://sites.google.com/site/fgcomp2013/
[2] http://www.image-net.org/challenges/LSVRC/2013/

Table 1. Descriptors sets and combinations used in the evaluation procedure.

(a) Descriptors sets

Descriptors Set	Based on	k	# Dimensions
GIST 960	GIST	–	960
GIST 05-100	GIST	5	100
GIST 25-100	GIST	25	100
GIST 50-100	GIST	50	100
GIST 100-100	GIST	100	100
BAG 960	BAG	–	960
BAG 05-100	BAG	5	100
BAG 25-100	BAG	25	100
BAG 50-100	BAG	50	100
BAG 100-100	BAG	100	100

(b) Tested combinations

Combination	Categ.Level Desc.	Obj.Level Desc.
GB 960	GIST 960	BAG 960
GG 960	GIST 960	GIST 960
BB 960	BAG 960	BAG 960
BG 960	BAG 960	GIST 960
GB 05-100	GIST 05-100	BAG 05-100
GG 05-100	GIST 05-100	GIST 05-100
BB 05-100	BAG 05-100	BAG 05-100
BG 05-100	BAG 05-100	GIST 05-100
GB 25-100	GIST 25-100	BAG 25-100
GG 25-100	GIST 25-100	GIST 25-100
BB 25-100	BAG 25-100	BAG 25-100
BG 25-100	BAG 25-100	GIST 25-100
GB 50-100	GIST 50-100	BAG 50-100
GG 50-100	GIST 50-100	GIST 50-100
BB 50-100	BAG 50-100	BAG 50-100
BG 50-100	BAG 50-100	GIST 50-100
GB 100-100	GIST 100-100	BAG 100-100
GG 100-100	GIST 100-100	GIST 100-100
BB 100-100	BAG 100-100	BAG 100-100
BG 100-100	BAG 100-100	GIST 100-100

descriptor is calculated for each image using an implementation[3] that produces a 960-dimensional feature vector. For BAG, the visual vocabulary size is also set to 960. Besides, the image dataset was also described using different semantic vocabularies: the number of concepts k was set to 5, 25, 50, or 100; and the size of semantic visual vocabulary n was set to 100. Table 1(a) shows information about all the sets of descriptors, while Table 1(b) presents the combinations used in the experiments. In order to refer to all combinations that use GIST at the category level and BAG at the object level, hereafter we will use GB (similarly, GG, BB, and BG will be used for other combinations).

Both tasks (image classification and clustering) are evaluated in our experiments. For image classification, a 5-nearest neighbor (5-NN) classifier was evaluated with different radius values. We also implement three others 5-NN classifiers based on the retrieval results of a single Slim-tree, so called: ST, ST_B and ST_G. The former, ST, was constructed using an extended descriptor obtained from the concatenation of GIST 960 and BAG 960, while the others, ST_B and ST_G, were constructed using only BAG 960 and GIST 960, respectively. The F-Score (*i.e.*, an harmonic mean of precision and recall) was used to assess the image classification results. For evaluating image clustering, we adopt pair counting (or concordance) approach [5], which allows us to compute F-Score. Finally, we have also applied a *K-Means clustering* algorithm in order to compare to the clustering results obtained by the proposed hierarchical model. In this case, we set the number of clusters to the same number of groups generated during the construction of the corresponding two-level hierarchical structure and used the same descriptor adopted at category level.

Table 2 presents the number of clusters and F-Score values for image classification and image clustering – both using the two-level hierarchical model; and the F-Score values obtained by *K-Means clustering* algorithm The results are

---

[3] http://lear.inrialpes.fr/software

Table 2. F-Score values for image classification and image clustering experiments.

(a) GIST

Cat. Rad.	# Clust.	GB Class.	GB 960 Clust.	GG Class.	GG 960 Clust.	KM with GIST
1.00	41651	**0.886**	0.000	0.886	0.000	0.000
1.30	17176	0.860	0.006	0.863	0.006	0.001
1.50	5813	0.836	0.040	0.847	0.040	0.002
1.65	2529	0.818	0.067	0.834	0.067	0.004
1.85	978	0.793	0.266	0.843	0.266	0.007
2.05	406	0.779	0.563	0.859	0.563	0.015
2.25	198	0.859	**0.600**	0.870	**0.600**	0.027
2.50	82	0.761	0.553	0.883	0.553	0.061
2.65	45	0.760	0.526	0.885	0.526	0.101
2.80	24	0.759	0.526	**0.887**	0.526	0.176
2.90	21	0.759	0.522	0.885	0.522	0.202
3.00	16	0.759	0.522	0.886	0.522	0.238
3.10	10	0.760	0.521	**0.887**	0.521	0.298
3.20	8	0.760	0.521	**0.887**	0.521	**0.335**
		GB 05-100		GG 05-100		
1.00	48250	**0.811**	0.000	0.811	0.000	0.000
2.25	7176	0.788	0.010	0.778	0.010	0.001
3.00	1274	0.781	0.075	0.777	0.075	0.004
4.65	99	0.787	0.559	0.812	0.559	0.045
5.65	35	0.780	**0.586**	0.825	**0.586**	0.111
		GB 25-100		GG 25-100		
1.00	48626	**0.868**	0.000	**0.868**	0.000	0.000
2.25	36373	0.862	0.000	0.862	0.000	0.000
3.00	8666	0.827	0.007	0.823	0.007	0.001
4.65	167	0.805	0.286	0.826	0.286	0.028
5.65	36	0.791	**0.527**	0.851	**0.303**	0.121
		GB 50-100		GG 50-100		
1.00	48630	**0.860**	0.000	**0.860**	0.000	0.000
2.25	37447	0.859	0.000	0.859	0.000	0.000
3.00	9465	0.826	0.007	0.824	0.007	0.001
4.65	172	0.796	0.231	0.827	0.231	0.027
5.65	32	0.789	**0.527**	0.848	**0.527**	0.128
		GB 100-100		GG 100-100		
1.00	48628	**0.855**	0.000	**0.855**	0.000	0.000
2.25	36285	0.852	0.000	0.853	0.000	0.000
3.00	8304	0.815	0.005	0.814	0.005	0.001
4.65	147	0.786	0.192	0.822	0.192	0.031
5.65	27	0.785	**0.505**	0.841	**0.505**	0.144

(b) BAG

Cat. Rad. ($\times 10^3$)	# Clust.	BB Class.	BB 960 Clust.	BG Class.	BG 960 Clust.	KM with BAG
0.05	42706	0.747	0.014	0.769	0.014	0.000
0.10	22263	0.736	0.155	0.798	0.155	0.000
0.15	10983	0.743	**0.610**	0.832	**0.610**	0.001
0.25	4412	0.750	0.534	0.869	0.534	0.002
0.35	1741	0.751	0.563	0.877	0.563	0.004
1.00	163	0.758	0.523	0.886	0.523	0.046
5.00	11	**0.760**	0.521	**0.887**	0.521	0.424
10.00	5	**0.760**	0.521	**0.887**	0.521	**0.590**
15.00	3	**0.760**	0.521	**0.887**	0.521	0.527
22.50	3	**0.760**	0.521	**0.887**	0.521	0.527
		BB 05-100		BG 05-100		
0.10	20936	0.751	0.108	0.789	0.108	0.000
0.35	2010	0.766	**0.527**	0.829	**0.527**	0.003
5.00	20	**0.776**	0.520	**0.834**	0.520	0.281
10.00	6	**0.776**	0.521	**0.834**	0.521	0.476
18.50	3	**0.776**	0.521	**0.834**	0.521	**0.587**
		BB 25-100		BG 25-100		
0.10	23881	0.764	0.033	0.799	0.033	0.000
0.35	2512	0.867	**0.546**	0.867	**0.546**	0.002
5.00	20	**0.796**	0.520	0.873	0.520	0.267
10.00	6	**0.796**	0.521	0.873	0.521	0.484
18.50	3	**0.796**	0.521	**0.874**	0.521	**0.575**
		BB 50-100		BG 50-100		
0.10	23864	0.758	0.043	0.792	0.043	0.000
0.35	2604	0.782	**0.536**	0.859	**0.536**	0.002
5.00	18	**0.792**	0.520	**0.866**	0.520	0.303
10.00	4	**0.792**	0.520	**0.866**	0.521	**0.597**
18.50	3	**0.792**	0.521	**0.866**	0.521	0.570
		DD 100-100		DG 100-100		
0.10	23480	0.741	0.026	0.779	0.026	0.000
0.35	2586	0.766	**0.521**	0.848	**0.521**	0.002
5.00	20	0.776	0.520	**0.863**	0.520	0.262
10.00	4	0.776	**0.521**	**0.863**	0.521	**0.601**
18.50	3	**0.777**	0.521	**0.863**	0.521	0.581

presented for all 20 combinations and for different values of category radius r. It is also worth to mention that the F-Score values for image classifiers based on structures ST, ST_B and ST_G were 0.7505, 0.7599 and 0.8874, respectively, while the best result for *K-Means* using GIST – called KM_G – was 0.335; and the best result for *K-Means* using BAG – called KM_B – was 0.601.

For image classification task, the results of the proposed model were very close to the best F-Score (0.8874) obtained by the structure ST_G, but in contrast to ST_G our method also solves the image clustering task. The best results were obtained by GG 960 (0.887). The combinations of semantic descriptions represent good alternatives for scenarios with restrictions on computer power and/or on storage space, since they were more economical ($\approx$ one tenth, in our

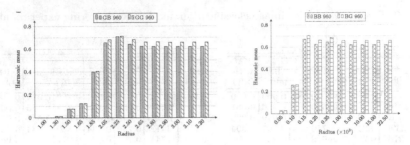

Fig. 1. Harmonic mean of F-Scores for GB 960, GG 960, BB 960 e BG 960.

experiments), but they were able to obtain quite competitive results. For image clustering task, KM_G was worst than all the results obtained by GB/GG combinations. For BB/BG combinations, KM_B was superior in some cases, especially for scenarios with a small number of categories. But, the best clustering results (0.610) obtained by BB 960 and BG 960 were greater than KM_B.

Again, the proposed model is able to deal with both tasks (image classification and clustering). So, in order to evaluate which combination is better in both tasks at the same time, the harmonic mean of the F-Score for classification and for clustering was calculated considering each combination. The harmonic mean for GG 960 was 0.710 for a radius of 2.25; and for BG 960 it was 0.686 for radius of 350 (see Fig. 1). Most of the combinations presented a stable result for the harmonic mean greater than 0.6 (for radius values above 2.00 for GB and GG and for radius above 350 for BB and BG). The results of the proposed model are directly related to the radius values. For GB 960 and GG 960, the best results were associated with a radius values greater than 2.05; while for BB 960 and BG 960, the best results were related to radius values greater than 150. For combinations of semantic descriptions, best results were obtained for radius values greater than 4.65 and 350 for GB/GG and for BB/BG, respectively (see Fig 2). Those results seem to be related to the distribution of distances between descriptors, since best results are generally associated with radius values which are greater than 60%~70% of the actual distances between descriptors. If we consider the results for classification and for clustering separately, GB 960, GG 960, BB 960 and BG 960 presented a superior performance when compared to

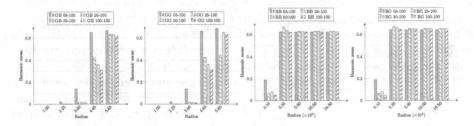

Fig. 2. Harmonic mean of F-Scores for combinations generated from semantic visual vocabularies.

combinations of semantic descriptions. However, when the combined performance (on both task) is taken into account, the combinations with a reduced
number of dimensions generated using semantic visual vocabularies become
interesting options to be explored – especially for those with severe restrictions
of computer power and/or storage space. Although the construction time for
different combinations are almost stable, the time spent during 5-NN search has
varied from 6 to 183 times greater for GB 960, GG 960, BB 960 and BG 960
when compared to the other combinations with a reduced number of dimensions.

5   Conclusion

Image classification and image clustering are two important tasks related to
image analysis. This work proposes a two-level hierarchical model for solving
both tasks using a hierarchical combination of image descriptors. The construction of a latent semantic representation for images is presented and its impact
on the results of both tasks for the two-level hierarchical model is evaluated.

Test results have confirmed the superior performance attained by the hierarchical combination of descriptors when compared to a simple concatenation
of them or to the use of single descriptors. The hierarchical combination of
semantic representations has presented results similar to the other hierarchical
combinations, using only a small fraction of the time and space needed by others, which is interesting specially for those with restrictions of computer power
and/or storage space. Future works should investigate the use of different latent
space models for image representation and their impact on the results of the
simultaneous solution for both tasks (image classification and clustering).

References

1. Andrade, F.S.P., Almeida, J., Pedrini, H., da S.Torres, R.: Fusion of local and global
   descriptors for content-based image and video retrieval. In: Alvarez, L., Mejail, M.,
   Gomez, L., Jacobo, J. (eds.) CIARP 2012. LNCS, vol. 7441, pp. 845–853. Springer,
   Heidelberg (2012)
2. Chen, S., Shi, W., Lv, X.: Feature coding for image classification combining global
   saliency and local difference. Pattern Recognition Letters **51**, 44–49 (2015)
3. Deerwester, S.C., Dumais, S.T., Landauer, T.K., Furnas, G.W., Harshman, R.A.:
   Indexing by latent semantic analysis. Journal of the American Society for Information Science **41**(6), 391–407 (1990)
4. Farahzadeh, E., Cham, T.J., Sluzek, A.: Scene recognition by semantic visual words.
   Signal, Image and Video Processing (October 2014) http://dx.doi.org/10.1007/
   s11760-014-0687-7
5. Pfitzner, D., Leibbrandt, R., Powers, D.: Characterization and evaluation of similarity measures for pairs of clusterings. Knowledge and Information Systems **19**(3),
   361–394 (2009)
6. Wang, X.Y., Zhang, B.B., Yang, H.Y.: Content-based image retrieval by integrating color and texture features. Multimedia Tools and Applications **68**(3), 545–569
   (2014)
7. Yue, J., Li, Z., Liu, L., Fu, Z.: Content-based image retrieval using color and texture
   fused features. Mathematical and Computer Modelling **54**(3–4), 1121–1127 (2011)

Kernel Combination Through Genetic Programming for Image Classification

Yuri H. Ribeiro, Zenilton K.G. do Patrocínio Jr.[✉],
and Silvio Jamil F. Guimarães

Pontifícia Universidade Católica de Minas Gerais, Belo Horizonte, Brazil
yuri.ribeiro@sga.pucminas.br, {zenilton,sjamil}@pucminas.br

Abstract. Support vector machine is a supervised learning technique which uses kernels to perform nonlinear separations of data. In this work, we propose a combination of kernels through genetic programming in which the individual fitness is obtained by a K-NN classifier using a kernel-based distance measure. Experiments have shown that our method KGP-K is much faster than other methods during training, but it is still able to generate individuals (*i.e.*, kernels) with competitive performance (in terms of accuracy) to the ones that were produced by other methods. KGP-K produces reasonable kernels to use in the SVM with no knowledge about the distribution of data, even if they could be more complex than the ones generated by other methods and, therefore, they need more time during tests.

Keywords: Genetic programming · Support vector machines · Kernel combination · Image classification

1   Introduction

Support vector machine (SVM) is a supervised learning technique conceived by [2] as a binary linear classifier. Given a vector space H and a set of data such as $S = (x_i, y_i)$ in which $x_i \in H, y_i \in \pm 1$, a SVM calculates an optimal hyperplane that separates the data from two classes.

However, according to [9], such hyperplane might not exist since a single outlier in the training data can impact negatively on the calculation of the optimal hyperplane. Therefore, it is desirable that SVM tolerates a certain degree of error to deal with outliers. In order to cope with this issue, the authors in [2] introduced slack variables during the calculation of the optimal hyperplane in order to relax the separation constraints. Since large values of those variables could lead to trivial solutions, they also proposed the use of a margin weight to control the size of the margin.

Since SVM is a linear classifier, in order to perform nonlinear separations of data, kernel functions can be used to transform the given data to a higher

The authors are grateful to PUC Minas, CNPq, CAPES and FAPEMIG for the partial financial support of this work.

© Springer International Publishing Switzerland 2015
A. Pardo and J. Kittler (Eds.): CIARP 2015, LNCS 9423, pp. 314–321, 2015.
DOI: 10.1007/978-3-319-25751-8_38

dimensional feature space in which they are linearly separable. A kernel function (represented by $k(\cdot, \cdot)$) are continuous symmetrical functions. According to [10], it is difficult to identify if a function is a kernel, thus any function that satisfies Mercer's theorem [6] could be used. Moreover, a closure property for some operations between kernels could also be explored to generate new kernels [9,10].

Although there are ways of solving efficiently the primal form of the SVM problem (i.e., the calculation of the optimal hyperplane) [8], most of the literature addresses the following dual form of the SVM problem, which is considered more conveniently solvable, as follows

$$\underset{\alpha \in \mathbb{R}^m}{\text{maximize}} \; W(\alpha) = \sum_{i=1}^{m} \alpha_i - \frac{1}{2} \sum_{i,j=1}^{m} \alpha_i \alpha_j y_i y_j k(x_i, x_j), \qquad (1)$$

$$\text{subject to} \qquad\qquad\qquad\qquad\qquad\qquad\qquad\qquad\qquad (2)$$

$$\sum_{i=1}^{m} \alpha_i y_i = 0 \qquad\qquad\qquad (3)$$

$$0 \le \alpha_i \le \frac{C}{m} \;\;, \forall i = 1, \ldots, m \qquad\qquad (4)$$

in which W is the vector of hyperplane coefficients, C and ξ are the aforementioned margin weight and slack variables, respectively, and α is the vector of dual variables corresponding to each separation constraint. According to [3], the decision function can be written as

$$f(x) = sgn \left(\sum_{i=1}^{m} \alpha_i y_i k(x_i, x) + b \right) \qquad\qquad (5)$$

in which b is the bias of the separating hyperplane.

In general, the choice of an appropriate kernel is one important design decision when SVM is used; however, that task is nontrivial. The usual approach is based on a set of predefined kernels from the literature when there is no knowledge about the distribution of data for a given application. Another way is to analyze the application data in order to obtain insights about their distribution. Either ways the usage of SVM gets to be limited.

Evolutionary algorithms (EAs) have presented good results in evolving kernels by making combinations of kernels or searching for kernel parameters in diverse applications [3,10]. In [10], the authors proposed the combination of kernels through genetic programming in which the fitness of each individual (representing a kernel function) is set to the accuracy of a SVM classifier, i.e., at each iteration of their evolutionary method – hereafter called KGP, they have trained and evaluated each kernel function using part of the dataset. However, in [10] training sets are small and the execution time is neglectable, thus it is not possible to infer the consequences of using KGP over large (web scale) datasets.

In this work, we also propose the use of genetic programming (GP) to combine kernels, but, in our GP method, the fitness of each individual is obtained by a K-Nearest Neighbor (K-NN) classifier using a kernel-based distance measure. Experiments have shown that our method, so-called KGP-K, is much faster than KGP during training, but it is still able to generate individuals (i.e., kernels) with competitive performance (in term of accuracy) to the ones that were produced by other methods.

This work is organized as follows. Section 2 discussed genetic programming and presents its use for kernel combination. Our proposed method is presented in Section 3. Some experimental results performed on a well known image dataset are given in Section 4. Finally, in Section 5, some conclusions are drawn and future works are pointed out.

2 Kernel Genetic Programming

Genetic programming (GP) [4], similar to genetic algorithm (GA), is an evolutionary method based upon the principles of biological evolution. The major difference between GP and GA is that GP individuals are generally represented by trees whose size constantly change during execution.

In those, a number of solutions (or individuals) to a given problem are randomly generated, and they together are called a population. The individuals are made in a way such that two operations – called genetic operators – can be applied to then: *mutation* and *crossover*. In the first, a randomly selected part of an individual is exchanged by a new one that is randomly generated; in the latter, randomly selected parts of two different individuals are exchanged between them. The algorithm runs for a number of iterations (each one is called a *generation*). In each generation, the individuals are evaluated in some way (which is dependent on the application domain). The result of such evaluation is called *fitness* and it is used to determine to which individuals the genetic operators will be applied and which of them are the best from their generation (*i.e.*, the best solutions to the problem). The algorithm stops when some condition is reached, such as a certain value of fitness, a maximum number of generations, or both. Fig. 1(a) shows an example of mutation operator, while Fig. 1(b) illustrates a crossover operator.

The KGP algorithm proposed in [10] uses GP to generate valid kernels. It starts with a set of Mercer's kernels randomly generated and uses the aforementioned closure property to produce new kernels. The operations used are exponential, addition or multiplication by another kernel and the multiplication by a real number. Each individual has its fitness set to the accuracy a SVM classifier that is generated by using the kernel represented by the individual itself.

3 Proposed Method

Given a training dataset, whose classes are known, and an observation of unknown class. A K-NN classifier decides the class of the observation based on the classes of the K nearest neighbors in the training set by using some statistic such as the mode. In order to generate a K-NN classifier, we only need a distance measure between the data elements.

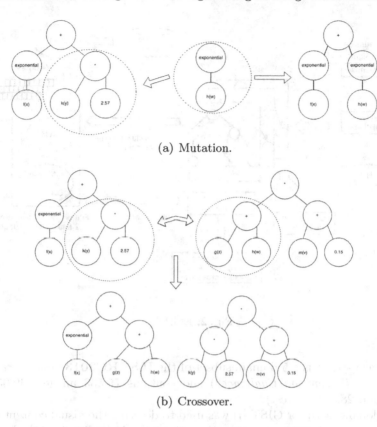

(a) Mutation.

(b) Crossover.

Fig. 1. Examples of genetic operator of GP.

A kernel distance [12] is a distance measure between objects based on a kernel. Given a definite positive kernel function k and two points p and q, a kernel distance d_k is given by:

$$d_k(p, q) = k(p, p) + k(q, q) - 2k(p, q) \tag{6}$$

Therefore, the K-NN classifier using the kernel distance d_k can be used to obtain a fitness for each individual during KGP algorithm. Since there is no off-line learning in the K-NN classifier, its use is expected to be inferior to the use of SVM in terms of accuracy. But since the calculations of a K-NN classifier are simpler, it is also expected to be faster. A simplified diagram of the process can be seen in Fig. 2

4   Experiments and Results

In this section, we present the results of experiments made to assess the performance of the proposed method. During experiments, the **FGComp2013**[1]

---
[1] https://sites.google.com/site/fgcomp2013/

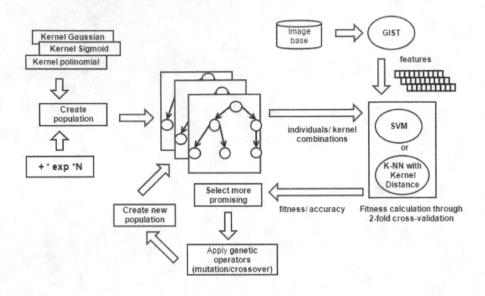

Fig. 2. KGP

dataset was used. It is a 5-domain subset of the **ILSVRC2013** (*Imagenet Large Scale Visual Recognition Challenge*[2]) and contains 75,533 images (49,052 for training and 28,481 for test).

The global descriptor GIST [7] was used to describe the visual content of the images x_i in H addressing the semantic perception. According to [11], the GIST can be defined as a feature vector g, in which each component g_k is given by

$$g_k = \sum_{x,y} w_k(x,y) \times |I(x,y) \otimes h_k(x,y)|, \qquad (7)$$

in which $\otimes$ and $\times$ denote convolution and multiplication of values related to the pixels, respectively; $I(x,y)$ is the luminance channel for the input image; $h_k(x,y)$ is a multiscale Gabor filter bank and $w_k(x,y)$ is a spatial window which is used for computing the average energy of each filter in different positions at the image.

In order to compare our method to [10], we implement it using ECJ [5]. For individual evaluation, we use both LIBSVM [1], so-called KGP, and our own implementation of K-NN using kernel distance, so-called KGP-K (which considers 5 nearest neighbors). In both cases, we have 5 generations and 30 individuals for GP, with a probability of 0.9 for crossover operation and a probability of 0.1 for mutation. We also take advantage of multicore technology and explore the parallelization during individual evaluation using 10 threads to do that (which generates a processor occupancy of almost 90%).

---

[2] http://www.image-net.org/challenges/LSVRC/2013/

Table 1. Experimental results for train step

	Accuracy		Time (in min)	
	average	Δ	average	Δ
KGP	93.86	0.08	2131	211
KGP-K	89.24	0	230	35
Grid	93.69	0	471	0
Random Walk	92.83	0.41	1080	49
Monte Carlo	93.36	0.10	1305	390

We have also compare KGP and KGP-K to: (i) a Grid search of LIBSVM, which is a strategy to explore multiple combinations of C and γ for the Gaussian kernel using cross validation and takes the best as the solution; (ii) a Monte Carlo's method which generates 150 random kernel combinations and takes the best one as the solution; and (iii) a Random Walk method using 30 random combinations of two kernels, followed by a test to choose the best as "current kernel combination". In our experiments, due to restriction of time, we have only three runs for each method in training and test steps (*e.g.*, KGP has taken an average time of one day and a half during training step).

Table 1 presents the average and standard deviation concerning the train step, while Table 2 presents the average and standard deviation for the test step. The experiments were done by using a Core i7 5820k with 16G of memory running Windows 8.1. It is worth to mention that, during training with KGP and KGP-K, each kernel (*i.e.*, individual) is evaluated (*i.e.*, has its fitness calculated) using a 2-fold cross validation over the training data with a SVM classifier and a K-NN classifier, respectively. At end of the training step, the best kernel should be tested, and we do that using a 2-fold cross validation over the testing data with a SVM classifier for both: KGP and KGP-K.

The results of Grid and KGP are very similar. The proposed method KGP-K is inferior during training but it presents a great improvement during tests. It is worth to notice that KGP-K spends a very short time in training. Monte Carlo

Table 2. Experimental results for test step

	Accuracy		Time (in min)	
	average	Δ	average	Δ
KGP	95.34	0.07	433	107
KGP-K	94.82	0.12	626	47
Grid	95.38	0	246	0
Random Walk	94.74	0.18	989	138
Monte Carlo	95.11	0.15	606	376

is superior to KGP-K in terms of accuracy but it spends more time than KGP-K during training. Finally, KGP-K represents a feasible alternative for kernel evolution in scenarios that training time is an important issue. KGP-K produces reasonable kernels to use in the SVM with no knowledge about the distribution of data, but they could be more complex than the ones generated by KGP and, therefore, they need more time during tests.

5　Conclusion

In this work, we propose the combination of kernels through genetic programming in which the individual fitness is obtained by a K-NN classifier using a kernel-based distance measure. Experiments have shown that KGP-K is much faster than KGP during training, but it is still able to generate individuals (*i.e.*, kernels) with competitive performance (in term of accuracy) to the ones that were produced by other methods.

Thus, KGP-K represents a feasible alternative for kernel evolution in scenarios that training time is an important issue. KGP-K produces reasonable kernels to use in the SVM with no knowledge about the distribution of data, but they could be more complex than the ones generated by KGP and, therefore, they need more time during tests.

In future works, we will explore ways to control the individuals during the evolutionary process to prevent the generation of complex (and time-consuming) individuals. It will be also interesting to assess the impact on our method of descriptors with more semantic information about the problem domain.

References

1. Chang, C.C., Lin, C.J.: LIBSVM: A library for support vector machines. ACM Transactions on Intelligent Systems and Technology **2**, 27:1–27:27 (2011)
2. Cortes, C., Vapnik, V.: Support-vector networks. Machine Learning **20**(3), 273–297 (1995)
3. Gönen, M., Alpaydın, E.: Regularizing multiple kernel learning using response surface methodology. Pattern Recognition **44**(1), 159–171 (2011)
4. Koza, J.R.: Genetic programming: on the programming of computers by means of natural selection, vol. 1. MIT press (1992)
5. Luke, S.: Ecj 13: A java EC research system (2005)
6. Mercer, J.: Functions of positive and negative type, and their connection with the theory of integral equations. Philosophical Transactions of the Royal Society of London. Series A, Containing Papers of a Mathematical or Physical Character **209**, 415–446 (1909)
7. Oliva, A., Torralba, A.: Modeling the shape of the scene: A holistic representation of the spatial envelope. International Journal of Computer Vision **42**(3), 145–175 (2001)
8. Shalev-Shwartz, S., Singer, Y., Srebro, N., Cotter, A.: Pegasos: Primal estimated sub-gradient solver for SVM. Mathematical Programming **127**(1), 3–30 (2011)
9. Smola, A.J., Schölkopf, B.: Learning with kernels. Citeseer (1998)

10. Sullivan, K.M., Luke, S.: Evolving kernels for support vector machine classification. In: Proceedings of the 9th Annual Conference on Genetic and Evolutionary Computation, pp. 1702–1707. ACM (2007)
11. Torralba, A., Murphy, K., Freeman, W.: Using the forest to see the trees: exploiting context for visual object detection and localization. Communications of the ACM **53**(3), 107–114 (2010)
12. Wu, G., Chang, E.Y., Panda, N.: Formulating distance functions via the kernel trick. In: Proceedings of the Eleventh ACM SIGKDD International Conference on Knowledge Discovery in Data Mining, pp. 703–709. ACM (2005)

A Complex Network-Based Approach to the Analysis and Classification of Images

Geovana V.L. de Lima, Thullyo R. Castilho, Pedro H. Bugatti,
Priscila T.M. Saito, and Fabrício M. Lopes$^{(\boxtimes)}$

Federal University of Technology - Paraná, Cornelio Procopio, Brazil
{geovanalima,tcastilho}@alunos.utfpr.edu.br,
{pbugatti,psaito,fabricio}@utfpr.edu.br

Abstract. Complex network is a topic related with a plurality of knowledge from various areas and has been applied with success in all of them. However, it is a recent area considering its application in image pattern recognition. There are few works in the literature that use the complex networks for image characterization following its analysis and classification. An image can be interpreted as a complex network wherein each pixel represents a vertex and the weighted edges are generated according to the location and intensity between two pixels. Thus, the present paper aims to investigate this type of application and explore different measurements that can be extracted from complex networks to better characterize an image. One special type of measure that we applied were those based on motifs, which are employed in several areas. However, to the best of our knowledge, motifs were never explored in complex networks representing images. The results demonstrate that our proposed methodology presented great potential, reaching up to 89.81% of accuracy for the classification of public domain image texture datasets.

Keywords: Complex networks · Motifs · Pattern recognition · Image processing

1 Introduction

In the last decade, there was a great interest regarding the potential of complex data (e.g. image, videos, among others). In several areas, these types of data are daily generated, increasing in a great extent their volume. Thus, to cope with such data deluge, it is important to propose techniques capable to automatically characterize and classify them. To perform such task, a classical theory based on complex networks has been emerged as a notable paradigm. For instance, the use of complex networks to perform image characterization and recognition is becoming highly relevant [2]. However, there is still a lot to be explored considering the complex network theory applied to images.

Hence, the present paper proposes a new methodology based on complex networks to better characterize an image. To do so, we consider an image as a complex network wherein each pixel represents a vertex and the weighted edges

© Springer International Publishing Switzerland 2015
A. Pardo and J. Kittler (Eds.): CIARP 2015, LNCS 9423, pp. 322–330, 2015.
DOI: 10.1007/978-3-319-25751-8_39

are generated according to the location and intensity between two pixels. Over the generated complex network, special measures based on motifs were exploited to describe the images. It is important to highlight that the experiments testify the notable results achieved by the proposed methodology.

2   Background

The Complex Network theory is a topic related with a diversity of knowledge from several areas. Besides, it has been applied with success in all of them, due to its flexibility and generality, allowing the representation of different structures as a graph [1,3,10,16,17]. The network can be analyzed, classified and modeled through its topology and measurements [4,7]. The network features can be used as descriptors to distinguish different patterns, and thereby originating pattern recognition techniques.

2.1   Complex Networks Measurements

There are several measures in the literature that can be applied to describe an complex network. The main measures are explained in the present section, where $e_{i,j}$ is an edge connecting the vertices i and j, and $|V|$ is the total number of vertices in the network.

- **Vertex Degree:** the degree of a given vertex i is the number of vertices connected to it (i.e. its neighbors).
- **Average Degree:** the average degree (ϕ_μ) is the sum from the graph's number of edges divided by its number of vertices.
- **Histogram of Degrees:** the histogram, largely employed as image descriptor to obtain the frequency of a given pixel intensity, can also be applied to describe a complex network. In this case computes how many vertices exist in each bin of the connectivity histogram $(p(\phi))$.
- **Average Minimum Path:** the average minimum path is the average of all the minimum paths of the network.
- **Mean Centrality:** the mean centrality is the measurement that indicates the mean of central vertices, i.e., significant vertex for the minimum paths of the network.
- **Transitivity:** the transitivity measures the mean probability of which if the vertices i and j are connected to the vertex f, they will also be connected between themselves.
- **Number of Communities:** considering a graph $G(V, E)$, a community in this graph is a subgraph $G'(V', E')$ in which the vertices are strongly connected. There are different ways to measure a subgraph, because there are different definitions of the community structures. The most accepted definition requires that all nodes of a community must be connected between themselves. This obligation leads to the definition of a clique. A clique is the densest subgraph between three or more vertices, i.e., each graph vertex

needs to be connected to another vertex, in a way that does not exist other ones adjacent between them. This definition can be extended to an n-clique, in which requires that the biggest geodesic distance between two subgraphs vertices can not be bigger than n. In the definition of 2-clique the vertices do not need to be all connected between themselves, but can only have an intermediary vertex between them. The 3-clique can have two intermediary vertices between them, and so on [4].

- **Motifs:** the first hypothesis about motifs in complex networks were found in social networks [22]. Milo et al. [18] expanded the use of motifs in complex networks to cases of networks based on gene regulation, neurons, food chains, logic circuits and the world wide web. Motifs are small interconnection patterns that occur in a directed or non-directed graph with a frequency significantly bigger than the expected in its random version (i.e., in a graph with the same number of nodes, edges and average degree as the real network, but the edges are distributed in a random manner) [15]. The significance degree of a given motif M in the graph G is defined by the $Z - score$ and is calculated through the Equation 1 [4].

$$Zscore_M = \frac{n_M - <n_M^{rand}>}{\delta_{n_M}^{rand}}, \tag{1}$$

where n_M is the number of times that the subgraph M appears in the graph G; $<n_M^{rand}>$ and $\delta_{n_M}^{rand}$ are, respectively, the average and the standard deviation of the number of times that this subgraph (M) appears in the random network.

2.2 Texture

An image can be described by primitive low level features based on color, texture and shape patterns[5]. The texture is one of the most important in several contexts. Texture is an intuitive term and does not possess a precise definition, being found numerous definitions [12,21]. Besides, the texture recognition process, made intuitively by humans, commonly requires a high computational complexity [19].

3 Methodology

The methodology is mainly composed by four steps: (1) modeling image as a graph; (2) extraction of measures; (3) learning and training; (4) classification using supervised classification methods. This sequence can be seen in Figure 1.

In the proposed methodology the image is characterized by a complex network, where each pixel is considered a vertex of the network (i.e. graph). To make the connections between the vertices was adopted the creation of a lattice adjacency connected by a given radius. In this method all the vertices that represent the neighbor pixels, which are inside a given radius r, are connected. This method makes easier the local affinity relation over different regions.

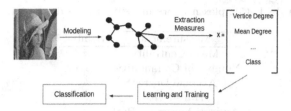

Fig. 1. Pipeline of the proposed methodology.

Initially it is performed a sweep pixel by pixel over the image, for each pixel selected it is calculated the Euclidean distance between its neighbors pixels. As formally defined by Equation 2, if the Euclidean distance between two pixels $p = (i, j) \in P$ and $p' = (i', j') \in P$ is not bigger than a given radius r (e.g. r = 5) the two vertices corresponding to the pixels are connected by an edge.

For each edge $e \in E$ from the graph G is associated an weight which is calculated by means of the coordinates from the two pixels that formed the edge and theirs respective intensities, as seen in Equation 3. Therefore, it is generated a new graph $G = (P, E)$ that is non-oriented, weighted and without loops.

The weight value of the edges $w(e)$ can assume a big value scale. Therefore, because this fact it is performed a weight normalization to guarantee that the weights will be into range 0 and 1, as it is seen in the Equation 4.

It can be noted that each vertex has a similar number of connections and the graph presents a regular behavior. However a graph with regular behavior is not considered a complex network, and so it does not has any relevant property to be extracted [2]. Thus it is necessary to accomplish a behavioral analysis of the graph. An efficient way to do this task is the analysis of the derived graphs. We called this analysis as δ transformations. In each transformation is applied a threshold t in the set of edges E of the graph, in order to select a subset E^*, $E^* \subset E$, in which each edge from E^* must have the weight less or equal to t, as seen in Equation 5.

$$E = \left\{ ((i, j), (i', j')) \in P x P | \sqrt{(i - i')^2 + (j - j')^2} \leq r \right\} \qquad (2)$$

$$d(e) = (i - i')^2 + (j - j')^2 + (v_{ij} - v_{i'j'})^2 \; \forall \; e = \{(i, j), (i', j')\} \in E \qquad (3)$$

$$w(e) = \frac{d(e)}{maxPixelIntensity^2 + r^2} \qquad (4)$$

$$E^* = \delta_t(E) = \{e \in E | w(e) \leq t\} \qquad (5)$$

The threshold t is incremented by a regular interval, obtaining $T = [t_1, t_2, \ldots, t_L]$, where the initial threshold is 0.005, the final is 0.165 and the increment is 0.005. For each incremented t is obtained a new subgraph from the original graph. This approach can be interpreted as the acquisition several samples of the complex network. Considering the measurements that can be extracted from the network (see Section 2), a feature vector was generated

326   G.V.L. de Lima et al.

Table 1. Complex network measurements - descriptors.

Measurement	Symbol
Mean Centrality	bi_μ
Number of Communities	N_C
Average Degree	ϕ_μ
Transitivity	C
Average Minimum Path	ℓ
Motifs	M
Connectivity Histogram	$p(\phi)$

for each image. Table 1 shows which measurements were used as descriptors to compose the feature vectors.

It was used *motifs* of sizes 3 and 4 and in the connectivity histogram the value of ϕ varied from 0 to 20. For each yielded graph by the δ transformations are extracted the complex network measurements showed in Table 1. The feature subvector regarding each transformation is composed according to Equation 6. Then the feature subvectors are concatenated to create the final feature vector.

$$\psi_{t_L} = [bi, N_C, \phi\mu, C, \ell, M, p(\phi)] \tag{6}$$

4 Experiments

In this section, we describe the datasets (Section 4.1) and scenarios (Section 4.2) used in the experiments as well as the results obtained (Section 4.3).

4.1 Datasets

The experiments were conducted on two well-known texture datasets. The first one is the Brodatz dataset, obtained from [6], which consists of 112 different textures of size (640x640) pixels. Each texture is partitioned into 25 (128x128) non-overlapping subimages, such that 2800 images were considered. Figure 2a displays samples from this dataset.

The second image dataset is referred to the KTH-TIPS, which is an extent of the CUReT dataset [9]. KTH-TIPS dataset, obtained from [13], consists of 10 texture classes with 81 images per class. Images, 200x200 pixels in size, were captured at nine scales, viewed under three different illumination directions and three different poses. Figure 2b displays samples from this dataset.

(a)   (b)

Fig. 2. Examples of images from the datasets. (a) Brodatz. (b) KTH-TIPS.

4.2   Scenarios

For the extraction of the network descriptors from each dataset, we used the *software* R [20] with the package iGraph [8]. In order to evaluate the performance of the proposed methodology, we considered three different scenarios. Initially, for the first experiment, we have used the learning methods: k-Nearest Neighbors (kNN), Decision Tree (DT), Naïve Bayes (NB), Support Vector Machines (SVM) and Multilayer Perceptron (MP). We have used the implementation of those learning methods available in the WEKA data mining library with the default parameters, unless stated otherwise [11]. For the kNN method, we used the IBK algorithm with $k = 1$. For the Decision Tree method, we used the J48 and Random Forest (RF) algorithms. For the SVM method, we used the LibSVM algorithm with a linear kernel configuration. In this paper, we consider a q-fold cross-validation protocol for all experiments, where $q = 10$.

Recent researches have shown that the discriminating power of the learning methods has been affected by irrelevant and redundant information. Therefore, for the second experiment, in order to identify and remove as much irrelevant and redundant training information as possible, we perform Correlation-based feature selection, as proposed in [11]. It was selected 28 features, including measures of: connectivity histogram, transitivity, average minimum path, subgraphs, motifs of size 4 similar to Figure 3A and motifs of size 4 similar to Figure 3B.

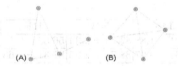

Fig. 3. Relevant motifs for classification.

From the results obtained in the two previous experiments, it was observed (Figure 4) the absence of a pattern in the classification from the Brodatz dataset. It was related to the heterogeneity of some images, due to the pre-processing method (used to construct the dataset) results in the samples of the same class whose textures and patterns are completely different. Therefore, the samples were re-organized using the k-means algorithm [14]. Experiments were conducted with 100 and 50 clusters. With 100 clusters, the average of samples per class was 27.76. With 50 clusters, the average of samples per class was 55.52.

Fig. 4. Heterogeneous images in the Brodatz dataset.

Table 2. Average accuracies ± standard deviations on the two datasets obtained by the classifiers for the first experiment without feature selection.

Dataset	IBK	J48	NB	RF	SVM	MP
KTH-TIPS	50.61 ± 3.54	59.5 ± 5.73	39.63 ± 3.51	**69.01±3.70**	*	57.53 ± 3.52
Brodatz	**75.14±1.65**	67.00 ± 2.75	73.19 ± 2.63	**75.28±1.85**	64.08 ± 2.79	*

Table 3. Average accuracies ± standard deviations on the two datasets obtained by the classifiers for the first experiment with feature selection.

Dataset	IBK	J48	NB	RF	SVM	MP
KTH-TIPS	58.02 ± 3.61	63.58 ± 5.05	42.22 ± 5.30	**70.62±5.64**	49.01 ± 4.75	63.58 ± 4.49
Brodatz	79.93 ± 1.47	70.28 ± 2.30	79.61 ± 2.07	80.76 ± 1.15	*	**87.32±2.10**

Table 4. Average accuracies ± standard deviation on the Brodatz dataset obtained by the classifiers for the third experiment, with and without the Feature Selection (FS) algorithm, using 100 clusters.

Features	IBK	J48	NB	RF	SVM	MP
Without FS	85.62 ± 1.42	72.11 ± 2.56	**86.41±2.16**	82.24 ± 1.89	59.15 ± 2.91	26.66 ± 2.17
With FS	85.84 ± 1.34	72.83 ± 2.34	86.09 ± 2.11	83.89 ± 2.36	79.36 ± 1.57	86.27 ± 2.31

Table 5. Average accuracies ± standard deviation on the Brodatz dataset obtained by the classifiers for the third experiment, with and without the Feature Selection (FS) algorithm, using 50 clusters.

Features	IBK	J48	NB	RF	SVM	MP
Without FS	76.33 ± 2.38	89.01 ± 1.88	87.24 ± 2.34	56.59 ± 2.15	51.51 ± 3.01	88.53 ± 2.62
With FS	89.08 ± 1.23	76.98 ± 3.07	88.76 ± 2.05	87.31 ± 1.63	50.79 ± 3.20	**89.81 ±2.21**

4.3   Results

The results of the three experiments are shown in the Tables 2-5. The fields with * indicate that it was not possible to classify the data with such algorithm, due to the lack of enough computer resources given the Weka algorithm implementations. Regarding to the first experiment, one can observe (Table 2) that the results were underperforming, reaching about 75% of classification accuracy for the Brodatz dataset and less than 70% for the KTH-TIPS.

The second experiment, using the feature selection (FS) algorithm, presents better results (see Table 3), due to the identification and removal of noise generated by irrelevant and redundant features. MP classifier achieves an accuracy above 87% for Brodatz, and RF classifier achieves above 70% for KTH-TIPS.

Tables 4-5 shows the results from the third experiment, using 100 and 50 clusters, respectively. In general, we obtained gains with the use of the clustering. The highest gains are highlighted in bold in Tables 4 and 5. With 100 clusters (Table 4), NB classifier reached 86.41% of accuracy without feature selection algorithm, obtaining a gain of 13.22% in relation to the results presented without the clustering (see NB classifier with 73.19% of accuracy in Table 2). With 50 clusters (Table 5), J48 classifier achieved 89.01% of accuracy without feature selection algorithm, obtaining a gain of 24.01% compared to the results presented without the clustering (see J48 classifier with 65.00% of accuracy in Table 2).

5 Conclusion

In this paper, we presented a new methodology to describe images through complex networks measurements. In addition, the motifs, a special type of measure, were applied resulting in higher accuracies. It is important to highlight that, to the best of our knowledge, motifs were never explored in complex networks representing images. The experiments performed show that the proposed methodology reached up to 89.81% of accuracy for the classification of public domain image texture datasets, increasing it in a great extent. These results testify the notable applicability of our methodology to the characterization of images.

Acknowledgments. This work was supported by CNPq, Fund. Araucária and UTFPR.

References

1. Albert, R., Barabási, A.L.: Statistical mechanics of complex networks. Reviews of Modern Physics **74**(1), 47 (2002)
2. Backes, A.R., Casanova, D., Bruno, O.M.: A complex network-based approach for texture analysis. In: Bloch, I., Cesar Jr, R.M. (eds.) CIARP 2010. LNCS, vol. 6419, pp. 354–361. Springer, Heidelberg (2010)
3. Barabási, A.L., Bonabeau, E.: Scale-free networks. Scientific American (2003)
4. Boccaletti, S., Latora, V., Moreno, Y., Chavez, M., Hwang, D.U.: Complex networks: Structure and dynamics. Physics Reports **424**(4–5), 175–308 (2006)
5. Brilhador, A., Colonhezi, T.P., Bugatti, P.H., Lopes, F.M.: Combining texture and shape descriptors for bioimages classification: a case of study in ImageCLEF dataset. In: Ruiz-Shulcloper, J., Sanniti di Baja, G. (eds.) CIARP 2013, Part I. LNCS, vol. 8258, pp. 431–438. Springer, Heidelberg (2013)
6. Brodatz, P.: Textures: A Photographic Album for Artists and Designers, vol. 66. Dover, New York (1966)
7. Da Costa, L.F., Rodrigues, F.A., Travieso, G., Villas-Boas, P.R.: Characterization of complex networks: a survey of measurements. Adv. Phys. **56**(1), 167–242 (2007)
8. Csardi, G., Nepusz, T.: The iGraph software package for complex network research. InterJournal Complex Systems 1695 (2006), http://igraph.org
9. Dana, K., Van-Ginneken, B., Nayar, S., Koenderink, J.: Reflectance and Texture of Real World Surfaces. ACM Transactions on Graphics (TOG) **18**(1), 1–34 (1999)
10. Dorogovtsev, S.N., Mendes, J.F.: Evolution of networks. Adv. Phys. **51**(4), 1079–1187 (2002)
11. Hall, M., Frank, E., Holmes, G., Pfahringer, B., Reutemann, P., Witten, I.H.: The weka data mining software: an update. ACM SIGKDD **11**(1), 10–18 (2009)
12. Haralick, R.M.: Statistical and structural approaches to texture. Proceedings of the IEEE **67**(5), 786–804 (1979)

13. Hayman, E., Caputo, B., Fritz, M., Eklundh, J.-O.: On the significance of real-world conditions for material classification. In: Pajdla, T., Matas, J.G. (eds.) ECCV 2004. LNCS, vol. 3024, pp. 253–266. Springer, Heidelberg (2004)
14. Jain, A.K.: Data clustering: 50 years beyond k-means. Pattern Recognition Letters **31**(8), 651–666 (2010)
15. Konagurthu, A.S., Lesk, A.M.: On the origin of distribution patterns of motifs in biological networks. BMC Systems Biology **2**(1), 73 (2008)
16. Lopes, F.M., Cesar-Jr, R.M., Da Costa, L.F.: Gene expression complex networks: Synthesis, identification, and analysis. J. Comput. Biol. **18**(10), 1353–1367 (2011)
17. Lopes Jr, F.M., Martins Jr, D.C., Barrera, J., Cesar Jr, R.M.: A feature selection technique for inference of graphs from their known topological properties: Revealing scale-free gene regulatory networks. Information Sciences **272**, 1–15 (2014)
18. Milo, R., Shen-Orr, S., Itzkovitz, S., Kashtan, N., Chklovskii, D., Alon, U.: Network motifs: simple building blocks of complex networks. Science **298**(5594), 824–827 (2002)
19. Parker, J.R.: Algorithms for image processing and computer vision. John Wiley & Sons (2010)
20. R Development Core Team: R: A Language and Environment for Statistical Computing (2008)
21. Sklansky, J.: Image segmentation and feature extraction. IEEE Transactions on Systems, Man and Cybernetics **8**(4), 237–247 (1978)
22. Wasserman, S., Faust, K.: Social Network Analysis: Methods and Applications. Cambridge University Press, Structural Analysis in the Social Sciences (1994)

Assessing the Distinctiveness
and Representativeness of Visual Vocabularies

Leonardo Chang[1,2]($\boxtimes$), Airel Pérez-Suárez[1], Máximo Rodríguez-Collada[1],
José Hernández-Palancar[1], Miguel Arias-Estrada[2], and Luis Enrique Sucar[2]

[1] Advanced Technologies Application Center (CENATAV),
7A # 21406, Siboney, Playa, CP 12200 Havana, Cuba
{lchang,asuarez,mrodriguez,jpalancar}@cenatav.co.cu
[2] Instituto Nacional de Astrofísica, Óptica y Electrónica (INAOE),
Luis Enrique Erro # 1, Tonantzintla, CP 72840 Puebla, Mexico
{lchang,ariasmo,esucar}@ccc.inaoep.mx

Abstract. Bag of Visual Words is one of the most widely used
approaches for representing images for object categorization; however,
it has several drawbacks. In this paper, we propose three properties and
their corresponding quantitative evaluation measures to assess the ability of a visual word to represent and discriminate an object class. Additionally, we also introduce two methods for ranking and filtering visual
vocabularies and a soft weighting method for BoW image representation.
Experiments conducted on the Caltech-101 dataset showed the improvement introduced by our proposals, which obtained the best classification
results for the highest compression rates when compared with a state-of-
the-art mutual information based method for feature selection.

Keywords: Bag of visual words · Visual vocabulary · Object categorization · Object recognition

1 Introduction

One of the most widely used approaches for representing images for object categorization is the Bag of Words (BoW) approach. BoW-based methods have
recently obtained good results and they even attained the best results for several classes in the recent PASCAL VOC Challenge 2011 on object classification.

The key idea of BoW approaches is to discretize the entire space of local
features (e.g., SIFT, SURF) extracted from a training set at interest points or
densely sampled in the image. With this aim, clustering is performed over the set
of features extracted from all the images of the training set in order to identify
features that are visually equivalent. Each cluster is interpreted as a visual word,
and all clusters form a so-called visual vocabulary. Later, in order to represent
an image from the training set, each feature extracted from the image is assigned
to a visual word of the visual vocabulary; from which a histogram of occurrences
of each visual word in the image is obtained. When an unseen image arrives, it is
represented using the visual vocabulary and then it is processed by the classifier.

© Springer International Publishing Switzerland 2015
A. Pardo and J. Kittler (Eds.): CIARP 2015, LNCS 9423, pp. 331–338, 2015.
DOI: 10.1007/978-3-319-25751-8_40

One of the main limitations of the BoW approach is that the visual vocabulary is built using features that belong to both the object and the background. This implies that the noise extracted from the image background is also considered as part of the object class description. Also, in the BoW representation, every visual word is used and they contribute in the same way to the histogram of an image, regardless of their low representative and discriminative power. All these elements may limit the quality of further classification processes.

Several methods have been proposed in the literature to overcome the limitations of the BoW approach. These include recent works aimed to build more discriminative and representative visual vocabularies. Authors in [1–3] use the class labels of images in the vocabulary training stage in order to obtain a more discriminative vocabulary. Also, since with a typical hard assignment features that lie near Voronoi boundaries are not well-represented by the visual vocabulary, researchers have explored multiple assignments and soft weighting strategies to address this problem. E.g., [4,5] proposed methods for multiple assignment where a feature is matched to k nearest terms in the vocabulary and these terms are weighted by a scaling function such that the nearest terms obtain a higher value. The related work that is closest to ours is the recent work of Zhang *et al.* [6]. In their paper authors propose a supervised Mutual Information (MI) based feature selection method. Their algorithm uses MI between each dimension of the image descriptor and the image class label to compute the dimension importance. Finally, using the highest importance values, they reduce the image representation size. Their method achieve higher accuracy than feature compression methods such as Product Quantization [7] and BPBC [8].

In this paper, we propose three properties to assess the ability of a visual word to represent and discriminate an object class in the context of the BoW approach. We define three measures in order to quantitatively evaluate each of these properties. Besides, we propose two methods for ranking and filtering the visual vocabulary and a new soft weighting method for representing an image from this vocabulary. One of the ranking methods is based on a *tf.idf* weighting scheme while the other one as well as the soft weighting method are based on the above mentioned measures. Experiments conducted on the Caltech-101 [9] dataset showed the improvement introduced by our proposals, which obtained the best classification results for the highest compression rates when compared with a state-of-the-art mutual information based method.

The paper is organized as follows: Section 2 introduces the proposed properties and measures for the evaluation of the representativeness and distinctiveness of visual words, the methods for ranking and filtering the visual vocabulary as well as the soft weighting method for image representation. The performance of our proposed methods on the Caltech-101 dataset and a discussion of the obtained results are presented in Section 3. Finally, Section 4 concludes the paper with a summary of our findings and a discussion of future work.

2   Proposed Method

In this section we propose three properties and their corresponding quantitative evaluation measures to assess the ability of a visual word to represent and discriminate an object class. Besides, we propose two ranking and filtering methods, one based on the above mentioned measures and the other one, based on a *tf.idf* weighting scheme. Finally, we propose a new soft weighting method for image representation which is also based on the proposed measures.

2.1   Inter-class Representativeness Measure

A visual word could be comprised of features from different object classes, representing visual concepts or parts of objects common to those different classes. These common parts or concepts do not have necessarily to be equally represented inside a visual word because, even when similar, object classes should also have attributes that differentiate them. Therefore, we can say that, in order to represent an object class the best, a property that a visual word must satisfy is to have a high representativeness of this class. In order to measure the representativeness of a class c_j in visual word k, the measure $\mathcal{M}_1$ is proposed:

$$\mathcal{M}_1(k, c_j) = \frac{f_{k,c_j}}{n_k}, \tag{1}$$

where f_{k,c_j} represents the number of features of class c_j in visual word k and n_k is the total number of features in visual word k.

2.2   Intra-class Representativeness Measure

A visual word could be comprised of features from different objects, many of them probably belonging to the same object class. Even when different, object instances from the same class should share several visual concepts. Taking this into account, we can state that a visual word best describes a specific object class while more balanced are the features from that object class comprising the visual word, with respect to the number of different training objects belonging to that class. Therefore, we could say that, in order to represent an object class the best, a property that a visual word must satisfy is to have a high generalization or intra-class representativeness over this class.

To measure the intra-class representativeness of a visual word k for a given object category c_j, the measure μ is proposed:

$$\mu(k, c_j) = \frac{1}{O_{c_j}} \sum_{m=1}^{O_{c_j}} \left| \frac{o_{m,k,c_j}}{f_{k,c_j}} - \frac{1}{O_{c_j}} \right|, \tag{2}$$

where O_{c_j} is the number of objects (images) of class c_j in the training set, o_{m,k,c_j} is the number of features extracted from object m of class c_j in visual word k, and f_{k,c_j} is the number of features of class c_j that belong to visual word k.

The term $1/O_{c_j}$ represents the ideal ratio of features of class c_j, that guarantees the best balance, i.e., the case where each object of class c_j is equally represented in visual word k.

The measure μ evaluates how much a given class deviates from its ideal value of intra-class variability balance. In order to make this value comparable with other classes and visual words, μ could be normalized using its maximum possible value, which is $\frac{2 \cdot O_{c_j} - 2}{O_{c_j}^2}$. Taking into account that μ takes its maximum value in the worst case of intra-class representativeness, the measure $\mathcal{M}_2$ is defined to take its maximum value in the case of ideal intra-class variability balance and to be normalized by $\max(\mu(k, c_j))$:

$$\mathcal{M}_2(k, c_j) = 1 - \frac{O_{c_j}}{2 \cdot (O_{c_j} - 1)} \sum_{m=1}^{O_{c_j}} \left| \frac{o_{m,k,c_j}}{s_{k,c_j}} - \frac{1}{O_{c_j}} \right|. \tag{3}$$

2.3 Inter-class Distinctiveness Measure

$\mathcal{M}_1$ and $\mathcal{M}_2$ provide, under different perspectives, a quantitative evaluation of the ability of a visual word to describe a given class. However, we should not build a vocabulary just by selecting those visual words that best represent each object class, because this fact does not directly imply that the more representative words will be able to differentiate well one class from another, as a visual vocabulary is expected to do. Therefore, we can state that, in order to be used as part of a visual vocabulary, a desired property of a visual word is that it should have high values of $\mathcal{M}_1(k, c_j)$ and $\mathcal{M}_2(k, c_j)$ (represents well the object class), while having low values of $\mathcal{M}_1(k, \{c_j\}^C)$ and $\mathcal{M}_2(k, \{c_j\}^C)$ (misrepresents the rest of the classes), i.e., it must have high discriminative power.

In order to quantify the distinctiveness of a visual word for a given class, the measure $\mathcal{M}_3$ is proposed. $\mathcal{M}_3$ expresses how much the object class that is best represented by visual word k is separated from the other classes in the $\mathcal{M}_1$ and $\mathcal{M}_2$ rankings.

Let $\Theta_{\mathcal{M}}(K, c_j)$ be the set of values of a given measure $\mathcal{M}$ for the set of visual words $K = \{k_1, k_2, ..., k_N\}$ and the object class c_j, sorted in descending order of the value of $\mathcal{M}$. Let $\Phi(k, c_j)$ be the position of visual word $k \in K$ in $\Theta_{\mathcal{M}}(K, c_j)$. Let $P_k = \min_{c_j \in C}(\Phi(k, c_j))$ be the best position of visual word k in the set of all object classes $C = \{c_1, c_2, ..., c_Q\}$. Let $c_k = \arg\min_{c_j \in C}(\Phi(k, c_j))$ be the object class where k has position P_k. Then, the inter-class distinctiveness (measure $\mathcal{M}_3$), of a given visual word k for a given measure $\mathcal{M}$, is defined as:

$$\mathcal{M}_3(k, \mathcal{M}) = \frac{1}{(|C| - 1)(|K| - 1)} \sum_{c_j \neq c_k} (\Phi(k, c_j) - P_k). \tag{4}$$

2.4 On Ranking and Reducing the Size of Visual Vocabularies

In this subsection, we present two methods for ranking and reducing the size of the visual vocabularies, towards more reliable and compact image representations. The first one, named MMM, is based on the measures proposed in

Sections 2.1-2.3. Let $\Theta^{\mathcal{M}_1}(K)$ and $\Theta^{\mathcal{M}_2}(K)$ be the rankings of vocabulary K, using measures $\mathcal{M}_3(K, \mathcal{M}_1)$ and $\mathcal{M}_3(K, \mathcal{M}_2)$, respectively. $\Theta^{\mathcal{M}_1}(K)$ and $\Theta^{\mathcal{M}_2}(K)$ provide a ranking of the vocabulary based on the distinctiveness of visual words according to inter-class and intra-class variability, respectively.

In order to find a consensus, $\Theta(K)$, between both rankings $\Theta^{\mathcal{M}_1}(K)$ and $\Theta^{\mathcal{M}_2}(K)$, a consensus-based voting method can be used; in our case, we decided to use the Borda Count algorithm [10] although any other can be used as well. The Borda Count algorithm obtains a final ranking from multiple rankings over the same set. Given $|K|$ visual words, a visual word receive $|K|$ points for a first preference, $|K| - 1$ points for a second preference, $|K| - 2$ for a third, and so on for each ranking independently. Later, individual values for each visual word are added and a final ranking obtained. From this final ranking a reduced vocabulary can be obtained by selecting the first N visual words.

The second ranking and filtering method we propose is based on a $tf.idf$ weighting scheme, named FRM (Frequency-based Ranking Method). Our proposal is based on the definitions introduced in [11]. Traditionally, $tf.idf$ has been used as a weighting scheme for image representation. However, in our proposal we use $tf.idf$ for ranking and/or filtering the set of visual words. Let $D = \{m_1, m_2, \cdots, m_N\}$ be the image training set from which the visual vocabulary has been built. According to [11], the *term frequency* and the *inverse document frequency* of a visual word v_i in an image m_j, denoted by tf_{v_i,m_j} and idf_{v_i,m_j}, respectively, are defined by the following expressions:

$$tf_{v_i,m_j} = \frac{K_1 \cdot O_{ij}}{O_{ij} + K_2 \cdot \left(1 - b + b \cdot \left(\frac{|\{v_q|O_{qj} > 0\}|}{V_{avg}}\right)\right)} \qquad idf_{v_i,m_j} = \log \frac{|D| - |D_{v_i}| + 0.5}{|D_{v_i}| + 0.5}, \qquad (5)$$

where K_1, K_2 and b are constants, O_{ij} is the occurrence of v_i in m_j, V_{avg} is the average number of visual words representing the images of the training set, and D_{v_i} is the set of images in which the occurrence of v_i is greater than zero.

Taking into account the way in which the histogram of occurrences of the visual words is built for each image, it will be highly probable that any visual word *occurs* in almost all images. This will have a negative influence in the computation of the *idf* expression. For solving this issue, we propose to redefine D_{v_i} as the set of images in which the occurrence of v_i is greater than the average occurrence of v_i in all the images of the training set.

Using the *tf* expression and the new definition of *idf*, we can build for each visual word v_i, a vector containing the product of tf_{v_i,m_j} and idf_{v_i,m_j}, in each image $m_j \in D$. The average of the values contained in this vector, will constitute the ranking of v_i. From this ranking a reduced vocabulary can be obtained by selecting the first N visual words.

2.5 Soft Weighting for Image Representation

Once the visual vocabulary is built, the images are represented through a histogram of the occurrences of the visual words. For building this histogram, the distinctiveness and representativeness of visual words are not taken into account during the histogram construction. Following, we propose a new soft weighting method for image representation, named SWIR, that tackles the negative effect that the above mentioned problem have over the histogram of occurrences.

Let $\Theta(N)$ be the final raking values of the N selected visual words that constitute the visual vocabulary, obtained using one of the ranking and filtering methods proposed in section 2.4. Let assume these values are normalized such that they are in $[0,1]$. We will use these values for supporting the presence of the highly discriminative visual words as well as for penalizing the presence of those with low descriptive power. With this aim, we first compute a *pivot* element, denoted as $P_{\Theta(N)}$, as the average raking value of the N visual words. The *contribution weight* of a visual word v_i, denoted as cw_{v_i}, is computed as follows:

$$cw_{v_i} = 1 - P_{\Theta(N)} + \Theta_{v_i}, \qquad (6)$$

where Θ_{v_i} is the ranking value of v_i in $\Theta(N)$.

For obtaining the representation of an image m_j, we propose to multiply the occurrences of the visual words in the histogram of m_j by their respective contribution weights. Those visual words having a ranking over $P_{\Theta(N)}$ are considered as more representative and discriminative, and consequently, their presence in the histogram is rewarded (i.e., it is increased). On the other hand, visual words with rankings under the pivot are penalized by reducing their presence in the histogram of occurrences.

3   Experimental Results

The main goal of the experiments we present in this section is to quantitatively evaluate the improvement introduced by our proposals to the BoW-based image representation and to compare with the MI-based method proposed in [6], which obtains the best classification results among the feature selection and compression methods of image representation for object categorization. The experiments were conducted on the well-known Caltech-101 [9] dataset. All the experiments were done on a single thread of a 3.4 GHz Intel i7 processor and 8GB RAM PC.

In the experiments presented here, we used for image representation a BoW-based schema with PHOW features (dense multi-scale SIFT descriptors) [12] and spatial histograms as image descriptors. Elkan's K-means [13] with four different K values (K= 512, 1024, 2048 and 4096) was used to build the visual vocabularies; these vocabularies constitute the baseline. Later, each of the baseline vocabularies is ranked using the MI-based method proposed in [6] and our two proposed ranking methods, MMM and FRM, with and without the new representation method, SWIR. Based on these rankings, nine new vocabularies are obtained by filtering each baseline vocabulary, leaving the 10%, 20%, ..., 90%, respectively. We tested the obtained visual vocabularies in a classification task, using a homogeneous kernel map to transform a χ^2 Support Vector Machine (SVM) into a linear one [14]. We follow the experimental setup of [15], namely, we train on 30 images per class and test on the rest, limiting the number of test images to 50 per class. The classification accuracy results are reported in Fig. 1.

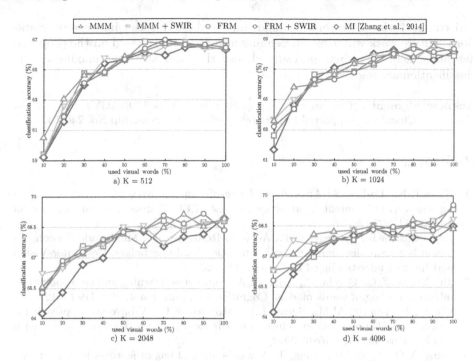

Fig. 1. Mean classification accuracy results on the Caltech-101 dataset.

As it can be seen in Fig. 1, for each value of K used in the experiment, our proposals obtain the best classification accuracy results for the highest compression rates (10, 20%), being MMM the best method. Moreover, for the other filtering sizes our proposals attain comparable and even better results than the MI-based method. Besides, in almost all values of K the combination of the MMM and FRM methods with SWIR method gets the highest classification accuracy results, being the combination between FRM and SWIR the best. Therefore, we can assert that taking into account the distinctiveness and representativeness of visual words in the image representation improves the accuracy of the classifier.

4   Conclusions

In this paper we have introduced three properties and their corresponding quantitative evaluation measures to assess the ability of a visual word to represent and discriminate an object class, in the context of the BoW approach. We also devised two methods for reducing the size of visual vocabularies that allow to obtain more distinctive and representative visual vocabularies for BoW image representation. Finally, we introduced a soft weighting method for image representation. The experiments conducted over the well-known Caltech-101 dataset showed that i) using the more discriminative and representative visual words, and ii) their properties quantitative measures it is possible to obtain more accurate and compact visual vocabularies and improved BoW-based image representations. Future work will focus on defining a method that, based on the proposed measures, help us to automatically choose the filter size that maximizes the classification accuracy.

Acknowledgments. This work was supported in part by CONACYT Project No. 215546. L. Chang was supported in part by CONACYT scholarship No. 240251.

References

1. Kesorn, K., Poslad, S.: An enhanced bag-of-visual word vector space model to represent visual content in athletics images. IEEE Transactions on Multimedia **14**(1), 211–222 (2012)
2. Lopez-Sastre, R., Tuytelaars, T., Acevedo-Rodriguez, F., Maldonado-Bascon, S.: Towards a more discriminative and semantic visual vocabulary. Computer Vision and Image Understanding **115**(3), 415–425 (2011)
3. Jiu, M., Wolf, C., Garcia, C., Baskurt, A.: Supervised learning and codebook optimization for bag of words models. Cognitive Computation **4**, 409–419 (2012)
4. Chang, L., Duarte, M.M., Sucar, L.E., Morales, E.F.: A bayesian approach for object classification based on clusters of sift local features. Expert Systems with Applications **39**, 1679–1686 (2012)
5. Jiang, Y.G., Ngo, C.W., Yang, J.: Towards optimal bag-of-features for object categorization and semantic video retrieval. In: CVIR, pp. 494–501. ACM (2007)
6. Zhang, Y., Wu, J., Cai, J.: Compact representation for image classification: To choose or to compress? In: CVPR 2014 (2014)
7. Jégou, H., Douze, M., Schmid, C.: Product quantization for nearest neighbor search. IEEE Pattern Analysis and Machine Intelligence **33**(1), 117–128 (2011)
8. Gong, Y., Kumar, S., Rowley, H.A., Lazebnik, S.: Learning binary codes for high-dimensional data using bilinear projections. In: CVPR 2013 (2013)
9. Fei-Fei, L., Fergus, R., Perona, P.: Learning generative visual models from few training examples: An incremental bayesian approach tested on 101 object categories. Comput. Vis. Image Underst. **106**(1), 59–70 (2007)
10. Emerson, P.: The original borda count and partial voting. Social Choice and Welfare **40**(2), 353–358 (2013)
11. Moulin, C., Barat, C., Ducottet, C.: Fusion of tf.idf weighted bag of visual features for image classification. In: Qunot, G. (ed.) CBMI, pp. 1–6. IEEE (2010)
12. Bosch, A., Zisserman, A., Munoz, X.: Image classification using random forests and ferns. In: ICCV, vol. **23**(1), pp. 1–8 (2007)
13. Elkan, C.: Using the triangle inequality to accelerate k-means. In: Fawcett, T., Mishra, N., (eds.) ICML, pp. 147–153. AAAI Press (2003)
14. Vedaldi, A., Zisserman, A.: Efficient additive kernels via explicit feature maps. Pattern Analysis and Machine Intellingence **34**(3) (2011)
15. Lazebnik, S., Schmid, C., Ponce, J.: Beyond bags of features: Spatial pyramid matching for recognizing natural scene categories. In: CVPR, pp. 2169–2178 (2006)

Image Coding, Processing
and Analysis

A Scale Invariant Keypoint Detector Based on Visual and Geometrical Cues

Levi O. Vasconcelos$^{(\boxtimes)}$, Erickson R. Nascimento, and Mario F.M. Campos

Department of Computer Science, Universidade Federal de Minas Gerais,
Belo Horizonte, Brazil
{leviovasconcelos,erickson,mario}@dcc.ufmg.br

Abstract. One of the first steps in a myriad of Visual Recognition and Computer Vision algorithms is the detection of keypoints. Despite the large number of works proposing image keypoint detectors, only a few methodologies are able to efficiently use both visual and geometrical information. In this paper we introduce KVD (Keypoints from Visual and Depth Data), a novel keypoint detector which is scale invariant and combines intensity and geometrical data. We present results from several experiments that show high repeatability scores of our methodology for rotations, translations and scale changes and also presents robustness in the absence of either visual or geometric information.

Keywords: Keypoint detector · Local features

1 Introduction

Over the years, the task of selecting a set of points of interest in images has been omnipresent in a large number of Visual Recognition and Computer Vision methodologies. A careful choice of points in images may avoid the inclusion of noisy pixels and enables the identification of regions that are rich in information, aiding an effective description of such regions. Additionally, the use of an image subset enables the tackling of cluttered backgrounds and occlusions in object recognition [7,3] and scene understanding applications. Moreover, the ever growing volume of data, which includes high resolution images, RGB-D data and the massive image repositories available in the web, makes the development of keypoint detectors crucial for a large number of image processing techniques.

In a common image representation pipeline for matching and classification tasks, before computing feature vectors for pixels, these pixels must be selected by a detector algorithm. Thus, while a descriptor algorithm is concerned with providing a discriminative identification for a keypoint by analyzing its vicinity, a detector is designed for finding informative image patches.

As stated, the detection of a set of points of interest, henceforth referred to as *keypoints*, consists in looking for points located in discriminative regions of

---

This work is supported by grants from CNPq, CAPES and FAPEMIG.

A. Pardo and J. Kittler (Eds.): CIARP 2015, LNCS 9423, pp. 341–349, 2015.
DOI: 10.1007/978-3-319-25751-8_41

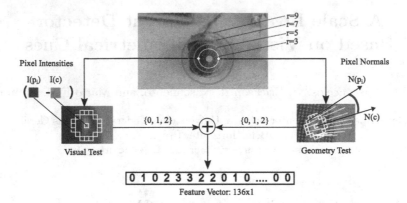

Fig. 1. The extraction and fusion of visual and geometrical features of KVD detector.

the image, that will account for good *repeatability*, which in turn may lead to smaller ambiguity. There is a vast body of literature on image keypoint detectors, of which [7,4,12,13] are well known representatives.

Broadly speaking, the main task of a keypoint detector is to assign a saliency score to each pixel of an image. This score is then used to select a (usually smaller) subset of pixels that presents the following properties: i) Repeatability; ii) Distinctiveness; iii) Locality and iv) Accurately localizable.

The main contribution of this paper is a scale invariant keypoint detector called KVD (Keypoints from Visual and Depth Data), which efficiently combines intensity and depth. Our method produces the best performing detector by combining visual and geometrical data, and presents a good performance and graceful degradation even in the absence of either one of them.

Related Work. Since the seminal paper of Morevec [10], where he presented one of the first corner detectors, a large number of keypoint detectors have been proposed. Harris detector [4], Harris-Laplacian [8], SIFT [7], SURF [1] are some of the most popular detectors for images.

A recent approach that has become popular in keypoint selection is based on machine learning techniques. Rosten and Drummond [12] proposed the FAST detector, which creates a feature vector that is used by a decision tree to classify the pixel as a keypoint. The Roten and Drummond's technique was improved by Rublee et. al [13]. They presented the ORB detector which uses a scale pyramid to add scale invariance and measures the cornerness of each keypoint candidate by computing Harris corner. Another recent methodology also based on machine learning technique is presented in [5]. The authors proposed a keypoint detection from depth maps by using Random Forest which is trained to maximize the repeatability score.

Extracting data from images can usually provide rich information on the object features. The main drawback is the sensitiveness of these feature to illumination changes. Geometrical information produced by 3D sensors based on structured lighting or time of flight, in its turn, is less sensitive to visible lighting conditions. Three-dimensional data has been successfully used by algorithms such as NARF [15] and on 3D detectors implementations derived from 2D approaches [14] such as SIFT3D, HARRIS3D and HARRIS6D.

Despite the growing popularity of techniques that combine both visual and geometric informations to build descriptors [11,17] and their use in recognition tasks, this fusion is not a common approach for keypoint detection. In this work, we present a novel keypoint detector, which simultaneously takes into account both visual and geometrical information to detect keypoints.

We show that using both visual and geometric information at the detection level improves the quality and performance of higher level visual processes.

2 Methodology

The input for our algorithm is a pair (I, D), which denotes the output of a typical RGB-D device. For each pixel $\mathbf{x}$, $I(\mathbf{x})$ is the pixel's intensity, $D(\mathbf{x})$ is depth for that pixel, $P(\mathbf{x})$ is the corresponding 3D point, and $N(\mathbf{x})$ is its normal vector.

Our technique is built upon a supervised training approach, with a training step where a decision tree is created to classify points into keypoints and non-keypoints. There are three steps: the feature vector extraction and fusion, the model training and the non-maximal suppression.

Feature Extraction. The first step of the detection process creates a feature vector for every keypoint candidate. Figure 1 depicts the feature vector construction. Given an image pixel coordinates $\mathbf{c} \in \mathbb{R}^2$, we consider its vicinity as the image patches that contain the circles centred at $\mathbf{c}$ with radii varying in $r \in \mathcal{S}$. Each circle is defined by the function $B(r, \mathbf{c})$ which we denote as $B_r(\mathbf{c})$:

$$B_r(\mathbf{c}) : \mathbb{R}^3 \rightarrow \{\mathbf{p}_1, \mathbf{p}_2, ..., \mathbf{p}_n\}. \tag{1}$$

The $B_r(\mathbf{c})$ function outputs all pixels $\mathbf{p}_i$ lying in the Bresenham's circle with radius equals to r. Thus, the vicinity considered consists of the concatenation of all vectors $B_r(\mathbf{c}), \forall r \in \mathcal{S}$. We define the vicinity of a central pixel $\mathbf{c}$ as:

$$\mathcal{V}_c = \{B_{r_1}(\mathbf{c}), B_{r_2}(\mathbf{c}), ..., B_{r_{|\mathcal{S}|}}(\mathbf{c})\}, \quad \forall r_i \in \mathcal{S}. \tag{2}$$

Whereas in this work, we used $\mathcal{S} = \{3, 5, 7, 9\}$. Thus, we compute visual features using fast intensity difference tests [12]. For each pixel $p \in \mathcal{V}_c$ and a given threshold t_v we evaluate:

$$\tau_v(\mathbf{c}, \mathbf{p}_i) = \begin{cases} 2 & \text{if } I(\mathbf{p}_i) - I(\mathbf{c}) < -t_v \\ 1 & \text{if } I(\mathbf{p}_i) - I(\mathbf{c}) \geq t_v \\ 0 & \text{otherwise.} \end{cases} \tag{3}$$

We embed geometric cues into the feature vector computed by the function τ_v to increase robustness both to illumination changes and to the lack of texture in the scenes. The geometric feature extraction $\tau_g(.)$ function is based on two invariant geometric measurements: i) the normal displacement, and ii) the surface's convexity. The normal displacement test evaluates if the dot product between the normals $N(\mathbf{c})$ and $N(\mathbf{x_i})$ is smaller than a given displacement threshold t_g, and the convexity test computes the local curvature indicator, κ as:

$$\kappa(\mathbf{c}, \mathbf{p}_i) = \langle P(\mathbf{c}) - P(\mathbf{p}_i), N(\mathbf{c}) - N(\mathbf{p}_i) \rangle, \tag{4}$$

where $\langle . \rangle$ is the dot product, and $P(\mathbf{c})$ is the $3D$ spatial point associated with pixel $\mathbf{c}$ and depth $D(\mathbf{c})$. The κ function captures the convexity of geometric features and also unambiguously characterizes the dot product between surface normals. Thus, the geometrical features are computed as:

$$\tau_g(\mathbf{c}, \mathbf{p}_i) = \begin{cases} 2 & \text{if } \langle N(\mathbf{p}_i), N(\mathbf{c}) \rangle < t_g \wedge \kappa(\mathbf{c}, \mathbf{p}_i) > 0 \\ 1 & \text{if } \langle N(\mathbf{p}_i), N(\mathbf{c}) \rangle < t_g \wedge \kappa(\mathbf{c}, \mathbf{p}_i) < 0 \\ 0 & \text{otherwise.} \end{cases} \tag{5}$$

Scale invariance is endowed to our detector by using the geometry information available in the depth map to weigh the influence of each circle. We analyze the geometrical vicinity encompassed by each Bresenham's circle $B_r(\mathbf{c})$ in the $3D$ scene by computing the minimum Euclidean distance:

$$\mathbf{d_r} = \min_{p_i} |P(\mathbf{c}) - P(\mathbf{p_i})|, \forall \mathbf{p_i} \in B_r(\mathbf{c}), \tag{6}$$

where $P(\mathbf{c})$ and $P(\mathbf{p_i})$ are the $3D$ points corresponding to the central pixel $\mathbf{c}$ and the pixels composing the Bresenham's circle $\mathbf{p_i} \in B_r(\mathbf{c})$. The distance d_r is weighted by the Gaussian

$$\mathbf{w_r} = \exp\left(-\frac{(\mu - \mathbf{d_r})^2}{\sigma^2}\right) \tag{7}$$

in order to penalize circles which its estimated radii in the 3D scene are distant from $\mu = 0.02$ meters. We then build a feature vector from a Bresenham's circle of radius $\mathbf{r}$ centered at $\mathbf{c}$ as a row vector $\mathbf{v_r} = \begin{bmatrix} f_1 \cdots f_{|B_r(\mathbf{c})|} \end{bmatrix}$ where:

$$f_i(\mathbf{c}, \mathbf{r}) = \mathbf{w_r} * (\tau_v(\mathbf{c}, \mathbf{p_{i,r}}) + \tau_g(\mathbf{c}, \mathbf{p_{i,r}})), \tag{8}$$

where $\mathbf{p_{i,r}}$ is the ith element of the Bresenham's circle $B_r(\mathbf{c})$. The final feature vector F is generated by concatenating all the feature vectors $\mathbf{v_r}$ as, in this work:

$$F = \begin{bmatrix} \mathbf{v_3} \ \mathbf{v_5} \ \mathbf{v_7} \ \mathbf{v_9} \end{bmatrix}. \tag{9}$$

Decision Tree Training. In the training step, we create a keypoint model by training a decision tree using the ID3 algorithm [2]. We generated a training set by extracting a total of $160,144$ points from the RGB-D Berkeley 3-D Object Dataset (B3DO) [6]. This dataset is composed of a large number of real world scenes with several different objects, geometry and visual data.

We used 66% points to train, and the remaining points ($54,449$) to test the quality of the final decision tree. Both sets were equally divided into positive and negative samples. In order to define positive labels for keypoints, we computed the curvature of several, manually selected, keypoints. We have found the value of 0.09 based on the average of these curvatures. Thus, all points with curvature larger than 0.09 were labeled as a positive sample for the keypoint class. To take into account texture features, we added keypoints detected by ORB as positive examples. The classification accuracy obtained in the test was equal to 0.91.

Non-maximal Suppression. In the last step of our methodology we perform a non-maximal suppression. We compute a response value $R_p(\mathbf{c}, \mathbf{r})$ based on the feature values of each circle. For each radius $\mathbf{r} \in \mathcal{S}$,

$$R_p(\mathbf{c}, \mathbf{r}) = \max_{X \in \{X_{rc_1}, X_{rc_2}\}} \frac{1}{|X|} \sum_{x_i \in X} D_v(\mathbf{c}, \mathbf{x_i}) + \lambda D_g(\mathbf{c}, \mathbf{x_i}), \qquad (10)$$

where $D_v(\mathbf{c}, \mathbf{x}) = |I(\mathbf{x}) - I(\mathbf{c})|$ gives the visual response and $D_g(\mathbf{c}, \mathbf{x}) = 1 - \langle N(\mathbf{x}), N(\mathbf{c}) \rangle$ provides the geometrical response. The factor λ is used to define the contribution of the geometrical information in the final response. The set $X_{rc_k} = \{\mathbf{p_i} : \mathbf{p_i} \in B_r(c) \wedge (\tau_v(\mathbf{c}, \mathbf{p_i}) = k \vee \tau_g(\mathbf{c}, \mathbf{p_i}) = k)\}$ is composed of all pixels which bin has value k.

We rank the maximal points by using both absolute difference between intensities and normal surface angles for the pixels in the contiguous set of the Bresenham's circle. The final response of each candidate is defined as the maximum response among all radii:

$$R_f(\mathbf{c}) = \max_r R_p(\mathbf{c}, \mathbf{r}), \forall r \in \{3, 5, 7, 9\}. \qquad (11)$$

We divide the image into smaller patches with size $w \times w$ (in this work, $w = 5$) and for each patch we select the pixel with the larger response, Equation 11.

3 Experiments

We compared our approach against standard detectors for two-dimensional images: SIFT [7] and ORB [13], for geometric data HARRIS3D [14] (a 3D version of Harris corner detector), SIFT3D [1], and the HARRIS6D [14]. The HARRIS6D detector, similarly to our methodology, uses both visual and geometrical data to detect keypoints. In our experiments, we used the RGB-D SLAM Dataset [16]. This dataset contains several RGB-D data of real world sequences and for each acquisition it provides the ground truth for the camera pose. For our experiments, we used the sequences containing only translation motions (*freiburg2_xyz*) and rotation of the camera (*freiburg2_rpy*).

To evaluate each detector, we applied the repeatability score, which measures the ability of a detector to find the same set of keypoints on images acquired of a scene from different view points or different conditions. For details the reader is referred to [9]. In our experiments, we used the parameter $\epsilon = 0.6$.

---

[1] available in the Point Cloud Library: www.pointclouds.org

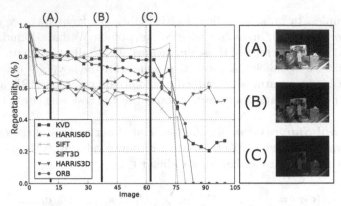

Fig. 2. The poor illumination experiment. We captured a total of 104 images of a cluttered room starting at dusk (on the right three examples of the used images). One can notice that KVD is the only method which uses visual information, that remains providing reliable keypoints once the intensity image is nearly lost (C image).

For the parameter settings, to choose a value for t_g, we ran the learning and testing for 15, 30 and 60 degrees using the RGB-D Berkeley 3-D Object Dataset (B3DO) [6]. We used a fraction of the dataset for validation purposes and the remaining part for training, the large accuracy was returned by using $t_g = 15$.

Robustness. We performed experiments to evaluate the repeatability for images acquired with changes in translation, rotation, scale, and illumination. We used offsets ranging from 0.03 meters to 0.75 meters (horizontal direction) for translational tests and for scale tests we select a set of frames with the camera moving away from the scene up to 0.35 meters. In the illumination change experiments we captured a total of 104 images of a cluttered room starting at dusk (partial illumination) at an interval of one minute between acquisitions. Figure 2 shows three frames of this sequence.

Figure 3 shows the results of the repeatability tests. Our detector provides the highest repeatability rate when there are large translational movements (0.8 meters) and large angular rotations (50 degrees). Also in Figure 3 (d),(e) we can see that only KVD, HARRIS6D and HARRIS3D were still capable to provide keypoints from heavily corrupted images under illumination changes and noise, and KVD presented the highest repeatability rate. It is worth noticing that in the illumination change experiment (Figure 2), KVD was the only method which uses visual information that was capable of still provide keypoints after the visual information vanishes (about image 80).

To perform brightness changes, we gradually increased the value of each pixel by adding an increasingly higher constant β using images from *freiburg2_xyz* sequence. To test the robustness to image noise, we used a Gaussian additive noise with zero mean. In Figure 3 one may readily see that our detector presents the largest repeatability rate, thanks to the visual and geometric information fusion of our detection methodology.

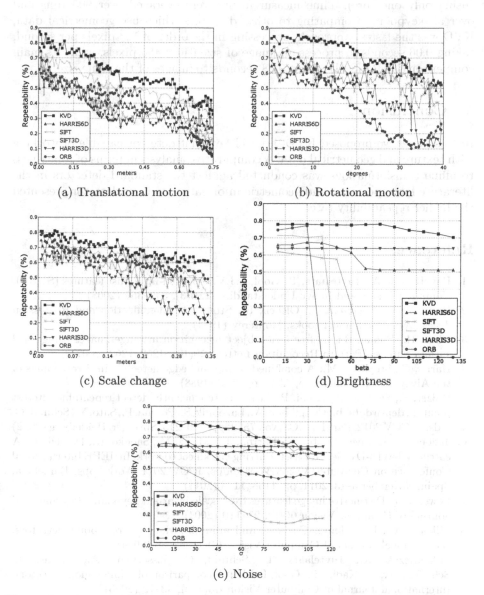

(a) Translational motion

(b) Rotational motion

(c) Scale change

(d) Brightness

(e) Noise

Fig. 3. Results for the repeatability experiment. (a) Horizontal translation camera motion; (b) Rotational movement around the yaw axis; (c) Scale changing; (d) Brightness changing and (e) Gaussian Noise. Our method (KVD) is represented by the blue curve. One can readily see that KVD, among all methods which uses visual information (including HARRIS6D), is the one which continues to identify the most reliable keypoints even when strongly corrupted intensity images are given as input.

Time Performance. The time experiments ran on an Intel Core i7 3.5GHz (using only one core). Time measurements were averaged over 900 runs and over all keypoints. Comparing to other detectors which use geometrical data, KVD was the fastest approach, processing in the order of 10^6 pixels per second, taking 0.06 seconds to process an image of size 640×480 pixels, while its main competitor (HARRIS 6D) takes 0.08 seconds to images of the same size.

4 Conclusion

In this paper we proposed KVD, a novel keypoint detector capable of working with texture and geometrical data. A comparative analysis in terms of robustness to affine transformations was conducted against the standard detectors in the literature for appearance and geometric information and our detector presented the higher repeatability rate.

References

1. Bay, H., Ess, A., Tuytelaars, T., Gool, L.J.V.: Speeded-up robust features (SURF). Computer Vision and Image Understanding **110**(3), 346–359 (2008)
2. Breiman, L., Friedman, J., Olshen, R., Stone, C.: Classification and Regression Trees. Wadsworth and Brooks, Monterey (1984)
3. Chen, H., Bhanu, B.: 3D free-form object recognition in range images using local surface patches. Pattern Recognition Letters **28**(10), 1252–1262 (2007)
4. Harris, C., Stephens, M.: A combined corner and edge detector. In: Proceedings of the Alvey Vision Conference, AVC, pp. 1–6 (1988)
5. Holzer, S., Shotton, J., Kohli, P.: Learning to efficiently detect repeatable interest points in depth data. In: Fitzgibbon, A., Lazebnik, S., Perona, P., Sato, Y., Schmid, C. (eds.) ECCV 2012, Part I. LNCS, vol. 7572, pp. 200–213. Springer, Heidelberg (2012)
6. Janoch, A., Karayev, S., Jia, Y., Barron, J.T., Fritz, M., Saenko, K., Darrell, T.: A category-level 3-D object dataset: Putting the kinect to work. In: IEEE International Conference on Computer Vision Workshops, ICCV 2011 Workshops, Barcelona, Spain, November 6–13, 2011, pp. 1168–1174 (2011)
7. Lowe, D.G.: Distinctive image features from scale-invariant keypoints. International Journal of Computer Vision **60**(2), 91–110 (2004)
8. Mikolajczyk, K., Schmid, C.: Scale and affine invariant interest point detectors. International Journal of Computer Vision **60**(1), 63–86 (2004)
9. Mikolajczyk, K., Tuytelaars, T., Schmid, C., Zisserman, A., Matas, J., Schaffalitzky, F., Kadir, T., Gool, L.J.V.: A comparison of affine region detectors. International Journal of Computer Vision **65**(1–2), 43–72 (2005)
10. Moravec, H.P.: Towards automatic visual obstacle avoidance. In: Proceedings of the 5th International Joint Conference on Artificial Intelligence, p. 584 (1977)
11. do Nascimento, E.R., Oliveira, G.L., Vieira, A.W., Campos, M.F.M.: On the development of a robust, fast and lightweight keypoint descriptor. Neurocomputing **120**, 141–155 (2013)
12. Rosten, E., Porter, R., Drummond, T.: Faster and better: A machine learning approach to corner detection. IEEE Trans. Pattern Anal. Mach. Intell. **32**(1), 105–119 (2010)

13. Rublee, E., Rabaud, V., Konolige, K., Bradski, G.R.: ORB: an efficient alternative to SIFT or SURF. In: IEEE International Conference on Computer Vision, ICCV 2011, Barcelona, Spain, November 6–13, pp. 2564–2571 (2011)
14. Rusu, R.B., Cousins, S.: 3D is here: Point cloud library (PCL). In: IEEE International Conference on Robotics and Automation, ICRA (2011)
15. Steder, B., Rusu, R.B., Konolige, K., Burgard, W.: Point feature extraction on 3D range scans taking into account object boundaries. In: IEEE International Conference on Robotics and Automation, ICRA 2011, Shanghai, China, May 9–13, pp. 2601–2608 (2011)
16. Sturm, J., Magnenat, S., Engelhard, N., Pomerleau, F., Colas, F., Burgard, W., Cremers, D., Siegwart, R.: Towards a benchmark for RGB-D SLAM evaluation. In: Proc. of the RGB-D Workshop on Advanced Reasoning with Depth Cameras at Robotics: Science and Systems Conf (2011)
17. Zaharescu, A., Boyer, E., Varanasi, K., Horaud, R.: Surface feature detection and description with applications to mesh matching. In: IEEE Conference on Computer Vision and Pattern Recognition (CVPR), pp. 373–380 (2009)

Efficient Polynomial Implementation of Several Multithresholding Methods for Gray-Level Image Segmentation

David Menotti[1]($\boxtimes$), Laurent Najman[2], and Arnaldo de A. Araújo[3]

[1] Federal University of Paraná, Curitiba, PR, Brazil
menotti@inf.ufpr.br
[2] Groupe ESIEE Paris, Université Paris-Est, Noisy-le-Grand, France
[3] Federal University of Minas Gerais, Belo Horizonte, MG, Brazil

Abstract. Multithresholding consists of segmenting a histogram of image in classes by using thresholds. Many researchers avoid the exponential space problem of possible thresholds combinations of a given criteria function. In this work, we present a polynomial easy-to-implement dynamic programming algorithm to find the exact optimum thresholds of three well-known criteria functions for multithresholding: the maximum of histogram between class-variance (Otsu's method); the maximum histogram entropy (Kapur *et al.*'s method), and minimum histogram error (Kittler and Illingworth's method). The algorithm, that has been used to optimum quantization, has $O((K-1)L^2)$ time complexity, where K and L stand for the number of desired classes and the number of gray levels in the image, respectively. Experiments showed that the exact optimum thresholds for gray-level image segmentation can be found in less than 160 milliseconds in a Pentium 4-2GHz, in whatever the number of classes.

Keywords: Segmentation · Multithresholding · Dynamic programming

1 Introduction

Threshold selection is the simpler image segmentation method [6]. This method consists of selecting a threshold value in a histogram of image, which separates the objects from the background. In many applications of image processing and pattern recognition, the gray-level of pixels belonging to the object are substantitally different from those belonging to the background. Hundreds works were developed based on this assumption [6].

A class of threshold selection methods consists of finding the threshold value on histogram which optimizes a given function. In the following, we cite three well-known methods of this class. Otsu [5] proposed to maximize the separability of the resultant thresholded histogram classes, by using the between-class variance criterion associated with them. Kapur *et al.*[1] proposed a method based on information theory concepts to find a suitable threshold set such that the maximum entropy can be obtained by the segmented histogram classes. Based on

© Springer International Publishing Switzerland 2015
A. Pardo and J. Kittler (Eds.): CIARP 2015, LNCS 9423, pp. 350–357, 2015.
DOI: 10.1007/978-3-319-25751-8_42

assumption that the probability distributions of gray-level objects in an image are Gaussianly distributed, Kittler and Illingworth [2] proposed the minimum error thresholding method. The optimum threshold is the one which minimizes the error rate of the resultant thresholded histogram classes with the desired mixtures of Gaussian distributions. In the remainder of this work, due to space constrain and simplicity, we will only refer to Otsu, Kapur and Kittler methods.

Multiple threshold selection, or simply multithresholding, consisting of segmenting a histogram of image in classes by using thresholds. Several threshold selection methods can be directly extended to multiple threshold selection, such as the three ones cited earlier. Nevertheless finding the optimum thresholds for these extended multithresholding methods become computationally very expensive. One need to test all possible thresholds combinations, which increase exponentially as the number of desired classes increase. For instance, to find the seven optimum thresholds (which segment an image in eight classes) of a given criteria function of an image with 256 gray levels, we should test $256!/(256 - 7)!$ possible thresholds combinations. If we take a computer that can test 1 billion of threshold combinations by second, it shall take about two years to test all possible combinations. In Liao et al. [3] and Wu et al. [7]'s works, the time complexity order of the search algorithm to find the optimum thresholds for Otsu, Kapur and Kittler methods was decreased. However it still continue exponential.

In this paper, we present a polynomial easy-to-implement dynamic programming algorithm to find the optimum thresholds for these methods, which has $O((K-1)L^2)$ time complexity, where K and L stand for the number of desired classes and the number of gray levels in the image, respectively. Note that there are in the literature faster algorithms than ours [4], $O(KL)$, but their implementation are not straightforward.

The rest of this paper is organized as follows. Basic definitions are presented in Section 2. The criteria functions of three multithresholding methods are described in Section 3. Section 4 presents the polynomial dynamic programming (DP) algorithm and shows an implementation for it. Experiments concerning the run time of the algorithm for the three methods and a segmentation example are shown in Section 5. Finally, conclusions are pointed out in Section 6.

2   Basic Definitions

2.1   Images and Histograms

Let N denote the set of natural numbers. Let X be a subset of points $(x,y) \in \mathbb{N}^2$, such that $0 \le x < m$, and $0 \le y < n$, where m and n denote the dimensions of X. Let $|Y|$ denote the the cardinality of a set $Y \subseteq \mathbb{N}^2$. Note that $|X| = m \times n$. A mapping I, from X to Z_L, where $Z_L = \{0, ..., L-1\}$, is called an *image*. In applications, L is typically 256. For a point $(x,y) \in X$, $l = I(x,y)$ is called the *level* of the point (x,y) on I.

Let X_l be a subset of X, such that for all $(x,y) \in X_l \subseteq X$, we have $I(x,y) = l$. Let $H(l)$ be the *absolute frequency* of level l in image I, i.e. $H(l) = |X_l|$. Note that $H(l) = 0$ if there is no $(x,y) \in X$ such that $I(x,y) = l$. Let P_l denote the probability of one pixel having the gray-level l, i.e. $P_l = H(l)/(m \times n)$. Note that $\sum_{l=0}^{L-1} H(l) = m \times n$, and $\sum_{l=0}^{L-1} P_l = 1$. The mapping H from the levels of image I to its absolute frequency levels, i.e. $H : Z_L \to \mathbb{N}$, is called the *histogram* of image I.

2.2 Thresholding

Usually a multithresholding histogram-based method uses $K - 1$ thresholds (i.e. $T = \{t_0, t_1, ..., t_{K-2}\}$) to partition the histogram of an image in K classes. That is, the histogram is partitioned in classes $C_k = \{H(i)|s_k \leq i \leq f_k\}$ with $0 \leq k < K$, where s_k and f_k stand for the starting and the final histogram class boundaries, respectively. They are defined as: $s_k = 0$ if $k = 0$, and $s_k = t_{k-1} + 1$ otherwise; $f_k = L - 1$ if $k = K - 1$, and $f_k = t_k$ otherwise.

2.3 Histogram Statistics

Now let us present definitions that will help us to describe the thresholding methods and the DP algorithm. Let I be an image with L levels and let H be the corresponding histogram. We define the ath-order histogram statistics of the histogram class $H(p, q)$ as

$$S^a(p, q) = \sum_{l=p}^{q} l^a \times H(l). \tag{1}$$

By using this definition, let us define the cumulative probability and the mean of the histogram class $H(p, q)$ as

$$\omega(p, q) = S^0(p, q)/(m \times n), \tag{2}$$
$$\mu(p, q) = S^1(p, q)/S^0(p, q), \tag{3}$$

respectively.

Let us introduce one more definition, which will help us to simplify further explanations, the ath-order histogram statistics error of the histogram class $H(p, q)$ regarding to the level b, i.e.

$$E^a(p, q, b) = \sum_{l=p}^{q} |l - b|^a \times H(l). \tag{4}$$

Finally, we set the $H(p, q)$ histogram class variance as

$$\sigma^2(p, q) = \left(\sum_{l=p}^{q} |l - \mu(p, q)|^2 \times P_l \right) / \omega(p, q)$$
$$= E^2(p, q, \mu(p, q))/S^0(p, q). \tag{5}$$

Equations 1 and 4 (and consequently the other ones defined in this section) can be computed with $O(L^2)$ complexity for all possible $0 \leq p \leq q < L$ if we use a recursive definition as

$$\alpha(p, q) = \begin{cases} \beta & \text{if } p = q, \\ \beta + \alpha(p, q - 1) & \text{otherwise.} \end{cases} \tag{6}$$

where β stands for the last computation at the equation, namely, when $l = q$.

3   Thresholding Criterion Functions

In this section, we describe three well-known criteria functions ($\psi(T)$) of multi-thresholding methods for gray-level image segmentation: ($\psi_{BCV}(T)$) the between class variance [5], ($\psi_{Ent}(T)$) the maximum entropy [1], and ($\psi_{ME}(T)$) the minimum error [2] criteria. These functions can be represented and decomposed as histogram class factors, i.e. $\varphi(s_k, f_k)$.

The optimum threshold set T^* is obtained as the argument value which optimizes a given criteria function, i.e.

$$T^* = \underset{0 \leq T < L}{\arg \operatorname{opt}} \psi(T). \tag{7}$$

where opt is a extremum operator depending on criteria function. That is, max for Otsu and Kittler methods, and min for Kapur method.

3.1   The Between-Class Variance

In Otsu's work [5], three possible discriminant criterion functions based on ratios of the within-class, the between-class and that of total variance are presented. All of these are equivalent to each other for the evaluation of the optimum thresholding process. Otsu suggested to maximize the between-class variance because it is the simplest one for computation. The between-class variance criteria function can be computed as

$$\psi_{BCV}(T) = \sum\nolimits_{k=0}^{K-1} \varphi(s_k, f_k), \tag{8}$$

where the histogram class factor $\varphi(s_k, f_k)$ is

$$\varphi(s_k, f_k) = \omega(s_k, f_k)[\mu(s_k, f_k) - \mu(0, L-1)]^2. \tag{9}$$

3.2   The Maximum Entropy

In the maximum entropy-based thresholding, the optimum threshold is obtained by applying information theory. That is, the optimal threshold set (T_{Ent}) is the one that maximizing the information content of the histogram image. As derived from Kapur *et al.*'s work [1], the original gray-level distribution of the image is divided into a number of classes of probability distributions in the multilevel thresholding case. Then the entropies associated with these distributions are computed as

$$\varphi(s_k, f_k) = - \sum_{l=s_k}^{f_k} \frac{P_l}{\omega(s_k, f_k)} \log \frac{P_l}{\omega(s_k, f_k)}. \tag{10}$$

And, then the criteria function is defined as

$$\psi_{Ent}(T) = \sum\nolimits_{k=0}^{K-1} \varphi(s_k, f_k). \tag{11}$$

3.3   The Minimum Error

In the concept of minimum error thresholding, the gray-level histogram of the image is thought of as an estimate of the probability density function $p(l)$ of the mixture distribution, comprising the gray-level of several classes (i.e. objects and background). It is assumed that each of these class distributions $p(l|k)$ of the mixture follows a normal distribution, with a class standard deviation of σ_k, a class mean of μ_k, and a priori probability of ω_k; hence, the histogram can be approximated as:

$$p(l) = \sum_{k=0}^{K-1} \frac{\omega(s_k, f_k)}{\sigma^2(s_k, f_k)\sqrt{2\pi}} \exp^{-(l-\mu(s_k,f_k))^2/2\sigma^2(s_k,f_k)} \tag{12}$$

The optimum threshold (T_{ME}) can be determined by solving an resultant quadratic equation with respect to l [2]. However, the parameters $\omega(s_k, f_k)$, $\mu(s_k, f_k)$, and $\sigma^2(s_k, f_k)$ of the mixture density function $p(l)$ associated with the image are unknown. In order to overcome the difficulties of estimating the unknown parameters, Kittler and Illingworth [2] presented a criterion function $\psi_{ME}(T)$, which is given by:

$$\psi_{ME}(T) = 1 + 2\sum_{k=0}^{K-1} \varphi(s_k, f_k) \tag{13}$$

where

$$\varphi(s_k, f_k) = \omega(s_k, f_k)[\log\left(\sigma(s_k, f_k)\right) + \log\left(\omega(s_k, f_k)\right)] \tag{14}$$

4   Dynamic Programming Algorithm

Thanks to decomposition of the criteria functions in histogram class factors $\varphi(s_k, f_k)$ among other mathematical properties we can apply the polynomial DP algorithm to find the optimum thresholds for image segmentation which is described in this section. A proof of correctness of the algorithm is not show due to space constrain.

Let $\psi(p, q)$ be an optimum criteria function conceived on the $q+1$-first gray-levels of the histogram of image when segmented by p-first optimum thresholds $(t_0, t_1, ..., t_{p-1})$, which can be written as the sum of the histogram class factors φ's, i.e.

$$\psi(p, q) = \sum_{k=0}^{p} \varphi(s_k, f_k^{p,q}), \tag{15}$$

where $f_k^{p,q} = q$ if $k = p$, and $f_k^{p,q} = t_k$ otherwise.

Let us define $\psi(p, q)$ as a recurrence equation as follows. Initially, we are interested to know the optimum criteria conceived on the $q+1$-first gray-level of the histogram of image when no threshold is used to segmented the histogram, i.e. $\psi(0, q)$. It can be directly computed as the histogram class factor $\varphi(0, q)$, i.e

$$\psi(0, q) = \varphi(0, q) \tag{16}$$

Algorithm 1. Computing $\psi(K-1, L-1)$

Data: $\varphi(p,q)$ - histogram class contribution
Result: ψ - criteria function
Result: DPT - optimum thresholds matrix

1 **for** $q = 0 \ldots L-1$ **do** $\psi(0,q) \leftarrow \varphi(0,q)$;
2 **for** $p = 1 \ldots K-1$ **do**
3 $\quad$ $\psi(p,p) \leftarrow \psi(p-1, p-1) + \varphi(p,p)$;
4 $\quad$ $DPT(p,p) \leftarrow p-1$;
5 $\quad$ **for** $q = p+1 \ldots L-K+p$ **do**
6 $\quad\quad$ $\psi(p,q) \leftarrow -\infty$;
7 $\quad\quad$ **for** $l = p-1 \ldots q-1$ **do**
8 $\quad\quad\quad$ **if** $(\psi(p,q) > \psi(p-1,l) + \varphi(l+1,q))$ **then**
9 $\quad\quad\quad\quad$ $\psi(p,q) \leftarrow \psi(p-1,l) + \varphi(l+1,q)$;
10 $\quad\quad\quad\quad$ $DPT(p,q) \leftarrow l$;

Once we have the solution computed up to the level $p-1$, i.e. $\psi(p-1,q)$, for all possible q, we are interested in computing the $\psi(p,q)$. It can be computed as the optimum (e.g. most or least depending on criteria function) term composed by the optimum criteria function conceived on the $l-1$-first gray-levels of the histogram of image being segmented by $p-1$ thresholds ($\psi(p-1,l)$) and the histogram class factor $\varphi(l+1,q)$, i.e.

$$\psi(p,q) = \operatorname*{opt}_{p-1 \leq l < q} (\psi(p-1,l) + \varphi(l+1,q)) \tag{17}$$

for all $p \leq q$, with $0 \leq p < K$, and $0 \leq q < L$, and where opt stands for max or min depending on criteria function.

To recover the thresholds that yield the optimum criteria function, we have to store the thresholds obtained from the dynamic programming algorithm, for future backwards searching, as follows

$$DPT(p,q) = \begin{cases} p-1, & \text{if } p = q, \\ \arg \operatorname{opt}_{p-1 \leq l < q} (\psi(p-1,l) + \varphi(l+1,q)), & \text{otherwise,} \end{cases} \tag{18}$$

for all $p \leq q$, with $0 \leq p < K$, and $0 \leq q < L-1$. From $DPT(K-1, L-1)$ we can find the $K-1$ optimum thresholds, i.e. $T^* = \{t_0^*, t_1^*, \ldots, t_{K-2}^*\}$, as

$$t_{n-1}^* = DPT(n, X_n) \tag{19}$$

where, $X_n = L-1$ if $n = K-1$, and $X_n = t_n^*$ otherwise.

Algorithm 1 shows an implementation for the dynamic programming algorithm. It is composed of two main loops, where the second one is enchained by other two loops, which gives the cubic time complexity of the algorithm, i.e. $O((K-1)L^2)$. Note that the Algorithm 1 maximize the criteria function. If minimizitation is required (as for Kittler method), we have only to modify two lines. To use $+\infty$ in line 6, and $<$ in the comparison in line 8.

Fig. 1. From left to right, the classic lena image (512 × 512 pixels), its segmented images in eight classes (using seven thresholds) by Otsu (61 87 111 131 148 167 191), Kapur (60 87 112 136 159 180 202) and Kittler (64 89 115 135 149 163 184) methods, respectively.

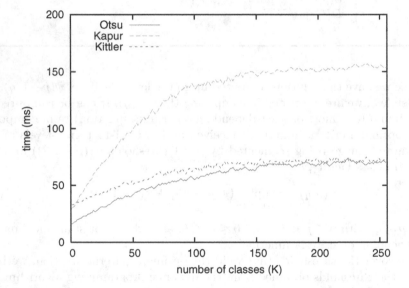

Fig. 2. Run time curves for Otsu, Kapur, and Kittler methods using lena image (512x512 pixels), by varing K from 1 up to 256.

5   Experiments

In this section, we show an experiment concerning the run time of the dynamic programming algorithm. We ran the algorithm using as input the classical lena image (with 512 × 512 pixels) for the three presented multithrehsolding methods. Fig. 2 shows the run time curves obtained from each method (using the DP algorithm) by varying the number of desired classes K from 1 up to 256. We can observe a significant difference among the response time of Kittler and Otsu methods regarding to Kapur method. This fact is due to an overhead on consistency verification of histogram class factors, i.e. φ, for Kapur method. By analyzing the upper-bound $O((K-1)L^2)$ and the curves shown in Fig. 2, we can say that the polynomial dynamic programming algorithm works (sub)linearly regarding to the number of classes K. In practice, our algorithm segments an image with 512×512 pixels in less than 160 milliseconds on a machine with architecture Pentium 4 - 2GHz, in whatever the number of classes.

Fig. 1 shows an example of segmentation: image of lena and its segmentation in eight (8) classes for Otsu, Kapur and Kittler methods. The optimum thresholds are shown in parenthesis. These images were segmented each one in less than 50 milliseconds in same architecture described above.

6   Conclusion

In this work, we presented and tested a polynomial algorithm to find the exact optimum threshold for three well-know methods: Otsu [5], Kapur [1], and Kittler [2]. This algorithm can be used to find the optimum thresholds of several other multithresholding methods. In a forthcoming work, we will establish the necessary and sufficient conditions which the criterion of a multithresholding method must respect to be solved by such polynomial algorithm. As future works, we want to join to the presented dynamic programming algorithm a divide-and-conquer strategy. This new algorithm to find the optimum thresholds will have $O(KN \log N)$ time complexity.

Acknowledgments. We thank UFPR, UFMG, FAPEMIG, CAPES, and CNPq for the support.

References

1. Kapur, J., Sahoo, P., Wong, A.: A new method for gray-level picture thresholding using the entropy of the histogram. Computer Vision, Graphics and Image Processing **29**, 273–285 (1985)
2. Kittler, J., Illingworth, J.: Minimum error thresholding. Pattern Recognition **1**(19), 41–47 (1986)
3. Liao, P.S., Chen, T.S., Chung, P.C.: A fast algorithm for multilevel thresholding. Journal of Information Science and Egineering **17**, 713–727 (2001)
4. Luessi, M., Eichmann, M., Schuster, G.: New results on efficient optimal multilevel image thresholding. In: IEEE Int. Conf. on Image Processing, pp. 773–776 (2006)
5. Otsu, N.: A threshold selection method from grey-level histograms. IEEE Transactions on Systems, Man and Cybernetics **9**(1), 41–47 (1979)
6. Sezgin, M., Sankur, B.: Survey over image thresholdintg techniques and quantitative performance evaluation. Journal of Electronic Imaging **13**(1), 146–165 (2004)
7. Wu, B.F., Chen, Y.L., Chiu, C.C.: Efficient implementation of several multilevel thresholding algorithms using a combinatorial scheme. International Journal of Computer and Applications **28**(3), 259–269 (2006)

Optimizing the Data Adaptive Dual Domain Denoising Algorithm

Nicola Pierazzo[1]($\boxtimes$), Jean-Michel Morel[1], and Gabriele Facciolo[1,2]

[1] CMLA, École Normale Supérieure de Cachan, Cachan, France
`nicola.pierazzo@cmla.ens-cachan.fr`
[2] IMAGINE/LIGM, École Nationale des Ponts et Chaussées,
Champs-sur-Marne, France

Abstract. This paper presents two new strategies that greatly improve the execution time of the DA3D Algorithm, a new denoising algorithm with state-of-the-art results. First, the weight map used in DA3D is implemented as a quad-tree. This greatly reduces the time needed to search the minimum weight, greatly reducing the overall computation time. Second, a simple but effective tiling strategy is shown to work in order to allow the parallel execution of the algorithm. This allows the implementation of DA3D in a parallel architecture. Both these improvements do not affect the quality of the output.

Keywords: Image denoising · Quad-tree · Parallel processing

1 Introduction

Image denoising is one of the fundamental image restoration challenges [18]. It consists in estimating an unknown noiseless image $\mathbf{y}$ from a noisy observation $\mathbf{x}$. We consider the classic image degradation model

$$\mathbf{y} = \mathbf{x} + \mathbf{n}, \tag{1}$$

where the observation $\mathbf{x}$ is contaminated by an additive white Gaussian noise $\mathbf{n}$ of variance σ^2. All denoising methods assume some underlying image regularity. Depending on this assumption they can be divided, among others, into transform-domain and spatial-domain methods.

Transform domain methods work by shrinking (or thresholding) the coefficients of some transform domain [7,14,25]. The Wiener filter [28] is one of the first such methods operating on the Fourier transform. Donoho et al. [5] extended it to the wavelet domain.

Space-domain methods traditionally use a local notion of regularity with edge-preserving algorithms such as total variation [24], anisotropic diffusion [19], or the bilateral filter [27]. Nowadays however spatial-domain methods achieve remarkable results by exploiting the self-similarities of the image [1]. These patch-based methods are non-local as they denoise by averaging similar patches

© Springer International Publishing Switzerland 2015
A. Pardo and J. Kittler (Eds.): CIARP 2015, LNCS 9423, pp. 358–365, 2015.
DOI: 10.1007/978-3-319-25751-8_43

in the image. Patch-based denoising has developed into attempts to model the patch space of an image, or of a set of images. These techniques model the patch as sparse representations on dictionaries [4,6,15,16,29], using Gaussian Scale Mixtures models [23,29,30], or with non-parametric approaches by sampling from a huge database of patches [12,13,17,21].

Current state-of-the-art denoising methods such as BM3D [3] and NL-Bayes [11] take advantage of both space- and transform-domain approaches. They group similar image patches and jointly denoise them by collaborative filtering on a transformed domain. In addition, they proceed by applying two denoising stages, the second stage using the output of the first one as its guide.

Some recently proposed methods use the result of a different algorithm as their guide for a new denoising step. Combining for instance, nonlocal principles with spectral decomposition [26], or BM3D with neural networks [2]. This allows one to mix different denoising principles, thus yielding high quality results [2,26].

DDID [9] is an iterative algorithm that uses a guide image (from a previous iteration) to determine spatially uniform regions to which Fourier shrinkage could be applied without introducing ringing artifacts. Several methods [8,10,20] use a single step of DDID with a guide image produced by a different algorithm. This yields much better results than the original DDID. Unfortunately, DDID has a prohibitive computational cost, as it paradoxically denoises a large patch to recover a single pixel. Moreover, contrary to other methods, aggregation of these patches doesn't improve the results since it introduces blur.

More recently, Data-Adaptive Dual Domain Denoising (DA3D) [22] was presented to address those issues. By using just a small fraction of the patches, it avoids unnecessary computations in the uniform areas of the image. Moreover, DA3D uses a more complex estimation of the image shape to reduce staircasing artifacts. In order to choose the patches to process, DA3D keeps track of the partial aggregation weights, and iteratively selects the patch with the smaller weight. The search for this patch can be expensive, especially on large images. Moreover, since the choice of a patch depends on the previous ones, there is no straight-forward method to parallelize this algorithm.

Contribution. This paper proposes an effective method to accelerate the search step of DA3D, and an approach to run the algorithm in a multi-processor environment. With these, DA3D can run in reasonable time even on medium-large images, making it even more interesting for real-world applications.

In order to accelerate the search step, a quadtree is used to store and update the minimum value. This decreases the complexity of the search from $O(n)$ to $O(\log n)$, where n is the number of pixels in the image.

To allow the execution of the algorithm on a multi-core architecture, it is noted that the simple strategy of dividing the images in stripes is effective and yields the same results than the single-process version of the algorithm.

Section 2 recalls the DA3D algorithm. Section 3 tackles the problems of tracking the minimum weight and of parallel execution. Section 4 shows some results and section 5 presents the conclusions.

2   Data-Adaptive Dual Domain Denoising

This section describes the DA3D algorithm, as presented in [22].

To denoise the area around the pixel p from the noisy image $\mathbf{y}$ DA3D extracts a 64×64 pixel block centered in p (denoted y) and the corresponding block g from the guide image $\mathbf{g}$. An affine model $P(q) = \langle \boldsymbol{\alpha}, q \rangle + \beta$ of the block is estimated computing a weighted least squares regression

$$\min_{P} \sum [y(q) - P(q)]^2 \cdot K_{reg}(q), \tag{2}$$

with the constraint $P(p) = g(p)$, where the sum is computed over the domain of y and K_{reg} is a bilateral weight function

$$K_{reg}(q) = \exp \left(-\frac{|g(q) - g(p)|^2}{\gamma_{rr}\sigma^2} - \frac{|q - p|^2}{2\sigma_{sr}^2} \right), \tag{3}$$

which selects the parts of the block that gets approximated by P. Once estimated, the local plane P is subtracted from the patch, effectively removing shades and gradients.

The blocks are processed to eliminate discontinuities that may cause artifacts in the subsequent frequency-domain denoising. To that end, a bilateral weight function k is derived from the guide g, to identify the pixels of the block belonging to the same object as the center p.

$$k(q) = \exp \left(-\frac{|g(q) - g(p)|^2}{\gamma_r\sigma^2} \right) \exp \left(-\frac{|q - p|^2}{2\sigma_s^2} \right). \tag{4}$$

The first term identifies the pixels belonging to the same structure as p, by selecting the ones with a similar color in the guide, while the second term removes the periodization discontinuities associated with the Fourier transform.

The weights in k are then used to modify y and g in order to remove their discontinuities and to obtain y_m and g_m (see lines 12-13 of Table 1). In this way the "relevant" part of the blocks (similar to the central pixel) is retained by k, and its average value is assigned to the rest. The modified block y_m is denoised by shrinkage of its Fourier coefficients using g_m as an oracle (lines 14-18 of Table 1). Then the "modification" of the patches is reverted and the regression plane P is added back to the block. The shrinkage assumes that the image y contains additive white Gaussian noise.

For color images, k is computed by using the Euclidean distance, while the shrinkage is done independently on each channel of the YUV color space.

Since the denoising remains valid for all pixels in the "relevant" part of the block, the processed blocks are aggregated to form the final result. The aggregation weights are the squares of the weights (4).

The image blocks to be processed are selected using a greedy approach. At each iteration a weight map $\mathbf{w}$ with the sum of the aggregation weights is updated. This weight map permits to identify the pixel in the image with the

Table 1. Pseudo-code for DA3D. Variables in **bold** denote whole images, while *italics* denote single blocks. Multiplication and division are pixel-wise.

Input: y (noisy image), **g** (guide)
Output: denoised image

1	**w** ← 0	
2	**out** ← 0	
3	**while** min(**w**) < τ **do**	
4	$p \leftarrow \arg\min(\mathbf{w})$	
5	$y \leftarrow \text{ExtractPatch}(\mathbf{y}, p)$	
6	$g \leftarrow \text{ExtractPatch}(\mathbf{g}, p)$	
7	$K_{reg} \leftarrow \text{ComputeKreg}(g)$ //	regression weight, eq. 3
8	$P \leftarrow \arg\min_P \sum [y(q) - P(q)]^2 \cdot K_{reg}(q)$ //	regression plane, eq. 2
9	$y \leftarrow y - P$ //	subtract plane from the block
10	$g \leftarrow g - P$ //	and from the guide
11	$k \leftarrow \text{ComputeK}(g)$ //	eq. 4
12	$y_m \leftarrow k \cdot y + (1-k)\left(\frac{\sum k(l)y(l)}{\sum k(l)}\right)$	
13	$g_m \leftarrow k \cdot g + (1-k)\left(\frac{\sum k(l)g(l)}{\sum k(l)}\right)$	
14	$Y \leftarrow \text{DFT}(y_m)$	
15	$G \leftarrow \text{DFT}(g_m)$	
16	$\sigma_f^2 \leftarrow \sigma^2 \sum k(q)^2$	
17	$K \leftarrow \begin{cases} 1 & \text{if } f = 0 \\ \exp\left(-\frac{\gamma_f \sigma_f^2}{\|G(f)\|^2}\right) & \text{otherwise} \end{cases}$ //	shrinkage
18	$x_m \leftarrow \text{IDFT}(K \cdot Y)$	
19	$x \leftarrow \left[x_m - (1-k)\left(\frac{\sum k(l)y(l)}{\sum k(l)}\right)\right] / k$ //	revert line 12
20	$x \leftarrow x + P$ //	add plane back to the block
21	$aggw \leftarrow k \cdot k$ //	aggregation weight
22	$\mathbf{w} \leftarrow \text{AddPatchAt}(p, \mathbf{w}, aggw)$ //	accumulate in the correct position
23	$\mathbf{out} \leftarrow \text{AddPatchAt}(p, \mathbf{out}, aggw \cdot x)$	
24	**return out/w**	

lowest aggregation weight, which will be selected as the center of the next block to process (line 4 of Table 1). The process iterates until the total weight for each pixel becomes larger than a threshold τ. The total number of processed blocks depends on the image complexity. The centers of the effectively processed blocks are concentrated on edges and details.

The parameters σ_{sr}, γ_{rr}, σ_s, γ_r, γ_f and τ are specific of the algorithm, and σ is the standard deviation of the noise.

3   Improvements

3.1   Tracking the Minimum Weight

In the implementation of DA3D the authors select the position with the lowest aggregation weight in **w** with a simple linear search. This approach shows its limit when the size of the image increases. In fact, for every processed block, the computation needed to find it is of the order of $O(n)$, with n the number of pixels of the image. Therefore, under the reasonable assumption that the number of processed blocks is a fraction of the total (from the original article, between 1% and 20%), and since the denoising of a block is performed in a bounded time, the complexity of the algorithm is $O(n^2)$. This is peculiar, because the algorithm appears local in its nature.

We propose to use a quad-tree to keep track of the minimum. The weight map $\mathbf{w}$ is in the leaves of the tree, and every node contains the minimum value of its four children. This can also be interpreted as a multi-scale version of $\mathbf{w}$, built using a *min* filter. The space complexity for this data structure is

$$\sum_{i=0}^{\log n} \frac{n}{4^i} \leq \frac{4}{3}n = O(n) \tag{5}$$

because every "layer" of the tree is 25% smaller than the previous one.

In order to retrieve the position of the minimum value, one has simply to traverse the tree from the root to the leaf, always choosing one of the children with the minimum value. This guarantees that the chosen pixel is a global minimum for $\mathbf{w}$, and has time complexity $O(\log n)$.

To update the tree, it suffices to update the appropriate leaves, and then recompute the minima in the upper nodes until the top. Since the aggregation is done one patch at a time, it is simple to calculate which nodes need to be updated, thus avoiding to recompute the values for areas in which $\mathbf{w}$ has not changed. The time complexity for this update is $O(k)$, where k is the number of pixels of the patch that is aggregated. Since k is constant, the aggregation does not increase the complexity of the algorithm.

One could be tempted to update the values one by one. Although this could be simpler to implement, it is slower, having a time complexity of $O(k \log n)$. Using this data structure instead, the total complexity of the algorithm becomes $O(n \log n)$, which allows to denoise bigger images.

3.2 Parallel Processing

Since DA3D selects the patches to denoise in a greedy fashion, it is impossible to know where the next patch will be prior to the aggregation step of the current one. This makes parallelization more complex than in other denoising algorithms.

In order to denoise a pixel p, the algorithm uses the other pixels inside a (64×64) window, all the pixels needed to denoise p are at a distance of at most 32. This makes the algorithm *local*, and allows to solve the problem of parallelism by just splitting the image in tiles. Each tile can be denoised separately, and then the results can be combined together.

It is clear that the patches chosen in this way will not correspond exactly with the patches chosen without parallelism. The main difference can be an oversampling of the areas near the edges, since the weights from a neighboring tile are not taken into account. This could result in a slight overhead in the processing time.

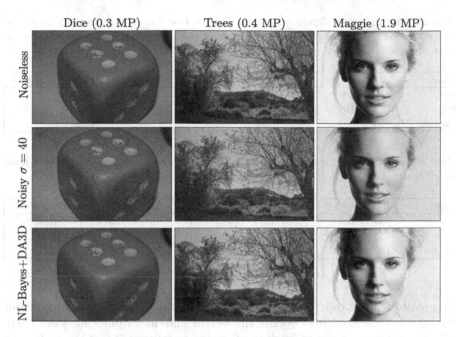

Fig. 1. Sample images, with noisy and denoised version. It is advised to zoom in on the digital version for more details. The results of the DA3D with the different improvements are visually identical.

However, the experiments show that the overhead is negligible, and the results of the simple and parallel versions of the algorithm are identical from a practical standpoint. With bigger images, the overlap area becomes smaller, therefore the factor of acceleration should become even closer to the number of processors.

4   Results

We tested the methods of Section 3 on the test images of Figure 1. We selected this set to be as varied as possible. Dice contains many smooth areas, Trees is mainly composed of texture and Maggie is a relatively large image, for which the improvement due to the quad-tree is more noticeable. On those images, we tested the DA3D algorithm with the suggested improvements, and we timed the execution on a dual-core laptop. The results are shown in Table 2.

The improvements do not change the output image significantly. The comparison of PSNR is shown in Table 3. Notice how the value of PSNR does not change among the different versions of the algorithm.

5   Conclusion

This paper presented two new strategies to improve the execution time of the DA3D Algorithm. First, a quad-tree structure was used as the weight map **w**.

Table 2. Runtimes for different versions of DA3D. Baseline represents the time of the original version. Notice how the improvement of the quad-tree is more prominent on bigger images.

Image	Baseline	Quad-Tree	Parallel (2 cpu)	Tree + Parallel
Dice	2.12s	1.51s	1.12s	0.92s
Trees	19.10s	12.78s	10.68s	8.56s
Maggie	28.05s	8.26s	15.03	5.36

Table 3. PSNR values for different versions of DA3D, also compared with Non-local Bayes[11].

Image	NL-Bayes	Baseline	Quad-Tree	Parallel	Tree + Par.
Dice	36.17 dB	37.90 dB	37.90 dB	37.90 dB	37.90 dB
Trees	23.49 dB	23.71 dB	23.71 dB	23.71 dB	23.71 dB
Maggie	33.48 dB	34.54 dB	34.54 dB	34.54 dB	34.54 dB

This greatly reduces the time needed to search for the minimum weight, without affecting the time needed to update the weight map in a significant way. Then, a tiling strategy is shown to work to allow the parallelization of the code with minimum overhead.

Acknowledgments. Work partly founded by Centre National d'Etudes Spatiales (MISS Project), European Research Council (advanced grant Twelve Labours), Office of Naval research (ONR grant N00014-14-1-0023), DGA Stéréo project, ANR-DGA (project ANR-12-ASTR-0035), FUI (project Plein Phare) and Institut Universitaire de France.

References

1. Buades, A., Coll, B., Morel, J.M.: A review of image denoising algorithms, with a new one. SIAM Mult. Model. Simul. **4**(2) (2006)
2. Burger, H.C., Schuler, C., Harmeling, S.: Learning how to combine internal and external denoising methods. In: Weickert, J., Hein, M., Schiele, B. (eds.) GCPR 2013. LNCS, vol. 8142, pp. 121–130. Springer, Heidelberg (2013)
3. Dabov, K., Foi, A., Katkovnik, V., Egiazarian, K.: Image denoising by sparse 3d transform-domain collaborative filtering. IEEE TIP **16**(82) (2007)
4. Dong, W., Shi, G., Li, X.: Nonlocal image restoration with bilateral variance estimation: A low-rank approach. IEEE TIP **22**(2) (2013)
5. Donoho, D.L., Johnstone, J.M.: Ideal spatial adaptation by wavelet shrinkage. Biometrika (1994)
6. Elad, M., Aharon, M.: Image denoising via sparse and redundant representations over learned dictionaries. IEEE TIP **15**(12) (2006)
7. Gnanadurai, D., Sadasivam, V.: Image denoising using double density wavelet transform based adaptive thresholding technique. IJWMIP **03**(01) (2005)
8. Knaus, C.: Dual-domain image denoising. Ph.D. thesis, Diss. Univ. Bern (2013)

9. Knaus, C., Zwicker, M.: Dual-domain image denoising. IEEE ICIP (2013)
10. Knaus, C., Zwicker, M.: Progressive image denoising. IEEE TIP **23**(7) (2014)
11. Lebrun, M., Buades, A., Morel, J.M.: Implementation of the "non-local bayes" (NL-bayes) image denoising algorithm. Image Processing On Line (2013)
12. Levin, A., Nadler, B.: Natural image denoising: Optimality and inherent bounds. IEEE CVPR (2011)
13. Levin, A., Nadler, B., Durand, F., Freeman, W.T.: Patch complexity, finite pixel correlations and optimal denoising. In: Fitzgibbon, A., Lazebnik, S., Perona, P., Sato, Y., Schmid, C. (eds.) ECCV 2012, Part V. LNCS, vol. 7576, pp. 73–86. Springer, Heidelberg (2012)
14. Li, H.Q., Wang, S.Q., Deng, C.Z.: New image denoising method based wavelet and curvelet transform. WASE ICIE **1** (2009)
15. Mairal, J., Bach, F., Ponce, J., Sapiro, G., Zisserman, A.: Non-local sparse models for image restoration. IEEE ICCV (2009)
16. Mairal, J., Sapiro, G., Elad, M.: Learning multiscale sparse representations for image and video restoration. SIAM Mult. Model. Simul. **7**(1) (2008)
17. Mosseri, I., Zontak, M., Irani, M.: Combining the power of internal and external denoising. IEEE ICCP (2013)
18. Motwani, M.C., Gadiya, M.C., Motwani Jr., R.C., Harris, F.C.: Survey of image denoising techniques. GSPX (2004)
19. Perona, P., Malik, J.: Scale-space and edge detection using anisotropic diffusion. IEEE TPAMI **12**(7) (July 1990)
20. Pierazzo, N., Lebrun, M., Rais, M., Morel, J.M., Facciolo, G.: Non-local dual image denoising. IEEE ICIP (2014)
21. Pierazzo, N., Rais, M.: Boosting shotgun denoising by patch normalization. IEEE ICIP (2013)
22. Pierazzo, N., Rais, M., Morel, J.M., Facciolo, G.: DA3D: Fast and data adaptive dual domain denoising. IEEE ICIP (2015)
23. Portilla, J., Strela, V., Wainwright, M.J., Simoncelli, E.P.: Image denoising using scale mixtures of gaussians in the wavelet domain. IEEE TIP (2003)
24. Rudin, L.I., Osher, S., Fatemi, E.: Nonlinear total variation based noise removal algorithms. Phys. D **60** (1992)
25. Starck, J.L., Candès, E.J., Donoho, D.L.: The curvelet transform for image denoising. IEEE TIP **11**(6) (2002)
26. Talebi, H., Milanfar, P.: Global image denoising. IEEE TIP **23**(2) (2014)
27. Tomasi, C., Manduchi, R.: Bilateral filtering for gray and color images. IEEE ICCV (1998)
28. Wiener, N.: Extrapolation, Interpolation, and Smoothing of Stationary Time Series. The MIT Press (1964)
29. Yu, G., Sapiro, G., Mallat, S.: Image modeling and enhancement via structured sparse model selection. IEEE ICIP (2010)
30. Zoran, D., Weiss, Y.: From learning models of natural image patches to whole image restoration. IEEE ICCV (November 2011)

Sub-Riemannian Fast Marching in SE(2)

Gonzalo Sanguinetti[1]([✉]), Erik Bekkers[2], Remco Duits[1,2],
Michiel H.J. Janssen[1], Alexey Mashtakov[2], and Jean-Marie Mirebeau[3]

[1] Department of Mathematics and Computer Science,
Eindhoven University of Technology, Eindhoven, The Netherlands
{G.R.Sanguinetti,R.Duits,M.H.J.Janssen}@tue.nl
[2] Department of Biomedical Engineering,
Eindhoven University of Technology, Eindhoven, The Netherlands
{E.J.Bekkers,A.Mashtakov}@tue.nl
[3] Laboratory Ceremade, CNRS, University Paris-Dauphine, Paris, France
mirebeau@ceremade.dauphine.fr

Abstract. We propose a Fast Marching based implementation for computing sub-Riemanninan (SR) geodesics in the roto-translation group $SE(2)$, with a metric depending on a cost induced by the image data. The key ingredient is a Riemannian approximation of the SR-metric. Then, a state of the art Fast Marching solver that is able to deal with extreme anisotropies is used to compute a SR-distance map as the solution of a corresponding eikonal equation. Subsequent backtracking on the distance map gives the geodesics. To validate the method, we consider the uniform cost case in which exact formulas for SR-geodesics are known and we show remarkable accuracy of the numerically computed SR-spheres. We also show a dramatic decrease in computational time with respect to a previous PDE-based iterative approach. Regarding image analysis applications, we show the potential of considering these data adaptive geodesics for a fully automated retinal vessel tree segmentation.

Keywords: Roto-translation group · Sub-riemannian · Fast marching

1 Introduction

In this article we study a curve optimization problem in the space of coupled positions and orientations $\mathbb{R}^2 \times S^1$, which we identify with roto-translation group $SE(2)$. We aim to compute the shortest curve $\gamma(t) = (x(t), y(t), \theta(t)) \in SE(2)$ that connects 2 points $\gamma(0) = (x_0, y_0, \theta_0)$ and $\gamma(L) = (x_1, y_1, \theta_1)$ with the restriction that the curve is "lifted" from a planar curve in the sense that the third variable θ is given by $\theta(t) = \arg(\dot{x}(t) + i\,\dot{y}(t))$, see Fig. 1. This restriction imposes a so-called sub-Riemannian (through the text we denote sub-Riemannian as SR)

G. Sanguinetti—The research leading to the results of this article has received funding from the European Research Council under the (FP7/2007-2014-)ERC grant ag. no. 335555 and from (FP7-PEOPLE-2013-ITN)EU Marie-Curie ag. no. 607643.

© Springer International Publishing Switzerland 2015
A. Pardo and J. Kittler (Eds.): CIARP 2015, LNCS 9423, pp. 366–374, 2015.
DOI: 10.1007/978-3-319-25751-8_44

metric that constrains the tangent vectors to the curve to be contained in a sub-space of the tangent space at every point. This subspace is a plane, which differs from point to point, and is the set of all possible tangents to curves in $SE(2)$ that are lifted from smooth planar curves. A SR-metric is a degenerated Riemannian metric in which one direction, the one perpendicular to the path in this case, is prohibited (i.e. it has infinite cost). On top of the SR-metric, we also consider a smooth external cost, which weights the metric tensor in every location and allows for data-adaptivity.

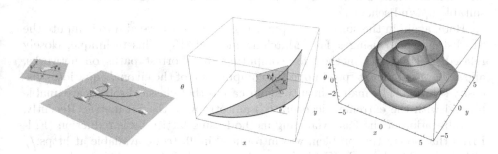

Fig. 1. Left: the sub-Riemannian problem in $SE(2)$ can be identified with that of a car with two controls (giving gas and steering the wheel). **Center:** the paths are "lifted" into curves in $SE(2) = \mathbb{R}^2 \times S^1$ with tangent vectors constrained to the plane spanned by the vector fields X_1 and X_2 (eq. (1)) associated with the controls. **Right:** the SR-spheres (for $t = 2, 4$ and 6) obtained via the FM-LBR method.

Essentially, the SR-problem in $SE(2)$ is that of a car that can go forward, backward and rotate (a so-called Reeds-Shepp car) so the possible states of the car form a 3D manifold given by the position (x, y) and the orientation θ of the car. Then, admissible trajectories of the car parametrized by only 2 control variables associated to the car moving along a straight line (giving gas) and to a change of direction (turning the steering wheel). The fact that the car cannot step aside infinitesimally imposes the SR-geometry. Finally, the curve optimization problem is to find among all possible trajectories between two given states, the one with minimal SR-length.

In image analysis the SR-geodesics in $SE(2)$ have been proposed in [4] as candidates for completion of occluded contours. Here, the geometrical structure is used as a model for the functional architecture of the primary visual cortex. This model has proven to be valuable in numerous applications [3–6], and it becomes powerful when combined with the orientation score theory [6] that allows for an invertible stable transformation between 2D images and functions on the $SE(2)$ group. The main advantage of considering this space of positions and orientations is that intersecting curves are automatically disentangled, and therefore the processing in the extended domain naturally deals with complex structures such as crossing.

Sub-Riemannian geodesics in the uniform cost case (the same cost for all the $SE(2)$ elements) were studied by several authors (e.g. [5,12]). Recently, a wavefront propagation method for computing SR-geodesics that also deals with the non-uniform cost case has been proposed in [1]. This method is an extension to the SR-case of a classical PDE-approach for computing cost-adaptive geodesics used in computer vision, where the metric tensor is induced by the image itself. The main idea is to consider propagation of equidistant surfaces described by level sets of the viscosity solution of an eikonal equation, while subsequent backtracking gives the geodesics. In order to solve the eikonal equation, the authors rely on a computationally expensive iterative approach based on a left-invariant finite-difference discretization of the PDE combined with a suitable upwind scheme.

Here, again in the spirit of computer vision methods, we aim to compute the SR-distance map using a Fast Marching method [13]. This technique, closely related to Dijkstra's method for computing the shortest paths on networks, allows for a significant speed up in the computation of the eikonal equation's viscosity solution. The main difficulty in our case is that classical solvers are unable to deal with the extreme (degenerated) anisotropy of the SR-metric. Recently, a modification of the Fast Marching method using lattice basis reduction (FM-LBR) that solves this problem was introduced in [9] (code available at https://github.com/Mirebeau/ITKFM). Then, the purpose of this paper is to show how the SR-curve optimization problem can be numerically solved using the FM-LBR method. The key aspects to consider are a Riemannian relaxation of the SR-problem and expressing the resulting metric tensor as a matrix-induced Riemannian metric in a fixed Cartesian frame. We develop these ideas in the Theory section. Then, two experiments are presented. The first one considers the uniform cost case ($\mathcal{C} = 1$) and shows that the FM-LBR based method presented here outperforms the iterative implementation in [1] in terms of CPU time, while keeping a similar accuracy. The advantages of considering data-adaptive SR-geodesics for extracting blood vessels in retinal images are illustrated in the second experiment.

2   Theory

Problem Formulation. Let $g = (x, y, \theta)$ be an element of $SE(2) = \mathbb{R}^2 \rtimes S^1$. A natural moving frame of reference in $SE(2)$ is described by the left-invariant vector fields $\{X_1, X_2, X_3\}$ spanning the tangent space at each element g:

$$X_1 = \cos\theta \partial_x + \sin\theta \partial_y, \; X_2 = \partial_\theta, \; X_3 = -\sin\theta \partial_x + \cos\theta \partial_y. \tag{1}$$

The tangents $\dot\gamma(t)$ along curves $\gamma(t) = (x(t), y(t), \theta(t)) \in SE(2)$ can be written as $\dot\gamma(t) = \sum_{i=1}^{3} u^i(t) \, X_i|_{\gamma(t)}$. Only the curves with $u^3 = 0$ are liftings of planar curves (see fig. 1). Then, the tangents to curves that are liftings of planar curves are expressed as $\dot\gamma(t) = u^1(t) \, X_1|_{\gamma(t)} + u^2(t) \, X_2|_{\gamma(t)}$ and they span the so-called distribution $\Delta = \mathrm{span}\{X_1, X_2\}$. Now, the triplet $(SE(2), \Delta, G_0)$ defines a sub-Riemannian manifold with inner product G_0 given by:

$$G_0(\dot\gamma, \dot\gamma) = \mathcal{C}(\gamma)^2 \left(\beta^2 |\dot x \cos\theta + \dot y \sin\theta|^2 + |\dot\theta|^2 \right). \tag{2}$$

In view of the car example (see Fig. 1), the parameter $\beta > 0$ balances between the cost of giving gas (the X_1 direction) and the turning of the wheel (the X_2 direction). A smooth function $\mathcal{C} : SE(2) \rightarrow [\delta, 1]$, $\delta > 0$ is the given external cost. In order to keep the notation sober during this paper, we do not indicate the dependence of G_0 on the cost $\mathcal{C}$ nor that it also depends on the curve γ. Note that the subindex 0 in the metric tensor recalls the SR-structure imposed by allowing null displacement in the X_3 direction (i.e. infinite cost for the car to move aside). This choice of notation will become clear later in the text. Now, optimal paths γ of the car in our extended position orientation space are solutions of the problem:

$$W(g) = d_0(g, e) = \min \left\{ \int_0^T \|\dot{\gamma}(t)\|_0 \, dt \ \middle| \ \dot{\gamma} \in \Delta, \gamma(0) = e, \gamma(T) = g, T \geq 0 \right\} \quad (3)$$

where $e = (0, 0, 0)$ is the origin, where $\|\dot{\gamma}(t)\|_0 = \sqrt{G_0(\dot{\gamma}(t), \dot{\gamma}(t))}$ is the SR-norm and d_0 is the SR-distance on $SE(2)$.

Riemannian Approximation. It is possible to obtain a Riemannian approximation of the SR-problem by expanding the metric tensor in eq. (2) to:

$$G_\epsilon(\dot{\gamma}, \dot{\gamma}) = G_0(\dot{\gamma}, \dot{\gamma}) + \epsilon^{-2} \mathcal{C}(\gamma)^2 \beta^2 |\dot{x} \sin \theta - \dot{y} \cos \theta|^2, \quad (4)$$

where ϵ determines the amount of anisotropy between X_3 and Δ. This definition bridges the SR-case, obtained at the limit $\epsilon \downarrow 0$, with the full Riemannian metric tensor when $\epsilon = 1$ (isotropic in the spatial directions X_1 and X_3). Actually, it is easy to verify that if $\mathcal{C} = 1$ and $\beta = \epsilon = 1$, then $G_1(\dot{\gamma}, \dot{\gamma}) = |\dot{x}|^2 + |\dot{y}|^2 + |\dot{\theta}|^2$. Also, by replacing G_0 with G_ϵ in eq. (3) we can construct a Riemannian norm $\| \cdot \|_\epsilon$ and a distance d_ϵ satisfying $\lim_{\epsilon \downarrow 0} \| \cdot \|_\epsilon = \| \cdot \|_0$ and $\lim_{\epsilon \downarrow 0} d_\epsilon = d_0$.

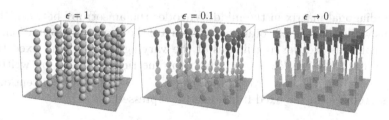

Fig. 2. Each ellipsoid represents the Tissot's indicatrix of the metric G_ϵ at different elements $g \in SE(2)$ (for the case $\mathcal{C}(g) = 1$ and $\beta = 1$). The parameter ϵ in eq. (4) bridges the Riemannian case with the SR-one. When $\epsilon = 1$ each direction has the same cost. At the limit $\epsilon \downarrow 0$, the direction X_3 has infinite cost and the distribution Δ appears.

Solution Via the Eikonal Equation. Now we can present the eikonal system that solves the problem (3) by computing the distance map $W(g)$ as proved in [1]. Following [4], let us introduce some differential operators that will simplify the notation of the remaining equations. Let U be a smooth function $U : SE(2) \to \mathbb{R}$. The Riemannian gradient ∇^ϵ, computed as the inverse of the metric tensor G_ϵ acting on the derivative, is given by:

$$\nabla^\epsilon U := G_\epsilon^{-1} dU = \mathcal{C}^{-2}\beta^{-2}(X_1 U)X_1 + \mathcal{C}^{-2}(X_2 U)X_2 + \epsilon^2 \mathcal{C}^{-2}\beta^{-2}(X_3 U)X_3. \quad (5)$$

Then, the norm of the gradient ∇^ϵ is given by:

$$\|\nabla^\epsilon U\|_\epsilon = \sqrt{\mathcal{C}^{-2}\beta^{-2}|X_1 U|^2 + \mathcal{C}^{-2}|X_2 U|^2 + \epsilon^2 \mathcal{C}^{-2}\beta^{-2}|X_3 U|^2}. \quad (6)$$

Thus, the eikonal system that characterizes the propagation of equidistant surfaces reads as:

$$\begin{cases} \|\nabla^\epsilon W(g)\|_\epsilon = 1, & \text{if } g \neq e, \\ W(e) = 0. \end{cases} \quad (7)$$

When $\epsilon \downarrow 0$ this system becomes the SR-eikonal system in [1, eq.3] where it was proved that the unique viscosity solution is indeed the geodesic distance map from the origin $W(g) = d_\epsilon(g, e)$. Then, SR-geodesics are the solutions $\gamma_b(t)$ of the following ODE system for backtracking:

$$\begin{cases} \dot{\gamma}_b(t) = -\nabla^\epsilon(W(\gamma_b(t))), & t \in [0, T] \\ \gamma_b(0) = g. \end{cases} \quad (8)$$

The Metric Matrix-Representation in the Cartesian Frame. A symmetric matrix M_ϵ representing the anisotropic metric in the frame $\{\partial_x, \partial_y, \partial_\theta\}$ can be obtained by a basis transformation from the varying frame $\{X_1, X_2, X_3\}$ (see [4, Sec.2.6]):

$$M_\epsilon = \begin{pmatrix} \cos\theta & 0 & -\sin\theta \\ \sin\theta & 0 & \cos\theta \\ 0 & 1 & 0 \end{pmatrix} \begin{pmatrix} \mathcal{C}^2\beta^2 & 0 & 0 \\ 0 & \mathcal{C}^2 & 0 \\ 0 & 0 & \epsilon^{-2}\mathcal{C}^2\beta^2 \end{pmatrix} \begin{pmatrix} \cos\theta & 0 & -\sin\theta \\ \sin\theta & 0 & \cos\theta \\ 0 & 1 & 0 \end{pmatrix}^T. \quad (9)$$

Here the diagonal matrix in the middle encodes the anisotropy between the X_i directions while the other 2 rotation matrices are the basis transformation. Note that the columns are the coordinates of the varying frame in the fixed frame, e.g. $X_1 = \cos\theta\partial_x + \sin\theta\partial_y + 0\partial_\theta$. Then, the metric tensor can be written as $G_\epsilon(\dot{\gamma}, \dot{\gamma}) = \dot{\gamma}(t) M_\epsilon \dot{\gamma}(t)$, with $\dot{\gamma}(t) = (\dot{x}(t), \dot{y}(t), \dot{\theta}(t))$. Using this convention, the eikonal system (7) in the fixed frame can be expressed as:

$$\begin{cases} \nabla^T W(g) M_\epsilon^{-1} \nabla W(g) = 1, & \text{if } g \neq e, \\ W(e) = 0, \end{cases} \quad (10)$$

where $\nabla = (\partial_x, \partial_y, \partial_\theta)^T$ is the usual Euclidean gradient. The same holds for the backtracking equation (8) which writes:

$$\begin{cases} \dot{\gamma}_b(t) = -M_\epsilon^{-1} \nabla W(\gamma_b(t)), & t \in [0, T] \\ \gamma_b(0) = g. \end{cases} \quad (11)$$

Note that when approaching the SR-case, the $\lim_{\epsilon \downarrow 0} M_\epsilon$ does not exist but the $\lim_{\epsilon \downarrow 0} M_\epsilon^{-1}$ is well defined in Eq. (11).

Anisotropic Fast Marching. We can now immediately identify Eq. (10) with [9, eq. 0.1] and then solve the eikonal system via the FM-LBR method. Our empirical tests show that $\epsilon = 0.1$, which gives an anisotropy ratio $\kappa = 0.01$ (see [9, eq. 0.5]), is already a good approximation of the SR-case and is the value used in the following experiments.

3 Experiments and Applications

Validation Via Comparison in Uniform Cost Case. The exact solutions of the SR-geodesic problem for the case $\mathcal{C} = 1$ are known (see [12] for optimal synthesis of the problem). Therefore, and similar to what is done in [1], we consider this case as our golden standard. Here, we want to compare both the computational time and the accuracy achieved in the calculation of the discrete SR-distance map $W(g)$, which is the solution of the eikonal system (7) when $\epsilon \downarrow 0$.

Let us set $\beta = 1$ and consider a grid $\mathcal{G}_s = \{(x_i, y_j, \theta_k) \in SE(2)\}$ with uniform step size s, where $x_i = is$, $y_j = js$, $\theta_k = ks$, the indices $i, j, k \in \mathbb{Z}$ such that $|x_i| \leq 2\pi$, $|y_j| \leq 2\pi$ and $-\pi + s \leq \theta_k \leq \pi$. Then we compute the discrete geodesic distance map $W(g)$ on $\mathcal{G}_s$ using the iterative method in [1] and the FM-LBR. In order to measure the accuracy of the achieved solutions we follow the method explained in detail in [1]. There, by solving the initial value problem from the origin e, a set of arc length parametrized SR-geodesics is computed such that SR-spheres of radius t are densely sampled. Then, the endpoints $g = (x, y, \theta)$ of each geodesic is stored in a list together with its length t. Finally, we define the max relative error as $E_\infty(t) = \max(|W(g) - t|/t)$ where the max is taken over all the endpoints g and where the value of $W(g)$ is obtained by bi-linearly interpolating the numerical solutions of eq. (7) computed on the grid $\mathcal{G}_s$. The results and comparisons are presented in Fig. 3. Here we solved the eikonal equation in increasingly finer grids $\mathcal{G}_s$ obtained by setting the step size $s = \pi/n, n \in \mathbb{N}^+$. Note that the size of $\mathcal{G}_s$ is then $(2n+1)(2n+1)(n-1)$. The graph in Fig. 3(left) shows the comparison of the accuracy achieved in the computation of the SR-sphere of radius $t = 4$ when n increases. The behaviour for SR-spheres of different radius is similar. The CPU time is compared in Fig. 3(center). The 3rd plot illustrates the method for computing the accuracy. The orange surface is the SR-sphere of radius $t = 4$ computed with the FM-LBR method on a grid corresponding to $n = 101$. The points are the geodesic endpoints, their color is proportional to the error of the FM-LBR (blue-low, green-medium, red-high error). The first observation is that even though the iterative method is more accurate, both methods seem to have the same order of convergence (the slope in the log-log graphs) when the grid resolution increases. This seems reasonable as both methods use first order approximations of the derivatives. Also, we hypothesise that the offset in favour of the iterative method is due to the Riemannian approximation of the SR-metric (i.e. selecting $\epsilon = 0.1$), but this needs further investigation. The second key observation is that the CPU time increases dramatically with n for the iterative method. Therefore, it is clear that we can achieve the same accuracy using the FM-LBR but with much less computational effort, which is of vital importance in the subsequent application.

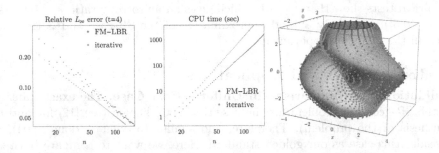

Fig. 3. Validation via comparison in the uniform cost case. The experiment (illustrated on the left, see the text) shows that even though the iterative method in [1] is more accurate we can still achieve with the FM-LBR method better results and with less CPU effort, just by increasing the grid sampling.

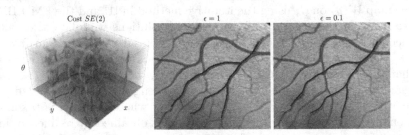

Fig. 4. Tracking of blood vessels in retinal images via cost adaptive SR-geodesics (see experiment details in [1]). **Left:** the cost obtained from the image (orange indicates locations with low cost). **Center:** Tracking in the full ($\epsilon = 1$) Riemannian case. **Right:** Tracking with the approximated ($\epsilon = 0.1$) SR-geodesics.

Application to Retinal Vessel Tree Extraction. The analysis of the blood vessels in images of the retina provides with early biomarkers of diseases such as diabetes, glaucoma or hypertensive retinopathy [7]. For these studies, it is important to track the structural vessel tree, a difficult task especially because of the crossovers and bifurcations of the vessels. Some existing techniques [1,10] rely on considering an extended (orientation and/or scale) domain to deal with this issue. Moreover, in [1] promising results were obtained by formulating the vessel extraction as a SR-curve optimization problem with external cost obtained through some wavelet-like transformation of the 2D images. In the previous experiment, we have shown that our proposed FM-LBR based implementation computes in practice the same geodesics as the iterative method in [1]. Therefore, by simply replacing the eikonal equation solver in [1] we can obtain the same results but with a dramatic decrease of the computational demands (both CPU time and memory). The example in Fig. 4 shows the advantages of considering the SR-metric in performing the vessel tree extraction. In this case (a patch of size 200x200 with 64 orientations considered) the iterative method computed the distance map in approximately 1 hour while the FM-LBR did the same in 20 seconds. For the experiments details we refer to [1], for more examples see www.bmia.bmt.tue.nl/people/RDuits/Bekkersexp.zip.

4   Conclusions

Over the last decade, some authors [4–6] have shown the advantages of considering the roto-translation group embedded with a SR-geometry as a powerful, rich tool in some image analysis related problems or for the geometrical modelling of the visual perception. In our opinion, 2 obstacles have prevented this framework to become more popular amongst engineers: the expensive computational demands involved (resulting of considering the extended orientation space) and the lack of efficient numerical methods able to deal with the extreme (degenerated) anisotropy imposed by the SR-metric. These obstacles are addressed by the main contribution of this work, which is solving (up to our knowledge for the first time) the SR-geodesic problem using a Fast Marching based implementation. To be able to achieve this, we rely on the FM-LBR solver recently introduced in [9] and show that even when relaxing the SR-restriction by a Riemannian approximation of the metric we achieve excellent numerical convergence, but much faster than with the approach in [1]. Regarding the retinal imaging application our promising preliminary studies suggest that it is at least feasible to aim for a full vessel tree segmentation as the solution of a single optimization problem, but this requires further investigation. Future work will pursue extension of this method to the 3D-rototranslation group $SE(3)$ and the applications in neuroimaging and 3D-vessel segmentation.

References

1. Bekkers, E., Duits, R., Mashtakov, A., Sanguinetti, G.: A PDE approach to Data-Driven Sub-Riemannian Geodesics. SIIMS (In press)
2. Benmansour, F., Cohen, L.D.: Tubular Structure Segmentation Based on Minimal Path Method and Anisotropic Enhancement. IJCV **92**(2), 192–210 (2011)
3. Ben-Yosef, G., Ben-Shahar, O.: A tangent bundle theory for visual curve completion. PAMI **34**(7), 1263–1280 (2012)
4. Citti, G., Sarti, A.: A Cortical Based Model of Perceptual Completion in the Roto-Translation Space. JMIV **24**(3), 307–326 (2006)
5. Duits, R., Boscain, U., Rossi, F., Sachkov, Y.: Association Fields via Cuspless Sub-Riemannian Geodesics in SE(2). JMIV **49**(2), 384–417 (2014)
6. Franken, E., Duits, R.: Crossing-Preserving Coherence-Enhancing Diffusion on Invertible Orientation Scores. IJCV **85**(3), 253–278 (2009)

7. Ikram, M.K., Ong, Y.T., Cheung, C.Y., Wong, T.Y.: Retinal Vascular Caliber Measurements: Clinical Significance, Current Knowledge and Future Perspectives. Ophthalmologica **229**, 125–136 (2013)
8. Li, H., Yezzi, A.: Vessels as 4-d curves: Global minimal 4-d paths to extract 3-d tubular surfaces and centerlines. IEEE TMI **26**, 1213–1223 (2007)
9. Mirebeau, J.-M.: Anisotropic Fast-Marching on cartesian grids using Lattice Basis Reduction. SIAM J. Num. Anal. **52**(4), 1573 (2014)
10. Péchaud, M., Peyré, G., Keriven, R.: Extraction of tubular structures over an orientation domain. In: Proc. IEEE Conf. CVPR, pp. 336–343 (2009)
11. Peyré, G., Péchaud, M., Keriven, R., Cohen, L.: Geodesic methods in computer vision and graphics. F. Trends in Comp. Graphics and Vision **5**(3–4), 197–397 (2010)
12. Sachkov, Y.L.: Cut locus and optimal synthesis in the sub-Riemannian problem on the group of motions of a plane. ESAIM: COCV **17**, 293–321 (2011)
13. Sethian, J.A.: Level Set Methods and Fast Marching Methods. Cambridge Univ. Press (1999)

Re-ranking of the Merging Order
for Hierarchical Image Segmentation

Zenilton Kleber G. do Patrocínio Jr.$^{(\boxtimes)}$ and Silvio Jamil F. Guimarães

Pontifícia Universidade Católica de Minas Gerais, Belo Horizonte, Brazil
{zenilton,sjamil}@pucminas.br

Abstract. Hierarchical image segmentation provides a set of image segmentations at different detail levels in which coarser detail levels can be produced from merges of regions belonging to finer detail levels. However, similarity measures adopted by hierarchical image segmentation methods do not always consider the homogeneity of the combined components. In this work, we propose a hierarchical graph-based image segmentation using a new similarity measure based on the variability of the merged components which is responsible for the re-ranking of the merging order that was originally established by the minimum spanning tree. Furthermore, we study how the inclusion of this characteristic has influenced the quality measures. Experiments have shown the superior performance of the proposed method on three well known image databases, and its robustness to noise was also demonstrated.

Keywords: Hierarchical image segmentation · Graph-based method · Similarity measure · Region-merging criterion

1 Introduction

The process of grouping perceptually similar pixels into regions is known as image segmentation. A hierarchical image segmentation is a set of image segmentations in which coarser detail levels can be produced from merges of regions belonging to finer detail levels. Thus, all segmentations at finer levels are nested with respect to those at coarser levels. Hierarchical methods have also the interesting property of preserving spatial and neighboring information among segmented regions. In this work, a hierarchical image segmentation in the framework of edge-weighted graphs is proposed, in which the image is equipped with an adjacency graph and the edge weight is given by a dissimilarity between two points of the image.

The use of minimum spanning tree (MST) for image segmentation was introduced in [6]. The method proposed by [4] was responsible to make popular the graph-based segmentation approach, but it does not provide a hierarchy. Some optimality properties of hierarchical segmentations have been studied in [3,7].

The authors are grateful to PUC Minas, CNPq, CAPES and FAPEMIG for the partial financial support of this work.

© Springer International Publishing Switzerland 2015
A. Pardo and J. Kittler (Eds.): CIARP 2015, LNCS 9423, pp. 375–382, 2015.
DOI: 10.1007/978-3-319-25751-8_45

Considering that, for a given image, one can tune the parameters of the well-known method [4] for obtaining a reasonable segmentation of this image. A framework to transform a non-hierarchical method to a hierarchical one has been proposed in [5].

The main contribution of this paper is the proposal of a new (dis)similarity measure based on the variability of the merged components in the context of graph-based hierarchical segmentation, which is responsible for the re-ranking of the merging order that was originally established by the MST. Moreover, similar to [5], instead of iteratively deciding whether two adjacent regions might be merged, we compute the scales for which the regions must be merged.

According to our experiments, the proposed method is statistically equivalent or better, in terms of paired t-test, than hGB [5]. Furthermore, since it is a hierarchical approach, the results of our algorithm satisfy both the locality principle and the causality principle (*i.e.*, the number of regions decreases when the scale parameter increases, and the contours do not move from one scale to another).

This work is organized as follows. Section 2 presents the new (dis)similarity measure. In Section 3, we present our hierarchical method for image segmentation. Some experimental results performed on three well known image databases are given in Section 4. Finally, in Section 5, some conclusions are drawn and future works are pointed out.

2 A New Dissimilarity Measure Based on a Weighted Observation Scale

Let us remember some definitions of the region-merging criterion used in [4]. The main idea is to measure the evidence for a boundary between two regions by comparing two quantities: one based on intensity differences across the boundary, and the other based on intensity differences between neighboring pixels within each region.

More precisely, two measures are considered: the *internal difference* $Int(X)$ of a region X and the *difference* $Diff(X,Y)$ between two neighboring regions X and Y. The *internal difference* $Int(X)$ of a region X is the highest edge weight among all the edges linking two vertices of X in the MST, while the *difference* $Diff(X,Y)$ between two neighboring regions X and Y is the smallest edge weight among all the edges that link X to Y. Thus, for merging two adjacent regions X and Y, it is necessary to verify the following region merging predicate:

$$\textbf{MergePred}(X,Y) = \begin{cases} \text{true} & , \text{if } Diff(X,Y) \leq MInt(X,Y) \\ \text{false} & , \text{otherwise} \end{cases} \quad (1)$$

in which the minimal internal difference $MInt(X,Y)$ is defined as:

$$MInt(X,Y) = \min\{Int(X) + \tau_a(X), Int(Y) + \tau_a(Y)\} \quad (2)$$

and the threshold function τ_a controls the degree to which the difference between two components must be greater than their internal differences in order to be considered as an evidence of a boundary between them. If X is a small component, $Int(X)$ may not estimate properly the local characteristics of the data (in the extreme case, when $|X| = 1$, we have $Int(X) = 0$). Therefore, in [4], a threshold function based on the size (or area) of the component is used, *i.e.*:

$$\tau_a(X) = \frac{k_a}{|X|} \qquad (3)$$

with a constant parameter k_a.

However, the adoption of this threshold function ignores the variability inside a region, since only its highest internal value and its area are considered. In order to cope with this problem, we propose the replacement, in the threshold function, of the component size by the region weight, *i.e.*:

$$\tau_w(X) = \frac{k_w}{\omega(X) + 1} \qquad (4)$$

in which, $\omega(X)$ is the sum of weights of all edges linking two vertices of X in the MST. Then, two regions X and Y should be merged when:

$$Diff(X, Y) \leq \min\left\{ Int(X) + \frac{k_w}{\omega(X) + 1}, Int(Y) + \frac{k_w}{\omega(Y) + 1} \right\} \qquad (5)$$

where k_w is a parameter used to prevent the merging of high variability regions (*i.e.*, larger k_w forces lower variability regions to be merged). Moreover, the value of the region weight $\omega(X)$ is implicitly related to its area, since one should expect that larger regions induce high variability values.

The merging criterion defined by Eq. (5) depends on the scale k_w at which the regions X and Y are observed. So, let us consider the *(weighted observation) scale $S_Y^w(X)$ of X relative to Y* as a measure based on the difference between X and Y, on the internal difference of X and on the region weight $\omega(X)$:

$$S_Y^w(X) = (Diff(X, Y) - Int(X)) \times (\omega(X) + 1). \qquad (6)$$

Therefore, the *(weighted) scale $S(X, Y)$* can be defined as:

$$S^w(X, Y) = \max(S_Y^w(X), S_X^w(Y)). \qquad (7)$$

And, finally, Eq. (5) can be rewritten as:

$$k_w \geq S^w(X, Y). \qquad (8)$$

So, two adjacent regions X and Y must be merged at scale k_w if their dissimilarity measure is smaller than or equal to k_w. In this work, differently from [4] in which k_a (or k_w) was fixed a priori, we want to compute the minimum value of k_a (or k_w) for which two adjacent regions should be merged.

3   A Hierarchical Graph Based Image Segmentation

Now, we describe the method $hGBw$ to compute a hierarchy of partitions based on scales as defined by Eq. (7). Apart of the dissimilarity measure based on weighted observation scale, it is important to note that the method for computing

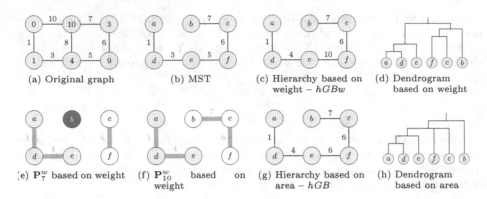

(a) Original graph   (b) MST   (c) Hierarchy based on   (d) Dendrogram
                                       weight – $hGBw$ based on weight

(e) $\mathbf{P}_7^w$ based on weight   (f) $\mathbf{P}_{10}^w$ based on   (g) Hierarchy based on   (h) Dendrogram
                                          weight   area – hGB based on area

Fig. 1. Example of re-ranking for merging order based on weight.

the hierarchy of partitions is similar to the method hGB [5], which has proposed a hierarchical strategy for the method GB [4].

It is possible to generate a partition $\mathbf{P}_\lambda^w$ of V induced by the connected components of the graph made from V and the edges whose weights are below λ, for every spanning tree T based on a set V of image pixels, for every weight map $w : E \to \mathbb{N}$ that relates a weight to each edge of T and for every threshold $\lambda \in \mathbb{N}$. It is well known [3,6] that, for any two values λ_1 and λ_2 such that $\lambda_1 \geq \lambda_2$, the partitions $\mathbf{P}_{\lambda_1}^w$ and $\mathbf{P}_{\lambda_2}^w$ are *nested* and $\mathbf{P}_{\lambda_1}^w$ is *coarser* than $\mathbf{P}_{\lambda_2}^w$. Hence, the set $\mathcal{H}^w = \{\mathbf{P}_\lambda^w \mid \lambda \in \mathbb{N}\}$ is a *hierarchy of partitions induced by the weight map* w. A detailed discussion about notions for handling hierarchies could be found in [3,6,7].

Similar to hGB, the proposed algorithm $hGBw$ does not produce a hierarchy of partitions, instead it produces a weight map L (*weighted observation scales*) from which the desired hierarchy $\mathcal{H}^L$ can be inferred for a given T. It starts from a minimum spanning tree T of the edge-weighted graph built from the image. For every edge e, the new weight map $L(e)$ is initialized to ∞; then, in order to compute the scale $L(e)$ associated with each edge e of T, the method $hGBw$ iteratively considers the edges of T in a non-decreasing order of their original weights w; and for each edge e linking two vertices x and y the following steps are performed:

(i) Find the region X of $\mathbf{P}_{w(e)}^w$ that contains x.
(ii) Find the region Y of $\mathbf{P}_{w(e)}^w$ that contains y.
(iii) Compute the hierarchical weighted observation scale $L(e)$.

At step (iii), $L(e)$ is calculated from the *hierarchical weighted scale* $S'_Y(X)$ of X relative to Y, which is the lowest *weighted* scale at which some sub-region of X, namely X^*, will be merged to Y. This can be computed as follows:

(1) Initialize the value of v to ∞.
(2) Decrement the value of v by 1.
(3) Find the region X^* of $\mathbf{P}_v^L$ that contains x.
(4) Repeat steps 2 and 3 while $S_Y^w(X^*) < v$.
(5) Set $S'_Y(X) = v$.

With the appropriate changes, the same algorithm allows $S'_X(Y)$ to be computed. Finally, the hierarchical weighted scale $L(e)$ is simply set to:

$$L(e) = \max\{S'_Y(X), S'_X(Y)\}. \tag{9}$$

Figure 1 illustrates the result of $hGBw$ on a simple graph. The hierarchical weighted scales are shown in Fig. 1(c). The whole hierarchy can be depicted as a dendrogram in Fig. 1(d), whereas two partitions of the hierarchy (at scales 7 and 10) are shown in Fig. 1(e) and Fig. 1(f). Observe the re-ranking of the merging order that was originally established by the MST, when compared to the result of hGB in Fig. 1(g) and Fig. 1(h).

4   Experiments

In order to provide a comparative analysis, we take into account the databases proposed in [1,2,8] and the measures presented in [2]. The database proposed in [1] is divided into two groups (single and two objects) containing 100 images each one. Hereafter, the group containg one object is called **WI1OBJ** and **WI2OBJ** for two objects. According to [1], their database was designed to contain a variety of images with objects that differ from their surroundings by either intensity, texture, or other low level cues. To avoid potential ambiguities it was selected images that clearly depict one object or two objects in the foreground.

Another database which is used for comparison is the Berkeley Segmentation Dataset [2], so-called **BSDS500**. This database is divided in three folds, *train*, *val* and *test*, containing 200, 100 and 200 images, respectively. In this work, the parameters are set according to the best F-measure value computed on *train* and *val* folds. In this database, a semantic segmentation is done, and sometimes, some images are under-segmented. Each image has 5 to 8 human-marked ground truths with a high degree of consistency between different human subjects but a certain variance in the level of details.

Finally, we also used the database proposed in [8], so-called **GRABCUT**. This database is originally used for detecting the contours of one object. Moreover, this database contains some images which also are in **BSDS500**.

The evaluation is based on the F-measure, which is the harmonic mean of precision and recall and it can be seen as a summary statistic of each method. In all cases, scores are optimal considering a constant scale parameter for the whole database (ODS) and a scale parameter varying for each image (OIS) [2]. Furthermore, main goal here is to study the behavior of $hGBw$ when compare to hGB [5] and GB [4] (which is a non-hierarchical version). To that end, there are different way to transforming the images into a graph. In this work, we will consider only two:

- the underlying graph is the one induced by the 8-adjacency pixel relationship with edge weights set to the color gradient computed by the Euclidean distance in the RGB space, so to identify this kind of graph we will use c followed by the name of the method (where c stands for color space);

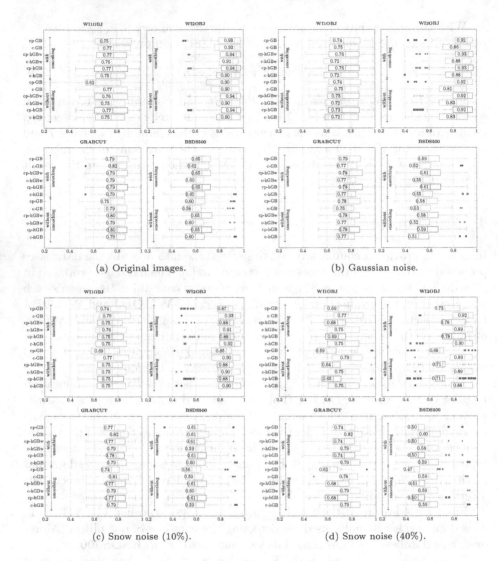

Fig. 2. Results for each dataset in which color-based and color-position-based graph creation are used as input of the compared methods. The upper part shows results with smoothing operation, while the lower part is without smoothing operation.

- the underlying graph is the one induced by the 10 nearest neighbors in RGBXY space with edge weights set to the Euclidean distance in the RGBXY space, so to identify this kind of graph we will use *cp* followed by the name of the method (where *cp* stands for color-position space). A connected graph must be guaranteed, thus the number of nearest neighbors will be increased to produce a connected graph if needed.

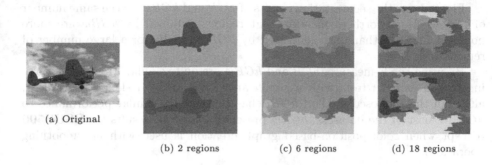

(a) Original   (b) 2 regions   (c) 6 regions   (d) 18 regions

Fig. 3. An example of segmentation results. In (b), (c) and (d) image segmentations with 2, 6 and 18 regions, respectively. Top row: threshold function is based on area – hGB. Bottom row: threshold function is based on weight – $hGBw$.

Table 1. Comparison our method $hGBw$ and the method hGB [5] according to paired Student t-test using F-measure and the scale parameter varying for each image (OIS).

Database	Methods	Smoothing	Confidence interval (5%)	The best method
WEIZMANN1OBJ	c-hGB × c-hGBw	no	[-0.0013,0.00423]	Equivalent
		yes	[-0.0071,0.00235]	Equivalent
	cp-hGB × cp-hGBw	no	[-0.00036,0.00529]	Equivalent
		yes	[-0.016,0.00067]	Equivalent
WEIZMANN2OBJ	c-hGB × c-hGBw	no	[-0.011,0.00728]	Equivalent
		yes	[-0.0035,0.00346]	Equivalent
	cp-hGB × cp-hGBw	no	[-0.009,0.00765]	Equivalent
		yes	[-0.003,0.000756]	Equivalent
BSDS500	c-hGB × c-hGBw	no	[-0.01,-0.00207]	c-hGBw
		yes	[-0.017,-0.00436]	c-hGBw
	cp-hGB × cp-hGBw	no	[-0.006,0.00161]	Equivalent
		yes	[-0.011,-0.00408]	cp-hGBw
GRABCUT	c-hGB × c-hGBw	no	[-0.0039,0.00162]	Equivalent
		yes	[-0.0063,0.00883]	Equivalent
	cp-hGB × cp-hGBw	no	[-0.0046,0.000847]	Equivalent
		yes	[-0.0015,0.00655]	Equivalent

Fig. 2(a) shows the results of experiments for each dataset when color-based and color-position-based graph creation are used with or without smoothing operation. While hGB and $hGBw$ present similar results that are superior to GB specially for the color-position-based graph, GB is the only one that seems to be greatly affected by the smoothing operation.

Fig. 2 also shows the results of experiments designed to assess the robustness of the compared methods to random impulse noises. From these experiments, we observe that all methods are affected by the smoothing operation specially for the color-position-based graph. Again, GB seems to be the most affected one for higher levels of noise. When color-position-based graph are used, GB presents 17% and 20% of improvement for **WI1OBJ** and **GRABCUT**, respectively (see Fig. 2(d)). For hGB and $hGBw$, the improvement obtained by the adoption of a smoothing operation is 10% at most.

382   Z.K.G. do Patrocínio Jr. and S.J.F. Guimarães

Fig. 3 shows the segmentation results of hGB and $hGBw$ for the same number of regions. It is worth to mention that regions obtained by $hGBw$ are more homogenous than than ones generated by hGB specially for a large number of regions (Fig. 3(d)).

By using the F-measure, hGB and $hGBw$ are quite similar. However according to the paired t-test (with a significance level of 0.05) shown in Table 1, although the proposed method $hGBw$ has presented a similar performance to hGB in most of the datasets, $hGBw$ presents a superior results for **BSDS500** (except when color-position-based graph creation is used with no smoothing operation).

5   Conclusion

This work proposes a hierarchical graph-based image segmentation using a new similarity measure based on the variability of the merged components which is responsible for the re-ranking of the merging order that was originally established by the MST. Furthermore, we study how the inclusion of this characteristic has influenced the quality measures.

Experiments have shown the superior performance of the proposed method on three well known image databases, and its robustness to noise was also demonstrated. Actually, the proposed method $hGBw$ is statistically equivalent or better than hGB [5].

For future works, we will study how to automatically choose a good hierarchical scale, and also, the real influence of filtering in our method. Another interesting work is related to visualize the hierarchy in terms of salience maps.

References

1. Alpert, S., Galun, M., Brandt, A., Basri, R.: Image segmentation by probabilistic bottom-up aggregation and cue integration. PAMI **34**(2), 315–327 (2012)
2. Arbelaez, P., Maire, M., Fowlkes, C., Malik, J.: Contour detection and hierarchical image segmentation. PAMI **33**, 898–916 (2011)
3. Cousty, J., Najman, L.: Incremental algorithm for hierarchical minimum spanning forests and saliency of watershed cuts. In: Soille, P., Pesaresi, M., Ouzounis, G.K. (eds.) ISMM 2011. LNCS, vol. 6671, pp. 272–283. Springer, Heidelberg (2011)
4. Felzenszwalb, P.F., Huttenlocher, D.P.: Efficient graph-based image segmentation. IJCV **59**, 167–181 (2004)
5. Guimarães, S.J.F., Cousty, J., Kenmochi, Y., Najman, L.: A hierarchical image segmentation algorithm based on an observation scale. In: SSPR/SPR, pp. 116–125 (2012)
6. Morris, O., Lee, M.J., Constantinides, A.: Graph theory for image analysis: an approach based on the shortest spanning tree. IEE Proceedings of Communications, Radar and Signal Processing **133**(2), 146–152 (1986)
7. Najman, L.: On the equivalence between hierarchical segmentations and ultrametric watersheds. JMIV **40**, 231–247 (2011)
8. Rother, C., Kolmogorov, V., Blake, A.: Grabcut -interactive foreground extraction using iterated graph cuts. ACM Trans. on Graphics **23**(3), 309–314 (2004)

A Novel Quality Image Fusion Assessment Based on Maximum Codispersion

Silvina Pistonesi[1]([✉]), Jorge Martinez[1], Silvia María Ojeda[2],
and Ronny Vallejos[3]

[1] Departamento de Matemática, Universidad Nacional del sur,
Av. Alem 1253, 2do Piso, B8000CPB Bahía Blanca, Argentina
{silvina.pistonesi,martinez}@uns.edu.ar
[2] Facultad de Matemática, Astronomía y Física, Universidad Nacional de Córdoba,
Ing. Medina Allende s/n, Ciudad Universitaria, CP 5000 Córdoba, Argentina
ojeda@mate.uncor.edu
[3] Departamento de Matemática, Universidad Técnica Federico Santa María,
Av. España 1680, Valparaíso, Chile
ronny.vallejos@usm.cl

Abstract. In this paper, we present a novel objective measure for image fusion based on the codispersion quality index, following the structure of Piella's metric. The measure quantifies the maximum local similarity between two images for many directions using the maximum codispersion quality index. This feature is not commonly assessed by other measures of similarity between images. To vizualize the performance of the maximum codispersion quality index we suggested two graphical tools. The proposed fusion measure is compared to image structural similarity based metrics of the state-of-art. Different experiments performed on several databases show that our metric is consistent with human visual evaluation and can be applied to evaluate different image fusion schemes.

Keywords: Image fusion-codispersion coefficient-image quality measure

1 Introduction

Image fusion is the process of combining information from two or more images of a scene into a single composite image, which is more informative and suitable for both visual perception and computer processing. Quality assessment of different image fusion schemes is traditionally carried out by subjective evaluations [5]. Even though this method is reliable, it is expensive and too slow for real world applications. Therefore, it is of great interest to provide an objective performance measure able to predict image fusion quality automatically and consistent with human visual perception. Several objective image quality measures for image fusion have been proposed and classified into four groups according to their characteristics: information theory based metrics, image feature based metrics, human perception inspired fusion metrics, and image structural similarity based

© Springer International Publishing Switzerland 2015
A. Pardo and J. Kittler (Eds.): CIARP 2015, LNCS 9423, pp. 383–390, 2015.
DOI: 10.1007/978-3-319-25751-8_46

metrics [2]. In the context of measures based on image structural similarity, Piella's metric [4], Cvejic's metric [1] and Yang's metric [9], were developed.

Recently, a new measure of similarity between images, based on the codispersion coefficient, was suggested by Ojeda et al. [3], namely, the CQ index. This measure takes into account the spatial association in a specific direction h between a degraded image and the original unmodified image. This performance allows a quantification of how well the important information in the source images is represented by the fused image.

In this work, we present a novel quality assessment metric for image fusion based on a modification of CQ index, in the same way as the universal image quality index (Q) is used in Piella's metric. In adition, motivated by the structural similarity index $(SSIM)$ map proposed by Wang et al. [8] and the codispersion map developed by Vallejos et al. [6], we presented two graphical tools to analize the performance of our quality index.

The rest of the paper is organized as follows: Section 2 gives a brief introduction of the CQ index, defines the maximum codispersion quality measure and presents two graphical tools. Section 3 presents an overview of the structural similarity based metrics for image fusion. Section 4 includes a description of the proposed metric, whereas Section 5 contains experimental results obtained by using the proposed metric. Finally, Section 6 presents the conclusion of the paper.

2   The Image Quality Metric

Let $x = \{x_{i,j} | 1 \leq i \leq N, 1 \leq j \leq M\}$ and $y = \{y_{i,j} | 1 \leq i \leq N, 1 \leq j \leq M\}$, with $N, M \in \mathbb{N}$, the original and test image signals, respectively. The quality index CQ was introduced by Ojeda et al. [3] and it is defined as follows:

$$CQ(h) = \widehat{\rho}(h)\, l(x,y)c(x,y), \tag{1}$$

where $\widehat{\rho} = \dfrac{\sum\limits_{s,s+h \in D} a_s b_s}{\sqrt{\widehat{V}_x(h)\,\widehat{V}_y(h)}}$, is the sample codispersion coefficient in the direction

h, with $s = (i,j)$, $h = (h_1, h_2)$, $D \subset Z^d$, D finite set, $a_s = x(i+h_1, j+h_2,) - x(i,j)$, $b_s = y(i+h_1, j+h_2,) - y(i,j)$, $\widehat{V}_x(h) = \sum\limits_{s,s+h \in D} a_s^2$, and $\widehat{V}_y(h) =$

$\sum\limits_{s,s+h \in D} b_s^2$. It is obvious that $|\widehat{\rho}(h)| \leq 1$. The codispersion coefficient captures

different levels of spatial similarity between two images by considering different directions in two-dimensional space. In (1), $l(x,y) = \dfrac{2\bar{x}\bar{y}}{\bar{x}^2 + \bar{y}^2}$ and $c(x,y) =$

$\dfrac{2S_x S_y}{S_x{}^2 S_y{}^2}$, are the luminance and contrast components, respectively, where $\bar{x}$ and $\bar{y}$ are the sample average values of images x and y, S_x, S_y and S_{xy} are the deviations of x and y and covariance between x and y, respectively.

2.1   Maximum Codispersion Quality Index: CQ_{max}

In this section, a novel measure to quantify similarity between two images is introduced. This measure is labeled the CQ_{max} index, and it is an intermediate and necessary step in the definition of our proposal to evaluate image fusion methods. In each evaluated window w, the CQ_{max} index, is defined as the maximum value of $CQ(h)$. This implies that CQ_{max} can seek the direction h that maximizes the CQ in the window w. Note that this direction may not be unique.

$$CQ_{max}(h|w) = \max_{\{h \,:\, p(h) \,\geq\, p_0\}} \widehat{\rho}(h|w)\, l(x,y|w) c(x,y|w), \qquad (2)$$

where $p(h)$ is the proportion of the pixels in the image corresponding to the direction h in the window w and p_0 is the threshold.

We propose to use a sliding window approach: starting from the top-left corner of the two images x, y, a sliding window of a fixed size block by block over the entire image until bottom-right corner is reached (for more details see [7]). Finally, CQ_{max} is determined by averaging all CQ local maximum quality indexes for all the windows $w \in W$

$$CQ_{max} = \sum_{w \in W} \frac{CQ_{max}(h|w)}{|W|}, \qquad (3)$$

with W the family of all windows and $|W|$ is the cardinality of W.

2.2   Graphical Tools: Visual Inspection of CQ_{max}

In order to describe the result of CQ_{max} application, we proposed two graphical tools: CQ_{max} *index map* and h *direction map*. The CQ_{max} *index map* allows to visualize locally the information about the quality degradation of the image. According to this map, the brightness indicates the magnitude of the local CQ_{max} index, and more brightness means better quality. The h *direction map*, depictes the direction h in which CQ_{max} reaches the maximum value considering the CIELab color space to represent the three components: h norm, h_1 and h_2. In this map two different situations may arise. First, CQ_{max} index values achieved in equal norm directions but different orientation correspond to equal lightness but different colors in CIELab space. In the second situation, directions with same orientation but different norm correspond to similar colors with different lightness. Note that if CQ_{max} is reached in two o more directions, we choose the lowest norm direction. See Fig. 1.

3   Image Fusion Metrics

In this section, a brief overview of state-of-the-art image structural similarity fusion metrics is presented.

3.1   Image Structural Similarity-Based Metrics

Wang's Metric $SSIM$: Wang et al. proposed the $SSIM$ index for the corresponding regions in images x and y, defined as [8]

$$
SSIM(x,y) = [l(x,y)]^{\alpha} [c(x,y)]^{\beta} [s(x,y)]^{\gamma}
$$
$$
= \left(\frac{2\bar{x}\bar{y} + C_1}{\bar{x}^2 + \bar{y}^2 + C_1} \right)^{\alpha} \left(\frac{2S_x S_y + C_2}{S_x^2 + S_y^2 + C_2} \right)^{\beta} \left(\frac{S_{xy} + C_3}{S_x S_y + C_3} \right)^{\gamma}, \quad (4)
$$

where $\bar{x}$ and $\bar{y}$ are the sample average values of images x and y, S_x, S_y and S_{xy} are the sample deviations and the sample covariance, respectively. The parameters α, β and γ, adjust the realtive importance of the three components. The constants C_1, C_2 and C_3 are included to avoid instability when denominators are very close to zero. In order to simplify the expression (4), Wang et al. set $\alpha = \beta = \gamma = 1$ and $C_3 = C_2/2$. This results in a specific form of the $SSIM$ index:

$$
SSIM(x,y) = \frac{(2\bar{x}\bar{y} + C_1)(2S_{xy} + C_2)}{(\bar{x}^2 + \bar{y}^2 + C_1)(S_x^2 + S_y^2 + C_3)}. \quad (5)
$$

A previus version of this approach is known as Q index and is written as [7]

$$
Q(x,y) = \frac{2\bar{x}\bar{y}}{\bar{x}^2 + \bar{y}^2} \frac{2S_x S_y}{S_x^2 + S_y^2} \frac{S_{xy}}{S_x S_y} = \frac{(4\bar{x}\bar{y}S_{xy})}{(\bar{x}^2 + \bar{y}^2)(S_x^2 + S_y^2)}. \quad (6)
$$

The following image structural similarity fusion metrics are based on (5) and (6) measures.

Piella's Metric Q_W: Piella and Heijmans proposed three fusion quality metrics based on Wang's Q index [4]. These are:

$$
Q_S(x,y,f) = \frac{1}{|W|} \sum_{w \in W} [\lambda(w) Q(x,f|w) + (1 - \lambda(w)) Q(y,f|w)], \quad (7)
$$

$$
Q_W(x,y,f) = \sum_{w \in W} c(w) [\lambda(w) Q(x,f|w) + (1 - \lambda(w)) Q(y,f|w)], \quad (8)
$$

$$
Q_E(x,y,f) = Q_W(x,y,f) \cdot Q_W(x',y',f')^{\alpha}, \quad (9)
$$

where the weight $\lambda(w)$ is defined as

$$
\lambda(w) = \frac{s(x|w)}{s(x|w) + s(y|w)}. \quad (10)
$$

where $s(x|w)$ and $s(y|w)$ are the local saliencies of the two input images x and y within the window w, respectively. In the Piella's implementation, $s(\cdot|w)$ is the variance of image within window w and the coefficient $c(w)$ in (8) is
$c(w) = \dfrac{\max\{s(x|w), s(y|w)\}}{\sum\limits_{w' \in W} \max\{s(x|w'), s(y|w')\}}$. In (9), $Q_W(x',y',f')$ is the Q_W calculated
with the edge images x', y' and f', and α is a parameter that weighs the edge contribution information.

Cvejic's Metric Q_C: Cvejic et al. defined a performance measure as [1]

$$Q_C(x, y, f) = \sum_{w \in W} \text{sim}\,(x, y, f|w) \cdot Q\,(x, f) + (1 - \text{sim}\,(x, y, f|w)) \cdot Q\,(y, f),\quad (11)$$

with $\text{sim}\,(x, y, f|w) = \begin{cases} 0, & \text{if } \dfrac{\sigma_{xf}}{\sigma_{xf} + \sigma_{yf}} < 0, \\ \dfrac{\sigma_{xf}}{\sigma_{xf} + \sigma_{yf}}, & \text{if } 0 \le \dfrac{\sigma_{xf}}{\sigma_{xf} + \sigma_{yf}} \le 1, \\ 1, & \text{if } \dfrac{\sigma_{xf}}{\sigma_{xf} + \sigma_{yf}} > 1. \end{cases}$. The weighting fac-

tor depends on the similarity in spatial domain between the input and fused image.

Yang's Metric Q_Y: Yang et al. proposed another way to used $SSIM$ for fusion assessment [9]:

$$Q_Y\,(x, y, f) = \begin{cases} \lambda\,(w)\,SSIM\,(x, f|w) + (1 - \lambda\,(w))\,SSIM\,(y, f|w), \\ \quad \text{if } SSIM\,(x, y|w) \ge 0.75, \\ \max\{SSIM\,(x, f|w), SSIM\,(y, f|w)\}, \\ \quad \text{if } SSIM\,(x, y|w) < 0.75. \end{cases} \quad (12)$$

the local weight $\lambda\,(w)$ is as the definition in (10).

4 Proposed Image Fusion Performance Metric CQ_M

We use the $CQ_{\max}$ index defined in (3) and following the structure of Piella metric's, (8), to define the quality index CQ_M for image fusion as

$$CQ_M(x, y, f) = \sum_{w \in W} c\,(w)\,[\lambda\,(w)\,CQ_{\max}(h|w)\,(x, f) +$$

$$(1 - \lambda\,(w))\,CQ_{\max}(h|w)\,(y, f)] . \quad (13)$$

The closer the $CQ_M(x, y, f)$ value to 1, the higher the quality of the fused image.

5 Experimental Results and Analysis

To test the performance of the proposed approach, we have carried out three experiments. In the first experiment, the $CQ_{\max}$ index was tested in different types of distortions (see Fig. 1) and compared to the results with Q index and the mean subjective rank (MSR) evaluation obtained from [7] (all images have equal mean square error (MSE)). Their $CQ_{\max}$ maps and h directions maps are presented. In the second and third experiments, the following image fusion algorithms were eva-luated, Laplacian Pyramid (LP), Ratio Pyramid (RP), Discrete Wavelet Trans-form (DWT), and Shift Invariant DWT (SIDWT), the performances of which were subjetively tested and accepted in the literature. For simulation of these methods, the "Image Fusion Toolbox", provided by Rockinger, is used (available from: http://www.metapix.de/toolbox.htm/). For the four image fusion algorithms, for both, the second and the third experiments, the approximation coefficients of the two input images averaged and the larger absolute values of the high sub-bands is selected. In the second experiment we performed a 3-level decomposition and in the third, a 4-level decomposition was used. For our metric, we set $p_0 = 0.75$, the minimum proportion of pixels that is necessary to capture spatial information in different directions, and w window size used was 8×8 pixels. For Piella's and Cvejic's metrics we used the same window size and for Yang's metric, $C_1 = C_2 = 2 \times 10^{-16}$ and the w window size used was 7×7 pixels[1] .

First Experiment: The $CQ_{\max}$ exhibits very consistent concordance with the Q results and with the MSR evaluation. The $CQ_{\max}$ index maps (Fig. 1, second row), show a consistency with perceived quality measurement.

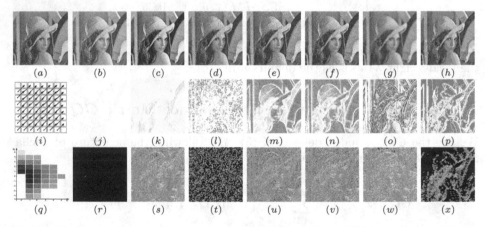

Fig. 1. (a) Original Lena image; image contaminated with: (b) Mean Shift, MSR = 1.59, $Q = 0.9894$, $CQ_{\max} = 0.9894$; (c) Contrast Stretching, MSR = 1.64, $Q = 0.9372$, $CQ_{\max} = 0.9378$; (d) Impulsive Salt Pepper Noise, MSR = 3.32, $Q = 0.6494$, $CQ_{\max} = 0.7765$; (e) Multiplicative Speckle Noise, MSR = 4.18, $Q = 0.4408$, $CQ_{\max} = 0.5249$; (f) Additive Gaussian Noise, MSR = 4.27, $Q = 0.3891$, $CQ_{\max} = 0.4859$; (g) Blurring, MSR = 6.32, $Q = 0.3461$, $CQ_{\max} = 0.4083$ and (h) JPEG Compression, MSR = 6.68, $Q = 0.2876$, $CQ_{\max} = 0.4037$; all images have equal MSE; (i) $h = (1,1)$ direction in a 8×8 window size, $p(h) = 62/64$; (j) − (p) $CQ_{\max}$ index map (brightness indicates better quality); (q) Reference of h direction map; (r) − (x) h direction maps.

The Mean Shift distortion, does not change the structure information of Lena image, therefore it corresponds to a very bright $CQ_{\max}$ index map. By contrast, the JPEG Compression contaminated image $CQ_{\max}$ index map

---

[1] The same setting that appears in [1],[4],[9].

(Fig. 1 (o)) exhibits many areas with dark pixels, showing a poor quality. In Fig. 1 (q) a black color covering the entire map except from a patch implies that in $h = (1, 0)$ or $h = (0, 1)$ the index reaches the maximum similarity. In Fig. 1 (u) and (v), the h direction maps present a similar appearance; they are predominant shades of fuchsia, indicating that the maximum similarities were reached, e.g. in $h = (3, -1)$ or $h = (4, -1)$.

Second Experiment: 32 sets of infrared (IR) and visual images (V) from "TNO UN Camp" database are used as source images (see Fig. 2). The evaluation results of the metrics for this image set are shown in Fig. 2 (g). In all schemes, the metrics assign the highest values to LP and SIDWT methods and the lowest to RP. The Kendall τ rank correlation coefficient reveals that CQ_M has reasonable agreement with Q_W ($\tau = 0.706$), Q_C ($\tau = 0.771$) and Q_Y ($\tau = 0.770$), respectively. These outcomes are consistent with those obtained by Lui et al. [2].

Third Experiment: "Medical" database including magnetic resonance imaging (MRI) and computed tomography (CT) images, and "Clock" database

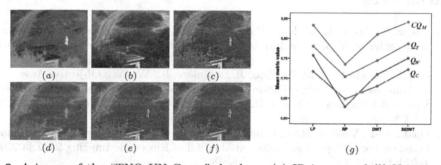

Fig. 2. A image of the "TNO UN Camp" database: (a) IR image and (b) V image; and $(c) - (f)$ fused image obtained by: LP, RP, DWT and SIDWT methods; (g) fusion metrics performance according to image fusion methods.

Table 1. Objective evaluations of different image fusion metrics for the fused images in "Medical" and "Clock" databases.

Image	Methods	Metric			
		Q_W	Q_C	Q_Y	CQ_M
"Medical" database	LP	**0.8089**	0.6247	**0.6874**	**0.8391**
	RP	0.6319	0.6053	0.6182	0.6903
	DWT	0.7314	0.6190	0.6368	0.7718
	SIDWT	0.7780	**0.6587**	0.6692	0.8169
"Clock" database	LP	**0.9272**	0.8284	0.8816	**0.9451**
	RP	0.7878	0.7564	0.7879	0.8257
	DWT	0.9139	0.7919	0.8471	0.9362
	SIDWT	0.9217	**0.8368**	**0.8853**	0.9413

containing multi-focus images are used. In both, as it is seen in Table 1, CQ_M assigns the highest values to LP and SIDWT methods, followed by DWT and the worst values correspond to RP method. The proposed measure has a coherent behavior with the perceptual evaluations.

6   Conclusion

In this paper, we have proposed an objective image fusion performance index based on maximum codispersion. The amount of information in image features, carried from the source images to the fused image, is considered as the measure of fusion algorithm performance. This amount is calculated by means of the maximum codispersion index, considering different directions which can be visually inspected through the two graphical tools proposed. Experimental results confirm that the novel measure gives good results when evaluating different fusion schemes, correlates well with the subjective criteria, and shows good agreement with the state-of-the-art metrics presented, rendering a considerable improvement over them.

References

1. Cvejic, N., Loza, A., Bull, D., Canagarajah, N.: A similarity metric for assessment of image fusion algorithms. International Journal of Signal Processing **2**(3), 178–182 (2005)
2. Liu, Z., Blasch, E., Xue, Z., Zhao, J., Laganière, R., Wu, W.: Objective Assessment of Multiresolution Image Fusion Algorithms for Context Enhancement in Night Vision: A Comparative Study. IEEE Trans. Pattern Anal. Mach. Intell. **34**(1), 94–109 (2012)
3. Ojeda, S.M., Vallejos, R.O., Lamberti, P.W.: Measure of similarity between images based on the codispersion coefficient. Journal of Electronic Imaging **21**(2), 023019-1–023019-5 (2012)
4. Piella, G., Heijmans, H.: A new quality metric for image fusion. In: Proc. Int. Conf. on Image Process (ICIP), vol. 3, pp. 173–176 (2003)
5. Toet, A., Franken, E.M.: Perceptual evaluation of different image fusion schemes. Displays **24**(1), 25–37 (2003)
6. Vallejos, R., Osorio, F., Mancilla, D.: The codispersion map: a graphical tool to visualize the association between two spatial variables. Statistica Neerlandica **69**(3), 298–314 (2015)
7. Wang, Z., Bovik, A.C.: A universal image quality index. IEEE Signal Processing Letters **9**(3), 81–84 (2002)
8. Wang, Z., Bovik, A.C., Sheikh, H.R., Simoncelli, E.P.: Image Quality Assessment: From Error Visibility to Structural Similarity. IEEE Transactions on Image Processing **13**(4), 600–612 (2004)
9. Yang, C., Zhang, J., Wang, X., Liu, X.: A Novel Similarity Based Quality Metric for Image Fusion. Inf. Fusion **9**(2), 156–160 (2008)

Magnetic Resonance Image Selection for Multi-Atlas Segmentation Using Mixture Models

Mauricio Orbes-Arteaga[1], David Cárdenas-Peña[1(✉)], Mauricio A. Álvarez[2], Alvaro A. Orozco[2], and Germán Castellanos-Dominguez[1]

[1] Signal Processing and Recognition Group,
Universidad Nacional de Colombia, Manizales, Colombia
dcardenasp@unal.edu.co
[2] Grupo de Investigación en Automática,
Universidad Tecnológica de Pereira, Pereira, Colombia

Abstract. In this paper, magnetic resonance image similarity metrics based on generative model induced spaces are introduced. Particularly, three generative-based similarities are proposed. Metrics are tested in an atlas selection task for multi-atlas-based image segmentation of basal ganglia structure, and compared with the mean square metric, as it is assessed on the high dimensional image domain. Attained results show that our proposal provides a suitable atlas selection and improves the segmentation of the structures of interest.

Keywords: Generative embedding · Fisher score · Magnetic resonance imaging · Multi-atlas segmentation · Template selection

1   Introduction

Brain magnetic resonance images (MRI) play an important role in the diagnosis and treatment of medical diseases. Applications such as disease progression, brain mapping, and surgery planning require of accurate brain structure segmentation [1]. However, such task is difficult to perform due to the presence of artifacts and low contrast between the tissues, mainly inside the subcortical region.

Atlas-based techniques are commonly used for dealing with the above constraints, as they allow to include shape and intensity distribution of any structure as *a priori* knowledge (atlas). To this end, the atlases are usually non-linearly mapped to the target image space and finally combined into a single labeling image using a procedure, known as atlas voting or label fusion. However, as brain shapes are not unimodal distributed, anatomically non relevant atlases can bias the achieved segmentation. Moreover, the computational cost linearly increases with the number of atlases to be registered. To overcome these issues, multi-atlas approaches have been proposed to properly select and combine the independent

© Springer International Publishing Switzerland 2015
A. Pardo and J. Kittler (Eds.): CIARP 2015, LNCS 9423, pp. 391–399, 2015.
DOI: 10.1007/978-3-319-25751-8_47

contributions of an atlas [2]. In this sense, proper selection of atlases allows to improve the resulting segmentation, while keeping the number of atlases as low as possible. Usually, the selection criterion is based on image similarity metrics [3], as mutual information or mean squares, being computed in a common image space [2] or in the target image space [4]. However, a large similarity value does not necessarily imply high quality propagated labels [5]. Moreover, as the metrics are computed in the original image space, the intrinsic image morphological properties may not be highlighted.

Hence, new methodologies have been introduced to find low dimensional spaces to map the images and assess the similarities. Techniques as manifold learning [6] and locality preserving projections [7] have been used in this regard. On the other hand, generative embeddings have proved to be efficient for representation and discrimination of high dimensional data structures [8]. These approaches take advantage of the low dimensional space induced by the generative model parameters or scores.

In this work, we propose to use the induced metrics from generative models as image similarity function in the atlas selection in a multi-atlas segmentation scheme. Our proposal uses generative models to represent MRI, so they are mapped into a more compact and discriminative space highlighting anatomical differences. In order to compute the image similarities, three probability based approaches are considered: Likelihood-based, Parameter-based, and Fisher score-based. Additionally, as the intensity probability distribution of the image is unknown, Gaussian and Student's t mixture models are used to estimate it. Obtained results show that the similarities in the new representation space achieve a more suitable selection of atlases improving the segmentation accuracy compared with metrics computed in the original image space, such as the means square.

2   Materials and Methods

2.1   Multi-atlas Based Segmentation

The input MRI space is described as follows: Let $\mathscr{X}=\{\boldsymbol{X}^n, \boldsymbol{L}^n : n=1,\dots,N\}$ be a labeled MRI dataset holding N image-segmentation pairs, where $\boldsymbol{X}^n=\{x_r^n \in \mathbb{R} : r \in \Omega\}$ is the n-th MR image, the value r indexes all spatial elements ($spel$), and $\boldsymbol{L}^n=\{l_r^n \in \{1, C\} : r \in \Omega\}$ is the provided image segmentation into $C \in \mathbb{N}$ classes. In the case of 3D-volume analysis, both, $\boldsymbol{X}^n$ and $\boldsymbol{L}^n$, have dimension $\Omega = \mathbb{R}^{T_a \times T_s \times T_c}$, with $\{T_a, T_s, T_c\}$ being the Axial, Sagittal, and Coronal sizes, respectively. Thus, the segmentation of each target image is accomplished by combining the subset holding the most similar labeled atlases of $\mathscr{X}$, which are selected by a given similarity criterion.

In addition, the majority vote strategy is used to carry out MRI segmentation. This straightforward procedure assigns the most agreed label among the selected atlases to each spel of the target image. So, let $\boldsymbol{X}^q$ be a target image and $\mathscr{X}_q=\{\boldsymbol{X}^t, \boldsymbol{L}^t : t=1,\dots,T\}$ be a subset of $\mathscr{X}_q \subset \mathscr{X}$ that holds $T \leq N$ selected atlases, which are ranked by the similarity measure $\kappa\{\cdot, \cdot\}$, so that

$\kappa\{X^q, X^t\} > \kappa\{X^q, X^{t+1}\}$. Also, let $\hat{L}^t$ be the provided segmentation of the t-th atlas after carrying out the deformable registration of the target image so that the matrix $\hat{L}^t$ assigns the label $\hat{l}^t_r$ to each spel r. Afterward, labeling from all atlases is gathered into a single estimated segmentation matrix $\hat{L}^q$ with elements:

$$\hat{l}^q_r = \arg\max_{c\in\{1,C\}} \sum_{t\in T} \delta(\hat{l}^t_r - c), \ \hat{l}^q_r \in \{1, C\}$$

where $\delta(\cdot)$ is the delta Dirac function. So, the image similarity function is crucial for selecting the closest templates to target images.

2.2   Generative Mixture Models for Extracting Image Features

Provided a set of parameters Θ, the intrinsic MRI features are proposed to be described by a generative model maximizing the conditional probability, $P(X|\Theta)$. For fitting parameters Θ to a given image $X=\{x_r\in\mathbb{R}: r\in\Omega\}$, this task is equivalent to the minimization of the negative log-likelihood cost function, $J=-\log P(X|\Theta)$, that under the assumption of independent and identically distributed spel intensities is written as:

$$\Theta^* = \arg\min_{\Theta}\left\{-\sum_{r\in\Omega}\log P(x_r|\Theta)\right\} \tag{1}$$

where $P(x_r|\Theta)$ is the probability that a pixel has intensity x_r, given the model parameters. Since the MR images may include several structures with different intensity ranges, we hypothesize that image features are better described by mixture models with K components and parameters $\Theta=\{\theta_k: k=1,\ldots,K\}$. Thus, the conditional probability is written as: $P(x_r|\Theta)=\sum_{k\in K}\omega_k P_k(x_r|\theta_k)$, subject to: $\sum_{k\in K}\omega_k=1$, where the mixture weight, $\omega_k\in\mathbb{R}^+$, stands for the prior probability of each spel to belong to the k-th component. $P_k(x_r|\theta_k)$ is the class conditional probability for the k-th component. We will discus the use of the following functions:

- *Gaussian Distribution*: $P_k(x_r|\theta_k)=\frac{1}{\sigma_k\sqrt{2\pi}}\exp\{-(x_r-\mu_k)^2/2\sigma_k^2\}$, where in the parameter set $\theta_k=\{\omega_k,\mu_k,\sigma_k\}$, $\mu_k\in\mathbb{R}$ is the mean and $\sigma_k\in\mathbb{R}^+$ is standard deviation.
- *Students't Distribution* ($\Gamma(\cdot)$ notates the Gamma function):

$$P_k(x_r|\theta_k)=\frac{\Gamma((\nu_k+1)/2)}{\Gamma(\nu_k/2)\sqrt{\pi\nu_k}\sigma_k}\left(1+\frac{1}{\nu_k}\left(\frac{x_r-\mu_k}{\sigma_k}\right)^2\right)^{-(\nu_k+1)/2}$$

Therefore $\theta_k=\{\omega_k,\mu_k,\sigma_k,\nu_k\}$, with $\nu_k\in\mathbb{R}^+$ as the degrees of freedom.

2.3   Generative-Model Based Measures of Pair-Wise Image Similarity

- *Likelihood-based similarity:* Due to the $\log P(X^m|\Theta^n)$ is the probability that the image X^m is generated by the model parameters Θ^n, the following log-likelihood measure of pairwise similarity is defined [8]:

$$\kappa\{X^n, X^m\} = \log P(X^m|\Theta^n) \tag{2}$$

– *Parameter-based similarity:* For better handling of size variant images, each image is represented by a concatenated parameter vector Θ that results from the model optimization, making the image characterization be only dependent on the size of the model parameters instead of the whole image domain:

$$\kappa\{X^n, X^m\} = f(\Theta^n, \Theta^m) \tag{3}$$

where $f(\Theta^n, \Theta^m)$ is a similarity function between the vectors Θ^n and Θ^m.

– *Fisher-score-based similarity:* For describing the direction in which the model parameters should be modified to better fit the data, the gradient of the log-likelihood in Eq. (1), $\nabla_\Theta \log P(X|\Theta)$ is used (termed the Fisher score [8]) as follows:

$$\kappa\{X^n, X^m\} = f(\nabla_{\Theta^n} J(X^n|\Theta^n), \nabla_{\Theta^m} J(X^m|\Theta^m)) \tag{4}$$

where $\nabla_\Theta J(X|\Theta) = \{\partial J/\partial\mu_k, \partial J/\partial\sigma_k\}_{k=1}^K$ for the case of the Gaussian mixtures, and $\nabla_\Theta J(X|\Theta) = \{\partial J/\partial\mu_k, \partial J/\partial\sigma_k, \partial J/\partial\nu_k\}_{k=1}^K$ for Student's t mixtures.

3   Experimental Set-Up

To evaluate the performance of the proposed measures of similarity between MRIs, a multi-atlas segmentation scheme is considered so that the atlases are ranked according to the degree of similarity with a target image. Also, the corresponding label images are combined through a majority voting scheme for estimating the final segmentation. Thus, the evaluation process have the following stages: *i)* Image preprocessing, *ii)* Generative model optimization, and *iii)* Similarity metric evaluation for the Atlas voting.

3.1   MRI Database and Image Preprocessing

The MRI collection used is a subset of the Open Access Series of Imaging Studies (OASIS) database that was proposed for the MICCAI 2012 *Multi-atlas labeling and Statical Fusion Challenge*. The dataset holds T1-Weighted structural MRI scans from 35 subjects (13 males and 22 females) aging from 18 to 90 years old. Each $256\times256\times287$ MRI volume has a voxel size of $1\times1\times1mm$. All images were expertly labeled for 26 structures. Due to our research interest in Parkinson surgery, only the following structures are considered: hypothalamus, amygdala, putamen, caudate nucleus, thalamus, and pallidum. Fig. 1 shows a sample image subject and its segmentation provided.

To measure image similarities within a single common image space, input MRI set is spatially normalized into the Talairach space using a rigid alignment to the MNI305 atlas. For the label propagation, every atlas image is also spatially mapped into the target image spatial coordinates with an elastic deformation (ANTS toolbox[1]).

---

[1] http://picsl.upenn.edu/software/ants

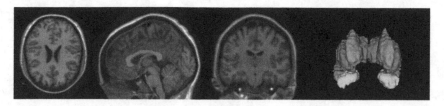

Fig. 1. Left to Right: Axial, Sagittal, Coronal views, and ground-truth segmented structures.

3.2 Generative Model Optimization

We use the Expectation-Maximization (EM) algorithm to find the parameter set of the generative mixture models representing an image (see Eq. (1)). Aiming each mixture to represent the same regions in all images, the EM at each of them is initialized as follows: i) k-means algorithm is performed over a subset of randomly taken spels from the input dataset. ii) Those resulting centroids are used further as seeds for the EM.

The ability of each distribution function considered for describing the input MRI set is analyzed by incrementing the number of mixtures $K=2,\ldots,16$ on the model as seen in Fig. 2 showing the average log-likelihood of the Gaussian mixture model. Fig. 2a relates the case when the whole image is fit, and Fig. 2b – when fitting only the region of interest (ROI) corresponding to the basal ganglia location. As a result, the former GMM fitting becomes more complex due to the larger amount of structures of the entire image. It is worth noting, for the ganglia region, that the larger is the number of mixtures, the better the fitting in the generative process. Nevertheless, the model can be over-fitted for a considerable number of mixtures.

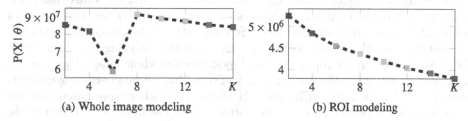

(a) Whole image modeling   (b) ROI modeling

Fig. 2. Gaussian Mixture Model fitting for several number of mixtures.

For the case of the Student's t mixture, we evaluate the image fitting by varying the degrees of freedom, $\nu=1,\ldots,20$. As seen on the top file in Fig. 3, the results achieved of the ROI modeling show that lower values of ν allow improving the generative model performance. The whole image modeling seems to have the same behavior but with worse consistency. Additionally, the bottom file in Fig. 3 show the degrees of freedom obtained from EM for a given number of mixtures. Thus, ν tends to be more stable when the number of components is increased. However, it is known that the Student's t resembles the Gaussian distribution for large values of ν.

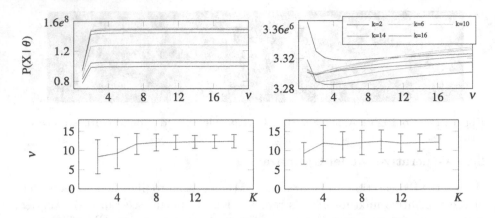

Fig. 3. Student's t parameter tuning. **Top:** Log-likelihood versus the degrees of freedom. **Bottom:** Degrees of freedom versus number of mixtures (subject mean and standard deviation depicted). **Left:** Whole image modeling. **Right:** ROI modeling.

3.3 Validation of Image Similarity in Multi-atlas-Based Segmentation Tasks

We assess the performance of the proposed similarity approaches within an atlas selection task, where all structures are segmented using the atlas-voting label propagation approach in the target image space. Specifically for the (see Eq. (3)) parameter-based and (Eq. (4)) Fisher score-based measures, we make use of the Gaussian kernel, $f(\Theta^n, \Theta^m) = \exp(\|\Theta^n - \Theta^m\|_2^2 / 2\sigma_f^2)$, as the similarity function between feature vectors, where the scale parameter $\sigma_f \in \mathbb{R}^+$ is tuned using the maximum dispersion criterion [9]. For the sake of comparison, we also assess as a similarity metric the voxel-wise Mean Squares (MS) in the image domain space.

Fig. 4 shows the results for multi-atlas segmentation using Gaussian distributions. As seen on the top file in Fig. 4 modeling the whole image, the accuracy achieved by all image similarities is not affected by the number of components used to model the input MRI space. However, the Fisher score-based measure outperforms the others. In turn, the bottom file in the figure Fig. 4 display the ROI-based modeling performance that improves the one achieved by the whole image modeling. Particularly, in Fig. 4 the bottom left figure shows that the larger the number of mixtures the lower the segmentation performance due to the model over-fitting at each image. Once again, the Fisher score-based selection outperforms the other strategies; this result may be explained since the derivatives take into account the degree of agreement between models.

Likewise, we estimate the accuracy using the Student's t distribution as seen in the top file in Fig. 5, showing a similar performance to the Gaussian distribution for the whole image modeling. For the ROI modeling, the parameter-based and Fisher score-based selection methods achieve the highest accuracy at a larger number of mixtures.

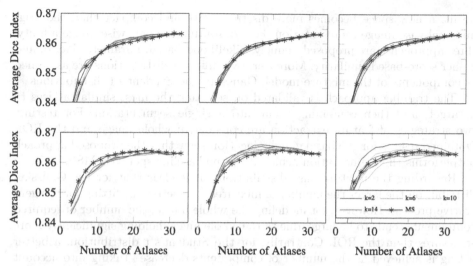

Fig. 4. Dice Index versus the number of atlases for all considered image similarities using Gaussian mixtures. **Top:** Whole image modeling. **Bottom:** ROI image modeling. **Left to Right:** Likelihood-based, Parameter-based and Fisher score-based atlas selection.

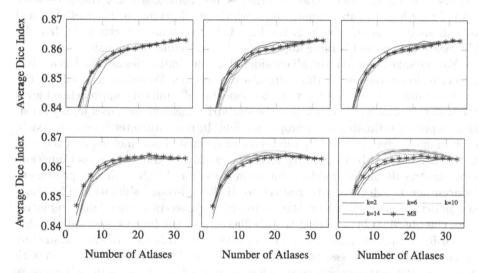

Fig. 5. Dice Index versus the number of atlases for all considered image similarities using Student's t mixtures. **Top:** Whole image modeling. **Bottom:** ROI image modeling. **Left to Right:** Likelihood-based, Parameter-based and Fisher score-based atlas selection.

4 Discussion

We introduce a new strategy for measuring MRI similarities supporting a multi-atlas segmentation scheme. The proposal allows computing pairwise similarities in a low dimensional space being induced by a generative model. As a result, a new space becomes more discriminative and compact than the original spel-wise image representation. For computing the pair-wise image affinity, three approaches are proposed, namely, Likelihood-based, Parameter-based, and Fisher score-based similarity. Moreover, two different distributions are asssumed as components of the mixture model: Gaussian and Student's t distributions.

The training approach is validated on selecting the most similar atlases to a target, and then combining them into a single segmentation. For testing, two strategies of feature extraction are considered: whole image and the ROI. Obtained results for the basal ganglia location show that the proposed approach outperforms the segmentation achieved by the baseline spel-wise MS metric.

Regarding the mixture base distributions, it is clear that for the Gaussian distribution the larger the number of mixtures, the better the fitting for the generative process. However, for modeling the whole image, the number of required components tends to be large, due to the whole image holding significantly more structures than the ROI. Contrarily, for the Student's t distribution, a better fitting is achieved as the number of components decrease. Taking into account that the degrees of freedom parameter, ν, allows to differentiate a Student's t from Gaussian like shapes, the tuning of such parameter is more complex than the location parameter and the scale parameter, at each mixture. This is mainly because the log-likelihood cost function is not convex. Hence, the parameter tuning may lead to suboptimal values, which are different to the ones obtained by exhaustive search, as seen in the Fig. 3. In this sense, we conclude that the Gaussian distribution is more appropriate for modeling the images.

For the sake of evaluation, all considered image similarities are used as a selection criterion in the multi-atlas segmentation scheme. According to results in the right column in Figs. 4 and 5, the likelihood-based similarity approach achieves the worst accuracy, this is because the similarity measure becomes highly sensitive to poorly estimated or improper models. In the parameter-based approach, each image is characterized by the vector of estimated parameters, and the similarity is measured by comparing vector pairs using a Gaussian kernel function. Obtained results in the middle columns in Figs. 4 and 5 show that improvement in accuracy is achieved with respect to likelihood-based similarity. Therefore, the information captured by the vector of parameters is more discriminative than the obtained by assessing the likelihood over the images, specially in high dimensional images. Also, in order to capture the influence of the parameters on the generative process, the gradient of the log-likelihood cost function with respect to the parameters is used as feature extraction. As a result this measure selects a more appropriate subset of atlases than the former introduced measures, achieving a higher accuracy respect to them, as seen in Figs. 4 and 5. Finally, aiming to compare the proposals against the conventional similarities, the well know Mean squares is used. In this case, the new similarities outperform the MS baseline in the atlas selection task, with the advantage of being only dependent on the number of parameters in the model, which is considerably smaller than the number of spels an image.

As a future work, other image generative models are to be tested (e.g. Markov Random Fields), where the spatial information is also taken into consideration, providing more robust estimation to the artifacts present on MR images. Other methods for model comparison, such as dissimilarities and kernel methods, will also be included.

Acknowledgments. This work was supported by Programa Nacional de Formación de Investigadores "Generación del Bicentenario", 2011/2012, the research projects 111065740687, 111056934461 and 20101008258 funded by COLCIENCIAS.

References

1. Despotovic, I., Vansteenkiste, E., Philips, W.: Brain volume segmentation in newborn infants using multi-modal mri with a low inter-slice resolution. In: 2010 Annual International Conference of the IEEE Engineering in Medicine and Biology Society, EMBC 2010, pp. 5038–5041 (2010)
2. Aljabar, P., Heckemann, R.A., Hammers, A., Hajnal, J.V., Rueckert, D.: Multi-atlas based segmentation of brain images: atlas selection and its effect on accuracy. NeuroImage **46**(3), 726–738 (2009)
3. Cárdenas-Peña, D., Orbes-Arteaga, M., Castellanos-Dominguez, G.: Supervised brain tissue segmentation using a spatially enhanced similarity metric. In: Vicente, J.M.F., Álvarez-Sánchez, J.R., de la Paz López, F., Toledo-Moreo, F.J., Adeli, H. (eds.) Artificial Computation in Biology and Medicine. LNCS, vol. 9107, pp. 398–407. Springer, Heidelberg (2015)
4. Artaechevarria, X., Munoz-Barrutia, A., Ortiz-de Solorzano, C.: Combination strategies in multi-atlas image segmentation: application to brain mr data. IEEE Transactions on Medical Imaging **28**(8), 1266–1277 (2009)
5. Langerak, T.R., Berendsen, F.F., Van der Heide, U.A., Kotte, A.N.T.J., Pluim, J.P.W.: Multiatlas-based segmentation with preregistration atlas selection. Medical Physics **40**(9), 091701 (2013)
6. Wolz, R., Aljabar, P., Hajnal, J.V., Hammers, A., Rueckert, D.: Leap: learning embeddings for atlas propagation. NeuroImage **49**(2), 1316–1325 (2010)
7. Cao, Y., Yuan, Y., Li, X., Turkbey, B., Choyke, P.L., Yan, P.: Segmenting images by combining selected atlases on manifold. In: Fichtinger, G., Martel, A., Peters, T. (eds.) MICCAI 2011, Part III. LNCS, vol. 6893, pp. 272–279. Springer, Heidelberg (2011)
8. Bicego, M., Murino, V., Figueiredo, M.A.T.: Similarity-based classification of sequences using hidden markov models. Pattern Recognition **37**, 2281–2291 (2004)
9. Álvarez Meza, A.M., Cárdenas-Peña, D., Castellanos-Dominguez, G. In: Progress in Pattern Recognition, Image Analysis, Computer Vision, and Applications SE - 41

Interleaved Quantization for Near-Lossless Image Coding

Ignacio Ramírez[✉]

Facultad de Ingeniería, Universidad de la República, Montevideo, Uruguay
nacho@fing.edu.uy

Abstract. Signal level quantization, a fundamental component in digital sampling of continuous signals such as DPCM, or in near-lossless predictive-coding based compression schemes of digital data such as JPEG-LS, often produces visible banding artifacts in regions where the input signals are very smooth. Traditional techniques for dealing with this issue include dithering, where the encoder contaminates the input signal with a noise function (which may be known to the decoder as well) prior to quantization. We propose an alternate way for avoiding banding artifacts, where quantization is applied in an interleaved fashion, leaving a portion of the samples untouched, following a known pseudo-random Beroulli sequence. Our method, which is sufficiently general to be applied to other types of media, is demonstrated on a modified version of JPEG-LS, resulting in a significant reduction in visible artifacts in all cases, while producing a graceful degradation in compression ratio.

Keywords: Predictive coding · Dithering · Quantization · Near-lossless compression · Image compression

1 Introduction

Predictive coding is one of the oldest, yet still most popular tools for signal sampling, coding and compression [1,2]. The basic idea is to encode data sequentially so that the value of a new sample is encoded differentially with respect to a causal prediction computed from previously encoded samples. This helps in decorrelating the signal, and the prediction errors to be encoded usually exhibit a distribution that is sharply peaked at 0 [3], for which efficient entropy coding methods such as Golomb-Rice are available [4,5,6].

The usual method for improving compression rates in predictive coding is to allow a small distortion in the encoded signal by quantizing the prediction errors in steps of size $\Delta = 2\delta + 1$, where δ is a positive integer [7]. For small values of δ, this method is often referred to as *near-lossless* compression, since the maximum per-sample distortion is guaranteed to be no more than δ.

There is, however, an important drawback of quantization which applies to all forms of digital representation of signals, including PCM, DPCM, and modern

---

Work partially supported by the ANII DT program.

© Springer International Publishing Switzerland 2015
A. Pardo and J. Kittler (Eds.): CIARP 2015, LNCS 9423, pp. 400–407, 2015.
DOI: 10.1007/978-3-319-25751-8_48

Fig. 1. 2D banding effect. This artifact is more evident (and detrimental to the visual quality) in areas with slowly varying intensity, such as the toy example shown in this figure. Top to bottom, left to right: undistorted image, proposed method (IQ) with $\delta = 1$ and no dithering, JPEG-LS with $\delta = 4$, IQ with $\delta = 4$ and $p = 0.9$ (The differences in the quantized output between JPEG-LS and IQ are due to a modified run length coding method in the latter). *Note: this figure is best appreciated on a computer screen.*

predictive coding: when the signals being encoded are very smooth, the quantization error sequence is highly correlated, creating "bands" or "staircases" which significantly affect the perceived quality of the reconstructed signals (see figures 1 and 3). In the case of predictive coding, this has the additional effect of being fed back into the predictor itself, creating more complex and perhaps even more annoying artifacts.

The technique of *dithering* was originally introduced in [8] precisely for reducing banding effects due to quantization in digital signal coding. In short, dithering introduces random noise in the signal, so that long sequences of smoothly varying samples are broken up, thus effectively avoiding the banding associated to such regions. Since then, dithering has become ubiquitous in all forms of digital signal coding, an enourmous body of work has been written on the subject, with several variants proposed (see [9] for a review for the case of digital images).

More closely related to our work, is the concept of *deterministic dithering*, where the "noise" to be added is a function known both to the encoder and the decoder. This idea was first proposed in the context of sampling theory in [10], using deterministic pseudo-random noise sequences to contaminate the input signal. The contaminated signal is then sampled and quantized (non-predictively) to one bit per sample. Under certain conditions on the dithering sequence and the sampling rate, the method is shown to reconstruct a wide range of signals. This idea was later extended in [11] to non-pseudo-random dithering functions such as sinusoids, again in a non-predictive sampling context.

As with the preceding cases, our motivation lies in the removal of banding artifacts due to quantization. However, contrary to all of the above methods, we break the bands by allowing a pseudo-randomly chosen set of samples to be encoded *losslessly*. In this way, not only bands are removed, but the quantization error feedback that produces them is effectively broken often and, more importantly, at random positions, thus avoiding the formation of banding patterns typical of near-lossless predictive coding.

We apply this technique to a simplified version of the JPEG-LS standard [6], with clearly positive results in terms of overall mean squared error (MSE) and visual quality, both perceived subjectively, and as given by the Structural SIMiliarity (SSIM) image quality index [12], at the cost of a small (and predictable) increase in file size (measured in average bits per pixel – BPP). Moreover, the technique allows one to vary the amount of dithering, thus allowing the user to select different trade-offs between visual quality and compressibility.

2   Background

2.1   Predictive Coding

Let $\mathbf{x}_1^n$ denote a sequence of n data samples to be encoded, where $\mathbf{x}_i^j$ is the sub-sequence from i to j; the sub-index may be omitted when $i = 1$. Coding of a new sample x_j is done by first computing a prediction of its value in terms of past samples, $\hat{x}_j = f(\mathbf{x}^{j-1})$, and then encoding (using some sort of Entropy coding) the prediction error $e_j = x_j - \hat{x}_j$. Since both the encoder and the decoder have access to the same information, the above procedure can be replicated at the decoder, so that only errors need to be transmitted.

Usual predictors include adaptive linear functions, $f(\mathbf{x}^{j-1}) = \sum_{k=1}^{p} a_k x_{j-k}$, for some $p \geq 1$, and simple fixed predictors such as the constant ($\hat{x}_j = x_{j-1}$), and linear ($\hat{x}_j = 2x_{j-1} - x_{j-2}$) ones. The latter two are popular in "low complexity" compression algorithms such as JPEG-LS, as they require very little hardware resources. In order to compensate for the simplicity and fixed nature of these predictors, an adaptive component is usually included in the form of a *bias correction term* $b_j = \frac{1}{j-1} \sum_{i=0}^{j-1} e_i$. In this way, the final error $e_j = \hat{e}_j + b_j$, where $\hat{e}_j$ is the output of the fixed predictor, has an empirical distribution centered at 0, which results in compression gains. As fixed predictors tend to exhibit different biases depending on the local shape of the sequence, bias correction is often made *context dependent*, where by context we mean some function of the past few samples which captures the shape of the signal near the sample being encoded.

2.2   Near-Lossless Coding

In this setting, prediction errors are quantized in steps of size $\Delta = 2\delta + 1$, for a maximum absolute per-sample distortion of δ between the original signal $\mathbf{x}^n$ and the one reconstructed at the decoder, which we denote by $\mathbf{y}^n$. The quantized error $\tilde{e}_j$ is obtained from e_j via,

$$\tilde{e}_j = q(e_j) = \text{sign}(e_j) \left\lceil \frac{|e_j| + \delta}{1 + 2\delta} \right\rceil,$$

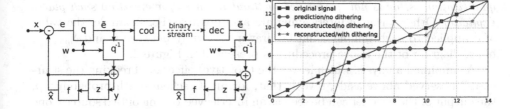

Fig. 2. Interleaved quantization encoding/decoding scheme. Here f stands for the predictor, q for the quantization block, q^{-1} for the inverse quantization block, $q^{-1}(\tilde{e}_j) = 2\delta \hat{e}_j$, and z for a delay block, whose output is its input delayed by one time step for $j > 1$, and 0 for $j \leq 1$ (time indexes are ommited for simplicity).

Fig. 3. Banding effect on lossy predictive coding of 1D signals, and the effect of dithering. Here $x_j = j - 1$, $\hat{x}_j = x_{j-1}$, and $\delta = 3$. The last curve, shown in cyan, corresponds to a pseudo-random interleaved quantization of the prediction errors with a quantization probability of $p = 0.7$.

where $[\cdot]$ denotes rounding to nearest integer. However, since both decoder and encoder must have the same data available when processing the j-th sample, on both sides the prediction $\hat{x}_j$ must be now based on the reconstructed samples $\mathbf{y}^{n-1}$, $\hat{x}_j = f(y^{j-1})$, and not on the original ones, $\mathbf{x}^{k-1}$. Therefore quantization affects not only the transmitted errors, but also the prediction itself. In regions of the input signal where $|x_j - x_{j-1}| \ll \delta$ for many consecutive samples, the corresponding regions in the reconstructed signal $\mathbf{y}^n$ will be "flattened out", as small consecutive errors will be quantized to 0. To illustrate the above situation, consider the simple zero order predictor $\hat{x}_j = f(y^{j-1}) = y_{j-1}$. In this case, the unquantized error will be $e_j = x_j - \hat{x}_j = x_j - y_{j-1}$. Now, if $e_j = x_j - y_{j-1} < \delta$ we have that $\tilde{e}_j = 0$, in which case $y_j = y_{j-1}$. This error feedback loop goes on until $|\hat{x}_j - x_j| \geq \delta$, at which point a jump of size Δ will occur. This is illustrated in Figure 3, along with the proposed method, to be discussed next.

3 Interleaved Quantization

We propose a simple modification to the lossy scheme presented in Section 2.2 where only a fraction $0 \leq p < 1$ of the prediction error samples are quantized. As can be seen in Figure 3 (cyan line), this is enough to break the staircase (1D banding) effect observed when no dithering is performed.

There are many possible ways to define the locations where quantization will occur. The algorithm that we present here, coined *interleaved quantization* (IQ) chooses such locations by generating a pseudo-random Bernoulli sequence $\mathbf{w}^n$ where $w_j \in \{0,1\}$, with $P(w_j = 1) = p$, and then quantizes the errors e_j at those locations j for which the corresponding $w_j = 1$. Although not truly random, the sequence $\mathbf{w}^n$ is sufficiently irregular to avoid generating visible artifacts in $\mathbf{y}^n$. *The key point here is that, given a fixed pseudo-random number generator, and a fixed seed, both the coder and the decoder know the exact places where quantization is, or is not, performed, without the need for encoding such places explicitly.* Other forms of interleaving are also possible. For example, the value of δ applied to each sample could be drawn uniformly between 0 and $\delta_{\max}$. A block diagram of the above procedure is presented in Figure 2.

A simplified analysis, which leaves the (positive) effect of "breaking the staircases" observed above aside, reveals that, for an IQ scheme with probability p, the output of the encoder can be seen as an interleaved coding of two sources: one corresponding to a lossy signal, and other to a lossless one. Therefore, if L_{lossy} is the codelength obtained for a given case with the fully lossy scheme ($p = 1$), and L_{lossless} is the one obtained in the lossless case, the resulting code length for the IQ scheme L_{iq} should be close to $pL_{\text{lossy}} + (1 - p)L_{\text{lossless}}$. Also ignoring the "staircase breaking effect", and with similar arguments, the distortion D_{iq} in the image reconstructed by IQ should be close to $pD_{\text{lossy}} + (1 - p)D_{\text{lossless}}$. As will be shown in Section 4, these simplified results are indeed quite accurate. In this way, p serves as an additional parameter to select a particular rate-distortion trade-off.

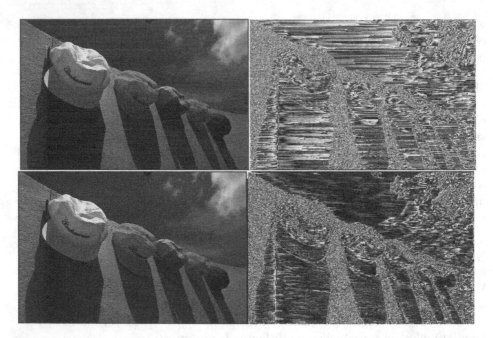

Fig. 4. Sample grayscale results. Here we show a grayscale version of the "kodim03" image from the Kodak dataset. The above pictures correspond to the near-lossless compression of kodim03 for $\delta = 10$ and no interleaved quantization $p = 1.0$ (0.86 bpp), and its absolute error with respect to the original undistorted image. The bottom row shows the same image, and its error, when compressed using interleaved quantization with $p = 0.9$ (0.96 bpp). In this case, the artifacts are dramatically reduced at a slight bitrate increase of 0.1 bpp.

We applied the IQ idea to a simplified version of JPEG-LS which we will refer to as "IQ" in the sequel. Its main difference with JPEG-LS lies in the way that it switches to *run coding mode*, which in IQ is analogous to the lossless case, whereas JPEG-LS takes into account quantization (a reasonably complete description of JPEG-LS is not possible given the space constraints; please refer to [6] for technical details on its definition). As JPEG-LS uses a very simple, fixed (2D) predictor together with a context-dependent bias correction term, the effect of quantization fits well within the simplified analysis of Figure 3, as the results below show.

4   Results and Discussion

The primary purpose of our algorithm is to improve upon the visual artifacts produced by current near-lossless prediction-based image coding techniques. Figures 4 and Figure 5 are examples for which such artifacts are clearly visible, even for small target distortions, on a very low dynamic range medium such as paper or even an ordinary computer monitor. It is important to underline that such effects are much more noticeable, at even smaller target distortions, on current commercial displays aimed at consumers in general. For a numerical evaluation of our method, we applied the IQ algorithm to a grayscale version of the "Kodak dataset"[1,2]. In Figure 6 we report these results in terms of the traditional Rate-Distortion curve, based on mean squared error (MSE), and on a Rate-Quality

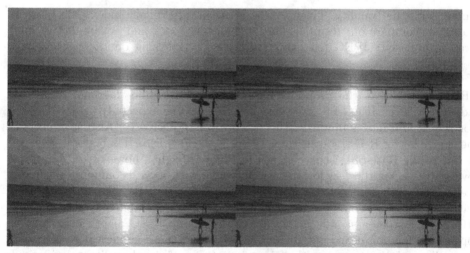

Fig. 5. Color example. Without quantization (left column) the banding effect is already noticeable for $\delta = 5$, is clearly visible for $\delta = 10$. Leaving only 10% unquantized already improves the visual quality significantly, as can be seen on the right column. *Note: this example is best appreciated on a computer screen.*

---

[1] Publicly available at http://r0k.us/graphics/kodak/

[2] Additional examples, as well as the source code, are available at http://iie.fing.edu.uy/~nacho/demos/iq/.

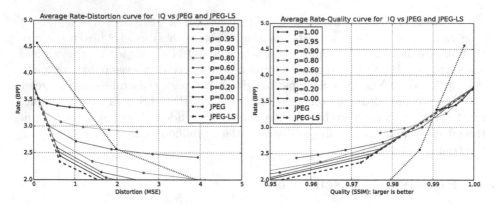

Fig. 6. Summary of results. Left: Rate-Distortion curves in terms of MSE for JPEG, JPEG-LS and IQ in the near-lossless region. Right: Rate-SSIM curves for the same algorithm. In both cases, the IQ curve is plotted for various values of the quantization probability p, each dot corresponding to a value of δ, starting with $\delta = 0$ (lossless, that is, MSE= 0 on the left, and SSIM= 1.0 on the right), in increments of 1. In the first case, the Rate-Distortion curves for IQ are above the JPEG-LS one for $p < 1.0$, meaning that the process of interleaving does not provide advantages over JPEG-LS in terms of quadratic Rate-Distortion. (It remains, however, below that of JPEG, for values of $\delta < 4$.) In the second case, where lower-right is better, IQ improves over JPEG-LS in the very low distortion region ($\delta \leq 3$). *Note: this is a color graph.*

curve, with the "quality" given by the Structural SIMiliary index [12]. In both cases, we compare our results against the classic (lossy, and not predictive, but transform-based) JPEG [13], and JPEG-LS [6], focusing on the near-lossless region ($\delta \leq 5$).

As can be seen in Figure 6(left), from a traditional quadratic Rate-Distortion (R-D) perspective, the proposed interleaved quantization does not offer any advantages over JPEG-LS; it essentially coincides (as expected) with JPEG-LS for $p = 1$, and moves upwards (this is worse) as p decreases. Also as expected, both give better R-D tradeoffs than JPEG in the low-distortion region shown. In terms of the Rate-SSIM curve shown in Figure 6(right), however, IQ improves over JPEG-LS in the very low distortion region, with several configurations lying below and to the right of the JPEG-LS curve (that is, higher SSIM at the same bitrate). At some point (here, below 3.00bpp), also as expected, both IQ and JPEG-LS lose by a significant margin to the classic JPEG algorithm, which is optimized for non-near lossy operation. Although these numerical results may seem dissapointing, we argue that the gain in terms of visual quality, as evidenced in figures 4 and 5, is much larger. Also, it is important to bear in mind that one of the advantages of near-lossless compression lies in its guaranteed maximum distortion, something which may be advantageous, from a legal standpoint, over traditional methods such as JPEG (example, medical imaging for diagnosis). In this sense, our method retains such advantages, while producing less visual artifacts, and at a small decrease in compression rate.

References

1. Elias, P.: Predictive coding-I. IRE Transactions on Information Theory **1**(1), 16–24 (1955)
2. Elias, P.: Predictive coding-II. IRE Transactions on Information Theory **1**(1), 24–33 (1955)
3. O'Neal, J.: Predictive quantizing systems (differential pulse code modulation) for the transmission of television signals. The Bell System Technical Journal **45**(5), 689–721 (1966)
4. Golomb, S.W.: Run-length encodings (corresp.). IEEE Transactions on Information Theory **12**(3), 399–401 (1966)
5. Rice, R.F.: Some practical universal noiseless coding techniques-part III. Technical report JPL-91-3, Jet Propulsion Laboratory (1991)
6. Weinberger, M., Seroussi, G., Sapiro, G.: The LOCO-I lossless image compression algorithm: Principles and standardization into JPEG-LS. IEEE Trans. IP **9** (2000)
7. Cutler, C.: Differential quantization of communication signals (1952). US Patent 2,605,361
8. Roberts, L.G.: Picture coding using pseudo-random noise. IRE Transactions on Information Theory **8**(2), 145–154 (1962)
9. Chen, J.S.: A comparative study of digital halftoning techniques. In: 1992 Proceedings of the IEEE 1992 National Aerospace and Electronics Conference, NAECON 1992, vol. 3, pp. 1139–1145 (1992)
10. Masry, E.: The reconstruction of analog signals from the sign of their noisy samples. IEEE Trans. IT **IT–27**(6), 735–745 (1981)
11. Cvetković, Z., Daubechies, I.: Single bit oversampled A/D conversion with exponential accuracy in the bit rate. In: Proc. Data Compression Conference (DCC) 2000, Snowbird, UT, pp. 343–352 (2000)
12. Wang, Z., Bovik, A.C., Sheikh, H.R., Simoncelli, E.P.: Image quality assessment: from error measurement to structural similarity. IEEE Trans. IP **13**(1) (2004)
13. Wallace, G.: The JPEG still picture compression standard. Communications of the ACM **34**(4), 30–44 (1991)

Image Edge Detection Based on a Spatial Autoregressive Bootstrap Approach

Gustavo Ulloa[1]([✉]), Héctor Allende-Cid[2], and Héctor Allende[1,3]

[1] Universidad Técnica Federico Santa María, Valparaíso, Chile
gulloa@alumnos.inf.utfsm.cl, hallende@inf.utfsm.cl
[2] Pontificia Universidad Católica de Valparaíso, Valparaíso, Chile
hector.allende@ucv.cl
[3] Universidad Adolfo Ibañez, Viña del Mar, Chile
hallende@uai.cl

Abstract. In this paper a new algorithm to perform edge detection based on a bootstrap approach is presented. This approach uses the estimated spatial conditional distribution of the pixels conditioned by their neighbors. The proposed algorithm approximates the original image by adjusting local 2D autoregressive models to different blocks of the image. The residuals are used in order to generate resampled images by using bootstrap techniques. The proposed algorithm applied to synthetic and real images generates as a result, a binary image, in which the detected edges can be observed.

Keywords: Spatial autoregressive models · Image procesing · Edge detection · Segmentation · Sieve bootstrap

1 Introduction

During the last decades, edge detection and image segmentation, have been two of the topics that have drawn more attention in the area of computer vision and other related areas. For example, in the topic of medical imaging, it is known that the features that determine the presence or absence of a disease, do not appear in the whole image, instead they appear in local regions of it [7]. Edge detection allows to locate and identify sharp discontinuities of an image. These discontinuities are due to abrupt changes in the pixel intensity which characterizes boundaries of objects in a scene. Due to this reason, edges give boundaries between different regions of an image, which can be used to identify objects with segmentation methods [1]. Many techniques for edge detection have been proposed, based in the compute of gradient by the first and second derivatives [1,4]. There are many edge detection operators available that identify vertical, horizontal, corner and step edges. The operators based in the first derivative are the Sobel, Prewitt and Robert, and the the main operators based on the

---

This work was supported by research grant Mecesup FSM 0707/Mineduc.

A. Pardo and J. Kittler (Eds.): CIARP 2015, LNCS 9423, pp. 408–415, 2015.
DOI: 10.1007/978-3-319-25751-8_49

second derivative are Zero Crossing, Laplacian of Gaussian (LoG) and Canny edge detector. These methods do not use an explicit spatial relation from the neighboord like the correlation information.

The two-dimensional autoregressive models are one way to represent the gray/intensity images based on the spatial linear relation of the pixels. Recently a segmentation and edge detection method based on an AR-2D models have been proposed [6]. The algorithm consists in locally fitting a two-dimensional autoregressive model to the original image. The image is divided into square region and an AR-2D model is fitted to each of these regions catching the linear relation in the image. For that, the residual image contains the non-linear relation present in the image. This makes that abrupt transitions between regions/object of the image and the areas with different textures are noticed. This algorithm highlights the location of the edges of the original image, but does not differentiate them in a unique way from the different areas, instead what it does, it uses the gray-scale transitions, which do not specify where one region ends and where the other starts. This is necessary in applications like image segmentation [9].

In this paper we focus our attention on edge detection of images based on the spatial information obtained by the estimation of the empirical conditional spatial distribution of the pixels of the image by means of the use of a AR-2D sieve bootstrap approach. This bootstrap approach is similar to the AR-1D sieve bootstrap in time series [2], with the difference that the index set, instead of being $\mathbb{R}|\mathbb{Z}$, corresponds to $\mathbb{Z}^2$ and an order relation can be defined.

The paper is presented as follows: In the next section we present an overview of the spatial AR processes. In Section 3 we describe our proposal. In Section 4 we show some simulation and real data results. In the last section we present some concluding remarks.

2   State of the Art

Spatial Linear Models

In all the following, all the random fields are indexed over $\mathbb{Z}^d$, with $d \geq 2$, and $\mathbb{Z}^d$ is endowed with the usual partial order, that is for $s = (s_1, \ldots, s_d)$, $u = (u_1, \ldots, u_d)$ in $\mathbb{Z}^d$, we write $s \leq u$ if for all $i = 1, \ldots d$, $s_i \leq u_i$. For $a, b \in \mathbb{Z}^d$, such that $a \leq b$ and $a \neq b$, the following indexing subsets in $\mathbb{Z}^d$, will be considered:

$$S[a, b] = \{x \in \mathbb{Z}^d | a \leq x \leq b\}, \quad S\langle a, b] = S[a, b] \backslash \{a\}, \tag{1}$$

$$S[a, \infty] = \{x \in \mathbb{Z}^d | a \leq x\}, \quad S = \langle a, \infty] = S[a, \infty] \backslash \{a\}, \tag{2}$$

Let $(X_s)_{s \in \mathbb{Z}^d}$ be a real valued square integrable random field. The random field (X_s) is said to be stationary or weakly stationary if

$$E(X_s) = \mu_X, \quad \forall s \in \mathbb{Z}^d, \tag{3}$$

$$\gamma(u, v) = E[(X_u - E(X_u))(X_v - E(X_v))] = \gamma(u + h, v + h), \quad \forall\, u, v, h \in \mathbb{Z}^d \tag{4}$$

It is strictly stationary, if for all $h \in \mathbb{Z}^d$, $(X_j)_{j \in S}$ and $(X_{j+h})_{j \in S}$ have the same joint distributions.

We say that a random field $(X_s)_{s\in\mathbb{Z}^d}$ is linear if for any s,

$$X_s = \sum_{j\in\mathbb{Z}^d} \psi_j \varepsilon_{s-j} \tag{5}$$

with $\sum |\psi_j| < \infty$ and where $(\varepsilon_s)_{s\in\mathbb{Z}^d}$ denotes a family of independent and identically distributed (i.i.d) centered random variables with variance $\sigma^2 > 0$.

Following [8], we say that a random field $(X_s)_{s\in\mathbb{Z}^d}$ is a spatial ARMA(p,q) with parameters $p, q \in \mathbb{Z}^d$, if it is weakly stationary and satisfies the following equation

$$X_s - \sum_{j\in S\langle 0,p]} \phi_j X_{s-j} = \varepsilon_s + \sum_{k\in S\langle 0,q]} \theta_k \varepsilon_{s-k} \tag{6}$$

where $(\phi_j)_{j\in S\langle 0,p]}$ and $(\theta_k)_{k\in S\langle 0,q]}$ denotes respectively the autoregressive and the moving-average parameters with $\phi_0 = \theta_0 = 1$. Notice that, if $p = 0$, the sum over $S\langle 0,p]$ is supposed to be zero, and the process is called a spatial autoregressive AR(p) random field. In the same sense, if $q = 0$ the process is called an MA(q) random field.

The ARMA random field is called causal if it has the following unilateral expansion

$$X_s = \sum_{j\in S[a,\infty]} \psi_j \varepsilon_{s-j}, \tag{7}$$

with $\sum_{j\in S[a,\infty]} |\psi_j| < \infty$.

Let $\phi(z) = 1 - \sum_{j\in S\langle 0,p]} \phi_j z^j$ and $\theta(z) = 1 + \sum_{j\in S\langle 0,q]} \theta_j z^j$ where $z = (z_1, \ldots, z_d)$.

Then, a sufficient condition [8] for the random field to be causal is that the autoregressive polynomial $\phi(z)$ has no zeros in the closure of the open disc D^d in $\mathbb{C}^d$.

The first study of this class of models was studied by Whittle in 1954 [11]. There exist several prediction windows that can be considered in the definition of a spatial ARMA process. A complete treatment of prediction windows and examples can be found in [3].

Spatial ARMA 2-dimensional

The 2D ARMA process is defined by the equation [5] with $s = (i,j) \in \mathbb{Z}^2$

$$\Phi(B_1, B_2)X(i,j) = \Theta(B_1, B_2)\varepsilon(i,j), \tag{8}$$

where the two dimensional backward operators $\Phi(B_1, B_2)$ and $\Theta(B_1, B_2)$ are given by

$$\Phi(B_1, B_2) = \sum_k \sum_l \phi(k,l) B_1^k B_2^l,$$

$$\Theta(B_1, B_2) = \sum_k \sum_l \theta(k,l) B_1^k B_2^l,$$

with $B_1 X(i,j) = X(i-1,j)$ and $B_2 X(i,j) = X(i,j-1)$ and $\varepsilon(i,j)$ are independent random variables with $\mathbb{E}[\varepsilon(i,j)] = 0$ and $Var[\varepsilon(i,j)] = \sigma^2$.

As in the time series case, there are conditions on the 2-dimensional polynomials to be stationary and to have invertibility. For stationarity, it is enough to assume that the complex valued polynomial $\Phi(z_1, z_2)$ is not zero for any z_1 and z_2, which simultaneously satisfies $|z_1| < 1$ and $|z_2| < 1$.

As in the one-dimensional case, if $\Phi(B_1, B_2) = 1$, then the process is called moving average, and if $\Theta(B_1, B2) = 1$, the process is called autoregresive.

Sieve Bootstrap

Sieve bootstrap is a bootstrap method to generate trajectories from the original time series maintaining its probabilistic structure. The sieve bootstrap method is based on resampling with replacement from the residuals obtained from estimating the stochastic process observed. It is important to highlight that the method is based on the approximation of an infinite dimensional or non parametric model by means of a sequence of finite dimensional parametric models, due that the model converges to infinity as $n \to \infty$ [2]. The sieve bootstrap method is based on the Wold theorem, which establishes that if we decompose a stationary stochastic process $\{X_s\}_{s \in \mathbb{Z}^d}$, and we take the stochastic part, it can be represented as a stochastic mean average stationary process $\{X_s\}_{s \in \mathbb{Z}^d}$ of order infinity or general linear model

$$X_s - \mu_X = \sum_{j=0}^{\infty} \psi_j \varepsilon_{s-j}, \qquad \psi_0 = 1, \, s \in \mathbb{Z}^2, \tag{9}$$

where $\{\varepsilon_s\}_{s \in \mathbb{Z}^2}$ is a i.i.d. process with $E[\varepsilon_s] = 0$ and $\sum_{j=0}^{\infty} \psi_j^2 < \infty$. This general linear representation plus some assumptions allows us to use the sieve method in linear and mean average autoregressive models.

If the observed process supports the linear general representation (9) and it is invertible, we can represent $\{X_s\}_{s \in \mathbb{Z}^2}$ as a one-side infinite-order autorgressive process

$$X_s - \mu_X = \sum_{j=0}^{\infty} \phi_j (X_{s-j} - \mu_X) + \varepsilon_s, \qquad \phi_0 = 1, \, s \in \mathbb{Z}^2, \tag{10}$$

with $\sum_{j=0}^{\infty} \phi_j^2 < \infty$. With this representation, it can be used as a AR-sieve approximation with $AR(p)$ models.

Sieve Bootstrap Confidence Intervals. The sieve bootstrap confidence intervals are built from the empirical quantiles obtained from the B bootstrap observations X_{S+h}^*. These observations, h steps ahead, are part of the B bootstrap trajectories generated by means of the sieve bootstrap algorithm for prediction intervals, with which we estimate the conditional distribution of X_{S+h}, given the known observations.

3 Proposed Method

In this paper we propose an edge detection algorithm for images which is based in the spatial relation estimated by means of an AR-2D sieve bootstrap approach. This algorithm consists in two main steps; The first consists in the estimation of the empirical conditional distribution of a pixel and the second step discriminates if a pixel is or not an edge pixel. Based on the imposed restriction that the real intensity pixel must be inside of a prediction interval if it shares a similar correlation structure with its neighborhood. Because of this, it is expected that a pixel belonging to a rough transition between two regions of the image (as the edges), should be outside the prediction interval.

The algorithm proposed is an extension of the algorithm proposed in [6] (Algorithm 1), which is the following and will be denoted as Algorithm 2.

Algorithm 1

1: Split image I in square blocks of dimesion $k \times k$.
2: Compute the autoregressive coeficient by least square estimators $\hat{\phi}_1, \hat{\phi}_2, \ldots \hat{\phi}_p$ or $\hat{\phi}_{0,1}, \hat{\phi}_{1,0}, \ldots \hat{\phi}_{1,1}$ of the two dimensional autoregressive model to each block.
3: Compute the residual image by means of the difference between the original image I and the estimated image $\hat{I}$.

The proposed algorithm is as follows:

Algorithm 2. Edge Detection

1: Use Algorithm 1.
2: Center the estimated residuals by means of

$$\tilde{\nu}_s = \left(\hat{\nu}_s - \frac{1}{N-p} \sum_{s=p+1}^{N} \hat{\nu}_s \right), \tag{11}$$

where s is the spatial coordinate $s = (i, j)$ of the residual pixel computed and N is the number of pixels in each block.
3: Generate a resample $\{\nu_s^*\}_{s=1}^T$ from $\hat{F}_{\tilde{\nu}, N}(y)$ of each block.
4: Generate a bootstrap sample of each block with

$$X_{i,j}^* = \hat{\phi}_{1,0} X_{i-1,j}^* + \hat{\phi}_{0,1} X_{i,j-1}^* + \hat{\phi}_{1,1} X_{i-1,j-1}^* + \varepsilon_{i,j}^*, \tag{12}$$

where $X_{i,j}^* = X_{i,j}$ for $i, j \leq 1$.
5: Generate a bootstrap prediction of the pixels in each block by means of

$$X_{i,j}^* = \hat{\phi}_{1,0} X_{i-1,j}^* + \hat{\phi}_{0,1} X_{i,j-1}^* + \hat{\phi}_{1,1} X_{i-1,j-1}^* + \varepsilon_{i,j}^*, \tag{13}$$

where $X_{i,j}^* = X_{i,j} \; \forall i, j \in S$.
6: Repeat Steps 3 to 5, B times for each block.

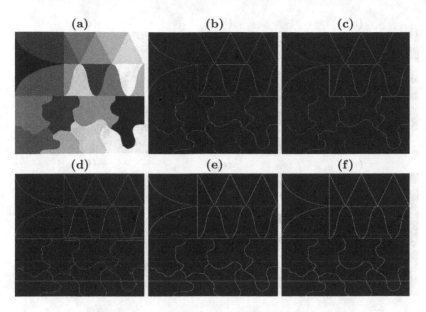

Fig. 1. (a) Original image, (b) Sobel edge detector, (c) Prewitt edge detector, (d) LoG edge detector, (e) Canny edge detector and (f) Image result of Algorithm 2.

7: Obtain a prediction interval of $(1 - \alpha)100\%$ for the real value of the pixel $X_{i,j}$ using $\hat{F}^*_{X_{i,j}}$.

$$\left[-\sqrt{H^*_{(1-\alpha)}}, \sqrt{H^*_{(1-\alpha)}}\right], h = 1, \cdots, s, \tag{14}$$

where $H^*_{(1-\alpha)}$ is the quantile $1 - \alpha$ of $\hat{F}^*_{X_{i,j}}$

8: Determine if the real value of the pixel $X_{i,j}$ belongs to the interval.

9: If $X_{i,j}$ does not belong to the interval, the pixel is considered as an edge.

4 Simulated and Real Image Results

In this section we present two experiments that illustrate the performance of the proposed algorithm for edge detection and other proposals widely studied in the literature like the follow operators: Sobel, Prewitt, LoG and Canny, which are based in the first and second estimate derivatives.

We consider simulated and real images of size 512×512, which were taken from the USC-SIPI image database http://sipi.usc.edu/database/. The order of the AR-2D model was $p = 3$. The number of bootstrap samples used in the experiment was $B = 300$. The sizes of the blocks was of 64×64, 128×128, 256×256 and 512×512. The selection of an especific pair of α of the $(1 - \alpha)100\%$ prediction intervals and size of blocks depended for each image, where was considered aspects like continuity of the edges and number of point misclassified.

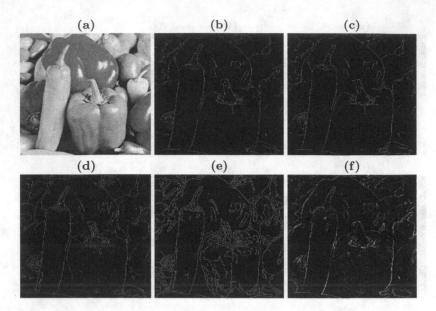

Fig. 2. (a) Original image, (b) Sobel edge detector, (c) Prewitt edge detector, (d) LoG edge detector, (e) Canny edge detector and (f) Image result of Algorithm 2.

In Figure 1 we can see the results of the diferent edge detection approaches applied to a synthetic image composed of many regions with different constant levels of gray intensity and shape of the boundaries. The approaches based in the first derivative did not detect all the boundaries and presented some discontinuitues (Figure 1(b) and 1(c)), which was partially solved by second derivative based approaches (Figure 1(d) and 1(e)). The LoG method (Figure 1(d)) presented spurious edges. The Canny approach (Figure 1(e)) presented discontinuities in some boundaries. Finally, the Boostrap approach (Figure 1(f)), outperforms all the clasic approaches, because it detected all the boundaries of the regions without discontinuities. The parameters of the Bootstrap approach were $\alpha = 0.05$ and a block size of 512×512.

In Figure 2 the results applied to the real image are presented. We can observe that all the clasic approaches obtained similar results, but with some differences related to the continuity of some boundaries and the presence of spurious edges, specifically in the Canny approach (Figure 2(e)). The parameters of the Bootstrap approach (Figure 2(f)), were $\alpha = 0.05$ and a block size of 256×256. The Bootstrap approach presents a good identification of the real edges, but it also shows the presence of many pixels inside of the regions missclasified as edges. Despite this, the Bootstrap approach seems to follow detect most of the real edges.

The results of the proposed method on both simulated and real images look promising, and the edges are clearly distinguishable.

5   Conclusions

In this paper we have introduced a new algorithm to perform edge detection based on a Bootstrap approach. This approach uses the spatial conditional distribution, estimated for each pixel, in order to obtain prediction intervals for them. This allows to classify as edges, pixels whose gray intensity are not within the intervals, i.e. those pixels that seem distant from the probabilistic structure of their neighbors, which is assumed to be similar inside a specific region.

The conditional Bootstrap estimation of the distribution of the pixels in a gray level image could open a new line of research in image analysis processing, which could be used not only in better edge detection algorithms, but also in segmentation algorithms or as a feature in more complex image analysis techniques.

As future work, it is planned to improve the current algorithm applying the propagation of the AR-2D process not only from the top-left corner of the image, but also from the other three corners. We assume that merging the information from 4 different directions could improve the edge detection of more types of edges, i.e. diagonal and lines placed in different layouts. We plan also to propose an extension of the algorithm to color or multi-spectral images.

We also consider future work, the robustification of the algorithm in order to work with contaminated images with additive and innovative noise based on the approach in AR-1D models presented in [10]. The latter work showed good results with innovative and additive noises, so we think it could be useful for this approach.

References

1. Bhardwaj, S., Mittal, A.: A survey on various edge detector techniques. Procedia Technology **4**, 220–226 (2012). 2nd International Conference on Computer, Communication, Control and Information Technology (C3IT-2012), February 25–26, 2012
2. Bühlmann, P.: Sieve bootstrap for time series. Bernoulli **2**(3), 123–148 (1997)
3. Guyon, X.: Random fields on a network. In: Modeling, Statistics and Applications. Springer (2005)
4. Khan, W.: Image segmentation techniques: A survey. Journal of Image and Graphics **1**(4), 166–170 (2013)
5. Martin, R.J.: Some results on unilateral arma lattice processes. Journal of Statistical Planning and Inference **50**, 395–411 (1996)
6. Ojeda, S., Vallejos, R.: A new image segmentation algorithm with applications to image inpainting. Computational Statistics and Data Analysis **54**(9), 2082–2093 (2010)
7. Rangaraj, M.: Biomedical Image Analysis. CRC Press (2005)
8. Tjostheim, D.: Statistical spatial series modelling. Adv. Appl. Prob. **10**, 130–154 (1978)
9. Uemura, T., Koutaki, G., Uchimura, K.: Image segmentation based on edge detection using boundary code. ICIC International **7**(10), 220–226 (2011)
10. Ulloa, G., Allende-cid, H., Allende, H.: Robust sieve bootstrap prediction intervals for contaminated time series. International Journal of Pattern Recognition and Artificial Intelligence **28** (2014)
11. Whittle, P.: On stationary processes on the plane. Biometrika **41**, 434–449 (1954)

Iterative Gradient-Based Shift Estimation: To Multiscale or Not to Multiscale?

Martin Rais[1,2]($\boxtimes$), Jean-Michel Morel[2], and Gabriele Facciolo[2]

[1] DMI, UIB, Palma, Majorca, Spain
martus@gmail.com
[2] CMLA, ENS-Cachan, Cachan, France

Abstract. Fast global shift estimation is a critical preprocessing step on many high level tasks such as remote sensing or medical imaging. In this work we deal with a simple question: should we use an iterative technique to perform shift estimation or should we use a multiscale approach. Based on the obtained results, both methodologies proved to lose accuracy as the noise increases, however this accuracy loss increases with the shift magnitude. The conclusion is that a multiscale strategy should be used when the shift magnitude is higher than approximately a fifth of a pixel.

Keywords: Shift estimation · Multiscale · Iterative

1 Introduction

Given two images shifted by some unknown displacement $\mathbf{v}$, the problem of shift estimation is to compute this displacement. Problems such as low SNR conditions, lack of image structure and quantization errors make this task non trivial. Several issues appear as well when seeking for accurate subpixel shifts. Nevertheless, precise and real-time shift estimation methods are required in many fields, such as remote sensing [4,11,15] or medical imaging [6,16].

As mentioned in [17], there are mainly four types of shift estimation methods that achieve subpixel accuracy: correlation interpolation, intensity interpolation, differential methods and phase correlation.

Correlation interpolation methods achieve subpixel accuracy by fitting an interpolation surface to the samples of a discrete correlation function, and then, the maximum of this surface is searched. This methodology not only implies calculating the discrete correlation between images, which is a resource consuming task, but also to interpolate it. A more straightforward way to achieve

During this work, the author had a fellowship of the Ministerio de Economia y Competividad (Spain), reference BES-2012-057113, for the realization of his Ph.D. thesis. This work was also partially supported by the Centre National d'Etudes Spatiales (MISS Project), the European Research Council (Advanced Grant Twelve Labours), the Office of Naval Research (under Grant N00014-97-1-0839), Direction Générale de l'Armement, Fondation Mathématique Jacques Hadamard and Agence Nationale de la Recherche (Stereo project).

© Springer International Publishing Switzerland 2015
A. Pardo and J. Kittler (Eds.): CIARP 2015, LNCS 9423, pp. 416–423, 2015.
DOI: 10.1007/978-3-319-25751-8_50

subpixel accuracy is to interpolate selected parts of the input images to create a much denser grid. Then, the task is to match these grids between images, which requires knowing beforehand which part of the input images to interpolate and then match, something which is not always available.

To date, there are mainly two fast and accurate shift estimation methods from which several branches have emerged. The first one is based on the phase correlation technique [3,5,12], in which the displacement is estimated using the cross-power spectrum between both images. This technique, although able to obtain quite accurate results, requires at least the computation of the DFT for both input images, a task that could be prohibitive depending on the context.

On the other hand, differential methods are normally faster than Fourier-based methods, since they do not require computing the DFT. By using a differential technique, the difference between two frames is related with the spatial intensity gradient of the first image. Given $I_1(x,y)$ and $I_2(x,y)$, and denoting the components of the translation between both images by v_x and v_y, we have

$$I_2(x,y) = I_1(x - v_x, y - v_y). \tag{1}$$

Using the first order Taylor expansion yields

$$I_1(x,y) - I_2(x,y) \approx v_x \frac{\partial I_1(x,y)}{\partial x} + v_y \frac{\partial I_1(x,y)}{\partial y} \tag{2}$$

which is a formula known under the name of optical flow equation [6]. Since the higher terms of the Taylor approximation were removed, this relation performs well only when the translation is small, in particular when it is less than one pixel. The unknown shift $\mathbf{v}$ is estimated by minimizing the error in this equation. This can be done by minimizing the L_2 norm. Using linear least squares is a classical solution, introduced by Lucas-Kanade [7], and has linear complexity.

This estimator, however, ignores the higher terms of the Taylor development and the fact that the underlying input images have noise, which biases the results. A complete study on this bias was performed by Robinson and Milanfar [13], followed by Pham *et al.* [9]. In these works, an explicit formula for the Lucas-Kanade estimator bias was derived. However, these authors address the bias in two completely different ways.

Robinson and Milanfar tried to reduce the influence of the estimator's bias by designing a gradient estimation filter (i.e. antisymmetric) which minimized its bias derivation in the Fourier domain based on the selection of pre-filters and on the prior knowledge of the image spectrum and some constraint about the shift [14]. Surprisingly, this article proposed to minimize the estimator bias by attacking the approximation error in the data model due to the linear signal approximation performed by the Taylor development, while completely ignoring the noise. In fact, low Signal-to-Noise Ratio situations are discarded since they claim that in many image registration applications, the effective SNR falls into a high SNR regime. For this reason, they achieve poor results on images with SNR lower than 20dB. Furthermore, none of these previous approaches work under aliased situations or badly sampled images, which are possible (yet undesired) in computer vision problems.

Pham *et al.*, on the other hand, derived a complete 2D gradient-based shift estimation bias in the spatial domain. However, instead of dealing with it explicitly, they note the linear dependence between the estimator's bias with both the shift magnitude and the noise. They also remark that the bias due to the noise is proportional to the shift magnitude as well. Thus, they propose to reduce the bias by iteratively computing the shift and resampling the second image onto the first. Based on their results, with only three iterations they are able to obtain an almost unbiased estimator. This iterative scheme was actually proposed by Lucas and Kanade in [7], and further refined in Baker *et al.* [1] in a complete study of the Lucas-Kanade estimator. However, this iterative scheme involves performing interpolation, which becomes an expensive computation.

A different iterative scheme, such as in Thevenaz *et al.* [16], consists in computing the image pyramid and to perform shift estimation on each level separately. Beginning by the coarser level, the estimated shift is then used to resample the second image on the next finer scale. Although this technique requires the construction of the pyramid, it can allow itself to use more complex interpolation techniques on lower scales due to its reduced cost. Most importantly, the shift estimation performed on each scale could also be made iterative, a price that can be payed when working on coarser scales.

Objective. Both iterative techniques (direct and multiscale) succeed in reducing the bias when enough iterations are applied. However, it is not straightforward, based on the shift magnitude and on the noise conditions of the input images, to estimate which methodology achieves better results on each condition. For example, if the shift magnitude is above one pixel, the multiscale approach will definitely be necessary. Furthermore, under noisy conditions, working on a coarser scale permits to reduce the noise influence, however less pixels (and thus equations) will be available to perform shift estimation.

In this article we evaluate both methodologies by varying the noise, the shift to estimate, the derivative kernels used, the amount of iterations and the underlying interpolation method in order to understand how each methodology performs. What is more, we answer the question of deciding between applying a multiscale approach or sticking to the original solution.

The rest of this paper is organized as follows. In section 2 both methodologies are explained in detail. In section 3 we evaluate each of them, under all possible conditions, and based on this we draw conclusions on section 4.

2   Methods

2.1   Iterative Lucas-Kanade Shift Estimation Method

The Lucas-Kanade algorithm is based on the optical flow equation:

$$I_t(x,y) \approx \nabla I_1(x,y)\mathbf{v}. \tag{3}$$

where $\nabla I_1(x, y) = \left[\frac{\partial I_1(x,y)}{\partial x}, \frac{\partial I_1(x,y)}{\partial y} \right]$ and $\mathbf{v} = \begin{bmatrix} v_x \\ v_y \end{bmatrix}$ is the unknown shift. Then, to estimate the global optical flow between both grayscale images I_1 and I_2, the Lucas-Kanade algorithm assumes a constant flow for the whole image, thus implying a unique translation vector $\mathbf{v}$ for every pixel. This assumption leads to the construction of an overdetermined system of equations, $\mathbf{Av} = \mathbf{b}$, where $\mathbf{A}$ is composed of spatial intensity derivatives and $\mathbf{b}$ has temporal derivatives

$$\mathbf{A} = \begin{pmatrix} \frac{\partial I_1}{\partial x}(p_1) & \frac{\partial I_1}{\partial y}(p_1) \\ \vdots & \vdots \\ \frac{\partial I_1}{\partial x}(p_n) & \frac{\partial I_1}{\partial y}(p_n) \end{pmatrix} \qquad \mathbf{v} = \begin{pmatrix} v_x \\ v_y \end{pmatrix} \qquad \mathbf{b} = - \begin{pmatrix} \frac{\partial I_1}{\partial t}(p_1) \\ \vdots \\ \frac{\partial I_1}{\partial t}(p_n) \end{pmatrix} \qquad (4)$$

and p_i with $i = 1 \ldots n$ represents the ith pixel and n the number of pixels. To solve this system, (v_x, v_y) is obtained by performing the linear least squares method, using the Moore-Penrose pseudo-inverse. Let I_x, I_y and I_t denote $\frac{\partial I_1}{\partial x}$, $\frac{\partial I_1}{\partial y}$ and $\frac{\partial I_1}{\partial t}$ respectively, the following linear system has to be solved

$$\mathbf{A}^T \mathbf{A} \mathbf{v} = \mathbf{A}^T \mathbf{b} \qquad (5)$$

where $\mathbf{A}^T \mathbf{A} = \begin{bmatrix} \sum I_x^2 & \sum I_x I_y \\ \sum I_x I_y & \sum I_y^2 \end{bmatrix}$ is the second moment matrix, and $\mathbf{A}^T \mathbf{b} = \begin{bmatrix} \sum I_t I_x \\ \sum I_t I_y \end{bmatrix}$ is a spatio-temporal gradient correlation term. To solve this system, the matrix $\mathbf{A}^T \mathbf{A}$ must be invertible in which case the solution is $(\mathbf{A}^T \mathbf{A})^{-1} \mathbf{A}^T \mathbf{b}$.

It is not a coincidence that the results of the method depend on the inversion of this second moment matrix since the determinant of this matrix is crucial for determining the limits on the estimation performance [9]. A study on this matrix before performing the shift estimation can be used to discard ill-posed cases. This happens for example when the gradient occurs on its majority on a single direction and therefore we are dealing with a potentially unsolvable situation, commonly known as the aperture problem. Last but not least, since the Taylor development is centered at 0, this method performs well only when the translation is small, i.e., shifts larger than 1 would not be correctly estimated.

Lucas and Kanade also suggest iterating the method to obtain better results and converge to the true displacement value. This algorithm is easily understood in the following lines:

```
1  i ← 0;  I_2(0) ← I_2;  w ← 0
2  while  i ≤ k  and  |v(i − 1) − v(i − 2)| ≥ min do
3        v(i) ← findshift(I_1, I_2(i))
4        w   ← w + v(i)
5        I_2(i + 1) ← Resample(I_2, −w)
6        i   ← i + 1
```

where $findshift$ uses Eq. (5) to solve for $v(i)$ and $Resample$ performs interpolation on the input images, which is a costly operation. In particular, if an inappropriate interpolation algorithm is used, it could lead to poor results, implying a non-negligible computational cost.

On the other hand, it was proved in Pham *et al.* [9] that this iterative method is able to significantly reduce the bias, provided an appropriate resampling method is used. Due to this reason, very poor results are obtained when dealing with highly aliased images, as shown in [10] when a single iteration outperforms the multi-iteration method. Nevertheless, with a correct resampling and with a sufficient number of iterations, this method is the only capable, to our best knowledge, of practically removing the bias.

2.2 Multiscale Lucas Kanade Shift Estimation Method

By building a pyramid representation of the input images, Eq. (5) can be applied on each scale to estimate the shift between images, and this estimated shift can in turn be used to resample the second image on the following level of the pyramid. In our case, a dyadic Gaussian pyramid approximation was used [2]. We also evaluated using an exact dyadic Gaussian pyramid [8], filtering with $\sigma = 1.4$ before subsampling, however the results were similar. Starting from the coarse image at scale $n > 1$, the method is summarized in the following lines:

1 $I_1^{1\ldots n} \leftarrow ComputeImagePyramid(I_1, n)$ // *Burt & Adelson's Gaussian Pyramid [2]*,
2 $I_2^{1\ldots n} \leftarrow ComputeImagePyramid(I_2, n)$ // *i.e.,* IMPYRAMID *function from Matlab*
3 $i \leftarrow n;\;\; w \leftarrow 0$
4 **while** $i > 0$ **do**
5       $v(i) \leftarrow findshift(I_1^i, I_2^i)$
6       $w \;\;\; \leftarrow w * 2 + v(i) * 2$
7       $I_2^{i-1} \leftarrow Resample(I_2^{i-1}, -w)$
8       $i \;\;\;\; \leftarrow i - 1$
9 $v(i) = findshift(I_1^1, I_2^1)$

3 Results

Both methodologies described in sections 2.1 and 2.2 were evaluated extensively under different noise conditions, shifts and gradient estimators. To show the most representative results, four SNR conditions were evaluated: noiseless, low noise ($\sigma = 5$), medium noise ($\sigma = 25$) and high noise ($\sigma = 50$). Each table is organized in groups of four lines corresponding to each of these four noise configurations. Also, the four most significant shifts in terms of results are shown: a big shift $(0.5, -0.9)$, a medium shift $(0.2, -0.2)$, a small shift $(0.024, 0.052)$ and no shift.

The performance of each algorithm under each condition was evaluated by simulating shifted images obtained from a high resolution satellite image of 10000×10000 pixels. For each noise and shift, 100 experiments were averaged, and each experiment was performed by shifting the large image using Fourier interpolation and taking a 50×50 subimage from a random position away from the edges to avoid ringing artifacts followed by adding white Gaussian noise and evaluating all the methods (Fig. 1). The results shown were later validated using the Cramer-Rao bound (verifying that both $var(\hat{v_x})$ and $var(\hat{v_y})$ are lower than 0.01) so that the averaged values contain only valid shift estimations.

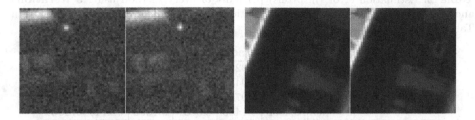

Fig. 1. Two problems: a noisy and an almost unidimensional gradient situation

Table 1. Estimation error (in pixels) per shift of every method using **2 iterations** and **bicubic** interpolation from valid estimations. For each shift and estimation method, four SNR conditions were tested. The first three columns are for the iterative method (IT) while the last three are for the multiscale approach (MS) with a single iteration per scale. In each case, three gradient estimation methods were used: backward difference and Gaussian derivative with $\sigma = 1$ and with $\sigma = 0.3$ respectively.

Shift (px)	Noise	IT2G1	IT2G2	IT2G3	MS2G1	MS2G2	MS2G3
(0.5000,-0.9000)	$\sigma = 0$	0.0514	0.0818	0.0472	0.0387	0.1600	**0.0316**
	$\sigma = 75$	0.1375	0.1053	0.1103	0.0744	0.1808	**0.0582**
	$\sigma = 150$	0.2875	0.1414	0.2305	0.1267	0.2130	**0.1009**
	$\sigma = 300$	0.4927	0.2327	0.4292	0.2319	0.2872	**0.1909**
(0.0000,0.0000)	$\sigma = 0$	**0.0000**	0.0000	0.0000	0.0000	0.0000	0.0000
	$\sigma = 75$	**0.0114**	0.0188	0.0132	0.0164	0.0188	0.0175
	$\sigma = 150$	**0.0168**	0.0330	0.0219	0.0300	0.0326	0.0313
	$\sigma = 300$	**0.0191**	0.0539	0.0307	0.0527	0.0549	0.0573
(0.2000,-0.2000)	$\sigma = 0$	0.0115	0.0117	0.0154	**0.0115**	0.0360	0.0159
	$\sigma = 75$	0.0249	0.0267	0.0223	**0.0192**	0.0470	0.0225
	$\sigma = 150$	0.0652	0.0424	0.0487	0.0360	0.0591	**0.0358**
	$\sigma = 300$	0.1295	0.0765	0.1103	0.0738	0.0899	**0.0694**
(0.0240,0.0520)	$\sigma = 0$	0.0040	**0.0019**	0.0052	0.0039	0.0073	0.0054
	$\sigma = 75$	**0.0122**	0.0181	0.0138	0.0156	0.0189	0.0166
	$\sigma = 150$	**0.0198**	0.0326	0.0231	0.0296	0.0326	0.0311
	$\sigma = 300$	**0.0300**	0.0543	0.0354	0.0547	0.0564	0.0581
Avg.	$\sigma = 0$	0.0167	0.0238	0.0170	0.0135	0.0508	**0.0132**
	$\sigma = 75$	0.0465	0.0422	0.0399	0.0314	0.0664	**0.0287**
	$\sigma = 150$	0.0973	0.0624	0.0811	0.0556	0.0843	**0.0498**
	$\sigma = 300$	0.1678	0.1043	0.1514	0.1033	0.1221	**0.0939**

In tables 1 and 2 results are shown for 2 iterations and bicubic interpolation and for 3 iterations with spline interpolation respectively. From these results several conclusions can be drawn. First, as expected, the multiscale method is much more robust when the shift magnitude is high. In fact, even at a shift of (0.2,-0.2) it is recommendable to use the multiscale method instead of the standard iterative version. Second, when no shift or a small shift is present, the non-multiscale methods achieve much better accuracies. Apparently, the multi-

Table 2. Estimation error (in pixels) per shift of every method using **3 iterations** and **spline** interpolation from valid estimations. Table configuration is the same as in Table 1.

Shift (px)	Noise	IT3G1	IT3G2	IT3G3	MS3G1	MS3G2	MS3G3
(0.5000,-0.9000)	$\sigma = 0$	0.0156	0.0238	**0.0065**	0.0114	0.1007	0.0086
	$\sigma = 75$	0.0646	0.0437	0.0437	0.0293	0.1194	**0.0251**
	$\sigma = 150$	0.1869	0.0727	0.1326	0.0533	0.1488	**0.0497**
	$\sigma = 300$	0.4092	0.1480	0.3337	0.1093	0.2143	**0.1001**
(0.0000,0.0000)	$\sigma = 0$	**0.0000**	0.0000	0.0000	0.0000	0.0000	0.0000
	$\sigma = 75$	**0.0116**	0.0199	0.0133	0.0261	0.0330	0.0260
	$\sigma = 150$	**0.0194**	0.0357	0.0246	0.0468	0.0547	0.0467
	$\sigma = 300$	**0.0250**	0.0621	0.0391	0.0980	0.1065	0.1001
(0.2000,-0.2000)	$\sigma = 0$	**0.0027**	0.0045	0.0043	0.0206	0.0205	0.0235
	$\sigma = 75$	0.0201	0.0229	**0.0182**	0.0304	0.0430	0.0334
	$\sigma = 150$	0.0475	0.0395	**0.0373**	0.0483	0.0593	0.0489
	$\sigma = 300$	0.1096	**0.0718**	0.0913	0.0982	0.1195	0.0977
(0.0240,0.0520)	$\sigma = 0$	**0.0007**	0.0009	0.0013	0.0068	0.0041	0.0080
	$\sigma = 75$	**0.0120**	0.0188	0.0132	0.0219	0.0283	0.0225
	$\sigma = 150$	**0.0207**	0.0348	0.0248	0.0471	0.0548	0.0464
	$\sigma = 300$	**0.0313**	0.0622	0.0412	0.1011	0.1056	0.1001
Avg.	$\sigma = 0$	0.0047	0.0073	**0.0030**	0.0097	0.0313	0.0100
	$\sigma = 75$	0.0271	0.0263	**0.0221**	0.0269	0.0559	0.0268
	$\sigma = 150$	0.0686	**0.0457**	0.0548	0.0489	0.0794	0.0479
	$\sigma = 300$	0.1438	**0.0860**	0.1263	0.1017	0.1365	0.0995

scale algorithms are not suited for such small shifts since their poor performance on lower scales results in less accurate results. This result contradicts several state-of-the-art methods and is worth remarking. Third, regarding the amount of iterations/scales to use, in presence of high noise, performing more iterations in the original scale or using more scales in the multiscale approach gives worse results in terms of accuracy. When dealing with a noisy situation, the resampling operation proved to be negative for the shift estimation algorithm. This result is more accentuated for the multiscale approach. Finally, the multiscale algorithm proved to be a better contender when dealing with noise in general, although this factor is greatly influenced by the shift magnitude. However, except when the shift magnitude is lower than a fifth of a pixel, its use is recommended. Moreover, its computational cost is lower than the iterative counterpart since the resampling is performed on lower resolution images.

4   Conclusions

In this paper we dealt with a simple question never answered in the community: should we use a multiscale strategy to perform gradient based shift estimation or should we directly attack the problem by simply iterating in the original scale. The answer of this question was shown to depend heavily on the shift magnitude more than the SNR of the images. Under small shift magnitudes, performing a multiscale strategy achieves poorer results, in particular due to the lack of displacement on the lower scales that makes the method less accurate. However, when dealing with shifts higher than one fifth of a pixel, the multiscale strategy showed strong improvements over traditional iterative Lucas-Kanade shift estimation. Last but not least, in situations under low SNR, we concluded that performing fewer iterations or using fewer scales achieves improved accuracy, and this result is even more remarked in the multiscale approach. As a future work, experimentation is planned on a larger dataset of images with different characteristics, and by testing several other interpolation methods for image resampling when iterating the algorithm.

References

1. Baker, S., Matthews, I.: Lucas-kanade 20 years on: A unifying framework. Int. J. Comput. Vision **56**(3), 221–255 (2004)
2. Burt, P.J., Adelson, E.H.: The Laplacian pyramid as a compact image code. IEEE Transactions on Communications **31**(4), 532–540 (1983)
3. Foroosh, H., Zerubia, J., Berthod, M.: Extension of phase correlation to subpixel registration. IEEE TIP **11**(3), 188–200 (2002)
4. Goshtasby, A., Stockman, G., Page, C.: A Region-Based Approach to Digital Image Registration with Subpixel Accuracy. IEEE Transactions on Geoscience and Remote Sensing **GE-24**(3) (1986)
5. Guizar-Sicairos, M., Thurman, S.T., Fienup, J.R.: Efficient subpixel image registration algorithms. Opt. Lett. **33**(2), 156–158 (2008)
6. Horn, B.K., Schunck, B.G.: Determining optical flow (1981)
7. Lucas, B.D., Kanade, T.: An iterative image registration technique with an application to stereo vision. In: Proceedings of the 7th International Joint Conference on Artificial Intelligence, vol. 2, pp. 674–679 (1981)
8. Morel, J.M., Yu, G.: Is sift scale invariant? Inverse Problems and Imaging **5**(1), 115–136 (2011)
9. Pham, T.Q., Bezuijen, M., Van Vliet, L.J., Schutte, K., Luengo Hendriks, C.L.: Performance of optimal registration estimators. In: Proc. SPIE, vol. 5817, pp. 133–144 (2005)
10. Pham, T., Duggan, M.: Bidirectinal bias correction for gradient-based shift estimation. In: IEEE ICIP, pp. 829–832, Oct 2008
11. Rais, M., Thiebaut, C., Delvit, J.M., Morel, J.M.: A tight multiframe registration problem with application to earth observation satellite design. In: 2014 IEEE International Conference on Imaging Systems and Techniques, pp. 6–10 (2014)
12. Reddy, B., Chatterji, B.: An FFT-based technique for translation, rotation, and scale-invariant image registration. IEEE TIP **5**(8), 1266–1271 (1996)
13. Robinson, D., Milanfar, P.: Fundamental performance limits in image registration. IEEE TIP **13**(9), 1185–1199 (2004)
14. Robinson, D., Milanfar, P.: Bias minimizing filter design for gradient-based image registration. Signal Processing: Image Communication **20**(6), 554–568 (2005). Special Issue on Advanced Aspects of Motion Estimation
15. Sabater, N., Leprince, S., Avouac, J.P.: Contrast invariant and affine sub-pixel optical flow. In: IEEE ICIP, pp. 53–56 (2012)
16. Thévenaz, P., Ruttimann, U.E., Unser, M.: A pyramid approach to subpixel registration based on intensity. IEEE TIP **7**(1), 27–41 (1998)
17. Tian, Q., Huhns, M.N.: Algorithms for subpixel registration. Comput. Vision Graph. Image Process. **35**(2), 220–233 (1986)

A Study on Low-Cost Representations for Image Feature Extraction on Mobile Devices

Ramon F. Pessoa$^{(\boxtimes)}$, William R. Schwartz, and Jefersson A. dos Santos

Department of Computer Science, Universidade Federal de Minas Gerais (UFMG),
Belo Horizonte, Minas Gerais 31270-901, Brazil
{ramon.pessoa,william,jefersson}@dcc.ufmg.br

Abstract. Due the limited battery life and wireless network band-width limitations, compact and fast (but also accurate) representations of image features are important for multimedia applications running on mobile devices. The main purpose of this work is to analyze the behavior of techniques for image feature extraction on mobile devices by considering the *triple trade-off problem* regarding effectiveness, efficiency, and compactness. We perform an extensive comparative study of state-of-the-art binary descriptors with bag of visual words. We employ a dense sampling strategy to select points for low-level feature extraction and implement four bag of visual words representations which use hard or soft assignments and two most commonly used pooling strategies: average and maximum. These mid-level representations are analyzed with and without lossless and lossy compression techniques. Experimental evaluation point out ORB and BRIEF descriptors with soft assignment and maximum pooling as the best representation in terms of effectiveness, efficiency, and compactness.

1 Introduction

In 2014, the number of smartphone users worldwide achieved around 1.75 billion. Recent forecasts indicate that the growth of smart mobile devices usage should increase even more the next years [1]. Many challenges and opportunities have emerged concerning image/video processing tasks, such as annotation, categorization, detection and retrieval. The challenges in image processing in mobile devices include constraints such as memory and computing resources which may be very limited [2]. Due the limited battery life of mobile devices, energy usage is also a critical issue [2]. Regarding feature extraction from images, those constraints configure a *trade-off* among effectiveness, efficiency and compactness.

In this work, we deal with the *feature extraction triple trade-off problem* in mobile devices by evaluating low-cost feature representations. We concentrate our efforts in three main fronts: (1) binary low-level descriptor selection; (2) mid-level representations; and (3) feasibility analysis of data compression techniques. Binary descriptors are interesting options because they provide effective and compact representation [3]. Mid-level representations based on Bag of Visual Words (BoVW, or just BoW) are also good alternative since they provide suitable

© Springer International Publishing Switzerland 2015
A. Pardo and J. Kittler (Eds.): CIARP 2015, LNCS 9423, pp. 424–431, 2015.
DOI: 10.1007/978-3-319-25751-8_51

representation for the amount of local features extracted. Finally, we analyze the use of well-known compression algorithms to reduce as most as possible the size of the final feature representation. To study low-cost representations for image feature extraction on mobile devices, we have adopted a content-based image retrieval (CBIR) application protocol.

Content-Based Image Retrieval (CBIR) applications on mobile devices have been typically modeled using a client-server architecture [2]. Girod et al. [2] present a low latency interactive visual search system. They use interest point detection, compressed histogram of gradients (CHoG) descriptor and a mid-level representation. However, due to the complexity of spatial sub-block assignment scheme, the extraction of the CHOG is not fast enough. In addition, the quality of features is also influenced by the detection of interest points, which does not receive much attention by the CHOG. In [3], lossless compression of binary image features is proposed to be used in a mobile CBIR enviroment. The coding solution exploits the redundancy between descriptors of an image by sorting the descriptors and applying differential pulse coded modulation (DPCM) and arithmetic coding. They do not use mid-level representation, just apply lossless compression on binary features before sending them to a server side. Each binary descriptor is computed from a patch around a detected keypoint. They propose a lossless predictive coding scheme for binary features.

Our work differs from the literature in several aspects. First, to the best of our knowledge, there is no works in the literature that evaluate (or use) low-cost mid-level representation based on dense sampling in mobile applications and it has been shown that dense sampling is more accurate than interest point detection to compute bag-of-visual-word features [4]. Second, there is no work that evaluates the state-of-the-art binary descriptor called BinBoost [6] for image feature extraction on mobile devices. Finally, we evaluate many compression techniques and different assignment/pooling strategies to obtain compact representations.

2   Evaluation Methodology

We aim at evaluating binary low-level descriptors in different mid-level representations to find the most suitable setups in terms of effectiveness, efficiency, and compactness. As mentioned earlier, we have adopted a CBIR process which is composed by offline and online phases.

In the *Offline phase*, after extracting local feature vectors from the image dataset, the feature space is quantized and each region corresponds to a visual word. We use the codebook to create bag-of-word representations for all images in the database. Whereas, in the *Online phase*, given a query image, its local feature vectors are computed and then assigned to the visual words in the dictionary. Finally, the local assignment vectors are summarized by a pooling strategy, which creates the bag-of-visual-words representation. A compression step may be processed to reduce the feature vector size.

In the similarity search, a distance function (Euclidean) is used as similarity measure to rank the database images.

2.1 Low-Level Feature Extraction

Five well-known binary descriptors are used to encode low-level local properties: (1) BRIEF [7]; (2) ORB [8]; (3) BRISK [9]; (4) FREAK descriptor [10]; and (5) BinBoost descriptor [6]. We used a dense sampling (6 pixels, as in [5]) strategy to select points for low-level feature extraction.

2.2 Mid-Level Representation

We evaluated two codeword assignment strategies with two different pooling approaches (average and maximum). To summarize, we use *Hard assignment* where the local feature descriptors of the image are matched with visual words of the vocabulary (the nearest one). A histogram of the visual descriptors is populated by the corresponding bins. We also use *Soft assignment*. In this case, instead of assigning a descriptor to a single corresponding visual word, we assign it to k bins in a soft manner. More specifically, for every descriptor, we add a quantity q to the bins of the k top nearest visual words. This quantity q is the Gaussian kernel (Radial Basis Function) distance of the descriptor and the visual word.

2.3 Data Compression

Data compression is classified into two categories: lossless and lossy.

In this paper, we have used two approaches of lossless compression: Huffman Encoding and Error Enconding + Huffman. The first one, *(Huffman encoding)* is based on frequency of occurrence for each possible value of common symbols which are generally represented using fewer bits than less common symbols. We use the variation of Huffman called byte-oriented Huffman Code [11] where a sequence of bytes is assigned to bin values of a BoW representation. In the second approach, we use *Error Enconding* witch is the difference between bin values. The first bin is the maximum error and have their own value. In this paper, we applied this technique to try get repeated differences of bin values and get a better compression using Huffman encoding.

Two approaches of lossy compression were tested in the Bag of Words using Soft-Assignment with Maximum Pooling approach (BoW Soft-MAX). In *Soft-MAX Truncated*, instead of sending float values, all numbers expressed in floating-point were truncated and transformed in integer values. As a result, we use the approach *Soft-MAX using Ranges*. In this lossy compression, we created fixed features vectors with values in ranges of 5 or 10 or 15 or 20 or 25 or 30. We choose values after looking for the minimum and maximum in all values of the features of Soft-MAX. The idea is activate a bin if the value of the Soft-MAX Truncated is next to the central point in the range.

3 Experimental Setup

The experiments were conducted in two public available image datasets: Caltech-101 [12] and The PASCAL VOC 2007 [13]. Caltech-101 dataset contains

9,144 images. The complete dataset size is 138.6 MB. The PASCAL VOC 2007 dataset consists of 9,963 images. It has multiple objects per image. The complete PASCAL VOC 2007 size is 875.5 MB.

We used the $P@10$ metric (a well known and widely used metric of information retrieval) to evaluate *effectiveness*. This measure is called precision at N or $P@N$. The *efficiency* was evaluated by computing the feature extraction and representation time, in seconds. Finally, we have used the representation size (in bytes) and the Compression Ratio (CR) as measures for evaluating the *compactness*. In this aspect, our baseline is the size of all images in the datasets. Thus, we always divide images size per image representation size. If CR is high, the compression ratio is better because the resulting image representation is smaller.

4 Results and Discussion

In this section, we present the experimental results and the discussion. Our analysis is organized in three main parts. Section 4.1 presents the effectiveness evaluation, Section 4.2 presents the efficiency evaluation of each representation approach and Section 4.3 evaluates different compression techniques.

4.1 Effectiveness Evaluation

Table 1 (a) and (b) show the $P@10$ for each binary descriptor with four different BoW-based mid-level representations. Regarding the Caltech 101 dataset, the Soft-Assignment with Max Pooling (Soft-MAX) achieved the best results for all tested descriptors. For the VOC Pascal 2007 dataset, Soft-MAX achieved high $P@10$ values for BinBoost, BRIEF and ORB descriptors. Soft-AVG and Hard-AVG mid-level representation also yield very high results for some descriptors.

Although, in the Caltech 101 dataset, FREAK descriptor with Hard-MAX has similar $P@10$ as in FREAK with Soft-AVG or Soft-MAX, all mid-level representations with FREAK descriptor yields low precision ($P@10$) comparing with the other binary descriptors.

Table 1. $P@10$ for each descriptor with different mid-level representations (H = Hard, S = Soft, BB = BinBoost, BF = BRIEF, BK = BRISK, FK = FREAK, OB = ORB). $P@10$ reported with a confidence of 95%.

	(a) Caltech 101				(b) Pascal VOC 2007			
	S-AVG	**S-MAX**	**H-MAX**	**H-AVG**	**S-AVG**	**S-MAX**	**H-MAX**	**H-AVG**
BB	15.8 ± 0.3	$\mathbf{24.4 \pm 0.4}$	17.6 ± 0.3	$\mathbf{23.0 \pm 0.4}$	40.2 ± 0.2	$\mathbf{44.9 \pm 0.2}$	42.4 ± 0.2	43.6 ± 0.2
BF	16.0 ± 0.3	$\mathbf{26.3 \pm 0.4}$	18.2 ± 0.3	18.6 ± 0.3	39.8 ± 0.2	$\mathbf{44.6 \pm 0.2}$	39.6 ± 0.2	$\mathbf{44.6 \pm 0.2}$
BK	19.7 ± 0.3	$\mathbf{26.7 \pm 0.4}$	18.1 ± 0.3	20.0 ± 0.3	$\mathbf{43.3 \pm 0.2}$	42.0 ± 0.2	39.0 ± 0.2	42.2 ± 0.2
FK	$\mathbf{18.5 \pm 0.3}$	$\mathbf{18.5 \pm 0.3}$	$\mathbf{18.5 \pm 0.3}$	17.2 ± 0.3	41.1 ± 0.2	37.7 ± 0.2	37.9 ± 0.2	$\mathbf{41.1 \pm 0.2}$
OB	14.1 ± 0.2	$\mathbf{26.2 \pm 0.4}$	17.1 ± 0.3	17.7 ± 0.3	39.7 ± 0.9	$\mathbf{45.7 \pm 0.2}$	38.8 ± 0.2	42.3 ± 0.2

4.2   Efficiency Evaluation

Figure 1(a) presents the computational time required for each descriptor to extract features for all images in Caltech 101 and Pascal VOC 2007 combined. According to the results, while BinBoost and BRISK are the most expensive descriptors, BRIEF, FREAK and ORB can be considered good choices since they are very fast. For this experiment, we extracted each descriptor five times per image and the results are reported with a confidence of 95% ($\alpha=0.05$).

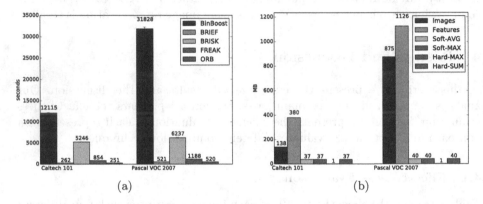

(a)   (b)

Fig. 1. (a) Time (in seconds) spent for feature extraction of all images of Caltech 101 and VOC 2007 using different descriptors. (b) Size (MB) of the Images, Features and ORB' Mid-Level Representations in the datasets Caltech 101 and Pascal VOC 2007.

To evaluate each descriptor in both effectiveness and efficiency aspects, we present the scatter plot in Figure 2, which shows the relation between P@10 and time in seconds (in log scale) for the best descriptors in the Caltech 101 (Figure 2(a)) and VOC 2007 (Figure 2(b)) datasets. In this scenario, the most suitable representations are "BRIEF + Soft-MAX" and "ORB + Soft-MAX" for Caltech 101 and "ORB + Soft-MAX", "BRIEF + Soft-MAX", and "BRIEF + Hard-AVG" for VOC 2007.

4.3   Compactness Evaluation

In this section, we evaluate the feature representation compactness aiming at finding the most suitable descriptors concerning their feature vector size. As it can be seen in Figure 1(b), it is better to transfer mid-level representation to be processed in the server side instead of images or low-level features because mid-level representation are more compact.

Lossless Compression: Figures 3(a) and 3(b) present the relation between P@10 and Compression Ratio (CR) for the most suitable feature representations in the Caltech 101 and Pascal VOC 2007 datasets, respectively.

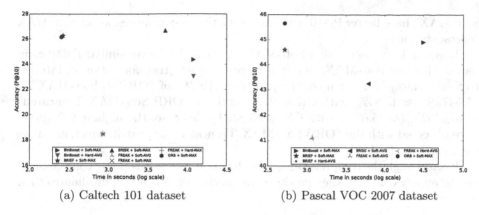

(a) Caltech 101 dataset   (b) Pascal VOC 2007 dataset

Fig. 2. Relation of Accuracy (P@10) versus Time in seconds (log scale) for the most accurate descriptors (See Table 1).

According to the results "BRIEF + Soft-MAX" and "ORB + Soft-MAX" can be considered the most suitable approaches for the Caltech 101 dataset. For the Pascal VOC 2007 dataset, the best ones are "ORB + Soft-MAX", "BRIEF + Soft-MAX", "BRIEF + Hard-AVG" and "BRIEF + Hard-AVG + Huffman". BinBoost and BRISK are time consuming and have been discarded.

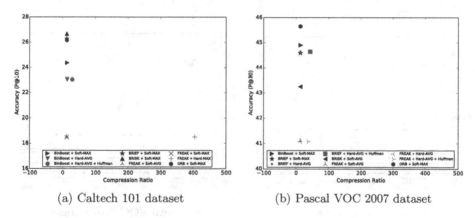

(a) Caltech 101 dataset   (b) Pascal VOC 2007 dataset

Fig. 3. Relation between P@10 and Compression Ratio (CR) for the most suitable feature representations in Table 1 and/or using lossless compression.

Lossy Compression: Figure 4(a) and 4(b) present the relation between P@10 and Compression Ratio (CR) for the Lossy compression of Soft-MAX representation in the Caltech 101 and Pascal VOC 2007 datasets, respectively.

In the Caltech 101 dataset, we have included the best Soft-MAX representation to compare its performance with the compact ones. In the Pascal VOC 2007 dataset, we also have included the "BRIEF + Hard-AVG" and "BRIEF + Hard-AVG + Huffman". In both datasets, "ORB + Soft-MAX" and "BRIEF +

Soft-MAX" have better P@10 compared with the lossy compression of Soft-MAX representations.

It is worth to observe that Soft-MAX Truncated achieves similar P@10 compared with raw Soft-MAX, but it is more compact (transformation of interger to float values). For example, the precision (P@10) of "ORB + Soft-MAX" is 45,6471% ($\approx$ 45.65%) with CR = 21.41 and the "ORB Soft-MAX Truncated" is 45.6492% ($\approx$ 45.65%) with CR = 85.83. In this case, the highest CR values were observed with the "ORB Soft-MAX Truncated" approach, which are more compact (See Table 2).

Even though the compression approaches that use ranges (lossy compression) are extremely compact, they produce low precision rates, which invalidates their use.

Table 2. Compression Ratio (CR) of "BRIEF + Soft-MAX", "BRIEF + Soft-MAX Truncated", "ORB + Soft-MAX" and "ORB + Soft-MAX Truncated" in the datasets Caltech 101 and Pascal VOC 2007.

	Caltech 101	Pascal VOC 2007
BRIEF + Soft-MAX	3.69	21.3
BRIEF + Soft-MAX Truncated	14.9	85
ORB + Soft-MAX	3.75	21.41
ORB + Soft-MAX Truncated	15.07	85.83

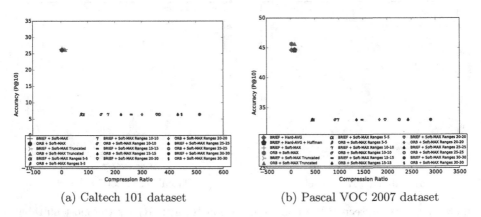

(a) Caltech 101 dataset   (b) Pascal VOC 2007 dataset

Fig. 4. Relation between P@10 and Compression Ratio (CR) for the lossy compression of Soft-MAX representation. The best representations in Figure 3 have been included only for comparison.

5   Conclusions and Future Work

In this paper, we conducted extensive evaluation of low-cost mid-level representation approaches by exploiting binary local descriptors in the context of feature extraction on mobile devices. The experimental results pointed out that the most suitable representations in terms of effectiveness, efficiency, and compactness are ORB and BRIEF descriptors with Soft assignment and MAX pooling. In addition, even though the BinBoost is an accurate descriptor, it produces a larger feature vector and together with BRISK descriptor spends much more time to extract features. Another good alternative to have an acceptable accuracy rate gaining a better compression ratio is to use the descriptors ORB or BRIEF with Soft-MAX Truncated instead of Soft-MAX. As future work, we intend to investigate the use of algorithms for detection of interest points. We also plan to use more datasets and more mid-level representations and test the impact of using different distance metrics on the final CBIR ranking.

Acknowledgments. This work was partially financed by Brazilian National Research Council – CNPq (Grant 477457/2013-4 and 449638/2014-6), Minas Gerais Research Foundation – FAPEMIG (Grants APQ-01806-13, APQ-00567-14 and APQ-00768-14), and Coordination for the Improvement of Higher Education Personnel – CAPES.

References

1. Cisco. Cisco visual networking index: Global mobile data traffic forecast update, 20142019, Tech. Rep., (2015)
2. Girod, B., Chandrasekhar, V., Chen, D.M., Cheung, N.-M., Grzeszczuk, R., Reznik, Y., Takacs, G., Tsai, S.S., Vedantham, R.: Mobile visual search. Signal Processing Magazine **28**(4), 61–76 (2011)
3. Ascenso, J., Pereira, F.: Lossless compression of binary image descriptors for visual sensor networks. In: DSP, pp. 1–8 (2013)
4. Chatfield, K., Lempitsky, V., Vedaldi, A., Zisserman, A.: The devil is in the details: an evaluation of recent feature encoding methods (2011)
5. Penatti, O., Silva, F.B., Valle, E., Gouet-Brunet, V., Torres, RdS: Visual word spatial arrangement for image retrieval and classification. Pattern Recognition **47**(2), 705–720 (2014)
6. Trzcinski, T., Christoudias, M., Fua, P., Lepetit, V.: Boosting binary keypoint descriptors. In: CVPR, pp. 2874–2881 (2013)
7. Calonder, M., Lepetit, V., Strecha, C., Fua, P.: BRIEF: binary robust independent elementary features. In: Daniilidis, K., Maragos, P., Paragios, N. (eds.) Computer Vision – ECCV 2010. LNCS, vol. 6314, pp. 778–792. Springer, Heidelberg (2010)
8. Rublee, E., Rabaud, V., Konolige, K., Bradski, G.: Orb: an efficient alternative to sift or surf. In: ICCV, pp. 2564–2571 (2011)
9. Leutenegger, S., Chli, M., Siegwart, R.Y.: Brisk: binary robust invariant scalable keypoints. In: ICCV, pp. 2548–2555 (2011)
10. Alahi, A., Ortiz, R., Vandergheynst, P.: Freak: fast retina keypoint. In: CVPR, pp. 510–517 (2012)
11. Silva de Moura, E., Navarro, G., Ziviani, N., Baeza-Yates, R.: Fast and flexible word searching on compressed text. ACM Transactions on Information Systems **18**(2), 113–139 (2000)
12. Fei-Fei, L., Fergus, R., Perona, P.: Learning generative visual models from few training examples: An incremental bayesian approach tested on 101 object categories. Computer Vision and Image Understanding **106**(1), 59–70 (2007)
13. Everingham, M., Van Gool, L., Williams, C.K.I., Winn, J., Zisserman, A.: The PASCAL Visual Object Classes Challenge 2007 (VOC 2007) Results. https://web.archive.org/web/20140815083700/http://pascallin.ecs.soton.ac.uk/challenges/VOC/voc2007/index.html

Segmentation, Analysis of Shape and Textur

Multiscale Exemplar Based Texture Synthesis by Locally Gaussian Models

Lara Raad$^{(\boxtimes)}$, Agnès Desolneux, and Jean-Michel Morel

CMLA, Ecole Normale Supérieure de Cachan, Cachan, France
lara.raad@cmla.ens-cahchan.fr

Abstract. In exemplar based texture synthesis methods one of the major difficulties is to synthesize correctly the wide diversity of texture images. So far the proposed methods tend to have satisfying results for specific texture classes and fail for others. Statistics-based algorithms present good results when synthesizing textures that have few geometric structures and are able to preserve a complex statistical model of the sample texture. On the other hand, non-parametric patch-based methods have the ability to reproduce faithfully highly structured textures but lack a mechanism to preserve its global statistics. Furthermore, they are strongly dependent on a patch size that is decided manually. In this paper we propose a multiscale approach able to combine advantages of both strategies and avoid some of their drawbacks. The texture is modeled at each scale as a spatially variable Gaussian vector in the patch space, which allows to fix a patch size fairly independent of the texture.

Keywords: Texture synthesis · Locally gaussian · Multiscale · Patch size

1 Introduction

Exemplar based texture synthesis is a well known problem that has many applications in computer graphics, computer vision and image processing, for example for fast scene generation, inpainting, and texture restoration. It is defined as the process of generating from an input texture sample a perceptually equivalent larger one. Texture synthesis algorithms are generally divided into two categories, the statistics-based [5,7,13] and the non-parametric patch-based [1–3,10–12,17]. The first category models a given texture sample by estimating statistical parameters that characterize the underlying stochastic process. Although these methods can faithfully reproduce some of the global statistics of the sample and synthesize micro and pseudo-periodic textures, they generally do not yield high quality visual results for more structured ones, in particular when the sample is small and contains large objects. The second category rearranges local neighbourhoods of the input sample in a consistent way. These methods provide efficient algorithms able to reproduce highly structured textures. Even though they yield visual satisfactory results, they often turn into practising verbatim copies of large parts of the input sample.

© Springer International Publishing Switzerland 2015
A. Pardo and J. Kittler (Eds.): CIARP 2015, LNCS 9423, pp. 435–443, 2015.
DOI: 10.1007/978-3-319-25751-8_52

Statistics-based methods are generally done in two steps: analysis and synthesis. The analysis step consists in identifying a set of global statistics from the input texture and the synthesis process generates an image satisfying the estimated set of statistics. These methods were inspired from Julesz [9], who discovered that many texture pairs having the same second-order statistics would not be preattentively discerned by humans. The success of Julesz first model can be checked in [5] where the authors propose to synthesize textures by randomizing the Fourier phase of the sample image while maintaining its Fourier modulus, thus preserving the second order statistics of the sample. These statistics are enough to synthesize micro-textures that can be characterized by their Fourier modulus but they fail for more structured ones as can be seen in [6]. Heeger and Bergen [7] initiated more sophisticated statistics-based methods describing the input sample by the histograms of its wavelet coefficients. A new texture is then created by enforcing these statistics on a white noise image. The results are satisfying for a small class of textures. Indeed the proposed statistics miss important correlations between scales and orientations, as can be verified in [8]. In [13] Portilla and Simoncelli extended [7] by estimating autocorrelations, cross-correlations and statistical moments of the wavelet coefficients of the texture sample. Compared to the previous statistical attempts, convincing results are observable on a very wide range of textures. Although this method represents the state of the art for psychophysically and statistically founded algorithms, the results nevertheless often present blur and phantoms effects.

Non-parametric patch-based methods were initialized by Efros and Leung [3] who extended to images Shannon's Markov random field model initially devised to simulate text. The synthesized texture is constructed pixelwise. For each new pixel, a patch centered at the pixel is compared to all patches with the same size in the input sample. The nearest matches help predict the pixel value in the reconstructed image. Several works [1,17] have extended and accelerated this method. Still these pixelwise algorithms are not always satisfactory. They are known to grow "garbage" when the compared patches are too small, or may lead to verbatim copies of significant parts of the input sample for large patches as can be verified in [4]. To overcome these drawbacks more recent methods stitch together entire patches instead of performing a synthesis pixel by pixel. The question then is how to blend a new patch in the existing texture. In [12] this is done by a smooth transition. Efros and Freeman [2] refined this process by stitching each new patch along a minimum cost path across its overlapping zone with the texture under construction. Kwatra et al. in [11] extended the stitching procedure of [2] by a graph cut approach redefining the edges of the patches. In [10] the authors propose to synthesize a texture image by sequentially improving the quality of the synthesis by minimizing a patch-based energy function. These non-parametric patch-based approaches often present satisfactory visual results. However, the risk remains of copying verbatim large parts of the input sample. Furthermore, a fidelity to the global statistics of the initial sample is not guaranteed, in particular when the texture sample is not stationary. See [18] for an extensive overview of the different neighbourhood-based methods.

More recently methods such as [15,16] combine patch-based and statistics-based methods to overcome the previous drawbacks. In [15] the author proposes to use a patch-based approach where all the patches of the synthesized image are created from a sparse dictionary learnt on the input sample. In [16] Tartavel et al. extend the work in [15] by minimizing an energy that involves a sparse dictionary of patches combined with constraints on the sample's Fourier spectrum. With the same motivation of avoiding verbatim-copies of the input sample and providing a statistical model of it, in [14] the authors proposed an algorithm that involves a local multivariate Gaussian texture model in the patch space.

Macro-textures show information at different scales that cannot be captured with a unique patch size. This motivates the extension of patch-based methods to a multiscale framework in the spirit of [1,16]. In this way the method is more robust to the patch size and avoids the blending step of patch-based approaches.

The rest of this paper is structured as follows. In Section 2 the multiscale approach is presented. In Section 3 two experiments are shown. The first one presents multiscale results and explores the impact of the scale interval on their efficiency. The second experiment shows how to combine two different synthesis methods: the multiscale locally Gaussian and the Portilla-Simoncelli statistical method [13]. Conclusions are presented in Section 4.

2   A Multiscale Algorithm

Macro textures have the particularity to present details at different scales: a coarse one containing the global structure and finer ones containing the details. On the one hand small patch sizes may capture the finer details of the input, yet if an algorithm is based only on them, the resulting texture will lack global coherence. On the other hand big patch sizes tend to a better respect of the global configuration but risk of a "copy-paste" effect. Furthermore, it becomes impossible to model the variability of large patches by curse of dimensionality: a texture sample will generally not contain enough patch samples. This is for example apparent in [14]. Multiscale approaches instead permit to contemplate several patch sizes within one synthesis (capture the different level of details).

In this section the potential of a multiscale approach is illustrated by improving the method in [14]. This approach can be summarized in a few sentences. The method begins by a synthesis in the coarsest scale ($k = K - 1$) using [14] where the quilting step is replaced by a simple average of the overlapping patches. For the remaining scales ($k = K - 2, \ldots, 0$) a synthesis is performed by using the result of the previous scale ($k + 1$) and the input of corresponding resolution. At each scale the synthesis is done patch by patch in a raster-scan order. Each new patch, added to the synthesized image, overlaps part of the previously synthesized patch and is the combination of a low resolution patch and a high resolution one sampled from a multivariate Gaussian distribution. The Gaussian distribution of the high frequencies of a given patch is estimated from the high frequencies of its m nearest neighbours in the corresponding scale input image. The synthesis result of the finer scale is the desired output image.

Notations

- $u_0 : \Omega \to \mathbb{R}$: input texture image. $\Omega = I_M \times I_N$ of size $M \times N$ where I_c is the discrete interval $[0, \ldots, c-1]$
- $w_0 : \Omega_r \to \mathbb{R}$: output texture image. $\Omega_r = I_{rM} \times I_{rN}$ of size $rM \times rN$
- r: ratio (size of output image w_0)/(size of input image u_0)
- $n \times n$: patch size
- m: number of nearest neighbours used to learn the Gaussian distribution
- K: number of scales (maximum factor of zoom out is $K-1$)
- $u_k : \Omega^k \to \mathbb{R}$: zoom out of u_0 by a factor 2^k. $\Omega^k = I_{2^{-k}M} \times I_{2^{-k}N}$ of size $2^{-k}M \times 2^{-k}N$ for $k = 1 \ldots K-1$
- $w_k : \Omega_r^k \to \mathbb{R}$: synthesized texture at scale k. $\Omega_r^k = I_{r2^{-k}M} \times I_{r2^{-k}N}$ of size $r2^{-k}M \times r2^{-k}N$ for $k = 0 \ldots K-1$
- $v_k : \Omega_r^k \to \mathbb{R}$: zoom in of w_{k+1} by a factor 2 for $k = 0 \ldots K-2$
- G_σ: Gaussian kernel centered of standard deviation σ
- $L_{u_k} : \Omega^k \to \mathbb{R}$: low resolution of u_k. $L_{u_k} = u_k * G_\sigma$, $k = 0 \ldots K-2$
- $L_{w_k} : \Omega_r^k \to \mathbb{R}$: low resolution of w_k. $L_{w_k} = w_k * G_\sigma$, $k = 0 \ldots K-2$
- $H_{w_k} : \Omega_r^k \to \mathbb{R}$: high resolution of w_k. $H_{w_k} = w_k - w_k * G_\sigma$, $k = 0 \ldots K-2$
- $p_u^{(x,y)}$: square patch of size $n \times n$ from an image u of size $M \times N$ at position (x, y). $p_u^{(x,y)} = \{u((x,y)+(i,j)), (i,j) \in [0, \ldots, n-1]^2\}$, $(x,y) \in \mathcal{V}_u = I_{M-n+1} \times I_{N-n+1}$
- $\mathcal{Z}_2^{out}(u)$: zoom out by a factor 2 of image u performed as a smooth frequency cutoff followed by a sub-sample of factor 2
- $\mathcal{Z}_2^{in}(u)$: zoom in by a factor 2 of image u performed by a zero padding of the discrete Fourier transform of u

Distance Between Patches

To estimate the parameters of the Gaussian distribution of the patch being processed, denoted by $p_{w_k}^{(x',y')}$, the set $\mathcal{U}$ of m nearest patches in u_k to $p_{w_k}^{(x',y')}$ is considered. These patches are those minimizing the distance to $p_{w_k}^{(x',y')}$ defined in (1) for $k = K-1$ and in (2) for the remaining scales $k = K-2, \ldots, 0$.

The size of patch overlap is fixed to half the patch size $n/2$. Depending on the stage of the synthesis three different cases of overlap can be observed: vertical (first row of raster-scan)(VO), horizontal (first column of raster-scan)(HO) and L-shape (everywhere else)(LO). The overlap area of a patch $p_u^{(x,y)}$ is denoted as $Op_u^{(x,y)} = \{u((x,y)+(i,j)), (i,j) \in \mathcal{O}\}$ where

$$\mathcal{O} = \begin{cases} [0, \ldots, n-1] \times [0, \ldots, \frac{n}{2}-1] & \text{if VO} \\ [0, \ldots, \frac{n}{2}-1] \times [0, \ldots, n-1] & \text{if HO} \\ [0, \ldots, \frac{n}{2}-1] \times [0, \ldots, n-1] \cup [\frac{n}{2}, \ldots, n-1] \times [0, \ldots, \frac{n}{2}-1] & \text{if LO} \end{cases}$$

When $k = K-1$ the m nearest neighbours in u_{K-1} to the patch $p_{w_{K-1}}^{(x',y')}$ are those minimizing the L^2 distance restricted to the overlap area (1).

$$d(p_{u_{K-1}}^{(x,y)}, p_{w_{K-1}}^{(x',y')})^2 = \frac{1}{|\mathcal{O}|} \sum_{(i,j)\in\mathcal{O}} (u_{K-1}(x+i, y+j) - w_{K-1}(x'+i, y'+j))^2$$

(1)

When $k = K - 2, \ldots, 0$ the nearest neighbours in u_k to the patch $p_{w_k}^{(x',y')}$ are those minimizing a distance (2) similar to (1) with an additional term taking into account the low resolution v_k (the synthesis result of the previous scale $k + 1$). Is is important to notice that when comparing $Op_{u_k}^{(x,y)}$ and $Op_{w_k}^{(x',y')}$ the low and the high resolution must be considered jointly, they are not independent.

$$d(p_{u_k}^{(x,y)}, p_{w_k}^{(x',y')})^2 = \frac{1}{|\mathcal{O}|} \sum_{(i,j)\in\mathcal{O}} (u_k(x+i, y+j) - w_k(x'+i, y'+j))^2$$
$$+ \frac{1}{n^2} \sum_{i,j=0}^{n-1} (Lu_k(x+i, y+j) - v_k(x'+i, y'+j))^2$$

(2)

The Gaussian Model and the Blending Process

Every patch $p_{w_k}^{(x',y')}$ in w_k for $k = 0, \ldots, K - 1$ is sampled from a multivariate Gaussian distribution in the spirit of [14]. The parameters (μ, Σ) of the distribution of $p_{w_k}^{(x',y')}$ are estimated on the set $\mathcal{U} = \{p_{u_k}^{(x_1,y_1)}, \ldots, p_{u_k}^{(x_m,y_m)}\}$ as in (3). Here $p_{u_k}^{(x_i,y_i)}$, for $i = 1, \ldots, m$, are the m nearest patches to $p_{w_k}^{(x',y')}$ in u_k for the distances in (1) and (2).

$$\mu = \frac{1}{m} \sum_{i=1}^{m} q_{u_k}^{(x_i,y_i)}, \quad \Sigma = \frac{1}{m} QQ^t$$

(3)

In (3) $q_{u_k}^{(x_i,y_i)}$ is the patch $p_{u_k}^{(x_i,y_i)}$ in vector form and Q is the matrix whose columns are $(q_{u_k}^{(x_i,y_i)} - \mu)$, $i = 1, \ldots, m$. Sampling a patch $\tilde{p} \sim G(\mu, \Sigma)$ comes down to sampling m independent normal variables as can be seen in (4).

$$\tilde{q} = \frac{1}{m} Q^t Q W D q' + \mu$$

(4)

Here $\tilde{q}$ is the vector form of $\tilde{p}$, $q' \sim G(0, I_m)$, W is a matrix whose columns are the eigenvectors of $Q^t Q$ and D is a diagonal matrix with its eigenvalues.

The blending process consists in simply averaging the values across the overlap area as in (5). This step is applied only for the synthesis at scale $k = K - 1$.

$$w_k(x'+i, y'+j') = \begin{cases} \frac{1}{2}\left(\tilde{p}(i,j) + p_{w_{K-1}}^{(x',y')}\right) & \text{if } (i,j) \in \mathcal{O} \\ \tilde{p}(i,j) & \text{if } (i,j) \in I_n^2 - \mathcal{O} \end{cases}$$

(5)

Synthesizing Patches at Scales $k = K - 2, \ldots, 0$

At each scale k a patch $p_{w_k}^{(x',y')}$ is synthesized as the combination of a low resolution patch with a high resolution one. It can be decomposed as follows

$$p_{w_k}^{(x',y')} = p_{w_k*G_\sigma}^{(x',y')} + (p_{w_k}^{(x',y')} - p_{w_k*G_\sigma}^{(x',y')}) = p_{v_k}^{(x',y')} + (p_{w_k}^{(x',y')} - p_{v_k}^{(x',y')})$$
$$= p_{L_{w_k}}^{(x',y')} + p_{H_{w_k}}^{(x',y')}.$$

The set $\mathcal{U}$ define the Gaussian distribution of $p_{L_{w_k}}^{(x',y')} \sim G(\mu_L, \Sigma_L)$ and $p_{H_{w_k}}^{(x',y')} \sim G(\mu_H, \Sigma_H)$ and therefore the distribution of the patch $p_{w_k}^{(x',y')} \sim G(\mu, \Sigma)$ where $\mu = \mu_H + \mu_L$ and $\Sigma = \Sigma_L + \Sigma_H + \mathbb{E}(p_{L_{w_k}}^{(x',y')}(p_{H_{w_k}}^{(x',y')})^t) + \mathbb{E}(p_{H_{w_k}}^{(x',y')}(p_{L_{w_k}}^{(x',y')})^t)$. Instead of sampling $p_{L_{w_k}}^{(x',y')}$ from its Gaussian distribution, $p_{v_k}^{(x',y')} \sim G(\mu_L, \Sigma_L)$ is kept to conserve the low resolution synthesis from the previous scale. The high frequency patch $p_{H_{w_k}}^{(x',y')}$ is sampled form $G(\mu_H, \Sigma_H)$ and then added to $p_{v_k}^{(x',y')}$. In this way the correlations between high and low resolution pixels are respected, using the low resolution synthesis v_k as initialization.

3   Experiments

All the texture examples in Figures 1 and 2 can be found at http://dev.ipol.im/ ~lraad/ciarp_2015/. The experiments shown in Figure 1 compare the multiscale method using one, two and three scales. This is performed for micro- and macro-textures. For all the experiments the side patch size is fixed to $n = 20$ and the number of nearest neighbours to $m = 20$. Figure 1 shows that using a single scale is not enough to reproduce faithfully the global structure of the input example. Naturally to achieve satisfying synthesis results for $K = 1$ a bigger patch size should be considered. Still this would lead to limitations on the Gaussian model [14]. A fix patch size was sufficient to achieve satisfying results on all examples shown. Another positive aspect of using smaller patches is that one can find more reliable examples in the input sample to build the multivariate Gaussian distributions. Finally complex quilting steps like those used in [2,10,11] is no longer necessary. It can be replaced by an average of the values along the overlap zone for the synthesis of the coarsest scale. This is possible since at $k = K-1$ the images are smoother and an average is then well suited. In general it is enough to average the overlapping parts only at the coarser scales.

In Figure 1 the experiments show that for the three different cases ($K = 1, 2, 3$) the Gaussian synthesis entails a slight blur. To recover these fine details at scale $k = 0$ an additional step can be applied to the multiscale synthesis result. The output image w_0 is combined to Portilla and Simoncelli's method [13]. In [13] the synthesis image is initialized with a white noise. For this experiment Portilla and Simoncelli's method is initialized with the result of the multiscale method instead of a random noise. In Figure 2 the result of the multiscale approach is compared to the results of combining the algorithms and to those of [13]. They show that the granularity of the input texture is globally recovered. The resulting texture respects the global statistics of the input imposed by [13] while maintaining the structures that are lost if the method is initialized with a white noise. Some of the example images in Figures 1 and 2 were provided from [13].

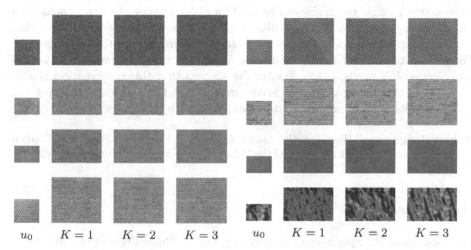

u_0 $K = 1$ $K = 2$ $K = 3$ u_0 $K = 1$ $K = 2$ $K = 3$

Fig. 1. Synthesis results for $K = 1, 2, 3$ scales. The parameters were fixed to $n = 20$ and $m = 20$. *It is recommended to zoom in the images by a factor 400% to evaluate texture details.*

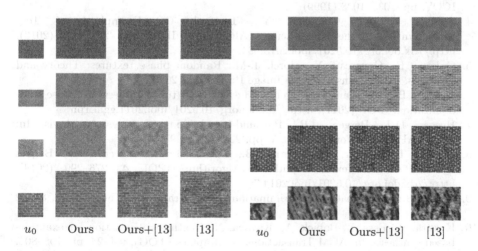

u_0 Ours   Ours+[13]   [13] u_0 Ours   Ours+[13]   [13]

Fig. 2. Comparison of several texture synthesis algorithms: ours, ours combined to [13] and [13]. The parameters were fixed to $n = 20$, $m = 20$ and $K = 3$. *It is recommended to zoom in the images by a factor 400% to evaluate texture details.*

4   Conclusion

In this paper a multiscale approach of the locally Gaussian texture synthesis algorithm [14] was proposed. A first synthesis is performed at the coarsest scale to generate the global structure of the synthesized image. For the remaining scales the corresponding finer details are added on the low resolution result of the previous scale and so on until the finer scale is reached. The experiments showed that a single patch size can be used for different type of textures achieving satisfying visual results. A second observation is that due to the use of Gaussian models the synthesis results lose some resolution compared to the input sample. To recover its granularity the multiscale algorithm was combined with Portilla and Simoncelli's method [13]. The results showed that this combination is able to preserve the strong geometric structures and at the same time respect the global statistics of the sample that are imposed with [13].

Acknowledgments. Work partly founded by the European Research Council (advanced grant Twelve Labours) and the Office of Naval research (ONR grant N00014-14-1-0023).

References

1. Ashikhmin, M.: Synthesizing natural textures. In: Proceedings of the 2001 Symposium on Interactive 3D graphics, pp. 217–226. ACM (2001)
2. Efros, A.A., Freeman, W.T.: Image quilting for texture synthesis and transfer. In: SIGGRAPH, pp. 341–346 (2001)
3. Efros, A.A., Leung, T.K.: Texture synthesis by non-parametric sampling. In: IEEE ICCV, pp. 1033–1038 (1999)
4. Aguerrebere, C., Gousseau, Y., Tartavel, G.: Exemplar-based Texture Synthesis: the Efros-Leung Algorithm. IPOL **3**, 223–241 (2013). http://dx.doi.org/10.5201/ipol.2013.59
5. Galerne, B., Gousseau, Y., Morel, J.-M.: Random phase textures: Theory and synthesis. IEEE Transactions in Image Processing (2010)
6. Galerne, B., Gousseau, Y., Morel, J.-M.: Micro-Texture Synthesis by Phase Randomization. IPOL (2011). http://dx.doi.org/10.5201/ipol.2011.ggm_rpn
7. Heeger, D.J., Bergen, J.R.: Pyramid-based texture analysis/synthesis. In: SIGGRAPH, New York, NY, USA, pp. 229–238 (1995)
8. Briand, T., Vacher, J., Galerne, B., Rabin, J.: The Heeger and Bergen Pyramid Based Texture Synthesis Algorithm. IPOL **4**, 276–299 (2014). http://dx.doi.org/10.5201/ipol.2014.79
9. Julesz, B.: Visual pattern discrimination. IEEE Trans. Inf. Theory **8**(2), 84–92 (1962)
10. Kwatra, V., Essa, I., Bobick, A., Kwatra, N.: Texture optimization for example-based synthesis. In: ACM Transactions on Graphics (TOG), vol. 24, pp. 795–802. ACM (2005)
11. Kwatra, V., Schödl, A., Essa, I., Turk, G., Bobick, A.: Graphcut textures: image and video synthesis using graph cuts. In: ACM Transactions on Graphics (TOG), vol. 22, pp. 277–286. ACM (2003)

12. Liang, L., Liu, C., Xu, Y.-Q., Guo, B., Shum, H.-Y.: Real-time texture synthesis by patch-based sampling. ACM Transactions on Graphics **20**(3), 127–150 (2001)
13. Portilla, J., Simoncelli, E.P.: A parametric texture model based on joint statistics of complex wavelet coefficients. IJCV **40**(1), 49–70 (2000)
14. Raad, L., Desolneux, A., Morel, J.M.: Locally gaussian exemplar based texture synthesis. In: 2014 IEEE International Conference on Image Processing (ICIP), pp. 4667–4671. IEEE, October 2014
15. Peyré, G.: Sparse modeling of textures. Journal of Mathematical Imaging and Vision **34**(1), 17–31 (2009)
16. Tartavel, G., Gousseau, Y., Peyré, G.: Variational texture synthesis with sparsity and spectrum constraints. Journal of Mathematical Imaging and Vision (2014)
17. Wei, L.-Y., Levoy, M.: Fast texture synthesis using tree-structured vector quantization. In: SIGGRAPH, pp. 479–488 (2000)
18. Wei, L.Y., Lefebvre, S., Kwatra, V., Turk, G.: State of the art in example-based texture synthesis. In: Eurographics 2009, State of the Art Report, EG-STAR, pp. 93–117. Eurographics Association (2009)

Top-Down Online Handwritten Mathematical Expression Parsing with Graph Grammar

Frank Julca-Aguilar[1]([⊠]), Harold Mouchère[1], Christian Viard-Gaudin[1], and Nina S.T. Hirata[2]

[1] University of Nantes, Nantes, France
faguilar@ime.usp.br
[2] University of São Paulo, São Paulo, Brazil

Abstract. In recognition of online handwritten mathematical expressions, symbol segmentation and classification and recognition of relations among symbols is managed through a parsing technique. Most parsing techniques follow a bottom-up approach and adapt grammars typically used to parse strings. However, in contrast to top-down approaches, pure bottom-up approaches do not exploit grammar information to avoid parsing of invalid subexpressions. Moreover, modeling math expressions by string grammars makes difficult to extend it to include new structures. We propose a new parsing technique that models mathematical expressions as languages generated by graph grammars, and parses expressions following a top-down approach. The method is general in the sense that it can be easily extended to parse other multidimensional languages, as chemical expressions, or diagrams. We evaluate the method using the (publicly available) CROHME-2013 dataset.

Keywords: Mathematical expression recognition · Graph grammar · Top-down parsing · Bottom-up parsing

1 Introduction

An online handwritten mathematical expression consists of a sequence of strokes, usually collected using a touch screen device. For example, in Figure 1, the expression is composed of five strokes, that is $(str_1, \ldots, str_5)$, where str_i is the ith stroke, considering the input order. Recognition of online handwritten mathematical expressions involves three processes: (1) symbol segmentation, (2) symbol classification and (3) structural analysis. The first process groups strokes that form a same symbol; the second identifies which mathematical symbol represents each group of strokes and the third identifies relations between symbols – as the *superscript* relation between symbols "a" and "b" in the expression "$a^b c$".

The recognition process is usually handled by a parsing technique [1,2,8,10]. In these techniques, a grammar defines the mathematical language (valid symbols and structures) to be recognized and a parse algorithm determines the structure of the expression, in accordance with the grammar. Reasons to use

© Springer International Publishing Switzerland 2015
A. Pardo and J. Kittler (Eds.): CIARP 2015, LNCS 9423, pp. 444–451, 2015.
DOI: 10.1007/978-3-319-25751-8_53

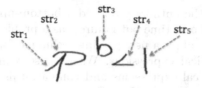

Fig. 1. Online handwritten mathematical expression composed of five strokes: $(str_1, \ldots, str_5)$.

parsing techniques include: (1) they generate an structured result that can be further processed, (2) the grammar represents our understanding or model of the object to be recognized and (3) missing information can be completed using syntactic or contextual information [3]. For example, in an expression "(1+1)", if all symbols but the closing parenthesis are already recognized, a parse algorithm can determine that the missing symbol is actually a closing parenthesis. Contextual information is useful when dealing with handwritten expressions as ambiguous recognition cases can be generated.

Parsing techniques have been successfully applied in recognition of strings, where symbols or words are arranged horizontally (there is only one relation type between symbols). Those approaches generate a parse tree as result; and according to how the parse tree is built, the techniques can be divided into two types: top-down and bottom-up. Top-down techniques determine first high level structures (subexpressions), then low level structures (symbols). The bottom-up approaches perform the inverse process. According to the literature, top-down techniques or bottom-up techniques with a top-down component are needed to build powerful parsers [3]. A main advantage of the top-down components is the fact that it avoids to parse some subexpressions that do not generate valid parsing results [3,5].

Most grammars used to represent mathematical expressions are based on grammars to parse strings [1,5,8,10]. However, as these grammars were originally designed to represent only horizontal relations between symbols, it is difficult to extend the model to represent languages with multiple relation types. About the parse algorithms, most approaches follow a pure bottom up parsing; for instance, different adaptations of the CYK algorithm can be seen in [1,8,10].

Graph grammars [7] can provide a more natural model to represent mathematical expressions: sentences (mathematical expressions) can be represented as labeled graphs, where vertices represent (terminal) symbols and edges represent relations among symbols. As arbitrary relations can be expressed as edges, the model provides a flexible representation, so that it is easy to extend a particular grammar to define new structures. On the other hand, if no strong constraints are imposed, a similar parsing technique can be used to recognize other multidimensional languages, as handwritten chemical expressions and diagrams. However, the general representation of graph grammars can generate a considerable increase on the computational cost of the parse algorithm. As an example, a tentative to use graph grammars for mathematical expressions recognition can be found in [2], where the authors proposed a bottom-up parse algorithm; but even with a small grammar, time out failure was a problem.

In this work, we introduce a new parsing technique for recognition of online handwritten mathematical expressions. We propose a graph grammar model to represent mathematical expressions and compare this approach with grammars used in other approaches (Section 2.1). To cope with the complexity problem, we process input strokes so that symbol and relation hypotheses are pre-calculated and used to limit the subexpressions evaluated by the parse algorithm (Section 2.2). The proposed parse algorithm follows a top-down approach and can be extended to parse other multidimensional languages. To evaluate the proposed method, we used the CROHME-2013 dataset [6] (Section 3).

2   Top-Down Graph Grammar Parsing Method

The proposed method consists of three components: a context-free graph grammar, a *symbol hypotheses relational graph* (SHRG) and a top-down parse algorithm. The graph grammar defines the valid mathematical symbols, subexpressions and relations among them. The SHRG defines the groups of strokes that will be evaluated to determine if they can be interpreted as a symbol or subexpression. Finally, the top-down parse algorithm uses the grammar to determine valid interpretations of all subexpressions and symbols given by the SHRG.

2.1   Context-Free Graph Grammar

A graph grammar is defined by a tuple $M = (N, T, I, R)$, where N is a set of non-terminal symbols (or non-terminals); T is a set of terminal symbols (or terminals), such that $N \cap T = \emptyset$; I is an initial or start graph and R is a set of production or rewriting rules [7]. Figure 2 shows a graph grammar example.

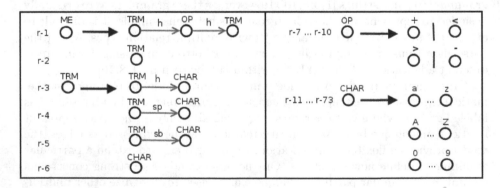

Fig. 2. Graph Grammar example: N={ME, TRM, OP, CHAR}, T = {+,-, <, >, a, ...,z, A, ..., Z, 0, ..., 9}. I corresponds to the left hand side graph of rule r-1 and R = {r-1, ..., r-73}.

We denote a rule as $r = (A, B)$ to indicate a replacement of a graph A by a graph B. In addition, we call A the left hand side (LHS) grammar graph of r $(A = LHS(r))$, and B the right hand side (RHS) graph of r $(B = RHS(r))$. Both, A and B, are digraphs. As it can be seen in Figure 2, vertices and edges of the rule graphs are labeled. For a given rule graph $G = (V, E)$, we define vertex labels by a mapping function α: $V_G \rightarrow N \cup T$, and edge labels by a mapping function β: $E_G \rightarrow SR$, where SR is a set of mathematical relation labels. In Figure 2, SR includes the following labels: "sp" (superscript), "sb" (subscript) and "h" (horizontal).

A context-free graph grammar is a graph grammar such that for each rule (A, B), A is a single vertex graph – as in the case of Figure 2. To clarify the further explanations, we assume that a grammar is defined only with two types of rules: *terminal* and *non-terminal*. In a terminal rule the RHS graph is a single vertex graph , whose vertex is labeled with a terminal symbol – rules from r-7 to r-73 of Figure 2 for instance. A non-terminal rule refers to a rule whose RHS graph contains one or more vertices, labeled only with non-terminal symbols – as r-1 of Figure 2. In addition, we will refer to the non-terminal of the start graph as *start symbol*.

As mentioned above, most approaches for recognition of mathematical expressions extend the grammars used for strings. Figure 3 shows a comparison of a grammar model proposed in [5] and one used in our approach. The grammar proposed in [5] defines production rules of the form: $A \xrightarrow{r} A_1 A_2 \ldots A_k$, where r indicates a relation between adjacent elements in the RHS. As the model defines a unique relation type between consecutive elements, rules that include different relation types must be split into several rules (as shown in Figure 3(a)). Further, when a CYK parse algorithm is used (as in [1, 8, 10]), the grammar needs to be transformed to a Chomsky Normal Form, which requires the grammar to have no more than two elements the RHS. As a result, grammar rules with more than two elements in the RHS must be split, incrementing the total number of rules. These restrictions make difficult to extend string grammars to model multidimensional languages.

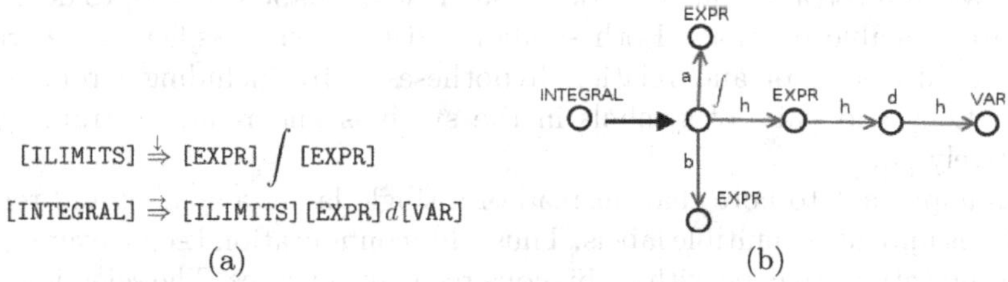

Fig. 3. Integration rule example used in [5] (a) and its corresponding representation using graph grammar (b). "a" and "b" edge labels indicate above and below relations respectively.eps

2.2   Symbol Hypotheses Relational Graph

A symbol hypothesis is a set of strokes that can be interpreted as a terminal symbol. Each symbol hypothesis is assigned a label set defined by a function $\gamma : SH \rightarrow P(L)$, where SH is a set of symbol hypotheses, L is a set of symbol labels, and $P(L)$ is the power set of L.

A Symbol hypothesis relational graph is a digraph (V, E), where V is a set of symbol hypotheses and E is a set of spatial relation hypotheses, defined over pairs of *compatible* symbol hypotheses [1]. As in the case of symbol hypotheses, we define a function $\delta : E \rightarrow P(SR)$, where SR is a set of relation labels (as defined in Section 2.1), and $P(SR)$ is the power set of SR. Figure 4 shows an example of a SHRG.

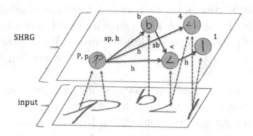

Fig. 4. SHRG example. Edge labels indicate relation types: sp = *superscript*, h = *horizontal*.

To compute symbol hypotheses, we built a 3-nearest neighbor graph from a graph with the bounding box center of the input strokes as vertices and euclidean distances as edge weights. Then, for each stroke, we generate all combinations of the stroke with its neighbors. Each combination defines a symbol hypothesis. For each symbol hypothesis, its corresponding labels are calculated by a neural network classifier that uses shape context and online features, as defined in [4].

To calculate relation hypotheses, we evaluate all pairs of compatible symbol hypotheses and use a neural network classifier, with shape features, to determine the most probable relations. Both symbol and relation classifiers were trained to reject false symbol and relation hypotheses – by including wrong stroke combinations and pairs of symbols in the symbols and relations training sets respectively [4].

It is important to note that, instead of a single label, a symbol and relation hypothesis may have multiple labels. Thus, this configuration keeps several possible interpretations to cope with ambiguous recognition cases. The selection of the most probable labels is based on recognition scores calculated by the classifiers. Given a hypothesis h (symbol or relation) and a set of probable labels $(l_1, \ldots, l_m)$, sorted in descending order by their likelihood score, $score(l_i), for\, i = 1, \ldots, m$,

---

[1] Two symbol hypotheses sh_i, sh_j are compatible if $sh_i \cap sh_j = \emptyset$.

we select k labels, such that: $\sum_{i=1}^{k} score(l_i) > tr$, where tr is a threshold defined experimentally.

2.3 Top-Down Parse Algorithm

The proposed algorithm considers that the input to the algorithm is a set of strokes, denoted as $str = \{str_1, \ldots, str_n\}$ [2]. Given str, a graph grammar M, and a SHRG G, the algorithm calculates recursive partitions of str according to the rules of M, starting from the rules derived by the start symbol of G, until generating partitions derived by terminal rules. For a given rule r, we consider only partitions of str derived by minors of G^3 that are isomorphic to RHS(r).

Figure 5 illustrates the parsing process of the input expression and SHRG of Figure 4 and graph grammar of Figure 2. The process starts by determining partitions of the complete set of strokes (top of the image), according to the rules derived by the non-terminal **ME** (the start symbol of the grammar). Two partition candidates are found, one using rule r-1 and the other using rule r-2. Each partition is actually a minor graph isomorphic to the RHS graph of the rule that generates the partition. A graph that defines a partition is called **instantiated graph**. The strokes of each vertex of each instantiated graph are further partitioned using the rules derived by their corresponding non-terminals. For example, in the instantiated graph derived by rule r-1, the strokes of the subexpression "p^b" are partitioned according to the rules derived by the non-terminal **TRM**.

As it is shown in Figure 5, for a given set of strokes str and a non-terminal NT, several instantiated graphs may be generated. Those results are recorded in a table denoted as T, where $T(str = \{str_1, \ldots, str_n\}, NT) = \{(g_1, r_1), \ldots, (g_q, r_q)\}$, g_i is an instantiated graph and r_i is the rule that "generated" g_i. The use of the parse table T is usually used in strings parsing [3] to calculate parse results only once (memoization).

The partial results recorded in table T define a parse forest– set of different interpretations of the input. A tree of the parse forest represents a particular interpretation of the input and is defined by a sequence of partitions calculated from the start symbol to terminals. For instance, Figure 5 shows a total of 8 interpretations or parse trees and one of those may be composed by the partitions indicated with red arrows. The tree corresponds to the interpretation "P^b4".

Once the parse forest is built, the final step consists on extracting a tree that better represents the input, according to a given measure. To do that, we defined a ranking function $p : t \rightarrow \mathbb{R}$, where t is a parse tree. Currently, we calculate

---

[2] We denote a set as a braced list of elements, that is $set = \{element_1, \ldots, element_n\}$ and a sequence (ordered set) as a bracketed list of elements, that is $sequence = (element_1, \ldots, element_n)$, where $element_i$ is the ith element considering a particular order.

[3] A graph H is a *minor* of a graph G if H can be obtained from a **subgraph** of G by contracting edges [9].

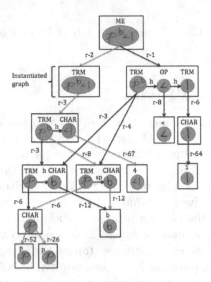

Fig. 5. Recursive partitions calculated by the top-down parse algorithm.eps

p(t) with the geometric mean of the relations and classification scores given by the symbol and relations classifiers to the partitions that compose t.

3   Experimentation

We evaluated the proposed methods using the CROHME 2013 competition dataset [6]. The dataset includes 101 symbol classes and 6 relation types: superscript, subscript, horizontal, above (for example, between a fraction bar and its numerator), below (fraction bar with denominator), and inside (between the radical symbol and its radicand). Using the training part of the dataset, the threshold tr, was fixed in 0.98 for the symbol classifier and 0.95 for the relations classifier.

Table 1 shows our results compared to those of the two best systems (out of five) that used only the CROHME dataset for training (the systems are identified by numbers, as in [6]). The used metrics are: recognition rate (percentage of mathematical expressions correctly recognized), symbol segmentation and symbol and relation recognition rates. The tree rel. metric measures the percentage

Table 1. Comparison of our method with results of CROHME-2013 competition

System	recognition rate	segmentation recall	precision	classification recall	precision	tree rel. recall	precision
IV	23.40	84.97	87.4	73.94	75.77	49.73	51.48
II	19.97	80.70	86.35	66.41	71.06	22.44	27.00
ours	**21.61**	**75.70**	**83.41**	**62.63**	**69.00**	**44.67**	**49.73**

of pairs of correctly segmented and classified symbols from the total number of relations between adjacent symbols. While our system obtained comparable results in terms of recognition rate, it obtained better results in terms of relations detection than in symbols detection.

4 Conclusions and Further Work

In this paper, we describe a new parsing technique for recognition of online handwritten mathematical expressions. The proposed method provides comparable results to those of the best systems of the CROHME-2013 competition. Results show that the use of symbol and relation hypotheses to define valid subexpressions is an effective method to reduce the parsing complexity. In addition, the graph grammar modeling of the proposed method provides a general framework to parse other multidimensional languages, as chemical expressions, or diagrams.

Future work includes the optimization of the symbol and relation classification modules. New features should be explored and evaluated in the context of the complete system performance.

References

1. Álvaro, F., Sánchez, J.A., Benedí, J.M.: Recognition of on-line handwritten mathematical expressions using 2d stochastic context-free grammars and hidden markov models. Pattern Recognition Letters (2012)
2. Celik, M., Yanikoglu, B.: Probabilistic mathematical formula recognition using a 2d context-free graph grammar. In: 2011 International Conference on Document Analysis and Recognition (ICDAR), pp. 161–166, September 2011
3. Grune, D., Jacobs, C.J.H.: Parsing Techniques: A Practical Guide, 2nd edn. Springer (2008)
4. Julca-Aguilar, F., Viard-Gaudin, C., Mouchère, H., Medjkoune, S., Hirata, N.: Mathematical symbol hypothesis recognition with rejection option. In: 14th International Conference on Frontiers in Handwriting Recognition (2014)
5. MacLean, S., Labahn, G.: A new approach for recognizing handwritten mathematics using relational grammars and fuzzy sets. International Journal on Document Analysis and Recognition (IJDAR) **16**(2), 139–163 (2013)
6. Mouchère, H., Viard-Gaudin, C., Garain, U., Kim, D.H., Kim, J.H., Zanibbi, R.: Icdar 2013 crohme: Competition on recognition of online handwritten mathematical expressions @ONLINE, April 2013
7. Pflatz, J., Rosenfeld, A.: Web grammars. In: Proc. First International Joint Conference on Artificial Intelligence, pp. 193–220 (1969)
8. Simistira, F., Katsouros, V., Carayannis, G.: Recognition of online handwritten mathematical formulas using probabilistic SVMs and stochastic context free grammars. Pattern Recognition Letters **53**, 85–92 (2015)
9. Wagner, K.: Über eine eigenschaft der ebenen komplexe. Mathematische Annalen **114**(1), 570–590 (1937). http://dx.doi.org/10.1007/BF01594196
10. Yamamoto, R., Sako, S., Nishimoto, T., Sagayama, S.: On-line recognition of handwritten mathematical expressions based on stroke-based stochastic context-free grammar. In: International Workshop on Frontiers in Handwriting Recognition (2006)

Shape Analysis Using Multiscale Hough Transform Statistics

Lucas Alexandre Ramos[1]($\boxtimes$), Gustavo Botelho de Souza[2],
and Aparecido Nilceu Marana[1]

[1] Faculty of Sciences, UNESP, Bauru, SP 17033–360, Brazil
lucasramosunesp@outlook.com
[2] Department of Computing, UFSCar, São Carlos, SP 13565–905, Brazil

Abstract. With the widespread proliferation of computers, many human activities entail the use of automatic image analysis. The basic features used for image analysis include color, texture, and shape. In this paper, we propose MHTS (Multiscale Hough Transform Statistics), a multiscale version of the shape description method called HTS (Hough Transform Statistics). Likewise HTS, MHTS uses statistics from the Hough Transform to characterize the shape of objects or regions in digital images. Experiments carried out on MPEG-7 CE-1 (Part B) shape database show that MHTS is better than the original HTS, and presents superior precision–recall results than some well-known shape description methods, such as: Tensor Scale, Multiscale Fractal Dimension, Fourier, and Contour Salience. Besides, when using the multiscale separability criterion, MHTS is also superior to Zernike Moments and Beam Angle Statistics (BAS) methods. The linear complexity of the HTS algorithm was preserved in this new multiscale version, making MHTS even more appropriate than BAS method for shape analysis in high-resolution image retrieval tasks when very large databases are used.

1 Introduction

Shape is one of the basic features used for image analysis, together with color and texture. According to Costa and Júnior [1], the concept of *shape* can be understood as any visual singular entity or an object as a whole defined by a single set of connected points (either in a discrete or continuous space).

During the process of image analysis, it is of utmost importance to consider that certain information only makes sense under certain viewing conditions, such as the scale [2,3]. In shape recognition, which can be part of image analysis, the scale of observation can be crucial.

However, the choice of the most appropriate scale of observation is not a trivial task, and it is initially impossible to predict the optimal scale representation. So, one must consider all possible scales, hence the concept of multiscale representation, an approach used widely in various applications and signal processing (including images) [2,3].

© Springer International Publishing Switzerland 2015
A. Pardo and J. Kittler (Eds.): CIARP 2015, LNCS 9423, pp. 452–459, 2015.
DOI: 10.1007/978-3-319-25751-8_54

Multiscale shape description methods can be found in the literature. Some examples are Multiscale Fractal Dimension [4], Multiscale Fourier Descriptor [5,6], and Curvature Scale-Space (CSS) [7].

In this paper, we propose MHTS (Multiscale Hough Transform Statistics), a multiscale version of the shape description method called HTS (Hough Transform Statistics), proposed by Souza and Marana [8,9]. Experimental results showed that the MHTS presents better recognition rates than HTS and some other traditional shape description methods, such as: Tensor Scale (TS) [14], Multiscale Fractal Dimension (MFD) [4], Fourier [15], Contour Salience (CS) [16] and Zernike Moments [17]. Furthermore, the MHTS algorithm, likewise HTS, has complexity $\Theta(n)$, being n the number of points of the silhouette, which is an important requirement for content based image retrieval of high resolution images from large databases.

2   HTS - Hough Transform Statistics

Souza and Marana [8,9] showed that the use of statistics from the Hough Transform [10] for shape description is worthwhile, since, as shown in Figure 1, the Hough Transform of silhouettes of objects of the same class are similar, whereas the silhouettes of objects from different classes are quite different.

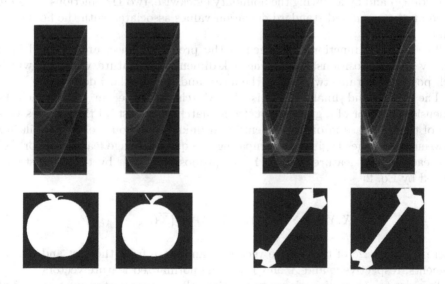

Fig. 1. Hough Transforms of two apples and two bones silhouettes from the MPEG-7 CE-1 (Part B) database [12]. One can observe that the Hough Transforms of silhouettes from the same class are similar, whereas Hough Transforms of silhouettes from distinct classes are quite different.

In the first phase of the HTS shape description method, the boundary points of an object image are extracted. Then, in the second phase, when the Hough Transform is calculated, each boundary point is mapped on an accumulator · matrix, by means of sinusoidal curves given by the Eq. 1, as proposed in [11], varying θ from 0° to 179°:

$$round(\rho) = x \times \cos(\theta) + y \times \sin(\theta) \tag{1}$$

In the Hough Transform space, following a sinusoidal curve r that represents a given boundary point p in the image space, it is possible to find the number $h(\theta)$ of all sinusoidal curves that intersect r at position h. By the end of this process, the calculated histogram h is associated with the boundary point p. The value $h(\theta)$ indicates the number of boundary points that are collinear to p in the direction $\theta + 90°$. Based on this, one can observe that boundary points that belong to straight line segments in the object boundary present histograms with high values (peaks) at certain positions and a high standard deviation, while in rounded shapes all boundary points will present equalized histograms. Therefore, its worthwhile to use the number of intersections and their distribution (histograms) as a shape descriptor

After associating a histogram to each boundary point, the next step is the Feature Extraction phase, in which for each boundary point it is calculated the first and second moments (mean and standard deviation, respectively) from its associated histogram. Given an initial boundary point (the top leftmost point, for instance) and by following the boundary clockwise, two 1D functions are built based on the mean and standard deviation values associated with the boundary points.

The two 1-D functions, obtained in the previous phase, are sampled in k equally spaced positions, generating a k-dimensional feature vector in which each position contains two values, the mean and the standard deviation.

The third, and final phase, is the Matching phase, in which each k-dimensional vector of a given silhouette is matched against all the features vectors of the database in order to identify an unknown silhouette. The similarity between two images is given by comparing the query's image feature vector (X) with each gallery feature vector (Y), as proposed in [13], by the $L1$ distance defined by Eq. 2:

$$L1(X,Y) = \sum_{i=1}^{k} |\overline{X}(i)_f - \overline{Y}(i)_f| + |\overline{X}(i)_s - \overline{Y}(i)_s| \tag{2}$$

where k is the size of the feature vectors, f and s are from the first and second moments, respectively, and $\overline{X}$ and $\overline{Y}$ are the normalized feature vectors.

In order to achieve invariance to rotation, the feature vector must be shifted k times and, after each shift, be compared with the other feature vector. The similarity will be the minimum distance obtained after the k comparisons.

After calculating the distances between the query feature vector and each gallery feature vector, the unknown object is classified as belonging to the same class of the gallery feature vector that results in the minimum L1 distance.

The three HTS phases are summarized below:

Preprocessing: In this phase, likewise the BAS method [13], given an image of an unknown object, it is binarized and an edge detection algorithm is applied in order to segment the boundary of the object. Then, a sequence of boundary points is obtained by starting from the top leftmost boundary point and following the boundary clockwise until complete a full turn around the shape;

Feature Extraction: This phase begins by calculating the Hough Transform of all boundary points of the shape. Next, for each boundary point p, its histogram is calculated by taking all the values found in the Hough space in the positions given by the correspondent sinusoidal curve. Then, the first and second order moments are computed from the histograms calculated for each boundary point, generating two 1D moment functions. Finally, the two 1D functions are sampled in equally spaced k points (where k is defined by the user), generating the feature vector associated with the object being analyzed;

Matching: The query feature vector X, extracted from the unknown object, is compared with each gallery feature vector Y using the $L1$ distance. To achieve invariance to rotation, likewise the BAS method, the feature vector X is shifted (rotated) to the left (always copying the values in the first position to the last) k times. Each new configuration of the shifted query feature vector is compared with the gallery feature vector Y. The final distance between the two feature vectors is taken as the minimum distance obtained for all k comparisons. The unknown object is then classified as belonging to the same class of the nearest (most similar) object in the database.

3   MHTS - Multiscale Hough Transform Statistics

The basic idea behind a multiscale approach is to create a family of derivate signals (pictures) whose structures are successively simplified. Lower scales structures should represent simplifications of the corresponding structures at higher scales, i.e, they cannot simply be something created by the multiscale method. Thus, it is possible to analyze the different levels of representation and using only those that exhibit characteristics of interest.

A major reason for representing information already present in the original signal in multiples levels is that the successive simplification removes unwanted details, such as noise or non-significant structures, facilitating the processing of future tasks. Moreover, by explicitly dealing with the scale parameter, this approach allows the handling of significant image structures which become explicit in each level. Associated with the fact that the decrease of the scale is related to reducing the amount of information, this also implies an increase in computational efficiency.

Regarding the monoscale HTS, the θ and ρ parameters vary from 0° to 179° and from 0 to max_ρ, with increments of $\Delta_\theta = 1$ and $\Delta_\rho = 1$, respectively.

In the multiscale HTS (MHTS), n Hough Spaces are calculated for n scales, given by different Δ_θ and Δ_ρ parameter values $((\Delta_\theta = 1, \Delta_\rho = 1), (\Delta_\theta = 2, \Delta_\rho = 2), \ldots, (\Delta_\theta = n, \Delta_\rho = n))$. Figure 2 illustrates the Hough Transforms obtained for $n = 5$ scales.

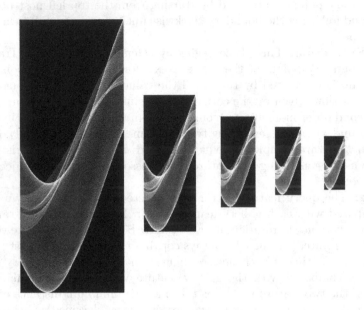

Fig. 2. Hough Transforms obtained for $n = 5$ different scales, given by the parameters $(\Delta_\theta = 1, \Delta_\rho = 1), (\Delta_\theta = 2, \Delta_\rho = 2), \ldots, (\Delta_\theta = 5, \Delta_\rho = 5)$.

In this new multiscale approach, each shape image is represented by n Hough Transform spaces, one per each scale.

In order to obtain the shape descriptors from this multiscale representation, the following approach was adopted: the n Hough Transforms had their 1D functions calculated, sampled, and finally concatenated, thus generating one single feature vector.

4   Experimental Results

In order to evaluate the performance of the new MHTS shape descriptor, some experiments were carried out, and the obtained results were compared with HTS, as well as with some well-referenced shape description methods: Tensor Scale (TS) [14], Multiscale Fractal Dimension (MFD) [4], Fourier [15], Contour Salience (CS) [16], Zernike Moments [17], and Beam Angle Statistics (BAS) [13]. The performances were compared using the precision–recall and the multiscale separability criterion. The precision is the fraction of retrieved instances that are relevant, while the recall (or sensitivity) is the fraction of relevant instances that are retrieved.

MPEG-7 CE-1 (Part B) shape dataset [12] was used in the experiments. This dataset is composed of 1400 images (divided into 70 classes, each class with 20 images), where the background is black and the silhouette is white.

Figure 3 (left) shows the precision–recall curves of MHTS, with some different scale combinations. One can notice that using only the first three scales (1,2, and 3) MHTS presented a better result than when all five scales (1, 2, 3, 4, and 5) were used. This shows that not all scales may be relevant to the image descriptor, but it is important to analyze them all. When using the first, third and fifth scale (1, 3, and 5) the result was close to the monoscale HTS version, proving that the fifth scale may not be relevant for the descriptors construction in this database, and may even impair the results.

Figure 3 (right) shows the best results obtained for the MHTS method and the other methods using the MPEG-7 CE-1 (Part B) shape database [12]. Despite of MHTS presenting, in this experiment, a worse performance in terms of precision-recall than Zernike Moments and BAS, the MHTS method outperformed all other shape description methods assessed in this work, including HTS.

For the methods that presented the best performances regarding the precision-recall curves in the previous experiment we also analyzed their performance regarding the search radius versus separability (multiscale separability) criterion, which has been considered by some authors as a metric to compare shape description methods [16]. Multiscale separability indicates how clusters of

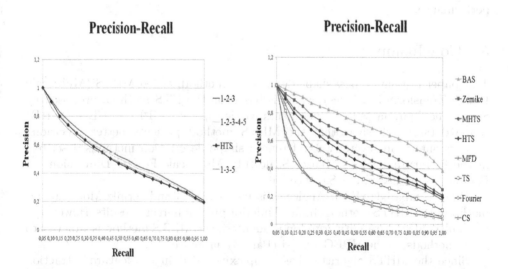

Fig. 3. (Left)Precision–Recall curves of MHTS method, with three different scale combinations: {1,2,3,4,5}, {1,2,3}, {1,3,5} and the monoscale HTS. (Right)Precision–Recall curves of the descriptors for the MPEG-7 CE-1 (Part B) database: BAS (Beam Angle Statistics), Zernike Moments, MHTS (Multiscale HTS), HTS, Multiscale Fractal Dimension (MFD), Tensor Scale (TS), Fourier, and Contour Salience (CS).

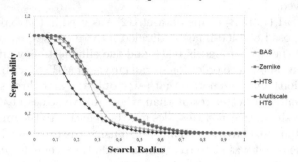

Fig. 4. Search radius versus separability (multiscale separability) curves for the MPEG-7 CE-1 (Part B) database. The MHTS obtained the best performance.

different classes are distributed in the feature space (the more separated the clusters, the better is the descriptor). The higher the multiscale separability curve obtained by the method, the better its performance is.

The best shape descriptors for the MPEG-7 CE-1 (Part B) dataset [12] in terms of precision–recall results were: BAS, Zernike, MHTS, and HTS. The multiscale separability curves of these methods, for the same dataset, are shown in Figure 4. As one can observe, for this criterion MHTS obtained the best performance.

5   Conclusion

This paper presents a new shape description method, called MHTS (Multiscale Hough Transform Statistics), which is based on the HTS method, proposed by Souza and Marana [8,9]. Experiments carried out on MPEG-7 CE-1 (PartB) shape dataset [12] show that the MHTS method presents better precision–recall results than several well-referenced shape description methods described in the literature, such as: Tensor Scale [14], Multiscale Fractal Dimension [4], Fourier [15], and Contour Salience [16].

When compared to Beam Angle Statistics (BAS) [13] and Zernike Moments [17] methods, the MHTS method obtained inferior precision–recall results. However, if the multiscale separability criterion is adopted, the MHTS method is superior to these methods, in the MPEG-7 CE-1 (Part B) database [12].

Since the MHTS algorithm has complexity $\Theta(n)$ in the feature extraction and matching phases, it is much faster than BAS, whose complexity is $\Theta(n^2)$.

Therefore, from the obtained results, we can conclude that for shape recognition based tasks using large images stored in very large databases, which is more and more common nowadays, the MHTS method can outperform the BAS descriptor regarding the processing time, while presenting accuracy rates almost similar to the BAS method and superior to several other well-known shape descriptors found in the literature, including HTS (its monoscale version).

Acknowledgment. The authors thank Fapesp for the financial support (Process: 2014/10611-0).

References

1. Costa, L.F., Júnior, R.M.C.: Shape Analysis and Classification - Theory and Practice. CRC Press, New York (2000)
2. Witkin, A. P.: Scale-space filtering: a new approach to multi-scale description. In: Image Understanding. Ablex, pp. 79–95 (1984)
3. Lindeberg, L.: Scale-space theory: A basic tool for analysing structures at different scales. Journal of Applied Statistics **21**, 25–270 (1994)
4. Backes, A.R., Bruno, O.M.: Implementação e Comparação de Métodos de Estimativa da Dimensão Fractal e sua Aplicação á Análise e Processamento de Imagens. Universidade de São Paulo (USP), São Carlos-SP (2006)
5. Kunttu, L., Lepistöl, L., Rauhama, J., Visa, A.: Multiscale fourier descriptor for shape classification. In: Proceedings of 12th International Conference on Image Analysis and Processing, Mantova, Italy, September 17–19, pp. 536–541 (2003)
6. Kunttu, L., Lepistöl, L., Rauhama, J., Visa, A.: Multiscale fourier descriptor for shape-based image retrieval. In: Proceedings of 17th International Conference on Pattern Recognition, Cambridge, UK, vol. 2, pp. 765–768 (2004)
7. Mokhtarian, F., Mackworth, A.: Scale-based Description and Recognition of planar curves and two-dimensional objects. IEEE Transactions on Pattern Analysis and Machine Intelligence **8**, 34–43 (1986)
8. Souza, G.B., Marana, N.: HTS and HTSn: New shape descriptors based on Hough transform statistics. Computer Vision and Image Understanding **127**, 43–56 (2014). Academic Press Inc. Elsevier Science, San Diego
9. Souza, G.B., Marana, N.: HTS: a new shape descriptor based on Hough transform. In: 2013 IEEE International Symposium on Circuits and Systems (ISCAS), pp. 974–977 (2013)
10. Hough, P.V.C.: A method and means for recognizing complex patterns, U.S. Patent 3069654 (1962)
11. Duda, R.O., Hart, P.E.: Use of the Hough transformation to detect lines and curves in pictures. Commun. ACM **15**, 1–15 (1972)
12. Jeannin, S., Bober, M.: Description of core experiments for MPEG-7 motion/shape, Technical report ISO/IECJTC1/SC29/WG11 MPEG99/N2690 (1999)
13. Arica, N., Vural, F.T.Y.: BAS: a perceptual shape descriptor based on the beam angle statistics. Pattern Recogn. Lett. **24**, 1627–1639 (2003)
14. Miranda, P.A.V., Torres, R.S., Falcão, A.X.: TSD: a shape descriptor based on a distribution of tensor scale local orientation. In: Brazilian Symposium on Computer Graphics and Image Processing, pp. 139–146 (2005)
15. Zhang, D., Lu, G.: A comparative study on shape retrieval using Fourier descriptors with different shape signatures. In: International Conference on Intelligent Multimedia and Distance Education, pp. 1–9 (2001)
16. Torres, R.S., Falcão, A.X.: Contour salience descriptors for effective image retrieval and analysis. Image and Vision Computing **25**, 3–13 (2007)
17. Teague, M.R.: Image analysis via the general theory of moments. J. Opt. Soc. Am. **70**, 920–930 (1980)

Inference Strategies for Texture Parameters

Jorge Martinez[1], Silvina Pistonesi[1], and Ana Georgina Flesia[2]([⊠])

[1] Departamento de Matemática, Universidad Nacional Del Sur,
Avenida Alem 1253, 2do Piso, B8000CPB Bahía Blanca, Argentina
{martinez,silvina.pistonesi}@uns.edu.ar
[2] Facultad de Matemática, Astronomía y Física, Universidad Nacional de Córdoba,
Ing. Medina Allende S/n, Ciudad Universitaria, 5000 Córdoba, Argentina
flesia@famaf.unc.edu.ar

Abstract. The Autobinomial model is a commonplace in Bayesian image analysis since its introduction as a convenient image model. Such model depends on a set of parameters; their value characterize texture allowing to perform classification of the whole image into regions with uniform properties of the model.

This work propose a new estimator of the parameter vector of the Autobinomial model based on Conditional Least Square minimization via Real Coded Genetic Modeling and analyze its performance compared to the classical linear approximation, which exchanges the CLS equation with a reduced Taylor equation prior to minimization. Our simulation study shows that the genetic modeling approach gives more accurate estimations when true data is provided. We also discuss its influence in a set of classification experiments with multispectral optical imagery, estimating the scalar vector parameter with our estimator and the classical linear one. Our experiments show promising results, since our approach is able to distinguish image features that the classical approach does not.

Keywords: Real coded genetic algorithm · Conditional least squares method · Gibbs Markov random field · Autobinomial model · Parameter estimation

1 Introduction

The Gibbs Markov Random Field model (GMRF) is a powerful tool for the extraction of spatial information contained in an image. It provides a convenient and consistent way for modeling context dependence of image pixels. In many applications of this type of stochastic models, the estimation of parameters plays an important role. Classical estimators are constructed as solution of optimization problems, obtained with techniques such as Newton Raphson (NR), Simulated Annealing (SA) and Iterated Conditional methods, among others.

However, optimal estimation of these parameters from one or more realizations of the GMRF is often difficult in real situations. Metaheuristics approaches have been widely recognized as efficient approaches for many hard optimization problems [2]. Genetic Algorithms (GAs) are included in this context. They are general purpose population based search techniques which mimic the principle

© Springer International Publishing Switzerland 2015
A. Pardo and J. Kittler (Eds.): CIARP 2015, LNCS 9423, pp. 460–467, 2015.
DOI: 10.1007/978-3-319-25751-8_55

of natural selection and natural genetics laid by Charles Darwin. The concept of GAs was introduced by John Holland in 1975. The approach works by creation of a population of candidate solutions (chromosomes) which evolve through the so called genetic operations of selection, crossover and mutation until some stopping criteria are met. Traditionally, candidate points (chromosomes) in genetic algorithms are represented by binary coded strings; for a survey in the field see [4] and references therein.

In recent years, real coded genetic algorithms (RCGAs) have been used to solve continuous optimization problems [7],[8],[1]. In real coded GA (RCGA), real-valued genes are used instead of the conventional bit-string encoding, i.e. it treats chromosomes as vectors of real-valued numbers. It then adapts the genetic operators of the binary coded GA accordingly.

In this paper, we introduce a new estimator of the Autobinomial GMRF parameters (ABM) solving the Conditional Least Square (CLS) equations with a RCGA design and study its accuracy under ABM simulation and its performance in a classification experiment.

The paper is structured as follows. In the next section, we briefly review the framework of GMRF, Autobinomial Model, CLS equations and define our RCGA based estimator. In the Experiments section we analyze the accuracy of our estimate via Monte Carlo simulation of the true ABM, comparing it with a linear model estimation (LM), Schröder's approximate solution based on a linear Taylor approximation to the CLS equations, [11]. We also present a (Landsat 5 TM) classification example, to explore and visualize the power of our estimate in the image classification context. Conclusions are left to the last section.

2   Image Context Characterization

This section introduces some basic concepts related to the MRF models and a particular class of MRF that will be used in this paper: Autobinomial. For a more detailed discussion on the subject we refer to [6].

We model the images as being configurations of a Gibbs field with a certain neighborhood potential. For a single pixel site x_s this approach results in a conditioned distribution

$$P\left(x_s/\mathcal{N}_s;\theta\right) = \frac{\mathrm{e}^{-H(x_s,\mathcal{N}_s;\theta)}}{Z_s},$$

with local energy function $H(x_s,\mathcal{N}_s;\theta)$, parameter vector θ, and Z_s a normalization constant, called "partition function of the distribution". The parameter vector θ, weighs the contributions of the different cliques in the neighborhood $\mathcal{N}_s$. In the following we only use a second order homogeneous and isotropic neighborhood.

Autobinomial Model. The ABM is a discrete Markovian model with energy function defined as

$$H\left(x_s,\mathcal{N}_s;\theta\right) = \ln\binom{M}{x_s} + x_s\eta_s \tag{1}$$

where M is the maximum grey value and $\binom{M}{x_s}$ denote the binomial coefficients. The quantity

$$\eta_s = \alpha + \beta_{11}\frac{x_t + x_{t^*}}{M} + \beta_{12}\frac{x_u + x_{u^*}}{M} + \beta_{21}\frac{x_r + x_{r^*}}{M} + \beta_{22}\frac{x_z + x_{z^*}}{M} \quad (2)$$

reflects the joint influence of the neighbors with the parameter vector $\theta = (\alpha, \beta_{11}, \beta_{12}, \beta_{21}, \beta_{22})^T$, see Fig. 1. The partition function of the distribution is given by:

$$Z = \sum_{z_s=0}^{M} e^{H(z_s, \mathcal{N}_s; \theta)} = \left(1 + e^{-\eta_s}\right)^M$$

Consequently the conditional probability distribution function is written as:

$$P(x_s/\mathcal{N}_s; \theta) = \binom{M}{x_s} \omega_s^{x_s} (1 - \omega_s)^{M-x_s} \quad \forall x_s = 0, 1, \ldots, M \quad (3)$$

where $\omega_s = \frac{1}{1+e^{-\eta_s}}$.

Thus, the random variable X_s modeling the intensity of the image at the pixel s has a conditional binomial distribution with parameters M and ω_s. The expected value and the variance of X_s are respectively:

$$E[X_s] = M\omega_s = \frac{M}{1+e^{-\eta_s}} \quad V[X_s] = M\omega_s(1-\omega_s) = M\frac{e^{-\eta_s}}{(1+e^{-\eta_s})^2} \quad (4)$$

For $\eta = 0$, $E[X_s] = \frac{M}{2}$ and $V[X_s] = \frac{M}{4}$.

Parameter Estimation with the CLS Method. The Conditional Least Square (CLS) estimator is defined as the argument that minimizes the equation:

$$\hat{\theta} = \arg\min_\theta \sum_{s\in S} (x_s - E[X_s])^2. \quad (5)$$

From Equation (4), the Equation (5) can be rewritten as:

$$\hat{\theta} = \arg\min_\theta \sum_{s\in S} \left(x_s - \frac{M}{1+e^{-\eta_s}}\right)^2. \quad (6)$$

Thus the vector minimizing the quadratic cost function of Equation (6) is the Conditional Least Square estimator. This approach attempts to minimize the error between the observed image and the expected image. Classical solutions are obtained with solvers as Newton-Raphson and other gradient descent algorithms. Schröder et al. [11] proposed to exchange this equation with a reduced Taylor expansion, which leaded to a linear model estimation (LM).

Our Proposal: (RCGA) Based Estimator. In this paper, we propose a new estimator of the ABM parameter vector as a solution of the CLS equation obtained with a real coded genetic algorithm. GA has been frequently used for parameter estimation in many studies, solving non-convex optimization problems, like ours. However, the application of GA's for estimating the parameters of the ABM has not been explored yet. Over the many options of GA algorithms, we selected a version with integrated crossover rule and local technique due to Kaelo and Ali [9]. Our proposal is then outlined in Algorithm 1:

Algorithm 1. RCGA for ABM parameter estimation

Step 1) **Initialization.** Generate N uniformly distributed random points from the search region Ω and store the points and their corresponding function values in S.

Step 2) **Stopping rule based on the best and the worst point.** Find the best and worst points in S, x_l and x_h, where the best point x_l has the lowest function value f_l and the worst point x_h has the highest function value f_h. If the stopping condition (e.g., $|f_h - f_l| \leq \epsilon$) is achieved, then stop.

Step 3) **Generation of offsprings:** The following rules are repeated until m offsprings are generated.

   – 3.1 *Tournament selection using two players:* two points are chosen at random from the set S and the better of the two is taken as a parent for crossover.

   – 3.2 *Crossover Rule:* two offsprings are produced at a time using three parents x_1, x_2 and x_3 selected using tournament of two players. The first offspring y_1 is created mating the parents by using $y_1^i = \frac{x_1^i + x_2^i}{2} + \sigma_i \left(\frac{x_1^i + x_2^i}{2} - x_3^i \right)$, where y_1^i is the ith component of y_1, σ_i is a uniform random number in $[0, 1]$ for each i, and x_3 is the worst parent.
   The second offspring y_2 is created mating the parents using $y_2^i = x_1^i + F_i \left(x_1^i + x_3^i \right)$, where F_i are uniform random numbers in $[0.4, 1]$.

   – 3.3 *Mutation:* The offsprings produced in the crossover step are mutated with probability p_m, by applying the non-uniform mutation rule, suggested by Michalewicz [10].

Step 4) **Update S.** The worse m points in S are replaced with the m offsprings. Set $k = k + 1$. If no point is better than the best point in the previous generation go to Step 2; else continue to Step 5.

Step 5) **Local technique.** Select a point y at random from the set S, different from the current best x_l. Find a trial point $\bar{x}$ using the current best point, x_l, in S and a randomly drawn point y from S, different from x_l. The point $\bar{x}$ then competes with the current worst point in S. The rule for the local technique is: $\bar{x}^i = \left(1 + \gamma^i \right) x_l^i - \gamma^i y^i$, where $\bar{x}^i$ is the ith component of $\bar{x}$, and γ^i are uniform random numbers, say in [-0.5, 1.5], different for each i. The point $\bar{x}$ is biased towards the best point x_l. If $f(\bar{x}) < f_h$ then replace x_h and f_h by $\bar{x}$ and $f(\bar{x})$ in S respectively. Repeat Step 5 l_r times. Go to Step 2.

---

3 Experiments

In all our experiments, the structural parameters of our RCGA estimator were chosen as follows: the number of chromosomes (parameter N) used was set to 100, the maximum number of allowed generations (parameter T) was set to 10000, and $m = 10$ (offsprings). The mutation was performed with probability $p_m = 0.001$, and the parameter b of the non-uniform mutation rule was set to $b = 5$. These are standard suggestions, see [10] for details. The stopping rule focuses on the difference between the best and the worst chromosome in the population in order to decide for termination. The algorithm terminates when $|f_h - f_l| \leq \epsilon = 10^{-4}$ or the maximum number of generations (T) was reached.

First Experiment: Monte Carlo Simulation Study. We designed this experiment to study the accuracy of the proposed estimator (mean square norm (MSN) of the difference with the true value) and its empirical distribution. The benchmark estimator for this model is the LM approach of Schröder et al. [11]. Thus, we study the error statistics and empirical distributions of LM as well over the same database and discuss the diferencies. Our Monte Carlo database was comprised of 500 synthetic images (128×128 sized) with 256 grays levels, generated for each specified vector parameter: (i) $\theta = (0,0,0,0,0)^T$, (ii) $\theta = (3,0,0,0,-3)^T$, (iii) $\theta = (-2,1,1,-0.6,-0.6)^T$, (iv) $\theta = (3,0,0,-3,0)^T$, (v) $\theta = (-2,1,-0.5,-0.5,2)^T$ and (vi) $\theta = (0,1,1,-1,-1)^T$. See Fig. 1.

Fig. 1. From left to right, neighbourhood of the pixel x_s and textures under study for cases (i), (ii), (iii), (iv), (v) and (vi) respectively.

We restricted the parameter domain to be in $[-4, 4]^5$ as suggested by Chen and Dubes [5], generating the textures with the Gibbs sampler algorithm. We report the estimators empirical distributions of all cases as boxplots in Fig. 3. For the case (i), very noisy texture, all parameters equal to zero, both estimators exhibits the same behavior. In all other cases, RCGA has overall good accuracy, and at least one parameter has better accuracy than LM. Also, the RCGA estimator shows a lower or almost equal standard deviation than LM in all cases.

In cases (ii), (iv) and (v), the parameters β_{21} and β_{22} which control the diagonal texture structure were estimated better by RCGA than LM. The SN empirical distribution for each estimator is reported in Fig. 2. Schröeder et al. experiments have also shown the problems of the LM estimator to compute accurately the diagonal parameters.

In the case (iii) the value of the autocorrelation parameter, α, was under-estimated by LM. In the (vi) case, β_{21} and β_{22}, were underestimated, and the parameters that control the vertical and horizontal texture structure, β_{11} and β_{12}, were overestimated by LM, see Fig. 3. For each case, according to Mann-Whitney U Test, statistically significant differences were reported ($p < 0.01$) between LM and RCGA in the parameter that determines the orientation of the texture: β_{22} case (ii), β_{21} case (iv), β_{11} case (v), β_{21} case (vi) and the same result was reach in α case (iii).

Second Experiment: Landsat 5 TM Data Classification. In this section we present an example to analyze the behavior of the RCGA estimator in the context of supervised texture classification in remote sensing images.

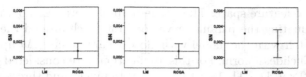

Fig. 2. From left to right: SN error boxplot of the (ii), (iv) and (v) cases, respectively. For the others cases, (i), (iii) and (vi), the lower value of MSN was obtained by RCGA: 0.0076, 0.0026, 0.0040 against LM estimator: 0.0077, 0.0028, 0.0041, respectively.

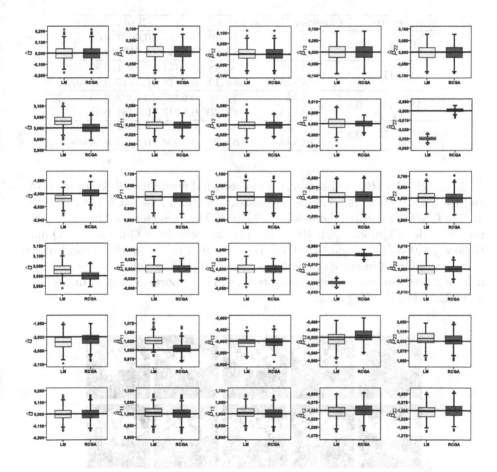

Fig. 3. Performance of LM and RCGA using CLS criterion. From left to right, top to bottom, boxplot depict estimations of parameters $\alpha, \beta_{11}, \beta_{12}, \beta_{21}, \beta_{22}$ for cases (i) -(vi) respectively. The horizontal line indicated specified parameter value for each case.

A scene of a Landsat 5 TM image (courtesy of CONAE-Argentina), shown in Fig. 4, with spatial resolution 30 m, was selected and the ABM assumed a valid model. We estimated the vector of parameters θ in a selected training area for each class and employed the outcome as a texture characterization vector in a five-dimensional feature space. The image map of classes was obtained labeling a pixel by estimating the parameter vector in a patch around the image pixel, tagging the patch with the model with closest parameters ($\Delta\theta$ up to threshold T) using the Euclidean norm. For this application were considered four different window sizes: 9×9, 11×11, 13×13 and 15×15 pixels, and threshold $T = k/10$, with $k : 1, \ldots, 40$.

Table 1. Results of classification obtained by LM and RCGA.

Window sizes	T	Classifier Method	OA (%)	$\widehat{\kappa}$	CI of κ (95%)
9×9	2.5	LM	85.70	0.6175	$(0.6077, 0.6274)$
		RCGA	**85.92**	0.6266	$(0.6170, 0.6364)$
11×11	1.4	LM	83.48	0.5673	$(0.5571, 0.5777)$
		RCGA	**84.11**	0.5948	$(0.5747, 0.5950)$
13×13	0.8	LM	82.38	0.5407	$(0.5302, 0.5514)$
		RCGA	**82.40**	0.5492	$(0.5388, 0.5597)$
15×15	0.8	LM	81.55	0.5133	$(0.5024, 0.5244)$
		RCGA	**82.21**	0.5308	$(0.5273, 0.5488)$

Image classification performance was evaluated with Overall Accuracy (OA) and Kappa statistical measures. For the study, we used Landsat 5 TM $(228 - 88)$ data in GeoTIFF format, dated March 3, 2011. The scene selected in experiment was Bajo de la Quinta, with 190×190 pixels. Bajo de la Quinta ("La Quinta Hollow") ($40°56'14''$ S and $64°20'34''$ W) is located in the northern coast of the San Matías Gulf, Province of Río Negro, Argentina. The hollow is covered by a field of active sand-dunes (approximately $7 \, \text{km}^2$). A portion of sand-dunes zone was selected as training area.

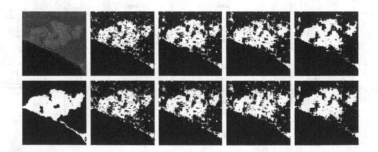

Fig. 4. First column: Bajo de la Quinta scene, Landsat 5 TM image and Ground Truth. Second to Fifth column: Classification map obtained by LM and RCGA, for 9×9, 11×11, 13×13 and 15×15 windows sized, respectively.

According to the scale established by Landis and Koch the values of Kappa reveal a level of agreement "substantial" when 9×9 window sized is used and "moderate" on the rest, between the ground truth image and the class maps obtained by LM and RCGA. All Kappa coefficients were statistically significant

$(p < 0.01)$, confirming significant concordance between the maps compared. The behavior of the classifier methods was similar, although the RCGA reaches slightly higher classification accuracy than LM. Closer look at the class maps outputs revealed that a portion of the sand dunes next to water was misclassified by LM while RCGA gives better edge data. Grounds verification were carried out using the aid of topographic map and the printed satellite imagery showing the observed site and surrounding area. The maps are shown in Fig. 4.

4   Conclusion

We introduced a new estimator of the ABM parameters using a RC Genetic Modeling approach to solve the CLS equations. Our simulation experiments show that our estimator is more accurate than the benchmark estimator in at least one parameter in all cases, specially on directional parameters, and our experiment in land classification shows it use feasible in real applications. In fact, the better use of directional information gives better edge definition to the classification map.

References

1. Ali, M.M., Törn, A.: Population set-based global optimization algorithms: some modifications and numerical studies. Computers and Operations Research **31**(10), 1703–1725 (2004)
2. Boussad, I., Lepagnot, J., Siarry, P.: A survey on optimization metaheuristics. Information Sciences **237**, 82–117 (2013). Prediction, Control and Diagnosis using Advanced Neural Computations
3. Cariou, C., Chehdi, K.: Unsupervised texture segmentation/classification using 2-d autoregressive modeling and the stochastic expectation-maximization algorithm. Pattern Recognition Letters **29**(7), 905–917 (2008)
4. Coello, C.: An updated survey of GA-based multiobjective optimization techniques. ACM Computing Surveys **32**(2), 109–143 (2000)
5. Chen, C.C., Dubes, R.C.: Experiments in fitting discrete markov random fields to textures. In: IEEE Proceedings of Conference on Computer Vision and Pattern Recognition, number MSU-CPS-88-09, San Diego, CA, USA, pp. 298–303 (1989)
6. Gaetan, C., Guyon, X.: Spatial Statistics and Modeling. Springer Series in Statistics. Springer (2010)
7. Herrera, F., Lozano, M.: Two-loop real-coded genetic algorithms with adaptive control of mutation step sizes. Applied Intelligence **13**(3), 187–204 (2000)
8. Herrera, F., Lozano, M., Sánchez, A.M.: A taxonomy for the crossover operator for real-coded genetic algorithms: An experimental study. International Journal of Intelligent Systems **18**, 309–338 (2003)
9. Kaelo, P., Ali, M.M.: Integrated crossover rules in real coded genetic algorithms. European Journal of Operational Research **176**(1), 60–76 (2007)
10. Michalewicz, Z.: Genetic algorithms + data structures = evolution programs, 3rd edn. Springer, London (1996)
11. Schröder, M., Rehrauer, H., Seidel, K., Datcu, M.: Spatial information retrieval from remote sensing images: Part b. gibbs markov random fields. IEEE Transaction on Geoscience and Remote Sensing **36**, 1446–1455 (1998)

Texture Characterization via Automatic Threshold Selection on Image-Generated Complex Network

Thiago P. Ribeiro, Leandro N. Couto, André R. Backes[(⊠)],
and Celia A. Zorzo Barcelos

Faculdade de Computação, Faculdade de Matemática,
Universidade Federal de Uberlândia, Uberlândia, MG, Brazil
{tpribeiro,leandro,arbackes,celiazb}@ufu.br

Abstract. This work presents an automated approach to texture characterization through complex networks. By applying an automatic threshold selection for network degree map generation, we managed to achieve significant reduction in the number of descriptors used. The method is adaptive to any image database, because it is based on the analysis of the energy value of the degree histogram of the complex networks generated particularly from each database. Experiments using the proposed method for texture classification using databases from literature show that the proposed method can not only reduce feature vector size, but in some cases also improve correct classification rates when compared to other state of the art methods.

Keywords: Texture characterization · Complex networks · Automatic threshold selection

1 Introduction

Texture is one of many attributes by which an image can be characterized. The advancement of modern image processing techniques and the richness of information provided by texture analysis resulted in the use of the texture attribute in several different image processing and computer vision tasks: content based image retrieval (CBIR) [1], image segmentation [2], [3], image synthesis [4], clustering and classification [5,6]. Practical applications can also be found in many important fields, such as security and event detection [7], medical image analysis [8] and social behaviour analysis [9], to cite a few examples.

Literature presents a wide range of methods for texture description and classification. These methods can be divided into four basic categories: statistical methods [10], geometric properties-based methods, filtering and transform-based methods (or signal processing-based methods) and model-based methods [11,12].

These methods generate comparable data based upon information extracted from the visual data. Whether it is statistics, quantified geometric properties or the resulting data after a transform is applied to the image, the information

© Springer International Publishing Switzerland 2015
A. Pardo and J. Kittler (Eds.): CIARP 2015, LNCS 9423, pp. 468–476, 2015.
DOI: 10.1007/978-3-319-25751-8_56

works as a descriptor for that texture. The key to a good descriptor (i.e., one that presents good precision for a wide variety of datasets, while also being robust enough to offer good recall, even against image transformations such as rotation) is to extract appropriate information from the image. Finding which features results in a better discrimination of textures from different classes is a complex problem that has been the topic of extensive research.

Images can be modeled as complex networks for many different applications. Complex networks, in turn, can be computationally represented by graphs [13]. There are several different methods available for statistical and topological analysis and characterization of complex networks [14]. Using this process, a texture can yield information through the use of complex network description metrics, which works well given that the periodic nature of the texture means they usually yield networks with relevant and representative statistics and topologies [15]. One category of methods for complex network description is degree histogram analysis. The histogram offers simple and concise statistics on the complex network, and many features can be derived from it. The work on [13] successfully uses statistics from the degree histogram of a complex network generated from an image to characterize textures, showing that the histogram can be a powerful tool for such tasks. However, the success of the method depends on the appropriate choice of parameters; specifically, the quality of the graph generated from the texture, that is, how discriminating it can be, strongly depends on the choice of the threshold value that determines connections (or lack thereof) between the complex network's nodes. Different thresholds yield very different graphs. Better results were achieved when acquiring statistics from networks obtained using different thresholds and combining the results into a bigger descriptor.

This work presents an improvement on the previous method by greatly reducing descriptor size by intelligently choosing thresholds to compose the feature vector. This is done through analysis of statistical measures yielded by the networks of different thresholds and using that information to judge the significance of threshold values and selected the most relevant ones. Data from similar thresholds usually have high dependence, which means some of them can be discarded without significantly decreasing the classification results (and sometimes improving them). Experiments were performed comparing the method to other state-of-the-art texture analysis methods, on commonly used datasets.

2   Graph Approach for Texture Analysis

2.1   Graph Modelling

In order to analyze a texture using graph properties, we must first model the texture as a graph which emphasizes some desirable properties related to the pixels neighborhood. To accomplish that, we modeled the texture as an undirected graph $G = (V, E)$ by associating each image pixel $I(x, y)$, $x = 1 \dots M$, $y = 1 \dots N$, as a vertex $v \in V$ [13]. An edge $e \in E$ connects two vertices when the Euclidean distance between them is no longer than a radius value r:

$$E = \left\{ e = (v, v') \in V \times V \mid \sqrt{(x - x')^2 + (y - y')^2} \leq r \right\},$$ (1)

where x and y are the coordinates of the pixel $I(x, y)$ associated to the vertex v. We also associate a weight to each edge $e \in E$. This weight $w(e)$ is defined as

$$w(e) = \frac{(x - x')^2 + (y - y')^2 + r^2 \frac{|I(x,y) - I(x',y')|}{255}}{r^2 + r^2}$$ (2)

where $I(x, y) = g$, $g = 0, \ldots, 255$ is the gray value associated to the image pixel and $r^2 + r^2$ is the maximum weight value. This weight function considers both pixels distance and difference of intensities in its calculus. Since the pixels intensities present a wider range of values than its position, we decided to normalize it in function of the radius r to avoid the dominance of this attribute in the calculus. Notice that we also normalized the weight function according to the square of the radius r, so that, the $0 \leq w(e) \leq 1$.

Once we modelled the texture sample as a graph, we are able to compute its properties. One simple property is the degree of each graph vertex. We define the degree of a vertex v as:

$$deg(v) = |\{v' \in V | (v, v') \in E\}|.$$ (3)

where $|A|$ is the count of the number of items in the set A. From the degree of each graph vertex, we obtain the histogram degree $h(i)$

$$h(i) = \sum_{v \in V} \delta(deg(v) - i)$$ (4)

where $\delta(j, i)$ is the Kronecker's delta

$$\delta(i) = \begin{cases} 1, & i = 0 \\ 0, & i \neq 0 \end{cases}$$ (5)

and the probability density function $p(i)$

$$p(i) = \frac{h(i)}{\sum_{i=0}^{k} h(i)}$$ (6)

where $k = \max_{v \in V} deg(v)$ is the maximum degree of the graph G.

2.2 Dynamic Evolution of the Graph

The graph obtained from a texture image is a regular graph. This is because each vertex is connected to the same number of other vertices of the graph and this number of vertices is limited by the value of the radius r. Thus, the degree of its vertices does not hold any desirable information for the characterization of the graph/texture.

A interesting tool for investigating a graph behavior comes from the complex networks theory and its called dynamic evolution[13]. It aims to investigate the graph properties as a function of time, i.e., it considers that the graph is changing along the time as well as its properties. This process enables to study how the properties change and their trajectories, and use them as additional information to analyze and classify a graph.

Although the graph obtained from a texture does not change along the time, it is possible to emulate this process by applying a threshold t over the set of edges E in order to select a subset E_t, $E_t \subseteq E$. In this work, we propose to select edges from $e \in E$ to compose E_t where the weight of the edge, $w(e)$, is equal to or smaller than the threshold t:

$$E_t = \delta_t(E) = \{e \in E | w(e) \leq t\}. \tag{7}$$

By considering the original set of vertices V, we are able to obtain a new graph $G_t = (V, E_t)$ representing an intermediary stage in the graph evolution.

The degree of a node bears information on how the corresponding pixel relates to its neighbours. Let D_t be the matrix of degrees of the nodes $v_{x,y} \in V$ for a given t. Every $v_{x,y}$ has a corresponding $D_t(x, y) \in D_t$, where $D_t(x, y) = deg(v_t(x, y))$. Energy, entropy and contrast are extracted from these degree matrices to compose the feature vector used to characterize the texture sample

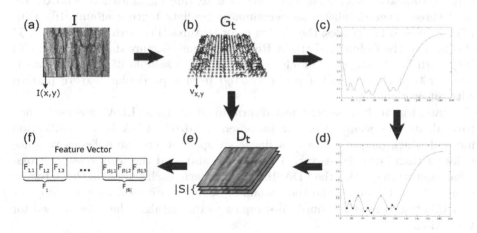

Fig. 1. Stages of the proposed method: (a) Input image; (b) Complex network generated for each threshold value t and texture sample in the dataset; (c) Average energy histogram; (d) Thresholds selected; (e) Degree distribution from the texture sample for each selected threshold; (f) Feature vector composed by energy, entropy and contrast.

3   Automatic Threshold Selection

The work in [13] set the threshold t consisting of an initial threshold $t_{initial} = 0.005$, which was gradually increased by a value $t_{incr} = 0.015$, until it achieved a maximum threshold $t_{final} = 0.530$. This values were obtained empirically.

We propose a method to automatically select thresholds for the set t. By analyzing the empirical thresholds previously proposed, we observed that by varying the texture databases the results obtained were not the best. Instead of setting a fixed range for the thresholds, the proposed method selects N thresholds from the set of thresholds T, which is created by the following parameters: $t_{initial} = 0.005$, $t_{incr} = 0.005$ and $t_{final} = 0.950$.

Figure 1 illustrates the stages for automatic selection of the thresholds. Initially we create a complex network for each texture image and threshold t. In the sequence, we compute the energy for each degree's histograms and generate the average energy histogram of all images in the texture database. From this average histogram we select all the local peaks and valleys. This results in a new set S of thresholds, $S \subset T$, containing the thresholds t which will be used to model the texture pattern into a complex network. Then, for each network generated using a threshold $T \in S$ we calculate the energy, entropy and contrast of its degree's histograms. This measurements will be concatenated to compose the feature vector.

4   Experiments and Results

In order to evaluate our automatic threshold selection approach, the image feature vectors were calculated and used in a texture classification context. We used three image databases as benchmark: Brodatz texture album [16], with 1776 images in 111 classes; the VisTex color textures [17], with 864 images in 54 classes; and the Columbia-Utrecht Reflectance and Texture database (CUReT) [18], with 5612 images in 61 classes. Each image sample of any database is 200×200 pixels size and it was extracted from a particular texture pattern without overlapping.

Statistical analysis using linear discriminant analysis (LDA) was performed to evaluate the accuracy of our proposed approach. LDA is a classification method which projects data in a linear subspace where inter-classes variance is larger than intra-classes variance [19]. We also used the *leave-one-out cross-validation* strategy with the LDA. In this approach, each sample in the database is used for validation while the remaining samples are used as a training set and this test is repeated until all samples in the database have been used for validation.

Before applying our threshold selection approach, some parameters must be defined in order to compute the complex networks from a texture sample. To model the network, we used a radius $r = 3$, which resulted in a maximum node $v_{x,y}$ degree of 28.

Table 1. Comparison of the mean and median classification results.

Method	Brodatz		Vistex		CUReT	
	Dim.	Success rate (%)	Dim.	Success rate (%)	Dim.	Success rate (%)
Mean	36	93.30	**48**	**96,88**	**48**	**78.90**
Median	**54**	**94.14**	54	96,64	42	77.08

In order to efficiently apply our approach on texture analysis we must first select the best set of thresholds. As previously stated, we propose to evaluate the variation on the energy of the degree distribution obtained for a set of threshold values to select the most discriminative ones. Thus, for each texture sample, we compute the energy of the degree distribution for each threshold in a set of 190 different threshold values defined by the following equation: $t(i) = 0.005 + 0.005(i - 1), i = 1, \ldots, 190$. Then, we compute the average curve from the curves obtained of all textures. This average curve shows how the energy levels are distributed over the textures in the entire database. To compute this curve, we evaluated two approaches: mean and median. In the sequence, we selected the thresholds which correspond to the peaks and valleys of the average curve as the parameters of the graph descriptors (Section 3). Table 1 show the results achieved for the two approaches (mean and median) on three different image sets.

We notice that each approach achieves a different number of thresholds for each image set. This is expected as the average curve represents the variation of energy levels over the textures. In general, we achieve the best success rate by using the mean instead of the median. The only exception is in the Brodatz dataset. However, this result presents the largest difference in the number of thresholds selected between mean and median.

We also performed a comparison with traditional and state of art texture analysis methods. Table 2 presents the results yielded for each method. For this comparison, we considered the mean measurement to compute the average curve used to select the best thresholds, as shown in Table 2. We must emphasize that we were not able to implement all compared approaches due to the complexity of the method or missing information in their respective papers. Thus, for methods that lack results for one or more datasets, these results correspond to the ones presented in their respective paper. We also compared our approach with the traditional implementation of the complex network method, where the thresholds are manually selected [13].

Table 2. Results yelded for all compared methods.

Method	Number of descriptors	Success rate (%) Brodatz	Vistex	CUReT
First Order	5	40.20	52.66	57.78
Wavelets	36	70.27	72.11	58.52
LBP	25	89.58	88.89	74.07
Gabor	64	82.49	91.67	80.12
Backes et. al[13]	108	**95.27**	86.76	84.32
Zhang et. al[20]	100	94.90 ± 0.7	-	-
Crosier and Griffin [21]	1,296	-	-	**98.6 ± 0.2**
Perea & Carlsson[22]	215	-	-	95.66 ± 0.45
Varma and Zisserman [23]	2,440	-	-	97.43
Zhang et al. [24]	6,561	-	-	92.44 ± 1.04
Zhang et al. [25]	648	-	-	94.44 ± 1.13
Proposed approach	36, 48, 48	93.30	**96.88**	78.90

Results indicate that our approach presents a consistent high performance in all texture datasets. It is able to yield the highest success rate in Vistex dataset and the third best result in Brodatz dataset. In this case, its results in 1.97% smaller than the best results, but using less than half the number of descriptors. The worst performance of our approach is in the CUReT dataset. However, methods with higher success rate present from 4 to 136 times more descriptors than our proposed approach.

5   Conclusions

Descriptor size is an important characteristic to consider in a mathematical modelling method, specially in recent times in which lower cost embedded systems and big data problems have become so relevant. If two descriptors offer similar classification rates, a method presenting a much smaller feature vector size would be preferable. A smaller feature vector takes up less storage and memory space and is generally faster to process and apply a classifier to. The method proposed in this work yields feature vectors smaller than other state of the art methods, while keeping on par with those methods' results in terms of classification rates over several image databases, as was shown by the experiments performed. This work also further showcases how complex network measures can be a powerful tool in adequately describing texture. In this case, statistical analysis of the degree histogram yielded information not only on the overall nature of the data, but also about the thresholds that are the most significant. Through automated threshold selection, the proposed method can also adapt to the particularities of each specific set of data through customized threshold selection. The dimensionality reduction is therefore based on the complexity of the data. Future work on this approach could be exploring this relation between the statistical measures of the degree histogram, used for dimensionality reduction, and what they can inform about the nature and complexity of the data.

Acknowledgments. André R. Backes gratefully acknowledges the financial support of CNPq (National Council for Scientific and Technological Development, Brazil) (Grant #301558/2012-4). Celia A. Zorzo Barcelos gratefully acknowledges the financial support of CNPq (National Council for Scientific and Technological Development, Brazil) (Grant #207513/ 2014-7, #475819/2012-8 and #305812/2013-0). The authors gratefully acknowledge the financial support of CNPq, FAPEMIG and PROPP-UFU.

References

1. Hiremath, P.S., Pujari, J.: Content based image retrieval using color, texture and shape features. In: International Conference on Advanced Computing and Communications, ADCOM 2007, Guwahati, Assam, pp. 780–784. IEEE (2007)
2. Belongie, S., Carson, C., Greenspan, H., Malik, J.: Color- and texture-based image segmentation using EM and its application to content-based image retrieval. In: Sixth International Conference on Computer Vision, Bombay, pp. 675–682. IEEE (1998)
3. Goncalves, W.N., Bruno, O.M.: Dynamic texture analysis and segmentation using deterministic partially self-avoiding walks. Expert Systems with Applications 40(11), 4283–4300 (2013)
4. Efros, A.A., Leung, T.K.: Texture synthesis by non-parametric sampling. In: The Proceedings of the Seventh IEEE International Conference on Computer Vision, vol. 2, pp. 1033 1038 (1999)
5. Serra, G., Grana, C., Manfredi, M., Cucchiara, R.: Covariance of covariance features for image classification. In: Proceedings of International Conference on Multimedia Retrieval, ICMR 2014, pp. 411:411–411:414. ACM, New York (2014)
6. Zhao, Y., Jia, W., Hu, R.X., Min, H.: Completed robust local binary pattern for texture classification. Neurocomputing 106, 68–76 (2013)
7. Ma, Y.M.Y., Cisar, P.: Event detection using local binary pattern based dynamic textures. In: 2009 IEEE Computer Society Conference on Computer Vision and Pattern Recognition Workshops (2009)
8. Kassner, A., Thornhill, R.E.: Texture analysis: a review of neurologic MR imaging applications. American Journal of Neuroradiology, AJNR 31(5), 809–816 (2010)
9. Ghidoni, S., Cielniak, G., Menegatti, E.: Texture-based crowd detection and localisation. In: Lee, S., Cho, H., Yoon, K.-J., Lee, J. (eds.) Intelligent Autonomous Systems 12. AISC, vol. 193, pp. 725–736. Springer, Heidelberg (2012)
10. Haralick, R.M.: Statistical and structural approaches to texture. Proc. IEEE 67(5), 786–804 (1979)
11. Jain, A., Tuceryan, M.: HandBook of Pattern Recognition and Computer Vision. In: Chen, C.H., Pau, L.F., Wang, P.S.P. (eds.), pp. 207–248. World Scientific Publishing Co. Inc., River Edge (1998)
12. Chetverikov, D., Renaud, P.: A brief survey of dynamic texture description and recognition. In: International Conference on Computer Recognition Systems, pp. 17–26 (2005)
13. Backes, A.R., Casanova, D., Bruno, O.M.: Texture analysis and classification: a complex network-based approach. Information Sciences 219, 168–180 (2013)
14. Costa, L.D.F., Rodrigues, F.A., Travieso, G., Boas, P.R.V.: Characterization of complex networks: a survey of measurements. Advances in Physics 56(1), 78 (2005)
15. Backes, A.R., Casanova, D., Bruno, O.M.: A complex network-based approach for texture analysis. In: Bloch, I., Cesar Jr, R.M. (eds.) CIARP 2010. LNCS, vol. 6419, pp. 354–361. Springer, Heidelberg (2010)
16. Brodatz, P.: Textures: a photographic album for artists and designers. Dover pictorial archives. Dover Publications (1966)
17. VisTex: Vision Texture Database (2009)
18. Dana, K.J., van Ginneken, B., Nayar, S.K., Koenderink, J.J.: Reflectance and texture of real-world surfaces. ACM Trans. Graph. 18(1), 1–34 (1999)
19. Duda, R.O., Hart, P.E., Stork, D.G.: Pattern Classification, 2nd edn. Wiley-Interscience (2000)

20. Zhang, J., Marszalek, M., Lazebnik, S., Schmid, C.: Local features and kernels for classification of texture and object categories: a comprehensive study. In: Conference on Computer Vision and Pattern Recognition Workshop, CVPRW 2006, p. 13 (2006)
21. Crosier, M., Griffin, L.D.: Using basic image features for texture classification. International Journal of Computer Vision **88**(3), 447–460 (2010)
22. Perea, J.A., Carlsson, G.: A klein-bottle-based dictionary for texture representation. International Journal of Computer Vision **107**(1), 75–97 (2014)
23. Varma, M., Zisserman, A.: Unifying statistical texture classification frameworks. Image and Vision Computing **22**(14), 1175–1183 (2004)
24. Zhang, J., Liang, J., Zhao, H.: Local energy pattern for texture classification using self-adaptive quantization thresholds. IEEE Transactions on Image Processing: A Publication of the IEEE Signal Processing Society **22**(1), 31–42 (2013)
25. Zhang, J., Liang, J., Zhang, C., Zhao, H.: Scale invariant texture representation based on frequency decomposition and gradient orientation. Pattern Recognition Letters **51**, 57–62 (2015)

A RFM Pattern Recognition System Invariant to Rotation, Scale and Translation

Selene Solorza-Calderón$^{(\boxtimes)}$ and Jonathan Verdugo-Olachea

Facultad de Ciencias, Universidad Autónoma de Baja California,
Km. 103, Carretera Tijuana-Ensenada, 22860 Ensenada, B.C., México
selene.solorza@uabc.edu.mx

Abstract. In this paper a rotation, scale and translation (RST) invariant pattern recognition digital system based on 1D signatures is proposed. The rotation invariance is obtained using the Radon transform, the scale invariance is achieved by the analytical Fourier-Mellin transform and the translation invariance is realized through the Fourier's amplitude spectrum of the image. Once, the RST invariant Radon-Fourier-Mellin (RFM) image is generated (a 2D RST invariant), the marginal frequencies of that image are used to build a RST invariant 1D signature. The Latin alphabet letters in Arial font style were used to test the system. According with the statistical method of bootstrap the pattern recognition system yields a confidence level at least of 95%.

Keywords: Pattern recognition · Radon-Fourier-Mellin Images · 1D RST invariant signature · Radon transform · Analytical Fourier-Mellin transform

1 Introduction

In the pattern recognition field, the feature extraction process to generate a descriptor invariant to geometric transformations of the object (translation, rotation, scale, noise, illumination and others) is not a trivial problem. Since the first optical experiments in the middle of last century, the features extraction has been a subject of interest and a great progress were done since the introduction of the classical joint transform correlator by Vander Lugt [1], that is the classical matched filter (CMF). Due to the fact that the CMF filter has low response to additive Gaussian noise other filters were generated, just as the phase-only filter (POF), the synthetic discriminant function filter (SDF) and others. In general, the filters are specialized to solve specific problems, for example the filter could have an excellent performance in the discrimination step and the signal-to-noise ratio but low efficiency under non-homogeneous illumination [2]. Although composite filters are being used, the RST invariant image classification problem is an active field due to its intrinsic complexity[3–7].

Actually, with the great advance in technology, the pattern recognition via digital images is a very productive area. A lot of methodologies in digital images

© Springer International Publishing Switzerland 2015
A. Pardo and J. Kittler (Eds.): CIARP 2015, LNCS 9423, pp. 477–484, 2015.
DOI: 10.1007/978-3-319-25751-8_57

features extraction based on joint transforms correlators are developed. T.V. Hoang and S. Tabbone [8] uses the Radon and the 1D Fourier-Mellin transform to build a 2D RST invariant classifier. However, the classification step is realized by the use of the 2D cross-correlation of the target and the problem images. On the other hand, the 2D Fourier-Mellin transform (FMT) are used to design 2D RST invariant classifiers. Because of the factor $\frac{1}{r}$ in this transform, generally the translation invariance is done in the spatial domain using the centroid or the center of mass of the objects, but removing a small disk around the centroid or the center of mass to reduce the large effect of the factor $\frac{1}{r}$ [9]. Ghorbel [10] propose the analytical Fourier-Mellin transform (AFMT), where the images are weighted by the factor r^σ with $\sigma > 0$ to eliminate the influence of $\frac{1}{r}$ in the FMT. However, this transform not preserves the rotation and scale invariance. Derrode [9] propose a normalization of the AFMT by two of the AFMT harmonics to obtain a RST invariant descriptor together with the Euclidean distance for the classification mechanism.

In this work a 1D RST invariant Radon-Fourier-Mellin (RFM) digital image pattern recognition system is designed. Moreover, a methodology to generate one and only one classifier output plane is proposed, instead of the multiple classifier output planes obtained with the correlator pattern recognition systems [5–8]. The work is organized as follows: Section 2 explains the mathematical foundations of the RST invariant images and the methodology to obtain the 1D signature. Section 3 exposes the procedure to construct the classifier output plane of 95% confidence level. Finally, conclusions are given in section 5.

2   Digital System Invariant to Rotation, Scale and Translation

In the Radon-Fourier-Mellin (RFM) digital image pattern recognition, the first step is obtain the shift invariance. This is achieved using the amplitude spectrum $A(u, v)$ of the Fourier transform [12]. Fig. 1 shows the Fourier's amplitude spectrums for black and white 257×257 pixel images of: the image with the A Arial font letter without geometric transformations, called I_1; the image with the A Arial font letter with a rotation angle of 315° and scaling of -25%, named I_2; the image with the B Arial font letter without geometric transformations, denominated I_3. Also, Fig. 1 shows that $A_3(x, y) = |\mathcal{F}\{I_3(x, y)\}|$ is different of $A_1(x, y) = |\mathcal{F}\{I_1(x, y)\}|$ and $A_2(x, y) = |\mathcal{F}\{I_2(x, y)\}|$. Moreover, in Fig. 1 is seen that A_2 presents the same rotation angle of I_2 and it has a stretch deformation due to the scale variation.

The next step of the RMF system is the scale invariance, which is given via the fast analytical Fourier-Mellin transform (AFMT),

$$M(k, \omega) = \mathcal{M}\{A(e^\rho, \theta)\} = \frac{1}{2\pi} \int_{-\infty}^{\infty} \int_0^{2\pi} A(e^\rho, \theta) e^{\rho\sigma} e^{-i(k\theta + \rho\omega)} d\theta d\rho, \quad (1)$$

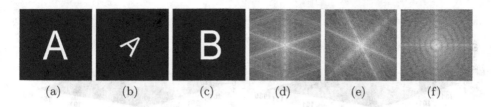

Fig. 1. Fourier's amplitude spectrum examples. (a) Image I_1: the A Arial font letter without geometric transformations. (b) Image I_2: the A Arial font letter with a rotation angle of $315°$ and scaled -25%. (c) Image I_3: the B Arial font letter without geometric transformations. (d) $A_1(u,v) = |\mathcal{F}\{I_1(x,y)\}|$. (e) $A_2(u,v) = |\mathcal{F}\{I_2(x,y)\}|$. (f) $A_3(u,v) = |\mathcal{F}\{I_3(x,y)\}|$.

where $\rho = \ln(r)$ and $\sigma > 0$. Eq. (1) is not an invariant to scale and rotation, but normalizing the AFMT by its dc-value the amplitude spectrum is a scale invariance [9], that is

$$S(k,\omega) = \left| \frac{M(k,\omega)}{M(c_x,c_y)} \right| , \qquad (2)$$

where (c_x, c_y) is the central pixel of the image. Fig. 2(d), Fig. 2(e) and Fig. 2(f) present $S_1(k,\omega)$, $S_2(k,\omega)$ and $S_3(k,\omega)$ images, respectively. These are the normalized analytical Fourier-Mellin amplitude spectrums of $A_1(e^\rho,\theta)e^{\rho\sigma}$, $A_2(e^\rho,\theta)e^{\rho\sigma}$ and $A_3(e^\rho,\theta)e^{\rho\sigma}$ (Fig. 2(a), Fig. 2(b) and Fig. 2(c)), respectively. The images are not rotation invariant yet. Fig. 2(a) and Fig. 2(b) show the circular shift in the angular variable.

Finally, the rotation invariant is obtained by the Radon transform [8] of the normalized analytical Fourier-Mellin amplitude spectrum $S(k,\omega)$, that is

$$R(r,\theta) = \mathcal{R}\{S(k,\omega)\} = \int_{-\infty}^{\infty} \int_{-\infty}^{\infty} S(k,\omega)\delta(r - k\cos\theta - \omega\sin\theta)dk d\omega , \quad (3)$$

where $r \in (-\infty,\infty)$, $\theta \in [0,\pi)$ and δ is the Dirac delta function. Fig. 3(a), Fig. 3(b) and Fig. 3(c) show the RFM images invariant to rotation, scale and translation associated to Fig. 1(a), Fig. 1(b) and Fig. 1(c), respectively. Practically,

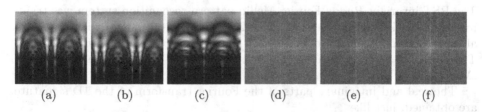

Fig. 2. Normalized analytical Fourier-Mellin spectrum with $\sigma = 0.5$. (a) $A_1(e^\rho,\theta)e^{\rho\sigma}$. (b) $A_2(e^\rho,\theta)e^{\rho\sigma}$. (c) $A_3(e^\rho,\theta)e^{\rho\sigma}$. (d) The $S_1(k,\omega)$ of Fig. 2(a). (e) The $S_2(k,\omega)$ of Fig. 2(b). (f) The $S_3(k,\omega)$ of Fig. 2(c).

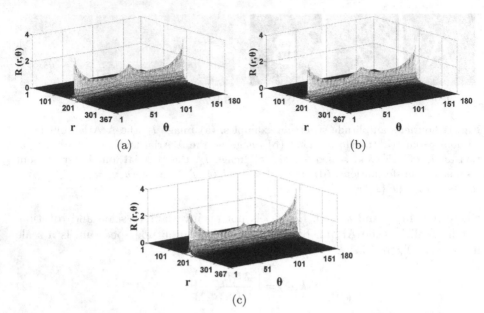

Fig. 3. The Radon transform examples. (a) The $R(r,\theta)$ of Fig. 2(d). (b) The $R(r,\theta)$ of Fig. 2(e). (c) The $R(r,\theta)$ of Fig. 2(f).

Fig. 3(a) and Fig. 3(b) are equal, the former is obtained from the image with the A Arial font letter without geometric distortions and the latter is generated with the A Arial font letter rotated and scaled. Fig. 3(c) is different to the others two images, this is associated to the B Arial font letter without distortions.

To reduce the computational time cost, the marginal frequencies are used in the 1D RST invariant signature construction, that is

$$V(x) = \sum_y R(x,y) \, . \tag{4}$$

3   The Confidence Level

The RST invariant Radon-Fourier-Mellin pattern recognition system was training using black and white (BW) 257×257 pixel digital images with the Latin alphabet letters in Arial font style, each image was rotated $360°$ with $\Delta\theta = 1°$. Thereafter, each of those images were scaled $\pm 25\%$ with a scale step size of $\Delta k = \pm 1\%$.

The real and imaginary parts of the Fourier transform of the 1D signature are obtained, just like

$$R_V(u) + iI_V(u) = F(u) = \mathcal{F}\{V(x)\} = \int_{-\infty}^{\infty} V(x)e^{-i2\pi ux}dx \, , \tag{5}$$

to determine the signature's power by

$$P_R = \frac{1}{N_R} \sum R_V^2 , \tag{6}$$

$$P_I = \frac{1}{N_I} \sum I_V^2 , \tag{7}$$

where N_R and N_I are the length of the signatures R_V and I_V, respectively. A database of target images should be established to train the RFM pattern recognition system. The P_R and P_I of those images are obtained to determine the 95% confidence interval (CI) by the statistical method of bootstrap using a replacement constant $B = 1,000$ and normal distribution [11]. Fig. 4(a) shows the output plane for the 26 Arial font letter of the Latin alphabet. Each letter image was rotated 360° ($\Delta\theta = 1°$) and then scaled ±25% ($\Delta k = ±1\%$), therefore 18,360 images for each letter were created. Then, each CI is built from 18,360 values. In Fig. 4(a), the horizontal and vertical axes represent the CI for the P_R and P_I values, respectively. A rectangle area is assigned to each image (Fig. 4(b) displays an amplification zone of the output plane to observe the rectangle area assigned to some letters). Because those rectangles are not overlapped, the RFM pattern recognition system has a confidence level at least of 95% in the digital image classification. Therefore, a one and only one classifier output plane was used, instead of the multiple classifier output planes (one for each reference image in the database) for correlator systems[6–8] or distance systems [5,9]. For example, in the case of the latin alphabet letters the correlator systems [6,7] uses 26 output planes. In [8], the classification step is realized by the use of the 2D cross-correlation of the target and the problem images. Because the Radon transform generates a circular shift in the angular variable, 180 2D cross-correlation values are calculated for each pair of images, employing a lot of computation time in the classification process. Therefore, the single output plane methodology reduces the investment computational time considerably.

4 Noise Analysis

To test the performance of the system when images have additive Gaussian noise, the similarity coefficient was used, it is defined like

$$SC = 1 - \frac{||S_T - S_{TN}||_\infty}{||S_T - S_{FN}||_\infty} , \tag{8}$$

where $||\mathbf{x}||_\infty = max\{|x_1|, |x_2|, \ldots, |x_n|\}$, S_T is the signature of the image, S_{TN} is the signature of the image with noise and S_{FN} is the signature of the background image with noise. When S_T and S_{TN} are similar the $||S_T - S_{TN}||_\infty \to 0$, then $SC \approx 1$. On the other hand, when the problem image has to much noise that it looks like the background image with noise, the S_T and S_{FN} are similar and $||S_T - S_{FN}||_\infty \to 0$, thus $SC < 0$. For the sake of comparison, the performance of

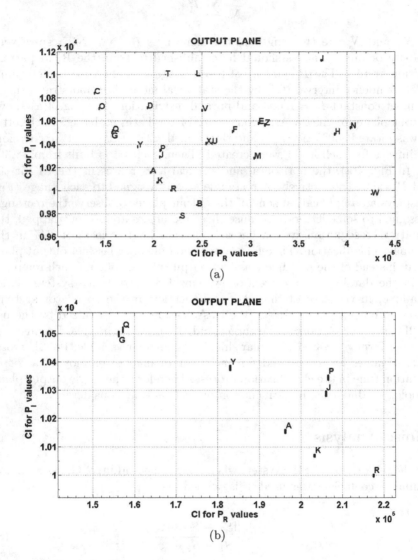

Fig. 4. (a) The classifier output plane. (b) Amplification zone of the classifier output plane.

SURF methodology when the images have noise is included, but here the results are given in terms of the repeatability parameter r,

$$r = \frac{C(T, PI)}{mean(N_T, N_{PI})},\tag{9}$$

where $C(T, PI)$ represents the number of the common detected points in the target T and the problem image PI; N_T and N_{PI} are the number of points detected in T and PI, respectively. Fig. 5 presents the graphs of the mean of the SC response for the RFM system and the repeatability analysis (r values) for the SURF algorithm. The images were altered with additive Gaussian noise of media zero and variance from zero to 0.3, using 40 images per sample. In Fig. 5 is shown that RFM system has a better response under this kind of noise than the SURF methodology.

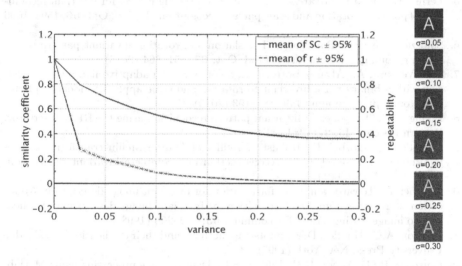

Fig. 5. The RFM and SURF pattern recognition systems performance when images have additive Gaussian noise with variance σ from 0 to 0.3 and step size of $\Delta\sigma = 0.025$.

5   Conclusions

This work presents a RFM pattern recognition system using a 1D signature invariant to rotation, scale and translation (RST) based on the analytical Fourier-Mellin and Radon transforms. The system presents a confidence level at least of 95% in the pattern recognition of rotated, scaled and translated black and white images with the Latin alphabet letters in Arial font style. Moreover, this RST invariant Radon-Fourier-Mellin methodology generates a single classifier output plane to reduce the computational cost time of the classification procedure.

Acknowledgments. This work was partially supported by CONACyT under grant No. 169174. Jonathan Verdugo-Olachea is a student in the Math program offered by the Facultad de Ciencias, Universidad Autónoma de Baja California and he is supported by a CONACyT scholarship under the research proyect No. 169174.

References

1. Van der Lugt, A.: Signal detection by complex spatial filtering. IEEE Trans. Inf. Theory **IT–10**, 139–145 (1964)
2. Vijaya Kumar, B.V.K., Hassebrook, L.: Performance measures for correlation filters. Appl. Opt. **29**, 2997–3006 (1990)
3. Lowe, D.G.: Distinctive image features from scale-invariant key points. IJCV **60**, 91–110 (2004)
4. Bay, H., Essa, A., Tuytelaars, T., Van Gool, L.: Speeded-Up Robust Features (SURF). CVIU **110**, 346–359 (2008)
5. Lerma-Aragón, J.L., Álvarez-Borrego, J.: Vectorial signatures for invariant recognition of position, rotation and scale pattern recognition. J. Mod. Opt. **56**, 1598–1606 (2009)
6. Solorza, S., Álvarez-Borrego, J.: Translation and rotation invariant pattern recognition by binary rings masks. J. Mod. Opt. **62**, 851–864 (2015)
7. Solís-Ventura, A., Álvarez-Borrego, J., Solorza, S.: An adaptive nonlinear correlation with a binary mask invariant to rotation and scale applied to identify phytoplankton. Opt. Commun. **339**, 185–193 (2015)
8. Hoang, T.V., Tabbone, S.: Invariant pattern recognition using the RFM descriptor. Pattern Recogn. **45**, 271–284 (2012)
9. Derrode, S., Ghorbel, F.: Robust and efficient Fourier-Mellin transform approximations for gray-level image reconstruction and complete invariant description. CVIU **83**, 57–78 (2001)
10. Ghorbel, F.: Towards a unitary formulation for invariant image description; Application to Towards a unitary formualtion for invariant image description. Application to image coding. Ann. Telecommun. **53**, 242–260 (1998)
11. Davison, A.C., Hinkley, D.V.: Bootstrap methods and their application. Cambridge University Press, New York (1997)
12. Gonzalez, R.C., Woods, R.E., Eddins, S.L.: Digital image processing using Matlab. Gatesmark Publishing, MA (2009)

Texture Analysis by Bag-Of-Visual-Words of Complex Networks

Leonardo F.S. Scabini[(⊠)], Wesley N. Gonçalves, and Amaury A. Castro Jr.

Federal University of Mato Grosso Do Sul, CPPP, Ponta Porã, MS 79907-414, Brazil
leonardo.f.scabini@gmail.com, {wesley.goncalves,amaury.junior}@ufms.br

Abstract. The texture is an important property of images, and it has been widely used to image characterization and classification. In this paper, we propose a novel method for texture analysis based on Complex Network theory. Basically, we show how to build networks from images, and then construct a vocabulary of visual words with Bag-Of-Visual-Words method. To build the vocabulary, the degree and strength of each vertex are extracted from the networks. The feature vector is composed by the visual word occurrence, unlike most traditional Complex Network works that extract global statistical measures of vertices. We show through experiments in four databases the effectiveness of our approach, which has overcome traditional texture analysis methods.

Keywords: Texture analysis · Complex networks · Bag-Of-Visual-Words

1 Introduction

When we look at images, an important characteristic that can be noted is its texture. Although texture can be easily interpreted by humans, designing an automatic tool to perform the same role is a difficult and challenging task. Despite the importance for images, there is no concise definition in literature to the term texture [18]. Nevertheless, it can be described as a repeating pattern of intensity levels in a region of the image.

Through the years, many methods to texture analysis have been proposed in the literature. They can be divided into the following categories: spectral analysis [1,15], statistical analysis [12,13] and complexity analysis [17]. Regardless of the approach, the goal of a texture analysis method is to extract relevant features that present both local and global information of the pixels, ensuring that the whole pattern is correctly represented. In this context, Complex Networks theory (CN) is a strong approach with such properties, and recently some works on texture analysis based on CN has emerged [3,6,10,11]. However, previous works

L.F.S. Scabini — Grateful to the program NERDS da Fronteira, and PET - Fronteira to the financial support and physical space granted to the development of the research and experiments.

© Springer International Publishing Switzerland 2015
A. Pardo and J. Kittler (Eds.): CIARP 2015, LNCS 9423, pp. 485–492, 2015.
DOI: 10.1007/978-3-319-25751-8_58

extract global measurements from the CN, which in some cases, is not effectively in texture analysis. Moreover, CN is still underexplored in images because CN theory itself is a new area that has emerged in the past decade.

This work presents a new method to texture analysis based on CN theory. The main idea is to build networks from images, and then apply the Bag-Of-Visual-Words (BOVW) method over them. Instead of extracting global statistical measures from CN, like previous works, measurements of each vertex based on its degree and strength are extracted. This information is used to build a vocabulary of visual words with BOVW, and the feature vector is composed by the visual word occurrence in the image. Results on four datasets have shown the effectiveness of the proposed method.

The next sections of this paper describe every step to represent a texture with CN and BOVW. In Section 2, a brief review of CN theory is presented. Section 3 presents the proposed method to build networks from textures and characterize them using BOVW. In Section 4, the parameters of the proposed method are evaluated, and a comparison with traditional texture methods is performed. Finally in Section 5, a brief conclusion of the work and future works.

2   Complex Network Theory

The CN theory is an intersection between graph theory and statistical mechanisms, which emerge from physics. The popularity of CN rise from its flexibility to model and represent many problems, resulting in a wide range of applications [8]. Works using CN usually have two main steps: modeling the problem as networks and extracting measurements from them. To build a CN, a weighted and undirected graph $C = (V, E)$ is defined, where $V = \{v_1, ..., v_n\}$ is a set of vertices and $E = \{e_{v_i, v_j}\}$ a set of edges.

To characterize the structure of CN, recent works focused in exploring topological features [4,7]. Usually, most of the traditional works use information of vertex properties, such as degree and strength. The vertex degree is the number of its connections, and the vertex strength is the sum of its edges. Most of the works focuses in the analysis of vertices degree and strength, evaluating statistical measures of global distribution, such as the average vertex degree.

3   Proposed Method

3.1   Texture Representation with Complex Networks

The first step of the proposed method is to model an image I with $w \times h$ pixels and gray levels between 0 and 255 as a network $G = \{V, E\}$, where $V = \{v_1, ..., v_{w*h}\}$ is the set of vertices such that each vertex corresponds to one pixel and $E = \{e_{v_i, v_j}\}$ is the set of edges. Two vertices v_i and v_j are connected if the Euclidean distance of their corresponding pixels p_i and p_j is smaller than a radius r. The edge weight is given by the pixel distance multiplied by the difference between their intensities. This allows us to include spatial and intensity information into the connections. So, an edge connecting two vertices v_i and v_j is defined by:

$$e_{v_i,v_j} = \begin{cases} \frac{1}{r}|I(v_i) - I(v_j)|d(v_i, v_j), & \text{if } d(v_i, v_j) \leq r \\ \emptyset, & \text{otherwise} \end{cases} \qquad (1)$$

where $I(v_i)$ and $I(v_j)$ are the gray level intensity of the pixels corresponding to the vertices v_i and v_j, respectively, and $d(v_i, v_j)$ is the Euclidean distance. The multiplication by $\frac{1}{r}$ is a normalization factor that keeps the edge weight between 0 and 255 for any radius r.

Initially, the network has the same number of connections, presenting a regular topology. In order to transform the regular network, a function $G^{t,r} = C(G, t)$ is applied over the original network, where edges that have weight greater than t is discarded. A new t-scaled network $G^{t,r}$ is obtained using radius r to connect vertices, where its edges were redefined according to the threshold t. The threshold affects directly the topology, and can result in networks with dense or sparse connections. Fig. 1 illustrates two networks transformed with different thresholds. It can be observed that vertices with similar gray level intensities are connected, and the threshold controls the level of similarity.

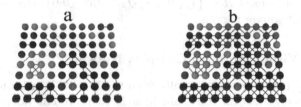

Fig. 1. Networks $G^{t_1,r}$ and $G^{t_2,r}$ transformed using two thresholds $t_1 < t_2$. The network was built from an image with 10x8 pixels, using radius $r = \sqrt{2}$. (a) t_1. (b) t_2

3.2 Vertex Measurements

Given a network $G^{t,r}$, the degree and strength of each vertex v_i can be calculated as:

$$k^{t,r}(v_i) = \sum_{v_j} \begin{cases} 1, & \text{if } e_{v_i,v_j} \in E \\ 0, & \text{otherwise} \end{cases} \qquad (2)$$

$$s^{t,r}(v_i) = \sum_{v_j} \begin{cases} e_{v_i,v_j}, & \text{if } e_{v_i,v_j} \in E \\ 0, & \text{otherwise} \end{cases} \qquad (3)$$

To characterize different properties of the network topology, to each vertex v_i a vector of measurements is extracted using a set of thresholds $T = \{t_1, \ldots, t_{nt}\}$ and radiuses $R = \{r_1, \ldots, r_{nr}\}$:

$$\psi(v_i) = [k^{t_1,r_1}, s^{t_1,r_1}, \ldots, k^{t_{nt},r_{nr}}, s^{t_{nt},r_{nr}}] \qquad (4)$$

This allows evaluating the evolution of the network since its creation (little thresholds) to its stabilization (high thresholds). To define these sets, first it is found the range of threshold $[t_1, t_{nt}]$ and then, this range is divided into nt intervals. In order to find the range of thresholds, it is estimated the mean μ and standard deviation σ of edges of networks built from training images P (Equation 5 and 6).

$$\mu = \frac{1}{|P| * |E|} \sum_{I \in P} \sum_{v_i \in V_I} e_{v_i, v_j}, \forall j \tag{5}$$

$$\sigma = \frac{1}{(|P| * |E|) - 1} \sum_{I \in P} \sum_{v_i \in V_I} (e_{v_i, v_j} - \mu)^2, \forall j \tag{6}$$

With the distribution μ and σ, the initial and the final thresholds are defined by $t_1 = max(3, \ \mu - 3\sigma)$ and $t_{nt} = min(255, \ \mu + 3\sigma)$. The initial threshold is limited to prevent that networks have enough connections and the final threshold is limited to the maximum possible weight. The parameters μ and σ model the distribution of the edges weight, and according to the Gaussian properties, the initial and final thresholds ensure a cover of 99.8% of the network edges. To the set of radiuses, it is used $R = \{1, \sqrt{2}, \sqrt{8}, \sqrt{18}, \sqrt{32}, \sqrt{50}\}$, that is those which covers a different square regions.

3.3   Bag-Of-Visual-Words of Complex Networks

The BOVW [9] method came originally from the Bag-Of-Words method applied to document categorization. Its main idea is to represent documents with a histogram of words occurrence along the text. In BOVW, the same idea is used, but instead of words literally, features of pixels are used. Therefore, a visual word represents a region of pixels with similar properties. To train these visual words, several features of the image can be extracted, and then it is performed a clustering (usually with K-Means) to build the vocabulary of visual words.

In the context of CN, the image features are the vertex vectors $\psi(v_i)$ described in the previous section. To build the vocabulary, K-Means is performed in a set $D = [\psi(v_i)] \ \forall \ v_i$ composed by vertex vectors of each image of the training set P. The algorithm is initialized randomly and performs a clustering based on the Euclidean distance of the vectors, returning $C = \{c_1, ..., c_k\}$ centroids corresponding to each visual word. With the centroids, it is possible to assign a visual word to each vertex by its Euclidean distance:

$$w(v_j) = \arg\min_{i=1}^{k} \ dist(\psi(v_j), c_i) \tag{7}$$

where arg min returns an index between 1 and k. Fig. 2 shows a sample of the assignment of visual words in three different textures.

The feature vector used in the classification is composed by the visual words occurrence $h(w_i)$ (Equation 8). With these measurements, the proposed method

Fig. 2. Samples of visual words assignment on three different textures. It was used $k = 50$, and each color represent a different visual word, according to the scale 1 to 50.

combines both local (information of each vertex) and global (occurrence of visual words) information of the texture.

$$\varphi = [h(w_1), \ldots, h(w_k)] \tag{8}$$

4 Experiments and Results

In this section, we perform an analysis of each parameter and also a comparison with traditional texture analysis methods. In the classification, the K-Nearest Neighbors classifier (KNN) is used, with the 10-fold cross-validation. We have chosen a simple classifier rather than a sophisticated one in order to highlight the importance of texture descriptors.

In the experiments, four traditional databases were used in order to ensure a large variety of images and evaluate the invariance to scale, illumination, etc. The four databases are: Brodatz [5] with 111 classes with 10 samples of 200x200 pixels, Vistex [16] with 54 classes with 16 samples of 128x128 pixels, Usptex [2] with 191 classes with 12 samples of 128x128 pixels and KTH - Tips [14] with 11 classes with 432 samples of varied dimensions.

4.1 Parameter Analysis

As previously discussed, the three main parameters of the proposed method are the set of thresholds $T = \{t_1, ..., t_{nt}\}$, radiuses $R = \{r_1, ..., r_{nr}\}$ and number of visual words k. Three configurations were evaluated, using 10 thresholds and different radius sets. We have defined empirically the set P, the number of visual words k and nt. It was evaluated other numbers of thresholds, but that does not critically affect the results, and $nt = 10$ was fixed as standard. Fig. 3 (A) presents the accuracy rate for three configurations using different number of visual words k in the Vistex database. The first configuration $R = \{1, \sqrt{2}, \sqrt{8}\}$ achieved good accuracy rates, but the second one, using $R = \{1, \sqrt{2}, \sqrt{8}, \sqrt{18}\}$, has improved the results. The third configuration, which is composed by $R = \{1, \sqrt{2}, \sqrt{8}, \sqrt{18}, \sqrt{32}\}$, decreased the accuracy rate. Therefore, the second configuration is defined as standard, where the number of features used to each vertex is 80 ($nt * nr *$ number of measures $= 10 * 4 * 2$).

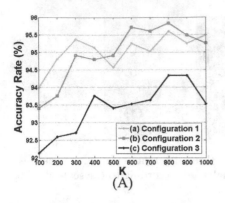 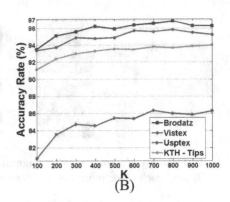

(A)   (B)

Fig. 3. (A) Results on Vistex database using three radius configurations and $nt = 10$ thresholds. (B) Classification results in each database using Configuration 2.

Although we have found the best parameters on Vistex database, this configuration was used in all four databases and showed the best results. Due to the wide variety of these databases, we believe that this configuration presents satisfactory results for a large range of images. Fig. 3 (B) shows the results of classification in all databases with k ranging from 100 to 1000. It is important to notice that the best results were achieved using k between 700 and 1000. However, using $k = 100$ the proposed method overcomes all the compared methods in Vistex and Usptex databases (see Table 1 in the next sub-section).

4.2   Comparison with Traditional Methods

We have compared the proposed method with the following traditional methods: Fourier Descriptors [1], Gabor Filters [15], Co-occurrence Matrix [13], Dense SIFT with BOVW [9], Local Binary Patterns-Variance (LBPV) [12] and Local Fractal Dimension [17]. To each method, the parameters used are those that present the best result. Table 1 shows the accuracy rate and the number of features to each method in all databases. For the proposed method, we show the results using 100 visual words and the number of visual words that provided the best result.

On Brodatz database, the best results were achieved by the proposed method with 96.85% against 94.05% of Dense SIFT and Local Fractal dimension. Using 100 visual words, the proposed method reached 93.51%, the same performance of LBPV. In the Vistex database, the proposed method overcomes LBPV using 100 visual words, with 93.40% against 91.32% and provided its best result of 95.83% using 800 visual words. The Usptex database proved to be the most difficult to the methods, in general, due to its large amount of classes. In this database, the proposed method presented the best performance that has overcome LBPV with 86.34% against 78.01% that is a difference of almost 9%. Finally, in the KTH - Tips database, the proposed method also achieved the best result, reaching 94.00% with 1000 visual words against 93.77% of the Local fractal dimension. This result shows that the proposed method is robust against many variations

Table 1. Results achieved by texture analysis methods in each database. Each column presents the number of features, the accuracy rate and standard deviation (in brackets).

Method	Brodatz	Vistex	Usptex	KTH - Tips
Fourier	99 features 70.72%(±3.85)	63 features 72.09%(±4.89)	63 features 49.78(±3.13)	63 features 80.09(±1.82)
C. Matrix	40 features 86.49(±2.69)	40 features 87.74(±2.72)	40 features 63.73(±2.71)	40 features 86.36(±1.12)
Gabor	40 features 89.01 (±1.52)	40 features 86.11 (±1.75)	40 features 73.62 (±2.68)	40 features 93.29(±1.04)
L. Fractal	5550 features 94.05 (±2.69)	2700 features 80.08 (±5.07)	9550 features 30.28 (±1.85)	550 features 93.77(±0.77)
Dense SIFT	500 features 94.05(±2.13)	300 features 75.92(+2.85)	300 features 53.23(±3.37)	500 features 89.84(±1.18)
LBPV	54 features 93.51(±1.89)	54 features 91.32(±2.27)	54 features 78.01(±2.68)	54 features 91.58(±1.32)
P. Method	**100 features** **93.51%(±2.43)**	**100 features** **93.40%(±1.56)**	**100 features** **80.76%(±2.48)**	**100 features** **91.01%(±1.37)**
P. Method	**800 features** **96.85%(±2.05)**	**800 features** **95.83%(±0.98)**	**700 features** **86.34%(±1.92)**	**1000 features** **94.00%(±1.61)**

present in KTH - Tips database, such as changes in scale, color, illumination and even dimension of the images.

As the results show, the proposed method has overcome traditional texture analysis methods including the Dense SIFT with BOVW. These experiments ensure that the method has good invariance and generalization power, keeping excellent results in the four databases. This method shows that the combination between CN and BOVW provides a high level of texture discrimination.

5   Conclusion

In this work, a novel method to texture analysis was proposed. Using two approaches (Complex Networks and Bag-Of-Visual-Words), it was possible to extract texture descriptors based on the degree and strength of each vertex. CN theory allows to representing texture as networks, and BOVW build a vocabulary of visual words based on CN topology properties. Results show that the proposed method overcomes traditional methods in four widely used databases.

As future works, we intend to extract information only to relevant vertices, instead of the whole network. This will ensure an improvement in the computational cost, and can result in a reduction in the number of visual words.

References

1. Azencott, R., Wang, J.P., Younes, L.: Texture classification using windowed fourier filters. IEEE Transactions on Pattern Analysis and Machine Intelligence **19**(2), 148–153 (1997)

2. Backes, A.R., Casanova, D., Bruno, O.M.: Color texture analysis based on fractal descriptors. Pattern Recognition **45**(5), 1984–1992 (2012)
3. Backes, A.R., Casanova, D., Bruno, O.M.: Texture analysis and classification: A complex network-based approach. Information Sciences **219**, 168–180 (2013)
4. Boccaletti, S., Latora, V., Moreno, Y., Chavez, M., Hwang, D.U.: Complex networks: Structure and dynamics. Physics Reports **424**(4), 175–308 (2006)
5. Brodatz, P.: Textures: a photographic album for artists and designers. Dover Pubns (1966)
6. Chalumeau, T., Meriaudeau, F., Laligant, O., Costa, L.D.F.: Complex networks: application for texture characterization and classification. In: ELCVIA: Electronic Letters on Computer Vision and Image Analysis, vol. 7, pp. 093–100 (2008)
7. Costa, L.D.F., Rodrigues, F.A., Travieso, G., Villas Boas, P.R.: Characterization of complex networks: A survey of measurements. Advances in Physics **56**(1), 167–242 (2007)
8. Costa, L.D.F., Oliveira Jr, O.N., Travieso, G., Rodrigues, F.A., Villas Boas, P.R., Antiqueira, L., Viana, M.P., Correa Rocha, L.E.: Analyzing and modeling real-world phenomena with complex networks: a survey of applications. Advances in Physics **60**(3), 329–412 (2011)
9. Csurka, G., Dance, C., Fan, L., Willamowski, J., Bray, C.: Visual categorization with bags of keypoints. In: ECCV International Workshop on Statistical Learning in Computer Vision, pp. 1–22 (2004)
10. Gonçalves, W.N., Machado, B.B., Bruno, O.M.: A complex network approach for dynamic texture recognition. Neurocomputing, 211–220 (2015)
11. Gonçalves, W.N., de Andrade Silva, J., Bruno, O.M.: A rotation invariant face recognition method based on complex network. In: Bloch, I., Cesar Jr, R.M. (eds.) CIARP 2010. LNCS, vol. 6419, pp. 426–433. Springer, Heidelberg (2010)
12. Guo, Z., Zhang, L., Zhang, D.: Rotation invariant texture classification using LBP variance (lbpv) with global matching. Pattern Recognition **43**(3), 706–719 (2010)
13. Haralick, R.M., Shanmugam, K., Dinstein, I.H.: Textural features for image classification. IEEE Transactions on Systems, Man and Cybernetics **6**, 610–621 (1973)
14. Hayman, E., Caputo, B., Fritz, M., Eklundh, J.-O.: On the significance of real-world conditions for material classification. In: Pajdla, T., Matas, J. (eds.) ECCV 2004. LNCS, vol. 3024, pp. 253–266. Springer, Heidelberg (2004)
15. Jain, A.K., Farrokhnia, F.: Unsupervised texture segmentation using gabor filters. In: Proceedings of the IEEE International Conference on Systems, Man and Cybernetics, 1990, pp. 14–19. IEEE (1990)
16. Pickard, R., Graszyk, C., Mann, S., Wachman, J., Pickard, L., Campbell, L.: Vistex database. Media Lab., MIT, Cambridge, Massachusetts (1995). http://vismod. media.mit.edu/vismod/imagery/VisionTexture/vistex.html
17. Varma, M., Garg, R.: Locally invariant fractal features for statistical texture classification. In: IEEE 11th International Conference on Computer Vision, ICCV 2007, pp. 1–8. IEEE (2007)
18. Zhang, J., Tan, T.: Brief review of invariant texture analysis methods. Pattern Recognition **35**(3), 735–747 (2002)

Bregman Divergence Applied to Hierarchical Segmentation Problems

Daniela Portes L. Ferreira[1]([✉]), André R. Backes[1], and Celia A. Zorzo Barcelos[2]

[1] Faculdade de Computação, Universidade Federal de Uberlândia, Uberlândia, Brazil
[2] Faculdade de Matemática, Universidade Federal de Uberlândia, Uberlândia, Brazil
daniela.portes@iftm.edu.br

Abstract. Image segmentation is one of the first steps in any process concerning digital image analysis and its accuracy will go on to determine the quality of this analysis. A classic model used in image segmentation is the Mumford-Shah functional, which includes both the information to pertaining the region and the length of its borders. In this work, by using the concept of loss in Bregman Information a functional is defined which is a generalization of the Mumford-Shah functional, once it is obtained from the proposed function by means of the Squared Euclidean distance as a measure of similarity. The algorithm is constructed by using a fusion criterion, which minimizes the loss in Bregman Information. It is shown that the proposed hierarchical segmentation method generalizes the algorithm which minimizes the piecewise constant Mumford-Shah functional. The results obtained through use of the *Generalized I-Divergence*, *Itakura-Saito* and *Squared Euclidean* distance, show that the algorithm attained a good performance.

Keywords: Hierarchical segmentation · Mumford-Shah functional · Fusion region

1 Introduction

The segmentation of images is one of the first steps in any process concerning digital image analysis and its accuracy determines the quality of this analysis. The main goal of segmentation is to subdivide an image into homogeneous groups called regions. Homogeneity can be measured in terms of color, texture, motion, depth, etc. For the purpose of this study, it is measured through the similarity of the gray levels. Thus, the regions are formed by pixels, connected or not, and which are grouped by a criterion that determines the similarity or dissimilarity of their values, thereby generating a single partition [1].

Determining how image segmentation should be performed is not an easy task to solve, since the level of detail to which it is accomplished will depend

C.A.Z. Barcelos—The authors gratefully acknowledge the financial support of CNPQ (National Council for Scientific and Technological Development, Brazil) (Grants ♯207513/2014 − 7, ♯305812/2013 − 0, ♯475819/2012 − 8).

A. Pardo and J. Kittler (Eds.): CIARP 2015, LNCS 9423, pp. 493–500, 2015.
DOI: 10.1007/978-3-319-25751-8_59

on the observer along with the complexity of the problem to be solved. The representation of all possible regions pertaining to the image is called Hierarchical Partition $\mathcal{H}$ of the image. Image segmentation is obtained from the $\mathcal{H}$ Hierarchy constructed by selecting a partition from the set. This approach allows regions to be selected at different scales or sections of the image, [4].

A classic model used in segmentation of an image I is the Mumford- Shah functional, [6]. The segmentation procedure that uses this variational model partitions I into X_i sets obtained by the agglomeration of regions, considering both the information of the region and the length of its boundaries.

In this paper, the authors propose the use of the concept of Bregman Information, presented by Banerjee et al. [2] as an alternative to the construction of the hierarchy $\mathcal{H}$. The proposed method is a development of the minimization algorithm in discrete form the Mumford-Shah functional presented in [5], differentiated by the fusion criterion and also the widespread similarity measure through the concept of Bregman Information. Thus, $\mathcal{H}$ is obtained by a fusion algorithm in which the loss in Bregman Information is minimized. The Bregman Information used for the functional can be defined using different metrics derived from the Bregman divergence.

2   Bregman Information

2.1   Bregman Divergence

Definition: *Given a convex function* $\varphi : \mathbb{R}^n \to \mathbb{R}$ *the corresponding Bregman Divergence between* x *and* $y \in dom(\varphi)$ *is given by:*

$$d_\varphi(x,y) = \varphi(x) - \varphi(y) - \langle \nabla\varphi(y), x - y \rangle$$

where $\nabla\varphi(y)$ *is the gradient vector of* φ *in* y *[3].*

A low mathematical accuracy of this definition is presented in Fig.1.

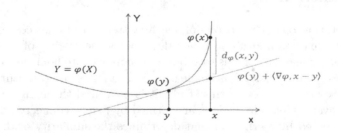

Fig. 1. Geometric interpretation of Bregman Divergence.

Different choices for the convex function f induces different metrics, Table 1 contains some convex functions f with their respective Bregman Divergences [2].

In [2], the authors use the divergence of Bregman to measure the distortion rate of Shannon, thus introducing the concept of Bregman Information.

Table 1. Convex Functions x Bregman Divergence.

Domain	$\varphi(x)$	$d_\varphi(x,y)$	Distance
$\mathbb{R}^d$	$\mathbf{x}^2$	$\mathbf{x} - \mathbf{y}^2$	Squared Euclidean Distance
$\mathbb{R}_{++}$	$-\log x$	$\frac{x}{y} - \log(\frac{x}{y}) - 1$	Itakura-Saito Distance
d-Simplex	$\sum_{j=1}^d x_j \log_2 x_j$	$\sum_{j=1}^d x_j \log_2(\frac{x_j}{y_j})$	KL-Divergence
$\mathbb{R}_+^d$	$\sum_{j=1}^d x_j \log x_j$	$\sum_{j=1}^d x_j \log(\frac{x_j}{y_j}) - \sum_{j=1}^d (x_j - y_j)$	Generalized I-Divergence

From this concept, the problem of finding a partition and its representatives is presented as a problem of minimizing the loss in Bregman Information. In the following sections, a summary of these concepts is presented, with a more detailed study established in [2].

2.2 Bregman Information

Definition: *Let X be a random variable with values in* $X = \{x_i\}_{i=1}^n \subset S \subset \mathbb{R}^n$ *with a discrete probability distribution* $v = \{v_i\}$. *Given the divergence of Bregman* d_φ, *the Bregman Information of the X, in relation to* φ *is given by:*

$$I(X) = \min_{s \in ri(S)} \sum_{i=1}^n v_i d_\varphi(x_i, s).$$

The vector s, which makes the above mentioned functional minimal will be called the **Bregman Representative of X**. This representative does not depend on the choice of Bregman divergence and it is the value expected for the random variable X, [2]. So taking $s = \mu = \sum_{i=1}^n v_i x_i$ one has:

$$I(X) = \sum_{i=1}^n v_i d_\varphi(x_i, \mu). \tag{1}$$

2.3 Loss in Bregman Information

Let $\mathbf{X}$ be a random variable that take values in a finite set $X = \{x_i\}_{i=1}^n \subset S \subset \mathbb{R}^n$ following a probability measure v. Let $\wp = \{R_h\}_{h=1}^k$ be a partitioning of X with their respective Bregman representatives. If $M = \{\mu_h\}_{h=1}^k$ is the set of those representatives and $p = \{p_h\}_{h=1}^k$ with $p_h = \sum_{x_i \in R_h} v_i$ as a measure of probability in M, it has the variable induced $\mathbf{M}$ with values in M and the probability of distribution p. Thus $\mathbf{R_h}$ is a random variable with values in R_h following the probability distribution $\frac{v_i}{p_h}$ to $x_i \in R_h$, [2].

Note that $I_\varphi(\mathbf{X})$ is the "Bregman Total Information" while $I_\varphi(\mathbf{M})$ is the "Bregman Information between regions". The difference $L_\varphi(\mathbf{M}) = I_\varphi(\mathbf{X}) - I_\varphi(\mathbf{M})$ is called **Loss in Bregman Information** and represents the "Bregman Information within regions",[2]. Applying Bregman Information definition given in (1), it follows that:

$$L_\varphi(\mathbf{M}) = \sum_{h=1}^k \sum_{i=1}^n v_i d_\varphi(x_i, \mu_h). \tag{2}$$

$L_\varphi(\mathbf{M})$ measures the Information Loss occurred when performing the partition of X. Thus, the smaller the loss in Bregman Information better will be the performed partition.

If $k = n$, i.e., the number k of regions is equal to the size of X, then there is no loss of information. On the other hand if all elements of the set X are grouped into a single set, the loss of information is given by the Bregman Information of the **X**, in other words, $L_\varphi(\mathbf{M}) = I_\varphi(\mathbf{X})$ where $M = \{\mu\}$ and μ is the Bregman representative of the **X**.

Based on the above definitions presented, the problem of determining a partition for a given image $I = \{x_i\}_{i=1}^n$ may be formulated as an optimization problem of $L_\varphi(\mathbf{M})$. The goal is to determine $M = \{\mu_h\}_{h=1}^k$ such that $L_\varphi(\mathbf{M})$ is minimal.

3 Proposed Method

The main idea of the proposed method is to combine Bregman Information of regions with boundaries, to obtain a hierarchical partition. With the hierarchical structure constructed, the problem of targeting becomes the locating of the desired partition in the hierarchy, which can be performed by establishing a threshold for the number of end regions.

Let $I = \{x_i\}$ be all the pixels of a given image, $\wp = \{R_h\}_{h=1}^k$ an I partition with their respective Bregman representatives, $M = \{\mu_h\}_{h=1}^k$ and K the set of all the boundaries between the regions obtained by the partition. For the construction of the hierarchical structure a region merging algorithm is used, whose purpose is to determine the sets of representatives M and boundaries K, which minimize the functional defined by:

$$E_\varphi(M, K) = \sum_{h=1}^k \sum_{x_i \in X_h} v_i d_\varphi(x_i, \mu_h) + \lambda l(K) = L_\varphi(\mathbf{M}) + \lambda l(K). \qquad (3)$$

where:

- $E_\varphi(M, K)$ is the energy of the functional in function of the image $X = \{x_i\}_{i=1}^n$ and the K boundaries between regions.
- $l(K)$ is the length of the boundaries K.
- λ is a scale parameter [7].

Note that the segmentation of the functional defined in equation (3) is a problem of minimizing the loss in Bregman Information $L_\varphi(\mathbf{M})$, plus a regularization term that controls the length of boundaries K that divide regions.

Due to the large quantity of points in image I, for a hierarchical partition, we constructed the Region Adjacency Graph (RAG) for the pixels in the image. Thus, the fusion is performed only to neighboring regions that meet the criteria of similarity. For each graph edge, there is associated a minimum value α which indicates the cost of fusion. Later, the regions are merged iteratively following the criterion of fusion, usually this criterion involves minimizing the cost of the fusion. Each time a pair of regions is joined, a new node is created in the tree. This new node is attached to the pair of nodes, that are now called "children nodes", and a new value α is assigned to the "father node". The algorithm stops when there is only one region in RAG. The cost and fusion criteria used in this study are presented below.

3.1   Fusion Cost

Merging two adjoining regions is interesting if its result is better than the previous representation, that is, if the energy $E_\varphi(X)$, considering the joined regions, is less than when these were separated. From this statement the criterion used in the fusion algorithm is constructed.

Consider the adjacent regions $R_1 = \{x_1, ..., x_l\}$ and $R_2 = \{x_{l+1}, ..., x_m\}$ such that $R = \{x_1, ..., x_m\}$. If $\mathbf{X_u}$ is a random variable with values in X_u following the probability distribution v_i the Bregman representative of $\mathbf{X_u}$ is $\mu = \sum_{i=1}^m v_i x_i$.

Note that $X_d = \{R_1, R_2\}$ is a partition from X_u and $M = \{\mu_h\}_{h=1}^2$ the respective set of Bregman representatives. Considering $p = \{p_h\}_{h=1}^2$ with $p_h = \sum_{x_i \in R_h} v_i$ as a probability measure in M, we have the induced variable $\mathbf{M}$ with values in M and the probability distribution p. The regions $\mathbf{R_h}$ are random variables with values in R_h following the probability distributions $\frac{v_i}{p_h}$ for each $x_i \in R_h$. Bregman representatives of the variables $\mathbf{R_1}$ and $\mathbf{R_2}$ are given by: $\mu_1 = \sum_{i=1}^l \frac{v_i}{p_1} x_i$ and $\mu_2 = \sum_{i=l+1}^m \frac{v_i}{p_2} x_i$, respectively.

The Bregman representative s, from $\mathbf{M}$, is the expected value of $\mathbf{M}$, these means: $s = \sum_{h=1}^2 p_h \mu_h = p_1 \sum_{i=1}^l \frac{v_i}{p_1} x_i + p_2 \sum_{i=l+2}^m \frac{v_i}{p_2} x_i = \sum_{i=1}^m v_i x_i = \mu$.

From definition (1) one has:

$$I_\varphi(\mathbf{M}) = \sum_{h=1}^2 p_h d_\varphi(\mu_h, \mu) = p_1 d_\varphi(\mu_1, \mu) + p_2 d_\varphi(\mu_2, \mu). \tag{4}$$

One also observes that the loss in Bregman Information given by the X_d partition is $L_\varphi(M) = I_\varphi(\mathbf{X_u}) - I_\varphi(\mathbf{M})$.

In order to define the fusion criterion the difference between the energy obtained by considering the fusion regions, $E_\varphi(M_u, K_u)$, and that obtained when they remain separate, $E_\varphi(M, K)$, should be calculated. If there is no partition to X_u, the set K_u is empty. Therefore, $l(K_u) = 0$. In this manner one obtains from equation (3) that

$$E_\varphi(M_u, K_u) = L_\varphi(\mathbf{M_u}) + \lambda l(K_u) = L_\varphi(\mathbf{M_u}) = I_\varphi(\mathbf{X_u}); \tag{5}$$

Let K be a unitary set whose element is the boundary between R_1 and R_2.

$$E_\varphi(M, K) = L_\varphi(\mathbf{M}) + \lambda l(K); \tag{6}$$

Thus, using equations (4), (5) and (6), a definition is made as follows, the cost of the fusion $\Delta_\varphi(R_1, R_2)$ of the regions R_1 and R_2 are defined in the following.

Definition: Let φ a relatively convex and differentiable function, $R_1 = \{x_1, ..., x_l\}$ and $R_2 = \{x_{l+1}, ..., x_m\}$ two adjacent subsets of X with Bregman representatives, μ_1 and μ_2 respectively. Let $M = \{\mu_1, \mu_2\}$ be an interior set of $dom(\varphi)$. Consider $\mathbf{X}$ as a random variable with values in X following the probability distribution v_i. Being $p = \{p_h\}_{h=1}^2$ with $p_h = \sum_{x_i \in R_h} v_i$ a probability measure on M and K being a unitary set whose element is the boundary between R_1 and R_2. Then,

$$\Delta_\varphi(R_1, R_2) = E_\varphi(M_u, K_u) - E_\varphi(M, K), \text{ or}$$
$$\Delta_\varphi(R_1, R_2) = p_1 d_\varphi(\mu_1, \mu) + p_2 d_\varphi(\mu_2, \mu) - \lambda l(K). \tag{7}$$

Note that the fusion cost is calculated using only the Bregman representatives of the regions instead of all the elements of R_1 and R_2. This procedure is analogous to that shown in [8].

One observes that if $\mathbf{X}$ follows a uniform probability distribution, this means $p_1 = \sum_{x_i \in R_1} v_i = \sum_{i=1}^l \frac{1}{m} = \frac{l}{m}$ and $p_2 = \sum_{x_i \in R_2} v_i = \sum_{i=l+1}^m \frac{1}{m} = \frac{m-l}{m}$.
Hence,

$$\Delta_\varphi(R_1, R_2) = \frac{l}{m} d_\varphi(\mu_1, \mu) + \frac{m-l}{m} d_\varphi(\mu_2, \mu) - \lambda l(K). \tag{8}$$

Considering the convex and differentiable function $\varphi = \|.\|_2$, the Bregman divergence is the Euclidean distance, which is, $d_\varphi(x, y) = \|x - y\|_2^2$. Therefore,

$$\Delta_\varphi(R_1, R_2) = \frac{l}{m} \|\mu_1 - \mu\|_2^2 + \frac{m-l}{m} \|\mu_2 - \mu\|_2^2 - \lambda l(K), \text{ where} \tag{9}$$

$$l = |R_1| \text{ and } m - l = |R_2|. \tag{10}$$

Furthermore:

$$\|\mu_1 - \mu\|_2 = \frac{|R_2| \|\mu_1 - \mu_2\|_2}{|R_1| + |R_2|} \text{ and } \|\mu_2 - \mu\|_2 = \frac{|R_1| \|\mu_1 - \mu_2\|_2}{|R_1| + |R_2|}. \tag{11}$$

Replacing the equations (10) and (11) in (9) one has:

$$\Delta_\varphi(R_1, R_2) = \frac{|R_1| |R_2|}{|R_1| + |R_2|} \|\mu_1 - \mu_2\|_2^2 - \lambda l(K). \tag{12}$$

Equation (12) is the discretized form of the Mumford-Shah functional, one of the most robust methods used in image segmentation [5].

The decision to merge two regions is not made based on the simple comparison of the two regions, but considering if the union results in a better approximation, that is, a consideration is made as to how much $\Delta_\varphi(R_i, R_j)$ is less than zero. In this manner, the fusion of (R_i, R_j) occurs if for each R_i with $\Delta_\varphi(R_i, R_.) < 0$, $\Delta_\varphi(R_i, R_j)$ is minimal.

3.2 Algorithm

Let $I = \{x_i\}$ be the set of pixels in a given image and $\wp = \{R_k\}$ a partition from I. The initial partition can be obtained by considering each pixel as an image region, that is, causing $R_i = x_i, \forall i$.

1. Set the $\wp$ initial partition;
2. Input a value for the scale parameter λ;

3. While $|\wp| > 1$
   (a) Calculate cost $\Delta_\varphi(R_i, R_j)$ as defined in (7) for each pair of adjacent regions the fusion;
   (b) Find the set C of all pairs of adjacent regions in which $\Delta_\varphi(R_i, R_j) < 0$;
   (c) While a pair $C_{ij} \in C$ is selected
      i. Select the pair $C_{ij} = (R_i; R_j)$ following the fusion criterion;
      ii. Replace in $\wp$, R_i and R_j with the union of these regions;
      iii. Remove from C all pairs containing R_i or R_j;
   (d) End-While;
   (e) Increase λ;
4. End-While;

The λ increment can be linear, polynomial or exponential. The algorithm performs a multi-scale segmentation, depending on this parameter. The increase in λ value enables the fusion of regions that will remain separated with lower values of this parameter.

4   Obtained Results

In the experiments, one observed the ability of the described method to capture the regions using different choices of Bregman Divergence. The performance was analyzed for the methods of three Bregman Information definitions given by the divergence: *Generalized I-divergence*, *Itakura-Saito* and *Squared Euclidean*. The last, as previously shown, generates the discretized form of the Mumford-Shah functional(MS).

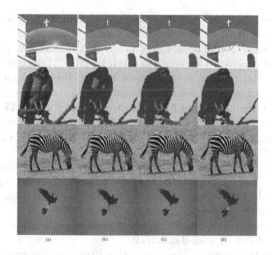

Fig. 2. (a) original images, (b) segmented images using *Squared Euclidean* distance, (c) segmented images using *Generalized I-divergence* , (d) segmented images using *Itakura-Saito*.

The parameter λ as well as the method used for increasing the λ depends on the choice of Bregman Divergence. In this work for *Generalized I-divergence* and *Itakura-Saito*, the parameter was increased linearly while for the *Squared Euclidean* an exponential increase was chosen. Fig. 2 shows the results obtained using the Bregman divergences mentioned above. One observes that the algorithm performed well in all models. Methods using the divergences *Generalized I-divergence* and *Itakura-Saito* have similar results to the discrete model of MS.

5 Concluding Remarks

The applicability of systems involving the search for similarity depends on the distance chosen. Moreover, in many applications it is not clear which is the most appropriate metric. Thus, several studies have been conducted in order to develop methods that are efficient for a family of distance functions that share similar properties. In this sense, we propose a functional which generalizes the Mumford-Shah Funcional. We propose the use the Bregman Information concept as an alternative to constructing a hierarchical segmentation method. From this concept, the method allows the use of different similarity measures as well as it allowing to update E_φ, during the merging process, with a computational cost that does not depend of the size of the intervening regions.

The results presented herein were obtained using the *Generalized I-divergence*, *Itakura-Saito* and *Squared Euclidean*, which demonstrate the good performance of the algorithm for these different choices.

References

1. Burrus, N., Thierry, M.B., Jolion, J.M.: Image segmentation by a contrario simulation. Pattern Recognition **42**(7), 1520–1532 (2009)
2. Banerjee, A., Merugu, S., Dhillon, I.S., Ghosh, J.: Clustering with Bregman divergences. Journal of Machine Learning Research **6**, 1705–1749 (2005)
3. Bregman, L.M.: The relaxation method of finding the common point of convex sets and its application to the solution of problems in convex programming. USSR, Computational Mathematics and Mathematical Physics **200–217** (1967)
4. Cardelino, J., Bertalmio, M., Caselles, V., Randall G.: A contrario hierarchical segmentation. In: 16th IEEE International Conference Image Processing (ICIP), pp. 4041–4044 (2009)
5. Koepfler, G., Lopez, C., Morel, J.M.: A multi scale algorithm for image segmentation by variational method. SIAM Journal on Numerical Analysis **31**(1), 282–299 (1994)
6. Mumford, D., Shah, J.: Optimal approximations by piecewise smooth functions and associated variational problems. Pure Appl. Math. (1989)
7. Petitot, J.: An introduction to the Mumford-Shah segmentation model. Journal of Physiology, Paris **97**(2–3), 335–342 (2003)
8. Telgarsky, M. and Dasgupta, S.: Agglomerative Bregman clustering. In: Proc. ICML (2012)

SALSA – A Simple Automatic Lung Segmentation Algorithm

Addson Costa and Bruno M. Carvalho$^{(\boxtimes)}$

Departamento de Informática e Matemática Aplicada,
Federal University of Rio Grande do Norte, Natal, RN 59078-970, Brazil
addson.costa@gmail.com, bruno@dimap.ufrn.br

Abstract. This work proposes the use of SALSA (*A Simple Automatic Lung Segmentation Algorithm*), a simple and fast algorithm for the segmentation of Computerized Tomography lung volumes. The algorithm is composed by the application of several simple image processing operations. The algorithm was tested on the database provided by LOLA11, a lung segmentation challenge that took part during the MICCAI 2011. The obtained results put SALSA's accuracy rate very close to the accuracy rates of the methods on the top of the LOLA11 ranking. We are currently at the stage of developing the method for segmenting the lung lobes, a more challenging task.

Keywords: Image segmentation · Lung segmentation · Cut adjustment

1 Introduction

Since its invention, the usage of Computerized Tomography (CT) images for diagnostic purposes has revolutionized the medical practice. However, the analysis of pulmonary tomographic images is a demanding task due to the high amounts of data involved, that have to be segmented. There are several semi-automatic and automatic methods for performing this task, with varying computational efficiency and accuracy values. The method proposed in this work uses several simple and well known image processing operations, such as the 3D FloodFill algorithm [1], to segment the volumes based on the voxel intensities and their relationship with their neighborhoods.

The Computer Aided Diagnostic (CAD) is an application area that is going through a fast expansion due to the the ever growing requirements of obtaining fast diagnostics when working with large and complex data volumes. In Pulmonology, the lung segmentation is the first step in obtaining the diagnostic for a patient. The segmentation algorithm must be robust to several problems that may be present in the CT volumes, such as the presence of artifacts, noise or the abnormal formation of the lungs, as can be seen in Figure 1.

This paper is organized as follows: This section introduces the problem and contextualizes it, while Section 2 briefly summarizes some of the related work. Section 3 describes in detail the proposed method, whose results are discussed in Section 4. Finally, Section 5 shows comments about the work done and points out the future developments associated with this work.

© Springer International Publishing Switzerland 2015
A. Pardo and J. Kittler (Eds.): CIARP 2015, LNCS 9423, pp. 501–508, 2015.
DOI: 10.1007/978-3-319-25751-8_60

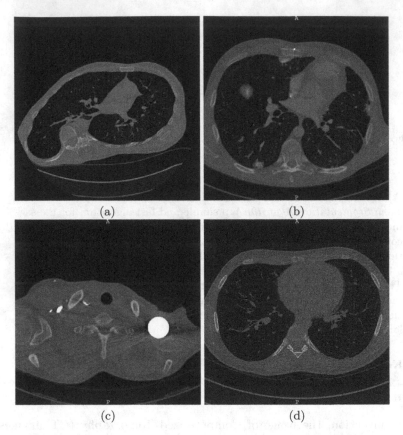

(a)   (b)

(c)   (d)

Fig. 1. Examples of volumes with anomalies in the LOLA11 database [9]: (a) Bad formation of lungs, (b) Lung with a disease (c) CT volume with metal artifacts (d) Volume with high level of noise.

2   Related Work

The task of performing semi or fully automatic lung segmentation is one that has been successfully approached before [6], even though it had not been thoroughly evaluated in some cases. In 2011, during the 14th International Conference on Medical Image Computing and Computer Assisted Intervention (MICCAI), a challenge of lobe and lung segmentation (LOLA11) [9] was held as a part of the Workshop on Pulmonary Analysis. The intent was to set up a database with common as well as challenging CT chest volumes for analyzing the performance and robustness of lung and lobe segmentation algorithms.

The LOLA11 database consists of 55 volumes of varied sizes, with the cans coming from different sources and representing a variety of clinically common scanners and protocols. The scans were selected such that the lung segmentation is classified as *easy* in approximately half of the scans, and *hard* in the other half.

The results produced by the proposed methods are submitted to a web server, that analyzes the accuracy of the methods against manually segmented ground truth volumes and ranks them on the LOLA11 web site[1]. To ensure consistent evaluation, the organizers of the workshop and maintainers of the web site do not make available the reference (ground truth) segmentations.

Up to the time of the writing of this paper, other 16 groups have had their results published in the LOLA11 web site. We now briefly describe some of these methods.

The group labeled *Human* uses a second human observer to manually segment all images and analyzes the variability between these segmentations and the ground truth provided by LOLA11 [9].

The method proposed by Lassen et al. [7] uses a low resolution version of the volume to detect the lungs and determine an appropriate threshold. Then, a region growing method is used on the high resolution volume. The trachea is found by looking for appropiate 2D objects in slices. After that, the method employs a watershed to enhance the lung separation, as well as other operations to remove leakages and to include blood vessels. The technique proposed by Weinheimer et al. [12] starts the processing by looking for the trachcobronchial tree. Then, a 3D region growing method searches for low density structures (lungs) and the result of this operation is processed by a hole filling algorithm to include high density structures, e.g. blood vessels, in the segmented object. If a single component is found, a lung separation operation is performed by using a method that searches for a minimum separation between the lungs.

The method proposed by Pinho et al. [8] is divided into 4 main steps: background removal, trachea localization, airway tree segmentation, and graph cut segmentation to separate the lungs. Morphological operations of opening and closing are then used to produce the final result. The method proposed by Korn et al. [5] employs a region growing method based on density, geometry and shape information. The method is divided into 4 steps by first segmenting the lungs, followed by the refinement of this segmentation, the segmentation of the trachea and bronchi, and the refinement of the separation between the lungs, where all of this steps are performed by growing or shrinking objects based on geometrical shape or density information surrounding the analyzed voxels.

The method of Sun et al. [11] uses an algorithm of rib detection to initialize two active shape models to approximately segment the lungs, and then adapts the model to the data by using an algorithm that also receives as input a segmentation of the trachea and main bronchi, to find optimal surfaces of the lungs. The method of Gu et al. [2] executes an initial approximated lung segmentation, and then proceed to detect correct problems in the segmentation by detecting know landmarks, such as ribs, lung bottom boundaries and using an elastic registration method to match the detected landmarks to a predefined template.

The method of Hosseini-Asl et al. [3] first removes the background surrounding the patient's body. Then, the visual appearance of the 3D volume is modeled using an Incremental Sparse Non-negative Matrix Factorization (ISNMF), gen-

---

[1] http://www.lola11.com/

erating a voxel distribution in a feature space. The volume is then segmented by clustering the voxels in this space using K-means. Finally, the 3D segmented regions are refined through a connected component analysis.

3   SALSA

In this paper, we prose the algorithm SALSA (Simple Automatic Lung Segmentation Algorithm), that is formed by composing several simple image processing operations to perform the lung segmentation task. The work flow of the algorithm can be seen in Figure 3 and it is described below.

After the original image is loaded, we apply a thresholding operation followed by the search of seed voxels in each lung (Figure 3a). The threshold is set at $-239HU$ which was enough to guarantee that all lung voxels are selected. Small variations of this value do not affect the overall results produced by the algorithm. Then, the seed search step looks for voxels on the same y line on an axial slice which have the most lung voxels between them. This process is repeated for all slices that have lung voxels, while also estimating the maximum width and height of the lungs on axial slices.

The seeds found in the previous step are used to perform an intensity based growing boundary search, to segment the respiratory system (Figure 3b). This task is performed by analyzing the $5 \times 5 \times 5$ neighborhoods of all neighbors of the

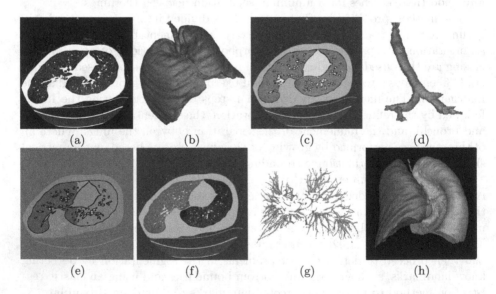

Fig. 2. Work flow of the SALSA algorithm: (a) Thresholded image; (b) Boundary object delineating the respiratory system; (c) Background detection (d) Detected trachea; (e) Initial lung cut definition; (f) Final cut adjustment using Sobel operator; (g) Detected vessel tree; and (h) Final 3D rendering of left and right lungs.

seed voxels. An analyzed voxel is also labeled as boundary voxel and included in the processing queue if its neighborhood contains more than a certain number of background voxels, where this number is determined varies according to the estimated noise level. This process is repeated until the processing queue is empty. This detected boundary includes the lungs and trachea objects, but not the vessels. We then use the 2D FloodFill algorithm to segment the background outside the 2D axial boundary of the previous step (pink and reddish hues of Figure 3c) and the background inside the 2D axial boundary of the previous step (yellow hue of Figure 3c).

The trachea is found based on its anatomy, as we search for a tubular structure. Since some of the volumes are ordered in the opposite direction (equivalent to upside down), we search for it in both directions. This search is performed by looking for connected components in 3D and comparing the areas of the connected component on adjacent slices. If these areas do not vary much throughout the structure, it is assumed to be a tubular structure, and if its height is larger than a threshold, the trachea is detected and segmented. A result can be seen in Figure 3d.

At this point, we have the segmented the background and the trachea and we need to check if the lungs touch each other, and separate them, if necessary. To avoid leakages, we make a cut in the image based on the position of the two seeds found before, producing an initial separation (Figure 3e). After that, the cuts are analyzed and adjusted by optimizing the cut area using a local search [10], such that we have the smallest possible number of voxels of a lung traversing the cut. Several independent cuts can be moved in different directions on each image, since the lungs may be connected in several points. We also use the result of the application of a Sobel filter to guide those cuts, producing cleaner cuts, as can be seen in Figure 3f. Note that, since these leakages occur in small localized areas and the initial cuts are close to the optimal cuts, it is more efficient to look for local adjustments of these cuts instead of running a mincut/maxflow algorithm to globally optimize the cut.

After the last step, we need to include the voxels that belong to vessels. We do that by adding all voxels that touch the computed boundary and belong to a tubular object (Figure 3g). Then, we paint the lungs according to the standard set by the LOLA11 Challenge [9], producing the result seen on Figure 3h.

4   Experiments

The validation of the proposed method was performed using the database provided by the LOLA11 Challenge [9], containing 55 CT chest images, with approximately half of them being considered hard.

The LOLA11 Challenge web site allows somebody to submit the segmentation results following their instructions, and computes the *Maximum Overlap* (accuracies) of the submitted results against their manually labeled ground truth. The Maximum Overlap rate is computed by translating the submitted results a few voxels on each axis, computing the intersection between them and the ground truth references, and keeping the highest score for each volume.

The results below were obtained by applying SALSA to all 55 images of the LOLA11 database, using a notebook with a I5-3337U CPU running at 1.8Ghz, with 4Gb of RAM DDR3-1600 and an SS disk.

The Table 1 shows the Maximum Overlap rates of the segmented volumes against the LOLA11 ground truth volumes, where *mean* indicates the mean value, *std* the standard deviation, *min* the minimum value, *Q1* the first quartile, *med* the median, *Q3* the third quartile, and *max* maximum values for the 55 volumes.

Table 1. Maximum Overlap rates for the 55 volumes of the LOLA11 Challenge database.

obj	mean	std	min	Q1	med	Q3	max
LL	0.959	0.108	0.213	0.968	0.985	0.989	0.994
RL	0.957	0.135	0.015	0.978	0.986	0.991	0.995
score	0.958						

The execution times for all volumes averaged approximately 44s, ranging from 10 to 248 seconds when applied to the 55 volumes. We can see in Figure 4 an example of the segmentation of a lung with an abnormality produced by SALSA. The images were generated using the ITK-SNAP software [4].

We now summarize the results of the automatic segmentation methods submitted to LOLA11 [9] website. Weinheimer et al. [12] achieved a Maximum Overlap of 0.964 (without morphological closing) and 0.97 (with morphological closing). The average execution time on a computer with an Intel Xeon processor running at 2.83 GHz with 4GB RAM was 7.3 minutes without and 11.4 minutes with the morphological closing. Lassen et al. [7] achieved Maximum Overlap of 0.973 running on a standard quad-core Windows computer with 8 GB de RAM, taking about 1 minute per case, on average, with the individual times ranging from 0.5 to 3 minutes.

Pinho et al. [8] achieved Maximum Overlap of 0.948, Gu et al. [2] achieved Maximum Overlap of 0.939 and Hosseini et al. [3] achieved Maximum Overlap of 0.965. They did not provide execution times.

Korn et al. [5], achieved Maximum Overlap of 0.949 and reported an average execution time was 12.6 minutos on a notebook Dell with an Intel Core2 Duo T9600 CPU running at 2.8Ghz with 4GB RAM, while Sun et al. [11], achieved Maximum Overlap of 0.949 with average execution time of about 6 minutos, but the computer used in the experiments was not described.

In the LOLA11 Challenge [9], the best result was achieved by the Human segmentation, that produced manually annotated segmentations following the protocol defined by the challenge, resulting in a Maximum Overlap rate of 0.984.

O SALSA achieved better Maximum Overlap rates than seven algorithms, such as Gu et al. [2], Pinho et al. [8], Korn et al. [5], Sun et al. [11], and worse rates than seven algorithms, such as Weinheimer et al. [12], Lassen et al. [7] and

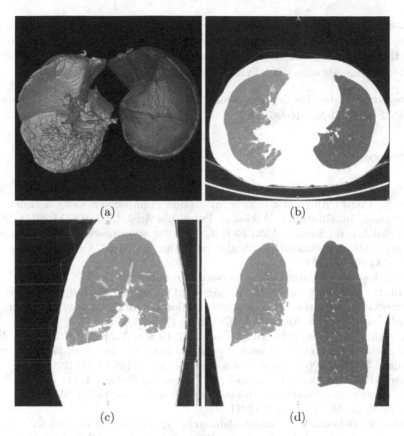

(a)   (b)

(c)   (d)

Fig. 3. Segmentation of a lung with an abnormality (lola11-02 sample): (a) Surface rendering of the lungs, (b) Axial, (c) Sagital, and (d) Coronal slices of the volume.

Hosseini et al. [3]. However, our average result is only 0.022 points (2.2%) below the Maximum Overlap average rate of the best automatic segmentation method.

Since the execution times were measured on different machines, we cannot compare the absolute values directly. However, considering that SALSA took an average $0.435\mu s$ per voxel, we believe that our algorithm will compare favorably against the other submitted algorithms.

5   Conclusion

In this work, we propose the SALSA algorithm, a simple and fast automatic lung segmentation algorithm, that works well for a good range of protocols and presence of noise and artifacts on CT chest scans. The algorithm is comprised of several simple image processing operations that can be implemented efficiently.

The algorithm was tested on the database provided by LOLA11, a lung segmentation challenge that took part during the MICCAI 2011. The proposed method achieved the average accuracy rate of 0.958 (95.8%) on the 55 volume database of the LOLA11 Challenge. We are currently tuning the algorithm to produce results with higher accuracies. Future work will include the segmentation of the lung lobes, a much more challenging problem, due to the low contrast that the thin membranes that divide the lobes present in CT exams.

Acknowledgements. The authors would like to thank the support of the grant FAPERN PRONEM No 610006/2010.

References

1. Gonzalez, R., Woods, R.: Digital Image Processing, 2nd edn. Prentice Hall (2002)
2. Gu, S., Pu, J.: Automatic lung segmentation improvement using a registration framework. In: Fourth Int. Works. on Pulm. Im. Anal. (at MICCAI 2011) (2011)
3. Hosseini-Asl, E., Zurada, J.M., El-Baz, A.: Lung segmentation using incremental sparse NMF. In: Fourth Int. Works. on Pulm. Im. Anal. (in conjunction with MICCAI 2011) (2011)
4. ITK: Itk-snap. www.itksnap.org (acessed November 2014)
5. Korn, R., Kim, J., Schmidt, G., Binnig, G.: Description of a fully automatic lung segmentation algorithm based on the cognition network tecnology. In: Fourth Int. Works. on Pulm. Im. Anal. (at MICCAI 2011) (2011)
6. Kuhnigk, J.M., Hahn, H.K., Hindennach, M., Dicken, V., Krass, S., Peitgen, H.O.: Lung lobe segmentation by anatomy-guided 3D watershed transform. In: SPIE. Medical Imaging 2003: Image Processing, vol. 4, pp. 1482–1490 (2003)
7. Lassen, B., Kuhnigk, J.M., Schmidt, M., Krass, S., Peitgen, H.O.: Lung and lung lobe segmentation methods at fraunhofer mevis. In: Fourth Int. Works. on Pulm. Im. Anal. (at MICCAI 2011) (2011)
8. Pinho, R., Delmon, V., Vandemeulebroucke, J.: Keuhkot: a method for lung segmentation. In: Fourth Int. Works. on Pulm. Im. Anal. (at MICCAI 2011) (2011)
9. van Rikxoort, E., van Ginneken, B., Kerkstra, S.: Lobe and lung analysis 2011. http://www.lola11.com/ (acessed June 2015)
10. Russell, S.J., Norvig, P.: Artificial Intelligence: A Modern Approach, 3rd edn. Prentice Hall (2009)
11. Sun, S., Bauer, C., Beichel, R.: Robust active shape model based lung segmentation in CT scans. In: Fourth Int. Works. on Pulm. Im. Anal. (at MICCAI 2011) (2011)
12. Weinheimer, O., Achenbach, T., Heussel, C.P., Düber, C.: Automatic lung segmentation in MDCT images. In: Fourth Int. Works. on Pulm. Im. Anal. (at MICCAI 2011) (2011)

Segmentation of Urban Impervious Surface Using Cellular Neural Networks

Juan Manuel Núñez[✉]

Centro de Investigación en Geografía y "Ing. Jorge L. Tamayo",
A.C. Contoy 137, Lomas de Padierna, Tlalpan 14240, Mexico D.F., Mexico
jnunez@centrogeo.org.mx

Abstract. In this paper an automatic segmentation technique for endmember detection to urban impervious surface with the help of the Biophysical Composition Index (BCI) and the segmentation based on Cellular Neural Network (CNN) was proposed. In particular, we focused in the derivation of BCI through of Landsat-8 Operational Land Imager (OLI) images, to proceed to the CNN segmentation through the threshold auto-select for impervious surface estimation as a linear decision given by a linear activation function. After some simulations based on the proposed technique, the obtained results, traditional single threshold-based segmentation and Otsu algorithm are assessed in terms of accuracy achieved through a stratified sample taken of a Very High Resolution image (VHR) of WorldView-2 (WV-2) with the same date as Landsat-8 OLI.

The accuracy assessment from a stratified random sample showed that the CNN segmentation was the most accurate method followed by the traditional single threshold-based segmentation.

Keywords: Urban impervious surface · Cellular Neural Network · Urban biophysical composition · Endmember detection · Segmentation · Landsat-8

1   Introduction

Urban impervious surfaces are defined mainly as artificial structures and surfaces, such as buildings, pavements and car parks that seal the soil and prevent many essential ecosystem services (e.g., production of food, habitat for plants, micro-climate regulation); so that knowledge about their characteristics and changes in composition, magnitude, location, geometry and morphology is significant for a high range of practical applications at local and global scales [1]. The estimation of urban impervious surface can be seen as a problem of end members selection at the pixel level, one procedure widely employed in many fields to account for mixed pixels in remote sensing imagery [2]. In the determination of endmembers, the within-class and between-class variations can exert profound influences on the accuracy of estimation of impervious surface area, since an inappropriate endmember set could severely affect the accuracy of fractional impervious surface areas [3].

The within-class variability refers to relative differences in spectral signature within the same land cover class, while the between-class variation suggests spectral

© Springer International Publishing Switzerland 2015
A. Pardo and J. Kittler (Eds.): CIARP 2015, LNCS 9423, pp. 509–516, 2015.
DOI: 10.1007/978-3-319-25751-8_61

variations between two or more different land cover classes (e.g. soil and impervious surfaces). To reduce the impacts of endmember variability, different approaches have been developed to solve this problem. Some of them included the reduction of within-class variation and/or the enhancement of between-class variation, and others that test all potentially feasible endmember combinations by the trial-and-error method trying to find the best-fit model [4]. With all this, the problem of endmember selection between "purest" endmembers that can be selected with relative ease but that do not always yield optimal results, or the selection of the most "representative" endmembers but very difficult to estimate with a simple linear combination of spectral signatures of typical homogeneous materials, has not yet been fully solved [5]. In an attempt to expand and improve existing techniques for reducing variability endmember, some improved methods to extract endmembers take advantage of spatial and spectral relationships between a target pixel and its neighboring pixels to exclude unwanted pixels along the processing steps [6].

This paper proposes the developing an automatic segmentation technique for endmember detection to urban impervious surface with the help of the biophysical composition index (BCI) and the segmentation based on Cellular neural network (CNN) [7, 8]. Because they exclusively have a degree of local connectivity, CNN is particularly suitable for segmentation tasks. The pattern of their interaction with their near neighbors originates perform functions of extraction and hollow fill of small segments to merge them with larger regions. Taking advantage of the spectral and spatial relationships, it is intended that the proposal technique can both enhance between-class variation and decrease within-class variation for the urban impervious surfaces estimated. The paper is organized as follows: Section 2 introduce the fundamentals of the proposed technique; then, in Section 3, for the studio area, the datasets used and major processing steps are presented; in Section 4, the accuracy assessment results for the impervious surface estimations are presented and discussed; finally, concluding remarks about the proposal are presented in Section 5.

2   Background

2.1   BCI Derivation

BCI is a quantitative spectral indicator designed for characterizing biophysical composition of urban environments, that spectrally can moderately separate better bare soil from impervious surfaces, and it has significantly higher correlations with vegetation and impervious surface fractions when compared to other widely used indices in the endmember extraction techniques, including normalized difference vegetation index (NDVI), normalized difference built-up index (NDBI) and normalized difference impervious surface index (NDISI) [7]. BCI is derived by a review of the Tasseled Cap (TC) transformation [9], as shown in Eqs. (1) to (4)

$$BCI = \frac{(H + L)/2 - V}{(H + L)/2 + V} \tag{1}$$

with

$$H = \frac{TC1 - TC1_{min}}{TC1_{max} - TC1_{min}} \tag{2}$$

$$L = \frac{TC2 - TC2_{min}}{TC2_{max} - TC2_{min}} \tag{3}$$

$$V = \frac{TC3 - TC3_{min}}{TC3_{max} - TC3_{min}} \tag{4}$$

where   H is "high albedo", L is "low albedo", and V is "vegetation"; TCi (i = 1,2,3) are the first three TC components; TCi_{min} and TCi_{max} are the minimum and maximum values of the respective TC component. Because different forms of TC transformation have been proposed for a series of remote sensing sensors with various spatial and spectral resolutions, is also possible apply BCI to imagery from various remote sensors with multiple resolutions.

2.2   CNN Segmentation

The cellular neural network (CNN) is a large-scale nonlinear artificial circuit that possesses real-time signal processing ability. Originally developed by Chua and Yang [8], recently has been introduced in the context of satellite images, due to use of local connectivity's property in solving geospatial tasks [10, 11]. The standard CNN is formed by connected cells in a two-dimensional network structure. The state and output equations of each cell could be expressed as below [8]:

$$\dot{X}_{ij}(t) = -X_{ij}(t) + \sum_{C(k,l) \in N_r(i,j)} A(i,j;k.l) y_{kl}(t) + \sum_{C(k,l) \in N_r(i,j)} B(i,j;k,l) u_{kl} + Z_{ij} \tag{5}$$

$$y_{ij}(t) = f\left(X_{ij}(t)\right) = \tfrac{1}{2}(|X_{ij}(t) + 1| - |X_{ij}(t) - 1|) \tag{6}$$

where $X_{ij}(t)$, u_{ij} and $y_{ij}(t)$ are the state, the input and the output of the cell. $A(i,j;k.l)$ and $B(i,j;k,l)$ are feedback and control templates, and Z_{ij} represent the bias current value of the cell. $|u_{ij}| \leq 1$ and $X_{ij}(0) = 0$ are the constraint conditions.

Each cell in CNN only connects to its neighborhood $N_r(i,j)$ (r stands for neighborhood radius, usually r = 1) and interacted with each other directly, but the disconnected cells interacted with each other through continuous dynamic propagation effect. Cell neighborhood could be expressed as [8]:

$$N_r(i,j) = \{C(k,l) := max(|k - i|, |l - j|) \leq r, 1 \leq k \leq M, 1 \leq 1 \leq N\} \tag{7}$$

Real-time signal processing capability and exclusively local connections are properties that have beginning to be used in tasks of digital image processing such as: feature extraction, edge detection, image segmentation, moving object detection and image fusion [12]. Image segmentation aims at divide the image into homogeneous regions with the better borders position estimation. So, after image segmentation, the digital images are partitioned into disjoint homogeneous regions. There are several ways to define homogeneity of a region that are based on a particular objective in the segmentation process [13]. In the CNN approach, segmentation is based on a threshold template selection and the most important essential point of CNN threshold is to find a set of accurate template. In this paper we work with the adaptive threshold method [14]. According to this method, the threshold template has the form:

$$A = \begin{bmatrix} 0 & 0 & 0 \\ 0 & a & 0 \\ 0 & 0 & 0 \end{bmatrix}, \qquad B = \begin{bmatrix} 0 & 0 & 0 \\ 0 & 0 & 0 \\ 0 & 0 & 0 \end{bmatrix}, \qquad Z = z^* \qquad (8)$$

where $a > 1$ and $z^* \in \mathbb{R}$. If the initial activation $x_{ij}(t)$ is contained in the interval [-1, 1], then $y_{ij}(t) = x_{ij}(t)$ so the activation function indicates that:

$$U = \frac{z}{1 - A_{ij}} \qquad (9)$$

where $A_{ij} = a > 1$ is supposed and U is threshold value in the input image. $Z > 0$ sets a negative threshold U, meanwhile $Z < 0$ sets a positive threshold U.

3 Materials and Methods

3.1 Study Area and Data Used

The study area is the city of Merida, located at Northwestern Peninsula of Yucatan, Mexico. Merida is known for its cultural heritage and for being one of the safest cities in the country; however, also it faces major challenges in urban issues, such as pollution of aquifers related to expansion of impervious surface [15].

Multispectral Imagery. A Landsat-8 OLI image with multispectral bands (at 30 m spatial resolution) acquired on January 2014 was used in this study. The FLAASH method embedded in the ENVI software, based on the MODTRAN radiation transfer code, was applied to all multispectral bands. Uniform parameters were specified for the image: tropical atmospheric model, the rural aerosol model, and the 2-Band aerosol retrieval method. Atmospheric correction to obtain reflectance information is necessary for derived good estimates of biophysical variables like a TC transformation and BCI. In addition to the Landsat-8 OLI scene, a Very High Resolution (VHR) satellite image acquired by WorldView-2 (WV-2) in April 2014 (at 2 m spatial resolution) was used to assess the performance of the urban impervious surface estimation. The multispectral image at 2 m spatial resolution was then orthorectified using the rational polynomial coefficients provided by the image supplier.

3.2   Proposed Procedure

Once the atmospherically corrected surface reflectance of Landsat-8 OLI is obtained, the proposed procedure is the following:

a) *TC Transformation Calculation.* For the six Landsat-8 OLI bands (2 to 7) were applied the TC transformation parameters [16], resulting in the three firsts TC components: brightness, greenness and wetness.

b) *BCI Derivation.* BCI indicator is calculated and the results are contained in the range [-1, 1]. Impervious surfaces are associated with higher and positive values; vegetation has lower and negative values and bare soil have intermediate values, and can be separable from impervious surfaces.

c) *Segmentation for Endmember Detection.* To automatically extract endmember candidates of impervious surface, an optimal selection of threshold to extract low and high albedo was used according to [4]. The selection of this value is related to the largest number of features retained when the traditional single-threshold segmentation is applied. After CNN threshold template is applied by a linear activation function. For this case $a = 2$ is supposed, so the threshold value determines directly the quality of the resultant impervious surface estimation.

d) *Accuracy Assessment.* To evaluate the performance of segmentation methods, ground references of impervious surfaces were derived by visual interpretation and manual digitization from the WV-2 satellite image. Two segmentation classes were assessed: impervious surfaces associated with higher and positive BCI values; and others linking vegetation, related with lower and negative values, bare soil and mixed lands (e.g., bare soil and vegetation in residential areas). A stratified random sample of 180 reference sampling points was performed in the ENVI software for assessed each of the three segmentation methods. The selected samples were grouped in a 90×90 m size for to reduce impact of geometric error between multi-source remote sensing images.

4   Results

For the six Landsat-8 OLI reflectance bands (2 to 7), the three firsts TC components (brightness, greenness and wetness) were derived through method described in [16] and BCI image was calculated applying Eqs. (1) to (4). The chosen threshold value used to characterize endmember of impervious surface was fixed in -0.04, searching the preservation of the largest number of features. Single-threshold segmentation, CNN segmentation, and OTSU algorithm [17] were presented to illustrate the effectiveness of the proposed method.

Fig. 1 shows in an upper-left image, a natural color band combination in RGB for the orthorectified VHR WV-2 image. Upper-right image shows the results of segmentation between single-threshold segmentation; low-left the CNN segmentation; and lower-right image the OTSU algorithm result.

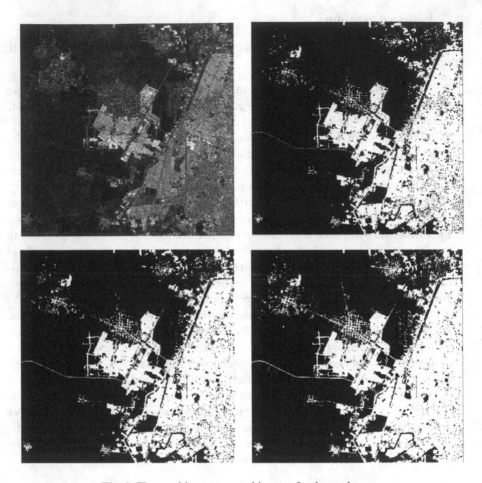

Fig. 1. The resulting segmented images for the study area

Segmentation accuracy was assessed using the testing set obtained of the orthorectified VHR WV-2 image. Results indicated that CNN was the most accurate segmentation method followed by the traditional single threshold and OTSU with an overall
accuracy of 82.2%, 80.6% and 73.3%, respectively.

In the confusion matrices, CNN segmentation presented the higher value of identified pixels with urban impervious surface and when looking the per-class user and
producer accuracies, CNN showed consistently the best performance for the urban
impervious surface class. In other words, although 97.8% of the pixels have been
correctly identified as urban impervious surface, only 75% of the pixels called impervious surface are actually urban areas. The confusion matrices are shown in Table 1.

Table 1. Confusion matrices for each segmentation method tested (a) traditional single threshold-based segmentation, (b) CNN segmentation, (c) Otsu algorithm.

(a)

Class	Other	Impervious surface	Row total	User's accuracy (%)
		Reference		
Classified				
Other	94	9	103	91.3
Impervious	26	51	77	66.2
Column total	120	60	180	
Producer's accuracy (%)	78.3	85.0		Overall 80.6

(b)

Class	Other	Impervious surface	Row total	User's accuracy (%)
		Reference		
Classified				
Other	58	2	60	96.6
Impervious	30	90	120	75.0
Column total	88	92	180	
Producer's accuracy (%)	65.9	97.8		Overall 82.2

(c)

Class	Other	Impervious surface	Row total	User's accuracy (%)
		Reference		
Classified				
Other	72	0	72	100.0
Impervious	48	60	108	55.5
Column total	120	60	180	
Producer's accuracy (%)	60.0	100.0		Overall 73.3

Obtained results showed that the CNN segmentation showed the highest accuracy over traditional single threshold-based segmentation and Otsu algorithm. The CNN segmentation accuracy reflects that connected pixels, have been accurately extracted to estimate better urban impervious surfaces. With this improved method, one may identify urban impervious surfaces with an accuracy as high as 80% which is an enough accuracy. Some confusions occurred between bare soil and certain impervious surfaces (grass/bare soil and water/dark impervious surfaces) for the other evaluated methods, especially in the Otsu algorithm.

5   Conclusions

Estimating the distribution of urban impervious surface is important in monitoring urban areas and understanding human activities. In this paper, a combination of methods was proposed for detecting urban impervious surface by combining an urban biophysical composition indicator and an improved segmentation method based in the CNN approach. Within CNN approach, segmentation can be considered in terms of the local connectivity between pixels given by the linear activation function of threshold. So, threshold value determines directly the quality of the resultant output segmented image, thereby improving the results of the traditional single threshold-based segmentation in terms of less within-class and between-class variations.

References

1. Scott, D., Petropoulos, G.P., Moxley, J., Malcolm, H.: Quantifying the Physical Composition of Urban Morphology throughout Wales Based on the Time Series (1989–2011) Analysis of Landsat TM/ETM+ Images and Supporting GIS Data. Remote Sensing **6**(12), 11731–11752 (2014)
2. Wu, C., Murray, A.T.: Estimating impervious surface distribution by spectral mixture analysis. Remote Sensing of Environment **84**(4), 493–505 (2003)
3. Somers, B., Asner, G.P., Tits, L., Coppin, P.: Endmember variability in spectral mixture analysis: A review. Remote Sensing of Environment **115**(7), 1603–1616 (2011)
4. Deng, C., Wu, C.: A spatially adaptive spectral mixture analysis for mapping subpixel urban impervious surface distribution. Remote Sensing of Environment **133**, 62–70 (2013)
5. Plaza, A., Martinez, P., Perez, R., Plaza, J.: Spatial/spectral endmember extraction by multidimensional morphological operations. IEEE Transactions on Geoscience and Remote Sensing **40**, 2025–2041 (2002)
6. Roessner, S., Segl, K., Heiden, U., Kaufmann, H.: Automated differentiation of urban surfaces based on airborne hyperspectral imagery. IEEE Transactions on Geoscience and Remote Sensing **39**(7), 1525–1532 (2001)
7. Deng, C., Wu, C.: BCI: A biophysical composition index for remote sensing of urban environments. Remote Sensing of Environment **127**, 247–259 (2012)
8. Chua, L.O., Yang, L.: Cellular neural networks: theory. IEEE Transactions on Circuits and Systems **35**(10), 1257–1272 (1988)
9. Kauth, R.J., Thomas, G.S.: The Tasseled Cap— A graphic description of the spectral-temporal development of agricultural crops as seen by Landsat. In: Proceedings of the Symposium on Machine Processing of Remotely Sensed Data, pp. 41–51 (1976)
10. Núñez, J.M.: Edge detection for Very High Resolution Satellite Imagery based on Cellular Neural Network. Advances in Pattern Recognition **96**, Special issue in Research in Computing Science; CIC-IPN, 55–64. ISSN: 1870-4069 (2015)
11. Gazi, O.B., Belal, M., Abdel-Galil, H.: Edge Detection in Satellite Image Using Cellular Neural Network. International Journal of Advanced Computer Science & Applications **5**(10) (2014)
12. Goraş, L., Vornicu, I., Ungureanu, P.: Topics on cellular neural networks. In: Bianchini, M., Maggini, M., Jain, L.C. (eds.) Handbook on Neural Information Processing. ISRL, vol. 49, pp. 97–141. Springer, Heidelberg (2013)
13. Guo, M., Feng, D.: Improved method for image segmentation based on cellular neural network. In: Wang, X., Wang, F., Zhong, S. (eds.) Electrical, Information Engineering and Mechatronics 2011. LNEE, pp. 671–678. Springer London, Heidelberg (2012)
14. Medina Hernandez, J.A., Castaneda, F.G., Cadenas, J.A.M.: A method for edge detection in gray level images, based on cellular neural networks. In: 52nd IEEE International Midwest Symposium on Circuits and Systems, MWSCAS 2009, pp. 730–733. IEEE, August 2009
15. Iracheta, A., Bolio, J.: Mérida Metropolitana: Una propuesta integral para su desarrollo. Fundación Plan Estratégico de Yucatán, COMEY, Centro EURE, Mérida, Yuc. Pascual, Josep María, 379 p. (2007)
16. Baig, M.H.A., Zhang, L., Shuai, T., Tong, Q.: Derivation of a tasselled cap transformation based on Landsat 8 at-satellite reflectance. Remote Sensing Letters **5**(5), 423–431 (2014)
17. Otsu, N.: A threshold selection method from gray-level histograms. Automatica **11** (285–296), 23–27 (1975)

Signals Analysis and Processing

Adaptive Training for Robust Spoken Language Understanding

Fernando García[✉], Emilio Sanchis, Lluís-F. Hurtado, and Encarna Segarra

Departament de Sistemes Informàtics i Computació, Universitat Politècnica de
València, Valencia, Spain
{fgarcia,esanchis,lhurtado,esegarra}@dsic.upv.es

Abstract. Spoken Language Understanding, as other areas of Language
Technologies, suffers from a mismatching between the conditions of the
training of the models and the real use of the systems. If the semantic models are estimated from the correct transcriptions of the training corpus, when the system interacts with real users, some recognition
errors can not be recovered by the understanding system. To achieve
an improvement in real environments we propose the use of the output
sentences from the recognition process of the training corpus in order to
adapt the models. To estimate these models, a labeled and segmented
corpus is needed. We propose an algorithm for the automatic segmentation and labeling of the recognized sentences considering the correct
segmented and labeled data as reference. Experiments with a spoken dialog corpus show that this approach outperforms the approach based on
correct transcriptions.

Keywords: Spoken language understanding · Learning from noisy
data · Adaptive training

1 Introduction

In many applications of language technologies, a mismatch may occur between
the conditions of the training of the models and the real use of the systems. This
problem can appear in statistical models, which are some of the most common
models used to represent the knowledge sources involved in oral communication.
Statistical models have the advantage that they can be trained by using automatic learning algorithms and they can accurately represent the variability of
many linguistic components, such as acoustic-phonetic, syntactic, or semantic
components [11],[4]. However, in many cases it is not possible to have a training
corpus that contains all of the linguistic variability necessary to estimate good
linguistic components.

To address this problem, some approaches have been proposed in the literature depending on the kind of models to learn or the possibility of obtaining

This work is partially supported by the Spanish MEC under contract TIN2014-
54288-C4-3-R and FPU Grant AP2010-4193

© Springer International Publishing Switzerland 2015
A. Pardo and J. Kittler (Eds.): CIARP 2015, LNCS 9423, pp. 519–526, 2015.
DOI: 10.1007/978-3-319-25751-8_62

accurate training samples [5]. For example in Automatic Speech Recognition (ASR), the acoustic-phonetic models must be adapted to noisy environments and the language models must also be adapted to deal with the problems of coverage. In Spoken Language Understanding (SLU), the lack of enough training data is also a common problem.

One possibility for tackling unobserved inputs in real environments is to supply lattices or graphs of linguistic units as input to the systems in order to represent more variability according to similarities between words or phonemes, for instance Word Confusion Networks are used for robust semantic parsing in [14]. Another way to adapt systems to unobserved inputs in real environments is to use active learning techniques [12], in which some real utterances/sentences are selected to dynamically adapt the models.

In the specific case of SLU, one of the main problems is to obtain a semantically labeled corpus [2], that is large enough to train the semantic models. In most cases, even though the training corpus is obtained through real speech interactions, the semantic labeling is generated by considering the correct transcriptions of the utterances. Therefore, even though the semantic labeled training corpus takes into account the variability associated to spontaneous speech, the noise generated by the speech recognition errors is not considered. With semantic models trained in that way, when the system interacts with real users, some ASR errors cannot be recovered by the understanding module. Similar problems occur when a multilingual SLU is designed. In that case the input sentences to the understanding module are corrupted not only by the recognition process but also by the translation process. Solutions to this problem can be found in [3], where the translation process is enriched by the combination of several translators and generating a graph of words that represents multiple hypotheses, or in [9], where the training samples are translated from the original language to the user language and then translated back to the original language. This way they have a training corpus that includes the specific characteristics of the translation process.

In this paper, we present an adaptive training approach to SLU that uses the output sentences from the ASR process of the training corpus in order to adapt the SLU models to the characteristics of the ASR process. In order words, we use the noisy training data, which is obtained from the recognition process, to estimate the semantic models. We have applied this approach to the DIHANA task [1] with information about train timetables and fares in Spanish, and we have studied the behavior of the system by considering three different ASR engines: an open domain (Google recognizer), and two in-domain recognizers (HTK and Loquendo) where both the language model and the vocabulary must be provided. Our training approach is based on the automatic segmentation and labeling of the ASR output taking the correct semantically segmented/labeled data as reference. To do this, an algorithm that segments and labels the ASR output using the Levenshtein distance to the correct transcription has been developed. Two approaches to SLU have been studied: a Conditional Random Field (CRF) approach [10] and a Two-level stochastic model [13], which is based on Stochastic Finite-State Automata. Experiments with the DIHANA corpus show that this enriched learning approach outperforms the classical approach based on clean (the correct transcriptions) training data.

2   Semantic Representation for the DIHANA Task

The domain of the DIHANA task is an information system about railway timetables, fares, and services in Spanish. The DIHANA corpus consists of 900 dialogs that were acquired from 225 users using the Wizard of Oz technique. Thus many characteristcs of spontaneous speech are present in the user utterances. The number of user turns acquired was 6,280 and the vocabulary size was 823 words. The semantic representation chosen for the task is based on frames. A total of 25 semantic labels were defined for the DIHANA task, consisting of 10 types of frames (Affirmation, Negation, Price, Hour, Departure-time..) and 15 attributes (City, Origin-City,Destination-City, Class, Train-Type...).

An example of the semantic representation translated from the original Spanish DIHANA corpus is shown below:

> *"I want to know the timetable on Friday*
> *to Barcelona, on June 18th"*
> (HOUR)
> Destination-City: Barcelona
> Departure-Date: (Friday)[18-06]

3   The Understanding System

Our understanding system works in two phases (see Figure 1) [13]. The first phase consists of a sequential transduction of the input sentence in terms of an intermediate semantic language. In the second phase, a set of rules transduces this intermediate representation in terms of frames. Since the intermediate language is close to the frame representation, this phase only requires a small set of rules to construct the frame. This second phase consists of the following: the deletion of irrelevant segments of the input sentence, the reordering of the relevant concepts and attributes that appeared in the user sentence following an order which has been defined a priori, the instantiation of certain task-dependent values, etc.

In order to represent the meaning of the sentences in terms of the intermediate semantic language, a set of 64 semantic units was defined. Each semantic unit represents the meaning of words (or sequences of words) in the sentences. For example, the semantic unit *query* can be associated to *"can you tell me"*, *"please tell me"*, *"what is"*, etc. This way, an input sentence (sequence of words) has a semantic sentence (sequence of semantic units) associated to it, and there is an inherent segmentation. An example is shown in Figure 1.

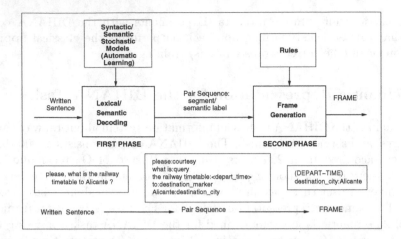

Fig. 1. The understanding process in two phases.

3.1 Semantic Models

Two different SLU techniques have been studied to implement the first phase, a generative technique (the Two-level) and a discriminant technique (a classical CRF).

To apply the Two-level technique [13],[6], we assume that each user turn in the training set has a sequence of concepts (semantic units) associated to it, each of these concepts represents a piece of meaning of the user turn, and there is a segment (sequence of consecutive words) in the user sentence that is associated to each of these concepts. This approach consists of learning two types of finite-state models from the training set of pairs (u, c), where u is the sequence of segments and c is the corresponding sequence of concepts.

A model A_s for the *semantic language* is estimated from the sequences of concepts c that are associated to the input sentences. A set of models, *concept models* A_{c_i} (one for each concept c_i), is estimated from all the segments of words associated to this concept. The semantic model A_s represents the semantic information provided by the training data, and each concept model A_{c_i} represents the lexical and syntactic information for the corresponding concept c_i.

For the understanding process, all the models must be combined in order to take advantage of all the lexical, syntactic, and semantic constraints. To do this, the states of the stochastic automaton A_s are substituted by the corresponding stochastic automaton A_{c_i}. Once this integrated automaton A_t is built, the understanding process consists of finding the best path in this automaton given the input sentence. In the experimentation, we used a 2-gram model for the A_s automaton and for the A_{c_i} automata.

CRFs have been successfully used for SLU tasks [7]. We defined a set of basic features that includes only lexical information, setting a window such as incorporates the two previous and the two posterior words. A more complete set of features could be defined for applying the CRFs to SLU tasks [7], however, in this work we have not done a depth study of the best combination of features.

4 Alignment Process

In order to learn the SLU system from noisy samples (that is, with the sentences obtained by the ASR engine) it is necessary to segment and label these new sentences for both approaches, the Two-level and CRFs.

To do this without manual effort, we translate the labeling and segmentation of the correct transcribed sentences to the recognized sentences. This is done by obtaining the Levenshtein distance between the two sentences, which not only supplies the distance but also supplies the word alignment associated to this distance.

Once we have a word-to-word alignment, we can translate the segmentation and labeling to this new sentence. Then, we can learn the concept models by using the original clean data, the new noisy data obtained by the ASR, or a combination of the two. These concept models will be used in the SLU system (Figure 2).

It should be noted that, in SLU, there are some words that are keywords (very relevant) to some concepts, and systematic errors in these specific words can generate many errors in the semantic interpretation. For example in the following sentence:

$$Correct: \quad qu\acute{e}\,|\,tipo\,|\,de\,|\,tren\,|\,es\,|\,el\,|\,m\acute{a}s\,|\,r\acute{a}pido$$
$$ASR\ output: \quad que\,|\,tipo\,|\,de\,|\,tres\,|\,-\,|\,el\,|\,m\acute{a}s\,|\,r\acute{a}pido$$

$$qu\acute{e}\ tipo\ de\ tren\ es : <tipo\_tren>$$
$$el\ m\acute{a}s\ r\acute{a}pido : tipo\_tren$$

$$que\ tipo\ de\ tres : <tipo\_tren>$$
$$el\ m\acute{a}s\ r\acute{a}pido : tipo\_tren$$

there is an ASR error in the word "*tren*" (train) that has been recognized as the word "*tres*" (three) due to the acoustic similarity in Spanish. If we include the output of the ASR as a semantic training sample, the segment "*que tipo de tres*" will be associated to the concept "*tipo_tren*". This way, it is possible for a similar error to be recovered during the understanding process.

This also occurs with some words specific to the task, such as "*moviendo*" (moving) instead of "*volviendo*" (returning); or "*rosario*" (rosary) instead of "*horario*" (timetable).

5 Experiments

In order to evaluate the effectiveness of the approach we carried out some experiments with the DIHANA corpus. The corpus was split into a training set of 4,887 turns and a test set of 1,340 turns.

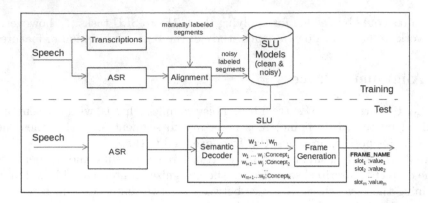

Fig. 2. Scheme of our approach

We studied the behavior of the proposed approach with three different ASR engines: the open domain Google recognizer, and two in-domain recognizers (Loquendo and HTK). The acoustic and language models were learned as follows. In the case of the Google ASR system, there were no options to adapt the models because it is an open domain ASR system with its own acoustic and language models. In the case of Loquendo, which has its own acoustic models, only the language model was learned by using the DIHANA corpus. And in the case of HTK, the acoustic and language models were in-domain models that were learned from the DIHANA training corpus.

For the generation of the semantic corpus using the output sentences from the ASR engines, we have worked in different ways. In the case of Google, since it is an open domain ASR, the new sentences were obtained by just recognizing all the utterances of the corpus. In the case of the other two engines, the language model (LM) was estimated from a part of the training corpus. If we had used the LM obtained from the whole training corpus to recognize it, the ASR results would have been very good, and we would not have a corpus with typical recognition errors. In order to obtain conditions in the new training corpus similar to conditions in the test corpus, we split the training corpus into 10 subsets. Each subset was processed by an ASR system with a LM estimated from the rest of the training sentences. After 10 iterations we had a corpus of sentences that were recognized in conditions similar to the test corpus.

After that, the new recognized sentences were segmented and semantically labeled following the process described in Section 4. The Word Error Rate for the Google recognizer was 27.11, for the Loquendo recognizer was 20.21, and for the HTK recognizer was 17.66. As expected, the more capability to adapt the models to the domain, the less error rate obtained.

We defined two measures to evaluate the accuracy of the models in the SLU process, the percentage of correct semantic units (%csu) and the percentage of correct frame slots (frame name and its attributes) (%cfs), which is equivalent to concept accuracy.

The %*csu* measure allows us to evaluate the first phase of our understanding system. This measure is calculated in the same way as the word accuracy used in speech recognition. The %*cfs* measure evaluate the overall understanding system and have already been used by other authors [8]. As shown in Section 2, the semantic representation of a sentence is one or more frames. Each frame consists of a name and a sequence of attribute-value pairs. The %*cfs* measure is the frame slot accuracy, that is, the number of correctly understood units (frame name and its attribute-value pairs) divided by the number of units in the reference.

Table 1. Results obtained using the different ASR engines.

ASR	Two-level						CRFs					
	Google		Loquendo		HTK		Google		Loquendo		HTK	
SLU model	%csu	%cfs	%csu	%cfs	%csu	%cfs	%csu	%cfs	%csu	%cfs	%csu	%cfs
clean	62.0	72.8	73.8	82.5	80.4	85.6	74.1	77.0	80.3	85.7	84.7	87.8
noisy	76.8	82.6	77.2	85.2	81.3	86.1	83.3	85.2	82.6	87.5	85.3	88.4
clean+noisy	76.8	82.4	77.2	85.3	82.0	86.5	83.9	85.5	82.2	87.4	85.5	89.0

Table 1 shows the results of the understanding process for the test corpus and for the two SLU approaches (Two-level and CRFs). As can be observed, in all the recognizers and in all the understanding systems the results for the %*cfs* measure outperforms those of the %*csu*. That is because in the %*cfs* measure irrelevant segments are not considered. These kind of segments are syntactically complex and in the training set there are few samples of each possible realization of them.

The results of SLU systems estimated from noisy data (*noisy* in Table 1) outperform the results obtained by the SLU systems estimated from clean data (*clean* in Table 1) for all the measures defined in both SLU approaches. This differences are more significant for the ASR engines with higher WER; for instance, the *Google noisy* results outperform the *Google clean* results by 9.8 points in the %*cfs* metric for Two-level approach and 8.2 points for CRFs approach. The *noisy* results for the ASR with the lowest WER (HTK) only outperform the *clean* results by 0.5 points in the %*cfs* metric for Two-level and 0.6 for CRFs approach. As expected, the improvement in SLU is more significant in the ASR engines with lower performance, which scope for improvement is bigger.

Finally, the use of the combined models (*clean+noisy*) returned very similar results to those obtained with *noisy* models. We think that a more sophisticated way of combining *noisy* and *clean* data, for instance using some interpolation techniques, would obtain better results.

6   Conclusions

We have presented an approach for the development of SLU systems by adapting the models to the errors generated in the previous phase of ASR. It is based on the automatic generation of a new segmented and semantically labeled corpus from the original utterances. Some experiments were performed with the Spanish DIHANA corpus using three different ASR systems and two SLU approaches. The results show that this learning approach can recover and deal with errors generated in the ASR process.

As future work, it would be interesting to study how to better combine models obtained with *clean* training data with models obtained with *noisy* training data.

Acknowledgements. This work is partially supported by the Spanish MEC under contract TIN2014-54288-C4-3-R and FPU Grant AP2010-4193.

References

1. Benedí, J.M., Lleida, E., Varona, A., Castro, M.J., Galiano, I., Justo, R., López de Letona, I., Miguel, A.: Design and acquisition of a telephone spontaneous speech dialogue corpus in Spanish: DIHANA. In: LREC 2006, pp. 1636–1639 (2006)
2. Bonneau-Maynard, H., Rosset, S., Ayache, C., Kuhn, A., Mostefa, D.: Semantic annotation of the french media dialog corpus. In: Ninth European Conference on Speech Communication and Technology (2005)
3. Calvo, M., García, F., Hurtado, L.F., Jiménez, S., Sanchis, E.: Exploiting multiple hypotheses for multilingual spoken language understanding. In: CoNLL (2013)
4. De Mori, R., Bechet, F., Hakkani-Tür, D., McTear, M., Riccardi, G., Tür, G.: Spoken language understanding: A survey. IEEE Signal Processing Magazine **25**(3), 50–58 (2008)
5. Deng, L., Li, X.: Machine learning paradigms for speech recognition: An overview. IEEE Transactions on Audio, Speech, and Language Processing **21**(5) (2013)
6. García, F., Hurtado, L., Segarra, E., Sanchis, E., Riccardi, G.: Combining multiple translation systems for spoken language understanding portability. In: Proc. of IEEE Workshop on Spoken Language Technology (SLT), pp. 282–289 (2012)
7. Hahn, S., Lehnen, P., Heigold, G., Ney, H.: Optimizing CRFs for SLU tasks in various languages using modified training criteria. In: INTERSPEECH (2009)
8. Hahn, S., Lehnen, P., Raymond, C., Ney, H.: A comparison of various methods for concept tagging for spoken language understanding. In: LREC (2008)
9. He, X., Deng, L., Tür, D.H., Tür, G.: Multi-style adaptive training for robust cross-lingual spoken language understanding. In: IEEE International Conference on Acoustics, Speech, and Signal Processing (ICASSP), May 2013
10. Lafferty, J., McCallum, A., Pereira, F.: Conditional random fields: probabilistic models for segmenting and labeling sequence data. In: International Conference on Machine Learning, pp. 282–289. Citeseer (2001)
11. Raymond, C., Riccardi, G.: Generative and discriminative algorithms for spoken language understanding. In: Proceedings of Interspeech 2007, pp. 1605–1608 (2007)
12. Riccardi, G., Hakkani-Tür, D.: Active learning: theory and applications to automatic speech recognition. IEEE Transactions on Speech and Audio Processing **13**(4), 504–511 (2005)
13. Segarra, E., Sanchis, E., Galiano, M., García, F., Hurtado, L.: Extracting Semantic Information Through Automatic Learning Techniques. IJPRAI **16**(3) (2002)
14. Tur, G., Deoras, A., Hakkani-Tur, D.: Semantic parsing using word confusion networks with conditional random fields. In: INTERSPEECH (2013)

The Effect of Innovation Assumptions on Asymmetric GARCH Models for Volatility Forecasting

Diego Acuña[1]([⊠]), Héctor Allende-Cid[2], and Héctor Allende[3]

[1] Universidad Técnica Federico Santa María, Valparaíso, Chile
diego.acuna@usm.cl
[2] Pontificia Universidad Católica de Valparaíso, Valparaíso, Chile
hector.allende@ucv.cl
[3] Universidad Adolfo Ibáñez, Viña Del Mar, Chile
hallende@uai.cl

Abstract. The modelling and forecasting of volatility in Time Series has been receiving great attention from researchers over the past years. In this topic, GARCH models are one of the most popular models. In this work, the effects of choosing different distribution families for the innovation process on asymmetric GARCH models are investigated. In particular, we compare A-PARCH models for the IBM stock data with Normal, Student's t, Generalized Error, skew Student's t and Pearson type-IV distributions. The main findings indicate that distributions with skewness have better performance than non-skewed distributions and that the Pearson IV distribution arises as a great candidate for the innovation process on asymmetric models.

Keywords: Financial markets · GARCH models · Asymmetry · Innovation processes

1 Introduction

In financial markets, the volatility of an asset is considered to be a metric of the risk associated with the asset itself, so its estimation is crucial in pricing models and in Value-at-Risk (VaR) calculations. Due to the large amount of research in this topic, stylized facts about the volatility of financial assets have emerged and been confirmed over the years [6], such as the mean reversion property, persistence and the asymmetric impact of innovations on the volatility. It should be expected that a good volatility model must be able to capture these stylized facts. One of the most successful systems for volatility modelling is the GARCH methodology developed by Engle et. al. [2,5] which is able to encompass many of those stylized facts. Nevertheless, in the original formulation of GARCH models, the asymmetry effect was not addressed. As a workaround,

Funded by CONICYT-PCHA/Magíster Nacional/2014 - 22141595.

A. Pardo and J. Kittler (Eds.): CIARP 2015, LNCS 9423, pp. 527–534, 2015.
DOI: 10.1007/978-3-319-25751-8_63

many extensions to this system have been proposed, being one of the most successful ones the asymmetric power ARCH model (A-PARCH) of Ding et. al. [4]. This model outperforms other classical GARCH[1] formulations for equity markets where asymmetry is a necessity [9]. Due to this reason, it is going to be the preferred volatility formulation in this work.

Since the first works of Mandelbrot [13] and Fama [7] the distribution of financial asset returns have been known to be non-Gaussian and negatively skewed [10] with heavy tails, but there is few research on the probability density function (pdf) scheme of the innovations of a GARCH process with the ability to capture the properties described before. The Normal distribution has been widely used since the first work on ARCH models [5], but it obviously fails on accounting fat tails. Also, the Student's t [2] and the generalized error distribution (GED) [15] have received some attention mainly because they are more flexible than the Normal distribution regarding fat tails and skewness. More recently, Stavroyiannis et. al. [18] proposed the use of the Pearson type-IV distribution (see [14] for a detailed study on the distribution) due to its flexibility to approximate pdfs with fat tails [12], obtaining good results for standard GARCH models compared to Student's t and skewed Student's t (s-Student) distributions in the sense of Fernandez and Steel [8].

The aim of this paper is to make a formal study on the effect of the selection of the family distribution used in the innovation part of a GARCH model for the modelling of asymmetric process. In particular, it is of interest the analysis of Normal, Student's t, GED and Pearson IV distributions on A-PARCH models, regarding the performance of the model in tasks of forecasting volatility. The results should give researchers guidelines to the correct specification of a volatility model for a financial process. The remainder of this paper is organized as follows: Section 2 explains the A-PARCH model and the distributions used for the innovation process. In Section 3, the methodology of the study and the data used for experimentation is presented. Section 4 reports the results and the analysis of the study. Finally, in Section 5 we give some concluding remarks.

2   A-PARCH Model and the Innovation Process

Lets P_t denote an asset price at time t and its continuously compounded return over the period $t-1$ to t as $r_t = ln(P_t) - ln(P_{t-1})$. Following Engle's formulation [6] we can define both the conditional mean and variance as:

$$m_t = E_{t-1}[r_t] \tag{1}$$

$$h_t = E_{t-1}[(r_t - m_t)^2] \tag{2}$$

where $E_{t-1}[u]$ is the conditional expectation of u given the information set $\mathcal{F}$ at time $t-1$ (sometimes denoted as $E[u|\mathcal{F}_{t-1}]$). The return process R_t can be defined as:

---

[1] The term GARCH is generally used in literature (and in this work) to refer to the entire family of GARCH models when no conflict exist.

$$R_t = m_t + \sqrt{h_t}\epsilon_t, \quad \text{where } E_{t-1}[\epsilon_t] = 0 \text{ and } Var_{t-1}[\epsilon_t] = 1 \qquad (3)$$

As a general assumption, $\{\epsilon_t\} \sim i.i.d.\,F()$ for some distribution function F. The GARCH methodology focuses on providing an expression for the conditional variance h_t. As stated before, in this work h_t will follow the formulation of an A-PARCH(p,q) process:

$$h_t^\delta = \alpha_0 + \sum_{i=1}^{p} \alpha_i (|R_{t-i}| - \gamma_i R_{t-i})^\delta + \sum_{j=1}^{q} \beta_j h_{t-j}^\delta, \quad \text{where}$$

$$\begin{aligned}
&\alpha_0 > 0, \delta \geq 0, \\
&\alpha_i \geq 0, i = 1, \ldots, p, \\
&-1 < \gamma_i < 1, i = 1, \ldots, p, \\
&\beta_j \geq 0, j = 1, \ldots, q.
\end{aligned} \qquad (4)$$

This model imposes a Box-Cox transformation on h_t with order δ. The asymmetry is handled by the parameter γ. If $\gamma = 0$ there is no asymmetry and with $\delta = 2$ the model behaves as a standard GARCH model. Since we are interested on the asymmetry, in general γ will not be equal to zero.

2.1   The Innovation Process

Engle [5] proposed the use of the standard Normal distribution for the specification of ϵ_t. As explained before, the distribution of the returns tends to have fat tails, so the use of a Normal distribution is a strong assumption that needs to be revisited. Bollerslev [2] and Nelson [15] showed that the innovations with Student's t and GED distributions obtained better results than the Normal one. Later, several studies reported good results using skewed versions of Normal and Student's t distributions in contrast of the non-skewed versions on asymmetric models [1,16]. Recently, Stavroyiannis et. al. [18] used the Pearson type-IV distribution in a standard GARCH model outperforming skewed Student's t versions of the innovation process. So, it is of interest to perform a general study of those distributions for the innovation process on asymmetric models. As seen on equation (3) one of the requirements over the distribution used for ϵ is being specified as a zero mean and one variance process ($0 - 1$ from now on). Next, we show how to get a $0 - 1$ version for non-obvious distributions.

Generalized Error Distribution. The density of a $0-1$ GED random variable z is given by [15]:

$$f(z) = \frac{\nu \cdot exp[-\frac{1}{2}|\frac{z}{\lambda}|^\nu]}{\lambda \cdot 2^{(1+1/\nu)}\Gamma(\frac{1}{\nu})}, \quad \text{where}$$

$$\lambda = \left[2^{\frac{-2}{\nu}} \frac{\Gamma(\frac{1}{\nu})}{\Gamma(\frac{3}{\nu})} \right]^{\frac{1}{2}}, \quad \text{for} -\infty < z < \infty \text{ and } 0 < \nu \leq \infty. \qquad (5)$$

where $\Gamma(\cdot)$ is the gamma function and ν is a tail-thickness parameter. Note that when $\nu = 2$, z behaves as the standard Normal distribution.

Skewed Distributions by Inverse Scale Factors. It is possible to introduce skewness into unimodal and symmetric distributions by using inverse scale factors in the positive and negative orthant [8]. Briefly, the procedure is as follows: given a skew parameter ξ, the density of a random variable z can be represented as:

$$f(z|\xi) = \frac{2}{\xi + \xi^{-1}} \left[f(\xi z)H(-z) + f(\xi^{-1}z)H(z) \right] \tag{6}$$

where $\xi \in \mathbb{R}^+$ and $H(\cdot)$ is the Heaviside function. The mean and variance are defined as:

$$\begin{aligned}
E[z] &= M_1(\xi - \xi^{-1}) \\
V[z] &= (M_2 - M_1^2)(\xi^2 - \xi^{-2}) + 2M_1^2 - M_2
\end{aligned} \tag{7}$$

where $M_r = 2 \int_0^\infty z_r f(z)dz$.

It is possible to standardize skewed versions of the Normal, Student's t and GED distributions using the conditions given above.

Pearson Type-IV Distribution. A normalized version of the Pearson type-IV distribution is given by [18] using a modern form for the distribution obtained by Nagahara [14]. For a random variable z:

$$\begin{aligned}
f(x) &= \frac{\hat{\sigma} \cdot \Gamma(\frac{m+1}{2})}{\sqrt{\pi} \cdot \Gamma(\frac{m}{2})} \left| \frac{\Gamma(\frac{m+1}{2} + i\frac{\nu}{2})}{\Gamma(\frac{m+1}{2})} \right|^2 \frac{1}{(1+x^2)^{\frac{m+1}{2}}} \exp(-\nu \cdot \tan^{-1}x), \text{ where} \\
x &= \hat{\sigma}z + \hat{\mu} \\
\hat{\mu} &= -\frac{\nu}{m-1} \quad \text{and} \\
\hat{\sigma}^2 &= \frac{1}{m-2} \left[1 + \frac{\nu^2}{(m-1)^2} \right].
\end{aligned} \tag{8}$$

for $m > 1/2$, m controls the kurtosis and ν the asymmetry of the distribution.

3   Methodology

3.1   Data Description

The data set consist of continuously compounded returns of IBM stocks, where the estimation period spans from January 1, 1990 to January 1, 2015 (6300 observations) and the out-of-sample evaluation period spans from January 2, 2015 to May 12, 2015 (90 observations). On Figure 1 two plots of the stock price and return value for IBM are shown.

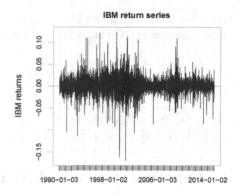

Fig. 1. IBM stock and return values.

3.2   The Model and Performance Evaluation

From a previous study of IBM return series and its autocorrelation and partial autocorrelation function, an A-PARCH(1,1) model was used for the conditional variance:

$$h_t^\delta = \alpha_0 + \alpha_1(|R_{t-1}| - \gamma_1 R_{t-1})^\delta + \beta_1 h_{t-1}^\delta \tag{9}$$

The five distributions (Normal, Student-t, GED, Skewed Student-t and Pearson type-IV) used for the innovation process ϵ_t have mean 0 and variance 1. The shape parameter for Student-t, GED, Skewed Student-t and Pearson type-IV distributions is equal to ν. The skew parameter for the Skewed Student-t distribution is ξ and for the Pearson type-IV is m. For the estimation phase, the preferred algorithm is maximum likelihood as usual in GARCH literature. For the evaluation of the models, an out-of-sample evaluation is going to be used with the second period of the data. Since there is no a preferred loss function for GARCH models [9], we are going to use the following performance measures:

$$MSE = n^{-1} \sum_{t=1}^{n} (\sigma_t - h_t)^2 \tag{10}$$

$$MAE = n_{-1} \sum_{t=1}^{n} |\sigma_t - h_t| \tag{11}$$

$$Logloss = -n^{-1} \sum_{t=1}^{n} (\sigma_t ln(h_t) + (1 - \sigma_t)ln(1 - h_t)) \tag{12}$$

where n is the sample size. As we need a measure for the volatility (σ_t in each loss function), a historical estimator for it is going to be needed. In particular, the Garman-Klass estimator [11] has shown to be very efficient, provided that there are no destabilizing large values [17] and it will be used in this study. The expression for the Garman-Klass estimator consists of:

$$\hat{\sigma}_t^2 = \frac{1}{2}\left(ln\frac{H_t}{L_t}\right) - (2 \cdot ln2 - 1)\left(\frac{C_t}{O_t}\right) \tag{13}$$

where O_k and C_t are the opening and close price in day t, and, H_t and L_t are the highest and lowest price of the asset in study in time t.

4   Experimentation and Analysis

The parameters estimation for the A-PARCH(1,1) model are given in Table 1 grouped by the distribution used on the innovation process. Also, below each value, in parenthesis we give the standard error for the estimated value.

Table 1. Parameters estimated for the volatility model

Innovation	μ	ω	α_1	γ_1
Normal	3.042e-04	1.018e-03	7.856e-02	4.735e-01
	(9.706e-05)	(1.452e-04)	(5.902e-03)	(4.922e-02)
Student	2.380e-04	5.872e-04	7.509e-02	0.4154
	(1.119e-04)	(1.368e-04)	(7.371e-03)	(6.166e-02)
GED	2.055e-04	7.439e-04	7.594e-02	0.4431
	(1.342e-04)	(1.533e-04)	(7.290e-03)	(6.173e-02)
s-Student	2.565e-04	5.934e-04	7.53553e-02	0.4142
	(1.461e-04)	(1.388e-04)	(7.390e-03)	(6.196e-02)
Pearson IV	2.838e-04	5.917e-04	7.544e-02	0.4123
	(1.697e-04)	(1.387e-04)	(7.399e-03)	(6.193e-02)
Innovation	β_1	δ	shape	skew
Normal	9.279e-01	6.406e-01	-	-
	(5.466e-03)	(8.009e-02)	-	-
Student	0.9344	0.6932	5.1893	-
	(6.848e-03)	(0.1050)	(0.3170)	-
GED	0.9319	0.6737	1.2744	-
	(6.8529e-03)	(0.1012)	(2.771e-02)	-
s-Student	0.9342	0.6913	5.1859	1.0156
	(6.8692e-03)	(0.1050)	(0.3164)	(1.808e-02)
Pearson IV	0.9341	0.6914	5.1835	-0.0874
	(6.8844e-03)	(0.1055)	(0.3161)	(0.1203)

It is interesting to note that, for the Student's t, skewed Student's t and the Pearson IV distributions the shape parameter is practically the same. The difference between those three distribution is given by the skewness: the Student's t is symmetric, where the skewed Student's t and Pearson IV are asymmetric distributions. In Table 2, we show the performance measures (loss function) used.

For all cases from the out-of-sample evaluation the Pearson IV distribution gave the best results. For the log-likelihood of the estimation phase, the skewed Student's t distribution obtained the best result. Those results show that the skewness for the innovation process plays a fundamental role in the volatility modelling.

Table 2. Loss functions and Log Likelihood for each model estimated (in bold each value which is the best measure for the selected loss function)

Innovation	MSE	MAE	Log Loss	Log Likelihood
Normal	7.4849e-06	2.19496e-03	6.44927e-02	-8849.456
Student	3.6194e-06	1.42859e-03	6.43533e-02	17541.49
GED	3.6519e-06	1.43351e-03	6.43545e-02	-8583.458
s-Student	3.6167e-06	1.42848e-03	6.43531e-02	**17541.91**
Pearson IV	**3.5970e-06**	**1.42641e-03**	**6.43524e-02**	17541.83

For the forecast made (in table 2) we can observe that the best distributions for the innovation process were the Pearson type-IV followed by the skewed Student's t distribution. A corrected Diebold-Mariano test [3] for checking the statistical significance of the better forecast obtained from Pearson IV was made. The results are presented in table 3 where it can be seen that for the MSE, it is clear that the Pearson IV distribution has statistically different forecast accuracy than the skewed Student's t and because it has lower MSE in this case we choose the Pearson IV innovation. For the MAE loss function we cannot reject the null hypothesis so statistically the two forecast have the same accuracy.

Table 3. Diebold Mariano test statistic (DM) for forecast comparison using skewed Student's t and Pearson IV distributions.

Innovation used in forecast	Test result	MSE	MAE
s-Student vs Pearson IV	DM	2.3176	0.6521
	p-value	0.0277	0.5195

5   Conclusion

The election of the distributions used for the disturbances in GARCH asymmetric volatility modelling has shown to be an important phase on the construction, estimation and forecasting in volatility financial markets models. In particular, we have concluded that the model with skewed distributions outperforms the model with non-skewed distributions in the forecast of the IBM stock time series in terms of the performance measures MSE, MAE and Log Loss.

We tested the introduction of the Pearson type-IV distribution for the disturbances on an A-PARCH model. The results obtained in IBM stock time series are encouraging (similar than for standard GARCH models [18]). The proposal was also validated with the S&P-500 time series obtaining similar results (available upon request). Future work will deal with the validation of this formulation with other well-known time series.

References

1. Alberg, D., Shalit, H., Yosef, R.: Estimating stock market volatility using asymmetric GARCH models. Applied Financial Economics **18**(15), 1201–1208 (2008)
2. Bollerslev, T.: Generalized autoregressive conditional heteroskedasticity. Journal of Econometrics **31**, 307–327 (1986)
3. Diebold, F.X., Mariano, R.S.: Comparing predictive accuracy. Journal of Business & Economic Statistics **20**(1), 134–144 (2002)
4. Ding, Z., Granger, C.W.J., Engle, R.F.: A long memory property of stock market returns and a new model. Journal of Empirical Finance **1**(1), 83–106 (1993)
5. Engle, R.F.: Autoregressive conditional heteroscedasticity with estimates of the variance of United Kingdom inflation. Econometrica: Journal of the Econometric Society **50**(4), 987–1007 (1982)
6. Engle, R.F., Patton, A.J.: What good is a volatility model. Quantitative Finance **1**(2), 237–245 (2001)
7. Fama, E.F.: The Behavior of Stock-Market Prices **38**(1), 34–105 (1965)
8. Fernandez, C., Steel, M.F.J.: On Bayesian Modeling of Fat Tails and Skewness. Journal of the American Statistical Association **93**(441), 359–371 (1998)
9. Hansen, P.R., Lunde, A.: A forecast comparison of volatility models: Does anything beat a GARCH(1,1)? Journal of Applied Econometrics **20**(7), 873–889 (2005)
10. Jondeau, E., Poon, S.H., Rockinger, M.: Financial modeling under non-Gaussian distributions. Springer Science & Business Media (2007)
11. Klass, M.J., Mark, B.G.: On the Estimation of Security Price Volatility from Historical Data. The Journal of Business **53**, 67–78 (1980)
12. Magdalinos, M.A., Mitsopoulos, G.P.: Conditional heteroskedasticity models with pearson family disturbances. The Refinement of Econometric Estimation and Test Procedures, Finite Sample and Asymptotic Analysis, 1–33 (2007)
13. Mandelbrot, B.: The Variation of Certain Speculative Prices (1963)
14. Nagahara, Y.: The PDF and CF of Pearson type IV distributions and the ML estimation of the parameters. Statistics & Probability Letters **43**(3), 251–264 (1999)
15. Nelson, D.B.: Conditional heteroskedasticity in asset returns: A new approach. Econometrica: Journal of the Econometric Society **59**, 347–370 (1991)
16. Peters, J.P.: Estimating and forecasting volatility of stock indices using asymmetric GARCH models and (Skewed) Student-t densities. Preprint, University of Liege, Belgium (2001)
17. Poon, S.H.: A practical guide to forecasting financial market volatility. Wiley Finance (2005)
18. Stavroyiannis, S., Makris, I., Nikolaidis, V., Zarangas, L.: Econometric modeling and value-at-risk using the Pearson type-IV distribution. International Review of Financial Analysis **22**, 10–17 (2012)

Blind Spectrum Sensing
Based on Cyclostationary Feature Detection

Luis Miguel Gato, Liset Martínez, and Jorge Torres[✉]

Department of Telecommunications and Telematics, José Antonio Echeverría,
Superior Polytechnic Institute, 114. 11901, 19390 Havana, La Habana, Cuba
lmiguelgato@gmail.com, {liset,jorge.tg@electrica.cujae.edu.co}
http://www.cujae.edu.cu

Abstract. Cognitive Radio has emerged as a promising technology to improve the spectrum utilization efficiency, where spectrum sensing is the key functionality to enable its deployment. This study proposes a cyclostationary feature detection method for signals with unknown parameters. We develop a rule of automatic decision based on the resulting hypothesis test and without statistical knowledge of the communication channel. Performance analysis and simulation results indicate that the obtained algorithm outperforms reported solutions under low SNR regime.

Keywords: Cognitive radio · Cyclostationarity · Feature detection · Blind spectrum sensing

1 Introduction

A new paradigm for wireless communication devices called *Cognitive Radio* [1] has emerged to optimize the employment of the radio spectrum. Through the use of vacant channels it is possible to improve the spectrum utilization [2]. Several current technologies operate in this way, for example: *Bluetooth* (WPAN – IEEE 802.15.1) [3], WLAN – IEEE 802.11k [4], and WRAN – IEEE 802.22 [5]. In this regard, spectrum sensing techniques represent a key component of these systems.

From the perspective of signals detection, the spectrum sensing techniques can be classified as *coherent detection* or *non-coherent detection* [6]. In the former case, the signal of interest (SoI) is detected using a generated signal, this is conformed taking into account the modulation parameters like the carrier frequency and phase, order of the modulation, shape and duration of pulses, etc. Matched filter provides the optimal solution in terms of the output signal-to-noise-ratio (SNR). However, prior knowledge of the SoI is required [6]. On the other hand, non-coherent detection also referred as blind detection, does not require prior knowledge of the primary signals modulation parameters. Energy detection (ED) is the most widely used technique for blind detection [7]. Nevertheless, the incapability of distinguishing between different types of signals, the vulnerability to uncertainty in noise variance estimation, and the poor performance under low

© Springer International Publishing Switzerland 2015
A. Pardo and J. Kittler (Eds.): CIARP 2015, LNCS 9423, pp. 535–542, 2015.
DOI: 10.1007/978-3-319-25751-8_64

SNR regimes, represent an important limitation in practice [8]. On the other hand, the use of cyclostationarity detection (CD) is reported to mitigate the limitations of ED [9]. By means of CD, the performance in terms of reliability under low SNR and fading conditions overcomes the main disadvantages in regard to the ED [8,9]. Although this technique is considered by many authors as a coherent technique, there have been several attempts to use CD detectors in blind detection [10,11]. Jang in [11] gives a method to compute the cycle frequencies profile of the spectral correlation density (SCD). Using that method, the author proposes a threshold for automatically signal detection, which is the maximum estimated magnitude of SCD that rejects null hypothesis. The evaluation method used was Monte Carlo simulations, under multi-path fading and low SNR.

The rest of this paper is organized as follows. The CD model for blind detection is described in Section 2. In Section 3, the main results are discussed. Finally, the conclusions are drawn in Section 4.

2   Cyclostacionary Feature Detection

The spectrum sensing problem can be stated in terms of a binary hypothesis test, where $\mathcal{H}_0$ represents the hypothesis corresponding to the absence of the signal, and $\mathcal{H}_1$ to the presence of the signal. These hypotheses are given by:

$$\begin{aligned} \mathcal{H}_0 &: x[n] = \omega[n] \\ \mathcal{H}_1 &: x[n] = s[n] \otimes h[n] + \omega[n] \end{aligned} \qquad n = 0, 1, ..., N-1 \qquad (1)$$

where $x[n]$ and $s[n]$ represent the received signal and the SoI, respectively. The impulse response of the channel ($h[n]$) is conformed taking into account fading conditions and it is modeled to be statistically independent from the additive white Gaussian noise (AWGN) of the channel ($w[n]$). The operation $\otimes$ indicates convolution product over N. The main difference between detection techniques is the statistic used to discriminate the hypotheses. The spectral correlation density function is the statistic used in cyclostationary feature detection.

2.1   Cyclostationary Processes

Cyclostacionarity[1] is an inherent property of the communication signals. This feature is present in sinusoidal carriers, train pulses, spreading codes, hopping sequences, cyclic prefixes and preambles, sampling and propagation phenomena [13]. For these signals, the autocorrelation function is periodic and can be obtained by a set of basis functions called *cyclic autocorrelation function* (CAF). The CAF is a generalization of the autocorrelation function, and allows to distinguish cyclic features from stationary noise. Extrapolating Wiener-Khinchin's

---

[1] In the proposed model, only *wide sense cyclostationary processes* are considered. Further mathematical details can be found in [12].

theorem [14] to cyclostationary signals, the Fourier transform of the CAF stands for the *cyclic spectrum*, also referred as *spectral correlation density function* (SCD). The SCD can be estimated for each cyclic frequency α by the *cyclic periodogram* as:

$$I^\alpha[n, f] \triangleq \frac{1}{N} X_N[n, f] X_N^*[n, f - \lfloor \alpha N \rfloor]] \equiv S_{x_N}^\alpha[n, f] \qquad (2)$$

where $X_N[n, f]$ indicates the short-time Fourier transform (STFT) of $x[n]$ at n over N samples, and $\lfloor \cdot \rfloor$ stands for the integer part of the number. The symbol $(^*)$ indicates complex conjugate. From (2) a classical spectral analysis could be made setting $\alpha = 0$ (no periodicities at all). This particular case corresponds to the power spectral density function (PSD), derived from the wide sense stationary processes theory.

Figures 1(a) and 1(b) show[2] the PSD and the SCD, respectively, of a BPSK signal contaminated with AWGN. From the PSD, it is difficult to distinguish the set of spectral frequencies corresponding to a SoI, due to the overlapping between signal and noise. On the other hand, the cyclic spectral analysis avoids this effect, since the SoI exhibits periodicities and the noise does not. For example, it is easier to detect a peak in the cycle frequency at $\alpha = 2f_c$ (where there is not overlapping noise) than in $\alpha = 0$, that corresponds to the traditional PSD. It should be noted that, for every $\alpha \neq 0$, the SCD of noise ($S_\omega^\alpha[f]$) is zero due to it's stationarity.

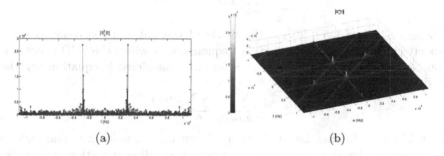

(a)   (b)

Fig. 1. Spectral analysis of a BPSK signal ($f_c = 2886$ Hz, $R_b = 260$ bits/s, $N = 1024$ samples) contaminated with AWGN (SNR = 3 dB). (a) Power spectral density (PSD), $S_x^0[f]$. (b) Spectral correlation density (SCD), $S_x^\alpha[f]$.

2.2 Impact of Channel Fading and Doppler Shift on the Cyclostationary Features

According to the results presented by Bkassiny [15], cyclostationary features in communication signals are preserved even in the presence of channel fading. The

---

[2] Cyclic and spectral frequencies are specified in Hz, it is easily done from the sampling frequency, $f_s = 22050$ Hz in this example.

channel can be considered as wide sense stationary as long as the mobile device covers a distance about a few tens of the wavelength of the carrier signal, this in an observation period. An acceptable approximation is to consider the channel as wide sense stationary with uncorrelated scattering (WSSUS), a commonly used model for dealing frequency selective channels [15]. In this case, the autocorrelation function of the received signal is also periodic with the same period than the SoI. Hence, the received signal is also cyclostationary with the same cycle components than the transmitted signal. As a result, when fading channels are considered as general linear time-variant systems, the cyclostationary features of the SoI are not modified. This is why the blind detection technique presented in this work is robust under practical scenarios.

If the channel is also characterized by Doppler effect, the cyclic spectrum of the SoI is convolved by the Doppler power spectral density. Let f_{max} be the maximum Doppler shift, the convolution causes the cyclic spectrum to spread at most $\pm f_{max}$ for every cycle frequency. However, Doppler shifting is irrelevant in blind spectrum sensing performance, given that the parameters of the signal are not used in the detection procedure. The cyclic features do not vanish, so it is still possible to perform detection.

2.3   Detection Statistic

In case of cyclostationary signals in AWGN, an approximate sufficient statistic for the *maximum likelihood detector* [16], called *multicycle detector*, is given by:

$$Y_{ML} = \sum_{\alpha \in A} \sum_f S_s^\alpha[f] S_{x_N}^{*\alpha}[f] \tag{3}$$

where $S_s^\alpha[f]$ and $S_{x_N}^\alpha[f]$ are the SCD[3] of the SoI and the received signal, respectively, and A is the set of cycle frequencies for which the SCD is not zero. If only cycle frequencies different from zero are considered in equation (3), then $S_x^\alpha[f] = S_s^\alpha[f]$, and

$$Y_{ML} = \sum_{\alpha \in A, (\alpha \neq 0)} \sum_f |S_{x_N}^\alpha[f]|^2 \tag{4}$$

Under blind conditions, the set A of cycle frequencies is unknown. The *radiometer*, or energy detector, is a common solution of blind detection, and it is a particular case of equation (3) when $\alpha = 0$ is considered:

$$Y^0 = \sum_f |S_{x_N}^0[f]|^2 \tag{5}$$

Let $Y^\alpha = \sum_{\alpha \in A} \sum_f |S_{x_N}^\alpha[f]|^2$, then the maximum likelihood detection criterion in equation (4) can be stated in term of Y^0 and Y^α by:

$$Y_{ML} = Y^\alpha - Y^0 \tag{6}$$

---

[3] From now on, the time parameter in the SCD is omitted for simplicity. Hence, $S_{x_N}^\alpha[f] \equiv S_{x_N}^\alpha[n, f]$ is always treated as the SCD estimated using equation (2).

From the interpretation of the cyclic spectrum as a spectral correlation function [11], Y^α is also given by:

$$Y^\alpha = \lim_{N \to \infty} \frac{1}{2N+1} \sum_{\alpha \in A} Y[\lfloor \alpha N \rfloor] \otimes Y^*[-\lfloor \alpha N \rfloor] \qquad (7)$$

where $Y[f] = X_N[f]X_N^*[f]$.

Given the statistic $Z[\lfloor \alpha N \rfloor] = Y[\lfloor \alpha N \rfloor] \otimes Y^*[-\lfloor \alpha N \rfloor]$, it is easy to verify that Z is an estimator of $|S_{x_N}^\alpha[f]|^2$ for every cycle frequency [11]. Besides, $Z[\lfloor \alpha N \rfloor] = \mathcal{F}\{y[n]y^*[n]\}$, and $y[n] = x_N[n] \otimes x_N[-n]$. The sequence $y[n]$, can be obtained applying the inverse DFT to $|X_N[f]|^2$, in order to avoid the convolution. This can be performed in a very efficient way if an FFT (Fast Fourier Transform) algorithm is used.

As Jang proposed in [11], the accumulative value of Z can be used to avoid missing features due to the lack of cycle frequency resolution.

$$G[\lfloor \alpha N \rfloor] = \sum_{\beta=0}^{\lfloor \alpha N \rfloor} Z[\beta] \qquad (8)$$

An equivalent and more efficient way to obtain this magnitude is attainable through the following convolution:

$$G[\lfloor \alpha N \rfloor] = Y[\lfloor \alpha N \rfloor] \otimes Y^*[-\lfloor \alpha N \rfloor] \otimes u[\lfloor \alpha N \rfloor]$$
$$= \mathcal{F}\left\{y[n]y^*[n] \times \mathcal{F}^{-1}\{u[\lfloor \alpha N \rfloor]\}\right\} \qquad (9)$$

where the notation $u[\cdot]$ indicates a unit step sequence. Hence, the statistic Z can be efficiently computed by the following difference equation:

$$Z[\lfloor \alpha N \rfloor] = G[\lfloor \alpha N \rfloor] - G[\lfloor \alpha N \rfloor - 1] \qquad (10)$$

for every $\alpha \in A$. The resulting set of values correspond to the cycle frequencies profile of the SCD [11]. The block diagram of the proposed algoritm for obtaining the cylic profile is shown in Figure 2.

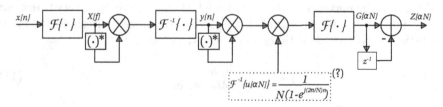

Fig. 2. Block diagram of the proposed algoritm for obtaining the cylic profile. The inverse DFT of unit step is not computed during the procedure, it's assumed to be previously caculated.

2.4 Detection Threshold Setting

The main parameters that characterize any detector's performance are: the probability of detection (P_d) and the probability of false alarm (P_{fa}) [17]. The value of γ that maximizes the P_d for a fixed P_{fa}, can be obtained from the Neyman-Pearson's Theorem, also known as *likelihood ratio test* [17]. However, it is required to know the probability density functions of the detection statistic under both hypotheses $\mathcal{H}_0$ and $\mathcal{H}_1$. Therefore, under blind conditions, an empirical criteria for establishing a detection threshold is demanded.

Figure 3(a) shows the normalized Z statistic (Z_u), obtained using the method described in Figure 2, corresponding to the same signal of Figure 1. The histogram of Z_u is shown in Figure 3(b). When the SoI is present, most of the samples of Z_u are related with noise[4]. In order to select a threshold, a confidence criteria C must be defined. The detection threshold for a confidence C, denoted by γ_c, corresponds to the magnitude of Z_u for which the $C * 100$ percent of samples are lower than γ_c. However, the proposed criteria is valid only under the hypothesis $\mathcal{H}_1$. If there is not a signal present (and γ_c is close to 1), there will always be samples above this value. Hence, both the probability of detection and the probability of false alarm would be one, and this detector would not be useful.

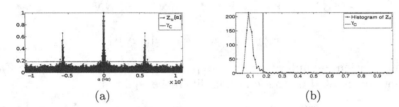

(a)   (b)

Fig. 3. Establishing the detection threshold (C = 0.95). (a) Normalized detection statistic for the BPSK signal of Figure 1. (b) Histogram corresponding to (a).

Another parameter is defined for avoiding this problem: the *tolerance level* (T), defined as the maximum value of γ_c for which $\mathcal{H}_0$ is rejected. Every threshold below T indicates detected signal. Finally, the normalized threshold for blind cyclostationary feature detection can be stated as follows:

$$\gamma = \begin{cases} \gamma_c , & \text{if } \gamma_c \leq T \\ 1 , & \text{otherwise.} \end{cases} \tag{11}$$

If $\gamma_c > T$ $(\gamma = 1)$, then hypothesis $\mathcal{H}_0$ will never be rejected.

---

[4] This noise is not channel noise properly, but estimation error from the periodogram in equation (2). According to the *central limit theorem* [17], this error can be modeled as a normally distributed random variable.

3 Results

The proposed detector was verified through Monte Carlo simulations, as suggested by Kay [17]. For each hypothesis, 2000 iterations were conducted in order to obtain reliable results. BPSK, QPSK, BFSK and MSK signals with length $N = 1024$ samples were analyzed. As an additional condition, fading and Doppler effects were considered, which parameters were randomly selected from trial to trial.

Receiver Operating Characteristics (ROC). An effective way to summarize the detector performance is to represent P_d versus P_{fa} [17]. A set of ROCs curves corresponding to the detection of different signals are showed in Figure 4(a). In Figure 4(b) another representation of the simulations results are shown for several types of signals. Similar representations are shown for the conventional ED and the enhanced version using sliding window, obtained from their analytical expressions presented in [10]. Note that the performance of the ED is independent of the modulation detected. Although the performance of the classical ED is poor under low SNR regimes, about 10 dB gain can be obtained if a sliding window of length 70 samples is used. However, the complexity of the detector is increased. Even using this enhanced version, the proposed CD method overcomes the ED for all the signals analyzed and $P_d = 0.9$.

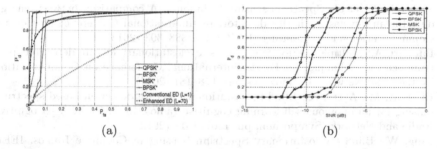

(a)   (b)

Fig. 4. Comparison between the ED and the proposed technique. (a) ROC curves for SNR $= $ -5 dB. (b) Curves of P_d vs. SNR for $P_{fa} = 0.1$. * Results obtained by simulations using the proposed technique.

4 Conclusions

The method proposed in this paper takes advantage of the cyclic features commonly presented in communication signals, in order to perform spectrum sensing. Conventional cyclostationary feature detection techniques are not well posed if the signal parameters are unknown. Under these conditions, a decision criteria for blind detection of primary signals is proposed based on practical assumptions.

Considering the trade-off between implementation complexity and performance, our proposed method stands as a good compromised solution for blind spectrum sensing. Low SNR regimes, presence of a fading channel and Doppler effect were considered in simulations. It was shown that the proposed method has a better performance than other solutions based on energy detection.

The proposed solution represents a useful technique for cognitive radio devices that operate as secondary users. It allows to detect idle channels for increasing spectrum utilization efficiency.

References

1. Haykin, S.: Cognitive Radio: Brain-empowered wireless communications. IEEE Journal on Selected Areas in Communications **23**(2), 201–220 (2005)
2. McHenry, M.: Frequency agile spectrum access technologies. In: FCC Workshop on Cognitive Radio, pp. 1–4 (2003)
3. Yucek, T., Arslan, H.: A survey of spectrum sensing algorithms for Cognitive Radio applications. IEEE Communications Surveys and Tutorials **11**(1), 116–130 (2009)
4. Panaousis, E.: Optimizing the Channel Load Reporting Process in IEEE 802.11k-enabled WLANs. Dept. of Computer Science of the Athens University of Economics and Business (2008)
5. Shellhammer, S.: Spectrum sensing in IEEE 802.22. Qualcomm Inc., pp. 1–6 (2010)
6. Sklar, B.: Digital communications: Fundamental and applications, 2nd edn. Prentice Hall (2001)
7. Bagwari, A., Tomar, G.: Improved spectrum sensing technique using multiple energy detectors for Cognitive Radio networks. International Journal of Computer Applications **62**(4), 11–21 (2013)
8. Satheesh, A., et al.: Spectrum sensing techniques. A comparison between energy detector and cyclostationarity detector. In: International Conference on Control Communication and Computing (ICCC), pp. 388–393 (2013)
9. Bagwari, A.: Multiple energy detection vs. cyclostationary feature detection spectrum sensing technique. In: Fourth International Conference on Communication Systems and Network Technologies, pp. 178–181 (2014)
10. Bkassiny, M., Avery, K.: Blind cyclostationary feature detection based spectrum sensing for autonomous self-learning cognitive radios. In: IEEE ICC - Cognitive Radio and Networks Symposium, pp. 1507–1511 (2012)
11. Jang, W.: Blind Cyclostationary Spectrum Sensing in Cognitive Radios. IEEE Communications Letters **18**(3), 393–396 (2014)
12. Boyles, R., Gardner, W.: Cycloergodic properties of discrete parameter non-stationary stochastic processes. IEEE Transactions on Information Theory **29**, 105–114 (1983)
13. Gardner, W., Napolitano, A., Paura, L.: Cyclostationarity: Half a century of research. IEEE Signal Processing **86**, 639–697 (2006)
14. Peebles, P.: Probability principles, random variables and random signals, 4th edn. Mc Graw Hill (2006)
15. Bkassiny, M., et al.: Wideband spectrum sensing and non-parametric signal clasification for autonomous self-learning cognitive radios. IEEE Transactions on Wireless Communications **11**(7), 2596–2605 (2012)
16. Gardner, W.: Signal interception: a unifying theoretical framework for feature detection. IEEE Transactions on Communications **36**(8), 897–906 (1988)
17. Kay, S.: Fundamentals of Statistical Signal Processing. Detection theory, vol. 2. Prentice-Hall (1987)

Language Identification
Using Spectrogram Texture

Ana Montalvo[1]([✉]), Yandre M.G. Costa[2], and José Ramón Calvo[1]

[1] Advanced Technologies Application Center, Havana, Cuba
amontalvo@cenatav.co.cu
http://www.cenatav.co.cu/
[2] Department of Informatics, State University of Maringá, Maringá, Brazil

Abstract. This paper proposes a novel front-end for automatic spoken language recognition, based on the spectrogram representation of the speech signal and in the properties of the Fourier spectrum to detect global periodicity in an image. Local Phase Quantization (LPQ) texture descriptor was used to capture the spectrogram content. Results obtained for 30 seconds test signal duration have shown that this method is very promising for low cost language identification. The best performance is achieved when our proposed method is fused with the i-vector representation.

Keywords: Spoken language recognition · Texture image descriptors · Low cost language identification

1 Introduction

The process of automatically recognize the presence of a given spoken language in a speech segment, is commonly referred to as spoken language recognition. The existing language recognition systems rely on features derived through short-time spectral analysis, many of such systems are based solely on acoustic models, trained using spectral/cepstral features.

In many approaches that apply prosody to spoken language recognition, extracted features are based on statistics of pitch and energy contour segments [1]. Our texture-based spoken language recognition system is motivated by a fundamental hypothesis, which states that different languages can be distinguished using texture descriptors over the speech signal spectrogram, we also consider a big component of that discriminative information is prosody, known as the music of language [2].

The present paper is organized as follows. After this introduction, Section 2 reviews what an spectrogram is and how texture descriptor is used in this work. In Section 3 a theory about the prosodic nature of textural characteristics found in the spectrogram, is discussed. Furthermore in Section 4 are presented all the experimental details. Finally Section 5 is devoted to the results analysis, followed by Section 6 with the conclusions and research perspective.

© Springer International Publishing Switzerland 2015
A. Pardo and J. Kittler (Eds.): CIARP 2015, LNCS 9423, pp. 543–550, 2015.
DOI: 10.1007/978-3-319-25751-8_65

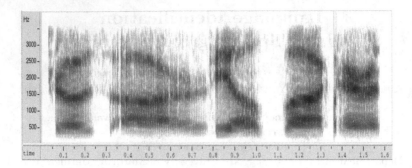

Fig. 1. Wideband spectrogram example.

2   Texture Descriptors Over the Spectrogram

Spectrogram is a visual representation of the spectrum of frequencies in a sound [3].

As shown in Figure 1, texture is the most noticeable visual content in a spectrogram image. Taking this into account, we have explored a texture descriptor presented in image processing literature in order to capture information to describe this content.

The literature shows us a long story of research in texture representation but recent works have shown that Local Phase Quantization (LPQ) [4] appear to be a very interesting alternative to textural content description. LPQ has been successfully applied to different problems achieving promising results, including in works related to audio classification tasks [5–7].

The next subsections describe some details about it.

2.1   Local Phase Quantization (LPQ)

This texture operator was originally created to describe the textural content on blurred images. However, it has shown a good performance even when applied to clear images. LPQ, the acronym for Local Phase Quantization, is a spectral texture approach which extracts frequency components that characterizes the underlying structures in the images taking into account the blur invariance of the Fourier Transform Phase.

The phase of 2D Short Term Fourier Transform (STFT) is used to find the blur insensitive information for each pixel over a rectangular window on its neighbourhood [4].

A rectangular window N_x, of size M-by-M is taken from each image pixel position x of an image $f(x)$ to calculate the local phase information using STFT:

$$F(u, x) = \sum_{y \in N_x} f(x - y)e^{-2\pi u^T y} = w_u^T f_x \qquad (1)$$

where w_u is the basis vector of the 2-D DFT at frequency u, and f_x is a vector containing all M^2 image samples from N_x.

The following four vectors are considered on the LPQ operator: $u_1 = [a, 0]^T$, $u_2 = [0, a]^T$, $u_3 = [a, a]^T$, and $u_4 = [a, -a]^T$, where a is sufficiently small to satisfy the blur invariance condition, therefore

$$F_x = W f_x. \tag{2}$$

For the purpose of maximally preserve the information, the coefficients need to be decorrelated, quantized and turn in integers ranging from 0 to 255. Thus, a feature vector is composed of these integer values in order to be used in classification tasks.

3   Language Long Term Cues

The basic appeal of long-term approach is that it aims to describe the spectral characteristics of speech as a whole, by taking into account the contribution of all the individual speech sounds in the considered time interval [8].

Indeed, modelling prosody is still an open problem, mostly because of the suprasegmental nature of the prosodic features [9].

The variation of pitch provides some recognizable melodic properties to speech. This controlled modulation of pitch is referred as intonation and it can be observed in the spectrogram between 80-400 Hz as a dark line, in the voiced phonemes interval [10].

Some syllables or words may be made more prominent than others, resulting in linguistic stress. This property is reflected in the spectrogram as darker zones.

The sound units gets shortened or lengthened in accordance to some underlying pattern giving certain rhythm to speech. The spectrogram provides visual clues that delimit the temporal boundaries between phonemes and words, also between speech and silence intervals. That is why, if a sentence is represented with an spectrogram, is possible to obtain information about its rhythm.

So prosodic cues might live in different frequency zones of the spectrogram, and they could be modelled using textural information.

3.1   Prosody, The Music of Language and Speech

Acoustically, speech and music are fundamentally similar. Both use sound, and so are received and analysed by the same organs. Many of their acoustical features are similar, although used in different ways [11].

Musical genres are categorical descriptions that are used to describe music. A particular musical genre is characterized by statistical properties related to the instrumentation, rhythmic structure and form of its members Different reasons had motivated research on automatic music genre classification, and spite of all efforts done during the last years, such task still remains an open problem [5].

Motivated by the similarities between the perceptual characteristics that define musical genre and the prosody of languages, we decided to evaluate an effective method of automatic recognition of musical genre, to identify spoken language. [6].

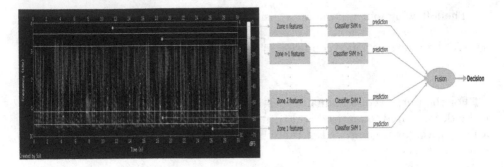

Fig. 2. Methodology used for classification.

4 Experimental Design and Implementation

The experiments were conducted over predefined training and evaluation sets, using for all this purposes the data defined as evaluation set by the National Institute of Standardization Technologies for the 2009 Language Recognition Evaluation (NIST LRE-2009). For training each language model, were used no more than 2 and a half hours, this is why we call it a low cost method, regarding the low resource demand. The 5 target languages involved were English, French, Mandarin, Russian and Spanish. The evaluation corpus were two balanced sets of 250 signals each, one including 3 seconds duration samples and the other of 30 seconds duration.

Frequency spectrograms were obtained from the 8 kHz signals by applying 256-point Discrete Fourier Transform to Hanning windowed frames at a 10 ms frame rate. Taking into account that the texture produced by the spectrograms is not uniform in frequency, and that previous results described in [5,6] suggest that spectrogram image zoning, in order to preserve local feature, could help to achieve good results, we decided to segment the spectrogram image in $n = 10$ frequencies sub-bands. Figure 2 depicts this strategy, here called linear zoning.

Once the spectrograms were generated we proceeded the texture feature extraction from these images. We used LPQ and LBP texture operators to capture the image content in each sub-band [12,13].

In LPQ representation, quantized coefficients are mapped as integer values using binary coding. These binary codes will be generated and accumulated in a histogram to be used as the feature vector, 256-bin histogram.

The classifier used in this work was the Support Vector Machine (SVM) introduced by Vapnik in [14]. Normalization was performed by linearly scaling each attribute to the range $[-1, 1]$. For the SVM a Gaussian kernel was used and the parameters cost and gamma were tuned using a grid search.

Each training sample is represented by a spectrogram, saved as an image, and then divided into 10 small images corresponding to 10 frequency zones. Each image thumbnail is represented with a texture descriptor and those descriptors are used to train a SVM multiclass by zone.

The same procedure was used to obtain the test descriptors for utterances of 3 and 30 seconds, of each target language.

Each SVM classifier was trained using 1500 descriptors (300 utterances of each language). With this amount of classifiers ($n = 10$), we used estimation of probabilities to proceed the combination of outputs in order to get a final decision. In this situation, is very useful to have a classifier producing a posterior probability $P(class|input)$. Here, we are interested in estimation of probabilities because we want to try different fusion strategies like Product and Sum, both presented by Kittler et al. in [15].

4.1 Baseline System Description

In order to validate this approach we attempt to evaluate a state-of-the-art system implemented by us, over the designed experimental setup. It wouldn't be fair to quote the results observed in the literature for language identification since they are built using much more data.

The TV space is estimated over the training set of target languages (72 hours of data) using a Gaussian Mixture Model-Universal Background Model (GMM-UBM) [16] with 512 Gaussian components trained over around 200 hours of 40 languages.

Table 1. Performance obtained for each zone created with linear zoning.

Zone Id.	Frequency band (Hz)	Accuracy (%)	
		LPQ_{30}	LPQ_3
1	**0-400**	**86**	**63.8**
2	400-800	76	53.6
3	800-1200	66.8	42.8
4	1200-1600	62	41.6
5	1600-2000	53.2	42.4
6	2000-2400	52.8	39.6
7	2400-2800	54.8	44.8
8	2800-3200	52	38.8
9	3200-3600	48	40.8
10	3600-4000	46.8	37.2

Table 2. Results obtained by the 5 class system, merging all zone predictions.

Fusion rule	LPQ_{30}		LPQ_3	
	Acc.	EER	Acc.	EER
Sum	86%	**7.3** %	65%	17.2%
Product	88%	8%	66%	**16.8**%

The dimension of the i-vector is set to 400 [17], and intersession compensation is applied to remove the nuisance in i-vectors using linear discriminant analysis (LDA)[18], a popular dimension reduction method in the machine learning community. The dimension of the i-vectors after LDA is 4.

Each target language model is obtained by taking the mean of the corresponding compensated i-vectors, over a set of 4 hours of balanced data per language.

Given a test utterance, the score for a target language is estimated using the cosine similarity measure between the target i-vector and the test i-vector.

5   Results and Analysis

Two different evaluations were made: training and testing with 30 seconds speech utterances, and training and testing with 3 seconds speech utterances.

Table 1 shows the performance obtained for each zone created with linear zoning. Here the notation LPQ_{30}, refers to the experiment that uses LPQ texture descriptors and 30 seconds duration signals to train and test.

The performance measures used for this evaluation are the accuracy and the equal error rate (EER). The accuracy reflects the percentage, of the 250 test signals, that were correctly classified. The EER represents the system performance when the false acceptance probability (detecting the wrong language for a given test segment) is equal to the missed detection probability (rejecting the correct language).

To apply LPQ features over a spectrogram, has a lot in common with extracting MFCC features to the speech signal, besides most state-of-the-art speech processing systems use some form of MFCC as their acoustic feature representation, because of their spectral nature.

Table 2 shows the fused classification scores. It is worth noting how merging all zones predictions improves the performance of the best individual SVM classifier (from zone 1). Another important issue was to verify that to discharge the worst zones -upper ones- does not always help to increase the final recognition. Even zone 10, provided useful information when classifiers were merged.

Spoken language recognition over short duration ($\leq 3sec$) speech segments is one of the ongoing challenges, our method is also susceptible to this phenomenon (Table 2).

5.1   Comparison with the TV Approach

Trying to reproduce a state-of-the-art method for language recognition over our own experimental setup, we developed an i-vector framework taking the risk of a bad performance due to its nature of high demanding resources method.

Comparing the results with the baseline, is remarkable how the proposed method obtained comparable results with the TV state of the art approach (Table 3).

However the most important outcome is the significant EER reduction when both systems scores are merged. Notice how the fusion itself is a result that competes with state of the art systems, however using much less data [17].

We could also say that both representations, textural representation of the speech and total variability, complement each other based on the improvement

Table 3. Comparison between LPQ system, i-vector baseline and their fusion, in terms EER (%) and demanded data (hours).

System	30 sec	3 sec	Model data	UBM-TV data
LPQ	7.3 %	17.2%	2.5 h/target	-
i-vector	7.6 %	22.8%	4 h/target	72 h
Fusion	**4.8 %**	**14.29%**	-	-

their fusion brought. Besides it is quit known that long term approaches are able to convey information sometimes impossible to reflect in the short term based ones.

6   Conclusion

The most interesting and original result is the experimental demostration of how the spectrogram texture discriminates the musical genre and it is also useful to identify languages.

In this study, we proposed a framework to model textural characteristics of speech spectrograms, which as we showed, indirectly model prosodic cues.

It was described a technique of visual data interpretation for spoken language recognition, and as main outcomes of this innovative approach we could mention:

- a new methodology to extract language features from spectrogram representation was developed,
- a new framework for using suprasegmental information in spoken language recognition was presented,
- a low dimensional vector representation which brings a comprehensive framework for futures subsystem merging,
- a representation with complementary information to the TV space [19].

Remains as challenges:

- to find an optimal fusion rule, probably a trained fusion function,
- to try this method in closely related language sets.

References

1. Sangwan, A., Mehrabani, M., Hansen, J.H.L.: Language identification using a combined articulatory prosody framework. In: Proc. International Conference on Acoustics, Speech and Signal Processing, pp. 4400–4403. IEEE (2011)
2. Schuller, B., Steidl, S., Batliner, A., Burkhardt, F., Devillers, L., Müller, C.A., Narayanan, S.: Paralinguistics in speech and language - state-of-the-art and the challenge. Computer Speech & Language **27**(1), 4–39 (2013)
3. Rabiner, L., Schafer, R.: Theory and Applications of Digital Speech Processing, 1st edn. Prentice Hall Press, Upper Saddle River (2010)

4. Ojansivu, V., Heikkilä, J.: Blur insensitive texture classification using local phase quantization. In: Elmoataz, A., Lezoray, O., Nouboud, F., Mammass, D. (eds.) ICISP 2008 2008. LNCS, vol. 5099, pp. 236–243. Springer, Heidelberg (2008)
5. Costa, Y.M.G., de Oliveira, L.E.S., Koerich, A.L., Gouyon, F., Martins, J.G.: Music genre classification using LBP textural features. Signal Processing **92**(11), 2723–2737 (2012)
6. Costa, Y., Oliveira, L., Koerich, A., Gouyon, F.: Music genre recognition using gabor filters and LPQ texture descriptors. In: Ruiz-Shulcloper, J., Sanniti di Baja, G. (eds.) CIARP 2013, Part II. LNCS, vol. 8259, pp. 67–74. Springer, Heidelberg (2013)
7. Costa, Y., Oliveira, L., Koerich, A., Gouyon, F.: Music genre recognition based on visual features with dynamic ensemble of classifiers selection. In: 20th International Conference on Systems, Signals and Image Processing, pp. 55–58, July 2013
8. luc Rouas, J.: Modeling long and short-term prosody for language identification. In: Proc. Int. Conf. on Spoken Language Processing (2005)
9. Rouas, J.L.: Automatic prosodic variations modelling for language and dialect discrimination. IEEE Transactions on Audio, Speech, and Language Processing **15**(6), 1904–1911 (2007)
10. Mary, L.: Extraction and Representation of Prosody for Speaker, Speech and Language Recognition. Springer Briefs in Electrical and Computer Engineering. Springer (2012)
11. Wolfe, J.: Speech and music, acoustics and coding, and what music might be for. In: Proc. 7th International Conference on Music Perception and Cognition, pp. 10–13 (2002)
12. Heikkilä, J., Ojansivu, V., Rahtu, E.: Improved blur insensitivity for decorrelated local phase quantization. In: 20th International Conference on Pattern Recognition, Istanbul, Turkey, pp. 818–821, August 23–26, 2010
13. Ojala, T., Pietikäinen, M., Mäenpää, T.: Multiresolution gray-scale and rotation invariant texture classification with local binary patterns. IEEE Trans. Pattern Anal. Mach. Intell. **24**(7), 971–987 (2002)
14. Vapnik, V.N.: The Nature of Statistical Learning Theory. Springer (1995)
15. Kittler, J., Hatef, M., Duin, R.P.W., Matas, J.: On combining classifiers. IEEE Trans. Pattern Anal. Mach. Intell. **20**(3), 226–239 (1998)
16. Torres-Carrasquillo, P.A., Singer, E., Kohler, M.A., Greene, R.J., Reynolds, D.A., Deller Jr., J.R.: Approaches to language identification using gaussian mixture models and shifted delta cepstral features. In: Proc. International Speech Communication Association Conference (2002)
17. Dehak, N., Torres-Carrasquillo, P.A., Reynolds, D.A., Dehak, R.: Language recognition via i-vectors and dimensionality reduction. In: Proc. International Speech Communication Association Conference, pp. 857–860 (2011)
18. McLaren, M., van Leeuwen, D.A.: Source-normalized LDA for robust speaker recognition using i-vectors from multiple speech sources. IEEE Transactions on Audio, Speech & Language Processing **20**(3), 755–766 (2012)
19. Jiang, B., Song, Y., Wei, S., McLoughlin, I.V., Dai, L.: Task-aware deep bottleneck features for spoken language identification. In: 15th Annual Conference of the International Speech Communication Association, pp. 3012–3016 (2014)

Combining Several ASR Outputs in a Graph-Based SLU System

Marcos Calvo, Lluís-F. Hurtado, Fernando García[⊠], and Emilio Sanchis

Departament de Sistemes Informàtics i Computació, Universitat Politècnica de València, Valencia, Spain
{mcalvo,lhurtado,fgarcia,esanchis}@dsic.upv.es

Abstract. In this paper, we present an approach to Spoken Language Understanding (SLU) where we perform a combination of multiple hypotheses from several Automatic Speech Recognizers (ASRs) in order to reduce the impact of recognition errors in the SLU module. This combination is performed using a Grammatical Inference algorithm that provides a generalization of the input sentences by means of a weighted graph of words. We have also developed a specific SLU algorithm that is able to process these graphs of words according to a stochastic semantic modelling.The results show that the combinations of several hypotheses from the ASR module outperform the results obtained by taking just the 1-best transcription.

Keywords: Graph of words · Graph of concepts · Spoken language understanding

1 Introduction

Advances in speech technologies have allowed voice-driven human-computer interaction systems to be ubiquitous in our lives. All these systems have many features in common, and one of them is that they have to understand what the user said in order to provide a suitable answer. Spoken Language Understanding (SLU) aims to provide a semantic representation of the user's utterance.

The input to the SLU system is usually the 1-best transcription of the utterance provided by the ASR [6]. However, this approach makes it impossible to correct the mistakes made in the recognition stage. In recent years, there has been a growing interest in overcoming the limitations derived from using a single decoding of the utterance as the input to the SLU system by exploiting the information contained in the ASR lattices [7],[11]. Another way to address this problem is to combine a set of sentences provided by one or more ASRs, in order to reduce the effect of the errors introduced by any single sentence. One way to perform this combination is to use a voting algorithm [5], to obtain a new output that is made of segments corresponding to the original sentences. Another

This work is partially supported by the Spanish MEC under contract TIN2014-54288-C4-3-R and FPU Grant AP2010-4193

A. Pardo and J. Kittler (Eds.): CIARP 2015, LNCS 9423, pp. 551–558, 2015.
DOI: 10.1007/978-3-319-25751-8_66

option, which is the one explored in this paper, is to build a graph of words from the set of sentences by using a Grammatical Inference method. This way, a set of extra sentences made up from chunks of the original sentences are represented in the graph of words along with the original sentences.

Many successful SLU systems are based on statistical models [3],[10],[8],[4]. This kind of modelization is able to represent the variability of the lexical realizations of concepts (meanings) as well as the different ways in which concepts can be arranged. Another important aspect of these models is that they can be learned from corpora. The training corpora must be large enough to allow an accurate estimation of the probabilities, and it must represent the lexical and syntactic variability that is used in the language to express the semantics as much as possible. Nevertheless, the training corpus may not be large enough to contain all the variability, and it is also important to have information about the errors that can be generated in the recognition process [11]. Since this information is ASR dependent, it is not usually included in the training process. For this reason, it can be a good approach to learn semantic models from a clean corpus and to enrich the input to the semantic decoding by means of multiple hypotheses. We have explored this approach and we have applied it to a task of an information system about railway timetables and fares in Spanish.

2   System Description

Spoken Language Understanding is usually addressed as the task of finding the best sequence of concepts $\hat{C}$, given an utterance A:

$$\hat{C} = \underset{C}{\operatorname{argmax}}\, p(C|A) \tag{1}$$

By introducing the sequence of words W underlying the utterance Equation 1 can be written as:

$$\hat{C} = \underset{C}{\operatorname{argmax}} \underset{W}{\max}\, p(A|W) \cdot p(W|C) \cdot p(C) \tag{2}$$

In this work, we have used a decoupled modular architecture (see Figure 1). The key aspects of this architecture are the use of a Grammatical Inference

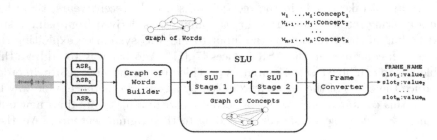

Fig. 1. Scheme of the architecture of our system.

algorithm to combine and generalize the outputs of one or more ASRs and a specific SLU algorithm that is able to take graphs of words as input.

In this architecture, the first module is dedicated to speech recognition. Since we want to combine and generalize multiple sentences provided by this module, its output will be either the n-best list provided by a single ASR or a set of 1-best decodifications provided by several ASRs working in parallel.

The second module combines the sentences provided by the first step by using a Grammatical Inference algorithm. The idea of Grammatical Inference is to generate a language (usually represented as an automaton or a graph of words) that generalizes a set of sentences that are provided as its input. Also, the algorithm that we have developed assigns a probability to each sentence of the new generalized set by means of a Maximum Likelihood criterion. This probability can be seen as a re-estimation of the distribution $p(A|W)$.

Next, the semantic decoding is carried out by means of a SLU module that is able to deal with graphs of words. For this system, we have developed a semantic decoding methodology that works in two stages. First, the graph of words is converted into a graph of concepts in which both syntactic and semantic information is included in the arcs of the graph. To build this graph of concepts, the first stage of the SLU algorithm uses both the graph of words and a set of Stochastic Finite State Automata (SFSA), which modelize the lexicalizations of the concepts of the task. Then the algorithm searches for matchings between the sequences of words that are represented in the graph of words and in each of the SFSA. The matchings of maximum probability become arcs in the graph of concepts. The weights of each arc in this graph are $p(A|W_i^j) \cdot p(W_i^j|c)$, where W_i^j stands for a chunk of a sentence represented between nodes i and j in the input graph of words and c is the concept it represents.

Then, this graph of concepts is processed in a second stage. In this stage, the algorithm searches for the best path in the graph based on the probabilities represented in both the graph of words and in a model that represents how the concepts are chained. The path of the maximum combined probability fulfills Equation 2. However, the output of this stage is not only the best sequence of concepts, it is also the underlying sequence of words and its segmentation in terms of the concepts.

Finally, the segmentation provided by the previous module is processed to extract and normalize the relevant semantic information and convert it into a frame representation.

3   A Grammatical Inference Algorithm to Build Graphs of Words

The goal of our Grammatical Inference algorithm is to generalize the syntactic structures of the sentences supplied by one or more ASRs by building a weighted graph of words. A graph of words represents a set of recognition alternatives that are built from the individual transcriptions of the utterance. This way, the SLU

Correct utterance: *me puede decir horarios de trenes a Alicante*
(could you tell me train timetables to Alicante)

MSA Matrix with multiple ASR outputs:

me	puede	decir	horarios	de	trenes	–	Alicante
–	puede	decir	horas	de	trenes	–	Alicante
me	puede	decir	hola	–	trenes	a	Alicante

Graph of words:

Fig. 2. Method to build a graph of words from multiple ASR outputs.

module can search among them for the most accurate sentence based on semantic constraints.

Our algorithm for building this weighted graph of words works in two steps. First, the different recognition alternatives are aligned using a Multiple Sequence Alignment (MSA) algorithm [1]. To carry out this process, we have modified the ClustalW [9] Multiple Sequence Alignment software.

The MSA process builds an alignment matrix. Each row in this matrix represents awords different sentence, and each column represents the alignment of each symbol. When a symbol cannot be aligned to any other symbol of any other sentence, the special symbol '-' is used (non-alignment points).

The second step consists of building a weighted directed acyclic graph of words from the information contained in the MSA alignment matrix. The graph construction algorithm starts creating as many nodes as columns in the alignment matrix, plus one for the initial state. Then, for each cell in the matrix that contains a symbol different to '-', we create an arc in the graph of words. Each arc is labeled with the word attached to the cell and has a counter of the number of times it is used. Finally, we weight the arcs by normalizing the counters attached to them. The final node of the graph is the node that represents the last column of the matrix.

Figure 2 shows an example of how the graph-builder algorithm works. As shown, this graph represents not only the input sentences, but also a set of sentences of similar characteristics. For example, the correct sentence *me puede decir horarios de trenes a Alicante* (could you tell me train timetables to Alicante) was not among the transcriptions provided, but it can be recovered using this mechanism. Furthermore, any full path from the initial to the final node in the graph represents an alternative transcription of the original utterance, and its probability is the product of the probabilities of the individual arcs of the path. Hence, this graph provides a re-estimation of the probability distribution $p(A|W)$, considering only a generalization of the individual transcriptions provided by the ASR module and weighting them according to a Maximum Likelihood criterion.

4 Semantic Decoding

Our SLU method works in two stages, both of which use stastistical semantic models. The first stage converts a graph of words into a graph of concepts using the information provided by the semantic model about the lexical structures that are associated to each concept. The graph of concepts has the same nodes as the graph of words. However, each arc represents a path in the graph of words whose underlying sequence of words is associated to a concept. Hence, each arc is labeled with the corresponding sequence of words and the concept it is attached to. Each arc is also weighted using a combination of the probabilities represented in the graph of words and those provided by the semantic model. The second stage finds the best sequence of concepts by searching for the best path in the graph of concepts, based also on the information about the concatenation of concepts included in the semantic model. The method for building the graph of concepts finds paths between any pair of nodes in the graph of words that represent sequences of words that are associated to any of the concepts of the task. To modelize the probability of a sequence of words for a given concept, we train a bigram Language Model (LM) for every concept. Thus, given a sequence of words W_i^j induced by a path from node i to node j in the graph of words, the LM associated to concept c computes the probability $p(W_i^j|c)$.

An n-gram LM can be represented as a Stochastic Finite State Automaton (SFSA). Hence, the problem of searching for relevant sequences of words in the graph of words for each concept can be stated as the search for common paths in both the graph of words and the automaton that represents the LM for each concept. However, due to the nature of this problem, we can add two restrictions to this statement. Let LM_c be the LM attached to the concept c and let q_c be a state of this automaton. The first restriction is that any path in LM_c must start at its initial state, but it can end at any state q_c. The second restriction is related to the second stage of the semantic decoding process. We search for the best path in the graph of concepts and the score for any path is the product of the probabilities of its edges combined with the score provided by a LM of sequences of concepts. Hence, in the first stage, for any pair of nodes i, j and any concept c, only the path in the graph of words that maximizes the score $p(A|W_i^j) \cdot p(W_i^j|c)$ becomes an arc in the graph of concepts. Therefore, the graph of concepts can be built by using the following Dynamic Programming algorithm[1]:

$$M(i,j,q_c) =$$

$$\begin{cases} 1 & \text{if } i = j \wedge q_c \text{ is the initial state of } LM_c \\ 0 & \text{if } i = j \wedge q_c \text{ is not the initial state of } LM_c \\ 0 & \text{if } j < i \\ \max\limits_{\substack{\forall a \in E_{GW}: \text{dest}(a)=j \\ \forall (q_c', \text{wd}(a), q_c) \in LM_c}} M(i, \text{src}(a), q_c') \cdot p(q_c', \text{wd}(a), q_c) \cdot \text{wt}(a) \\ \qquad\qquad \text{otherwise} \end{cases}$$

(3)

---

[1] We say that for every two nodes i, j in the graph of words, it holds that $i < j$ if i comes before j in the topological order of the nodes of the graph.

where dest(a) stands for the destination node of the arc a in the graph of words, src(a) refers to its source node, and wd(a) and wt(a) refer to the word and the weight attached to the arc, respectively. Also, $(q'_c, \text{wd}(a), q_c)$ represents a transition from the state q'_c to the state q_c labeled with wd(a) in the SFSA that represents LM_c. In consequence, $M(i, j, q_c)$ represents the best path in the graph of words that starts in the node i, ends in the node j, and whose underlying sequence of words reaches the state q_c in LM_c.

The second SLU stage searches for the best path in the graph of concepts, taking into account a bigram LM of sequences of concepts, which modelizes the probability distribution of the sequences of concepts $p(C)$. This search is performed via Dynamic Programming. The result is the best sequence of concepts as well as the underlying sequence of words and its segmentation in terms of the concepts.

Finally, this segmentation is converted into a frame representation (Table 1), which involves deleting irrelevant segments, reordering concepts and attributes, and automatically instantiating certain task-dependent values, among others.

Table 1. Example of semantic segmentation and its frame.

Input utterance	*hola quería saber los horarios para ir a Madrid* *(hello I'd like to know the timetables to go to Madrid)*
Semantic segments	*hola* : courtesy *quería saber* : query *los horarios para ir* : \<time\> *a Madrid* : destination_city
Frame	(TIME?) DEST_CITY : Madrid

5 Experimental Results

To evaluate the proposed approach, we have performed a set of experiments using the DIHANA task [2]. This task consists of a telephone-based information system for trains in Spanish. It has a corpus of 900 dialogs of spontaneous telephonic speech (which were acquired using the Wizard of Oz) that amount to 6,229 user turns from 225 speakers. This set of user turns was split into a subset of 4,889 utterances for training and 1,340 for testing. The orthographic transcriptions of all the user turns are available and are semi-automatically segmented and labeled using a set of 30 concepts.

We used the HTK, Loquendo, and Google ASRs. Table 2 shows if the Acoustic Model and the Language Model of each ASR were trained with the information from the training corpus. It also shows the resulting Word Error Rates (WERs). As expected, the greater the amount of information provided to the ASR from the corpus, the lower the WER.

In order to validate our approach, we performed three types of SLU experiments. The first type constitutes the baseline and consists of taking the 1-best of each ASR separately. In the second type, we took the n-best from the Google

Table 2. Information of the task provided to each ASR.

ASR	Acoustic Model	Lang. Model	WER
HTK	yes	yes	17.55
Loquendo	no	yes	20.12
Google	no	no	29.73

ASR since it is the one that best modelizes a real-world situation, and we built graphs of words using them. Finally, we took the 1-best from each ASR and combined them into a graph of words. To evaluate each experiment we measured the WER, the Concept Error Rate (CER), and the Frame-Slot Error Rate (FSER), which refers to errors in the semantic frames.

The results obtained in our experiments are shown in Table 3. These results show that, in terms of FSER, the combination of multiple hypotheses from the ASR module outperformed the respective baselines. The same happened for CER, except when comparing the CER achieved using the combination of the sentences from all the ASRs with the one obtained using the 1-best sentence from HTK. The reason for this is related to the data we used for training each ASR. The LMs for HTK and Loquendo were trained with data from the task, while the Google ASR had no information from the task. This way, it was easier for HTK and Loquendo to recognize in-vocabulary words, but when an out-of-vocabulary word appeared they failed, while the Google ASR could provide the correct transcription. Thus, when we combined the three ASRs, the Google ASR helped to identify some semantic segments with important keywords (which may have been out-of-vocabulary words), but in some cases it generated more variability in the graph due to its transcription errors. The results also show that in most cases the FSER is lower than the CER, which means that most of the errors were done in semantically irrelevant segments, such as courtesies. In terms of WER, the quality of the transcription achieved using a combination of several hypotheses and the proposed semantic decoding method was better than the respective baselines in all cases. This helped to improve the FSER, as the values of the frame slots were better recognized. Thus, we confirm our hypothesis that the sentences obtained through a generalization process by means of a Grammatical Inference algorithm lead to an improvement in the overall behavior of the system.

Table 3. Results obtained using the different compositions of ASR outputs as well as the individual 1-bests.

Input graphs of words	WER	CER	FSER
HTK 1-best	17.55	14.15	12.81
Loquendo 1-best	20.12	24.10	22.65
Google 1-best	29.73	32.50	32.69
Google 3-best	27.04	24.28	23.77
Google 5-best	26.85	23.85	23.00
HTK + Google + Loquendo 1-bests	14.87	15.58	10.48

6 Conclusions

In this work, we have presented an approach to SLU based on the combination of several ASR outputs in a graph-based system. We have developed a Grammatical Inference algorithm that takes several recognitions provided by the ASR module and builds a graph of words that represents a generalization of the original sentences. We have also developed a two-stage SLU method, which is based on Dynamic Programming algorithms. We have evaluated this approach using the Spanish DIHANA task. The results show that an appropiate combination and generalization of the transcriptions provided by the ASR module improves the overall behavior of the system.

Acknowledgement. This work is partially supported by the Spanish MEC under contract TIN2014-54288-C4-3-R and FPU Grant AP2010-4193.

References

1. Bangalore, S., Bordel, G., Riccardi, G.: Computing consensus translation from multiple machine translation systems. In: ASRU, pp. 351–354 (2001)
2. Benedí, J.M., Lleida, E., Varona, A., Castro, M.J., Galiano, I., Justo, R., de Letona, I.L., Miguel, A.: Design and acquisition of a telephone spontaneous speech dialogue corpus in Spanish: DIHANA. In: LREC, pp. 1636–1639 (2006)
3. Bonneau-Maynard, H., Lefèvre, F.: Investigating stochastic speech understanding. In: IEEE Automatic Speech Recognition and Understanding Workshop (ASRU), pp. 260–263 (2001)
4. Calvo, M., García, F., Hurtado, L.F., Jiménez, S., Sanchis, E.: Exploiting multiple hypotheses for multilingual spoken language understanding. In: CoNLL, pp. 193–201 (2013)
5. Fiscus, J.G.: A post-processing system to yield reduced word error rates: recognizer output voting error reduction (ROVER). In: 1997 IEEE Workshop on Automatic Speech Recognition and Understanding, pp. 347–354 (1997)
6. Hahn, S., Dinarelli, M., Raymond, C., Lefèvre, F., Lehnen, P., De Mori, R., Moschitti, A., Ney, H., Riccardi, G.: Comparing stochastic approaches to spoken language understanding in multiple languages. IEEE Transactions on Audio, Speech, and Language Processing **6**(99), 1569–1583 (2010)
7. Hakkani-Tür, D., Béchet, F., Riccardi, G., Tür, G.: Beyond ASR 1-best: Using word confusion networks in spoken language understanding. Computer Speech & Language **20**(4), 495–514 (2006)
8. He, Y., Young, S.: Spoken language understanding using the hidden vector state model. Speech Communication **48**, 262–275 (2006)
9. Larkin, M.A., Blackshields, G., Brown, N.P., Chenna, R., McGettigan, P.A., McWilliam, H., Valentin, F., Wallace, I.M., Wilm, A., Lopez, R., Thompson, J.D., Gibson, T.J., Higgins, D.G.: ClustalW and ClustalX version 2.0. Bioinformatics **23**(21), 2947–2948 (2007)
10. Segarra, E., Sanchis, E., Galiano, M., García, F., Hurtado, L.: Extracting Semantic Information Through Automatic Learning Techniques. IJPRAI **16**(3), 301–307 (2002)
11. Tür, G., Deoras, A., Hakkani-Tür, D.: Semantic parsing using word confusion networks with conditional random fields. In: INTERSPEECH (2013)

EEG Signal Pre-processing for the P300 Speller

Martín Patrone$^{(\boxtimes)}$, Federico Lecumberry,
Álvaro Martín, Ignacio Ramirez, and Gadiel Seroussi

Facultad de Ingeniería, Universidad de la República, Montevideo, Uruguay
{mpatrone,fefo,almartin,nacho,gseroussi}@fing.edu.uyi

Abstract. One of the workhorses of Brain Computer Interfaces (BCI) is the P300 speller, which allows a person to spell text by looking at the corresponding letters that are laid out on a flashing grid. The device functions by detecting the Event Related Potentials (ERP), which can be measured in an electroencephalogram (EEG), that occur when the letter that the subject is looking at flashes (unexpectedly). In this work, after a careful analysis of the EEG signals involved, we propose a preprocessing method that allows us to improve on the state-of-the-art results for this kind of applications. Our results are comparable, and sometimes better, than the best results published, and do not require a feature (channel) selection step, which is extremely costly, and which must be adapted to each user of the P300 speller separately.

Keywords: EEG · ERP · BCI · P300 speller · SSVEP

1 Introduction

Brain signals detected using non-invasive methods such as electroencephalograms (EEG) (Figure 1) provide a very rough summary of the overall activity of the brain at different locations of the scalp. Event Related Potentials (ERP) are relatively strong signals that can be detected when an event that is significant to the subject occurs. The P300 ERP (which stands for Positive peak at 300ms) is thought to occur when such event is both relevant to the task that the subject is performing, and unexpected. This principle has been applied to construct the so-called "P300 speller" (see Figure 2), which allows a subject to spell text by focusing on each individual letter, one at a time, and waiting for it to flash on a screen. If such flashes are unpredictable, a P300 occurs, which hints the device as to which letter the subject is looking at. In practice, the signal to noise ratio is very low, thus P300 events are very hard to detect. Therefore, each letter must usually be flashed several times before an automatic decision can be made. Some devices arrange the letters on a rectangular grid and flash entire rows and columns at a time, which increments the number of times that each letter is flashed per time unit.

This work was supported by the CSIC 2012 I+D project 519, and the CSIC "Iniciación a la Investigación" program.

© Springer International Publishing Switzerland 2015
A. Pardo and J. Kittler (Eds.): CIARP 2015, LNCS 9423, pp. 559–566, 2015.
DOI: 10.1007/978-3-319-25751-8_67

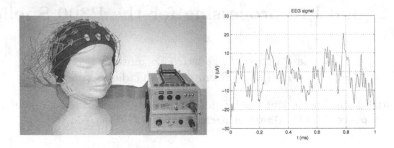

Fig. 1. Left: sample EEG measurement device. Right: typical EEG signal from one channel.

In 2006, an open challenge called the BCI Competition III was proposed. Its goal was to obtain the best possible performance (in correct letter classification) on a dataset obtained using a speller on two different subjects. The winner of the competition was the method proposed in [1], which combines several mainstream machine learning techniques. The method will be described in full detail in Section 2.

In this work, we perform an in-depth signal processing-oriented analysis of the EEG signals produced in P300 speller systems. In particular, we focus on the ones obtained from the BCI Competition.[1] The driving question behind our work is: how much can we simplify and/or robustify a speller system by applying a priori knowledge about the EEG signals involved? The result of this work is twofold: first, we are able to improve on the state-of-the-art by exploiting such prior information instead of relying on a pure black-box approach such as [1]; second, we provide evidence supporting the hypothesis that there is a significant amount of underlying information, beyond the P300 ERPs, that is needed for a successful discrimination between positive and negative events. The latter conclusion is obtained by classical signal-theoretic results from synchronous detection theory.

2   Background

In this section we describe common aspects of EEG signals, the P300 speller, and the approach followed in [1] to infer a letter to be spelled from the EEG signals read from the scalp of the subject.

Figure 1 shows a typical EEG measurement device. The EEG signal is captured by several electrodes distributed over the scalp of a subject. These electrodes measure the electromagnetic field, at various points on the surface of the scalp, that is produced by the neural activity of the brain. The distribution of such points varies from device to device although some standards exist. The system discussed in this work adheres to the 10-20 standard for EEG electrode location [2]. The signal measured at each electrode is called a *channel*. Due to

---

[1] Dataset available at http://www.bbci.de/competition/iii.

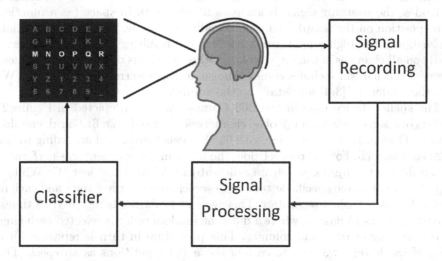

Fig. 2. P300 speller diagram. All possible letters are laid out on a square grid, displayed on a computer screen. All rows and colums are flashed, one at a time, in random order, while the subject stares at the desired letter. Meanwhile, the neural activity of the subject is captured using an EEG device, pre-processed, and then fed to a classification system which infers the letter that the subject is looking at.

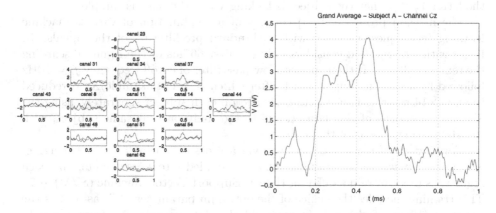

Fig. 3. Average P300 waveform for subject A. Left: on all 64 channels. Right: detail for the Cz channel, which is one channels where the P300 ERP manifests itself with more strength. In this case, on the Cz channel, the maximum potential is not achieved at 300ms, but rather at 450ms. However, the overall peak seems to be centered around 300ms.

the conductive interface between the signal to be measured and the transducing electrodes, the resulting signal is low-pass filtered both in space (as a function of the position on the scalp), and time. Finally, due to the very small potentials involved, and the high amplification needed, the resulting signal to noise ratio (SNR) on all channels is usually very low. Other problems derived from the measurement mechanism includes common noise accross electrodes (channels). (We refer the reader to [3,4] for details on the subject.)

The speller device used in the BCI Competition III (depicted in Figure 2) consists of a screen with a set $\mathcal{Y}$ of 36 characters arranged on a 6×6 grid, coupled to an EEG measurement machine with 64 channels distributed according to the 10-20 standard [2]. For the competition, the following experiment was performed on two different subjects, which we call "subject A" and "subject B". While a subject stares at some specific letter on the screen, each of the 6 rows and each of the 6 columns is flashed separately. This cycle of 12 flashes is repeated 15 times, for a total of 12×15 flashes, where a different random order is selected each time for the flashing of rows and columns. This procedure in turn is repeated for a series of 185 letters; we refer to each of these 185 repetitions as an *epoch*. The first 85 epochs are reserved for training; the remaining 100 are exclusively for testing.

Beginning with each flash, the EEG signal of the 64 channels is sampled for a duration of one second, at a precision of 12 bits per channel, at a sampling frequency of 240Hz. The resulting matrix of 240×64 signal samples constitutes one *data sample*, which we denote by $\mathbf{X} = \{x_{ik}\}$, with x_{ik} being the voltage measured for channel k at discrete time i (relative to the beginning of the flash). Each data sample $\mathbf{X}_j$ (where j denotes a data sample time index) is labeled with the letter $Y_j \in \mathcal{Y}$ that the subject is looking when the data is sampled.

The method proposed in [1] consists of a combination of various machine learning techniques, together with a standard pre-filtering of the signals. To begin with, the method considers only the first 667ms of the signal, discarding the remainig 333ms. It then applies a low-pass filter of cutoff frequency $f_c = 10$Hz followed by a subsampling of 12 : 1, after which each data sample $\mathbf{X}_j$ is reduced to an 64×14 matrix. The system is trained on each subject separately, using the 85 training epochs of the dataset, and tested, only on that same subject, with the 100 testing epochs of the dataset.

Training of all parameters is done via a cross-validation[5]/classifier aggregation variant where the training subset is divided into 17 segments, and each segment is used to train a different (linear) Support Vector Machine (SVM) [6,7]. This training includes the choice of the optimum parameter "C", as well as the optimum subset of channels (columns of the data samples $\mathbf{X}$) from which to train the SVM, and of course the best SVM for that setting.

Training proceeds as follows. The subset of channels is chosen via backward selection. In turn, for each candidate subset, differen SVMs are trained using different values of C, and the best one is kept. In all cases, the cost function to be minimized is the error rate on the remaining 16 subsets.

Finally, the best 17 SVMs are combined into one classifier by linearly adding their scores, and selecting the letter with the highest associated cumulative score.

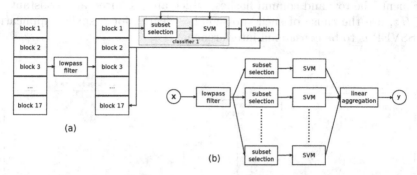

Fig. 4. Classifier architecture proposed in [1]. a) The training dataset is divided into 17 equal-sized, non-overlapping subsets, and 17 SVMs are trained with each one of them. The parameters of each SVM, including the selection of the best subset of channels on which to apply the SVM, is learned independently, using the other 16 subsets as validation data. b) For classification, the output of all 17 SVMs is linearly added to produce an average score, which is then used to select the candidate letter.

A diagram of the architecture just described is shown in Figure 4.

From the above description, two things should be immediatly clear. First, the training procedure is notoriously costly, as each step in the backward selection of each SVM consists in turn of the training and testing of several SVMs. (Once trained, however, detection is very fast, as only a few linear operations are required). Second, the total number of parameters is quite high, which makes the obtained detector extremely overfitted to a particular user. Although cross-performance between subjects was not the goal of the competition, it is nevertheless interesting to see how universal such system could be.

3   Adding a-priori Information to Improve P300 Spellers

As mentioned in the introduction, the focus of this work is on a priori information about EEG signals for P300 speller detection. The a priori information that is usually assumed about EEG signals (see [4] for a review on the subject) includes, as is generally the case, a characterization of what is signal, and what is noise. The noise, as in most applications, is assumed white and uncorrelated. The signal of interest, on the other hand, is considered a band-limited linear superposition of various sub-signals related to specific neural phenomena such as alpha and beta waves, electrooculomotor (EOG) impulses, and ERPs.

In the case of P300 spellers, as their name suggests, the main hypothesis behind their design is that positive events (that is, "the row or column that the user is looking at flashes") produce a positive ERP 300ms after the flash occurs.

Incidentally, another component that is usually present in P300 speller systems is the so-called Steady State Visual Evoked Potential (SSVEP), which occurs in response to a periodic visual stimulus. In the case of the BCI Competition speller experiment, the row and column flashes, which are produced at a constant rate of $5.7 Hz$, are the cause of such sub-signals. Clearly, for a speller application, such SSVEP is to be considered interference.

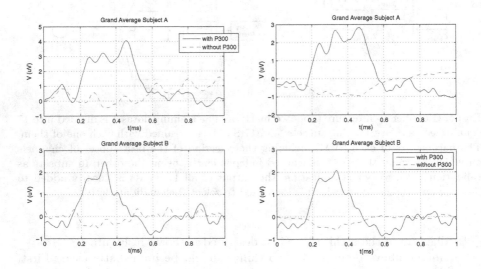

Fig. 5. Removal of SSVEP: Left: Average positive (blue, continuous) and negative (red, dotted) signals for subjects A (above) and B (below). Right: same signals after SSVEP removal. The SSVEP can be clearly seen as a periodic component on the average negative signals on both graphs on the left. Notice that both the average P300, as well as the SSVEP, vary significantly between both subjects.

According to the above scenario, and using [1] as the reference method, we propose three approaches to exploit the existing (or assumed) a priori information about EEG signals, with the hope to improve the speller performance:

1. A synchronous detector of the P300 pulse waveform
2. Pre-filter the signal using the P300 waveform as a matched filter and feed the result to the speller of [1]
3. Remove the SSVEP from the EEG signal and feed the result to the speller of [1]

In the first case, we constructed a synchronous detector by modeling the overall P300 pulse waveform (one per channel) from the grand average of all positive events (see Figure 3). Denote by $\mathcal{Y}^r$ the characters of $\mathcal{Y}$ on the r-th row, and by $\mathcal{Y}_c$ the characters on the c-th column. Denote by $r_j \in \{0, 1, 2, \ldots, 6\}$ and $c_j \in \{0, 1, 2, \ldots, 6\}$ the index of the row or column flashed during sample j

(if a row is flashed, we let $c_j = 0$ and vice versa). The P300 waveform is estimated as the average signal measured each time either $\mathcal{Y}^r$ or $\mathcal{Y}_c$ contains Y_j:

$$\mathbf{Z} = \sum_j \mathbf{X}_j \mathbf{1}\left(\{Y_j \in \mathcal{Y}^{r_j}\} \cup \{Y_j \in \mathcal{Y}_{c_j}\}\right), \tag{1}$$

where $\mathbf{1}(\cdot)$ denotes the indicator function associated to an event.

Note that we are making a strong assumption here: that the shape and position of the pulse is always the same. Deviations from such assumptions may deteriorate the estimation of the matched filter $\mathbf{Z}$. The detection procedure, according to synchronous detection theory, is to measure the filter response at the peak of the matched filter. Note that the filter $\mathbf{Z}$ is multi-channel, each column of it being a classical one-dimensional matched filter (for example, the one corresponding to the Cz channel is shown in Figure 3 on the right):

$$\zeta_j = \sum_k \sum_{i=1} (\mathbf{X}_j)_{ik} \mathbf{Z}_{ik}. \tag{2}$$

Denote by J a given epoch. Similar to (1), the overall score for a candidate letter Y occuring during epoch J is given by

$$\zeta(Y) = \sum_{j \in J} \zeta_j \mathbf{1}\left(\{Y_j \in \mathcal{Y}^{r_j}\} \cup \{Y_j \in \mathcal{Y}_{c_j}\}\right). \tag{3}$$

As evidenced by the results in Table 1, the above procedure yields very poor results, which point out the weaknesses behind the basic assumptions about the P300 ERP in its role for detecting significant events. This may occur at two levels: either the P300 ERP is too variable itself (besides what can be assumed interference) to be summarized as an average waveform, either in shape or in location, or there is more information besides what may be called "P300" that is related to a positive event. The second detector proposed, which pre-filters the EEG signals prior to introducing it into the machinery proposed in [1], supports the above conclusion. Although synchronicity is not required in this case, variations in the occurence of the P300 peak may introduce a significant blur in the resulting matched filter, with a negative impact on the overall process.

The third variant is based on the observation that the periodic flashes that occur throughout the entire experiment induce a Steady State Visual Evoked Potential, which manifests itself as a periodic waveform of the same frequency as the flashing rate; this is clearly visible in Figure 5, left column. We remove this interference by estimating the periodic component of the signal with period $5.7Hz$ and then substracting that component from the original signal. The result can be observed on the left column of Figure 5.

4   Results, Discussion and Conclusions

By performing the aforementioned operation as a pre-processing step to the speller of [1], we observe gains in several aspects. The most important one is

Table 1. Summary of results, given as the number of correct letter identification obtained on the BCI Competition III testing dataset, which consists of 100 epochs. A: results from [1]; B: synchronous detector results, C: results obtained with [1] when the matched P300 filter is used to pre-filter the input; D: method from [1] when the SSVEP component is removed from the input; E: [1] with no channel selection; F: [1] with no channel selection, with the SSVEP component removed from the input.

Subject	A	B	C	D	E	F
A	97	33	83	96	94	**98**
B	**96**	34	61	95	92	94

that we are able to significantly improve upon the performance of [1] when no channel selection is performed (and all channels are used); to give some perspective, using the implementation provided by the authors of [1], this reduces the training time from over an entire day to a few minutes. Moreover, for subject A, we even improve on the *best* result that can be obtained after the selection procedure. For subject B, the performance drops slightly (only two more samples are missclassified). When combining our pre-filtering with the full training of [1], we maintain the performance on subject A, and come closer to that of subject B. As such small differences could easily be due to random fluctuations, we conclude that the pre-filtering method proposed is able to produce essentially the same results as the original algorithm, while reducing its training time dramatically. Given that this training must be performed on each new subject, such reduction is clearly welcome.

References

1. Rakotomamonjy, A., Guigue, V.: BCI Competition III: Dataset II - ensemble of SVMs for BCI P300 speller. IEEE Trans. Biomed. Eng. (2007)
2. American Electroencephalographic Society: Guidelines for standard electrode positionnomenclature. J. Clin. Neurophysiol. **8**, 200–202 (1991)
3. Vidal, J.: Toward direct brain-computer communication. Annual Review of Biophysics and Bioengineering **2**, 157–180 (1973)
4. Wolpaw, J., Birbaumer, N., Heetderks, W., McFarland, D., Peckham, P., Schalk, G., Donchin, E., a Quatrano, L., Robinson, C., Vaughan, T.: Brain-computer interface technology: a review of the first international meeting. IEEE Trans. on Rehabilitation Eng. **8**, 164–173 (2000)
5. Kohavi, R.: A study of cross-validation and bootstrap for accuracy estimation and model selection. In: IJCAI1995 Proceedings of the 14th International Joint Conference on Artificial Intelligence, Vol. 2, pp. 1137–1143. Morgan Kaufmann (1995)
6. Cortes, C., Vapnik, V.: Support-vector networks. Machine Learning **20**(3), 273–297 (1995)
7. Smola, A., Schölkopf, B.: A tutorial on support vector regression. Statistics and Computing **14**, 199–222 (2004)

Audio-Visual Speech Recognition Scheme Based on Wavelets and Random Forests Classification

Lucas Daniel Terissi$^{(\boxtimes)}$, Gonzalo D. Sad,
Juan Carlos Gómez, and Marianela Parodi

Laboratory for System Dynamics and Signal Processing, Universidad Nacional de
Rosario CIFASIS-CONICET, Rosario, Argentina
{terissi,sad,gomez}@cifasis-conicet.gov.ar

Abstract. This paper describes an audio-visual speech recognition system based on wavelets and Random Forests. Wavelet multiresolution analysis is used to represent in a compact form the sequence of both acoustic and visual input parameters. Then, recognition is performed using Random Forests classification using the wavelet-based features as inputs. The efficiency of the proposed speech recognition scheme is evaluated over two audio-visual databases, considering acoustic noisy conditions. Experimental results show that a good performance is achieved with the proposed system, outperforming the efficiency of traditional Hidden Markov Model-based approaches. The proposed system has only one tuning parameter, however, experimental results also show that this parameter can be selected within a small range without significantly changing the recognition results.

Keywords: Speech recognition · Audio-visual speech · Random forests · Wavelet analysis

1 Introduction

Communication among humans is inherently a multimodal process, in the sense that, for the transmission of an idea, not only is important the acoustic signal but also the facial expressions and body gestures [9]. For instance, a significant role in spoken language communication is played by lip reading. This is essential for the hearing impaired people, and is also important for normal listeners in noisy environments to improve the intelligibility of the speech signal. This correlation between the acoustic and visual information during speech has motivated, in the last decades, several research activities associated with audio-visual speech recognition [14]. This research has demonstrated that recognition rates in noisy acoustic conditions can be significantly improved in comparison with only-acoustic recognition systems [12].

For audio-visual speech recognition, several kinds of pattern recognition methods have been adopted in the literature such as Linear Discriminant Analysis, Artificial Neural Networks (ANN) [12], matching methods utilizing dynamic programming, K-Nearest Neighbors (K-NN) algorithms [13], Support Vector

© Springer International Publishing Switzerland 2015
A. Pardo and J. Kittler (Eds.): CIARP 2015, LNCS 9423, pp. 567–574, 2015.
DOI: 10.1007/978-3-319-25751-8_68

Machine classifiers (SVM) [16] and Hidden Markov Models [7][8][11]. The most widely used classifiers are traditional HMMs that statistically model transitions between the speech classes and assume a class-dependent generative model for the observed features. In general, these recognition systems require a calibration stage to tune the parameters of the classifier in order to obtain an adequate performance in the recognition. This calibration is often performed by testing different combinations of the classifier's tuning parameters, which is usually a time consuming procedure. In addition, the optimal values for the parameters could depend on the particular visual features data set being employed.

In this paper, a novel audio-visual speech classification scheme based on wavelets and Random Forests (RF) [4] is proposed. Wavelet multiresolution analysis is used to model the sequence of audio and visual parameters. The coefficients associated with these representations are used as features to model the audio-visual speech information. Speech recognition is then performed using these wavelet-based features and a Random Forests classification method. Random Forests [4] have very good discriminative capabilities, run efficiently on large databases, can handle thousands of input variables avoiding the need for variable selection, are fast and can grow as many trees as it is necessary without overfitting. These good characteristics are inherited by the proposed audio-visual recognition scheme. The performance of the proposed speech classification scheme is evaluated over two different isolated word audio-visual databases.

The rest of this paper is organized as follows. In section 2 the proposed classification scheme for audio-visual speech recognition is presented. The different visual databases employed to evaluate the proposed system are described in section 3. In section 4 experimental results are presented, and the accuracy of the proposed method is compared to the corresponding to traditional Hidden Markov Model-based approaches, over the same databases. Finally, some concluding remarks are given in section 5.

2   Proposed System

A schematic representation of the proposed speech classification scheme is depicted in Fig. 1. In a first stage, Discrete Wavelet Transform (DWT) is applied to the input parameters. The idea is to perform a multilevel decomposition of the time varying input parameters using the DWT and then use the approximation coefficients to represent them. Resampling of the time functions, prior to the DWT decomposition, is needed in order to have a fixed-length feature vector. In this way, independently of the number of frames associated with each word, a resulting fixed length feature vector is obtained. To have a fixed-length feature vector represents an advantage since it makes the comparison between two feature vectors easier. This method is also independent of the kind of input, in this paper the method is evaluated using acoustic and fused audio-visual input parameters. The wavelet-based feature vector computation scheme is depicted in Fig. 2.

In the wavelet decomposition block, a multilevel decomposition of the time functions is performed, and only the approximation coefficients are retained to

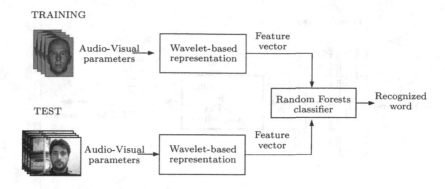

Fig. 1. Schematic representation of the proposed audio-visual speech classification system.

represent them. The approximation accuracy is determined by the chosen resolution level, which also determines the length of the resulting feature vector. Since this length has to be kept reasonably small, there will be a trade-off between accuracy and feature vector length. The design parameter is then the length of the feature vector, which determines the resolution level to be used. The widely used **db4** wavelet [5] is employed for the representation of the time functions.

In the second stage, a classification based on Random Forests (RF) is performed. Random Forests is an ensemble of decision trees. The ensemble construction strategy is focused in increasing the diversity among the trees. Decision trees are very unstable (generally a small change in the dataset results in large changes in the developed model [3]), then the diversity among the trees in the ensemble is increased by fitting each tree on a bootstrap replicate (random subset of the available data, of the same length, taken with replacement) of the whole data. In addition, more diversity is introduced during the growing of each tree. For each node the method selects a small random subset of P attributes (from the total number of attributes available) and use only this subset to search for the best split. The combination of these two sources of diversity produces an ensemble with good prediction performance. This performance will depend on the correlation between any two trees in the forest and on the strength of each individual tree. The stronger the individual trees are and the less correlated they are, the better error rate the classifier will achieve. The parameters to adjust for a Random Forests classifier are the number of trees to grow and the number of randomly selected splitting variables to be considered at each node. The number of trees to grow does not strongly influence the results as long as it is kept large (generally, 1000 trees are enough). Then, in practice, the only tuning parameter of the model is the number of randomly selected splitting variables to be considered at each node.

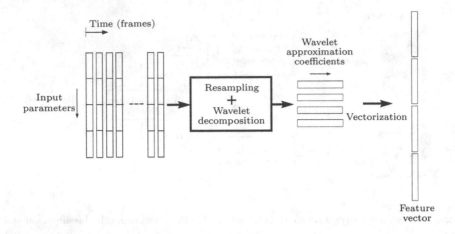

Fig. 2. Schematic representation of the method proposed for computing the wavelet-based feature vector. In this example, the input features are composed by 4 parameters.

3   Audio-Visual Databases

The performance of the proposed classification scheme is evaluated over two isolated word audio-visual databases, *viz.*, a database compiled by the authors, hereafter referred as AV-UNR database and the Carnegie Mellon University (AV-CMU) database (now at Cornell University) [1].

I) *AV-UNR* database: The AV-UNR database consists of videos of 16 speakers, pronouncing a set of ten words (*up, down, right, left, forward, back, stop, save, open* and *close*) 20 times. The audio features are represented by the first eleven non-DC Mel-Cepstral coefficients, and its associated first and second derivative coefficients. Visual features are represented by three parameters, *viz.*, mouth height, mouth width and area between lips.

II) *AV-CMU* database: The AV-CMU database [1] consists of ten speakers, with each of them saying the digits from 0 to 9 ten times. The audio features are represented by the same parameters as in AV-UNR database. To represent the visual information, the weighted least-squares parabolic fitting method proposed in [2] is employed in this paper. Visual features are represented by five parameters, *viz*, the focal parameters of the upper and lower parabolas, mouth's width and height, and the main angle of the bounding rectangle of the mouth.

4   Experimental Results

The proposed audio-visual speech recognition system is tested separately on the databases described in section 3. To evaluate the recognition rates under noisy acoustic conditions, experiments with additive Babble noise, with SNRs ranging from -10 dB to 40 dB, were performed. Multispeaker or Babble noise environment is one of the most challenging noise conditions, since the interference is speech from other speakers. This noise is uniquely challenging because of its highly time evolving structure and its similarity to the desired target speech [10]. In this paper, Babble noise samples were extracted from *NOISEX-92* database, compiled by the Digital Signal Processing (DSP) group at Rice University [6]. To obtain statistically significant results, a two nested 5-fold cross-validation (CV) is performed over the whole data in each of the databases, to compute the recognition rates.

For each database, the evaluation is carried out considering speech data represented by only-audio information on one side and by fused audio-visual information on the other, resulting in four different experiments. Independently of the database being considered, audio-visual features are extracted from videos where the acoustic and visual streams are synchronized. The audio signal is partitioned in frames with the same rate as the video frame rate. For the case of considering audio-visual information, the audio-visual feature vector at frame t is composed by the concatenation of the acoustic parameters with the visual ones.

The tuning parameters of the system are the ones associated with the audio-visual feature representation block and the ones corresponding to the RF classifier. Regarding the wavelet-based representation, the tuning parameters are the normalized length of the resampled time functions, the mother wavelet and the resolution level for the approximation. In the experiments over the two databases presented in this paper, these parameters are remained fixed. In particular, the normalized length was set to 256, the wavelet resolution level was set to 3, and the widely used **db4** was chosen as the mother wavelet. Regarding the RF classifier, the parameters to adjust are the number of trees to grow and the number of randomly selected splitting variables to be considered at each node. However, the number of trees to grow does not strongly influence the performance of the classifier as long as it is kept large. In particular, in the experiments presented in this paper this value is set to 1000 trees. Thus, the only tuning parameter of the proposed recognition scheme is the number of randomly selected splitting variables to be considered at each node, hereafter denoted as α.

4.1   Results

The recognition rates of the proposed method over the two audio-visual databases are presented in this subsection. In addition, these results are compared with the ones obtained with a speech recognition system based on Hidden Markov Models (HMMs) over the same databases. Hidden Markov Model approaches have been extensively proposed in the literature for speech recognition [8], and proved to be highly efficient for this task, even on noisy conditions [15]. For comparison purposes, the performance of the HHMs based recognition system was computed for each database, using also two nested 5-fold cross-validation. In particular, the HMMs were implemented using N-state left-to-right models and considering continuous symbol observation, represented by the linear combination of M Gaussian distributions.

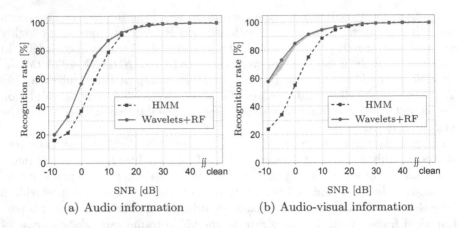

Fig. 3. Recognition rates for different SNRs for the cases of considering (a) only-audio and (b) fused audio-visual information over the AV-UNR database. The performance of the proposed recognition scheme is depicted in solid line (green), while the corresponding to the HMM-based approach is in dashed line (blue). The grey area corresponds to the performances obtained by selecting α in the range from 2 to 6.

AV-UNR database: The results obtained for the cases of considering speech data represented by only-acoustic and audio-visual information over the AV-UNR database are depicted in Fig. 3(a) and 3(b), repectively. It can be seen that for this database, with the proposed approach (solid green line) satisfactory results are obtained, outperforming the HMM-based classification approach (dashed blue line).

AV-CMU database: In Fig. 4(a) and 4(b), the recognition rates obtained over the AV-CMU database are depicted for the cases of considering audio-only and audio-visual information, respectively. As expected, the performance in the recognition task deteriorates as the SNR decreases. For both cases, it can be seen that with the proposed classification scheme (solid green line) good performance is achieved. In particular, in comparison with traditional HMMs approach (dashed blue line), the proposed method leads to significant improvements in the recognition rates for middle and low range SNRs.

The results depicted in Fig. 3 and 4 shows that the proposed method performs well, yielding better performance in comparison with HMM-based methods. As stated before, these experiments were performed by selecting the value for the only tuning parameter, that is the number of randomly selected splitting variables to be considered at each node, via validation procedure (inner CV). However, these experiments also show that this parameter can be selected within a range without significantly affecting the performance of the recognition task. This situation is depicted in Fig. 3 and 4, where the gray areas corresponds to the performances of the system when using α in the range from 2 to 6. Thus, these results indicate that the system can be employed using a fixed setup, *i.e.*, the same wavelet-based representation and RF classifier parameters in all the

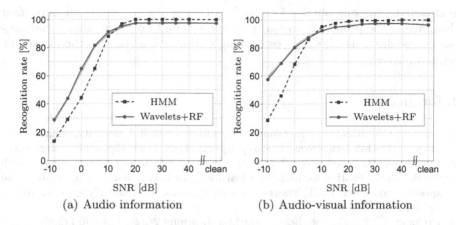

Fig. 4. Recognition rates for different SNRs for the cases of considering (a) only-audio and (b) fused audio-visual information over the AV-CMU database. The performance of the proposed recognition scheme is depicted in solid line (green), while the corresponding to the HMM-based approach is in dashed line (blue). The grey area corresponds to the performances obtained by selecting α in the range from 2 to 6.

experiments, and the performance will be similar to the one obtained through a tuning stage. This is an important advantage of the proposed approach in comparison to other methods that necessarily require a usually time consuming optimization stage of the classifiers' metaparameters.

5   Conclusion

An audio-visual speech classification scheme based on wavelets and Random Forests have been proposed in this paper. The sequences of input acoustic and visual parameters are represented via wavelet multilevel decomposition, where only the approximation coefficients are retained to represent them. The proposed representation method leads to a fixed length feature vector, independently of the number of frames associated with each word. This method is also independent of the kind of input feature, either audio-only or fused audio-visual, being considered. These fixed-length wavelet-based feature vectors are then used to model the speech information. Speech recognition is then performed using these wavelet-based features and a Random Forests classification method. The performance of the proposed recognition scheme is evaluated over two different isolated word audio-visual databases. Experimental results show that a good performance is achieved with the proposed system, outperforming the efficiency of traditional Hidden Markov Model-based approaches. The proposed system has only one tuning parameter which can be selected within a small range without significantly changing the recognition results. The experimental results show that the system can be employed using a fixed setup, *i.e.*, the same wavelet-based representation and RF classifier parameters in all the experiments, and the performance will be similar to the one obtained through a tuning stage. This is an important advantage of the proposed approach in comparison to other methods that necessarily require a usually time consuming optimization stage of the classifiers' metaparameters.

References

1. Advanced Multimedia Processing Laboratory. Cornell University, Ithaca, NY. http://chenlab.ece.cornell.edu/projects/AudioVisualSpeechProcessing/
2. Borgström, B., Alwan, A.: A low-complexity parabolic lip contour model with speaker normalization for high-level feature extraction in noise-robust audiovisual speech recognition. IEEE Transactions on Systems, Man and Cybernetics 38(6), 1273–1280 (2008)
3. Breiman, L.: Bagging predictors. Machine Learning 26(2), 123–140 (1996)
4. Breiman, L.: Random forests. Machine Learning 45(1), 5–32 (2001)
5. Daubechies, I.: Ten Lectures on Wavelets. SIAM, Pennsylvania (1992)
6. NOISEX-92 database. Digital Signal Processing (DSP) group. Rice University, Houston, TX
7. Dupont, S., Luettin, J.: Audio-visual speech modeling for continuous speech recognition. IEEE Trans. Multimedia 2(3), 141–151 (2000)
8. Estellers, V., Gurban, M., Thiran, J.: On dynamic stream weighting for audiovisual speech recognition. IEEE Transactions on Audio, Speech, and Language Processing 20(4), 1145–1157 (2012)
9. Jaimes, A., Sebe, N.: Multimodal human-computer interaction: A survey. Computer Vision and Image Understanding 108(1–2), 116–134 (2007)
10. Krishnamurthy, N., Hansen, J.: Babble noise: Modeling, analysis, and applications. IEEE Transactions on Audio, Speech, and Language Processing 17(7), 1394–1407 (2009)
11. Papandreou, G., Katsamanis, A., Pitsikalis, V., Maragos, P.: Adaptive multimodal fusion by uncertainty compensation with application to audiovisual speech recognition. Transactions on Audio, Speech, and Language Processing 17(3), 423–435 (2009)
12. Potamianos, G., Neti, C., Gravier, G., Garg, A., Senior, A.W.: Recent advances in the automatic recognition of audio-visual speech. Proceedings of the IEEE 91, 1306–1326 (2003)
13. Shin, J., Lee, J., Kim, D.: Real-time lip reading system for isolated korean word recognition. Pattern Recognition 44(3), 559–571 (2011)
14. Shivappa, S., Trivedi, M., Rao, B.: Audiovisual information fusion in human computer interfaces and intelligent environments: A survey. Proceedings of the IEEE 98(10), 1692–1715 (2010)
15. Terissi, L.D., Sad, G., Gómez, J.C., Parodi, M.: Noisy speech recognition based on combined audio-visual classifiers. Lecture Notes in Computer Science 8869, 43–53 (2015)
16. Zhao, G., Barnard, M., Pietikäinen, M.: Lipreading with local spatiotemporal descriptors. IEEE Transactions on Multimedia 11(7), 1254–1265 (2009)

Fall Detection Algorithm Based on Thresholds and Residual Events

Fily M. Grisales-Franco[1]([✉]), Francisco Vargas[2], Álvaro Ángel Orozco[3],
Mauricio A. Alvarez[3], and German Castellanos-Dominguez[1]

[1] Signal Processing and Recognition Group, Universidad Nacional de Colombia,
Manizales, Colombia
{fmgrisalesl,cgcastellanosd}@unal.edu.co
[2] SISTEMIC, Faculty of Engineering, Universidad de Antioquia UdeA,
Medellín, Colombia
jesus.vargas@udea.edu.co
[3] Grupo de Investigacion En Automatica, Universidad Tecnologica de Pereira,
Pereira, Colombia
{aaog,malvarez}@utp.edu.co

Abstract. Falling is a risk factor of vital importance in elderly adults, hence, the ability to detect falls automatically is necessary to minimize the risk of injury. In this work, we develop a fall detection algorithm based in inertial sensors due its scope of activity, portability, and low cost. This algorithm detects the fall across thresholds and residual events after that occurs, for this it filters the acceleration data through three filtering methodologies and by means of the amount of acceleration difference falls from Activities of Daily Living (ADLs). The algorithm is tested in a human activity and fall dataset, showing improves respect to performance compared with algorithms detailed in the literature.

1 Introduction

The elderly people are facing risk factors as are the falls that can lead to suffer minor, serious and even fatal injuries. It is estimated that each year about one-third of adults over 65 years old suffer falls, and the likelihood of falling increases substantially with advancing age [9]. When a fall occurs, it is possible to minimize the risk of injury depending largely on the response, rescue and timely care. Therefore, an appropriate system for falls detection on real time of elderly people is a problem of interest, which has been approached from different fields based on video [3], acoustic [12], inertial sensors [4] or mobile phone technology [7].

Existing fall detection approaches can be explained and categorized into three different classes, which are: camera, environment sensor, and wearable device based approaches [5]. Fall detection through cameras (vision) or environment sensors (audio, vibration) requires expensive equipment that limits the scope of activity for the person being monitored and can compromise his privacy because these sensors commonly are in indoors. In contrast, fall detection through wearable devices has been increasing because the scope of activity is relatively unrestricted, the device may be easily attached to the body, and its cost is low; this

© Springer International Publishing Switzerland 2015
A. Pardo and J. Kittler (Eds.): CIARP 2015, LNCS 9423, pp. 575–583, 2015.
DOI: 10.1007/978-3-319-25751-8_69

approach is based on embedded inertial sensors to detect the body movement and they are divided into two classes: the first class only analyzes the acceleration to detect falls (accelerometers), and the second class uses the acceleration and the body orientation (accelerometers and gyroscopes) [7].

A key factor to fall detect is the ability that possess the methodologies to acquire, manage, process and get useful information from the inertial sensor raw data, hence, the methodologies must be able to discover accurately features that differentiate a fall from the ADLs. But the raw data generated by the sensors are affected for several sources: some related to intentional movement of the body as human and gravitational acceleration (low frequency signals) and others that may add noise as external vibrations and mechanical resonance (high frequency signals), that should be attenuated by adequate filtering techniques [2].

The fall detection paradigm can be interpreted as a binary classification problem between falls and ADLs, some works implement complex inference techniques as in [9] that use hidden Markov models to analyze acceleration data, but they are inappropriate for falls detection because they spend excessive amounts of computational resources and a fast response is essential. Therefore, most solutions with wearable devices use threshold-based algorithms for detection of falls events because the processing capacity is lower [4].

In this work, we present a fall detection algorithm based on thresholds and residual events after the fall occurs, through an accelerometer worn on the human body. The algorithm uses three filtering methodologies to attenuate the sources that affect the data (Median filter, High pass Finite Impulse Response (FIR) filter, and Soft thresholding), it also uses one feature that measures the amount of acceleration to differentiate falls from ADLs (Signal Magnitude Area). To evaluate the proposed algorithm we implement two algorithms detailed in the literature and we test them using The MobilFall Dataset available online [11]. The results are presented like the capacity to detect or not detect a fall in terms of sensitivity, specificity and hit rate, showing that the proposed algorithm improvement the fall detection regarding algorithms of the literature.

2   Methods

Generality the output of the accelerometer has three signals $A = (x(t), y(t), z(t))$ that represent the tri-axial acceleration x,y,z due to the motion and gravity.

Preprocessing: In the preprocessing step is used a median filter that refers to the replacement of a point A_i by the median values of the signal in a segment $M_e\{A_{(i,j)}\}$ this filter eliminates most of the signal generated by noise, keeping the low frequency components as are the body motion and the gravitational acceleration. Also is used a high pass filter that eliminates the low frequency corresponding to acceleration due to gravity, removing the offset from the signal to give a dynamic acceleration.

To generate a signal and to do more representative the fall with respect to ADLs considering the residual movement, is formulate the Soft Thresholding [6], that is an optimization problem of the form:

$$\underset{B}{\mathrm{argmin}}\{||\boldsymbol{A} - \widehat{\boldsymbol{A}}||_2^2 + \lambda||\widehat{\boldsymbol{A}}||_1\}$$

where $\widehat{\boldsymbol{A}} = (\widehat{\boldsymbol{x}}(t), \widehat{\boldsymbol{y}}(t), \widehat{\boldsymbol{z}}(t))$ are the estimation to be determined from the observe $\boldsymbol{A}$ signals. The regularization term $\lambda||\widehat{\boldsymbol{A}}||_1$ is chosen to promote sparsity of the solution $\widehat{\boldsymbol{A}}$. The Soft Thresholding allows depending on the regularization parameter λ selected to ensure that the noise variance is reduced to a specified fraction of its original value.

Feature Extraction: The algorithms for fall detection use the acceleration and/or orientation data to detect sequential stages to determine a fall, if the sequence is met the fall is confirmed. The sequence of stages may include: start of fallen, velocity, change of orientation and posture monitoring. To such detection the accelerometer signals are characterized through the Signal Magnitude Area (SMA) [13]:

$$SMA = \sum_i |x_i| + \sum_i |y_i| + \sum_i |z_i|,$$

where x_i, y_i, z_i are the ith sample of the $\boldsymbol{x}, \boldsymbol{y}, \boldsymbol{z}$ axis respectively. This feature is independent of the orientation of the device and corresponds to the amount of acceleration that an user has exerted on the accelerometer.

Fall Detection Algorithm: The fall detection algorithm operates in a series of steps represented in the Algorithm 1. First over an observation window in the accelerometer data three preprocessing methods (a median filter, a high pass FIR filter and finally the Soft Thresholding) are applied in order to make more representative the fall. After the Signal Magnitude Area (SMA) is calculated to get the accumulated acceleration and to evaluate if the accumulated acceleration exceeds an acceleration threshold empirically determined, meaning the user is engaged in a high energy activity like running, jumping or a possible fallen. So, if this upper acceleration threshold is exceeded the window is moved a determinate time (sliding windows) and over it is applied again the three preprocessing methods and is calculated the Signal Magnitude Area (SMA), finally if this SMA value no exceeds a lower acceleration threshold empirically determined, it means the user is in a low energy activity and the fall is detected.

3 Experiments

Usually for falls detection through portable devices are used the methodology presented in Fig. 1, our work emphasizes on the stage of data preprocessing and fall detection.

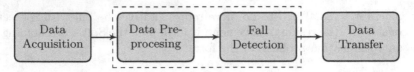

Fig. 1. Framework for fall detection.

The data set used called The MobilFall Dataset (second version) [11] was recorded on the Biomedical Informatics & eHealth Laboratory, at the Department of Informatics Engineering of the Technological Educational Institute of Crete. Data from the accelerometer and gyroscope sensor of a smartphone were recorded with sampling period $7.6ms$ at $87Hz$ mean sampling frequency for the accelerometer and $0.3ms$ at $200Hz$ mean sampling rate for the gyroscope. The MobilFall Dataset contains data from 24 volunteers: seventeen males (age: $22-47$ years, height: $1.69-1.89m$, weight: $64-103kg$) and seven females (age: $22-36$ years, height: $1.60-1.72m$, weight: $50-90kg$). Nine participants performed falls and ADLs, while fifteen performed only the falls, discriminated as shown in the table Table 1.

To build the fall detection algorithm we use the following parameters based on the basic trade-off between detecting all falls and avoiding false positives: The windows length is $l = 2$ seconds, the first acceleration threshold is $11m/s^2$, the second acceleration threshold is a value close to zero, and the wait time is equivalent to $n = 1$ second. In the preprocessing step we use the follow set of values to ensure good filtering as they do in [1]: for the median filter we determine

---

Algorithm 1. Fall Detection

Input acceleration: $\boldsymbol{A} \in \mathbb{R}^{3 \times t}$, Windows length: l and Thresholds: $\zeta_u, \zeta_l \in \mathbb{R}^+$.
Initialize the windows $\boldsymbol{A}_{(i,j)}$ where $l = |i - j|$.
while Fall is not detected **do**
    Apply the Median Filter, the High Pass Filter, and the Soft Thresholding.
    Calculate $\boldsymbol{A}_{SMA} = SMA\{\boldsymbol{A}_{(i,j)}\}$
    if $\boldsymbol{A}_{SMA} > \zeta_u$ **then**
        wait n samples and set $\boldsymbol{A}_{(i+n,j+n)}$
        Apply the Median Filter, the High Pass Filter, and the Soft Thresholding.
        Calculate $\boldsymbol{A}_{SMA} = SMA\{\boldsymbol{A}_{(i+n,j+n)}\}$
        if $\boldsymbol{A}_{SMA} < \zeta_l$ **then**
            Fall is detected
        else
            Fall is not detected
        end if
    else
        Fall is not detected
    end if
    Increment the windows.
end while

Table 1. The MobiFall Dataset.

	Type	Trials	Time	Description
FOL	Forward-lying	3	10s	Fall Forward from standing, use of hands to dampen fall
FKL	Front-knees-lying	3	10s	Fall forward from standing, first impact on knees
SDL	Back-sitting-chair	3	10s	Fall backward while trying to sit on a chair
BSC	Sideward-lying	3	10s	Fall sidewards from standing, bending legs
STD	Standing	1	5m	Standing with subtle movements
WAL	Walking	1	5m	Normal walking
JOG	Jogging	3	30s	Jogging
JUM	Jumping	3	30s	Continuous jumping
STU	Stairs up	6	10s	Stairs up (10 stairs)
STN	Stairs down	6	10s	Stairs down (10 stairs)
SCH	Sit chair	6	6s	Sitting on a chair
CSI	Car-step in	6	6s	Step in a car
CSO	Car-step out	6	6s	Step out a car

Table 1 Shows the Falls (FOL, FKL, SDL, BSC) and the ADLs (STD, WAL, JOG, JUM, STU, STN, SCH, CSI, CSO) recorded in the MobiFall Dataset.

a filter of order 13, in the high pass FIR filter we use a order of 35, with stop frequency of $0.5Hz$. And to select the regularization parameter λ in the Soft Thresholding we set a series of values and select the value that gives better results in the methodology respect to the Hit Rate, Sensitivity and Specificity, as shows the Fig. 2, that value corresponds to $\lambda = 0.1$.

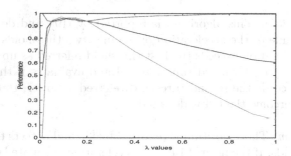

Fig. 2. Performance against λ, respect to Hit Rate, Sensitivity, Specificity.

The Fig. 3 shows an example of how the preprocessing step with the three filter methods affects the accelerometer signals to generate a representation more suitable of a fall taking into account the residual events. The Fig. 3(a) shows a fall of type FOL. The Fig. 3(b) shows the fall signal after of apply the median filter. The Fig. 3(c) shows the fall signal filtered Fig. 3(b) after of apply the high pass FIR filter. And the Fig. 3(d) shows the fall signal filtered Fig. 3(c) after of apply the Soft Thresholding.

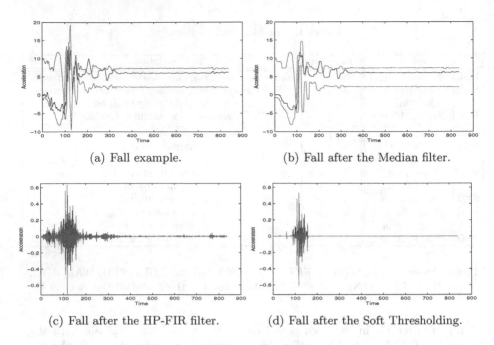

(a) Fall example.   (b) Fall after the Median filter.

(c) Fall after the HP-FIR filter.   (d) Fall after the Soft Thresholding.

Fig. 3. Example of the preprocessing step in a fall signal. x axis, y axis, z axis.

In order to compare the proposed algorithm we implement two algorithms detailed in the literature:

Panagiotis Algorithm: This algorithm is reported by [10], and detects the fall when the magnitude of the acceleration overcomes two thresholds. If the magnitude of the acceleration exceeds the first threshold referred as upper, then the algorithm waits a predetermined time interval and evaluates if the magnitude of acceleration exceeds the second threshold referred as lower, thus, if the two thresholds are overcome the fall is detected.

Suleman Algorithm: This algorithm is reported by [8], and detects the fall evaluating two thresholds. If the norm $L1$ of the acceleration calculated every second exceeds a first threshold of acceleration, the algorithm waits a predetermined time and checks the orientation through the tilt angle, and if a second threshold of angle is overcome by the tilt angle, this means that the user is not standing and has fallen.

To evaluate properly the fall detection algorithm the results are presented in terms of sensitivity, specificity and hit rate as shown in the table 2, the results are represented like the capacity of detect or no a fall, so, the sensitivity represents the capacity to detect falls, the specificity represents the capacity of only detect falls and ignore non fall events, and the hit rate represents the proportion of true results among the population.

Table 2. Results of the four fall detection algorithms.

Activity	Type	Panagiotis Alg [10] Sensitivity	Specificity	Suleman Alg [8] Sensitivity	Specificity	Proposed Alg Sensitivity	Specificity
Fall	FOL	0,9722		0,9306		0,9583	
	FKL	0,9306		0,9861		0,9722	
	SDL	0,9444		0,9722		0,9722	
	BSC	0,9722		0,9167		0,9583	
ADL	STD		1,0000		1,0000		1,0000
	WAL		0,1111		1,0000		1,0000
	JOG		0,7037		0,7037		1,0000
	JUM		1,0000		0,3333		1,0000
	STU		0,6481		1,0000		1,0000
	STN		0,5556		1,0000		0,9074
	SCH		1,0000		1,0000		0,9444
	CSI		1,0000		0,6296		0,8889
	CSO		1,0000		1,0000		0,9444
Total		0,9549	0,8275	0,9514	0,8655	**0.9653**	**0,9503**
Hit Rate		0,8857		0,9048		**0,9571**	

4 Discussion and Conclusion Remarks

In the present work, we implement a fall detection algorithm based on thresholds to detect sequential stages in inertial sensor data, the MobilFall Dataset (second version) was used in order to evaluate the fall detection algorithm comparing it against two algorithms detailed in the literature. The result presents in the table 2 show the strengths and weaknesses of each one of the algorithms with respect to the different types of fall and ADLs.

As seen in the Fig. 3 for a fall detection algorithm in the step of preprocessing an adequate filtering techniques allows detect patterns corresponding to a fall and give acceleration signals more suitable to the classification step to decide between a fall and an ADL. Therefore the median filter Fig. 3(b) reduces the noise in the accelerometer signal and provide to the High Pass FIR filter a cleaner signal. The High Pass FIR filter Fig. 3(c) is used to remove the offset from the signals and obtain a dynamic acceleration. The Soft Thresholding Fig. 3(d) promotes sparsity to the acceleration signal representing the low energy activities as zero, necessary in the algorithm to decide whether there has been a fall, since in the moment of detect the fall is important to consider the residual events, like they are: the user direction, the energy activity, and the normal acceleration values.

In the table 2 we see that the Panagiotis algorithm [10] presents better capacity of detect falls that of ignore non fall events, higher sensitivity than specificity. It works better for falls of type FOL, BSC than for FKL and SDL; on the other hand the algorithm works well for ADLs as STD, SCH, CSI, CSO. Commonly these activities do not exceed the upper threshold and if exceed it, they do not exceed the lower threshold. Unlike the algorithm does not perform well with WAL, JOG, STU and STN that are higher energy activities that they can exceed the upper and lower thresholds. We see also that the Suleman algorithm [8] has less sensitivity and higher specificity with respect to Panagiotis algorithm, this algorithm present more sensitivity for falls of type FKL and SDL than for FOL and BSC falls; at the ADLs the algorithm presents more specificity for STD, WAL, STU, STN, SCH, CSO than for JOG, JUM, CSI; as the algorithm works with the subject direction these three ADLs present more intensity that affects the device direction.

The results in the table 2 shows with respect to the Hit Rate, the total of sensitivity and specificity that the proposed algorithm performs better than the Panagiotis and Suleman algorithms that are detailed in the literature. For falls we see that our algorithm in terms of sensitivity compared to the Suleman algorithm improves in FOL, BSC and keeps in SDL and in terms of specificity it is equal in STD, WAL, and STU because these activities do not exceed the first threshold in the two algorithms. For ADLs the proposed algorithm has more specificity in JOG, JUM, and CSI because it does not take into account the direction (in these ADLs the Suleman algorithm presents the lowest values of specificity), our algorithm has less specificity in STN, SCH, and CSO; probably It detects them as a fall, because these activities present a moment of high energy where the first threshold could be overcome, followed by a moment of low energy where the second threshold could be not overcome.

As future work, it is important to test the proposed algorithm in others data sets, and find automatically the optimal regularization parameter λ in the Soft Thresholding.

Acknowledgments. This work was supported by the project *"Plataforma tecnológica para los servicios de teleasistencia, emergencias médicas, seguimiento y monitoreo permanente a los pacientes y apoyo a los programas de promoción y prevención"*, code "Ruta-N: 512C-2013"; the research project 16882 funded by Universidad Nacional de Colombia and Universidad de Caldas; and the the research projects 111065740687, 111056934461 funded by COLCIENCIAS.

References

1. de Alba, S.G., Clifford, M., Reyna, R., Palomera, E., Gonzalez, R.: Human fall detection using 3-axis accelerometer (2005)
2. Figo, D., Diniz, P.C., Ferreira, D.R., Cardoso, J.M.P.: Preprocessing techniques for context recognition from accelerometer data. Personal Ubiquitous Comput. **14**(7), 645–662 (2010)
3. Ke, S.R., Thuc, H.L.U., Lee, Y.J., Hwang, J.N., Yoo, J.H., Choi, K.H.: A review on video-based human activity recognition. Computers **2**(2), 88–131 (2013)
4. Li, Q., Stankovic, J., Hanson, M., Barth, A., Lach, J., Zhou, G.: Accurate, fast fall detection using gyroscopes and accelerometer-derived posture information. In: Sixth International Workshop on Wearable and Implantable Body Sensor Networks, BSN 2009, pp. 138–143 (2009)

5. Mubashir, M., Shao, L., Seed, L.: A survey on fall detection: Principles and approaches. Neurocomputing **100**, 144–152 (2013). special issue: Behaviours in video
6. Chen, P.-Y., Selesnick, I.W.: Overlapping group shrinkage/thresholding and denoising. In: ASEE 2014 Zone I Conference, September 2012
7. Hwang, S.-Y., Ryu, M.-H., Yang, S.Y., Lee, N.B.: Fall detection with three-axis accelerometer and magnetometer in a smartphone. In: Computer Science and Technology, pp. 65–70 (2012)
8. Kazi, S.B., Sikander, S., Yousafzai, S.: Fall detection using single tri-axial accelerometer. In: ASEE 2014 Zone I Conference, April 2014
9. Tong, L., Song, Q., Ge, Y., Liu, M.: Hmm-based human fall detection and prediction method using tri-axial accelerometer. Sensors Journal, IEEE **13**(5), 1849–1856 (2013)
10. Torrent, J., Kostopoulos, P., Nunes, T., Salvi, K., Deriaz, M.: Increased fall detection accuracy in an accelerometer-based algorithm considering residual movement. In: ICPRAM 2015, 4th International Conference on Pattern Recognition Applications and Methods, January 2015
11. Vavoulas, G., Pediaditis, M., Spanakis, E., Tsiknakis, M.: The mobifall dataset: an initial evaluation of fall detection algorithms using smartphones. In: 2013 IEEE 13th International Conference on Bioinformatics and Bioengineering (BIBE), pp. 1–4, November 2013
12. Yazar, A.: Multi-sensor based ambient assisted living (2013)
13. He, Y., Li, Y., Chuan, Y.: Falling-incident detection and alarm by smartphone with multimedia messaging service (mms). Computer Science & Communications, ETSN **1**(1), 1–5 (2012)

Digital Filter Design with Time Constraints Based on Calculus of Variations

Karel Toledo, Jorge Torres$^{(\boxtimes)}$, and Liset Martínez

Higher Polytechnic Institute José Antonio Echeverría,
114. 11901, 19390 La Habana, Cuba
karel.tdlg@gmail.com, {jorge.tg,liset}@electrica.cujae.edu.cu
http://www.cujae.cu

Abstract. Digital filter design with short transient state is a problem encountered in many fields of signal processing. In this paper a novel low-pass filter design technique with time-varying parameters is introduced in order to minimize the rise-time parameter. Through the use of calculus of variations a methodology is developed to write down the optimal closed-form expression for varying the parameters. In this concern, two cases are addressed. The ideal case in which infinite bandwidth is required and a solution of finite bandwidth. The latest is obtained by means of a proper restriction in the frequency domain. The proposed filter achieves the shortest rise-time and allows better preservation of the edge shape in comparison with other reported filtering methods. The performance of the proposed system is illustrated with the aid of simulations.

Keywords: Filter design · Rise-time · Time-varying parameters · Calculus of variations

1 Introduction

Time constraint filter design is widely used for receiving signal involving rectangular pulses. Several configurations are based on the displacement of poles over particular curves in the S plane with regard to the Butterworth design, in order to obtain a reduction of rise-time. For instance, some designs use the parabola [12], the ellipse [16] or the catenary curves [7].

Other solutions modify the equations formula of a given design by a parameter. In this respect, a modification of the Bessel filter is considered in [8], and the rise-time is decremented through the increase of a given parameter. However, the cutoff frequency is also shifted, which represent a trade-off for this type of solution. Moreover, a method for the synthesis of the wide-band amplifier transfer function can be developed by using the direct performance parameter in the time domain, known as delay to rise-time ratio [5].

On the other hand, the eigenfilter method represents an approach in a least square sense [11]. This design is implemented with time and frequency constraints in order to minimize the rise-time and overshoot of the step response

© Springer International Publishing Switzerland 2015
A. Pardo and J. Kittler (Eds.): CIARP 2015, LNCS 9423, pp. 584–592, 2015.
DOI: 10.1007/978-3-319-25751-8_70

simultaneously. In a similar way, the linear programming has been applied to filter design. In this methodology the ease of implementation is remarkable and the convergence to a unique-solution is generally guaranteed [9].

Furthermore, by means of several analytic definitions of rise-time parameter, closed-form relations can be obtained for the filter coefficients. These coefficients are established looking for the minimum value of the rise-time. A first approach for defining the rise-time analytically, given in [4], is based on the standard deviation of the impulse response. A second approach, described in [3], is obtained under the constraint of a given noise bandwidth. Finally, after considering restrictions in the bandwidth, optimal expressions of the filter coefficients are suggested in [15].

However, when a constant cutoff frequency is specified in advance, the indeterminacy principle establishes a lower bound for the rise-time. In order to overcome this issue, the variation of parameters in time is considered in [10,14]. This solution has been implemented in many fields of signal processing as: seismic data processing, navigation systems, speech analysis and measurement of evoked potentials of the human brain [10].

The contribution of this paper is focused on obtaining the optimal close-form expression for the characteristic frequency function, in order to minimize the rise-time. This solution is motivated by the work presented in [10]. A practical approximation and the digital implementation of the proposed time-varying system are also discussed. The results show to possess many advantages over the above-mentioned time-varying systems.

2 Filter Conception

2.1 Problem Formulation

Analog second order systems are described by the following transfer function:

$$H(s) = \frac{k}{\frac{1}{\omega_0^2}s^2 + \frac{2\beta}{\omega_0}s + 1} \tag{1}$$

where k, β and ω_0 represent the gain, the damping factor and the characteristic frequency, respectively. In addition, β and ω_0 are related to the step response. The larger values of β and ω_0 are, the smaller the output oscillations and the rise-time become.

Besides, the step response of the second-order filter [10] is given by:

$$g(t) = 1 - \left[\cos\left(\omega_0 t \sqrt{1 - \beta^2}\right) + \frac{1}{\sqrt{1 - \beta^2}} \sin\left(\omega_0 t \sqrt{1 - \beta^2}\right) \right] \cdot e^{-\beta\omega_0 t} \tag{2}$$

Usually, the rise-time is defined as the time interval T_R between $g(t) = 0.1$ and $g(t) = 0.9$. Moreover, it is known as the time required for the step response to increase from 10 to 90 percent of its final value [1]. However, to establish an analytic expression of T_R from this definition is not possible. An alternative rise-time definition [4] is shown in Fig. 1 taking into account the impulse response $h(t)$. This definition is applied in particular fields as indicated in [2]. The quantity is directly related to the standard deviation of the impulse response $h(t)$ and is equaled to:

$$T_R = \sqrt{2\pi \left[\int_0^\infty t^2 h(t) \mathrm{d}t - T_D^2 \right]} \tag{3}$$

where T_D is the time-delay and can be defined as the centroid of area of the curve $h(t)$ [4], i.e.:

$$T_D = \int_0^\infty t \cdot h(t) \mathrm{d}t \tag{4}$$

An expression for varying the ω_0 parameter in time for the second order system given in (2) is proposed in [10]. This dynamic system allows a reduction of rise-time. However, the optimal relations are not derived, which in turn demands further analysis. The next Section addresses a method for solving the above problem based on the definition given in (3) and the use of calculus of variations.

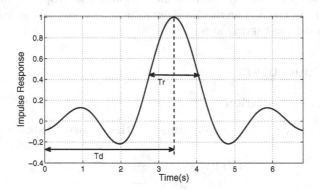

Fig. 1. Impulse response of a generic system.

2.2   Ideal Case with Infinite Bandwidth

The aforementioned close-form expression of rise-time in (3) can be considered as the functional of a variational problem [17] of the form:

$$I(\omega_0(t)) = \int_0^\infty F(\omega_0(t), \omega_0'(t), t) \mathrm{d}t \tag{5}$$

where

$$F(\omega_0(t), \omega_0'(t), t) = t^2 \cdot h(\omega_0(t), \omega_0'(t), t) \qquad (6)$$

and $T_D = 0$ for minimizing the time-delay parameter simultaneously. The impulse response of second-order systems with time-varying characteristic frequency is $h(\omega_0(t), \omega_0'(t), t)$. This term is represented by the inverse Laplace transform of the equation (1) or the derivative of the step response (2) as follows:

$$h(t) = \frac{R}{2}\left[(P_{2t} + jP_{1t})e^{P_2+jP_1} + (P_{2t} - jP_{1t})e^{P_2-jP_1}\right] \qquad (7)$$

where

$$R = \sqrt{\frac{2-\beta^2}{1-\beta^2}}, \quad P_1 = \omega_0(t)\sqrt{1-\beta^2}t + \tan^{-1}\left(\frac{-1}{\sqrt{1-\beta^2}}\right) \qquad (8)$$

$$P_2 = -\omega_0(t)\beta t, \quad P_{1t} = \sqrt{1-\beta^2}(\omega_0(t) + \omega_0'(t)t), \quad P_{2t} = -\beta(\omega_0(t) + \omega_0'(t)t)$$

The integrand given in (5) is related to the definition of T_R in (3). The number $I(\omega_0(t))$, defined in (5), gives a measure of rise-time, with lower $I(\omega_0(t))$ the rise-time assumes a lesser value. The main idea is to find an optimal expression of $\omega_0(t)$, denoted by $\overline{\omega_0}(t)$, in order to obtain the optimal value of the T_R parameter. This solution must satisfy the Euler-Lagrange equation written as [17]:

$$\frac{\partial F}{\partial \omega_0}\left(\overline{\omega_0}(t), \frac{d\overline{\omega_0}}{dt}(t), t\right) - \frac{d}{dt}\left(\frac{\partial F}{\partial \omega_0'}\left(\overline{\omega_0}(t), \frac{d\overline{\omega_0}}{dt}(t), t\right)\right) = 0 \qquad (9)$$

By writing out the derivatives, the following condition arises:

$$- 2t^2 Re^{P_2}\beta \cos(P_1) = 0 \qquad (10)$$

in which the solution is given by $P_1 = (2k+1)\frac{\pi}{2}$. Finally, through the definition of P_1 in (8) the final expression of $\overline{\omega_0}(t)$ is described as:

$$\overline{\omega_0}(t) = -\frac{(2k+1)\frac{\pi}{2} + \tan^{-1}\left(\frac{1}{\sqrt{1-\beta^2}}\right)}{\sqrt{1-\beta^2}t} \qquad t \neq 0 \qquad (11)$$

The time-varying solution given in (11), for the characteristic frequency, goes to infinity when t approach to zero, that is, the system can not be implemented by any practical system in hardware. However, a solution can be addressed adding an expression of energy restriction for the $\overline{\omega_0}(t)$ curve. This is described in the next Section.

2.3   Proposed Method with Finite Bandwidth

The class of problem in which the required functional is expressed with integral restrictions is called isoperimetric [17]. The isoperimetric problem allows to establish conditions for obtaining bounded solutions. In this case, the constraint introduced is described as:

$$E_{\omega_0} = \int_0^\infty \omega_0^2(t)\mathrm{d}t = constant \tag{12}$$

The condition (12) ensures a bounded solution for the variational problem in (5). The new expression for the functional can be rewritten as follows:

$$F(\omega_0(t), \omega_0'(t), t) = t^2 \cdot h(\omega_0(t), \omega_0'(t), t) + \lambda\omega_0^2(t) \tag{13}$$

where λ is the undetermined Lagrangian multiplier whose values must be determined. Thus, according to the Euler-Lagrange equation given in (9) with the functional described in (13), the following condition must be satisfied:

$$-t^2 R\beta \cos\left(\overline{\omega_0}(t)\sqrt{1 - \beta^2}t + \tan^{-1}\left(\frac{1}{\sqrt{1 - \beta^2}}\right)\right)e^{-\overline{\omega_0}(t)\beta t} + \lambda\overline{\omega_0}(t) = 0 \tag{14}$$

From (14) the obtaining of a closed-form expression for $\overline{\omega_0}(t)$ is not affordable and the solution is investigated by numerical methods. For each value of t, $\overline{\omega_0}(t)$ represents the root of the function defined in the left member of (14). Fig. 2 shows a plot of the $\overline{\omega_0}(t)$ encountered by a combination of bisection, secant, and inverse quadratic interpolation methods [6] when t is varied from 0 to $65.7596 \cdot 10^{-5}$ in steps of $2.2676 \cdot 10^{-5}$ seconds having a precision of $1.1102 \cdot 10^{-16}$ Hertz.

A family of curves is obtained for each different value of λ specified in Fig. 2. The value of λ controls the peak of the curve, higher peaks demand higher bandwidth and produce lower rise-time. The curves on Fig. 2 illustrates the bounded behavior specified by the isoperimetric condition.

3   Digital Implementation

The digital implementation of the proposed filter with varying parameters is carried out using the bilinear transformation $s = 2f_s(\frac{1-z^{-1}}{1+z^{-1}})$ in order to avoid the aliasing effect [13]. Consequently, the analog filter shown in (1) is transformed into a digital filter as follow:

$$H(z) = \frac{b_0 + b_1 z^{-1} + b_2 z^{-2}}{a_0 + a_1 z^{-1} + a_2 z^{-2}} \tag{15}$$

where:

$$b_0 = \overline{\omega_0}^2, \quad b_1 = 2\overline{\omega_0}^2, \quad b_2 = \overline{\omega_0}^2 \tag{16}$$
$$a_0 = 4f_s^2 + 4f_s\beta\overline{\omega_0} + \overline{\omega_0}^2, \quad a_1 = 2\overline{\omega_0}^2 - 8f_s^2, \quad a_2 = 4f_s^2 - 4f_s\beta\overline{\omega_0} + \overline{\omega_0}^2$$

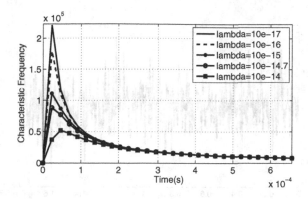

Fig. 2. Characteristic Frequency for particular values of λ.

From the relation given in (15) the following difference equation is obtained after applying the inverse z-Transform:

$$y[n] = \frac{b_0}{a_0}x[n] + \frac{b_1}{a_0}x[n-1] + \frac{b_2}{a_0}x[n-2] - \frac{a_1}{a_0}y[n-1] - \frac{a_2}{a_0}y[n-2] \qquad (17)$$

Moreover, the coefficients of the difference equation given in (17) are updated based on the time-varying characteristic frequency described by $\overline{\omega_0}(t)$. In regard to hardware complexity, the scheme for implementing the proposed system is conformed by two blocks, one for the synchronization procedure and one for the digital system $H(z)$. In this respect, a similar behavior compared to the system presented for Kaszynski-Piskorowski [10] is obtained.

4   Results

In order to illustrate the performance of the given design graphical results are obtained in a noisy environment. Figure 3 depicts the rectangular impulse signal at the input of the proposed filter. In this case, the signal-to-noise ratio (SNR) parameter is equaled to 5 dB. A filter with time-varying characteristic frequency is implemented based on the curve obtained in Fig. 2 and sampling frequency $f_s = 44100$ Hz. In this case, a value of $\lambda = 10^{-14.7}$ is chosen in order to reduce the oscillations at the output. However, an optimum value of λ must be investigated.

For comparing the output filtered signals, three different systems are analyzed: traditional filter of constant parameter given in (2), time-varying parameters filter presented for Kaszynski and Piskorowski [10,14], and the proposed method based on calculus of variations.

The first simulation is made by equaling the peaks of $\overline{\omega_0}(t)$ of both methods, the proposed solution and the Kaszynski-Piskorowski method. Besides, a value of $d = 10$ is assumed in [10] in order to evaluate the methods in similar conditions. The filter of constant parameter is implemented having $\beta = 0.866$ and $\omega_0 = 10^4$ rad/s.

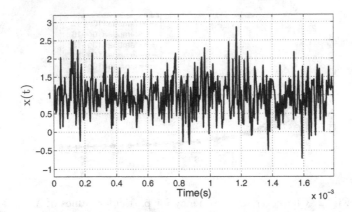

Fig. 3. Rectangular impulse of SNR equaled to 5 dB.

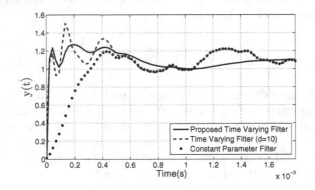

Fig. 4. Output filtered signals by three different systems.

Fig. 4 shows similar behavior of the systems analyzed taking into account the rise-time. The proposed solution, the Kaszynski-Piskorowski method and the constant parameter filter exhibit values of T_R equals to $1.7857 \cdot 10^{-5}$, $1.8714 \cdot 10^{-5}$ and $30.0904 \cdot 10^{-5}$ seconds, respectively. The proposed solution improves the T_R parameter in comparison to the Kaszynski-Piskorowski method.

The rise-time parameter is incremented to $4.1211 \cdot 10^{-5}$ seconds choosing a value of $d = 5$. This value is selected in order to minimize the oscillations for the Kaszynski-Piskorowski method [10,14]. According to this, the proposed filter, developed in Section 2, allows shorter transient state and smaller overshoot than any of the other time-varying parameter techniques reported.

On the other hand, the second simulation is performed by using the input signal with step changes and $SNR = 10$ dB, as shown in Fig. 5. This allows to evaluate the case in which rectangular impulses with certain levels are introduced in the proposed system, Fig. 6 depicts the results.

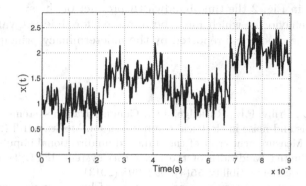

Fig. 5. Signal with step changes and $SNR = 10$ dB.

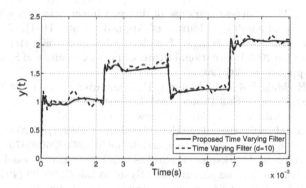

Fig. 6. Filtered signal with step changes.

From Fig. 6 it can be observed that the proposed filter is superior to the Kaszynski-Piskorowski method in the preservation of the pulse shape. In this regard, the rise-time parameter is similar in both of these methods, but the oscillations are smaller in the proposed filter.

5 Conclusion

In this paper a new filter with time-varying parameter is given, which describes an optimal solution for the characteristic frequency by means of calculus of variations. In order to minimize the rise-time parameter, an ideal method and a practical approximation are presented. The digital system is implemented using a bilinear transformation and the result shows a reduction in the rise-time parameter with regard to others reported methods. This methodology allows overshoot and undershoot due to the variation in the spectral properties, however the oscillations exhibit better behavior in comparison with the solution given in [10]. In particular, the trade-off between rise-time and overshoot is an open issue in the frame of calculus of variations and time-varying parameters. Finally, for each value of λ in Fig. 2 the time-bandwidth product of the system is already specified, the behavior of which must be analyzed for different values of λ in comparison to the theoretical reported by the indeterminacy principle.

References

1. Carlson, A.B., Crilly, P.B., Rutledge, J.C.: Communication systems: an introduction to signals and noise in electrical communication. McGraw-Hill (2002)
2. Carobbi, C.: Measurement error of the standard unidirectional impulse waveforms due to the limited bandwidth of the measuring system. IEEE Transactions on Electromagnetic Compatibility 55(4), 692–698 (2013)
3. Chen, H.: On minimum step response rise time of linear low-pass systems under the constraint of a given noise bandwidth. Proceedings of the IEEE 70(4), 404–406 (1982)
4. Elmore, W.C.: The transient response of damped linear networks with particular regard to wideband amplifiers. Journal of Applied Physics 19(1), 55–63 (1948)
5. Filanovsky, I.: One class of transfer functions with monotonic step response. In: Proceedings of the 2003 International Symposium on Circuits and Systems, ISCAS 2003, vol. 1, pp. I-389-I-392 (2003)
6. Forsythe, G.E., Malcolm, M.A., Moler, C.B.: Computer Methods for Mathematical Computations. Prentice Hall Professional Technical Reference (1977)
7. Ghausi, M.S., Adamowicz, M.: A new class of filters for pulse applications. Journal of the Franklin Institute 282(1), 20–30 (1966). http://www.sciencedirect.com/science/article/pii/0016003266903759
8. Johnson, J., Johnson, D., Boudra, P., Stokes, V.: Filters using bessel-type polynomials. IEEE Transactions on Circuits and Systems 23(2), 96–99 (1976)
9. Johnson, A.T.J.: Optimal linear phase digital filter design by one-phase linear programming. IEEE Transactions on Circuits and Systems 37(4), 554–558 (1990)
10. Kaszynski, R., Piskorowski, J.: Selected structures of filters with time-varying parameters. IEEE Transactions on Instrumentation and Measurement 56(6), 2338–2345 (2007)
11. Kok, C.W., Law, Y.M.: Constrained eigenfilter design without specified transition bands. In: 2004 Proceedings of the IEEE International Conference on Acoustics, Speech, and Signal Processing, (ICASSP 2004), vol. 2, pp. ii-401-4 (2004)
12. Mullick, S.: Pulse networks with parabolic distribution of poles. IRE Transactions on Circuit Theory 8(3), 302–305 (1961)
13. Oppenheim, A.V., Schafer, R.W.: Discrete-time signal processing, Third edition. Prentice Hall (2010)
14. Piskorowski, J.: Phase-compensated time-varying butterworth filters. Analog Integrated Circuits and Signal Processing 47(2), 233–241 (2006). http://link.springer.com/article/10.1007/s10470-006-5255-9
15. Roy, S.: Transient response characteristics of a third-order filter. IEEE Transactions on Circuit Theory 15(1), 69–71 (1968)
16. Scanlan, J., Lim, J.: Phase response and ripple in minimum-phase broadband equalizers. IEEE Transactions on Circuit Theory 11(4), 507–508 (1964)
17. Weinstock, R.: Calculus of Variations: With Applications to Physics and Engineering. Courier Dover Publications (1974)

Theory of Pattern Recognition

Discriminative Training for Convolved Multiple-Output Gaussian Processes

Sebastián Gómez-González$^{(\boxtimes)}$, Mauricio A. Álvarez, Hernan F. García,
Jorge I. Ríos, and Alvaro A. Orozco

Faculty of Engineering, Universidad Tecnológica de Pereira, Pereira, Colombia
segomez@utp.edu.co

Abstract. Multi-output Gaussian processes (MOGP) are probability distributions over vector-valued functions, and have been previously used for multi-output regression and for multi-class classification. A less explored facet of the multi-output Gaussian process is that it can be used as a generative model for vector-valued random fields in the context of pattern recognition. As a generative model, the multi-output GP is able to handle vector-valued functions with continuous inputs, as opposed, for example, to hidden Markov models. It also offers the ability to model multivariate random functions with high dimensional inputs. In this paper, we use a discriminative training criteria known as Minimum Classification Error to fit the parameters of a multi-output Gaussian process. We compare the performance of generative training and discriminative training of MOGP in subject recognition, activity recognition, and face recognition. We also compare the proposed methodology against hidden Markov models trained in a generative and in a discriminative way.

1 Introduction

A growing interest within the Gaussian processes community in Machine learning has been the formulation of suitable covariance functions for describing multiple output processes as a joint Gaussian process. Examples include the semi-parametric latent factor model [17], the multi-task Gaussian process [5], or the convolved multi-output Gaussian process [1, 6]. Each of these methods uses as a model for the covariance function either a version of the linear model of coregionalization (LMC) [9] or a version of process convolutions (PC) [11]. Different alternatives for building covariance functions for multiple-output processes have been reviewed by [3].

Multiple output GPs have been used for supervised learning problems, specifically, for multi-output regression [5], and multi-class classification [7,16]. The interest has been mainly on exploiting the correlations between outputs to improve the prediction performance, when compared to modeling each output independently. In particular, a Gaussian process is used as a prior over vector-valued functions $\mathbf{f}(\mathbf{x})$ mapping from $\mathbf{x} \in \mathbb{R}^p$ to $\mathbf{f}(\mathbf{x}) \in \mathbb{R}^D$. Components of $\mathbf{f}(\mathbf{x})$ may be continuous or discrete.

© Springer International Publishing Switzerland 2015
A. Pardo and J. Kittler (Eds.): CIARP 2015, LNCS 9423, pp. 595–602, 2015.
DOI: 10.1007/978-3-319-25751-8_71

In this paper, we advocate the use of multi-output GPs as generative models for vector-valued random fields, this is, we use multi-output GPs to directly modeling $p(\mathbf{f}(\mathbf{x}))$. Afterwards, we use this probabilistic model to tackle a classification problem. An important application area where this setup is of interest is in multivariate time series classification. Here the vector-valued function $\mathbf{f}$ is evaluated at discrete values of $\mathbf{x}$, and it is typically modeled using an unsupervised learning method like a hidden Markov model (HMM) or a linear dynamical system (LDS) [4]. Notice that by using a multi-output GP to model $\mathbf{f}(\mathbf{x})$, we allow the vector-valued function $\mathbf{f}(\mathbf{x})$ to be continuous on the input space. Furthermore, we are able to model multivariate random functions for which $p > 1$. It is worth mentioning that the model we propose here, is different from classical GP classification as explained for example in [15]. In standard GP classification, the feature space is not assumed to follow a particular structure, whereas in our model, the assumption is that the feature space may be structured, with potentially correlated and spatially varying features.

As a generative model, the multi-output Gaussian process can be used for classification: we fit a multi-output GP for every class independently, and to classify a new vector-valued random field, we compute its likelihood for each class and make a decision using Bayes rule. This generative approach works well when the real multivariate signal's distribution is known, but this is rarely the case. Notice that the optimization goal in the generative model is not a function that measures classification performance, but a likelihood function that is optimized for each class separately.

An alternative is to use discriminative training [12] for estimating the parameters of the multi-output GP. A discriminative approach optimizes a function classification performance directly. Thus, the results of the discriminative training procedure are usually better for classification problems. There are different criteria to perform discriminative training, including maximum mutual information (MMI) [10], and minimum classification error (MCE) [13].

In this paper we present a discriminative approach to estimate the hyper-parameters of a multi-output Gaussian Process (MOGP) based on minimum classification error (MCE). In section 2 we review how to fit the multi-output GP model using the generative approach, and then we introduce our method to train the same MOGP model with a discriminative approach based on MCE. In section 3 we show experimental results, with both the generative and discriminative approaches. Finally, we present conclusions on section 4.

2   Generative and Discriminative Training of MOGPs

In our classification scenario, we have M classes. We want to come up with a classifier that allows us to map the matrix $\mathbf{F}(\mathbf{X})$ to one of the M classes. Columns of matrix $\mathbf{X}$ are input vectors $\mathbf{x}_n \in \mathbb{R}^p$, and columns of matrix $\mathbf{F}$ are feature vectors $\mathbf{f}(\mathbf{x}_n) \in \mathbb{R}^D$, for some n in an index set. Rows for $\mathbf{F}$ correspond to different entries of $\mathbf{f}(\mathbf{x}_n)$ evaluated for all n. For example, in a multi-variate time series classification problem, $\mathbf{x}_n$ is a time point t_n, and $\mathbf{f}(\mathbf{x}_n)$ is the multi-variate time series at $\mathbf{x}_n = t_n$. Rows of the matrix $\mathbf{F}$ are the different time series.

The main idea that we introduce in this paper is that we model the class-conditional density $p(\mathbf{F}|\mathbf{X}, \mathcal{C}_m, \boldsymbol{\theta}_m)$ using a multi-output Gaussian process, where $\mathcal{C}_m$ is the class m, and $\boldsymbol{\theta}_m$ are hyperparameters of the multi-output GP for class m. By doing so, we allow correlations across the columns and rows of $\mathbf{F}$. We then estimate $\boldsymbol{\theta}_m$ for all m in a generative classification scheme, and in a discriminative classification scheme using minimum classification error. Notice that a HMM would model $p(\mathbf{F}|\mathcal{C}_m, \boldsymbol{\theta}_m)$, since vectors $\mathbf{f}_n$ would be already defined for discrete values of $\mathbf{x}$. Also notice that in standard GP classification, we would model $p(\mathcal{C}_m|\mathbf{F})$, without any particular correlation assumptions over $\mathbf{F}$.

Available data for each class are matrices $\mathbf{F}_m^l$, where $m = 1, \ldots, M$, and $l = 1, \ldots, L_m$. Index l runs over the instances for a class, and each class has L_m instances. In turn, each matrix $\mathbf{F}_m^l \in \mathbb{R}^{D \times N_m^l}$ with columns $\mathbf{f}_m^l(\mathbf{x}_n) \in \mathbb{R}^D$, $\mathbf{x}_n \in \mathbb{R}^p$, and $n = 1, \ldots, N_m^l$. To reduce clutter in the notation, we assume that $L_m = L$ for all m, and $N_m^l = N$ for all m, and l. Entries in $\mathbf{f}_m^l(\mathbf{x}_n)$ are given by $f_d^{l,m}(\mathbf{x}_n)$ for $d = 1, \ldots, D$. We define the vector $\hat{\mathbf{f}}_d^{l,m}$ with elements given by $\{f_d^{l,m}(\mathbf{x}_n)\}_{n=1}^N$. Notice that the rows of $\mathbf{F}_m^l$ are given by $(\hat{\mathbf{f}}_d^{l,m})^\top$. Also, vector $\mathbf{f}_m^l = [(\hat{\mathbf{f}}_1^{l,m})^\top \ldots (\hat{\mathbf{f}}_D^{l,m})^\top]^\top$. We use $\mathbf{F}_m$ to collectively refer to all matrices $\{\mathbf{F}_m^l\}_{l=1}^L$, or all vectors $\{\mathbf{f}_m^l\}_{l=1}^L$. We use $\mathbf{X}_m^l$ to refer to the set of input vectors $\{\mathbf{x}_n\}_{n=1}^N$ for class m, and instance l. $\mathbf{X}_m$ refers to all the matrices $\{\mathbf{X}_m^l\}_{l=1}^L$. Likewise, Θ refers to the set $\{\boldsymbol{\theta}_m\}_{m=1}^M$.

2.1 Generative Training

In the generative model, we train separately a multi-output GP for each class. In our case, training consists of estimating the kernel hyperparameters of the multi-output GP, $\boldsymbol{\theta}_m$. Let us assume that the training set consists of several multi-output processes grouped in $\mathbf{F}_m$ and drawn independently, from the Gaussian process generative model given by $p(\mathbf{f}_m^l|\mathbf{X}_m^l, \mathcal{C}_m, \boldsymbol{\theta}_m) = \mathcal{N}(\mathbf{f}_m^l|\mathbf{0}, \mathbf{K}_m)$, where $\mathbf{K}_m$ is the kernel matrix for class m. In order to train the generative model, we maximize the log marginal likelihood function with respect to the parameter vector $\boldsymbol{\theta}_m$, assuming that the different instances of the multi-output process are generated independently given the kernel hyperparameters. We use a gradient-descent procedure to perform the optimization.

To predict the class label for a new matrix $\mathbf{F}_*$ or equivalently, a new vector $\mathbf{f}_*$, and assuming equal prior probabilities for each class, we compute the marginal likelihood $p(\mathbf{F}_*|\mathbf{X}_*, \mathcal{C}_m, \boldsymbol{\theta}_m)$ for all m. We predict as the correct class that one for which the marginal likelihood is bigger.

2.2 Discriminative Training

In discriminative training, we search for the hyperparameters that minimize some classification error measure for all classes simultaneously. In this paper, we chose to minimize the minimum classification error criterion as presented in [13]. A soft version of the $\{0,1\}$ loss function for classification can be written as

$$\ell_m(\mathbf{f}) = \frac{1}{1 + \exp(-\gamma_1 d_m(\mathbf{f}) + \gamma_2)}, \tag{1}$$

where $\gamma_1 > 0$ and γ_2 are user given parameters, and $d_m(\mathbf{f})$ is the *class classification error measure*, given by

$$d_m(\mathbf{f}) = -g_m(\mathbf{f}) + \log \left[\frac{1}{M-1} \sum_{\substack{\forall k \\ k \neq m}} e^{g_k(\mathbf{f})\eta} \right]^{\frac{1}{\eta}}, \tag{2}$$

where $\eta > 0$, and $g_m(\mathbf{f}) = a \log p(\mathbf{f}|\mathbf{X}, \mathcal{C}_m, \boldsymbol{\theta}_m) + b = a \log \mathcal{N}(\mathbf{f}|\mathbf{0}, \mathbf{K}_m) + b$. Parameters $a > 0$, and b are again defined by the user. Expression $g_m(\mathbf{f})$ is an scaled and translated version of the log marginal likelihood for the multi-output GP of class m. We scale the log marginal likelihood to keep the value of $g_m(\mathbf{f})$ in a small numerical range such that computing $\exp(g_k(\mathbf{f})\eta)$ does not overflow the capacity of a double floating point number of a computer. Parameters γ_1 and γ_2 in equation (1) have the same role as a and b in $g_m(\mathbf{f})$, but the numerical problems are less severe here and setting $\gamma_1 = 1$ and $\gamma_2 = 0$ usually works well.

Expression in equation (2) converges to $-g_m(\mathbf{f}) + \max_{\forall k: k \neq m} g_k(\mathbf{f})$ as η tends to infinity. For finite values of η, $d_m(\mathbf{f})$ is a differentiable function. The value of $d_m(\mathbf{f})$ is negative if $g_m(\mathbf{f})$ is greater than the "maximum" of $g_k(\mathbf{f})$, for $k \neq m$. We expect this to be the case, if $\mathbf{f}$ truly belongs to class $\mathcal{C}_m$. Therefore, expression $d_m(\mathbf{f})$ plays the role of a discriminant function between $g_m(\mathbf{f})$ and the "maximum" of $g_k(\mathbf{f})$, with $k \neq m$.[1] The classification error measure is a continuous function of $\boldsymbol{\Theta}$, and attempts to model a decision rule. Notice that if $d_m(\mathbf{f}) < 0$ then $\ell_m(\mathbf{f})$ goes to zero, and if $d_m(\mathbf{f}) > 0$ then $\ell_m(\mathbf{f})$ goes to one, and that is the reason as why expression (1) can be seen as a soft version of a $\{0,1\}$ loss function. The loss function takes into account the class-conditional densities $p(\mathbf{f}|\mathbf{X}, \mathcal{C}_m, \boldsymbol{\theta}_m)$, for all classes, and thus, optimizing $\ell_m(\mathbf{f})$ implies the optimization over the set $\boldsymbol{\Theta}$.

Given some dataset $\{\mathbf{X}_m, \mathbf{F}_m\}_{m=1}^M$, the purpose is then to find the hyperparameters $\boldsymbol{\Theta}$ that minimize the cost function that counts the number of classification errors in the dataset,

$$\mathcal{L}(\{\mathbf{X}_m\}_{m=1}^M, \{\mathbf{F}_m\}_{m=1}^M, \boldsymbol{\Theta}) = \sum_{m=1}^M \sum_{l=1}^L \ell_m(\mathbf{f}_m^l). \tag{3}$$

We can compute the derivatives of equation (3) with respect to the hyperparameters $\boldsymbol{\Theta}$, and then use a gradient optimization method to find the optimal hyperparameters for the minimum classification error criterion.

Computational Complexity. As part of the inference process, we need to invert each matrix $\mathbf{K}_m$, with dimensions $DN \times DN$. The computational complexity of each optimization step is then $O(LMD^3N^3)$, this could be very slow

---

[1] We use quotes for the word maximum, since the true maximum is only achieved when η tends to infinity.

for many applications. In order to reduce computational complexity, in this paper we resort to low rank approximations for the covariance matrix appearing on the likelihood model. In particular, we use the partially independent training conditional (PITC) approximation, and the fully independent training conditional (FITC) approximation, both approximations for multi-output GPs [2].

3   Experimental Results

In this section we show results for different experiments that compare the following methods: hidden Markov models trained in a generative way using the Baum-Welch algorithm [14], hidden Markov models trained in a discriminative way using minimum classification error [13], multi-output GPs trained in a generative way using maximum likelihood (this paper), and multi-output GPs trained in a discriminative way using minimum classification error (this paper). We use the CMU MOCAP database to identify subjects from their walking styles and to classify different activities like walking and running. For this experiment, we also try different frame rates for the training set and validation set to show how the multi-output GP method adapts to this case. We also experiment with a problem of face recognition, to show that our method is not constrained to time series (to model $\mathbf{f}(t)$), but can be used in a general Markov field scenario (to model $\mathbf{f}(\mathbf{x})$, where $\mathbf{x}$ has more than one dimension).

We assume that the HMMs have a Gaussian distribution per state. The number of hidden states of a HMM is shown in each of the experiments in parenthesis, for instance, HMM(q) means a HMM with q hidden states

3.1   Subject and Activity Identification in MOCAP

For this experiment we used the CMU MOCAP database.[2] To perform subject identification by walking style, we took the first 8 repetitions of the walking sequences for subject 7, subject 8, and subject 35. Then, for each subject, we took four instances for training, and other four for validation. For the activity identification experiment, we classified between running and walking. We used instances from ten different subjects (subjects 2,7,8,9,16,35,39,127,141,143) with a total of 37 repetitions for running, and 42 repetitions for walking.

We also studied the scenario where the frame rate for the motions used in training could be different from the frame rate for the motions used in testing. This configuration simulates the scenario where cameras with different recording rates are used to keep track of human activities. Notice that HMMs are not supposed to adapt well to this scenario, since the Markov assumption is that the current state depends only on the previous state. However, the Gaussian process captures the dependencies of any order, and encodes those dependencies in the kernel function, which is a continuous function of the input variables. Thus, we can evaluate the GP for any set of input points, at the testing stage, without the need to train the whole model again.

---

[2] The CMU Graphics Lab Motion Capture Database was created with funding from NSF EIA-0196217 and is available at http://mocap.cs.cmu.edu.

Table 1. Classification accuracy rates (mean and standard deviation) of subject and activity identification on the CMU-MOCAP database. The table on the left shows the accuracy on an experiment where the camera frame rates of the training and validation cameras is the same. The table on the right shows the scenario when the validation camera frame rate is different from the training camera.

Method	Generative	Discriminative
FITC	60.68 ± 3.98	95.71 ± 2.98
PITC	76.40 ± 12.38	93.56 ± 5.29
HMM (3)	96.70 ± 2.77	97.95 ± 2.23
HMM (5)	94.69 ± 4.36	96.32 ± 0.82
HMM (7)	92.24 ± 4.49	99.77 ± 0.99

(a) Activity identification

Method	Accuracy
FITC Gen	93.28 ± 3.76
PITC Gen	93.28 ± 3.76
FITC MCE	94.96 ± 4.60
PITC MCE	94.96 ± 4.60
HMM Gen (7)	33.33 ± 0.00
HMM MCE (7)	83.33 ± 16.6

(b) Subject identification

Table 1 shows the results of these experiments. The table on the left shows the results for activity identification, for the case where the training and validation cameras have the same frame rate. Notice that in this case the HMMs have a good performance both in the generative and the discriminative case. On the other hand, the results for the Gaussian processes are much better with our proposed discriminative method than with the generative method. The table on the right shows the results for the subject identification experiment, and also the scenario where the camera used in training and in validation have different frame rates. Notice that since a MOGP models $\mathbf{f}(t)$ for a continuous time variable t, it is easy to adapt our model to this case by simply scaling the time accordingly to the ratio of the frame rates of the training and validation camera without the need to train the model again. The HMMs do not adapt well to this scenario as we said before. The results show that the performance of the multi-output GP is clearly superior to the one exhibited by the HMM in this case. Although the results for the HMM in Table 1 (right) were obtained fixing the number of states to seven, we also performed experiments for three and five states, obtaining similar results. This experiment is an example where our model is useful to solve a problem that a HMM does not solve satisfactorily.

3.2   Face Recognition

The goal of this experiment is to show an example where the vector-valued function is dependent on input variables with dimensionality greater than one, functions of multi-dimensional inputs like space $(f(\mathbf{x}_0), f(\mathbf{x}_1), ..., f(\mathbf{x}_n))$. We do not present results with HMMs for this experiment since they are not meant to model these multidimensional-input random fields. In this problem we work with face recognition from pictures of the Georgia Tech database.[3] This database, contains images of 50 subjects stored in JPEG format with 640×480 pixel resolution. For each individual 15 color images were taken, considering variations

---

[3] Georgia Tech Face Database, http://www.anefian.com/research/face_reco.htm

in illumination, facial expression, face orientations and appearance (presence of faces using glasses). For each subject we took 8 images for training and 7 images for validation.

Here we did two experiments. The first experiment was carried out taking 5 subjects of the Georgia Tech database that did not have glasses. For the second experiment we took another 5 subjects of the database that had glasses. In both experiments, each image was divided in a given number of regions of equal aspect ratio. For each region n we computed its centroid $\mathbf{x}_n$ and a texture vector $\mathbf{f}_n$. Notice that this can be directly modeled by a multi-output GP where the input vectors $\mathbf{x}_n$ are two dimensional. Table 2 show the results of this experiment

Table 2. Face recognition accuracy (mean and standard deviation) using a grid of size BX=4, BY=7.

Method	Gen	Disc	Method	Gen	Disc
FITC	61.57 ± 3.50	86.84 ± 0.01	FITC	54.73 ± 6.55	81.57 ± 3.7
PITC	64.72 ± 2.34	95.78 ± 8.03	PITC	64.21 ± 9.41	81.57 ± 7.2
FITC*	66.71 ± 3.82	96.84 ± 7.06	FITC*	60.53 ± 0.02	90.52 ± 9.41
PITC*	73.68 ± 5.88	96.30 ± 3.00	PITC*	69.47 ± 9.41	77.36 ± 8.24

(a) Faces without glasses	(b) Faces with glasses

with the discriminative and the generative training approaches. The number of divisions in the X and Y coordinates are BX and BY respectively. The features extracted from each block are mean RGB values and Segmentation-based Fractal Texture Analysis (SFTA) [8] of each block. The SFTA algorithm extracts a feature vector from each region by decomposing it into a set of binary images, and then computing a scalar measure based on fractal symmetry for each of those binary images.

The results show high accuracy in the recognition process in both schemes (faces with glasses and faces without glasses) when using our proposed discriminative training method. For all the settings, the results of our discriminative training method are better than the results of the generative training method. This experiment shows the versatility of the multi-output Gaussian process to work in applications that go beyond time series classification.

4   Conclusions

In this paper, we advocated the use of multi-output GPs as generative models for vector-valued random fields. We showed how to estimate the hyperparameters of the multi-output GP in a generative way and proposed a method to find these parameters in a discriminative way. Through different experiments we could see that the performance of our framework is equal or better than its natural competitor, the HMM.

For future work, we would like to study the performance of the framework using alternative discriminative criteria, like Maximum Mutual Information (MMI) using gradient optimization or Conditional Expectation Maximization [12]. We would also like to compare our method against supervised classification techniques for functional data.

References

1. Álvarez, M.A., Lawrence, N.D.: Sparse convolved Gaussian processes for multi-output regression. In: Koller, D., Schuurmans, D., Bengio, Y., Bottou, L. (eds.) NIPS, vol. 21, pp. 57–64. MIT Press, Cambridge (2009)
2. Alvarez, M.A., Lawrence, N.D.: Computationally efficient convolved multiple output Gaussian processes. The Journal of Machine Learning Research **12**, 1459–1500 (2011)
3. Álvarez, M.A., Rosasco, L., Lawrence, N.D.: Kernels for vector-valued functions: a review. Foundations and Trends® in Machine Learning **4**(3), 195–266 (2012)
4. Bishop, C.M.: Pattern Recognition And Machine Learning (Information Science And Statistics). Springer (2007). http://www.openisbn.com/isbn/9780387310732/
5. Bonilla, E.V., Chai, K.M., Williams, C.K.I.: Multi-task Gaussian process prediction. In: Platt, J.C., Koller, D., Singer, Y., Roweis, S. (eds.) NIPS, vol. 20. MIT Press, Cambridge (2008)
6. Boyle, P., Frean, M.: Dependent Gaussian processes. In: Saul, L., Weiss, Y., Bouttou, L. (eds.) NIPS, vol. 17, pp. 217–224. MIT Press, Cambridge (2005)
7. Chai, K.M.: Variational multinomial logit Gaussian process. Journal of Machine Learning Research **13**, 1745–1808 (2012)
8. Costa, A., Humpire-Mamani, G., Traina, A.J.M.: An efficient algorithm for fractal analysis of textures. In: 2012 25th SIBGRAPI Conference on Graphics, Patterns and Images (SIBGRAPI), pp. 39–46, August 2012
9. Goovaerts, P.: Geostatistics For Natural Resources Evaluation. Oxford University Press, USA (1997)
10. Gopalakrishnan, P., Kanevsky, D., Nádas, A., Nahamoo, D.: An inequality for rational functions with applications to some statistical estimation problems. IEEE Transactions on Information Theory **37**, 107–113 (1991)
11. Higdon, D.M.: Space and space-time modelling using process convolutions. In: Anderson, C., Barnett, V., Chatwin, P., El-Shaarawi, A. (eds.) Quantitative Methods for Current Environmental Issues, pp. 37–56. Springer-Verlag (2002)
12. Jebara, T.: Machine Learning: Discriminative and Generative. Springer (2004)
13. Juang, B.H., Hou, W., Lee, C.H.: Minimum classification error rate methods for speech recognition. IEEE Transactions on Speech and Audio Processing **5**(3), 257–265 (1997)
14. Rabiner, L.: A tutorial on hidden Markov models and selected applications in speech recognition. Proceedings of the IEEE **77**(2), 257–286 (1989)
15. Rasmussen, C.E., Williams, C.K.I.: Gaussian Processes for Machine Learning. MIT Press, Cambridge (2006)
16. Skolidis, G., Sanguinetti, G.: Bayesian multitask classification with Gaussian process priors. IEEE Transactions on Neural Networks **22**(12), 2011–2021 (2011)
17. Teh, Y.W., Seeger, M., Jordan, M.I.: Semiparametric latent factor models. In: Cowell, R.G., Ghahramani, Z. (eds.) AISTATS 10, pp. 333–340. Society for Artificial Intelligence and Statistics, Barbados, 6–8 January 2005

Improving the Accuracy of CAR-Based Classifiers by Combining Netconf Measure and Dynamic−K Mechanism

Raudel Hernàndez-Leòn[✉]

Centro de Aplicaciones de Tecnologías de Avanzada (CENATAV),
7a ♯ 21406 e/214 and 216, Rpto. Siboney, Playa, 12200 La Habana, Cuba
rhernandez@cenatav.co.cu

Abstract. In this paper, we propose combining Netconf as quality measure and Dynamic−K satisfaction mechanism into Class Association Rules (CARs) based classifiers. In our study, we evaluate the use of several quality measures to compute the CARs as well as the main satisfaction mechanisms ("Best Rule", "Best K Rules" and "All Rules") commonly used in the literature. Our experiments over several datasets show that our proposal gets the best accuracy in contrast to those reported in state-of-the-art works.

Keywords: Supervised classification · Satisfaction mechanisms · Class association rules

1 Introduction

Associative classification, introduced in [2], integrates Association Rule Mining (ARM) and Classification Rule Mining (CRM). This integration involves mining a special subset of association rules, called Class Association Rules (CARs), using some quality measures (QM) to evaluate them. A classifier based on this approach usually consists of an ordered CAR list l, and a satisfaction mechanism for classifying unseen transactions using l [2,3,6].

Associative classification has been applied to many tasks including prediction of consumer behavior [17], automatic error detection [19], breast cancer detection [15], and prediction of protein-protein interaction types [16], among others.

In associative classification, similar to ARM, a set of items $I = \{i_1, \ldots, i_n\}$, a set of classes C, and a transactional dataset T, are given. Each transaction $t \in T$ is represented by a set of items $X \subseteq I$ and a class $c \in C$. A lexicographic order among the items of I is assumed. The Support of an itemset $X \subseteq I$, denoted as $Sup(X)$, is the fraction of transactions in T containing X (see Eq. 1).

$$Sup(X) = \frac{|T_X|}{|T|} \tag{1}$$

where T_X is the set of transactions in T containing X and $|\cdot|$ represents the cardinality.

© Springer International Publishing Switzerland 2015
A. Pardo and J. Kittler (Eds.): CIARP 2015, LNCS 9423, pp. 603–610, 2015.
DOI: 10.1007/978-3-319-25751-8_72

A CAR is an implication of the form $X \Rightarrow c$ where $X \subseteq I$ and $c \in C$. The most commonly used measures to evaluate CARs are Support and Confidence. The rule $X \Rightarrow c$ is held in T with certain Support s and Confidence α, where s is the fraction of transactions in T that contains $X \cup \{c\}$ (see Eq. 2), and α is the probability of finding c in transactions that also contain X (see Eq. 3), which represents how "strongly" the rule antecedent X implies the rule consequent c. A CAR $X \Rightarrow c$ satisfies or covers a transaction t if $X \subseteq t$.

$$Sup(X \Rightarrow c) = Sup(X \cup \{c\}) \tag{2}$$

$$Conf(X \Rightarrow c) = \frac{Sup(X \Rightarrow c)}{Sup(X)} \tag{3}$$

However, in [4], the authors analyzed several measures (Conviction, Lift, and Certainty factor), as an alternative to the Support and Confidence measures, for estimating the strength of an association rule.

The rest of the paper is organized as follows. The related work is described in next section. Our proposal is presented in section three. In the fourth section the experimental results are shown. Finally, conclusions are given in section five.

2   Related Work

In general, CAR-based classifiers could be divided in two groups according to the strategy used for computing the set of CARs:

1. Two Stage classifiers. In a first stage, all CARs satisfying the Support and Confidence values (or other measures) are mined and later, in a second stage, a classifier is built by selecting a small subset of CARs that fully covers the training set, CBA [2] and CMAR [3] follow this strategy.
2. Integrated classifiers. In these classifiers a small subset of CARs is directly generated using different heuristics, CPAR [6], TFPC [9] and DDPMine [13] follow this strategy.

Regardless of the strategy used for computing the set of CARs, in order to build the classifier we need to sort the CARs. In the literature, there are six main strategies for ordering CARs:

a) CSA (Confidence - Support - Antecedent size): First, the rules are sorted in a descending order according to their Confidence. In case of ties, CARs are sorted in a descending order according to their Support, and if the tie persist, CSA sorts the rules in ascending order according to the size of their rule antecedent. This strategy has been used by the CBA classifier [2].
b) ACS (Antecedent size - Confidence - Support): This strategy is a variation of CSA, but it takes into account the size of the rule antecedent as first ordering criterion followed by Confidence and Support. The classifier TFPC [9] follows this ordering strategy.

c) SrQM (Specific rules (Sr) - Quality Measure (QM)): First, the rules are sorted in a descending order according to the size of the CARs and in case of tie, the tied CARs are sorted in a descending order according to their QM value. CAR-IC classifier follows this ordering strategy [18].

d) WRA (Weighted Relative Accuracy): The WRA rule ordering strategy assigns to each CAR a weight and then sorts the set of CARs in a descending order according to the assigned weights [12,14]. The WRA has been used to order CARs in two versions of the TFPC classifier [12,14]. Given a rule $X \Rightarrow Y$ the WRA is computed as follows:

$$WRA(X \Rightarrow Y) = Sup(X)(Conf(X \Rightarrow Y) - Sup(Y))$$

e) LAP (Laplace Expected Error Estimate): LAP was introduced by Clark and Boswell [1] and it has been used to order CARs in CPAR classifier [6]. Given a rule $X \Rightarrow Y$, in [6] the LAP is defined as follows:

$$LAP(X \Rightarrow Y) = \frac{Sup(X \Rightarrow Y) + 1}{Sup(X) + \mid C \mid}$$

where C is the set of predefined classes.

f) χ^2 (Chi-Square): The χ^2 rule ordering strategy is a well known technique in statistics, which is used to determine whether two variables are independent or related. After computing an additive χ^2 value for each CAR, this value is used to sort the CARs in a descending order in the CMAR classifier [3].

In [18], the authors show that the $SrQM$ rule ordering strategy obtains the best results of all strategies mentioned above. Once the classifier has been built, we need to select a satisfaction mechanism for classifying unseen transactions. Four main satisfaction mechanisms have been reported [2,3,14,21]:

1. **Best Rule:** It selects the first ("best") rule in the order that satisfies the transaction to be classified, and then the class associated to the selected rule is assigned to this transaction [2].
2. **Best K Rules:** It selects the best K rules (per each class) that satisfy the transaction to be classified and then the class is determined using these K rules, according to different criteria [14].
3. **All Rules:** It selects all rules that satisfy the transaction to be classified and use them to determine the class of the new transaction [3].
4. **Dynamic−K:** It is similar to the "Best K Rules" mechanism but the value of K may change for each transaction to be classified [21].

Classifiers following the "Best Rule" mechanism could suffer biased classification or overfitting since the classification is based on only one rule. On the other hand, the "All Rules" mechanism includes rules with low ranking for classification and this could affect the accuracy of the classifier. The "Best K Rules" mechanism has been the most used satisfaction mechanism for CAR-based classifiers, reporting the best results. However, in [21] the authors mention some limitations of this mechanism. Also in [21], the authors proposed the Dynamic−K

satisfaction mechanism, which does not have the drawbacks of the other three mechanisms (see next section).

In this paper, we propose to combine the Dynamic$-K$ satisfaction mechanism and the Netconf quality measure into CAR-based classifiers. In order to show the suitability of our proposal, we evaluate several quality measures as well as the other reported satisfaction mechanisms. Experiments over several datasets show that our proposal gets the best performance in contrast to those reported in state-of-the-art works.

3   Our Proposal

In the next subsections we describe the Dynamic$-K$ satisfaction mechanism (subsection 3.1) as well as the Netconf measure (subsection 3.2). Based on the advantages of Dynamic$-K$ over the other satisfaction mechanisms and based on the characteristics of Netconf measure, we propose in this paper to improve the accuracy of CAR-based classifiers by combining them.

3.1   Dynamic$-K$ Satisfaction Mechanism

As we mentioned in related works, the main satisfaction mechanisms reported have limitations that can affect the classification accuracy. In general, the "Best K Rules" mechanism has been the most widely used for CAR-based classifiers, reporting the best results [11]. However, in [21] the authors show that using this mechanism could affect the classification accuracy. Ever more when most of the best K rules were obtained extending the same item, or when there is an imbalance among the numbers of CARs with high measure values, per each class, that cover the new transaction (see some examples in [21]).

In order to overcome these drawbacks, the Dynamic$-K$ mechanism was proposed in [21]. First, Dynamic$-K$ sorts the CARs using the SrQM rule ordering strategy. Later, it selects, for each class $c \in C$, the set of rules $X \Rightarrow c$ covering the new transaction t and satisfying the following conditions:

- $X \Rightarrow c$ is a maximal rule.
- for all $i \in I$, with i lexicographically greater than all items of X, $QM(X \cup \{i\} \Rightarrow c) < QM(X \Rightarrow c)$ holds.

Thereby they included more large rules with high quality measure values in the classification, avoiding redundancies and including more different items in the antecedents of the selected CARs.

Let N_i be the set of maximal CARs of class c_i that were selected for Dynamic$-K$ mechanism. After selecting all N_i (for $i = 1$ to $|C|$), Dynamic$-K$ assigns the class c_j such that the QM average of all rules of N_j is greater than the QM average of the top $|N_j|$ rules of each N_i, with $i \neq j$ and $|N_i| \geq |N_j|$. In case of tie among classes with different number of CARs, the class with less number of CARs is preferred because the CARs are sorted in descendent order according to their sizes (SrQM rule ordering strategy); in case of tie among classes with equals number of CARs, the class with greater Support is selected, if the tie persist the class is selected randomly.

Resuming, the Dynamic$-K$ mechanism does not have the drawbacks of the other existent mechanisms since:

- It selects the maximal rules with high QM values, avoiding redundancies and allowing the inclusion of more different items in the antecedents of the selected CARs, thereby CARs of low quality are not included for classifying.
- The result is not affected when there is an imbalance among the numbers of CARs with high QM values, for each class, that cover the new transaction, this happens because to classify a new transaction, Dynamic$-K$ considers the average of the same amount of CARs.
- It considers all good quality CARs that cover the new transaction and not only the best one. Thereby, Dynamic$-K$ does not fall on the mistake of assuming that the best rule is going to classify correctly all transactions that it covers.

3.2 Main Quality Measures

In [4], the authors analyzed several measures (Conviction, Lift, and Certainty factor), as an alternative to the Confidence measure, for estimating the strength of an association rule. As an important result, they show that some of these measures overcome the drawbacks of the Confidence. However, in case of Lift and Certainty factor, they have other limitations.

The Lift measure (see Eq. 4) has a not bounded range [4], therefore differences among its values are not meaningful and for this reason, it is difficult to define a Lift threshold.

$$Lift(X \Rightarrow Y) = \frac{Sup(X \Rightarrow Y)}{Sup(X)Sup(Y)} \tag{4}$$

On the other hand, Certainty factor is defined by Eq. 5.

$$CF(X \Rightarrow Y) = \begin{cases} \frac{Conf(X \Rightarrow Y) - Sup(Y)}{1 - Sup(Y)} & if \ Conf(X \Rightarrow Y) > Sup(Y) \\ \frac{Conf(X \Rightarrow Y) - Sup(Y)}{Sup(Y)} & if \ Conf(X \Rightarrow Y) < Sup(Y) \\ 0 & otherwise \end{cases} \tag{5}$$

Negative values of Certainty factor mean negative dependence, while positive values mean positive dependence and 0 means independence. However, the value that Certainty factor takes depends on the Support of the consequent (the class in our case). When $Conf(X \Rightarrow Y)$ is close to $Sup(Y)$, even if the difference of $Conf(X \Rightarrow Y)$ and $Sup(Y)$ is close to 0 but still positive, the Certainty factor measure shows a strong positive dependence when $Sup(Y)$ is high (close to 1).

In [7], the authors introduced a measure to estimate the strength of an association rule, called Netconf. This measure, defined in equation 6, has among its main advantages that it detects misleading rules produced by the Confidence.

$$Netconf(X \Rightarrow Y) = \frac{Sup(X \Rightarrow Y) - Sup(X)Sup(Y)}{Sup(X)(1 - Sup(X))} \tag{6}$$

As a simple example, suppose that $Sup(X) = 0.4$, $Sup(Y) = 0.8$ and $Sup(X \Rightarrow Y) = 0.3$, therefore $Sup(\neg X) = 1 - Sup(X) = 0.6$ and $Sup(\neg X \Rightarrow Y) = Sup(Y) - Sup(X \Rightarrow Y) = 0.5$. If we compute $Conf(X \Rightarrow Y)$ we obtain 0.75 (a high Confidence value) but Y occurs in 80 % of the transactions, therefore the rule $X \Rightarrow Y$ does worse than just randomly guessing, clearly, $X \Rightarrow Y$ is a misleading rule [4]. For this example, $Netconf(X \Rightarrow Y) = -0.083$ showing a negative dependence between the antecedent and the consequent.

4 Experimental Results

In this section, we present the result of combining the Netconf measure and the Dynamic$-K$ satisfaction mechanism into a CAR-based classifier. These results are compared with those obtained by the other three satisfaction mechanisms: "Best Rule" [2], "Best K Rules" [14] and "All Rules" [3]. Additionally, we show the result of combining different measures and the four satisfaction mechanisms.

For the experiment showed in Table 1, the four satisfaction mechanisms were implemented inside the CAR-IC classifier [18], using the Netconf threshold set to 0.5, as it was reported in other works [20]. All our experiments were done using ten-fold cross-validation reporting the average over the ten folds, the same folds were used for all satisfaction mechanisms. All the tests were performed on a PC with an Intel Core 2 Duo at 1.86 GHz CPU with 1 GB DDR2 RAM. Similar to other works [2,3,8,13,20], we used several datasets, specifically 20. The chosen datasets were originally taken from the UCI Machine Learning Repository [10], and their numerical attributes were discretized by Frans Coenen using the LUCS-KDD [5] discretized/normalized CARM Data Library.

For the experiment showed in Table 2, we used the Confidence threshold set to 0.5, the Certainty Factor threshold set to 0 and for Lift and Conviction, the threshold set to 1, as their authors suggested. It is important to highlight that both Lift and Conviction are not bounded range [4], therefore differences among its values are not meaningful. Therefore, the authors suggest to use for these measures, the threshold set to 1; values greater than 1 mean positive dependence between antecedent and consequent. In case of Certainty Factor, positive dependence is obtained for values greater than 0.

In Table 1, we can see that the combination of Dynamic$-K$ mechanism and Netconf measure yields an average accuracy higher than the combination of Netconf and all other reported mechanisms, having a difference of 2.4 % with respect to the mechanism in the second place ("Best K Rules" with K set to 5, the same value used in other works [6,11,12,14]). Additionally, Dynamic$-K$ wins in 19 of the 20 datasets and ties in the other one.

From the results show in Table 2, we can conclude that the Dynamic$-K$ mechanism obtains the best results independent of the quality measure used to compute the set of CARs, being Netconf the best of all evaluated measures.

Table 1. Classification accuracy using Netconf and the different mechanisms.

Dataset	Best rule	All rules	Best K rules	Dynamic K
adult	83.17	82.15	84.50	**87.33**
anneal	92.74	91.89	95.38	**96.42**
breast	85.48	84.58	85.43	**87.65**
connect4	56.95	55.95	62.18	**67.09**
dermatology	79.48	78.28	79.66	**80.39**
ecoli	83.01	81.40	84.01	**86.92**
flare	87.03	86.44	86.45	**88.58**
glass	69.07	68.23	68.92	**72.13**
heart	54.26	53.20	57.34	**61.92**
hepatitis	85.51	84.60	87.02	**87.60**
horseColic	83.51	82.81	83.56	**86.41**
ionosphere	85.03	83.96	86.02	**86.93**
iris	97.10	97.04	96.67	**97.72**
led7	73.67	72.37	75.88	**78.18**
letRecog	74.20	73.56	73.42	**75.70**
mushroom	99.48	98.80	**99.52**	**99.52**
pageBlocks	92.88	92.19	94.93	**97.81**
penDigits	78.80	77.36	78.32	**84.03**
pima	76.38	75.65	78.53	**79.67**
waveform	74.11	73.18	75.22	**79.07**
Average	80.59	79.68	81.65	**84.05**

Table 2. Average accuracy of different quality measures over the tested datasets, for different satisfaction mechanisms.

Measure	Best rule	All rules	Best K rules	Dynamic$-K$
Certainty Factor	74.28	73.39	72.08	77.68
Lift	75.49	74.64	73.21	77.88
Conviction	79.53	78.32	79.21	81.16
Confidence	79.59	78.68	80.60	81.52
Netconf	**80.59**	**79.68**	**81.65**	**84.05**

5   Conclusions

In this paper, we have proposed to improve the accuracy of CAR-based classifiers by combining Netconf measure and Dynamic$-K$ satisfaction mechanism. From the experimental results, we can conclude that the Dynamic$-K$ satisfaction mechanism obtains the best results independent of the quality measure used to compute the set of CARs, being Netconf the best of all evaluated measures.

References

1. Clark, P., Boswell, R.: Rule induction with CN2: some recent improvments. In: Proc. of European Working Session on Learning, pp. 151–163 (1991)
2. Liu, B., Hsu, W., Ma, Y.: Integrating classification and association rule mining. In: Proc. of the KDD, pp. 80–86 (1998)
3. Li, W., Han, J., Pei, J.: CMAR: accurate and efficient classification based on multiple class-association rules. In: Proc. of the ICDM, pp. 369–376 (2001)
4. Berzal, F., Blanco, I., Sánchez, D., Vila, M.A.: Measuring the accuracy and interest of association rules: A new framework. Intelligent Data Analysis **6**(3), 221–235 (2002)

5. Coenen, F.: The LUCS-KDD discretised/normalised ARM and CARM Data Library (2003). http://www.csc.liv.ac.uk/~frans/KDD/Software/LUCS-KDD-DN

6. Yin, X., Han, J.: CPAR: Classification based on predictive association rules. In: Proc. of the SIAM International Conference on Data Mining, pp. 331–335 (2003)

7. Ahn, K.I., Kim, J.Y.: Efficient Mining of Frequent Itemsets and a Measure of Interest for Association Rule Mining. Information and Knowledge Management 3(3), 245–257 (2005). Hanoi, Vietnam

8. Wang, J., Karypis G.: HARMONY: Efficiently mining the best rules for classification. In: Proc. of SDM, pp. 205–216 (2005)

9. Coenen, F., Leng, P., Zhang, L.: Threshold Tuning for improved classification association rule mining. In: Ho, T.-B., Cheung, D., Liu, H. (eds.) PAKDD 2005. LNCS (LNAI), vol. 3518, pp. 216–225. Springer, Heidelberg (2005)

10. Asuncion, A., Newman D.J.: UCI Machine Learning Repository (2007). http://www.ics.uci.edu/~mlearn/MLRepository.html

11. Wang, Y.J., Xin, Q., Coenen, F.: A novel rule weighting approach in classification association rule mining. In: International Conference on Data Mining Workshops, pp. 271–276 (2007)

12. Wang, Y.J., Xin, Q., Coenen, F.: A novel rule ordering approach in classification association rule mining. In: Perner, P. (ed.) MLDM 2007. LNCS (LNAI), vol. 4571, pp. 339–348. Springer, Heidelberg (2007)

13. Cheng, H., Yan, X., Han, J., Yu, P.S.: Direct discriminative pattern mining for effective classification. In: Proc. of the ICDE, pp. 169–178 (2008)

14. Wang, Y.J., Xin, Q., Coenen, F.: Hybrid Rule Ordering in Classification Association Rule Mining. Trans. MLDM 1(1), 1–15 (2008)

15. Karabatak, M., Ince, M.C.: An expert system for detection of breast cancer based on association rules and neural network. Expert Syst. Appl. 36, 3465–3469 (2009)

16. Park, S.H., Reyes, J.A., Gilbert, D.R., Kim, J.W., Kim, S.: Prediction of protein-protein interaction types using association rule based classification. BMC Bioinformatics 10(1) (2009)

17. Bae, J.K., Kim, J.: Integration of heterogeneous models to predict consumer behavior. Expert Syst. Appl. 37, 1821–1826 (2010)

18. Hernández, R., Carrasco, J.A., Fco, M.J., Hernández, J.: Classifying using specific rules with high confidence. In: Proc. of the MICAI, pp. 75–80 (2010)

19. Malik, W.A., Unwin, A.: Automated error detection using association rules. Intelligent Data Analysis 15(5), 749–761 (2011)

20. Hernández, R., Carrasco, J.A., Fco, M.J., Hernández, J.: CAR-NF: A Classifier based on Specific Rules with High Netconf. Intelligent Data Analysis 16(1), 49–68 (2012)

21. Hernández-León, R.: Dynamic K: a novel satisfaction mechanism for CAR-based classifiers. In: Ruiz-Shulcloper, J., Sanniti di Baja, G. (eds.) CIARP 2013, Part I. LNCS, vol. 8258, pp. 141–148. Springer, Heidelberg (2013)

Local Entropies for Kernel Selection and Outlier Detection in Functional Data

Gabriel Martos[✉] and Alberto Muñoz

Department of Statistics, University Carlos III, Madrid, Spain
{gabrielalejandro.martos,alberto.munoz}@uc3m.es

Abstract. An important question in data analysis is how to choose the kernel function (or its parameters) to solve classification or regression problems. The choice of a suitable kernel is usually carried out by cross validation. In this paper we introduce a novel method consisting in choosing the kernel according to an optimal entropy criterion. After selecting the best kernel function we proceed by using a measure of local entropy to compute the functional outliers in the sample.

Keywords: Local entropy · Functional data · Kernel selection · Outlier detection

1 Introduction

Outlier detection is a common task in Statistics and Data Analysis. When one deals with functional data, this problem becomes difficult since it is not obvious how to translate functional data into the traditional statistical framework. In recent works [2,6] and references therein, several authors propose to consider depth measures to capture the atypical functional data. As we will show, these measures fails to capture the depth but extreme in shape functional observations.

In this paper we use a finite dimensional representation of functional data in order to transform the (infinite dimensional) functional data objects to finite dimensional data points that possess a 'traditional' probability distribution. For this aim, we need first to select a suitable kernel function and/or its adequate parameters. We address this problem by using a minimal entropy criterion. Next, given a suitable kernel based representation of the functional data at hand, we determine if there are functional outliers in the data by using a local entropy measure for functional data.

The article is organized as follows: In Section 2 we propose a measure of local entropy and present a consistent estimator for it. In Section 3 we describe the procedure to choose a suitable kernel to represent functional data and how to address the problem of outlier detection using a local entropy measure. In Section 4 we show the performance of the proposed method with two experiments.

© Springer International Publishing Switzerland 2015
A. Pardo and J. Kittler (Eds.): CIARP 2015, LNCS 9423, pp. 611–618, 2015.
DOI: 10.1007/978-3-319-25751-8_73

2 Local Entropies

We consider a measure space $(X, \mathcal{F}, \mu)$, where X is a sample space (here a compact set of $\mathbb{R}^d$), $\mathcal{F}$ a σ-algebra of measurable subsets of X and $\mu : \mathcal{F} \rightarrow \mathbb{R}^+$ the ambient σ-additive measure, the Lebesgue measure. A probability measure (PM) $\mathbb{P}$ is a σ-additive finite measure absolutely continuous w.r.t. μ that satisfies the three Kolmogorov axioms. By Radon-Nikodym theorem, there exists a measurable function $f_{\mathbb{P}} : X \rightarrow \mathbb{R}^+$ (the density function) such that $\mathbb{P}(A) = \int_A f_{\mathbb{P}} d\mu$, and $f_{\mathbb{P}} = \frac{d\mathbb{P}}{d\mu}$ is the Radon-Nikodym derivative.

The family of α-Entropies, proposed by Rényi [10], plays an important role in several statistical and data analysis problems. Next we present this family of uncertainty measures to later extend this concept to a measure of local entropy.

Definition 1 (α-Entropy). *Let $\mathbb{P}$ be a probability measure defined in a measure space $(X, \mathcal{F}, \mu)$ and let $f_{\mathbb{P}}$ be the respective density function. For $\alpha \geq 0$ and $\alpha \neq 1$, the α-Entropy of the PM $\mathbb{P}$ is computed as follows:*

$$H_{\alpha}(\mathbb{P}) = \frac{1}{1-\alpha} \log\left(V_{\alpha}(\mathbb{P})\right) = \frac{1}{1-\alpha} \log\left(\int_X f_{\mathbb{P}}^{\alpha}(x)dx\right),$$

where $V_{\alpha}(\mathbb{P}) = ||f_{\mathbb{P}}||_{\alpha} = \mathbb{E}_{\mathbb{P}}(f_{\mathbb{P}}^{\alpha-1})$.

Several renowned entropy measures in the statistical literature are particular cases in the family of α-Entropies. For instance, when $\alpha = 0$ we obtain the Hartley entropy, when $\alpha \rightarrow 1$ then H_{α} converges to the Shannon entropy and when $\alpha \rightarrow \infty$ then H_{α} converges to the Min-entropy measure.

Let $x \in X$ be a point in the support of the PM $\mathbb{P}$ and let $B(x, r_{\delta})$ be the ball with center in x and radius r_{δ} that fulfils the following condition:

$$\delta = \int_{B(x,r_{\delta})} f_{\mathbb{P}}(x)dx,$$

the δ-**Neighbors** of the point x, denoted as $n_{\delta}(x)$, is the open set $n_{\delta}(x) = X \cap B(x, r_{\delta})$. Let us introduce the new entropy:

Definition 2 (δ-Local α-Entropy). *Let $x \in X$ be a point in the support of the PM $\mathbb{P}$ and let $n_{\delta}(x)$ be the set of its δ-neighbors. For $\alpha \geq 0$ and $\alpha \neq 1$, the δ-local α-entropy of the point x is defined as:*

$$h_{\alpha,\delta}(x) = \frac{1}{1-\alpha} \log\left(v_{\alpha,\delta}(x)\right) = \frac{1}{1-\alpha} \log\left(\int_{n_{\delta}(x)} f_{\mathbb{P}}^{\alpha}(x)dx\right).$$

The H_{α} entropy of a PM $\mathbb{P}$ can be estimated by means of the local entropy measures. Given a partition of the support of the PM $\mathbb{P}$ into a suitable sequence of non overlapping regions, that is a collection of points $\{x_1, \ldots, x_n\}$ and a proper δ such that $X = \bigcup_{i=1}^{n} n_{\delta}(x_i)$ and $n_{\delta}(x_i) \cap n_{\delta}(x_j) = \varnothing \ \forall i \neq j$, then:

$$V_{\alpha}(\mathbb{P}) = \int_X \sum_{i=1}^{n} \mathbb{1}_{[x \in n_{\delta}(x_i)]}(x) f_{\mathbb{P}}^{\alpha}(x)dx = \sum_{i=1}^{n} \int_{n_{\delta}(x_i)} f_{\mathbb{P}}^{\alpha}(x)dx = \sum_{i=1}^{n} v_{\alpha,\delta}(x_i),$$

where $\mathbb{1}_{[x \in n_\delta(x_i)]}$ stands for the indicator function that takes the value 1 when $x \in n_\delta(x_i)$ and 0 otherwise. Therefore, the entropy of a PM $\mathbb{P}$ can be computed as the sum of local entropies:

$$H_\alpha(\mathbb{P}) = \frac{1}{1-\alpha} \log\left(V_\alpha(\mathbb{P})\right) = \frac{1}{1-\alpha} \log\left(\sum_{i=1}^{n} v_{\alpha,\delta}(x_i)\right). \qquad (1)$$

Next we propose a general method to estimate the δ-Local α-Entropy, and using Equation 1 the α-Entropy of a probability measure.

2.1   Entropy Estimation

Usually the available data are given as a finite sample. We consider a *iid* sample $s_n(\mathbb{P}) = \{x_i\}_{i=1}^{n}$ drawn from a PM $\mathbb{P}$. In first place we propose a method to estimate the δ-Local α-Entropy and later, by aggregation, an estimator of the α-Entropy. For this aim, we consider **asymptotic $f_\mathbb{P}$-monotone** functions.

Definition 3 (asymptotic $f_\mathbb{P}$-monotone functions). *Consider a random sample $S_n = \{x_i\}_{i=1}^{n}$ drawn from a PM $\mathbb{P}$ with density function $f_\mathbb{P}$. A function $g(x, S_n) : X \times S_n \to \mathbb{R}$ is asymptotically $f_\mathbb{P}$-monotone if:*

$$f_\mathbb{P}(x) \geq f_\mathbb{P}(y) \Rightarrow \lim_{n \to \infty} P\left(g(x, S_n) \geq g(y, S_n)\right) = 1 \ \forall x, y \in X.$$

Examples of asymptotic $f_\mathbb{P}$-monotone functions are $g_1(x, S_n) \propto \hat{f}_{S_n}(x)$, where $\hat{f}_{S_n}$ is a consistent estimator of the density $f_\mathbb{P}$ and $g_2(x, S_n, k) = e^{-d_{S_n,k}(x)}$, our choice in this article, where $d_{S_n,k}(x)$, is the distance from the point x to its kth-nearest neighbour. The asymptotic $f_\mathbb{P}$-monotone functions are natural plug-in estimators of the δ-Local α-Entropy:

$$\hat{h}_\alpha(x) = \frac{1}{|1-\alpha|} \log\left(g(x, S_n)^{-\alpha}\right) \text{ for } \alpha > 0 \text{ and } \alpha \neq 1.$$

Proposition 1 (Consistency). *The proposed estimator $\hat{h}_\alpha$ of the δ-local α-entropies is consistent.*

Proof. Let g be an asymptotic $f_\mathbb{P}$-monotone function used as a plug-in estimator of $h_{\alpha,\delta}$. If $f_\mathbb{P}(x) \geq f_\mathbb{P}(y)$ then for a sufficiently small δ is always true that $h_{\alpha,\delta}(x) \leq h_{\alpha,\delta}(y)$ (and equivalently $v_{\alpha,\delta}(x) \leq v_{\alpha,\delta}(y)$). By Definition 3 then:

$$f_\mathbb{P}(x) \geq f_\mathbb{P}(y) \Rightarrow \lim_{n \to \infty} P\left(\hat{h}_\alpha(x) \leq \hat{h}_\alpha(y)\right) = 1 \ \forall x, y \in X.$$

With the decomposition given in Equation 1, we are able to propose the following estimator for the α-Entropy.

Definition 4 (α-Entropy estimator). *Given a random sample $S_n = \{x_i\}_{i=1}^{n}$ drawn from a PM $\mathbb{P}$ and an asymptotically $f_\mathbb{P}$-monotone function $g(x, S_n)$, the plug-in α-Entropy estimator of the distribution $\mathbb{P}$ is defined as:*

$$\widehat{H}_\alpha(\mathbb{P}) = \frac{1}{1-\alpha} \log\left(\sum_{i=1}^{n} \hat{v}_{\alpha,\delta}(x_i)\right) = \frac{1}{1-\alpha} \log\left(\sum_{i=1}^{n} g(x_i, S_n)^{-\alpha}\right).$$

In next section with the aid of $\widehat{H}_\alpha(\mathbb{P})$ we will be able to compare the entropy associated to different kernel representations. The δ-Local α-Entropy estimations will be used to find functional outliers in the sample.

2.2 Estimation of Minimum Entropy Regions for Outlier Detection

Consider an *iid* sample $s_n(\mathbb{P}) = \{x_i\}_{i=1}^n$ drawn from the PM $\mathbb{P}$. To estimate which points in the sample belong to high density regions, we solve the following optimization problem:

$$
\begin{aligned}
\min_{\chi_1,\dots,\chi_n} \quad & \sum_{i=1}^n \chi_i \hat{h}_{\alpha,\delta}(x_i) + C \sum_{i=1}^n \xi_i \\
\text{s.t.} \quad & \hat{h}_{\alpha,\delta}(x_i) \leq H + \xi_i, \\
& \xi_i \geq 0, \qquad\qquad\qquad i = 1,\dots,n,
\end{aligned}
\tag{2}
$$

where $\chi_i \in \{0,1\}$ for $i = 1,\dots,n$ are auxiliary and binary variables, H is a threshold parameter and C is a regularization constant.

The local entropy measure can be seen as a projection of the sample points to a new coordinate system where the less locally entropic points are projected near to the origin and the most entropic far away from the origin. The solution of the problem stated in Equation 2 is an optimal hyperplane that isolates the points projected near the origin, that is the set of points that belongs to a high density (low entropy) region in the support of the distribution.

3 Kernel Selection and Outlier Detection

Most functional data analysis approaches choose an orthogonal basis of functions $B = \{\phi_1,\dots,\phi_N\}$ ($N \in \mathbb{N}$), where each ϕ_i belongs to a general function space $\mathcal{H}$ (usually $L_2(X)$ being X a compact real vector space) and then represent each functional datum by means of a linear combination in the $\text{Span}(B)$ [4, 9]. A usual choices is to consider $\mathcal{H}$ as a Reproducing Kernel Hilbert Space (RKHS) of functions [1]. In this case, the elements in the spanning set B are the eigenfunctions associated to the (positive-definite and symmetric) kernel K that generates $\mathcal{H}$. Let f be a curve in $\mathcal{H}$ sampled in $S_f^n = \{(x_i, f(x_i)) \in X \times \mathbb{R}\}_{i=1}^n$, by using the Mercer's decomposition, the function f can be approximated as:

$$
f(x) \approx \sum_{i=1}^n \alpha_i K(x, x_i) = \sum_{i=1}^n \alpha_i \sum_{j=1}^d \lambda_j \phi_j(x_i)\phi_j(x),
$$

where λ_j is the eigenvalue corresponding to the eigenvector ϕ_j of the kernel matrix $K_{S_f} = (K(x_i, x_j))_{i,j}$ for all $(x_i, x_j) \in S_f^n$ and $d = \min(n, \text{range}(K_S))$. We represent each functional datum $f \in \mathcal{H}$ as a point in $\mathbb{R}^d$ by using the expansion coefficients $\{\lambda_1^*,\dots,\lambda_d^*\}$ associated to f, where $\lambda_j^* = \lambda_j \sum_{i=1}^n \alpha_i \phi_j(x_i)$. This representation is stable as is demonstrated in Theorem 2 in [8].

3.1 Kernel Selection Based on a Minimum Entropy Criterion

The choice of the kernel and its best parameters is usually carried out using a cross-validation criterion. Our approach consist in select the kernel parameter(s) such that the H_α entropy associated to the point representation of the functional data (using the coefficients $\{\lambda_1^*, \ldots, \lambda_d^*\}$) is optimal. In this way the dimension (complexity) [5] of the feature space is established at the point where the decrements in the H_α entropy is stabilized.

3.2 Functional Outlier Detection Method

Given the best finite dimensional representation of the functional data, we proceed by using the δ-Local α-Entropy to solve the problem stated in Equation 2 in order to capture the most local entropic functional data (Max-local entropy).

4 Experimental Section

Artificial Experiment: In the first experiment we show how to choose the best kernel parameter to represent functional data and how to detect functional outliers in the sample. For this aim, we simulate 100 curves as follows:

$$f_i(t) = \sin(t) + \cos(t + \varepsilon_i) + a_i + b_i t^2 \quad i = 1, \ldots, 95,$$

$$f_i(t) = \sin(t) + \cos(t + \varepsilon_i) + \frac{1}{2}(\sin(5\pi t) + \cos(5\pi t + \varepsilon_i)) + a_i + b_i t^2 \quad i = 96, \ldots, 100,$$

where $t \in [0, 2\pi]$, and the random coefficients ε_i, a_i, b_i, are independently and normally distributed with means: $\mu_\varepsilon = 0$, $\mu_a = 5$ and $\mu_b = 1$ and variances $\sigma_\varepsilon^2 = \sigma_b^2 = 0.25$ and $\sigma_a^2 = 0.2$. The curves are represented in Figure 1.

For this experiment we consider a polynomial kernel $K_\rho(x_i, x_j) = \langle x_i, x_j \rangle^\rho$, where $\rho = 1, \ldots, 10$. In Figure 2-left we shown the entropy for different kernel degree parameters ρ. We choose the parameter $\rho = 7$ (the elbow of the plot)

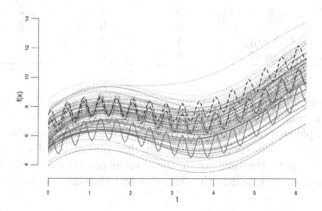

Fig. 1. The 100 curves generated for the experiment.

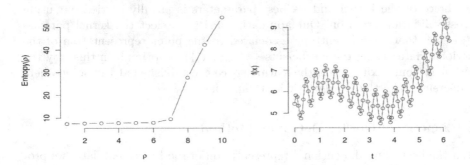

Fig. 2. Entropy evolution according to ρ (left) and functional representation of a curve based on a SVM Polynomial Kernel with $\rho = 7$ (right).

as it is the value where the changes in the entropy stabilizes. In Figure 2-right we show an outlier curve approximated using a Support Vector Machine (SVM) with $K_{\rho=7}$ to shown that the entropy criterion is adequate to fit the ρ parameter to represent functional data.

After fixing the best parameter $\rho = 7$ for representing the simulated functional data, we proceed to detect the outliers in the sample. We use a battery of different algorithms (already implemented in R) [3] to identify contaminated points (outliers) in the simulated data. The results are summarized in Table 1.

Table 1. Number of outlier, false-Positive and false-Negative identifications.

Metric/Technique	True outliers captured	Positives-false (Type I error)	Negative-false (Type II error)
Out-Trim	0	5	5
FM-depth	0	5	5
Out-Mode	0	0	5
Out-RP	0	5	5
Out-RProy	0	5	5
Out-Double R. Proy.	1	4	4
Max-local entropy ($K_{p=7}$)	**5**	**0**	**0**

The proposed method (Max-local entropy) works very well in the detection of the contaminated (outliers) curves. Our method is able to detect all the outliers in the sample without any positive-false nor negative-false detections. More sophisticated techniques, such as Out-Trim that made use of a bootstrapping procedure to compute the outliers or the double projection method that uses multiple depth measures, fails in the task of detect the simulated extreme curves.

Real Data Experiment. The real data example considers the detection of outliers in a sample of non-linear profiles. These data come from the manufacture of engineered woodboards [11]. In Figure 3-left we shown the set of 24 curves, each one corresponding to a vertical density profile. In a previous work [7], the authors identify 3 outliers profiles that are highlighted in red in Figure 3-right. The aim of this experiment is to demonstrate that the proposed method is also able to detect the outliers in the sample of non-linear profiles. For this experiment

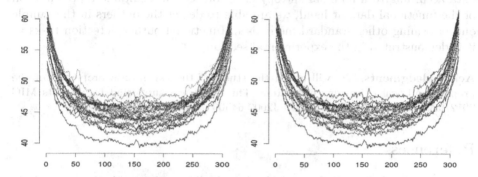

Fig. 3. The 24 density profiles and the 3 otulier profiles in red on the right.

we consider a RBF kernel $K_\sigma(x_i, x_j) = \exp^{-\frac{(x_i - x_j)^2}{2\sigma}}$, when σ is the complexity parameter. When σ increases then the RBF kernel tends to behaves like the linear kernel. In the other way around, when σ decreases the dimension of the feature space increases. In Figure 4-left we shown the entropy for different σ-parameter, we choose the value $\sigma = 20$ as it is the point where the changes in the entropy stabilizes. The representation of one profile obtained for $K_{\sigma=20}$ is presented in Figure 4-center. In Figure 4-right, we present a boxplot of the local entropies. The 3 outlier points in this plot correspond to the 3 non-linear outlier profiles [7] highlighted in red in Figure 3-right.

Regarding the competitor depth measures, the only metric that it is able to detect the 3 outlier in the sample is Out-Trim, that makes use of a bootstrapping procedure to determine the extreme values in the sample. The remaining metrics, also used in the artificial experiment, are able to capture only two outliers (the two most depth curves in the sample) but not the outlier in shape.

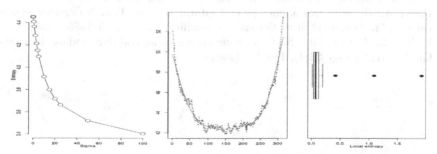

Fig. 4. Entropies associated to different σ values (left). An example of an adjusted profile using $K_{\sigma=20}$ (center). The distribution of the local entropies ($\sigma = 20$)(right).

5 Conclusions

In this work we introduce a new measure, the local entropy, that can be additively used to compute the entropy of a distribution. A consistent estimator for the local entropy is also introduced. Using a finite dimensional representation for functional data, we select suitable kernel parameters for representing functional data according to a minimal entropy criterion. Given a suitable representation of the functional data at hand, we are able to detect the outliers in the sample outperforming other standard methods in functional outlier detection tasks as it is demonstrated in the experimental section.

Acknowledgments. We will afford the study of the asymptotic properties of the proposed δ-Local α-Entropy estimators. This work was supported by projects MIC 2012/00084/00, ECO2012-38442, SEJ2007-64500.

References

1. Aronszajn, N.: Theory of reproducing kernels. Transactions of the American Mathematical Society **68**, 337–404 (1950)
2. Febrero, M., Galeano, P., González-Manteiga, W.: Outlier detection in functional data by depth measures, with application to identify abnormal nox levels. Environmetrics **19**(4), 331–345 (2008)
3. Febrero-Bande, M., de la Fuente, M.O.: Statistical computing in functional data analysis: the r package fda. usc. Journal of Statistical Software **51**(4), 1–28 (2012)
4. Ferraty, F., Vieu, P.: Nonparametric Functional Data Analysis: Theory and Practice. Springer, New York (2006)
5. Sathiya Keerthi, S., Lin, C.: Asymptotic behaviors of support vector machines with gaussian kernel. Neural computation **15**(7), 1667–1689 (2003)
6. López-Pintado, S., Romo, J.: On the concept of depth for functional data. Journal of the American Statistical Association **104**(486), 718–734 (2009)
7. Moguerza, J.M., Muñoz, A., Psarakis, S.: Monitoring nonlinear profiles using support vector machines. In: Rueda, L., Mery, D., Kittler, J. (eds.) CIARP 2007. LNCS, vol. 4756, pp. 574–583. Springer, Heidelberg (2007)
8. Muñoz, A., González, J.: Representing functional data using support vector machines. Pattern Recognition Letters **31**(6), 511–516 (2010)
9. Ramsay, J.O.: Functional Data Analysis. Wiley, New York (2006)
10. Rényi, A.: On measures of entropy and information. In: Fourth Berkeley Symposium on Mathematical Statistics and Probability, vol. 1, pp. 547–561 (1961)
11. Walker, E., Paul Wright, S.: Comparing curves using additive models. Journal of Quality Technology **34**(1), 118–129 (2002)

Improving Optimum-Path Forest Classification Using Confidence Measures

Silas E.N. Fernandes[1], Walter Scheirer[2], David D. Cox[2],
and João Paulo Papa[3](✉)

[1] Department of Computing, Federal University of São Carlos - UFSCar Rodovia
Washington Luís, Km 235 - SP 310, São Carlos-SP 13565-905, Brazil
silasfernandes@ieee.org
[2] Department of Molecular & Cellular Biology, Harvard University, 52 Oxford St.,
Cambridge, MA 02138, USA
[3] Department of Computing, Univ Estadual Paulista - UNESP,
Av. Eng. Luiz Edmundo Carrijo Coube, 14-01, Bauru-SP 17033-360, Brazil
papa@fc.unesp.br

Abstract. Machine learning techniques have been actively pursued in
the last years, mainly due to the great number of applications that make
use of some sort of intelligent mechanism for decision-making processes.
In this work, we presented an improved version of the Optimum-Path
Forest classifier, which learns a score-based confidence level for each
training sample in order to turn the classification process "smarter",
i.e., more reliable. Experimental results over 20 benchmarking datasets
have showed the effectiveness and efficiency of the proposed approach for
classification problems, which can obtain more accurate results, even on
smaller training sets.

Keywords: Optimum-path forest · Supervised learning · Confidence
measures

1 Introduction

Pattern recognition techniques aim at learning decision functions that separate
a dataset in clusters of samples that share similar properties. Supervised techniques are known to be the most accurate, since the amount of information
available about the training samples allows them to learn class-specific properties, as well as one can design more complex learning algorithms to improve
the quality of the training data. The reader can refer to some state-of-the-art
supervised techniques, such as Support Vector Machines (SVMs) [4], Artificial
Neural Networks (ANNs) [8], Bayesian classifiers, and the well-known k-nearest
neighbours (k-NN), among others. The reader can refer to Duda et al. [6] for a
wide discussion about such methods.

Although we have very sophisticated and complex techniques, it is always
important to keep an open mind for different approaches that may lead us to

© Springer International Publishing Switzerland 2015
A. Pardo and J. Kittler (Eds.): CIARP 2015, LNCS 9423, pp. 619–625, 2015.
DOI: 10.1007/978-3-319-25751-8_74

better results. Simple ideas can improve the effectiveness of some well-known techniques. Ahmadlou and Adeli [1], for instance, proposed the Enhanced Probabilistic Neural Networks, being the idea to avoid the influence of noisy samples when computing the covariance matrix of each class. This simple idea has shown to be very effective in some situations. Later on, Guo et al. [7] presented a simple heuristic to reduce SVM computational load while maintaining its good generalization over unseen data. Their approach is based on the computation of the lowest margin instances, which are than used as support vector candidates.

Some years ago, Papa et al. [10,11] presented a graph-based supervised pattern recognition technique called Optimum-Path Forest (OPF), which has demonstrated interesting results in terms of efficiency and effectiveness, being some of them comparable to the ones obtained by SVMs, but faster for training. The idea of OPF is to model the pattern recognition task as a graph partition problem, in which a set of key samples (*prototypes*) acts as being the rulers of this competition process. Such samples try to conquer the remaining ones offering to them optimum-path costs: when a sample is conquered, it receives the label of its conqueror. An interesting property stated by Souza et al. [12] concerns with OPF error bounds, which are the same as k-NN when all training samples are prototypes and a path-cost function that computes the maximum arc-weight along a path is employed. Such statement is very interesting, since a recent work by Amancio et al. [3] showed strong evidences that, in practice, k-NN may perform so well as SVMs.

The approach proposed by Papa et al. [10,11] elects the prototype nodes as being the nearest samples from different classes, which can be found out through a Minimum Spanning Tree (MST) computation over the training graph: the connected samples in the MST are marked as being the prototype nodes. In case of multiple MSTs in large datasets, the current OPF implementation, although the values of the possible optimum-paths that are going to be offered for a given graph node may be the same from samples from different classes, the one which reaches that node first will conquer it. The main problem concerns with the "tie-regions", i.e., the regions in which we have a set of training samples that offer the same optimum-path cost to a given node. Therefore, this scenario may lead OPF to be more prone to errors in the training set.

In this paper, we propose to consider not only the optimum-path value from a given sample in the classification process, but also its *confidence value*, which is measured by means of a score index computed through a learning process over a validating set. The idea is to penalize the training samples that do not have "reliable" confidence values. We have shown this approach can overcome traditional OPF in several datasets, even when we learn on smaller training sets, as well as it can perform training faster than its na "ive version when using the same amount of data.

The remainder of the paper is organized as follows. Sections 2 and 3 present the OPF background theory and the proposed approach for score-based confidence computation, respectively. Section 4 describes the methodology and the experimental results. Finally, conclusions and future works are stated in Section 5.

2   Optimum-Path Forest

Let $\mathcal{D}(\mathcal{X}, \mathcal{Y})$ be a dataset, in which $\mathcal{X}$ and $\mathcal{Y}$ stand for the set of samples (feature vectors) and the set of their labels, respectively. The OPF classifier models D as being a weighted graph $G(\mathcal{V}, \mathcal{A}, d)$, such that the set of samples are now the graph nodes, i.e., $\mathcal{V} = \mathcal{X}$, and the arcs are defined by the adjacency relation $\mathcal{A}$. In addition, the arcs are weighted by a distance function $d : \mathcal{V} \times \mathcal{V} \rightarrow \Re^{+}$.

Similarly to the process of ordered communities generation, in which group of individuals are originated based on the connectivity relations among their leaders, the OPF classifier employs a competition process among some key samples in order to partition the graph into optimum-path trees (OPTs) according to a predefined path-cost function. Analogously, the population is partitioned into communities, where each individual belongs to a group that has offered him the best reward.

Besides, the dataset $\mathcal{D}$ can be partitioned in two or three subsets according to the set of possible approaches. In the situation we need two subsets, we have that $\mathcal{D} = \mathcal{D}_1 \cup \mathcal{D}_2$, in which $\mathcal{D}_1$ and $\mathcal{D}_2$ stand for the training and testing sets, respectively. Therefore, the graph-based formulations of the training and testing sets are given by $G_1(\mathcal{V}_1, \mathcal{A}_1, d)$ and $G_2(\mathcal{V}_2, \mathcal{A}_2, d)$, respectively. However, without loss of generality, OPF usually uses the same adjacency relation for both sets. Thus, we can redefine both graphs as $G_1(\mathcal{V}_1, \mathcal{A}, d)$ and $G_2(\mathcal{V}_2, \mathcal{A}, d)$. Notice the standard OPF classifier uses a complete graph, which means all pairs of nodes are connected.

Let π_s be a path in the graph $\mathcal{G}_1$ with terminus in the sample $s \in \mathcal{D}_1$, and $(\pi_s \cdot \langle s, t \rangle)$ be the concatenation between π_s and the arc $\langle s, t \rangle$, such that $t \in \mathcal{D}_1$. Let $\mathcal{S} \subseteq \mathcal{V}_1$ be the set of prototype nodes from all classes. Roughly speaking, the idea of OPF is to minimize $f(\pi_t), \forall t \in \mathcal{D}_1$, where $f(\cdot)$ is defined as the path-cost function given by:

$$
f(\langle s \rangle) = \begin{cases} 0 & \text{if } s \in \mathcal{S} \\ +\infty & \text{otherwise,} \end{cases}
$$
$$
f(\pi_s \cdot \langle s, t \rangle) = \max\{f(\pi_s), d(s, t)\}, \tag{1}
$$

in which $d(s, t)$ denotes the distance between nodes s and t. Particularly, an optimal set of prototypes $\mathcal{S}^*$ can be found exploiting the theoretical relation between the MST and the minimum spanning forest generated by OPF using $f(\cdot)$, as stated by Alléne et al. [2]. By computing an MST in G_1, we obtain an acyclic graph whose nodes are the samples in $\mathcal{D}_1$ and the arcs are non-directed and also weighted by the distance function d. Besides that, every pair of nodes in the MST is connected by a simple path, which is optimum with respect to $f(\cdot)$. In addition, this minimum spanning tree encodes an optimum-path tree for each root (prototype) node. Thus, the optimum prototypes are defined as the nearest elements in the MST with different labels in $\mathcal{D}_1$.

In the classification phase, for each sample $r \in \mathcal{D}_2$, we consider all arcs connecting r to every $s \in \mathcal{D}_1$. If we take into account all possible paths from S^* to r, we can find the optimum path π_r^*, i.e., the one that minimizes $f(r)$ as follows:

$$f(r) = \min_{\forall s \in \mathcal{D}_1} \{\max\{f(s), d(s,r)\}\}. \qquad (2)$$

Let $s^* \in \mathcal{D}_1$ be the sample that satisfies Equation 2. The OPF classification step simply assigns the label of s^* as being that of r.

3   Learning Score-Based Confidence Levels

The classification using the confidence level supports the idea of assigning a score to all training nodes by means of a learning process over a validation set. In order to extract the confidence level, we need to partition the dataset $\mathcal{D}$ in three subsets, say that $\mathcal{D} = \mathcal{D}_1 \cup \mathcal{D}_v \cup \mathcal{D}_2$, in which $\mathcal{D}_1$, $\mathcal{D}_v$ and $\mathcal{D}_2$ stand for the training, validation and testing sets, respectively.

The proposed approach for learning scores aims at training OPF classifier over $\mathcal{D}_1$ for further classification of $\mathcal{D}_v$, using the same methodology described in Section 2. The main difference now is that we associate to each training sample a *reliability* level $\phi(\cdot)$, which is computed by means of its individual performance in terms of its recognition rate over the validation set. However, considering the aforementioned approach, a sample $t \in \mathcal{D}_1$ that did not participate from any classification process, would be scored as $\phi(t) = 0$, and may be penalized, since the higher the score the most reliable that sample is. Therefore, for such samples we have set $\phi(t) \to 1$ to give them a chance to perform a good job during the classification over the unseen (test) data. Thus, at the and of the classification process over the validation set $\mathcal{D}_v$, we have a score measure $\phi(s) \in [0,1], \forall s \in \mathcal{D}_1$, which can be used as a *confidence level* of that sample. In short, there are three possible confidence levels:

- $\phi(s) = 0$: it means sample s did not perform a good work on classifying samples, since it has misclassified all samples. Therefore, samples with score equals to 0 *may not be reliable*;
- $0 < \phi(s) < 1$: it means sample s has misclassified samples, as well as it has also assigned correct labels to some of them. Notice the larger the errors, the lower is a sample's reliability. Samples with scores that fall in this range, *may be reliable*; and
- $\phi(s) = 1$: it means either sample s did not participate in any classification process, or s assigned the correct label to all its conquered samples, which means s is a *reliable sample* according to our definition.

After learning the confidence levels for each training sample, one needs to modify the naïve OPF classification procedure in order to consider this information during the label assignment. In order to fulfill this purpose, we proposed a modification in the OPF classification procedure (Equation 2) as follows:

$$f(r) = \min_{\forall s \in \mathcal{D}_1} \left\{ \left(\frac{1}{\phi(s) + \epsilon} \right) * \max\{f(s), d(s, r)\} \right\}, \tag{3}$$

where $\epsilon = 10^{-4}$ is employed to avoid numerical instabilities. Therefore, the idea of the first term in the above equation is to penalize samples with *low confidence* values by increasing their costs. In short, the amount of penalty is inversely proportional to a sample's confidence level.

4   Methodology and Experimental Results

In order to evaluate the efficiency and effectiveness of the proposed confidence-based approach for OPF classifier, we perform experiments over 20 classification datasets (real and synthetic datasets)[1,2,3,4]. Due to the lack of space, instead of showing characteristics individually for these datasets, we append in Table 1 which also presents the mean accuracies. The choice of these datasets was motivated by their level of complexity (overlapped samples), which turns the classification process more sensible to misclassification. The experiments were conducted on a computer with a Pentium Intel Core $i3^{\circledR}$ 3.07Ghz processor, 4 GB of memory RAM and Linux Ubuntu Desktop LTS 12.04 as the operational system.

For each dataset, we conducted a cross-validation procedure with 15 runnings, being each of them partitioned as follows: 30% of the samples were used to compose the training set, being the validation and testing sets ranged from $10\% - 60\%, 20\% - 50\%, \ldots, 50\% - 20\%$. These percentages have been empirically chosen, being more intuitive to provide a larger validation set for *confidence learning*.

In Table 1 is included average accuracy over all datasets. In order to provide a robust analysis, we performed the non-parametric Friedman test, which is used to rank the algorithms for each dataset separately. In case of Friedman test provides meaningful results to reject the null-hypothesis (h_0: all techniques are equivalent), we can perform a post-hoc test further. For this purpose, we conducted the Nemenyi test, proposed by Nemenyi [9] and described by Demšar [5], which allows us to verify whether there is a critical difference (CD) among techniques or not. Due to the lack of space, instead of showing all diagrams for each dataset, we highlighted the best techniques in bold according to Nemenyi test.

We can observe OPFc has obtained the best results in 7 out 20 datasets, and with results very close to the best ones in other 7 datasets. The very worst results were obtained over "duke-breast-cancer" and "Leukemia", since these are small datasets, thus providing a validation set that was not enough to learn good confidence levels. However, even in these datasets, OPFc recognition rate was close to standard OPF one. As OPF* has employed bigger datasets, it was expected more accurate results.

---

[1]   http://mldata.org
[2]   http://archive.ics.uci.edu/ml
[3]   http://pages.bangor.ac.uk/~mas00a/activities/artificial_data.htm
[4]   http://lrs.icg.tugraz.at/research/aflw

Table 1. Mean accuracy results: the bold values stand for the most accurate techniques. The recognition rates were computed according to [11], which consider unbalanced datasets.

Dataset	OPF	OPF*	OPFc	# samples	# features	# classes
a1a	65.74	65.59	**69.05**	32,561	123	2
aloi	95.31	**96.92**	95.09	108,000	128	1,000
connect-4	**63.32**	63.05	63.10	67,557	126	3
synthetic1	50.69	**50.78**	50.72	100,000	100	1,000
synthetic2	85.29	85.56	**87.33**	100,000	4	4
synthetic3	89.55	89.70	**91.14**	100,000	4	4
synthetic4	53.05	52.44	**56.14**	500	2	2
dmoz-web-directory-topics	59.16	**62.06**	56.72	1,329	10,629	5
dna	83.80	**88.99**	85.02	5,186	180	3
duke-breast-cancer	80.37	**91.15**	79.46	86	7,129	2
ijcnn1	93.78	**96.46**	94.13	191,681	22	2
Statlog-Letter	97.31	**98.58**	97.58	35,000	16	26
Leukemia	71.47	**76.90**	69.63	72	7,129	2
mushrooms	93.68	92.61	**96.93**	8,124	112	2
scene-classification	66.04	**67.78**	66.60	2,407	294	15
shuttle	94.48	**97.25**	95.09	101,500	9	7
usps	97.24	**97.93**	97.28	9,298	256	10
w1a	80.54	80.15	**80.68**	49,749	300	4
yahoo-web-directory-topics	50.54	51.77	**56.36**	1,106	10,629	4
aflw	88.00	**89.48**	88.93	8,193	4,096	2

It was not possible to establish some specific situation (considering the dataset configuration, such as the number of classes and the number features, for instance) in which OPFc might be better than OPF and OPF*, although it seems the proposed approach has obtained the top results in high-dimensional datasets, except for "dmoz-web-directory-topics". If we consider an error margin of around 3%, the proposed approach obtained similar results in 17 out 20 datasets, thus being considered a very suitable approach to improve OPF classifier.

The above assumption can be strengthened if we consider the computational effort of the techniques. As expected, standard OPF has been faster than OPFc and OPF* with respect to the training (training+learning scores) step, since it does not need to compute the confidence level for every training sample. However, the Nemenyi statistical test pointed out OPFc has been faster than OPF* for training (Figure 1a), being similar to it with respect to the classification step, as displayed in Figure 1b. On average, i.e., considering all 20 datasets, standard OPF has been about 2.108 times faster than OPFc and OPF*.

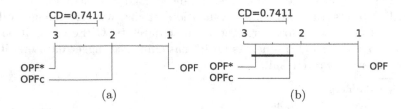

(a)   (b)

Fig. 1. Nemenyi statistical test regarding the (a) training (training + learning scores) and (b) testing computational load. Groups of similar approaches are connected to each other.

5   Conclusions and Future Works

In this work, we introduced a confidence-based learning algorithm to improve OPF classification results. The idea is to penalize training samples that misclassify others in a classification process over a validation set. The proposed algorithm aims at learning confidence levels for each training sample to be further used in a modified version of the standard classification procedure employed by OPF.

Experiments over 20 datasets showed the robustness of the proposed approach, which obtained the best results in 7 datasets, as well as very close recognition rates in other 7 datasets. Additionally, OPFc can improve standard OPF results even with smaller training sets, being also faster than OPF trained over training+validation sets.

Acknowledgments. The authors would like to thank CAPES for their financial support, and FAPESP grants #2013/20387-7 and #2014/16250-9, as well as CNPq grants #47057162013-6, #303182/2011-3 and #306166/2014-3.

References

1. Ahmadlou, M., Adeli, H.: Enhanced probabilistic neural network with local decision circles: A robust classifier. Integrated Computer-Aided Engineering **17**(3), 197–210 (2010)
2. Allène, C., Audibert, J.Y., Couprie, M., Keriven, R.: Some links between extremum spanning forests, watersheds and min-cuts. Image and Vision Computing **28**(10), 1460–1471 (2010)
3. Amancio, D.R., Comin, C.II., Casanova, D., Travieso, G., Bruno, O.M., Rodrigues, F.A., Costa, L.F.: A systematic comparison of supervised classifiers. PLoS ONE **9**(4), e94137 (2014)
4. Cortes, C., Vapnik, V.: Support-vector networks. Machine Learning **20**(3), 273–297 (1995)
5. Demšar, J.: Statistical comparisons of classifiers over multiple data sets. J. Mach. Learn. Res. **7**, 1–30 (2006). http://dl.acm.org/citation.cfm?id=1248547.1248548
6. Duda, R.O., Hart, P.E., Stork, D.G.: Pattern Classification, 2nd Edition. Wiley-Interscience (2000)
7. Guo, L., Boukir, S.: Fast data selection for SVM training using ensemble margin. Pattern Recognition Letters **51**, 112–119 (2015)
8. Haykin, S.: Neural Networks: A Comprehensive Foundation, 3rd edn. Prentice-Hall Inc., Upper Saddle River (2007)
9. Nemenyi, P.: Distribution-free Multiple Comparisons. Princeton University (1963)
10. Papa, J.P., Falcão, A.X., Albuquerque, V.H.C., Tavares, J.M.R.S.: Efficient supervised optimum-path forest classification for large datasets. Pattern Recognition **45**(1), 512–520 (2012)
11. Papa, J.P., Falcão, A.X., Suzuki, C.T.N.: Supervised pattern classification based on optimum-path forest. International Journal of Imaging Systems and Technology **19**(2), 120–131 (2009)
12. Souza, R., Rittner, L., Lotufo, R.A.: A comparison between k-optimum path forest and k-nearest neighbors supervised classifiers. Pattern Recognition Letters **39**, 2–10 (2014). Advances in Pattern Recognition and Computer Vision

Multiple Kernel Learning for Spectral Dimensionality Reduction

Diego Hernán Peluffo-Ordóñez[1], Andrés Eduardo Castro-Ospina[2]([✉]),
Juan Carlos Alvarado-Pérez[3,4], and Edgardo Javier Revelo-Fuelagán[5]

[1] Universidad Cooperativa de Colombia – Pasto, Pasto, Colombia
[2] Research Center of the Instituto Tecnologico Metropolitano, Medellin, Colombia
andrescastro@itm.edu.co
[3] Universidad de Salamanca, Salamanca, Spain
[4] Universidad Mariana, Pasto, Colombia
[5] Universidad de Nariño, Pasto, Colombia

Abstract. This work introduces a multiple kernel learning (MKL) approach for selecting and combining different spectral methods of dimensionality reduction (DR). From a predefined set of kernels representing conventional spectral DR methods, a generalized kernel is calculated by means of a linear combination of kernel matrices. Coefficients are estimated via a variable ranking aimed at quantifying how much each variable contributes to optimize a variance preservation criterion. All considered kernels are tested within a kernel PCA framework. The experiments are carried out over well-known real and artificial data sets. The performance of compared DR approaches is quantified by a scaled version of the average agreement rate between K-ary neighborhoods. Proposed MKL approach exploits the representation ability of every single method to reach a better embedded data for both getting more intelligible visualization and preserving the structure of data.

Keywords: Dimensionality reduction · Generalized kernel · Kernel PCA · Multiple kernel learning

1 Introduction

The aim of dimensionality reduction (DR) is to extract a lower dimensional, relevant information from high-dimensional data, being then a key stage within the design of pattern recognition and data mining systems. Indeed, when using adequate DR stages, the system performance can be enhanced as well as the data visualization can become more intelligible. The range of DR methods is diverse, including those classical approaches such as principal component analysis (PCA) and classical multidimensional scaling (CMDS), which are respectively based on variance and distance preservation criteria [1]. Recent methods of DR are focused

---

This work is supported by the Faculty of Engineering of Universidad Cooperativa de Colombia-Pasto, and the ESLINGA Research Group.

A. Pardo and J. Kittler (Eds.): CIARP 2015, LNCS 9423, pp. 626–634, 2015.
DOI: 10.1007/978-3-319-25751-8_75

on the data topology preservation. Mostly such a topology is driven by graph-based approaches where data are represented by a non-directed and weighted graph. In this connection, the weights of edge graphs are certain pairwise similarities between data points, the nodes are data points, and a non-negative similarity (also affinity) matrix holds the pairwise edge weights. Spectral methods such as Laplacian eigenmaps (LE) [2] and locally linear embedding (LLE) [3] were the pioneer ones to incorporate similarity-based formulations. Also, given the fact that the rows of the normalized similarity matrix can be seen as probability distributions, divergence-based methods have emerged (i.e., stochastic neighbor embedding (SNE) [4]). Spectral approaches for DR have been widely used in several applications such as relevance analysis [5,6], dynamic data analysis [7,8] and feature extraction [9,10]. Because of being graph-driven methods and involving then similarities, spectral approaches can be easily represented by kernels [11], which means that a wide range of methods can be set within a Kernel PCA framework [12]. At the moment to choose a method, aspects such as nature of data, complexity, aim to be reached and problem to be solved should be taken into consideration. In this regard, as mentioned above, there exists a variety of DR spectral methods making the selection of a method a nontrivial task. Also, some problems may require the combination of methods so that the properties of different methods are simultaneously taken into account to perform the DR process and the quality of resultant embedded space is improved.

The purpose of this work is to provide a multiple kernel learning (MKL) approach allowing for both selecting a DR method, and combining different methods to exploit the representation ability of every single method to reach a better embedded space than the one obtained when using only one method. This approach starts with kernel representations of conventional spectral methods as explained in [11]. Then, a generalized kernel is calculated by means of a linear combination of kernel matrices whose coefficients are estimated by an adapted variable relevance approach proposed in a previous work [6]. Similar approaches have been applied on dynamic data clustering [13] and image segmentation [14]. The experiments are carried out over well-known data sets, namely an artificial Spherical shell, a Swiss roll toy set, and MNIST image bank [15]. The DR performance is quantified by a scaled version of the average agreement rate between K-ary neighborhoods as described in [16].

The rest of this paper is organized as follows: Section 2 outlines the proposed MKL approach for dimensionality reduction. Section 3 describes the experimental setup as well as section 4 presents the results and discussion. Finally, some final remarks are drawn in section 5.

2   Multiple kernel Learning for Dimensionality Reduction

In mathematical terms, the goal of DR is to embed a high dimensional data matrix $\boldsymbol{Y} \in \mathbb{R}^{D \times N}$ into a low-dimensional, latent data matrix $\boldsymbol{X} \in \mathbb{R}^{d \times N}$, being $d < D$. Then, observed data and latent data matrices are formed by N data points, denoted respectively by $\boldsymbol{y}_i \in \mathbb{R}^D$ and $\boldsymbol{x}_i \in \mathbb{R}^d$, with $i \in \{1, \ldots, N\}$.

Kernel PCA, as PCA, maximizes a variance criterion, which can be seen as an inner product criterion when data matrix is centered. Let $\boldsymbol{\Phi} \in \mathbb{R}^{D_h \times N}$ be an unknown high dimensional representation space such that $D_h \ggg D$, and $\phi(\cdot)$ be a function that maps data from the original dimension to a higher one, such that $\phi(\cdot) : \mathbb{R}^D \rightarrow \mathbb{R}^{D_h}, \boldsymbol{y}_i \mapsto \phi(\boldsymbol{y}_i)$.

Given this, we can write the i-th column vector of matrix $\boldsymbol{\Phi}$ as $\boldsymbol{\Phi}_i = \phi(\boldsymbol{y}_i)$. Consequently, the inner product on the high-dimensional vector space is $\phi(\boldsymbol{y}_i)^\top \phi(\boldsymbol{y}_j) = k(\boldsymbol{y}_i, \boldsymbol{y}_j) = k_{ij}$, where $k(\cdot, \cdot)$, followed from Mercer's condition, is a kernel function. In matrix terms, we get that the kernel matrix is $\boldsymbol{K} = \boldsymbol{\Phi}^\top \boldsymbol{\Phi}$.

Since Kernel PCA is developed under the condition that matrix $\boldsymbol{\Phi}$ has zero mean, we must ensure this condition by centering the kernel matrix as follows:

$$
\begin{aligned}
\boldsymbol{K} \leftarrow &\boldsymbol{K} - \frac{1}{N}\boldsymbol{K}\mathbf{1}_N\mathbf{1}_N^\top - \frac{1}{N}\mathbf{1}_N\mathbf{1}_N^\top\boldsymbol{K} + \frac{1}{N^2}\mathbf{1}_N\mathbf{1}_N^\top\boldsymbol{K}\mathbf{1}_N\mathbf{1}_N^\top \\
&= (\boldsymbol{I}_N - \mathbf{1}_N\mathbf{1}_N^\top)\boldsymbol{K}(\boldsymbol{I}_N - \mathbf{1}_N\mathbf{1}_N^\top),
\end{aligned} \tag{1}
$$

where $\mathbf{1}_N$ and $\boldsymbol{I}_N$ are N-dimensional all ones vector and identity matrix, respectively.

The aim of our MKL approach is to get a generalized kernel $\widetilde{\boldsymbol{K}} \in \mathbb{R}^{N \times N}$ from a linear combination of a set of kernels $\{\boldsymbol{K}^{(1)}, \ldots, \boldsymbol{K}^{(M)}\}$ to input a DR approach based on kernels. Ensuring linear independency, the generalized kernel can be written as:

$$
\widetilde{\boldsymbol{K}} = \sum_{m=1}^{M} \alpha_m \boldsymbol{K}^{(m)}. \tag{2}
$$

Here, we propose to estimate the coefficients by using an adapted version of the variable ranking approach proposed in [6]. In [13], authors apply MKL based on a ranking vector to cluster time-varying data in a sequence of frames. A cumulative kernel is calculated to track the dynamic behavior, having each kernel a corresponding data matrix (one per frame). Unlike, in this approach we have a single data matrix, and then the ranking vector should be calculated using directly the kernel matrices. Define a matrix $\mathcal{K} \in \mathbb{R}^{N^2 \times M}$ holding the vectorization of the kernel matrices. Likewise, suppose that a lower-rank representation $\widehat{\mathcal{K}} \in \mathbb{R}^{N^2 \times M}$ of matrix $\widehat{\mathcal{K}}$ is known. Regarding any othonormal matrix $\boldsymbol{U} = [\boldsymbol{u}^{(1)} \cdots \boldsymbol{u}^{(c)}] \in \mathbb{R}^{M \times c}$, we can write the lower-rank matrix as

$$
\widehat{\mathcal{K}} = \mathcal{K}\boldsymbol{U}. \tag{3}
$$

So, the full-rank matrix can be then estimated as $\mathcal{K} = \widehat{\mathcal{K}}\boldsymbol{U}^\top$. Similarly to the feature extraction problem stated in [5,9], here we propose to maximize the variance of $\widehat{\mathcal{K}}$ by solving the following optimization problem:

$$
\max_{\boldsymbol{U}} \ \mathrm{tr}(\boldsymbol{U}^\top \mathcal{K}\mathcal{K}\boldsymbol{U}) \tag{4a}
$$

$$
\text{s. t.} \ \ \boldsymbol{U}^\top\boldsymbol{U} = \boldsymbol{I}_c. \tag{4b}
$$

As demonstrated in [6], previous problem has a dual version that can be expressed as

$$\min_{U} \|\mathcal{K} - \widehat{\mathcal{K}}\|_F^2 \tag{5a}$$

$$\text{s. t.} \quad U^\top U = I_c, \tag{5b}$$

where $\| \cdot \|_F$ stands for Frobenius norm. Since this formulation is a quadratic problem subject to orthonormal constraints, a feasible solutions is selecting U as the eigenvectors related to the c largets eigenvalues of $\mathcal{KK}$.

Finally, the coefficients α_m of the linear combination to calculate the generalized kernel are the ranking values quantifying how much each column of matrix $\mathcal{K}$ (each kernel) contributes to minimizing the cost function given in (5a). Again, applying the variable relevance approach presented in [6], we can calculate the ranking vector $\alpha = [\alpha_1, \ldots, \alpha_M]$ using:

$$\alpha = \sum_{m=1}^{c} \lambda_m u^{(m)} \circ \alpha^{(m)}, \tag{6}$$

where $\circ$ denotes Hadamard (element-wise) product. Given the problem formulation, possitivenes of α is guaranteed and then can be directly used to perform the linear combination.

3   Experimental Setup

Databases. Experiments are carried out over three conventional data sets. The first data set is an artificial spherical shell ($N - 1500$ data points and $D = 3$). The second data set is a randomly selected subset of the MNIST image bank [15], which is formed by 6000 gray-level images of each of the 10 digits ($N = 1500$ data points –150 instances for all 10 digits– and $D = 24^2$). The third data set is a toy set here called Swiss roll ($N = 3000$ data points and $D = 3$). Figure 1 depicts examples of the considered data sets.

Kernels for DR. Three kernel approximations for spectral DR methods [11] are considered. Namely, classical multidimensional scalling (CMDS), locally linear embedding (LLE), and graph Laplacian eigenmaps (LE). CMDS kernel is the double centered distance matrix $D \in \mathbb{R}^{N \times N}$ so

$$K^{(1)} = K_{CMDS} = -\frac{1}{2}(I_N - 1_N 1_N^\top)D(I_N - 1_N 1_N^\top), \tag{7}$$

where the ij entry of D is given by $d_{ij} = \|y_i - y_j\|_2^2$ and $\| \cdot \|_2$ stands for Euclidean norm.

A kernel for LLE can be approximated from a quadratic form in terms of the matrix $\mathcal{W}$ holding linear coefficients that sum to 1 and optimally reconstruct observed data. Define a matrix $M \in \mathbb{R}^{N \times N}$ as $M = (I_N - \mathcal{W})(I_N - \mathcal{W}^\top)$ and λ_{max} as the largest eigenvalue of M. Kernel matrix for LLE is in the form

$$K^{(2)} = K_{LLE} = \lambda_{max} I_N - M. \tag{8}$$

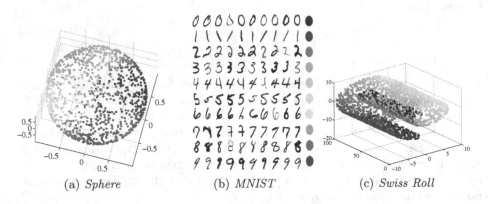

(a) *Sphere*   (b) *MNIST*   (c) *Swiss Roll*

Fig. 1. The three considered datasets.

Since kernel PCA is a maximization problem of the covariance of the the high-dimensional data represented by a kernel, LE can be expressed as the pseudo-inverse of the graph Laplacian L:

$$K^{(3)} = K_{LE} = L^{\dagger}, \tag{9}$$

where $L = D - S$, S is a similarity matrix and $D = \text{Diag}(S1_N)$ is the degree matrix. All previously mentioned kernels are widely described in [11]. The similarity matrix S is formed in such a way that the relative bandwidth parameter is estimated keeping the entropy over neighbor distribution as roughly $\log K$ where K is the given number of neighbors as explained in [17]. The number of neighbors is established as $K = 30$.

As well, a RBF kernel is also considered: $K^{(4)} = K_{RBF}$ whose ij entry are given by $\exp(-0.5\|y_i - y_j\|/\sigma^2)$ with $\sigma = 0.1$. For all methods, input data is embedded into a 2-dimensional space, then $d = 2$.

Accordingly, the MKL approach is performed considering $M = 4$ kernels. The generalized kernel provided $\tilde{K}$ here as well as the individual kernels $K^{(1)}, \ldots, K^{(M)}$ are tested on kernel PCA as explained in [12].

Performance Measure: To quantify the performance of studied methods, the scaled version of the average agreement rate $R_{NX}(K)$ introduced in [16] is used, which is ranged within the interval $[0, 1]$. Since $R_{NX}(K)$ is calculated at each perplexity value from 2 to $N-1$, a numerical indicator of the overall performance can be obtained by calculating its area under the curve (AUC). The AUC assesses the dimension reduction quality at all scales, with the most appropriate weights.

Notwithstanding, it is important to note that kernels approximations are suboptimal and input parameters are not properly set, which means that under other settings, the quality measure and resultant embedding data might be significantly different. Here, just basic settings are considered in order to show the benefit of MKL rather than the individual methods.

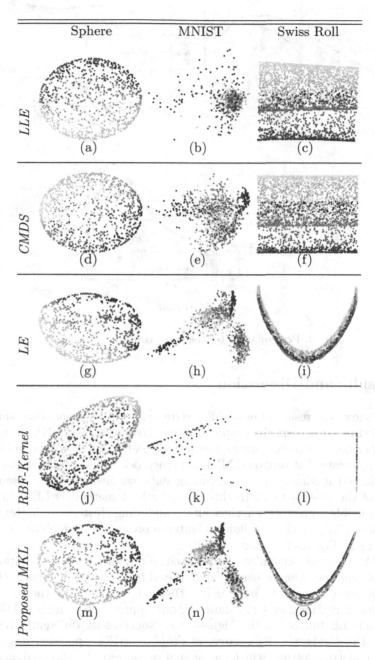

Fig. 2. 2D representations for selected methods over all data sets.

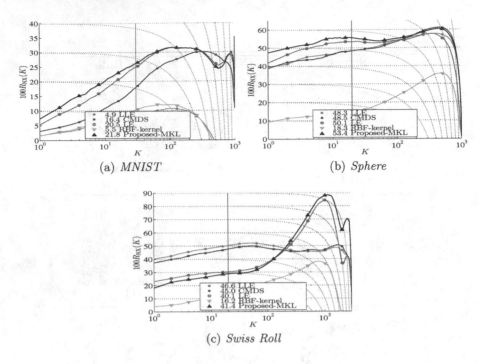

(a) *MNIST*   (b) *Sphere*

(c) *Swiss Roll*

Fig. 3. Performances for the three considered datasets.

4   Results and Discussion

Figure 2 shows the resultant embedding data using the corresponding kernels of
the studied methods, and the proposed generalized kernel for MKL. Comparing
resultant embedding representations with the $R_{NX}(K)$ curves shown in Figure 3,
we can appreciate that proposed MKL approach determines the best one among
the considered methods, since embedding data reached by MKL resemble to
the one of the best method. In this case, the best method is LE, which gets
more intelligible representation since either underling clusters are better formed
(see Figure 2(h)), or the manifold is better represented -resembling an object
unfolding (see Figures 2(g) and 2(i)).

Additionally, the generalized kernel used in a kernel PCA may improve the
quality of representation as can be appreciated from Figure 3. Indeed, the area
under the curve reached by our MKL is the highest for two of the tested data
sets. Particularly, for *Swiss roll* data set, our approach gets higher AUC than
the baseline LE but is not the highest one. Nonetheless, differently the other
considered methods, the R_{NX} curve of proposed MKL approach has a right-
sided asymmetric plotting, which means that our approach is focused on specific
structures of data -in this case, the global structure.

5 Conclusions and Future Work

In this work, a multiple kernel learning approach for dimensionality reduction tasks is presented. The core of this approach is the generalized kernel that is calculated by means of a linear combination of kernel matrices representing spectral dimensionality reduction methods, where the coefficients are obtained from a variable ranking based on a variance criterion. Proposed approach improves both data visualization and preservation by exploiting the representation ability of every single technique.

As future work, new multiple kernel learning approaches will be explored by combining kernel representations arising from other dimensionality reduction methods, aimed at reaching a good trade-off between preservation of data structure and intelligible data visualization.

References

1. Borg, I.: Modern multidimensional scaling: Theory and applications. Springer (2005)
2. Belkin, M., Niyogi, P.: Laplacian eigenmaps for dimensionality reduction and data representation. Neural Computation 15(6), 1373–1396 (2003)
3. Roweis, S.T., Saul, L.K.: Nonlinear dimensionality reduction by locally linear embedding. Science 290(5500), 2323–2326 (2000)
4. Hinton, G.E., Roweis, S.T.: Stochastic neighbor embedding. In: Advances in Neural Information Processing Systems, pp. 833–840 (2002)
5. Wolf, L., Bileschi, S.: Combining variable selection with dimensionality reduction. In: 2005 IEEE Computer Society Conference on Computer Vision and Pattern Recognition, CVPR 2005, vol. 2, pp. 801–806, June 2005
6. Peluffo, D.H., Lee, J.A., Verleysen, M., Rodríguez-Sotelo, J.L., Castellanos-Domínguez, G.: Unsupervised relevance analysis for feature extraction and selection: a distance-based approach for feature relevance. In: International Conference on Pattern Recognition, Applications and Methods - ICPRAM 2014
7. Langone, R., Alzate, C., Suykens, J.A.: Kernel spectral clustering with memory effect. Statistical Mechanics and its Applications, Physica A (2013)
8. Maestri, M., Cassanello, M., Horowitz, G.: Kernel PCA performance in processes with multiple operation modes. Chemical Product and Process Modeling 4(5), 7 (2009)
9. Wolf, L., Shashua, A.: Feature selection for unsupervised and supervised inference: The emergence of sparsity in a weight-based approach. Journal of Machine Learning 6, 1855–1887 (2005)
10. Unsupervised feature relevance analysis applied to improve ECG heartbeat clustering. Computer Methods and Programs in Biomedicine (2012)
11. Ham, J., Lee, D.D., Mika, S., Schölkopf, B.: A kernel view of the dimensionality reduction of manifolds. In: Proceedings of the Twenty-first International Conference on Machine learning, p. 47. ACM (2004)
12. Peluffo-Ordóñez, D., Lee, J., Verleysen, M.: Generalized kernel framework for unsupervised spectral methods of dimensionality reduction. In: IEEE Symposium Series on Computational Intelligence (2014)

13. Peluffo-Ordónez, D., Garcia-Vega, S., Langone, R., Suykens, J., Castellanos-Dominguez, G., et al.: Kernel spectral clustering for dynamic data using multiple kernel learning. In: The 2013 International Joint Conference on Neural Networks (IJCNN), pp. 1–6. IEEE (2013)
14. Molina-Giraldo, S., Álvarez-Meza, A.M., Peluffo-Ordoñez, D.H., Castellanos-Domínguez, G.: Image segmentation based on multi-kernel learning and feature relevance analysis. In: Pavón, J., Duque-Méndez, N.D., Fuentes-Fernández, R. (eds.) IBERAMIA 2012. LNCS, vol. 7637, pp. 501–510. Springer, Heidelberg (2012)
15. LeCun, Y., Bottou, L., Bengio, Y., Haffner, P.: Gradient-based learning applied to document recognition. Proceedings of the IEEE 86(11), 2278–2324 (1998)
16. Lee, J.A., Renard, E., Bernard, G., Dupont, P., Verleysen, M.: Type 1 and 2 mixtures of Kullback-Leibler divergences as cost functions in dimensionality reduction based on similarity preservation. Neurocomputing (2013)
17. Cook, J., Sutskever, I., Mnih, A., Hinton, G.E.: Visualizing similarity data with a mixture of maps. In: International Conference on Artificial Intelligence and Statistics, pp. 67–74 (2007)

Indian Buffet Process for Model Selection in Latent Force Models

Cristian Guarnizo$^{(\boxtimes)}$, Mauricio A. Álvarez, and Alvaro A. Orozco

Engineering PhD Program, Universidad Tecnológica de Pereira,
Colombia, South America
{cdguarnizo,malvarez,aaog}@utp.edu.co

Abstract. Latent force models (LFM) are an hybrid approach which combines multiple output Gaussian processes and differential equations, where the covariance functions encode the physical models given by the differential equations. LFM require the specification of the number of latent functions used to build the covariance function for the outputs. Furthermore, they assume that the output data is explained by using the entire set of latent functions, which is not the case in many real applications. We propose in this paper the use of an Indian Buffet process (IBP) as a way to perform model selection over the number of latent Gaussian processes in LFM applications. Furthermore, IBP allows us to infer the interconnection between latent functions and the outputs. We use variational inference to approximate the posterior distributions, and show examples of the proposed model performance over artificial data and a motion capture dataset.

Keywords: Indian buffet process · Latent force models · Gaussian processes · Regression

1 Introduction

Latent force models (LFM) are an hybrid approach of Gaussian processes (GP), where the covariance function is built from a convolution. This convolution is performed using the Green's function of a differential equation [1]. Hence, latent functions may represent a physical quantity, like the action of a protein for transcription regulation of a gene or a latent force in a system involving masses, springs and dampers (see [1]). Despite its success for prediction, it is still unclear how to select the number of latent functions and, how to unveil the interactions between the latent functions and the output variables that are being modelled [5]. Several methods have been proposed in the literature for the problem of model selection in related areas of multiple output Gaussian processes. For example in multi-task learning, a Bayesian multi-task learning model capable to learn the sparsity pattern of the data features base on matrix-variate Gaussian scale mixtures is proposed in [11]. Also, in [7], Robot inverse dynamics are approximated by a multi-task Gaussian Process where a Bayesian information criterion is used

© Springer International Publishing Switzerland 2015
A. Pardo and J. Kittler (Eds.): CIARP 2015, LNCS 9423, pp. 635–642, 2015.
DOI: 10.1007/978-3-319-25751-8_76

for model selection. In a closely related work in multi-task Gaussian processes [15], the problem of model selection was approached using the spike and slab distribution as prior over the weight matrix of a linear combination of Gaussian processes latent functions. The inference step is performed using a variational approach.

In this paper, we use an Indian Buffet Process (IBP) [9,10] for model selection in latent force models. The IBP is a non-parametric prior over binary matrices, that imposes an structure over the sparsity pattern of the binary matrix. It has previously been used for introducing sparsity in linear models [12]. We formulate a variational inference procedure for inferring posterior distributions over the structure of the relationships between output functions and latent processes, by combining ideas from [4] and [8]. We show examples of the model using artificial data and motion capture data.

2   Latent Force Models

In a multi-variate regression setting the likelihood model for each output can be expressed as $y_d(t) = f_d(t) + w_d(t)$, where $t \in \mathbb{R}^+$ is the input time, $\{y_d(t)\}_{d=1}^D$ is the collection of D outputs, $w_d(\cdot)$ is an independent noise process and each $f_d(t)$ is given by

$$f_d(t) = \sum_{q=1}^{Q} S_{d,q} \int_0^t G_d(t - \tau') u_q(\tau') \, d\tau', \qquad (1)$$

where $G_d(\cdot)$ is a smoothing function or smoothing kernel, $\{u_q(t)\}_{q=1}^Q$ are orthogonal processes, and the variables $\{S_{d,q}\}_{d=1,q=1}^{D,Q}$ measure the influence of the latent function q over the output function d. We assume that each latent process $u_q(t)$ is a Gaussian process with zero mean function and covariance function $k_q(t,t')$.

2.1   Covariance Functions

Due to the linearity in expression (1), the set of processes $\{f_d(t)\}_{d=1}^D$ follows a joint Gaussian process with mean function equal to zero, and covariance function given by $k_{f_d,f_{d'}}(t,t') = \sum_{q=1}^{Q} S_{d,q} S_{d',q} k_{f_d^q, f_{d'}^q}(t,t')$, where $k_{f_d^q, f_{d'}^q}(t,t')$ is defined as

$$k_{f_d^q, f_{d'}^q}(t,t') = \int_0^t \int_0^{t'} G_d(t - \tau) G_{d'}(t' - \tau') k_q(\tau, \tau') \, d\tau \, d\tau'. \qquad (2)$$

For some forms of the smoothing kernel $G_d(\cdot)$, and the covariance function $k_q(\cdot)$, the covariance functions $k_{f_d^q, f_{d'}^q}(t,t')$ can be worked out analytically. Additionally, we assume the following form for $k_q(t,t')$

$$k_q(t,t') = \exp\left(-\frac{(t - t')^2}{l_q^2}\right), \qquad (3)$$

where l_q is the length-scale associated to latent function q. Next, we briefly describe two different smoothing kernels used in this work.

Gaussian Smoothing (GS) Function. If we assume that the smoothing kernel $G_d(\cdot)$ has the following form

$$G_d(t, t') = \frac{p_d^{1/2}}{(2\pi)^{1/2}} \exp\left[-\frac{p_d}{2}(t - t')^2\right],$$

where p_d is a precision value. Although we refer to this function as GS function, it has been shown by [2] that this Green's function can be derived from a particular form of a partial differential equation that represents a diffusion process.

Second Order Differential Equation (ODE2). In this scenario, we assume that the data can be explained using a second order differential equation related to a mechanical system

$$m_d \frac{\mathrm{d}^2 f_d(t)}{\mathrm{d}t^2} + C_d \frac{\mathrm{d} f_d(t)}{\mathrm{d}t} + B_d f_d(t) = \sum_{q=1}^{Q} S_{d,q} u_q(t), \tag{4}$$

where $\{m_d\}_{d=1}^{D}$ are mass constants, $\{C_d\}_{d=1}^{D}$ are damper constants, and $\{B_d\}_{d=1}^{D}$ are spring constants. Without loss of generality, the value of the mass m_d, for all d, is set to one. Now, assuming initial conditions equal to zero, the solution for the Green's function associated to (4) is given by $G_d(t - t') = \frac{1}{\omega_d} \exp\left[-\alpha_d(t - t')\right] \sin\left[\omega_d(t - t')\right]$, where α_d is the decay rate and ω_d is the natural frequency. Both variables are defined as $\alpha_d = C_d/2$ and $\omega_d = \sqrt{4B_d - C_d^2}/2$, as explained in [2]. In next section, we describe the proposed method for model selection in latent force models.

3   Model

The model selection approach presented here follows ideas from the variational formulation for convolved multiple output Gaussian processes presented in [4], and the variational formulation for the Indian Buffet Process proposed in [8]. We start by defining the likelihood as $p(\mathbf{y}|u, \mathbf{X}, \boldsymbol{\theta}, \mathbf{S}, \mathbf{Z}) = \prod_{d=1}^{D} \mathcal{N}(\mathbf{y}_d|\mathbf{f}_d, \boldsymbol{\Sigma}_{\mathbf{w}_d})$, where $\boldsymbol{\Sigma}_{\mathbf{w}_d}$ is the covariance matrix associated to noise process at output d, $u = \{u_q\}_{q=1}^{Q}$, $\mathbf{S} = [S_{d,q}] \in \mathfrak{R}^{D \times Q}$, $\mathbf{Z} = [Z_{d,q}] \in \{0,1\}^{D \times Q}$ and each output vector $\mathbf{f}_d$ is defined as

$$\begin{bmatrix} f_d(\mathbf{x}_1) \\ \vdots \\ f_d(\mathbf{x}_N) \end{bmatrix} = \begin{bmatrix} \sum_{q=1}^{Q} Z_{d,q} S_{d,q} \int_{\mathcal{X}} G_{d,q}(\mathbf{x}_1 - \mathbf{z}) u_q(\mathbf{z}) d\mathbf{z} \\ \vdots \\ \sum_{q=1}^{Q} Z_{d,q} S_{d,q} \int_{\mathcal{X}} G_{d,q}(\mathbf{x}_N - \mathbf{z}) u_q(\mathbf{z}) d\mathbf{z} \end{bmatrix}.$$

For each latent function $u_q(\cdot)$, we define a set of auxiliary variables or inducing variables $\mathbf{u}_q \in \mathbb{R}$, obtained when evaluating the latent function u_q at a set of M inducing inputs $\{\mathbf{z}_m\}_{m=1}^{M}$. We refer to the set of inducing variables using

$\mathbf{u} = \{\mathbf{u}_q\}_{q=1}^Q$. Following ideas used in several computationally efficient Gaussian process methods, we work with the conditional densities $p(u|\mathbf{u})$, instead of the full Gaussian process $p(u)$, as in [3]. The conditional density of the latent functions given the inducing variables can be written as

$$p(u|\mathbf{u}) = \prod_{q=1}^Q \mathcal{N}(u_q | \mathbf{k}_{u_q,\mathbf{u}_q}^\top \mathbf{K}_{\mathbf{u}_q,\mathbf{u}_q}^{-1} \mathbf{u}_q, k_{u_q,u_q} - \mathbf{k}_{u_q,\mathbf{u}_q}^\top \mathbf{K}_{\mathbf{u}_q,\mathbf{u}_q}^{-1} \mathbf{k}_{u_q,\mathbf{u}_q}),$$

with $\mathbf{k}_{u_q,\mathbf{u}_q}^\top = [k_{u_q,u_q}(\mathbf{z},\mathbf{z}_1), k_{u_q,u_q}(\mathbf{z},\mathbf{z}_2), \ldots, k_{u_q,u_q}(\mathbf{z},\mathbf{z}_M)]$. The prior over $\mathbf{u}$ has the following form $p(\mathbf{u}) = \prod_{q=1}^Q \mathcal{N}(\mathbf{u}_q | \mathbf{0}, \mathbf{K}_{\mathbf{u}_q,\mathbf{u}_q})$. For the elements of $\mathbf{S}$ we use an spike and slab prior as follows [12]

$$p(S_{d,q}|Z_{d,q},\gamma_{d,q}) = Z_{d,q}\mathcal{N}(S_{d,q}|0,\gamma_{d,q}^{-1}) + (1 - Z_{d,q})\delta(S_{d,q}),$$

where $Z_{d,q}$ are the elements of the binary matrix $\mathbf{Z}$ that follows an Indian Buffet Process Prior. Thus, the prior for $Z_{d,q}$ is given by $p(Z_{d,q}|\pi_q) = \text{Bernoulli}(Z_{d,q}|\pi_q)$. With $\pi_q = \prod_{j=1}^Q v_j$ and $p(v_j) = \text{Beta}(\alpha,1)$. To apply the variational method, we write the joint distribution for $\mathbf{Z}$ and $\mathbf{S}$ as

$$p(\mathbf{S},\mathbf{Z}|\boldsymbol{v},\boldsymbol{\gamma}) = \prod_{d=1}^D \prod_{q=1}^Q [\pi_q \mathcal{N}(S_{d,q}|0,\gamma_{d,q}^{-1})]^{Z_{d,q}} [(1-\pi_q)\delta(S_{d,q})]^{1-Z_{d,q}},$$

where hyperparameters $\gamma_{d,q}$ follow $p(\boldsymbol{\gamma}) = \prod_{d=1}^D \prod_{q=1}^Q \text{Gamma}(\gamma_{d,q}|a_{d,q}^\gamma, b_{d,q}^\gamma)$. According to our model, the complete likelihood follows as

$$p(\mathbf{y},\mathbf{X},u,\mathbf{S},\mathbf{Z},\boldsymbol{v},\boldsymbol{\gamma},\boldsymbol{\theta}) = p(\mathbf{y}|\mathbf{X},u,\mathbf{S},\mathbf{Z},\boldsymbol{v},\boldsymbol{\gamma},\boldsymbol{\theta})p(u|\boldsymbol{\theta})p(\mathbf{S},\mathbf{Z}|\boldsymbol{\gamma},\boldsymbol{v})p(\boldsymbol{v})p(\boldsymbol{\gamma}),$$

where $\boldsymbol{\theta}$ are the hyperparameters regarding the type of covariance function.

3.1   Variational Inference

For the variational distribution, we use a mean field approximation, and assume that the terms in the posterior factorize as $q(\mathbf{u}) = \prod_{q=1}^{Q_+} q(\mathbf{u}_q)$, $q(\mathbf{S},\mathbf{Z}) = \prod_{d=1}^D \prod_{q=1}^{Q_+} q(S_{d,q}|Z_{d,q})q(Z_{d,q})$, $q(\boldsymbol{\gamma}) = \prod_{d=1}^D \prod_{q=1}^{Q_+} q(\gamma_{d,q})$, $q(\boldsymbol{v}) = \prod_{q=1}^{Q_+} q(v_q)$. where Q_+ represents the level of truncation, this indicates that the number of latent functions Q is estimated from the range $[1,Q_+]$ (see [8], for details). Following the same formulation used by [3], the posterior takes the form $q(u,\mathbf{u},\mathbf{S},\mathbf{Z},\boldsymbol{v},\boldsymbol{\gamma}) = p(u|\mathbf{u})\, q(\mathbf{u})\, q(\mathbf{S},\mathbf{Z})\, q(\boldsymbol{\gamma})q(\boldsymbol{v})$. Thus, the lower bound $F_V(q(\mathbf{u}),q(\mathbf{S},\mathbf{Z}), q(\boldsymbol{\gamma}), q(\boldsymbol{v}))$ that needs to be maximized, is given as [6]

$$\int q(u,\mathbf{u},\mathbf{S},\mathbf{Z},\boldsymbol{v},\boldsymbol{\gamma}) \log \left\{ \frac{p(\mathbf{y},\mathbf{X},u,\mathbf{S},\mathbf{Z},\boldsymbol{v},\boldsymbol{\gamma},\boldsymbol{\theta})}{q(u,\mathbf{u},\mathbf{S},\mathbf{Z},\boldsymbol{v},\boldsymbol{\gamma})} \right\} du\, d\mathbf{u}\, d\mathbf{S}\, d\mathbf{Z}\, d\boldsymbol{v}\, d\boldsymbol{\gamma}.$$

Updates for moments of each variational distribution are obtained by calculating the derivative of the expression above with respect to each moment and setting the derivative equal to zero.

4   Results

In this section, we show results from different datasets, including artificial data and motion capture data. For the artificial dataset, we are interested in recovering the known interconnection matrix ($\mathbf{Z}$) between the latent functions and outputs. For the real datasets, we analyse the regression performance compared to its non-sparse version.

4.1   Synthetic Data

To show the ability of the proposed method to recover the underlying structure between the output data and the latent functions, we apply the method to a toy multi-output dataset. Toy data is generated from the model explained in section 3, with the GS smoothing kernel, $D = 3$, $Q = 2$ and $\alpha = 1$. For GS smoothing kernel, we set the precision values to $p_1 = 0.01$, $p_2 = 1/120$, and $p_3 = 1/140$. We use the following values for matrices $\mathbf{Z}$, and $\mathbf{S}$,

$$\mathbf{Z} = \begin{bmatrix} 0 & 1 \\ 1 & 0 \\ 1 & 0 \end{bmatrix}, \quad \mathbf{S} = \begin{bmatrix} 0 & 1.48 \\ -3.19 & 0 \\ 6.87 & 0 \end{bmatrix}.$$

For the covariance functions $k_q(t, t')$ of the latent functions, we choose the length-scales as $l_{1,1} = 0.1$ and $l_{2,1} = 0.2$. Next, we sample the model and generate 30 data points per output, evenly spaced in the interval $[0, 1]$. We assume that each process $w_d(t)$ is a white Gaussian noise process with zero mean, and standard deviation equal to 0.1. The approximate model is then estimated using the proposed variational method with $Q_+ = 4$ and $\alpha = 1$. Additionally, for the variational distribution of latent functions, we set $M = 15$ inducing points evenly space along the output interval. Fig. 1 shows the results of model selection for this experiment. Hinton diagram (Fig. 1a) shows that $\mathbb{E}[\mathbf{Z}]$ approximates well $\mathbf{Z}$. Moreover, the posterior mean functions for each output closely approximate the data, as shown in Figures 1b to 1d.

4.2   Human Motion Capture Data

In this section, we evaluate the performance of the proposed method compared to the Deterministic Training Conditional Variational (DTCVAR) inference procedure proposed in [3]. DTCVAR also uses inducing variables for reducing computational complexity within a variational framework, but assumes that $Z_{d,q} = 1$, for all q, and d. Hyperparameters for kernel functions are learned using scaled conjugate gradient optimization. In this case, we use the Carnegie Mellon University's Graphics Lab motion-capture motion capture database [1]. Specifically, we consider the movements "walking" and "balance" from subject 02 motion 01 and subject 49 motion 18, respectively. From the 62 channels, we select 15 for

---

[1] This dataset is available at http://mocap.cs.cmu.edu

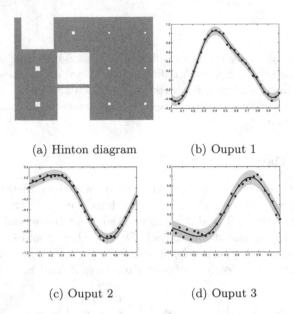

(a) Hinton diagram   (b) Ouput 1

(c) Ouput 2   (d) Ouput 3

Fig. 1. Results for model selection for example 1. Hinton diagram for $\mathbb{E}[Z_{d,q}]$ and, mean and two standard deviations for the predictions over the three outputs.

this experiment. We assume a level of truncation $Q_+ = 9$, and make a comparison between the GS and the ODE2 covariance functions. The latter covariance function is used because human motion data consists of recordings of an skeleton's joint angles across time, which summarize the motion. For performance comparison purposes, we use standardized mean square error (SMSE) and mean standardized log loss (MSLL) as defined in [14]. Table 1 shows the performance comparison, where best performance is obtained using the method proposed here. Figure 2 shows the Gaussian process mean and variance for the predictive

Table 1. Standardized mean square error (SMSE) and mean standardized log loss (MSLL) for different models and different kernel functions.

Subject		ODE2	IBP + ODE2	GS	IBP + GS
02	SMSE	0.5463	0.2087	0.5418	**0.1790**
	SMLL	-0.6547	**-1.2725**	-0.7863	-1.1993
42	SMSE	0.9448	**0.1013**	-	-
	SMLL	-0.0295	**-1.5939**	-	-

distribution of six outputs from subject 02 using IBP + ODE2. In most of the predictions, the model explains the testing data points with adequate accuracy, taking into account that the number of latent functions inferred by our approach is 2, while DTCVAR approach uses 9 latent functions.

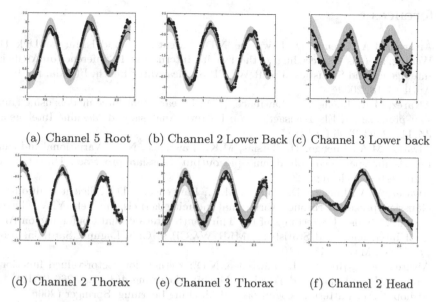

(a) Channel 5 Root   (b) Channel 2 Lower Back (c) Channel 3 Lower back

(d) Channel 2 Thorax   (e) Channel 3 Thorax   (f) Channel 2 Head

Fig. 2. Mean (solid line) and two standard deviations (gray shade) for predictions over six selected outputs from IBP + ODE2 trained model. Data points are represented by dots.

5 Conclusions

We have introduced a new variational method to perform model selection in latent force models. Our main aim was to identify the relationship between the latent functions and the outputs in LFM applications. The proposed method achieved comparable results to the DTCVAR method, in which, a full connectivity between latent functions and output functions is assumed. This makes our method suitable to applications where the complexity of the model should be reduced. The proposed model selection method can be applied in other applications that involve the use of a covariance function based on differential equations, such as inferring the biological network in gene expression microarray data (e.g. see [13]).

Acknowledgments. Authors would like to thank Convocatoria 567 of Colciencias, and Banco Santander for the support received under the program "Scholarship for Young Professors and Researchers Iberoamérica". The authors would also like to acknowledge the support from British Council and Colciencias under the research project "Sparse Latent Force Models for Reverse Engineering of Multiple Transcription Factors" and Universidad Tecnológica de Pereira for support under the research project Human motion synthesis through physically-inspired machine learning models, with code 6-15-3. The authors of this manuscript would like to thank Professor Fernando Quintana from Pontificia Universidad Católica de Chile, for his valuable comments over the model proposed here.

References

1. Álvarez, M.A., Luengo, D., Lawrence, N.D.: Latent force models. In: van Dyk, D., Welling, M. (eds.) Proceedings of the Twelfth International Conference on Artificial Intelligence and Statistics. JMLR W&CP 5, Clearwater Beach, Florida, pp. 9–16, April 16–18, 2009
2. Álvarez, M.A., Luengo, D., Lawrence, N.D.: Linear latent force models using gaussian processes. IEEE Transactions on Pattern Analysis and Machine Intelligence **35**(11), 2693–2705 (2013)
3. Álvarez, M.A., Luengo, D., Titsias, M.K., Lawrence, N.D.: Variational inducing kernels for sparse convolved multiple output gaussian processes. University of Manchester, Tech. rep. (2009)
4. Álvarez, M.A., Luengo, D., Titsias, M.K., Lawrence, N.D.: Efficient multioutput Gaussian processes through variational inducing kernels. In: Teh, Y.W., Titterington, M. (eds.) Proceedings of the Thirteenth International Conference on Artificial Intelligence and Statistics. JMLR W&CP 9, Chia Laguna, Sardinia, Italy, pp. 25–32, May 13–15, 2010
5. Álvarez, M.A., Rosasco, L., Lawrence, N.D.: Kernels for vector-valued functions: a review. Foundations and Trends in Machine Learning **4**(3), 195–266 (2012)
6. Bishop, C.M.: Pattern Recognition and Machine Learning. Springer (2006)
7. Chai, K.M., Williams, C., Klanke, S., Vijayakumar, S.: Multi-task Gaussian Process Learning of Robot Inverse Dynamics. In: NIPS 2008 (2009). http://eprints.pascal-network.org/archive/00004640/
8. Doshi-Velez, F., Miller, K., Van Gael, J., Teh, Y.W.: Variational inference for the indian buffet process. In: AISTATS (2009), pp. 137–144 (2009)
9. Griffiths, T.L., Ghahramani, Z.: Infinite latent feature models and the indian buffet process. In: NIPS, pp. 475–482. MIT Press (2005)
10. Griffiths, T.L., Ghahramani, Z.: The indian buffet process: an introduction and review. Journal of Machine Learning Research **12**, 1185–1224 (2011)
11. Guo, S., Zoeter, O., Archambeau, C.: Sparse bayesian multi-task learning. In: Shawe-Taylor, J., Zemel, R., Bartlett, P., Pereira, F., Weinberger, K. (eds.) Advances in Neural Information Processing Systems 24, pp. 1755–1763. Curran Associates, Inc. (2011). http://papers.nips.cc/paper/4242-sparse-bayesian-multi-task-learning.pdf
12. Knowles, D.A., Ghahramani, Z.: Nonparametric Bayesian sparse factor models with application to gene expression modelling. Annals of Applied Statistics **5**(2B), 1534–1552 (2011)
13. Olsen, C., Fleming, K., Prendergast, N., Rubio, R., Emmert-Streib, F., Bontempi, G., Haibe-Kains, B., Quackenbush, J.: Inference and validation of predictive gene networks from biomedical literature and gene expression data. Genomics **103**(5–6), 329–336 (2014)
14. Rasmussen, C.E., Williams, C.K.I.: Gaussian Processes for Machine Learning. MIT Press, Cambridge (2006)
15. Titsias, M.K., Lázaro-Gredilla, M.: Spike and slab variational inference for multi-task and multiple kernel learning. In: NIPS 2011, pp. 2339–2347 (2011)

SPaR-FTR: An Efficient Algorithm for Mining Sequential Patterns-Based Rules

José Kadir Febrer-Hernández[1]([⊠]), Raudel Hernández-León[1],
José Hernández-Palancar[1], and Claudia Feregrino-Uribe[2]

[1] Centro de Aplicaciones de Tecnologías de Avanzada (CENATAV),
7a # 21406 E/ 214 and 216, Rpto. Siboney, C.P. 12200 Playa, La Habana, Cuba
{jfebrer,rhernandez,jpalancar}@cenatav.co.cu
[2] Instituto Nacional de Astrofísica, Óptica y Electrónica (INAOE),
Luis Enrique Erro No. 1, Sta. María Tonantzintla,
CP:72840 Puebla, Mexico
cferegrino@ccc.inaoep.mx

Abstract. In this paper, we propose a novel algorithm for mining Sequential Patterns-based Rules, called SPaR-FTR. This algorithm introduces a new efficient strategy to generate the set of sequential rules based on the interesting rules of size three. The experimental results show that the SPaR-FTR algorithm has better performance than the main algorithms reported to discover frequent sequences, all they adapted to mine this kind of sequential rules.

Keywords: Data mining · Sequential patterns · Rule mining

1 Introduction

An important part of the Sequential Patterns-based Classification (SPaC) is the process of mining the set of classification rules, called SPaRs (Sequential Patterns-based Rules). These rules are mined from a class-transaction dataset, where a SPaR describes an implicative co-occurring relationship between a sequence α and a class c.

It is very common to confuse sequences of items with itemsets. In itemsets, an item can occur at most once but in a sequence, an itemset can occur multiple times. Additionally, in itemset mining, $(abc) = (cba)$ but in sequence mining, $\langle (ab)\, c \rangle \neq \langle c\, (ab) \rangle$.

Sequential Patterns-based Classification has been used in different tasks, for example: text classification [1], document-specific keyphrase extraction [2], text segmentation [3,4], web document classification [5,6], determination of DNA splice junction types [7], e-learning [8], automatic image annotation [9], among others.

In SPaC, it is assumed that a set of items $I = \{i_1,\, i_2,\, ...,\, i_l\}$, a set of classes C, and a set of transactions T are given, where each transaction $t \in T$ consists of a sequence $\langle \alpha_1\, \alpha_2\, ...\, \alpha_n \rangle$, so that $\alpha_i \subseteq I$, and a class $c \in C$. The Support of

© Springer International Publishing Switzerland 2015
A. Pardo and J. Kittler (Eds.): CIARP 2015, LNCS 9423, pp. 643–650, 2015.
DOI: 10.1007/978-3-319-25751-8_77

a sequence α, denoted as $Sup(\alpha)$, is the fraction of transactions in T containing α (see Eq. 1).

$$Sup(\alpha) = \frac{|T_\alpha|}{|T|} \tag{1}$$

where T_α is the set of transactions in T containing α (see Def. 1) and $|\cdot|$ is the cardinality operator.

Definition 1. *Let $\alpha = \langle \alpha_1\ \alpha_2\ ...\ \alpha_n \rangle$ and $\beta = \langle \beta_1\ \beta_2\ ...\ \beta_m \rangle$ be sequences, we will say that α is contained in β if there exists integers $1 \leq j_1 < j_2 < ... < j_n \leq m$ such that $\alpha_1 \subseteq \beta_{j_1}$, $\alpha_2 \subseteq \beta_{j_2}$, ..., $\alpha_n \subseteq \beta_{j_n}$, with $\beta_{j_i} \in \beta$.*

A SPaR is an implication of the form $\alpha \Rightarrow c$ where α is a sequence and $c \in C$. The size of a SPaR is defined as its cardinality, a SPaR containing k itemsets (including the class) is called a k-SPaR. The rule $\alpha \Rightarrow c$ is held in T with certain Support and Confidence (see Eqs. 2 and 3). If both Support and Confidence values of a SPaR $r : \alpha \Rightarrow c$ are greater than to the user-specified thresholds, r is declared to be an interesting SPaR.

$$Sup(\alpha \Rightarrow c) = Sup(\alpha \otimes \langle c \rangle) \tag{2}$$

where $\otimes$ is the concatenation operator (see Def. 2).

$$Conf(\alpha \Rightarrow c) = \frac{Sup(\alpha \Rightarrow c)}{Sup(\alpha)} \tag{3}$$

Definition 2. *Let $\alpha = \langle \alpha_1\ \alpha_2\ ...\ \alpha_n \rangle$ and $\beta = \langle \beta_1\ \beta_2\ ...\ \beta_m \rangle$, we will call the sequence $\langle \alpha_1\ \alpha_2\ ...\ \alpha_n\ \beta_1\ \beta_2\ ...\ \beta_m \rangle$ the concatenation of α and β, and we will use the operator $\otimes$ to indicate it.*

In this paper, we introduce an efficient strategy to generate the set of SPaRs based on the interesting rules of size three. The rest of the paper is organized as follows. The next section describes the related work. Our proposal are presented in Section three. In the fourth section the experimental results are shown. Finally, the conclusions and future works are given in section five.

2   Related Work

In the last decades, some works have used sequential patterns to increase the accuracy of classifiers. In these works, the extracted sequential patterns are considered to be important features and are used to build the classification model. However, there are not reported algorithms (with pseudo code or source code included) that directly compute the set of SPaRs. We assume that this is due to these algorithms can be obtained from the sequential pattern mining algorithms, without any algorithmic complications.

In general, most of the sequential pattern mining algorithms can be split into two main groups: (1) apriori-like algorithms (AprioriAll, AprioriSome and

DynamicSome [10], GSP [11], SPIRIT [12]) and (2) pattern-growth based algorithms (PrefixSpan [13], LAPIN [14], PRISM [15]).

In [11], the authors proposed the GSP algorithm, which includes time constrains and taxonomies in the mining process. In the experiments, the authors show that GSP runs 2 to 20 times faster than apriori-like algorithms [10]. Following similar ideas, the use of regular expressions was introduced in the SPIRIT algorithm [12].

The PrefixSpan algorithm, proposed in [13], is based on recursively constructing the patterns by growing on the prefix, and simultaneously, restricting the search to projected datasets. This way, the search space is reduced at each step, allowing for better performance in the presence of small support thresholds.

PRISM, the algorithm introduced by Karam Gouda in [15], uses a vertical approach for enumeration and support counting, based on the novel notion of primal block encoding, which is based on prime factorization theory.

The LAPIN (LAst Position INduction) algorithm [14] uses an item-last-position list and a prefix border position set instead of the tree projection or candidate generate-and-test techniques introduced so far.

Our proposal also stores a list of occurrence positions but unlike LAPIN that stores the last position of each single item in each transaction, SPaR-FTR stores for each interesting sequence α, and for each transaction t, a list with the occurrence positions of α in t.

3   SPaR-FTR Algorithm

In this section, we describe the SPaR-FTR algorithm, which uses the Support and Confidence measures to evaluate the candidate SPaRs and generates all candidate SPaRs from the set of interesting 3-SPaRs. Let $r : \alpha \Rightarrow c$ be an interesting SPaR and T be a transactional dataset, SPaR-FTR stores for each $t \in T$, a list L_t with the occurrence positions of α in t (see Def. 3).

Definition 3. *Let $\alpha = \langle \alpha_1\ \alpha_2\ ...\ \alpha_n \rangle$ and $\beta = \langle \beta_1\ \beta_2\ ...\ \beta_m \rangle$ be sequences such that α is contained in β (i.e. exists integers $1 \leq j_1 < j_2 < ... < j_n \leq m$ such that $\alpha_1 \subseteq \beta_{j_1}$, $\alpha_2 \subseteq \beta_{j_2}$, ..., $\alpha_n \subseteq \beta_{j_n}$), we will call occurrence position of α in β (occP(α, β)) to:*

- *the set of positions of all possible β_{j_n} in β, if $|\alpha| \leq 2$;*
- *the least position of all possible β_{j_n} in β, if $|\alpha| > 2$.*

In Table 1, five transactions and the occurrence positions of three sequences of different sizes are shown. Notice that when $|\alpha| > 2$ (e.g. $\langle a\ f\ b \rangle$ in transaction 2) we could also have several β_{j_n} (e.g. $(b : 4)$ and $(b : 6)$) but the proposed strategy to generate the candidate rules, only require the least of all.

Similar to the reported algorithms for frequent sequence mining [10, 13–15], in a first step, SPaR-FTR computes all the interesting 2-SPaRs using the Support and Confidence measures to evaluate them. As we mentioned above, SPaR-FTR stores for each interesting SPaR $r : \alpha \Rightarrow c$ (of any size) and for each transaction

Table 1. Example of five transactions and the occurrence positions of three sequences off different sizes.

Tid	Sequence	$\langle b \rangle$	$\langle a\ f \rangle$	$\langle a\ f\ b \rangle$
1	$\langle a\ b \rangle$	(b:2)		
2	$\langle cd\ a\ ef\ b\ cd\ ab \rangle$	(b:4), (b:6)	(f:3)	(b:4)
3	$\langle af\ f \rangle$		(f:2)	
4	$\langle af\ ef\ bf \rangle$	(b:3)	(f:2), (f:3)	(b:3)
5	$\langle b \rangle$	(b:1)		

$t \in T$, a list with the occurrence positions of α in t. Later, in a second step, SPaR-FTR obtains the set of 3-SPaRs (see Alg. 1) by combining the 2-SPaRs belonging to the same class. Unlike the reported algorithms mentioned above, which generates the k-SPaRs either by combining the interesting $(k-1)$-SPaRs with a common $k-2$ prefix or using a depth first search strategy, SPaR-FTR computes the k-SPaRs $(k > 3)$ by combining the interesting $(k-1)$-SPaRs and the interesting 3-SPaRs obtained in the second step (see Alg. 2).

Algorithm 1. Pseudo code for computing the interesting 3-SPaRs.

Input: Transactional dataset T, Support threshold $minSup$ and Confidence threshold $minConf$.
Output: Set of interesting 3-SPaRs.

```
1  L₁ ← {twoInterestingSPaR(T)}
2  L₂ ← ∅
3  foreach c ∈ C do
4      foreach (r₁ : ⟨i⟩ ⇒ c) ∈ L₁ and (r₂ : ⟨j⟩ ⇒ c) ∈ L₁ do
5          foreach t ∈ T do
6              if ∃op₁ > op₂ (op₁ ∈ occP(⟨j⟩,t) and op₂ ∈ occP(⟨i⟩,t)) then
7                  r₃ ← ⟨i⟩ ⊗ ⟨j⟩ ⇒ c
8                  Computes support Sup and confidence Conf of r₃
9                  if (r₃.Sup > minSup) and (r₃.Conf > minConf) then
10                     L₂ ← L₂ ∪ {r₃}
11                 end
12             end
13         end
14     end
15 end
16 return L₂
```

The main differences between algorithms 1 and 2 are in lines 4 and 6. In line 4 of Algorithm 1, the 2-SPaRs of the same class are combined to generate the candidate 3-SPaRs while in Algorithm 2, the $(k-1)$-SPaRs are combined with

---

Algorithm 2. Pseudo code for computing the interesting k-SPaRs

---

Input: Set of interesting $(k-1)$-SPaRs, set of interesting 3-SPaRs, Support
    threshold $minSup$ and Confidence threshold $minConf$.
Output: Set of interesting k-SPaRs.

1 $L_1 \leftarrow (k-1)$-SPaRs
2 $L_2 \leftarrow$ 3-SPaRs
3 $L_3 \leftarrow \emptyset$

4 **foreach** $c \in C$ **do**
5   **foreach** $(r_1 : \langle \alpha_1 \dots \alpha_{k-1} \rangle \Rightarrow c) \in L_1$ **and** $(r_2 : \langle \alpha_{k-1}\ \beta \rangle \Rightarrow c) \in L_2$ **do**
6   **foreach** $t \in T$ **do**
7   **if** $\exists op_1\ (op_1 \in occP(\langle \alpha_{k-1}\ \beta \rangle, t)$ **and** $op_1 > occP(\langle \alpha_1 \dots \alpha_{k-1} \rangle, t))$
                 then
8                   $r_3 \leftarrow \langle \alpha_1 \dots \alpha_{k-1} \rangle \otimes \langle \beta \rangle \Rightarrow c$
9   Computes support Sup and confidence $Conf$ of r_3
10   **if** $(r_3.Sup > minSup)$ **and** $(r_3.Conf > minConf)$ **then**
11                      $L_3 \leftarrow L_3 \cup \{r_3\}$
12   **end**
13   **end**
14   **end**
15   **end**
16 **end**

17 **return** L_3

---

the 3-SPaRs to generate the candidate k-SPaRs. In case of line 6, the difference is a direct consequence of the definition of occurrence position (see Def. 3 in this section).

4 Experimental Results

In this section, we present the results of our experimental comparison between SPaR-FTR and the main sequence mining algorithms reported in the literature (GSP [10], PrefixSpan [13], LAPIN [14] and PRISM [15]), all them adapted to compute the interesting SPaRs. All codes (implemented in ANSI C standard) were provided by their authors and adapted by us to compute the interesting SPaRs.

The experiments were conducted using several document collections, three in our case: AFP (*http://trec.nist.gov*), TDT (*http://www.nist.gov*) and Reuter (*http://kdd.ics.uci.edu*). The characteristics of these datasets are shown in Table 2. Our tests were performed on a PC with an Intel Core 2 Quad at 2.50 GHz CPU with 4 GB DDR3 RAM, running on Windows 7 system.

In the same way as in other works [10], for all used datasets, sentences are distinguished and ordered in each document. This means that the document is

Table 2. Tested datasets characteristics.

Dataset	#instances	#classes
AFP	711	22
TDT	2978	92
Reuter	21578	115

considered as being an ordered list of sentences. Each sentence is considered as being an unordered set of words. If we compare the market basket analysis problem with our approach, then a document plays the role of a client, the sentences from a document play the role of all the transactions for this client, the position of the sentence within the document plays the role of the date, and the set of words from a sentence plays the role of a list of bought items. Therefore, we represented the document as a sequence of itemsets where each one corresponds with the set of words of each sentence.

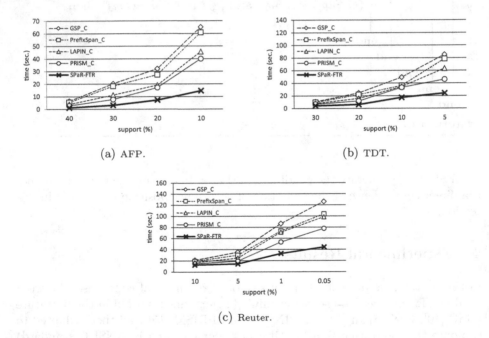

(a) AFP.   (b) TDT.

(c) Reuter.

Fig. 1. Runtime comparison using AFP, TDT and Reuter document collections.

In order to evaluate the performance of the SPaR-FTR algorithm, we process the three document collections with different support thresholds. In general, document collections are very sparse (with low transaction overlapping degree). Therefore, low Support thresholds are required, mainly in Reuter collection, where there are 21578 transactions and 115 classes.

In figures 1(a), 1(b) and 1(c), we show the result of all evaluated algorithms using different Support thresholds and a Confidence threshold set to 0.5. We do not test different Confidence values because the volume of the SPaRs depends on the Support threshold and we are evaluating the efficiency of our algorithm to generate the set of SPaRs. Notice that we add the characters "_C" to the name of the algorithms to specify that they are the adaptation of the original sequence mining algorithms mentioned above.

In the three experiments, the SPaR-FTR algorithm shows the best performance of all evaluated algorithms. The main reason of this result is that the candidates generation strategy, introduced in SPaR-FTR, generates less candidate rules than the other algorithms. As another experiment, we count the number of candidate SPaRs generated for each evaluated algorithm. In Table 3, we show the approximate results, in thousands, obtained on Reuter collection.

Table 3. Approximate number of candidate SPaRs, in thousands, obtained on Reuter collection.

Algorithms	Support thresholds (%)			
	10	5	1	0.05
GSP_C	25.3	46.2	80.9	112.3
PrefixSpan_C	23.9	41.1	73.6	104.2
LAPIN_C	21.3	37.4	68.7	97.5
PRISM_C	19.3	34.6	64.6	91.2
SPaR-FTR	16.2	28.8	52.1	71.9

Notice that SPaR-FTR generates 15 % less candidate rules (for all Support thresholds) than PRISM_C algorithm, which has the second better performance. Therefore, based on our experiments we can conclude that SPaR-FTR has good scalability with respect to the number of transactions and with respect to the decreasing of the Support threshold.

5   Conclusions

In this paper, we have proposed a novel algorithm for mining Sequential Patterns-based Rules, called SPaR-FTR, which introduces a new efficient strategy to generate the set of SPaRs based on the interesting rules of size three. The experimental results show that the SPaR-FTR algorithm has better performance than the main algorithms reported to discover frequent sequences, all they adapted to mine this kind of sequential rules.

As future work, we are going to study the problem of producing SPaRs with multiple labels, it means rules with multiple classes in the consequent. This kind of rules could be useful for problems where some documents can belong to more than one topic.

References

1. Buddeewong, S., Kreesuradej, W.: A new association rule-based text classifier algorithm. In: Proceedings of the 17th IEEE International Conference on Tools with Artificial Intelligence, pp. 684–685 (2005)

2. Xei, F., Wu, X., Zhu, X.: Document-specific keyphrase extraction using sequential patterns with wildcards. In: Proceedings of the IEEE 14th International Conference on Data Mining (2014)
3. Cesario, E., Folino, F., Locane, A., Manco, G., Ortale, R.: Boosting text segmentation via progressive classification. Knowl. Inf. Syst. **15**(3), 285–320 (2008)
4. García-Hernández, R.A., Martínez-Trinidad, J.F., Carrasco-Ochoa, J.A.: A fast algorithm to find all the maximal frequent sequences in a text. In: Sanfeliu, A., Martínez Trinidad, J.F., Carrasco Ochoa, J.A. (eds.) CIARP 2004. LNCS, vol. 3287, pp. 478–486. Springer, Heidelberg (2004)
5. Shettar, R.: Sequential Pattern Mining from Web Log Data. International Journal of Engineering Science and Advanced Technology **2**, 204–208 (2012)
6. Haleem, H., Kumar, P., Beg, S.: Novel frequent sequential patterns based probabilistic model for effective classification of web documents. In: 2014 International Conference on Computer and Communication Technology (ICCCT), pp. 361–371 (2014)
7. Berzal, F., Cubero, J.C., Sánchez, D., Serrano, J.M.: ART: A Hybrid Classification Model. Mach. Learn. **54**(1), 67–92 (2004)
8. Faghihi, U., Fournier-Viger, P., Nkambou, R., Poirier, P.: A generic episodic learning model implemented in a cognitive agent by means of temporal pattern mining. In: Chien, B.-C., Hong, T.-P., Chen, S.-M., Ali, M. (eds.) IEA/AIE 2009. LNCS, vol. 5579, pp. 545–555. Springer, Heidelberg (2009)
9. Teredesai, A.M., Ahmad, M.A., Kanodia, J., Gaborski, R.S.: CoMMA: A Framework for Integrated Multimedia Mining Using Multi-relational Associations. Knowl. Inf. Syst. **10**(2), 135–162 (2006)
10. Agrawal, R., Srikant, R.: Mining sequential patterns. In: Proceedings of the Eleventh International Conference on Data Engineering, pp. 3–14 (1995)
11. Srikant, R., Agrawal, R.: Mining sequential patterns: generalizations and performance improvements. In: Proceedings in the 5th International Conference Extending Database Technology, pp. 3–17 (1996)
12. Garofalakis, M., Rastogi, R., Shim, K.: SPIRIT: Sequential pattern mining with regular expression constraints. In: Proceedings of the 25th International Conference on Very Large Data Bases, pp. 223–234 (1999)
13. Pei, J., Han, J., Mortazavi-asl, B., Pinto, H., Chen, Q., Dayal U., Hsu, M.: PrefixSpan: Mining sequential patterns efficiently by prefix-projected pattern growth. In: Proceedings of the 17th International Conference on Data Engineering, pp. 215–224 (2001)
14. Yang, Z., Wang, Y., Kitsuregawa, M.: LAPIN: effective sequential pattern mining algorithms by last position induction for dense databases. In: Kotagiri, R., Radha Krishna, P., Mohania, M., Nantajeewarawat, E. (eds.) DASFAA 2007. LNCS, vol. 4443, pp. 1020–1023. Springer, Heidelberg (2007)
15. Gouda, K., Hassaan, M., Zaki, M.J.: Prism: An effective approach for frequent sequence mining via prime-block encoding. J. Comput. Syst. Sci. **76**(1), 88–102 (2010)
16. Yu, X., Li, M., Lee, D.G., Kim, K.D., Ryu, K.H.: Application of closed gap-constrained sequential pattern mining in web log data. In: Zeng, D. (ed.) Advances in Control and Communication, LNEE, vol. 137, pp. 649–656. Springer, Heidelberg (2012)
17. Liao, V., Chen, M.: An efficient sequential pattern mining algorithm for motifs with gap constraints. In: Proceedings of the 2012 IEEE International Conference on Bioinformatics and Biomedicine (BIBM) (2012)

Online Kernel Matrix Factorization

Andrés Esteban Páez-Torres$^{(\boxtimes)}$ and Fabio A. González

MindLab Research Group, Universidad Nacional de Colombia, Bogotá, Colombia
{aepaezt,fagonzalezo}@unal.edu.co

Abstract. Matrix factorization (MF) has shown to be a competitive machine learning strategy for many problems such as dimensionality reduction, latent topic modeling, clustering, dictionary learning and manifold learning, among others. In general, MF is a linear modeling method, so different strategies, most of them based on kernel methods, have been proposed to extend it to non-linear modeling. However, as with many other kernel methods, memory requirements and computing time limit the application of kernel-based MF methods in large-scale problems. In this paper, we present a new kernel MF (KMF). This method uses a budget, a set of representative points of size $p \ll n$, where n is the size of the training data set, to tackle the memory problem, and uses stochastic gradient descent to tackle the computation time and memory problems. The experimental results show a performance, in particular tasks, comparable to other kernel matrix factorization and clustering methods, and a competitive computing time in large-scale problems.

Keywords: Feature space factorization · Kernel matrix factorization · Large-scale learning

1 Introduction

Matrix factorization (MF) is a popular method in machine learning. The goal of matrix factorization is to find two (or more) matrices, which multiplied better approximate an original input matrix. There different approaches to perform MF, which include principal component analysis (PCA), non-negative matrix factorization (NMF) [9], singular value decomposition (SVD), and independent component analysis (ICA) [7]. All of them have proved their good performance in different machine learning problems such as dimensionality reduction, manifold learning, dictionary learning and clustering. However, the majority of MF methods are linear methods, which is an important limitation when dealing with data exhibiting non-linear dependencies. Kernel methods are an important class of machine learning methods, which address the problem of non-linear pattern modeling by first mapping the data to a higher dimensional feature space induced by a kernel, and then finding linear patterns that correspond to non-linear patterns in the original space. Methods like the support vector machines are widely used and show a very high performance, compared to other supervised methods. Many linear methods can take advantage of kernels by means of the kernel trick.

© Springer International Publishing Switzerland 2015
A. Pardo and J. Kittler (Eds.): CIARP 2015, LNCS 9423, pp. 651–658, 2015.
DOI: 10.1007/978-3-319-25751-8_78

Kernel matrix factorization methods such as kernel matrix factorization (KMF) [6,19], kernel PCA (KPCA) [14], kernel SVD (KSVD) [16], have demonstrated their capability extracting non-linear patterns that is translated in better performance when compared to their linear counterparts. The drawback of such kernel methods is their high computational cost, the time and space required to compute kernel matrices is quadratic in terms of the number of examples. This leads to the impossibility of directly using these methods when the number of samples is large. The purpose of this paper is to present *online kernel matrix factorization* (OKMF), a KMF algorithm that is able to handle the matrix factorization in a kernel induced feature space with large-scale data sets, under a reasonable amount of time and storage resources. OKMF addresses the memory problem imposing a budget restriction, this is, restricting the number of samples needed to represent the feature space base. With respect to the computation time, OKMF uses a stochastic gradient descent (SGD) strategy for optimizing its cost function [2]. SGD has proven to be a fast alternative to solve optimization problems when the amount of samples is large. The method was evaluated in a clustering task of 5 data sets that range from medium to large-scale. We compared OKMF with other kernel and large-scale clustering methods. The paper is organized as follows, the next section present the related work to KMF. In section 3 we present OKMF derivation and algorithm. In section 4, we present the experiments, results and their analysis. Finally, in section 5 we present the conclusions of the work.

2   Related Work

This section shows a short review of the current development of kernel matrix factorization. Basically KMF methods extend the linear matrix factorization methods with kernels in order to achieve a factorization able tot extract non-linear patterns. As with SVM, the kernel trick allows to extend linear methods to work in a high-dimensional space, called feature space, without calculating an explicit mapping to that space. One of the first methods to extend MF with kernels is the work of Zhang et al. [19] that considers a factorization of the form $\phi(X)^T\phi(X) = \phi(X)^T W_\phi H$. This method uses a modification of the multiplicative rules proposed by Lee et al. [9]. In the field of recommender systems the work of Rendle et al. [13] propose to use a regularized kernel matrix factorization in order to create a recommender system. Jun et al. [8] proposed two methods, P-NMF and KP-NMF, which are projective variations of NMF [9] and KMF [19]. Another of the seminal works in the field of KMF is the method proposed by Ding et al. [6], this method uses a different factorization of the form $\Phi(X) = \Phi(X)WG^T$. An et al. [1] proposes a method for multiple kernel factorization. The work of Pan et al. [12] proposes a method with a self-constructed kernel that preserves the non-negativity restriction in feature space. The article presented by Li et al. [10] uses a similar approach to Ding et al., but constructs a new kernel that represent, in a non-supervised approach, the manifold of the feature space. The work of Li and Ngom [11] provides some modifications to classical KMF [6,19], in order to simplify the calculations. Xia et al. [18] propose a robust kernel matrix factorization using the same factorization as in [6], but instead the cost function uses a different norm. All the mentioned works use the complete kernel matrix to compute the KMF, and therefore, they are inapplicable to large scale problems. This motivates the development of of a kernel matrix factorization method capable of dealing with large scale problems. Selecting a sample of the data, is one of the most common approaches for reducing time and memory requirements for machine learning methods. This approach has been used to improve the scalability of kernel methods through a strategy called *learning in a budget* [4]. In this strategy, the budget is a representative set of the training set with only $p \ll n$, samples, where n is total number of samples in the training data set. The kernel is then calculated between the training set and the budget, reducing the size from $O(n^2)$ to $O(np)$. Following this approach, Wang et al. proposed ECKF a KMF method [17]. This method uses a subset of the data in order to compute a KMF. Another related method is presented the work of Chen and Cai on spectral clustering[3], which uses a subset of data samples called landmarks to calculate a sparse representation of data based on kernels.

3   Online Kernel Matrix Factorization

In the following discussion we assume a kernel function $k : \mathcal{X} \times \mathcal{X} \to \mathbb{R}$, which induces a mapping $\Phi : \mathcal{X} \to \mathcal{F}$ from the problem space, $\mathcal{X}$, to a feature space, $\mathcal{F}$. For simplicity's sake, we assume $\mathcal{X} = \mathbb{R}^m$ and $\mathcal{F} = \mathbb{R}^n$. Also, a set of l samples in the problem space is noted as X corresponding to a matrix in $\mathbb{R}^{m \times l}$, and a subset, called a budget, is noted as $B \in \mathbb{R}^{m \times p}$.

To understand OKMF, let's consider a factorization of the feature space into a product of a linear combination of feature space vectors and a low-dimensional latent space representation.

$$\Phi(X) = \Phi(B)WH \tag{1}$$

where $\Phi(X) \in \mathbb{R}^{n \times l}$ is the mapping of all data into a feature space , $\Phi(B) \in \mathbb{R}^{n \times p}$ is the mapping of the budget B into the feature space and B satisfies the budget restriction, i.e, $|B| \ll |X|$. $W \in \mathbb{R}^{p \times r}$ is a weight matrix . Finally, $H \in \mathbb{R}^{r \times l}$ is the latent space representation for every element of $\Phi(X)$.

The previous factorization lead us to the following optimization problem:

$$\min_{W,h_i} J_i(W, h_i) = \min_{W,h_i} \frac{1}{2} \|\Phi(x_i) - \Phi(B)Wh_i\|^2 + \frac{\lambda}{2}\|W\|_F^2 + \frac{\alpha}{2}\|h_i\|^2 \tag{2}$$

To find the optimization rules for SGD, the partial derivatives of the cost in equation 2 with respect W and h_i.

$$\frac{\partial J_i(W, h_i)}{\partial h_i} = W^T\Phi(B)^T\Phi(x_i) - W^T\Phi(B)^T\Phi(B)Wh_i + \alpha h_i \tag{3}$$

654   A.E. Páez-Torres and F.A. González

$$\frac{\partial J_i(W, h_i)}{\partial W} = \Phi(B)^T \Phi(x_i) h_i^T - \Phi(B)^T \Phi(B) W h_i h_i^T + \lambda W \qquad (4)$$

In the previous equations we can replace $\Phi(B)^T \Phi(B)$ by the matrix $k(B, B) \in \mathbb{R}^{p \times p}$ defined as $k(B, B) = \{k(b_i, b_j)\}_{i,j}$, where $b_i \in \mathbb{R}^m$ corresponds to the i-th column of B. In the same way we can replace $\Phi(B)^T \Phi(x_i)$ by $k(B, x_i)$ defined in a similar way. This means that we can avoid computing the explicit mapping of data into feature space and use the more common kernel-trick approach. The update rule for h_t is a closed formula resulting from equating the derivative in equation 3 to zero.

$$h_t = (W_{t-1}^T k(B, B) W_{t-1} - \alpha I)^{-1} W_{t-1}^T k(B, x_t) \qquad (5)$$

The update rule for W_t is the standard SGD rule

$$W_t = W_{t-1} - \gamma(k(B, x_t) h_t^T - k(B, B) W_{t-1} h_t h_t^T + \lambda W_{t-1}) \qquad (6)$$

With the rules found in equation 5 and equation 6 we can design an algorithm to compute the feature space factorization. It takes as arguments the data matrix, budget matrix, the learning rate γ, regularization parameters λ and α. The output correspond to the matrix W.

Algorithm 1. Online kernel matrix factorization

procedure OKMF$(X, budget, W, \gamma, \lambda, \alpha)$
    $KB \leftarrow k(budget, budget)$
    for all $x_i \in X$ **do**
        $kxi \leftarrow k(budget, x_i)$
        $h_i \leftarrow (W^T KBW - \alpha I)^{-1} W^T kxi$
        $W \leftarrow W - \gamma(kxi h_i^T - KBW h_i h_i^T + \lambda W)$
    end for
    return W
end procedure

The use of a budget poses a new problem which is the selection of this budget. To tackle this problem, two approaches were used. The first was randomly picking p instances of the data set. The second one is computing a k-Means clustering with $k = p$, the resulting k cluster centers can be viewed as a prototype set of the data.

4 Experiments

One of the applications of matrix factorization is clustering, hence we choose it as the task to evaluate OKMF. The columns of the factors matrix, $\Phi(B)W$, can be viewed as a set of cluster centers in feature space. In turn, the latent space representation matrix H contains the information of the membership of each element to each cluster.

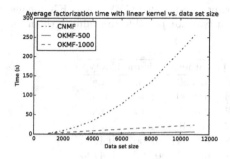

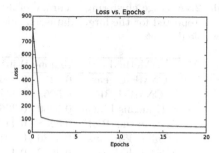

Fig. 1. Average factorization time of 30 runs vs. data set size (left) and OKMF average loss vs. epochs(right)

Table 1. Datasets Characteristics

Name	# of Samples	# of Classes	# of Attributes
Abalone	4,177	3	8
WineQ	4,898	3	11
Synthetic	5,000	2	2
Seismic	98,528	3	50
Covtype	581,012	7	54

Two kinds of data sets were used, medium-scale and large-scale, the characteristics of the data sets is presented in Table 1. The performance measure selected is the clustering accuracy, which is the fraction of correctly clustered points, showed in equation 7.

$$AC = \frac{\sum_{i=1}^{N} \delta(cf_i, map(c_i))}{N} \tag{7}$$

Where cf_i is the found label and c_i the ground truth, N the number of data points. $\delta(\cdot)$ is 1 when the found label cf_i matches c_i. $map(\cdot)$ is the best match of the found clusters and the ground truth computed using the Hungarian Algorithm. The compared algorithms are kernel k-Means [5], kernel convex non-negative matrix factorization [6] and online k-Means [15]. The kernels used in the experiments are linear and Gaussian (RBF). A parameter exploration was performed to find parameters of OKMF and the σ parameter of the RBF kernel. 30 tests were conducted and average accuracy and average time are reported. Finally the budget size was fixed to 500. The randomly picked budget is labeled as OKMF-R in the results, the strategy using k-Means cluster centers is labeled as OKMF-K. All algorithms were implemented in Python using Anaconda's MKL Extension on a computer with Intel Core i5 with four cores at 3.30GHz and 8GB of memory. Given kernel k-Means and CNMF methods require to have the whole kernel matrix in main memory, it is not feasible to use them to cluster the Seismic and Covtype data sets.

Table 2. Average clustering accuracy of 30 runs. Results for CNMF and KK-means are not reported for the larger datasets, since it was not possible to evaluate them on the whole dataset.

Method	Abalone	WineQ	Synthetic	Seismic	Covtype
CNMF-Linear	0.5253	0.3966	0.6369	n.a.	n.a.
CNMF-RBF	0.5269	0.4488	0.9800	n.a.	n.a.
K K-means-Linear	0.5280	0.3962	0.6377	n.a.	n.a.
K K-means-RBF	0.5268	0.4487	1.000	n.a.	n.a.
Online k-means	0.5286	0.3918	0.6494	0.4007	0.4276
OKMF-K-Linear	0.3658	0.4261	0.5041	0.3923	0.4405
OKMF-K-RBF	0.5188	0.4447	0.6230	0.5000	0.4875
OKMF-R-Linear	0.3658	0.4276	0.5033	0.3918	0.4300
OKMF-R-RBF	0.5331	0.4410	0.6925	0.5000	0.4876

4.1 Analysis

Table 2 show the results of the different methods and the different data sets. Our method performs very well in the task of clustering. Also the capability of using kernels enhance the performance of the accuracy without incurring in large memory usage or time to compute the factorization. Also the accuracy is not greatly affected by the budget selection scheme, given there is not a large difference between the performance of OKMF-R and OKMF-K.

Table 3 presents the clustering times, online k-means is the fastest algorithm, it outperforms by much the other algorithms. However, OKMF is faster than the CNMF factorization algorithm. The figure 1 shows a comparison between CNMF and OKMF with 500 and 1000 budget size, whilst CNMF average time behaves quadratic, OKMF average time behaves linear, also shows that OKMF converges within 2 to 5 epochs. Figure 2 shows the impact of budget size on clustering accuracy, this support the idea of having a small budget and achieve good performances.

Table 3. Average clustering time of 30 runs. Results for CNMF and KK-means are not reported for the larger datasets, since it was not possible to evaluate them on the whole dataset.

Method	Abalone	WineQ	Synthetic	Seismic	Covtype
CNMF-Linear	35.91	52.26	49.92	n.a.	n.a.
CNMF-RBF	37.15	50.88	50.95	n.a.	n.a.
K K-means-Linear	1.10	1.55	1.54	n.a.	n.a.
K K-means-RBF	2.35	2.84	3.04	n.a.	n.a.
Online k-means	0.06	0.06	0.05	0.41	1.90
OKMF-K-Linear	3.06	3.22	3.62	45.45	422.21
OKMF-K-RBF	4.54	4.84	5.18	82.65	648.59
OKMF-R-Linear	1.23	1.33	1.20	34.18	396.94
OKMF-R-RBF	2.72	3.14	3.76	70.23	635.67

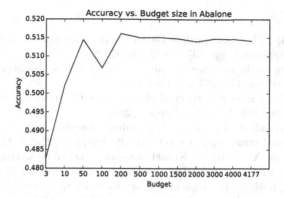

Fig. 2. Average clustering accuracy of 30 runs vs. budget size

5 Conclusions

We presented a novel kernel matrix factorization method that uses a budget restriction to tackle the memory issue and computation time. Using a budget leads to OKMF save memory, given it is not necessary to store the complete kernel matrix of size $n \times n$, but a smaller kernel matrix of the budget of size $p \times p$, which is a significant reduction if $p \ll n$. However, this leads to two problems, the budget size selection and the selection of the budget itself. The first problem can be solved by the exploration of this budget size in order to minimize the reconstruction error. To solve the second problem, we studied two ways, the first is randomly pick p instances of the original data, the second is applying k-means fixing k to the budget size. Also, in the task of clustering our method performs as well as other kernel matrix factorization methods, including CNMF. OKMF has low memory requirements, because it depends directly on the budget size, so having millions of samples, doesn't affect the memory usage. Using SGD as the method to optimize also implies a memory saving when performing the KMF, instead of keeping in memory a kernel matrix of the budget against all the data with a size of $p \times n$, OKMF only needs a kernel vector of the budget against the current instance of size $p \times 1$. Besides OKMF has an advantage in the time required to process large number of instances, because it converges with a small number of epochs and the time factorization takes grows linearly with the number of instances. As future work, other strategies for the budget selection can be studied and the application of OKMF in other tasks different from clustering.

References

1. An, S., Yun, J.M., Choi, S.: Multiple kernel nonnegative matrix factorization. In: 2011 ICASSP Conference, pp. 1976–1979. IEEE (2011)
2. Bottou, L.: Large-scale machine learning with stochastic gradient descent. In: COMPSTAT 2010, pp. 177–186. Springer (2010)
3. Chen, X., Cai, D.: Large-scale spectral clustering with landmark-based representation. In: Twenty-Fifth AAAI Conference (2011)
4. Crammer, K., Kandola, J., Singer, Y.: Online classification on a budget. In: Advances in Neural Information Processing Systems, pp. 225–232 (2004)
5. Dhillon, I.S., Guan, Y., Kulis, B.: Kernel k-means: spectral clustering and normalized cuts. In: Tenth ACM SIGKDD Conference, pp. 551–556. ACM (2004)
6. Ding, C., Li, T., Jordan, M.I.: Convex and semi-nonnegative matrix factorizations. IEEE Transactions on Pattern Analysis and Machine Intelligence $32(1)$, 45–55 (2010)
7. Hyvärinen, A., Karhunen, J., Oja, E.: Independent component analysis, vol. 46. John Wiley & Sons (2004)
8. Jun, Y., Jintao, M., Xiaoxu, L.: A kernel based non-negative matrix factorization. In: Second IITA-GRS Conference, vol. 1, pp. 376–379. IEEE (2010)
9. Lee, D.D., Seung, H.S.: Learning the parts of objects by non-negative matrix factorization. Nature $401(6755)$, 788–791 (1999)
10. Li, P., Chen, C., Bu, J.: Clustering analysis using manifold kernel concept factorization. Neurocomputing 87, 120–131 (2012)
11. Li, Y., Ngom, A.: A new kernel non-negative matrix factorization and its application in microarray data analysis. In: 2012 CIBCB Symposium, pp. 371–378. IEEE (2012)
12. Pan, B., Lai, J., Chen, W.S.: Nonlinear nonnegative matrix factorization based on mercer kernel construction. Pattern Recognition $44(10)$, 2800–2810 (2011)
13. Rendle, S., Schmidt-Thieme, L.: Online-updating regularized kernel matrix factorization models for large-scale recommender systems. In: 2008 ACM RecSys Conference, pp. 251–258. ACM (2008)
14. Schölkopf, B., Smola, A., Müller, K.-R.: Kernel principal component analysis. In: Gerstner, W., Hasler, M., Germond, A., Nicoud, J.-D. (eds.) ICANN 1997. LNCS, vol. 1327, pp. 583–588. Springer, Heidelberg (1997)
15. Sculley, D.: Web-scale k-means clustering. In: WWW 2010 Conference, pp. 1177–1178. ACM (2010)
16. Shawe-Taylor, J., Cristianini, N.: Kernel methods for pattern analysis. Cambridge University Press (2004)
17. Wang, L., Rege, M., Dong, M., Ding, Y.: Low-rank kernel matrix factorization for large-scale evolutionary clustering. IEEE Transactions on Knowledge and Data Engineering $24(6)$, 1036–1050 (2012)
18. Xia, Z., Ding, C., Chow, E.: Robust kernel nonnegative matrix factorization. In: 12th ICDMW Conference, pp. 522–529. IEEE (2012)
19. Zhang, D., Zhou, Z.-H., Chen, S.: Non-negative Matrix Factorization on Kernels. In: Yang, Q., Webb, G. (eds.) PRICAI 2006. LNCS (LNAI), vol. 4099, pp. 404–412. Springer, Heidelberg (2006)

From Local to Global Communities in Large Networks Through Consensus

Mariano Tepper$^{(\boxtimes)}$ and Guillermo Sapiro

ECE, Duke University, Durham, USA
{mariano.tepper,guillermo.sapiro}@duke.edu

Abstract. Given a universe of local communities of a large network, we aim at identifying the meaningful and consistent communities in it. We address this from a new perspective as the process of obtaining *consensual* community detections and formalize it as a bi-clustering problem. We obtain the *global* community structure of the given network without running expensive global community detection algorithms. The proposed mathematical characterization of the consensus problem and a new bi-clustering algorithm to solve it render the problem tractable for large networks. The approach is successfully validated in experiments with synthetic and large real-world networks, outperforming other state-of-the-art alternatives in terms of speed and results quality.

1 Introduction

The inference of global community structure in networks (i.e., finding groups of nodes such that intra-group connections are denser than inter-group ones) has become a topic of great interest in the data analysis scientific community [4,5,15,24]. However, the best way to establish the community structure is still disputed [7]. This is particularly true for large networks, as the vast majority of community detection algorithms, e.g., modularity maximization [15], require the network to be completely known. A family of algorithms aims at finding communities by analyzing the network locally [1,4,22,24]. But how can we go from a collection of such *local* communities to *global* community structure? Addressing this efficiently for large networks is the topic of this work.

Let $G = (V, E, \psi)$ be the graph to analyze, where V is the set of m nodes, E is the set of edges, and $\psi : E \to \mathbb{R}^+$ is a weighting function on the edges (in the following we use the terms graph and network interchangeably). Generically, we consider that a local community-detection algorithm provides a candidate community $C \subset V$. Let us consider that we are provided with a pool (universe) $\{C_k\}_{k=1}^n$ of n such candidates. These candidates might come from a combination of running (a) different local community-detection algorithms, (b) one local algorithm with different parameters or initializations, and/or (c) one local algorithm on different modalities of the same network, by changing the set of edges and/or the function ψ (this case includes a network that changes over time).

Work partially supported by NSF, ONR, NGA, ARO, and NSSEFF.

A. Pardo and J. Kittler (Eds.): CIARP 2015, LNCS 9423, pp. 659–666, 2015.
DOI: 10.1007/978-3-319-25751-8_79

Given the pool $\{C_k\}_{k=1}^n$, how do we stitch these local communities together to obtain a *coherent* and *global* structure of the network G? Consensus/ensemble clustering is a well known family of techniques used in data analysis to solve this type of problem when we have a pool of partitions (instead of single communities as we have here). Typically, the goal is to search for the partition that is most similar, on average, to all input partitions. See [21] for a survey of the subject.

The most common form of consensus clustering for the case of a pool of single communities involves creating an $m \times m$ co-occurrence matrix $\mathbf{B}$, such that

$$\mathbf{B} = \tfrac{1}{c}\sum_{i=1}^{n}\mathbf{B}_k \qquad \text{where} \qquad (\mathbf{B}_k)_{ij} = \begin{cases} 1 & \text{if } i,j \in C_k; \\ 0 & \text{otherwise.} \end{cases} \tag{1}$$

There are many algorithms for analyzing $\mathbf{B}$, from simple techniques such as applying a clustering algorithm to it (e.g., k-means or hierarchical clustering), to more complex techniques [13]. Consensus for community detection was addressed in [3] and [8] within the standard formulation just described.

The mentioned aggregation process used to build $\mathbf{B}$ involves losing information contained in the individual matrices $\mathbf{B}_k$. In particular, only pairwise relations are conserved, while relations involving larger groups of nodes might be lost. In addition, using the average of several partitions might not be robust if some of them are of poor quality.

Contributions. We propose a novel formal framework and perspective for reaching consensus community detection by posing it as a bi-clustering problem [20]. We also introduce a new bi-clustering algorithm, fit for the type of matrices we analyze. The core novelty of this work is the use of a consensus framework for stitching local communities together, produced by algorithms that do not necessarily analyze large/huge networks as a whole. This allows to integrate this partial and seemingly disaggregated information into a coherent and global structural description of large networks. Our framework does not require a community quality measure to make decisions but can use of it if it is available.

Organization. In Section 2 we present the proposed approach. In Section 3 we discuss the experimental results. We provide some closing remarks in Section 4.

2   Consensus Community Detection

The input of the consensus algorithm is a pool $\mathcal{U} = \{C_k\}_{k=1}^n$ of candidates. We also assign a weight $w_k \in \mathbb{R}^+$ to each community candidate C_k. From V (the set of nodes) and $\mathcal{U}$, we define the $m \times n$ preference matrix $\mathbf{A}$. The element $(\mathbf{A})_{ik} = w_k$ if the i-th node belongs to the k-th local community, and 0 otherwise.

The community weights indicate the importance assigned to each candidate and can take any form. The simplest form uses uniform weights $(\forall k)\ w_k = 1$, in which case $\mathbf{A}$ becomes a binary matrix. In this case, no prior information is used about the quality of the input community candidates. If we have such information, it can be freely incorporated in these weights.

We are interested in finding clusters in the product set $V \times \mathcal{U}$. The main contribution of this work is to establish the formal connection between bi-clustering the preference matrix $\mathbf{A}$ (as a complete representation of $\mathcal{U}$) and the extraction of global community structure from local communities. This provides a very intuitive rationale: for each bi-cluster, we are jointly selecting a subset of nodes and local communities such that the former belongs to the latter.

2.1 Solving the Bi-clustering Problem

Among many tools for bi-clustering, see [16] and references therein, the Penalized Matrix Decomposition [23] and the Sparse Singular Value Decomposition [12] have shown great promise, mainly due to their conceptual and algorithmic simplicity. Correctly setting the parameters of these methods is crucial, since they determine the size of the bi-clusters [12,18,23]. In our experiments, finding the correct values for these parameters has proven extremely challenging, since each experiment needs a specifically tuned set of values.

We propose to follow a different path for solving the bi-clustering problem at hand. For $1 \leq q \leq \min\{m, n\}$, we define

$$\min_{\mathbf{X} \in \mathbb{R}^{m \times q}, \mathbf{Y} \in \mathbb{R}^{q \times n}} \|\mathbf{A} - \mathbf{XY}\|_1 \quad \text{s.t.} \quad \mathbf{X}, \mathbf{Y} \geq 0. \quad \text{(L1-NMF)}$$

$\mathbf{A}$ is, in our application, a sparse non-negative matrix. Notice that the positivity constraints on $\mathbf{X}, \mathbf{Y}$ have a sparsifying effect on them. The intuition behind this is that when approximating a sparse non-negative matrix, the non-negative factors will only create a sparse approximation if they are themselves sparse. We thus obtain sparse factors $\mathbf{X}, \mathbf{Y}$ without introducing any (difficult to set) parameters. With the L1 fitting term, we are aiming at obtaining a "median" type of result instead of the mean, providing robustness to poor group candidates present in the pool (i.e., spurious columns of $\mathbf{A}$).

A challenge with NMF is that q is not an easy parameter to set. To avoid a cumbersome decision process, we propose to set $q = 1$ and inscribe the L1-NMF approach in an iterative loop, find one rank-one at a time. The rank-one factorization $\mathbf{XY}$ will thus approximate a subset of $\mathbf{A}$ (because of the sparsity-inducing L1-norm), correctly detecting a single bi-cluster. Let $\mathcal{R}, \mathcal{Q}$ be the active sets (non-zero entries) of $\mathbf{X}$, $\mathbf{Y}$, respectively: $\mathcal{R}$ selects rows (nodes), while $\mathcal{Q}$ selects columns (local communities).

Algorithm 1 summarizes the proposed non-negative bi-clustering approach. Notice that instead of subtracting the product $\mathbf{XY}$ from $\mathbf{A}$, we set the corresponding rows and columns to zero, enforcing disjoint active sets between the successive $\mathbf{X}_t$ and $\mathbf{Y}_t$, and hence orthogonality. This also ensures that non-negativity is maintained throughout the iterations. If the bi-clusters are allowed to share nodes, we do not change the rows of $\mathbf{A}$. This is an important feature for community detection since overlapping communities are ubiquitous. The proposed algorithm is very efficient, simple to code, and demonstrated to work well in the experimental results that we will present later.

Algorithm 1. Bi-clustering algorithm.

input : Preference matrix $\mathbf{A} \in \mathbb{R}^{m \times n}$, stopping parameters τ_R and τ_C.
output: Bi-clusters $\{(\mathcal{R}_t, \mathcal{Q}_t)\}_{t=1}^T$

1 $t \leftarrow 0$;
2 **while** $\mathbf{A} \neq \mathbf{0}$ **do**
3       $t \leftarrow t + 1$;
4   Solve Problem (L1-NMF) for $\mathbf{X}_t, \mathbf{Y}_t$ with $q = 1$;
5       $\mathcal{R}_t \leftarrow \{i \mid i \in [1, m], (\mathbf{X}_t)_{i,1} \neq 0\}$; $\mathcal{Q}_t \leftarrow \{j \mid j \in [1, n], (\mathbf{Y}_t)_{1,j} \neq 0\}$;
6   **if** $|\mathcal{R}_t| \leq \tau_R \vee |\mathcal{Q}_t| \leq \tau_C$ **then** $t \leftarrow t - 1$;   **break**;
7   **if** *non-overlapping biclusters are desired* **then**
8           $(\forall i,j)\ i \in \mathcal{R}_t, j \in [1, n], (\mathbf{A})_{ij} \leftarrow 0$;
9       $(\forall i,j)\ i \in [1, m], j \in \mathcal{Q}_t, (\mathbf{A})_{ij} \leftarrow 0$;
10 $T \leftarrow t$;

The iterations should stop (1) when $\mathbf{A}$ is empty (line 2), or (2) when $\mathbf{A}$ contains no structured patterns. The second case is controlled by τ_R and τ_C (line 6), which determine the minimum size that a bi-cluster should have. Note that these parameters are intuitive, related to the physics of the problem, and easy to set. In all experiments in this paper, we set $\tau_R = 3$ and $\tau_C = 2$.

Implementation and Scalability. Any NMF algorithm can be adapted to use the L1 norm and solve (L1-NMF); in this work, we use the method in [20]. Following [14], it is relatively straightforward to implement any NMF algorithm in a MapReduce framework, making it completely scalable.

2.2 Extracting Local Communities

For community detection in large networks, algorithms that analyze the network locally are becoming popular [1,4,22,24]. These algorithms are extremely fast and can be adapted to optimize a wide range of different local quality measures. However this partial and seemingly disaggregated information does not provide a description of the full large network. We use our framework to integrate these local communities, obtaining such a coherent and global structural description.

In particular, given a single member s of an unknown community S, we aim at discovering S itself. To address this task, we use the PageRank-Nibble method [1,24], mainly because of its efficiency. Its computational cost is independent of the network size and proportional to the size of the detected community (think about how many friends you have in Facebook versus the total number of Facebook users). The key idea of PageRank-Nibble is to obtain a local spectral clustering algorithm by computing random walks starting from a single seed node s [1]. The PageRank scores give a measure of how well connected are the nodes around s. Algorithm 2 summarizes the overall procedure.

Conductance is the scoring function of choice in [24]. Communities are identified as local minima of $\{f(S_1) \ldots f(S_h)\}$. In our experiments, we found that

---

Algorithm 2. Community detection from a seed node

---

input : Graph $G(V,E)$, seed node s, community scoring function f, threshold ε.
output: A community $S_{k_{\mathrm{ext}}} \subset V$ containing the seed node s.
1 Compute random walk scores r_u from seed node s using PageRank-Nibble [1];
2 Compute the sweep vectors set $\{S_k\}_{k=1}^h$ [1], where
$S_k = S_{k-1} \cup \{\mathrm{argmax}_{u \notin S_{k-1}, r_u \geq \varepsilon} \frac{r_u}{d(u)}\}$, $S_1 = s$, and $d(u)$ is the degree of u;
3 Find the index k_{ext} corresponding to the extremum of $\{f(S_1) \ldots f(S_h)\}$;

---

conductance does not produce robust local minima; we use an alternative function. Modularity [15], the standard community scoring measure, is not effective for assessing small communities in large networks [7]. However, if we restrict the computation to the subgraph induced by the set $\{u \in V \mid r_u \geq \varepsilon\}$, modularity becomes effective. We name this measure local modularity. This choice is not critical in our framework and any other suitable scoring function can be used instead, e.g. [4].

In our experiments, we extract a single community per seed (notice again that this is not critical in our framework). We thus identify the local community around a seed node s as the sweep vector with maximum local modularity.

The pool of candidates is the set of all local communities, using every node as a seed. Alternatively, we could randomly sample the set of nodes, in a Monte Carlo fashion. Moreover, any local community detection algorithm, e.g., [4,22], or even a combination of several of them, can be used with our framework. In this work, we use a binary preference matrix, i.e., uniform weights.

3   Experimental Results

We begin by testing the proposed framework in synthetic networks with ground truth communities, see Table 1. The performance of the consensus solution is on par with what is achieved by analyzing the ground truth and then picking the best local communities in the pool of candidates. The consensus community structure is obtained without tuning parameters nor accessing the ground truth.

We tested the proposed approach on four real-world networks (Amazon, DBLP, Youtube, and Orkut) with a functional definition of ground-truth [24] (http://snap.stanford.edu/). The ground-truth contains the top 5,000 ground-truth communities of each network. To run the simulations with these large networks, we accelerate our computations by pruning, from the preference matrix, the columns (local communities) whose local modularity is below a threshold γ (for Amazon, DBLP, Youtube, and Orkut $\gamma = 0.22, 0.2, 0.22, 0.09$, respectively).

We compare the proposed approach with other state-of-the-art methods both in terms of speed and quality of the results. The stochastic variational inference (SVI) algorithm [6] was particularly designed to work with large networks. However, the number of communities is an input to the method and the author's code does not scale well with this quantity: trying to discover more than 500

Table 1. Results with synthetic networks (m is the number of nodes and δ the average node degree), produced with a standard benchmark generator [10]. In each experiment, we compute generalized normalized mutual information scores [9] over 100 different synthetic instances. For this comparison, we created a small subset of the local communities that fit more closely each of the T_{GT} ground truth communities. By picking the best and the median in this subset we obtain each of the T_{GT} best local communities and each of the T_{GT} good local communities, respectively. The consensus solution is always competitive with the best base solution and outperforms the good base solution, both found by using the ground truth and thus providing idealized performances (hardly achievable in practice). Our result is achieved by only looking at the base local communities.

		Mean	STD	Median	Min	Max
	Consensus	0.879	0.171	0.964	0.336	1.000
$m = 10^2, \delta = 10$	T_{GT} best local communities	0.872	0.126	0.926	0.446	1.000
	T_{GT} good local communities	0.654	0.159	0.676	0.256	0.924
	Consensus	0.705	0.217	0.707	0.289	1.000
$m = 10^2, \delta = 15$	T_{GT} best local communities	0.733	0.198	0.779	0.239	1.000
	T_{GT} good local communities	0.664	0.175	0.701	0.255	0.917
	Consensus	0.812	0.053	0.818	0.665	0.922
$m = 10^3, \delta = 10$	T_{GT} best local communities	0.844	0.036	0.850	0.749	0.924
	T_{GT} good local communities	0.790	0.047	0.795	0.648	0.879
	Consensus	0.661	0.066	0.659	0.536	0.841
$m = 10^3, \delta = 15$	T_{GT} best local communities	0.683	0.041	0.681	0.566	0.798
	T_{GT} good local communities	0.611	0.044	0.609	0.506	0.713
	Consensus	0.618	0.067	0.622	0.332	0.773
$m = 10^4, \delta = 30$	T_{GT} best local communities	0.455	0.070	0.457	0.171	0.633
	T_{GT} good local communities	0.307	0.075	0.306	0.117	0.577

communities led to out-of-memory issues. We thus set this number to 500 for all experiments. The global consensus algorithm (LF) in [8] allows to use different base community detection algorithms; we used OSLOM [11], Infomap [19], Louvain [2], and Label Propagation (LP) [17]. All tests were performed on a desktop computer with an Intel i7-4770 CPU, 32 GB of RAM, and Ubuntu Linux 12.04.

Our method outperforms the alternatives in all the evaluated networks, see Table 2. In the Amazon network, our method is 3 minutes slower than LF+Louvain but obtains a performance gain of 34% over it; it is one order of magnitude faster than LF+Infomap with a performance gain of 8%. These comparisons are much more favorable to our method in the DBLP network. Our method is 4 times faster and almost 3 times better than LF+Louvain; it is also 68 times faster than LF+OSLOM with a performance boost of 48%.

Figure 1 presents two examples of the results of our bi-clustering algorithm. First, we observe that the proposed approach clearly organizes the data contained in the preference matrix, detecting an almost block-diagonal structure in it (albeit with overlaps and a small amount of noise in the preference matrix itself). Another important observation is that the detected bi-clusters share nodes (see the zoomed-in details), thus detecting overlapping consensus communities.

Table 2. Comparison of the efficiency and accuracy of the proposed approach against other community detection methods. We compare with the stochastic inference algorithm (SVI) [6], and with the *global* consensus algorithm (LF) [8], using different base community detection algorithms. Our approach achieves top precision performances in minimum time (respectively measured as the fraction of retrieved communities that the ground truth and in minutes). V and E are the set of vertices and edges of the networks, respectively.

Algorithms	Amazon $\#V \approx 3 \times 10^6$ $\#E \approx 9 \times 10^6$		DBLP $\#V \approx 3 \times 10^6$ $\#E \approx 1 \times 10^7$		Youtube $\#V \approx 1 \times 10^7$ $\#E \approx 3 \times 10^7$		Orkut $\#V \approx 3 \times 10^7$ $\#E \approx 1 \times 10^9$	
	Time	Prec.	Time	Prec.	Time	Prec.	Time	Prec.
LF [8] + OSLOM [11][1]	263.15	0.837	660.68	0.664	_[3]	–	_[3]	–
LF [8] + Infomap [19][1]	179.83	0.900	407.43	0.616	_[3]	–	_[3]	–
LF [8] + Louvain [2][1]	8.10	0.724	41.55	0.347	_[4]	–	_[3]	–
LF [8] + LP [17][1]	23.37	0.792	172.40	0.406	_[3]	–	_[3]	–
SVI [6][2]	58.88	0.409	28.22	0.388	78.63	0.271	_[4]	–
Our approach	11.12	0.976	9.70	0.984	11.42	0.981	67.45	0.718

[1] https://sites.google.com/site/andrealancichinetti/
[2] https://github.com/premgopalan/svinet
[3] No results after more than 6 days of execution (> 8700 minutes).
[4] Presented out-of-memory problems and was terminated by the operating system.

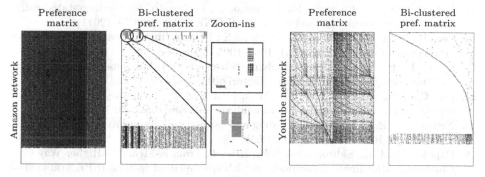

Fig. 1. Examples of bi-clustering the preference matrix for two real-world networks using the proposed approach. We permute rows and columns of the bi-clustered preference matrix to ease its visualization. The structural simplification obtained with our consensus approach is clear in the block-diagonal (plus overlaps) structure of the preference matrix.

4 Conclusions

We analyzed for the first time the process of generating a global community structure from locally-extracted communities and formalized it as a bi-clustering consensus problem. This offers a new perspective for this important problem. Our consensus algorithm stitches the local communities together, obtaining a coherent and global community structure for large networks. The approach is successful in several experiments with synthetic and large real-world networks.

References

1. Andersen, R., Chung, F., Lang, K.: Local graph partitioning using PageRank vectors. In: FOCS (2006)

2. Blondel, V., Guillaume, J.L., Lambiotte, R., Lefebvre, E.: Fast unfolding of communities in large networks. J. Stat. Mech. **2008**(10), P10008+ (2008)
3. Campigotto, R., Guillaume, J.L., Seifi, M.: The power of consensus: random graphs have no communities. In: ASONAM (2013)
4. Clauset, A.: Finding local community structure in networks. Phys. Rev. E **72**, 026132 (2005)
5. Girvan, M., Newman, M.E.J.: Community structure in social and biological networks. Proc. Natl. Acad. Sci. U.S.A. **99**(12), 7821–7826 (2002)
6. Gopalan, P., Blei, D.: Efficient discovery of overlapping communities in massive networks. Proc. Natl. Acad. Sci. U.S.A. **110**(36), 14534–14539 (2013)
7. Lancichinetti, A., Fortunato, S.: Limits of modularity maximization in community detection. Phys. Rev. E **84**(6), 066122+ (2011)
8. Lancichinetti, A., Fortunato, S.: Consensus clustering in complex networks. Sci. Rep. **2** (2012)
9. Lancichinetti, A., Fortunato, S., Kertész, J.: Detecting the overlapping and hierarchical community structure in complex networks. New J. of Phys. **11**(3), 033015 (2009)
10. Lancichinetti, A., Fortunato, S., Radicchi, F.: Benchmark graphs for testing community detection algorithms. Phys. Rev. E **78**(4) (2008)
11. Lancichinetti, A., Radicchi, F., Ramasco, J., Fortunato, S.: Finding statistically significant communities in networks. PLoS ONE **6**(4), e18961+ (2011)
12. Lee, M., Shen, H., Huang, J.Z., Marron, J.S.: Biclustering via sparse singular value decomposition. Biometrics **66**(4), 1087–1095 (2010)
13. Li, T., Ding, C., Jordan, M.I.: Solving consensus and semi-supervised clustering problems using nonnegative matrix factorization. In: ICDM (2007)
14. Liu, C., Yang, H., Fan, J., He, L., Wang, Y.: Distributed nonnegative matrix factorization for web-scale dyadic data analysis on mapreduce. In: WWW (2010)
15. Newman, M.E.J., Girvan, M.: Finding and evaluating community structure in networks. Phys. Rev. E **69**, 026113 (2004)
16. Papalexakis, E.E., Sidiropoulos, N.D., Bro, R.: From K-Means to Higher-Way Co-Clustering: Multilinear decomposition with sparse latent factors. IEEE Trans. Signal Process. **61**(2), 493–506 (2013)
17. Raghavan, U.N., Albert, R., Kumara, S.: Near linear time algorithm to detect community structures in large-scale networks. Phys. Rev. E **76**, 036106 (2007)
18. Ramírez, I., Tepper, M.: Bi-clustering via MDL-based matrix factorization. In: Ruiz-Shulcloper, J., Sanniti di Baja, G. (eds.) CIARP 2013, Part I. LNCS, vol. 8258, pp. 230–237. Springer, Heidelberg (2013)
19. Rosvall, M., Bergstrom, C.: Maps of random walks on complex networks reveal community structure. Proc. Natl. Acad. Sci. U.S.A. **105**(4), 1118–1123 (2008)
20. Tepper, M., Sapiro, G.: A bi-clustering framework for consensus problems. SIAM J. Imaging Sci. **7**(4), 2488–2525 (2014)
21. Vega-Pons, S., Ruiz-Shulcloper, J.: A survey of clustering ensemble algorithms. Int. J. of Pattern Recognit Artif. Intell. **25**(03), 337–372 (2011)
22. Wang, L., Lou, T., Tang, J., Hopcroft, J.: Detecting community kernels in large social networks. In: ICDM (2011)
23. Witten, D.M., Tibshirani, R., Hastie, T.: A penalized matrix decomposition, with applications to sparse principal components and canonical correlation analysis. Biostatistics **10**(3), 515–534 (2009)
24. Yang, J., Leskovec, J.: Defining and evaluating network communities based on ground-truth. In: MDS (2012)

A Feature Selection Approach for Evaluate the Inference of GRNs Through Biological Data Integration - A Case Study on *A. Thaliana*

Fábio F.R. Vicente[1,2], Euler Menezes[1], Gabriel Rubino[1],
Juliana de Oliveira[3], and Fabrício Martins Lopes[1(✉)]

[1] Federal University of Technology, Cornélio Procópio, Paraná, Brazil
{fabiofernandes,fabricio}@utfpr.edu.br
[2] Institute of Mathematics and Statistics, University of São Paulo, São Paulo, Brazil
[3] Department of Biological Sciences Faculty of Sciences and Letters of Assis - FCLA,
University of São Paulo State - UNESP,
Av. Dom Antonio, 2100, Parque Universitrio 19806-900, Assis, São Paulo, Brazil
juliana@assis.unesp.br

Abstract. The inference of gene regulatory networks (GRNs) from expression profiles is a great challenge in bioinformatics due to the curse of dimensionality. For this reason, several methods that perform data integration have been developed to reduce the estimation error of the inference. However, it is not completely formulated how to use each type of biological information available. This work address this issue by proposing feature selection approach in order to integrate biological data and evaluate three types of biological information regarding their effect on the similarity of inferred GRNs. The proposed feature selection method is based on sequential forward floating selection (SFFS) search algorithm and the mean conditional entropy (MCE) as criterion function. An expression dataset was built as an additional contribution of this work containing 22746 genes and 1206 experiments regarding *A. thaliana*. The experimental results achieve 39% of GRNs improvement in average when compared to non-use of biological data integration. Besides, the results showed that the improvement is associated to a specific type of biological information: the cellular localization, which is a valuable and information for the development of new experiments and indicates an important insight for investigation.

Keywords: Gene regulatory networks · Feature selection · Data integration · Bioinformatics · *Arabidopsis thaliana*

1 Introduction

One of the main challenges in bioinformatics is to perform the reverse engineering of GRNs (gene regulatory networks) from expression profiles [2]. Since the genes and their corresponding proteins are only *part* of a whole biological system, it is important to discover the network of interactions between the cell components to

© Springer International Publishing Switzerland 2015
A. Pardo and J. Kittler (Eds.): CIARP 2015, LNCS 9423, pp. 667–675, 2015.
DOI: 10.1007/978-3-319-25751-8_80

better understand how the systems work. Furthermore, such knowledge can be useful to perform intervention and control of the system[23]. The development of techniques such as DNA microarrays, SAGE and RNA-Seq [29] allowed studying the dynamic of the cell in a scale that was unfeasible with the previous methods. Since the interaction between the genes works as a network that produces the observed expression, the idea is to perform a reverse engineering in order to recover the network from the expression profiles.

The search space of possible networks is huge. Thus, the inference can be modeled as a feature selection problem, where a criterion function is used to evaluate a subset of predictor genes (features) that better classify the state of a given target gene based on the expression values [16,17]. In this way, the inference consists in searching for a subset of predictors for each target.

A GRN can be modeled as Bayesian Networks [12], Boolean Networks [8], Probabilistic Boolean Networks (PBN) [25] or Probabilistic Genetic Network (PGN) [3]. Also, distinct *criterion function* can be used for inference. Some criterion function as Pearson correlation [26] are limited to the evaluation of pairs of genes and the combinatorial regulation of multiple predictors cannot be assessed. The Coefficient of Determination (CoD) [13] is not limited to a number of variables and allows to model the multivariate nature of the regulation. Other criterion functions are based on information theory such as Mutual Information [22], Tsallis Entropy [19] and Mean Conditional Entropy (MCE) [18].

One of the main limitations of the inference is the high dimensionality. For this reason, it is important the development of new methods that take into account other *information* than the expression profiles in order to reduce the intrinsic estimation error of the inference and to recover plausible biological networks.

Distinct approaches have been proposed to implement data integration in GNs. Some works evaluate the data integration in biological networks [20,21,28]. Other methods perform a clustering analysis to identify groups of genes related to some particular property [7]. Other methods include known information about the topological properties of the network such as degree of connectivity, average path length and other local and global characteristics [16,27].

However, a methodology to define how to select the biological information in order to reduce error on inference is still not completely formulated. Moreover, the study of distinct biological information can reveal the contribution of each one in the inference and favor the discovery of new biological knowledge such as biological information that are decisive to characterize the network together with the system dynamic. This work proposes a feature selection approach in order to evaluate a GRNs inference model based on a criterion function that encodes multivalued biological features applied on the *A. thaliana* organism.

2   Materials and Methods

2.1   Gold Standard Network

The gold standard network is the directed graph with the known physical direct interactions between each predictor (TF) and their target genes. The *Arabidopsis thaliana* gold standard network (AtRegNet) was obtained from AGRIS (The Arabidopsis Gene Regulatory Information Server) [30] on which each interaction is verified in at least one experimental approach. The graph has 8154 genes of which 67 are predictors and 8131 are target genes, comprising 11481 edges.

Expression Data. All expression data were obtained from GEO [4] and only samples of the platform GPL198 (*Affymetrix Arabidopsis ATH1 Genome Array*) were selected. The chip contains 22810 *probe sets* that were mapped to genes through annotation data from TAIR [15], Gene Ontology [1] and TIGR [5]. A probe set is a collection of sequences (probes) used to identify a gene sequence and to measure its expression.

The GEO files containing the expression samples were obtained through the R Bioconductor, GEOquery and Biobase [6]. The files in SOFT format were acquired in three types: GDS (GEO Dataset, 13 files), GSE (GEO Series, 58 files) and GSM (GEO Samples, 109 files), each one with a set of expression experiments. The files were preprocessed to obtain the expression values and to filter out samples with missing data. Thus the 180 files resulted on a table with 22746 genes and 1206 experiments.

Biological Information. A set of features associated to each probe set in the expression data where obtained from TAIR, KEGG [14] and NCBI [11]. For each probe set a corresponding *locus identifier* (TAIR) and a *NCBI gene id* were obtained. Then, the biological information associated to the NCBI gene id were obtained from the NCBI and features associated to the locus identifier were obtained from TAIR and KEGG. The dataset contains 23593 annotated elements and 15 features related to several biological aspects.

2.2   GRNs Inference

To infer the GRN it is necessary determine the best subset of predictors for each target gene. Thus, in a dataset with n transcription factors there are 2^n possible subset of predictors for each gene. Since the search space is huge, the sequential forward floating selection (SFFS)[24] algorithm was adopted to search for the best solution. The criterion function evaluates each subset by taking into account both the expression values and the biological information on the dataset. The expression value part is evaluated computing the mean conditional entropy (MCE) [18]. The MCE is computed as the average of the entropies of a target gene Y given the values of the predictors X (Eq. 1).

$$H(Y|X) = \sum_{x \in X} H(Y|x) P(x). \tag{1}$$

The MCE take into account only the expression values. Because the small number of samples it is common the occurrence of many ties between distinct set of predictors. Thus, only the expression data is commonly insufficient to determine a suitable solution. For this reason, the proposed criterion function includes a term related to another type of feature, i.e., a biological information.

$$F(Y, X) = \alpha[H(Y|X)] + \beta[D(Y, X)], \tag{2}$$

where $D(Y, X)$ is equals to 1 when the biological information of the gene Y is equals to X in the biological data set D. The parameters α and β defines the weight of each type of information where $\beta \in (0, 1)$ and $\alpha = 1 - \beta$. Thus, with the proposed feature selection approach the SFFS will search for the subset of predictors that not just minimize the entropy, but also for those that are coherent to the other biological aspects of the target gene.

3   Results and Discussion

Data Preprocessing. The expression data are represented in a table with the variables (genes) in rows and the expression samples $s(i)$ in columns. The expression values of the genes of each sample $s(i)$, $s(i) \in \mathbb{R}$, were normalized by the *normal transformation*, defined as follows:

$$\eta[s(i)] = \frac{s(i) - E[s(i)]}{\sigma[s(i)]}, \tag{3}$$

where $\sigma[s(i)]$ is the standard deviation of $s(i)$ and $E[s(i)]$ is the expectation of $s(i)$. The normalized data where discretized into three levels $\{-1, 0, +1\}$ through a threshold mapping

$$s(i) = \begin{cases} -1 & \alpha < l \\ 0 & l \le \alpha \le h \\ +1 & \alpha > h \end{cases} \tag{4}$$

where, α is the expression value of the sample s, of the gene g.

Biological Features. The annotation of genes on public databases makes available several types of information, which refer to distinct aspects. They can be descriptive, some times adopting conventional terms to classify the gene as belonging to a category, for example, to a specific biological pathway, a known function, to cite but a few. Thus, in this work were adopted three features related to *physical* aspects and to the *activity* of the gene: (i) cellular location, (ii) pathway and (iii) function. Then, since all annotated features into the databases are attributes of type *nominal*, the value of each feature was indexed by an integer value resulting on a dataset with 20817 unique annotated pairs (*probe set, gene locus*) Table 1.

Intersection Between Datasets. To evaluate the proposed approach, the subset of genes in the intersection of the three datasets (gold standard network, expression and biological information) was adopted, resulting on 5974 Gene locus (Table 2).

Table 1. Biological information available on public databases.

Database	Feature	Number of distinct values
TAIR	function	121
TAIR	located in	6
KEGG	pathway	128

Table 2. The validation dataset comprises 5974 genes.

Dataset	Description	Quantity
Gold standard network	Edges	8589
Expression data	Samples	1206
Biological features	Features	3

Evaluation of the Inference. In order to measure the effectiveness of the proposed approach it was adopted the *Similarity* between the gold standard and the inferred network, which was presented by [9] and is widely used for validation of methods of GNs inference. The validation is based on a confusion matrix, as described in Table 3. The *Similarity* is computed as presented in (Eq. 5) and the normalized value relative to the inference based only on expression data($\alpha = 1$), defined as follows:

Table 3. Confusion matrix. TP = true positive, FN = false negative, FP = false positive, TN = true negative.

Edge	Inferred	Not Inferred
Present	TP	FN
Absent	FP	TN

$$\text{Similarity} = \sqrt{\text{precision} \times \text{recall}} = \sqrt{\frac{TP}{TP + FP} \times \frac{TP}{TP + FN}}. \quad (5)$$

The experimental results have presented distinct performance for the three types of biological information (Figure 1(a)). In particular, the *localization* improves the similarity while *pathway* and *function* increased the error of the inference. For *cellular localization*, the curve increases from β varying from 0.1 to 0.7 and decreases for values greater than 0.7. This indicates that the expression combined to cellular localization can improve the similarity and that the use of only one type of data can limit the inference. The improvement varies according to the threshold, being higher for small values. The average improvement when the same weight is given to both expression and biological information (i.e. $\beta = 0.5$) is 39.1%.

The other two biological information presented a negative effect in similarity. A possible explanation is that the gold standard regulatory network refers to *physical* interactions and metabolic pathway and gene function refers to other type of relationship. The localization refers to a physical space on the cell where genes acts, metabolic pathway is more generic than localization and refers to the biological pathway the genes are related (not necessarily the genes are in

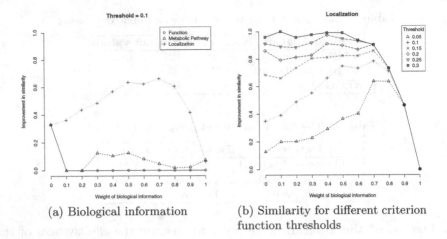

(a) Biological information

(b) Similarity for different criterion function thresholds

Fig. 1. Evaluation of the data integration of three types of biological information: Function, Metabolic pathway and Cellular localization. Weight = 0 means only expression. Weight = 1 means only biological information.

the same local or interacts physically each other) and, an even more generic than metabolic pathway is the gene function. Thus, several proteins can have the same molecular function or acts in common metabolic pathways and can be an explanation for the decreasing in similarity. This points to the importance of the correct feature selection that can reduce the estimation error, specially in this type of multilevel data integration.

Figure 1(b) shows the improvement in similarity. Results show the similarity increases more and faster for lower thresholds and that both expression and localization are important. For weight of biological information over 0.7 the similarity decreases faster despite of the threshold.

Another important issue is the validation of GNs inference. Here, we adopted the validation regarding to a know network, which useful to evaluate the *inferential* perspective as pointed by [10]. The validation of methods of data integration is still an problem to be solved in GNs inference.

4   Conclusions

This work presented a feature selection approach for integration of distinct datasets based on expression data and biological information for the inference of gene regulatory networks, which is based on SFFS search algorithm and MCE criterion function. An expression dataset was built as an additional contribution of this work containing 22746 genes and 1206 experiments regarding *A. thaliana*. The dataset was composed with a gold standard network, expression data and biological features were assembled and the proposed approach was applied on the composed dataset. The results showed the increasing on the similarity (average

39%) of the recovered network when the criterion function is based on cellular localization. Also, the results showed that the performance is better when expression and cellular localization are combined instead of the use of each one only, which is a valuable information for the development of new experiments and indicates an important insight for investigation.

The evaluation of GNs inference is commonly performed based on the know links of a gold-standard network. However, other biological information could be also used to validate the inference methods. Thus, as future work it is suggest the investigation of validation measures that take into account distinct biological data. Also, the inclusion of more types of biological information and to perform the proposed approach using these biological information can be considered as a further work. Moreover, would be also important to evaluate the best set of the parameters (weight of biological information and the threshold of the criterion function).

Acknowledgments. This work was supported by FAPESP grant 2011/50761-2, UTFPR, CNPq, Fundação Araucária, CAPES and NAP eScience - PRP - USP.

References

1. Ashburner, M., Ball, C.A., Blake, J.A., Botstein, D., Butler, H., Cherry, J.M., Davis, A.P., Dolinski, K., Dwight, S.S., Eppig, J.T., Harris, M.A., Hill, D.P., Issel-Tarver, L., Kasarskis, A., Lewis, S., Matese, J.C., Richardson, J.E., Ringwald, M., Rubin, G.M., Sherlock, G.: Gene ontology: tool for the unification of biology. Nat. Genet. **25**(1), 25–29 (2000)
2. Baralla, A., Mentzen, W.I., de la Fuente, A.: Inferring gene networks: dream or nightmare? Annals of the New York Academy of Sciences **1158**, 246–56 (2009)
3. Barrera, J., Cesar Jr., R.M., Martins Jr., D.C., Vencio, R.Z.N., Merino, E.F., Yamamoto, M.M., Leonardi, F.G., Pereira, C.A.B., Portillo, H.A.: Constructing probabilistic genetic networks of Plasmodium falciparum, from dynamical expression signals of the intraerythrocytic development cycle. In: McConnell, P., Lin, S.M., Hurban, P. (eds.) Meth. of Microarray Data Analysis, pp. 11–26. Springer (2007)
4. Barrett, T., Wilhite, S.E., Ledoux, P., Evangelista, C., Kim, I.F., Tomashevsky, M., Marshall, K.A., Phillippy, K.H., Sherman, P.M., Holko, M., Yefanov, A., Lee, H., Zhang, N., Robertson, C.L., Serova, N., Davis, S., Soboleva, A.: NCBI GEO: Archive for functional genomics data sets - Update. NAR **41**(D1), 991–995 (2013)
5. Childs, K.L., Hamilton, J.P., Zhu, W., Ly, E., Cheung, F., Wu, H., Rabinowicz, P.D., Town, C.D., Buell, C.R., Chan, A.P.: The tigr plant transcript assemblies database. Nucleic Acids Research **35**(suppl. 1), D846–D851 (2007)
6. Davis, S., Meltzer, P.: Geoquery: a bridge between the gene expression omnibus (geo) and bioconductor. Bioinformatics **14**, 1846–1847 (2007)
7. De Haan, J., Piek, E., van Schaik, R., de Vlieg, J., Bauerschmidt, S., Buydens, L., Wehrens, R.: Integrating gene expression and go classification for pca by preclustering. BMC Bioinformatics **11**(1), 158 (2010)
8. D'haeseleer, P., Liang, S., Somogyi, R.: Genetic network inference: from coexpression clustering to reverse engineering. Bioinformatics **16**(8), 707–726 (2000)

9. Dougherty, E.R.: Validation of inference procedures for gene regulatory networks. Current Genomics **8**(6), 351–359 (2007)

10. Dougherty, E.R.: Validation of gene regulatory networks: scientific and inferential. Briefings in Bioinformatics **12**(3), 245–252 (2011)

11. Edgar, R., Domrachev, M., Lash, A.E.: Gene Expression Omnibus: NCBI gene expression and hybridization array data repository. Nucleic Acids Research **30**(1), 207–210 (2002)

12. Friedman, N., Linial, M., Nachman, I., Pe'er, D.: Using bayesian networks to analyze expression data. Journal of Computational Biology **7**(3–4), 601–620 (2000)

13. Hashimoto, R.F., Kim, S., Shmulevich, I., Zhang, W., Bittner, M.L., Dougherty, E.R.: Growing genetic regulatory networks from seed genes. Bioinformatics **20**(8), 1241–1247 (2004)

14. Kanehisa, M., Goto, S.: KEGG: Kyoto Encyclopedia of Genes and Genomes. Nucleic Acids Research **28**(1), 27–30 (2000)

15. Lamesch, P., Berardini, T.Z., Li, D., Swarbreck, D., Wilks, C., Sasidharan, R., Muller, R., Dreher, K., Alexander, D.L., Garcia-Hernandez, M., Karthikeyan, A.S., Lee, C.H., Nelson, W.D., Ploetz, L., Singh, S., Wensel, A., Huala, E.: The arabidopsis informtion resource (TAIR): improved gene annotation and new tools. NAR (2011)

16. Lopes, F.M., Martins Jr., D.C., Barrera, J., Cesar, Jr., R.M.: A feature selection technique for inference of graphs from their known topological properties: Revealing scale-free gene regulatory networks. Information Sciences **272**, 1–15 (2014)

17. Lopes, F.M., Martins Jr., D.C., Barrera, J., Cesar Jr., R.M.: SFFS-MR: A floating search strategy for grns inference. In: Dijkstra, T.M.H., Tsivtsivadze, E., Marchiori, E., Heskes, T. (eds.) PRIB 2010. LNCS, vol. 6282, pp. 407–418. Springer, Heidelberg (2010)

18. Lopes, F.M., Martins Jr., D.C., Cesar Jr., R.M.: Feature selection environment for genomic applications. BMC Bioinformatics **9**(1), 451 (2008)

19. Lopes, F.M., de Oliveira, E.A., Cesar Jr., R.M.: Inference of gene regulatory networks from time series by Tsallis entropies. BMC Systems Biology **5**(1), 61 (2011)

20. Lopes, F.M., Ray, S.S., Hashimoto, R.F., Cesar Jr., R.M.C.: Entropic biological score: a cell cycle investigation for GRNs inference. Gene **541**(2), 129–137 (2014)

21. Lu, L.J., Xia, Y., Paccanaro, A., Yu, H., Gerstein, M.: Assessing the limits of genomic data integration for predicting protein networks. Gen. Res. **15**(7), 945–53 (2005)

22. Margolin, A., Basso, K.N., Wiggins, C., Stolovitzky, G., Favera, R., Califano, A.: ARACNE: An algorithm for the reconstruction of gene regulatory networks in a mammalian cellular context. BMC Bioinformatics **7**(suppl. 1), S7 (2006)

23. Pavlopoulos, G.A., Secrier, M., Moschopoulos, C.N., Soldatos, T.G., Kossida, S., Aerts, J., Schneider, R., Bagos, P.G.: Using graph theory to analyze biological networks. BioData mining **4**(1), 10 (2011)

24. Pudil, P., Novovičová, J., Kittler, J.: Floating search methods in feature-selection. Pattern Recognition Letters **15**(11), 1119–1125 (1994)

25. Shmulevich, I., Dougherty, E.R., Kim, S., Zhang, W.: Probabilistic boolean networks: a rule-based uncertainty model for gene regulatory networks. Bioinformatics **18**(2), 261–274 (2002)

26. Stuart, J.M., Segal, E., Koller, D., Kim, S.K.: A gene-coexpression network for global discovery of conserved genetic modules. Science **302**(5643), 249–255 (2003)

27. da Rocha Vicente, F.F., Lopes, F.M.: SFFS-SW: A feature selection algorithm exploring the small-world properties of GNs. In: Comin, M., Käll, L., Marchiori, E., Ngom, A., Rajapakse, J. (eds.) PRIB 2014. LNCS, vol. 8626, pp. 60–71. Springer, Heidelberg (2014)
28. Vicente, F.F.R., Lopes, F.M., Hashimoto, R.F., Cesar Jr., R.M.: Assessing the gain of biological data integration in gene networks inference. BMC Genomics 13(suppl. 6), S7 (2012)
29. Wang, Z., Gerstein, M., Snyder, M.: RNA-Seq: a revolutionary tool for transcriptomics. Nat. Rev. Genet. 10(1), 57–63 (2009)
30. Yilmaz, A., Mejia-Guerra, M.K., Kurz, K., Liang, X., Welch, L., Grotewold, E.: Agris: the arabidopsis gene regulatory information server, an update. Nucleic Acids Research 39(suppl. 1), D1118–D1122 (2011)

Semi-supervised Dimensionality Reduction via Multimodal Matrix Factorization

Viviana Beltrán, Jorge A. Vanegas$^{(\boxtimes)}$, and Fabio A. González

Mindlab Research Group, Universidad Nacional de Colombia, Bogotá, Colombia
{lvbeltranb,javanegasr,fagonzalezo}@unal.edu.co

Abstract. This paper presents a matrix factorization method for dimensionality reduction, semi-supervised two-way multimodal online matrix factorization (STWOMF). This method performs a semantic embedding by finding a linear mapping to a low dimensional semantic space modeled by the original high dimensional feature representation and the label space. An important characteristic of the proposed algorithm is that the new representation can be learned in a semi-supervised fashion. So, annotated instances are used to maximize the discrimination between classes, but also, non-annotated instances can be exploited to estimate the intrinsic manifold structure of the data. Another important advantage of this algorithm is its online formulation that allows to deal with large-scale collections by keeping low computational requirements. According with the experimental evaluation, the proposed STWOMF in comparison with several linear supervised, unsupervised and semi-supervised dimensionality reduction methods, presents a competitive performance in classification while having a lower computational cost.

1 Introduction

Multimedia information presents many opportunities due to the richness of its high-dimensional information, but also implies many computational challenges mainly related with the well-known "curse of dimensionality" [3] that dramatically affects the speed of machine learning algorithms. Dimensionality reduction allows to eliminate the redundancy and the noise present in the manifold structure of the original high dimensional feature representation and tackles the curse of dimensionality by compressing the representation in a more expressive reduced set of variables that preserve the most important characteristics of the initial set. This is done by finding a transformation that does not alter the information presented by the initial data set. Dimensionality reduction is a technique widely used today in many machine learning tasks such as regression, annotation, classification, clustering, pattern recognition, information retrieval among others [1]. This technique would be used in unsupervised as well as supervised approaches. Unsupervised dimensionality reduction is mainly used with the aim of exploring the data structure and extracting meaningful information from data without any prior information. In contrast, in supervised dimensionality reduction specific targets (labeled instances) of interest are used to guide the process

© Springer International Publishing Switzerland 2015
A. Pardo and J. Kittler (Eds.): CIARP 2015, LNCS 9423, pp. 676–682, 2015.
DOI: 10.1007/978-3-319-25751-8_81

of dimensionality reduction. Even though supervised approaches can exploit the labeled data in order to improve classification performance, they require every training instance to be labeled. But a proper annotation of a whole dataset is an arduous process, and for large-scale real-world collections is infeasible to ensure a reliable annotation for each instance. So, in many cases we are in a situation where we have a big quantity of potential data for training our algorithms but only a small fraction with annotations can be used. Even so, non annotated data present valuable information about the manifold structure of the data that should be exploited in some way. This paper presents a semi-supervised dimensionality reduction method based on matrix factorization that can be used in training datasets that are not fully annotated by using the information from annotated instances to preserve the separability between elements from different classes, but also using the non-annotated elements to estimate the intrinsic manifold structure of the data.

The rest of this paper is organized as follows: Section 2, presents a comprehensive revision of related works in linear dimensionality reduction; in Section 3, details about of the proposed method are explained; Section 4, presents an evaluation of the proposed method in comparison with several state-of-the-art linear methods in dimensionality reduction; and finally, Section 5 presents some concluding remarks.

2   Related Work

There are a high number of linear techniques that perform dimensionality reduction by embedding the data to a lower semantic space, among the unsupervised approaches stand out principal component analysis (PCA) [10], factor analysis (FA) and independent component analysis (ICA) [13]. Other approaches like locality preserving projection (LPP) [11] and neighborhood preserving embedding (NPE) [9] try to preserve the local neighborhood structure. Some dimensionality reduction techniques can take into account domain knowledge. This domain knowledge can be expressed in different forms, such as, class labels, pairwise constraints or another kind of prior information. Fisher's linear discriminant analysis (LDA) [8] was one of the first techniques to take advantage of class observation to preserve the separability of the original classes. Also, there are semi-supervised alternatives that learn from a combination of both labeled and unlabeled data. For instance, semi-supervised discriminant analysis (SDA) [5] and the soft label based linear discriminant analysis SL-LDA [16] use the labeled data to maximize the separability between classes and uses the unlabeled data to estimate the intrinsic manifold structure of the data. Also, there are some non-linear alternatives (isometric feature mapping [14], locally linear embedding [12] and Laplacian Eigenmaps [2], among others). Unfortunately the modeling of these non-linearities leads to high computational complexities that make them prohibitive to use in large-scale collections. The method introduced in this paper, presents two characteristics that make it highly scalable: first, it is based on linear transformations, and second, its algorithm is formulated as an online-learning approach, which only needs to keep small portions of the training data in main memory and requires little time to reach a predefined expected risk.

3   Semi-supervised Two-Way Multimodal Online Matrix Factorization

We can represent an entire collection by a matrix $X \in \mathbb{R}^{n \times k}$, where k is the total number of instances in a training set and n is the number of features that represent each instance. In a similar way, we can represent the associated classes by a binary matrix $T \in \mathbb{R}^{m \times k}$, where m is the total number of classes in the collection, and a 1 in the j-th position $(1 \leq j \leq m)$ of the i-th column defines the membership of the i-th instance in the j-th class. This paper presents a semi-supervised dimensionality reduction framework based on TWOMF (Two-way Multimodal Online Matrix Factorization) [15], which simultaneously finds a mapping from the feature representation and from the class representation to an r-dimensional common semantic space, where $n \gg r$, and additionally, back-projection functions that reconstruct from this low r-dimensional space to the original feature and class representations are learned. These mappings are modeled for encoder and decoder matrices that perform linear transformations to and from the semantic space. So, the feature representation can be projected to the semantic space by an encoder matrix $W_x \in \mathbb{R}^{r \times n}$ and reconstructed back by a decoder matrix $W_x^{'} \in \mathbb{R}^{n \times r}$ such that $H \approx W_x X$ and $X \approx W_x^{'} H$. And, in a similar way, a reconstruction for the label representation is defined by $H \approx W_t T$ and $T \approx W_t^{'} H$, where, $W_t \in \mathbb{R}^{r \times m}$, and $W_t^{'} \in \mathbb{R}^{m \times r}$ are the encoder and decoder matrices for the label representation. Finally, a mapping between the original features and label representation, forcing an alignment of the semantic projections, is expressed by: $T \approx W_t^{'} W_x X$. All these previous conditions are put together and the problem is solved as an optimization problem by minimizing the following loss function:

$$
L = \alpha \sum_{i=1}^{k} \left\| x_i - W_x^{'} W_x x_i \right\|_F^2 + (1 - \alpha) \sum_{i=1}^{l} \left\| t_i - W_t^{'} W_t t_i \right\|_F^2
$$

$$
+ \delta \sum_{i=1}^{l} \left\| t_i - W_t^{'} W_x x_i \right\|_F^2 + \beta \left(\| W_v \|_F^2 + \left\| W_v^{'} \right\|_F^2 + \| W_t \|_F^2 + \left\| W_t^{'} \right\|_F^2 \right) \tag{1}
$$

where, x_i is the feature vector of the i-th instance in the data collection X and t_i is the corresponding binary label vector, α controls the relative importance between the reconstruction of the instance representation and the label representation, δ controls the relative importance of the mapping between instance features and label information and β controls the relative importance of the regularization terms, which penalize large values for the Frobenius norm of the transformation matrices. In this paper, we are interested in scenarios where we have a large number of instances for training (k instances), but only a restricted l number of them are properly labeled. The loss function (Eq. 1) takes advantage of both annotated and non-annotated instances. The first term in the loss function uses all the instances to model the low semantic space and the second and third terms use only the annotated instates to model the semantic space and the mapping between features and label information. The final algorithm uses stochastic gradient descent learning [4], by updating the transformation matrices at each iteration with a mini-batch of instances with their corresponding features and label representation that are randomly sampled from the training set, due to the fact that samples in a minibatch are discarded after the minibatch is processed, it is possible to scan large datasets without memory restrictions.The algorithm ends when a predefined maximum number of epochs is reached. Once the learning process is completed, the projection to the low-rank semantic representation can be performed by multiplying the original high-dimensional feature representation by the coding W_x matrix ($h_i = W_x x_i$).

4   Experiments and Results

In this section, we evaluate our algorithm in comparison with several widely-used datasets for dimensionality reduction, manifold learning and classification tasks (the details of each dataset are shown in Table 1). We evaluate the performance of our algorithm by calculating classification accuracy in each one of these datasets. We compare our method with other linear supervised, semi-supervised and unsupervised dimensionality reduction methods. These methods include SVM (Support Vector Machines) with a linear kernel [7], LDA [8], SRDA (spectral regression discriminant analysis) [6], SDA [5] and PCA [10]. For determining the parameters of each method, we perform an exploration by using 5-fold cross-validation. For our method, we need to determine five parameters, including, the learning rate, the mini-batch size and the α, β and δ parameters present in the cost function.

Table 1. Dataset information and data partition for each dataset

Dataset	Original dataset partitions		Low-scale partitions		Large-scale evaluation		#Dim	#Class
	Train	Test	Train	Test	Train	Test		
Covtype		581012	8000	8000	100000	2000	54	7
MNIST	60000	10000	8000	8000	60000	10000	784	10
Letters		20000	8000	8000	–		16	26
USPS	4649	4649	4649	4649	–		256	10

For all algorithms, except for the supervised, i.e, SVM, LDA and SRDA, we use the projected training set to construct a nearest neighborhood classifier (1NN) for evaluating the classification accuracy of the projected test set, in a similar setup as in [16]. In this evaluation, we explore the performance for different percentage of randomly selected annotated instances in training set. Table 2 reports the average accuracies for 10 runs in each configuration in the four datasets using the low-scale partitions (see Table 1). As we can see, the

STWOMF presents competitive results in comparison with all other algorithms when the dimensionality of the semantic representation coincides with the number of classes (r=C). Furthermore, when the dimensionality increases (r=C+10), STWOMF over performs the other algorithms (in our experiments, a further increase of the dimensionality did not contribute to improve the performance of the algorithm).

An evaluation with the two largest datasets using different sizes of training set was performed in order to verify the capability of the proposed method to deal with large-scale collections. Figure 1 presents the average classification accuracies and times for different sizes of the training set (the reported results are the average of 10 runs for each configuration). The STWOMF is compared against the SDA which is another semi-supervised method that also uses the unlabeled data to estimate the manifold structure of the data. For all training sizes only 30% of instances are annotated, so we can see that both methods are able to learn from labeled and unlabeled instances and both can improve their performance as more training instances are available. However, STWOMF presents two advantages: first, unlike SDA, in STWOMF we can increase the dimensionality of the semantic space resulting in an improvement in the performance. For instance, in the MNIST dataset, the STWOMF using 17 latent factor (STWOMF-r17) presents a gain in accuracy of about 6 points over the same STWOMF using only 7 latent factor (STWOMF-r7) and the SDA; and second, STWOMF presents a little increase in the time required for training as more training instances are used, leading to a speedup of about 3.5x-7x over SDA in MNIST and about 8x in CovType. The main reason for the short time used in training phase by STWOMF is that, thanks to its online formulation for large datasets, a few number of epochs are required until the algorithm converges (convergence in all algorithms is verified by means of a minimum threshold required to improve the reconstruction error in each epoch). In fact, for both datasets MNIST and CovType only two epochs are required to achieve convergence.

Table 2. Classification accuracy for different percentages of annotated instances in training set using low-scale partitions. Reported results are the average of 10 runs for each configuration (r = number of latent factors, C = number of classes in the dataset).

METHOD		STWOMF r=C	STWOMF r=C+10	SDA	LDA	SVM	SRDA	PCA r=C	PCA r=C+10
COVTYPE	100%	0.725 1.0e-2	0.770 1.0e-2	0.735 0.0	0.708 3.5e-3	0.674 3.3e-16	0.698 3.3e-16	0.707 3.3e-16	0.763 3.3e-16
	60%	0.720 1.9e-2	0.755 1.0e-2	0.719 3.3e-16	0.704 7.6e-3	0.679 3.3e-16	0.685 3.3e-16	0.683 3.3e-16	0.724 0.0
	30%	0.686 1.7e-2	0.712 1.0e-2	0.687 3.3e-16	0.707 7.6e-3	0.667 3.3e-16	0.653 0.0	0.639 3.3e-16	0.679 0.0
MNIST	100%	0.882 0.0	0.939 0.0	0.870 0.0	0.897 0.0	0.839 0.0	0.856 0.0	0.874 0.0	0.938 0.0
	60%	0.864 0.0	0.930 0.0	0.870 0.0	0.890 0.0	0.817 0.0	0.833 0.0	0.863 0.0	0.929 0.0
	30%	0.848 0.0	0.916 0.0	0.850 0.0	0.881 0.0	0.780 0.0	0.786 0.0	0.842 0.0	0.910 0.0
LETTERS	100%	0.946 1.5e-2	0.946 1.6e-3	0.950 3.3e-16	0.699 0.0	0.701 3.3e-16	0.936 0.0	0.940 0.0	0.940 0.0
	60%	0.933 1.9e-3	0.923 0.0	0.940 3.0e-4	0.694 3.3e-16	0.699 0.0	0.919 3.3e-16	0.913 3.8e-3	0.914 0.0
	30%	0.905 3.5e-3	0.885 6.1e-3	0.917 4.4e-4	0.680 3.3e-016	0.697 3.3e-16	0.893 0.0	0.872 2.5e-3	0.872 3.1e-3
USPS	100%	0.936 9.2e-3	0.966 3.3e-3	0.925 6.7e-3	0.943 3.3e-16	0.914 6.6e-16	0.921 6.6e-16	0.930 0.0	0.963 0.0
	60%	0.927 3.4e-3	0.957 1.0e-3	0.917 0.0	0.939 0.0	0.901 0.0	0.906 6.6e-16	0.921 6.6e-16	0.953 0.0
	30%	0.910 4.9e-3	0.942 2.4e-3	0.903 3.3e-16	0.926 6.6e-16	0.883 3.3e-16	0.884 0.0	0.903 3.3e-16	0.938 3.3e-16

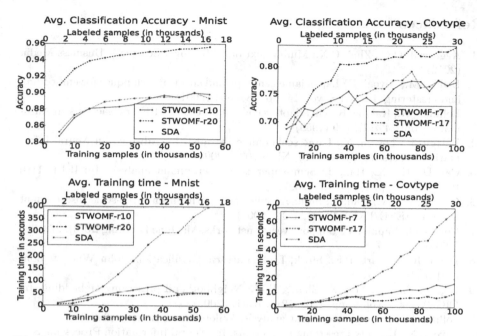

Fig. 1. Average classification accuracy (top) and average required time for training (bottom) in MNIST (left) and CovType (right) datasets using different number of training instances. For all training sizes only 30% of instances are annotated.

5   Conclusions

We presented an approach for dimensionality reduction that takes advantage of annotated data to model a semantic low-space representation that preserves the separability of the original classes. Furthermore, this method has the ability to exploit unlabeled instances for modeling the manifold structure of the data and use it to improve its performance in classification. The experimental evaluation shows that the proposed method presents competitive results in terms of classification accuracy in comparison with several unsupervised, semi-supervised and supervised linear dimensionality reduction methods, but with the advantage of its online learning formulation that allows it to deal with large collections of data by achieving a significantly reduction in computational requirements, in terms of memory consumption and required time for training.

Acknowledgments. This work was partially funded by projects *Diseño e implementación de un sistema de cómputo sobre recursos heterogéneos para la identificación de estructuras atmosféricas en predicción climatológica* number 1225-569-34920 through Colciencias contract number 0213-2013 and Multimodal Image Retrieval to Support Medical CaseBased Scientific Literature Search, ID R1212LAC006 by Microsoft Research/LACCIR. Jorge A. Vanegas thanks for doctoral grant supports Colciencias 617/2013 and Viviana Beltrán also thanks to Colciencias grant 645 *Jóvenes Investigadores e Innovadores de Colciencias* 2014.

References

1. Aggarwal, C.C., Zhai, C.X.: Mining text data. Springer Science & Business Media (2012)
2. Belkin, M., Niyogi, P.: Laplacian eigenmaps and spectral techniques for embedding and clustering. In: NIPS, vol. 14, pp. 585–591 (2001)
3. Bellman, R., Kalaba, R.: On adaptive control processes. IRE Transactions on Automatic Control **4**(2), 1–9 (1959)
4. Bottou, L., LeCun, Y.: Large scale online learning. In: Advances in Neural Information Processing Systems 16, NIPS 2003 (2003)
5. Cai, D., He, X., Han, J.: Semi-supervised discriminant analysis. In: IEEE 11th ICCV 2007, pp. 1–7. IEEE (2007)
6. Cai, D., He, X., Han, J.: Srda: An efficient algorithm for large-scale discriminant analysis. IEEE TKDE **20**(1), 1–12 (2008)
7. Cortes, C., Vapnik, V.: Support-vector networks. Machine Learning **20**(3), 273–297 (1995)
8. Duda, R.O., Hart, P.E., Stork, D.G.: Pattern classification. John Wiley & Sons (2012)
9. He, X., Cai, D., Yan, S., Zhang, H.-J.: Neighborhood preserving embedding. In: CICCV 2005, vol. 2, pp. 1208–1213. IEEE (2005)
10. Jolliffe, I.: Principal component analysis. Wiley Online Library (2002)
11. Niyogi, X.: Locality preserving projections. In: Neural Information Processing Systems, vol. 16, p. 153. MIT (2004)
12. Roweis, S.T., Saul, L.K.: Nonlinear dimensionality reduction by locally linear embedding. Science **290**(5500), 2323–2326 (2000)
13. Stone, J.V.: Independent component analysis: an introduction. Trends in Cognitive Sciences **6**(2), 59–64 (2002)
14. Tenenbaum, J.B., De Silva, V., Langford, J.C.: A global geometric framework for nonlinear dimensionality reduction. Science **290**, 2319–2323 (2000)
15. Vanegas, J.A., Beltran, V., González, F.A.: Two-way multimodal online matrix factorization for multi-label annotation. In: ICPRAM, pp. 279–285, January 2015
16. Zhao, M., Zhang, Z., Chow, T.W., Li, B.: A general soft label based linear discriminant analysis for semi-supervised dimensionality reduction. Neural Networks **55**, 83–97 (2014)

Fine-Tuning Convolutional Neural Networks Using Harmony Search

Gustavo Rosa[1], João Papa[1(✉)], Aparecido Marana[1], Walter Scheirer[2], and David Cox[2]

[1] São Paulo State University, Bauru, São Paulo, Brazil
{gustavo.rosa,papa,nilceu}@fc.unesp.br
[2] Harvard University, Cambridge, MA 02138, USA
{wscheirer,davidcox}@fas.harvard.edu

Abstract. Deep learning-based approaches have been paramount in the last years, mainly due to their outstanding results in several application domains, that range from face and object recognition to handwritten digits identification. Convolutional Neural Networks (CNN) have attracted a considerable attention since they model the intrinsic and complex brain working mechanism. However, the huge amount of parameters to be set up may turn such approaches more prone to configuration errors when using a manual tuning of the parameters. Since only a few works have addressed such shortcoming by means of meta-heuristic-based optimization, in this paper we introduce the Harmony Search algorithm and some of its variants for CNN optimization, being the proposed approach validated in the context of fingerprint and handwritten digit recognition, as well as image classification.

1 Introduction

One of the biggest computer vision problems consists in producing good intern representations of the real world, in such way that these descriptions can allow a machine learning system to detect and classify objects in labels [3]. The problem still persists when faced with situations where there exist variations of luminosity in the environment, as well as different perspectives in the image acquisition process and problems related to rotation, translation and scale.

Traditional machine learning approaches intend to tackle the aforementioned situation by extracting feature vectors with the purpose to feed a classifier by means of a training set, and thereafter classify the remaining images. Thereby, although the feature learning problem has received great attention in the last decades, a considerable effort has been dedicated to the study of deep learning techniques [2,5,9]. Despite the fact that there are several deep learning techniques out there, one of the most widely used approaches is the Convolutional Neural Networks (CNN) [9]. These neural networks are composed of different stages and architectures, which are responsible for learning different kinds of information (e.g., images and signals).

© Springer International Publishing Switzerland 2015
A. Pardo and J. Kittler (Eds.): CIARP 2015, LNCS 9423, pp. 683–690, 2015.
DOI: 10.1007/978-3-319-25751-8_82

The main problem related to such deep learning techniques concerns with the high amount of parameters used to adjust these neural networks to their best performance. Meta-heuristic techniques are among the most used for optimization problems, since they provide simple and elegant solutions in a wide range of applications. Nonetheless, the reader may face just a few and very recent works that handle the problem of CNN optimization by means of meta-heuristic techniques. Fedorovici et al. [6], for instance, employed Particle Swarm Optimization and Gravitational Search Algorithm to select parameter in CNN aiming to cope with optical character recognition applications.

Although some swarm- and population-based optimization algorithms have obtained very promising results in several applications, they may suffer from a high computational burden in large-scale problems, since there is a need for optimizing all agents at each iteration. Some years ago, Geem [7] proposed the Harmony Search (HS) technique, which falls in the field of meta-heuristic optimization techniques. However, as far as we know, Harmony Search and some of its variants have never been applied for CNN optimization.

Therefore, the main contributions of this paper are twofold: (i) to introduce HS and some of its variants to the context of CNN fine-tuning for handwritten digits and fingerprint recognition, as well as for image classification, and (ii) to fill the lack of research regarding CNN parameter optimization by means of meta-heuristic techniques. The remainder of this paper is organized as follows. Sections 2 and 3 present the Harmony Search background theory and the methodology, respectively. Section 4 discusses the experiments and Section 5 states conclusions and future works.

2   Harmony Search

Harmony Search is a meta-heuristic algorithm inspired in the improvisation process of music players. Musicians often improvise the pitches of their instruments searching for a perfect state of harmony [7]. The main idea is to use the same process adopted by musicians to create new songs to obtain a near-optimal solution according to some fitness function. Each possible solution is modeled as a harmony, and each musical instrument corresponds to one decision variable.

Let $\phi = (\phi_1, \phi_2, \ldots, \phi_N)$ be a set of harmonies that compose the so-called "Harmony Memory" (HM), such that $\phi_i \in \Re^M$. The HS algorithm generates after each iteration a new harmony vector $\hat{\phi}$ based on memory considerations, pitch adjustments, and randomization (music improvisation). Further, the new harmony vector $\hat{\phi}$ is evaluated in order to be accepted in the harmony memory: if $\hat{\phi}$ is better than the worst harmony, the latter is then replaced by the new harmony. Roughly speaking, HS algorithm basically rules the process of creating and evaluating new harmonies until some convergence criterion.

In regard to the memory consideration step, the idea is to model the process of creating songs, in which the musician can use his/her memories of good musical notes to create a new song. This process is modeled by the Harmony Memory Considering Rate ($HMCR$) parameter, which is the probability of choosing one value from the historic values stored in the harmony memory, being $(1-HMCR)$ the probability of randomly choosing one feasible value[1], as follows:

$$\hat{\phi}^j = \begin{cases} \phi_A^j & \text{with probability } HMCR \\ \theta \in \Phi_j & \text{with probability } (1 - HMCR), \end{cases} \qquad (1)$$

where $j \in \{1, 2, \ldots, M\}$, $A \sim \mathcal{U}(1, 2, \ldots, N)$, and $\Phi = \{\Phi_1, \Phi_2, \ldots, \Phi_M\}$ stands for the set of feasible values for each decision variable[2].

Further, every component j of the new harmony vector $\hat{\phi}$ is examined to determine whether it should be pitch-adjusted or not, which is controlled by the Pitch Adjusting Rate (PAR) variable, according to Equation 2:

$$\hat{\phi}^j = \begin{cases} \hat{\phi}^j \pm \varphi_j \varrho & \text{with probability } PAR \\ \hat{\phi}^j & \text{with probability } (1\text{-}PAR). \end{cases} \qquad (2)$$

The pitch adjustment is often used to improve solutions and to escape from local optima. This mechanism concerns shifting the neighbouring values of some decision variable in the harmony, where ϱ is an arbitrary distance bandwidth, and $\varphi_j \sim \mathcal{U}(0, 1)$.

2.1   Improved Harmony Search

In the last years, several researches have attempted to develop variants based on the original HS [1] in order to enhance its accuracy and convergence rate. Some works have proposed different ways to dynamically set the HS parameters, while others suggested new improvisation schemes. Mahdavi et al. [11], for instance, proposed a new variant called Improved Harmony Search (IHS), which taps a new scheme that improves the convergence rate of the Harmony Search algorithm. In other words, the IHS algorithm differs from traditional HS as it updates dynamically its PAR and distance bandwidth values during every new improvisation step.

As stated before, the mainly difference between IHS and traditional HS algorithm is how they adjust and update their PAR and bandwidth values. In order to pursue this goal and to eradicate the handicaps that come up with fixed values of PAR and ϱ, the IHS algorithm changes their values according to the iteration number.

2.2   Global-Best Harmony Search

Some concepts of swarm intelligence algorithms, as the ones presented in Particle Swarm Optimization (PSO) [4,8], have been used to enhance the Harmony

---

[1] The term "feasible value" means the value that falls in the range of a given decision variable.

[2] Variable A denotes a harmony index randomly chosen from the harmony memory.

Search algorithm in order to improve its effectiveness on either discrete and continuous problems. The so-called Global-best Harmony Search (GHS) [12] applies this technique by modifying the pitch-adjustment step of the IHS, so that its new harmony value is represented by the best harmony found in the Harmony Memory. Thereby, the distance bandwidth parameter ϱ is deserted off the improvisation step, so that the decision variable j of the new harmony is computed as follows:

$$\hat{\phi}^j = \phi^j_{best},$$ (3)

where *best* stands for the index of the best harmony in the HM.

2.3   Self-Adaptive Global-Best Harmony Search

Unlikely and inspired by its predecessor (i.e., GHS), the self-adaptive Global-best Harmony Search (SGHS) algorithm [13] applies a new improvisation method and some fine-tuning adaptive parameter procedures. During the memory consideration step, in order to avoid getting trapped at a local optimum solution, Equation 1 is replaced as follows:

$$\hat{\phi}^j = \begin{cases} \phi^j_A \pm \varphi_j \varrho & \text{with probability } HMCR \\ \theta \in \Phi_j & \text{with probability } (1 - HMCR). \end{cases}$$ (4)

Since $HMCR$ and PAR variables are dynamically updated during the iteration process by recording their previous values in accordance to the generated harmonies, we assume their values are drawn from normal distributions, i.e., $HMCR \sim \mathcal{N}(HMCR_m, 0.01)$ and $PAR \sim \mathcal{N}(PAR_m, 0.05)$. The variables $HMCR_m$ and PAR_m stand for the average values of $HMCR$ and PAR, respectively.

In order to well-balance the algorithm exploitation and exploration processes, the bandwidth parameter ϱ is computed as follows:

$$\varrho(t) = \begin{cases} \varrho_{max} - \frac{\varrho_{max} - \varrho_{min}}{T} \times 2t & \text{if } t < T/2 \\ \varrho_{min} & \text{if } t \geq T/2. \end{cases}$$ (5)

3   Methodology

3.1   Experimental Setup

In this work, we proposed the fine-tuning of CNN parameters using Harmony Search-based algorithms, as well as using a random initialization of the parameters (RS). We have employed three HS variants: (i) Improved Harmony Search [11], (ii) Global-best Harmony Search [12], and (iii) Self-adaptive Global-best Harmony Search [13]. In order to provide a statistical analysis by means of Wilcoxon signed-rank test [15], we conducted a cross-validation with 10 run-nings. Finally, we employed 15 harmonies over 250 iterations for convergence considering all techniques. Table 1 presents the parameter configuration for each optimization technique[3].

Table 1. Parameter configuration.

Technique	Parameters
HS	$HMCR = 0.7$, $PAR = 0.5$, $\varrho = 0.1$
IHS	$HMCR = 0.7$, $PAR_{MIN} = 0.0$ $PAR_{MAX} = 1.0$, $\varrho_{MIN} = 0.0$ $\varrho_{MAX} = 0.1$
GHS	$HMCR = 0.7$, $PAR_{MIN} = 0.1$ $PAR_{MAX} = 1.0$
SGHS	$HMCR_m = 0.98$, $PAR_m = 0.9$ $\varrho_{MIN} = 0.0$, $\varrho_{MAX} = 0.1$ $LP = 100$

3.2 Datasets

In regard to the parameter optimization experiment, we employed two datasets, as described below:

- MNIST dataset[4]: it is composed of images of handwritten digits. The original version contains a training set with $60,000$ images from digits '0'-'9', as well as a test set with $10,000$ images[5].
- CIFAR-10 dataset[6]: is a subset image database from the "80 million tiny images" dataset, collected by Alex Krizhevsky, Vinod Nair, and Geoffrey Hinton. Composed by $60,000$ 32x32 colour images in 10 classes, with $6,000$ images per class. It is also divided into five training batches and one test batch, each one containing $10,000$ images. Therefore we have $50,000$ images for training purposes and $10,000$ for testing duties.

In regard to the source-code, we used the well-known Caffe library[7] [16], which is developed under GPGPU (General-Purpose computing on Graphics Processor Units) platform, thus providinga more efficient implementations.

4 Experimental Results

In this section, we present the experimental results over MNIST and CIFAR-10 datasets. We employed the very same architecture proposed by Caffe[8] to handle

---

[3] Notice these values have been empirically chosen.
[4] http://yann.lecun.com/exdb/mnist/
[5] The images are originally available in gray-scale with resolution of 28×28.
[6] http://www.cs.toronto.edu/~kriz/cifar.html
[7] http://caffe.berkeleyvision.org
[8] http://caffe.berkeleyvision.org/gathered/examples/mnist.html

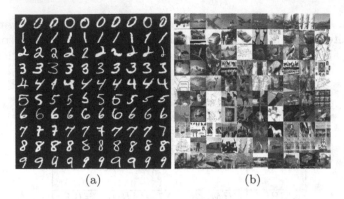

(a)   (b)

Fig. 1. Some training examples from (a) MNIST and (b) CIFAR-10 datasets.

MNIST dataset, which is composed of two layers with convolution and pooling operations.

Table 2 presents the mean accuracy and the standard deviation over the testing set using the best parameters found out by HS-based algorithms, random search (RS) and the set of parameters employed by Caffe library itself. According to the Wilcoxon signed-rank test, we have bolded the most accurate techniques in Table 2. Additionally, we also show the number of calls to the CNN learning procedure to give us an idea about the computational burden of each technique.

Table 2. Experimental results concerning MNIST dataset.

Technique	Final Accuracy (test set)	#calls
Caffe	99.07%±0.03	1
RS	98.70%±0.56	1
HS	99.23%±0.04	265
IHS	**99.24%±0.03**	**265**
GHS	**99.24%±0.08**	**265**
SGHS	**99.29%±0.06**	**265**

Considering the experimental results, we can drive some conclusions here: HS-based techniques seem to be very suitable for CNN optimization, since they achieved better results than a simple random search algorithm. This statement is very interesting, since most part of works employ a random search to fine-tune CNNs. Other conclusion concerns with the HS variants, for example, IHS: it seems to be slightly more important to update the PAR parameter dynamically regarding to the vanilla harmony search algorithm, but is still also better to consider the best harmony's values when creating the new harmony memory, as employed by GHS and SGHS.

Currently, the best error rate we have obtained was around 0.63% with SGHS technique, being one of the best errors up to date obtained by the work of

Wan et al. [14] (0.21%). However, their work employed a different technique of the one applied in this paper. Thereafter, we are not concerned in improving the top results, but to stress we can turn the results better by using meta-heuristic techniques instead of a random search. We have shown here we can improve the results obtained by Caffe library itself by means of a proper selection of the CNN parameters.

In regard to "CIFAR-10 Dataset" experiments, we employed the CIFAR-10 quick model[9], which is composed of three layers with one convolution and one pooling operation each. We bolded the most accurate techniques in Table 3 according to the Wilcoxon signed-rank test. Once again, SGHS has obtained the top results concerning CNN fine-tuning, which can be a promising indicator of the suitability of this technique to this context.

Table 3. Experimental results concerning CIFAR-10 dataset.

Technique	Final Accuracy (test set)	#calls
Caffe	71.51%±0.77	1
RS	66.97%±1.39	1
HS	**72.28%±0.37**	**265**
IHS	71.54%±0.09	265
GHS	71.86%±0.10	265
SGHS	**72.43%±0.19**	**265**

5 Conclusions

In this paper, we dealt with the problem of CNN model selection by means of meta-heuristic techniques, mainly the ones based on the Harmony Search. We conducted experiments in two public datasets for CNN fine-tuning considering HS and three variants, as well a random search and the set of parameters suggested by the open-source code we have used. The results highlighted here allow us to conclude that HS-based techniques are a suitable approach for CNN optimization, since they outperformed other techniques compared in this work.

Acknowledgments. The authors are grateful to FAPESP grants #2013/20387-7, #2014/09125-3, #2014/16250-9 and #2014/24491-6, and CNPq grants #303182/2011-3 and #470571/2013-6.

References

1. Alia, O., Mandava, R.: The variants of the harmony search algorithm: an overview. Artificial Intelligence Review **36**, 49–68 (2011)

---

[9] http://caffe.berkeleyvision.org/gathered/examples/cifar10.html

 2. Arel, I., Rose, D., Karnowski, T.: Deep machine learning - a new frontier in artificial intelligence research [research frontier]. IEEE Computational Intelligence Magazine **5**(4), 13–18 (2010)
 3. Bishop, C.: Neural networks for pattern recognition. Oxford University Press (1995)
 4. Eberhart, R.C., Kennedy, J.: A new optimizer using particle swarm theory. In: Proceedings of the Sixth International Symposium on Micromachine and Human Science, pp. 39–43 (1995)
 5. Farabet, C., Couprie, C., Najman, L., LeCun, Y.: Learning hierarchical features for scene labeling. IEEE Transactions on Pattern Analysis and Machine Intelligence **35**, 1915–1929 (2013)
 6. Fedorovici, L.O., Precup, R.E., Dragan, F., Purcaru, C.: Evolutionary optimization-based training of convolutional neural networks for ocr applications. In: 2013 17th International Conference on System Theory, Control and Computing (ICSTCC), pp. 207–212, October 2013
 7. Geem, Z.W.: Music-Inspired Harmony Search Algorithm: Theory and Applications, 1st edn. Springer Publishing Company, Incorporated (2009)
 8. Kennedy, J., Eberhart, R.C.: Particle swarm optimization. In: Proceedings of the IEEE International Joint Conference on Neural Networks, pp. 1942–1948. IEEE Press (1995)
 9. LeCun, Y., Bottou, L., Bengio, Y., Haffner, P.: Gradient-based learning applied to document recognition. Proceedings of the IEEE **86**(11), 2278–2324 (1998)
10. LeCun, Y., Kavukcuoglu, K., Farabet, C.: Convolutional networks and applications in vision. In: Proceedings of 2010 IEEE International Symposium on Circuits and Systems, pp. 253–256 (2010)
11. Mahdavi, M., Fesanghary, M., Damangir, E.: An improved harmony search algorithm for solving optimization problems. Applied Mathematics and Computation **188**(2), 1567–1579 (2007)
12. Omran, M.G., Mahdavi, M.: Global-best harmony search. Applied Mathematics and Computation **198**(2), 643–656 (2008)
13. Pan, Q.K., Suganthan, P., Tasgetiren, M.F., Liang, J.: A self-adaptive global best harmony search algorithm for continuous optimization problems. Applied Mathematics and Computation **216**(3), 830–848 (2010)
14. Wan, L., Zeiler, M., Zhang, S., Cun, Y.L., Fergus, R.: Regularization of neural networks using dropconnect. In: Dasgupta, S., Mcallester, D. (eds.) Proceedings of the 30th International Conference on Machine Learning. vol. 28, pp. 1058–1066. JMLR Workshop and Conference Proceedings (2013), http://jmlr.org/proceedings/papers/v28/wan13.pdf
15. Wilcoxon, F.: Individual comparisons by ranking methods. Biometrics Bulletin **1**(6), 80–83 (1945)
16. Jia, Y., Shelhamer, E., Donahue, J., Karayev, S., Long, J., Girshick, R., Guadarrama, S., Darrell, T.: Caffe: Convolutional architecture for fast feature embedding (2014). arXiv preprint arXiv:1408.5093

Genetic Sampling k-means for Clustering Large Data Sets

Diego Luchi[(✉)], Willian Santos, Alexandre Rodrigues,
and Flávio Miguel Varejão

Federal University of Espírito Santo,
Av. Fernando Ferrari, 514, Goiabeiras, Vitória, ES, Brazil
diego.lucchi@gmail.com
http://ninfa.inf.ufes.br/

Abstract. In this paper we present a sampling approach to run the k-means algorithm on large data sets. We propose a new genetic algorithm to guide sample selection to yield better results than selecting the individuals at random and also maintains a reasonable computing time. We apply our proposal in a public mapping points data set from the 9th DIMACS Implementation Challenge.

Keywords: Cluster analysis · k-means · Resampling · Meta-heuristics

1 Introduction

In many applications of different fields the task of identifying sets of similar elements is required. In such applications the objective is to find groups so that objects belonging to the same group are similar to each other and dissimilar to objects of other groups. The concept of similarity is subjective and may vary from one application to another. A widely used and well-known criteria for similarity is the sum of squared errors (SSE). The problem is to partition the observations into groups so the SSE is minimum, which is NP-hard for most cases [1]. As it is unlikely that there is an exact algorithm that runs in polynomial time, unless $P = NP$, the use of heuristic and approximate methods is justified.

Depending on the metric(criteria), the data distribution, size of the data set and number of groups, some clustering methods are better than others. One of the most popular clustering method is the k-means algorithm [10,11]. The k-means is very well known for its speed and accuracy when the metric to be met is the SSE. In fact, the k-means is a local search algorithm for the minimum SSE that always finishes running in a local minimum [10]. Despite having been applied to many problems with good results, the traditional k-means algorithm is unfeasible for very large data sets. To solve this problem, there are numerous approaches, like initializing methods for the clusters centroids [2,13], dimension reduction [8,12,14] and others [3,6,7].

In this paper we try to solve the k-means algorithm for clustering large data sets by searching a good sample using a genetic algorithm (GA) [9]. Other works

© Springer International Publishing Switzerland 2015
A. Pardo and J. Kittler (Eds.): CIARP 2015, LNCS 9423, pp. 691–698, 2015.
DOI: 10.1007/978-3-319-25751-8_83

did a similar approach [3,6], improving the execution time of the k-means by randomly sampling a subset of the original data to estimates the centroids. In this paper we propose a genetic algorithm (GA) [9] to guide the individuals selection to obtain a better sample to perform k-means, yielding a better estimation of centroids and, consequently, lower SSE.

The paper is organized as follows: in the Section 2 we discuss how to determine which sample is better and the intuition behind this idea; Section 3 presents the genetic algorithm to perform the re-sampling of the original data set; in Section 4 we apply our method on public mapping points data set from the 9th DIMACS Implementation Challenge and compare the results with the ones from two other algorithms, and we present our findings and observations in Section 5.

2   Sampling k-means

One of the most used approach to undertake the k-means algorithm on very large data sets is sampling. The centroids are estimated based on a representative sample of the entire data set. The obvious choice is to pick a random sample and carry out the k-means algorithm to obtain estimates of the true centroids. We call the true centroids a set of points that will give us the lowest SSE in the complete data set. Our experiments revealed that the sample size is expected to grow in proportion to the number of groups to maintain quality. This result is in line with the one reported in [3]. We ran the random k-means on the NY data set from the 9th DIMACS implementation challenge [5] two times, one varying the sample size linearly with the number of clusters and another with a sample size fixed. Figure 1 shows how the quality of the results is affected by the sample size. Let 1 be the best known solution, note that as the number of centroids (clusters) increases the quality diminishes if we keep the sample size fixed. Therefore, it is unfair to compare results between methods with different sample sizes.

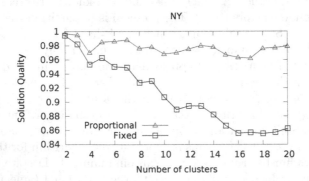

Fig. 1. Influence of the sample size in the solution quality (NY data set).

Given an arbitrary sample size, we propose an algorithm to guide the selection of individuals to compose the sample. Our proposal tries to find the set of observations that results in the highest sample SSE. Although this sounds counterintuitive, since we want to minimize the SSE in the original data set, our results show that our proposal outperforms the traditional random sampling. The intuition behind our approach is that if we remove a point close to a centroid its position will change a little. The further from a centroid a point to be removed is, the further the centroid will be repositioned. Following this thought, it is noticeable that the points in the cluster edge will have a greater impact on the centroid position and if we want to choose a set of points to remove from the data set, choosing the points with less contribution to SSE, and consequently with less impact on the centroid position, would be a good idea.

In this paper we seek for a sample that result the highest sample SSE. The basic idea would be to discard points near the centroid and pick up new ones to replace them, keeping the sample size unchanged. After that, run the k-means algorithm in the new sample and repeat the procedure with the new centroids. Repeat this until you can not get a higher SSE, and at this stage the selected points in the last sample must be away from the centroids, on the edge of the clusters (Fig. 2). Rather than implement the algorithm described above, we have implemented a meta-heuristic to accomplish this task. In the next section we detail the genetic algorithm utilized to re-sampling the data set.

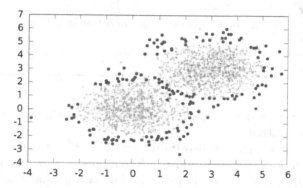

Fig. 2. Final selected points on the edge of the clusters.

3   Genetic Sampling

The genetic algorithm is a search and optimization technique that mimics the natural selection process [9]. Through inheritance (crossover) and mutation of individuals we can simulate a survival of the fittest environment. The fitness of the individuals is measured by the quality criteria, ranging from problem to problem. In our problem, the individuals (samples) with larger SSE are more likely to survive and produce offspring for future generations.

At first, a population of individuals (samples) and the centroids are initialized at random. Then, the parents are selected through a roulette wheel, a well-known way to perform selection, with selection probabilities proportional to the quality (SSE), so that more adapted individuals will have a better chance of generating

---

Algorithm 1. Genetic Algorithm Framework

---

function GASAMPLER($P, K, Sample, Pop$)
   for each individual in population **do**   ▷ Initialization and evaluation
      individual ← a random sample of *Sample* points of P
      fitness ← FITNESS(*individual*)
   end for
   while not stop condition **do**   ▷ Main Loop
      while Population Size $< 2 \cdot Pop$ **do**
         Using roulette wheel select the parents   ▷ Selection
         Offspring ← CROSSOVER(*parent1, parent2*)   ▷ Crossover
         if RANDOM $\leq$ mutation probability **then**   ▷ Mutation
            MUTATION(*Offspring1*)
         end if
         if RANDOM $\leq$ mutation probability **then**   ▷ Mutation
            MUTATION(*Offspring2*)
         end if
         Population ∪ Offspring
      end while
      for each individual in population **do**   ▷ Initialization and evaluation
         fitness ← FITNESS(*individual*)   ▷ Evaluation
      end for
      Remove from the population the *Pop* less fittest individuals
   end while
   return The best individual of the population
end function

---

offspring to the next generation. The basic framework utilized in this work can be seen in the algorithm 1.

The parameters used in the algorithm 1 are: $P \subset \mathbb{R}^d$, set of data points to be clustered. Like in k-means algorithm the K parameter is used to represent the number of groups in the final solution. The last two parameters, *Sample* and *Pop* are the sample size used for each individual and how many individuals will compose the population (the size of the population) in the genetic algorithm, respectively.

The function that calculates fitness of the individuals is straight forward. Given an individual, we run the k-means algorithm and return the SSE of the solution. The two operators (crossover and mutation) are described in the algorithms 2 and 3.

Commonly, the crossover operator cuts the chromosome of parents in one or two points and generates two new individuals using pieces of each chromosome. However, in our problem the chromosome is a collection of objects (a sample of the original data set), and the order of the elements in the chromosome does not influence the quality of the sample. To allow any combining output between the two individuals we shuffle the chromosome before cut.

The mutation operator is responsible for adding new information on population. In our case, those observations of the data set that were not selected in

---

Algorithm 2. Crossover operator

---

function CROSSOVER(*individual1, individual2*)
    individual1 ← shuffle individual1
    cut ← a random integer between 0 and individual size
    newIndividual1 ← elements before the cut *individual1* ∪ elements after the cut
of *individual2*
    newIndividual2 ← elements before the cut *individual2* ∪ elements after the cut
of *individual1*
    return newIndividual1, newIndividual2
end function

---

the random start would not be in any individual. After all, the crossover operator only generates new individuals within the elements that already exist in the population. The idea of mutation operator is simple, we remove an element of an individual and choose, from the full data set, a new element to replace it. However, we introduce a bias in this random selection. This kind of bias does not normally exist, but our tests showed good results. We use a mechanism similar to the selection (roulette wheel), with probabilities of points removal proportional to the distance to the nearest centroid, since those points contribute little to the SSE.

Algorithm 3. Mutation operator

---

function MUTATION(*individual*)
    using roulette wheel selection to select a point from the sample to swap
    select a random point from the population not in the sample
    swap the two points
end function

---

4 Experimental Results

In this section the results of the experiments are presented and discussed. First, the data sets used to validate the algorithm are presented, after that we explain how the algorithm was set up and the test environment configuration. At last, the results are presented.

We have used twelve real data sets varying from small to very large number of points. They are all mapping points from the 9th DIMACS Implementation Challenge [5]. We didn't fixed the number of clusters, instead we have varied it from 2 to 20.

4.1 Algorithm Set Up

In Table 1 we show the parameters choice for the genetic algorithm. All tests were run on a Intel(R) Core(TM) i5-3570 CPU @ 3.40GHz with 8 Gb of available physical memory. The algorithms were implemented using Python in a LINUX environment.

Table 1. Parameters used in the algorithm

Parameter	Value	Description
P	-	One of the data sets on the previous subsection
K	2-20	Number of clusters
Sample	510	Size of each sample [4]
Pop	20	Size of the population of samples
generations	50	Number of iterations of the genetic algorithm

4.2   Tests Results

Figure 3 shows the comparison the running times of our genetic proposal and the full k-means algorithm for the NY and LKS data sets (the other data sets result on similar figures). As we expected, the full k-means algorithm is not recommended for application on very large data sets and high values of k. Since the proposed method works with a fixed number of samples, the size of the original data set does not influence the computational cost of the algorithm. Moreover, as the number of clusters goes up, the time consumed to finish the k-means algorithm increases substantially, whereas the runtime for our proposal scales well (sublinear). These two facts show that the proposed method is suitable for large data sets.

Figure 4 presents the average quality based on 30 replications of our proposal. Remind that the solution quality 1 represents best known solution, obtained by carrying out the full k-mean algorithm. For comparison, we also show the average quality of the sampling k-means based on a random sample of size 510. The genetic algorithm searches for a sample whose elements are in the cluster edge, instead of picking any at random. As a result it outperforms the random, specially for large values of k. The results for the data sets not showed in this paper follow the same pattern to the ones presented here.

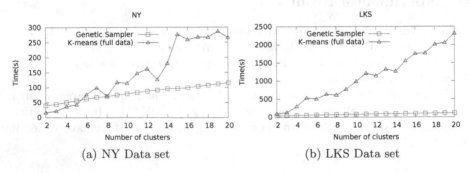

(a) NY Data set   (b) LKS Data set

Fig. 3. Average runtime of the k-means (full data set) and GA Sampler.

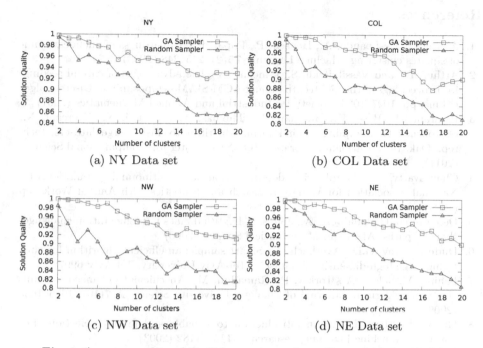

Fig. 4. Average quality of the GA sampler and a uniform random sampler.

5   Conclusion

From the results shown we can conclude that the Genetic Algorithm is a viable option for clustering large databases. It performs right between the full k-means and the random sampling on time and solution quality.

As future work, we intented to improve the quality drop when the number of clusters goes up. We conjecture that increasing the sample size linearly with the number of clusters would mantain the results of our proposal comparable with the ones form the full k-means algorithm. In addition, it is important to compare how this sampling technique performs next to other algorithms for clustering large data sets. So, it is in our plans to compare the Genetic Sampling k-means against the most popular algorithms for clustering large data sets.

Acknowledgments. We gratefully acknowledge the financial support provided by FAPES, without which the present study could not have been completed.

References

1. Aloise, D., Deshpande, A., Hansen, P., Popat, P.: Np-hardness of euclidean sum-of-squares clustering. Machine Learning **75**(2), 245–248 (2009)
2. Arthur, D., and Vassilvitskii, S.: k-means++: The advantages of careful seeding. In: Proceedings of the eighteenth annual ACM-SIAM symposium on Discrete algorithms, pp. 1027–1035. Society for Industrial and Applied Mathematics (2007)
3. Bejarano, J., Bose, K., Brannan, T., Thomas, A., Adragni, K., Neerchal, N., Ostrouchov, G.: Sampling within k-means algorithm to cluster large datasets. Tech. rep., Oak Ridge National Laboratory (ORNL); Center for Computational Sciences (2011)
4. Chakravarty, S.: Sample size determination for multinomial population. In: National Association for Welfare Research and Statistics 39th Annual Workshop (1999)
5. Demetrescu, C., Goldberg, A., Johnson, D.: 9th dimacs implementation challenge-shortest paths. American Mathematical Society (2006)
6. Dudu Lazarov, G.D., Averbuch, A.: Smart-sample: an efficient algorithm for clustering large high-dimensional datasets. Tel-Aviv University, Tel-Aviv 69978
7. Fahim, A., Salem, A., Torkey, F., Ramadan, M.: An efficient enhanced k-means clustering algorithm. Journal of Zhejiang University Science A **7**(10), 1626–1633 (2006)
8. Guyon, I., Elisseeff, A.: An introduction to variable and feature selection. The Journal of Machine Learning Research **3**, 1157–1182 (2003)
9. Holland, J.H.: Adaptation in natural and artificial systems: an introductory analysis with applications to biology, control, and artificial intelligence. U Michigan Press (1975)
10. Jain, A.K.: Data clustering: 50 years beyond k-means. Pattern Recognition Letters **31**(8), 651–666 (2010)
11. Lloyd, S.: Least squares quantization in PCM. IEEE Transactions on Information Theory **28**(2), 129–137 (1982)
12. Sarwar, B., Karypis, G., Konstan, J., Riedl, J.: Item-based collaborative filtering recommendation algorithms. In: Proceedings of the 10th International Conference on World Wide Web, WWW 2001,, pp. 285–295. ACM, New York (2001)
13. Su, T., Dy, J.: A deterministic method for initializing k-means clustering. In: 16th IEEE International Conference on Tools with Artificial Intelligence, ICTAI 2004, pp. 784–786. IEEE (2004)
14. Wold, S., Esbensen, K., Geladi, P.: Principal component analysis. Chemometrics and Intelligent Laboratory Systems **2**(1), 37–52 (1987)

Analysing the Safe, Average and Border Samples on Two-Class Imbalance Problems in the Back-Propagation Domain

Roberto Alejo[1]([✉]), Juan Monroy-de-Jesús[2], J. Horacio Pacheco-Sánchez[3],
Rosa María Valdovinos[4], Juan A. Antonio-Velázquez[1],
and J. Raymundo Marcial-Romero[4]

[1] Tecnológico de Estudios Superiores de Jocotitlán, Carretera Toluca-Atlacomulco
KM. 44.8, Ejido de San Juan y San Agustín, 50700 Jocotitlán, Mexico
ralejoll@hotmail.com
[2] University Center UAEM Atlacomulco, Universidad Autónoma del Estado de
México, Carretera Toluca-Atlacomulco KM. 60, Atlacomulco, México
[3] Instituto Tecnológico de Toluca, Av. Tecnólgico s/n Ex-Rancho La Virgen,
52140 Metepec, México
[4] Faculty of Engineering, Universidad Autónoma del Estado de México,
Cerro de Coatepec s/n, Ciudad Universitaria, C.P. 50100 Toluca, México

Abstract. In this work, we analyze the training samples for discovering what kind of samples are more appropriate to train the back-propagation algorithm. To do this, we propose a Gaussian function in order to identify three types of samples: Border, Safe and Average samples. Experiments on sixteen two-class imbalanced data sets where carried out, and a non-parametrical statistical test was applied. In addition, we employ the SMOTE as classification performance reference, i.e., to know whether the studied methods are competitive with respect to SMOTE performance. Experimental results show that the best samples to train the back-propagation are the average samples and the worst are the safe samples.

Keywords: Two-class imbalance · Border · Average and safe samples · SMOTE · Back-propagation

1 Introduction

Class imbalance is a type of problem in the Pattern Recognition, where some classes are highly under-represented compared with other classes. It has been considered one of the ten challenging problems in Data Mining research, and in the last years it has been received a great attention for the research community on machine learning and Pattern Recognition [10,19].

This work has been partially supported under grants of: Projects 3072/2011 from the UAEM, ROMEP/103.5/12/4783 from the Mexican SEP and SDMAIA-010 of the TESJO, and by the UAEM 3834/2014/CIA project.

A. Pardo and J. Kittler (Eds.): CIARP 2015, LNCS 9423, pp. 699–707, 2015.
DOI: 10.1007/978-3-319-25751-8_84

The back-propagation multilayer perceptron is a very popular artificial neural network (ANN), and is affected by the class imbalance in the same way that the other standard classifiers,, which become slow to converge to the expected solution [1–3]. In this way, several techniques for dealing with class imbalance problem through the appropriate selection of the samples to train the ANN are proposed. For example, in Ref. [16] a selection mechanism was presented, which pay more attention to the samples that are "difficult" to classify. Similarly, other authors suggest to give more priority to the samples close to the decision borderline or to the samples which are harder to learn [9,11,13].

On the other hand, about the class imbalance problem several researches propose to improve the classification performance [2,4,15] eliminating the samples that are hard to learn or close to the decision borderline, because they could be "noise" or "overlapped" samples. The edition techniques as the Edited Nearest Neighbor Rule or Tomek links have been widely used [10,19]. So the question pendent is: What it is best for the back-propagation? to eliminate samples that are hard to learn or close to the decision borderline? or to pay more attention on these samples?

In this paper, we empirically analyze these scenarios in order to identify which samples are the best for training the back-propagation on two-class imbalanced domains. We propose a novel function which uses the output of the neural network for identifying each kind of samples: border, safe and average samples. Experiments on sixteen two-class imbalanced data sets show the adequate distinction of the samples and how the neural network behavior is increased.

2   Theoretical Framework

In the specialized literature about the class imbalance problem, it is rived the interest of finding the best samples to build the classifiers, eliminating those samples with high probability to be noise or overlapped samples [2,4,14,15], or focusing in those close to the borderline decision [9,11,13] (the latter has been less explored). So, in these literature, we identify basically three categories of samples:

– Noise and rare or outliers samples. The first ones are instances with error in their labels [17] or erroneous values in theirs features that describe them, and the last ones are minority and rare samples located inside of the majority class [20].
– Border or overlapped samples, are those samples located where the decision boundary regions are intersected [2].
– Safe samples are those with high probability to be correctly labeled by the classifier and they are surrounded by samples of the same class [20].

However, there are other samples that might be of interest, those samples situated close to the borderline decision and far of the safe samples. These samples are known as *average samples*. In this paper, we are interested in identifing what samples could be the best for training the back-propagation multilayer perceptron when this is trained in a two-class imbalance context. Bearing this in mind, we analyze only three kinds of samples: the *border*, the *safe* and the *average* samples. We use the neural network output to analyze the training samples using a Gaussian function γ (Eq. 1) for identifying the kind of sample. The function proposed is:

$$\gamma(diff) = exp(-\frac{||diff - \mu||^2}{2\sigma^2}), \tag{1}$$

Variable *diff* is the normalized difference between the real ANN outputs for a sample q,

$$diff = \frac{z_{min}^q}{\sqrt{(z_{min}^q - z_{maj}^q)^2}} - \frac{z_{maj}^q}{\sqrt{(z_{min}^q - z_{maj}^q)^2}}, \tag{2}$$

where z_{min}^q and z_{maj}^q are the real ANN outputs corresponding to minority and majority classes (respectively) for a q sample. Variable μ is computed under the following consideration: the target ANN outputs are usually codified in 0 and 1 values. For example, for a two-class problem (class A and class B) the desired ANN outputs is codified as $((1; 0)$ and $(0; 1))$ respectively. These values are the target ANN outputs, and the expected final values are emitted by the ANN after training. So, in accordance with this understanding, the expected values by μ are:

- $\mu = 1.0$ for safe samples, because it is expected that the ANN classifies with high accuracy level, it is expected that the ANN output for all neurons will be values close to $(0,1)$ or $(1,0)$. So, if we apply Eq. 2 the expected value (ideally) is 1.0, at which the γ function (Eq. 1) has its maximum value.
- $\mu = 0.0$ for border samples, because it is expected that the classifier do not classifies correctly, i.e., the expected ANN outputs for all neurons are values close to $(0.5, 0.5)$, so the *diff* (Eq. 2) is approximately 0.0, at which the γ function (Eq. 1) has its maximum value for these samples.
- $\mu = 0.5$ for average samples, because it is expected that ANN classifies with less accuracy. In addition, the average samples are between safe $(\mu = 1.0)$ and border $(\mu = 0.0)$ samples.

The γ function (Eq. 1) is in this work proposed to give a certain degree of priority to each type of samples. The goal is to identify each type of sample for that μ value. The Eq. 1 gives high values to samples when its *diff* (Eq. 2) is close to μ and low values when the *diff* is far to μ. That is to say, how the neural network output depends on certain sample evaluated in some moment, the samples closed to the desired output (more similar)

Basically, the process to select the samples was the next: Before the ANN training, the training data set is balanced at 100% through an effective oversampling technique. In this work we use the SMOTE [6]. During training, the proposed method select the samples using the Eq. 1 to update the neural network weights, it chooses from the balanced training data set only the samples to use in the neural network train.

3   Experimental Set-Up

In this section, we will describe the techniques, data sets and experimental frame-work used in this paper. Firstly, for the experimental stage we chose two real-world remote sensing data bases: Cayo and Feltwell. The Cayo data set comes from a particular region in the Gulf of Mexico [1], and it has eleven classes, four features and 6019 samples. The Feltwell data set represents an agricultural area near the village of Fetwell (UK) [5] with fifteen features, five classes and 10945 samples. However, as we are interested in to study two-class imbalance problems, we decompose the multi-class problem into multiple two-class classification problems. We proceed as follow: we take one class (c_j) from original database (DB) to integrate the minority class (c^+) and the rest of classes were joined to shape the majority class (c^-), so we integrate the two-class dabase DB_j ($j = 1, 2, ..., J$, and J is the number of classes in DB). In other words, $DB_j = c^+ \cup c^-$. So we obtain J two-class imbalanced data sets. The main characteristics of the new produced benchmarking data sets are shown in Table 1.

Table 1. A brief summary of the main characteristics of a new produced benchmarking data set. The $\mathbf{C}_j$ and $\mathbf{F}_j$ databases corresponding to subsets of Cayo and Feltwell respectively.

Databases	#Minority class samples	#Majority class samples	Imbalance Ratio
C_1	838	5181	6.18
C_2	293	5726	19.54
C_3	624	5395	8.65
C_4	322	5697	17.69
C_5	133	5886	44.26
C_6	369	5650	15.31
C_7	324	5695	17.58
C_8	722	5297	7.34
C_9	789	5230	6.63
C_{10}	833	5186	6.23
C_{11}	772	5247	6.80
F_1	3531	7414	2.10
F_2	2441	8504	3.48
F_3	896	10049	11.22
F_4	2295	8650	3.77
F_5	1781	9164	5.15

On the other hand, the sequential back-propagation algorithm was used in this work, the ten-fold cross-validation method was applied on all data sets shown in Table 1, and the weights were ten times randomly initialized for each training process. Therefore, the results of classifying the test samples were averaged between the ten folds and the ten different weights initialization. The learning rate (η) was set to 0.1 and the stopping criterion was established at 500 epoch or if the MSE value is lower than 0.001. A single hidden layer was used. The number of neurons in the hidden layer was set in four. Finally, the Area Under the Receiver Operating Characteristic Curve (AUROC) [7] was used as a measure criteria for the classifiers performance, because it is one of most widely-used and accepted technique for the evaluation of binary classifiers in imbalanced domain [10].

4   Results and Discussion

Here we present the main experimental results of this research. We have used a well known and effective over-sampling technique (SMOTE [6]) to deal with the class imbalance problem, as classification performance reference, to know if the studied methods show competitive performing. Table 2 shows the AUC obtained in the classification stage for each dataset in accordance to the type samples, when the back-propagation gives priority to the border, safe and average samples (see section 2). The values in bold type represents the best result in each data set.

Table 2. Back-progation classification performance measured using AUC and average rank.

Databases	$\mu = 0$	$\mu = 0.5$	$\mu = 1$	SMOTE	Standard
C_1	0.9421	0.9774	0.9365	**0.9780**	0.9335
C_2	0.9652	**0.9688**	0.9378	**0.9688**	0.7520
C_3	0.9622	0.9664	0.9577	**0.9670**	0.9490
C_4	0.8883	0.9789	0.8306	**0.9818**	0.9406
C_5	0.9182	**0.9688**	0.9543	0.9669	0.8458
C_6	0.8603	0.9478	0.8452	**0.9514**	0.7720
C_7	0.9108	0.9788	0.9647	**0.9813**	0.8303
C_8	0.9766	**0.9903**	0.9879	0.9895	0.9853
C_9	0.9353	0.9645	0.8519	**0.9679**	0.9350
C_{10}	0.9018	0.9021	0.8666	**0.9185**	0.8337
C_{11}	0.8683	**0.9698**	0.8491	0.9667	0.9219
F_1	0.9774	0.9779	0.9721	**0.9781**	0.9773
F_2	0.9700	0.9735	0.9497	**0.9748**	0.9651
F_3	0.9687	**0.9767**	0.9553	0.9748	0.8900
F_4	0.9741	**0.9774**	0.9657	0.9765	0.9705
F_5	0.9821	**0.9852**	0.9702	0.9820	0.9676
Average Rank	3.3125	1.5625	4.1875	**1.5**	4.4375

In Table 2 we observe that the best classification performance is presented by SMOTE and by the back-propagation with $\mu = 0.5$ (when the ANN is trained with average samples). In addition, it is noted that the worst performance is obtained for the safe samples ($\mu = 1.0$) and the standard back-propagation. The back-propagation classification performance when $\mu = 0$ is close to the safe samples performance, but it is better, in agreement with the Friedman ranks and the AUC values. In other words, we observe that the best samples to the training at the back-propagation are the average samples, i.e., those that are not in the overlap region but are close to them and near to the area where the safe samples are.

On the other hand, the classification performance of the back-propagation with $\mu = 0.5$ is very similar to the SMOTE performs, they exhibit virtually the same results. However, the number of samples used by back-propagation with $\mu = 0.5$ is approximately 38% (to F_j and C_j) of the total samples used by SMOTE and 68% of samples employed by standard back-propagation (see Table 3). Moreover, we do not despite the $\mu = 0$ results, because using approximately only 2.3% of the samples on SMOTE algorithm, it obtains results with few

Table 3. Number of samples used in the training process in accordance to the μ values (see section 2). Remembering we used the ten-fold-cross-validation method and the resulting number showed correspondence to the training fold.

Databases	$\mu = 0$	$\mu = 0.5$	$\mu = 1$	SMOTE	Standard
C_1	142	4007	7796	9327	5418
C_2	287	3408	8166	10309	5418
C_3	269	3646	7959	9711	5418
C_4	228	3632	5962	10255	5418
C_5	224	3378	8720	10595	5418
C_6	246	3949	6373	10171	5418
C_7	259	4027	8549	10253	5418
C_8	182	3611	8340	9535	5418
C_9	91	3105	6741	9415	5418
C_{10}	838	4418	6671	9335	5418
C_{11}	233	3577	6007	9445	5418
F_1	258	5232	11389	13343	9850
F_2	294	6576	12758	15305	9850
F_3	256	6515	14887	18087	9850
F_4	284	5854	13135	15567	9850
F_5	283	5431	14032	16495	9850
Average	**273**	**4397**	**9217**	**11696**	**6803**

differences in its performance. Table 3 shows the number of samples used in the training stage for several μ values.

From sizes shown in the Table 3, we observe that when the back-propagation is trained with $\mu = 0$ the number of samples used is much less than with the other values of μ. However, the classification performance obtained with this value is worst than SMOTE and back-propagation with $\mu = 0.5$. So, when the $\mu = 1.0$ the number samples used is close to the SMOTE and the back-propagation performance is the worst among all studied methods. According to the results shown in this section, we consider necessary to make a statistical analysis. For this, we apply the Friedman and Iman–Davenport test in order to detect whether differences in the results exist. Both test are applied with a level of confidence $\gamma = 0.05$, and we use the KEEL software. If the null-hypothesis is rejected, we use a post-hoc test in order to find the particular pairwise comparisons that produce statistical significant differences. The Holm-Shaffer post-hoc tests are applied in order to report any significant difference between individual methods here used. The Holm procedure rejects the hypotheses (H_i) one at a time until no further rejections can be done [12]. Holm method ordains the p-values from the smallest to the largest, i.e., $p_1 \leq p_2 \leq p_{k-1}$, and the sequence $H_1, H_2, ..., H_{k-1}$ being the corresponding hypotheses. After the Holm procedure rejects H_1 to H_{i-1} if i is the smallest integer such that $p_i > \alpha/(k-i)$. This procedure starts with the most significant p-value. As soon as a certain null-hypothesis cannot be rejected, all the remaining hypotheses are retained as well [18]. The Shaffer method follows a very similar procedure to that proposed by Holm, but instead of rejecting H_i when $p_i \leq \alpha/(k-i)$, it rejects H_i if $p_i \leq \alpha/t_i$, where t_i is the maximum number of hypotheses which can be true given that any $(i-1)$ hypotheses are false [8].

Considering reduction performance distributed according to chi-square with 4 degrees of freedom Friedman statistic is to set at 50.5, and p-value computed by Friedman Test is 3.1355E-10. Now, considering reduction performance distributed according to F-distribution with 4 and 60 degrees of freedom, Iman and Davenport statistic is 56.1111, and p-value computed by Iman and Daveport Test is 1.3086E-19. So the null hypothesis is rejected, both Friedman's and Iman-Davenport's tests indicate that significant differences exist in the results. Due to these results, a post-hoc statistical analysis is required. We have to compute and ordain the corresponding statistics and p-values. Table 4 presents the family of hypotheses ordered by their p-values and the adjustment by Holm's and Shaffer's statistics procedures. In Table 4 we can see that the Holm-Shaffer test agrees in that do not exist statistical significant differences between the back-propagation with $\mu = 0.5$ and the SMOTE back-propagation, but there is difference between the back-propagation $\mu = 0.1$ and the SMOTE back-propagation. The classification performance of the back-propagation with $\mu = 0.5$ is very competitive with the SMOTE back-propagation, using much less samples in the training stage than the SMOTE algorithm (see Table 3). In same way, results from the Table 4 confirm that the worst samples to train the back-propagation are those far to decision borderline: the back-propagation with $\mu = 1.0$.

Table 4. P-values for $\alpha = 0.05$. Holm and Shaffer test rejects those hypotheses that have unadjusted p-value $\leq p-Holm$ and p-value $\leq p-Shaffer$ respectively. The rejected null hypothesis are typed in bold.

Methods	$z = (R_0 - R_i)/SE$	p	$p-Holm$	$p-Shaffer$
10 SMOTE vs. Standard	5.25476	0	**0.005**	**0.005**
9 $\mu = 0.5$ vs Standard	5.142956	0	**0.005556**	**0.008333**
8 $\mu = 1.0$ vs SMOTE	4.807546	0.000002	**0.00625**	**0.008333**
7 $\mu = 0.5$ vs $\mu = 1.0$	4.695743	0.000003	**0.007143**	**0.008333**
6 $\mu = 0.0$ vs SMOTE	3.242299	0.001186	**0.008333**	**0.008333**
5 $\mu = 0.0$ vs $\mu = 0.5$	3.130495	0.001745	**0.01**	**0.0125**
4 $\mu = 0.0$ vs Standard	2.012461	0.044171	0.0125	0.0125
3 $\mu = 0.0$ vs $\mu = 1.0$	1.565248	0.117525	0.016667	0.016667
2 $\mu = 1.0$ vs Standard	0.447214	0.654721	0.025	0.025
1 $\mu = 0.5$ vs SMOTE	0.111803	0.910979	0.05	0.05

5   Conclusion

In this paper we study the performance of the backpropagation algorithm when it is trained with samples in different points of the representation space, specifically, in the borderline, average and safe area. The proposal follows three goals: firstly, identify the nature of the samples which are more appropriate for training the back-propagation algorithm while the computational cost is diminished without sacrificing performance; secondly, provide a method for handling the imbalance problem in data sets with two-classes using the neural network; finally, analyze the competitiveness of the proposal here made respect to use a resampling method which avoid the imbalance problem in the data set, but increase significantly the amount of samples used, SMOTE.

For the identification of the nature of the samples we propose to include a Gaussian function in the decision step of the back-propagation algorithm. The results obtained show that the best samples for training the back-propagation are the average samples, i.e., those close to the borderline decision that are not in the overlap region. With this, the back-propagation needs less samples in the training stage than the SMOTE, obtaining a similar classification performance.

Future work will extend this study, we are interested in to generalize this study to multiples classes domains and to dip in problems where the dataset shows a large size and an extreme class imbalance.

References

1. Alejo, R., García, V., Pacheco-Sánchez, J.H.: An efficient over-sampling approach based on mean square error back-propagation for dealing with the multi-class imbalance problem. Neural Processing Letters, 1–16 (2014)
2. Alejo, R., Valdovinos, R.M., García, V., Pacheco-Sanchez, J.H.: A hybrid method to face class overlap and class imbalance on neural networks and multi-class scenarios. Pattern Recognition Letters **34**(4), 380–388 (2013)
3. Anand, R., Mehrotra, K., Mohan, C., Ranka, S.: An improved algorithm for neural network classification of imbalanced training sets. IEEE Trans. on Neural Networks **4**, 962–969 (1993)
4. Batista, G.E.A.P.A., Prati, R.C., Monard, M.C.: Balancing strategies and class overlapping. In: Famili, A.F., Kok, J.N., Peña, J.M., Siebes, A., Feelders, A. (eds.) IDA 2005. LNCS, vol. 3646, pp. 24–35. Springer, Heidelberg (2005)
5. Bruzzone, L., Serpico, S.: Classification of imbalanced remote-sensing data by neural networks. Pattern Recognition Letters **18**, 1323–1328 (1997)
6. Chawla, N.V., Bowyer, K.W., Hall, L.O., Kegelmeyer, W.P.: Smote: Synthetic minority over-sampling technique. Journal of Artificial Intelligence Research **16**, 321–357 (2002)
7. Fawcett, T.: An introduction to roc analysis. Pattern Recogn. Lett. **27**, 861–874 (2006)
8. García, S., Herrera, F.: An Extension on "Statistical Comparisons of Classifiers over Multiple Data Sets" for all Pairwise Comparisons. Journal of Machine Learning Research **9**, 2677–2694 (2008)
9. Han, H., Wang, W.-Y., Mao, B.-H.: Borderline-SMOTE: A new over-sampling method in imbalanced data sets learning. In: Huang, D.-S., Zhang, X.-P., Huang, G.-B. (eds.) ICIC 2005. LNCS, vol. 3644, pp. 878–887. Springer, Heidelberg (2005)
10. He, H., Garcia, E.: Learning from imbalanced data. IEEE Transactions on Knowledge and Data Engineering **21**(9), 1263–1284 (2009)
11. He, H., Bai, Y., Garcia, E.A., Li, S.: Adasyn: Adaptive synthetic sampling approach for imbalanced learning. In: IJCNN, pp. 1322–1328 (2008)
12. Holm, S.: A simple sequentially rejective multiple test procedure. Scandinavian Journal of Statistics **6**(2), 65–70 (1979)
13. Inderjeet, M., Zhang, I.: knn approach to unbalanced data distributions: a case study involving information extraction. In: Proceedings of Workshop on Learning from Imbalanced Datasets (2003)
14. Laurikkala, J.: Improving identification of difficult small classes by balancing class distribution. In: Quaglini, S., Barahona, P., Andreassen, S. (eds.) AIME 2001. LNCS (LNAI), vol. 2101, pp. 63–66. Springer, Heidelberg (2001)
15. Lawrence, S., Burns, I., Back, A., Tsoi, A.C., Giles, C.L.: Neural network classification and prior class probabilities. In: Orr, G.B., Müller, K.-R. (eds.) NIPS-WS 1996. LNCS, vol. 1524, pp. 299–314. Springer, Heidelberg (1998)

16. Lin, M., Tang, K., Yao, X.: Dynamic sampling approach to training neural networks for multiclass imbalance classification. IEEE Trans. Neural Netw. Learning Syst. **24**(4), 647–660 (2013)
17. López, V., Fernández, A., García, S., Palade, V., Herrera, F.: An insight into classification with imbalanced data: Empirical results and current trends on using data intrinsic characteristics. Inf. Sci. **250**, 113–141 (2013)
18. Luengo, J., García, S., Herrera, F.: A study on the use of statistical tests for experimentation with neural networks: Analysis of parametric test conditions and non-parametric tests. Expert Systems with Applications **36**(4), 7798–7808 (2009)
19. Prati, R.C., Batista, G.E.A.P.A., Monard, M.C.: Data mining with imbalanced class distributions: concepts and methods. In: Proceedings of the 4th Indian International Conference on Artificial Intelligence, IICAI 2009, Tumkur, Karnataka, India, December 16–18, pp. 359–376 (2009)
20. Stefanowski, J.: Overlapping, rare examples and class decomposition in learning classifiers from imbalanced data. In: Ramanna, S., Howlett, R.J. (eds.) Emerging Paradigms in ML and Applications. SIST, vol. 13, pp. 277–306. Springer, Heidelberg (2013)

Improving the Accuracy of the Sequential Patterns-Based Classifiers

José K. Febrer-Hernández[1](✉), Raudel Hernández-León[1],
José Hernández-Palancar[1], and Claudia Feregrino-Uribe[2]

[1] Centro de Aplicaciones de Tecnologías de Avanzada (CENATAV), 7a # 21406 E/
214 and 216, Rpto. Siboney, C.P. 12200 Playa, La Habana, Cuba
{jfebrer,rhernandez,jpalancar}@cenatav.co.cu
[2] Instituto Nacional de Astrofísica, Óptica y Electrónica (INAOE), Luis Enrique
Erro No. 1, Sta. María Tonantzintla, CP:72840 Puebla, Mexico
cferegrino@ccc.inaoep.mx

Abstract. In this paper, we propose some improvements to the Sequential Patterns-based Classifiers. First, we introduce a new pruning strategy, using the Netconf as measure of interest, that allows to prune the rules search space for building specific rules with high Netconf. Additionally, a new way for ordering the set of rules based on their sizes and Netconf values, is proposed. The ordering strategy together with the "Best K rules" satisfaction mechanism allow to obtain better accuracy than SVM, J48, NaiveBayes and PART classifiers, over three document collections.

Keywords: Data mining · Supervised classification · Sequential patterns

1 Introduction

Classification based on Sequential Patterns (CSPa), introduced in [6], integrates Classification Rule Mining [1] and Sequential Pattern Mining [2]. This integration involves mining a subset of Sequential Patterns-based Rules (SPaRs). Sequential patterns-based classification has been used in different tasks, for example: text classification [3], document-specific keyphrase extraction [4], and web document classification [5], among others.

CSPa aims to mine a set of SPaRs from a class-transaction dataset. A classifier based on this approach usually consists of an ordered SPaR list l, and a mechanism for classifying new transactions using l. It is common to confuse sequences with itemsets. Unlike an itemset, in which an item can occur at most once, in a sequence an itemset can occur multiple times. Additionally, in itemset mining, $(abc) = (cba)$ but in sequence mining, $\langle (ab) \, c \rangle \neq \langle c \, (ab) \rangle$. In CSPa, it is assumed that a set of items $I = \{i_1, i_2, ..., i_n\}$, a set of classes C, and a set of transactions T are given, where each transaction $t \in T$ consists of a sequence

© Springer International Publishing Switzerland 2015
A. Pardo and J. Kittler (Eds.): CIARP 2015, LNCS 9423, pp. 708–715, 2015.
DOI: 10.1007/978-3-319-25751-8_85

$\langle \alpha_1 \ \alpha_2 \ ... \ \alpha_n \rangle$, so that $\alpha_i \subseteq I$, and a class $c \in C$. The Support of a sequence α, denoted as $Sup(\alpha)$, is the fraction of transactions in T containing α (see Eq. 1).

$$Sup(\alpha) = \frac{|T_\alpha|}{|T|} \tag{1}$$

where T_α is the set of transactions in T containing α (see Def. 1) and $|\cdot|$ is the cardinality operator.

Definition 1. *Let $\alpha = \langle \alpha_1 \ \alpha_2 \ ... \ \alpha_n \rangle$ and $\beta = \langle \beta_1 \ \beta_2 \ ... \ \beta_m \rangle$ be sequences, we will say that α is contained in β if there exists integers $1 \leq j_1 < j_2 < ... < j_n \leq m$ such that $\alpha_1 \subseteq \beta_{j_1}, \ \alpha_2 \subseteq \beta_{j_2}, \ ..., \ \alpha_n \subseteq \beta_{j_n}$, with $\beta_{j_i} \in \beta$.*

A SPaR is an implication of the form $\alpha \Rightarrow c$ where α is a sequence and $c \in C$. The size of a SPaR is defined as its cardinality, a SPaR containing k itemsets (including the class) is called a k-SPaR. The rule $\alpha \Rightarrow c$ is held in T with certain Support and Confidence (see Eqs. 2 and 3). If the measure values used to compute and evaluate a SPaR $r : \alpha \Rightarrow c$ are greater than to a user-specified threshold, r is declared to be an interesting SPaR.

$$Sup(\alpha \Rightarrow c) = Sup(\alpha \otimes \langle c \rangle) \tag{2}$$

where $\otimes$ is the concatenation operator (see Def. 2).

$$Conf(\alpha \Rightarrow c) = \frac{Sup(\alpha \Rightarrow c)}{Sup(\alpha)} \tag{3}$$

Definition 2. *Let $\alpha = \langle \alpha_1 \ \alpha_2 \ ... \ \alpha_n \rangle$ and $\beta = \langle \beta_1 \ \beta_2 \ ... \ \beta_m \rangle$, we will call the sequence $\langle \alpha_1 \ \alpha_2 \ ... \ \alpha_n \ \beta_1 \ \beta_2 \ ... \ \beta_m \rangle$ the concatenation of α and β, and we will use the operator $\otimes$ to indicate it.*

The accuracy of the sequential patterns-based classifiers depend on four main elements: (1) the quality measure used to generate the SPaRs, (2) the pruning strategy, (3) the ordering strategy and (4) the mechanism used for classifying unseen transactions. Therefore, any of the main sequential patterns mining algorithms (GSP [6], PrefixSpan [7], LAPIN [8] and PRISM [9]) can be adapted to generate the SPaRs.

Currently, all classifiers based on sequential patterns use the Support and Confidence measures for computing and ordering the set of SPaRs. However, several authors have pointed out some drawbacks of these measures [10], for example, Confidence detects neither statistical independence nor negative dependence among items (misleading rules).

Many studies [2,6] have indicated the high number of rules that could be generated using a small Support threshold. To address this problem, recent works [11] prune the rules search space each time that a rule satisfies both Support and Confidence thresholds, it means that rules satisfying both thresholds are not extended anymore. Using this strategy, it is more frequent the generation of general (short) rules than the generation of specific (large) rules, some of which could be more interesting.

In order to overcome these drawbacks, in this paper we propose some general improvements to the sequential patterns-based classifiers. The rest of the paper is organized as follows. The next section describes the related work. Our proposal are presented in section three. In the fourth section the experimental results are shown. Finally, the conclusions are given in section five.

2   Related Work

In the last decades, some works have used sequential patterns to increase the accuracy of classifiers. The sequential pattern mining algorithms can be split into two main groups: (1) apriori-like algorithms (GSP [6]) and (2) pattern-growth based algorithms (PrefixSpan [7], LAPIN [8], PRISM [9]).

Once the SPaRs are generated, these are ordered. For this task there are six main strategies reported in the literature: Confidence-Support-Antecedent, Antecedent-Confidence-Support, Weighted Relative Accuracy, Laplace Expected Error Estimate, Chi-Square and L^3. In [12], the authors show that the L^3 rule ordering strategy obtains the best results of all strategies mentioned above. However, all these ordering strategies are based on Confidence measure.

Once a SPaR-based classifier has been built, usually presented as a list of sorted SPaRs, there are three main mechanisms for classifying unseen data [11].

- **Best rule**: This mechanism assigns the class of the first ("best") rule in the order that satisfies the transaction to be classified.
- **Best K rules**: This mechanism selects the best K rules (for each class) that satisfy the transaction to be classified and then the class is determined using these K rules, according to different criteria.
- **All rules**: This mechanism selects all rules that satisfy the unseen transaction and then these rules are used to determine their class.

Since the "Best K rules" mechanism has been the most widely used for rule-based classification, reporting the best results, we will use it in our experiments.

3   Our Proposal

In the next subsections we describe a procedure, called SPaRs-Gen, to generate the set of interesting SPaRs (subsection 3.3), which uses the Netconf measure to evaluate the candidate SPaRs (subsection 3.1) and applies a new pruning strategy (subsection 3.2).

3.1   Netconf Measure

All classifiers based on sequential patterns use the Support and Confidence measures for mining the set of SPaRs. However, several authors have pointed out some drawbacks of these measures that could lead us to discover many more rules than it should [10]. In particular, the presence of items with high Support can lead us to obtain misleading rules (see Ex. 1) because higher-Support items appear in many transactions and they could be predicted by any itemset.

Example 1. *Without loss of generality, let us assume that $Sup(X) = 0.4$, $Sup(Y) = 0.8$ and $Sup(X \Rightarrow Y) = 0.3$, therefore $Sup(\neg X) = 1 - Sup(X) = 0.6$ and $Sup(\neg X \Rightarrow Y) = Sup(Y) - Sup(X \Rightarrow Y) = 0.5$. If we compute $Conf(X \Rightarrow Y)$ we obtain 0.75 (a high Confidence value) but Y occurs in 80% of the transactions, therefore the rule $X \Rightarrow Y$ does worse than just randomly guessing. In this case, $X \Rightarrow Y$ is a misleading rule.*

On the other hand, in [13] the authors proposed a measure, called Netconf (see Eq. 4), to estimate the strength of a rule. In general, this measure solves the main drawbacks of the Confidence measure, reported in other works [10].

$$Netconf(X \Rightarrow Y) = \frac{Sup(X \Rightarrow Y) - Sup(X)Sup(Y)}{Sup(X)(1 - Sup(X))} \tag{4}$$

The Netconf has among its main advantages that it detects the misleading rules obtained by the Confidence. For the Ex. 1, $Netconf(X \Rightarrow Y) = -0.083$ showing a negative dependence between the antecedent and the consequent. Therefore, in this paper we propose to use the Netconf measure instead of Support and Confidence for computing and ordering the set of interesting SPaRs.

3.2   Pruning Strategy

Most of the algorithms in SPaR-based classification [6] prune the SPaRs search space each time a SPaR satisfying the defined thresholds is found, it produces general (small) rules reducing the possibility of obtain specific (large) rules, some of which could be more interesting. Besides, since the defined threshold(s) must be satisfied, many branches of the rules search space could be explored in vain.

In our proposal, instead of pruning the SPaR search space when a SPaR satisfies the Netconf threshold, we propose the following pruning strategy:

- If a SPaR r does not satisfy the Netconf threshold $minNF$ ($r.NF \leq minNF$) we do not extend it anymore avoiding to explore this part of the SPaR search space in vain.
- Let $r_1 : \alpha \Rightarrow c$ and $r_2 : \beta \Rightarrow c$ be SPaRs, if the SPaR $r : \langle \alpha \otimes \beta \rangle \Rightarrow c$ satisfies the Netconf threshold but $r.NF < r_1.NF$ and $r.NF < r_2.NF$ then we prune r avoiding to generate SPaRs with less quality than their parents.

The intuitive idea (or hypothesis) behind this pruning strategy is that specific rules with high values of quality measure are better to classify than general rules with high values of quality measure.

3.3   Generating and Ordering the SPaRs

In this section, we describe the procedure (called SPaRs-Gen) to generate de set of interesting SPaRs, which uses the Netconf measure to evaluate the candidate SPaRs and applies the pruning strategy introduced in section 3.2.

Let $\alpha \Rightarrow c$ be an interesting SPaR and T be a set of transactions, SPaRs-Gen stores for each $t \in T$, a list with the occurrence positions of α in t (see Def. 3).

Definition 3. *Let* $\alpha = \langle \alpha_1\ \alpha_2\ ...\ \alpha_n \rangle$ *and* $\beta = \langle \beta_1\ \beta_2\ ...\ \beta_m \rangle$ *be sequences such that* α *is contained in* β *(i.e. exists integers* $1 \leq j_1 < j_2 < ... < j_n \leq m$ *such that* $\alpha_1 \subseteq \beta_{j_1}$, $\alpha_2 \subseteq \beta_{j_2}$, ..., $\alpha_n \subseteq \beta_{j_n}$*), we will call occurrence position of* α *in* β *(occP(α, β)) to the least position of all possible* β_{j_n} *in* β, *if* $| \alpha | > 2$, *and the set of positions of all possible* β_{j_n} *in* β, *if* $| \alpha | \leq 2$.

Similar to the reported algorithms for frequent sequence mining [6–9], in a first step, SPaRs-Gen obtains the set of 3-SPaRs by combining the 2-SPaRs belonging to the same class. The pseudo code of the 3-SPaRs generation is not described for simplicity. However, is valid to remember that, as we mentioned above, SPaRs-Gen stores for each interesting SPaR $\alpha \Rightarrow c$ (of any size) and for each transaction $t \in T$, a list with the occurrence positions of α in t. Unlike the reported algorithms, which generate the k-SPaRs either by combining the interesting $(k-1)$-SPaRs with a common $k-2$ prefix or by using a depth first search strategy, SPaRs-Gen computes the k-SPaRs $(k > 3)$ by combining the interesting $(k-1)$-SPaRs and the interesting 3-SPaRs (see Alg. 1).

Algorithm 1. Pseudo code for computing the interesting k-SPaRs

---

Input: Set of interesting $(k-1)$-SPaRs, set of interesting 3-SPaRs and Netconf threshold $minNF$.
Output: Set of interesting k-SPaRs.
1 $L_1 = (k-1)$-SPaRs, $L_2 = $ 3-SPaRs, $L_3 = \emptyset$
2 **foreach** $c \in C$ **do**
3   **foreach** $(r_1 = \langle \alpha_1\ ...\ \alpha_{k-1} \rangle \Rightarrow c) \in L_1$ **and** $(r_2 = \langle \alpha_{k-1}\ \beta \rangle \Rightarrow c) \in L_2$ **do**
4   **foreach** $t \in T$ **do**
5   **if** $\exists op_1\ (op_1 \in occP(\langle \alpha_{k-1}\ \beta \rangle, t)$ **and** $op_1 > occP(\langle \alpha_1\ ...\ \alpha_{k-1} \rangle, t))$ **then**
6                  $r_3 = \langle \alpha_1\ ...\ \alpha_{k-1} \rangle \otimes \langle \beta \rangle \Rightarrow c$
7   Computes the Netconf NF of r_3
8   **if** $(r_3.NF > minNF)$ **and**
9                      $(r_3.NF \geq r_1.NF$ **or** $r_3.NF \geq r_2.NF)$ **then**
10 | $L_3 = L_3 \cup \{r_3\}$
11   **end**
12   **end**
13   **end**
14   **end**
15 **end**
16 **return** L_3

In line 3 of Algorithm 1, the $(k-1)$-SPaRs are combined with the 3-SPaRs to generate the candidate k-SPaRs. In line 5, the definition of occurrence position is applied. Finally, the candidate SPaRs are built in line 6, their Netconf values computed in line 7 and, the pruning strategy verified in lines $8 - 9$.

Once the set of SPaRs has been generated, it is sorted. As mentioned in section 3.2, for classifying, we propose to use specific (large) rules with high Netconf; for this purpose, we sort the set of SPaRs in a descending order according to their sizes (the largest first) and in case of tie, we sort the tied SPaRs in a descending order according to their Netconf (the highest values first).

The intuitive idea behind this ordering strategy is that large rules should be preferred before short rules because in general more specific rules have a higher

Netconf than general rules. In case of tie in size, rules with high Netconf values should be preferred before rules with low Netconf values.

For classifying unseen transactions, we decided to follow the "Best K rules" mechanism, because the "Best rule" mechanism could suffer biased classification since the classification is based on only one rule; and the "All rules" mechanism takes into account rules with low ranking, which could affects the accuracy.

4   Experimental Results

In this section, we report some experimental results where our proposal, called SPaC-NF, is compared, over three document collections, against other classifiers as NaiveBayes, PART [14], J48 [1], Support Vector Machines [15] and against a classifier (SPaC-MR) built with the Main Results obtained in SPaR-based classification. All these classifiers, with the exception of SPaC-NF and SPaC-MR, were evaluated using Weka (http://www.weka.net.nz/).

The experiments were done using ten-fold cross-validation, reporting the average over the ten folds. Our tests were performed on a PC with an Intel Core 2 Quad at 2.50 GHz CPU with 4 GB DDR3 RAM, running on Windows 7 system. Similar to other works, experiments were conducted using several document collections, three in our case: AFP (http://trec.nist.gov), TDT (http://www.nist.gov) and Reuter (http://kdd.ics.uci.edu). The characteristics of these datasets are shown in table 1.

Table 1. Tested datasets characteristics.

Dataset	#instances	#classes
AFP	711	22
TDT	2 978	92
Reuter	21 578	115

In the same way as in other works, for all used datasets, sentences are ordered in each document. This means that the document is considered as being an ordered list of sentences and each sentence is considered as being an unordered set of words. Therefore, we represented the document as a sequence of itemsets where each one corresponds with the set of words of each sentence.

In the experiments, different parameters for each classify were used. In case of SVM classify, the weka default parameter values and a polynomial kernel were used. For J48 and PART classifiers we used the confidence factor set to 0.25 and the minimum number of objects set to 2, as their authors suggested in [1]; additionally, for PART classifier we used the seed value set to 1. In SPaC-MR we used the Confidence threshold set to 0.5 as was proposed in other works [12]. Finally, in SPaC-NF we used the Netconf threshold set to 0.5 (equivalent to 75 % if we map Netconf from $[-1; 1]$ to $[0; 1]$) based on the study performed in [16].

In Table 2, the results show that SPaC-NF yields an average accuracy higher than the other evaluated classifiers, having in average a difference in accuracy of 3.2 % with respect to the classifier in the second place (SVM classifier).

Table 2. Comparison against other sequential patterns-based classifiers.

Dataset	SVM	J48	NaiveBayes	PART	SPaC-MR	SPaC-NF
AFP	88.7	81.5	83.6	78.3	89.5	93.8
TDT	89.6	86.2	80.8	75.4	87.1	91.9
Reuter	82.5	79.3	78.2	75.7	80.3	84.7
Average	86.9	82.3	80.8	76.4	85.6	90.1

In Table 3, we show the impact of our improvements. For this, we compare our approach (SPaC-NF) that uses the Netconf measure and obtains large rules against a SPaR-based classifier (SPaC-MR) that uses the Confidence measure and obtains short rules. Additionally, for both classifiers, we evaluate the best rule ordering strategy reported (L^3) and the strategy proposed by us, based on their rule sizes (largest first) and Netconf values.

Table 3. Impact of the different improvements in a general SPaC-based classifier.

	SPaC-MR		SPaC-NF	
Dataset	L^3	Size & NF	L^3	Size & NF
AFP	89.5	90.9	92.4	93.8
TDT	87.1	88.6	90.3	91.9
Reuter	80.3	81.8	83.5	84.7
Average	85.6	87.1	88.7	90.1

To show the better performance of sequential patterns-based classifiers over the Class Association Rules (CARs) based classifiers in tasks of texts classification, in Table 4 we compare our approach against the main CAR-based classifiers. The results show how the own nature of the sequences, where the order is important, make them more appropriated than CARs for texts classification.

Table 4. Comparison against the main CAR-based Classifiers.

Dataset	CBA	CMAR	HARMONY	CAR-NF	SPaC-NF
AFP	72.8	74.2	76.3	77.5	93.8
TDT	74.2	74.3	72.4	74.8	91.9
Reuter	74.9	73.7	73.6	74.1	84.7
Average	73.9	74.1	74.1	75.5	90.1

5 Conclusions

In this paper, we have proposed some improvements to the Sequential Patterns-based Classifiers. Firstly, we introduced a new pruning strategy for computing SPaRs, using the Netconf as measure of interest. This pruning strategy allows to obtain specific rules with high Netconf. Besides, we proposed a new way for ordering the set of SPaRs using their sizes and Netconf values. The experimental results show that SPaC-NF classifier has better performance than SVM, J48, NaiveBayes, PART and SPaC-MR classifiers, over three document collections.

References

1. Quinlan, J. R.: C4.5: Programs for Machine Learning. Published by Morgan Kaufmann Publishers Inc. (1993)
2. Mannila, H., Toivonen, H., Verkamo, A.: Discovery of Frequent Episodes in Event Sequences. Data Min. Knowl. Discov. 1(3), 258–289 (1997)
3. Buddeewong, S., Kreesuradej, W.: A new association rule-based text classifier algorithm. In: Proceedings of the 17th IEEE International Conference on Tools with Artificial Intelligence, pp. 684–685 (2005)
4. Xei, F., Wu, X., Zhu, X.: Document-Specific Keyphrase Extraction Using Sequential Patterns with Wildcards. In: Proceedings of the IEEE 14th International Conference on Data Mining (2014)
5. Haleem, H., Kumar, P., Beg, S.: Novel frequent sequential patterns based probabilistic model for effective classification of web documents. In: 2014 International Conference on Computer and Communication Technology (ICCCT), pp. 361–371 (2014)
6. Srikant, R., Agrawal, R.: Mining Sequential Patterns: Generalizations and Performance Improvements. In: Proceeding in the 5th International Conference Extending Database Technology, pp. 3–17 (1996)
7. Pei, J., Han, J., Mortazavi-asl, B., Pinto, H., Chen, Q., Dayal U., Hsu, M.: PrefixSpan: Mining Sequential Patterns Efficiently by Prefix-Projected Pattern Growth. In: Proceedings of the 17th International Conference on Data Engineering, pp. 215–224 (2001)
8. Yang, Z., Wang, Y., Kitsuregawa, M.: LAPIN: effective sequential pattern mining algorithms by last position induction for dense databases. In: Kotagiri, R., Radha Krishna, P., Mohania, M., Nantajeewarawat, E. (eds.) DASFAA 2007. LNCS, vol. 4443, pp. 1020–1023. Springer, Heidelberg (2007)
9. Gouda, K., Hassaan, M., Zaki, M.J.: Prism: An effective approach for frequent sequence mining via prime-block encoding. J. Comput. Syst. Sci. 76(1), 88–102 (2010)
10. Steinbach, M., Kumar, V.: Generalizing the Notion of Confidence. In: Proceedings of the ICDM, pp. 402–409 (2005)
11. Wang, Y., Xin, Q., Coenen, F.: Hybrid Rule Ordering in Classification Association Rule Mining. Trans. MLDM 1(1), 1–15 (2008)
12. Hernández, R., Carrasco, J.A., Martínez, JFco, Hernández, J.: Combining Hybrid Rule Ordering Strategies Based on Netconf and a Novel Satisfaction Mechanism for CAR-based Classifiers. Intell. Data Anal. 18(6S), S89–S100 (2014)
13. Ahn, K.I., Kim, J.Y.: Efficient Mining of Frequent Itemsets and a Measure of Interest for Association Rule Mining. Information and Knowledge Management 3(3), 245–257 (2004)
14. Frank, E., Witten, I. H.: Generating Accurate Rule Sets Without Global Optimization. In: Proceedings of the 15th International Conference on Machine Learning, pp. 144–151 (1998)
15. Cortes, C., Vapnik, V.: Support-Vector Networks. Mach. Learn. 20(3), 273–297 (1995)
16. Hernández, R., Carrasco, J.A., Martínez, JFco, Hernández, J.: CAR-NF: A classifier based on specific rules with high netconf. Intell. Data Anal. 16(1), 49–68 (2012)

A Mixed Learning Strategy for Finding Typical Testors in Large Datasets

Víctor Iván González-Guevara[1], Salvador Godoy-Calderon[1],
Eduardo Alba-Cabrera[2(✉)], and Julio Ibarra-Fiallo[2]

[1] Instituto Politécnico Nacional, Centro de Investigación en Computación (CIC),
Av. Luis Enrique Erro S/N, Unidad Profesional Adolfo López Mateos, Zacatenco,
Delegación Gustavo A. Madero, 07738 Ciudad de Mexico, Mexico
{vgonzalez,sgodoyc}@cic.ipn.mx
[2] Colegio de Ciencias e Ingenierías, Departamento de Matemáticas, Universidad San
Francisco de Quito (USFQ), Diego de Robles y Vía Interoceanica, Quito, Ecuador
{ealba,jibarra}@usfq.edu.ec
http://www.springer.com/lncs

Abstract. This paper presents a mixed, global and local, learning strategy for finding typical testors in large datasets. The goal of the proposed strategy is to allow any search algorithm to achieve the most significant reduction possible in the search space of a typical testor-finding problem. The strategy is based on a trivial classifier which partitions the search space into four distinct classes and allows the assessment of each feature subset within it. Each class is handled by slightly different learning actions, and induces a different reduction in the search-space of a problem. Any typical testor-finding algorithm, whether deterministic or metaheuristc, can be adapted to incorporate the proposed strategy and can take advantage of the learned information in diverse manners.

Keywords: Feature selection · Testor theory · Algorithms

1 Introduction

Feature Selection is a well known branch of Pattern Recognition responsible for identifying those features, describing objects under study, that provide relevant information for classification purposes. Testor Theory is one of the common tools used for such task. During the last decade several algorithms have been designed for finding the set of all typical testors in a dataset [5,7,9]. Unfortunately, the time complexity of computing all typical testors has an exponential growth with respect to the number of features describing objects. Also, recent research has unveiled different elements that also have effect over the complexity of that problem, such as the number of rows in the initial basic matrix, the density

Mexican authors wish to thank CONACyT and SIP-IPN for their support of this research, particularly through grant SIP-20151393. Also, Ecuatorian authors wish to thank the financial support received from USFQ-Small Grants.

© Springer International Publishing Switzerland 2015
A. Pardo and J. Kittler (Eds.): CIARP 2015, LNCS 9423, pp. 716–723, 2015.
DOI: 10.1007/978-3-319-25751-8_86

of that matrix, and the number of typical testors within it or the underlying structure of the basic matrix $Agregarcitaaartculo4delrevisorMemo$. All those factors severely complicate finding typical testors in large datasets. Moreover, some of the empirical results found in carefully designed benchmarks like the one on [2], add up to the intuition that no single typical testor-finding algorithm can be found to have the best possible behavior for any given problem. This kind of *No-Free-Lunch* intuition, taken from the field of evolutionary and bio-inspired algorithms, encourages researching techniques that allow increased algorithm performance and solving the problem of finding typical testors in large datasets with the least possible computational cost.

With that goal in mind, this paper proposes a mixed learning strategy designed to allow typical testor-finding algorithms to reduce the search space of any problem. The proposed strategy will be responsible for identifying and storing the pertinent local and global information for the stated purpose, while the underlying typical testor-finding algorithm (a search algorithm) decides when and how it makes use of the learned information.

2   Theoretical Framework

Several research papers have more than exhaustively presented the fundamental definitions of Testor Theory. Here we quickly outline the context for our particular research, and advise the reader who requires a thorough review of those concepts to refer to [4] and [6].

All known typical testor-finding algorithms have a comparison matrix as input. That matrix, called Basic Matrix, contains the summary information about the comparison of all objects belonging to different classes within a given supervision sample. When the original supervision sample is a partition, and all comparisons have been evaluated with a boolean difference function, then the basic matrix (BM) is binary and its rows conform a *Sperner* family. Within such matrix, a *Testor* is defined as a subset τ of columns (or features) such that no zero-row can be found in $BM|_\tau$ (called the τ-restricted matrix). Also, a *Typical Testor* is defined as an irreducible testor (i.e. a testor such that none of its subsets is a testor). As a consequence of its irreducibility, typical testors are identified by the property that each feature in $BM|_\tau$ has at least one *Typical Row*, where the corresponding column contains a 1, and all other columns in that row contain a 0.

In practical terms, typical testors are characterized by being the only feature subsets that fulfill the two following conditions:

1. $BM|_\tau$ has no zero-rows (so τ is a testor)
2. Each column in $BM|_\tau$ has at least one typical row (so τ is typical)

Largely, the complexity of finding typical testors in big matrices lies in the analysis of restricted matrices in search for the fulfillment of both conditions. In order to minimize that effort, and as the basis for our proposed learning strategy we briefly introduce the following concepts:

2.1   Masks and Assessment Indices

The following definitions are introduced in [5]:
Let B be a basic matrix, and let τ be any feature subset in B, then

Definition 1. *The Acceptance Mask of τ (am(τ)) is a binary tuple in which the ith element is 1 if the ith row in $B|_\tau$ has at least a 1 in the columns of features in τ, and 0 otherwise.*

Definition 2. *The Compatibility Mask of τ (cm(τ)) is a binary tuple in which the ith element is 1 if the ith row in $B|_\tau$ has only a 1 in the column of a feature in τ and 0 otherwise.*

To the previous definitions, we add the following,

Definition 3. *The Typicity Mask of τ (tm(τ)) is an integer tuple in which the ith element is the number of typical rows that feature x_i has in $B|_\tau$.*

The defined masks allow the characterization of all feature subsets, either as a Testor or as a Typical. For that task we define the following indexes:

Definition 4. *The Testor Error index of subset τ in B ($e_T(\tau)$), is the number of zero rows in $B|_\tau$ (i.e. the number of zero entries in am(τ)).*

Definition 5. *The Typical Error index of subset τ in B ($e_{Ty}(\tau)$), is the number of features in τ that do not have at least one typical row in $B|_\tau$ (i.e. the number of zero entries in tm(τ)).*

For algorithmic purposes, both error indexes are interpreted as the number of changes a particular feature subset has to undergo in order to become a testor or a typical testor.

2.2   The Classifier

By using the error indexes defined in previous subsection we define a trivial classifier that effectively partitions the search space (i.e. the power set of all feature subsets) in four classes: *Testors*, *Typicals*, *TypicalTestors*, and *Incompatibles* (See Fig.1).

The first three classes have already been presented: *Testors*, *Typicals* and *Typical Testors* are characterized by the conditions discussed in section 2. *Incompatibles*, on the other hand, are those feature subsets whose restricted matrix contains one or more zero-rows, and where not all features have a typical row.

Often, the reason why a particular feature fails to have a typical row, is because another feature, in the same subset, damages its potential typical rows by having a 1 in the same row. We call that condition an *incompatibility* between those two features, and have identified it as one of the most important phenomena to be learned. When, during the search for typical testors, an incompatibility is found within a feature subset, the search algorithm can safely ignore the analysis of any other feature subset containing the identified pair of incompatible features.

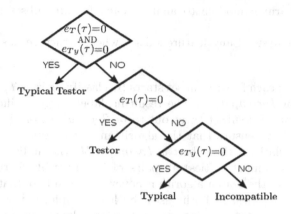

Fig. 1. The feature subset classifier

3   Learning Strategy

By *learning* we mean the process by which any piece of information (knowledge), relevant for the solution of a problem, is identified and stored to be used later. So, as stated before, the goal of the proposed strategy is to provide some additional knowledge to enable any typical testor-finding algorithm for a more efficient search process.

All typical testor-finding algorithms proceed iteratively by analyzing one or more feature subsets from the search space on each iteration, and then deciding which other elements in the search space are to be, or not to be analyzed next. This decision is made by a set of rules that follow a pre-defined order in which the search space is to be traversed (even a random order). Deterministic algorithms such as those in [5, 7, 9] generally analyze one subset at a time, while metaheuristic algorithms like those in [1, 3, 8] tend to analyze more than one subset on each iteration.

When a typical testor-finiding algorithm is adapted to use this strategy, the learning module learns all that can be learned from each feature subset the search algorithm analyzes. The resulting knowledge can then be used as a form of *taboo list* that allows the algorithm to skip the analysis of some subsets with the guarantee that no typical testor is going to be missed by the overall process. The specific way in which the proposed learning strategy can be adapted to any algorithm is briefly described in the next subsection.

3.1   Adapting the Strategy

Regardless of the specific order that a typical testor-finding algorithm follows, there are only two specific modifications that it needs to undergo in order to adapt the proposed learning strategy:

1. Allow the learning module to analyze each feature subset the algorithm selects,
2. Avoid the analysis of any feature subset whose structure has already been learned,

The analysis of each feature subset starts by classifying it as *Testor*, *Typical*, *TypicalTestor* or *Incompatible*. The resulting label triggers different learning actions. If the analyzed subset turns out to be *TypicalTestor* the whole subset is learned globally to ensure that the algorithm never tests any of its subsets or supersets. Similarly, if the subset is *Incompatible* (i.e. it has zero-rows and includes feature incompatibilities) all pairs of incompatible features are globally learned so that the search algorithm never tests a subset that includes any of those incompatibilities. In both cases the learned information is considered global in the sense that it remains constant during the whole run of the search algorithm. Locally learned information, on the other hand, only stores information that serve as a reference point for deciding which subsets not to analyze. This kind of knowledge is updated as the algorithm runs. Such is the case for subsets labeled as *Testor* or as *Typical* which have one important property in common: either their *Testor Error index*, or their *Typical Error index* evaluates to zero. By following that line of reason, it quickly becomes clear that finding a *Testor* immediately rules out the analysis of any of its supersets, while finding a *Typical* rules out the analysis of any of its subsets.

Any known typical testor-finding algorithm can be adapted to incorporate the proposed strategy. Figure 3 presents a tiny example where the proposed learning strategy is used to analyze several feature subsets and generate their descendants.

4   Pseudo-Code and Sample Experiments

In this section we present the algorithmic form of the proposed strategy as well as some experiments performed with it.

4.1   Pseudo-Code

Let B be a basic matrix with columns labeled with the elements of set R (a complete feature set). We call *descendants* of τ any feature subset within the search space whose analysis is not ruled out after analyzing τ. Also, let $Incomp(\tau)$ be a procedure that finds and returns all pairwise incompatibilities in subset τ. Figure 2 outlines the proposed learning strategy in the form of a function that receives a $\tau \subset R$ as input, and returns its filtered descendants. Two auxiliary functions were used for clearly stating the pseudocode in Figure 2, those functions are:

1. *Classify*(): Receives a feature subset as input, and outputs the corresponding class label (See Figure 1).
2. *FilterWithGlobalLearning*(): Receives a family of feature subsets as input, and uses any previously stored global learning information to filter the set.

Learning Strategy.

Input: A feature subset τ
 Output: The filtered descendants of τ

label $= Classify(\tau)$
Case label of
      Testor do
          Store: τ and $e_{Ty}(\tau)$
          Descendants $= \{\sigma \subset \tau \mid e_{Ty}(\sigma) < e_{Ty}(\tau)\}$
      Typical do
          Store: τ and $e_T(\tau)$
          Descendants $= \{\sigma \supset \tau \mid e_{Ty}(\sigma) = 0 \ \wedge \ e_T(\sigma) < e_T(\tau)\}$
      Typical Testor do
          Store: τ
          Descendants $= \{\sigma \in \wp(R) \mid \sigma \not\subseteq \tau \ \wedge \ \sigma \not\supseteq \tau)\}$
      Incompatible do
          Store: τ, $e_T(\tau)$, $e_{Ty}(\tau)$, and $Incomp(\tau)$
          Descendants $= \{\sigma \in \wp(R) \mid e_T(\sigma) \leq e_T(\tau) \}$
   endCase
Descendants $= FilterWithGlobalLearning(\text{Descendants})$

Fig. 2. Pseudocode for the proposed learning strategy

In order to ilustrate the mechanics of the learning strategy, Table 1 shows a tiny basic matrix (called the Ms matrix). Some feature subsets from the Ms matrix are analyzed following the the pseudo-code in Figure 1. The results are summarized in Table 2.

Table 1. The Ms matrix used for illustrating the learning strategy

a	b	c	d	e	f
1	0	0	0	1	0
1	1	0	0	0	1
0	0	1	0	0	1
1	0	0	1	0	1

4.2 Sample Experiments

We adapted the well-known BR-algorithm [5] to use the proposed learning strategy, and compared the number of tested subsets (labeled as $Hits$) and the execution time between the original algorithm and the adapted one. Input matrices for these experiments were designed by applying the ϕ, θ, and γ operators, over the Ms matrix, following the specifications and method described in [2]. Table 3 summarizes the experiments performed showing the number of rows, columns and typical testors ($TTestors$) of each input matrix.

Table 2. Some examples of four different cases

τ	$e_T(\tau), e_{Ty}(\tau)$	Label	Learning	Descendants
$\tau_1 = \{a,c,e\}$	$e_T(\tau_1) = 0$ $e_{Ty}(\tau_1) = 1$	Testor	$[\{a,c,e\},1]$	$\{\{a,c\}\}$
$\tau_2 = \{b,c\}$	$e_T(\tau_2) = 2$ $e_{Ty}(\tau_2) = 0$	Typical	$[\{b,c\},2]$	$\{\{b,c,d\},\{b,c,e\},\{b,c,d,e\},\{b,c,d,f\}\}$
$\tau_3 = \{a,f\}$	$e_T(\tau_3) = 0$ $e_{Ty}(\tau_3) = 0$	Typical Testor	$[\{a,f\}]$	$\{\{b\},\{c\},\{d\},\{e\},\{a,b\},\{a,c\},\{a,d\},$ $\{a,e\},\{b,c\},\{b,d\},\{b,e\},\{b,f\},\{c,d\},$ $\{c,e\},\{c,f\},\{d,e\},\{d,f\},\{e,f\},\{a,b,c\},$ $\{a,b,d\},\{a,b,e\},\{a,c,d\},\{a,c,e\},$ $\{a,d,e\},\{b,c,d\},\{b,c,e\},\{b,c,f\},$ $\{b,d,e\},\{b,d,f\},\{b,e,f\},\{c,d,e\},$ $\{c,d,f\},\{c,e,f\},\{d,e,f\},\{a,b,c,d\},$ $\{a,b,c,e\},\{a,b,d,e\},\{a,c,d,e\},$ $\{b,c,d,e\},\{b,c,d,f\},\{b,c,e,f\},$ $\{b,d,e,f\},\{c,d,e,f\},\{a,b,c,d,e\},$ $\{b,c,d,e,f\}\}$
$\tau_4 = \{b,c,d,f\}$	$e_T(\tau_4) = 1$ $e_{Ty}(\tau_4) = 4$	Incompatible	$[\{b,c,d,f\},1,4$ $(b,f),(c,f),(d,f)]$	$\{\{a,c\},\{a,f\},\{e,f\},\{a,b,c\},\{a,c,d\},$ $\{a,c,e\},\{a,e,f\},\{a,b,c,d\},\{a,b,c,e\},$ $\{a,c,d,e\},\{b,c,d,e\},\{a,b,c,d,e\}\}$

Table 3. Performance of the adapted BR-algorithm

Matrix	Rows	Cols	TTestors	Original BR		Adapted BR	
				Hits	Time	Hits	Time
Id_5	5	5	1	16	0.001	16	0.001
Id_{15}	15	15	1	16384	1.582	16384	1.580
$\phi^2(Ms)$	4	12	28	180	0.002	68	0.001
$\phi^3(Ms)$	4	18	108	2361	0.03	222	0.006
$\theta^2(Ms)$	16	12	8	617	0.011	216	0.013
$\theta^3(Ms)$	64	18	12	30979	3.986	4196	1.157
$\gamma^2(Ms)$	8	12	16	352	0.007	252	0.037
$\gamma^3(Ms)$	16	24	256	166252	152.617	111132	22.305

As it can be seen, the proposed strategy cannot improve the search process in the case of identity matrices. However, the number of hits is notoriously reduced in all other cases, effectively reducing the problem's search space. Also note that the execution time is not always reduced proportionally, since the internal structure of the input matrix can sometimes severely complicate the calculation of masks and error indices.

5 Conclusions

A general mixed learning strategy for finding typical testors in large datasets was presented. The proposed strategy uses both globally and locally learned information to calculate the descendants of the currently analyzed feature subset, effectively reducing the search space for any problem. The host search algorithm however, must decide the order in which the search space is analyzed, as well as the size of its population. The interaction and dependence between the host algorithm and the learning module determines, for the most part, the performance yield by any experiment. Since there are no current means for predicting the optimum order for traversing a search space or for maximizing the use of learned information, the intuition that no single algorithm can be found to optimally solve any problem instance is strengthened.

Evidently the problem of finding typical testors still stands as not solvable in polynomial time; however, the proposed strategy is enough to cut out from the analysis all feature subsets that neither have real possibilities of being typical testors, nor contribute to the rest of the search process.

References

1. Alba-Cabrera, E., Santana, R., Ochoa-Rodriguez, A., Lazo-Corts, M.: Finding typical testors by using an evolutionary strategy. In: Proceedings of the 5th Ibero American Symposium on Pattern Recognition, p. 267 (2000)
2. Alba-Cabrera, E., Ibarra-Fiallo, J., Godoy-Calderon, S.: A theoretical and practical framework for assessing the computational behavior of typical testor-finding algorithms. In: Ruiz-Shulcloper, J., Sanniti di Baja, G. (eds.) CIARP 2013, Part I. LNCS, vol. 8258, pp. 351–358. Springer, Heidelberg (2013)
3. Diaz-Sanchez, G., Piza-Davila, I., Sanchez-Diaz, G., Mora-Gonzalez, M., Reyes-Cardenas, O., Cardenas-Tristan, A., Aguirre-Salado, C.: Typical testors generation based on an evolutionary algorithm. In: Yin, H., Wang, W., Rayward-Smith, V. (eds.) IDEAL 2011. LNCS, vol. 6936, pp. 58–65. Springer, Heidelberg (2011)
4. Lazo-Cortés, M., Ruiz-Shulcloper, J., Alba-Cabrera, E.: An overview of the evolution of the concept of testor. Pattern Recognition 34(4), 753–762 (2001)
5. Lias-Rodríguez, A., Pons-Porrata, A.: BR: a new method for computing all typical testors. In: Bayro-Corrochano, E., Eklundh, J.-O. (eds.) CIARP 2009. LNCS, vol. 5856, pp. 433–440. Springer, Heidelberg (2009)
6. Martnez-Trinidad, J.F., Guzmán-Arenas, A.: The logical combinatorial approach to pattern recognition, an overview through selected works. Pattern Recognition 34(4), 741–751 (2001)
7. Sanchez-Diaz, G., Lazo-Cortes, M., Piza-Davila, I.: A fast implementation for the typical testor property identification based on an accumulative binary tuple. International Journal of Computational Intelligence Systems 5(6), 1025–1039 (2012)
8. Sanchez-Diaz, G., Diaz-Sanchez, G., Mora-Gonzalez, M., Piza-Davila, I., Aguirre-Salado, C., Huerta-Cuellar, G., Reyes-Cardenas, O., Cardenas-Tristan, A.: An evolutionary algorithm with acceleration operator to generate a subset of typical testors. Pattern Recognition Letters 41, 34–42 (2014)
9. Santiesteban-Alganza, Y., Pons-Porrata, A.: LEX: A new algorithm for calculating typical testors. Revista Ciencias Matematicas 21(1), 85–95 (2003)

A Bag Oversampling Approach for Class Imbalance in Multiple Instance Learning

Carlos Mera[1]($\boxtimes$), Jose Arrieta[1], Mauricio Orozco-Alzate[2], and John Branch[1]

[1] Universidad Nacional de Colombia, Sede Medellín, Colombia
{camerab,jmarrietar,jwbranch}@unal.edu.co
[2] Universidad Nacional de Colombia, Sede Manizales, Colombia
morozcoa@unal.edu.co

Abstract. Multiple Instance Learning (MIL) is a relatively new learning paradigm which allows to train a classifier with weakly labelled data. In spite that the community has been developing different methods to learn from this kind of data, there is little discussion on how to proceed when there is an imbalanced representation of the classes. The class imbalance problem in MIL is more complex compared with their counterpart in single-instance learning because it may occur at instance and/or bag level, or at both. Here, we propose an oversampling approach at bag level in order to improve the representation of the minority class. Experiments in nine benchmark data sets are conducted to evaluate the proposed approach.

Keywords: Multiple instance learning · Class imbalance · Oversampling · Bag oversampling

1 Introduction

In pattern recognition, a supervised classifier is trained to assign a class label to an object based on its feature vector. In this approach, also known as Single-Instance Learning (SIL), each object is represented by a single feature vector which has a unique class label associated to it. However, in many applications, this representation is insufficient to describe complex objects (e.g. a forest) consisting of different parts (e.g trees, mountains, sky and lake). In such applications, the parts of the objects are important to differentiate among them (e.g. to discriminate between a forest and a beach). A relatively new learning paradigm named Multiple-Instance Learning (MIL) allows to describe a complex object (termed a *bag*) using multiple feature vectors (termed *instances*). Based on it, a learning algorithm is trained on a set of bags which can potentially preserve more information of the objects, compared with a single feature vector representation [1].

The authors would like to thank *Fondo de Movilidad Académica* from Facultad de Minas at Universidad Nacional de Colombia, Sede Medellín.

A. Pardo and J. Kittler (Eds.): CIARP 2015, LNCS 9423, pp. 724–731, 2015.
DOI: 10.1007/978-3-319-25751-8_87

MIL problems are often considered as two-class ones, where bags in the *positive* class are those containing the target concept to be recognized, while bags in the *negative* class do not contain it. In the above-mentioned example, positive bags correspond to images of forests and negative bags could be images of beaches, cities and deserts. The standard assumption claims that positive bags contain at least one positive instance (the target concept), whereas negative bags contain only negative (or background) instances. Nevertheless, other assumptions might be considered [7].

An important issue in SIL is the class imbalance problem [9]. This is related with the unequal representation of classes in a training data set. Several studies have shown that, with imbalanced training data sets, Bayesian decision algorithms give strongly biased solutions towards the majority class (the less important in most applications), getting poor performance in the minority one (typically, the most important one) [12]. In MIL, the problem of class imbalance also appears; however, it is more complex because the imbalance can occur at either instance or bag levels, or at both [13]. As in SIL, the majority class influences MIL algorithms in order to build decision boundaries biased in favor of this. Despite the importance of the problem in pattern recognition applications, there is still a little discussion about it. Then, in this paper we explain in short the imbalance problem and propose an oversampling approach to balance MIL data sets at bag level.

2   Related Work

2.1   Multiple Instance Learning

MIL, as defined by Dietterich et al. [6], allows us to represent complex objects through a collection (named *bag*) of feature vectors (named *instances*). A mutiple instance (MI) data set, in a two-class problem, has the form $B = \{(B_1, y_1), \ldots, (B_N, y_N)\}$ where, $y_i \in \Omega = \{+1, -1\}$ is the label for the bag $B_i = \{\mathbf{x}_{i1}, \ldots, \mathbf{x}_{in_i}\} \in \mathbb{R}^\chi$, containing n_i instances from the instance space χ. This way, the goal of MIL algorithms is to learn a mapping function $F(B) : \mathbb{R}^\chi \to \Omega$. This function returns a bag label by classifying its instances and combining their hidden labels (y_{ij}) using, for example, the noisy-or rule [7],

$$F(B_i) = \frac{p(y = 1|B_i)}{p(y = -1|B_i)} = \frac{1 - \prod_{j=1}^{n_i}(1 - p(y_{ij} = 1|\mathbf{x}_{ij}))}{\prod_{j=1}^{n_i}(p(y_{ij} = -1|\mathbf{x}_{ij}))} \tag{1}$$

which represents the standard assumption that a bag is positive if and only if at least one of the instances is positive.

Several MIL algorithms have been developed over the past years. One of the earliest works is Axis-Parallel Rectangles (APR) [6]. This approach tries to isolate the target concept by building an hyper-rectangle in the instance space χ, which only contains instances from positive bags. Another related approach, named Diverse Density (DD) [11], aims to find the most positive point in the input space with the maximum diverse density. Few years later, motivated by the high computation requirements of the DD algorithm, Zhang & Goldman proposed the EM-DD algorithm [21], which uses the Expectation Maximization (EM) approach to speed up the optimization process of the DD algorithm. Other methods try to model the target concept through density models, and then, they use a discriminative approach to separate the concept and background instances. Two examples of these approaches are MI-SVM [2] and MIL-Boost [18]. In contrast, other authors have proposed to embed each bag into a new feature space using a representative set of instances selected from the training bags and then learn a single-instance classifier in this new feature space; a salient example of these embeddings is MILES [4]. For a more detailed description of these and other approaches, readers can refer to [1,7].

2.2   The Class Imbalance Problem

In SIL, the class imbalance problem occurs when the samples of one class (the majority) outnumber the samples of the other class (the minority). Bayesian decision algorithms optimize a decision rule by minimizing the overall risk in the classification. In other words, they look for a function $f(\mathbf{x})$ such that:

$$f(\mathbf{x}) = \arg \min_{\omega_k \in \Omega} \sum_{k=1}^{C} L_{kj} p(\mathbf{x}|\omega_k) P(\omega_k) \tag{2}$$

where, L_{kj} is the loss (or cost) function of confusing ω_j with ω_k, $p(\mathbf{x}|\omega_k)$ is the conditional probability and $P(\omega_k)$ is the *prior* probability for the class ω_k. When it is assumed that costs of misclassifications are equal for all classes, the optimal decision rule is to select the class with the highest *posterior* probability, as shown in (3) for a two-class problem.

$$f(\mathbf{x}) = \begin{cases} 1, & \frac{p(\mathbf{x}|y=1)}{p(\mathbf{x}|y=-1)} > \frac{P(y=-1)}{P(y=1)} \\ -1, & \text{otherwise} \end{cases} \tag{3}$$

Accordingly, learning algorithms trained with imbalanced data sets draw decision boundaries biased in favor of the majority class. As a result, samples from the majority class are classified with high precision, while samples from the minority class (usually the most important one) tend to be misclassified.

Several approaches have been proposed to face the class imbalance problem in SIL [9,14]. Among them, sampling algorithms to change the class distributions [3], cost-sensitive learning algorithms [17], one-class learning algorithms [10] and approaches based on classifier ensembles [8]. However, these approaches can not be directly applied to MIL data sets because they are designed to work on individual instances rather than on bags.

2.3   The Class Imbalance Problem in MIL

The MIL paradigm has been attracting attention in the pattern recognition community because it can be applied in practical problems where the training data sets are weakly labelled. However, in many real-world problems the training samples are imbalanced, e.g. automatic inspection involves class imbalance between defects (the minority class) and non-defects (the majority class); similarly, in face recognition for video surveillance applications, the same drawback appears since there are few samples of the target (positive) class compared with the background (the negative one).

As in SIL, MIL algorithms could be biased for the majority class. However in MIL the problem is more complex because the imbalance can be at instance level, bag level, or both [13,20]. Following the taxonomy presented in [1], MIL algorithms fall in one of the following paradigms: Instance-Space (IS) paradigm, in which the discriminative learning process occurs at the instance-level; the Bag-Space (BS) paradigm, where each bag is treated has a whole entity and the learning process discriminates between entire bags; and finally, the Embedded-Space (ES) paradigm, where each bag is mapped into a single feature vector that summarizes the relevant information about the whole bag, so a classifier is learned in the new embedded space.

Based on that, if the imbalance is present at the instance level, MIL algorithms which fall in the IS paradigm will be biased by the negative class. It happens because the number of real positive instances in positive bags are few compared with the negative ones in both, positive and negative bags. Therefore, discriminative algorithms which build a decision boundary based on the Bayesian framework, will be biased in favor of the negative class. On the other hand, algorithms in the ES paradigm could be skewed by the imbalance if the function used to map a bag into a single feature vector is prone to be affected by the imbalance rate. An example is the average mapping function, which excludes the relevant information in positive bags, if the number of positive instances in the bag is very low compared with the negative ones. Similarly, if the imbalance is present at bag level, MIL algorithms which fall in the BS paradigm will also be biased for the negative class.

In the literature there is a little discussion about this problem in MIL. Wang et al. presented in [19] a cost-sensitive approach based on AdaBoost where different costs are considered for the misclassification of bags. The same authors proposed in [20] an oversampling approach which uses SMOTE [3] to increase the number of both, instances and bags in the positive class. However, this approach does not care whether the instances used for the oversampling are negative instances in positive bags, which could increase the ambiguity in the data set. Finally, authors in [13] proposed an instance level strategy to improve the representation of the positive class by oversampling true positive instances and undersampling the negative ones.

3   An Oversampling Approach for Bags

As done in [13], we take advantage of the standard MIL assumption and use Kernel Density Estimation (KDE) [15] to model the negative population in order to look for the most positive instances in positive bags. In this way, if instances in negative bags $\{x_i\} \in B^-$ are i.i.d. data drawn from an unknown density $p(x|B^-)$, it can be estimated by KDE according to:

$$\hat{p}\left(x|B^-\right) = \frac{1}{r^- \, h^d} \sum_{i=1}^{r^-} k\left(\frac{x - x_i}{h}\right) \tag{4}$$

where h is a tunable smoothing parameter, d is the dimensionality of x, $k(\cdot)$ is the kernel of the estimator, and r^- is the number of negative instances of all negative bags. Here, we take the typical choice of using a Gaussian kernel.

If we use $\hat{p}\left(x|B^-\right)$ as a quantitative measure of the degree of negativity for each instance, then we can claim that the farther x is away from B^-, the higher is the probability that x is positive according to B^-. Similarly, we assume that the target concept, responsible for the positive label, in a positive bag is represented by the most positive instances, i.e. the farthest instance from the model of the negative population. Once the most positive instances have been identified, we can use SMOTE to create new synthetic positive instances and then create new positive bags in order to strength the target concept in the training data set. As a result, the number of positive instances increases as well as the number of positive bags. Algorithm 1 shows the details of the proposed approach.

Algorithm 1. Informative_Bag_SMOTE(P, N)

1:   P: average instances per bag
2:   N: number of synthetic bags to be generated
3:   **for** $i = 1$ to N **do**
4:      $B_{new}^i \leftarrow$ Create a new empty bag with positive label
5:
6:      ▷ Generate a new positive instance for B_{new}^i:
7:      $(B_1^+, B_2^+) \leftarrow$ select 2 positive bags from the training data set at random
8:      $x_{1j}^+ \leftarrow \arg\min_{j=1,\dots,n_i} \hat{p}(x_{1j}|B^-)$ ▷ Select the most positive instance in B_1^+
9:      $x_{2j}^+ \leftarrow \arg\min_{j=1,\dots,n_i} \hat{p}(x_{2j}|B^-)$ ▷ Select the most positive instance in B_2^+
10:     $x_{i1} \leftarrow x_{1j}^+ + (x_{2j}^+ - x_{1j}^+) * \alpha$, where $\alpha \in [0,1]$ at random
11:     $Append(x_{i1}, B_{new}^i)$
12:
13:     ▷ Generate new negative instances for B_{new}^i:
14:     $x_{1j}^- \leftarrow \arg\max_{j=1,\dots,n_i} \hat{p}(x_{1j}|B^-)$ ▷ Select the most negative instance in B_1^+
15:     **for** $j = 2$ to P **do**
16:        $x_{2j}^- \leftarrow$ get a negative instance from B_2^+ at random
17:        $x_{ij} \leftarrow x_{1j}^- + (x_{2j}^- - x_{1j}^-) * \alpha$, where $\alpha \in [0,1]$ at random
18:        $Append(x_{ij}, B_{new}^i)$
19:     **end for**
20: **end for**

This approach is different from the Bag_SMOTE algorithm presented in [20] because ours makes an informative oversampling always considering the most positive instances in positive bags. Therefore, our approach creates synthetic bags containing synthetic positive instances, which helps to reinforce the target concept in the data set.

4   Experiments and Discussion

We use nine standard MIL benchmark data sets [5] to test our method. Table 1 lists the data sets and their characteristics. We choose these data sets because they are well known in the MIL literature, come from diverse pattern recognition applications, and have different rates of imbalance at bag level.

Adopting a standard evaluation procedure, we repeat the experimental process by 5 runs with different random selected training and testing sets using 10-fold cross-validation. We report the area under the receiver-operating curve (AUC) and G-Mean, which are standard measures in class imbalance problems [9]. Additionally, we compare different state-of-the-art MIL algorithms, however, we only report the one with the best average results in the original dataset, i.e. before applying the resampling techniques. Afterwards, we use it for comparison. A list of the used algorithms, together with their parameters, is below. All of them are available from the MIL toolbox [16].

- APR with a threshold $t = 0.1$
- Citation k-NN with $k = 3$ (named C-kNN)
- mi-SVM with a radial kernel and a regularization parameter $C = 10$
- MILBoost with 100 reweighting rounds

The average of the AUC performances and the average of the G-Mean are shown in Table 2. Each column reports the measure for each data set. The MIL algorithm used for the classification for each data set appears in brackets under its name. Through the rows, the table is split into two blocks: in the first block we report the results for the AUC measure and, in the second block, we report the results for the G-Mean. Each block is subdivided in four parts: the first part (named Original) shows the performance measures achieved by MIL classifiers with the original version of the data sets. The second part (named **B-Bags***) shows the performance measures for the MIL algorithms after oversampling the positive bags with the approach proposed in this paper. The third part (named Bag-SMOTE) shows the performance of the bag oversampling approach presented in [20]. The fourth one (named B-Instances) shows the performance for the MIL algorithms after resampling using the instance approach in [13].

Table 1. Details of standard MIL benchmark data sets used in the experiments

Data set	Size	Features	Positive Bags	Negative Bags	Positive Instances	Negative Instances	%Minority Bags
Musk2	6598	166	39	63	1017	5581	38,20
Muta2	2132	7	13	29	660	1472	30,95
Bird (BRCR)	10232	38	197	351	4759	5473	35,95
Bird (WIWR)	10232	38	109	439	1824	8408	19,89
Web1	2212	5863	17	58	488	1724	22,66
Web2	2219	6519	18	57	499	1720	22,66
Corel(African)	7947	9	100	1900	484	7463	5,00
Corel(Horses)	7947	9	100	1900	389	7558	5,00
Corel(Cars)	7947	9	100	1900	493	7454	5,00

Table 2. Performance Results for the AUC(x100) and the G-Mean(x100). Best results are highlighted in boldface and the proposed method is indicated with the symbol ∗

	Musk2	Muta2	Bird (BRCR)	Bird (WIWR)	Web1	Web2	Corel (African)	Corel (Horses)	Corel (Cars)
	[APR]	[mi-SVM]	[MILBoost]	[C-kNN]	[mi-SVM]	[MILBoost]	[C-kNN]	[C-kNN]	[C-kNN]
AUC									
Original	84,40	71,21	75,18	**94,52**	83,62	**75,77**	90,60	95,94	82,83
B-Bags*	81,00	**73,52**	**75,87**	94,34	79,23	69,46	86,04	**97,10**	**86,56**
Bag-SMOTE	84,39	67,49	74,75	94,05	84,25	65,53	89,87	95,96	82,66
B-Instances	**85,36**	73,22	75,02	94,06	**84,56**	74,66	85,73	93,55	81,15
G-Mean									
Original	84,00	61,33	66,12	84,55	71,08	**64,23**	56,09	87,00	60,31
B-Bags*	80,30	**68,71**	**68,58**	88,09	71,69	61,12	**76,18**	**92,29**	**77,92**
Bag-SMOTE	83,82	57,74	68,24	86,22	73,94	50,38	71,23	90,56	67,60
B-Instances	**84,90**	56,75	68,38	**89,89**	**74,44**	60,12	49,84	78,30	58,30

Several observations can be made from this table. First, in most datasets the use of a resampling technique (whether at bag level or at instance level) improves the performance achieved by the algorithms in one of the measures. It empirically confirms that MIL algorithms are prone to be affected by the class imbalance problem, therefore, the use of resampling techniques contributes in the increase of the algorithm's performances. Second, the proposed method in this paper (B-Bags) achieved better performance in four of the datasets. Furthermore, it gets better results, for the G-Mean measure, when the imbalance rate between the positive and negative class is high, as in Corel datasets. Finally, comparing B-Bags (our approach) with Bag-SMOTE, we can see that B-Bags gets better performance in most data sets. It can be explained because our approach has a higher probability of generating at least one positive instance in synthetic bags, compared with Bag-SMOTE, which only generates new synthetic instances without taking care of replicating the true positive ones.

5   Conclusions

In this paper an informative bag oversampling approach for MIL data sets has been proposed. This approach uses a model of the negative population in order to find the most positive instances in the minority class (the positive one). In contrast to other approaches, the oversampling is conducted for those most positive instances, therefore, the new synthetic bags help to strength the target concept in the positive class. Additionally, experiments empirically confirm that MIL algorithms are prone to be affected by the class imbalance problem, therefore, the use of resampling techniques can help to increase the prediction performance of the minority class. Our future work will be conducted in order to design a resampling approach that includes a bag undersampling approach in order to reduce both, the ambiguity among bags and the size of the data set.

References

1. Amores, J.: Multiple Instance Classification: Review, taxonomy and comparative study. Artif. Intell. **201**, 81–105 (2013)
2. Andrews, S., Tsochantaridis, I., Hofmann, T.: Support vector machines for Multiple-Instance Learning. In: Adv. Neural Inf. Process. Syst. App., vol. 15, pp. 561–568. MIT Press (2002)
3. Chawla, N.V., Bowyer, K.W., Hall, L.O., Kegelmeyer, W.P.: SMOTE: synthetic minority over-sampling technique. J. Artif. Intell. Res. **16**(1), 321–357 (2002)
4. Chen, Y., Bi, J., Wang, J.: MILES: Multiple-Instance Learning via embedded instance selection. IEEE Trans. Pattern Anal. Mach. Intell. **28**(12), 1931–1947 (2006)
5. Cheplygina, V., Sørensen, L., Tax, D.M.J., Pedersen, J.H., Loog, M., de Bruijne, M.: Classification of COPD with Multiple Instance Learning. In: International Conference on Pattern Recognition, pp. 1508–1513 (2014)
6. Dietterich, T.G., Lathrop, R.H., Lozano-Pérez, T.: Solving the Multiple Instance problem with axis-parallel rectangles. Artif. Intell. **89**(1–2), 31–71 (1997)
7. Foulds, J., Frank, E.: A review of Multi-Instance Learning assumptions. Knowl. Eng. Rev. **25**(1), 1–25 (2010)
8. Guo, H., Viktor, H.L.: Learning from imbalanced data sets with boosting and data generation: the DataBoost-IM approach. SIGKDD Explor. Newsl. **6**(1), 30–39 (2004)
9. He, H., Garcia, E.: Learning from imbalanced data. IEEE Trans. on Knowl. and Data Eng. **21**(9), 1263–1284 (2009)
10. Lee, Hyoung-joo, Cho, Sungzoon: The novelty detection approach for different degrees of class imbalance. In: King, Irwin, Wang, Jun, Chan, Lai-Wan, Wang, DeLiang (eds.) ICONIP 2006. LNCS, vol. 4233, pp. 21–30. Springer, Heidelberg (2006)
11. Maron, O., Lozano-Pérez, T.: A Framework for Multiple-Instance Learning. In: Adv. Neural Inf. Process. Syst. App., pp. 570–576. MIT Press (1998)
12. Martino, M., Fernández, A., Iturralde, P., Lecumberry, F.: Novel classifier scheme for imbalanced problems. Pattern Recogn. Lett. **34**(10), 1146–1151 (2013)
13. Mera, Carlos, Orozco-Alzate, Mauricio, Branch, John: Improving representation of the positive class in imbalanced multiple-instance learning. In: Campilho, Aurélio, Kamel, Mohamed (eds.) ICIAR 2014, Part I. LNCS, vol. 8814, pp. 266–273. Springer, Heidelberg (2014)
14. Nguyen, G., Phung, S.L., Bouzerdoum, A.: Learning pattern classification tasks with imbalanced data sets. In: Pattern Recognition, pp. 193–208. InTech (2009)
15. Parzen, E.: On estimation of a probability density function and mode. Ann. Math. Stat. **33**(3), 1065–1076 (1962)
16. Tax, D.M.J.: MIL: A Matlab toolbox for multiple instance learning (2015). http://prlab.tudelft.nl/david-tax/mil.html
17. Thai-Nghe, N., Gantner, Z., Schmidt-Thieme, L.: Cost-sensitive learning methods for imbalanced data. In: Proc. Int. Jt. Conf. Neural. Netw. pp. 1–8 (2010)
18. Viola, P., Platt, J., Zhang, C.: Multiple Instance boosting for object detection. In: Adv. Neural Inf. Process. Syst., pp. 1417–1426. MIT Press (2005)
19. Wang, Xiaoguang, Matwin, Stan, Japkowicz, Nathalie, Liu, Xuan: Cost-sensitive boosting algorithms for imbalanced multi-instance datasets. In: Zaïane, Osmar R., Zilles, Sandra (eds.) Canadian AI 2013. LNCS, vol. 7884, pp. 174–186. Springer, Heidelberg (2013)
20. Wang, X., Liu, X., Japkowicz, N., Matwin, S.: Resampling and cost-sensitive methods for imbalanced multi-instance learning. ICDM **2103**, 808–816 (2013)
21. Zhang, Q., Goldman, S.A.: EM-DD: An improved Multiple-Instance Learning technique. In: Adv. Neural Inf. Process. Syst. App., pp. 1073–1080. MIT Press (2001)

Video Analysis, Segmentation
and Tracking

Supervised Video Genre Classification Using Optimum-Path Forest

Guilherme B. Martins[1], Jurandy Almeida[2], and Joao Paulo Papa[1](✉)

[1] Department of Computing, São Paulo State University – UNESP,
Bauru, SP 17033-360, Brazil
guilherme-bm@outlook.com, papa@fcunesp.br
[2] Institute of Science and Technology, Federal University of São Paulo – UNIFESP,
São José dos Campos, SP 12247-014, Brazil
jurandy.almeida@unifesp.br

Abstract. Multimedia-content classification has been paramount in the last years, mainly because of the massive data accessed daily. Video-based retrieval and recommendation systems have attracted a considerable attention, since it is a profitable feature for several online and offline markets. In this work, we deal with the problem of automatic video classification in different genres based on visual information by means of Optimum-Path Forest (OPF), which is a recently developed graph-based pattern recognition technique. The aforementioned classifier is compared against with some state-of-the-art supervised machine learning techniques, such as Support Vector Machines and Bayesian classifier, being its efficiency and effectiveness evaluated in a number of datasets and problems.

Keywords: Video classification · Optimum-Path Forest · Supervised learning

1 Introduction

Advances in data transmission and storage have allowed a continuous growth of large digital libraries and multimedia databases [7]. In this context, genre-based video classification is often required to classify the dataset in order to allow a faster retrieval response. Video recommendation systems also make use of automatic classification of multimedia content, since each video genre might be associated with a certain profile of consumer.

A number of video classification solutions are based on machine learning techniques [4], being the main purpose of such approaches to predict the genre of a given input video. In the last years, several methods for genre-based video retrieval/classification have been proposed, in which textual [4,20], audio-based [13] and mostly low-level visual features [3,4,7,20,22] are among the most widely used tools for video description. Huang and Wang [14], for instance, employed the well-known Support Vector Machines (SVMs) together with a Self-Adaptive Harmony Search optimization algorithm to classify movie genres,

© Springer International Publishing Switzerland 2015
A. Pardo and J. Kittler (Eds.): CIARP 2015, LNCS 9423, pp. 735–742, 2015.
DOI: 10.1007/978-3-319-25751-8_88

and You et al. [21] proposed a semantic-oriented approach for video analysis based on Hidden Markov Models and a Bayesian classifier.

Later on, Hamed et al. [11] presented a video classification approach based on the Weighted Kernel Logistic Regression classifier, and Karpathy et al. [15] employed a Convolutional Neural Network for the same purpose. Dammak and Ben-Ayed [9] also employed SVMs for video classification, but now using signal processing-based feature extraction approaches. Recently, Ekenel and Semela [10] employed audio-visual and cognitive features to automatic classify videos of TV programs and YouTube.

Some years ago, Papa et al. [17,18] proposed the Optimum-Path Forest (OPF) classifier, which models the pattern recognition task as a graph partition problem. Basically, the dataset samples (feature vectors) are represented by graph nodes, which are connected to each other through an adjacency relation. After that, some key nodes (*prototypes*) rule a competition process among themselves in order to conquer the remaining samples offering to them optimum-path costs. When a sample is conquered, it receives the very same label of its conqueror, as well as the cost it has been offered. The OPF classifier has gained popularity in the last years, since it has obtained similar results to SVMs, but with a faster training step. Some of its main advantages are: (i) it does not make assumption samples separability in the feature space, (ii) it has no parameters, and (iii) it can be designed in a number of different ways.

However, to the best of our knowledge, OPF has never been employed in the context of genre-based video classification. Therefore, the main goal of this work is to introduce OPF for video classification tasks using video properties obtained from Bag-of-Visual Words, Bag-of-Scenes and Histogram of Motion Patterns, as well as to compare OPF against with some state-of-the-art pattern recognition techniques, such as Support Vector Machines, k-nearest neighbours (k-NN), Artificial Neural Networks with Multilayer Perceptrons (ANN-MLP), and a Bayesian classifier (BC).

The remainder of this work is organized as follows. Section 2 presents the theory related to the Optimum-Path Forest classifier, and Section 3 discusses the methodology used in this work. The experimental section is further described in Section 4, and Section 5 states conclusions and future works.

2 Optimum-Path Forest Classification

The OPF framework is a recent highlight to the development of pattern recognition techniques based on graph partitions. The nodes are the data samples, which are represented by their corresponding feature vectors, and are connected according to some predefined adjacency relation. Given some key nodes (prototypes), they will compete among themselves aiming at conquering the remaining nodes. Thus, the algorithm outputs an optimum path forest, which is a collection of optimum-path trees (OPTs) rooted at each prototype. This work employs the OPF classifier proposed by Papa et al. [17,18], which is explained in more details as follows.

Let $\mathcal{D} = \mathcal{D}_1 \cup \mathcal{D}_2$ be a labeled dataset, such that $\mathcal{D}_1$ and $\mathcal{D}_2$ stands for the training and test sets, respectively. Let $\mathcal{S} \subset \mathcal{D}_1$ be a set of prototypes of all classes (i.e., key samples that best represent the classes). Let $(\mathcal{D}_1, A)$ be a complete graph whose nodes are the samples in $\mathcal{D}_1$, and any pair of samples defines an arc in $A = \mathcal{D}_1 \times \mathcal{D}_1$[1]. Additionally, let π_s be a path in $(\mathcal{D}_1, A)$ with terminus at sample $s \in \mathcal{D}_1$.

The OPF algorithm proposed by Papa et al. [17,18] employs the path-cost function f_{max} due to its theoretical properties for estimating prototypes (Section 2.1 gives further details about this procedure):

$$f_{max}(\langle s \rangle) = \begin{cases} 0 & \text{if } s \in S \\ +\infty & \text{otherwise,} \end{cases}$$
$$f_{max}(\pi_s \cdot \langle s, t \rangle) = \max\{f_{max}(\pi_s), d(s, t)\}, \tag{1}$$

where $d(s, t)$ stands for a distance between nodes s and t, such that $s, t \in \mathcal{D}_1$. Therefore, $f_{max}(\pi_s)$ computes the maximum distance between adjacent samples in π_s, when π_s is not a trivial path. In short, the OPF algorithm tries to minimize $f_{max}(\pi_t)$, $\forall t \in \mathcal{D}_1$.

2.1 Training

We say that S^* is an optimum set of prototypes when OPF algorithm minimizes the classification errors for every $s \in \mathcal{D}_1$. We have that S^* can be found by exploiting the theoretical relation between the minimum-spanning tree and the optimum-path tree for f_{max} [1]. The training essentially consists of finding S^* and an OPF classifier rooted at S^*. By computing a Minimum Spanning Tree (MST) in the complete graph $(\mathcal{D}_1, A)$, one obtain a connected acyclic graph whose nodes are all samples of $\mathcal{D}_1$ and the arcs are undirected and weighted by the distances d between adjacent samples. In the MST, every pair of samples is connected by a single path, which is optimum according to f_{max}. Hence, the minimum-spanning tree contains one optimum-path tree for any selected root node.

The optimum prototypes are the closest elements of the MST with different labels in $\mathcal{D}_1$ (i.e., elements that fall in the frontier of the classes). By removing the arcs between different classes, their adjacent samples become prototypes in S^*, and the OPF algorithm can define an optimum-path forest with minimum classification errors in $\mathcal{D}_1$.

2.2 Classification

For any sample $t \in \mathcal{D}_2$, we consider all arcs connecting t with samples $s \in \mathcal{D}_1$, as though t were part of the training graph. Considering all possible paths from S^* to t, we find the optimum path $P^*(t)$ from S^* and label t with the class $\lambda(R(t))$ of its most strongly connected prototype $R(t) \in S^*$ ($\lambda(\cdot)$ is a function that assigns the true label for any sample in the dataset). This path can be identified incrementally, by evaluating the optimum cost $C(t)$ as follows:

$$C(t) = \min\{\max\{C(s), d(s, t)\}\}, \ \forall s \in \mathcal{D}_1. \tag{2}$$

---

[1] The arcs are weighted by the distance between their corresponding nodes.

Let the node $s^* \in \mathcal{D}_1$ be the one that satisfies Equation 2 (i.e., the predecessor $P(t)$ in the optimum path $P^*(t)$). Given that $L(s^*) = \lambda(R(t))$, the classification simply assigns $L(s^*)$ as the class of t. An error occurs when $L(s^*) \neq \lambda(t)$, being $L(\cdot)$ the predicted label of a given sample.

3   Methodology

This section describes the methodology employed in this work, which is composed of two main steps: (i) a *feature extraction* module based on three different methods (Section 3.1), and then (ii) the *genre classification* (Section 3.2). Also, a briefly description about the standardized dataset used in this work is presented in Section 3.3.

3.1   Feature Extraction

We employed three main approaches to encode the visual properties of a video: "Bag-of-Visual-Words" [5], "Bag-of-Scenes" [19] and "Histogram of Motion Patterns" [2]. The former two approaches are based on video frames and disregard transitions between them, whereas the latter one is based on motion information, and it considers the transitions between video frames. The quoted approaches are briefly described as follows:

Bag-of-Visual-Words (BoVW)
   It represents visual content with statistical information of local patterns, encoding the occurrences of quantized local features. For this, a visual dictionary or visual codebook is created from the feature-space quantization [5]. Here, the BoVW features were extracted considering the Pooling over Pooling (PoP) technique proposed in [3]. We used a dictionary of 1,000 visual words for the local features, and average pooling to compute the BoVW for each frame. Finally, max-pooling was then performed to combine those frames.

Bag-of-Scenes (BoS)
   BoS is an approach for encoding video visual properties [19] based on a dictionary of scenes, and it carries more semantic information than the traditional dictionaries based on local descriptions. Here, multiple configurations were considered for computing the BoS of a video, like varying the dictionary size, using hard or soft assignment and average or max pooling.

Histogram of Motion Patterns (HMP)
   This structural and statistical combined visual feature was introduced in [2] and designed to compare videos based on partial decoding of a video stream, motion feature extraction and signature generation.
   For each group of pictures (GOP) of a video stream, only the I-frames are selected due to their lossless information property. Then, those frames are divided into 8×8 pixel blocks, for subsequent extraction of 64 coefficients to obtain the four DC luminance terms of each macroblock. Thereafter, ordinal

measures are calculated for the macroblocks, and each possible combination of those measures is treated as a 16-bit individual pattern. At the end, the spatio-temporal patterns obtained from all macroblocks of the video stream are accumulated to compose a normalized histogram.

3.2   Genre Classification

In order to perform the video classification task, the OPF classifier was compared against with three well-known classifiers: Artificial Neural Networks with Multilayer Perceptron (ANN-MLP) [12], k-Nearest Neighbors (k-NN) [8] and Support Vector Machines (SVM) [6]. It is noteworthy that a polynomial (SVM-POLY) and a Radial Basis Function (SVM-RBF) kernel were used for SVM classifier, as well as SVM parameters have been optimized through cross-validation.

For each classifier, we performed 12 different experiments considering the visual features encoded with BoVW, BoS, and HMP. Table 1 presents in more details the experimental setup.

Table 1. Experimental setup.

Experiment	Descriptor	Setup
1	BoVW	Hard assignment – average pooling – 1000 visual words
2	BoS	Hard assignment – average pooling – 1000 scenes
3	BoS	Hard assignment – max pooling – 1000 scenes
4	BoS	Soft assignment – average pooling – 1000 scenes
5	BoS	Soft assignment – max pooling – 1000 scenes
6	BoS	Hard assignment – average pooling – 100 scenes
7	BoS	Hard assignment – max pooling – 100 scenes
8	BoS	Soft assignment ($\sigma = 1$) – average pooling – 100 scenes
9	BoS	Soft assignment ($\sigma = 1$) – max pooling – 100 scenes
10	BoS	Soft assignment ($\sigma = 2$) – average pooling – 100 scenes
11	BoS	Soft assignment ($\sigma = 2$) – max pooling – 100 scenes
12	HMP	6075 motion patterns

3.3   Dataset

In this work, we employed a benchmarking dataset provided by the MediaEval 2012 organizers for the Genre Tagging Task [20]. The dataset is composed of 14,838 videos divided into a development set (5,288 videos) and a test set (9,550 videos), comprising a total of 3,288 hours of video data.

The videos were collected from the blip.tv[2], and they are distributed among 26 video genre categories assigned by the blip.tv media platform, namely (the numbers in brackets are the total number of videos): Art (530), Autos and Vehicles (21), Business (281), Citizen Journalism (401), Comedy (515), Conferences

---

[2] http://blip.tv (as of May, 2015).

and Other Events (247), Documentary (353), Educational (957), Food and Drink (261), Gaming (401), Health (268), Literature (222), Movies and Television (868), Music and Entertainment (1148), Personal or Auto-biographical (165), Politics (1107), Religion (868), School and Education (171), Sports (672), Technology (1343), The Environment (188), The Mainstream Media (324), Travel (175), Videoblogging (887), Web Development and Sites (116), and Default Category (2349, which comprises videos that cannot be assigned to any of the previous categories). The main challenge of this scenario is the high diversity of video genres, as well as the high variety of visual contents within each genre category.

4   Experiments and Results

In this section, we present the experiments conducted to assess the robustness of OPF classifier in the context of genre-based video classification. In order to evaluate the results, we consider two performance measures: (i) the Mean Average Precision (MAP) and (ii) a recognition rate proposed by Papa et al. [18], which considers unbalanced data, as well as we compute the computational load for both training and classification steps. Figures 1(a) and 1(b) depict the results considering MAP and accuracy measures, respectively.

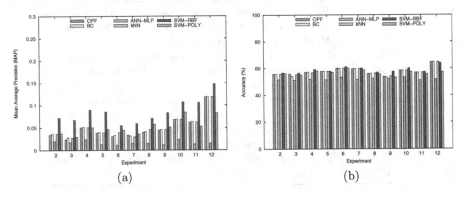

Fig. 1. Recognition results in terms of (a) MAP and (b) accuracy measures.

In regard to both measures, the experiment number 12 has showed the best results for all classifiers (except for ANN), which might be due to the robustness of HMP to several transformations, besides being suitable for very large collections of video data [2], which is in accordance with the MediaEval 2012 dataset used in our experiments. In terms of MAP, OPF has been placed in second or third in most cases, while for the accuracy measure OPF obtained the first or second position in most part of the experiments.

If we consider the computational load displayed in Figures 2(a) and 2(b) for the training and test steps, respectively, we shall observe OPF has been the fastest classifier for training in almost all experiments, as well as the second

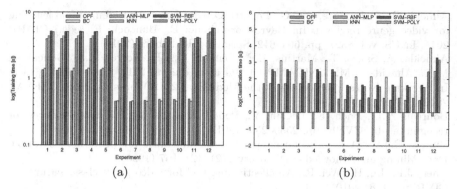

Fig. 2. Computational load for (a) training and (b) classification steps.

fastest classifier considering the classification time. In light of those results, we may conclude OPF is a suitable technique for the automatic classification of videos based on visual information, since it has obtained good recognition rates in a smaller amount of time when compared to the other techniques (except for ANN-MLP). Such skill might be very interesting in online classification and recommendation systems, in which a high trade-off between effectiveness and efficiency is extremely desired.

5 Conclusions

In this work, we introduced the OPF classifier for the task of automatic genre-based video classification. Three different video descriptors have been used together with six classifiers to provide a robust experimental analysis, in which OPF obtained good recognition rates (considering both MAP and accuracy) in all problems, as well as it required a low computational load for both training and classification steps when compared to the other techniques. Such skills allow OPF to be employed for online video retrieval and recommendation systems, in which a good trade-off between efficiency and effectiveness is highly desired. Future work includes the use of other features and/or summarization methods [16].

Acknowledgments. The authors are grateful to FAPESP grants #2013/20387-7 and #2014/16250-9, as well as to CNPq grants #306166/2014-3 and #470571/2013-6. We also thank Otávio A. B. Penatti for the BoVW and BoS features extracted from the videos.

References

1. Allène, C., Audibert, J.Y., Couprie, M., Keriven, R.: Some links between extremum spanning forests, watersheds and min-cuts. Image Vision Computing **28**(10), 1460–1471 (2010)
2. Almeida, J., Leite, N.J., Torres, R.S.: Comparison of video sequences with histograms of motion patterns. In: ICIP, pp. 3673–3676 (2011)

3. Almeida, J., Pedronette, D.C.G., Penatti, O.A.B.: Unsupervised manifold learning for video genre retrieval. In: Bayro-Corrochano, E., Hancock, E. (eds.) CIARP 2014. LNCS, vol. 8827, pp. 604–612. Springer, Heidelberg (2014)
4. Almeida, J., Salles, T., Martins, E.F., Penatti, O.A.B., Torres, R.S., Gonçalves, M.A., Almeida, J.M.: UNICAMP-UFMG at mediaeval 2012: genre tagging task. In: Working Notes Proceedings of the MediaEval 2012 Workshop (MEDIAEVAL 2012) (2012)
5. Boureau, Y.L., Bach, F., LeCun, Y., Ponce, J.: Learning mid-level features for recognition. In: CVPR, pp. 2559–2566 (2010)
6. Burges, C.J.C.: A tutorial on support vector machines for pattern recognition. Data Mining and Knowledge Discovery 2(2), 121–167 (1998)
7. Chen, J.F., Lu, H., Wei, R.: An effective method for video genre classification. In: CIVR, pp. 1–8 (2010)
8. Cover, T., Hart, P.: Nearest neighbor pattern classification. IEEE Transactions on Information Theory 13(1), 21–27 (2006)
9. Dammak, N., Ben-Ayed, Y.: Video genre categorization using support vector machines. In: Advanced Technologies for Signal and Image Processing (ATSIP 2014), pp. 106–110 (2014)
10. Ekenel, H.K., Semela, T.: Multimodal genre classification of tv programs and youtube videos. Multimedia Tools and Applications 63(2), 547–567 (2013)
11. Hamed, A.A.M., Li, R., Xiaoming, Z., Xu, C.: Video genre classification using weighted kernel logistic regression. Advances in Multimedia 2013, 1–6 (2013)
12. Hassoun, M.H.: Fundamentals of Artificial Neural Networks. MIT Press (1995)
13. Hradis, M., Reznícek, I., Behun, K.: Brno university of technology at mediaeval 2011 genre tagging task. In: Working Notes Proceedings of the MediaEval 2011 Workshop (MEDIAEVAL 2011) (2011)
14. Huang, Y.-F., Wang, S.-H.: Movie genre classification using SVM with audio and video features. In: Huang, R., Ghorbani, A.A., Pasi, G., Yamaguchi, T., Yen, N.Y., Jin, B. (eds.) AMT 2012. LNCS, vol. 7669, pp. 1–10. Springer, Heidelberg (2012)
15. Karpathy, A., Toderici, G., Shetty, S., Leung, T., Sukthankar, R., Fei-Fei, L.: Large-scale video classification with convolutional neural networks. In: CVPR, pp. 1725–1732 (2014)
16. Martins, G.B., Afonso, L.C.S., Osaku, D., Almeida, J., Papa, J.P.: Static video summarization through optimum-path forest clustering. In: Bayro-Corrochano, E., Hancock, E. (eds.) CIARP 2014. LNCS, vol. 8827, pp. 893–900. Springer, Heidelberg (2014)
17. Papa, J.P., Falcão, A.X., Albuquerque, V.H.C., Tavares, J.M.R.S.: Efficient supervised optimum-path forest classification for large datasets. Pattern Recognition 45(1), 512–520 (2012)
18. Papa, J.P., Falcão, A.X., Suzuki, C.T.N.: Supervised pattern classification based on optimum-path forest. International Journal of Imaging Systems and Technology 19(2), 120–131 (2009)
19. Penatti, O.A.B., Li, L.T., Almeida, J., da Torres, R.S.: A visual approach for video geocoding using bag-of-scenes. In: ICMR, pp. 1–8 (2012)
20. Schmiedeke, S., Kofler, C., Ferrané, I.: Overview of mediaeval 2012 genre tagging task. In: Working Notes Proceedings of the MediaEval 2012 Workshop (MEDIAEVAL 2012) (2012)
21. You, J., Liu, G., Perkis, A.: A semantic framework for video genre classification and event analysis. Signal Processing: Image Communication 25(4), 287–302 (2010)
22. Zhou, H., Hermans, T., Karandikar, A.V., Rehg, J.M.: Movie genre classification via scene categorization. In: ACM-MM, pp. 747–750 (2010)

Annotating and Retrieving Videos of Human Actions Using Matrix Factorization

Fabián Páez$^{(\boxtimes)}$ and Fabio A. González

MindLab Research Group, Universidad Nacional de Colombia, Bogotá, Colombia
fmpaezri@unal.edu.co

Abstract. This paper presents a method for annotating and retrieving videos of human actions based on two-way matrix factorization. The method addresses the problem by modeling it as the problem of finding common latent space representation for multimodal objects. In this particular case, the modalities correspond to the visual and textual (annotations) information associated with videos, which are projected by the method to the latent space. Assuming this space exists, it is possible to map between input spaces, i.e. visual to textual, by projecting across the latent space. The mapping between the spaces is explicitly optimized in the cost function and learned from training data including both modalities. The algorithm may be used for annotation, by projecting only visual information and obtaining a textual representation, or for retrieval by indexing on the latent or textual spaces. Experimental evaluation shows competitive results when compared to state-of-the-art annotation and retrieval methods.

1 Introduction

Video analysis is a task that has gained a lot of attention by the research community due to the growing amount of video content on the web. Having such large video repositories, e.g. YouTube, poses the problem of efficiently managing and accessing them. A system able to correctly annotate videos is useful for searching, categorizing and understanding applications. This work focuses on video annotation with a predefined number of human actions, according to their presence in the video. For this, only visual information is available at test time, but more information sources may be used during model training, such as action annotations or related audio.

For the current experimentation, the focus is given to the annotation model. The representation problem is not approached, and a state-of-the-art representation is used. The chosen model is two way matrix factorization [10], which has been also used for image annotation. The basic idea of the algorithm is to obtain a common latent space, which embeds the information content of the different modalities. Every modality has two projection matrices, one that allows to map from the original modality space to the latent space, and another one which maps back from the latent space to the original modality space. By means of this matrices, one could project from a desired input space to another modal

A. Pardo and J. Kittler (Eds.): CIARP 2015, LNCS 9423, pp. 743–750, 2015.
DOI: 10.1007/978-3-319-25751-8_89

space, e.g. from visual to textual by first mapping from visual to latent and finally from latent to textual.

After training the model for the annotation task, we also evaluate it in an information retrieval setup using the same dataset. For retrieval, the query-by-example method is used so only visual information is available as input query. The approach maps the input query visual representation to one of the available spaces, e.g. textual, latent, visual, and the collection videos to be retrieved are also mapped to that space. Having both query and collection in the same representation space, a particular similarity measure could be used to rank videos according to their similarity with the query. The collection videos are then presented to the user according to the ranking. The results show a competitive performance in both tasks when compared to an annotation model and a query by semantic example retrieval mode, both based on linear support vector machines (SVM).

This document is organized as follows: first, a short review of previous work is given on Sec. 2; then, the selected annotation model is described in Sec. 3; finally, experimental results are presented in Sec. 4 and conclusions in Sec. 5.

2   Previous Work

The evaluation in [14] compares different types of video features and interest point detectors using Bag of Features (BoF) and nonlinear SVM. The most important finding of the evaluation was that dense sampling improved action classification over interest point detectors, with the drawback of large number of features to process. This motivated the proposal of Dense Trajectory Features (DTF) [12] and Improved Dense Trajectories (IDT) [13]. The main idea of these features is to extract four descriptors along volumes aligned with tracked pixels.

These features have achieved state-of-the-art performance on various action recognition datasets. The IDT proposal used Fisher vectors [2] instead of BoF to encode the features and generate a video representation. Fisher vectors generate a high dimensional representation based on the gradient of local features with respect to the parameters of a generative model of the features.

By the time trajectory features were proposed, Convolutional Neural Networks (CNN) [5] were causing a revolution on image representation. These networks benefited from training deep models with large amounts of data, which allowed to learn complex features and avoid overfitting. Inspired by this trend, many video representations based on CNNs have been proposed. Among them is the work of Simonyan et al. [8], were an appearance and a motion CNN are combined to generate features which are aggregated with average pooling to generate a video representation, achieving a competitive result over IDT. Instead of average or max-pooling, Xu et al. [15] propose to use Fisher vectors to encode CNN features. This proposal achieved excellent results at the event detection task by means of appearance information only.

As IDT have the drawback of large number of generated features and long processing times, Motion Flow (MF) was proposed in [4], which reduces drastically the extraction time by exploiting the flow generated by the MPEG4 video encoding. This features are fast to compute, but achieve a lower performance compared to IDT.

In [14] and [12], a nonlinear SVM was used to assign single actions to a previously segmented video, represented using BoF. The nonlinear kernel in those cases was χ^2. Where multiple descriptors were available, such as for IDT, the kernels were aggregated by addition before applying the exponential function.

Representations with Fisher vectors generate high dimensional vectors, which achieve good performance with linear models, and so linear SVMs are used in [13] and [15].

3 Annotation Model

Two Way Matrix Factorization (TWMF) is a latent space method in which the cost function to optimize has no explicit mention of the latent space, and the objective is to obtain the most accurate reconstruction of the modalities when projected through the latent space and back. The basic assumption is that there exists a linear projection matrix between two information modalities, e.g. textual and visual. This projection first maps one modality to the latent space, and then projects from that space to the other modality. Lets assume we have vectorial representations $v_i \in \mathbb{R}^{D_v}$ and $t_i \in \mathbb{R}^{D_t}$ of the two modalities (v, t) for a given entity i. Each of the modalities has a projection matrix to the latent space, $W_t \in \mathbb{R}^{r \times D_t}$ and $W_v \in \mathbb{R}^{r \times D_v}$ respectively, where r is the dimension of the latent space. After projecting, a latent representation $h_i \in \mathbb{R}^{r \times 1}$ is obtained for the entity.

$$h_i = W_t t_i . \tag{1}$$
$$h_i = W_v v_i . \tag{2}$$

Each of the modalities has also a back-projection matrix, $W_t' \in \mathbb{R}^{D_t \times r}$ and $W_v' \in \mathbb{R}^{D_t \times r}$, which maps back from the latent space to the respective modality.

$$t_i = W_t' h_i . \tag{3}$$
$$v_i = W_v' h_i . \tag{4}$$

To express the relationship between modalities we can combine the previous expressions to obtain crossmodal mappings that don't explicitly use the latent space:

$$t_i = W_t' W_v v_i . \tag{5}$$
$$v_i = W_v' W_t t_i . \tag{6}$$

Assuming we have both representations for a number n of entities, the data for a modality can be conveniently represented in a matrix were each column represents an entity. Following our naming convention, these matrices are called $V \in \mathbb{R}^{D_v \times n}$ and $T \in \mathbb{R}^{D_t \times n}$. In the case of projecting from the "visual" to the "textual" modality, we would have

$$T = W_t' W_v V . \tag{7}$$

To obtain the projection and back-projection matrices we use Stochastic Gradient Descent implemented in Pylearn2 [1]. A cost function is minimized by letting the library calculate gradients. For the annotation task, the interest is in assigning labels based on visual content. The main term of the cost is based on least squares reconstruction of the textual modality from the projection through the latent space of the visual modality

$$\arg\min_{W_t', W_v} ||T - W_t' W_v V||_F^2 . \tag{8}$$

What this means is that we want a model that reconstructs as accurately as possible the textual modality from the visual modality.

Additional terms can be added to control model complexity, overfitting and sparsity among others. The initial formulation in [10] adds a regularization term of the projection matrices and reconstruction of each modality after passing through the latent space and back (one way), resulting in the following optimization problem:

$$\arg\min_{W_t, W_t', W_v W_v'} \begin{pmatrix} \delta||T - W_t' W_v V||_F^2 + \\ \alpha||V - W_v' W_v V||_F^2 + \\ (1-\alpha)\,||T - W_t' W_t T||_F^2 + \\ \beta\left(||W_t'||_F^2 + ||W_v||_F^2 + ||W_t||_F^2 + ||W_v'||_F^2\right) \end{pmatrix} . \tag{9}$$

4   Experiments

4.1   Annotation Task and Dataset Description

The goal of the task is to recognize the action or actions present in a video from a predefined set of actions. For the experimental evaluation we used two publicly available datasets: UCF101 [9] and THUMOS 2014 [3]. The UCF101 dataset contains realistic videos where each clip has exactly one action and has been segmented in time to have the best fit to the action. The dataset comprises 101 different actions, each action with several example videos. The THUMOS 2014 dataset includes videos belonging to the same 101 actions, but without time segmentation, so a single video can have more than one execution of multiple activities and also frames from activities different to the 101 actions set. There are two tasks and the current evaluation is performed on the first task: recognition. The second task is temporal segmentation.

The dataset has a training partition of 13320 trimmed videos from UCF101 dataset, a validation partition of 1010 untrimmed videos from THUMOS 2014 and a test partition of 1574 untrimmed videos also from THUMOS 2014. Validation data may be used as part of training data to generate test results. The objective is for each test video to generate a score for each of the 101 actions present in the training set. In the case of untrimmed videos, more than one action may be present in each sequence. Results are evaluated using Mean Average Precision (MAP).

Two models are evaluated: linear SVMs and TWMF. Models are trained using only training data, and evaluated on validation and test data. In the THU-MOS data, a score must be generated for each action. For TWMF, the textual projection value is used as score and for linear SVM, Platt scaled scores. The SVM implementation is from Scikit-Learn [6].

Visual and Textual Representation. As visual features we use IDT, extracted using the implementation provided by the IDT author and encoded using Fisher vectors using the pipeline described in [7]. The resulting Fisher Vectors are l^2 and power normalized as it is a recommended practice. The Fisher Vector implementation used is VlFeat [11]. The size of the resulting visual representation using Fisher Vectors when concatenating the 4 descriptors is 101,376.

The textual information consists of a binary 101-dimensional vector. Each dimension represents an action, and a 1 value indicates presence, while a 0 indicates absence, of the action.

Two Way Matrix Factorization Cost Components Evaluation. To select the algorithm parameters, we performed experiments using only parts of the cost function and evaluating its influence on the validation set MAP and training set cost value during each epoch. As textual information has a stronger semantic content, it has a higher importance and therefore the highest possible weight

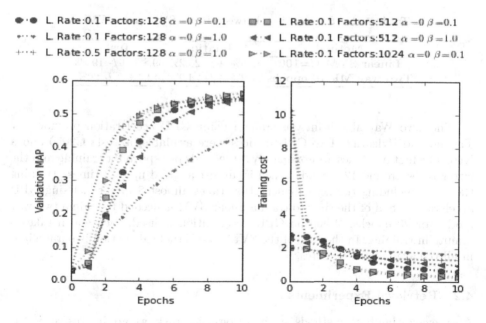

Fig. 1. Validation MAP and training cost when using all reconstruction terms and regularization of all projection matrices

(i.e. $\delta = 1$) is given to the two way term so that textual annotations are correctly reconstructed from the visual information. The most important term after the two way reconstruction is the one way reconstruction which speeds up convergence. Giving high importance to the regularization slows convergence. The results when the complete cost is used are presented in Fig. 1. It includes one experiment with a learning rate of 0.5. Other experiments using that learning rate showed a faster convergence rate but instability problems when the validation MAP was saturated. The specific case in the figure seem to have converged due to the high regularization. Only experiments with $\alpha = 0$ are presented as giving importance to reconstructing the one way visual term slowed convergence and in some cases produced instabilities. This behavior is attributed to the fact that the visual matrix is dense and is also made of high dimensional (101,376) Fisher vectors, so reconstructing such a large amount of information is a harder task.

Results. The MAP results for linear SVM and TWMF are presented in Tab. 1. The C parameter of the SVM was selected using the validation set and the best value was $C = 100$, which matches the best value reported by [13]. TWMF obtains an improvement over linear SVM. Both algorithms show a performance drop on test data with respect to validation data. This may be due to the fact that training segments have only one label, while test segments have, in general, multiple labels.

Table 1. MAP comparison between linear SVM and TWMF.

Method	Validation	Test
Linear SVM C=100	52.6% +/- 25.2%	39.8% +/- 19.9%
Two-way MF 10 epochs	57.2% +/- 24.9%	42.4% +/- 20%

The Two Way algorithm was trained using GPU acceleration provided by Theano and Pylearn2. Two GPU devices were available: a Tesla C2050 and a K40. The first one takes approximately 30 seconds per epoch for training and the latter takes around 12 seconds which is almost a speed up of 3 times. Training the SVM including the kernel calculation takes almost 8 minutes. Using GPU acceleration, half of the time to train a linear SVM is needed to train a two-way model for 20 epochs. When no GPU acceleration is used, each epoch takes a minute in training. In the case of the SVM, the kernel calculation is parallelized in all the available CPU cores.

4.2   Retrieval Experiments

After evaluating both methods on the recognition task, we are interested on the retrieval task. The setup for the retrieval experiments consists on taking a partition of the dataset as the collection used by the system to retrieve documents, and the remaining documents as queries. In this case query-by-example is used, so each query visual representation is used as input to the system, and the aim is that the system generates a ranked list of relevant documents. Documents are considered relevant if they share at least one of the actions in the query document. To generate the ranked results, both query and collection are mapped to a semantic space. Using a similarity measure, the semantic representation of the query is compared to the semantic representation of each of the documents in the collection. The similarity value is used to generate the ranking. The semantic spaces considered are the textual space, corresponding to the action labels, and the latent space. Following previous work, we compare retrieval using TWMF with pure visual retrieval and QBSE using the learned linear SVM. The similarity measure is dot product in all cases, and the evaluation metric is also Mean Average Precision (MAP). The results are presented in Tab. 2.

Table 2. Comparison of retrieval results for visual retrieval, QBSE and TWMF using the latent and textual spaces.

Method	Validation	Test
Visual	11.8%	9.4%
QBSE SVM	51.5%	39.6%
Two Way MF Textual 10 epochs	52.5%	39.5%
Two Way MF Latent 10 epochs	52.5%	39.4%
Two Way MF Textual 20 epochs	57.9%	43.5%
Two Way MF Latent 20 epochs	58.4%	43.6%

5   Conclusions

The TWMF algorithm is an efficient method for annotation and retrieval of videos containing actions. Its online nature allows to train on large datasets without huge memory requirements and achieving task performance competitive or even better than using linear SVM. By means of GPU acceleration, the algorithm also achieves shorter training times compared to the linear SVM implementation which is also accelerated but with CPU parallelization of the kernel calculation.

The state of the art on the THUMOS dataset is achieved by combining IDT features with CNN features. Including CNN features as an additional modality or simply concatenating them with IDT is part of the future work. Nevertheless, the linear SVM baseline with IDT features is a good enough baseline when the comparison is focused not on the features but on the learning model.

References

1. Goodfellow, I.J., Warde-Farley, D., Lamblin, P., Dumoulin, V., Mirza, M., Pascanu, R., Bergstra, J., Bastien, F., Bengio, Y.: Pylearn2: a machine learning research library. arXiv preprint arXiv:1308.4214 (2013)

2. Jaakkola, T., Haussler, D., et al.: Exploiting generative models in discriminative classifiers. In: Advances in Neural Information Processing Systems, pp. 487–493 (1999)
3. Jiang, Y.G., Liu, J., Zamir, A.R., Toderici, G., Laptev, I., Shah, M., Sukthankar, R.: THUMOS challenge: Action recognition with a large number of classes (2014). http://crcv.ucf.edu/THUMOS14/
4. Kantorov, V., Laptev, I.: Efficient feature extraction, encoding, and classification for action recognition. In: 2014 IEEE Conference on Computer Vision and Pattern Recognition (CVPR), pp. 2593–2600. IEEE (2014)
5. Krizhevsky, A., Sutskever, I., Hinton, G.E.: Imagenet classification with deep convolutional neural networks. In: Advances in Neural Information Processing Systems, pp. 1097–1105 (2012)
6. Pedregosa, F., Varoquaux, G., Gramfort, A., Michel, V., Thirion, B., Grisel, O., Blondel, M., Prettenhofer, P., Weiss, R., Dubourg, V., Vanderplas, J., Passos, A., Cournapeau, D., Brucher, M., Perrot, M., Duchesnay, E.: Scikit-learn: Machine learning in Python. Journal of Machine Learning Research **12**, 2825–2830 (2011)
7. Peng, X., Wang, L., Wang, X., Qiao, Y.: Bag of visual words and fusion methods for action recognition: Comprehensive study and good practice (2014). arXiv preprint arXiv:1405.4506
8. Simonyan, K., Zisserman, A.: Two-stream convolutional networks for action recognition in videos. In: Advances in Neural Information Processing Systems, pp. 568–576 (2014)
9. Soomro, K., Zamir, A.R., Shah, M.: Ucf101: A dataset of 101 human actions classes from videos in the wild (2012). arXiv preprint arXiv:1212.0402
10. Vanegas, J.A., Beltran, V., González, F.A.: Two-way multimodal online matrix factorization for multi-label annotation. In: International Conference on Pattern Recognition Applications and Methods, pp. 279–285, January 2015
11. Vedaldi, A., Fulkerson, B.: VLFeat: An open and portable library of computer vision algorithms (2008). http://www.vlfeat.org/
12. Wang, H., Klaser, A., Schmid, C., Liu, C.L.: Action recognition by dense trajectories. In: 2011 IEEE Conference on Computer Vision and Pattern Recognition (CVPR), pp. 3169–3176. IEEE (2011)
13. Wang, H., Schmid, C.: Action recognition with improved trajectories. In: 2013 IEEE International Conference on Computer Vision (ICCV), pp. 3551–3558. IEEE (2013)
14. Wang, H., Ullah, M.M., Klaser, A., Laptev, I., Schmid, C.: Evaluation of local spatio-temporal features for action recognition. In: BMVC 2009-British Machine Vision Conference, pp. 124.1–124.11. BMVA Press (2009)
15. Xu, Z., Yang, Y., Hauptmann, A.G.: A discriminative CNN video representation for event detection. In: Proceedings of the IEEE Conference on Computer Vision and Pattern Recognition, pp. 1798–1807 (2015)

Recognition of Non-pedestrian Human Forms Through Locally Weighted Descriptors

Nancy Arana-Daniel$^{(\boxtimes)}$ and Isabel Cibrian-Decena

Universidad de Guadalajara, Centro Universitario de Ciencias Exactas e Ingenierías,
Blvd. Marcelino García Barragán # 1421, Guadalajara, Jalisco, Mexico
nancyaranad@gmail.com

Abstract. To recognize human forms in non-pedestrian poses presents a high complexity problem due mainly to the large number of degrees of freedom of the human body and its limbs. In this paper it is proposed a methodology to build and classify descriptors of non-pedestrian human body forms in images which is formed with local and global information. Local information is obtained by computing Local Binary Pattern (LBP) of key-body parts (head-shoulders, hands, feet, crotch-hips) detected in the image in a first stage of the method, and then this data is coupled in the descriptor with global information about euclidean distances computed between the key-body parts recognized in the image. The descriptor is then classified using a Support Vector Machine. The results obtained using the proposed recognition methodology show that it is robust to partial occlusion of bodies, furthermore the values of sensitivity, accuracy and specificity of the classifier are high enough compared with those obtained using other state of the art descriptors.

Keywords: Human detection · Non-pedestrian pose · Local Binary Pattern (LBP) · Support Vector Machine (SVM)

1 Introduction

There is a lot of interest concerning to the research and development of algorithm of human forms recognition due to the importance of its applications; such as surveillance, search and rescue, security, among others. This is the main reason of the existence in the literature of several approaches to recognize human forms: In [7], the authors present a mathematical model of the human body and in [9], [6], [13], they propose human detectors based on finding candidate body segments, and then constructing assemblies of body parts (part-based model). In [9], pictures of naked people were used, with uniform color background and without partial occlusions. Their approach assumes that an image of a human can be decomposed into a set of distinctive segments (torso, left/right upper arm, left/right lower arm, left/right upper leg, left/right lower leg) and then constructing assemblies of body segments [9]. In [5], a human detector is presented, which captures the local form information for the contour of the body silhouette

© Springer International Publishing Switzerland 2015
A. Pardo and J. Kittler (Eds.): CIARP 2015, LNCS 9423, pp. 751–759, 2015.
DOI: 10.1007/978-3-319-25751-8_90

in images of 128 by 64 pixels. In [10], is proposed a pose-invariant descriptor for humans, in standing pose, using part-template detections and segmenter of shape and pose, with 128 by 64 pixel images. In [18], is presented a descriptor robust to partial occlusion in images of people that are usually standing. In [19], depth data from a Xbox 360 Kinect is used to identify people in all poses. This method has affordable and low computational cost but has high dependency on head detection. In [16], the region with greater weight or importance is detected using Bag-of-Words (BoW); the method is robust to partial occlusion and different pose types, but only detects the region where the blue person could be located and does not indicate pose type. This method can not deal with images that do not contain human forms.

In pedestrian detection [15], a pedestrian template is learned from examples and then used for classification with a Support Vector Machine (SVM). In [6] they present a part-based model motivated by the pictorial structure models (Fischler and Elschlager) and developed a system that can estimate the pose of the human bodies. Among the major descriptors developed for various applications are Speed up Robust Features (SURF) [4]. This descriptor is invariant to rotation and scale, focused on the histogram of local oriented gradients within the interest point neighborhood. The Histogram of Oriented Gradient (HOG) is one of the best descriptors to capture the edge or local shape appearance, but achieves poor results with noisy backgrounds and it's not invariant to rotation and scale [5]. The Local Binary Pattern (LBP) is a simple and efficient texture descriptor, highly discriminative, invariant to rotation and gray scales, computationally efficient, but sensitive to noise [14]. LBP works successfully in texture classification [20], human detection [18], and face detection [1]. SURF, despite being scale invariant, is a sparse descriptor, as it uses only some features extracted from the image. LBP is a dense descriptor and, as mentioned above, it has proved to be successful in many applications.

In this paper, a descriptor of human forms in images is proposed, constructed through a part-based model of four key-body parts, see Fig. 1. In a first stage of the process of recognition, the LBP of the key-body parts is computed and four SVMs are trained in order to recognize and locate them in an image. A global descriptor is then built with the LBP and Euclidean distances computed between the key-body parts that are recognized in the image to train a SVM to recognize the whole human form (second stage). SVM has been proved to be very effective for classification of linear and nonlinear data [17]. The method has proved to be robust to partial occlusion of bodies and to reach high rates of recognition, as shown in Section 4.

a)   b)

Fig. 1. a) Model of the human body by Hanavan; b) blue shades indicate the body parts used.

This paper is organized as follows: The next Section will present a brief introduction to LBP. Then, in Section 3, the proposed approach based on LBP and part-based model is described. In Section 4, experimental results are given and Subsection 4.1 shows comparisons between our approach and some of the state-of-the-art descriptors; while Section 5 is devoted to conclusions.

2 LBP

The local binary pattern (LBP) [14], is a gray-scale invariant texture measure. In [14], Ojala *et al*, propose to use the LBP for rotation invariant texture classification. The original LBP operator (Eq. 1) is a binary code that describes the local texture with the eight-neighbors of a pixel, using the value of the center pixel as a threshold and then the thresholded values is multiplying with weights given to the corresponding pixels and summing up the result, see Fig. 2.

$$LBP_{P,R} = \sum_{p=0}^{P-1} s\left(g_p - g_c\right) 2^P \tag{1}$$

where

$$s(x) = \begin{cases} 1, x \geq 0 \\ 0, x < 0. \end{cases} \tag{2}$$

where P is the number of neighbors, g_c is the gray value of the center pixel, $g_p\,(p=0,...,p-1)$ is the value of its neighbors on a circle of radius R.

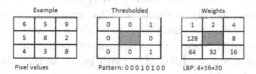

Fig. 2. The original LBP code

In [14], an extension of the original LBP is presented: uniform patterns (Eq. 3). They introduced a uniformity measure $U\,(pattern)$, which designates patterns that have U value of almost 2 as uniform if it contains at most two *0-1* or *1-0* transition in the pattern. For example, proposed the patterns 11111111_2 have U value of 0 and 00011110_2 have U value 2. *(Ojala, 2002)* propose the following operator for gray-scale and rotation invariant texture description.

$$LBP_{P,R}^{riu2} = \begin{cases} \sum_{p=0}^{P-1} s\left(g_p - g_c\right), U(G_P) \leq 2 \\ P+1, otherwise. \end{cases} \tag{3}$$

where the superscript *riu2* stands the use of rotational invariant uniform patterns and U(G_p) is defined as follows:

$$U(G_P) = |s(g_{P-1} - g_c) - s(g_0 - g_c)| + \sum_{p=0}^{P-1} |s(g_p - g_c) - s(g_{p-1} - g_c)| \qquad (4)$$

In this work the extension of the original LBP is used in order to have a descriptor which is rotational invariant.

3   Non-pedestrian Human Descriptor and Classifier

As it was mentioned above, this method involves two main processes or stages, in order to obtain a fully automated system for recognizing human forms. In a first off-line stage, five SVMs are used; the first four are trained using extended LBPs (Eq. 3) of the key-body parts, head-shoulders, left/right hand, left/right foot, i.e. one SVM is used for each body part, and therefore one SVM learns to recognize both, left and right hands and another one is used to recognize left and right foot. This is one of the advantages of using the extended version of LBP. We call these SMVs the key-body parts recognizers (KBPR). The fifth SVM (the whole body recognizer WBR) is trained using a whole human body descriptor which is constructed using the LBPs of the six body parts (counting two hands and two feet) and the Euclidean distance computed between these body parts in order to add information that helps to discriminate if the recognized body parts belong to the same body. The descriptor is shown in Fig. 5 and the off-line stage of this process is illustrated in Fig. 3.

In a second on-line stage, the four KBPR are executed while a window of size $m \times n$, proportionally sized to the image's size, is moved across the image(whatever the size of the image, $m \times n$ is calculated so that the window can cover every part of the body of a person occupying an area of 35% in the image). On each movement, an LPB of the sub-image in the window is computed and it is provided as input test vector data to the four previously trained KBPR. If a KBPR recognizes a one body part, the LBP is stored in the corresponding

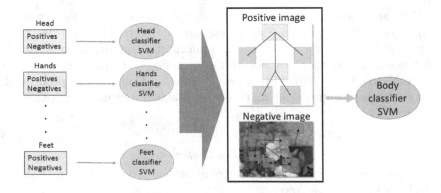

Fig. 3. Off-line stage of the process.

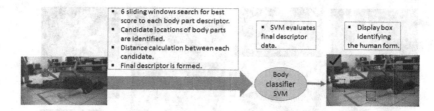

Fig. 4. On-line stage of the process.

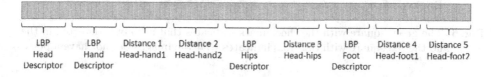

LBP	LBP	Distance 1	Distance 2	LBP	Distance 3	LBP	Distance 4	Distance 5
Head	Hand	Head-hand1	Head-hand2	Hips	Head-hips	Foot	Head-foot1	Head-foot2
Descriptor	Descriptor			Descriptor		Descriptor		

Fig. 5. The full descriptor of the whole human body constructed with the six LBPs of key-body parts and the distances between them, it is called 6PD-LBP descriptor.

part of the descriptor of Fig. 5. Once the window is moved on the whole image the distances between the recognized body parts can be computed to build the descriptor of Fig. 5, using the Eq. 5. The on-line stage of the process is shown in Fig. 4.

$$D(P_1, P_2) = \frac{\sqrt{(x_2 - x_1)^2 + (y_2 - y_1)^2}}{base} \qquad (5)$$

where "base" is the Euclidean distance of the first two local features (body parts). We normalize the distance dividing by 10, so all distances are proportional, no matter the size of the image.

4   Results

Tests showed that a human form that occupies $20 - 35\%$ of the image can be detected by this descriptor. The tolerance to small changes in scale is another advantage of using the extended version of LBP. In Fig. 6 we can see some results of using the final descriptor and LBP as a local descriptor (6PD-LBP). In Fig. 7, we can see the result of 6PD-LBP on the same rotated original image and the parts dispersed body, but are the same descriptors used in the images a) and b) detects that these descriptors are not one person, by the distance between their local descriptors. It's important to note that our approach can deal with images with different resolution.

Fig. 6. The green square with the check mark indicates that a body is detected in the image and the red square with the cross indicates that the image does not have a body.

Fig. 7. a)Rotated image, b)Original image, c)Dispersed body parts.

We used INRIA statical data set, introduced by Navneet DALAL, and is publicly available for research purposes from http://lear.inrialpes.fr/data, and some images by test from MPII Human Pose dataset [3]. SVMs were used, trained with gaussian kernels.

4.1 Comparisons

Three comparisons were performed to validate the effectiveness of our descriptor. Firstly, a full body LBP descriptor of the human form was computed. Then a SVM was trained with positive (images with a body on them) and negative (images without human bodies) images. Finally, the obtained detection results of that descriptor an ours are compared; the results are shown in Figs. 8, 9(a), and in the Table 1. The second comparison experiment consisted in computing part-based descriptors using the same six body parts as in our approach and descriptors such as: Histogram of Oriented Gradients (6PD-HOG) and SURF (6PD-SURF) descriptors to construct the whole descriptor shown in Fig. 5. Recognition rates obtained were compared against those obtained using 6PD-LBP. Images incorrectly classified were those that had much noise, or because of the body position, or where body parts were incorrectly detected.

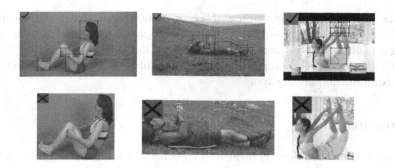

Fig. 8. Comparison between 6PD-LBP and LBP full body.

The following table shows the performance of classifiers using LBP, HOG and SURF as descriptors of texture and LBP full body descriptor. The number of training data is 505, where 253 are positive and 252 are negative. Meanwhile, the test total number of vectors is 279, where 134 are positive and 145 are negative.

Table 1. Evaluating performance of the classifier on train and test set.

Model	Train			Test		
	Accuracy	Sensitivity	Specificity	Accuracy	Sensitivity	Specificity
LBP full body	0.8201	0.9011	0.8015	0.6838	0.6940	0.7034
6PD-LBP	**0.8947**	0.9407	**0.8888**	0.8206	**0.8880**	0.8206
6PD-SURF	0.8791	**0.9486**	0.8690	**0.8814**	0.8880	**0.8896**
6PD-HOG	0.8726	0.9209	0.8650	0.8582	0.8582	0.8689

The following graphs, Fig. 9, are the ROC curve of the 4 classifiers with the performance curve for the classifier. The reader can note that higher rates of true positive patterns are obtained using the 6PD-LBP descriptor.

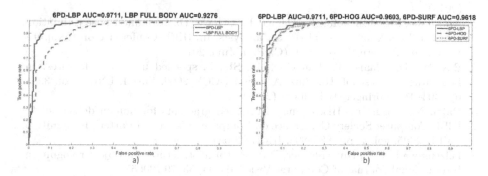

Fig. 9. a) ROC curves for SVMs classifiers trained with 6PD-LBP descriptor and the full body LBP descriptor as input data. b) ROC curves obtained for SVMs classifiers trained using part-base model descriptors 6PD-LBP, 6PD-SURF and 6PD-HOG.

In the performance of classifiers, if we need more sensitivity, the specificity is sacrificed. The reader should note that our approach has good results in the training set getting good generalization. However, in the testing set, our approach is slightly exceeded, while regarding the methodology of each local descriptor, LBP is computationally cheaper.

5   Conclusions

In this work, a methodology is presented to construct a part-based human body descriptor, that achieves non-pedestrian pose recognition. As it can be seen in the ROC curves and in the tables presented in the previous Section, our method obtains higher recognition rates compared with those approaches that use one descriptor with global information about the whole human body (full body LBP); even when this descriptor is rotational invariant. The part-based method proved to be robust to occlusion, although to reach good performance in experimental tests, at least four of the six body parts have to be recognized and included in the full descriptor. As future work, the sensitivity of our method will be proved statistically and implemented in an on-board computer of a flying robot, controlled with neural networks [8],[2], using omnidirectional cameras [12],[11] in order to obtain an intelligent UAV prototype.

Acknowledgments. This work was partially supported by grants CONACYT-CB-106838, 103191, 156567, 129079, INFR-229696 and scholarship grant CVU-556068.

References

1. Ahonen, T., Hadid, A., Pietikainen, M.: Face description with local binary patterns: Application to face recognition. IEEE Transactions on Pattern Analysis and Machine Intelligence **28**(12), 2037–2041 (2006)
2. Alanis, A.Y., Ornelas-Tellez, F., Sanchez, E.N.: Discrete-time inverse optimal neural control for synchronous generators. Eng. Appl. Artif. Intell. **26**(2), 697–705 (2013)
3. Andriluka, M., Pishchulin, L., Gehler, P., Schiele, B.: 2d human pose estimation: new benchmark and state of the art analysis. In: IEEE Conference on Computer Vision and Pattern Recognition (CVPR), June 2014
4. Bay, H., Tuytelaars, T., Van Gool, L.: SURF: speeded up robust features. In: Leonardis, A., Bischof, H., Pinz, A. (eds.) ECCV 2006, Part I. LNCS, vol. 3951, pp. 404–417. Springer, Heidelberg (2006)
5. Dalal, N., Triggs, B.: Histograms of oriented gradients for human detection. In: IEEE Computer Society Conference on Computer Vision and Pattern Recognition, CVPR 2005, vol. 1, pp. 886–893. IEEE (2005)
6. Felzenszwalb, P.F., Huttenlocher, D.P.: Pictorial structures for object recognition. International Journal of Computer Vision **61**(1), 55–79 (2005)
7. Hanavan Jr., E.P.: A mathematical model of the human body. Technical report, DTIC Document (1964)

8. Hernandez-Gonzalez, M., Alanis, A.Y., Hernandez-Vargas, E.A.: Decentralized discrete-time neural control for a quanser 2-dof helicopter. Applied Soft Computing **12**(8), 2462–2469 (2012)

9. Ioffe, S., Forsyth, D.A.: Probabilistic methods for finding people. International Journal of Computer Vision **43**(1), 45–68 (2001)

10. Lin, Z., Davis, L.S.: A pose-invariant descriptor for human detection and segmentation. In: Forsyth, D., Torr, P., Zisserman, A. (eds.) ECCV 2008, Part IV. LNCS, vol. 5305, pp. 423–436. Springer, Heidelberg (2008)

11. López-Franco, C., Arana-Daniel, N.: A geometric algebra model for the image formation process of paracatadioptric cameras. Journal of Mathematical Imaging and Vision **43**(3), 214–226 (2012)

12. López-Franco, C., Arana-Daniel, N., Alanis, A.Y.: Visual servoing on the sphere using conformal geometric algebra. Advances in Applied Clifford Algebras **23**(1), 125–141 (2013)

13. Mikolajczyk, K., Schmid, C., Zisserman, A.: Human detection based on a probabilistic assembly of robust part detectors. In: Pajdla, T., Matas, J.G. (eds.) ECCV 2004. LNCS, vol. 3021, pp. 69–82. Springer, Heidelberg (2004)

14. Ojala, T., Pietikainen, M., Maenpaa, T.: Multiresolution gray-scale and rotation invariant texture classification with local binary patterns. IEEE Transactions on Pattern Analysis and Machine Intelligence **24**(7), 971–987 (2002)

15. Oren, M., Papageorgiou, C., Sinha, P., Osuna, E., Poggio, T.: Pedestrian detection using wavelet templates. In: Proceedings of the 1997 IEEE Computer Society Conference on Computer Vision and Pattern Recognition, pp. 193–199. IEEE (1997)

16. Tani, Y., Hotta, K.: Robust human detection to pose and occlusion using bag-of-words. In: 2014 22nd International Conference on Pattern Recognition (ICPR), pp. 4376–4381. IEEE (2014)

17. Vapnik, V.: The nature of statistical learning theory. Springer Science & Business Media (2000)

18. Wang, X., Han, T.X., Yan, S.: An hog-lbp human detector with partial occlusion handling. In: 2009 IEEE 12th International Conference on Computer Vision, pp. 32–39. IEEE (2009)

19. Xia, L., Chen, C.-C., Aggarwal, J.K.: Human detection using depth information by kinect. In: 2011 IEEE Computer Society Conference on Computer Vision and Pattern Recognition Workshops (CVPRW), pp. 15–22. IEEE (2011)

20. Zhao, Y., Jia, W., Rong-Xiang, H., Min, H.: Completed robust local binary pattern for texture classification. Neurocomputing **106**, 68–76 (2013)

Automatic Video Summarization Using the Optimum-Path Forest Unsupervised Classifier

César Castelo-Fernández(✉) and Guillermo Calderón-Ruiz

School of Systems Engineering, Santa María Catholic University, Arequipa, Peru
{ccastelo,gcalderon}@ucsm.edu.pe

Abstract. In this paper a novel method for video summarization is presented, which uses a color-based feature extraction technique and a graph-based clustering technique. One major advantage of this method is that it is parameter-free, that is, we do not need to define neither the number of shots or a consecutive-frames dissimilarity threshold. The results have shown that the method is both effective and efficient in processing videos containing several thousands of frames, obtaining very meaningful summaries in a quick way.

Keywords: Optimum-path forest classifier · Video summarization · Shot detection · Clustering · Video processing

1 Introduction

Nowadays, huge amounts of multimedia information exist thanks to the popularization of smart portable devices like cell phones or tablets, which have cameras capable of recording high quality pictures and videos.

Such volume of information makes it necessary to have software capable of summarizing this information, allowing us to store only the most important parts of the videos. For example, 24-hour surveillance videos, that need to be analyzed daily, could be summarized into few-minutes clips. This problem could be solved using video processing and computer vision techniques.

To perform the analysis of the video's content, we need to extract features from each frame of it, more specifically, we need to characterize the color, texture and shape of the images composing the video. Then, the video is splitted into scenes and shots, which are the parts that compose it. This process is known as shot detection and it is the most important part of this kind of systems.

On the other hand, traditional approaches for shot detection consider the analysis of the level of dissimilarity between consecutive frames, setting a new shot when the dissimilarity is higher than a certain threshold. The problem with this approach is determining a suitable threshold for each video.

This paper presents a new approach for automatic video summarization, based on the application of the Optimun-Path Forest unsupervised classifier, a graph-based clustering technique known for being both fast and accurate.

© Springer International Publishing Switzerland 2015
A. Pardo and J. Kittler (Eds.): CIARP 2015, LNCS 9423, pp. 760–767, 2015.
DOI: 10.1007/978-3-319-25751-8_91

Moreover, this new approach does not need to know a priori the number of shots and scenes as other techniques do.

The rest of the document is organized as follows. Section 2 presents the main concepts of video summarization systems, Section 3 explains the techniques used for the proposed method, while Sections 4 and 5 present the evaluation and the conclusions, respectively.

2   Video Summarization

Formally speaking, a video can be defined as a set $V = \langle f_1, f_2, \ldots, f_n \rangle$ of frames f_i, that are images of M x N pixels. A video is made of the union of shots, which are separated by transitions. A transition T_i between the shots S_i and S_{i+1} can be represented by the pair $(s, t), s < t$, which are the indexes of the frames that form the transition, such that, $S_i = \langle \ldots, f_{s-1}, f_s \rangle$ and $S_{i+1} = \langle f_t, f_{t+1}, \ldots \rangle$. These transitions can be abrupt, when $t = s + 1$ (i.e. one shot starts immediately after the other) or gradual, when $t > s + 1$ (i.e. the two shots are superposed), being that the latter have edition effects, like fades or dissolutions.

In addition, the set of shots is grouped into scenes, which could be seen as a set of related shots developed in the same environment, also known as shots taken by the same camera.

The work developed by Chen et al. [2] presents an algorithm to detect the transitions in a video by using a threshold for the distance (dissimilarity measure) between two consecutive frames. This algorithm is very fast but it is very difficult to choose a suitable threshold, because it can be very different among videos.

Jadhav and Jadhav [4] developed a video summarization method that uses higher order color moments as the feature extraction technique. This method aims at the detection of shot boundaries by computing different statistics with the frames. However, it needs several thresholds for the shot boundary detection.

The method proposed by Ejaz et al. [3] uses an adaptive correlation scheme of color-based features which aims at the detection of key frames by using a threshold for the correlation level among them. The main drawback of this method is choosing a suitable threshold for the correlation levels.

Ren et al. [6] proposed a fuzzy approach that is able to classify the frames in the video according to the transitions present between them and according to camera motion analysis. The main idea is to generate a summary of the video according to the activities being performed inside it. One drawback is the use of a threshold to determine the final size of the summary generated.

Finally, Zhou et al. [9] proposed a video summarization method based on the use of a fuzzy c-means algorithm together with audio-visual features extracted from the video. The main problem of this technique is determining a suitable value for c (number of shots).

3   Automatic Video Summarization by Optimum-Path Forest

The method proposed in this paper relies on the use of a clustering algorithm to divide the video into shots.

We let the frames form groups in a natural way, that is, every group contains the most similar frames to each other. The reason for this is that a video is nothing more than a sequence of very similar pictures placed one next to the other at a certain frame rate. However, this is true for portions of the video (shots), not for the entire video, i.e., all the frames inside a shot are very similar to each other and they are different to frames in other shots.

This is the reason for using clustering. A clustering algorithm tries to find an optimal partition inside a group of objects, following the rule that every group has the highest level of similarity among their elements and the lowest level of similarity to the objects in the other clusters.

To perform this task, we need the objects to be represented numerically, more specifically as a feature vector, that it, a set of N numbers that represent the object as a point in a N-dimensional space. It is able to dictate whether two given images are similar or dissimilar. For the case of videos, they are obtained by applying one or more image processing techniques (i.e. feature extraction), which aim at the representation of the color, texture and shape of the frames.

Among the feature extraction techniques, we could mention color histograms, Gabor filters or Fourier descriptors, which are focused on representing color, texture and shape, respectively. Then, some distance function is needed to compute the level of dissimilarity between two vectors (e.g. Euclidean distance or Mahalanobis distance). Moreover, a very interesting option, and the one chosen for this work, is *Border-Interior Pixel Classification (BIC)*. This technique was chosen because it is both accurate for representing the color and fast enough to process the frames in the videos.

Regarding the clustering techniques, the most used approaches in the literature are the *k-means* algorithm and its variants *fuzzy k-means* or *k-medians*, which are all partition-based approaches. Also, we can mention probability-based approaches like *Mean-Shift*, *DBSCAN* and *Expectation-Maximization*. And, between others, we can also talk about graph-based approaches, like the ones based on the *Minimum-Spanning Tree (MST)* or the *Optimum-Path Forest (OPF)*, which is the one chosen for this work. We chose the OPF algorithm, because it is a threshold-free approach and it is both accurate and fast enough to find the shots in the video in a very short amount of time.

3.1   Feature Extraction Through Border/Interior Pixel Classification

Border-Interior Pixel Classification (BIC) [8] is a color-based technique proposed to address the well-known issue of global color representation presented by the traditional color histograms. This problem raises when we have two very different images with a very similar color distribution, i.e., two very different images will have very similar feature vectors.

As a solution, BIC performs a previous step of pixel classification into two possible kind of pixels, border and interior. For this, a quantization process has to be performed, transforming the color range of the pixels from, say, 256 gray levels (original image) to, say, 4 or 8 gray levels. Thus, an interior pixel is the one that is surrounded by pixels of the same (quantized) color and a border pixel is the one that is surrounded by at least one different color pixel. In other words, the interior pixels are the homogeneous regions of the image and the border pixels are the edges surrounding them. Then, separate histograms are computed for both interior and border pixels and the union of them is the final vector.

Furthermore, an improved distance measure is used instead of the traditional euclidean distance. This distance is called *dLog* and uses a logarithmic scale instead of a decimal one, aiming at the dissipation of the effect of very large values in the histograms (e.g. the image's background). It is defined by the Equation 3.1.

$$dLog(q,d) = \sum_{i=0}^{i<M} |f(q[i]) - f(d[i])| \qquad (3.1)$$

where M is the dimension of the vectors q and d and f is defined as:

$$f(n) = \begin{cases} 0 & \text{if } x = 0 \\ 1 & \text{if } 0 < x \leq 1 \\ log_2 x + 1 & \text{otherwise} \end{cases} \qquad (3.2)$$

3.2 Clustering Through the Optimum-Path Forest Unsupervised Classifier

The *Optimum-Path Forest (OPF)* [7] algorithm's main goal is to find an optimal partition of the training set with the help of a graph, which is used to represent the samples being grouped. For this, every sample is mapped to a node in the graph, representing it as a feature vector. The optimal partition OPF seeks for is represented as a forest of optimal trees rooted in specially-chosen samples called *prototypes*. A cluster is made of one or more trees.

OPF uses a searching algorithm which aims at finding an optimum path for every sample in the training set, which starts in one of the chosen prototypes. In this sense, this algorithm could be seen as a multiple-source and multiple-end shortest-path algorithm, defined by Equation 3.3.

$$\mathcal{V}(t) = \max_{\forall \pi_t^s \in (\mathcal{N}, \mathcal{A})} \{f(\pi_t^s)\} \qquad (3.3)$$

where π_t^s is the path from the node $s \in \mathcal{S}$ (set of prototypes) to the node t, $(\mathcal{N}, \mathcal{A})$ is the set of nodes (as defined by the adjacency relationship $\mathcal{A}$) and f is a function that measures the cost of the path π_t^s.

The set of prototypes $\mathcal{S}$ is chosen by computing a *Probability Density Function (PDF)* over the training set and then finding the maxima of this PDF. However, this PDF does not use the traditional (radial) Gaussian function to weight the relationship between every sample and its neighbors. It uses a modified version of the Gaussian function that uses the k nearest neighbors to every sample s instead of considering all the neighbors that are inside a certain radius. This approach has the advantage of better dealing with arbitrary-shape clusters by not assuming that all clusters has a circular shape, but allowing them to be represented in its natural way. Equation 3.4 dictates how the PDF is computed.

$$\rho(s) = \frac{1}{\sqrt{2\pi\sigma^2}|\mathcal{A}(s)|} \sum_{t \in \mathcal{A}(s)} \exp\left(\frac{-d^2(s,t)}{2\sigma^2}\right) \tag{3.4}$$

which computes a gaussian function centered on s where $\mathcal{A}$ is the adjacency function defined by k and σ is defined as: $\sigma = \max_{\forall(s,t)\in A}\left\{\frac{d(s,t)}{3}\right\}$.

While we need to enter the number k of neighbours used to create the k-nn graph, it can be computed automatically by measuring the quality of the graph cut and then optimizing this value for $[1, k_{max}]$, as proposed by Rocha et al. [7]. Finally, after finding the PDF maxima, we need to reduce the number of clusters found by using β to avoid very small clusters, as explained by Rocha et al. [7].

3.3 Shot and Scene Detection Through Two-Level Clustering

The clustering process explained above is performed using the feature vectors obtained from the video's frames. The result is a set of groups which correspond to the shots of the video. Then, we would like to choose one frame for each shot that better represents it. This frame is called the key-frame and corresponds to the centroid of the cluster.

Furthermore, after computing all the key-frames, we use them to perform the last process of our method, namely, the scene detection process. Based on the same principles behind the use of clustering to find the shots, we perform a new clustering process using only the key-frames. As a result, the groups found in this task will correspond to the scenes of the video.

Finally, we also compute the scene key-frames for this clusters and use them to generate the summary of the video. For this, we extract a small set of frames before and after each scene key-frame and put them together according to the time position of each key-frame. According to the job developed by Pfeiffer et al. [5], the minimum size a scene should have is 3.25 seconds in order to be analyzed properly by a person.

4 Evaluation

The validation process of the proposed method was initially made using commercial videos of different sizes. Table 1 summarizes the characteristics of the videos. A manual inspection process was performed to obtain the shot detection ground-truth for each video.

Regarding the statistical approach used to compare our method with other methods, we used the ROC curve, the most used method to compare information

Table 1. Videos used for the tests.

Video name	Resolution	Length	Frames	FPS	Shots
Taboo	480x320	04:52 min.	7008	24	201
Say it right	480x320	03:56 min.	5664	24	216
Crazy Frog	352x288	03:20 min.	5006	25	82
Bendita tu luz	480x320	04:10 min.	6007	24	146
Destino de fuego	480x360	03:59 min.	7191	30	175

retrieval algorithms. A ROC curve allows us to evaluate the global behavior of a technique, i.e., it is not biased by a particular choice of parameters.

We chose the threshold-based method proposed by Chen et al. [2] and also we chose a similar work, developed by Castelo [1], where a k-means algorithm is used to perform the clustering process. Furthermore, a threshold-based method is used in this work to determine the value of k.

Figure 1 presents the ROC curves obtained for the three methods, our OPF-based method, the threshold-based method and the k-means-based method.

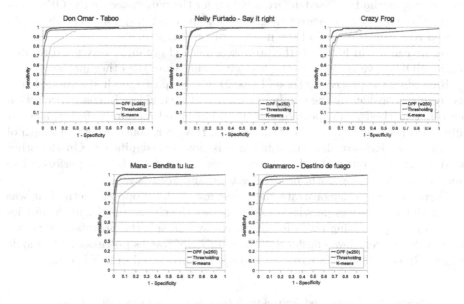

Fig. 1. ROC curves for the three methods, using the test videos. Here: $1 \leq k \leq 20, 0 \leq \beta \leq 500$ (OPF) y $0 \leq \mu \leq 0.99, 0 \leq \delta \leq 0.99$ (Thresholding and k-means).

Table 2 summarizes the ROC curves computed and presents, for each technique, the combination of parameters that lead to the better results according to the ROC curve.

We used different threshold values for both methods to create the ROC curve (thresholds μ and δ are used to detect abrupt and gradual transitions separately)

Table 2. False Positive Rate, True Positive Rate, Accuracy and Execution Time (seconds) for the three methods.

Video	Method	k/μ	β/δ	FPR	TPR	Acc.	Exec.Time
	OPF	7	160	**0.04**	**0.99**	**0.97**	0.564 ± 0.077
Taboo	Thresh.	0.00	0.04	**0.04**	0.97	0.96	**0.001 ± 0.001**
	k-means	0.05	0.05	0.08	0.82	0.87	1.193 ± 2.048
	OPF	6	40	0.07	0.98	**0.96**	0.438 ± 0.062
Say it right	Thresh.	0.04	0.12	**0.06**	**0.99**	**0.96**	**0.001 ± 0.001**
	k-means	0.09	0.05	0.09	0.86	0.88	1.184 ± 1.619
	OPF	14	340	**0.03**	**0.96**	**0.97**	0.396 ± 0.057
Crazy Frog	Thresh.	0.04	0.20	0.04	0.89	0.93	**0.001 ± 0.001**
	k-means	0.09	0.05	0.09	0.93	0.92	0.495 ± 1.021
	OPF	15	100	**0.02**	**0.97**	**0.97**	0.463 ± 0.065
Bendita tu luz	Thresh.	0.64	0.04	0.04	0.95	0.95	**0.001 ± 0.001**
	k-means	0.09	0.05	0.06	0.79	0.87	0.732 ± 1.556
	OPF	14	20	**0.03**	**0.95**	**0.96**	0.605 ± 0.085
Destino de fuego	Thresh.	0.00	0.04	0.04	0.94	0.95	**0.001 ± 0.001**
	k-means	0.05	0.05	0.06	0.82	0.88	1.078 ± 1.708

and, for our method, we used different values for the parameters of the OPF algorithm (the number k of nearest neighbors for the k-nn graph and the threshold β, used to automatically find the number of prototypes).

As we can see in Figure 1, the proposed method obtained very good results, i.e., its ROC curve is closer to the top left corner than the other methods'.

Regarding the processing time (Table 2), the proposed method obtained very fast results, considering the number of frames of each video. In comparison with the other methods, as expected, the threshold-based method is faster, since it only performs a lineal analysis of the frames. However, considering the length of the videos we can say that the difference is not very significant. On the other hand, comparing our method with the k-means-based method, it performed so much better regarding both, processing time and accuracy.

Furthermore, to demonstrate the efficiency of the proposed method, it was used with longer videos (movies). Table 3 shows the characteristics of the movies used and the processing times for them. As we can see, the processing time for the movies are very low, considering the number of frames processed. The movie "Ghost Rider" (158572 frames), for example, is processed in 23.85 seconds.

Table 3. Movies used for the time tests with their processing times.

Video	Resolution	Length	Frames	FPS	Processing Times
Batman Forever	320x240	01:56:34 h.	174869	25	27.99
Ghost Rider	320x240	01:50:13 h.	158572	25	23.85
Starship Troopers	320x240	02:08:28 h.	192712	25	36.06

As future work, we will compare the proposed method to a wider range of clustering algorithms.

5 Conclusions

In this work, a novel method for video summarization was presented. This method is based on the use of clustering techniques to find groups inside the video, which correspond to the shots and scenes. As was shown, the method is better than the two methods used for comparison. BIC, the feature extraction technique chosen, has proved to be both effective and efficient since it helped us to obtain low processing times with good accuracy. Overall, the proposed method is very effective to summarize videos, having obtained the best results looking at the ROC curves. Regarding the processing time needed to perform the analysis, our method is very efficient, considering the number of frames in the videos. It only needed 24 seconds to process a video with more than 158000 frames. Furthermore, one strong point of our method is that it does not need to know a priori the number of groups to perform the cluster analysis.

References

1. Castelo-Fernández, C.: Content-based video retrieval through wavelets and clustering. In: Proceedings of the IV Workshop de Visão Computacional, Bauru, São Paulo, Brasil. UNESP (2008)
2. Chen, L.H., Su, C.W., Mark Liao, H.Y., Shih, C.C.: On the preview of digital movies. Journal of Visual Communication and Image Representation (2003)
3. Ejaz, N.: Tayyab Bin Tariq, and Sung Wook Baik. Adaptive key frame extraction for video summarization using an aggregation mechanism. Journal of Visual Communication and Image Representation $23(7)$, 1031–1040 (2012)
4. Jadhav, P.S., Jadhav, D.S.: Video summarization using higher order color moments (vsuhcm). Procedia Computer Science 45, 275–281 (2015). International Conference on Advanced Computing Technologies and Applications (ICACTA)
5. Pfeiffer, S., Lienhart, R., Fischer, S., Effelsberg, W.: Abstracting digital movies automatically. Journal of Visual Communication and Image Representation $7(4)$, 345–353 (1996)
6. Ren, J., Jiang, J., Feng, Y.: Activity-driven content adaptation for effective video summarization. Journal of Visual Communication and Image Representation $21(8)$, 930–938 (2010). Large-Scale Image and Video Search: Challenges, Technologies, and Trends
7. Rocha, L.M., Cappabianco, F.A.M., Falcão, A.X.: Data clustering as an optimum-path forest problem with applications in image analysis. Int. J. Imaging Syst. Technol. 19, 50–68 (2009)
8. Stehling, R.O., Nascimento, M.A., Falcão, A.X.: A compact and efficient image retrieval approach based on border/interior pixel classification. In: Proceedings of the Eleventh International Conference on Information and Knowledge Management, CIKM '02, pp. 102–109 (2002)
9. Zhou, H., Sadka, A.H., Swash, M.R., Azizi, J., Sadiq, U.A.: Feature extraction and clustering for dynamic video summarisation. Neurocomputing $73(10–12)$, 1718–1729 (2010). Subspace Learning/Selected papers from the European Symposium on Time Series Prediction

A Shuffled Complex Evolution Algorithm
for the Multidimensional Knapsack Problem

Marcos Daniel Valadão Baroni$^{(\boxtimes)}$ and Flávio Miguel Varejão

Universidade Federal Do Espírito Santo,
Av. Fernando Ferrari, 514, Goiabeiras, Vitória, ES, Brazil
marcosdaniel.baroni@gmail.com
http://ninfa.inf.ufes.br/

Abstract. This work addresses the application of a population based evolutionary algorithm called shuffled complex evolution (SCE) in the multidimensional knapsack problem. The SCE regards a natural evolution happening simultaneously in independent communities. The performance of the SCE algorithm is verified through computational experiments using well-known problems from literature and randomly generated problem as well. The SCE proved to be very effective in finding good solutions demanding a very small amount of processing time.

Keywords: Multidimensional knapsack problem · Meta-heuristics · Artificial intelligence

1 Introduction

The multidimensional knapsack problem (MKP) is a strongly NP-hard combinatorial optimization problem which can be viewed as a resource allocation problem and defined as follows:

$$\text{maximize} \sum_{j=1}^{n} p_j x_j$$

$$\text{subject to} \sum_{j=1}^{n} w_{ij} x_j \leqslant c_i \quad i \in \{1, \ldots, m\}$$

$$x_j \in \{0, 1\}, \quad j \in \{1, \ldots, n\}.$$

The problem can be interpreted as a set of n items with profits p_j and a set of m resources with capacities c_i. Each item j consumes an amount w_{ij} from each resource i, if selected. The objective is to select a subset of items with maximum total profit, not exceeding the defined resource capacities. The decision variable x_j indicates if j-th item is selected.

Research supported by Fundação de Amparo à Pesquisa do Espírito Santo.

A. Pardo and J. Kittler (Eds.): CIARP 2015, LNCS 9423, pp. 768–775, 2015.
DOI: 10.1007/978-3-319-25751-8_92

The multidimensional knapsack problem can be applied on budget planning scenarios and project selections [8], cutting stock problems [7], loading problems [10], allocation of processors and databases in distributed computer programs [6].

The problem is a generalization of the well-known knapsack problem (KP) in which $m = 1$. However it is a NP-hard problem significantly harder to solve in practice than the KP. Due its simple definition but challenging difficulty of solving, the MKP is often used to to verify the efficiency of novel metaheuristics. A good review for the MKP is given by [5].

In this paper we address the application of a metaheuristic called shuffled complex evolution (SCE) to the multidimensional knapsack problem. The SCE is a metaheuristic, proposed by Duan in [3], which combines the ideas of a controlled random search with the concepts of competitive evolution and shuffling. The SCE algorithm has been successfully used to solve several problems like flow shop scheduling [11] and project management [4].

The reminder of the paper is organized as follows: Section 2 presents the shuffled complex evolution algorithm and proposes its application on the MKP. Section 3 comprises several computational experiments. In section 4 we make our concluding remarks about the experimental results.

2 The Shuffled Complex Evolution for the MKP

The shuffled complex evolution is a population based evolutionary optimization algorithm that regards a natural evolution happening simultaneously in independent communities. The algorithm works with a population partitioned in N complexes, each one having M individuals. In the next Subsection the SCE is explained in more details. In the later Subsection the application of SCE to the multidimensional knapsack problem is considered.

2.1 The Shuffled Complex Evolution

In the SCE a population of $N*M$ individuals is randomly taken from the feasible solution space. After this initialization the population is sorted by descending order according to their fitness and the best global solution is identified. The entire population is then partitioned (shuffled) into N complexes, each containing M individuals. In this shuffling process the first individual goes to the first complex, the second individual goes to the second complex, individual N goes to N-th complex, individual $M + 1$ goes back to the first complex, etc.

The next step after shuffling the complexes is to evolve each complex through a given fixed amount of K' steps. The individuals in each complex is sorted by descending order of fitness quality. In each step a subcomplex of P individuals is selected from the complex using a triangular probability distribution, where the i-th individual has a probability $p_i = \frac{2(n+1-i)}{n(n+1)}$ of being selected. The use of triangular distribution is intended to prioritize individuals with better fitness, supporting the algorithm convergence rate.

After the selection of the subcomplex, its worst individual is identified to be replaced by a new generated solution. This new solution is generated by the crossing of the worst individual and an other individual with better fitness. At first the best individual of the subcomplex is considered for the crossing. If the new solution is not better than the worst one, the best individual of the complex is considered for a crossing. If the latter crossing did not result in any improvement, the best individual of whole population is considered. Finally, if all the crossing steps couldn't generate a better individual, the worst individual of the subcomplex is replaced by a new random solution taken from the feasible solution space. This last step is important to prevent the algorithm becoming trapped in local minima. Fig. 1(b) presents the evolving procedure described above in a flowchart diagram.

After evolving all the N complexes the whole population is again sorted by descending order of fitness quality and the process continues until a stop condition is satisfied. Fig. 1(a) shows the SCE algorithm in a flowchart diagram.

2.2 The Shuffled Complex Evolution for the MKP

As it can be noted in its description the SCE is easily applied to any optimization problem. The only steps needed to be specified is (a) the creation of a new random solution and (b) the crossing procedure of two solutions. These two procedures are respectively presented by Algorithm. 1 and Algorithm 2.

Algorithm 1. Generation of a new random solution for the MKP.

```
 1: procedure NEW RANDOM SOLUTION
 2:     v ← shuffle(1, 2, . . . , n)
 3:     s ← ∅                                           ▷ empty solution
 4:     for i ← 1 : n do
 5:         s ← s ∪ {v_i}                               ▷ adding item
 6:         if  s is not feasible then          ▷ checking feasibility
 7:             s ← s − {v_i}
 8:         end if
 9:     end for
10:     return s
11: end procedure
```

To construct a new random solution (Algorithm 1) the items are at first shuffled in random order and stored in a list (line 2). A new empty solution is then defined (line 3). The algorithm iteratively tries to fill the solution's knapsack with the an item taken from the list (lines 4-9). The feasibility of the solution is then checked: if the item insertion let the solution unfeasible (line 6) its removed from knapsack (line 7). After trying to place all available items the new solution is returned.

The crossing procedure (Algorithm 2) takes as input the worst solution taken from the subcomplex $x^w = (x_1^w, x_2^w, \ldots, x_n^w)$, the selected better solution

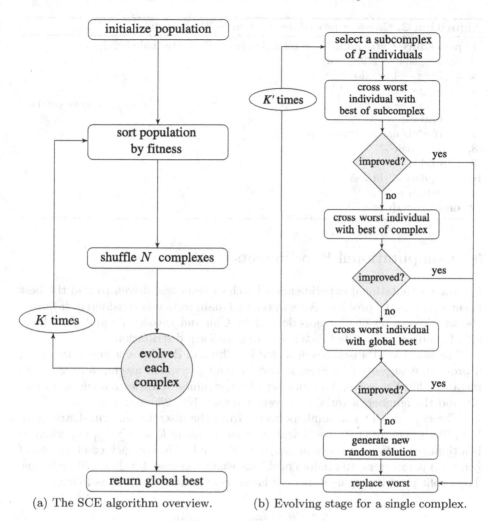

(a) The SCE algorithm overview.   (b) Evolving stage for a single complex.

Fig. 1. Flowchart representing the shuffled complex evolution algorithm.

$x_b = (x_1^b, x_2^b, \ldots, x_n^b)$ and the number c of genes that will be carried from the better solution. The c parameter will control how similar the worst individual will be from the given better individual. At first the items are shuffled in random order and stored in a list (line 2). Then c randomly chosen genes are carried from the better individual to the worst individual (line 5). At the end of steps the feasibility of the solution is checked (line 7) and the solution is repaired if needed. The repair stage is a greedy procedure that iteratively removes the item that less decreases the objective function. Finally the fitness of the generated solution is updated (line 10) and returned (line 11).

Algorithm 2. Crossing procedure used on SCE algorithm.
_____
1: **procedure** CROSSING(x^w : worst individual, x^b : better individual, c)
2:     $v \leftarrow$ shuffle$(1, 2, \ldots, n)$
3:     **for** $i \leftarrow 1 : c$ **do**
4:         $j \leftarrow v_i$
5:         $x_j^w \leftarrow x_j^b$ ▷ gene carriage
6:     **end for**
7:     **if** s^w is not feasible **then**
8:         repair s^w
9:     **end if**
10:    update s^w fitness
11:    return s^w
12: **end procedure**
_____

3   Computational Experiments

For the computational experiments a batch of tests was driven to find the best
parameters for the problem. Afterwards two main tests was considered: (a) using
the well-known set of problems defined by Chu and Beasley [2] and (b) a large
set of randomly generated instances using uniform distribution.

The set of MKP instances provided by Chu and Beasley was generated using
a procedure suggested by Freville and Plateau [5], which attempts to generate
instances hard to solve. The number of constraints m varies among 5, 10 and
30, and the number of variables n varies among 100, 250 and 500.

The w_{ij} were integer numbers drawn from the discrete uniform distribution
$U(0, 1000)$. The capacity coefficient c_i were set using $b_i = \alpha \sum_{j=1}^{n} w_{ij}$ where α
is a tightness ratio and varies among 0.25, 0.5 and 0.75. For each combination of
(m, n, α) parameters, 10 random problems was generated, totaling 270 problems.
The profit p_j of the items were correlated to w_{ij} and generated as follows:

$$p_j = \sum_{i=1}^{m} \frac{w_{ij}}{m} + 500q_j \qquad j = 1, \ldots, n$$

The second set of instances is composed by problems generated using a similar
setup. The only differences is that the profit p_j is also drawn from a discrete
uniform distribution $U(0, 1000)$. For each combination of (m, n, α) parameter,
600 random problems was generated, totaling 16200 problems.

All the experiments was run on a Intel Core i5-3570 CPU @3.40GHz computer with 4GB of RAM. The SCE algorithm for MKP was implemented in C
programming language. For the set of random instance all best known solution
was found by the solver SCIP 3.0.1 running for at least 10 minutes. SCIP [1] is an
open-source integer programming solver which implements the branch-and-cut
algorithm [9].

After a previous test batch parameters for SCE was defined as shown in
Table 1 and used in all executions of SCE.

Table 1. Parameters used in SCE algorithm.

Parameter	Value	Description
N	20	# of complexes
M	20	# of individuals in each complex
P	5	# of individuals in each subcomplex
K	300	# of algorithm iterations
K'	20	# of iterations used in the complex evolving process
c	$n/5$	# of genes carried from parent in crossing process

Table 2 shows the performance of the SCE on the Chu-Beasley set of instance. Each instance in the set was executed 10 times on SCE. The *SCE t* column shows the average execution time of SCE. The *gap* column shows the average ratio of the solution found by SCE and the best known solution of each instance. It can be observed that the SCE has a fast convergence speed, achieving high quality solutions in few seconds.

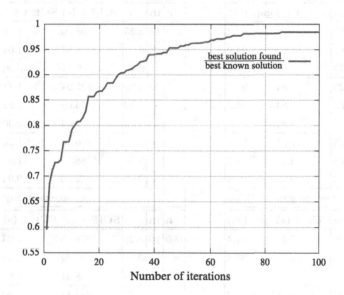

Fig. 2. Convergence process of SCE for MKP for a problem with $n = 500$, $m = 30$ and $t = 0.50$.

The fast convergence speed of SCE for MKP can be noticed in Fig. 2. The figure shows for each iterations step, the quality of best solution found for the first 100 iterations. The problem instance used was taken from the second set of problem (random instances). The best known solution was found with 600s of execution on SCIP solver and the execution of the SCE algorithm expended 1.1 seconds.

Table 2. SCE performance on Chu-Beasley problems.

Table 3. SCE performance on the random generated problems.

n	m	α	SCE t (s)	gap (%)
100	5	0.25	0.79	96.5
		0.5	0.81	97.4
		0.75	0.83	98.9
	10	0.25	0.75	95.7
		0.5	0.93	96.7
		0.75	0.89	98.5
	30	0.25	1.01	95.4
		0.5	1.07	96.4
		0.75	0.99	98.2
		average gap		97.1

n	m	α	SCE t (s)	gap (%)
250	5	0.25	1.72	93.2
		0.5	1.75	94.9
		0.75	1.78	97.6
	10	0.25	1.84	93.1
		0.5	1.84	94.6
		0.75	1.81	97.2
	30	0.25	2.21	93.2
		0.5	2.21	94.2
		0.75	2.31	96.6
		average gap		95.0

n	m	α	SCE t (s)	gap (%)
500	5	0.25	3.16	91.4
		0.5	3.18	93.4
		0.75	3.34	96.4
	10	0.25	3.39	91.7
		0.5	3.37	93.1
		0.75	3.44	96.2
	30	0.25	3.83	91.4
		0.5	3.90	92.6
		0.75	3.99	96.0
		average gap		93.6

n	m	α	SCIP t (s)	SCE t (s)	gap (%)
100	10	0.25	0.93	0.41	98.3
		0.50	0.28	0.39	99.3
		0.75	0.09	0.37	99.8
	20	0.25	3.15	0.41	98.2
		0.50	0.71	0.40	99.3
		0.75	0.16	0.37	99.8
	30	0.25	7.26	0.42	98.3
		0.50	1.47	0.42	99.3
		0.75	0.25	0.38	99.8
		average gap			99.1

n	m	α	SCIP t (s)	SCE t (s)	gap (%)
250	10	0.25	58.20	1.10	97.2
		0.50	8.51	1.04	98.9
		0.75	0.51	0.90	99.7
	20	0.25	227.94	1.11	97.6
		0.50	43.69	1.02	99.0
		0.75	1.59	0.90	99.8
	30	0.25	270.48	1.20	97.7
		0.50	88.73	1.09	99.0
		0.75	2.90	0.94	99.8
		average gap			98.7

n	m	α	SCIP t (s)	SCE t (s)	gap (%)
500	10	0.25	278.85	2.23	96.1
		0.50	177.32	2.14	98.4
		0.75	8.47	1.87	99.6
	20	0.25	284.11	2.30	96.7
		0.50	275.68	2.16	98.6
		0.75	33.67	1.90	99.7
	30	0.25	283.78	2.50	96.9
		0.50	283.54	2.32	98.7
		0.75	71.66	1.96	99.7
		average gap			98.3

4   Conclusions and Future Remarks

In this work we addressed the application of the shuffled complex evolution (SCE) to the multidimensional knapsack problem and investigated it performance through several computational experiments.

The SCE algorithm, which combines the ideas of a controlled random search with the concepts of competitive evolution proved to be very effective in finding good solution for hard instances of MKP, demanding a very small amount of processing time to reach high quality solutions for MKP.

Future work includes the investigation of different crossing procedures and the use of local search in the process of evolving complexes.

References

1. Achterberg, T.: Scip: Solving constraint integer programs. Mathematical Programming Computation **1**(1), 1–41 (2009). http://mpc.zib.de/index.php/MPC/article/view/4
2. Chu, P.C., Beasley, J.E.: A genetic algorithm for the multidimensional knapsack problem. Journal of Heuristics **4**(1), 63–86 (1998). http://dx.doi.org/10.1023/A:1009642405419
3. Duan, Q., Sorooshian, S., Gupta, V.: Effective and efficient global optimization for conceptual rainfall-runoff models. Water Resources Research **28**(4), 1015–1031 (1992)
4. Elbeltagi, E., Hegazy, T., Grierson, D.: A modified shuffled frog-leaping optimization algorithm: applications to project management. Structure and Infrastructure Engineering **3**(1), 53–60 (2007)
5. Freville, A., Plateau, G.: An efficient preprocessing procedure for the multidimensional 0–1 knapsack problem. Discrete Applied Mathematics **49**(1), 189–212 (1994)
6. Gavish, B., Pirkul, H.: Allocation of data bases and processors in a distributed computing system (1982)
7. Gilmore, P.C., Gomory, R.E.: The Theory and Computation of Knapsack Functions. Operations Research **14**, 1045–1074 (1966)
8. McMillan, C., Plaine, D.: Resource allocation via 0–1 programming. Decision Sciences **4**, 119–132 (1973)
9. Padberg, M., Rinaldi, G.: A branch-and-cut algorithm for the resolution of large-scale symmetric traveling salesman problems. SIAM Review **33**(1), 60–100 (1991)
10. Shih, W.: A Branch and Bound Method for the Multiconstraint Zero-One Knapsack Problem. Journal of The Operational Research Society **30**, 369–378 (1979)
11. Zhao, F., Zhang, J., Wang, J., Zhang, C.: A shuffled complex evolution algorithm with opposition-based learning for a permutation flow shop scheduling problem. International Journal of Computer Integrated Manufacturing (ahead-of-print), 1–16 (2014)

Pedestrian Detection Using Multi-Objective Optimization

Pablo Negri[1,2](✉)

[1] CONICET, Av. Rivadavia 1917, Buenos Aires, Argentina
pnegri@uade.edu.ar
[2] INTEC-UADE, Lima 717, Buenos Aires, Argentina

Abstract. Pedestrian detection on urban video sequences challenges classification systems because of the presence of cluttered backgrounds which drop their performances. This article proposes a Multi-Objective Optimization (MOO) technique reducing this limitation. It trains a pool of cascades of boosted classifiers using different positive datasets. A Pareto Front is obtained from the locally non-dominated operational points of the Receptive Objective Curve (ROC) of those classifiers. Using information about the dynamic of the scene, different pairs of operational points from the Pareto Front are employed to improve the performance of the system. Results on a real sequences outperform traditional detector systems.

Keywords: Multi-Objective Optimization · Pedestrian detection

1 Introduction

The behavior of object detection systems using image processing is controlled by fixing constrains or establishing performance criterias. Two numerical variables which can define this behavior are: Correct Detections (CD) and False Alarms (FA). CD computes objects successfully identified on the image, while FA are the erroneous outputs of the detector.

In some applications the CD ratio would be very important to identify an object or situation. For example, a buried land mines system detector should be very sensible to CD and would validate a position if there exists a slight doubt. Considering that a non detected land mine can take away a human life, a great number of FA is not relevant. On the other hand, an herbicide system using vision which has high FA ratio imply an economic waste when it fumigates unnecessarily the farmland. Minimizing the number of FA implies that not all the weeds would be eliminated. Even though, a low quantity of weed does not represent a danger for the crop. Thus, finding a balance between CD and FA will define the behavior of the system which is closely related with the application.

This article addresses a people detector using the Movement Feature Space (MFS) [8,9] on video sequences captured at a street corner, as show fig. 1(a). These kind of outdoors images with non controlled environments have numerous

© Springer International Publishing Switzerland 2015
A. Pardo and J. Kittler (Eds.): CIARP 2015, LNCS 9423, pp. 776–784, 2015.
DOI: 10.1007/978-3-319-25751-8_93

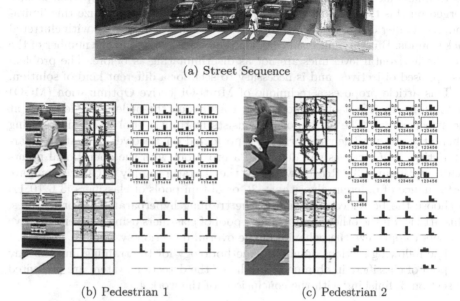

(a) Street Sequence

(b) Pedestrian 1   (c) Pedestrian 2

Fig. 1. Fig. (a) shows a capture of the street sequence. Figs. (b) and (c) represent non detected pedestrians and the features obtained from the MFS.

factors harming the performance of state of the art pedestrians detectors [4,5]. This is mainly due to: other moving objects on the scene, abrupt changes of the illumination, and a cluttered background.

Figures 1(b) and 1(c) show two examples of non detected pedestrians using MFS classifier. Second column represents the orientations matrix O_t of the MFS, and the third column shows the Histograms of Level Lines (HO2L) computed inside each patch of the grid (see [7,8] for details).

The HO2L features of the background without the Pedestrian 1 on fig. 1(b) are mostly composed of level lines with horizontal orientation: $bin = 4$. When the person is in front of the vehicle, their presence changes the histograms, but there is a high predominance of the horizontal orientation. It can be considered that their features are absorbed by the background features. Then, they are hardly noticeable by the classifier which would not detect the pedestrian. Pedestrian 2, fig. 1(c), shows a cluttered background generated by the shadows of the trees, producing moving level lines on the MFS until they became part of the background model. During this period, pedestrians walking in front of this background are not detected. The immersion effect is similar to the example 1, but less noticeable.

It can be stated that the problem is related with the presence of horizontal features. Actually, a person hardly generates this kind of features [5]. Therefore, on the training stage of a pedestrian classifier, this orientation becomes a discriminant factor that easily eliminates FA. However, when a person is submerged on this type of background, it is not detected. To minimize this limitation, a classifier can be trained using a greater number of persons with cluttered backgrounds. But this will result in an exponential increase in the number of the FA: the horizontal level lines are not as discriminating as before. The problem has opposed objectives, and is necessary to seek for a different kind of solution.

This article proposes a technique of Multi-Objective Optimization (MOO) to minimize the effect of the horizontal features on the pedestrian detectors at the street corner. The methodology consists to train a pool of classifiers using different datasets. Their performances projected on Receiver Operating Characteristics (ROC) curves will define a Pareto Front with the operational points locally optimums [3]. Recent works of the literature apply MOO to compare performance of different algorithms [2], or obtain pools of classifiers [3,6,10,11] to choose the better combination of the training hyperparameters or features. This article, on the other hand, trains a pool of classifiers using different positive datasets to optimize the behavior of the overall detection system.

The following sections details the methodology for the training and the way the pool of classifiers in obtained. Results of the detection system are presented on section 3, finishing with the conclusions of the work 4.

2   Methodology

2.1   ROC Front Construction

Pareto optimization gives a framework where solutions of the problem coexist with opposed objectives. This pool of solutions Ψ are the different classifiers trained by our system. The vector solution $\mathbf{x} = [x_1, ..., x_n]^T \in \Re^n$ is composed of all the decision variables x_i. The l objective functions are defined as $f_i(\mathbf{x}), i = 1, ..., l$. Then, the solution $\mathbf{x}^i$ domminates solution $\mathbf{x}^2$ ($\mathbf{x}^1 \leq \mathbf{x}^2$), if and only if $\mathbf{x}^1$ is better than $\mathbf{x}^2$ on one objective and is not worst on the others [11]:

$$\forall i : f_i(\mathbf{x}^1) \leq f_i(\mathbf{x}^2) \land \exists j : f_j(\mathbf{x}^1) < f_j(\mathbf{x}^2) \tag{1}$$

Using this dominance concept, the purpose of the MOO algorithm consists to find the set of all dominant solutions applying the objective functions to the system. This set is denominated Pareto Front.

This work relates the objective functions $f_j(\mathbf{x}^1)$ to the ratio CD/FA obtained from the ROC curve [3]. The ROC curve is generally employed to choose an operational point for a classifier [1]. To obtain the ROC for a two class problem, a classifier is applied on a dataset composed of positives and negatives samples using different validation thresholds. The use of each threshold would result on a CD and FA point which is employed to construct the ROC curve. This curve evaluates the sensibility and specificity of the classifier.

Fig. 2(b) represents and example of two ROC curves belonging to different classifiers. The objective functions f look for CD maximization and FA minimization points. Curve ROC1 locally dominates ROC2 for high values of CD,

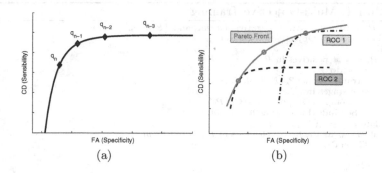

Fig. 2. Figure shows: (a) ROC curve for a Cascade of Boosted Classifiers and their operational points q_i, (b) Pareto Front using two ROC curves.

while ROC2 dominates ROC1 for low values of CD. The selection of locally dominant operational points defines the Pareto Front, which is draw on fig. 2(a) as the exterior bounding curve.

2.2   Classifiers Training

Cascade of Boosted Classifiers. This section details the methodology to combine the training of the Cascade of Boosted Classifiers, and the Multi-Objective Optimization technique. The training of a Cascade of Boosted Classifiers $\mathbf{C}$ requires a dataset P composed of positive samples of the class (pedestrians in this case), and a negative dataset N composed of non-class samples. It is also necessary to define some training parameters as: the maximum number of stages E in $\mathbf{C}$, the minimum percentage of correct detections d_{min} and the maximum percentage of false alarms f_{max} allowed at each stage [12].

The resulting Cascade $\mathbf{C} = \{C_1, C_2, ..., C_n\}$ is a set of n boosted classifiers C_i of growing complexity. Those C_i are applied sequentially on an test image to detect the positive class. The behavior of $\mathbf{C}$ is strongly related by the choose of all the training parameters and the datasets: $\{P, N, E, d_{min}, f_{max}\}$.

The ROC curve of $\mathbf{C}$ is computed employing the methodology proposed by Viola & Jones [12], considering the individual thresholds T_i of each stage C_i obtained on the training. The ROC curve is composed of the concatenation of the ROC segments calculated for each stage of the cascade. A segment j of the curve, corresponding to the C_j classifier of $\mathbf{C}$, results by applying a validation threshold to the dataset from $-\infty$ to the T_j value. Fig. 2(a) draws an example where q_n denotes the operational point of the last classifier C_n using T_n as value for their threshold, q_{n-1} corresponding to the C_{n-1} classifier, and so on.

Iterative Selection of P. The behavior of $\mathbf{C}$ will be strongly related by the positive samples populating the training set P. If the dataset P is highly homogeneous, through the training of $\mathbf{C}$ the positive samples projected on the classification space are easily grouped on kernels. Dissimilar samples of the mean

Algorithm 1. Multi-Objective Training

Require: P positive dataset, N negative dataset, and $\{E, d_{min}, f_{max}\}$
Ensure: Pool of Multi-Objective Cascades $\mathcal{C}_{MOO}$
1: $k \leftarrow 1$
2: $P_k \leftarrow P$, $p \leftarrow \#$ positives in P
3: **while** $k \leq \mathcal{N}$ **do**
4:     $\mathbf{C}_k \leftarrow$ TrainCascade$(P_k, N, E, d_{min}, f_{max})$
5:     $n \leftarrow \#$ of stages in $(\mathbf{C}_k)$
6:     $s, idx \leftarrow$ ComputeOutputScores$(\mathbf{C}_k, P_k)$
7:     $oidx \leftarrow$ SortIndexIncreassingOrder(s, idx)
8:     Update p: $p \leftarrow ((d_{min})^n \cdot p)$
9:     Create P_{new} as the first p elements of P_k sorted by $oidx$
10:     Save $\mathbf{C}_k$ in $\mathcal{C}_{MOO}$
11:     $k \leftarrow k + 1$
12:     $P_k = P_{new}$
13: **return** $\mathcal{C}_{MOO}$

---

class, called outliers, which are projected far away from those kernels, can be considered as negatives. The result of this kind of classifiers is a not so high ratio of CD, but a very low ratio of FA. Curve ROC2 in fig. 2(b) designs this kind of behavior. When P is heterogeneous, Adaboost has a hard work grouping the positive samples on the classification space, generating largest boundaries. This results on a highest ratio of CD and, at the same time, an increase of the FA. Curve ROC1 in fig. 2(b) illustrate this behavior compared to ROC2.

Algorithm 1 trains a pool of $\mathcal{N}$ Cascades of Boosted Classifiers: $\mathcal{C}_{MOO} = \{\mathbf{C}_1, ..., \mathbf{C}_{\mathcal{N}}\}$. Function $TrainCascade()$ on line 4 follows the guidelines of [12] to train all $\mathbf{C}_i$. It uses as input argument positive datasets P_k with growing heterogeneity as i goes from 1 to $\mathcal{N}$. Therefore, $\mathbf{C}_{\mathcal{N}}$ will have wider boundaries on the classification space than $\mathbf{C}_1$. It can be done by removing from P_k the positive samples placed at the center of the kernels on the classification space by $\mathbf{C}_k$. Functions $ComputeOutputScores()$ and $SortIndexIncreassingOrder()$ obtain and sort the scores of all the samples in P_k using $\mathbf{C}_k$, placing the highest scores at the end of the list $oidx$. Variable p, which represents the number of positive samples, is decreased on line 8 by a factor or d_{min}^n ($d_{min} < 1$). Then, P_{new} dataset is created by the first p samples of list $oidx$, and will be the next positive dataset to train $\mathbf{C}_{k+1}$.

3   Experiments and Results

Training and Test Datasets. The positive dataset $\mathcal{P}$ employed on the training procedure is composed of rectangular images containing a person from video sequences captured at a street corner, as shown fig. 1(a). 6,726 positive samples were obtained by flipping the patches on the vertical axis.

The negative set used to train the classifiers is the PASCALVOC 2012 dataset composed of 7,166 images without persons. The INRIA person negative set (1,570 images) is also employed but for the construction of the ROC curves and the definition of the Pareto Front.

The pedestrian detection systems are tested on the GSDatasets, which consist of view of a street corner capturing pedestrians while crossing the street.

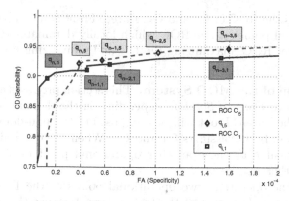

Fig. 3. The figure shows ROC curves from $\mathbf{C}_1$ and $\mathbf{C}_5$, and the operational points $q_{i,1}$ for cascade $\mathbf{C}_1$ and $q_{i,5}$ for cascade $\mathbf{C}_5$.

The datasets are public and available at http://pablonegri.free.fr/Downloads/ GSdataset-PANKit.htm. They consist on two sequences of two minutes where each pedestrian on the sight has its bounding box and a unique label. This sets can be employed to test detection and tracking systems on outdoors sequences. In sequence GS06, there are five persons crossing the street, generating 1,157 position to detect for the classifier. Sequence GS54 has 3,644 positive positions generated by 16 persons which cross the street. The remaining pedestrians of both sequences are not evaluated by the detection system.

The training was performed using a 3 fold-cross validation technique. The total positive base $\mathcal{P}$ is divided randomly in three datasets $\{\mathcal{P}_1, \mathcal{P}_2, \mathcal{P}_3\}$. Each training of $\mathcal{C}_{MOO}$ employs two of those sets to construct the positive dataset P. The remaining set, it can be denominated as V, is employed to compute the ROC curve in order to characterize the behavior of $\mathcal{C}_{MOO}$.

For each $\mathcal{C}_{MOO}$ were trained $\mathcal{N} = 5$ $\mathbf{C}_i$ following algorithm 1. This value of $\mathcal{N}$ was chosen based on the number of positive samples that were discarded at each iteration. It depends on variable d_{min} that is equals to 0.995 in our experiments. For $\mathcal{N} = 5$, the remaining number of positive samples is enough to train the last cascade $\mathbf{C}_5$: the number of positives training $\mathbf{C}_1$ is 4,484, and 3,253 for $\mathbf{C}_5$. The variable f_{max} has a value of 0.4.

A modification to the $TrainCascade()$ function of alg. 1 was introduced to train $\mathbf{C}$. The *regular* version uses the same positive dataset on the Adaboost algorithm for training and validating the strong classifier. This set changes at each stage of the Cascade training. On the modified version *fix*, the positive dataset is split on two sets for the training and the validation. The validation set is the same (is 'fixed') during all the training of $\mathbf{C}$.

The architecture of *regular* $\mathbf{C}_1$ has 12 stages C_i, while the *fixed* $\mathbf{C}_1^{fx}$ has 20 stages. The stage number of both versions of the Cascades increase within the training of the pool, because the heterogeneity of the positive datasets.

Figure 3 draws ROC curves obtained from a set $\mathcal{C}_{MOO}$ using dataset V (2,242 positive samples) and 100,000 negative patches from INRIA negative person set.

This figure shows the ROC of $\mathbf{C}_1$ and $\mathbf{C}_5$. Pareto Front can be estimated choosing the operational points of one ROC which locally dominates the operational points of the other ROC, maximizing the DC and minimizing FA.

Implementation of the MOO System. This section proposes a methodology to select the *Pareto Optimal Solution* depending on the dynamic of the scene.

From fig. 3 the Pareto Front will be composed of the non-dominanted operational points from both classifiers $\mathbf{C}_1$ and $\mathbf{C}_5$. When the dynamic of the scene changes, it is possible to chose another operational point of the same $\mathbf{C}_i$ or change for the other classifier.

To simplify the operation, two operational points of the Pareto Front are applied depending on the state of the traffic light. Because the objective is to increase the detection of pedestrians walking in front of the stopped vehicles the classifier should have wide boundaries on the classification space, and high CD rate. However, the continual use of this operational point on the Pareto Front, which also has high FA rate, will droops the performance of the detection system. When pedestrians stop crossing the street because the vehicles are circulating, the Pareto Solution can change for another operational point which belong to a classifier with narrow boundaries on the classification space. As the dynamic of the vehicles is governed by their traffic light, the change of the operational point on the Pareto Front will also be determined by their states:
- Green Traffic Light: operational point $q_{green} \rightarrow \mathbf{C}_1\{q_{n,1}\}$ to minimize FA.
- Red Traffic Light: operational point $q_{red} \rightarrow \mathbf{C}_5\{q_{n,5}\}$ or $\mathbf{C}_5\{q_{n-1,5}\}$, or $\mathbf{C}_5\{q_{n-2,5}\}$, to maximize DC.

The performance is evaluated using: *CD* as the number of pedestrians correctly detected, the *Miss Rate* as the percentage of non-detected pedestrians, *FA* the total amount of false alarms on the set, and the *Average Precision Ratio* (AP) obtained from the Precision-Recall curve at the choose operational point.

Table 1 presents the results of the MOO system compared to the regular Cascade of Boosted Classifiers $\mathbf{C}$, and the 'fixed' version $\mathbf{C}^{fx}$. The results depicted on table 1 of both versions of $TrainCascade()$ function, exhibit that the 'fixed' version has a better performance, and the implementation of the MOO system shows a better performance than the classic implementation.

Table 1. Detection results using different systems.

Detector	GS06 (1,157 positives)				GS54 (3,644 positives)			
	CD	Miss Rate (%)	FA	AP	CD	Miss Rate (%)	FA	AP
$\mathbf{C}$	790	31.7	160	67.8	2194	39.8	408	58.1
$\mathbf{C}^{fx}$	836	27.7	354	70.5	2468	32.2	749	64.9
$\mathcal{C}_{MOO}\{q_{n,1}, q_{n,5}\}$	805	30.4	238	67.7	2308	36.6	471	60.5
$\mathcal{C}_{MOO}\{q_{n,1}, q_{n-1,5}\}$	812	29.8	323	68.1	2345	35.6	611	60.9
$\mathcal{C}_{MOO}\{q_{n,1}, q_{n-2,5}\}$	817	29.3	474	68.0	2389	34.4	775	61.4
$\mathcal{C}_{MOO}^{fx}\{q_{n,1}, q_{n,5}\}$	852	**26.3**	460	**71.7**	2554	29.9	**842**	67.1
$\mathcal{C}_{MOO}^{fx}\{q_{n,1}, q_{n-1,5}\}$	854	26.1	523	71.6	2570	29.4	907	67.3
$\mathcal{C}_{MOO}^{fx}\{q_{n,1}, q_{n-2,5}\}$	854	26.1	562	71.5	2581	29.1	956	67.4

As expected, MOO systems maximize the number of CD, minimizing the Miss Rate, while the number of FA increase within acceptable values. For example, $\mathcal{C}_{MOO}^{fx}\{q_{n,1}, q_{n-1,5}\}$ system increases the number of CD by 18 samples on the GS06 dataset, and the FAs grows about 100, meaning one FA each 10 frames. The advantage of the MOO system is better appreciated on the GS54 dataset, while the FAs increase, again, by 100 samples, the system detect almost one hundred additional pedestrians, representing 2.5 % in comparison with the classic implementation. For detection systems, a greater number of CD is more significant as shown the highest values of AP. Thus, this combination can be choose as the best for this application.

4   Conclusions

This article proposes a Multi-Objective Optimization System applied to pedestrian detection on outdoor scenes complexes with cluttered backgrounds. A pool of classifiers is trained using different combination of positives datasets. Depending on the dynamic of the scene, different operational points corresponding to locally non-dominated solutions of the Pareto Front are applied to improve the system performance. The perspectives will be oriented to develop a methodology to optimize the choose of the positive samples to train the pool of classifiers.

Acknowledgments. This work was funded by the ACyT A14T24 (UADE), and the PICT-BICENTENARIO 2283 (FONCYT).

References

1. Bradley, A.: The use of the area under the roc curve in the evaluation of machine learning algorithms. PR **30**, 1145–1159 (1997)
2. Cabezas, I., Trujillo, M.: A method for reducing the cardinality of the pareto front. In: Alvarez, L., Mejail, M., Gomez, L., Jacobo, J. (eds.) CIARP 2012. LNCS, vol. 7441, pp. 829–836. Springer, Heidelberg (2012)
3. Chatelain, C., et al.: A multi-model selection framework for unknown and/or evolutive misclassification cost problems. PR **43**(3), 815–823 (2010)
4. Dalal, N., Triggs, B.: Histograms of oriented gradients for human detection. CVPR **1**, 886–893 (2005)
5. Felzenszwalb, P., Girshick, G., McAllester, D., Ramanan, D.: Object detection with discriminatively trained part-based models. PAMI **32**(9), 1627–1645 (2010)
6. Li, W., Liu, L., Gong, W.: Multi-objective uniform design as a svm model selection tool for face recognition. Expert Systems with Applications **38**, 6689–6695 (2011)
7. Negri, P.: Estimating the queue length at street intersections by using a movement feature space approach. IET IP **8**(7), 406–416 (2014)
8. Negri, P., Goussies, N., Lotito, P.: Detecting pedestrians on a movement feature space. PR **47**(1), 56–71 (2014)

9. Negri, P., Lotito, P.: Pedestrian detection using a feature space based on colored level lines. In: Alvarez, L., Mejail, M., Gomez, L., Jacobo, J. (eds.) CIARP 2012. LNCS, vol. 7441, pp. 885–892. Springer, Heidelberg (2012)

10. Rosales-Pérez, A., Gonzalez, J.A., Coello-Coello, C.A., Reyes-Garcia, C.A., Escalante, H.J.: Evolutionary multi-objective approach for prototype generation and feature selection. In: Bayro-Corrochano, E., Hancock, E. (eds.) CIARP 2014. LNCS, vol. 8827, pp. 424–431. Springer, Heidelberg (2014)

11. Rosales-Pérez, A., et al.: Surrogate-assisted multi-objective model selection for support vector machines. Neurocomputing **150**, 163–172 (2015)

12. Viola, P., Jones, M.: Rapid object detection using a boosted cascade of simple features. CVPR **1**, 511–518 (2001)

Author Index

Printed in the United States
By Bookmasters